VNR'S ENCYCLOPEDIA

of

HOSPITALITY

and

TOURISM

Edited by

Mahmood A. Khan
*Virginia Polytechnic Institute
and State University*

Michael D. Olsen
*Virginia Polytechnic Institute
and State University*

Turgut Var
Texas A&M University

VNR VAN NOSTRAND REINHOLD
_____ New York

Copyright © 1993 by Van Nostrand Reinhold
Library of Congress Catalog Card Number 92–40238
ISBN 0–442–00346–3

Printed in the United States of America.

Van Nostrand Reinhold
115 Fifth Avenue
New York, New York 10003

Chapman and Hall
2–6 Boundary Row
London, SE1 8HN, England

Thomas Nelson Australia
102 Dodds Street
South Melbourne 3205
Victoria, Australia

Nelson Canada
1120 Birchmount Road
Scarborough, Ontario M1K 5G4, Canada

16 15 14 13 12 11 10 9 8 7 6 5 4 3 2 1

Library of Congress Cataloging-in-Publication Data
VNR's encyclopedia of hospitality and tourism/[edited by] Mahmood A.
  Khan, Michael D. Olsen, Turgut Var.
      p. cm.
    ISBN 0–442–00346–3
    1. Hospitality industry—Encyclopedias. 2. Food service
management—Encyclopedias. 3. Hotel management—Encyclopedias.
4. Tourist trade—Encyclopedias. I. Khan, Mahmood A. II. Olsen,
Michael D. III. Var, Turgut.
TX905.V57 1992
647.94'03—dc20   92–40238

Contents

Preface

This volume is the premier and pioneer effort at publishing an encyclopedia covering the wide range of interrelated disciplines in the fields of hospitality and tourism. Obviously, it has been a tremendous undertaking, partly because of the multidisciplinary nature of the topics and partly because of the desire to present information useful to readers in a single publication. Although a seemingly impossible task at the start, with the help of a worldwide selection of distinguished experts from the many disciplines, we feel we've been successful in accomplishing our aims.

VNR's *Encyclopedia of Hospitality and Tourism* covers three major topics: foodservice, lodging, and tourism. The entries for each topic were selected by the editorial board members, written by experts in those special areas, and refereed by peer scholars in the respective fields, an approach unparalleled by any in the fields of hospitality and tourism. The intent is to provide complete information in a format that is readily comprehensible and useful. Every effort was made to include as many specific topics as possible, but, of course, space limitations had to be taken into consideration. We hope to rectify omissions and expand coverage of the topics in a supplemental volume.

The first section, Foodservice Management, covers foodservice management in general and food preparation and service in particular. Issues range from "back of the house" to "front of the house" topics for any type of foodservice operation. The foodservice and restaurant industry's rapid growth is highlighted, while specialized topics focus on the latest innovations and developments in foodservice. Other entries cover purchasing, market feasibility, foodservice operation, types of foodservices, food preparation, food sanitation, and service. Each entry provides an introduction and descriptive information, uses tables and figures to illustrate essential components, and adds case studies whenever necessary.

Hotel Management, the next section, provides basic information on the most common service and operational functions that make up the day-to-day activities of a traditional hotel. Basic managerial functions—such as finance, marketing, human resources, and operations—are presented first so that a proper grounding in these concepts is established. Using these concepts as the basic foundation for understanding how hotels work, subsequent entries build upon this base and explain in detail how various tasks and activities are carried out. Front office, maintenance, security, safety, and conference activities are among the topics covered.

The final section, Travel and Tourism, includes selections that represent the breadth and depth of tourism, from the definition to the psychology of tourism, from the traditional to the newly related disciplines. It was compiled in line with the recognition of the economic and social importance of tourism that has resulted in a remarkable increased momentum in tourism research. According to the WTO (the World Tourism Organization of the United Nations), worldwide travel and tourism revenue at the beginning of 1990 exceeded $2.4 trillion. During the same year the United States spent nearly $377 billion on travel and tourism, while in 1991, although still a preliminary figure, U.S receipts from foreign tourists totaled nearly $57 billion, a figure much larger than the total U.S. exports of agricultural goods. It is also estimated that, in 1990, tourism supported more than 850,000 jobs and generated $5.5 billion in federal, state, and local taxes. These figures clearly show the magnitude and importance of tourism for the world in general and the United States in particular.

The section begins with basic concepts and definitions and continues with entries on the sociology, psychology, anthropology, and economics of tourism to assist in the understanding of more complex topics such as ethnocentrism and seasonality. Other entries cover tourism law, infrastructure and development, and need assessment through brainstorming and the nominal group technique. We have attempted to emphasize authenticity and travel motivation, as well as to stress the sustainability and preservation of culture and environment. Many entries are devoted to the measurement and analysis of tourism-related data. The interdisciplinary nature of tourism is addressed in entries on global information technologies in airlines and the linkage between airlines and tourism. The final entry in the section provides the addresses and phone numbers of important tourism and travel-related organizations, publications, and data sources, as well as other valuable information for the interested reader.

Acknowledgments

We are grateful to all of the authors for their contributions, and to the referees for their valuable reviews, without which it would have been impossible to compile this publication. Likewise we are deeply appreciative of the help provided by the associate editors: Kevin B. Boberg of New Mexico State University, Las Cruces; William P. Fisher of the National Restaurant Association; Donald Getz of the University of Calgary; Michael Heywood of the University of Guelph; David Kirk of Queen Margaret College; Joseph E. Lavin of Choice International Hotels; Robert C. Lewis of the University of Guelph; Carl D. Riegel of Washington State University, Seattle; Pauline Sheldon of the University of Hawaii; Paul Slattery of Leisure Industries; Marian C. Spears of Kansas State University; John Stefanelli of the University of Nevada—Las Vegas; W. Terry Umbreit of Washington State University, Seattle; Carlton Van Doren of Texas A&M University; and Thomas E. Walsh of Iowa State University. We also wish to acknowledge the support from Van Nostrand Reinhold throughout the publication process. In particular, Judy Joseph, Pam Chirls, and Julie Markoff were instrumental in channeling the heavy influx of manuscripts and their reviews.

Mahmood A. Khan
Michael D. Olsen
Turgut Var

Contributors

Barbara A. Almanza
Department of Restaurant, Hotel, Institutional,
and Tourism Management
Purdue University
West Lafayette, Indiana

Sue Baker
Department of Hospitality Management
Hong Kong Polytechnic
Hung Hom, Kowloon, Hong Kong

James A. Bardi
School of Hotel, Restaurant, and Institutional
Management
The Pennsylvania State University—Berks Campus
Reading, Pennsylvania

Raphael Raymond Bar-On
Israel Ministry of Tourism
Jerusalem, Israel

Melvin N. Barrington
Department of Hotel, Restaurant, and Tourism
Administration
University of South Carolina
Columbia, South Carolina

Thomas W. Blaine
College of Parks and Recreation
Texas A&M University
College Station, Texas

Kevin B. Boberg
College of Business Administration and Economics
New Mexico State University
Las Cruces, New Mexico

Frank D. Borsenik
College of Hotel Administration
University of Nevada—Las Vegas
Las Vegas, Nevada

John Bowen
Bond University
School of Business
Gold Coast, Queensland, Australia

Russell E. Brayley
Faculty of Physical Education and Recreation Studies
University of Manitoba
Winnepeg, Manitoba, Canada

Key-Sung Chon
College of Hotel Administration
University of Nevada—Las Vegas
Las Vegas, Nevada

Erik Cohen
Department of Sociology and Social Anthropology
The Hebrew University of Jerusalem
Mount Scopus, Israel

Linda J. Cox
Agricultural and Resource Economics
University of Hawaii
Honolulu, Hawaii

Simon Crawford-Welch
Service Associates
Division of Strategic Yield Management, Inc.
Las Vegas, Nevada

John L. Crompton
Department of Recreation, Park, and Tourism
  Sciences
Texas A&M University
College Station, Texas

L. Taylor Damonte
Department of Restaurant, Hotel, and Tourism
  Administration
University of South Carolina
Columbia, South Carolina

Graham M. S. Dann
Faculty of Social Sciences
The University of West Indies
Bridgetown, Barbados

Frederick J. DeMicco
School of Hotel, Restaurant, and Recreation
  Management
The Pennsylvania State University
University Park, Pennsylvania

Chekitan Dev
School of Hotel Administration
Cornell University
Ithaca, New York

Kadir H. Din
Department of Geography
National University of Malaysia
Selangor, Malaysia

Monika Echtermeyer
Department of Tourism and Geography
Universitat Trier
Trier-Tarforst, Germany

Raymond C. Ellis, Jr.
American Hotel and Motel Association
Washington, D.C.

Howard Feiertag
Department of Hotel, Restaurant, and Institutional
  Management
Virginia Polytechnic Institute and State University
Blacksburg, Virginia

Daniel R. Fesenmaier
Department of Leisure Studies
University of Illinois
Champaign, Illinois

William P. Fisher
National Restaurant Association
Washington, D.C.

Morton Fox
School of Travel Industry Management
University of Hawaii
Honolulu, Hawaii

Paul R. Gamble
Department of Management Studies for Tourism
  and Hotel Industry
University of Surrey
Guildford Surrey, United Kingdom

Donald Getz
World Tourism Education and Research Center
University of Calgary
Calgary, Alberta, Canada

Frank M. Go
Department of Hospitality Administration
Hong Kong Polytechnic
Hong Kong

Charles R. Goeldner
College of Business and Administration
University of Colorado at Boulder
Boulder, Colorado

Claudia Gill Green
Foods, Nutrition, and Foodservice Management
University of North Carolina
Greensboro, North Carolina

Clare A. Gunn
Department of Recreation, Park, and Tourism
  Sciences
Texas A&M University
College Station, Texas

Lee Anne R. Hagan
Department of Park, Recreation, and Tourism
  Management
Clemson University
Clemson, South Carolina

Keith Hollinshead
Department of Recreation, Park, and Tourism
  Sciences
Texas A&M University
College Station, Texas

Nor K. Ishak
School of Hotel and Catering Management
MARA Institute of Technology
Selangor, Malaysia

Giles Jackson
Department of Hotel, Restaurant, and Institutional
Management
Virginia Polytechnic Institute and State University
Blacksburg, Virginia

Peter Jones
Service Sector Management
Brighton Polytechnic
East Bourne
Sussex, United Kingdom

James Kaiser
School of Hotel, Restaurant, and Recreation
Management
The Pennsylvania State University
University Park, Pennsylvania

Ronald A. Kaiser
Department of Recreation, Park, and Tourism
Sciences
Texas A&M University
College Station, Texas

Michael L. Kasavana
School of Hotel, Restaurant, and Institutional
Management
Michigan State University
East Lansing, Michigan

Robert V. Kemper
Department of Anthropology
Southern Methodist University
Dallas, Texas

Mahmood A. Khan
Department of Hotel, Restaurant, and Institutional
Management
Virginia Polytechnic Institute and State University
Blacksburg, Virginia

David Kirk
Department of Hospitality Studies
Queen Margaret College
Edinburgh, Scotland

Francis A. Kwansa
Department of Hotel, Restaurant, and Institution
Management
Virginia Polytechnic Institute and State University
Blacksburg, Virginia

Carolyn U. Lambert
School of Hotel, Restaurant, and Recreation
Management
The Pennsylvania State University
University Park, Pennsylvania

Harold Lane
Department of Hotel and Food Administration
Boston University—Metropolitan College
Boston, Massachusetts

Robert B. Lane
Food and Beverage Standards
Marriott Hotels and Resorts
Washington, D.C.

Joseph E. Lavin
Development, Choice Hotels
Silver Springs, Maryland

Choong-Ki Lee
Sejong University
Seoul, Korea

Neil Leiper
Department of Management Systems
Massey University
Palmerston North, New Zealand

Robert C. Lewis
School of Hotel and Food Administration
University of Guelph
Guelph, Ontario, Canada

Dallas Steve Lunceford
Choice Hotels
Silver Springs, Maryland

Craig C. Lundberg
School of Hotel Administration
Cornell University
Ithaca, New York

James R. MacGregor
Senior Tourism Consultant
Lavalin Corporation
Vancouver, British Columbia, Canada

Norman G. Marriott
Department of Food Science and Technology
Virginia Polytechnic Institute and State University
Blacksburg, Virginia

Robert J. Martin
College of Hotel Administration
University of Nevada—Las Vegas
Las Vegas, Nevada

Ken W. McCleary
Department of Hotel, Restaurant, and Institutional
Management
Virginia Polytechnic Institute and State University
Blacksburg, Virginia

Audrey McCool
College of Hotel Administration
University of Nevada—Las Vegas
Las Vegas, Nevada

Robert W. McLellan
Department of Parks, Recreation, and Tourism
Management
Clemson University
Clemson, South Carolina

Robert Christie Mill
School of Hotel and Restaurant Management
University of Denver
Denver, Colorado

Ady Milman
Dick Pope Institute for Tourism Studies
University of Central Florida
Orlando, Florida

Golam Mohammed
Department of Maritime Administration
Texas A&M University
Galveston, Texas

Peter E. Murphy
School of Business, Tourism Management Program
University of Victoria
Victoria, British Columbia, Canada

Suzanne K. Murrmann
Department of Hotel, Restaurant, and Institutional
Management
Virginia Polytechnic Institute and State University
Blacksburg, Virginia

Bvsan Murthy
Department of Hotel, Restaurant, and Institutional
Management
Virginia Polytechnic Institute and State University
Blacksburg, Virginia

Eddystone C. Nebel III
Department of Restaurant, Hotel, Institutional
and Tourism Management
Purdue University
West Lafayette, Indiana

Leland L. Nicholls
Department of Hospitality and Tourism
University of Wisconsin—Stout
Menomonie, Wisconsin

Michael Olsen
Department of Hotel, Restaurant, and Institutional
Management
Virginia Polytechnic Institute and State University
Blacksburg, Virginia

Philip L. Pearce
Department of Behavioural Sciences
James Cook University of North Queensland
Townsville, Australia

Laurel J. Reid
Department of Recreation and Leisure Studies
Brock University
St. Catherines, Ontario, Canada

Linda A. Riley
College of Business Administration and Economics
New Mexico State University
Las Cruces, New Mexico

Denney G. Rutherford
Hotel and Restaurant Administration
Washington State University
Seattle, Washington

Raymond S. Schmidgall
School of Hotel, Restaurant, and Institutional
Management
Michigan State University
East Lansing, Michigan

Martin Senior
Hotel and Catering Training Company
London, United Kingdom

Margaret Shaw
School of Hotel and Food Administration
University of Guelph
Guelph, Ontario, Canada

John E. H. Sherry
College of Hotel Administration
Cornell University
Ithaca, New York

Valene L. Smith
Department of Anthropology
California State University—Chico
Chico, California

Mary and David Snepenger
College of Business
Montana State University
Bozeman, Montana

Oscar Pete Snyder, Jr.
Hospitality Institute of Technology and Management
St. Paul, Minnesota

Marian C. Spears
Hotel, Restaurant, Institutional Management
and Dietetics
Kansas State University
Manhattan, Kansas

Charles A. Stansfield, Jr.
Department of Geography
Rowan State University
Glassboro, New Jersey

John Stefanelli
College of Hotel Administration
University of Nevada—Las Vegas
Las Vegas, Nevada

William P. Stewart
Department of Recreation, Park, and Tourism
Sciences
Texas A&M University
College Station, Texas

William B. Stronge
Department of Economics
Florida Atlantic University
Boca Raton, Florida

Deborah H. Sutherlin
Department of Home Economics and Family Living
Western Kentucky University
Bowling Green, Kentucky

Cheri Becker Suttle
Department of Hotel, Restaurant, and Institutional
Management
Virginia Polytechnic Institute and State University
Blacksburg, Virginia

Skip Swerdlow
Department of Hotel Administration
University of Nevada—Las Vegas
Las Vegas, Nevada

Richard Teare
Department of Service Industries
Bournemouth University
Fern Barrow, Dorset, United Kingdom

Eliza Ching-Yick Tse
Department of Hotel, Restaurant, and Institutional
Management
Virginia Polytechnic Institute and State University
Blacksburg, Virginia

Seoho Um
Department of Tourism and Recreation
Kyonggi University
Suwon-Shi, Kyonggi-Do, South Korea

Muzaffer M. Uysal
Department of Hotel, Restaurant, and Institutional
Management
Virginia Polytechnic Institute and State University
Blacksburg, Virginia

Pierre L. van den Berghe
Department of Sociology
University of Washington
Seattle, Washington

Tom Van Dyke
    Department of Hotel, Restaurant, and Institutional
        Management
    Indiana University of Pennsylvania
    Indiana, Pennsylvania

Turgut Var
    Department of Recreation, Park, and Tourism
        Science
    Texas A&M University
    College Station, Texas

Christine A. Vogt
    Department of Recreation and Park Administration
    Indiana University
    Bloomington, Indiana

Salah E. A. Wahab
    Cairo, Egypt

Mickey Warner
    Lantana, Florida

Carson E. Watt
    Department of Recreation, Park, and Tourism
        Sciences
    Texas A&M University
    College Station, Texas

Diane Welland
    National Restaurant Association
    Washington, D.C.

Peter Williams
    Centre for Tourism Policy and Research
    Simon Fraser University
    Burnaby, British Columbia, Canada

Stephen F. Witt
    European Business Management School
    University of Wales
    Swansea, United Kingdom

PART 1

Foodservice Management

1

The Restaurant
and Foodservice Industry

William P. Fisher

The restaurant and foodservice industry provides food and beverages prepared outside of the home for public consumption. It includes hotels, restaurants, lunchrooms, fast-food operations, catering services, schools, hospitals, industrial and military foodservice, and vending machines.

Since 1970 industry sales figures have climbed from $42.8 billion to $241.3 billion in 1990. Contemporary life-styles require food prepared away from home, and on a typical day 45 percent of adults patronize foodservice establishments.

With over eight million employees, the industry is the nation's largest retail employer. The number of foodservice employees is expected to increase to over 11 million by the year 2000. Foodservice establishments will realize the greatest numerical job growth of all industries from 1986 to 2000, adding 2.5 million jobs.

Women are enjoying increased career opportunities through the foodservice industry; of foodservice industry employees 57 percent are women as opposed to 45 percent for all industries. Minority groups are also discovering new career options in the foodservice industry: In 1988, 13 percent of all employees in the industry were black and another 10 percent were Hispanic.

Commercial Foodservice

As eating out becomes a necessity instead of a treat reserved for special occasions, restaurants and lunchrooms continue to grow. Estimated sales for these two commercial foodservice components in 1990 reached $77.2 billion, an increase of 5.4 percent over 1989.

The behavior patterns of the public continue to change, with a need for convenience and quick service. There are increasing numbers of two-career households, and couples are turning more and more to the ease of eating out or to takeout and delivery.

The fast-food segment is the industry leader in growth. Fast-food or limited-menu restaurant sales increased 7.4 percent in 1990 to $70.4 billion.

Another segment of the commercial foodservice group is cafeterias. The 1990 sales for this segment rose 5 percent over 1989 to $4.4 billion. The long-term outlook for cafeterias is positive and these establishments will enjoy increased sales as they undergo renovations, provide takeout services, and update their promotional campaigns.

Ice cream and frozen custard stands are also included in the commercial category. This group ranked third in overall performance among eating places in 1990, with sales reaching $2.2 billion, a 7.2 percent gain over 1989.

Catering has found its niche among the two-career households for couples who wish to entertain without spending a great deal of time preparing food. Social caterers saw a 7.8 percent increase in sales in 1990 to $2.2 billion.

Another sector of the commercial foodservice industry includes food contractors. These contractors provide foodservice to industrial plants, office buildings, hospitals, schools, airlines, and recreational centers that do not operate their own foodservice. Food contractors generated sales of over $14 billion in 1990.

Institutional Foodservice

Institutional foodservice, another category of foodservice operation, encompasses those school, government, business, health-care, or recreational facilities that provide their own foodservice. This group grew 5 percent from 1989 to 1990 with combined sales of over $26 billion.

The trends in the institutional foodservice sector are usually determined by the growth and change in the host institution. Educational foodservice is a good example. After years of declining enrollment in schools, which followed the graduation of the baby-boom generation, enrollment is expected to increase as the children of this population begin to enter school. Primary, secondary, and postsecondary institutions are expecting greater enrollment with predicted growth in foodservice operations.

Educational foodservice has the constant challenge of creating meals of high nutritional value that are attractive to students. Educational foodservice programs are emphasizing healthier food by lowering the sugar and salt content, using whole wheat breads, and serving more fish and chicken entrées. Today's lunchrooms have salad bars and à la carte options, and even kindergarten children have self-serve lunch lines where they may decide between various color-coded selections that show the food group from which the menu item is derived. Schools have introduced items reflecting the popularity of fast-food fare with their own versions of fast food, such as chicken nuggets and miniburgers.

About 24 million students are fed via the National School Lunch Program daily. Government funding of the program has been cut in recent years, lowering the number of free and reduced-price lunches served.

Colleges are shifting from mandated meal programs to retail and à la carte programs as well. University foodservice has expanded into multifaceted dining halls with some areas designated for lighter, low-calorie food and others for grilling hot dogs and hamburgers. Some colleges have food courts with fast-food chains represented, and several have pizza and sandwich delivery establishments on campus.

Innovations in foodservice are also apparent in health-care facilities. Hospitals and other health-care facilities need to monitor costs closely, but they also must serve nutritious, appetizing food to persons who may be so ill they have little enthusiasm for eating.

In 1990 health-care foodservice sales increased 1.9 percent over 1989. The demand for long-term care will continue to grow. By the year 2000, 35 million Americans will be over age 65 and the number of those over 85 will double from its present level.

Today's health-care facilities offer a broad range of services. Some have 24-hour room service, nutritional counseling, and menus from which patients can choose their meals.

Another sector of institutional foodservice is employee foodservice. Sales in this area totaled $7.2 billion in 1990. Some companies have installed elegant, upscale restaurants in their buildings where employees can have business lunches. Almost all programs are emphasizing nutrition and have salad bars, more fish and chicken entrées, and use less salt and sugar.

Vendors at baseball games have added more items to their usual offerings of hot dogs and soft drinks. Today at sports centers fans may buy salads, baby back ribs, cheese steaks, fajitas, steamed shrimp, oysters, sushi, and knishes as well as the traditional pretzels, beer, and hot dogs.

There are a variety of eating options at amusement parks. Many have food courts with fast-food chains plus upscale dining restaurants and cafeterias. Recreational foodservice will continue to grow with the anticipated increase in visits to parks, both national and theme, and in attendance at sports events.

Military Foodservice

Feeding military personnel is another area of the foodservice industry. It includes feeding troops and officers in clubs, dining halls, and military hospitals, as well as in the field. The number of those in the military was affected by the reduction in defense spending and grew by only 0.3 percent in 1990. Military foodservice sales reached $1.1 billion in 1990.

Many technological advances bring state-of-the-art foodservice to the military. Troops do not eat out of tin cans anymore, but receive their food rations in plastic-and-foil pouches called MREs, or meals-ready-to-eat. The traditional field commissaries have been usurped by mobile field kitchens that can be run by just two people, and bulk food supplies have been replaced by preportioned, precooked food packed in trays, which are reheated in boiling water.

For those not in the field, the clubs and dining halls have adopted modern decor with an emphasis on lighter, yet filling fare. Budget cuts in recent years have led to consolidation of some of the military eating establishments into a few units at each base that can be converted into different eating operations. In one location there might be a fast-food option, a midscale family restaurant that could also serve as a banquet/conference center and a nightclub/casual dining option.

History of Restaurant and Commercial Foodservice

From Inns and Taverns to Self-Service

The foodservice industry has its roots in the inns and taverns of the colonial period. Inns in America were patterned after those in England. Samuel Cole of Boston opened the first American tavern, the Coles Ordinary, in Boston in 1634.

Taverns and inns became informal gathering places where patrons could discuss politics and community gossip over ale and food. In 1740, the first stagecoaches began traveling from Boston and made roadside inns even more accessible and popular. The American Revolution ended the reign of the roadside inns as they went out of fashion along with the British. French cuisine became popular in government and society circles, with even Presidents Washington and Jefferson serving French dishes to their guests.

In France the first restaurant where customers could choose from a selection of items presented on a menu was opened in 1765 by A. Boulanger. He placed a sign scripted in Latin over his establishment that translated to: "Come to me all whose stomachs cry out in anguish and I shall restore you." Thus the word restaurant was derived from the word restore.

In the 1820s the first American restaurants opened in New York. Among those history makers were Niblo's Garden, Sans Souci, and Delmonico's. With these establishments began the era of "fashionable" restaurants where dining was a social event and an indulgence in fine food surrounded by lush decor, some featuring nightingales and elaborate fountains.

In the early 1900s, as more and more people entered the work force and were unable to eat at home, they needed a place to eat lunch. For men there evolved "free lunches" in saloons where, for 5 cents, customers could buy a beer and receive a complimentary lunch.

But the shift in the American economy from agrarian to industrial offered work options to many women and, as they poured into the work force, they also needed eating places. Since it was not acceptable at that time for women to eat in saloons, they found their haven in drug stores.

Drug store owners, renowned for their tasty elixirs and phosphates, responded to the need of working women by adding sandwiches to their menus. These soda fountains became extremely popular with working women by day and provided a place for couples to meet at night.

The Volstead Act of 1919, which began prohibition and ended free lunches and saloons, was a boon to soda fountains as they continued to do big business and added a variety of hot entrees to their menus. Prohibition also marked the advent of speakeasies, illegal saloons that served their clientele food as well as bathtub gin. During Prohibition many hotel dining rooms and other restaurants closed, but the speakeasies thrived. After the repeal of Prohibition during the Great Depression in the 1930s, many speakeasies developed into successful restaurants.

Tearooms that served the requisite tea plus finger sandwiches to women before Prohibition enjoyed greater popularity with both sexes during that period. In their heyday, some of these establishments served over one thousand people in a day. The leisurely pace and refined setting of the tearooms lost their appeal, however, as the public clamored for quicker service and lower prices.

The idea for a cafeteria was allegedly conceived by John Krueger who derived the concept from a smorgasbord. The first cafeteria is said to have appeared in California during the Gold Rush, but it became a widespread concept in the early 1900s. The perceived cleanliness, convenience, and respectable atmosphere of cafeterias attracted a large portion of both working women and men.

Cafeteria operators discovered the advantages of this type of restaurant as they gained savings by not needing table service and using simplified food preparation.

The creation of midscale luncheon restaurants with lighter fare on their menus caused cafeteria popularity to wane. As people began to accept cold offerings for lunch, luncheon operations gave them sandwiches and salads. During the depression, these restaurants became fiercely competitive and turned toward advertising and merchandising to win over consumers.

Self-service proliferated as the United States entered World War II in 1941. Labor shortages and rationing led to the creation of a thriving black market that provided much sought-after meats and sugar to the restaurateurs. Despite these hardships, the foodservice industry continued to grow and demand increased from 20 million meals a day to over 60 million.

Franchising and Fast-Food Restaurants

When Roy Allen and Frank Wright opened a root beer stand in 1919 they did not realize they would be pioneers of the franchise concept. That first stand grew to 2,500 A & W units, of which most were franchised.

The franchise concept is a way of marketing or distributing goods through an individual unit that has been granted the right to produce a product by the original or parent company. By the year 2000, franchise sales will comprise one half of all retail sales.

Over the years, fast-food chains have continued to spread the franchise concept. One of the largest chains originated in a San Bernardino, California, restaurant opened in the 1940s by Maurice and Richard McDonald. They developed a streamlined system for producing their hamburgers and french fries which helped them keep up with customer demand. Ray Kroc, a sales-man, visited their operation and was impressed with their system and the im-maculate condition of their restaurant. He convinced them to offer franchises, which he would sell for them and then split the profits with the McDonalds.

Kroc first opened a McDonald's pilot unit in Des Plaines, Illinois, in 1955. He worked on improving the McDonalds' already efficient production methods. He continued to sell the hamburgers for 50 cents and emphasized quick service and clean surroundings. By the time Kroc had finished refining his test site, he had a uniform product that could be reproduced and adver-tised around the country. Then he began selling franchises, giving con-sumers fast food and franchising as it is known today.

There were 37 McDonald's in 1957; by 1970 there were 1,500. By 1985 a new unit opened an average of every 12 hours. System-wide sales for McDonald's in 1990 generated $18 billion. The power of the fast-food chains in influencing the foodservice industry can be exemplified by their ability to provide uniformity of taste and service styles in any of their units, thus at-tempting to guarantee customers that what they order will be similar to the fast foods they have had before.

Other chains also helped to make the franchise concept an integral part of foodservice today, such as Kentucky Fried Chicken, Domino's, Burger King, Dunkin' Donuts, Holiday Inn, Pizza Hut, Bonanza, Wendy's and many, many more. Some of these operations also have international units; McDonald's added a Moscow unit to its operation in 1990.

Drive-thrus were also popularized by the chains. From the days of drive-ins with carhops on rollerskates serving customers in their cars, fast-food restaurants have progressed to double-drive-thrus and drive-thru-only opera-tions. Burgers and fries are not the only foods available through windows: Italian, Mexican, and Cajun foods, chicken, and pizza are offered.

The chains today are offering more extensive menus; McDonald's now has over 60 menu items. Most of the larger chains have tried to incorpor-ate a variety of offerings including salads and fish and are emphasizing less salt and fat in their production following the consumer trend toward more health-conscious eating. A 1989 National Restaurant Association survey of chain operators showed that 70 percent of fast-food and family-chain operators had entrée salads or salad bars, reduced-calorie dressing, fruit juices, and low-fat milk among their menu items.

History of Institutional Foodservice

Educational Foodservice

Institutional foodservice, like the first restaurant, can also be traced to Europe. The first school lunch programs began in 1849 in French Cantines Ecoliers and Victor Hugo is said to have provided hot meals for nearby school children in his home.

School foodservice began in the United States in 1853 when the Children's Aid Society of New York offered food to those children who attended their industrial school. In the early 1900s, those who fed children were mostly volunteers, but schools nationwide began providing meals to students by 1918.

School lunch programs grew considerably during the depression as federal funds became available to finance operations. Thirty-nine states were receiving government funding by 1934. In 1935 menus, recipes, and procedures began to be standardized by the Works Progress Administration (WPA). By 1941 the WPA had expanded to every U.S. state and 23,000 schools dished up almost 2 million lunches daily.

After the end of World War II, school administrators were not hesitant to install lunch programs in their school systems. President Harry Truman approved the National School Lunch Act in 1946 and studies were undertaken on nutrition. Community groups actively campaigned to get lunch programs in every school and greater numbers of students began participating in the program. The number of children in school lunch programs increased from 8.6 million in 1950 to 14 million in 1960.

In 1960 further legislation that strengthened the school lunch program was enacted. In 1964 the Economic Opportunity Act was passed, which started feeding programs for preschool children through Head Start projects. In 1966 the Child Nutrition Act created more funding for these programs. Through several newspaper and television reports in the late 1960s, the public became aware of the poverty and hunger that existed in some areas of the United States. In 1969, money was allocated to provide reduced-price and free lunches in school foodservice programs.

The largest increase in the number of schools participating in the National School Lunch Program occurred between 1970 and 1971. Foodservice in schools has changed considerably since the Type A lunch with its five mandatory parts: protein, bread, two servings of vegetables or fruit, and milk. This meal formula was not used after 1979.

University and college foodservice has changed a great deal. In the early days of colleges, students received food and board from hostels run by a faculty member or the students themselves. Colonial colleges began providing residence halls and dining rooms for the students, which featured "family-style" meals where students were assigned to a table and plates of food were passed around among them.

When these institutions became interested in the German educational procedure, which did not include housing or feeding, many schools stopped providing food and board. Then, sororities and fraternities took on the responsibility of feeding and housing students who were members of their organizations. With the return of the GIs after World War II, schools began to emphasize more individualized eating with several smaller tables where students gathered without preassignment. When cafeteria-style service was developed it was quickly put into use in the nation's colleges. This provided a quick, easy method to feed growing numbers of students who might have varying class and work schedules and needed to set their own timetables.

Postsecondary and vocational schools continued to grow with over 6,000 such institutions currently. Some contract with for-profit management companies, others offer only vending machines or buffet options, and some provide students with an array of foodservice programs.

Health-Care Foodservice   The first hospital in the United States, Philadelphia General, opened in 1751 and it provided the basics in foodservice. The staff produced its own milk, butter, pork, and soap for use by the patients. The patient menu consisted of mush and molasses with oxtail soup and black bread on occasion—diet had yet to play a controlling part in hospital foodservice.

In 1854 Florence Nightingale began stressing the importance of a proper diet in a patient's recovery and became the first hospital dietitian. Hospitals in the United States took notice of the nutritive effects of a proper diet and implemented dietary regimens that would aid the patient's recovery. In 1917 Lulu Graves founded the American Dietetic Association. The association began to distribute information about proper nutrition and provided cooking classes for diabetic patients as they left the hospital so they would be able to prepare food at home in accordance with their diets. Hospital foodservice was decentralized in all but the very small health-care facilities half a century ago.

In 1934, Presbyterian Hospital in Chicago closed the ward kitchens and used a centralized tray service. The patients were no longer disturbed by the noise and smells from the ward kitchens. The trays were assembled in a central kitchen and then delivered to the patients. The first meal carts were not heated or refrigerated so that the meal was often hot when it was meant to be cold and vice versa. Over the years insulated containers in electrically refrigerated or heated carts were developed.

In the 1930s, all hospitals had diet kitchens and many different types of patient diets available. Stainless steel equipment was put into use in the late thirties. In the 1940s, frozen food was introduced to hospital kitchens. In the 1950s, Kaiser Hospitals in California developed the "kitchenless kitchen" method of feeding patients. They used frozen entrees which they heated and then served.

Most health-care facilities used to have separate dining rooms for staff and employees but this practice later gave way to one dining room for all with a cafeteria and vending machines.

Long-term care and maintenance-care facilities became distinct operations in 1935 when federal funds to pay for nursing home care were made available through the Social Security Act. Recognizing that mealtime interaction can be therapeutic, these facilities, and many hospitals, now have dining rooms for ambulatory patients and patients who use wheelchairs.

Today's health-care facilities include hospitals, long-term care facilities, intermediate-care facilities, and skilled-nursing units and all are primary users of the foodservice industry. The role diet plays in the recuperation and general health of the patients and residents is of utmost concern to health-care providers.

Employee Foodservice   Industrial or employee foodservice, another area of institutional foodservice, began in the 1800s as many employers began providing meals for their workers. In 1815 Robert Owen set aside a large storeroom where his workers and their families could eat, and in 1834 the Bowery Savings Bank of New York started an employee foodservice program. Banks were some of the earliest employers to offer foodservice to their employees.

Employees began selling food to other workers in the 1930s and soon others, not associated with the company, began selling food to employees. But employee foodservice did not really grow until after World War II, when manufacturing plants producing materials for the war discovered that nutritious, well-balanced meals helped keep their employees healthy and on the job. In 1955 the coffee machine was invented, adding vending possibilities to industrial foodservice.

Cafeterias were still popular with industrial foodservice providers in the early 1960s and 1970s. The single-serving lines could move employees through rapidly and provide them with a variety of food. Today, cafeterias are still present in some industrial foodservice programs, but cafes, elegant dining rooms and fast-food restaurants may also be available. Some offices have food courts with many different food chains represented as well as restaurants where employees may hold business lunches.

History of Military Foodservice

In the 1700s, an American soldier had to rely on himself for daily sustenance by hunting or scavenging for berries and other edibles. On November 4, 1775, Congress developed the first legislation covering army rations. There was a heavy concentration on meat, flour, and beans, but General George Washington's men were not rationed any vegetables, nor were any other soldiers for many years.

Many times during the early years of the military, troops suffered from malnutrition and drew close to starvation; Valley Forge and Yorktown are two examples. In an effort to alleviate the food shortages, several legislative acts were passed governing military rations, which were kept as simple as possible.

In early 1800, military personnel consulted with medical professionals on rationing requirements. One consultant drew their attention to the value of oranges and lemons for preventing scurvy and suggested fresh fruits should be used whenever possible. The War of 1812 again saw troops at the point of starvation, so Congress made a provision for contractors to supply troops with food. Unfortunately, this system did not function as it should have, and the troops still faced uncertain ration supply. In 1818 the President signed a bill that created the position of Commissary General to oversee the feeding of the troops.

During the middle 1800s, the canning process was brought to America from England and a canning plant was established in Boston. These advances, coupled with the development of a procedure for producing condensed or evaporated milk in 1856 by Gail Borden, helped the state of military foodservice.

In 1875, rations were again analyzed and improved by adding green vegetables, dried fruits, milk, and cheese to the provisions. Travel rations, which contained three meals to be carried along with other provisions, were given to soldiers in 1889. The Quartermaster Corps was created in 1912 and began implementing changes in the foodservice system. Cooking and baking schools were established and field bakeries and rolling kitchens began operating. The Surgeon General's Office had its Food Division research the military foodservice, and improvements were made based on the findings of these studies.

The technological improvements and advances in food preservation meant a big difference in the rations the soldiers in World War I received. These advancements continued with World War II, and rations were constantly being revamped.

The A, B, C, and D rations were developed in 1940. The contents of these ranged from the A ration, which was composed of as many fresh ingredients as possible, to the D field ration, which contained three four-ounce bars of concentrated chocolate.

Over time, the energy and nutritional requirements of the troops, as well as the environment in which they must work, was taken into consideration during ration development. The creation of radiation, freeze-drying, dehydration, concentrated products, and streamlined packaging have played a large part in the advancements in military feeding.

The National Restaurant Association

The National Restaurant Association has been involved in the growth of the foodservice industry since it was founded on March 13, 1919, in Kansas City, Missouri. The founders wanted to establish an organization to help solve common problems of restaurant owners, to make their voice heard to the federal government, and to develop guidelines for sanitation procedures and maintaining food purity. The association has maintained those basic aims over the years while developing many more to serve and support the foodservice community.

The organization has origins in two business groups, the Kansas City Restaurant Association and the National Association of Rotary Clubs. The Rotary Club provided the professional principles upon which the association was founded and the Kansas City Restaurant Association provided the organizational structure.

The association's first convention was on December 1, 1919. In the early 1930s Chicago was chosen as the association's headquarters, and attendance at the convention in 1937 broke a record at over 10,000 people.

In 1979 the association moved to Washington, D.C. Today, because of concern about government intrusion into business, the association has developed a strong lobbying arm in order to protect its membership against hostile legislation and regulation. It encourages grassroots participation by members, arranges meetings between operators and their representatives and senators, lobbies on Capitol Hill and disseminates information among its members about upcoming legislation that could affect them.

The Educational Foundation of the National Restaurant Association arranges conferences and seminars and provides educational materials and scholarships for persons involved in the foodservice industry and for students seeking careers in the hospitality field. The Educational Foundation provides college-level courses, home-study programs, and seminars. It also offers video training programs, which can aid a restaurant operator in designing a training program or supplement the one already used. This section of the association awards the industry's largest scholarship and grant program and is dedicated to promoting career opportunities and recruiting new employees.

Returning once a year to Chicago, the association sponsors the National Restaurant Association's Restaurant, Hotel-Motel Show. Since the 1937 convention, attendance records have continued to be broken with the most recent show registering over 100,000 people. The show provides an opportunity for those in the foodservice industry to discover the latest trends in food, equipment, and cooking techniques from exhibitors, seminars, lectures, and management clinics.

The Future of the Foodservice Industry

Consumers' life-styles often govern eating habits, which in turn affect the food-service industry. As the 76 million baby boomers age, they will switch their focus more toward their families. It is projected that 80 percent of this group will have children by 1995 and they will begin saving for their children's education and their own retirement. The highlight on homelife will spur supermarkets and convenience stores to produce nutritious, pre-prepared food for these consumers. Restaurants are expected to continue the shift toward more nutritious menu items and increased delivery and takeout facilities.

Those already in retirement and in the senior market will be spending more. The 50 and older age group will grow by 18.5 percent between 1990 and 2000. These patrons will seek a quality dining experience with an emphasis on nutrition. The health-care market will expand for foodservice operators as more day-care centers and home-health programs are created for the growing senior population.

Women will become even more of a force in foodservice trends as they enter the work force in increasing numbers and continue to raise families. Takeout and delivery services will grow and provide more high-quality and healthy food.

Other future concerns for the foodservice industry include labor shortages and environmental issues. The shortage of employees will cause a growth in labor-saving technology, increased use of computers, and more self-service operations. Employers may also turn more and more to the senior population in order to ease the lack of employees.

Until comprehensive community solid-waste programs become reality, waste disposal will be an important consideration of the foodservice industry. America's landfills are becoming full and soon waste will have to be transported at great cost to other disposal areas. Recycling and source reduction will play integral roles in the industry's waste management. Concern over air pollution and the use of pesticides in food growing is also predicted to rise in the future. Many industries, including the foodservice industry, will begin working more closely with the Environmental Protection Agency and other environmental groups to find solutions to these problems.

Summary

The restaurant and foodservice industry is large and growing, contributing nearly 5 percent to the nation's gross domestic product (GDP), employing 8.5 million people, and accounting for $.43 of each dollar Americans spend for their food. With the tremendous variety of foods that are prepared and the number of choices available as to the style of dining desired (fast-food outlets, coffee shops, table service restaurants, cafeterias, and so forth), all economic projections point to continued growth of the industry well into the twenty-first century.

As more Americans eat their meals away from home, or eat food that is prepared away from home but is carried or delivered to the home, "dining out" is becoming more entrenched in our activities each day. Currently, on any given day, 50 percent of the adult population of the United States consumes a meal away from home. From any perspective, the restaurant and foodservice industry is a vital and dynamic component of the economic, employment, and social fabric of the nation.

Bibliography

Bowman, Jack, and Bob Gift. March 1989. Continuing to do well. *Food Management,* pp. 138–144.

Carlino, Bill. March 20, 1989. The new grade of food service. *Nation's Restaurant News,* pp. 15–24.

Carlino, Bill. April 13, 1989. Now at bat . . . speciality foods. *Nation's Restaurant News,* pp. 7–8, 13.

Chabrunn, Karen. May 20, 1988. Foodservice management: Beth Israel Medical Center. *Restaurant Business,* p. 86.

Emerson, Robert L. 1982. *Fast Food: The Endless Shakeout.* New York: Chain Store Publishing Corp.

Feeding students an education. February 1990. *Food Management,* p. 91.

50th Anniversary Issue: 1937–1987. November 11, 1987. *Restaurants and Institutions.*

Harger, Virginia F., Grace S. Shugart, and June Payne-Palacio. 1988. *Foodservice in Institutions,* 6th ed. New York: MacMillan.

Hooker, Richard J. 1981. *Food and Drink in America: A History.* New York: Bobbs-Merrill.

How school F/S is performing. June 15, 1990. *Food Service Director,* p. 52.

Iverson, Kathleen M. 1989. *Introduction to Hospitality Management.* New York: Van Nostrand Reinhold.

Keegan, Peter O. February 19, 1990. Campus feeding. *Nation's Restaurant News,* pp. 27, 30, 32.

Khan, Mahmood A. 1991. *Concepts of Foodservice Operations and Management,* 2d ed. New York: Van Nostrand Reinhold.

King, Paul. March 1988. Making special concessions. *Food Management,* pp. 136–142, 147.

King, Paul. April 1990. Out and about: breaking new ground. *Food Management,* pp. 123–125.

Klein, Roberta. August 10, 1989. PI in the sky. *Restaurant Business,* pp. 96, 98.

Lattin, Gerald W. 1989. *The Lodging and Food Service Industry.* Michigan: The Educational Institute of the American Hotel and Motel Association.

Levenstein, Harvey. 1988. *Revolution at the Table: The Transformation of the American Diet.* New York: Oxford University Press.

Liddle, Alan. April 2, 1990. Ballpark contractors unveil new battery of food items. *Nation's Restaurant News,* pp. 27, 30.

Luxenberg, Stan. 1985. *Roadside Empires: How the Chains Franchised America.* New York: Viking Peguin.

Mrak, Emil M., 1987. "Feeding the Combat Soldier." Paper read at Founder's Day, commemoration of 25 years of Army Research and Development for the Combat Soldier, 7–8 December 1987, at Natick, Mass.

National Restaurant Association. 1989. Survey of Chain Operators (unpublished study). Washington, D.C.

The role of school lunch. July 1990. *Restaurants and Institutions,* pp. 161–162.

Sapienza, Dunnovan L., James R. Abbey, and Jerome J. Vallen. 1977. *Readings on Managing Hotels/Restaurants/Institutions.* Rochelle Park, N.J.: Hayden Book Co.

75 years of foodservice history. May 1976. *Restaurant Business.*

Stephenson, Susie. May 13, 1988. Restaurant meals provide therapy too. *Restaurants and Institutions,* pp. 159, 161.

Tannahill, Reay. 1988. *Food in History.* New York: Crown Publishers.

Townsend, Rob. May 16, 1990. Self-serving attitudes pay off in cafeterias. *Restaurants and Institutions,* pp. 143, 146.

VanEgmond-Pannell, Dorothy. 1985. *School Foodservice.* 3d ed. Westport, Conn.: AVI Publishing.

Walkup, Carolyn. December 1989. Office-building restaurants doing big lunch business. *Nation's Restaurant News.*

Walkup, Carolyn. September 3, 1990. National school lunch program offers an education in nutrition. *Nation's Restaurant News*, pp. 25, 28.

Warner, Mickey. 1973. *Industrial Foodservice and Cafeteria Management*. Boston, Mass.: Cahners Publishing Co.

Whitcomb, Mildred. September 1963. How foodservice has changed in 50 years. *Modern Hospital*, pp. 163, 165.

2

Market Feasibility

Audrey C. McCool

The term *feasibility* refers to how practical a project or an idea is or how easily an objective might be accomplished. When considering a potential foodservice project—whether that project is developing a new restaurant, purchasing an existing property, changing the focus or direction of an existing restaurant, or bidding on a foodservice management contract—a marketing feasibility study must be completed prior to making the "go–no go" decision regarding the project.

The objective of a comprehensive marketing feasibility study is to determine whether the market potential is appropriate for a proposed project. The study is similar to a market research project in many ways and must be completed prior to the completion of a financial feasibility study that would be the basis for the final "go–no go" decision on the project. Essentially the market feasibility study should ask these questions: (1) Is there a market for this business in this area? (2) If so, how extensive is this market? and (3) What is the potential for capitalizing on this market at this location?

To answer these questions, a complete market feasibility study consists of the following components.

1. An analysis of the current market and the growth potential of the market area
2. An assessment of the potential site(s)
3. An analysis of the competition (both direct and indirect) relative to the total market potential
4. A determination of the facility concept (including type and size) that would best satisfy market demand

Ultimately, the decision regarding the project is based on the financial feasibility or the project's projected ability to generate a profit and provide a return to owners or investors on the funds they invest in the project. The comprehensive market feasibility study provides the data base for many of the estimates considered in the financial feasibility analysis.

Market Analysis

The location for a foodservice facility must be evaluated on the basis of the potential access it affords the operator to customers. The population available as potential customers must be described in such characteristics as population demographics, employment statistics, and major employers in the area. It is necessary to examine the market potential of the current population, but it is necessary to evaluate the future market, as well, if the market feasibility study is to be complete.

Trading Area

Generally a foodservice facility draws its customers from a particular geographic area, called the *trading area* for that operation. The size of a facility's trading area varies markedly. It may range from only the clientele of a particular organization housing the foodservice facility (that is, the children attending a particular school and eating in the school cafeteria) to a one- to three-mile radius that often defines the trading area for a fast-food facility or a family style restaurant. It may even extend to a 30- to 40-mile radius or more for a fine dining facility with an exceptional menu or an unusual and attractive location.

The trading area is usually divided into primary and secondary areas with the primary area generating at least 50 percent of the facility's business. Generally, unless the operation is located in or near a major traffic-generating location, such as a shopping mall or a hotel, about 50 percent of the foodservice's revenue will be generated by the population that is within a one-mile radius of the property. When preparing a market analysis for an existing property, the trading area can be determined from studies of the current patrons. A good approach for this analysis is to ask customers where they were just prior to coming to the foodservice facility and plotting their responses on a map of the area. In a new facility, however, it must be estimated from studies of the patrons of other operations.

Population Demographics

Once the trading area has been defined, the demographics, or the characteristics, of the population within that area must be identified and analyzed. The products and services offered by the foodservice facility must match the wants and expectations of the potential customers within the trading area if the operation is to be successful. Demographic data that should be collected for the study includes

1. Average age of the population
2. Average family size
3. Disposable income level
4. Educational levels
5. Ethnic backgrounds
6. Housing density
7. Housing values
8. Population density
9. Ratio of homeowners to renters
10. Ratio of males to females
11. Ratio of marrieds to singles
12. Types of housing
13. Types of occupations
14. Types of religions
15. Unemployment statistics
16. Types of employment

Neighborhood Descriptors

Many features of the neighborhood surrounding the proposed project site can significantly impact the market potential. Such features can also be important influences on the type of operation that would be successful in this trading area. Examples of these features include the following items:

Population Base Diversity and Stability. It may be difficult to find a product base that will be attractive to the required number of customers if the surrounding population is composed of very diverse ethnic groups, for example. Also, in a neighborhood that is experiencing rapid change, a popular concept today may be quickly rejected by the new population making the potential success of the foodservice facility short-lived. A stable, reasonably homogeneous population represents the most desirable population base.

The Neighborhood Appearance.   The appearance of the neighborhood may give some indication of the amount of discretionary funds available to the area population. Discretionary funds are the dollars persons have "left over" after paying for their fixed commitments such as rent or mortgage and utilities. These funds are available for them to spend as they wish, including for the purchase of food prepared outside the home. A neat, well kept neighborhood may indicate a population base with sufficient discretionary income to support a foodservice establishment.

Other Area Businesses and Activities.   The presence of other businesses or activities in the area is an indication of the type and amount of traffic flow that might be expected. Facilities such as retail shopping centers, athletic, cultural, or entertainment centers, and office or wholesale centers may bring potential customers to the trading area. In many instances, these businesses and activities may complement the products and services offered by the foodservice establishment.

Public Institutions.   Public institutions also influence the customer traffic in a trading area and should be considered in the market analysis. Public institutions are facilities such as schools, day care centers, colleges and universities, governmental services and buildings, and military bases. Public institutions not only influence the volume of customer traffic in the area, but they may also significantly determine many of the characteristics, such as age, educational background, or leisure time interests, of the potential customer population.

Psychographics   Psychographic considerations are those that picture the personality characteristics of the population. These considerations may also reflect the psychological factors that affect the population's behavior patterns. For example, considerations of concern to the market analysis would be the lifestyles of the trading area population and that population's spending patterns.

Much information is required for the market analysis as well as for the subsequent phases of the market feasibility study, and it is available from a variety of sources. Figure 1 lists some of the many sources that might be used to generate the statistics and other information needed for this study.

Environmental Scanning

Today's market environment is highly competitive and in a constant state of change. Yesterday's idea may be obsolete before it is fully implemented. "Today, looking ahead means reading the environment, understanding that change is constant, and developing the product that anticipates the needs and wants of the consumer." (Lewis and Chambers 1989:84) When collecting data for the market analysis, one cannot collect only the data that characterizes the trading area at the present time. Data must also be collected that will provide information regarding the future development of the area. For example, is there evidence of a new subdevelopment or a new shopping center? Is there a possibility that a new highway will be built bisecting the trading area in the next five to ten years?

Fig. 1. Data sources for market feasibility studies.
(Data from Stefanelli 1990; National Restaurant Association 1983.)

Reports from federal agencies such as the Bureau of the Census or the Department of Commerce

Reports from state and local agencies—commerce departments, economic development commission, zoning commission, business license bureau, county recorder, transportation department

Public libraries or area college and university libraries

Utility companies

Local newspaper files and reports

Local businesses such as mall or office building managers, real estate firms, foodservice purveyors, advertising agencies, billboard advertising firms, and media firms

Chamber of commerce

Convention, tourism, and visitors bureau

Industry publications

Research services of industry trade associations

University research institutes

Direct surveys of current and/or potential customers

Syndicated services that provide demographic and psychographic data

Tax authorities

State department of motor vehicles

Architects and construction contractors

Current owner of foodservice operation and existing key employees

Consultants and private research companies

Types of Environments

Changes could occur in one or more of several different environments surrounding the foodservice operation. These environments include the technological, political, economic, and sociocultural environments.

The Technological Environment.   The development of computers is an example of an advancement in the technological environment that has had a major impact on the operation and profitability of foodservice facilities. The many rapid advances in technology that impact the types of food products available, food preparation methods, and ordering and service procedures, as well as the consumers' expectations make the technological environment the most fluid of all the surrounding environments that might affect future market demand.

The Political Environment.   Political trends can have tremendous impact on a foodservice firm in terms of regulatory requirements, taxation, labor laws, and the stability of the operating environment. Examples of such impacts are the variances in requirements for sanitation inspections, minimum wage laws, and tip reporting requirements. The market analysis must consider trends appearing in the political environment and estimate how these trends might be reflected later in laws and regulations.

The Economic Environment.   Future economic trends such as recession periods, inflation, varying employment levels, personal income, and savings rates—to name a few—must be predicted and considered. The economic environment is closely related to the availability of discretionary income, and the environmental scan should indicate ways for the firm to capitalize on anticipated economic trends.

The Sociocultural Environment.   Foodservice establishments are entwined with the social and cultural practices of the populations they serve. Failure to adequately consider trends and changes in this area can be devastating for a facility. Examples of recent changes that have had significant impact on foodservice operations include the high proportions of two-income families and single person families as well as the increasing numbers of women traveling and eating out alone.

Steps in the Scanning Process   Environmental scanning and the subsequent development of long-range predictions regarding the trading area involves the following steps:

1. Watching for broad trends. Examples of recent trends include the changes in alcoholic beverage drinking patterns and the consumers' concerns with health and nutritional foods.

2. Determining which trends are relevant to the proposal. Not everything that happens in the environment is necessarily relevant to the particular foodservice operation under study.

3. Analyzing the impact of the change(s) in one or more of the environments. When an observed or anticipated trend seems relevant, the possible impact of that change, in both the short and long term, must be considered. Questions must be answered regarding the potential change's impact on the facility's product, price structure, target market, product cost, and employee attitude—to name only a few of the factors to be considered.

4. Predicting the direction of trends and changes in the future. Opportunities that might be developed for the firm as a result of these future developments should be identified and assessed. The outcomes of this scanning process are incorporated into the overall market analysis for the feasibility study.

Site Analysis

The selection of a good site within the trading area is critical. Ellsworth Statler, founder of the Statler Hotel chain, once said: "There are three factors necessary for the success of a hotel. They are location, location, and location" (Powers 1990:154) The same premise should be applied to the evaluation of a site for a foodservice operation. As Stefanelli (1990) has noted, the selection of a good location will not guarantee success, but the selection of a poor location will almost guarantee failure.

Firms today should consider the different types of locations available when selecting a site. The options available include the traditional freestanding site where the foodservice operation "stands alone." The firm is an individual operation not related to, or specifically relying on, any of the surrounding businesses or activities.

A second option that is becoming very popular with many different types of foodservices is location within another type of unit, such as a shopping mall or an office building. Persons coming to the host unit for other purposes provide a potential customer base that the foodservice establishment may be able to capitalize on. Thus, the firm may reduce its promotional costs while maintaining a steady customer base.

A third option that has also shown recent success is that of co-location.

Here a company pairs up with another noncompetitive foodservice operation or with another type of retail operation. Examples of these types of locations are an outlet of a cookie chain pairing with an ice cream outlet or a fast-food facility co-locating with a convenience store. Again, the foodservice facility anticipates increased customer traffic because of the traffic generated by the other firm with which it is paired.

When assessing the proposed site, consideration should be given to the volume of both pedestrian and automobile traffic in the area and to the proximity of both competitors and demand generators. Demand generators are facilities or activities that would encourage potential customers to come to the site as noted in the previous discussion of neighborhood descriptors.

It may be helpful to begin the site analysis by carefully studying the map of the trading area. Some of the characteristics that should be identified and analyzed are noted.

Major Traffic Arteries
The major thoroughfares, one-way streets, actual and effective speed limits, stop sign and traffic light locations, number of lanes in each street, median barriers, left turn lanes, traffic counts, ratio of commuter traffic to leisure traffic, proposed road alterations, and new road developments must be identified. Depending on the type of foodservice establishment, it may be important to determine the primary direction of the traffic flow at various times during the day. For example, a fast-food operation wanting to capitalize on the demand for dinner carry-out orders would want to be located so that the homebound traffic could make a right turn into the facility while an operation stressing breakfast service would want to be accessible to the inbound traffic flow. Fine dining facilities are concerned with the quality of the traffic flow as well as the quantity. A high volume of truck traffic, for example, would probably not yield customers interested in fine dining although such traffic may be excellent for a fast-food establishment.

Major Destinations
Major destinations include areas such as shopping malls, office buildings, or government installations. Potential customers are attracted to these points for other purposes and may then be enticed to patronize a conveniently located foodservice facility.

Direct Competitors
Direct competitors are the foodservice establishments that most closely resemble the project under consideration. They are the companies most likely to be focusing on the same market segment. Two fast-food outlets within three blocks of the proposed site would be direct competitors for a proposed new fast-food facility. The analysis must identify the location of all these competitors and the accessibility of those locations to the potential customers relative to the characteristics of the proposed site. This analysis will help to determine the potential impact of these direct competitors on the availability of trading area customers to the proposed project.

Indirect Competitors
The identification of indirect competitors is difficult. These competitors include the foodservice facilities competing for trading area customers that differ from the project under study in terms of the products and services offered, menu prices, appearance, and other operational factors. An employees' cafeteria in an office building, a family restaurant, and a fine dining restaurant may all be indirect competitors of a proposed fast-food facility. Nonfoodservice retailers may also be included in this category. For example, persons working in an office building may choose to shop in nearby stores

at noon rather than eat lunch. The retail shops, then, become indirect competitors for these persons' discretionary dollars.

The availability of a public transportation system must be considered. If such a system is available, a number of factors that would affect the flow of potential customers must be considered, including

1. Frequency of use by trading area residents
2. Frequency of use by persons outside the trading area
3. Proximity of stops to the proposed site
4. Frequency of scheduled runs
5. Cost to ride the system
6. System connections to and from the trading area
7. Public perception of the overall quality of the system
8. Ratio of public transportation to private transportation

A good public transportation network may be important when considering the availability of labor resources as well as for bringing potential customers to the site. Employees of foodservice establishments frequently do not live in the immediate area where they can readily get to the facility. If they do not have a personal automobile or they cannot drive for any number of reasons, some form of public transportation is necessary for their employment with the proposed firm.

Geographical Barriers Geographical barriers include both natural and artificial barriers that tend to restrict customer movement. People generally tend to conduct business and seek their leisure activities on one side of a geographical barrier unless something very attractive on the other side induces them to cross the barrier. Examples of such barriers include rivers, major highways, large real estate developments, dead-end streets, canyons, and schools. Direct and indirect competitors can sometimes function as geographical barriers as they can divert a customer who originally intended to visit a foodservice operation.

Social Barriers Social barriers may significantly affect potential customer traffic flows. People will not enter or cross areas where they do not feel comfortable. Examples of social barriers include industrial areas, slums or areas thought to have high crime rates, extremely affluent residential areas, and areas with congested traffic.

Size of the Site In the case of a new development or a proposal for a major renovation of an existing property, the site must be large enough to accommodate the building required to support the anticipated capacity as well as provide appropriate space for parking and other facilities, such as external storage areas, that may be required. If the project includes possible future expansion plans, space must be available for that as well.

Planning and Zoning Regulations This consideration is particularly important for new developments or major changes in the focus of an existing property. Project development is greatly facilitated if the site is already zoned for the proposed use for the project under consideration. Any possible zoning changes that may be required must be identified in the study, and the feasibility of getting such changes approved in the local political structure must be evaluated. Sometimes securing the necessary zoning changes can be very costly in terms of both time and money.

Site Visibility Good visibility can often provide an operation with a significant competitive advantage. Visibility is particularly important if the facility is located near a highway interchange or on a busy street with rapid traffic flow. In the case of a highway location, the facility, or its signage, should be visible from a sufficient distance to enable drivers to take the appropriate highway exit. On a busy street with congested signage for many retail outlets, the signage must stand out and be visible to drivers in time to allow them to get into the correct lane to make the appropriate turn into the operation's parking lot.

Site Topography Concern here is with the surface features of the site. Consideration should be given to the positioning of the building, particularly if the site is sloped. Where appropriate, the building should be positioned to take best advantage of the primary traffic flow, to enhance its visibility to potential customers, and to minimize the construction costs of access roads or entries from the street. Any required physical changes to the site, such as grading or landfills, should be identified. Soil tests should be made to identify the type of construction that can be supported. Consideration should also be given to the vegetation and the landscaping that will be required as well as to the types of vegetation that will flourish in the surrounding environment.

Land Costs A potential site may be eliminated from further consideration because of excessive costs. The base cost of the land or the lease cost for a site within another unit along with all related costs such as real estate tax charges, cost of licenses and permits, history of property appreciation, and the costs for improvements must be considered.

Taking the time to do a thorough analysis of the possible site options is imperative for the success of a project. A good site will not guarantee success, but a poor site will be very hard to overcome and is usually a major factor in a foodservice establishment's failure.

Analysis of the Competition

A thorough analysis of both direct and indirect competition must be completed. This analysis must consider such factors as

1. The type of establishment each competitor is operating
2. The ratio of direct to indirect competitors
3. The length of time the competitor has been in business
4. The attrition rate for new operations in this area
5. Ownership changes that have occurred for existing firms
6. The percentage of competitors who own their properties versus those who are franchise affiliates
7. Number of competitive properties for sale
8. Estimated number of future competitors
9. Quality of competitors' facilities—level of maintenance as well as original design quality
10. Distances of all competitors from the proposed project site
11. Operating factors such as seating capacities, seat turnover rates, check averages, estimated total sales volume, hours of operation, menus, menu prices, styles of service
12. Parking facilities
13. Drive-through, carry-out, and home delivery capability
14. Potential for nonfoodservice firms to be indirect competitors

The presence of competition (both direct and indirect) is not necessarily bad. A competitor's success may be an excellent indicator of the market potential of a site. What is important is consideration of the total volume of the market available in the trading area. The market must be large enough to continue to support the existing competition as well as the new, proposed operation.

The extent of the market support available can be calculated by the procedure outlined in Figure 2. If the net market support is positive, that figure can then be used to determine the number and size of new foodservice operations that would be feasible in this market. If the net market support is negative, there is already excess capacity in the market, and the proposed project would only be feasible *if* it could be reasonably expected to take a portion of the market away from existing competitors. When calculating the market support of a trading area, it is important to include any known facilities that are currently under development or that have been proposed as these facilities will also absorb some of the identified market potential.

The calculated market support of an area does not necessarily represent the sales level of the proposed project. The study must also determine the project's ability to capture its fair market share of the available demand. Fair market share may be defined as the ratio of the size of a proposed project in relation to the total competitive supply. For example, if the project under study represents one fifth of the total trading area's food services supply (as measured in seats or square footage), then the project's fair market share would be twenty percent of the possible customer base.

Fig. 2. Procedure for calculating available market support.
(*Data from Powers 1990:162–164.*)

P = Estimated population of the trading area

E = Trading area population's estimated per capita expenditure for food services

G = Gross estimated demand for food services within the trading area

L = Trading area leakage (population that goes outside its trading area)

O = Estimated dollar amount spent on food services outside the trading area by the trading area population

I = Estimated dollar amount spent on trading area food services by persons living outside the trading area

D = Net estimated demand for food services within the trading area

S = Average sales for individual trading area restaurants (estimated on facility's average sales per chair or per square foot)

N = number of food service facilities in the trading area

T = total food service sales in the trading area

M = Net market support available in the trading area

U = Number of additional food service facilities supportable by the trading area

Step 1. $G = P \times E$
Step 2. $L = O - I$
Step 3. $D = G - L$
Step 4. $T = S \times N$ (or $T = S$)
Step 5. $M = D - T$
Step 6. $U = M/S$

Facility Concept Determination

The information provided through the preceding steps should now form the basis for defining the concept of the proposed foodservice facility. A concept is "a combination of ideas that forms the foundation for a particular type of restaurant operation" (National Restaurant Association 1983:83). It includes factors such as the size, seating capacity, proposed menu, style of service, operating hours, atmosphere, and pricing structure. This concept should be developed in writing to facilitate visualizing the proposal relative to the developed market perspective.

By this point in the market feasibility study, the facility concept should be seen as a good one for the market area. Thus, the development of a written concept helps to define a project that is specifically oriented toward meeting local demand while optimizing the facility's profit potential. Since the facility concept integrates much of the data and many of the considerations of the earlier phases of the market feasibility study, it will become the basis for the preparation of developmental cost estimates as well as the development of the financial feasibility study.

Contract Foodservice Considerations

Market feasibility considerations for contract foodservice firms (foodservice management firms) are a special application of many of the concepts considered here. Contract foodservice firms are in the business of managing and operating foodservice facilities located within other organizations (parent firms) whose primary purpose is not the service of food and beverage. However, these foodservices are a requirement for the other organization (for example, a hospital or a prison) or would complement the activities of the other organization (for example, an office complex, sports arena, or amusement park).

The contracting firm usually acquires the right to operate the foodservice for the parent firm through a competitive bidding process. When considering whether to bid on, or to solicit, a possible contract, several factors should be considered by the foodservice management firm.

Size of the Institution, Organization, or Activity

Managing any foodservice operation requires at least some investment by the contracting firm even if all physical facilities and some payroll costs are provided by the parent firm. The size of the parent operation must be large enough to support the needed investment.

Opportunity to Expand the Range of Services or Add Other Contracts

If the initial operation is small, but represents a highly desirable location for the contracting firm, consideration should be given to possible expansion of the range of services that could be provided later or to the establishment of an initial base contract from which other contracts could be developed with other organizations at a later time. Even if the size of the initial contract is desirable, possible opportunities for other contracts in the market area should be explored and considered in the decision-making process regarding the contract opportunity under study.

Corporate Support Structure

The availability of needed corporate support structure, such as a regional or area office or personnel, in a nearby corporate contract operation must be considered. A comprehensive corporate support structure in an area means that a range of expertise is available to support a contract and may significantly reduce the size of a feasible operation. However, if there is no, or limited support available and the contracting firm must consider the development of a new market area as a part of the bidding process, other features of the contract must outweigh these additional development and continued support costs.

Type of Client to Be Served   The client offering the contract should be compatible with the service objectives and standards of the contracting firm. A partnership is the best relationship between the foodservice contractor and the parent firm. When the two partners have the same type of customer interests, the relationship is likely to work well and lead to a long-term, positive working relationship.

Once the contract potential has been surveyed in terms of these factors, the data collected must be integrated into a financial feasibility analysis. As indicated in the discussion of the general market feasibility study, the final "go–no go" decision regarding a contract opportunity under consideration is made on the basis of the findings of the financial feasibility analysis—a process that follows the completion of the market feasibility study.

Summary

Market feasibility analysis is a critical step toward the successful implementation of a potential foodservice project. A careful feasibility analysis draws together information on the market potential and that market's characteristics; the market environment; the site—its characteristics along with its strengths and weaknesses; and both the direct and indirect competition the project will face. Such information is essential for fully defining the concept of a proposed foodservice facility or for helping a contract firm make a decision regarding possible contract opportunity.

Without such information, project planning is based on intuition, invalidated assumptions, and guesswork, an inappropriate basis for project investment decisions today. The carefully completed market feasibility analysis may be the critical factor that determines the success or failure of a proposed project. As such, it should be given high-priority consideration in project development planning. For success, the planner must know the market, locate the appropriate site, understand the competition, and develop a competitive concept appropriate for the market needs at that site.

References

Lewis, R. C., and R. E. Chambers. 1989. *Marketing Leadership in Hospitality.* New York: Van Nostrand Reinhold.

National Restaurant Association. 1983. *Conducting a Feasibility Study for a New Restaurant.* Washington, D.C.: National Restaurant Association.

Powers, T. F. 1990. *Marketing Hospitality.* New York: John Wiley.

Stefanelli, J. 1990. *The Sale and Purchase of Restaurants.* New York: John Wiley.

Bibliography

Birchfield, J. C. 1988. *Design and Layout of Foodservice Facilities.* New York: Van Nostrand Reinhold.

Kazarian, E. A. 1988. *Foodservice Facilities Planning,* 3d ed. New York: Van Nostrand Reinhold.

Lundberg, D. E. 1989. *The Hotel and Restaurant Business,* 5th ed. New York: Van Nostrand Reinhold.

Marescotti, M. 1987. Cutting through the mystique of feasibility studies. *Foodservice and Hospitality* 20(2):84, 86.

McGuigan, R. 1987. Set your sights high when choosing a site. *Foodservice and Hospitality* 20(8):50, 52.

Rushmore, S. 1986. *How to Perform an Economic Feasibility Study of a Proposed Hotel/Motel.* Chicago: American Society of Real Estate Counselors of the National Association of Realtors.

Scanlon, N. L. 1990. *Marketing by Menu,* 2d ed. New York: Van Nostrand Reinhold.

3

Foodservice Operations Management

Peter Jones

A striking feature of the foodservice industry is just how many different types of foodservice operations there are. Customers are served food and meals almost anywhere they care to be—shopping malls, airplanes, hospitals, offices and factories, on the highway, in schools, and so on. This diversity raises interesting questions for the potential foodservice manager—just how different are these operations? If you can manage one type of restaurant can you also manage any other? Or would you have to learn whole new ways of doing things?

One of the best ways to examine the similarities and differences between foodservice operations is to analyze them as "systems." Systems analysis examines the exact nature of the interactions and processes that occur in any operation. Once the foodservice system is understood it is then possible to identify key issues that all operations managers face and relate these to the different systems.

In service industries such operations have been termed *service delivery systems* (SDS). A service delivery system has been defined (Pickworth 1988) as an "operation in which products/services are created and delivered to the customer almost simultaneously." In this case we are concerned about one specific kind of SDS, the foodservice delivery system (FDS). Some foodservice delivery systems can be identified as "dedicated." That is to say it is a FDS "which is designed to produce a specific range of menu items." Pickworth uses the example of fast-food chains. However in other cases, an FDS can be "multifaceted," so that it is a FDS "which is able to produce and serve a broad range of menu items." Thus in a dedicated FDS the expectation is that there would be one specific system, whereas in a multifaceted operation there may exist more than one specific system operating together. Multifaceted FDS may be found in hotels, hospitals, institutional foodservice, and so on.

Such service delivery systems are designed to carry out the basic function of changing *inputs*, principally food, through *processes*, such as cooking and serving, into desirable *outputs*, or meals. This system can be modeled as in Figure 1. The best way to analyze such systems is to look at the flow of raw materials.

Fig. 1. Basic systems model.

INPUTS ── PROCESSES ── OUTPUTS

The Traditional Foodservice System

The traditional foodservice system originated in large hotels in the late nineteenth century. This operation was based on inputs that comprised predominantly fresh raw materials processed by a large number of specialist personnel working in a production area or kitchen located as near to the service point as possible. Such an operation comprised eight distinct stages:

1. Storage—refrigerated or ambient storage of materials
2. Preparation—activities such as peeling, cutting, and so forth
3. Production (cooking)—methods such as frying, roasting, and so forth
4. Holding—storage between production and consumption
5. Service—style of delivering dishes/meals to consumers
6. Dining—consumption of meal by consumer in setting
7. Clearing—removal of equipment/food debris
8. Dishwash—cleansing of soiled equipment

The first four of these stages and the final stage occur back-of-house, that is to say out of sight and contact with the customer. The remaining three stages take place in the dining area. These eight stages have been illustrated (Cutliffe 1971) as shown in Figure 2. This shows a highly interactive system, with the back-of-house area shaded. Thus the basic FDS can be broken down into two subsystems conventionally identified as the food production system (back-of-house) and the foodservice system. The former is largely concerned with the preparation of food and beverage products into a state ready for consumption, and the latter is the methods used to deliver these products to

Fig. 2. Flow process chart of the traditional foodservice system. *(Source: G. Cutliffe, Analysing Catering Operations, 1971. London: Edward Arnold.)*

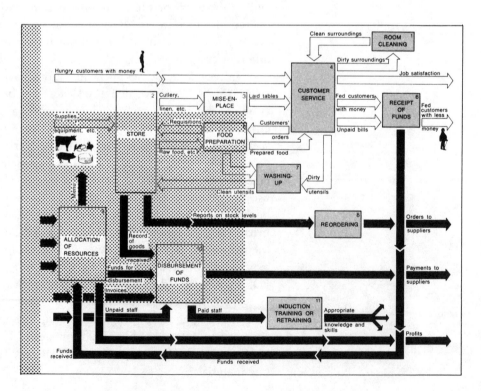

the consumer and restore the system to a state of readiness for the next consumer. Within these two main subsystems exist more specific subsystems, each designed for a single stage of the total process.

The complex model in Figure 2 can be simplified and be drawn as a flow diagram (Cousins and Foskett 1989). When the basic, traditional FDS is modeled in this way three alternative configurations emerge, essentially in the production system, as shown in Figure 3. Food can be cooked with or without preparation, it can be held prepared or cooked, or it can be served immediately after cooking or after holding.

Typically, à la carte menu items are served immediately after cooking. This system is sometimes called the *call order system*, which we shall call (A). Likewise, the *table d'hote* menu usually comprises dishes prepared in advance and held for a period of time before service (B). Where food is served without cooking, this is the *buffet* foodservice system (C).

(A) Storage–Preparation–Cooking–Service–Dining–Clearing–Dishwash
(B) Storage–Preparation–Cooking–Holding–Service–Dining–Clearing–Dishwash
(C) Storage–Preparation–Holding–Service–Dining–Clearing–Dishwash

These three systems are dedicated service delivery systems that derive from analyzing in detail the traditional FDS. But as Pickworth has suggested, there are very few "dedicated" systems. However so long as the majority of inputs flow through the FDS in the specific way identified then it can be considered as dedicated. It has been proposed (Huelin and Jones 1990) that the Pareto principle should be applied. Within each of these different FDS, at least 80 percent of the raw materials should flow through the system in the sequence of stages specified. However, up to 20 percent of raw materials may well follow other routes, bypassing some stages, going through additional stages, or following a different sequence.

Innovations in Foodservice Systems

Over the last one hundred years, there have been innovations that have enabled this basic model of three systems to be modified in a number of significant ways. There have been major changes in the *supply of raw materials* both in terms of increased shelf life (freezing, canning, and so on) and state of preparation (semiprepared, convenience products, fully finished products,

Fig. 3. Flow diagram of traditional foodservice delivery systems.
(Source: Adapted from Alan Huelin and Peter Jones, Foodservice systems: Generic types, alternative technology and infinite variation, Journal of Foodservice Systems 5(4), p. 303, 1990.)

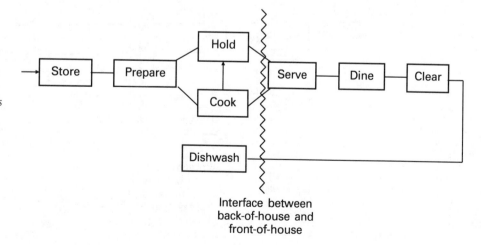

and so on). This now enables the complete avoidance of preparation and cooking stages back-of-house with the introduction of fully pre-prepared meals.

The second major innovation is at the *holding stage*. The introduction of cook-chill, cook-freeze and sous-vide technologies have extended the period of time that food can be held between the production stages and the service stages. In the case of cook-chill, individual dishes or meals are chilled to 3° C to be held in refrigerated storage for up to five days. Cook-freeze enables storage of meal products for up to three months. Sous-vide also entails chilling foods, as well as vacuum-packing the prepared dishes in sealed bags. This extends the shelf life to about twenty-one days.

These three innovations have made possible *decoupling*. This means that the two distinct areas of back-of-house and dining area do not need to be physically located next to each other. Also, quite clearly, food produced back-of-house is no longer consumed straight away, as is the case in the three FDS identified so far (A, B, and C).

Where these modern raw materials or technologies are used, there is the need for an additional stage of *regeneration* to be included. This stage takes the food from its purchased, chilled, or frozen state to make the food ready to eat. Secondly, where meals or dishes held in these ways are to be served in locations away from the point of production, there now also needs to be a *transportation* stage between holding and regeneration.

These two new stages can be added to the traditional eight to make a potential ten stage flow of raw materials through the system, illustrated in Figure 4, as follows:

Storage	Regeneration
Preparation	Service
Production (cooking)	Dining
Holding	Clearing
Transportation	Dishwash

Fig. 4. Flow diagram of modern foodservice delivery systems. *(Source: Adapted from Alan Huelin and Peter Jones, Foodservice systems: Generic types, alternative technology and infinite variation, Journal of Foodservice Systems 5(4), p. 304, 1990.)*

Ten Stages and Ten Dedicated FDS

Not all of these ten stages are necessarily present in all foodservice systems, nor are they necessarily discrete one from the other. An analysis of foodservice systems found in the industry suggests that these innovations have added

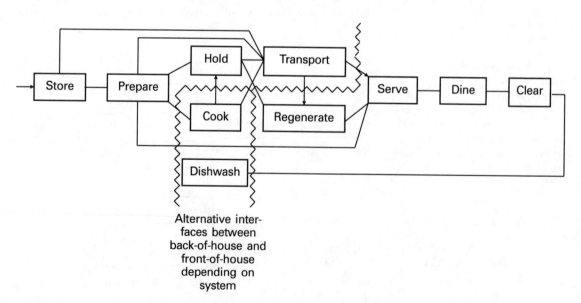

Alternative interfaces between back-of-house and front-of-house depending on system

a further seven new dedicated systems to the three already identified. These seven new *dedicated* service delivery systems are as follows:

- (D) Storage–Preparation–Cooking–Holding–Transport–Regeneration–Service–Dining–Clearing–Dishwash
- (E) Storage–Cooking–Holding–Transport–Regeneration–Service–Dining–Clearing–Dishwash
- (F) Storage–Cooking–Holding–Service–Dining–Clearing–Dishwash
- (G) Storage–Preparation–Cooking–Holding–Service–Dining–Clearing
- (H) Storage–Preparation–Cooking–Holding–Transport–Regeneration–Service–Dining–Clearing
- (I) Storage–Regeneration–Service–Dining–Clearing–Dishwash
- (J) Storage–Preparation–Cooking–Dining–Clearing–Dishwash

Each of the ten different dedicated FDS matches quite specific types of food-service operation, as follows:

A. Conventional à la carte restaurant using fresh commodities cooked to order
B. Conventional restaurant using fresh commodities cooked in advance
C. Foodservice outlet serving only uncooked foods, for example, buffet, sandwich bar
D. Conventional à la carte restaurants using fresh commodities and sous-vide
E. Conventional restaurants/cafeterias using convenience commodities and cook-chill
F. Conventional restaurant or cafeteria using convenience commodities served to order
G. Fast-food outlet
H. In flight foodservice
I. Restaurant/cafeteria/store buying all fully prepared meals from supplier
J. Japanese steakhouse concept using hibachi tables

To demonstrate that these FDS are really different from each other, it is possible to identify objective criteria for distinguishing the key features of food-service systems. Such criteria include type of raw materials used, inventory size, product range width and depth, capacity, production batch sizes, and flexibility (see Table 1). As one would expect, when analyzed each dedicated system has a unique combination of these criteria.

Key Issues

It has been suggested (Thompson 1967) that the ideal operation to manage would be one where "the market will absorb a single product at a continuous rate and as if the inputs flowed continously at a steady rate and with specified quality." In almost every case, every dedicated FDS does not match this ideal case. In the traditional systems (A, B, and C) there is a wide product range (menu) delivered noncontinuously (in response to customer orders) using inputs erratically with potentially variable quality (since cooking is an "art" rather than science). But the innovations in the design of FDS have shifted modern foodservice systems toward matching this ideal more closely. For instance, fast food has a greatly reduced product range (menu) thereby nearly having a "single product," and cook-chill and other technologies enable the batch production of food thereby creating a more continuous flow of production.

Table 1. *Comparison of characteristics of dedicated FDS*

	Raw materials type	Inventory size	Product range depth	Product range width	Capacity	Batch size	Flexibility
A	Fresh	High	High	High	Low	Low	High
B	Fresh	High	High	High	High	High	High
C	Fresh	High	High	Low	Low	Low	High
D	Fresh	High	High	High	Low	High	High
E	Convenience	High	High	High	High	High	High
F	Convenience	High	High	High	High	Low	High
G	Convenience	High	Low	Low	High	Low	Low
H	Fresh	High	Low	High	High	High	High
I	Convenience	Low	Low	Low	High	Low	Low
J	Fresh	Low	Low	Low	Low	Low	Low

One analysis (Jones 1988) proposes the difference between Thompson's ideal model and the majority of foodservice operations gives rise to three key issues in managing effective systems—productivity, capacity, and quality. These can be matched to the basic concept of the FDS as in Figure 5.

Productivity

Productivity is measured in terms of the level of output achieved by a given level of inputs. This definition of productivity is simple to state but complex to apply in the context of service industries in general, and the foodservice industry in particular. There are several problems. First, there are a very *large number* and *variety* of inputs/outputs that occur in the daily operation of

Fig. 5. Model of foodservice operations system and key result areas.
(Source: Peter Jones, Quality, capacity and productivity in service industries, International Journal of Hospitality Management 7(2), p. 107, 1988).

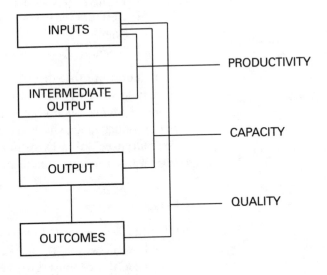

INPUTS = raw materials, labor, plant, equipment, energy, and all other resources need to provide the service/product.

INTERMEDIATE OUTPUT = the output achieved back-of-house to enable sales to be made (often termed *mise-en-place* in the foodservice industry) and capacity available front-of-house.

OUTPUT = actual sales of products/services, that is, the actual proportion of capacity achieved.

OUTCOMES = level of customer satisfaction with the experience.

a foodservice operation. In the manufacturing sector, the inputs needed to make a specific item of output, such as the parts needed to make a radio, are relatively easy to identify, measure, and account for. This is largely because the product is standardized, so that many hundreds or thousands of identical goods are manufactured. In foodservice, only the physical food items might be considered in this way, but even many products, such as flours, fat, and so on, have multiple uses in the kitchen. Many of the other features of the meal experience, such as service and atmosphere, are *intangible*, that is, difficult to see, touch, feel, or measure. Thus, most service transactions can be regarded as unique rather than standardized. One of the reasons why it is so difficult to standardize *all* inputs and to guarantee their impact on output is that the intangible components are complex and difficult to control. This intangibility has a further implication however—it is almost impossible to directly measure them. Thus attempts to measure inputs and outputs for productivity improvement reasons will almost always be difficult and the results are likely to be imprecise.

As we have seen the key characteristics of the "traditional" foodservice system are:

> Customized product
> Highly skilled craft people
> Complex flow of materials through a sequence of processes
> Clear differentiation between back-of-house "manufacture" and front-of-house "sales"
> Customer contact only with front-of-house
> Customer viewed as passive receiver of product/service

These characteristics and the complexities of the system, such as the multiple use of raw materials; the specialization of staff, their interactive approach to production; the allocation of overheads; and so on illustrate more specifically the reasons for the difficulties associated with monitoring and measuring productivity in this type of operation.

Although such traditional restaurant operations still exist in large numbers, there have been many changes to the way in which food is produced and served to the customer, as we have seen in the analysis of foodservice systems. Three main approaches to such innovation have been identified (Jones 1986). These three approaches to redesigning foodservice operations are production-lining (the fast-food system), decoupling, and increasing customer participation. In most cases innovations have initially lead to major productivity gains. But even with the more modern systems the problem of intangibles remains.

Whether it is a traditional system or a modern one, all foodservice managers need to improve productivity levels. Productivity improvement strategies can vary on the basis of formal and informal criteria. These should not be taken as separate from each other, but as two ends of a continuum. Formal criteria include the structure of the organization, delegation and authority, cost allocation, remuneration policy, and other aspects of the organization over which planning and control can be exercised. At the other end of the continuum are informal criteria that support productivity improvement, such as organizational climate and culture, involvement strategies, decision-making processes, and people development. Rather than change the organization to make productivity happen, these informal ideas change the attitudes and behavior of people within the organization. In addition, there are a range of specific techniques that can be used to measure, monitor, and identify productivity. Such techniques include time and motion studies, work measurement, method study, and so on.

Capacity

Managing capacity effectively is largely concerned with the issue of matching demand and supply. In Thompson's ideal model both of these were constant and predictable. In reality a FDS is a capacity constrained operation, that is to say it has a specific set of inputs that will enable a specified level of demand to be met. To put it another way, a restaurant has only a certain number of seats to serve people within the period of its opening hours. Although supply is fixed and relatively constant, demand is very variable in a number of ways.

Demand is typically very difficult to manage. There are four variables:

Volume—of demand, that is, total output over time
Variety—of services offered, that is, in foodservice the product range
Variation—of demand over time, that is, peaks and troughs in demand
Variability—the differential demand for different service/products

A key feature of foodservice operations management is the extent to which FDS matches different demand conditions. This is illustrated in Table 2. In addition, each manager of different types of FDS can adopt policies designed to match demand more closely with supply. Policies include sales promotion such as happy hours, differential pricing with price cuts during slack periods, employment of casual and part-time staff, modified opening hours, addition of take-out service, and so on.

Quality

Quality may be defined as "fitness for purpose." The operations manager is therefore concerned with ensuring that the customer gets what the customer expects. As with productivity, the intangibility factor presents major problems. There has been a great deal of research into what factors provide customer satisfaction in foodservice. This research is by no means complete, but a common feature emerging is the extent to which the total foodservice system needs to match the expectations of customers. This can be illustrated by the clear identification of speed of service as being essential to good customer service in the fast-food sector of the industry. But it is clear that customer needs are dynamic and changing and that the industry in terms of its system design and delivery needs to be adaptive to these changes. There are a number of ways the manager can approach quality.

The manager may consider all aspects of the system that *interface* with the consumer. Such interfaces can be physical or human. Physical interfaces

Table 2. *System innovation and capacity implications*

	System A, traditional restaurant	System E, cook-chill	System G, fast-food
Volume	Low	Medium to high	High
Variety	High	High	Low
Variation	High (difficult to forecast)	Low (predictable)	Low (easy to forecast)
Variability	High	High	Low

include the exteriors of service operations, their interior design, decor and layout, marketing material, and so on. In the foodservice context another key "physical" interface is the meal product itself. Human interfaces are all those staff who come into contact with the customer both directly and indirectly.

Despite innovations in foodservice system design, the industry continues to rely on a very large number of personnel to deliver its service/product. Clearly from the systems analysis above, different systems need different numbers of operatives with differing skill levels. The effective management of quality needs to match as closely as possible the needs of the system with all aspects of human resource management within the organization. This includes policies and procedures with regard to recruitment, selection, training, induction, remuneration and reward, and industrial relations. One common example of mismatch between operational objectives and human resource policy occurs over the issue of tipping. Employees who rely on tips are likely to take an extremely short-term view and focus on selling the highest price dish items since they receive a percentage of the customer's bill. This approach may mean that they are promoting dishes that are not the most profitable or cost effective and driving up the average spend which may deter return customers.

The formal organization structure, the style of management, and the delegation of authority also needs to match operational characteristics. For instance, it has increasingly been found that unit managers of chain restaurants and fast-food stores should have more autonomy than has previously been the case. As equally important are nonformal aspects of the organization commonly referred to as "organizational culture." This refers to the values and attitudes held by all members of the organization and the extent to which this fits with the overall strategy and operation of the business. There is growing evidence that a good match between an appropriate culture and service provision results in very high levels of performance from staff, with beneficial spin-offs for all the other key result areas.

Managing Foodservice Delivery Systems

In conclusion, using systems thinking to analyze the foodservice industry has identified ten basic types of foodservice systems. These ten systems are broadly similar inasmuch as they are alternative combinations of the ten possible stages in the foodservice process. But they are different in their use of people or technology to achieve the function of each stage. Therefore the manager needs to ensure that the total system or operation is balanced, has no bottlenecks, proceeds smoothly from one stage to the next and is able to respond to market circumstances, as well as understand in detail each specific stage of the system.

But management is far more than simply making the system work. Management takes place in the context of organizational goals. It is therefore important to look at outputs, as well as inputs and processes, if we are to fully understand operational management. In considering productivity capacity and quality, we have identified three main output goals. It has been proposed (Lockwood and Jones 1989) that an effective way to think of outputs is to consider them as *key result areas*. These are the things that a manager has to achieve for the operation to meet the strategic goals of the organization. They identify seven such key result areas, including the three we have examined in detail. These are:

1. Ensuring customer satisfaction
2. Maintaining employee performance
3. Protecting assets
4. Managing customer service
5. Maximizing productivity
6. Maximizing income and profit contribution
7. Managing quality

For any given type of foodservice operation the relative importance of these key result areas will be different. Indeed even within the same operation, their relative importance may vary over time. These key result areas do not exist in isolation from each other. Management action taken to improve performance in one area will inevitably affect one or more other areas.

By setting targets in each of these key result areas, the operations manager will be able to select the most appropriate way of resolving the issues of productivity, capacity, and quality identified above. These solutions are drawn not only from operations management thinking but depend also on human resource management, marketing, management science, and other management disciplines. The role of the manager is therefore to understand the system and integrate a wide body of knowledge into a coherent and appropriate set of policies and procedures designed to meet the organization's long-term objectives.

Summary

Using a systems approach, ten basic types of foodservice systems can be identified. These ten systems are broadly similar in as much as they are alternative combinations of the ten possible stages in the foodservice process. However, they are different in their use of people or technology to achieve the function of each stage. Management's task is to see that the total system or operation is well-balanced. There are several key result areas that should be considered by any manager to meet the strategic goals of the organization. By setting targets in each of these key result areas, the operations manager will be able to select the most appropriate way of resolving the issues of productivity, capacity, and quality. The role of the manager in understanding the system and integrating a wide body of knowledge in set policies and organizational objectives is very important.

References

Cousins, J. and D. Foskett. 1989. Curriculum development for food production operations teaching for the hospitality industry. *International Journal of Operations and Production Management* 9(5):77–87.

Cutliffe, G. 1971. *Analysing Catering Operations.* London: Edward Arnold.

Huelin, Alan, and Peter Jones. 1990. Foodservice systems: generic types, alternative technology and infinite variation. *Journal of Foodservice Systems* 5(4): 299–311.

Jones, Peter. 1986. The impact of trends in service operations on food service delivery systems. *International Journal of Operations and Production Management* 8(7):23–30.

Jones, Peter. 1988. Quality, capacity and productivity in service industries. *International Journal of Hospitality Management* 7(2):104–112.

Lockwood, Andrew, and Peter Jones. 1989. *The Management of Hotel Operations.* London: Cassell.

Pickworth, J. R. 1988. Service delivery systems in the foodservice industry. *International Journal of Hospitality Management* 7(1):43–62.

Thompson, J. D. 1967. *Organisation in Action,* New York: McGraw-Hill.

4

Food and Beverage Management

Robert B. Lane

This article provides an overview of the many considerations an operator of a food and beverage facility must plan on in the day-to-day management of the business, from the procurement of product to the accounting for its sale and profit. The primary emphasis is on the production of food, because it is the most difficult activity to manage and, yet, represents the most opportunity to make a profit. The information that follows is intended to provide the reader with an idea of the management strategies needed to survive.

The management of a food and beverage facility looks deceivingly simple to the customer, so that many people at one time or another are moved to speculate on whether they could operate a restaurant more efficiently than any they have seen in operation. Some of the more adventuresome go to a lot of trouble trying to prove it. That is one of the many fascinating facets of the business; it is an experience within the grasp of a relatively large number of people, particularly in a free market society. There is an old saying that anyone who eats three times a day can consider himself an expert, and that seems to be sufficient encouragement for some to dare to try opening a restaurant.

The opportunities are numerous and so are the pitfalls. Industry analysts have estimated over the years that as many as one out of four adults in the United States may have worked in the foodservice industry at one time or another. A more recent statistic is perhaps even more meaningful; four out of every five persons engaged in foodservice jobs want to leave the industry for another career, citing a variety of reasons. Those of us who have found our own niche may be surprised because, as many of us admit, something about it just "gets under your skin" and, although it is often a grueling challenge involving a greater than average level of commitment, the enjoyment and financial rewards can be tremendous.

Too often, because both a great number of people have grown up in the business or with the idea that it looks easy to the novice, these challenges are approached without regard to common sense planning and follow-through. Egos, emotions, and unfocused enthusiasm can eventually sap energy and capital, if there is not adequate planning and ongoing flexibility. At the same time, plans can be so thoroughly researched and articulated that they predestine failure. The fact is, the business changes so fast that even the experts are outguessed. The customer is fickle, and many a manager or owner and, sadly, the employee, are left to wonder what happened? Today's success can be tomorrow's statistic if, in fact, the food and beverage operation cannot turn on a dime and react to the changing marketplace.

Profiles of Successful Food and Beverage Managers

The typical food and beverage manager is atypical. No single profile can predetermine the most successful personality that would endure—and, yes, even thrive on—unusually long hours, hard physical work, dissatisfied guests, constant challenges with motivating a fairly free-moving labor market, legal liability and insurance concerns, and constant pressures from outside legal, governmental, charitable, and environmental influences, to say nothing of the well-placed concerns over shrinking food supplies, inflation, and threats of foodborne illness that, sooner or later, can become very personal nightmares. Yet, many who enter the business enjoy it immensely.

The most successful managers, certainly the leaders, have been successful not because of their technical backgrounds or depth of experience they offer, but more so for their love for the business, as exhibited by their affinity for their employees and guests, their penchant for detail, and their absolute desire to provide quality, value, and service to their market niche. Many of the best people in the business may not even choose to become managers; they are perfectly content with developing their specialized skills into strong role models, highly motivated to deliver successful experiences as they are called upon. The manager who recognizes and rewards this talent is special, as the greatest skill lies with those who know how to orchestrate and coach a great team.

The success stories of those who have become famous in the business probably run in the millions. One dinner experience, routine to the manager but unforgettable to the guests, can make a hero. And, the opportunities present themselves a million times a day.

If there was one test to be given to those considering a serious foodservice career, it should determine whether, and to what extent, they have an inborn desire to *serve* others. If not, then they don't belong in the business. The work is hard; the rewards are many. Motivating associates, recognizing effort and promoting advancement, training and encouraging the disabled and disadvantaged toward truly outstanding performance on behalf of satisfied guests, just as you would in your own home, provides an emotional high that just cannot be duplicated elsewhere.

The Importance of Having a Plan

As more countries opt for a free market society to move them toward the new century, there emerges a common language regarding the management of a capital venture which, realistically, should be the goal of any foodservice operation. *The acid test of leadership is the management of profitability.*

Management has to rely on a plan, and that plan must reflect a logical progression with a focus on profit. Too often, for reasons previously explained, some foodservice operations actually appear to be operating by the seat of their pants which, for many generations, has been their ultimate downfall. Overplanned, underestimated, overdramatized, and undercapitalized, the dismal failures defy a body count. They come and go, leaving a lot of damage in their wake. Owners and managers must exercise hands-on manage ment or be left behind in the dust.

The plan that most often escapes the operator is production, yet many operators choose to let instinct and bad habits prevail, guiding them into repeating the same errors over and over, rather than learning from their mistakes.

Elements of a Profitable Production Planning

Following an efficient chronology of planned food, beverage, labor, and equipment scheduling can eliminate or minimize many of the day-to-day operating problems that prevent owners and managers from even surviving, to say nothing of providing their guests a totally positive experience.

Essentially, the plan for production, the end objective of which is profit, can be broken down into a 10-step common sense sequence of inventory management.

1. Inventory and estimating of need
2. Purchasing/Ordering
3. Receiving of goods
4. Storage and issue
5. Preparation
6. Production
7. Service
8. Recovery
9. Accounting
10. Inventory verification

Inventory and Estimating of Need Whether it is capital funding and an elaborate marketing study, or simply somebody's favorite recipe and a dream, there has to be an inventory of resources on hand in order to open for business. In proper context for this section, however, let's address day-to-day management of goods on hand and the estimating of expected business.

Accurate estimates of anticipated business are usually taken from menu counts of previous business. Modern, sophisticated point of sale devices have replaced cash registers in most large food and beverage operations and the detailed output they provide in terms of items sold, customer flow by hour, average time spent filling an order, and other information, provide invaluable assistance to the manager. The most important of these, however, is the record of items sold, which is the base for planning and scheduling the next production effort.

Even before opening an operation for the very first time, management must have some idea of the business to be expected, as gleaned from observing market trends, competition, location, menu mix, customer profile, pricing, seasonality of food and similarly complex considerations. This is surely the most exciting part of the business, even after the operation is in full swing. Trying to predict what the customer will do is very challenging, fun at times and, perhaps, frustrating most of the time.

Accurate records of prior sales, adjusted for current needs, should guide the operator in planning and scheduling resources for future business.

Accurate inventories are an absolute necessity. They not only provide an insight into what materials have been used and now remain, but are the basis for profit accountability. Inventories must be thorough, preferably conducted at the same time each day and analyzed in detail for fine-tuning operational performance. Food is highly perishable; having too much on hand or worse yet, allowing it to be produced too far in advance, has a severe effect on its freshness, appearance, and flavor. Timing is a major flaw in most foodservice operations, but this will be addressed in further detail in the section on production.

The most effective managers always have their eyes on their inventory. Intimately familiar with the consumption of their goods on hand, they realize that it is more perishable than cash. The smaller the operation, the easier the task; the sheer size and number of people involved in a larger operation can make record keeping and communications a constant nightmare and can very negatively impact food quality.

Par stocks of food, beverages, and equipment can alleviate a lot of problems, but many operations are realistically limited by cash flow problems. Par stock maintenance is a dream out of reach if an operation cannot make its payroll. Practical inventory levels can be met with planning and flexibility, however, so this becomes an issue of effective management.

Inventory quantities are most often recorded to correspond with the original order quantity, or the quantity in which they are used in a particular recipe, or for a particular purpose, usually at the discretion of the operator. Whatever the quantity, amounts should be easily convertible to dollar costs, so that management is aware of food costs, sales trends, waste, and so forth.

Today, most operators, large and small, have developed their own formats for taking inventory, often supplemented by what their wholesalers/distributors make available to them in the way of forms, computerized order devices, price lists, and other means too numerous to detail here. Sophisticated, hand-held inventory devices are already in use by a few large operators, making obsolete the clerk with the pencil behind the ear.

Purchasing/Ordering — Purchasing for today's food and beverage environment requires a thorough knowledge of the products available, market conditions, and the rapid changes occurring. Experience is helpful, but it can lead to complacency instead of the innovation that is more of a necessity. There is much good information available and that, combined with experience and flexibility, can provide the basics.

The ordering of food, beverages, and equipment, in contrast, is much simpler, assuming that a procurement system of some kind is already in place. The smaller scale operator is at the mercy of the distributor for procurement information, but the larger company will most likely already have documented specifications, along with an established procurement system and policies of operation.

In either case, the daily operational task is managing the orders necessary to replenish stock. Following estimated needs, usage as documented by inventory, outside influences (weather, nearby events, and so on), the operator merely places the order with preestablished, approved suppliers.

Ordering involves the timely scheduling of goods to arrive within sufficient lead time to allow advance preparation, retain peak freshness (with perishable foods), and prevent needless rehandling and unnecessary waste of capital, space, and other resources. Scheduling of personnel follows these and other guidelines.

Receiving of Goods The manager's job only begins with placing the order—goods must be received in a timely manner and verified against written specifications, carefully marked with dates, and rotated in inventory. This step is crucial in the entire process. Unknowingly accepting less value than paid for can erode management's credibility with vendors and employees and seriously influence the quality of the finished product.

Specifications are usually established from written resources easily available in industry textbooks and from trade and marketing associations and continually refined until they are finely tuned to match market availability, seasonality, and customer preference. Every foodservice unit must include these in their strategy for operation, publish them, and regularly use them as a training resource.

Prices paid are checked against market quotes and price sheets furnished by vendors and substantiated by wholesale market price trends, competitive bids and routinely updated food cost computations, so that the operator is made aware of the need for menu price updates, where feasible.

Inventory rotation is usually accomplished in one of two systems, first-in/first-out (FIFO), or last-in/first-out (LIFO). Except in cases where logistics and special accounting methods encourage the LIFO system, most operations choose the FIFO method, if for no other reason than to assure use of the freshest product.

Cases or packages of product, depending on the practicality of marking, should reflect the date of receipt so that management is aware of how long the product has been on hand. This marking is extremely critical to ensure freshness and safe food handling, and some operations take the marking process a step further and include the price on each package to streamline their cost accounting methods and make employees more conscientious regarding the value of the company's assets that they are encouraged to help protect.

In most large operations, a purchasing agent or receiving clerk is delegated responsibility for both the ordering and receiving of product, but an effective check and balance system requires that these functions be separated. Even in a smaller operation, some degree of cross-check is recommended to protect the owner's investment. Thus, another reason for daily inventory verification of items sold versus goods on hand, as a key part of a check and balance system.

Although there is often a tendency on the part of management to delegate much of the receiving function, it is necessarily the ultimate responsibility of management. It is a critical step in cost accountability and quality control.

Storage and Issue The storage of goods on hand requires constant management vigilance, not necessarily from a need to over-control, but to ensure product turnover, discourage mishandling and over production, and deliver the freshest product to the guest.

Inventory accounting is streamlined if, to the greatest extent possible, the sequence of items on the inventory forms follow the storage arrangement of the various categories of food, beverage, and equipment.

Storage temperatures are crucially important to preserve freshness and discourage foodborne illness, and local health laws and common sense food handling precautions must take priority when establishing any storage procedures. Fresh meat, for instance, must be stored at the proper temperature to prevent further aging and deterioration of the product. As another example, the storage of raw foods of a dangerous nature, such as fresh eggs (risk of *Salmonella*) and even cleaned lettuce (cross-contamination from sinks and cutting boards), should be kept carefully covered and separated from other potentially hazardous foods, such as fresh chicken and seafood. Different foods, ideally, require different temperatures for storage in order to optimally protect freshness and flavor.

In addition, so many food safety concerns have received recent publicity because of their being attributed to foodborne outbreaks that they cannot be adequately addressed here. Again, it is the responsibility of management to be thoroughly aware of these dangers and constantly train and certify their personnel in food safety, in accordance with local laws and regulations.

State laws and company operating policies often govern the storage of alcoholic beverages, expensive food items, and chemicals, so their use is carefully controlled for both reasons of cost and potential danger. Federal laws covering an employee's "right to know," for instance, require that material safety data sheets be kept on hand for every potentially dangerous chemical, and training the employees on the use of these items is a challenge, particularly if many of the employees only know English as a second language.

Accurate and extensive inventories of key items are required either by the month or in conformance with other established accounting periods, and these records are carefully costed and used by the operation's accountants to determine the respective period's cost of sales. This inventory-taking is very time consuming and a well-organized storage arrangement can make it much easier.

Issue of Goods. The actual issue of goods in an efficient food and beverage operation of any even intermediate size is best done under a system of written requisition. Each person requiring food and/or beverages for their point of customer service routinely inventories (usually by informal spot checking) and "orders" by requisition, an inventory to replenish the par stock for their work area.

It is in management's best interest to routinely spot check these issues, to know how assets are used. Depending on the circumstances and the size of the operation, of course, the requisition system must be practical and should not be done purely to satisfy bureaucratic whims or unrealistic accounting procedures.

Long gone are the days when hotels and restaurants, for instance, could afford a crew of clerks and store persons to constantly rehandle food and process paperwork. Daily food cost accounting—once the norm for larger operations—is an unrealistic objective if there is no accurately costed daily inventory from which food cost is computed. Such tradition is also pointless because menu prices, recipes, and portions cannot be adjusted accordingly. But, if the information is relatively easy to calculate and provides a means whereby management can identify irregular variations in consumption, such a procedure may prove feasible.

Requisition forms may be handwritten or in the form of preprinted, itemized lists, and be costed to correspond with the unit of issue, which is particularly important if costs are needed and/or interdepartmental transfers are necessary to most accurately break out costs by a separate profit center, such as a banqueting department or cocktail lounge.

The relatively high cost, portability, and risks of handling alcoholic beverages requires special purchasing, receiving, storage, and issue controls. State and local laws, company policies, and internal control procedures should be stringent and almost always are, in terms of issue, usage and accounting reconciliation. A beverage cost comparison is usually kept separate from food so that management has available an ongoing analysis of cost trends, departmental expenses, transfers between outlets, and so forth. In larger hotels hosting banquet/catering functions, some guests, where local laws permit, may choose to bring in their own beverages and the hotel will charge an appropriate "corkage fee." Some liability with the hotel will still occur, as defined by laws.

Miscellaneous serving equipment, china, glassware, silver and flatware are usually not held in large reserves unless select items are returned after each use and then reissued for special occasions. Many operations establish a par stock for items and, once inventory is reduced to the minimum acceptable par stock level, management must consider replacement. One example of overkill promoted by vendors of computer software programs developed for food service operations is a feature whereby the computer will provide an automatic reorder level whenever inventories indicate that stock is below par. Realistically, however, most food and beverage operations are run with such tight budgets that management must weigh this decision along with many other capital intensive decisions. The name of the game, obviously, is to keep the cash flow moving, not to sit on investments of unused items. In very large and complex operations, such a program might be appropriate.

Other nonperishable controllable cost items, usually the expendable/ replaceable paper, plastic, chemicals, detergents, and cleaning products are routinely ordered and, more often than not, seldom analyzed in terms of use and cost. Rapidly increasing concerns about the environment and constant, escalating prices are making these products extremely expensive. The fact that they are disposable and so often considered expendable by employees and customers makes their use very expensive.

Whatever the size of the operation, some semblance of a written requisition system or inventory consumption accounting makes sense, so long as management uses it.

Preparation At least in the most perishable product line of food, production is the area where the operation is most vulnerable. It is often said that everyone who eats three times a day is an expert on food, and there are as many versions on how to prepare food as there are people who eat.

Management is ultimately responsible for not only deciding how food ought to be prepared (certainly in consultation with those who have the skill to actually do it), but also how it is freshly, attractively, wholesomely served and accounted for. Food preparation left to guesswork or to the whims of individuals provides no consistent base of quality or reputation.

The best system is a system of written recipes, regardless of the inclination on the part of many in the business who ridicule the use of written instructions for cooking. The fact is, written recipes are excellent training aids, provide the basis for product consistency, and hold people accountable for performance. They have been used for generations by the best chefs, including most of the world's famous chefs. The best recipes are those that have been refined again and again, until they are perfected. Additionally, recipes can serve as an important contract between management and employees to the effect that goods will be produced as specified. As with food specifications, management, acting on behalf of the customer, must establish the standard for the quality of the food and beverage served.

Certainly, one of the more notable characteristics of the new product quality movement bursting forth in recent years preaches empowerment for employees, encouraging them to do almost whatever is necessary in order to satisfy the guest. This is, indeed, a noble pursuit, as customers certainly deserve to be satisfied. However, allowing everybody involved in food preparation, for instance, to use their own discretion in modifying ingredients and altering recipe procedures, most often very negatively impacts food quality. There are many analogies; the new car customer, for instance, would not expect, or appreciate, an auto assembly line worker deciding to omit certain parts of a new car. The issue is quality and management must define what quality is.

The day-to-day preparation of food, in particular, must be well-planned and closely supervised at every stage, although there must be a dedicated effort to resist overcontrol. Historically, it is the nature of many managers to get caught up in the process without paying attention to what the final product tastes like. The proof exists in almost every restaurant in America, at one time or another, because one or more steps in the quality control process (such as tasting the food before it leaves the kitchen) were overlooked in the heat of business. Again, the best laid plans of the owner, manager, and chef fail unless the performance is managed.

One of the most important roles of management is making the necessary resources available that allow employees to effectively perform their work. In addition to having food on hand in sufficient time for it to undergo proper preparation, the typical operation is always short of adequate numbers of miscellaneous serving equipment, including knives, utensils, and such. These are the most important areas that need to be covered by par stocks, so there is always an adequate inventory on hand. There is always a tug-of-war between the people who need the items and the person responsible for remembering to order the item(s) and spend the money.

Many of those experienced in the business believe that the average foodservice employee is productive only 50 percent of the time, which has nothing to do with their personal performance. It is just the nature of the business; a lot of time is spent in getting ready and then, at least to some degree, waiting for the business. There is a special challenge in the manager discouraging overproduction, as the typical worker, learning early about the ever obvious shortage of labor, tends to work ahead in order to cover himself/herself. Consequently, much of the food is in danger of losing its freshness and flavor. On the other hand, timing is everything; many of the guest complaints an operation endures often occur because food has been on hand too long or prepared too far in advance. Without ongoing supervision, it is often served, and the customer who becomes dissatisfied never returns.

Indeed, the methods for preparation of food are very much guided by the objectives of the owners and/or managers, those other persons who are responsible for preparing it, many of whom have been hired for their expertise, ethnic influences, price/value marketing, locale, availability, and seasonality of food. All of these functions must be effectively managed in order to survive. Even then, the challenge is not over. In fact, it is just beginning.

Production   If the preparation phase of the production cycle represents the most vulnerable area for the operation to lose customers and profit, then the mismanagement of the ongoing production of food only worsens it. Preparation and production are different in the sense that production represents the ongoing availability, processing, set up, and re-storage of all prepared and ready-to-use foods.

Again, timing is everything. Once food is prepared, many food and beverage managers consider their work completed. This may be true for airline feeding, carry-out businesses, bakeries and for a minority of other types of businesses, but it is just the start for most other food and beverage facilities. Quite simply, in a quality operation, the food cannot be prepared all at once. As preparation can be made easier by the presence of recipe cards, a documented plan for production scheduling is a sensible step toward effective management and the reputation of the operation.

Consider several examples. A warm, limp salad can be a real disappointment, and it is usually the result of the green salad mixture being left out at room temperature, where it is more convenient for the server to prepare it as needed. If it is not the server, it might be a kitchen attendant, who prepared several dozen salads ahead, carefully crushing them in plastic wrap and putting them in the refrigerator when time permitted. Worse yet, it could have been made to order, from unwashed lettuce, or even "reworked" leftovers from a previous meal period. Thoroughly washing salad greens, storing them to both restore lost moisture and allow excess water to drain, will result in a product crisp and yet wet enough to provide the ideal surface for salad dressing to adhere to. Yet, salads often leave a kitchen under the least ideal circumstances. Another example of things taken for granted is the baked potato. It is convenient for the cook to bake them off all at one time, as it reduces the number of repetitive tasks that can be expected in the course of a typical day. The guest could care less, however, and is likely to be turned off by a hollow, dried-out, dark-colored potato that was cooked four or five hours ago. Wrapping the potato in foil doesn't help; it only causes it to steam and disintegrate and turn mealy from the inside. Besides, many operations only wrap them in foil so they don't have to wash them—a real turnoff for the guest who likes to eat the skin. *Fresh* chicken? Try soaking one in salted water for 30 minutes and see what floats out of it, then speculate how many restaurants take the trouble to wash it. What counts is whether they have washed your chicken. Stale odors and musty smelling butter on your table? This is evidence of leftover food being around for a long time, in and out of refrigerators, likely while unwrapped and exchanging odors with onions or fish.

Effective supervision of the production inventory helps safeguard the integrity of the original product. "You're only as good as the last meal you served," the saying goes, and the job is not over until you have served the best and freshest product possible. Shortcuts just won't do, particularly in the long run.

The best, most common sense solution is staggered production, although most foodservice preparation personnel tend to fight this. Thus, it becomes a management issue. Production has to continue on an ongoing basis, and each batch sampled as if it were critical to the operation's success. It is.

Certainly, a bartender would not mix drinks ahead as a matter of convenience, so why is the overproduction of food such a problem? The answer lies in human nature, and the effective manager must learn about and motivate a staff for quality through timely performance. Employees are, by no means, the problem. Much relates back to whether they have been given the tools to do their jobs, and the most important of these is an effective communication with management.

Simply put, production should occur as close as possible to the time of need.

Service   What counts to the customer is whether you can deliver what you have promised. Few operations are able to offer perfection in everything; quality, service, cleanliness, and value are what made McDonald's famous, and continue to be the goals they pursue—and every one of their managers understand that. Most other foodservice businesses don't even come close, particularly, those without strong leadership, as effective management starts at the top. If the people that put the food in front of the customer do not understand the company's overall culture, competition will eventually overwhelm them. Just think about how many foodservice companies and hundreds of thousands of restaurants have failed in the effort.

The nature of the hospitality business, overall, requires that a manager remind his or her employees of hundreds of things to do every day. Many of these are the finer points of service, because that is how the guest evaluates the operation. Human nature, obviously, makes this delivery diverse; often likely to be remembered as a once-in-a-lifetime experience or a miserable memory.

Of all the phases of production, service is pretty basic. There are many schools that teach it, and millions of those who have learned and modified it pass on what they think is important to remember. Most recently, customers are being asked (or expected) to serve themselves, as the labor market shrinks, inflation spirals, and operational problems cause owners and managers to look toward their customer for answers. Buffets, salad bars, self-service beverage centers, and condiment stations have brought the concept of the cafeteria into many other market segments.

The various styles of service are too numerous to mention here; information is abundantly available in reference books, which serve as the best base of information. The serious student should first rely on what is written and professionally recognized as authentic. Many who serve are under the impression that what they do is how it ought to be done, but that is not always the case. The most successful operations constantly train their people in how to serve. People who have decided to serve others as a profession should be absolutely dedicated to that effort. Above all, interested candidates must present themselves professionally and be willing and able to represent the customer's best interests. Otherwise, they are making the wrong career choice.

Recovery   After all of the food, beverages, and equipment necessary to perform a job is made available, used in whole or part and then put away, the entire process starts over again. Strict laws in nearly every country are meant to prohibit leftover food from being served, but only if it has been served to a previous guest; but there are no guarantees.

Beverage laws specifically prohibit one brand being substituted for another or product being diluted or otherwise adulterated. Federal law is stringently enforced. But, alas, more people eat than drink. If you think it is the law, you are only partially right. Much more is dependent upon the integrity of the individual foodservice manager.

More appropriately, however, *recovery* is really the restoration of the operation and, yes, the amount of food suitably (and permissibly, under the law) determined for later use. Somehow, the majority of people think of food as ultimately expendable and, therefore, fail to remember that it has to be managed just as any other asset. Protecting freshness and appearance, maintaining proper temperatures, and ensuring proper care in handling and re-storage are crucially important to protecting remaining assets. This is the inventory that allows the operation to continue.

Accounting How long the operation continues, however, is usually determined by the accountants. If there is no money leftover at the end of the day, then the foodservice unit cannot expect to survive for long.

Sophisticated point of sale information is helpful, but it does not adequately compute return on investment. And, a unit's owners or managers are often so busily engaged in taking care of the business that this information is overlooked until it is too late. Foodservice is an emotional business, full of proverbial optimists: tomorrow is always supposed to be better than today.

Accounting usually calls for key inventories to be done at the end of each major accounting period. Some operations, as previously mentioned, run daily food cost analyses, to provide an indication of cost trends. Many others, realistically, run a daily cost analysis to determine whether they can continue to stay in business.

Many in the business aspire to be their own boss, and many have done just that and been very successful. With the complexity of today's business, ever more obvious in a soft economy, this opportunity is out of reach for many. It is not as simple as selling the food, meeting the payroll, and banking the rest. Those who aspire also have to consider legal implications, zoning, taxes, liability and other forms of insurance, labor markets and the laws that cover them and, most recently, global politics, child care, increasing employee benefit costs, food safety, and product legislation. These all have to be considered in the accounting phase, beyond the day-to-day concerns.

Each day's success in a foodservice unit is usually measured in sales, covers and/or customer counts. Weekly, monthly, and semimonthly, it may also be food and beverage cost, payroll and benefits, controllable expenses for other goods, advertising, and a host of other budget line items on which each manager's performance is evaluated and each owner's survival determined.

Inventory Verification Once an operational cycle is complete, inventories of food, beverage, and equipment are not only calculated, but verified to form a basis for reorder. The most valuable "asset" of them all, the people who really form the character and personality of the operation, are part of the "inventory" that permits further success.

Summary

Timely execution is the backbone of the foodservice business. It is the strategic difference that will allow operators to survive. After costs of purchases and operating expenses are deducted and all other expenses allocated, there is much less "profit" available than most people outside the business might expect. Many operations make only a few cents on the dollar, and much of that is plowed right back into the business out of necessity.

Yet, foodservice is one of the most exciting businesses known. Long hours and ever-growing problems do not seem to deter the many who continue to enter the business each day. It is also a lot of fun, no two days are the same, and the opportunity to meet and please people is all the motivation a lot of people need in order to become successful.

"We're not in the food business serving people," one large foodservice corporation boasts, "but in the people business serving food." Both require tender, loving care, along with a similar passion for detail toward ultimate guest satisfaction. Long-term success begins with a thorough knowledge of food and its timely preparation and service.

5

Site Selection for a Foodservice Operation

David Kirk

General Principles

When considering the site for a foodservice operation, it is necessary to differentiate between the situation of an independent restaurant and that of a foodservice restaurant that is a part of another operation, whether it be a hotel, hospital, school, or factory.

In the former case, the site selection is largely related to marketing and customer-related issues. In the latter case, the site selection will be related to the primary function of the facility, with foodservice considerations occupying a secondary or supporting function. In this latter situation, the site of the foodservice operation is more related to client movement and accessibility of the foodservice facility within the total site.

We must also differentiate between new building construction and that of a location with an existing building being considered for conversion to a foodservice operation.

Market-Related Factors

General Trading Area   The selection of a suitable site is often a two-stage process. The first stage is to identify the general trading area for the business and the second stage is to identify a specific site within this trading area (Marquardt et al. 1983). Examples of important characteristics of a general trading area are shown in Table 1.

Current and projected population data for an area are of great value, particularly where the operation is to attract largely a local clientele. Social and economic characteristics of the population are also important in relation to the location of all types of restaurants.

Where the operation is designed to cater mainly to the motorist or commercial driver, information about traffic density and knowledge about new highway developments is helpful.

In relation to the market for a new foodservice operation, information

Table 1. *Characteristics of a general trading area*

Customer-related criteria	Community and environment
Current and projected population levels	Legislative and tax considerations
Current and projected income related factors	Competition within same market segment
Lifestyle and spending patterns	Local advertising channels
Demographic data: social class, age, sex, race, nationality, religion, etc.	Transportation provision
	Business infrastructure: banking, insurance, credit, etc.
	Pool of skilled and unskilled employees

about local competitors appealing to the same market segment as the proposed operation is essential.

Site Selection for a Freestanding Foodservice Operation

The factors governing the selection of a suitable site for a business, whether it be a product industry or a service industry, are the same. The aspect that changes is the relative weighting of the factors. These factors are (Dilworth 1989):

- Market related factors—locations of demand and completion
- Tangible cost factors—transportation, utilities, labor, taxes, site costs, construction costs
- Intangible cost factors—local attitudes toward industry, zoning and legal regulations, room for growth, climate, schools, churches, hospitals, recreational opportunities, and so on.

Undoubtedly for a service industry, such as foodservice, the market-related factors are those of prime importance. The other two groups of cost-related factors may be seen more in the way of constraints. As such, the economic and marketing factors related to a potential site are at the forefront of the decision-making process.

Site Selection within a General Trading Area

Once a general trading area has been identified, the next task is to evaluate sites within this area (Lewison and DeLozier 1986). Probably a number of possible sites will be identified. The strengths and weaknesses of each site must be compared, possibly using a weighted scoring system.

The site location may be

- On a freestanding site
- On an unplanned site, such as part of a business or downtown development
- On a planned site, such as a shopping center or mall.

A freestanding or isolated site may be located in a neighborhood area or on a highway. Because of its isolation from other businesses, a foodservice operation in this type of location must develop its own marketing and advertising program.

In the case of a highway location, visibility and access are critical to success and, in this respect, signposting from major highways can provide a major source of business. For similar reasons, accessibility from major traffic routes is important and sites close to major traffic intersections can be very effective. In this context traffic counts can be an important indicator of potential business (Keiser 1989). Account should also be taken of proposed highway developments.

An unplanned site may be part of a neighborhood or downtown shopping area, and may rely on pedestrian customers or public car parking. Alternatively it may be a strip development, with parking in front of the site (Bolen 1988). Signposting can be an important factor in attracting pedestrian and vehicular traffic. The frontage (that aspect of a building facing the main pedestrian or vehicular routes) of the restaurant can act as an important selling feature.

In the case of a planned site, access and parking are provided as a part of the development and a range of complementary shopping outlets are combined on the site in order to provide one-stop shopping. One of the critical factors for success in this type of a development is the location of the foodservice operation relative to main pedestrian traffic routes. Planned sites can vary in size from the neighborhood shopping center to the regional and super-regional mall developments. Foodservice operations may also form a part of specialty developments, such as the factory outlet center.

Nonmarket-Related Factors

Of great significance is the aspect of cost associated with the development of the site. This includes both the cost of purchase and the cost of site development, which covers factors such as building, landscaping, and the provision of associated facilities such as car parking and access roads.

Zoning of land use may restrict the choice of sites for a foodservice operation. Practice varies in different countries and even in geographical areas within the same country, but there is normally national, regional, and local control on any new developments. For example, planning applications for restaurants may be refused in residential areas where the noise and traffic associated with the restaurant can cause problems. Zoning may also have other implications for foodservice operations, such as limitations on the position, height, and size of signposts.

Access is a critical factor. Early consideration needs to be given to customer access and service access, garbage collection, and so on. The details of access requirements will depend on the major transport market segments from which customers are drawn—pedestrian, bus, train, or automobile. In the latter case, requirements also change where a drive-through facility is to be provided.

The geographical location of the site can be crucial to the success of a foodservice operation. Access must allow for customers and service vehicles and, ideally, these two access points should be different, or should be screened from each other. Noise from surrounding industry, traffic, or leisure activities can make a site unsuitable for a restaurant. Depending on the localized weather conditions, climate-related factors can be important, such as the direction of prevailing winds.

In relation to geographical location, the natural landscape of a site, or the potential for landscaping can do much to enhance a site. Landscaping can make the site more attractive and screen the site from roads and industrial sites. Alternatively, it can open up scenic or panoramic views.

Professional advice will be required if the full potential for landscaping is to be realized. The natural contours of the site must be assessed in terms of changing levels and slopes. Hard landscaping, for example using drives, paths, terraces, and walls, can improve the external appearance of the property to the arriving customer. Soft landscaping, using gardens, trees, and shrubs can be used similarly. Fountains, ponds, and other water features can also enhance a site. In addition to these positive aspects of landscaping, all types of landscaping can be used to screen delivery points and other eyesores. Garbage and trash storage areas can also be screened from customers.

A further aspect of the geographical location is the type of soil on a site, since this influences many design decisions and building costs. For a site requiring septic tanks, the natural drainage of the soil can be critical.

In most situations, car parking is an essential requirement for a freestanding foodservice operation. However, it is not just that car parking is required. The location of the car park is also critical in relation to access from roads and entrances to the building. It is likely that planning approval will, in some part, depend on the size and location of car parks and entrances and exits for vehicles. Landscaping can be used to obscure the car park and service roads from restaurant windows and entrances.

The external appearance of a building is constrained by the size and shape of the site, its contours, prospect, and vista. The external aspect of the building should be pleasing to the eye and should complement the foodservice theme and market.

The installation of utilities also has a cost implication. Initially of importance is the capital cost of the provision of utilities—gas, water, electricity, sanitary sewers, storm sewers. However, there are also running costs associated with the provision or lack of services. These two costs need to be balanced when evaluating a number of potential sites within the general trading area.

Selection of an Existing Building for Conversion to a Foodservice Facility

All of the previously mentioned factors are still important when considering the suitability of an existing building for conversion to a foodservice operation. However, the tangible and intangible cost factors change significantly when looking at the conversion of an existing building.

The marketing aspects of an existing property are identical to those for the new construction site. The major additional factors concern the development of an interesting and functional design within the physical constraints of an existing building, and the establishment of accurate cost figures for conversion costs and realistic conversion time estimates.

Local authority planning and zoning considerations can also be important when looking at the suitability of an existing building. For example, older or historically important buildings may be protected from changes to the structure and frontage. These restrictions may increase the cost of the conversion.

Site Selection within a Larger Facility

In this context, the larger facility may be a hotel, a hospital, school, college or university, a leisure or recreational facility, a shopping mall, or other facility. In these situations, the market is largely dictated by the prime function of the site.

The foodservice operation must be located in a position to maximize its market from within the customers or clients visiting the site. This situation may introduce an element of conflict with other occupants of the site. For example, in the case of a hospital, foodservice may be viewed by planners as a secondary or support function and therefore be given a low priority in terms of location. In commercial developments, such as shopping malls, key locations on the site are likely to be popular and may be reserved by major retailers or may carry a high cost premium.

Location of the foodservice facility is related to circulation of customers/clients. In determining the location of a foodservice operation, attention must be given to the identification of major pedestrian traffic routes, including routes from the car park to other parts of the facility.

Visibility and signposting also become key components of the site location. As with the case of freestanding sites, frontage of the site can be critical in attracting customers.

Access for customers, staff, and materials can often be problematic and may limit the choice of location, particularly where access is required for delivery vehicles.

Summary

Site selection is complex and involves balancing a range of marketing and cost related factors. In evaluating competing sites, some will be unacceptable because of weaknesses in either marketing or cost factors and can be easily eliminated. Other sites may be very similar in many respects but have varying advantages and disadvantages.

One approach to making a choice between a number of alternative sites is to use a weighted scoring system. Using this technique, a list of marketing and cost factors is developed and each item on the list is given a weighting based on its importance. Each site can then be scored on each of these factors and the scores summed to give an overall score. These scores can then be used to compare alternative sites and to choose between them.

References

Bolen, W. H. 1988. *Contemporary Retailing*, 3rd ed. Englewood Cliffs, N.J.: Prentice-Hall.

Dilworth, J. B. 1989. *Production and Operations Management-Manufacturing and Non-manufacturing*, 4th ed. New York: Random House, 552 p.

Keiser, J. R. 1989. *Principles and Practices of Management in the Hospitality Industry*, 2nd ed. New York: Van Nostrand Reinhold.

Lewison D. M., and M. W. DeLozier. 1986. *Retailing: Principles and Practices*, 2d ed. Columbus, Oh: C E Merrill Publishing Co.

Marquardt, R. A., J. C. Makens, and R. G. Roe. 1983. *Retail Management: Satisfaction of Consumer Needs*. Chicago: Dryden Press.

6

Restaurant Design

Carolyn U. Lambert

The success of a restaurant depends on many factors, but the success of the design depends on the attention given to the planning phases. Some restaurants may succeed with little planning, however, owners have found that planning is more important than any other factor in the facility's profitability. Planning can be divided into seven phases:

1. Idea, need, or opportunity
2. Concept development
3. Feasibility study
4. Financing arrangements
5. Design
6. Contract and construction
7. Approval and opening

First, an idea or need must be identified. The idea may stem from an individual, a group, or a corporation that decides to invest money in a restaurant. Once the idea is presented, a market survey should be conducted to determine consumer characteristics, such as age, income, location, sex, occupation, and life-style of the markets available. These data are used in the second phase, concept development.

The concept must be well defined so the planning team will understand the objectives of the project. The concept statement should describe the target market, type of restaurant, type of service, number of seats, square footage requirements, and menu plan. The menu becomes the focus of the design, as all other facility characteristics must be coordinated with the menu. Clearly, a Chinese menu would be incongruous in Southern Colonial decor. Menu items should be listed during this phase so the facility will be planned correctly. The target market should be defined by sex, age, income level, occupation, location, and buying behavior. If the specific location has not been selected, any site limitations, such as traffic accessibility, zoning codes, or landscaping restrictions should be itemized. These details must be known prior to conducting a feasibility study.

The feasibility study is the third and crucial phase and should be fully evaluated. It uses the information obtained in the concept development phase to determine the restaurant's profitability. While some owners conduct informal studies using industry rules of thumb, a professionally completed feasibility study may provide additional insights that will affect the profitability of the restaurant. Owners should be sure to hire an unbiased firm that will deliver an accurate and realistic study. The most common reason that a project fails is an overly optimistic or incorrect feasibility study.

Assuming that the feasibility study is positive, the next step is to secure financing. During this step, owners will be requesting cash to build and support the restaurant. This step is very important; many restaurants fail because of inadequate funding.

With financing, the owner is ready to determine the design of the facility. This step allows the owner to review the proposed menu and make any desired changes. Once the menu has been finalized, a space program can be written. First, the designer will use the menu to specify the necessary functional areas, such as storage, preparation, and service. Then, the designer writes a description of the general activities of each area, the equipment required for each activity, and the equipment requirements. For example, weighing, counting, and recording are activities that occur in receiving. Therefore that area should include a set of scales, a table, and a desk. After all function areas have been defined by activities and equipment needed, the designer can indicate the desired relationships between areas. With the relationships identified, schematic planning can begin. The relationship chart essentially defines the desired flow of food and personnel in the kitchen.

Scaled blueprints are developed from the schematic diagrams, showing all of the construction requirements, such as heating, ventilation, and air conditioning systems; electrical systems; and plumbing systems. All of the scaled blueprints and specifications are combined into a set of *construction documents*. The construction documents may be sent to prospective contractors to obtain construction bids. The building contract is usually awarded to the lowest bidder, however, the owner should be sure that the low bid meets the required specifications.

Construction is the sixth phase. This phase must be carefully supervised to ensure that the building is constructed according to the blueprints. Owners should also be prepared for construction delays due to errors, receipt of building permits, code inspections, and late equipment deliveries.

The last phase is the acceptance and opening phase. Owners may want to hold a grand opening as soon as the building inspector has signed the occupancy permit, but it is better to make sure that all equipment works and employees are trained. Therefore, most restaurants open for business without advertising for a few weeks. A grand opening is widely advertised once the "bugs" have been worked out.

A major segment of the design process is planning. The next section focuses on the major objectives in designing each function area.

Planning the Layout

The overall goals of the design are to ensure a smooth and straight flow of food, equipment, and employees, with no backtraffic or crosstraffic. Raw ingredients should enter the receiving area and follow an efficient logical path to the designated storage, preparation, and service areas. When food products must be carried from receiving to storage down long hallways or to different floor levels, the result is an increased labor cost. When employees must transport products across aisles, inefficiency occurs.

The flow can be translated into a preliminary bubble diagram in which the function areas are arranged in the desired locations. If the restaurant is new, the bubble diagram should represent the ideal. If the restaurant is located in an existing building, current physical constraints may influence the design. Figure 1 shows a bubble diagram for an ideal layout.

The designer can now begin to place workstations on the bubble diagram. Space requirement for aisles and equipment can be determined. Using typical measurements of three feet for equipment depth, three feet for work aisles, and four feet for traffic aisles, major workstations can be outlined. Specific equipment is not identified yet, as the objective for this step is to be sure that space is sufficient for all of the workstations. If all areas fit in the preliminary drawing, more detailed drawings can be made showing specific equipment. This plan should be evaluated to be sure the goals of a smooth and straight flow are met. Are all of the areas adjacent to appropriate workstations? Clearly, there could be more than one way to arrange the workstations, however, related tasks should be close to each other.

When the designer is satisfied with the overall arrangement of the workstations, the planning of each station can begin. Each station is unique and should be addressed carefully.

Receiving

Receiving is the first control point for the food and supplies and should be planned carefully. The receiving dock should be located at the back of the building, but with easy access from the street. If large tractor trailers will be delivering items, sufficient space must be allocated for turning. The height of the dock should be appropriate for the types of delivery trucks. If most deliveries arrive in tractor trailers, the platform should be elevated, however, if most deliveries arrive in small vans, the dock may be more appropriate at street level. The depth of the dock should provide enough space for a driver to easily unload a truck. The length of the dock will be determined by the number of trucks that will be unloading at the same time. Usually this number does not exceed two, as a receiving clerk cannot effectively handle more.

The dock should be protected from excessive temperatures, rain, and

Fig. 1. Bubble diagram illustrating relationships between areas.

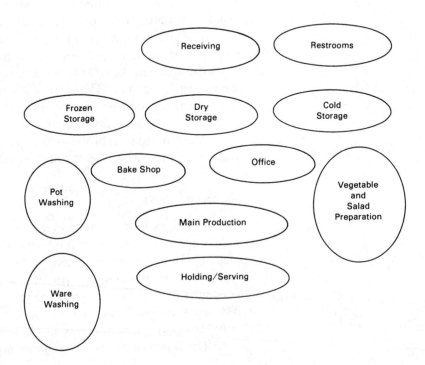

snow, so the dock should have a roof or be enclosed. Most restaurants use landscaping, foliage, or a wall to hide the receiving area from pedestrians and customers. Visibility of the area from either a receiving or manager's office is desirable.

The receiving area for checking, weighing, and counting should be located inside the facility. As products are carried inside, they should be examined for quality and quantity at the receiving table. This area should also be equipped with scales, hand trucks, utensils to open cases, a desk, and a computer to record products received.

Storage
Storage space for bulk products should be located within easy access of the receiving and production areas. The amount of space allocated for storage is a function of the number of meals served, the variety of menu items, the frequency of deliveries, and the management policies. Some managers prefer to maintain a large par stock of food items, whereas others seek to minimize the cash investment.

Dry Storage. The dry storage room should be dry, easy to clean, and well ventilated. Shelving should be arranged for easy access by employees. To allow an employee to use a cart, aisle widths should be 48 inches. The amount of necessary storage space needs to be determined for each facility. There are industry guidelines based on type of food operation, but each facility's needs will vary by menu, frequency of delivery, total volume, and purchasing policy.

Refrigerated and Frozen Storage. The size of walk-in refrigerator and freezers should be calculated on the basis of cubic feet of space required. This figure depends on specific menu items, frequency of delivery, and number of meals served. Walk-in refrigerators are used for long-term storage of raw ingredients or short-term storage of prepared foods. These storage units can be purchased in many configurations. Options include the type of doors, surface finish, shelving, and locking systems.

Paper and Cleaning Supplies. Space requirements for storing paper and disposables will be unique for each facility also. Some managers like to take advantage of price breaks by purchasing large quantities and therefore need to allocate ample space. Cleaning supplies must be stored in separate rooms from food products to avoid contamination. Space is required for dishmachine and pot-washing detergents and other cleaning items.

Production Areas
The main production area of the kitchen should be located between storage and service. Each area, such as preparation, hot food, cold food, and final preparation, should be designed according to the menu item requirements. If the owner anticipates making menu changes, equipment may be added. When equipment is selected without regard for the menu, it is difficult to produce the planned menu. In most cases, the equipment selected generically will not be the best pieces for a specific menu. For each area, the major consideration is the flow of food.

Equipment Configuration. Regardless of the specific workstation, equipment layouts usually follow one of five basic patterns: the straight-line, the L-shape, the U-shape, the parallel face-to-face, and the parallel back-to-back. Each layout has applications for different situations. The straight-line configuration

(Figure 2a) is best for low volume restaurants with limited menus. As the volume increases, the line may be broken into smaller workstations. This configuration is easily placed against a wall. The L-shape configuration (Figure 2b) is suitable when space is limited. This arrangement can minimize travel distances between major groups of equipment. The U-shape configuration

Fig. 2. Equipment configurations for foodservice areas.

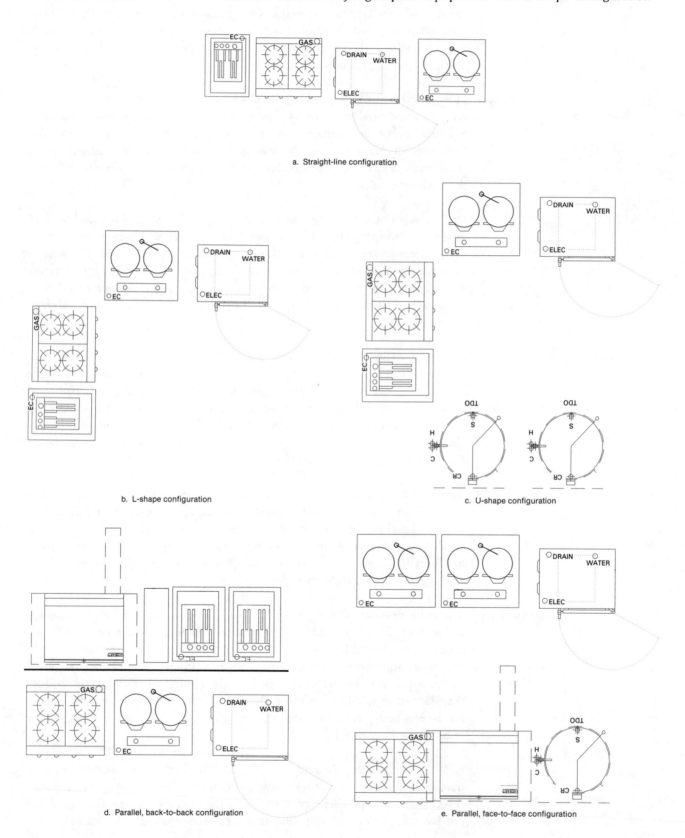

a. Straight-line configuration

b. L-shape configuration

c. U-shape configuration

d. Parallel, back-to-back configuration

e. Parallel, face-to-face configuration

(Figure 2c) is applicable when specific tasks need to be isolated, like baking or garde manger. This arrangement is best used for areas that do not require close supervision. Two parallel arrangements, face-to-face or back-to-back, offer different advantages. The parallel back-to-back (Figure 2d) can be used to minimize the cost of ventilation equipment, as only one hood is required. This arrangement also allows separation of workstations and employees. The parallel face-to-face (Figure 2e) is appropriate for large facilities where food distribution is separated from cooking. Two separate ventilation hoods are required. This arrangement is usually easier to supervise than the parallel back-to-back. The consequences of selecting a particular layout should be considered prior to finalizing the plans. For example, when a designer proposes an L-shape layout for a high volume production area, he or she may not realize that several employees will be working in that area. This plan will cause much confusion and frustration for employees.

Equipment Selection. Specific equipment should be selected carefully. The first decision is to determine the function of the equipment and if it is necessary for the facility. Other criteria for selection include the flexibility of the equipment, the use and abuse it may receive from employees, the construction materials, training required, energy requirements, and the costs associated with the purchase, such as installation, maintenance, and repair. The owner must also determine whether standard, modified standard, or custom equipment is needed. When custom equipment is desired, the owner will need to identify approved fabrication shops and then write specifications for the equipment. When standard equipment is acceptable, the equipment can be selected from equipment catalogs. Specifications can be written using the information from the catalogs.

Decisions on the capacity of the equipment should be made during the specification writing phase. Most equipment catalogs specify the dimensions and capacity of equipment, however, the capacity may be based on ideal conditions. The owner should calculate the actual capacity for specific products, rather than accepting the manufacturer's information.

Pre-Preparation
This area is for cleaning, peeling, chopping, mixing, and combining ingredients. Representative equipment includes food choppers, mixers, steam-jacketed kettles, vertical cutter mixers, and food processors. When the menu consists of items that are purchased already prepared, this area will be relatively small. Owners should consider the cost of square footage for this area plus the costs of purchasing raw ingredients and employees to process them versus the cost of purchasing preprocessed food items.

Cold Food
This area of the kitchen is used to assemble salads, appetizers, sandwiches, and desserts. Equipment specified for this area includes mixers, slicers, food processors, work tables, refrigerators, and utensils. As the facility size increases, this area may be sectioned into more than one workstation. The cold food area should be adjacent to the service area so employees can place finished items in the service refrigerators for waiters and waitresses.

Hot Food
The major section of the kitchen is devoted to producing entrees, soups, and vegetables. Workstations should be planned so each employee can work efficiently. Specific considerations include the volume required, production techniques, specialty items offered, style of service, and the skill level of employees. Equipment located here includes steamers, steam-jacketed kettles,

ovens, fryers, tilt-fryers, range tops, and grills. Extended-cooking equipment, like steam-jacketed kettles, tilt-fry pans, and ovens; and short-term cooking equipment, like deep-fat fryers, griddles, and broilers, should be grouped together. This arrangement allows the cooks to place items in extended-cooking equipment and then work in the short-term cooking area. If mobile equipment is selected, the cooking time can be rearranged as the menu changes.

Short-order Production. When the menu consists of several short-order items, such as french fries, hamburgers, and eggs, a short-order line may be needed. This line would include fryers, grills, and broilers. It is important to anticipate the volume so that equipment can be sized appropriately.

Bakery

If the manager or owner decides to offer a variety of baked products, a distinct area for baking is recommended. Decisions regarding the volume, production techniques, retail sales, and storage requirements for finished products will need to be made. Baking activities are not dependent on other food production areas, so the bakery can be located separate from these areas. The bakeshop should be located close to receiving and storage areas. If space is available adjacent to the food production area, equipment can be shared and supervision is easier.

Holding and Service

The service style planned for a facility is decided during the concept development phase. The service area should be designed to help servers perform their jobs efficiently. It should be planned with the dining sequence in mind. In small restaurants this area may only contain an overshelf with heat lamps and a refrigerator. In larger restaurants, a steam table with six to twelve inserts for pans is adequate. When the waiters and waitresses also bus dishes, the optimal service sequence is to enter the kitchen and drop off dirty dishes at the dishmachine, and then pick up cold food, hot food, beverages, and desserts. However, the precise layout should reflect the style of service and the number of courses offered.

Warewashing

The warewashing area should be located fairly close to the dining room and the main production areas. This placement allows the servers to drop off dishes as they enter the kitchen and for employees to replenish dishes to production areas. The problem of noise can be minimized by using double sets of doors or masonry walls between the dining room and kitchen.

The layout of the warewashing area is usually a straight-line, L-shape, or a U-shape arrangement. Warewashing machines vary from single-tank to three-tank flight type machines. The square footage required in a warewashing area depends on the quantity of dishes to be washed, method of transporting dishes to the area, and the storage requirements. To combat the uncomfortable nature of the activity, the area should be well-lighted, well-ventilated and equipped with a sound-absorbing ceiling.

Pot and Pan Area

Health department regulations dictate equipment requirements for the pot and pan area. A three-compartment sink is required in most communities. A three- to six-foot table is recommended on each end of the sinks. This area can be located close to the warewashing area or close to production. When the sinks are placed close to warewashing, employees can help out in both areas as needed. When the pot and pan area is located close to production, the cooks minimize the distance traveled to drop off dirty pots and obtain clean ones.

Office Areas Office spaces are needed to control the operation of the restaurant. Receiving clerks, chefs, and managers perform duties that require desk space in a separate area. Ideally, this office space should be located close to the area being supervised and provide some visibility of the area. A manager's office should also provide a private location for counseling employees, talking with salespeople, and completing financial records. Ideally, the manager's office should be located so that salespeople do not have to walk through the kitchen.

The amount of space allocated for offices depends on the space and funds available. This functional area may not be a high priority for designers and space is usually minimized.

The office environment is important to the type of work required. Management offices used for customer business should reflect the image the manager seeks to project. A nicely decorated office with carpeted floors and appropriate furniture will convey a different impression than a dimly-lit room, with a tiled floor and mismatched, scratched furniture.

Employee Areas Employee areas include locker rooms, break rooms, and restrooms. While these spaces do not directly generate revenue, personnel appreciate a manager who considers employee needs in the design. Locker rooms and restrooms should be provided for employees to store personal belongings, change clothes, and use the restroom without interfering with guests. These areas should be separate from production and storage areas. When employee areas are located close to exits and storage areas, pilferage problems may occur.

When employee break areas are provided, employees will be less likely to hang out on back docks, locker rooms, and in production areas. Break areas should be separate from production areas to allow employees a rest from the work. These areas should be maintained on a daily basis to ensure a clean, attractive area.

The Final Plan The final plan is an accumulation of all of the design ideas. After each workstation has been laid out, it can be placed into the plan. Adjustments will need to be made when equipment exceeds the allotted space or equipment duplications are noted.

The final plan should be evaluated prior to accepting the blueprints. Evaluation criteria include the flow of food, personnel, and equipment; the effective use of space, equipment, and personnel; safety and sanitation features, and the overall environment.

The key to a successful design is the attention devoted to each aspect of the plan. The designer must understand how a kitchen operates, and then use that knowledge to diagram the flow and arrange the function areas accordingly.

Summary

A restaurant's design has a major impact on the success of the operation, so planning the design should be completed carefully. The major goal of the design is to achieve a straight and smooth flow of resources. To ensure the optimum arrangement of workstations, a bubble diagram may be used. Each workstation is then laid out based on menu requirements. The final plan should be evaluated using design criteria of flow of food, personnel, and equipment; the use of space, equipment, and personnel; safety and sanitation features; and the overall physical environment.

Bibliography

Food service layouts. 1989. In *Commercial Kitchens*, ed. Robert A. Modlin, pp. 123–158. Arlington, Va.: American Gas Association.

Baraban, Regina S., and Joseph F. Durocher. 1989. *Successful Restaurant Design.* New York: Van Nostrand Reinhold.

Birchfield, John C. 1988. *Design and Layout of Foodservice Facilities.* New York: Van Nostrand Reinhold.

Pantano, Michael. 1987. Kitchen Design: A Practical Guide for the Non-Pro. *Lodging* 12(7):36–41, 57, 60.

Scriven, Carl R., and James W. Stevens. 1989. *Manual of Equipment and Design for the Foodservice Industry.* New York: Van Nostrand Reinhold.

7

Equipment Selection

Mahmood A. Khan

Selection of the proper equipment for each type of foodservice operation is extremely important. The type of equipment selected depends on the area in which it is to be used. Since equipment represents a fixed asset of a foodservice operation, which depreciates the moment it is purchased and installed, equipment selection requires careful planning and decision making. If improperly selected, equipment may tie up much needed cash and lead to the failure of the operation. There is a variety of foodservice equipment available with various modifications and a wide price range. Whether a particular piece of equipment is really needed and whether it is a good investment is the most difficult decision a foodservice manager is faced with. In addition to experience, careful calculations are needed before such a decision is made. The volume of food production and handling, employee productivity, and profitability of a foodservice operation directly depend on the type of equipment available at that facility.

Factors to Consider in Equipment Selection

Need This consideration is very important since it is obvious that need should dictate the purchase of any equipment. Need and planned use of equipment should be evaluated on the basis of whether the purchase or addition of that particular equipment will (1) result in desired or improved quality of food, (2) result in significant savings in labor and materials costs, (3) result in increased quantity of finished food products, and/or (4) contribute to the overall profitability of a foodservice operation.

Essential equipment should be given priority and preliminary selection should be based on the basic needs of an operation. Need for a particular piece of equipment should be assessed from different points of view as, for example, whether (1) the equipment will be used for prolonged periods of time, (2) it has the potential to meet the future needs of the foodservice operation, (3) the equipment will require maintenance, and (4) there exist alternate, less expensive versions of a similar piece of equipment that can adequately meet the demand of an operation. In other words, the need and essentiality should be calculated and well established. It is not financially advisable to buy expensive equipment or larger, more sophisticated equipment than what is essential for a foodservice operation.

Cost Several costs are incurred in the purchase, installation, and maintenance of any equipment in any type of foodservice operation. The major costs are (1) purchase or initial cost; (2) installation cost; (3) insurance costs; (4) repair and maintenance costs; (5) depreciation costs; (6) initial financing costs, interest, and other charges; (7) operating costs; and (8) costs of benefits and losses derived by addition of the equipment. Installation of equipment may require extensive remodeling that may be more expensive than the cost of the equipment itself.

Market prices of the equipment vary, based on the type of the equipment, the manufacturer, and the utility. A comparative assessment of these costs is essential before making any decision regarding equipment purchase. Expensive equipment, such as dishwashers, require more careful assessment than relatively less expensive equipment.

There are various methods of calculating the profitability of equipment based on costs. A foodservice manager may derive an equation that can be used for calculating the profitability of equipment based on factors most pertinent to that particular foodservice operation. A common equation used for calculations is:

$$E = \frac{A}{B + C + D}$$

where E = calculated value
A = savings in labor over the expected life of the equipment
B = cost of the equipment (including installation) minus the resale value of the equipment at the end of the expected life
C = cost of operation and maintenance of the equipment
D = interest or gains possible from investments instead of purchasing the equipment.

In the above calculations, if the value of E is 1.0 or more, then it is advisable to purchase the equipment, since it should more than pay for itself. If the value of E is more than 1.5, it is highly desirable—even necessary—to purchase that equipment. However, if the value of E is less than 1.0, it may not be advisable to purchase that particular equipment. Thus, the higher the value, the more potentially profitable it is to buy that equipment.

In the above-mentioned formula, the expected life of the equipment has to be included. Figures for the life expectancy of equipment are available from the manufacturer or the U.S. Internal Revenue Service. Normally, the life of common foodservice equipment ranges from 9 to 15 years. Various modifications of the formula may be made based on the factors directly pertaining to a particular foodservice operation. One such modification would be:

$$H = \frac{L(A + B)}{C + L(D + E + F) - G}$$

where H = calculated value
L = expected life of the equipment in years
A = savings in labor per year
B = savings in material per year
C = total cost of the equipment, including installation costs
D = cost of utilities per year
E = projected cost of maintenance and repair of the equipment per year

F = annual projected interest on the money in C, if invested elsewhere for the life of the equipment

G = turn-in value at the end of the life of the equipment.

As in the case of the previous formula, if the calculated value H is higher than 1.0, it is a good buy. Normally, the higher the value of H the more advisable it is to purchase that equipment.

The following example illustrates the application of the above formula. A restaurant owner is contemplating buying a steam-jacketed kettle for his operation. The data available indicates:

Expected life of the steam-jacketed kettle = 12 years (L)

Projected savings in labor per year due to the purchase of the equipment, $500 (A)

Projected savings in materials per year due to the purchase of the equipment, $300 (B)

Purchase and installation cost of the equipment, $3500 (C)

Projected costs of utilities per year to operate equipment, $57 (D)

Projected cost of maintenance per year for equipment, $15 (E)

Annual projected interest on the purchase and installation cost of the equipment (assuming rate of simple interest to be 6%) will be $3500 \times 6\% = $210 (F)

Projected turn-in value after 12 years, $200 (G)

The value of H may be calculated by substituting the data in the formula as follows:

$$H = \frac{12(500 + 300)}{3500 + 12(57 + 15 + 210) - 200}$$

$$= \frac{9600}{3500 + 3384 - 200} = 1.44 \text{ (Good Buy)}$$

This figure, as mentioned earlier, should preferably be higher than 1.0 but a foodservice operation management may decide to set this value to be much higher than 1.0. This will provide a standard basis for decision making when purchasing equipment. Also, the life expectancy of equipment may be much more than calculated, so the final value of H may be higher. A conservative figure should preferably be used for the expected life for equipment. On the other hand, equipment may not last as long as expected or may become outdated before the expiration of the projected life period.

Functional Attributes Since the equipment is selected to fulfill certain functions of a foodservice operation, it is necessary to evaluate each piece of equipment based on its functional attributes in the light of the desired needs. Performance of the equipment should be assessed based on the cost as well as the availability of other equipment. Maximum possible functions as compared to the costs should be given preference. The possibility of modifying the equipment by attachments and other changes should be considered as an asset. Both present and future anticipated menu changes will also dictate the type of equipment to be selected. If relatively large sums are being invested in the purchasing of equipment, future changes and development should definitely be taken into consideration. Functioning of equipment is also based on the type of energy required for its operation as well as the extent to which it is planned to be used.

Sanitation and Safety

Sanitation and safety are primary considerations in purchasing any equipment for a foodservice operation. Ease of cleaning and sanitation should be given high priority when selecting equipment. No matter how sophisticated a piece of equipment is, if it cannot be cleaned properly, it is not suitable for a foodservice operation. All materials used in the manufacture of the equipment, particularly food-contact surfaces, should be made of nontoxic materials. Equipment used in food production should be such that safe temperatures can be maintained easily and at all times. Sufficient accessories such as lights and dials should be integral parts to ensure that the proper temperatures are reached and maintained by the equipment. All parts should be easily accessible for cleaning. Wherever applicable and possible, the parts of the equipment should be able to be disassembled and reassembled easily and quickly to facilitate cleaning. Self-cleaning types of equipment are most preferable. The National Sanitation Foundation (NSF) certifies foodservice equipment that meets defined sanitary standards.

All equipment selected for a foodservice operation should have built-in safety feature(s). Electrical equipment should be used with proper voltage and should be free from any hazards. All moving and sharp parts should be properly protected. There should not be any rough or sharp edges on any pieces of equipment. Safety locks and devices should be used on all equipment wherever possible, such as in steamers, steam-kettles, and carts. Equipment should be free of crevices or holes, which may either harbor insects or microorganisms or hinder its proper cleaning and sanitation. All factors related to sanitation and safety should be checked before making any decision regarding the purchase of equipment.

Size, Appearance, and Design

The size of the equipment should be such that it can easily be accomodated in the space available in the layout and design of the facility. It may be difficult to place equipment where limited space is available. Improperly located equipment will be a continuous source of inconvenience and even a hazard. The doors and openings of the equipment should be designed such that they do not cause any problems or hazards.

The design and appearance of the equipment should be attractive and should perform the maximum functions with a minimum of problems. Durability of the equipment should be given consideration in the design, since the equipment used in foodservice operations is subjected to constant use and abuse. Although the functional characteristics should be given priority over the design, the design should be such that it facilitates smooth functioning of the equipment. The appearance of the equipment should be in line with the type of facility, with matching colors as much as possible.

Overall Performance

Foodservice equipment should also be selected on the basis of its overall performance, which includes such aspects as quietness of operation, easy mobility, remote control operations, computerized controls, variety of functions, availability of parts, and ease of maintenance. Those pieces of equipment known for their superior performance in a desired situation should be given priority when selecting equipment for any type of foodservice operation. It may be advisable to purchase equipment with proven efficiency rather than relatively new equipment with no history of use.

Types of Energy and Its Sources

Energy plays a very important role in the selection of equipment for use in foodservices. With increased emphasis on energy conservation, it is important to select energy efficient equipment. In order to understand energy, it is necessary to know its common sources as well as the common terminology used for the sources of energy.

Energy is available in different forms and can be transferred from one form to another. The common sources of energy primarily used in foodservices are electricity, gas, steam, and oil.

Electricity is the most common form of energy used in foodservices. It runs by a flow of electrons in an electric current, which is analogous to the flow of water in a pipe. As in the case of water, electricity can be quantitatively measured by the number of electrons flowing from a particular point at a given time. This flow of electrons per second is measured in amperes (amp or I). As the force of water from a pipe can be measured in pounds per square inch (psi), electricity can also be measured in volts (V).

A *volt* can be defined as the force required to push 1 amp of electricity by a given point in one second. Thus, the voltage is indicative of the force with which electricity is flowing. There are different ranges in voltages, such as 110–120 V and 220–240 V. The voltage requirement is an important consideration in the purchase of any equipment. Also, before plugging in any electric equipment, voltage should be checked, since serious damage may result by using improper voltage. Foodservice equipment is frequently available in different voltages and some comes with dual voltages, in which a switch is provided to change to the desired voltage.

The force behind the flow of electrical current (V) multiplied by the amount flowing (amp or I) gives the measure of electricity in watts (W). In other words, $W = V \times I$. This is an important relationship and can be used for different calculations pertaining to electricity:

$$W = V \times I$$
$$I = W/V$$
$$V = W/I$$

The required amperage can be calculated using the above relationship. For example, if 2000 W of electricity is on a 110-V line, the amperage requirement would be I/V, or 2000/110, which is equal to 18.2 amp. A 25 percent safety factor, for possible fluctuations in electric current, should be added to this figure. Thus a 25-amp fuse will be needed for this circuit. In planning electrical outlets for equipment use, these calculations are very helpful. It should be noted that as the voltage increases, amperage decreases. For example, if the voltage in the above example is 220, the amperage would be 2000/220 = 9.09.

The watts and voltage required for any electrical equipment are specified on a plate affixed to the equipment. For calculating the cost of the electricity, watts used per hour are used. Thus a watt-hour (Wh) is one watt of electricity flowing steadily for an hour. Since there are a large number of watts involved in the use of electricity, a kilowatt-hour (kWh) is used, which is 1000 W of electricity flowing steadily for an hour. Costs of electricity are usually given in cents per kilowatt-hour, from which energy costs of any equipment or electrical appliance may be calculated.

Many of the electrical appliances, particularly those used in foodservices, have a grounding system in them. Since electrons in electricity carry a negative charge, they can be attracted toward a positive charge. Electricity may become free (for various reasons) and flow to undesirable places. Thus, in order to provide for safety, measures are taken to ground negatively charged electrons by attracting them to a positive charge. It is advisable— even necessary—to use a grounding system. Usually the three-pronged plugs have grounding in them. In foodservice operations, all electrical equipment should be grounded for safety reasons.

When there is a resistance to the flow of water, there is an accumulation of water. Similarly, when there is a resistance to electricity, it accumulates to form heat. This principle is used when resistance elements are used for heating ovens, fryers, and similar equipment. Resistance (R) is set up against electricity by using certain metal wires, such as nickel, chromium, or their alloys. Resistance is measured in ohms. One ohm is equal to 1 amp at 1 V. Ohms can be calculated as:

$$R = V/I$$
$$I = V/R$$
$$V = IR$$

Electricity may exist as a direct current (DC), or as an alternating current (AC). The type of electricity in the United States is in the form of AC. An AC generator of electricity sweeps masses of electrons that are sent in alternating pulses. Most alternators in the United States set up 60 alternating pulses per second which is referred to as *cycles* (c) or *hertz* (Hz). Cycles are important for equipment that have motors or revolving parts, such as blenders and recorders. Their speed and performance are affected by the number of cycles. This information is usually provided by the manufacturer and is often placed on a plate on the equipment. For motors, the power is expressed in the form of horsepower (hp). One hp is equal to 746 W.

The flow of steam, which is another form of energy, is measured in pounds per square inch. Heat may be measured by the temperature or by the amount expressed in British thermal units (BTU) or calories. A BTU is the quantity of heat required to raise the temperature of one pound of water by 1°F. A calorie is the amount of heat required to raise the temperature of one gram of water by 1°C; it is equal to 3.968 Btu. This type of calorie should not be confused with the calorie used in nutritional sciences.

Once the energy requirements of all appliances and equipment are known, it is relatively easy to calculate the energy costs or to conduct an audit. In order to conserve energy, it is desirable to conduct energy audits at periodical intervals of time and to conserve energy wherever possible.

Summary

Equipment selection is one of the most important aspects in any foodservice operation. Because equipment is a fixed asset that begins to depreciate when it is installed, prior consideration should be given to the use and necessity of its purchase. The quantity of food produced, employee productivity, and financial success of a foodservice operation depends on the equipment selected and utilized. The basic considerations needed in the selection and purchase of equipment for a foodservice operation are described in depth in this article. Calculations for the cost effectiveness of the equipment are shown. Energy sources and its conservation are highlighted.

8

Kitchen Planning

David Kirk

Objectives of Kitchen Planning

The objectives of kitchen planning are

- To create a work area that can satisfy the requirements of the menu, staff skills, service style, and customer demand with the optimal use of resources
- To provide an efficient and effective work area in terms of movement of staff, equipment, and materials
- To minimize the risk of food poisoning through the provision of environmentally controlled storage areas and by the segregation of contaminated raw materials from finished product
- To provide a controlled environment for staff working in the kitchen together with adequate staff facilities
- To minimize the use of energy
- To provide adequate storage for raw materials, partially processed food materials, foods awaiting service, equipment, utensils, crockery and cutlery, and cleaning materials

The Planning Team

Kitchen planning is normally carried out by a team that includes an architect, a foodservice design consultant, a mechanical and electrical consultant(s), an interior designer, representatives of the client, and representatives of the foodservice equipment supply and installation company.

The planning team is normally coordinated by the architect or alternatively by the foodservice consultant. Other specialists may form a part of the team or may be consulted at various stages of the planning process. These include experts covering legal requirements, such as zoning, building and planning regulations, health and safety, fire prevention, and environmental health. In many cases, the foodservice equipment company is not selected until after a bidding process and therefore is not a part of the initial design team.

The first stage in the process is to develop a conceptual plan of the foodservice operation. From this is developed the physical plan, together with lists of equipment and specifications. These lists then go out to bid to select an equipment supplier and installer. This company is then responsible for the supply, installation, and commissioning of equipment. The final stage in the process is the hand-over to the client. This last stage includes familiarization and training on the equipment.

The Conceptual Plan

The conceptual plan provides the overall framework for the food production and service facility. The foodservice concept is developed by the foodservice consultant, working with the client to define the menu and food concept, food purchasing policy, the relationships between food production and service (degree of coupling), the style of service, and the method of financing.

Other factors that need to be taken into account include policies about the number of staff to be employed, skill levels of staff, particular space constraints related to the site, and financial and budgetary constraints.

The Menu and Food Concept The conceptual plan needs to provide detailed information about the type of menu to be used and information about food quantities to be served, together with a sales mix analysis. The sales mix analysis gives a breakdown of sales of each menu item throughout the hours of opening. This analysis can then be used to calculate total production volumes and peak production requirements. Both figures are required for equipment capacity calculations.

Food Purchasing Policy The food purchasing policy determines important space requirements for food storage and food preparation areas and indicates what food preparation equipment is necessary. For example, the mix of fresh, frozen, chilled, canned, and dried foods influences the type of storage required and the volume of storage for each type of food. Actual storage volume is related both to the rate of consumption and to the frequency of delivery.

Food preparation space and food preparation equipment are largely related to the nature of food raw materials. The greater the level of processing associated with the purchased form of a particular commodity, the smaller the space and equipment requirement within the operation.

Relationship between Food Production and Foodservice An important factor in foodservice design is to establish the link between production and service. This may be expressed as the degree of coupling between production and service. Where food is passed directly from production to service, with no storage or with minimal storage, there is said to be close coupling of production and service. Where a buffer stock is introduced between production and service, the buffer stock acts as a means of decoupling the two processes. The longer the high quality shelf life of the buffer stock, the greater the degree of decoupling possible.

It is possible to differentiate between a number of forms of foodservice systems based on the above relationships between production and service.

1. No buffer stock; all food production is initiated by the customer order.
2. Stock of partially prepared components; the production of menu items is initiated by the customer order.
3. Stock of completed ready-to-serve product; production is initiated by a fall in the level of buffer stock. Food is produced, in batches, to replenish the buffer stock.
4. Stock of shelf-stable ready-to-serve product; production is related

to schedule of requirements as part of a menu cycle. Food is produced in batches to meet the requirements of the production schedule.

It is important to establish which of the above procedures is appropriate for all of the items that appear on the menu, since this affects both preparation space and equipment requirements.

Style of Service

Style of service influences the kitchen plan in a number of ways. First, it is essential to distinguish between waiter service, self-serve, and counter service. Second, account must be taken of trends for cooking and preparation that the customer can see, introduced as a part of the theater or entertainment element of foodservice.

Finally, it is necessary to provide good communication between restaurant staff and kitchen staff. Good two-way communication between production and service areas is essential for a successful foodservice operation. At the peak of service activity, congestion can be avoided at the interface between production and service staff if thought is given to simplified means of communication. For example, electronic paging systems can be introduced to notify service staff that an order is ready for service. Similarly, printers in the kitchen can be linked to a terminal in the restaurant through which orders can be transmitted.

Other Constraints

Each design will be faced with a different set of constraints. Some of the typical problem areas include problems over obtaining staff (particularly skilled staff), constraints on the space allocated to foodservice, and limitations on the availability of investment capital.

Many tradeoffs can be made in the planning process to solve some of these problems. For example, if staff is hard to find, it is possible to substitute labor-saving equipment and technology for staff. Similarly, if skilled staff are expensive, it may be feasible to substitute equipment that has sophisticated (for example, computerized) control to reduce the skill requirements of staff. If there is a shortage of space, it is conceivable that high capacity equipment with a small footprint could be used to increase productivity from the limited floor area. However, all of these possible solutions have capital cost implications that need to be taken into account at the design stage.

Overall Space Requirements

The foodservice planner invariably must make decisions about the adequacy of total space provision and the allocation of space to the various functional areas. In most cases the total space availability is fixed by constraints imposed by the requirements of other aspects of the building, irrespective of whether we are dealing with new construction or with the conversion or renovation of an existing building.

Guidelines that indicate the space requirements for foodservice operations are available. These guidelines can be of great value to the foodservice planner, but great care is needed in their interpretation. For example, the trend over the last few years has been toward much greater space productivity, encouraged by better design, greater use of mechanized equipment, greater availability of convenience foods, and higher productivity of prime cooking equipment.

Dining Areas As a rough rule of thumb, seating and service areas range from 10 square feet (1 square meter) per customer for fast-food, banquet service, and industrial feeding, to 20 square feet (2 square meters) per customer for table service (Kotschevar and Terrell 1985).

Space allocation to dining areas depends largely on the style of service and the level of luxury and intimacy expected by the diners. For fine dining, or where it is desirable to provide intimate dining areas, a large amount of space is required compared with institutional foodservice operations. Fixed tables and chairs, as used in many fast-food operations, take up less space than tables with separate chairs. Similarly the shape of the table (round, square, or oblong) influences space requirements as does the number of diners per table.

The number of seats required is based on a knowledge of three factors: the number of customers to be served, the turnover rate (that is, the number of times a seat is used in one hour), and the allocation for empty seats. This allocation depends partly on the match between table types and party size, but is typically between 10 and 20 percent. Designing a restaurant with the correct mix of tables for two, four, six, and so on can reduce the allocation required for empty seats.

The use of trolleys by waiting staff for table work, dessert service, and similar activities, takes additional space. Typical space allocations for various types of food service are shown in Table 1.

Storage, Preparation, and Production Areas It is more difficult to estimate back-of-house space in foodservice because of the factors described above. The main factors involved are the volume of food produced, the method of production, and the rate of seat turnover.

There are no hard-and-fast rules about the amount of space required for production facilities for a foodservice operation. Any figures given are only a very rough guideline, but in practice these guidelines will vary greatly because of a number of factors. First, production areas must usually be accommodated in a space available, which is fixed by site and architectural constraints. Therefore, the kitchen designer must often show great ingenuity in fitting a kitchen, designed to produce a given quantity of food, into the available space. This space may be less than any guidelines or it may be a very awkward space in terms of good design principles. The food policy itself influences space requirement because of its effect on staffing levels, the amount of food preparation taking place on-site, and the capital available for labor saving devices. Other factors include allowances for the rate of seat turnover together with allowances for any take-away foodservice.

Second, all of the latest trends in equipment design and other labor saving techniques is leading to greater levels of space productivity (the number of meals that can be served per square foot or square meter of kitchen).

Table 1. *Space allocation for dining areas*

Type of facility	ft²	m²
Cafeteria (institutional)	9–15	0.9–1.4
Cafeteria (commercial)	15–18	1.4–1.7
Counter service	16–20	1.5–1.9
Banquet	10–12	0.9–1.1
Fine dining	15–20	1.4–1.9

Table 2. *Space allocation for storage, preparation and production*

Number of meals	ft²	m²
50–100	8	0.8
100–250	5	0.5
250–500	4	0.4
500–1000	3	0.3

This means that published guidelines are often an over-estimate of actual space necessary.

In spite of these concerns, guideline space figures are useful to the kitchen designer because they give an early indication of any particular space allocation problems. If a designer knows at an early stage in the design process that there are likely to be significant space constraints, he/she can both advise the clients of the problem and influence the establishment of a food and design policy that takes this constraint into account.

Kitchen allocations vary from 3 to 7 square feet (0.3 to 0.6 square meters) per customer where there is a single sitting and 10 to 20 square feet (1 to 2 square meters) where there is a single sitting (Lawson 1978). The space allocation per meal decreases as the number of meals served increases. In fast-food operations, an additional allocation of space is required for the take-away element of the business. Typical guideline figures for food storage, preparation, and production areas are shown in Table 2.

Allocation of Space within the Kitchen Area

As is the case with space guidelines, there are no hard-and-fast rules about the subdivision of space within the storage, preparation, and production area. Detailed consideration must be given to the menu, purchasing policy, methods of production, and method of service. Even the subdivisions of the kitchen areas will vary from one type of operation to another (Modlin 1989). Most foodservice operations will require the following areas:

> Goods reception
> Frozen food store
> Refrigerated storage
> Dry goods storage
> Preparation/production/cooking
> Serving
> Dining
> Dishwashing and potwashing
> Staff facilities: rest areas, toilets, showers

Once these areas have been allocated, they can be mapped onto a plan of the site. For kitchen planning work, a scale of ¼ inch = 1 foot or 1:50 is normally used. Initially the areas can be located on the plan, bearing in mind the need to establish efficient and hygienic work flows through the kitchen.

Basic Work Flow and Relationships between Work Centers

The flow of work within a foodservice kitchen is governed by both work design principles (Dilworth 1989) and hygiene requirements (Khan 1991).

The hygiene requirements call for a logical flow of food from its raw material state, through preparation and cooking, to service. There should be no chance of cross-contamination of food poisoning bacteria from raw foods to foods that are ready for service. There should be no cross-flow or back-tracking of food and utensils and equipment used for raw foods should not be used for prepared foods.

Work design principles dictate that work areas that are closely related in terms of frequent movement of materials and/or staff should be sited close together (Kazarian 1983). This is important in order to minimize the distances walked by staff and to minimize the total area required. Even in a well-planned kitchen, staff walk several miles in a day and, in a poorly planned kitchen, this distance can easily be doubled. Techniques are available to translate work study information about frequency of movement into layout bubble diagrams and layouts (Milson and Kirk 1980). Computer programs are also available to optimize layouts (Hales 1984), but it is usually not cost effective to do this for kitchens where the work flow is well established.

In practice, the difficulty is usually satisfying these requirements of work design and hygiene within the physical constraints of the building. With a new building, and if the catering consultant is involved at an early stage, these relationships are relatively easy to establish in the plan. If the foodservice consultant is only involved once the major structural details are finalized, or where the building already exists, the problem can become much more difficult.

In order to facilitate the design of the food preparation and production areas, it is normal to divide the activities of a kitchen into a number of work centers. A work center is a physical area within the kitchen where a particular type of operation is performed. This operation may be a particular process (such as vegetable preparation or broiling) or it may be the product preparation. Traditional restaurant and hotel kitchens are usually subdivided into process work centers (but with some product work centers such as the bakery). Fast-food kitchens are usually organized with product work centers.

A work center requires the equipment relevant to the particular products or processes of that work center. It also requires a space allocation for the number of staff working in that area, together with allowances for traffic aisles, opening of equipment doors, and passage of trolleys. Guideline figures for these space requirements are given in Table 3. It is important that main traffic aisles within a kitchen do not pass through work centers. This can be both inefficient and hazardous.

At this stage in the planning, detailed physical layouts of each work center are developed, based on the initial allocation of space. In order to aid the process, scaled templates are available from some manufacturers. As an alternative, many designers are now using symbol libraries supplied by manufacturers for incorporation into computer assisted design systems.

Choice of Equipment

The selection of equipment is based on an analysis of the menu together with information about production volumes and the relationships between production and service. This information is then related to the production capacity of relevant types of equipment. This may be expressed in a number of different ways (Fuller and Kirk 1991).

Table 3. *Space allocations for work centers*

Activity	Space allowance	
	inches	millimeters
Width of work table per employee	40–60	1000–1500
Working space in front of work space	36–48	900–1200
Allowance for doors, tilting equipment	24–36	600–900
Space for one person to pass	40–54	1000–1400
Main traffic aisle	60–70	1500–1700

Area of cooking surface: grills, griddles
Volume of cooking vessel: kettles, pans
Number of standard trays: steaming, convection and general purpose
      ovens, dishwashing machines
Weight of product per hour: fryers

The precise capacity depends upon the relationship between production and service. If producing to demand or to limited buffer stock, the capacity is related to the peak level of sales. If producing to longer term buffer stock, the capacity of equipment is related to optimal batch size. When producing shelf-stable buffer stock (chilled or frozen), food is produced to a production schedule related to the capacity of the chilling or freezing equipment.

Line balancing is also important in relation to equipment selection. This means matching items of preparation and cooking equipment to the capacity of chilling or freezing equipment in order to ensure that consistent batch sizes are used throughout the production process.

The choice of equipment can also influence the number of times that food must be transferred from one container to another. Manual handling of material can be reduced if equipment that utilizes the same tray or container size is chosen.

With a fixed menu, much more precise information is known about the product, such as its dimensions and optimal cooking conditions. Therefore, very precise decisions can be made about the amount of cooking equipment required. Also, there can be very precise matching between menu items and specialized pieces of equipment designed to cook that menu item in an optimal way.

In the case of cyclic or market menus, information is available about the broad structure of the menu, for example, the number of grilled, roast, or stewed items. The equipment must be more general in nature and the capacity cannot be accurately calculated.

Other factors involved in equipment selection include

Skill levels of staff
Duty of equipment
Services constraints (limitations on supplies of gas, electricity, water,
      drains, and ventilation)
Financial constraints
Energy management policy

Once the cooking method and capacity has been established for each menu, the completed list must be scrutinized to see if there is any redundancy in the list. For example, if three menu items require convection ovens, can two or all three of the items share one convection oven or are there constraints in terms of the time of day the oven is required? Are there flavor carry-over problems?

Decisions must also be made about the best method of providing equipment capacity. If it is estimated that 50 gallons of tilting kettle capacity is required, is this best provided by two kettles, each of 25 gallons capacity, or by a single kettle? In many situations, a number of smaller items gives greater flexibility than one large one.

It is very important that choice of equipment is not based solely on capital cost considerations. The total cost of the equipment, including energy, maintenance, and cleaning costs should be considered at the time of purchase (Pine 1989).

Summary

Kitchen planning is a complex process requiring the balancing of a number of factors. These factors include the utilization of resources such as physical space, foodservice equipment, foodservice staff (both the number of staff and their level of skill), and finance (capital and revenue). These factors must be balanced to produce and serve the quantity and quality of food demanded by the customers at the time it is required, while at the same time generating satisfactory profit margins. The design must also satisfy other constraints including legal requirements in relation to sanitation, food safety, health and safety, fire safety, and planning regulations.

The starting point for the kitchen plan is a clear identification of the foodservice concept. The foodservice concept identifies the market segmentation, potential customers, opening hours, type of menu, sales volume, profit margins, and the methods of production and service. This information is used to determine space allocation, work flows, and equipment requirements, all of which form the basis of the kitchen plan. The final plan is a compromise solution that satisfies the requirements of the foodservice concept within limits set by the constraints of capital and space availability.

References

Dilworth, J. B. 1989. *Production and Operations Management*, 4th ed. New York: Random House.

Fuller, J., and D. Kirk. 1991. *Kitchen Planning and Management*. London: Butterworth Heinemann.

Hales, L. 1984. *Computer-Aided Facilities Planning*. New York: Marcel Dekker.

Kazarian, E. A. 1983. *Foodservice Facilities Planning*, 2d ed. Westport, Conn.: AVI Publishing Co.

Khan, M. A. 1991. *Concepts of Foodservice Operations and Management*, 2d ed. New York: Van Nostrand Reinhold.

Kotschevar, L. H., and M. E. Terrell. 1985. *Foodservice Planning: Layout and Equipment*. New York: Wiley.

Lawson, F. 1978. *Principles of Catering Design*. London: Architectural Press.

Milson, A., and D. Kirk. 1980. *Principles of Design and Operation of Catering Equipment*. Chichester: Ellis Horwood.

Modlin, R. A. 1989. *Commercial Kitchens*. Arlington, Va.: American Gas Association.

Pine, R. 1989. *Catering Equipment Management*. London: Hutchinson.

9

Consumer Food Preferences

Barbara A. Almanza

It is relatively easy to define consumer food preferences but difficult to describe all the factors that influence their formation. A working definition of consumer food preferences would be "the desires of people that influence their menu selections when they are eating out." These preferences may be the same as when they are eating at home or may be different. For example, a person who is watching his or her calorie intake at home and avoiding desserts may wish to have a slice of cake when celebrating a birthday in a restaurant.

There is a difference between food liking, food preference, and food selection. Liking is a positive emotional response to food. It is associated with the taste of the food and may involve pleasant memories of eating that food. It plays a part in food preference but is not the same as food preference. A food preference represents one's desire when all *internal* factors influencing food choice are considered. These internal factors include personal interests in nutrition, health, taste, and variety, among others. Food liking is one of these internal factors.

Food selection is what is actually ordered when *external* factors are considered. These external factors might include the availability of the food, price of the food, and interactions with other people. Food selection may not exactly correspond to either food liking or food preference.

The following illustrates these three definitions: Even though most people enjoy the taste of chocolate cake (food liking), they realize that chocolate cake is not very nourishing as an evening meal and decide to order a beef or pork entrée (food preference). They find that the least expensive of these is a hamburger and decide to order that (food selection).

Formation of Preferences

An important question about food preferences is how much of these preferences are determined genetically and to what extent they are the result of learning. An understanding of this question would be helpful because it could explain the origin of food preferences and how to change undesirable food preferences. Research suggests the possibility of dual determination.

Genetic determinants have been suggested from studies that have shown the existence of a preference for sweet taste in newborns (Desor et al. 1973). Sweet fluids were presented to newborn infants and the amount measured. As the concentration of the sugar in those fluids was increased, infants consumed more of the fluids. The existance of a sweet preference at such an early age strongly suggests a genetic component in taste preference.

Genetic influence has been demonstrated from breeding experiments as well. It was determined many years ago that it is possible to selectively breed rats to have a greater or a lesser preference for sweet (Nachman 1959).

Genetic influence may also be expressed through its effect on the ability to digest certain foods. For example, genetically determined ability to digest lactose in milk has been shown. Most humans do not have complete ability to digest lactose as adults, with the exception of those people descended from cattle-herding, milk-drinking areas, such as northern Europe (Rozin et al. 1986). For those people lacking the genetically determined ability, small amounts of lactose may still be consumed, but large amounts are poorly tolerated.

The influence of learning has been suggested by the finding that the food preferences of close biological relatives are no more similar than the food preferences of people who do not share a common genetic background (Birch 1980). In another experiment, Birch and Marlin (1982) used two-year-old children and offered them novel cheeses and fruits between 0 and 20 times. In later choice tests, the children were found to prefer the foods to which they had received more exposure. This suggest the influence of learning in that the preferred foods were those which the child had been accustomed to eating.

Food preferences develop from childhood through adulthood. During this time, they may be influenced by a wide variety of factors including religious, cultural or ethnic, and geographic influences. In addition, individual characteristics such as health, sex, age, educational level, and socioeconomic status have been suggested to affect one's nutritional interests and food preferences.

Food preferences therefore may be a result of both genetics and learning. Biological differences in people may also influence food preference for individuals because of the effect on taste perception. For example, changes in taste and smell sensitivity may occur with age and may account for small changes in preference with aging (Cowart 1981; Schiffman 1979).

Certain illnesses and medications may have a biological effect on taste perception as well. Cancer is one of the more dramatic examples, as well as the chemotherapy that might be done for cancer. Loss of appetite and actual taste changes have been reported as well as other physical and psychological problems that can interfere with eating. For example, people with cancer sometimes report that sweet foods no longer taste as sweet to them and that other foods (particularly red meats) taste bitter (U.S. Department of Health and Human Services 1982).

Factors That Influence Food Preferences

An important part of understanding customer food preferences is an awareness of the factors that influence their development. Religion may play a significant role in some customers' food preferences. For example, Catholics may wish to avoid meats (beef, pork, lamb, poultry) on Fridays during Lent. Jews may avoid pork or pork-containing items. Seventh-Day Adventists believe that vegetarian diet and abstention from tea, coffee, alcoholic beverages, and tobacco is best for maintaining their health (Lowenberg et al. 1979). Muslims may wish to avoid eating pork or drinking wine or other alcoholic beverages. Hindus are strict vegetarians.

Most of these restrictions involve entrées rather than other menu items. Since these practices are highly individual, the most appropriate practice for a foodservice that is interested in accommodating people with differing beliefs is to provide a variety of selections and be knowledgeable in answering questions about ingredient content of foods.

Cultural or ethnic background may also play a role in determining food preference. The influence of food patterns from different countries is evident from the regional influence of immigrants in the United States. Czechoslovakian kolachies are found in parts of Iowa and Minnesota; lutefisk (cod), herring, and lefse from the Scandinavian countries are popular in Minnesota; chili con carne and tamales from Mexico are found in Texas; and German sausages and sauerkraut are popular in Pennsylvania and Wisconsin (Lowenberg et al. 1979).

Cultural or ethnic influence on food preference may be particularly evident in foods that provide a staple to the diet. This includes foods such as rice, potatoes, bread, or corn. Rice may be more typical of an accompaniment to a meal for someone of Asian background, in contrast to the southwestern United States with its Hispanic influence where corn dishes may be more typical. People from the midwestern United States often use potato dishes or bread to accompany the meal.

Cultural or ethnic background may even play a role in determinnig how often and when during a 24-hour period one may eat. In European societies, four meals a day is a typical pattern; two meals are common in sections of Africa such as with the Tiuv of Nigeria who eat at dawn and at dusk; and a single meal is eaten at irregular times by the Bemba of Central Africa (Bryant et al. 1985) and by people from Liberia. In North America, the three-meal-a-day pattern is considered traditional although people in the United States are often found to snack frequently so that they may be eating six to seven small meals a day (Bryant et al. 1985).

Ethnic influence on food preference can be significant in foods that are served at holidays. For example, lutefisk and lefse are traditional on Christmas Eve among families with Norwegian background; venison spread with sour cream and turkey stuffed with apples, raisins, and dark rye bread is popular with families of German background at Christmas; and borscht, braided Christmas bread, and stuffed cabbage rolls are traditional for families with Ukrainian background (Shenton et al. 1971).

Foodservices can and should consider these regional ethnic influences carefully in menu development and may even use them as part of the restaurant theme. According to the National Restaurant Association (1982), the favorite atmosphere restaurant for 16.9 percent of Americans is one that specializes in some type of ethnic food.

Beliefs in the long-term consequences of diet may also play a role in forming food preferences. Many researchers are reporting a growing awareness in diet/disease relationships and a subsequent growing interest in nutrition in customers. The public's interest has focused on the long-term effects of diet on obesity, heart disease, and cancer, although a study by the National Cancer Institute found that few people expressed willingness to make dietary changes to possibly prevent cancer (Ganem 1990). The link between changes in food selection and an ability to minimize one's risk for cancer may not be clear for customers and may be a reason why few people were willing to make dietary changes. In any case, it does appear that customers are becoming more aware of diet/disease relationships and are reporting a greater interest in nutrition.

The National Academy of Sciences report, *Diet and Health: Implications of Reducing Chronic Disease Risk* (Committee on Diet and Health, Food and Nutrition Board, National Research Council 1989), and *The Surgeon General's Report on Nutrition and Health* (Surgeon General's Office 1988) have suggested that the nutritional components of concern for most Americans are total calories, protein, total fat, saturated fat, cholesterol, complex carbohydrates, fiber, sodium, and calcium.

The percentage of Americans that report an interest in nutrition information is high, although the percentage of customers that actually use nutrition information appears to be smaller. In one study (Almanza 1989), customers in dormitory, university, hospital, and employee dining cafeterias were surveyed regarding their nutrition interests. Customers were first surveyed (group one), then nutrition information about the entrées was displayed and customers were again surveyed (group two). Sixty-nine percent of group one (which did not receive nutrition information) said they would be interested in nutrition information. The percentage of respondents from group two (which did receive nutrition information) that actually used nutrition information was smaller, however, at only seventeen percent.

Researchers have suggested that age, sex, health, educational level, and socioeconomic status are correlated with one's nutrition interest. More specifically, younger people, females, those with more education, and those in higher socioeconomic groups report a greater interest in nutrition (Carlson and Tabacchi 1986). People in these groups may be more likely to make dietary changes that influence their food selection when eating out. Even though many customers report an interest in nutrition, many factors appear to influence the actual food selection.

Food Consumption Patterns as a Reflection of Current Food Preferences

Food preferences do not appear to be static. When food consumption patterns are estimated for the American people as a group, food consumption patterns have clearly changed over the years (U.S. Department of Agriculture 1989). This suggests that food preferences may have also changed.

U.S. Department of Agriculture (USDA) studies have reported that in the last 20 years, there has been an increase in the consumption of the following groups: poultry, fish, vegetable fats and oils, fresh vegetables, fruits (particularly fresh), and flour and cereal products (USDA 1989). A decrease in consumption in the last 20 years was noted in meat, eggs, animal fats, refined sugar, coffee, tea, and cocoa (USDA 1989).

Menu items eaten away from home have reflected fairly similar trends as well. Reported changes included an increased demand for fish and seafood, poultry, fresh vegetables, fresh fruit, and salads (Ganem 1990).

From these studies, it can be seen that food consumption patterns for people as a group in the United States have changed. These changes may also be a possible reflection of changes in food preferences as well.

Summary

Consumer food preferences are the desires of people that influence their menu selections when they are eating out. Both genetics and one's environment affect the formation of preferences. Influences on food preferences include religion, cultural or ethnic background, and beliefs in the long-term consequences of diet. Food preferences may change with time. Foodservices should consider food preferences when planning menus. For example, some foodservices may wish to target particular market segments with specialized menus, whereas others may wish to accommodate different food preferences by providing a wide variety of selections.

References

Almanza, B. A. M. 1989. Change in consumer knowledge and response to foodservice entrees which are marketed as being lower in sodium, fat, cholesterol, and calories. (Doctoral dissertation, University of Illinois, 1989). *Dissertation Abstracts International*, 10, 4458B. (Order No. AAD89-24755)

Birch, L. L. 1980. The relationship between children's food preferences and those of their parents. *Journal of Nutrition Education* 12:14–18.

Birch, L. L. and D. W. Marlin. 1982. I don't like it; I never tried it: effects of exposure on two-year-old children's food preferences. *Appetite* 3:353–360.

Bryant C. A., A. Courtney, B. A. Markesbery, and K. M. DeWalt. 1985. *The Cultural Feast, An Introduction to Food and Society.* St. Paul: West Publishing Company.

Carlson, B. L. and M. H. Tabacchi. 1986. Meeting consumer nutrition information needs in restaurants. *Journal of Nutrition Education* 18:211–214.

Committee on Diet and Health, Food and Nutrition Board, National Research Council. 1989. *Implications for Reducing Chronic Disease Risk.* Washington, D.C.: National Academy Press.

Cowart, B. J. 1981. Development of taste perception in humans. Sensitivity and preference throughout the lifespan. *Psychological Bulletin* 90:43–73.

Desor, J. A., O. Mallor, and R. E. Turner. 1973. Taste in acceptance of sugars by human infants. *Journal of Comparative and Physiological Psychology* 84: 496–501.

Ganem, B. C. 1990. *Nutritional Menu Concepts for the Hospitality Industry.* New York: Van Nostrand Reinhold.

Lowenberg, M. E., E. N. Todhunter, E. D. Wilson, J. R. Savage, and J. L. Lubawski. 1979. *Food & People,* 3rd ed. New York: Wiley.

Nachman, M. 1959. The inheritance of saccharin preference. *Journal of Comparative and Physiological Psychology* 52:451–457.

National Restaurant Association. 1982. *How Consumers Make the Decision to Eat Out.* Washington, D.C.: National Restaurant Association.

Rozin, P., M. L. Pelchat, and A. E. Fallon. 1986. Psychological factors influencing food choice. In *The Food Consumer,* eds. C. Ritson, L. Gofton, and J. McKenzie, pp. 85–106. New York: Wiley.

Schiffman, S. 1979. Changes in taste and smell with age: psychophysical aspects. In *Sensory Systems and Communication in the Elderly,* eds. J. M. Ordy and K. Brizzee pp. 227–246, (Aging, Vol. 10). New York: Raven Press.

Shenton, J. P., A. M. Pellegrini, D. Brown, I. Shenker, and P. Wood. 1971. *American Cooking: The Melting Pot.* New York: Time-Life Books.

Surgeon General's Office. 1988. *The Surgeon General's Report on Nutrition and Health.* Washington, D.C.: U.S. Government Printing Office.

U.S. Department of Agriculture. 1989. *Food Consumption, Prices, and Expenditures, 1966–1987.* Statistical Bulletin No. 773. Washington, D.C.: U.S. Department of Agriculture.

U.S. Department of Health and Human Services. 1982. *Eating hints, recipes and tips for better nutrition during cancer treatment.* NIH Publication No. 82-2079. Bethesda, MD: National Cancer Institute.

10

Nutrition in the Foodservice Industry

Diane Welland

Two landmark studies published in the late 1980s, The Surgeon General's Report on Nutrition and Health and the National Research Councils' Report on Diet and Health, established dietary factors and particularly the overconsumption of certain nutrients, as major risk factors for developing chronic illnesses such as coronary heart disease and cancer (National Restaurant Association 1990b). These studies brought the issue of diet and health to the public's attention. Since then nutrition as a preventive health measure has been in the forefront of public health policy and a driving force behind America's changing food consumption patterns (National Restaurant Association 1992b).

Recommendations by national health organizations and governmental agencies stress the reduction of foods high in fat, saturated fat, and cholesterol and an increase in the consumption of complex carbohydrates and fiber (National Restaurant Association 1991b). Nutrition education initiatives aimed at the general public have been successful in increasing awareness and generating concern about nutrition when both eating at home and dining out. (National Restaurant Association 1990b; Henneberry and Charlet 1992). Consequently, U.S. Department of Agriculture (USDA) food consumption figures indicate Americans have decreased their intake of red meat, eggs, and some dairy products, while increasing their consumption of grains, pasta, rice, and fresh produce (National Restaurant Association 1991b; Putnam 1991).

According to a 1992 survey by the Food Marketing Institute, nutrition ranks second only to taste in importance when consumers shop for food (Food Marketing Institute 1992). In the foodservice sector, nutrition also plays an important role, particularly since money spent on away from home food purchases has steadily increased to about 43 percent of the food dollar in 1992 (National Restaurant Association 1992b).

Today, the average consumer eats out nearly four times per week and on a typical day about 50 percent of adults purchase food from a foodservice establishment (National Restaurant Association 1991a, 1992a). Furthermore, with the advent of dual income households and more working mothers, away-from-home dining is now viewed as a necessity rather than a special occasion indulgence. In fact, dining out continues to be an important component of the contemporary American lifestyle despite economic fluctuations. (National Restaurant Association, 1992b).

In light of these findings it is not surprising to find that many consumers are modifying their eating habits outside the home as well as inside. The increased frequency of routine dining out coupled with a heightened sense of nutrition awareness has resulted in a growing consumer demand for healthy menu items when dining out. Considering the foodservice industry is consumer-driven, this trend has had a great impact on many restaurateurs.

Nutrition Attitudes When Dining Out

In an effort to determine how consumers feel about nutrition when dining out, the National Restaurant Association conducted a 1989 Consumer Health and Nutrition survey. The survey found that when it comes to dining out, the U.S. adult population can be divided into three distinct groups: (1) unconcerned patrons, (2) committed patrons, and (3) vacillating patrons.

Unconcerned patrons are people who tend to describe themselves as meat and potato eaters. They eat whatever they want and their behavior is consistent with their attitudes. They are more likely than average to order rich desserts, steak and roast beef, fried fish, and premium ice cream. Unconcerned patrons represent 32 percent of the U.S. adult population.

Committed patrons believe that a good diet plays a role in the prevention of illness. They are committed to good nutrition and dedicated to eating well even when dining out. They are likely to order vegetables with lemon and herbs, poultry without skin, broiled or baked fish, lean meats, and fresh fruit. As a group committed patrons account for nearly 40 percent of the U.S. adult population.

Vacillating patrons are also concerned about health and nutrition but their eating out habits are not quite the same. Vacillators are taste and occasion driven, so the foods they are likely to order are inconsistent in terms of nutrition. Lean meats, rich desserts, steak and roast beef, food cooked without salt and premium ice cream are a few examples. They account for 29 percent of the U.S. adult population.

Compared to a similar study the association conducted in 1986, committed patrons increased 4 percentage points, from 35 percent in 1986 to 39 percent in 1989 and unconcerned patrons dropped 6 percentage points, from 38 percent of the U.S. adult population in 1986 to 32 percent in 1989. These data reveal that consumers who choose nutritious foods when dining out are clearly on the rise and no doubt will continue to grow in the future (National Restaurant Association 1990a).

Restaurant operators should be aware of the differences in the eating out behavior among the groups. Modification of a few menu items to improve their nutritive value could increase traffic for some operators by attracting customers who otherwise would not patronize their establishments (National Restaurant Association 1990b). Moreover, more healthy options on the menu could also increase frequency of customer visits because of a wider array of choices available.

Nutrition and the Chain Operator

Many restaurateurs have implemented changes to satisfy the needs of their health-conscious customers. Perhaps the most visible sector to respond to the nutrition trend has been the multiunit fast-food chains. The addition of healthy menu choices along with lower-fat product reformulations and available nutrition information are some of the ways these foodservice operators are adapting to a more nutrition-minded clientele.

A 1990 National Restaurant Association survey of fast-food and family restaurant chains with 350 units or more found that almost 90 percent of respondents use all vegetable oil and/or shortening for frying. This represents an increase of 27 percentage points from the association's 1989 survey, which found 62 percent of chain operators frying with all-vegetable oil and/or shortening (National Restaurant Association 1991c). The survey shows that many establishments have switched from frying french fries in animal lard to vegetable oil.

Other products that have been reformulated to reduce the fat or cholesterol content include shakes, hamburgers, ice cream desserts, and specialty sandwich items to name a few. In addition to modifying existing products many of these chains have taken the initiative to expand their menu choices and bring in new items geared toward the nutrition conscious.

The majority of the chains surveyed feature decaffeinated coffee (89 percent), entrée salads and/or salad bars (78 percent), poultry without the skin (78 percent), reduced or low-calorie salad dressing (74 percent), fruit juice (67 percent), and margarine (67 percent). Other popular items include grilled chicken sandwich (59 percent) and fresh vegetables (52 percent). These items represent a much wider selection than last year's offerings indicating that there has been much growth in healthy menu offerings for this sector. This growth is expected to continue as public nutrition awareness remains high (National Restaurant Association 1991c).

Nutrition and the Tableservice Operator

Tableservice restaurants have received little publicity regarding nutrition-oriented changes, but they have been no less active on the nutrition front and are eager to step up their nutrition efforts. According to a 1991 National Restaurant Association survey a vast majority of restaurants are willing to adapt menu items on request to satisfy nutritional concerns. In most cases all the customer needs to do is ask and the restaurant will

> Serve sauce on the side
> Serve salad dressing on the side
> Cook without salt
> Broil or bake rather then fry
> Prepare items using vegetable oil rather than butter
> Skin chicken before preparing (National Restaurant Association 1992d)

Modifying menu items upon request allows restaurants to create healthful items that suit their customer's taste. It also adds an element of personalized service most customers appreciate. Restaurateurs should consider these requests when adding healthy menu choices to the menu as a regular item.

Aside from altering existing menu items, a majority of tableservice restaurants offer special items for the health-conscious consumer. Examples of these include sugar substitutes, diet beverages, margarine, and reduced-calorie salad dressing. And, one-third to one-half of the tableservice operators surveyed feature menu items based on their nutritional benefits (National Restaurant Association 1992b). The interested consumer is also likely to find fresh fruit for dessert and whole grain breads, rolls, or crackers in about 8 out of 10 restaurants. In fact, nutrition has become so important that nearly half of the operators surveyed said they would be likely to contact a consulting registered dietitian about developing healthy menu choices (National Restaurant Association 1992d).

In general, both tableservice and chain operators offer nutritious options on the menu based on the wants and needs of the American public. Although not all items fit the bill for healthy fare, most often there are a few choices or modifications that can satisfy the health-conscious patron (Welland 1991).

Providing Nutrition Information

Providing accurate and easy-to-read nutrition information to the general public has also become an important component of public nutrition education programs and the impetus behind recent government regulatory activities. Although restaurants are not required by law to provide nutrition information on all their products, current Food and Drug Administration proposals recommend regulating restaurant use of nutrient descriptors (for example, low fat) and health claims (for example, heart-healthy).

Many of the multiunit chains are already voluntarily providing nutrition information for most of their products in order to satisfy customer demands. The ways in which these units supply this material varies according to type of establishment and the clientele served. The National Restaurant Association assessed the various ways the largest 25 fast-food chains provide nutrition information to individual restaurant units and restaurant patrons. They found that of the chains surveyed 84 percent have nutrition information available to consumers either through individual units, corporate headquarters, or both. All the chains not now providing nutrition information in any form are currently developing this type of material. In general, the most common nutrition information is in a pamphlet or booklet form, followed by wall posters, 800 numbers/consumer hotlines, and trayliners. One chain even has an interactive computer to answer consumer inquiries (National Restaurant Association 1992c).

Tableservice operators are also striving to provide nutrition information to their customers. However, these establishments provide this type of information in a very different manner compared to fast-food chains. For most restaurateurs the nature of the establishment dictates the way in which nutrition information is disseminated. Tableservice restaurants have a high level of customer/foodservice personnel interaction. This increased customer contact offers many opportunities to communicate nutrition information.

A carefully trained waitstaff that is well-versed regarding preparation methods and ingredients of dishes can easily answer customer inquiries when they arise. The waitstaff can also make suggestions or recommendations for the health-conscious customer.

Another possibility that some operators are now experimenting with includes printing an "invitation to ask" about the food preparation and ingredients on the menu. Examples of this approach include:

> "We will gladly provide information about our ingredients, just ask."
> "We will do our best to answer any questions about the contents of our food and preparation methods." (Welland 1991).

Although a well-trained waitstaff is desirable for this type of an approach it is not necessary, because nutrition information can be posted in the back-of-the-house and used as a reference or a handout to customers upon request.

In either case waitstaff should be knowledgeable enough to answer patron's questions quickly and accurately.

Future Alternatives

Appropriately chosen and properly promoted healthy menu items can be just as successful as standard fare. Creativity and flexibility are the keys to developing these types of items. Some opportunities available to the imaginative foodservice operator in the coming years include hiring chefs and other foodservice personnel trained in nutrition, working with registered dietitians, and using nutrition software to analyze recipes for nutrient content. Many restaurants are already experimenting with these types of options.

Another alternative is working with professional health organizations. Groups such as the American Cancer Society and the American Heart Association frequently design nutrition promotions specifically for the restaurateur. Many times these are offered free of charge. Local hospitals, clinics, and public health departments may also become involved with commercial restaurants and some companies have even started programs that cater to the healthy restaurateur niche. Although still a small minority, these types of services have begun appearing.

These are just a few of the innovative ways restaurants are addressing the needs of their health-conscious customers. In today's competitive environment, nutrition in restaurants will continue to hold a special appeal, and healthy choices will still be part of the menu mix. Extending menu choices provides the restaurant with the opportunity to satisfy all their customers' needs from the committed to the unconcerned (National Restaurant Association 1990; Welland 1991).

Summary

Growing public awareness about the importance of a healthy diet along with increased efforts in nutrition education have led to a shift in consumer eating patterns. As a result, many Americans are now concerned about nutrition when dining out. Foodservice operators have responded to this interest in nutrition in a number of ways. Many fast-food, family-restaurant chain, and tableservice operators have expanded their menus to include more healthy choices, and most establishments will alter existing menu items on request. In addition, nutrition information is becoming more and more available through either written material or verbal presentation. These trends are expected to continue as more opportunities arise for restaurateurs to work with registered dietitians and the nutrition community. In the future, healthy choices in foodservice establishments will continue to grow as customer demand increases.

References

Food Marketing Institute. 1992. *Trends and Consumer Attitudes at the Supermarket 1992.* Washington, D.C.: Food Marketing Institute.

Henneberry, S. R., and B. Charlet. 1992. A profile of food consumption trends in the United States. *Journal of Food Products Marketing* 1(1):3–23.

National Restaurant Association. 1990a. *Attitudes Toward Nutrition in Restaurants: Assessing the Marketplace.* Washington, D.C.: National Restaurant Association.

National Restaurant Association. 1990b. *Current Issues Report: Nutrition Awareness and the Foodservice Industry.* Washington, D.C.: National Restaurant Association.

National Restaurant Association. 1991a. *Foodservice Industry Pocket Factbook 1990–1991.* Washington, D.C.: National Restaurant Association.

National Restaurant Association. 1991b. *1991 National Restaurant Association Foodservice Industry Forecast.* Washington, D.C.: National Restaurant Association.

National Restaurant Association. 1991c. *1990 Survey of Chain Operators.* Washington, D.C.: National Restaurant Association.

National Restaurant Association. 1992a. *Foodservice Industry Pocket Factbook 1991–1992.* Washington, D.C.: National Restaurant Association.

National Restaurant Association. 1992b. *1992 National Restaurant Association Foodservice Industry Forecast.* Washington, D.C.: National Restaurant Association.

National Restaurant Association. 1992c. *Survey of Largest 25 Fast Food Chain Operators.* Washington, D.C.: National Restaurant Association.

National Restaurant Association. 1992d. *Tableservice Restaurant Trends: 1992.* Washington, D.C.: National Restaurant Association.

Putnam, J. J. 1991. Food consumption, 1970–1990. *Food Review* 14(3):2–12.

Welland, D. Meeting Nutrition Needs in the Restaurant Industry. Presentation at Center-of-the-Plate Conference, American Meat Institute, 16 April 1991, Chicago, IL.

11

Menus and Menu Planning

Mahmood A. Khan

The term *menu* refers to the list of food and beverage items served or the list of alternative items available for selection. It is usually in written form and often includes description and/or illustration and prices of the items or group of items served. Menus are the focal point around which all components of a foodservice system are centered. The success or failure of a foodservice operation primarily depends on the menu and how foods on it are selected and served. Profitability of an operation may also be dependent on the menu. Because menus play a key role in any foodservice system they must be very carefully planned. Menu planning is the process by which menus are planned, taking into consideration all factors such as food preferences of the clientele, nutritional qualities of foods, operational aspects involved in preparing and serving menu items, food costs, and labor costs. It involves selection of food and beverage items that are acceptable to both management and consumers.

Basic Considerations in Menu Planning

Careful menu planning will result in consumer satisfaction, employee motivation, and management success. The numerous factors that should be considered prior to and while planning menus may be considered from two aspects: the management's viewpoint and the consumers' viewpoint, as shown in Figure 1.

Management Viewpoint Considerations — *Organizational Goals and Objectives.* The primary consideration in menu planning is whether the menu conforms to the goals and objectives of the operation. For example, the menus planned for a hospital will be entirely different from the menus planned for a restaurant.

Budget. Budget is an extremely important factor in menu planning. The amount of money that can be spent depends on the income from food sales and the relative food cost percentage. In turn, the income from food sales depends on consumers' available disposable income (ADI), the location of the facility, the type of service, and several other dependent factors. Menu planning requires careful consideration of the relative costs of food, labor, and equipment. Careful planning with a blend of imagination, efficiency, and

Fig. 1. Factors to be considered in menu planning for a foodservice operation.

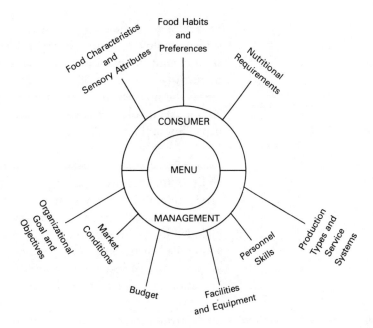

creativity is an important attribute for success in menu planning. Efficient utilization of all the available resources is essential for success in planning menus.

Depending on the type of foodservice, budgets are normally projected (1) on the basis of estimated costs for serving an actual number of residents, (2) by per capita allowances for the expected number of consumers, or (3) by forecasting the number of consumers during a specific period of time. The food cost percentage is also a very valuable tool in determining budgets. Also, precosted standardized recipes, when updated from time to time, help in the calculation of costs to be used in the formulation of budgets. Menu planning becomes very complex and difficult when a number of high and low cost items are included on a menu and when one or more of the items are offered as choices. Careful screening and selection of items are required in order to arrive at the desired combination that will result in a consistent average consumer check.

Food Market Conditions. Raw food products are subjected to seasonal fluctuations that have an enormous impact on the demand and supply. Favorable weather conditions may result in overabundance of a product and result in lower prices. On the other hand, adverse seasonal conditions may cause severe food product shortages and consequently higher prices. This factor is of primary importance when menus are planned, particularly for longer time periods. Fruits and vegetables are the food items most commonly affected by seasonal fluctuations. Menus should be planned to take maximum advantage of the seasonal availability or nonavailability of the food products.

Physical Facilities and Equipment. The physical facilities and available equipment dictate the type of menus that may be planned. Not only the availability of certain pieces of equipment but their number play an important role in the selection of menu items. Efficient menu planning requires a well-balanced approach toward the utilitization of materials, equipment, and employees. Available freezer and refrigerator space also determines the types of food items that can be stored prior to or after preparation.

Personnel Skills.   Efficient equipment and its layout will be of little value without skilled employees to handle them. Elegant menu items requiring specific skills cannot be included if trained food personnel are not available to make them. Any temporary or permanent lack of skilled personnel therefore restricts the number and type of menu items. In most restaurants, chefs play an important role in the success and popularity of the operation. Employees' capability and availability should be considered when planning menus.

Types of Production and Service Methods.   Time lag between production and service and the time required for service are very critical. In a conventional food production and delivery system, where foods are prepared, held at serving temperature, and served on the same day, relatively many choices may be included on the menu. On the other hand, in systems where food is cooked and chilled or frozen, there are limitations on the type of foods that can be prepared and served. Thus a menu item that is suitable for one foodservice operation may not be appropriate for another.

Consumer Viewpoint Considerations

Nutritional Requirements.   Meeting nutritional needs of the consumers in such institutions as hospitals, nursing homes, and schools, is extremely important and should be given top priority when planning menus. Commercial foodservices are also now beginning to give nutrition serious thought in the meals that they offer. An essential guide that is necessary for nutritional planning of menus is the table of *Recommended Daily Dietary Allowances* (RDA). Percentages of the daily RDA values should be taken into consideration when planning nutritionally well-balanced menus. On the basis of RDA, United States Recommended Dietary Allowances (USRDAs) are defined; they are primarily based on the average requirements, without taking into consideration the age or sex of the individuals. USRDAs are used primarily for *nutritional labeling.* Nutritional labels are printed on food packages and give information pertaining to calories per average serving; the amount of carbohydrates, proteins, and fats; and the percentage of nutrients provided in significant quantities by the specified normal serving of that food. The growing nutritional concerns among consumers warrants careful review of the portion sizes and the percentages of the RDAs derived from menu items. The salt, sugar, fiber, and overall carbohydrate contents provided by menu items need careful assessment when planning menus. Consumer's food preferences should also be taken into consideration since nutritional content alone does not guarantee a popular menu. The nutrient content of meals provided by school foodservice menus is restricted by the requirements of the National School Lunch Act, which provides guidelines for the nutritional adequacy of school lunches.

Providing nutritive foods by careful menu planning becomes absolutely necessary for hospital patients and nursing home residents. Closely associated with the selection of the items based on their nutrient contents are the different food groups, the most important of them being (1) meats, (2) fruits and vegetables, (3) milk and milk products, and (4) cereals and breads. The U.S. Department of Agriculture (USDA) has published various handbooks and tables that can be used in the calculation of the nutrient values of different foods.

Food Habits and Preferences.   No matter how sophisticated preparation methods are or how attractively foods are served, a menu is of little practical value if the foods in it are not liked by the consumer. In menu planning, food preferences and habits play a very important role. *Food preferences* may be defined as the selection of food items from choices available among acceptable foods. Patterns of food selection may emerge as a consequence of temporary or permanent food preferences. *Food habits* may be defined as the way in which individuals, in response to social and cultural pressures, select, consume, and utilize portions of the available food supply. Food preferences are based on sensory, social, psychological, religious, emotional, cultural, health, economic, preparation, and other related factors. Figure 2 summarizes these factors.

Intrinsic factors are those that are directly associated with food such as appearance, color, odor, texture, temperature, flavor, and quality. The manner in which food is presented (with both desirable or undesirable attributes), the way food is arranged on the plate, and the temperature at which it is served, all have an impact on food preferences. Standardized large-quantity food production may lead to a different food preference ranking than if similar foods are prepared at home. Variability in these intrinsic factors affect food preferences.

Extrinsic factors include the direct external factors that can affect food preferences as follows:

- *Environment.* Food preferences are affected by the environment in which the food is served. A good example is the hospital environment, which has a marked effect on the selection of food. On the other hand, the effect that a candlelight environment in a restaurant has on food preference compared to that in a fast-food restaurant is obvious.

Fig. 2. Factors affecting food habits, acceptance, and preferences.

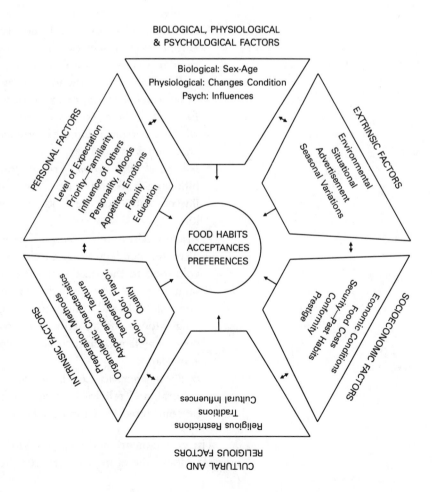

- *Situational Expectation.* The quality of food one expects is a function of the situation in which it is to be consumed. Food is expected to be good when it is associated with social, ritual, or religious occasions. Thus, the food served at a banquet or wedding party carries with it the expectation of something outstanding, in keeping with the occasion itself.
- *Advertising.* It is evident and many studies have proved that advertising can influence one's attitude toward food. Many foodservice operations use this vehicle for attracting consumers. Also, the consumers are tempted to try new food when it is properly advertised. Many places advertise the specialties on their menus.
- *Time and Seasonal Variations.* Food selections appear to be somewhat immune to the influence of certain natural phenomena such as seasonal variations, outdoor temperatures, and the day of the week. In addition, biological, physiological, and psychological factors can have a profound effect on food preferences by changing the appreciation, perception, or appetite toward food.

The individual and personal attributes that affect food choice are

- *Level of Expectation.* This has been shown to have a definite effect on food preferences and selection. For example, patients in hospitals have a low expectation regarding hospital food. When these patients find food better than they expected, the preference ratings are favorably affected. On the other hand, the level of expectation is much higher when dining at a restaurant. If the food is of lower quality than expected, the ratings can be adversely affected.
- *Priority.* This factor is indirectly related to the level of expectations. Airline foodservices or hospital foodservices are good examples of the consumers' priorities to reach their destination or recovery and well-being, rather than to have outstanding gourmet meals. Thus, other aspects are more likely to be critically evaluated than food.
- *Familiarity.* The conditions (both environmental and social) under which a person initially experiences food has an impact on acceptance behavior.
- *Influence of Other Persons.* Friends, relatives, and family members can influence food preferences. Even those being served on a cafeteria line can influence the food selection of a person behind them in the line.
- *Appetites, Moods, and Emotions.* These represent a complex intermingling of preference factors. A careless server may be spared for bringing cold food to the table when the consumer is in a good mood; the same may not be true if the consumer is in a bad mood. Moods are unpredictable and constantly change, which causes problems in planning. Moods and appetites are also influenced by physiological disorders, as well as such factors as satisfaction or dissatisfaction with work and salary.
- *Family Influence and Educational Status.* The impact of socioeconomical, cultural, and religious factors on food selection is evident and should be considered in planning menus.

The above-mentioned factors seldom have an impact singly. They are interrelated and therefore are very complex.

Food Characteristics. Probably the most important factor to be considered in menu planning is the food itself. Characteristics of foods, which include their organoleptic properties, play an important role in their acceptance. The most important aspects related to food characteristics are

- *Color.* Interesting and coordinating color combinations are very desirable and help in the acceptance of food and to an extent (indirectly) in stimulating appetite. Planning and arranging foods so that there is a good color combination, whether on a plate, tray, counter, or salad bar, are very important aspects of menu planning. Color also emphasizes the variety available for selection. When planning menus, different colored items should be included, and too many items with similar color should be avoided. In some printed menus, the visual aspects of the foods are enhanced by providing color pictures.
- *Texture and Shape.* These characteristics of foods also affect consumers' preferences. Certain foods are preferred because of their hard texture and some because of their soft texture. A desirable combination between the soft- and hard-textured items on the menu is essential. "Soft," "hard," "crispy," "crunchy," "chewy," "smooth," "brittle," and "grainy" are some of the adjectives used to describe food texture. A variety in texture in foods is highly desirable. Certain food items go well with a difference in texture. Soups are preferred with crispy crackers, soft-textured potatoes go well with chewy steaks, and casseroles are desirable with crisp vegetables. Foods in different colors and shapes add to the attraction of the menu as well as to eye appeal when the foods are served.
- *Consistency.* Consistency refers to the degree of viscosity or density of a product. Like texture, consistency provides for variety among the menu items. "Runny," "gelatinous," "pasty," "thin," "thick," "sticky," and "gummy" are the most common adjectives used to describe consistency. Food items on a particular menu should have varying consistencies. As a rule, items that have a hard texture should be complemented by items having a thin consistency. Relatively hard textured meats go well with thin gravies while nuts in thin items add a desirable combination of textures.
- *Flavor.* It is obvious that the flavor of foods is a very important consideration when planning menus. Simply stated, foods can have sweet, sour, bitter, or salty flavors, which can be present alone or in combination. In addition, there are various off-flavors or undesirable flavors specific to foods. A desirable blend of flavors is essential for creating uniqueness in the menu. The predominance of any one flavor is often undesirable. A contrast in the types of flavors and their intensity adds to the acceptability of menu items. Bland foods may be made more appetizing by adding pungent sauces or a blend of sweet and sour flavors may be added to a menu. The right combinations of spices and condiments are therefore essential in order to develop the right kinds of flavors.
- *Method of Food Preparation.* Consideration should be given to the method of preparation in menu planning. Food items can be prepared in several ways, and a variety in the methods of preparation is desirable. These methods include frying, baking, broiling, boiling, steaming, grilling, braising, or a combination of these methods. In each of these types of preparation, there may be variations based on the sauces or

gravies used or the equipment used, such as flame-broiled chicken with barbecue sauce or roast duck with gravy. From the management point of view, it is essential that there be a uniform distribution of the methods selected for food preparation. Optimum use of employee skills and equipment demands that there be a balanced distribution in preparation methods.

- *Serving Temperature.* This component is probably the least complex in planning menus based on food characteristics. Temperatures for food preferred by individuals vary with age and other personal factors. Both hot and cold foods are desirable items to be included on the menu. A chilled gazpacho appetizer is desirable with hot entrées, a cold salad may go well with hot bread, or a cold sandwich may be more desirable with hot food items.

- *Presentation Method.* The final appearance of food—whether on a plate, cafeteria counter, serving tray, take-out package, buffet table, or a display case—is a very important aspect in the final selection of the item. A three-dimensional appearance of the food adds to the attractiveness of the menu whether on paper or in actuality. A combination of tall, flat, and other shapes, when arranged in a symmetrical pattern, is eye appealing and should be considered when planning menus.

Menu Patterns and Types of Menus

A *menu pattern* is the outline of food items and choices to be included in each meal. Menu patterns are based on the types of foods to be included on the menu, considering all different factors. There are different kinds and styles of menus used in foodservice operations. However, menus may be divided based on the patterns into three principal types.

1. A *static* or *fixed menu* is one in which the same menu items are offered repeatedly. Many restaurants have static menus with a few limited choices. In many of the franchised restaurants static menus are offered.

2. *Cycle menu* refers to a series of menus, offering different items for a predetermined time period. The time period (daily, weekly, biweekly, monthly, quarterly, or other period) for which menus are planned may range from a few days to several weeks and is referred to as *menu cycle*. Menus are carefully planned and are rotated at selected fixed intervals of time. An advantage of using cycle menus is that they provide for changes based on seasonal variations. The food items selected should be adequately balanced throughout this cycle. The cycle may be short or long. Short cycles may be of three weeks' duration or less. Long cycles may range over an extended period of time, such as six-week cycles within a year or more. Cycle menus are commonly used in institutional foodservices, particularly hospitals and nursing homes. Where consumers are likely to utilize foodservices for a short period of time such as hospitals, shorter menu cycles are very appropriate. On the other hand, cycle menus may cause problems and may create monotony due to repetitions.

The advantages of the cycle menus may be summed up as follows: (1) If menus are carefully planned, cycle menus reduce the need for planning menus frequently, which avoids this tedious procedure and also frees much needed time for other management functions. (2) The frequent use of menu items in the cycle helps in standardizing production and service procedures. (3) The work loads of the employees and the equiment used may be evenly distributed on a long-term basis and can be uniformly balanced. (4) Food purchasing and inventory control are facilitated, since purchase orders are easy to make and the inventory can be controlled accordingly. Also, well-planned and formal methods of food purchasing may be utilized since the long-term needs are known. (5) Production forecasting and control becomes relatively easier. (6) Comparative evaluations of the cost of production can be made between menu cycles as well as between set periods within the cycles. (7) It is easy to make changes and troubleshoot any problems.

Certain disadvantages are associated with the use of cycle menus. The greatest problem is that the food items may become monotonous because of the lack of variability over a period of time. Also, if the cycles are not very carefully planned, the errors or problems keep repeating. Shorter cycles may result in too frequent repetitions and monotony. If the cycle is too long, planning and management may become too difficult and complicated. Therefore, the length of the menu cycle is extremely important and should be carefully assessed before and after its implementation.

Once the cycle menus are carefully planned and evaluated, they become established and provide all the above-mentioned advantages. Their proper use results in considerable savings, increases profitability, and facilitates overall management.

3. *Single-use menus* are planned only for special days or occasions and are not repeated.

Menus can also be categorized by choice(s): *No choice* or *nonselective menus* do not provide any choices among menu items. *Limited choice* menus provide selections for some menu items but offer no choices for others. For example, only a choice of entrées may be offered. *Choice menus* or *selective menus* offer a wide variety of choices among the items offered.

Mechanics of Menu Planning

Menu planning is one of the most important responsibilities of management. Thus the person(s) planning menus should be aware of all aspects of production and service.

Reference Materials Some of the reference materials that should be readily available for menu planning include

> Standardized recipe files, showing in detail method of preparation, portion sizes, portion costs, and nutrient content
> Copies of previous menus, if available
> Cookbooks
> Pictures of prepared foods, if available
> Food preference data, if available
> Market statements
> Consumer comments, if available
> Food delivery schedules
> A comprehensive list of menu items, preferably with their prices
> Food sales records
> Production records
> Professional and trade journals
> Organizational manual
> Other pertinent publications

An example of a menu planning form used on a weekly basis is shown in Figure 3. These menu forms, which may be modified to suit individual needs, are very useful since the food items selected are based on the type of the items included on the preceding day and the succeeding day. These interrelations should be considered on a day-to-day and week-to-week basis. A menu form should include meal pattern(s), number of meals, days of the week, and types of food items. When planning menus, care should be taken to avoid food leftovers as much as possible. In cycle menus, it will be difficult to utilize any leftovers until the cycle is repeated. It is advisable to keep a record of the leftover items and consider that when planning menus. The leftovers are also indicative of the nonpopularity of those items or the preferences for other menu choices.

Steps in Menu Planning   It is advisable to follow a sequence every time a menu is planned. The steps in menu planning, which have proven successful for many foodservice operations, are summarized on the following pages as examples.

Step 1. Select entrées, or main courses, of meal selection for entire menu cycle. In most cases, this selection would be dinner entrées, meat items, or their alternatives. These should preferably be selected first because (1) other food items for each meal are selected to complement the entrée choice, (2) they are often the most expensive items on the menu, (3) good balance among the menu items may be maintained by planning food items that complement the entrée, and (4) their cost will be indicative of the average meal price that can be expected. It is also recommended that the entrée selection be based on the cost of the item, maintaining a good balance between the high- and low-priced menu items. If the menu pattern does not provide for choices, a weekly menu should be planned using different entrée items from meats or meat substitutes, such as beef, chicken, fish, pork, and organ meats. Care should be taken to see that the same type of meat is not repeated on the preceding or succeeding day of the week, even if the preparation methods are different. If there are several choices provided for the same meal, combinations may be selected on the basis of consumer preferences. Variations in preparation methods should be provided for various days of the week. All factors discussed for menu selection should be taken into consideration.

Step 2. Select entrée for second most important meal of the day. In most cases this will be the entrée for lunch, except in the case of certain foodservice operations where the elderly or the employees are served. (In these cases, lunch is the most important meal of the day.) Most people prefer salads or light meals for lunch, and therefore these should be included on the menu. If choices are provided, there should be a balance among these items. Variety among type of meat, preparation methods, texture, and color should all be considered. Also, a balance should be maintained by selecting high-cost and the low-cost entrées. For example, if a high-cost entrée was selected for dinner, a relatively low-cost entrée may be selected for lunch, and vice versa.

Step 3. Select starchy foods. Starchy food such as potatoes, rice, pasta, and yams should be selected to complement the entrée, since they will provide variety in color, texture, consistency, shape, and flavor. These starchy foods should be coordinated with the entrée. If the entrées are relatively dry, moist and creamed dishes should be selected; on the other hand, if the meats have drippings or juice, bland foods such as mashed potatoes should be included to complement the flavor. Creamed or steamed items provide moistness when

Meal and Food Items	MONDAY	TUESDAY	WEDNESDAY	THURSDAY	FRIDAY	SATURDAY	SUNDAY
BREAKFAST							
Cereal							
1.							
2.							
Meat or							
Meat alternative (s)							
1.							
2.							
Breads							
1.							
2.							
Beverages/Fruit							
1.							
2.							
3.							
LUNCH							
Appetizer							
1.							
2.							
Entrées/Salads							
1.							
2.							
3.							
Vegetables							
1.							
2.							
3.							
Breads							
1.							
2.							
Desserts							
1.							
2.							
3.							
Beverages							
1.							
2.							
3.							
DINNER							
Appetizer							
1.							
2.							
Entrées							
1.							
2.							
3.							
Vegetables							
1.							
2.							
3.							
Breads							
1.							
2.							
Desserts							
1.							
2.							
3.							
Salads							
1.							
2.							
Beverages							
1.							
2.							

DATES: From _____ through _____   NAME OF THE OPERATION: _____

Fig. 3. Sample suggested form for use in menu planning of all meals for a week.

included with entrées that tend to be dry. Care should be taken to see that there are only a limited number of starchy items on the menu. It is quite possible that the entrée may be a casserole with starchy foods such as rice or potatoes; under these circumstances, this step should be totally excluded from the planning process.

Step 4. Select vegetable(s) for lunch and dinner. Vegetables should complement the entrée items and should be selected on the basis of color, shape, size, texture, preparation method, and flavor. The food characteristics discussed earlier should all be taken into consideration. In addition to contributing nutritive value, vegetables play a very important role in making the total meal attractive and appealing. The versatility in the types of vegetables that can be planned add to their desirability. Their colors, texture, and preparation methods provide for various possibilities and alternatives for the menu. They may be served as whole, halved, quartered, sliced, diced, cubed, julienne, or carved into attractive shapes. Carrots, broccoli, peas, cauliflower, beans, and other vegetables provide rich colors and interesting combinations. They may be prepared by using various methods such as steaming, boiling, and sautéing. Vegetables served should complement the entrée of the day. Highly seasoned entrées should be complemented with mild-flavored vegetables and vice versa. From the nutritional point of view, vegetables are a very important food group and more than one type of vegetable should therefore be included in any one menu.

Step 5. Select salads. Salads may consist of one or more combinations of vegetables, fruits, meats, fish, cheese, and gelatin molds. They may be accompanied by different kinds of dressings and garnishes. As in the case of vegetables, salads also add color, flavor, and texture to the meal. In the selection of salad items, entrées and vegetables for the meal should be considered in order to avoid any type of repetition. In general, if salads complement the entrées, smaller serving sizes are usually adequate. Although salads do not require elaborate equipment for their preparation, a good deal of hard labor is involved in their prepreparation, preparation, and arrangement. Also salads require more storage space as well as careful handling during holding and storage.

Step 6. Select soups and appetizers. Like salads, there are numerous types and kinds of appetizers and soups from which to choose. These items precede entrées or the main item of the meal. As is evident from their name, appetizers are for stimulating the appetite. Soups, to a great extent, serve the same function as appetizers. Since these foods are included to whet the appetite, it is essential to select recipes for soups that would increase the appetite for the main course of the meal. Soups and appetizers can be light or heavy based on their ingredients. A light appetizer should therefore be planned when heavy and filling entrées are offered and vice versa. Light entrées or sandwiches may be complemented by heavier soups. Leftover vegetables, juices, and drained syrups from canned foods may be effectively utilized in soups. Soups for the succeeding meal should be planned with consideration of possible leftovers and their utilization.

Step 7. Select desserts. Since the bulk of the menu items for the meals have already been selected, it should be easier to plan the desserts. It is always preferable to keep the dessert selection to the end. Desserts are very important since many patrons look forward to desserts, which not only add a final touch to the menu but also provide a lasting impression of the meal. Careful menu planning is therefore essential, as a well-planned meal may be spoiled by an unappealing dessert. It is primarily the taste of the dessert that is important rather than the quantity. A tasty small serving of a dessert is sufficient to leave a lasting impression of the meal. Desserts may consist of fruits (whole, part, or combination), cakes, pies, cheese, puddings, ice creams, and cookies. Many interesting combinations are possible with desserts. Since there is much concern regarding caloric value, it is important to consider that factor in menu planning. As in the case of other menu items, a light dessert should be planned with heavy meals and vice versa. There should be no duplication with any of the foods already included in the menu. The color, consistency/texture, and shape should be considered. A hot, spicy, entrée may be followed by an intensely sweet dessert, or a hot meat item may be followed by ice cream. Sweet and soft desserts also go very well with filling entrées. Entrées and desserts are usually the main items that the food patron considers when selecting items from the menus, and so they should be planned very carefully. Appearance of the desserts is very important when they are displayed on the dessert cart or in display cases. Nuts, condiments, and syrups add to the appeal of the desserts.

Step 8. Select bread items. Breads can be of many different kinds and shapes. Their preparation methods and final texture also vary considerably. Breads complement the entrée item and should be planned accordingly. Among the many varieties of breads are yeast, quick, sweet-dough, sourdough, flat, and several other specialty breads. Bland types of breads may be included when spicy and/or juicy items are on the menu. Breads may also be used in entrée items such as cheese rarebit on rye bread. In these situations bread duplication should be avoided. Also the shape, size, and texture of the bread should be taken into consideration.

Step 9. Select beverages. This is probably the easiest step in menu planning as there are several hot and cold beverages that are usually included on the menu. Beverages may be selected from alcoholic or nonalcoholic beverages, carbonated beverages, fruit juices, lemonade, coffee, milk shakes, hot tea, iced tea, and various types of milk products.

Step 10. Select breakfast menu. Breakfast items are relatively simple to plan. Normally, there are fixed breakfast items that need to be included on the menu, although variations in the preparation method are desirable. Juices, cereals, toasts, eggs, sausage, ham, and biscuits are among the popular breakfast items. Too much duplication and repetition of the items should be avoided as much as possible.

These steps outline the recommended procedure for menu planning. A final check is essential, taking into consideration all above-mentioned factors. Enough flexibility should be built into the menu to accommodate future changes and/or unexpected conditions. Examples of possible final checklists are provided (Figures 4 and 5).

Computers in Menu Planning

Several types of computer programs are available for use in menu planning. The menu planning process becomes extremely simplified if a computer is used. However, all factors should be considered and all applicable data should be included in the menu planning process. Data pertaining to consumer food

Fig. 4. Checklist for use in planning menus.

```
┌─────────────────────────────────────────────────────────────────────────┐
│ [  ] Is menu consistent with the management's goals and objectives?       │
│ [  ] Does the menu include all choices planned in the menu pattern?       │
│ [  ] Does the menu have a balance between the low-priced and high-priced items? │
│ [  ] Are all the equipment and facilities adequately utilized?            │
│ [  ] Are all the personnel skills effectively utilized?                   │
│ [  ] Are seasonal foods effectively used in the menu?                     │
│ [  ] Will there be sufficient time for production of all the menu items planned? │
│ [  ] Are the work loads balanced from the personnel and equipment point of view? │
│ [  ] Does the menu meet the desired nutritional requirements?             │
│ [  ] Is the menu well-balanced from the nutritional point of view?        │
│ [  ] Are the color combinations of the menu well-planned, attractive, and pleasing? │
│ [  ] Does the menu include items with varying consistencies and texture,  │
│      thereby providing well-balanced meals?                               │
│ [  ] Are attractive and appealing garnishes and accompaniments included wher- │
│      ever possible?                                                       │
│ [  ] Are the flavors well-selected to provide a well-balanced meal?       │
│ [  ] Are items selected of different shapes and sizes?                    │
│ [  ] Is there a balanced distribution of food items based on their preparation │
│      methods?                                                             │
│ [  ] Does the menu include hot and cold items distributed evenly?         │
│ [  ] Are choices provided according to food preferences or popularity?    │
│ [  ] Is the menu free of duplication, repetition, and blanks as to the food items │
│      included in the menu on the same day as well as the same week?       │
│ [  ] Does the overall menu represent high quality, wholesome, appealing, and │
│      manageable food and beverage items?                                  │
│                                                                           │
│ Comments: _____ │
│ _____ │
│ _____ │
│                                                                           │
│ Date: _____        Checked by: _____ │
└─────────────────────────────────────────────────────────────────────────┘
```

preferences, food characteristics, production time, labor needs, nutritional quality, overall costs, selling prices, inventory control, and/or forecasting are needed. Careful programming to include all of this information as well as the handling of data is necessary; this requires both skill and experience. The major advantages of using a computer for menu planning are

1. Storage of a voluminous amount of data. Inventory records, lists of recipes and ingredients, cost of ingredients and prepared menu items, serving sizes of menu items, nutritional and food preference data may all be stored in the computer and recalled for use in planning menus.

2. Financial savings. Computers may save significantly the costs incurred in planning menus.

3. Simplified calculations. Using a computer with stored data, it is relatively easy to calculate the cost of the menu items or the nutritional value of the menu.

4. Selection of menu items. Menu selection or choices at random can be facilitated if a sequential rating/ranking is provided.

5. Avoidance of human bias. Bias related to use of menu items and employee scheduling can be avoided by using computers.

6. RDA calculations. RDAs provided by meals can be very easily calculated by computers.

7. Cost calculations. Cost of the items, food cost percentages, selling price, percent profit, and other such calculations can be easily made.

Fig. 5. Final menu checklist.

Considerations	MON	TUES	WED	THURS	FRI	SAT	SUN
1. *Management's point of view*							
a. Conforms to the menu pattern							
b. Provides balance in the cost of items							
c. Meets nutritional adequacy							
d. Is based on seasonal fluctuations							
e. Provides optimum work load							
f. Provides optimum equipment load							
g. Utilizes personnel skills							
h. Facilitates production							
i. Facilitates fast and efficient service							
j. Appears promising and profitable							
2. *Consumer's point of view* Variety in:							
a. Color							
b. Texture							
c. Shape							
d. Flavor							
e. Consistency							
f. Preparation							
g. Other _____							
3. Conforms with food habits							
4. Is targeted toward consumers							
5. Overall acceptability							
6. Other aspects _____							
7. Remarks: _____							
Yes: ✔ No: x Needs Improvement: NI							

8. Forecasting. Forecasting can be done by using the stored data.
9. Consumer related data. Popularity of the menu items can be calculated from consumer demand data.
10. Illustrations. Graphs, charts, bar diagrams, pie diagrams, and tables produced almost instantly by computers are easier to interpret than raw data and can help in decision making.

Menu Design and Display

Menus can be written in two different formats for foodservice personnel and for consumers. Menus written for foodservice personnel are supplemented by such pertinent technical information as recipe file number, name of the recipe, production schedule (if not included separately), equipment usage, and prepreparation schedule. From the consumers' viewpoint menus are designed to "sell" and therefore menu items are described to attract consumers' attention. The descriptions are planned to create an appeal for the items served. Since the purpose of the menu is to communicate with the consumer, a good menu format is one that is effective in communicating the message to the intended consumer.

Menu design primarily depends on the type of the menu and foodservice facility. Menus that are à la carte allow for the selection of food items by the consumer from a list of foods presented on the menu with prices. Table d'hote menus offer complete meals at a fixed price. There may be choices provided in one or more categories. There are different sets of menus in hospitals for regular meals as well as for modified diets. Cafeteria and fast-food restaurant menus usually consist of a listing of items on a menu board or printed sheets. Some restaurants prefer to have two different sets of menus, one with prices to be given to the principal host and one without prices to be given to the rest of the customers in a party. Many places prefer adding special clip-ons to the menus. Foreign terms are often used in naming menu items.

Summary

Menus are the focal point around which all components of a foodservice system are centered. The success or failure of a foodservice operation depends primarily on the menu and how the foods on it are selected and served. Thus menu planning is one of the most important functions in a foodservice establishment. Careful menu planning results in consumer satisfaction, employee motivation, and success of the operation. Menu planning should be considered from the point of view of management as well as consumers and should be accomplished using a stepwise systematic approach. Computers have helped enormously in planning menus for different types of foodservice operations.

Bibliography

Eckstein, E. F. 1983. *Menu Planning*, 3rd ed. Westport, Conn.: AVI Publishing.

Food and Nutrition Board. National Research Council. 1989. *Recommended Dietary Allowances*, 9th ed. Washington, D.C.: U.S. Government Printing Office.

Khan, M. A. 1991. *Concepts of Foodservice Operations and Management*, 2d ed. New York: Van Nostrand Reinhold.

Kotchevar, L. H. 1987. *Management by Menu*. Chicago, Ill.: National Institute of the Foodservice Industry.

Kreck, L. A. 1975. *Menus: Analysis and Planning*. Boston, Mass.: Cahners Books.

Miller, J. E. 1987. *Menu Pricing and Strategy*, 2nd ed. New York: Van Nostrand Reinhold.

Miller, S. G. 1988. Creating menus with desktop publishing. *Cornell Hotel & Restaurant Administration Quarterly* 28(4):32–35.

Seaberg, A. G. 1973. *Menu Design, Merchandizing, and Marketing*, 3rd ed. Boston, Mass.: Cahners Books.

Spears, M. C., and A. G. Vaden. 1985. *Foodservice Organizations: A Managerial and Systems Approach*. New York: John Wiley.

U.S. Department of Agriculture. 1975. *Handbook No. 8 and No. 456, Nutritive Value of American Foods in Common Units*. Washington, D.C.: USDA.

West, B. B., L. V. Wood, V. Harger, and G. Shugart. 1977. Menu planning and food standards. In *Food Service in Institutions*, 5th ed. New York: John Wiley.

12

Foodservice Purchasing

John Stefanelli

All foodservice managers must perform many daily operations. Purchasing is a very important one because the quality of a restaurant's finished menu items depends on the raw ingredients used to produce them.

Purchasing is also very important because little can be done in the short run to correct a purchasing mistake. For instance, if the wrong product size is purchased, a finished menu item will not be consistent with its recipe requirements. The manager in this situation usually must choose between two equally disturbing options: serving a substandard menu item, or taking it off the menu, thereby risking customer disappointment.

Efficient and effective purchasing will minimize these types of mistakes. It will ensure that the foodservice operation achieves the primary purchasing objectives that all managers hope to attain: purchasing the right product, at the right time, for the right price, in the right amount, from the right supplier.

A smooth-running foodservice operation usually employs a management staff capable of implementing and performing the restaurant industry's generally accepted purchasing principles and procedures. These procedures include (1) developing specifications; (2) preparing an approved supplier list; (3) determining the appropriate order sizes and ordering procedures; and (4) establishing appropriate receiving and storage procedures.

Specifications

The first step in purchasing is developing appropriate specifications for each item that must be purchased from an outside supplier.

Specifications serve many purposes. They represent cost and quality control guidelines. They help avoid misunderstanding among suppliers, buyers, and people who use the purchased products. And they allow a manager to shop around for competitive price quotations from the suppliers who are able to fulfill the specifications.

The restaurant manager usually prepares product specifications, that is, formal statements of all the characteristics in a product required to fill specific needs. These statements note all necessary product characteristics, and in some cases also note additional information, such as the purchasing agent's desired delivery procedures, payment terms, and returns policy. When a product specification contains this additional information, it is sometimes referred to as a *purchase specification*.

A product specification is based primarily on the restaurant's production requirements. The characteristics necessary in a product will depend on the restaurant's recipes, menus, service style, cooking procedures, receiving and storage facilities, and budgetary constraints.

The typical product specification includes information such as

1. The exact name of the product
2. Its intended use
3. Quality desired
4. Product size
5. Usable yield percentage
6. Package size
7. Type of package
8. Packaging procedure
9. Preservation method
10. Point of origin
11. Degree of ripeness
12. Product form
13. Type of product processing
14. Color

Figure 1 shows a completed sample product specification for apples. Notice that it contains many factors. However, less information would be needed for some products, such as flour.

Approved Supplier List

Most restaurant managers develop an approved supplier list. In the typical multiunit restaurant company, the responsibility of developing such a list may be given to a corporate vice president of purchasing.

The primary purpose of the approved supplier list is to control a buyer's activities to some extent. Most supervisors and managers in foodservice operations have purchasing responsibilities. It would be very time consuming to expect each buyer to shop for merchandise every time he or she needed something. It also would generate a certain amount of inconsistent product quality and cost. By establishing an approved supplier list, the restaurant manager can streamline purchasing and achieve quality and cost control benefits. Furthermore, suppliers who want to be on the list usually are willing to grant price discounts if they are assured of repeat business.

Before a supplier can be added to a foodservice operation's approved supplier list, it must be accepted by the restaurant manager. Normally only a key member of management can add a supplier to the list. If, for example, an unapproved supplier approaches a chef, the chef would need to submit the supplier's name to his or her superior, who then would evaluate the supplier's suitability for inclusion on the list. This procedure ensures a certain degree of control in that it prevents buyers from entering into hidden, questionable business transactions.

Suppliers who want to be included on a restaurant's approved supplier list must be analyzed thoroughly. The restaurant manager should check a supplier's references in order to determine its performance capabilities. During

Red delicious apples
To be used for buffet service
U.S. Fancy government grade
From Washington State
72-count size
30- to 42-pound container
Moisture-proof container
Apples to be layered
 (cell cartons)
Whole, fresh, refrigerated
 apples
Fully ripened

Fig. 1. Sample product specification.

these reference checks, a manager should examine several selection criteria. The most important criteria are

1. Overall dependability
2. Service rendered
3. Quality offered
4. Quality consistency
5. Delivery schedule promised
6. The supplier's ability to adhere to its stated delivery schedule
7. Prices charged
8. Variety of products offered
9. Number of back orders
10. Number of product substitutions that must be made because of stockouts

Additional selection criteria that may be important to some restaurant companies are

1. Payment policy
2. Minimum order requirements
3. Required ordering procedure
4. Returns policy
5. The supplier's size and the length of time it has been in business

When a manager evaluates a potential approved supplier, he or she normally looks for consistency. The restaurant operator is very dependent on the supplier's performance. If the supplier makes a mistake, the restaurant may suffer production delays and disgruntled guests. The supplier who is unable or unwilling to accommodate the restaurant operator's needs will not survive in the competitive foodservice industry.

Order Sizes

Determining the appropriate order sizes is one of the most challenging duties faced by foodservice buyers. On the one hand, buyers do not want to overbuy because excess stock will increase the restaurant's storage costs. On the other hand, buyers do not want to underbuy because a stockout will lead to customer dissatisfaction.

It is difficult to compute proper order sizes because the typical restaurant's business is somewhat unpredictable. If the foodservice operation caters exclusively to banquet customers or to a captive audience, such as a school, it is relatively easy to determine how much to buy. Unfortunately, most restaurants do not have this luxury.

Before computing an order size, the buyer must know the supplier's delivery schedule. If, for example, the supplier delivers twice each week, the buyer can order enough stock to last one-half week, one week, one and one-half weeks, and so forth. Usually the restaurant operator prefers frequent deliveries if the items purchased are very expensive and/or if they are highly perishable.

Once the buyer determines the preferred ordering cycle, he or she must project product needs during that period. Generally, product needs are related to historical trends. For example, if a restaurant manager normally sells 250 steaks per day, and if the order size must be sufficient to accommodate three days, the minimum order will be 750 steaks less the number of steaks on hand. Given the unpredictability of the foodservice business, many buyers will tack on a safety stock in order to avoid stockouts and unhappy guests.

The order size computation can become a bit more complicated if the restaurant operation purchases products that must be trimmed before they can be served to guests. For instance, if a buyer purchases raw roast beef that has an edible yield of 75 percent, the 25 percent loss factor must be taken into account when computing the order size. To do this, the buyer must know the serving size per portion and the expected number of servings needed during the ordering cycle.

Assume that the restaurant expects to serve 500 6-ounce servings. How much raw roast beef must the buyer purchase? The calculations are as follows:

1 raw pound (16 oz) × Edible yield percentage (75%)
= Number of servable ounces per pound (12 oz)

Number of servable ounces per pound (12 oz) ÷ Serving size (6 oz)
= Number of servings per raw pound (2).

Number of customers (500) ÷ Number of servings per raw pound (2)
= Number of raw pounds to purchase (250 lbs)

Another method that can be used to compute the order size for this example is

Serving size (6 oz) ÷ Edible yield percentage (75 %)
= Amount of raw roast beef that must be purchased per serving (8 oz)

Number of raw ounces per serving (8 oz) × Number of customers (500)
= Order size (4,000 oz, or 250 lb)

Ordering Procedures

After the buyer computes the appropriate order sizes, he or she usually communicates the order to the approved supplier for that product line. If the approved supplier cannot accommodate the order size, normally there is an approved backup supplier.

Most buyers telephone in their orders. Some buyers give them to the sales representatives who visit the restaurants on a periodic basis. A few buyers mail formal purchase orders to the supplier (usually after they call them in). And some buyers prefer using the fax machine to enter their orders.

In some instances, a buyer could use a personal computer to tap into the supplier's computer. The buyer has the opportunity to enter all related order data and get immediate verification. This type of ordering procedure is very efficient, but most foodservice operators cannot afford it.

After the order is entered, the buyer must ensure that he or she has a copy of the order record. This is absolutely necessary, because this record will be used to check in the delivery.

Receiving Procedures

Some restaurant operators do not allow buyers to check in shipments. The general feeling in the industry is that a buyer should not be a receiver because this combination of duties allows an unscrupulous person an opportunity to defraud the company. However, some feel that the buyer is the logical nity to defraud the company. However, some feel that the buyer is the logical one to receive the shipment because he or she is most familiar with the merchandise.

The typical foodservice receiver uses the invoice receiving procedures. These procedures include

1. Compare the driver's invoice with the order record.
2. Compare the shipment with the driver's invoice and the order record.
3. Examine product quality.
4. Examine product quantity.
5. Arrange to return merchandise (if necessary).
6. Obtain credit slip for returns and allowances (if necessary).
7. Sign driver's copy of the invoice.
8. Keep restaurant's copy of the invoice and credit slip.
9. Send paperwork to bookkeeper (who will audit cost data and authorize payment).
10. Arrange storage for the shipment.

Storage Procedures

As soon as the receiver finishes checking the shipment, it must be placed in the proper storage facility. The merchandise must be secured, and it also must be stored under the proper temperature and humidity conditions.

The goal of storage management is to prevent the loss of merchandise due to theft, pilferage, and spoilage. Most restaurants store the expensive merchandise in a locked storage facility that can only be entered by the manager on duty. The remaining merchandise usually is stored in open storerooms, that is, the storerooms can be accessed by any authorized employee.

Product quality is maintained if products are stored in the proper environment. Improper environmental conditions can lead to spoilage or to products that, while technically not spoiled, have passed their peak of culinary quality and are not suitable for guest service. Either way, the restaurant's costs of doing business can increase significantly.

Summary

The quality and cost of finished menu items are influenced by the purchasing agent's performance. To ensure acceptable quality and cost, as well as consistency in production and service, the buyer must continually prepare and revise specifications, approved supplier lists, order sizes, ordering procedures, and receiving and storage techniques.

Bibliography

Coltman, M. 1990. *Hospitality Industry Purchasing.* New York: Van Nostrand Reinhold.
Dittmer, P. R., and G. G. Griffin. 1989. *Principles of Food, Beverage, and Labor Cost Controls for Hotels and Restaurants,* 4th ed. New York: Van Nostrand Reinhold.
Keister, D. C. 1990. *Food and Beverage Control,* 2d ed. Englewood Cliffs, N.J.: Prentice-Hall.
Kotschevar, L. H., and C. Levinson. 1988. *Quantity Food Purchasing,* 3d ed. New York: Macmillan.
National Association of Meat Purveyors. 1988. *Meat Buyers Guide.* McLean, Va.: National Association of Meat Purveyors.

NIFDA (National Institutional Food Distributor Associates, Inc. [Comsource]). 1985. *NIFDA Canned Goods Specifications Manual.* West Lafayette, Ind.: Purdue Research Foundation.

NIFDA. (National Institutional Food Distributor Associates, Inc. [Comsource]). 1985. *NIFDA Frozen Foods Specifications Manual.* West Lafayette, Ind.: Purdue Research Foundation.

The Produce Marketing Association. 1989. *The Produce Marketing Association Fresh Produce Reference Manual for Food Service.* Newark, Del.: Produce Marketing Association.

Stefanelli, J. 1992. *Purchasing: Selection and Procurement for the Hospitality Industry.* New York: Wiley.

Virts, W. B. 1987. *Purchasing for Hospitality Operations.* East Lansing, Mich.: The Educational Institute of the American Hotel & Motel Association.

Warfel, M. C., and M. L. Cremer. 1990. *Purchasing for Food Service Managers.* Berkeley, Calif.: McCutchan Publishing Corporation.

13

Food Production and Recipe Standardization

Deborah H. Sutherlin

Food production can be considered the core of the foodservice operation. There may be many differences in the type of operation, but basic similarities exist in the provision of food to consumers. In general, foodservice operations exist to provide products at an appropriate price, time, and level of quality for the given operation.

Foodservice systems have been classified in four main categories: traditional; commissary; ready-prepared; and assembly/serve (Unklesbay et al. 1977). These systems vary with respect to the degree of processing of purchased items, method of production, holding, and distribution.

Food production in traditional systems involves the procurement of ingredients to be processed, cooked, and served within individual foodservice units. These operations often maintain separate production centers such as baking, entrée preparation, and cold food production areas within the unit. To maintain labor costs and improve efficiency, a current trend in food production management is to procure foods in a more highly processed state. Traditional operations may purchase portioned or prepared meats, canned or frozen fruits and vegetables, and baked goods.

Commissary systems involve production of food items in a central facility. Menu items are partially or completely processed, then held frozen, chilled, or heated for distribution to satellite centers for final preparation and service. Large-scale operations may require equipment normally used by commercial food processing plants. These operations also require significant adjustments in recipes and food production procedures.

Ready-prepared foodservice systems have been developed in response to increasing labor costs and a critical shortage of skilled food production personnel (Spears 1991). Cook-chill and cook-freeze systems differ from traditional food preparation systems since menu items are prepared for inventory rather than for immediate service. In the cook-chill process, items are prepared and chilled in bulk. Foods are portioned and plated as much as a day before being served. In the cook-freeze process, items generally are stored frozen for 14 to 90 days. With both cook-chill and cook-freeze processes, menu items receive final heating just before service.

The increased availability of highly processed or fully prepared products has led to the development of assembly/serve systems. Use of prepared products requires mainly storage, portioning, assembly, heating, and service. Operations may use this approach exclusively or may incorporate fully prepared and portioned items with others that require greater degrees of processing.

Managing Food Production Systems

Foodservice operations are often described as systems. As such, the reliance on processes and the flow of materials helps explain the decisions made in planning for production. A major focus of foodservice management is the development and maintenance of procedures that predict and control the functions of the production system. Controls through menus, recipes, ingredient control, production forecasting, and production scheduling are key components of foodservice management.

Menu
The menu is a list of food products offered by the foodservice operation to the consumer. It is the foundation from which other functions of the system are based. In the initial stages of planning a foodservice operation, the menu guides the selection and layout of equipment. In operation, the menu controls other subsystems such as purchasing, storage, production, and service.

Menus are classified according to frequency of use (Spears 1991) and degree of choice (Spears 1991, Khan 1991). Within this classification, menus are described as fixed (static), cycle, or single-use and offer the consumer no choice, limited choice, or choice (Spears 1991). Figure 1 illustrates the types of foodservice operations that may be found in these various classifications. Depending upon the particular foodservice operation, the classification may fall in more than one category. In this example, *cafeteria* is shown in both the fixed and cycle menu category. Other classifications may also fall under more than one category, since foodservice operations of all types are becoming more conscious of consumer demands, which is reflected in an increasing number of choices offered.

Ingredient Control
Foodservice operations today have a wide variety of options in selection of products. Items may arrive as ingredients, semiprepared products, or ready-to-serve products. Ingredient control actually begins with the forecasting, purchasing, receiving, and storing of foods and continues through preparation and production (Spears 1991). Use of standardized recipes and accurate

Fig. 1. Menu classification.

	No Choice	Limited Choice	Choice
Fixed (static)		Quick-service restaurant	Full service restaurant Cafeteria
Cycle	Airline Nursing home	School food-service	Cafeteria
Single-use	Banquet	Catered luncheon	Buffet

forecasting of needed items facilitates the efficient processing of ingredients. The control of ingredients supports the major goals of product consistency and cost control.

Two approaches to ingredient control are common in foodservice operations. In traditional production systems, employees in production areas are often responsible for all processes relating to the preparation of specific items. Each employee must be trained in the proper use of measuring and processing equipment and ingredient handling. An alternative to this approach is training staff specifically assigned to the processes of ingredient control. With this approach, designated areas may be utilized for these procedures. This approach may involve arrangement in the kitchen or development of a separate room or area designed for ingredient preparation and distribution. An effective issue and assembly system controls all food and supplies from delivery to service by requiring authorization for distribution of products only in required amounts for production and service (Spears 1991).

The organization of an efficient ingredient control room or area requires considerations of location, equipment, and procedures. A location between storage and production areas facilitates the efficient flow of materials from ingredients to production. If initially planned in the foodservice operation, the ingredient control room should be the primary access to the main storage of items, including dry, refrigerated, and frozen storage areas. Provision of small refrigerated and frozen storage areas in or near the production areas should meet needs of temporary storage of some supplies. The following list indicates the major equipment needs of an ingredient control area.

Storage	Dry
	Refrigerated
	Frozen
Processing	Can opener
	Cutting board
	Knives
	Mixer
	Food chopper
Measuring	Scales
	Measuring cups
	Measuring spoons
	Ladles
Distributing	Various size containers
	Lids
	Steam table pans
	Sheet pans
	Carts
Other	Waste disposal
	Water supply

Actual equipment needs of a specific facility vary with layout, menu, and food production system. The development of standardized procedures for ingredient control and processing should be a priority of foodservice managers.

Forecasting models are a popular tool in projecting demand in foodservice operations. With the increased availablity of computer equipment, the use of more sophisticated techniques is possible. A basic premise of these models is the reliance on historical data and usage records. The assumption is that future needs will be similar to the past. The goal of evaluating usage is to analyze patterns or trends in the records. Consideration of issues of seasonality and changes in consumer demand or the business environment indicates the need for a subjective component in the determination of food production needs.

The most common forecasting methods are time series analyses, which are helpful in projecting short-term needs. The least complicated procedure is the moving average, useful for projecting needs for an individual item. The process described by Spears (1991), involves maintaining usage data for some time period, for example 5 to 10 days. The first step involves taking the average for the time period to determine the first data point. The second data point is determined by omitting the first usage point and determining the average usage for the next 5- to 10-day period.

An example of the usage of potatoes is illustrated in Figure 2. The process begins with the recording of usage of potatoes for 5 days. The first average is calculated by adding the usage for each of 5 days and dividing by 5. The first data point is 106 pounds. The second average is calculated by average use of potatoes for days 2 through 6. The second data point is 104 pounds. This procedure is repeated with each succeeding 5-day usage period. Evaluation of the *moving average* shows less change than is shown in the individual usage patterns. Use of average data values facilitates the ability of purchasing and production systems to plan for future needs. This technique would be most suited for those operations that utilized a fixed menu, since usage records would be more frequent and patterns more easily identified. However, this technique could be altered for those operations using cycle menus, since the same items would repeat, and historical data could be maintained and evaluated.

Scheduling production is an extension of the production forecast. Projections based on the expected number of portions of given menu items are the next step in ensuring appropriate amounts of food are prepared. Schedules define

Fig. 2. Moving average method for estimating demand for potatoes.

Day	Pounds of Potatoes	Average
1	120	
2	90	
3	105	
4	100	
5	115	106 (days 1–5)
6	110	104 (days 2–6)
7	105	107 (days 3–7)
8	95	105 (days 4–8)
9	120	109 (days 5–9)
10	115	109 (days 6–10)

the amount of each item to be prepared, time sequence, expected and actual yield, additional instructions, and employee assignments. In cook-chill and cook-freeze systems, accurate forecasting and scheduling is critical to maintain quality and avoid extended periods of holding. Figure 3 is an example of a format for scheduling production. As with standardized recipes, personalized formats should be developed for individual facilities to reflect the organization of food production and service.

The production schedule contains two basic types of information. Information regarding the projected needs for production are communicated through the production schedule to the employees. Information regarding the results of the production process is provided by the employee to the supervisor or manager. The correct use of a production schedule as a two-way communication tool is an excellent example of the feedback inherent in systems applications. Information from results can be important for management evaluation of planning and accuracy projections.

Recipe Standarization

The development and use of standardized recipes comprises one of the most important tools available to foodservice operations to control costs and ensure product consistency and quality. Consistent duplication of a food item is achieved with an accurate record of ingredients, amounts, and methods of combining ingredients and cooking. It is important that recipes be standardized for individual facilities since variation exists with equipment and temperature controls. The process of standardizing recipes results in instructions that have been tested in a specific operation with equipment and procedures that will be used in the production of the item. Recipes are tested for quality,

Fig. 3. Sample production schedule format.

| Date _____ |
| Meal _____ |
| Unit _____ |

Item/ Recipe	Quantity Needed	Actual Produced	Time	Leftover	Comments

Additional instructions

quantity, procedures, time, temperature, equipment, and yield. Items should be tested and results recorded until the product characteristics match the needs of the operation.

Standardized recipes offer the following advantages (Buchanan 1983):

- Promote uniform quality of foods produced
- Promote uniform quantity of foods served
- Save time for cooks, managers, or dietitians
- Save money by controlling waste and regulating inventories
- Simplify costing of menu items
- Simplify the training of new cooks
- Introduce a feeling of job security and satisfaction for foodservice workers

In cook-chill and cook-freeze systems, special recipes are required for many items due to changes that occur in storage. Flavor changes are common, especially in frozen items. The use of different ingredients or modification of storage time and temperature can be helpful in controlling these changes.

Developing a Program for Recipe Standardization

Selecting a basic format for recipes is an important first step in developing procedures for recipe standardization (Buchanan 1983). A block format is generally used in quantity foodservice operations. This method of portraying

---

Applesauce Cake

OVEN:	350° F	
BAKE:	25–30 minutes	
YIELD:	60 portions	
	1 18 × 26 × 2-inch pan	
PORTION:	Cut 6 × 10	

Ingredient	Amount	Procedure
Shortening, hydrogenated	1 lb	Cream shortening, sugar, and vanilla on medium speed using flat beater.
Sugar, granulated	2 lb	
Vanilla	1 Tbsp	
Eggs	8 each (14 oz)	Add eggs to creamed mixture and mix on medium speed for 3 minutes.
Applesauce	2 lb (4 cups)	Add applesauce and mix for 2 minutes.
Flour, cake	2 lb	Combine dry ingredients in a separate bowl.
Salt	1¼ tsp	
Baking powder	4 Tbsp	
Milk	1 cup	Add dry ingredients alternately with milk on low speed. Mix on medium speed 2–3 minutes.
		Pour batter into one greased 18 × 26 × 2-inch pan. Bake at 350° F for 25–30 minutes. Cool and frost.

Notes:
1. May be baked in 2   12 × 18 × 2-inch pans. Scale 4 lb 3 oz per pan. Portion 5 × 6 for 30 portions in each pan.

Fig. 4 Block format for recipes.

information categorizes the needed ingredients with amounts and procedures in visual "blocks" across columns (see Figure 4).

Information included in the recipe should also be determined for use in each operation. Generally, a recipe includes the following information:

Name of item
Total yield, portion size, and number of portions
Ingredients by count, weight, and/or measure
Procedures for combining ingredients
Cooking or baking equipment, temperatures, and time
Portioning information

Recipe Adjustment

Another important component of recipe standardization is the development of recipes that produce an appropriate number of portions for the operation. Foodservice operations may obtain recipes from a number of sources. Home recipes, published quantity recipes, or those prepared in the operation for which no written record exists are all examples of recipes that require adjustment. Two common methods of recipe adjustment are the factor method and the percentage method.

Factor Method. To simplify adjusting recipes, it is recommended that all ingredients, even liquids, be indicated by weight whenever possible. Using weight measurements is generally more accurate, especially with dry ingredients such as flour or baking powder, which can easily pack down in a volume measure. An additional adjustment can be made by converting all fractions (if they exist) to ounce portions of a pound. Figure 5 can be used to make this conversion.

The following four steps and example detail the factor method for recipe adjustment (Buchanan 1983).

Weight Measure		Decimal Unit	Volume Measure			Weight Measure		Decimal Unit	Volume Measure		
oz	lb		cup	qt	gal	oz	lb		cup	qt	gal
½		.03125	½			8½		.53125	8½		
1		.0625	1	¼		9		.5625	9	2¼	
1½		.093	1½			9½		.59375	9½		
2	⅛	.125	2	½		10	⅝	.625	10	2½	
2½		.156	2½			10½		.65625	10½		
3		.1875	3	¾		11		.6875	11	2¾	
3½		.218	3½			11½		.71875	11½		
4	¼	.25	4	1	¼	12	¾	.75	12	3	¾
4½		.281	4½			12½		.78125	12½		
5		.3125	5	1¼		13		.8125	13	3¼	
5½		.343	5½			13½		.84375	13½		
6	⅜	.375	6	1½		14	⅞	.875	14	3½	
6½		.40625	6½			14½		.90625	14½		
7		.4375	7	1¾		15		.9375	15	3¾	
7½		.46875	7½			15½		.96875	15½		
8	½	.5	8	2	½	16	1	1	16	4	1

Fig. 5 Weights and measures: decimal conversions.

Example: The base recipe yields 100 portions; production of 370 portions is needed

Step 1   Divide the desired yield by the known yield of the base recipe. The resulting figure of 3.7 is called the factor.

$$370 \div 100 = 3.7$$

Step 2   Multiply all recipe ingredients and the total recipe volume by the factor of 3.7 as shown.

Ingredients	100 Portions	Factor	370 Portions
dry chili beans	6.00 lb	× 3.7	22.20 lb
canned tomatoes	6.375 lb	× 3.7	23.5875 lb
chili powder	.25 lb	× 3.7	.925 lb
salt	.50 lb	× 3.7	1.85 lb
ground beef	20.00 lb	× 3.7	74.00 lb
chopped onions	1.50 lb	× 3.7	5.55 lb
flour	.75 lb	× 3.7	2.775 lb
total volume*	6.25 gal	× 3.7	23.124 gal

*In this example, the yield is given in gallons rather than pounds.

Step 3   Since it may be difficult for employees to interpret decimal amounts, reconverting these decimal units into pounds/ounces or quarts/cups may be desired.

Ingredients	370 Portions	Conversion from Decimal
dry chili beans	22.20 lb	22 lb 3 ½ oz
canned tomatoes	23.5875 lb	23 lb 9 ½ oz
chili powder	.925 lb	14 ½ oz
salt	1.85 lb	1 lb 13 ½ oz
ground beef	74.00 lb	74 lb
chopped onions	5.55 lb	5 lb 9 oz
flour	2.775 lb	2 lb 12 ½ oz
total volume	23.125 gal	23 gal 1 pt

If the total amount of an ingredient is	Round to	If the total amount of an ingredient is	Round to
	Weights	>½ cup but <¾ cup	closest full tsp or CW
<1 oz	stay in volume measures (Tbsp, tsp)	>¾ cup but <2 cups	closest full Tbsp or CW
>1 oz but <10 oz	closest ¼ oz	>2 cups but <2 qt	closest ¼ cup or CW
>10 oz but <2 lb 8 oz	closest ½ oz	>2 qt but <4 qt	closest ½ cup or CW
>5 lb	closest ¼ lb	>1 gal but <2 gal	closest full cup or CW
		>2 gal but <10 gal	closest full qt or CW
		>10 gal but <20 gal	closest ½ gal or CW
	Measures	>20 gal	closest full gal
<1 Tbsp	closest ⅛ tsp		
>1 Tbsp but <3 Tbsp	closest ¼ tsp	*Key:* > = greater than, < = less than, CW = convert to weight.	
>3 Tbsp but <½ cup	closest ½ tsp or CW		

Fig. 6   Weights and measures: guide for rounding off.

Step 4 The adjusted recipe ingredients may be in odd or unusual amounts and may require rounding. Basic guidelines for rounding in Figure 6 have been calculated to be within the limits of error normally introduced in the handling of ingredients in preparing quantity foods. Adjusted recipes should be reviewed for measurements or weights that would be difficult to handle with usual kitchen equipment. Using Figure 6, the sample recipe ingredients would be rounded in the following manner:

Ingredients	370 Portions	Rounded Amount
dry chili beans	22 lb 3½oz	22 lb 4 oz
canned tomatoes	23 lb 9½ oz	23 lb 8 oz
chili powder	14½ oz	14½ oz
salt	1 lb 13½ oz	1 lb 13½ oz
ground beef	74 lb	74 lb
chopped onions	5 lb 9 oz	5 lb 8 oz
flour	2 lb 12½ oz	2 lb 12 oz
total volume	23 gal 1 pt	23 gal 1 pt (no change)

Illustrated here is the process for rounding estimated amounts at the nearest 1/4 lb (dry chili beans, canned tomatoes), nearest 1/2 oz (chili powder, salt) and nearest full oz (flour).

Percentage Method. This method requires the conversion of ingredients to weights and the computation of the percentage of each ingredient of the total weight. Adjusting the ingredients for portion size or total yield is a simple process. The following step-by-step instructions describe recipe adjustment with the percentage method (McManis and Molt 1978):

Step 1 Convert all ingredients from measure or pounds and ounces to tenths of a pound. Make desired equivalent ingredient substitutions, such as frozen whole eggs for fresh or powdered milk for liquid.

Step 2 Total the weight of ingredients in a recipe after each ingredient has been converted to weight in the edible portion (EP). For example, the weight of carrots or celery should be the weight after cleaning and peeling. The recipe may show both AP (as purchased) and EP weights, but the edible portion is used in determining the total portion weight.

Step 3 Calculate the percentage of each ingredient in the recipe in relation to the total weight.

Formula:

$$\frac{\text{Individual ingredient weight}}{\text{Total weight}} \times 100 = \text{Percentage of each ingredient}$$

Step 4 Check the ratio of ingredients. Standards of ingredient proportions have been established for many items. The ingredients should be in proper balance before going further.

Step 5 Establish the weight needed to give the desired number of servings, which will be in relation to pan size, portion weight, or equipment capacity. Examples include the following:

- Total weight must be divisible by the weight per pan
- A cookie portion may weigh .14 lb per serving; therefore, .14 times the number of desired servings equals the weight needed
- Recipe total quantities should be compatible with mixing bowl capacity

Step 6 Cooking or handling loss must be added to the weight needed and may vary from 1 to 30 percent, depending on the product. Similar items produce predictable losses which with some experimentation can be accurately assigned. The formula for adding handling loss to a recipe is as follows:

$$100\% - \text{handling loss} = \text{yield \%}$$
$$(\text{yield \%})(\text{total quantity}) = \text{desired yield}$$
$$\text{total quantity} = \frac{\text{desired yield}}{\text{yield \%}}$$

Example: Yellow cake has a 1% handling loss. Desired yield is 80 lb of batter for 600 servings.

$$100\% - 1\% = 99\% \text{ or } .99$$
$$.99 \text{ of total quantity} = 80 \text{ lb batter}$$
$$\text{total quantity} = \frac{80 \text{ lb}}{.99}$$

Total quantity = 80.80 lb of ingredients for 80 lb available batter

Step 7 Multiply each ingredient percentage number by the total weight to give the exact amount of each ingredient needed. After the percentages of each ingredient have been established, any number of servings can be calculated and the ratio of ingredients to the total will be the same. As in the factor method, one decimal place on a recipe is shown unless the quantity is less than one pound, in which case two places are shown.

Comments on Recipe Adjustment

Adjusting and testing recipes are important but often overlooked processes in many foodservice operations. The process does require evaluation, recording of results, and multiple tests to ensure proper replication of menu items. In the aforementioned factor method, for illustration purposes, all ingredients were directly adjusted with the factor of 3.7. Testing adjusted recipes is needed, since such items as spices may not require direct adjustment. In this example, adjustments may be needed in the salt and chili powder in order to attain the desired flavor.

The increasing availability of computer programs for foodservice operations simplifies the conversion of recipes for various numbers of portions. However, the same rules apply in the testing and standardization of the recipe. Unfortunately, the computer is only a tool to develop information, not a tool that makes every operation equivalent. The sources of variation in equipment and temperature between foodservice operations still exist. The need for personalized instructions remains a key element in the development of standard products in foodservice.

Summary

Provision of products at an appropriate price, time, and level of quality for a given operation continues to be the goal of foodservice operations. Given the current concerns with cost containment and the availability of qualified employees, food production systems that utilize food processing technology or prepared products are becoming an important component of foodservice systems. In operations that are involved in food production, the implementation of procedures to develop standardized recipes provides a method to help ensure consistent quality. Regardless of the system, basic procedures that monitor the processes of the system continue to be required. Menus, ingredient control, forecasting, and scheduling continue to be important components of the successful management of food production and service.

References

Buchanan, P. W. 1983. *Quantity Food Preparation*, 2d ed. Chicago, Ill.: The American Dietetic Association.

Khan, M. A. 1991. *Concepts of Foodservice Operations and Management*, 2d ed. New York: Van Nostrand Reinhold.

McManis, H., and M. Molt. 1978. Recipe standardization and percentage method of adjustment. *NACUFS Journal 35.*

Spears, M. C. 1991. *Foodservice Organizations: A Managerial and Systems Approach*, 2d ed. New York: Macmillan.

Unklesbay, N., R. B. Maxcy, M. Knickrehm, K. Stevenson, M. Cremer, and M. Matthews. 1977. *Foodservice Systems: Product Flow and Microbial Quality and Safety of Foods.* North Central Regional Research Bulletin No 245. Columbia, Mo.: Missouri Agricultural Experiment Station.

14

The Cook-Chill Food Production Process

Claudia G. Green

Cook-chill is a ready food production process that involves conventional food preparation techniques using typical foodservice equipment followed by quick chilling and cold storage until service. The rapid chilling to 32–37°F is the feature that ensures an extended shelf life, reduces the opportunity for microbiological growth, and allows for the retention of the quality of a fresh product (Light and Walker 1991; Barnett 1987).

Organoleptic qualities of food such as taste, odor, texture, and appearance are better retained by chilling as opposed to freezing or canning (Light and Walker 1991). Moreover, the cook-chill has been found to result in operational cost benefits/savings. A disadvantage of cook-chill is that the total costs of installation of the production process including specialized equipment and structural modifications in the foodservice facility require a major financial commitment. Another disadvantage is the drying out of food during the chill and reheat process and the loss of crispness in selected pastries and battered foods.

Why Use Cook-Chill?

In the early 1970s, foodservice administrators were challenged to be innovative in directing changes by implementing new technology (processes) to existing circumstances (Donaldson 1971). More and more foodservice administrators began to explore alternative foodservice systems that would help cover and contain cost (Berkman 1980; Carroll 1980; Cipolla 1990; Franzese 1984, 1981; King 1989; Koncel 1977; Lippe 1983). Alternative systems (that is, convenience, cook-freeze, and cook-chill), thought to be able to address the operational problems of increasing costs as well as food product safety, product consistency, and low productivity, were introduced (Ridley et al. 1984; Rinke 1976). These systems met limited acceptance at that time due to the initial capital investment, seemingly limitless labor pool, and concerns regarding safety and consistency of foods prepared by these alternative foodservice systems (Lyman 1981).

In the early 1980s, foodservice administrators took steps to improve profitability by streamlining purchasing, increasing productivity, and marketing (Schuster 1980; Pickens and Shanklin 1985). These traditional cost containment procedures (Coltman 1989; Berkman 1980) by themselves, however, were no longer enough to address the escalating foodservice costs. In the 1980s many foodservice equipment companies advertised and promoted the financial benefits gained through the introduction of cook-chill (Bean 1985; King 1989).

Foodservice managers began to look at cook-chill as an alternative to solve operational problems including high labor cost and increasing food cost as well as customer demand for quality assurance in nutritive value, sensory characteristics, and food safety. Although the reason cited for the selection of cook-chill technology is primarily its labor and food cost savings/benefit, there is a lack of empirical research clearly supporting this cost benefit (Light and Walker 1991; Lough et al. 1978).

Labor Cost

Cook-chill technology has the capability to provide for increased productivity of employees and foodservice production equipment. These goals can be achieved by the inherent nature of cook-chill technology whereby food is produced in large quantities by skilled labor for inventory (Spears 1991) and later reheated and served by unskilled labor. Moreover, cook-chill technology introduces the principle of manufacturing with long production runs to the foodservice industry, which has had the reputation of having short production runs and low productivity. By increasing the productivity of the employee, fewer workhours are needed to prepare the food with the result being a reduction in production labor expense (Light and Walker 1991).

Food Cost

Cook-chill technology can contribute to lower food costs through elimination of overproduction. Cooking to inventory allows foodservice operations to develop a par stock level of chilled food products. Because food is held in a chilled state, it is easier to remove and rethermalize the exact amount needed to meet customer demand thereby reducing waste.

Large cook-chill operations that prepare food to be sent to satellite foodservice operations may realize reduction in food cost through centralized purchasing and central production. These cost savings may not be realized in smaller cook-chill operations.

Quality Assurance

Quality of food products prepared by cook-chill can be evaluated in terms of nutritive value, sensory value, and food safety. Consistent quality can be assured through the use of ingredient specifications, standard recipes and handling procedures, and attention to sanitation. Light and Walker (1991) found that successful cook-chill operations were more likely to have ongoing testing and modification of recipes to ensure the sensory quality of foods produced. Research studies support the belief that cook-chill does cause some loss of nutritional quality during chilled storage. Losses can be minimized when foods are handled according to standard guidelines.

The cook-chill process properly administered provides an opportunity for the systematic introduction of Hazard Analysis Critical Control Point (HACCP), a system that prevents the hazards associated with food procurement, food storage, food packaging, preprocessing, heat processing, food storage after heat processing, heat processing of precooked menu items, and service of food (Spears 1991). Although the safety of food prepared by cook-chill has been questioned by various experts in the literature, it has been found to be equally or more safe than food prepared and held using other production methods (Cremer 1981; Bunch et al. 1976). Strict guidelines were set in 1990 by the Food Safety and Inspection Service of the United States Department of Agriculture.

Use of Cook-Chill in the United States

Since 1980 a dramatic increase has occurred in the number of cook-chill production process installations in the United States. Statistics indicate that 1,400 cook-chill installations were made in a variety of institutional settings including hospitals, schools, nursing homes, college/universities, and prison systems in 1990. The expectation is that 3,400 installations will be in operation by 1995; most of the increase will be in hospital foodservices (Vulcan Hart 1991). A recent survey of 300 foodservice operators by *Foodservice Trendspotter,* a quarterly publication of the National Foodservice Panel, Incorporated, indicated that in the institutional market, large hospitals are still the most likely foodservice operations to adopt a cook-chill process followed by college/university foodservices and commercial restaurants. If the cook-chill process continues to be successful in the institutional foodservice sector in the 1990s, this process would obviously have other applications in institutional units and the entire foodservice industry.

The *Foodservice Trendspotter* survey revealed that only 71 percent of the respondents clearly understood the cook-chill process. Cook-chill is seen as an alternative to the other production processes (that is, conventional, convenience, and cook-freeze). To understand cook-chill food production more clearly, differences between the production processes should be compared and examined (see Figure 1).

Fig. 1. Food production processes.

Cook-chill	Conventional	Convenience	Cook-freeze
Receiving and storage	Receiving and storage	Receiving and storage	Receiving and storage
Ingredient cooking	Ingredient cooking	Rethermalization	Ingredient cooking
Rapid chill			Rapid freeze
Refrigerated storage			Freezer storage
Meal assembly	Meal assembly	Meal assembly	Meal assembly
Rethermalization			Rethermalization
Meal service	Meal service	Meal service	Meal service

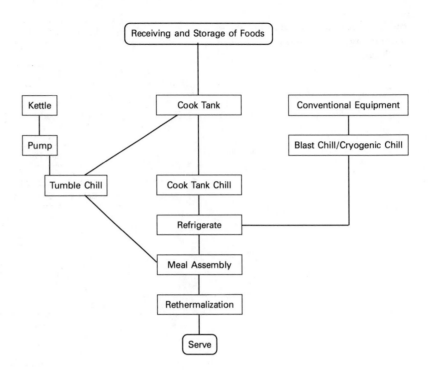

Fig. 2. Cook-chill food production technology.

Components of the Cook-Chill Process

In 1972 Cryovac Food Service System introduced the cook-chill process to the United States foodservice industry after five years of testing and development (Bean 1985). There are seven basic steps in the cook-chill process (Escueta et al. 1986; Jones and Heulin 1990) (see Figure 2):

1. Ingredient receiving and storage
2. Ingredient cooking
3. Rapid chilling
4. Refrigerated storage
5. Meal assembly
6. Rethermalization
7. Service

Sous-vide is a variation of the cook-chill process (Figure 3) in which raw or partially cooked foods are vacuum packed in a multilaminate plastic. The packaged food is then chilled and stored under refrigeration until service at which time the food is cooked to completion. Sous-vide technology is most easily applied to individually portioned foods (Light and Walker 1991).

Variations in Ingredient Cooking

The purpose of ingredient cooking is to change the texture of the food, enhance the flavor, and to kill organisms that may cause the food to spoil or become unsafe for consumption. Food products used in the cook-chill process should not be thoroughly cooked since additional cooking will occur during rethermalization (reheating). Critical factors in the cooking process are sanitation, cooking time, and length of time food is held.

Ingredients may be cooked using conventional equipment, cook-tanks, combined cooker/chillers, or conveyor thermal processing equipment. Conventionally prepared foods can be cooked in a convection oven, fryer, broiler, grill, braising pan, or such and then chilled. Cook tanks are kettles

Fig. 3. Sous-vide production technology: a variation of cook-chill.

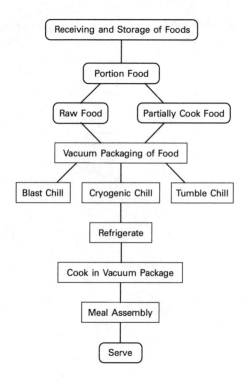

specifically designed for the cook-chill process. A cook tank is a hemispherical vessel designed to cook liquids and semiliquid foods. Cook tanks may be equipped with speed controls, timers, temperature indicators, programmable cooking cycles, a pump, and a stirring or agitation device. Cook tanks are linked with a pumping station that pumps the food from the kettle into the container or cryovac bag.

Cooker chillers combine the functions of cooking and chilling in a single piece of equipment thereby reducing product handling. Food, enclosed in cryovac packages, is placed in the tank of heated water and cooked. Once the food attains the desired internal temperature, the hot water is drained from the tank. The tank is then filled with cold water, which chills the food products to 32–37°F.

Conveyor belt production may be used in the cook-chill process and be linked with fryers, grills, or steamers. Food is loaded onto the conveyor belt at the cooking device and is unloaded at the end of the belt after passing through a blast chill chamber.

Variations in Chilling

Three variations of cook-chill technology include blast chiller, cryogenic chillers, and tumble chillers. With the blast chill method, chilled air is blown at a high velocity over hot food to chill the product as quickly as possible. A programmable control panel regulates the continuous flow of high velocity chilled air in order to chill the food as rapidly as possible. Blast chillers can be added to an existing conventional food production facility for easy integration of the cook-chill technology.

Cryogenic chilling, a process similar to blast chilling, circulates cold nitrogen or carbon dioxide gas to rapidly chill the food products. Use of nitrogen is more efficient because in the liquid form, nitrogen is −164°F. This fact means that a combined cook-chill/freeze operation can be set up with only one piece of equipment. Installation cost of the cryogenic method is greater than for blast chiller installation due to the requirement for on-site storage of liquid nitrogen.

Tumble chilling is simply the process of immersing the sealed food product in ice water. This method chills four times quicker than blast chilling with forced air. Tumble chillers are of two types: those equipped with a paddle device that agitates the bags of food or with a chamber that turns to rapidly move the water around.

The method of chilling determines the length of the shelf life of the food product. The shelf life of foods prepared by blast chill technology is five days counting the day of preparation, whereas the shelf life of foods prepared in kettles and pumped into bags, tumbled, and chilled may be up to three weeks. Foods consumed beyond the desirable shelf life may or may not be microbiologically safe but have been found to be consistently low in sensory acceptability.

Variations in Rethermalization

The process of rethermalization can be accomplished through bulk regeneration ovens, combination ovens, mobile regeneration trolleys, or microwave ovens. Bulk regeneration ovens use a forced hot air system of indirect heat with hot air circulating throughout the oven. Although bulk regeneration ovens are designed to reheat with minimal loss of moisture, the nature of this reheating system may cause products to dry out if not closely controlled. This system is best suited for products that need dry heat for crisping or browning.

Combination ovens provide cabinets that can use forced air dry heat and/or low pressure steam injection. These ovens may be used for initial cooking or for bulk regeneration with less drying of the food products.

Mobile rethermalization carts may be used exclusively for reheating items or for simultaneously reheating foods and for holding cold salads, beverages, and condiments at chilled temperatures.

A microwave oven is best suited for quick rethermalization of individual portions. While different densities and water content of various foods may create a problem with even heating by the microwave, this type of reheating can provide good results if proper procedures are followed.

Considerations in the Selection and Implementation of Cook-Chill

Current cook-chill foodservices are operating with varying degrees of productivity, profitability, and customer acceptance. Although the introduction of cook-chill technology seems straightforward, experience has shown it to be a complex, problematic process that could be simplified through systematic preplanning (Light and Walker 1991; Carroll 1980; Koncel 1977). There has been little research on cook-chill technology despite its worldwide use (Light and Walker 1991, Green and Weaver 1991; Greathouse et al. 1989). The first and only in-depth study regarding the introduction of cook-chill technology was based on a survey of 80 cook-chill operations in the United Kingdom (Light and Walker 1991). The findings of this survey of cook-chill operations in industrial operations, hotel/leisure facilities, hospitals, and educational institutions suggest ten key considerations in setting up and running a successful cook-chill operation:

1. Awareness and compliance with health and sanitation inspection guidelines
2. Awareness of the need for and operation of quality control
3. Training of all staff
4. Employment and stability in managers and decision makers
5. Strict control of time and temperatures
6. A universally accepted perception of a real need to introduce the system
7. Maintaining and developing an ongoing research and development program that includes ingredient as well as recipe modification and testing
8. Adequate capital expenditure and a plan for anticipated pay back period
9. Effective communication between customers and staff during the feasibility studies and installation
10. Extensive use of information from many resources during the process of making the decision to select cook-chill technology (Light and Walker 1991)

Advantages and Disadvantages of the Cook-Chill Production Process

The primary advantages of cook-chill are increased production labor and food cost control as well as the potential to be assured of product quality, consistency, and safety. At this point a brief discussion of each of these important issues may help clarify the advantages and disadvantages of the cook-chill production.

First, long runs result in lower labor hours and therefore lower labor costs by reducing production peaks and valleys. Second, cook-chill eliminates over production and subsequent waste that ultimately increases food costs. In large cook-chill operations, centralized purchasing and production also reduces the need for comprehensive or fully equipped kitchens at satellite foodservice units. These economies of scale, however, may not be seen in small cook-chill operations. The most important advantage of the cook-chill process is centralized control over aspects of product quality: nutritive value, sensory characteristics, and food safety through the use of strict quality assurance standards, standard recipes and handling procedures, and the Hazard Analysis Critical Control Point method, designed to ensure food safety.

One of the primary disadvantages of the cook-chill process is the initial capital investment in equipment. This investment may be substantial in the area of holding and chilling. Also, structural additions and installation modifications may be needed to adopt this new production process. Because it is widely accepted that there are numerous hazards in storing foods for extended time periods prior to service, the Federal Drug Administration has developed specific food safety guidelines for the use of the cook-chill process. There is an obvious need to maintain high standards of food sanitation in production, packaging, holding, distribution, and service. Operational disadvantages of the cook-chill process are the preparation of foods that are not considered "fresh" and the extensive attention to be given to this important consumer issue.

Summary

As foodservice administrators look for solutions to the problems of a dwindling supply of labor, spiraling food and labor cost, food safety, and production consistency, the cook-chill production process, which involves "cooking to inventory," becomes a viable alternative. The cook-chill process involves food production followed by rapid chilling and storage until use.

The cook-chill production process, which has been touted to reduce labor, food, and utility costs, increase efficiency, and improve food safety, has been used extensively throughout Europe since the mid-1960s. In the mid-1970s it was met with limited acceptance when it was initially introduced to the U.S. market. The reasons for the poor reception of this process were the plentiful supply of low-cost labor, little emphasis on cost containment, initial set-up costs for cook-chill, and lack of clarity with regard to food-safety issues.

Since 1980, however, there has been a dramatic increase in the acceptance of the cook-chill process as evidenced by the increasing number of cook-chill production process installations in the United States. Statistics indicate that there were 1,400 cook-chill operations in a variety of foodservice settings in 1990. It is expected that there will be 3,400 installations by 1995, with most of the increase in noncommercial foodservice operations.

References

Barnett, L. 1987. Simplifying operations: Using cook-chill. *School Foodservice Journal* 41(3):78–79.

Bean, R. L. 1985. System, system, who's got the system? *The Consultant* 18(2).

Berkman, J. 1980. Food service needs controls to contain costs. *Hospitals* (March 16):79–82.

Bunch, W. L., M. E. Matthews, and E. H. Marth. 1976. Fate of staphylococcus aureus in beef-soy loaves subjected to procedures used in hospital chill foodservice systems. *Journal of Food Science* 42(2):565–566.

Carroll, G. H. 1980. Case histories: a bulk pack chilled/frozen production system for a 500 bed hospital. *Journal of Foodservice Systems* 1:51–67.

Cipolla, M. M. 1990. Foodservice operators need systems for profitability, efficiency, and quality. *The Consultant.* 23:2.

Coltman, M. 1989. *Cost Control for the Hospitality Industry.* New York: Van Nostrand Reinhold.

Cremer, M. L. 1981. Sensory and microbiological qualities of beef loaf in four commissary foodservice treatments. *Journal of the American Dietetics Association* 78:483–489.

Donaldson, B. 1971. Food service. *Hospitals* 45:81–84.

Escueta, E. S., K. M. Fiedler, and A. Reisman. 1986. A new hospital foodservice classification system. *Journal of Foodservice Systems* 4:107–116.

Franzese, R. 1984. Food services survey shows delivery shift. *Hospitals* 58:16, 61–66.

Franzese, R. 1981. Survey examine hospitals' use of convenience foods. *Hospitals.* (Jan. 16):109–112.

Greathouse, K. R., M. B. Gregoire, M. C. Spears, V. Richards, and R. J. Nassar. 1989. Comparison of conventional, cook-chill, and cook-freeze systems. *Journal of the American Dietetics Association* 89(11):1606–1611.

Greene, C. A., and P. A. Weaver. 1991. Use of statistics in foodservice system literature. Unpublished manuscript. Virginia Polytechnic Institute and State University, Blacksburg, Va.

Jones, P. and A. Heulin. 1990. Foodservice systems—generic types, alternative technologies and infinite variation. *Journal of Foodservice Systems* 5:299–311.

King, P. 1989. Producing in a less costly foodservice. *Food Management.* May.

Koncel, J. A. 1977. Food service has vital role in overall hospital operations. *Hospitals* 51(Aug. 16):111–114.

Koncel, J. A. 1977. Planning pervaded conversion to cook/chill system. *Hospitals* 50(Nov. 16):87–92.

Light, N., and A. Walker. 1991. *Cook-Chill Catering: Technology and Management.* London: Elsevier Applied Sciences.

Lippe, D. 1983. Evaluation can be keen weapon for defending capital purchase. *Modern Healthcare* (Sept.):197–202.

Lough, J. B., J. M. Harper, G. R. Jansen, C. T. Shigetomi, and J. Anderson, 1978. Pilot study to evaluate food delivery systems used in school lunch program. *School Foodservice Research Review* 2(1):23–26.

Lyman, W. A. 1981. Cook-chill system for food service operations. *Proceedings of the 37th Conference of The Society for the Advancement of Foodservice Research.* April 2–4.

Pickens, C. W. and C. W. Shanklin. 1985. State of the art in marketing hospital foodservice departments. *Journal of the American Dietetics Association* 85(11):1474–78.

Ridley, S. J., M. E. Matthews, and L. M. McProud. 1984. Labor time code for assembling and microwave heating menu items in a hospital galley. *Journal of the American Dietetics Association* 84(6):648–654.

Rinke, W. J. 1976. Three major systems reviewed and evaluated. *Hospitals* 50(4):73–78.

Schuster, K. 1980. Survival of the fittest in hospital foodservice 1980–89. *Food Management* (Oct.):57:120.

Spears, M. C. 1991. *Foodservice Organizations: A Managerial and Systems Approach.* New York: Macmillan.

Vulcan Hart. 1991. *Cook-Chill Made Easy.* Seminar, Atlanta, Ga. April.

Bibliography

Bobeng, B. 1978. HACCP models for quality control of entree production in hospital foodservice systems. *Journal of the American Dietetics Association* 73:524.

Carroll, G. H. 1979. Labor time comparison of a cook-freeze and cook-service system of food production. *Journal of Canadian Dietetics Association* 40(1):39–49.

Cremer, M. L. 1977. Satellite foodservice system assessment in terms of time and temperature conditions and microbiological and sensory quality of spaghetti and chili. *Journal of Foodservice Systems* 42:225–227.

Dahl, C. and M. E. Matthews. 1979. Hospital cook/chill foodservice systems, *Journal of the American Dietetics Association.* 75:34–37.

Glew, G. 1973. The technology for improved service. *Hospitals* 47:51–52.

Goldberg, C. M., and M. Kohiligian. 1974. Conventional, convenience or ready food service. *Hospitals* (April 16):235–254.

Greathouse, K. R., and M. B. Gregoire. 1988. Variables related to selection of conventional, cook-chill, and cook-freeze systems. *Journal of the American Dietetics Association.* 88(4):476–478.

Harder, E. 1973. Convenience food decision: No! *Hospitals* 47:76–80.

Harper, J. M., G. R. Jansen, C. T. Shigetomi, and L. K. Fallis. 1972. Pilot study to evaluate food delivery systems used in school lunch programs I. Menu item acceptability. *School Foodservice Research Review* 1(1):20–24.

Herz, M. L., and J. J. Souder. 1979. Preparation systems have significant effect on cost. *Hospitals* (Jan.):89–92.

Koogler, G. H., and S. Nicholanco. 1977. Analysis of a decision framework for prepared food systems. *Hospitals* 5(4):95–98.

National Foodservice Panel, Inc. 1990. Interest in cook-chill is strong, but sous-vide still a mystery. *Foodservice Trendspotter* 1(3):1–9.

McLaren, A. 1980. Containing the costs of food service. *Hospitals* (March 16):75–77.

McProud, L. M. 1982. Reducing energy loss in food service. *Food Technology* 36(7):67–69.

Matthews, M. E. 1982. *Hospital Patient Feeding Systems.* Washington, D.C.:National Academy Press.

Matthews, M. E. 1982. Foodservice in health care facilities. *Food Technology* 36(7):53–71.

Matthews, M. E. 1977. Quality of food in cook-chill foodservice systems: a review. *School Foodservice Research Review* 1(1):15–19.

Matthews, M. E. 1975. Productivity studies reviewed, trends analyzed. *Hospitals* 49(Dec. 16):81–84.

Rappole, C. L. 1973. Institutional use of frozen entrees. *Cornell Hotel Restaurant Quarterly* 47:76–80.

Schuster, K. 1982. The state of healthcare foodservice 1982–83: Options and obstacles in the world of business. *Food Management* (Oct.):40–114.

15

Food Storage

John Stefanelli

Food storage is an extremely important activity performed daily by foodservice managers that can affect the cost and quality of finished menu items. Proper storage helps ensure customer satisfaction and consistent food costs, whereas inadequate storage can cause customer dissatisfaction and excessive costs due to waste, spoilage, and/or theft.

Storage usually is performed in conjunction with the receiving activity. When a food shipment arrives at the foodservice operation, someone must inspect it, sign for it, and see to it that it is stored in the proper location. Normally a manager or supervisor is entrusted with these tasks.

Sometimes the purchasing agent is responsible for buying, receiving, and storing. Some think that the purchasing agent is the logical person to receive and store because he or she knows exactly what was ordered and is most familiar with the products. However, most foodservice practitioners try to separate the buying from the receiving and storage functions because this combination of duties presents the buyer with a splendid opportunity to defraud the company.

In very large foodservice operations, especially those in large hotels, a separate storeroom manager is responsible for all storage-related activities. In fact, this manager may have several employees working for him or her; for instance, it is not unusual for a large hotel to have five or six persons working exclusively in the storeroom department.

The typical foodservice operation does not have a separate storeroom manager. Usually an assistant manager, or the manager on duty, shoulders the receiving and storage responsibilities. In most cases, the amount of time devoted to these activities during the typical working day does not exceed one to two hours.

Food Storage Objectives

The primary objectives of food storage are to prevent theft and pilferage; minimize food waste due to spoilage; and maintain a safe and sanitary food supply.

Theft is premeditated burglary whereas pilferage is less severe. Theft occurs when someone breaks into the storeroom and makes off with all the merchandise. Pilferage occurs whenever an employee, a delivery driver, or customer confiscates a small article: An employee sneaking off with a steak or two or a customer shoplifting a dinner plate are forms of pilferage.

Spoilage is an unhappy and unavoidable part of the foodservice industry. Generally, food products do not actually spoil in storage to the extent that they are inedible. They may be perfectly safe to eat; however, they may be well past their peak of quality. While at home we may not hesitate to serve lettuce that is a bit wilted, we can hardly expect customers to accept it and pay top dollar for it. Consequently, storage demands in the foodservice operation far exceed those that we place upon ourselves in our personal lives.

Foodservice managers are obliged to serve safe and sanitary food to their guests. Proper storage can help ensure that unwholesome foods are not served. Many unsafe foods do not always exhibit signs of spoilage or danger, for instance, an unsafe frozen product may appear perfectly acceptable. Therefore, the manager must follow the sanitation principles and procedures mandated by the local health authorities when planning and managing the food storage facilities. This will reduce the chance that customers and employees will consume foods that could cause foodborne illness.

Achieving the Food Storage Objectives

Achieving the food storage objectives begins in the planning stages of the foodservice operation. Before the facility is constructed, adequate space must be devoted to storage. Unfortunately, storage needs often give way to more pressing concerns, such as the need for more dining room space. However, inadequate space usually leads to excessive waste, spoilage, theft, and pilferage.

Inadequate space forces the manager to store foods in areas that are not designed to hold them. For example, foods should not be stored in hallways and under stairways. These environments are conducive to food loss. They also can cause foods to become contaminated which, if passed on to the customer, will cause unnecessary foodborne illness, several visits from the health officer, and probably a severe loss of future business.

Foods may not be stored in areas that are used to store soaps, chemicals, and other contaminants. Besides violating health regulations, foods will absorb odors from these products, thereby rendering them unfit to serve customers. Foods may not be stored in areas where there are overhead water and/or sewer pipes. These pipes can leak; at the very least, they will sweat occasionally. Any dripping can contaminate foods. It also will cause damp conditions that are conducive to vermin infestation as well as mold growth. Health regulations also prohibit food from being stored in restroom facilities or in rooms where garbage is stored.

Any food storage area must be well ventilated. While it cannot be damp and dingy, it also cannot be too dry. Excessive dryness will cause some foods to dehydrate. Dryness can also cause packaging to shrink, split, or tear, thereby causing the contents to spoil or lose culinary quality.

If foods are stored in areas not designed for food storage, chances are these areas are not secure. Theft and pilferage therefore, will be continuing problems for the foodservice manager. Ironically, the effort to save money by minimizing storage space during the planning phase of the restaurant's development will be lost many times over until the situation is rectified. Furthermore, insecure areas more than likely offer inviting targets, and easy access, to vermin.

Improper storage locations also tend to violate recommended temperature and humidity standards. Foods should be stored at temperatures and humidities that will preserve their shelf lives (Tables 1, 2, and 3). Appropriately designed dry storerooms, refrigerators, and freezers will maintain the ideal environmental conditions.

Health regulations require potentially hazardous foods, such as meats, seafood, and poultry, to be stored outside the temperature danger zone of 45°F to 140°F. Most microorganisms that can cause foodborne illness thrive in the danger zone. The foodservice operation must have adequate refrigeration and hot-holding equipment to store these foods or the local health officer will not allow it to remain open for business.

Nonfood items and nonhazardous food products, such as fresh produce, canned goods, and dried foods, usually have no government-mandated temperature and humidity requirements. Nevertheless, the foodservice manager should keep them in the ideal environment; anything less will result in severely shortened shelf lives.

Improper food storage areas also tend to violate health regulation shelving requirements. For instance, normally food products must be stored about four inches from walls, ceilings, and floors. Shelving conducive to air circulation, such as wire shelving, also must be used in most instances. Violations of these shelving requirements will reduce food shelf lives and create attractive locales for vermin.

Inappropriate storage areas probably are not located close to the receiving and food production areas. It is desirable to locate the receiving, storage, and food production departments next to each other and on the same floor level. This set up is the most efficient; it also ensures that foods are not out of their recommended temperature and humidity environments for excessive periods.

Table 1. *Shelf lives of some refrigerated foods*

Food	Recommended temperatures (°F/°C)	Maximum storage periods	Comments
Meat			
Roasts, steaks, chops	32–36/0–2.2	3 to 5 days	Wrap loosely
Ground and stewing	32–36/0–2.2	1 to 2 days	Wrap loosely
Variety meats	32–36/0–2.2	1 to 2 days	Wrap loosely
Whole ham	32–36/0–2.2	7 days	May wrap tightly
Half ham	32–36/0–2.2	3 to 5 days	May wrap tightly
Ham slices	32–36/0–2.2	3 to 5 days	May wrap tightly
Canned ham	32–36/0–2.2	1 year	Keep in can
Frankfurters	32–36/0–2.2	1 week	Original wrapping
Bacon	32–36/0–2.2	1 week	May wrap tightly
Luncheon meats	32–36/0–2.2	3 to 5 days	Wrap tightly when opened
Leftover Cooked Meats	32–36/0–2.2	1 to 2 days	Wrap or cover tightly
Gravy, Broth	32–36/0–2.2	1 to 2 days	Highly perishable
Poultry			
Whole chicken, turkey, duck, goose	32–36/0–2.2	1 to 2 days	Wrap loosely
Giblets	32–36/0–2.2	1 to 2 days	Wrap separate from bird

(continued)

Table 1. *Shelf lives of some refrigerated foods (continued)*

Food	Recommended temperatures (°F/°C)	Maximum storage periods	Comments
Poultry (Cont.)			
Stuffing	32–36/0–2.2	1 to 2 days	Covered container separate from bird
Cut-up cooked poultry	32–36/0–2.2	1 to 2 days	Cover
Fish			
Fatty fish	30–34/−1.1–1.1	1 to 2 days	Wrap loosely
Fish—not iced	30–34/−1.1–1.1	1 to 2 days	Wrap loosely
Fish—iced	32/0	3 days	Don't bruise with ice
Shellfish	30–34/−1.1–1.1	1 to 2 days	Covered container
Eggs			
Eggs in shell	40–45/4.4–7.2	1 week	Do not wash. Remove from container
Leftover yolks/whites	40–45/4.4–7.2	2 days	Cover yolks with water
Dried eggs	40–45/4.4–7.2	1 year	Cover tightly
Reconstituted eggs	40–45/4.4–7.2	1 week	Same treatment as eggs in shell
Cooked Dishes with Eggs, Meat, Milk, Fish, Poultry	32–36/0–2.2	Serve day prepared	Highly perishable
Cream-Filled Pastries	32–36/0–2.2	Serve day prepared	Highly perishable
Dairy Products			
Fluid milk	38–39/3.3–3.9	5 to 7 days after date on carton	Keep covered and in original container
Butter	38–40/3.3–4.4	2 weeks	Waxed cartons
Hard cheese (cheddar, parmesan, romano)	38–40/3.3–4.4	6 months	Cover tightly to preserve moisture
Soft cheese			
Cottage cheese	38–40/3.3–4.4	3 days	Cover tightly
Other soft cheeses	38–40/3.3–4.4	7 days	Cover tightly
Evaporated milk	50–70/10–21.1	1 year unopened	Refrigerate after opening
Dry milk (nonfat)	50–70/10–21.1	1 year unopened	Refrigerate after opening
Reconstituted dry milk	38–40/3.3–4.4	1 week	Treat as fluid milk
Fruit			
Apples	40–45/4.4–7.2	2 weeks	Room temperature till ripe
Avocados	40–45/4.4–7.2	3 to 5 days	Room temperature till ripe
Bananas	40–45/4.4–7.2	3 to 5 days	Room temperature till ripe
Berries, cherries	40–45/4.4–7.2	2 to 5 days	Do not wash before refrigerating
Citrus	40–45/4.4–7.2	1 month	Original container
Cranberries	40–45/4.4–7.2	1 week	
Grapes	40–45/4.4–7.2	3 to 5 days	Room temperature till ripe
Pears	40–45/4.4–7.2	3 to 5 days	Room temperature till ripe
Pineapples	40–45/4.4–7.2	3 to 5 days	Refrigerate (lightly covered) after cutting
Plums	40–45/4.4–7.2	1 week	Do not wash before refrigerating
Vegetables			
Sweet potatoes, mature onions, hard-rind squashes, rutabagas	60/15.6	1 to 2 weeks at room temp. 3 months at 60°F	Ventilated containers for onions
Potatoes	45–50/7.2–10	30 days	Ventilated containers
All other vegetables	40–45/4.4–7.2	5 days maximum for most; 2 weeks for cabbage, root vegetables	Unwashed for storage

Table 2. *Shelf lives of some frozen foods*

Food	Maximum storage period at −10° to 0°F (−23.3° to −17.7°C)
Meat	
Beef, roasts and steaks	6 months
Beef, ground and stewing	3 to 4 months
Pork, roasts and chops	4 to 8 months
Pork, ground	1 to 3 months
Lamb, roasts and chops	6 to 8 months
Lamb, ground	3 to 5 months
Veal	8 to 12 months
Variety meats (liver, tongue)	3 to 4 months
Ham, frankfurters, bacon, luncheon meats	2 weeks (freezing not generally recommended.)
Leftover cooked meats	2 to 3 months
Gravy broth	2 to 3 months
Sandwiches with meat filling	1 to 2 months
Poultry	
Whole chicken, turkey, duck, goose	12 months
Giblets	3 months
Cut-up cooked poultry	4 months
Fish	
Fatty fish (mackerel, salmon)	3 months
Other fish	6 months
Shellfish	3 to 4 months
Ice Cream	3 months. Original container. Quality maintained better at 10°F (−12.2°C)
Fruit	8 to 12 months
Fruit Juice	8 to 12 months
Vegetables	8 months
French-Fried Potatoes	2 to 6 months
Precooked Combination Dishes	2 to 6 months
Baked Goods	
Cakes, prebaked	4 to 9 months
Cake batters	3 to 4 months
Fruit pies, baked or unbaked	3 to 4 months
Pie shells, baked or unbaked	1½ to 2 months
Cookies	6 to 12 months
Yeast breads and rolls, prebaked	3 to 9 months
Yeast breads and rolls, dough	1 to 1½ months

Table 3. *Shelf lives of some dry storage foods*

Food	Recommended maximum storage period if unopened
Baking Materials	
Baking powder	8 to 12 months
Chocolate, baking	6 to 12 months
Chocolate, sweetened	2 years
Cornstarch	2 to 3 years
Tapioca	1 year
Yeast, dry	18 months
Baking soda	8 to 12 months
Beverages	
Coffee, ground, vacuum packed	7 to 12 months
Coffee, ground, not vacuum packed	2 weeks
Coffee, instant	8 to 12 months
Tea, leaves	12 to 18 months
Tea, instant	8 to 12 months
Carbonated beverages	Indefinitely
Canned Goods	
Fruits (in general)	1 year
Fruits, acidic (citrus, berries, sour cherries)	6 to 12 months
Fruit juices	6 to 9 months
Seafood (in general)	1 year
Pickled fish	4 months
Soups	1 year
Vegetables (in general)	1 year
Vegetables, acidic (tomatoes, sauerkraut)	7 to 12 months
Dairy Foods	
Cream, powered	4 months
Milk, condensed	1 year
Milk, evaporated	1 year
Fats and Oils	
Mayonnaise	2 months
Salad dressings	2 months
Salad oil	6 to 9 months
Vegetable shortenings	2 to 4 months
Grains and Grain Products	
Cereal grains for cooked cereal	8 months
Cereals, ready-to-eat	6 months
Flour, bleached	9 to 12 months
Macaroni, spaghetti, and other noodles	3 months
Prepared mixes	6 months
Rice, parboiled	9 to 12 months
Rice, brown or wild	Should be refrigerated
Seasonings	
Flavoring extracts	Indefinite
Monosodium glutamate	Indefinite
Mustard, prepared	2 to 6 months
Salt	Indefinite
Sauces (steak, soy, etc.)	2 years
Spices and herbs (whole)	2 years to indefinite
Paprika, chili powder, cayenne	1 year
Seasoning salts	1 year
Vinegar	2 years

(continued)

Table 3. *Shelf lives of some dry storage foods (continued)*

Food	Recommended maximum storage period if unopened
Sweeteners	
Sugar, granulated	Indefinite
Sugar, confectioners	Indefinite
Sugar, brown	Should be refrigerated
Syrups, corn, honey, molasses, sugar	1 year
Miscellaneous	
Dried beans	1 to 2 years
Cookies, crackers	1 to 6 months
Dried fruits	6 to 8 months
Gelatin	2 to 3 years
Dried prunes	Should be refrigerated
Jams, jellies	1 year
Nuts	1 year
Pickles, relishes	1 year
Potato chips	1 month

Food Storage Management Procedures

A well-run foodservice operation usually assigns one person to oversee the storage facilities. In most instances, this person also has other duties, such as food production or service management responsibilities. The full-time storeroom manager—typically found in the large foodservice operations—concentrates solely on running the storeroom and supervising storeroom employees.

Effective storeroom management begins when one person is assigned this responsibility. If the facilities are left to manage themselves, the foodservice operation can expect its food costs to be much higher than necessary.

Most foodservice operations have three types of storage facilities: (1) locked, central storage; (2) working storeroom; and (3) in-process storage.

Key, expensive food items usually are kept in locked, central storage. For instance, refrigerated and frozen meats, seafood, and poultry normally stay in these facilities until they are needed by the kitchen. Access is limited to authorized personnel. When needed, the foods are issued, with a record of the amount issued kept for control purposes. In larger foodservice operations, the typical record is a stock requisition (Figure 1) that food production and service department heads must complete before they are allowed to obtain issued stock.

Issuing follows the first-in, first-out (FIFO) principle. Food stock must be rotated every time a new shipment arrives and is stored. Some managers date and tag new items so the older stock can be recognized immediately.

Less expensive foods, such as condiments, juices, and spices, usually are kept in a working storeroom area. Employees are able to enter these areas and take what they need. Control is a bit more relaxed in these areas, although managers and supervisors do not neglect them entirely.

Foods that are kept in production or service areas are referred to as *in-process inventories*. There usually are several cabinets, reach-in refrigerators and

Figure 1. Typical stock requisition form.

| | | | FOOD REQUISITION | | No. XXXXX | |

FOOD REQUISITION

No. XXXXX

Dept. _____   Date _____, 19 ___

Quan.	Unit	Description	Issued	Unit Price	Amt.

Ordered by _____

Issued by _____

Received by _____

Distribution

White copy: Controller
Yellow copy: Storeroom
Pink copy: Chef

freezers, wall shelves, and hot-holding equipment to store them until they are used.

Other Storage Activities

The generally accepted storage management process involves stock rotation, standardized issuing procedures, restricted access, and control documentation. However, persons responsible for food storage usually undertake additional responsibilities. For instance, the facilities must be cleaned and maintained regularly. Unclean facilities will contaminate foods. And malfunctioning refrigerators and freezers will cause food spoilage. Inventories must be organized in a logical pattern. Usually the storeroom manager organizes them so that the more frequently used products are readily accessible, with the less popular items placed in less convenient areas.

The storeroom manager also may want to price code each food item as it is stored. This can be done when the foods are date coded. These price codes make it much easier to calculate food costs.

Usually the storeroom manager must maintain inventory counts so that the accountant or bookkeeper can calculate food costs. For example, it is common to take a month-end physical inventory of all food items (including those in the working storeroom and in-process inventories). This ending inventory will be priced out and will be used in the following formula to compute food costs:

> Beginning food inventory
> + Purchases
> − Ending inventory
> − Other credit (such as employee meals)
> = Cost of goods sold

Less frequently, the storeroom manager may need to maintain a perpetual inventory of some food products. For instance, it is common to keep a running account of the amount of a few key food items that should be in the restaurant. This procedure is part of food cost control, in that a manager will always know the usage rate of these key items, which then can be compared to the dining room sales records. Any discrepancies between the perpetual inventory record and the dining room sales records will be uncovered immediately. Food cost control problems therefore can be solved immediately, long before they become too serious.

Occasionally, the storeroom manager may need to pick up an emergency order. For instance, if there is a product shortage and the next scheduled shipment is two or three days away, someone will need to pick up enough supplies from the supplier's warehouse to fill the gap. Alternatively, if the restaurant is part of a chain operation, the storeroom manager may go to another unit in the chain and borrow the necessary stock.

The manager also would want to communicate food usage patterns to the purchasing agent so that he or she can revise the ordering procedures.

Finally, a storeroom manager disposes of any excess supplies. For instance, a menu change may cause a surplus of some food products. The storeroom manager may need to help the purchasing agent try to trade this stock for something else; failing that, he or she may donate it to a charitable organization.

Summary

The proper storage methods and procedures used in the foodservice industry are subject to a certain amount of opinion and discussion. Regardless of the type of foodservice operation, this article lists the most common attributes found in the well-run organization.

Bibliography

1992. *Applied Foodservice Sanitation*, 4th ed. Chicago, Ill.: The Educational Foundation of the National Restaurant Association.

Coltman, M. 1990. *Hospitality Industry Purchasing*. New York: Van Nostrand Reinhold.

Dittmer, P. R., and G. G. Griffin. 1989. *Principles of Food, Beverage, and Labor Cost Controls for Hotels and Restaurants*, 4th ed. New York: Van Nostrand Reinhold.

Keister, D. C. 1990. *Food and Beverage Control*, 2d ed. Englewood Cliffs, N.J.: Prentice-Hall.

Schwartz, W. C. 1989. Guess who's leaving with dinner. *Restaurants USA*. 9(8):26–29.

Stefanelli, J. 1992. *Purchasing: Selection and Procurement for the Hospitality Industry*, 3d ed. New York: Wiley.

Virts, W. B. 1987. *Purchasing for Hospitality Operations*. East Lansing, Mich.: The Educational Institute of the American Hotel & Motel Association.

Warfel, M. C., and M. L. Cremer. 1990. *Purchasing for Food Service Managers*. Berkeley, Calif.: McCutchan Publishing Corporation.

Fundamentals of Foodservice Sanitation

N. G. Marriott

The main goal of a foodservice sanitation program is to provide the customer a safe and wholesome product. During the second half of the 1980s, Bean and coworkers (1990) reported 2,397 outbreaks of foodborne illnesses representing 91,678 cases. Over 90 percent of the cases originated from bacteria that cause foodborne illness. Food was the source of 58 percent of the foodborne illnesses and 58 percent of the foodborne illness outbreaks were from food served in restaurants.

Proper sanitation in foodservice operations is essential to this industry since consumers spend approximately 50 percent of their food budget on meals outside of the home. As food production, handling, and preparation techniques and eating habits change, food remains the major source for microorganisms that can cause illness. An increase in preparation in centralized kitchens provides more opportunities for food to be contaminated with microorganisms that can cause foodborne illness. Mass feeding operations increase the number of people who may be affected by contamination. The challenge of protecting food from contamination has become more complicated and critical since microorganisms that cause foodborne illness are found in food preparation areas and on approximately 50 percent of the people who handle food.

Protection of Food against Contamination

Food spoilage and foodborne illness are caused by microorganisms that are present almost everywhere. Thus, the most effective strategy for protection against contamination is through hygienic practices that reduce contamination, an effective sanitation program to remove soil, and rigid temperature control of refrigerated foods to reduce growth of microorganisms that are the major contamination source.

Contamination Sources Foodservice products provide an ideal nutrition source for microbial growth. These items may be contaminated from insects, rodents, birds, soil, air, water, sewage, supplies, equipment, utensils, and employees. Refrigeration has been one of the most effective methods for reducing the effects of contamination through retarding the growth rate of microorganisms that cause food spoilage and foodborne illness. However, refrigeration is not a substitute for rigid sanitary practices to reduce contamination and remove soil from food production and storage areas.

Marriott (1989) reported that food products may transmit certain microorganisms causing foodborne illness that can be classified as infections or intoxications. Infection occurs through ingesting bacteria that cause foodborne illness. The infecting microorganism can multiply after ingestion and cause illness. Other bacteria produce toxins that can also cause vomiting, diarrhea, and other illnesses.

How Contamination May Be Reduced

Food items served in foodservice operations should not be touched by human hands if consumed uncooked or after cooking if such contact can be avoided. Contact from employees' hands can be reduced by use of disposable plastic gloves during food preparation and serving. Prepared foods in storage or ready for serving or holding should be covered with a close-fitting clean cover that will not collect dust, lint or other debris. Another sanitary approach is to place foods in an enclosed dust-free cabinet at the appropriate temperature. Foods served from a buffet should be protected with a steam table or ice tray, depending upon temperature requirements, and protected during display by a transparent shield over and in front of the food. Foodservice employees should be instructed to handle dishes and eating utensils in such a way that their hands do not touch any surface that will be in contact with food.

Storage facilities should provide protection against dust, insects, rodents, and other extraneous matter. Organized storage layouts with proper stock rotation can reduce contamination and facilitate cleaning. Clean and disinfected receptacles should be located in work areas for waste food particles. All receptacles should be washed and disinfected daily.

Role of Microorganisms in Sanitation

Effective sanitation is practiced to reduce contamination of food with microorganisms. Microorganisms (also called microbes and microbial flora) are found throughout the natural environment. A microorganism is a microscopic form of life found on all nonsterilized matter that can be decomposed. Most high moisture foods are highly perishable since they contain nutrients required for microbial growth. To reduce food spoilage and eliminate foodborne illness, microbial growth must be controlled. If proper sanitation practices are not followed during food preparation and serving, the rate and extent of the deteriorative changes that lead to spoilage will increase.

Applied Foodservice Sanitation by the National Restaurant Association Education Foundation (1992) suggests the need to recognize microorganisms as the enemy and be aware of the principal forms of microbial life that concern the foodservice manager in the storage, preparation, holding, and serving of food. The microorganisms that are most common and of greatest interest are bacteria, yeasts, molds, and viruses.

Bacteria are of most concern to foodservice personnel. These microbes are more commonly involved in food spoilage and foodborne illness than the other microorganisms mentioned. A bacterium is a living organism that contains only one cell. When viewed under the microscope, bacteria vary in shape from short and elongated rods to spherical or ovoid forms. Individual bacteria closely combine in various forms according to genera. Some sphere-shaped bacteria occur in clusters similar to a bunch of grapes (for example, staphylococci) while others are lined together to form a chain (for example, streptococci). Other genera of sphere-shaped bacteria form together in pairs such as pneumococci or appear as an individual bacterium.

Yeasts are generally unicellular and are larger than bacteria because they produce buds during the process of reproduction by division. Yeasts and molds can be spread through the air or other means and land on the surface of food. Large numbers of yeasts can cause a moist or a creamy white slimy appearance of food.

Molds contain more than one cell with a filamentous appearance. They can cause a variety of colors and are generally recognized by their mildewy or fuzzy, cottonlike appearance. Foods such as cheeses, nuts, and pastries that are low in moisture are more likely to spoil from mold growth.

Viruses are less likely to survive in a medium such as food. Illness from this microorganism is more likely to result from direct transmission from one person to another or from hot food. Viruses normally cause an infection instead of illness from ingestion of cold food. As stated in *Food Sanitation* by Guthrie (1988), human virus infection can be expected to occur only as a result of contact with another infected human. There are few viruses that are specific for more than one animal species.

Factors Affecting Microbial Growth

Bacteria multiply by splitting into two cells. This process continues as long as nutrients from dirty equipment and preparation areas exist and the temperature remains above freezing. An increase in temperature can dramatically increase growth rate. Some bacteria will multiply 10 times as fast at 38°F as 32°F. Under ideal conditions, bacterial growth follows a distinct pattern. After contamination by microorganisms, an acclimation period occurs when bacteria adjust to the new environment. Some of the microbes may not survive the change in environment, so for awhile there may be fewer microorganisms or no significant increase in number. The adaptation period is called the *lag phase* of microbial growth.

After a longer period of time, which may range from an hour to two or more days depending upon environmental conditions (including temperature), bacteria will start to multiply rapidly at a geometric rate, which is called the *logarithmic growth phase*. Since each microbe theoretically divides into two cells, the growth rate increases in a logarithmic pattern since each time that reproduction occurs the population size doubles. If two cells multiply the new population would be four; however the multiplication rate becomes more significant as illustrated by further multiplication: $4 \times 2 = 8$, $8 \times 2 = 16$, $16 \times 2 = 32$, $32 \times 2 = 64$, $64 \times 2 = 128$, $128 \times 2 = 256$, $256 \times 2 = 512$, $512 \times 2 = 1024$, $1024 \times 2 = 2048$, $2048 \times 2 = 4096$.

When the microbial population has increased to such large numbers that the bacteria compete for space, nutrients, and air, they no longer multiply so rapidly and some start dying. This period of competition is known as the *stationary growth phase*.

Lack of nutrients, effect of bacterial waste products, and competition from other microorganisms contribute to rapid death of microbial cells. This portion of the growth pattern, which is known as the *accelerated death phase*, is similar to the logarithmic growth phase in rate of population change except that the number of microbes are decreasing instead of increasing. The final phase of the growth pattern is the *reduced death phase*, which is nearly the opposite of the lag phase. A sustained accelerated death phase causes a decreased death rate. Figure 1 illustrates a typical growth curve (pattern) for bacteria.

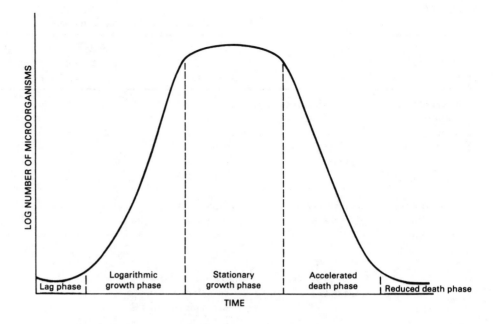

Fig. 1. A typical growth curve for bacteria (see text for details). (*Source: N. G. Marriott, Principles of Food Sanitation, 2d ed, p. 18, 1989. New York: Van Nostrand Reinhold.*)

Effects of Microorganisms on Food

Multiple handling of food increases the chance of microbial contamination. Spoilage microorganisms cause decomposition and putrefaction of food. Food is considered to be spoiled when it is unacceptable for human consumption. Other microorganisms can cause foodborne illness. *Foodborne illness* or a foodborne disease is an illness associated with or in which the cause is the ingestion of food. A *foodborne disease outbreak* is two or more persons experiencing a similar illness, usually related to the digestive system, after eating a common food if it is implicated as the source of the illness. Foodborne illness caused by a toxin produced from bacteria is called *food intoxication* while *food infection* is caused by the ingestion of infectious microorganisms. Table 1 provides a brief description of the major foodborne illnesses.

Health and Personal Hygiene

Humans are the major contamination source of food. They touch their environment with their hands, perspiration, and breath while spreading microorganisms. Unguarded coughs and sneezes transport microorganisms that can cause disease. Since poor hygiene can cause the distribution of disease-causing bacteria to food, humans are described in *Applied Foodservice Sanitation* (National Restaurant Association Education Foundation 1992) as the culprits and victims in foodborne illness incidents.

Ill employees should not be in contact with food or equipment and utensils used in preparing and serving food since they can transmit diseases of the respiratory tract such as the common cold, sore throat, pneumonia, and tuberculosis and intestinal disorders such as dysentery, typhoid fever, and infectious hepatitis. Major sources of contamination from ill or well humans are the skin, fingers, fingernails, hair, jewelry, mouth, nose and respiratory tract, and eyes. To ensure that employees are healthy, they should be given a physical examination periodically or be required to have a health card verifying that they have no transmissible diseases. Furthermore, it is desirable to provide employees training in foodservice sanitation and personal hygiene and require that they pass an examination over this material. All of these factors should be considered when selecting employees for assignment in foodservice.

Table 1. *Description of major foodborne illness*

Foodborne illness	Cause	Symptoms	Average time (hours) between consumption and illness	Preventive measures
Staphylococcal food poisoning	Enterotoxin produced by *Staphylococcus*	Nausea, vomiting, cramps	3–6	Proper sanitation and refrigeration
Salmonellosis	Ingestion of various species of *Salmonella*	Nausea, vomiting, diarrhea, fever, abdominal pain	6–24	Pasteurization of foods, proper sanitation of employees and operations, proper refrigeration
Clostridium perfringens food poisoning	Toxin produced by *Clostridium perfringens*	Nausea, vomiting, diarrhea, abdominal pain,	8–12	Prompt refrigeration of unconsumed cooked meats, heating of leftover food to original cooked temperature
Botulism	Toxins produced by *Clostridium botulinum*	Impaired swallowing, speaking, vision, coordination, and respiration	12–48	Proper sanitation and processing temperature during canning and smoking of foods
Travelers diarrhea	Enterotoxigenic *Escherichia coli*	Nausea, fever, diarrhea	4–12	Proper cleanliness and sanitation
Listeriosis	Ingestion of *Listeria monocytogenes*	Blood poisoning influenzalike symptoms, fever, interrupted pregnancy	6–72	Rigid sanitation and temperature control
Campylobacter	*Campylobacter enteritis* or *Campylobacter jejuni*	Diarrhea, abdominal pain, cramping, fever, headache, muscle pain, dizziness	72–120	Sanitary handling, processing, preparation, and storage of foods
Yersiniosis	*Yersinia enterocolitica*	Abdominal pain, fever, diarrhea, vomiting, skin rashes	24–36	Sanitary handling, processing, preparation, and storage of foods

Sanitary Facilities and Equipment

According to Marriott (1989), the primary requirement for sanitary design of foodservice facilities and equipment is cleanability. Cleanability suggests that an item or surface can be exposed for inspection or cleaning without difficulty and that it is constructed so that soil can be removed effectively by normal cleaning methods. Minimal inaccessible locations for soil, pests, and microorganisms to collect will enhance the maintenance of a clean establishment. A facility that is easier to clean can be maintained with less contamination.

With proper sanitary design and equipment layout, food being prepared is not readily contaminated by the facility or equipment. It is important that facility and equipment design create an environment where cleaning and sanitizing are easily accomplished.

Floors, walls, and ceilings should be constructed of material that is easily cleaned and maintained and is attractive in appearance. Materials to be used should be inert, durable, resistant to soil absorption, and smooth surfaced. Absorbency or porosity of floor material should be considered. When liquids are absorbed, flooring can be damaged and microbial growth is enhanced. Since nonabsorbent floor covering materials should be used in all food-preparation and storage areas, carpeting, rugs, and similar materials should not be installed.

Although flooring material is a critical aspect of sanitation, the way the floor is constructed is also important. Coving at a floor-wall joint facilitates cleaning by preventing accumulation of bits of food that attract insects and rodents. Concrete and terrazzo floors should be sealed to make the floors nonabsorbent and to reduce possible health hazards from cement dust.

Cleaning Steps   The basic steps for manual cleaning and sanitizing of a typical foodservice facility are:

1. Sinks and work surfaces should be cleaned before each use.
2. Heavy soil deposits should be scraped and presoaked to reduce gross deposits that contribute to deactivation of the cleaning compound. Items to be cleaned should be sorted and silverware and other utensils should be presoaked in a solution designated for that purpose.
3. Items to be cleaned should be washed in the first sink in a clean detergent solution at approximately 120°F, using a brush or dishmop to remove any residual soil.
4. The second sink should be designated for rinsing. It should contain clean, potable water that is 120–140°F for removal of all traces of soil and cleaning compound that may interfere with the activity of the sanitizing agent.
5. Utensils should be sanitized in the third sink by immersing items in hot water (180°F) for 30 seconds or in a chemical sanitizing solution for 1 minute. The sanitizing solution should be mixed to twice the recommended strength if items are immersed in water. Therefore, water carried from the rinse will not dilute the sanitizing solution below the minimum concentration required to be effective. Air bubbles should be avoided that could shield the interior from the sanitizer.
6. Sanitized utensils and equipment should be permitted to air dry since wiping can cause recontamination.
7. Clean utensils and equipment should be stored in a clean area more than 12" off the floor with protection from splash, dust, and contact with food.
8. The food-contact surfaces of fixed equipment should be covered when not in use.

Stationary Equipment   Stationary food-preparation equipment should be cleaned according to the manufacturer's instructions for disassembly and cleaning. General procedures include the steps that follow:

1. All electrically powered equipment should be unplugged.
2. Equipment should be disassembled, washed, and sanitized.
3. The balance of the food-contact surfaces should be washed and rinsed with a sanitizing solution mixed to twice the strength required for sanitizing by immersion.
4. All nonfood-contact surfaces should be wiped. Cloths used for wiping down stationary equipment and surfaces should be wrung out periodically in a sanitizing solution and kept separate from other wiping cloths.
5. All cleaned parts should be permitted to air dry before reassembly.

6. Stationary items that are designed to have detergent and sanitizing solutions pumped throughout should be cleaned according to the manufacturer's instructions. Sanitizing should involve spraying for 2–3 minutes with a double-strength solution of the sanitizer.

7. Although wooden cutting boards should not be used, if any exist, they should be scrubbed with a nontoxic detergent solution and stiff-bristled nylon brush (or a high pressure, low volume cleaning wand). A sanitizing solution should also be applied after every use. As cutting boards show wear from cuts and scars, they should be replaced with polyethylene boards. Wooden cutting boards should not be submerged in a sanitizing solution.

Cleaning Principles

It is beyond the scope of this publication to provide cleaning steps for all foodservice areas and equipment; however, this information is found in Marriott (1989). Yet cleaning principles for foodservice operations should be considered. Cleaning is more than the combination of soap, water, and labor. It is a practical application of chemistry. Cleaning is the removal of soil (matter out of place) from the foodservice operation. Longrée and Blaker (1982) place soil in two basic categories:

1. Water-soluble soils (such as sugar, juices, and salt)
2. Water-insoluble soils (such as grease, food particles, and other solid matter)

Cleaning involves the application of an appropriate cleaning compound on an unclean surface and the use of some form of mechanical energy (whether manual or through the use of cleaning equipment) to remove the soil. An effective cleaning technique is through the application of a cleaning compound on a soiled surface under sufficient pressure for a long enough time to penetrate the soil and remove it.

It has been a common practice to clean primarily with warm or hot water. However, debris can be removed more effectively through identification of the type of soil and matching the appropriate cleaning compound and equipment with the material to be removed. It is important to recognize that "like cleans like." Thus, organic matter and other alkaline soils are most effectively removed with alkaline cleaners, mineral soils with acid cleaners, and petroleum soils with solvent cleaners.

Classification of Cleaning Compounds   Since "like cleans like," it is important that the cleaning compound have characteristics similar to the type of soil. The following summary from Marriott (1989:81–84) relates to cleaning compound categories and the soils they remove most effectively.

Strongly Alkaline Cleaners.   These cleaners have strong dissolving powers and are very corrosive and irritating. Examples are caustic soda and silicates having high nitrous oxide:silicon dioxide ratios. These cleaners are used to remove heavy soils such as those from commerical ovens and smokehouses and have little effect on mineral deposits.

Heavy Duty Alkaline Cleaners.   These cleaners have moderate dissolving powers and are generally slightly noncorrosive. Examples are cleaners that contain active compounds such as sodium metasilicate, sodium hexametaphosphate, sodium pyrophosphate, and trisodium phosphate. These cleaners are frequently used with mechanized cleaning equipment and are excellent for removing fats and oils but of no value for mineral deposit control.

Mild Alkaline Cleaners. These cleaners are appropriate for hand cleaning lightly soiled areas. Examples of mild alkaline compounds are sodium carbonate, sodium sesquicarbonate, and tetrasodium pyrophosphate.

Strongly Acid Cleaners. These cleaners, which are highly corrosive, are used to remove encrusted surface matter and mineral scale. Strongly acid agents used in food operations are muriatic, hydrofluoric, sulfamic, sulfuric, and phosphoric acids.

Mildly Acid Cleaners. These compounds are mildly corrosive and are used to remove light mineral soils. Examples are hydroxyacetic, levulinic, acetic, and gluconic acids.

Sanitizing Principles

Removal of soil with a cleaning compound only eliminates the physical debris and leaves microbial flora on the area being cleaned. Thus, a sanitizer is needed to ensure that microbial contamination is removed. In foodservice operations, sanitizing is normally accomplished through the application of hot water or a chemical bactericide. Chemical sanitizing is done by immersing an object in the appropriate concentration of sanitizer for one minute; or by rinsing, swabbing, or spraying double the usual recommended concentration of the sanitizer on the surface to be sanitized. An exception is that quaternary ammonium sanitizers may not be sprayed at more than the recommended amount.

Thermal Sanitizing
This method is frequently convenient but is relatively inefficient because of the energy required. The two major sources for thermal sanitizing are steam and hot water.

Radiation Sanitizing
This method is most frequently used to sanitize processed food products. It is less practical for sanitizing equipment and areas since the light rays can be absorbed by dust, thin films of grease, and opaque or turbid solutions.

Chemical Sanitizing
This is the most economical method and can be effective if done properly.

Chlorine Sanitizers. These sanitizers are frequently used even though they may be corrosive, irritating to the skin, and relatively ineffective if the area being sanitized is not clean. These sanitizers are economical and provide rapid and effective kill of microorganisms. The chlorine sanitizers most frequently used are hypochlorites or chlorine dioxide.

Iodine Sanitizers. These sanitizers are more expensive than the chlorine compounds but they are less irritating and corrosive and less reactive to residual organic matter than chlorine. These sanitizers are more effective against viruses than the other chemical sanitizers. The most frequently used form of iodine sanitizers are iodophors.

Quaternary Ammonium Compounds (Quats). These sanitizers are being used more than in the past because of their residual characteristics and effectiveness against *Listeria monocytogenes*. The quats are less reactive to organic matter but are more expensive and selective in the microorganisms they destroy.

Acid Sanitizers. Acid sanitizers such as acetic, lactic, and propionic acids are being used more than in the past since their foam development has been reduced. They are effective against *Listeria monocytogenes* but do not effectively destroy *Salmonella*, can cause a slight odor on food surfaces, and are more expensive than the chlorine sanitizers. It appears that more acid-quat sanitizers will be used in the future because of their effectiveness against *Listeria monocytogenes*. All chemical sanitizers should be applied with the concentration recommended by the supplier.

Pest Control

A tidy foodservice operation should be free of insects, rodents, birds, and other pests. A foodservice facility can be more effectively protected against pests if their habits and points of vulnerability are known. Pests can carry disease-causing organisms and can cause extensive spoilage and waste. Elimination of shelters, rubbish, decaying material, discarded supplies, and equipment will discourage the presence of insects and rodents.

Insect Infestation

Cockroaches. Cockroaches are one of the most common pests among foodservice facilities. Many carry up to 50 different disease-causing microorganisms. Cockroaches will eat any food that humans consume in addition to human waste, decaying materials, dead insects, and some packaging materials. They are more active in dark areas at night. This pest can be detected by a strong oily odor that arises from a substance given off by certain glands and by small, black or dark brown and almost spherical droppings. The most effective control technique for cockroaches is rigid sanitation practices that involve their removal and the elimination of debris to attract them. Pyrid, Dursban, diazinon, and amidinohydrozone are effective against cockroaches.

Flies. Houseflies are a greater menace to human health than the cockroach. They are responsible for human diseases such as diarrhea, typhoid, and streptococcal and staphylococcal infections. The best method of fly control is a hygienic operation and a design that will not permit entry into the facility. Electric fly traps and sprays or fogs such as pyrethrins or Dichlorovos can aid in fly control.

Fruit Flies. These pests are attracted to decaying fruits. One of the most effective methods for control of these pests is to avoid the accumulation of rotting fruits and fermenting foods.

Rodent Infestation

Rats. Rats directly or indirectly transmit diseases such as leptospirosis, murine typhus, and salmonellosis. Rat populations shift as food becomes scarce in one location or a portion of the population starts to die from eradication methods, including trapping. A potential rodent deterrent can be created by the construction of a 4–5 feet wide band of white gravel or granite chips around the outside perimeter of a building. The most common rodenticides for rats are fumarin, warfarin, and pival.

Mice.   This rodent tends to exist where food scraps and a shelter are available. The eradication methods are effective cleaning to eliminate food sources and trapping.

Bird Infestation.   Birds are potential carriers of mites, *Salmonella*, and organisms that cause encephalitis and psittacosis. The best way to eliminate birds is to prevent their entry and use strychnine alkaloid to coat baits such as cereal grains.

Maintenance of a Sanitary Operation

It is the responsibility of management to maintain a sanitary foodservice operation. Sanitation must always be a high priority. After an effective sanitation program is established, it is important to monitor the operation. Monitoring is accomplished by inspection of the facility and the operation. Cleanliness is also monitored by analyzing microbial samples to determine the amount of contamination. The current and future monitoring technique is through hazard analysis critical control points (HACCP). This very important concept is discussed elsewhere in this encyclopedia.

Summary

Effective sanitation requires an understanding of contamination sources and the role of microorganisms in food spoilage and foodborne illness. Microorganisms cause food spoilage resulting in degradation of appearance and flavor; while foodborne illness occurs through the ingestion of food containing pathogenic microorganisms or their toxins.

To improve sanitation in foodservice establishments, the facility and equipment should be hygienically designed for cleanability. Food must be protected during storage, preparation, and serving from pests and microbial contamination, and handled with equipment and utensils that have been thoroughly cleaned and sanitized. It is important to select the cleaning compound with characteristics similar to the type of soil to be removed. Cleaning must be followed by sanitizing to remove microbial contamination.

References

Bean, N. H., P. M. Griffin, J. S. Goulding, and C. B. Ivey. 1990. Foodborne disease outbreaks, 5-year summary, 1983–1987. *J. Food Prot.* 53:711–728.

Guthrie, R. K. 1988. *Food Sanitation* 3d ed., pp. 24–87. New York: Van Nostrand Reinhold.

Longrée, K. and G. G. Blaker. 1982. *Sanitary Techniques in Foodservice* 2d ed., pp. 75–143. New York: Wiley.

Marriott, N. G. 1989. *Principles of Food Sanitation,* 2d ed., pp. 2–117, 177–199, 301–331. New York: Van Nostrand Reinhold.

National Restaurant Association Education Foundation. 1992. *Applied Foodservice Sanitation,* 4th ed., pp. 18–76. Washington, D.C.: National Restaurant Association.

17

Quality Assurance in Foodservice

Morton Fox

Quality assurance is a major subsystem of a foodservice operation and encompasses the entire operation. Thorner and Manning (1983) use quality assurance and quality control interchangeably and define the terms as an activity, procedure, method, or program that will ensure the maintenance and continuity of specifications and standards of a product within prescribed tolerances during all stages of handling, processing, preparation, and packaging, and will further ensure that all the original and desirable characteristics are sustained during storage, processing, or preparation and will remain unaltered until consumed. This definition emphasizes the complete control of the product from purchasing until it has been consumed by the customer.

Many restaurant operators consider foodservice quality assurance as a luxury that only the large fast-food and restaurant chains can afford. This assumption is incorrect! The large chains institute a quality control program because they know that it will make them money and save them money. The obvious reason for quality control is to produce a food product for sale that will be what the menu says it is, that will satisfy the expectation of the customers and that will offer an honest value for the price asked. If these objectives are obtained, the foodservice operator will experience repeat sales to old customers and sales to new customers who will hear about their fine quality operation through word-of-mouth—thus producing larger sales and more profit.

A less obvious and probably more financially beneficial reason for a quality assurance program would be the food and labor cost savings resulting from more exact procurement procedures and the use of quality-tested standardized recipes and streamlined food preparation procedures. The dollars saved here go directly into net profit and are therefore more powerful than the dollars received from increased sales.

Evolution of Quality Control in Foodservice

Historically, the control of quality in food parallels the history of food production. In this long history of quality control, the various attributes of quality were measured, and decisions made on the basis of sensory, that is human, evaluation (Kramer and Twigg 1970). Kramer and Twigg developed some of the principles of quality control for the food manufacturing industry that have been adapted by the foodservice industry. Quality assurance in all aspects of hospitality management has been expounded upon by Pearson and Glover (Pearson 1983; Glover and Briggs 1984).

In the foodservice industry, the multiunit fast-food organizations were at the forefront of installing effective quality assurance programs. Kirsch explains that quality control in a multiunit fast-food operation is no different than what it should be in any other foodservice operation (Kirsch 1981).

One of the most valuable results of an effective quality assurance program is the prevention of foodborne illnesses. A very successful system in helping prevent foodborne illnesses is one called Hazard Analysis Critical Control Point (HACCP), developed by major industrial food processors during the 1970s. The first step is to identify specific foods in danger of becoming contaminated. Then, for each food, the system sets control points to check for correct execution of procedures (Lydecker 1987). Snyder adapted HACCP for the foodservice industry and developed a course to train foodservice managers in the prevention of foodborne illnesses using HACCP (Snyder 1986).

Factors Affecting Quality Assurance in a Foodservice Operation

In general, poor quality foodservice can be attributed to the following factors:

- Poor quality raw material. A restaurant cannot start out with a poor quality raw product and end up with an acceptable quality finished product. The receipt of poor quality raw material can be reduced by having well-prepared specifications and a knowledgeable food buyer. Another important consideration is the selection of reliable suppliers.
- Inadequate inspection of purchased material. An important part of any foodservice quality assurance program is a knowledgeable and reliable receiving clerk. If incoming merchandise is not adequately inspected, then low-quality food products will slip through and the finished product will suffer accordingly.
- Improper handling and storage of food items. All foods are perishable; some are just more perishable than others. Consequently, they all need proper handling and storage. It is the responsibility of the storeperson to ensure that all food and beverage items are immediately placed under appropriate storage conditions, whether it be in the refrigerator, freezer, dry storeroom, or wine cellar. Without proper temperature control and ventilation, food products deteriorate rapidly with a corresponding reduction in quality.
- Malfunctioning equipment. Food preparation and cooking equipment that do not operate properly are not only a large inconvenience, they also contribute to a poor quality finished product. For example, if a gas oven is improperly maintained and cleaned some of its jets may become clogged resulting in insufficient heat in that part of the oven and thus uneven cooking. This situation is particularly disastrous when baking! The greatest potential danger to food quality and safety resulting from malfunctioning equipment exists when freezers and refrigerators are not operating properly. In the case of freezers where the temperature fluctuates out of control, there is a migration of ice crystals, which puncture the cells as they move back and forth, thus resulting in a breakdown of texture in most products and a loss of air in ice cream products. In malfunctioning refrigeration equipment, the results

can be more hazardous! If the temperature within the refrigerator rises, microorganisms are capable of growing and producing toxins; thus, not only is the quality of the food affected, but serious cases of food poisoning might result.

• Incorrect preparation. Poor quality resulting from incorrect preparation can be caused by several factors. One of the most common causes is the refusal of the cook to follow the recipe. It is up to management to ensure that cooks follow recipes explicitly, not only for quality control, but also for cost control. Another common fault in preparation is that many restaurants do not have proper measuring and weighing equipment. An effective quality assurance program must insist on having the proper quantitative tools that are accurate and periodically calibrated. Another reason for poor quality in food preparation is the carelessness of the cook. Cooks will, without thinking, prepare incompatible foods in the same fat or allow the cooking fat to remain too long in the deep fat fryer. Only through a systematic quality check can these types of mistakes be caught before the item reaches the consumer.

• Inappropriate service to the customer. No matter how excellent the quality of the raw material and how expertly prepared in the kitchen, if the menu item is not properly served the quality suffers. Good quality service includes pleasant and efficient waithelp, ensuring that the hot food is served hot and the cold food is served cold, and that the food is presented attractively on the plate since the customer's first evaluation of quality is the appearance of the dish.

• Poor sanitation. The quality of any food item is impaired with a piece of foreign material in it or on it. Another equally bad sign of poor sanitation that is disconcerting to a customer is to receive an improperly cleaned plate or piece of cutlery with some dried food on it. If a restaurant is in a general state of disarray, with unclean restrooms, dirty table tops, unswept floor, and so forth, the customers' perception of the quality of the eating experience in that restaurant has to be negatively affected.

Areas to Be Included in a Foodservice Quality Assurance Program

There is no easy way for a foodservice operation to install a quality assurance program. Most medium- and small-sized restaurants cannot afford to hire additional personnel just for quality control; so it must be accomplished with existing personnel.

Management must put forth a concerted effort to formalize quality controls through the entire operation. The primary task in formalizing a quality assurance program is establishing a proper state of mind in the employees. Every employee must be made aware of the importance of quality assurance and be motivated to practice quality control in all tasks performed. This can be accomplished through emphasis by supervisors at all levels, by proper training, and by writing quality assurance into all job descriptions and standing operating procedures.

It is better to bring all areas on line at one time in the quality assurance program rather than to do it piecemeal. Some of the actions that should be taken in bringing the different areas of quality assurance on line are as follows.

Purchasing The relationship between the purchasing function and quality assurance should be very close. In a small restaurant it may be as fundamental as the manager deciding on what quality food and beverage product to buy. In larger operations, normally someone other than the manager—possibly the chef or kitchen manager—is assigned the responsibility of determining what quality products to purchase. An important point to consider is that although quality assurance is a continual responsibility of the purchasing function, it should never be the ultimate responsibility of the buyer. There must be checks and balances.

In purchasing for a restaurant, the person responsible for buying food already uses quality as one of the basic criteria in determining what product to buy. To bring the purchasing function within the quality assurance program, the restaurant must have a complete library of specifications that represent the quality desired by management. In addition, the food buyer must conduct routine evaluations of suppliers to attempt to upgrade the quality and value of foods procured. An occasional taste testing panel to evaluate potential new products is also within the scope of the purchasing function.

Receiving and Inspecting

An effective quality assurance program has a well-organized receiving and inspecting system. Realistically, a small restaurant cannot afford to have one person do nothing but receive and inspect items from vendors, but the responsibility for receiving and inspecting should be delineated clearly so that there should be no question about who has the responsibility for accepting every shipment and verifying the quality and quantity of goods received. This might be the storeperson, a shift leader, or an assistant manager.

Management must provide training to the individual(s) responsible for receiving and inspecting incoming food products. This training can be conducted by the chef, other individuals within the organization who are knowledgeable in food quality, or by an outside source such as local vocational training schools.

It would be helpful if the receiving and inspecting section would have a set of illustrated color references depicting the items that are to be received and inspected. A detailed Standing Operating Procedure (SOP) or Receiving Manual is very beneficial to employees responsible for receiving and inspecting, especially to new and temporary personnel.

Management should spot check the effectiveness of the receiving and inspecting function by periodically evaluating the quality of incoming food items.

Storage

Improper storage is one of the most significant factors contributing to product quality breakdown in a foodservice operation. Consequently, adequate storage of food products must receive high priority in any quality control program.

One factor that contributes significantly to the rate of deterioration of food product is the storage temperature. The storeperson must know the appropriate storage temperatures for the different food commodities and ensure that the storage areas are maintained at these temperatures. This requires that all food storage areas have accurate thermometers located inside of them. This applies not only to freezers and refrigerated storage space, but also to dry storage areas where high temperatures can reduce the quality, nutritional value, and shelflife of canned and dried goods drastically over a period of time. These thermometers in the refrigerators and freezers should be checked at least two times per day—at the beginning of business and just prior to leaving in the evening. In the dry storage area once per day is sufficient, but in all cases these readings should be recorded and reviewed periodically by management.

Another very important principle in proper storage of foods is "First In, First Out" (FIFO). Food items that are received first in the storage area should be issued out first. In order to practice FIFO, the restaurant must have a systematic manner of receiving, marking, and storing all products received.

Regardless of whether the food product is frozen, refrigerated, or dry, certain physical storage principles must be considered in setting up a storage location. Adequate ventilation is of prime importance! All foods must be stored off the floor and away from walls and the ceiling to allow air to flow on all sides to remove heat. Storage areas must be maintained at high levels of cleanliness and constructed so that they may be washed down periodically with good drainage. Also of importance is good lighting so that items can be readily identified. Another consideration is the physical separation, during storage, of food items that emit and absorb odors.

Equipment Performance

Performance of food preparation and cooking equipment is a major aspect of any foodservice quality control program. Every item of new equipment is accompanied by an operating manual that explains operating procedures, capabilities of the equipment, and maintenance requirements. All maintenance personnel and operators should be required to read and understand this manual prior to working with the equipment.

It is management's responsibility to ensure that all control devices like thermometers, thermostats, timers, pressure gauges, and so forth are calibrated periodically to validate their accuracy. Ovens should be checked periodically for heat or energy distribution, to ensure uniform heating throughout the oven cavity. Other equipment has signal alarms like buzzers, bells, and lights which have to be checked periodically.

One way to ensure that equipment is working at maximum efficiency is through an effective preventive maintenance program. The key to a successful preventive maintenance program is the proper scheduling of the maintenance and the listing of all items that need to be checked. Preventive maintenance checklists should be prepared for each item of equipment and records should be maintained. During these maintenance checks, it is important that all control devices such as switches, fuses, alarms, and signal lights as well as the more obvious thermometers, thermostats, and timers be examined. Also check some of the more frequent trouble areas like gaskets around pressure cookers and refrigerators, latches, hinges, heating elements, and gas jets.

Food Preparation and Cooking

The kitchen is the domain of the chef or kitchen manager and consequently he/she is responsible for quality control in food preparation and cooking that takes place in the kitchen. One area in which the chef must take the full initiative is the premeal evaluation. All food items that are prepared for the serving line or otherwise for customer consumption must be quality evaluated prior to serving. This responsibility might lie with the preparing cook, the chef, the expediter, the waithelp, or some knowledgeable individual(s) appointed by management. It is a most important quality assurance responsibility that cannot be neglected!

Management can assist the chef by providing a knowledgeable individual or individuals (taste testing panel) periodically to evaluate the quality of the finished product. This individual(s) should critically compare the finished product with the approved standard. The items should be tested for proper seasoning, appropriate taste and aroma, attractive coloring and appearance, mouth feel, and other quality factors that influence the consumer's perception of quality. It is important that persons chosen for this task be knowledgeable in sensory evaluation.

The chef or kitchen manager, in carrying out these quality assurance responsibilities, must perform certain functions: (1) He/she must ensure that cooks are following the standard recipes to the letter; (2) He/she should frequently check spices and other additive ingredients to determine whether they have maintained their desired characteristics; (3) It is his or her responsibility to make sure that adequate scales, measuring devices, and proper cooking utensils are available; and (4) The chef has the important responsibility of ensuring that all kitchen personnel meet personal hygiene requirements and are dressed properly.

An effective method of keeping employees motivated and knowledgeable about quality assurance is through periodic training sessions where they should be brought up-to-date on the latest recipes, new equipment, new procedures, and new products recently introduced to the market. These training sessions would be an excellent time to improve their sensory evaluation skills through the training of taste testing panels.

Sanitation

Sanitation quality assurance is everyone's responsibility! Poor sanitation can reduce the overall quality of a foodservice establishment in many areas. Therefore, it is very important to control the quality of sanitation in a restaurant in addition to the quality of the food being served.

The first requirement for good sanitation is proper design of the foodservice facility. Facility design must allow easy access to all areas by cleaning personnel. The fewer inaccessible points in a foodservice operation, the less chance there is for a build-up of filth, insects, and microorganisms. When selecting the construction materials for walls, floors, and ceilings, a major consideration should be ease of cleaning and maintenance. Food-contact surfaces such as food-preparation tables and cutting boards should be made of highly impervious material that will not crack so that they will not harbor microorganisms.

Modern foodservice equipment is being manufactured with sanitation and ease of cleaning in mind thanks to standards established by a number of organizations and manufacturers. The National Sanitation Foundation recommends the following considerations when purchasing new foodservice equipment:

- Equipment should be easy to disassemble and to clean
- All materials should be nontoxic and impart no significant color, odor, or taste to food
- Internal corners and edges should be rounded off without the use of solder
- All surfaces should be smooth and free of pits, crevices, ledges, inside threads and shoulders, bolts and rivets
- Coating materials, especially those on food-contact surfaces, should resist cracking and chipping
- Waste and waste liquid should be easily removed.

One area that has a great potential influence on the sanitary quality assurance of a foodservice operation is the dishwasher. Every restaurant should have a quality control check on wares leaving the dishwasher. The pH of the water entering the dishwasher should be checked, and adjusted if required, to ensure optimum results. Rinse water should be checked for hardness since hard water sometimes causes films to form. An important factor to check is the temperature of the final rinse water, which should be hot enough to sanitize the wares coming out of the dishwasher; or if it is a low temperature, chemical assisted sanitizing, one must check the temperature of the water and the amount of residual chlorine in the water.

While the dining and food preparation areas have relatively high visibility, it is up to management to periodically check and ensure that locations like the refuse collection and disposal areas are maintained in a high state of sanitation. Garbage cans must be kept covered at all times, when not actually filling or emptying them, to discourage rodents and insects from frequenting them. In addition, they should be cleaned after each emptying and periodically disinfected.

A final sanitation consideration is that the proper control of rodents, insects, and vermin is best achieved through proper sanitation. If a persistent problem exists in this area, professional help should be obtained because the handling of poisonous insecticides and rodenticides around a foodservice establishment is a serious business. Under no circumstances should these poisons be stored in the vicinity of food items, and it is best to keep them locked in a safe place when not in use.

Customer Service
Customer service is the intangible factor that differentiates one foodservice operation from another. In order to get employees to practice good customer service, management must put forth a concerted effort to formalize quality controls in the service area. The primary task in formalizing a quality service program is establishing a proper state of mind in the employees. This can be accomplished by training and motivating employees to practice good customer service, and by writing the proper procedures into job descriptions and standing operating procedures. In all situations, good service must receive emphasis by supervisors at all levels.

One form of feedback that indicates whether good customer service is being provided is the customer complaint. Someone from management should personally investigate customer complaints to determine if they are valid complaints based on a breakdown in quality of the food or service, or if they are complaints stemming from the customers' personal ill-health or state of mind. The manager must have the experience and intelligence to evaluate the complaints to determine if corrective actions are required or if the complaint was not justified. In either case, the complaints must be handled tactfully with the customers, assuring them of corrective action to be taken and making remunerations where required. How guests feel when they leave an establishment will affect not only their decision to come back but what is said to others about the operation. When guests have a bad experience at a restaurant, they will tell two and one-half times more people than they would have had the experience been a good one. Repeat business is the key to success in the restaurant industry, which means that management should ensure that no dissatisfied customers should leave their restaurant until some corrective steps have been taken.

Summary

During the 1970s and 1980s, the food and beverage industry has started to realize the importance of quality assurance in foodservice. Quality assurance programs, which were initially developed by the large fast-food chains, are now being found in most quality foodservice operations. In this article the importance of quality assurance in increasing sales and in reducing production costs was discussed. The different factors that affect quality assurance in a foodservice operation were examined and areas to be included in an effective quality assurance program were discussed. Some of the more advanced hotel and restaurant schools are now including courses in quality assurance in their curricula, and consulting firms are available to assist restaurants in establishing their own quality assurance programs.

To maintain leadership in the world's food and beverage industry, U.S. restaurateurs and academia must work together to improve the quality of food and beverage products and services provided to guests. This must be a joint effort and must be based on developing and implementing effective quality assurance.

References

Glover, G., and A. Briggs. 1984. Productivity and quality assurance: A model for efficient and effective use of human resources. *The Bottomline* 12(4):3–12.

Kirsch, H. I. 1981. Quality control in multi-unit fast food operations. *Journal of Foodservice Systems* 1(2):137–147.

Kramer, A., and B. A. Twigg. 1970. *Quality Control for the Food Industry,* 3d ed. Westport, Conn.: AVI Publishing Co., Inc.

Lydecker, T. 1987. When foodborne illness strikes! *Restaurant and Institutions* Sept. 30:34–52.

Pearson, J. 1983. The baton raton hotel and club. *Lodging.* July:40–53.

Snyder, O. P. 1986. Applying the hazard analysis and critical points system in foodservice and foodborne illness prevention. *Journal of Foodservice Systems* 4(2):125–131.

Thorner, M. E., and P. B. Manning. 1983. *Quality Control in Foodservice,* 2d ed. Westport, Conn.: AVI Publishing Co., Inc.

Bibliography

Fox, M. 1984. An effective curriculum for a foodservice systems education. *Journal of Foodservice Systems* 3(1):17–31.

Fox, M. 1990. New food laboratories enhance foodservice management curriculum at University of Hawaii. *Journal of Foodservice Systems* 5(1):81–86.

Pedraja, R. R. 1986. The meaning and scope of quality assurance. *Environmental Management.* Feb./Mar.:25–28.

Snyder, O. P. 1986. Quality design for the foodservice industry. *Hospitality Institute of Technology.* Handout:1–10.

Walker, J. R., and T. T. Salemeh. 1990. The Q.A. payoff. *The Cornell H.R.A. Quarterly.* Feb.:57–59.

18

Cost Control in Foodservice

James Keiser

Control, one of the basic management functions, can be defined as helping to ensure performance and conform to plans, objectives, and goals. It can also be described as the essence of success. To be effective, these plans, objectives, and goals must be previously determined. Cost control is only one type of control a foodservice operation must utilize. Other controls can include control over quality, funds, physical assets, and personnel among others.

The larger and more sophisticated an operation becomes, the more the need for control. If one owned and operated a one-person hot dog stand, little control would be needed except an analysis of accounting data to see how the operation was doing and maintenance of purchasing price information. If the individual were to secure other hot dog stands and hire other individuals to operate them in different geographical areas, the need for control would be greatly increased since the owner could not be on hand at each stand to oversee operations, and the employees would not necessarily share the owner's goals and interests. In a sense, control could be considered a substitute for management presence. With foodservice having very tight profit margins and being such a hands-on situation (highly labor intensive, often encompassing many small transactions each of which must be handled properly) control is more important than in many other businesses.

Control works best when it is used with other management processes such as planning, organizing, directing, and evaluating. To have control an operation must

- Define its objectives or know what it wants to accomplish. These objectives can be financial, qualitative, or quantitative. You cannot just hope for success, but should have a realistic estimate of what this success should be.
- Have plans and programs to achieve the desired objectives since they will not automatically happen. Know what is realistic to achieve, and then plan how to achieve it.
- Provide resources to implement the plans. Resources can include proper personnel, equipment, and funds.
- Compare results with the desired results or objectives. If the desired objectives were not obtained, analyze why. In some cases, it may be necessary to redefine expected objectives or results.

Importance of Control

Control has been described as the essence of success. A commercial foodservice operation can only increase its profit by increasing sales, controlling or reducing costs, or a combination of both since sales minus costs equals profit. A noncommercial operation can, by controlling costs, provide better service to its patrons or do more of its primary mission if more funds are available from cost control measures.

Savings on cost can have a disproportionate effect on profit. Let us assume

Food sales	$300,000	100%
Food cost	$105,000	35%
Other costs	$180,000	60%
Profit	$ 15,000	5%

If management, by better cost control, can reduce its costs by 5% ($14,250), the profit is increased to $29,250; a 100% increase. The opposite is also true. If expenses had gone up by 5% and sales remained constant, the operation would have had only a $750 profit instead of $15,000.

Approaches to Control

There are two basic approaches to control. One is the behavioristic approach and the other is the traditional approach.

The traditional approach has two main aspects. One is directing personnel or keeping an eye on things or management by walking around (MBWA). If the manager sees or knows what is going on, he or she can correct things that are not right or that include cost control breakdowns. When the manager or owner is not on the scene, formal control procedures must cover this void.

The other aspect of traditional control is measurement of performance with that desired or deemed attainable. This is the comparison aspect of the management scheme, which is usually considered to have four parts.

1. Establishment of standards or goals. These can be expressed in different ways, for instance a budget figure, a percentage figure, or a performance figure such as meals served per server hour. Many industry standards are available for consideration by individual foodservice operations.
2. Measurement of performance. There must be some means of measuring performance. Usually it is a quantitative figure, such as a dollar amount, percentage, or standard such as meals served per server hour, that relates to standards.
3. Comparison and analysis. Once the standard or goal has been established and actual performance determined, it is possible to compare the two. The figures will rarely be the same, and the manager must decide how much variance is acceptable and how often the comparisons should be done or over what time periods.
4. Corrective action. Once a significant variation is determined, the manager must take corrective action. Such action might involve more observation, personnel changes, or different methods of operations, among many others. Or perhaps the standard is unrealistic and must be changed.

The behaviorist approach is based on the motivation of people toward the best interest of their employer. The theory stresses that the more positive the feelings employees have for an organization, the less likely they are to do something to harm the organization and thus will voluntarily work to keep costs down. If this is the feeling of employees generally, they will exert peer pressure on others to also control costs.

Management can do a number of things to implement the behaviorist approach and draw employees closer to the organization. Having better communication, encouraging socialization among employees, providing recognition and rewards, and treating the individual as a needed and valued part of the operation can all be important.

Although both approaches can be employed together, they may also conflict. The traditional theory depends on someone having responsibility for achieving certain goals and usually a boss-subordinate relationship with the boss being responsible for the subordinates achieving goals and for taking appropriate action when goals are not attained. This boss-subordinate can be at odds with everyone being equal and working together for mutual goals. If an adversarial relationship should develop, the employee may care less and the employer may then consider even more traditional type controls possibly aggravating the situation.

Most foodservice employers want good relations with their employees. However, most feel that traditional control systems are very necessary.

Using Percentages   One of the most widely used controls is the cost percentage or the dollar amount of the cost compared to sales for that cost. If food costs are $105,000 and food sales are $300,000, the food cost percentage is 35 percent. Food and labor cost percentages are the most frequently used and are considered prime costs. National percentages for various types of foodservice operations are available, and it can be helpful for a manager to compare his or her percentages with the standards.

However, there can be problems regarding the percentages. A low food cost percentage does not necessarily mean a higher profit. You would rather sell a steak dinner at $15 with a 50 percent food cost which grosses a $7.50 profit than a chicken dinner at $10 will a 40 percent food cost that only grosses a $6.00 profit. There is truth in the saying "You take dollars, not percentages, to the bank."

For the percentage to be realistic the selling price must be realistic. For example, if labor costs are 30 percent of sales and a 10 percent raise is given, the labor cost percentage becomes 33 percent. Even though the percentage has risen, the labor force may not be any less efficient. From a theoretical viewpoint it might be better to use percentages as a pricing mechanism rather than a cost control device.

Menu Pricing   Menu pricing is not a science although quantitative approaches can help. Factors that must be considered in menu pricing include

> Elasticity of demand, or whether a change in selling prices will have a significant effect on customer demand.
>
> Perception of value, or what a customer perceives the meal or food item is worth regardless of what it costs to produce.
>
> Effect of competition by which competition can hold selling prices down or lack of competition can allow higher prices than normal.
>
> Whether the operation might try to increase profit by using low selling

prices to increase volume or concentrate on higher unit profits with fewer unit sales.

Considering all costs. Early menu pricing schemes considered only food costs; newer pricing schemes also include labor and other cost considerations.

Menu Control

Control is essential to the menu in foodservice operations. Control aspects of the menu include

- The number of items. Generally the more items on a menu and the more sophisticated they are, the higher the costs. Higher costs include more, and perhaps higher priced, labor. More food is required for inventory, and there is more chance of overproduction and resulting waste.
- Leftover control. If an item is prepared in advance, there is always the chance of leftovers. Forecasting menu sales and planning to deliberately run out of an item can help alleviate this problem. For every item prepared in advance, management should determine in advance how any leftovers will be used. Such use might include resale, conversion into other items, or serving to staff. Management should have production quantities specified and the number of leftovers should be shown on the production sheet. Leftovers in storage should be dated.
- Cyclical menus. Some operations that change menus regularly employ cyclical menus where the same menu is rotated (usually not to fall on the same day of the week). There may be different cycles for different seasons of the year. By using cyclical menus, management can reduce the time necessary to write menus, simplify purchasing since the menu pattern is definite for the cycle period, and facilitate quantity purchasing. Since menus and workloads are known in advance, the number of employee hours can also be predetermined helping labor scheduling.

Forecasting Forecasting the number of food items that will be served and the staffing and preparation for this forecast are very important in cost control. Usually a first forecast is made for the number of customers expected. Factors involved include number of customers served the same period last year, current trends, and reasons for increased or decreased business. For example,

> Customers served same meal last year
> ± Current trends
> = Adjusted forecast
> ± Factors especially affecting customer count for this meal, such as a holiday
> = Final forecast

Once the total number of patrons is determined, it is necessary to forecast the quantity of each item on the menu that is expected to be sold. The meal is broken down by courses such as appetizers, entrées, and desserts. Total customers per meal may vary, but the percentage of customers having each course is usually constant. Thus, the number of items that are expected to be served for each course can be calculated. For example, if five hundred patrons are expected to be served and 60 percent normally eat desserts, three hundred dessert sales can be expected. After the number for each course is determined, the number of sales of each item listed in the course can be forecasted. Here past records are important. What percent of customers usually buy the item? If 20 percent of dessert customers usually buy apple pie and three hundred dessert sales are expected, apple pie should generate about sixty of these sales. Care should be taken when sales of an item can be influenced by other items on the menu. Another popular dessert item listed with apple pie might cause the apple pie percentage to change.

Cost Accounting Control

Cost accounting is designed to give timely information to management as to whether costs are in line. Foodservice cost accounting differs considerably from manufacturing cost accounting. A kitchen is a type of factory or manufacturing operation, but whereas a factory usually has long production runs of comparatively few items, a kitchen has more production runs of many items that can change throughout the day.

Usually foodservice cost accounting is of two types: percentage systems or standard costs. The percentage system relates the cost category in dollars to dollars sales. The resulting percentage is then judged as to its appropriateness. Although helpful and the state of the art for many operations, percentage cost accounting systems have failings previously discussed.

The other principal approach, standard costs, is based on determining the cost of an item or service in advance and comparing actual costs for all items sold (in the case of food) with the standard or projected costs. Assume it is calculated that a piece of apple pie costs 25 cents (food cost) to produce. If sixty pieces are sold the food cost should be $15.00. Further assume that the standard costs added together for all items served in a period are $1000. The actual food cost, including both direct purchases and food taken from prior inventory (food requisitions), is determined to be $1100. A variation or potential savings figure of $100 is revealed. Actual costs will usually be higher than standard costs because of waste, overproduction, and so forth, but the smaller the variance, the more efficient the operation. If actual costs should be lower than standard costs, management should be concerned about portions that are too small, using nonspecified ingredients, or, perhaps, inaccurate costing.

Actual costs	$ 1100
Standard costs	− 1000
Variation	$ 100

The variation may also be compared to sales to produce a percentage of variation. If food sales were $3000 and the variation $100, the percentage of variation would be 3.3 percent. The percentage figure is especially helpful when volumes vary, since a $100 variance could be acceptable with daily sales of $3000 but not with daily sales of $1500.

Food Cost Control

Food cost is one of the two major costs in a foodservice operation. Because it is a major cost, it is also one where significant savings can occur (or where excessive costs can also occur). It is also an area where savings can be made

Fig. 1. Aspects of food cost control.

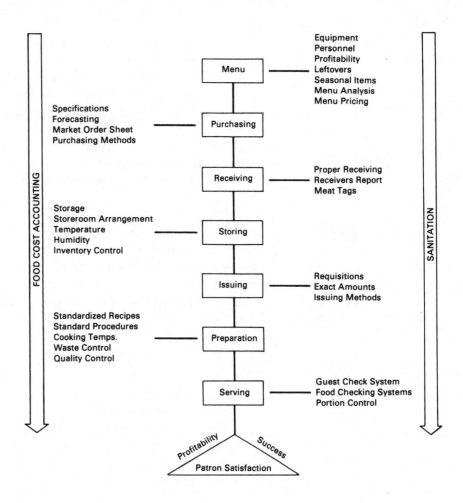

at no human cost. Labor cost control may involve fewer employees or fewer employee hours worked, which affects individual employees. In some cases, aspects of food control are necessary even though there appears to be no loss. An operation employs receiving controls even though there is no evidence of loss through receiving. What is unknown is the loss that could occur if no controls were utilized. Figure 1 shows various aspects of food cost control and their relationships.

Determining Food Costs   Over an extended period such as a year total food costs would probably approximate total food purchases for the year. Over a shorter period such as a week, weekly food purchases probably will not equal food cost since some purchases go into food inventory and some food is removed from prior inventory purchases and the two inventory transactions may not be equal. Daily (or a period's) food cost is generally considered to be food that is purchased directly for use that day (or period) and food taken from prior inventory, or

> Direct food purchases
> + <u>Food requisitions from prior inventory</u>
> = Food cost per day (or period)

This inventory fluctuation is also considered in the Statement of Income for a foodservice operation when calculating the cost of goods sold or cost of the food used.

Opening food inventory value
+ Food purchases during period
= Total value of available food
− Closing value of food inventory
= Value of food used during the period

Unless this inventory fluctuation is noted, food costs will be unusually high compared to food purchases when more food is put into inventory, and food costs will be understated when more food is drawn from inventory and not replaced.

Food Purchasing Procedures A goal of food purchasing is to have an appropriate but not excess amount on hand when needed. Modern practice is to have as little inventory on hand as possible since carrying inventory requires investment of money from working capital with no return on investment until the food is used. Higher inventory levels also increase storage costs.

Accurate forecasting of needs, predetermined specifications for the food to be purchased, and use of the best purchasing method for the operation are important in food purchasing. Traditionally, the food purchasing procedure is to

Write the menu
Forecast consumption
Prepare food product specifications
Determine necessary purchase quantities
Request prices from purveyors
Send orders to chosen purveyors

Although many food operators still follow this procedure, another procedure, sometimes called "one-stop purchasing," is being used more frequently. One-stop purchasing is arranging to buy all of a type of product from one purveyor with the assumption that with the volume, the purveyor will give the best deal. This concept has been helped by some developments in foodservice. Food purveyors are getting larger, expanding their product lines and geographical service areas. Total shopping capability is a goal for many. Rising delivery costs have made larger deliveries, which cost proportionately less, more desirable.

Advantages to the operator of one-stop shopping include chance for lower prices, less time spent with different sales personnel, less accounting work, more service from the chosen purveyor, and possibly use of the purveyor's computer. The larger one-stop purveyor may have more resources for, or more interest in, helping the operator financially if needed.

One-stop purchasing is only one method of food purchasing. Open market buying entails securing prices, usually by phone, from various purveyors and then giving item orders to those offering the best price for those items. A steward's market order sheet (Figure 2) may be used. This pre-lists usual items needed, has spaces for quantity on hand, quantity needed, and to write in the prices from various purveyors as they are called. After comparing the price quotations received, the buyer orders the desired items from each.

Sealed bid buying is used by institutions. In this process, the quantity needed by a period is determined, detailed specifications are prepared, and purveyors asked to submit sealed bids. Advantages of sealed bid buying include preventing favoritism, less frequent need for large-quantity purchasing, and the possibility of large quantity prices. This procedure can be cumber-

ON HAND	ARTICLE	WANTED	QUOTATIONS
	BEEF		
	Corned Beef		
	Corned Beef Brisket		
	Corned Beef Rump		
	Pig, Suckling		
	Corned Beef Hash		
	Beef Chipped		
	Beef Breads		
	Butts		
	Chuck		
	Fillets		
	Hip Short		
	Hip Full		
	Kidneys		
	Livers		
	Loin, Short		
	Strip		
	Shell Strip		
	Ribs Beef		
	Shins		
	Suet, Beef		
	Tails, Ox		
	VEAL		
	Breast		
	Brains		
	Feet		
	Fore Quarters		
	Hind Quarters		
	Head		
	Kidneys		
	Legs		
	Liver		
	Loins		
	Racks		
	Saddles		
	Shoulder		
	Sweet Breads		
	MUTTON		
	Fore Quarters		
	Kidneys		
	Legs		
	Racks		
	Saddles		
	Saddles, Hind		
	Shoulder		
	Suet		

ON HAND	ARTICLE	WANTED	QUOTATIONS
	Provisions (Cont'd)		
	Pig's Knuckles Fresh		
	Pig's Knuckles Corned		
	Pork, Fresh Loin		
	Pork, Larding		
	Pork, Spare Ribs		
	Pork, Salt Strip		
	Pork Tenderloin		
	Sausages, Country		
	Sausages, Frankfurter		
	Sausages, Meat		
	Shoulders, Fresh		
	Shoulders, Smoked		
	Shoulders, Corned		
	Tongues		
	Tongues, Beef Smoked		
	Tongues, Fresh		
	Tongues, Lambs		
	Tripe		
	POULTRY		
	Chickens		
	Chickens, Roast		
	Chickens, Broilers		
	Chickens, Broilers		
	Chickens, Supreme		
	Cocks		
	Capons		
	Ducks		
	Ducklings		
	Fowl		
	Geese		
	Goslings		
	Guinea Hens		
	Guinea Squabs		
	Pigeons		
	Poussins		
	Squabs		
	Turkeys, Roasting		
	Turkeys, Boiling		
	Turkeys, Spring		
	GAME		
	Birds		
	Partridge		
	Pheasant, English		
	Rabbits		

ON HAND	ARTICLE	WANTED	QUOTATIONS
	FISH (Cont'd)		
	Carp		
	Codfish, Live		
	Codfish, Salt Boneless		
	Codfish, Salt Flake		
	Eels		
	Finnan Haddie		
	Flounders		
	Flounders		
	Flounders, Fillet		
	Fluke		
	Haddock		
	Haddock, Fillet		
	Haddock, Smoked		
	Halibut		
	Halibut, Chicken		
	Herring		
	Herring, Smoked		
	Herring, Kippered		
	Kingfish		
	Mackerel, Fresh		
	Mackerel, Salt		
	Mackerel, Spanish		
	Mackerel, Smoked		
	Perch		
	Pickerel		
	Pike		
	Porgies		
	Pompano		
	Redsnapper		
	Salmon, Fresh		
	Salmon, Smoked		
	Salmon, Nova Scotia		
	Scrod		
	Shad		
	Shad Roes		
	Smelts		
	Sole, Boston		
	Sole, Lemon		
	Sole, English		
	Sturgeon		
	Trout, Brook		
	Trout, Lake		
	Trout, Salmon		
	Weakfish		
	Whitebait		
	Whitebait		
	Whitefish		
	Whitefish, Smoked		

ON HAND	ARTICLE	WANTED	QUOTATIONS
	Vegetables (Cont'd)		
	Extragon		
	Egg Plant		
	Garlic		
	Horseradish Roots		
	Kale		
	Kohlrabi		
	Lettuce		
	Lettuce, Ice Berg		
	Lettuce, Place		
	Leeks		
	Mint		
	Mushrooms		
	Mushrooms, Fresh		
	Okra		
	Onions		
	Onions, Yellow		
	Onions, Bermuda		
	Onions, Spanish		
	Onions, White		
	Onions, Scallions		
	Oyster Plant		
	Parsley		
	Parsnips		
	Peppermint		
	Peas		
	Peas, Green		
	Peppers, Green		
	Peppers, Red		
	Potatoes		
	Potatoes		
	Potatoes, Bermuda		
	Potatoes, Idaho		
	Potatoes, Idaho		
	Potatoes, Sweet		
	Potatoes, New		
	Potatoes, Yams		
	Pumpkins		
	Romaine		
	Radishes		
	Rhubarb, Fresh		
	Rhubarb, Hot House		
	Sage		
	Shallots		
	Sorrel		
	Sauerkraut		
	Spinach		
	Squash Crooked Neck		

ON HAND	ARTICLE	WANTED	QUOTATIONS
	FRUIT (Cont'd)		
	Dates		
	Figs		
	Gooseberries		
	Grapes		
	Grapes		
	Grapes		
	Grapes, Tokay		
	Grapes, Malaga		
	Grapes, Concord		
	Guavas		
	Limes, Florida		
	Limes, Persian		
	Lemons		
	Lemons		
	Lemons		
	Oranges		
	Oranges		
	Oranges		
	Oranges		
	Peaches		
	Peaches		
	Pears		
	Pears		
	Pears		
	Pears, Alligators		
	Pineapples		
	Plums		
	Plums		
	Pomegranates		
	Quinces		
	Raspberries		
	Strawberries		
	Strawberries		
	Tangerines		
	Watermelons		
	Watermelons		
	Watermelons		
	BUTTER		
	Print		
	Cooking		
	Sweet		
	EGGS		
	White		
	White		
	Brown		
	Mixed Colors		
	Pullets		

Fig. 2. Sample from a steward's market quotation list.

some and it does not allow operators to take advantage of pricing opportunities that may occur.

Cost-plus buying is making arrangements with a purveyor to pay a certain percentage to the purveyor over his cost. It usually involves ordering at a definite time, often in advance of when the purveyor does his buying, so the purveyor does not have to buy on the speculation that it will later be sold.

Co-op buying is a group of operations with similar needs banding together for mass purchasing. They may hire a manager who can spend more time on researching and negotiating the best buys than the individual operations can. Although selling prices may be lower for the purveyor, marketing costs are less since the purveyor need contact only the co-op and not its individual members.

Quantities to Purchase A problem in purchasing new perishable food items is how much to purchase at one time. Many factors, such as consumption rates, the time required for delivery after an order has been placed (lead time), the maximum quantity to be on hand at one time, quantity discounts, storage space available, and funds available for purchasing can enter into this decision. As mentioned, many operations seek to have as little on hand as possible with provisions for unexpected emergencies. Some very large foodservice operations have reduced their inventories by hundreds of thousands of dollars.

A quantitative help in ordering regularly stocked items is the economic order quantity (EOQ), the order quantity that minimizes purchase costs and inventory costs. It is about as easy to make a large order as a small one, so economies would suggest fewer larger orders. Doing so, however, requires more money tied up in inventory and increases the cost of maintaining this inventory. An EOQ attempts to find the best balance between these factors. The EOQ formula is

$$EOQ = \sqrt{\frac{2FS}{CP}}$$

where EOQ = the most efficient size order in terms of lowest purchasing costs and maintaining inventory costs

F = the fixed cost of making an order such as time, receiving, paper work, and so forth (let us assume $20)

S = sales or usage per year (let us assume 100 cases of canned tomatoes)

C = carrying cost, which represents the cost of money involved in carrying the inventory and the cost of maintaining the inventory space and security (let us assume 20 percent)

P = purchase price per unit or case (let us assume $20)

$$EOQ = \sqrt{\frac{2 \times 20 \times 100}{.20 \times 20}}$$

$$= \sqrt{\frac{4000}{4}}$$

$$= \sqrt{1000}$$

$$= 31.62$$

The EOQ would be about 32 cases.

A factor often considered in how much to purchase is par stocks. Par stocks are the amount of regularly used items management wants to have on hand. Management may decide that it wants twelve #10 cans of stewed tomatoes on hand. It will then purchase toward maintaining this amount.

Food Receiving Procedures

Receiving involves verifying that quantities received are actually the same as ordered and as on the invoice and that the items meet specifications. The kitchen is also informed of nondeliveries of expected foods.

Competent personnel are important in receiving. Often, something is delivered and anyone handy signs for it. The receiver should be conscientious in checking the food items and know what to look for. To be sure this type of person is on duty, some operations limit the times they will accept deliveries so they can have the best people available.

Tools for the receiver include accurate scales (check yours with a known weight), specifications detailing what is acceptable in the incoming items, and aids such as carts and counters. In some operations, management personnel occasionally take over the receiving function, often unannounced, just to keep an eye on things and to deter collusion between receiving and delivery personnel.

Receiving can include the following procedures:

A daily list of expected deliveries is prepared.
All incoming items are counted, weighed, and marked.
Purchase specifications are used to check for quality.
Invoice prices are checked against purchase orders or buyer quotation sheets.
The invoice is sometimes stamped similar to the following figure:

Date Received	
Quantity OK	____
Quality OK	____
Price OK	____
Entered	____
Paid	____

The date is written in and the individual(s) who checks quantity, quality, and prices initials in the proper space. Note is made when the bills are entered in accounts payable and the number of the check when paid.

Reports

The receiving clerk's Daily Report (Figure 3) has spaces for the receiver to describe what has come in, its value, and the vendor. There may also be three other columns listed under Purchase Journal Distribution. These are: Food Direct, Food Stores, and Sundries. These columns break down in dollars the value of food sent directly to the kitchen, presumably to be charged to that day's food cost, and the value of the food sent to the storeroom, which will be charged to food cost when issued from the storeroom. Sundries gives the value of nonfood items such as paper goods that may be received with food items but should not be included in food cost calculations. The food direct figure added with storeroom requisitions will provide the daily (or period) food cost.

Some operations use a Daily List of Deliveries. The purchaser prepares

	QUAN.	UNIT	DESCRIPTION	✔	UNIT PRICE	AMOUNT	TOTAL AMOUNT	PURCHASE JOURNAL DISTRIBUTION			
								FOOD DIRECT	FOOD STORES	SUNDRIES	

RECEIVING CLERK'S DAILY REPORT

NO. _____

DATE _____

_____
SIGNATURE

Fig. 3. Receiving clerk's daily report.

a daily list of what should be delivered each day including brands, sizes, weights, and prices. The receiver then checks off items as they arrive. This procedure also helps to pinpoint the nondelivery of expected items. Dating the goods as they arrive helps with receiving.

Food Storage Management, Issuing, and Inventory Control

Food storage management is concerned with spatial needs, location, security, temperature, arrangement of contents, and protection from vermin and insects.

Food stores are divided into two types: dry storage for nonperishables and refrigerated storage for perishables. Refrigerated storage also includes freezers.

Obviously the closer to the kitchen, the better for storage. Ideally receiving, storage, and kitchen would be in a direct line. At one time, an operation could not have too much storage. Now storage is purposely limited to prevent tying up money in inventory and proving the theory that if space is available, the space will be used whether really needed or not.

Security is limiting access to the storage areas. Problems can occur with maintenance and delivery personnel, as well as food personnel, who do not have reason to be in the storage area. A half door has proved helpful in keeping nonessential people out of the storeroom. Storage areas with ready access to outside entrances can be especially vulnerable.

Refrigerated storage may have different temperatures for different types of refrigerated items. Dry food storage should be on the cool side. One study showed that foods, in general, keep three times longer at 70°F than at 100°F. Relative humidity should be 50–60 percent.

There should be a planned arrangement of contents in storage, especially in dry storage areas. One scheme divides the dry storage space into areas for classes of foods such as beverages, canned vegetables, canned fruits, and so forth. Space is provided for each class of food, and the food items are arranged alphabetically in the class space. Exceptions can be made for fast moving, bulky, heavy, or seldom-used items. Care should be taken that the oldest items in storage are used first. This practice is sometimes called FIFO or first in, first out.

General cleanliness is important to help protect from vermin and insect infestation. Closed containers are also important. Means of entrance, such as holes in the wall (some mice can enter a half-inch hole), should be eliminated. Windows should have screens. Trash and garbage should never be left in storage areas.

Refrigerated storage has its own problems, but chief among them is allowing leftovers and opened packages to remain too long. This problem can be alleviated by dating the leftovers and, if necessary, identifying their contents. Some basic suggestions for improving storage are

- Use a thermometer to indicate excessively high temperatures.
- Date goods and use FIFO.
- Lock storeroom when not in use.
- Insist upon cleanliness.
- Keep goods from blocking evaporator coils and fans in refrigerated storage. Have an alarm to sound should temperatures become too high.

Inventory Control   Inventory control is becoming a more important part of food-cost control. Inventory control includes making the smallest investment possible in inventory, not running out of items, showing any variance between actual and calculated quantities, and providing an inventory dollar value showing usage of food items, pinpointing slow moving items, and alerting management when inventory replacements are needed.

Types of Inventories   There are two types of inventories. The physical inventory is the actual physical counting of items. A perpetual inventory keeps a continuing balance of the item. The balance can be in quantities or dollar value or both.

> Opening Balance + In − Out = Balance

A perpetual inventory has many advantages, but the cost and effort of maintaining such a system was usually too much for most operations until computerization made it feasible. Usually perpetual inventories are checked at least once a year with an actual or physical inventory.

A dollar opening and closing (which becomes the next opening) figure is necessary in preparing the income statement. Following are some helpful techniques for taking a physical inventory:

It is usually more efficient to have two people involved. One counts while the other records the data. If one of these persons is not involved in the storeroom operation, there is more control. There should be inventory sheets on which items are listed in the same order as they appear on the shelves or in the storeroom. Space can be left on the sheets for new items. Pricing is easier if prices have been marked on the items. If experience shows that most items do not fluctuate in their inventory counts, it may be necessary to count only expensive or fast moving items, although a complete inventory should be done at least once a year. The value of kitchen inventories should be added to the storeroom inventory figure.

Inventory Value   Management is always interested in the variance, or the difference between what should be in inventory and what is actually there, as shown by a physical inventory. Although there will always be some difference because of "shrinkage" or even overage, an excessive difference can be cause for concern. Is food walking out by itself? A too-high inventory value compared to food actually on hand can indicate food may be sent to the kitchen without proper recording of it. The formula for storeroom reconciliation is:

> Beginning inventory value
> + Food stores purchased
> = Total
> − Issues from storeroom
> = Balance
> ± Ending physical inventory value
> = Over (or short)

A figure that *some* operators find helpful is the inventory turnover figure or an average inventory figure divided into the cost of sales (or value of the food used). If the cost of goods sold is $20,000 and the average inventory figure is $4000, the inventory turnover is 5 times. Normally the higher the inventory turnover figure the better since management is tying up less working capital in inventory. An exception might be an operation that has insufficient funds and is buying hand-to-mouth and not getting the best prices.

Limited menu or fast service operations will have a higher turnover than a fine restaurant with a large and changing menu.

Issuing Control   Issuing involves supplying food to the preparation units after it has been in storage or in some cases after being received. Issuing control is necessary to see that no food is issued unless management wants it so and to provide a value of the food sent from the storeroom for accounting purposes.

Labor Cost Control

The other major cost in foodservice operations is labor. For many years not much thought was given to labor cost control. The peaks and valleys of activity in foodservice made labor costs high. Many workers were teenagers or adults who could not find other jobs and were not trained or motivated. Many foodservice operations were small with little management sophistication. However, labor shortages, strong competition, and pressure on the bottom line have caused management to seek ways to reduce labor costs. Some organizations are using outside-prepared (convenience) foods, which are prepared under factory conditions. Expansive menus have been cut back, and more self-service is sometimes employed. Technical advances such as more efficient equipment, better in-house communication devices, and developments in food processing and preservation have all helped.

Implicit in labor cost control are good personnel policies. Anything that draws employees closer to the operations may enhance their commitment to production and cost control so, employers should strive to create the best environment for their workers that they can.

One system for employee control and productivity has seven facets.

1. Have good personnel policies. Not only should the policies be fair but it is important to have policies so one employee is not treated differently from another. Personnel policies can cover many things including, but certainly not limited to, hiring practices, promotion, training, tardiness, absenteeism, family leave, discipline, drug use, and so forth. New discrimination legislation has made policies even more important.

2. Provide a two-part job analysis. One part is the job description, which describes what is performed on the job, duties, supervision, hours, and such. It is helpful in hiring, training, and eliminating overlapping work since, in describing the job, it is necessary to determine who should do what. The second part is the job specification, which lists the job requirements. It is most helpful in hiring since referring to the thought-out specification is better than making snap decisions on whether the applicant could or could not perform the job.

3. Simplify work to make the jobs or workers more productive. The jobs that have been described in the work specification may need new descriptions after better ways to perform them are developed. There is no one best way to perform a job, but there is always a better way. Improvements may involve different equipment, types of service, or menu items.

4. Use work production standards. Work production standards determine what to expect in production from an employee or positions per labor time impact. They can be expressed in units produced per time increment, such as customers served per server hour, or dollar amounts achieved per time increment, such as dollar sales generated per cook's hour. For work production standards, employees of a foodservice operation are usually divided

into four types: (1) those preparing food, or preparation; (2) those directly serving customers, or service; (3) those involved in sanitation or warewashing and clean up; and (4) administrative and general, which includes those not in the other categories. There may also be specialized groups such as valet parking attendants. Work production standards are prepared for each of the classes and the different jobs in each classification.

5. Forecast the anticipated number of customers for the meal or period, which has been described earlier.

6. Schedule, which is best done utilizing the forecasts and work production standards. If a cook's work production standard is eighty meals per work day and four hundred covers are expected, about five work days of cooks' time should be scheduled.

7. Generate control reports to tell management when and where costs are out of line. Usually the reports should include the labor cost percentage for each class of employees and how employees performed regarding work production standards. If an operation, such as hospital patient foodservice, does not have direct patron sales, work production standards become more necessary. Figure 4 shows a report that provides percentages of sales and covers per employee.

Work Production Standards

As previously mentioned, work production standards are simply the amount of work that workers in a specific job can be expected to perform during a specified time period. In using work production standards, workers can be considered to be either fixed or variable. A fixed employee is one who is needed regardless of changes in the number of patrons. One cashier may be necessary whether there are one hundred or two hundred patrons. Work production standards are not too useful for fixed type employees. A variable employee is one whose number varies with the number of patrons. Twice as many serving personnel are needed for four hundred as for two hundred patrons. Semivariable (or semifixed) positions vary but not in direct proportion to the number of patrons. For example, twice as many cooks may not be needed in this situation. Determining proper work production standards can be difficult, especially since customer count varies during a day. Sophisticated techniques such as time study can be used but basing work production standards on what an employee who is considered good at his or her job can produce in an average day or other time period is usually effective. Work production standards have an advantage over labor cost percentages since the percentage figure shows only the relationship between sales and labor cost whereas the work production standard is more objective and does not vary with changes in selling prices or wage rates.

Bar Charts

Bar charts or work activity graphs can be helpful in determining how well employees are scheduled in relation to work load. One approach plots the activity in a specific work area throughout the day (or period) against when workers are scheduled. This approach can reveal how workers are scheduled when their particular work area is busy or not so busy. Figure 5 plots scheduled times against activity.

As shown in Figure 6, another approach using bar charts is to observe individual employees and record how busy they are at various times. Different codings can be used to show this visually. If the chart shows that employees are not too busy at different times, schedule adjustments can be made.

Fig. 4. A payroll control Report.

ANALYSIS OF WEEKLY PAYROLL					
Week ending _____					
	Number of employees	Weekly payroll cost	Number of covers per employee	Sales per employee	Ratio of payroll to food sales
Administrative					
Manager	1	$400.00			
Bookkeeper	1	100.00			
Cashier	2	180.00			
Total	4	$680.00	760	$3200	7.5%
Preparation					
Cooks–					
cook's helper	4	$1000.00			
Baker	1	250.00			
Pantry	2	320.00			
Total	7	1570.00	434	$1828	12.3%
Service					
Host/hostess	1	$160.00			
Servers	10	890.00			
Busboy	2	300.00			
Total	13	$1350.00	234	$984	10.2%
Cleaning					
Dishwashers	2	$340.00			
Porter	1	170.00			
Total	3	$510.00	1,013	$381	4.0%
Grand Total	27	$4060.00	113		34.0%
Statistics					
Food sales	$12,800				
Covers served	3,040				
Average check	$ 4.21				

Foodservice Management Information Systems

Much of control is having information systems implemented that provide management with information for analysis. Such information must be accurate, timely, and relevant to enable managers to make changes when necessary. A number of computerized systems with different capabilities are available. The systems are made up of modules (defined as discreet and identifiable programs) that provide particular types of information. The information developed in one module can be used in another. For example, information developed in the forecasting module can be used in a purchasing or scheduling module.

Common modules include

• Forecasting. These modules develop and maintain a data base of historical data that can be used to forecast future business. The forecasting is usually done through the use of relatively simple mathematical models and can include moving average.

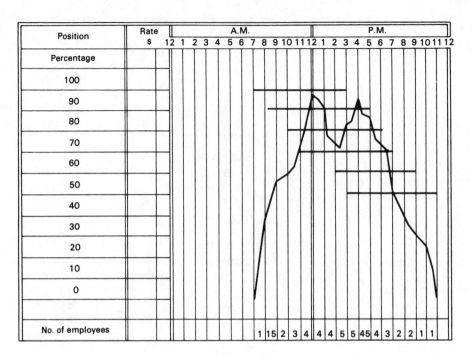

Fig. 5. Scheduling and kitchen production.

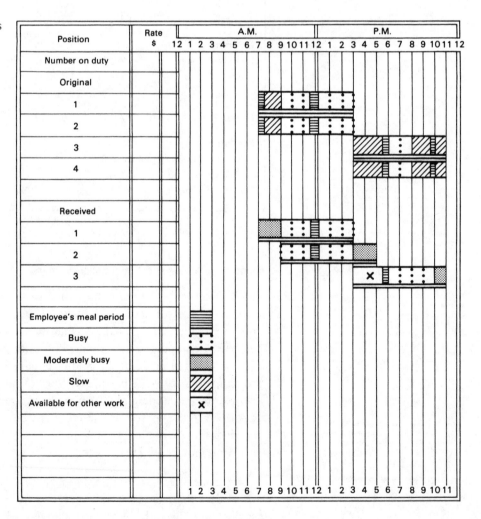

Fig. 6. Dishwasher's work schedule.

- Sales analysis. These modules can be used in a number of different ways. The costs of menu items and the resulting gross profit can be determined in advance. Managers can substitute various items to get a desired food cost before committing to production plans. They can track high and low sellers on the menu.
- Food production. Using data from the forecasting module and menu, production orders, storeroom requisitions, and recipes can be provided. These modules can then prepare requisitions for the amounts needed and adapt recipes to desired production quantities.
- Purchasing. These modules calculate the amounts of food to order, estimate par stock requirements, calculate inventory amounts on hand, and track purveyors' delivery capabilities in purchasing.
- Inventory. The two main purposes of the inventory module are to provide management with a perpetual inventory of items in storage and to calculate dollar values for these items. Other reports generated can include consumption reports and reorder flags.
- Labor cost analysis. In addition to keeping track of employee working time and wage rates, this module can analyze these data. Figures such as payroll costs compared to budget, covers served or income gained per labor input, labor cost per customer, and labor cost percentages can be generated. This system can also generate payroll records, payroll checks, and payroll taxes. One package also schedules workers according to need and other factors desired by management.

Helping the computerized systems are point of sale (POS) cash registers, which can be computers in themselves. In fact one definition of a POS is a computer that thinks it is a cash register. Foodservice management information systems have already given more dimension to foodservice cost control and promise to be even more sophisticated and helpful in the future.

Summary

Cost control is a vital part of foodservice management. The two major cost items, known as prime costs, are food and labor. There are two general approaches to cost control. One is behavioral, which stresses that if employees have positive feelings toward their employer, they will be less likely to try to increase costs for that employer. The traditional approach provides a desired standard and actual results are compared to that standard.

Food costs are controlled by concentrating the various aspects involved, such as purchasing, receiving, storage, inventorying, and issuing. There are a number of procedures that can be used in each of these areas to analyze and control costs.

Labor costs can be analyzed by using percentages, work production standards, and bar charts. Once the areas of excessive costs are identified, steps can then be taken to control the excesses.

Important to control are management information systems utilizing computers and point of sale registers. The formal computerized systems are made up of modules, and information developed in one module such as forecasting can be used in another module such as purchasing. Common modules are forecasting, sales analysis, food production, purchasing, inventory, and labor cost analysis.

19

Food Safety

Marian C. Spears

Many opportunities exist for food contamination in a foodservice operation making foodborne illness a major health problem in the United States today. All foods deteriorate, some more rapidly than others. Newspaper reporters and television newscasters are quick to inform the public when hundreds of conventioneers are taken to the hospital by ambulance after eating chicken at a hotel banquet; a foodborne illness outbreak on a cruise ship also can be a newsworthy item. Incidents such as these are not easily forgotten by customers who have every right to expect that the food served will be safe and wholesome. Food handling practices, beginning with purchasing and continuing through production and service, must be designed with the safety of the public in mind. Managers should remember that customers can initiate legal action against a foodservice operation for not protecting their safety (Spears 1991).

Major Types of Food Spoilage

Food spoilage generally denotes unfitness for human consumption due to chemical or biological causes. The major types of food spoilage are microbiological, biochemical, physical, and chemical. Contamination of some foods may be difficult to determine from appearance, odor, and taste. In other foods, however, mold, discolored or altered appearance, off-odors, or off-flavors are obvious signs of contamination.

Microbiological   The three most common microbiological organisms causing foodborne illness are bacteria, mold, and yeast and are found everywhere that temperature, moisture, and substrate favor life and growth. Some species are useful in preserving food, producing alcohol, or developing special flavors if they are specially cultured and used under controlled conditions. Other microbial activity, however, can be a primary cause of food spoilage.

Certain microorganisms and parasites are transmitted through food and may cause illnesses in people who ingest contaminated items. According to Longree and Armbruster (1987), microorganisms causing foodborne illnesses include bacteria, molds, yeast, viruses, rickettsiae, protozoa, and parasites. They state, however, that although most microorganisms producing foodborne illnesses are bacteria, less than one percent can be considered "enemies of man and many are his friends."

Bacteria.   Bacteria are microscopic, unicellular organisms of varying size and shape. In most instances, bacteria cannot be seen in food. Key factors affecting bacterial multiplication are type of organism, moisture, oxygen tension, pH, temperature, and presence of inhibitors. In general, multiplication of bacteria is affected by available moisture in food. Microorganisms vary in their response to oxygen; some require a definite minute quantity of oxygen.

The degree of a food's acidity or alkalinity, expressed as pH value, also affects bacterial growth. The *pH value* indicates the hydrogen ion concentration on a scale from 0 to 14, with 7 being neutral. Values below 7 indicate acidity and those above 7 indicate alkalinity. Bacteria grow best at a pH near neutral.

Specific temperatures are required for growth of bacteria. Various types respond differently to temperature. *Thermal death time* is the time required at a specified temperature to kill a specified number of bacteria under specific conditions. Time and temperature are important in preserving microbiological quality in food.

Various inhibitors have an effect on bacterial multiplication and death. Inhibitors may be integral in the food or be developed in the processing. Benzoic acid is a natural inhibitor in cranberries but alcohol produced in the growth and fermentation of yeast in fruit juice or in the production of wine is an example of an inhibitory substance that may accumulate and become toxic.

Molds and Yeasts.   Molds are larger than bacteria and grow on a wide range of substrates—moist or dry, acid or nonacid, high or low in salt or sugar. Molds also grow at various temperatures; optimum temperature is between 77°F and 86°F. Mold is colored and powdery and can be identified by the naked eye.

Viruses.   Viruses multiply in the living cells of food that is not cooked and are capable of causing diseases in plants, animals, and humans. They resemble bacteria because the right temperature, nutrients, moisture, and pH are necessary for growth and reproduction. The Norwalk virus is rapidly increasing as a health threat and outbreaks have occurred from contaminated water, shellfish, and many other foods as well as infected food handlers with poor sanitation habits.

Other Microorganisms.   Rickettsiae include typhus fever, Q fever, and Rocky Mountain spotted fever. Q fever is food related and may be transmitted to humans by cows infected with the organism through their milk if it has not been properly heat treated.

Protozoa may be carried by food and cause illness when ingested. Amoebic dysentery is caused by one of the pathogenic protozoa that can be spread by water and food. Animals and humans carry protozoa in their intestinal tracts, which has implications for food handling practices of foodservice personnel.

Parasites include trichinae, tapeworms, and roundworms. Trichinosis occurs when persons are served a trichinae-infested product, mainly pork. This disease is preventable if food is cooked to a proper end-point temperature. The United States Department of Agriculture (USDA), however, has developed processing methods for pork products that ensure a safe product. Pork should be purchased from approved sources and be adequately cooked.

Tapeworms may cause disease in humans when larva-infested beef or pork is ingested. Proper meat processing procedures are important to prevent contamination. Anasakis, a new source of tapeworm and roundworm infestation, is found in the currently popular raw seafood dishes such as sushi. The Food and Drug Administration (FDA) ruled in 1987 that fish that is not thoroughly cooked must be blast frozen to $-31°F$ or below for 15 hours or frozen to $-10°F$ or below for 7 days. In addition, the foodservice operator must keep a record of the process on file for 90 days.

Biochemical

Biochemical spoilage is caused by natural food enzymes, which are complex catalysts that initiate reactions in foods. Off-flavors, odors, or colors may develop in foods if enzymatic reactions are uncontrolled. An example is a peeled apple that is exposed to air; the surface of the apple turns brown because of enzyme activation by oxygen. Heat, cold, drying, addition of inhibiting chemicals, and irradiation are the principal means for inactivating natural food enzymes.

Physical

Physical spoilage of food may be caused by temperature changes, moisture, and dryness. Excessive heat, for example, dehydrates food and destroys certain nutrients. Severe cold also causes certain starches used in preparing sauces or gravies to break down at freezing temperatures.

Excessive moisture may cause the growth of mold and bacteria. It also may cause physical changes such as caking, stickiness, or crystallization thus affecting the quality of a food item. Powdered beverages may not dispense properly in a vending machine if the moisture level is too high.

Chemical

Numerous chemicals used in foodservice operations are toxic to humans. Cleaning supplies stored near food products have caused a number of public health problems. Herbicides, pesticides, and fungicides when ingested in large quantities may cause poisoning. These chemicals are used to kill undesirable weeds, plants, pests, fungi, or bacteria but may find their way into food. Tolerances of permissible residues are established by the Environmental Protection Agency (EPA) and are enforced by the FDA (Longree and Armbruster 1987).

Several food additives or preservatives, when used in excessive amounts, have caused illness in humans. Large concentrations of nitrites, used for stabilizing the normal red color of ham and bacon, are toxic in animals. Federal regulations are being prepared to reduce the amount to the minimum effective level. Sulfur dioxide was used to prevent food discoloration caused by oxidation. A number of food related allergies have been traced to sulfites in fresh fruits and vegetables, shrimp, and dried fruit. Proper labeling is required for packaged foods. FDA does not approve its use on fresh fruits and vegetables. Restaurants and supermarkets are now using lemon juice or citric acid for preserving color in these foods, especially on salad bars.

Too much monosodium glutamate (MSG) used as a flavor enhancer might cause flushing of the face, dizziness, headache, or nausea in susceptible consumers. These symptoms sometimes are referred to as the Chinese Restaurant Syndrome because MSG often is used in Oriental foods.

Foodborne Pathogens

Foodborne illnesses, which are outbreaks of gastroenteritis and are commonly called "food poisoning," are caused by microbial pathogens that multiply profusely in food. These illnesses are either *foodborne intoxications* caused by toxins formed in food prior to consumption or *foodborne infections* caused by the activity of large numbers of bacterial cells carried by food into the gastrointestinal system of the victim. Symptoms from ingesting toxin-containing food may occur within two hours; the incubation period of an infection, however, is usually longer than that of an intoxication.

Staphylococcus aureus

Staphylococcus aureus, which develops a toxin causing gastroenteritis when ingested, is one of the principal causative agents in foodborne illness. Symptoms include nausea, cramps, vomiting, and diarrhea and usually appear within two to three hours after ingestion of toxic food. The cells may survive for a long time in dust, soil, frozen foods, or on floors and walls. The human body is one of the most important sources of the organism. Because it thrives in infected skin abrasions, cuts, and pimples, foodservice employees with these problems should not be permitted to handle food.

Foods high in protein are likely to be involved in foodborne intoxication. Cream pies, custards, meat sauces, gravies, and meat salad can be the culprits. Appearance, flavor, or odor of the affected food items are not noticeably altered. The organism multiplies even under refrigeration, if temperatures are not sufficiently low or if the cooling process is not rapid enough. High protein foods should be kept very hot or very cold, never at room temperature.

Salmonella

Salmonella bacteria multiply in the intestinal tract of the victim and cause foodborne infections. The incubation period ranges from 6 to 72 hours and the symptoms include acute gastroenteritis with inflammation of the small intestine, nausea, vomiting, diarrhea, and frequently a moderate fever often preceded by headache and chills.

The primary source of *Salmonella* is the intestinal tract of carrier animals. The carrier appears to be well and shows no signs of illness but harbors causative organisms. Food animals are carriers, especially hogs, chickens, turkeys, and ducks. Salmonellosis, the disease caused by salmonellae, is spread largely by contaminated food and is believed to be one of the major communicable diseases in the United States.

Raw meat, poultry, shellfish, processed meats, egg products, and dried milk have been found to carry *Salmonella*. Meat mixtures, salad dressings, gravies, puddings, and cream-filled pastries are frequent causes of salmonellosis. Food handlers and poor sanitation practices often are associated with outbreaks. Holding food for longer periods at warm temperatures, slow cooling of large batches of food, and cutting on contaminated surfaces should be prevented in production, storage, or service.

The organism grows best in a nonacid medium and multiplication occurs over a wide range of temperatures, the optimum being the temperature of the human body. These organisms also have been shown to survive freezing and freezer storage.

Clostridium perfringens

Clostridium perfringens, a toxin, is considered the third most common cause of foodborne illness in the United States. It inhabits the intestinal tract of healthy animals and human beings and occurs in soil, sewage, water, and dust.

Symptoms usually begin 8 to 15 hours after ingestion and are similar to staphylococcus intoxication, yet milder, and also include nausea, cramping, and diarrhea.

Clostridium botulinum

Clostridium botulinum produces a toxin that affects the nervous system and is extremely dangerous. The disease called botulism is the food intoxication caused by bacteria. The illness is treated by administering an antitoxin. Improved food processing techniques have led to a greatly reduced number of incidents of botulism although inadequately processed home canned foods are frequently associated with the illness. Serving home canned food in either commercial or noncommercial foodservice operations is not permitted by local or state health departments.

Temperature and length of food storage also are factors influencing toxin production and growth. The toxin is stable in acid but unstable in alkalies. Meats, fish, and low-acid vegetables have been found to support toxin formation and growth. Soil grown vegetables, particularly potatoes, can be prime carriers of this toxin; toxic spores can get into the potato through its eyes. Precautions for avoiding botulism include purchasing food from safe sources, destroying canned foods with defects such as swells or leaks, storing foods under recommended conditions, and using appropriate methods for thawing frozen foods.

Streptococcus

Streptococcus faecalis inhabits the intestinal tract and may be discharged with feces. It is transmitted by the hands of food handlers and may contaminate food products. This bacterium is found in milk, cheese, and other unpasteurized dairy products. Longree and Armbruster (1987) stressed that clear distinction must be drawn between foodborne illness caused by sneezing and coughing of persons with strep infections and streptococcus disease transmission in which food might serve as a vehicle because it was handled by persons with unsanitary personal habits. Strep infections generally are transmitted by processed meats, cheese, cream pies, prepared puddings, and canned evaporated milk.

New Foodborne Pathogens

From 1982 to 1986, 31 percent of all foodborne outbreaks reported to the Centers for Disease Control (CDC) was of unknown etiology (Liston 1989). The reason for this is still unclear, but perhaps centralized production of food products and the use of refrigeration to hold fresh produce for long times could have contributed to the emergence of bacteria able to grow at low temperatures. According to Ryser and Marth (1989), within the past 15 years, several pathogenic bacteria have emerged, for example, *Listeria monocytogenes, Yersinia enterocolitica, Campylobacter jejuni, Vibrio cholerae,* and *Escherichia coli.* Of all these, *Campylobacter jejuni* is the most prevalent.

Campylobacter jejuni is recognized as one of the most common causes of gastroenteritis in humans. It is a pathogen of cattle, sheep, pigs, and poultry and is present in the flesh of these food animals. This pathogen is found in areas where raw meats and poultry are handled; sanitary handling techniques should be practiced in these areas. Raw milk also has been implicated in outbreaks of gastroenteritis caused by *Campylobacter.* Multiplication of the organism occurs in many different menu items including cake icings, eggs, poultry, and beef.

Sanitation Standards and Regulations

Governmental agencies at the federal, state, and local levels are responsible for the protection of the food supply available to the consumer. Key federal agencies involved in the wholesomeness and quality of food from producer to purchaser are the United States Public Health Service (PHS) and its subdivision, FDA, and the USDA. Thereafter, sanitation and service of food is controlled largely by state and local agencies and private organizations.

Role of Governmental Agencies

PHS. The PHS and its subdivision, FDA, both of which are agencies within the United States Department of Health and Human Services (HHS), are charged with promoting the health of every American and the safety of the nation's food supply. The CDC and FDA are related specifically to sanitation standards and regulation. CDC protects public health by providing leadership and direction in the control of diseases and other preventable hazards. It is responsible for providing assistance in identifying causes of disease outbreaks, including foodborne illnesses.

The mission of the FDA is to protect the nation's health against unsafe and impure foods other than meat, poultry, and fish; unsafe drugs and cosmetics; and other potential hazards. The National Marine Fisheries Service, under the Department of Commerce, offers a voluntary inspection program for fish and seafood. FDA, however, is responsible for inspection and sanitation of U.S. fish and seafood plants. FDA also is responsible for monitoring imports and interstate shipment of all food and for inspecting foodservice facilities on interstate carriers such as trains, airplanes, and ships. In addition, the FDA assists local agencies with their responsibility for inspecting foodservice establishments by developing model codes and ordinances and providing training and technical assistance.

Many state and local governments have adopted the PHS codes in establishing sanitation standards of performance for foodservice operations. Employees generally are required to have medical examinations to determine their qualifications to handle food safely and have a food handler's permit. Officials of state or local agencies make periodic inspections to compare performance of foodservice operations with standards of cleanliness and sanitation. Deficiencies must be corrected before the next inspection. The agency generally has the authority to close an operation that has many deficiencies.

The Environmental Protection Agency (EPA), another agency within HHS, also has responsibility in certain areas related to sanitation in foodservice establishments. EPA endeavors to comply with environmental legislation and control pollution. Of interest to the foodservice industry are programs on water standards, air quality, pesticides, noise abatement, and solid waste management.

USDA. USDA is authorized to make known and enforce food regulations by the Federal Meat Inspection Act, Poultry Product Inspection Act, Egg Products Inspection Act, and Agricultural Marketing Act. One of its most important functions, authorized by the Agricultural Marketing Act, is the grading, inspection, and certification of all agricultural products. The Food Safety and Inspection Service (FSIS) of the USDA is responsible for ensuring that meat and poultry products destined for interstate commerce and human consumption are wholesome, unadulterated, properly labeled, and do not pose any health hazards (National Restaurant Association 1989).

Controlling Microbiological Quality of Food

The goal of a sanitation program in a foodservice operation is to protect the customer from foodborne illness. Figure 1 shows possibilities for contamination of food before it is purchased including contaminated equipment, infected pests and animals, untreated sewage, unsafe water, and soil. After food is purchased, contamination can occur in storage, preparation, and service. Figure 2 shows possible transmission routes from infected persons through respiratory tract discharges, open sores, cuts, and boils, or through hands soiled with feces into food being prepared. The food is then eaten by other persons who become ill.

According to Ryser and Marth (1989), food handlers must take appropriate precautions to prevent cross-contamination between raw meat, poultry, seafood, and cooked foods or raw fruits and vegetables. According to the Educational Foundation of the National Restaurant Association (1985), contamination is the presence of harmful substances in food. Cross-contamination is the transfer of harmful microorganisms, such as *Salmonella,* from one food to another by means of contaminated equipment, utensils, or human hands. For example, chicken that is raw or not cooked to the proper temperature can contaminate a cutting board and knife. If the board and knife are not washed and sterilized, any food coming in contact with them also will be contaminated.

Time-Temperature Control   Contamination can be reduced by time-temperature control in the storage, production, and service of foods. Growth of harmful organisms can be slowed or prevented by refrigeration or freezing and organisms can be destroyed by sufficient heat. The minimum, maximum, and optimum temperatures vary for the various pathogenic microorganisms; in general, they flourish at temperatures between 40°F and 140°F as shown in Figure 3. This temperature range

Fig. 1. Transmission of a foodborne illness from an intermediate source to food and on to humans.
(*Source: The Educational Foundation of the National Restaurant Association, 1992, Applied Foodservice Sanitation, 4th ed. New York: John Wiley, p. 9.*)

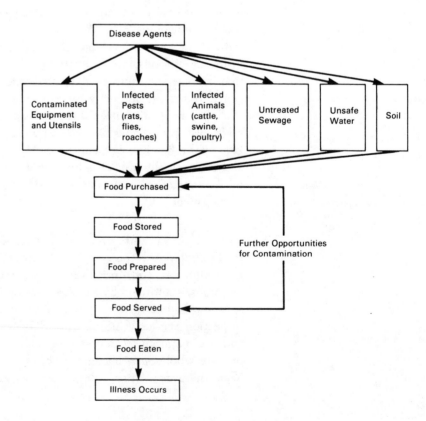

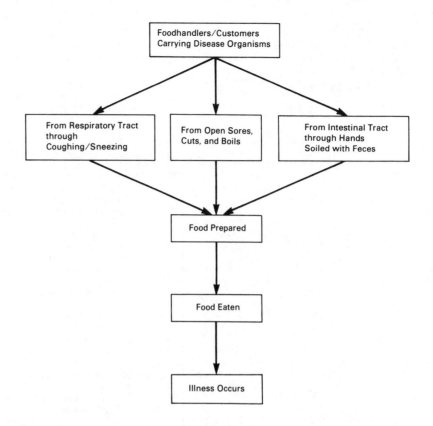

Fig. 2. Transmission of a foodborne illness from infected humans to food and back to other humans.
(Source: The Educational Foundation of the National Restaurant Association, 1985, Applied Foodservice Sanitation, 3d ed. New York: John Wiley, p. 17.)

is identified as the *food danger zone* because bacteria multiply rapidly within it. The longest period that food may safely remain in this zone is four hours, although food should not be in the 60°F to 100°F range longer than two hours. Safe temperatures, as applied to potentially hazardous food, are those of 40°F and below and 140°F and above. Both time and temperature are important in handling food to preserve microbiological quality.

Components of a Control System

Control of food safety must focus on the food itself; the people involved in handling food, either as employees or customers; and the facilities including both large and small equipment. The condition of food purchased must be considered as must be storage, production, and service. Employee hygiene and good food handling practices are basic to a sanitation program. Contamination from a customer is more difficult to control; a sneeze guard on a cafeteria service counter or salad bar helps. The design and construction of foodservice facilities and equipment will have an impact on the effectiveness of the sanitation program; moreover, maintenance of the facilities is also critical.

Critical Control Points

Bauman (1974) defined critical control points as those steps in production processing in which loss of control would result in unacceptable safety risk. Nine critical control points requiring monitoring for microbial quality and safety within foodservice operations have been identified (Unklesbay et al. 1977):

1. Food procurement
2. Food storage
3. Food packaging
4. Preprocessing
5. Heat processing
6. Food storage following heat processing

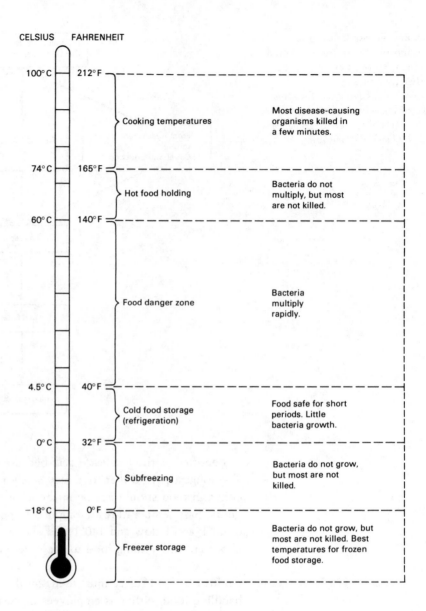

Fig. 3. Important temperatures in sanitation and food protection. *(Source: After Keeping food safe to eat, Home and Garden Bulletin No. 162, U.S. Department of Agriculture, 1970.)*

CELSIUS   FAHRENHEIT

Cooking temperatures — Most disease-causing organisms killed in a few minutes.

74°C   165°F — Hot food holding — Bacteria do not multiply, but most are not killed.

60°C   140°F

Food danger zone — Bacteria multiply rapidly.

4.5°C   40°F — Cold food storage (refrigeration) — Food safe for short periods. Little bacteria growth.

0°C   32°F — Subfreezing — Bacteria do not grow, but most are not killed.

−18°C   0°F — Freezer storage — Bacteria do not grow, but most are not killed. Best temperatures for frozen food storage.

7. Heat processing of precooked menu items
8. Food product distribution
9. Service of food

The type of delivery system used in a foodservice operation affects the number of areas requiring monitoring. In the majority of operations, food is prepared to serve immediately to the customer and monitoring through heat processing is all that is required. Chain operations, however, often have a commissary in which food items are prepared and then chilled or frozen for later distribution to individual restaurants. In these operations, all nine areas must be monitored.

Hazard Analysis Critical Control Point Models

The Hazard Analysis Critical Control Point (HACCP) concept refers to a system developed initially for quality control in the food processing industry, with special emphasis on microbial control. Critical control points are those steps in processing in which loss of control could result in a safety risk. HACCP is a preventive approach to quality control, identifying potential dangers for corrective action.

Snyder (1986) stated that in many ways a foodservice operation is a more complex food handling system than the large volume food production plant for which the HACCP model was designed. A menu often has from 100 to 150 food items and the normal production steps are numerous. In a food processing plant, a quality control laboratory for testing products before shipping is available. A foodservice operation does not have the trained personnel and laboratory equipment necessary for this type of program. Many operations, however, have established criteria for control of production and holding of highly hazardous products by monitoring time-temperature relationships, facility sanitation, and employee food handling techniques.

Protection of the Customer Infected meat, meat mixtures, and gravies invariably have been held at room temperature or refrigerated in large, deep pans for several hours. Leftover stews, gravies, and other meat mixtures should be put into small pots in an ice water bath and stirred often to bring the temperature down to 75°F or lower before refrigerating in small, shallow pans.

Overnight roasting of meat to avoid shrinkage also is hazardous and not recommended because low temperatures for many hours may contribute to the survival of toxins or bacteria such as *Salmonella, Clostridium perfringens,* and *Campylobacter jejuni,* especially in boned, rolled roasts. Chances for contamination of the boned, raw meat from hands, knives, and cutting surfaces are great. Careful reheating of leftover meat is recommended. The safest method for using leftover boned, rolled roasts is in stews and similar dishes for which a final temperature of at least 165°F is reached. Leftover roasts, which have not been boned, need to have the outside thoroughly heated to destroy toxins or bacteria. The bone-in roast, either whole or sliced, can be wrapped in foil and heated to 325°F in an oven. Slices of the roast also can be dipped in meat broth heated to 212°F.

Summary

Foodborne illness is a major health problem in the United States today. Food spoilage, denoting unfitness for human consumption, can be microbiological, biochemical, physical, and chemical. Microbiological spoilage is the most common and includes bacteria, molds and yeast, viruses, and others. Foodborne illnesses, commonly called "food poisoning," are caused by microbial pathogens that multiply in food and affect the gastrointestinal tract of humans.

Federal, state, and local governmental agencies are responsible for protecting the food supply available to consumers. Federal agencies involved in the wholesomeness and quality of food from producer to consumer are the U.S. Public Health Service and its subdivision, the Federal Drug Administration, and the U.S. Department of Agriculture.

The goal of a sanitation program in a foodservice operation is to protect the customer from foodborne illness. Time–temperature control in the storage, production, and service of foods is necessary. Food should never be left in the food danger zone, 40°F to 140°F, for more than 4 hours. Control of food safety depends on the food itself, the employees or customers handling food, and the facilities including both large and small equipment. Procurement, production, and service are critical control points in which loss of control could result in a safety risk. Two of the most critical risks are cross-contamination of food items and proper storage and reheating of leftovers.

Foodservice managers are becoming more aware of the importance of good sanitation practices and if a foodborne illness occurs, how to handle it.

Employee training in sanitation practices has been given top priority in many operations.

References

Bauman, H. E. 1974. The HACCP concept and microbiological hazard categories. *Food Technology* 28(9):30.

Educational Foundation of the National Restaurant Association. 1985. *Applied Foodservice Sanitation*, 3d ed. New York: Wiley.

Keeping food safe to eat. 1970. *Home and Garden Bulletin No. 162*. Washington, D.C.: U.S. Department of Agriculture.

Liston, J. 1989. Current issues in food safety—especially seafoods. *Journal of The American Dietetic Association* 89(7):911–913.

Longree, K., and G. Armbruster. 1987. *Quantity Food Sanitation*. New York: Wiley.

National Restaurant Association. 1989. A review of U.S. food grading and inspection programs. *Current Issues Report*. Washington, D.C.: National Restaurant Association.

Ryser, R. T., and E. H. Marth. 1989. "New" foodborne pathogens of public health significance. *Journal of The American Dietetic Association* 89(7):948–954.

Snyder, O. P. 1986. Applying the hazard analysis and critical control points system in foodservice and foodborne illness prevention. *Journal of Foodservice Systems* 4(2):125.

Spears, M. 1991. *Foodservice Organizations: A Managerial and Systems Approach*. New York: Macmillan.

Unklesbay, N. F., R. B. Maxcy, M. E. Knickrehm, K. E. Stevenson, M. L. Cremer, and M. E. Matthews. 1977. Foodservice Systems: product flow and microbial quality and safety of foods. *North Central Regional Research Bulletin No. 145*, pp. 21–25. Columbia, Mo.: Missouri Agricultural Experiment Station.

20

Hazard Analysis and Critical Control Point in Foodservice

O. P. Snyder, Jr.

What Is the Hazard Analysis and Critical Control Point (HACCP) Process?

HACCP is the systematic analysis of all process steps in a food production system from dealing with the contaminated ingredients from suppliers to consumption of food by the consumer, in order to acquire a detailed understanding of the hazards associated with each step. The analysis is then applied to the production steps to establish critical controls and eliminate hazardous conditions and procedures. Thus, operators can control food product quality and ensure its safety when it is consumed. The common microbiological, chemical, and hard-foreign-object contamination in food products can be kept at a safe level or eliminated when HACCP is applied. When HACCP is used by food production establishments, owner/managers can verify the self-control processes used to provide safe food products of specified quality. The foodservice industry's vital purpose for implementing HACCP-based precontrol programs is not only to comply with government regulations, but to prevent customer litigation and the disaster of public notoriety in case of a foodborne illness incident or outbreak.

Foodservice owners and managers are responsible for controlling the safety of all food items produced for consumption. All employees, from upper management to lowest level workers, must have a knowledge and understanding of the causes of foodborne illnesses in order to assess hazards and control the safety of food they prepare and serve.

Any food production process is never absolutely safe and there must always be a continual effort to reach the zero defect (absolute safety) goal. HACCP must include evolutionary improvement that continually addresses weaknesses in the process and reduces the chance of failure of the safety control system at each process step (critical control point).

History of HACCP and Application to Food Production

A hazard analysis procedure called HAZOPS (Hazard and Operability Study) was begun many years ago by the chemical processing industry. It includes the concept of failure mode analysis to determine how a hazard can cause a problem. Many points in a chemical process, just as in food processing, food preparation, and food distribution, rely on precise temperatures and times as well as functioning equipment and trained, alert personnel. If equipment is not maintained and functional, and if performance is not precise, a poor quality product is produced, or worse, a hazard is created. For example, in Bhopal, India in December 1984, 2,500 people were killed and perhaps 10 times that number were injured when a leak in a storage tank allowed the escape of deadly methyl isocyanate vapor. The most significant cause of the Bhopal disaster was the failure of personnel to monitor and maintain the safety equipment and instrumentation that would have detected the leak and prevented the tragic incident (Kletz 1985).

During the early 1960s the principle of hazard control was applied by the National Aeronautics and Space Administration (NASA) to ensure the safety of rockets designed to take astronauts to the moon. Another important component of space exploration was a supply of safe, nutritious food. Producers of this food were asked to use HACCP logic to formulate and produce space food that would not cause astronaut illness (Bourland et al. 1981).

A more general application of HACCP to food production began in the 1970s.

1971	April	National conference on HACCP.
	July	A person died after consuming underprocessed potato soup produced by Bon Vivant.
	August	The Campbell Soup Company underprocessed some chicken noodle soup. No one became ill.
	October	The president of Pillsbury implemented HACCP.
1972	September	Pillsbury conducted a FDA HACCP workshop. Critical control points were defined as
		Raw materials
		Processes
		Environment
		Personnel
		Finished product
		Distribution

As a result of the Bon Vivant soup incident and a few other commercial canning underprocessing episodes in the early 1970s, the FDA mandated that the commercial canning industry use HACCP in order to ensure an adequate retort process and commercial sterilization of canned food products. The government, working with the canning industry, completed a hazard analysis of commercial canning operations and then developed critical control points and procedures that ensure that all cans of food are given an adequate thermal process (Code of Federal Regulations [CFR 21], 1991). The canning industry requires a training and certification program for retort operators that is verified by government regulatory agencies (Food Processors Institute 1988).

Since then other food producing establishments both small and large and the government have recognized that implementation and maintenance of a HACCP system in food production facilities permits a fair degree of certainty that foodborne illness and diseases will be prevented.

The Need for HACCP: Foodborne Illness Outbreaks

Foodborne illness continues to be a major public health problem, as indicated by reports made to the Centers for Disease Control (CDC) in Atlanta, Georgia, the national agency responsible for disease surveillance. Foodborne illness incidents or outbreaks occur when there is lack of foodservice management concern and training, lack of employee training, lack of applied food safety knowledge, and lack of product procedural controls (for example, incorrect cooling times and inadequate holding temperatures for food items).

Table 1 is a tabulation of recorded, confirmed cases of food and water-borne illnesses in the United States. From these data it was calculated that an average of 11,514 cases of confirmed foodborne illness occurred annually during these years. Not all cases of foodborne illness are diagnosed, confirmed, and reported. Usually, the only cases reported to the CDC are those involving large numbers of people and gross mishandling of food. Sometimes, there can be two to three generations of infection (for example, Norwalk virus) from one initially infected person.

Table 2 shows the number of estimated annual cases of foodborne illness in the United States. This table attempts to indicate the number of people who become ill and never have their illnesses confirmed because they do not seek medical attention. The person-to-person transmission of foodborne disease is usually not reported in confirmed cases of many foodborne illnesses but is included in estimates. Hence, estimated numbers include people who become ill directly as a result of pathogens transmitted through food and others to whom the organism is subsequently transmitted through some kind of person-to-person fecal-oral contact.

Based on follow-up surveys conducted by the CDC after various disease outbreaks, it has been concluded that the ratio of estimated cases to those initially reported for all foodborne diseases is between 10:1 to 100:1. Todd (1989) estimated the probable number of foodborne disease cases in the United States to be 12.6 million per year.

Costs of Foodborne Illness

Todd (1989) estimated the cost of foodborne illness in the United States to be $8.4 billion. These figures include patient-related medical costs and lost wages. Other indirect costs resulting from product recalls, lost business, legal fees, and legal settlements may equal or even double the patient-related costs.

Table 1. *Number of reported cases of foodborne and waterborne illnesses in the United States 1983–1988[a]*

Year	Foodborne	Waterborne
1983	7,904	21,036
1984	8,193	1,800
1985	22,987	1,946
1986	5,804	1,569
1987	9,652	22,149
1988	14,000	2,128

Source: Based on data from Bean et al. 1990.
[a]These data probably represent only 1–10% of the actual number of cases occurring in these outbreaks.

Table 2. *Estimated number of cases of foodborne illness occurring annually in the United States*

Pathogen	Cases	Deaths
Bacillus cereus	84,000	0
Yersinia enterocolitica	5,000–20,000	0
Staphylococcus aureus	1,155,000	5–8
Salmonella spp. (nontyphi)	3,000,000	3,000
Campylobacter jejuni	2,100,000	2,100
Shigella spp.	300,000	600
Escherichia coli (enteric)	200,000	400
Clostridium perfringens	650,000	6–7
Vibrio cholera	13,000	1–2
Vibrio (noncholera)	10–30,000	300–900
Clostridium botulinum	100–200	3–4
Salmonella typhi	500–600	15–30
Listeria monocytogenes	25,000	1,000
Hepatitis A Virus	48,000	150
Norwalk Virus	181,000	0
Trichinella spiralis	100,000	1,000
Toxoplasma gondii	2,300,000	450
Taenia	1,000	>450
Giardia	7,000	0
Fish parasites	1,000	0

Source: Based on data from Bennett et al. 1987 and Todd 1989.

In 1985, Todd reported the cost of seventeen foodborne outbreaks (incidents) that resulted from inadequate or unsanitary food processing in Canada and the United States. For the seventeen incidents studied, total costs ranged from $16,690 to $1,053,205 per incident, with a median value of $108,615. The average cost per case was $788.00. Indirect costs were included, such as the value of pain, grief, suffering and death, and the loss of a housekeeper's productivity and leisure time.

Both food processors and foodservice establishments incur tremendous expenses when mishandling a food or food product results in a foodborne illness outbreak, especially when followed by lawsuits. The economic impact of a foodborne illness outbreak is generally greater for restaurants, hotels, and institutions than for catering establishments (see Table 3).

HACCP Assumes That the World Is Always Contaminated

HACCP accepts the fact that the world and our food will always be contaminated. The contamination must be kept below the illness-causing threshold for the consumer. Is there really a nonhazardous food? The answer seems to be no, if one looks at all of the foods that have been implicated in causing foodborne illnesses, as shown in Figure 1.

Food safety rules are written with conservative standards. Usually foodborne illness outbreaks occur when there is a blatant disregard for these rules and food is grossly mishandled. If raw, supplier-uncertified food is not heated to adequate pasteurization temperatures for adequate periods of time, pathogens from the wholesale system can survive and cause illness when people consume the food. For example, when persons consume uncooked or partially heated food such as raw oysters, rare hamburgers, and lettuce that has not been washed in flowing water, they may be ingesting large numbers of pathogenic microorganisms. There are no government inspection processes to verify the safety of raw foods. Therefore, buyers must know that their suppliers certify safe levels of foodborne illness agents in food products that are intended to be served raw or rare.

Employees carry infections and are capable of passing on these infections, both fecally and orally, days before they feel ill. It is imperative that all employees involved in the production and service of food be educated about the importance of washing their fingertips as well as hand surfaces with soap and water every time after using the toilet to prevent fecal contamination of food. Pimples and infected cuts on hands have been responsible for some very serious foodborne illness incidents. Employees must not be permitted to work with food if they have infected cuts on their hands or any other serious skin infections until these infections have healed.

A major mishandling error that is responsible for many foodborne illness incidents is slow cooling of food. When food is cooled slowly to 40°F (4.4°C) in 12 hours or more, time and temperature are adequate for bacterial pathogen growth in the food. The FDA 1976 Food Service Sanitation Manual (FDA Division of Retail Food Protection 1976) requires that hot food must be cooled within 4 hours to 40°F (4.4°C) or less.

Chemicals in food are also causes of foodborne illnesses. Incidents result when employees fail to measure correct amounts of food chemicals such as monosodium glutamate, nitrates, and sulfur containing compounds; acid foods are stored or heated in containers that release toxic metals into the food (for example, containers containing copper or lead); employees inadvertently or intentionally add cleaning, sanitizing, or pesticide chemicals to food. Employees must be taught to use chemicals (for example, detergents, insecticides, food chemicals) correctly and safely.

Components of a HACCP Program

The following approach is adapted from the seven components of a HACCP Program as now defined by the Food Safety Inspection Service of the USDA (USDA-FSIS, 1990).

1. Assessment of the microbiological, chemical, and hard-foreign-object hazards associated with each step in the product flow, from growing and harvesting raw materials and ingredients through consumption of the item. Determination is made of the levels at which these contaminants are safe and levels at which they become hazardous.
2. Determination of the step(s) or point(s) within the process at which the hazards can be most reliably controlled.
3. Completion of a failure mode analysis at each critical control point

Table 3. *Costs of foodborne illness outbreaks associated with foodservice establishments*

Type of establishment	Number of incidents	Median total cost per case (in $)
Restaurants and hotels	6	1,630
Institutions[a]	6	1,312
Catering establishments	5	439

Source: Based on data from Todd 1985.
[a]Includes hospitals, schools, rest homes.

Fig. 1. Foods associated with foodborne illness incidents.

Meat Beef: roasts, steaks, stews, pies, liver, tongue, gravy, processed products. Pork: ham, bacon, roasts, chops, spareribs, barbecued and processed pork products. Veal, lamb, goat, hamburger and other ground meats; frankfurters and other sausages; luncheon meats; game meats.

Marine Foods Fish: salmon (home canned, processed, eggs), tuna, herring, mackerel, sardines, trout, sole, cod. Shellfish: clams and clam chowder, shrimp, crab, lobster, oysters, scallops, squid, mussels, escargots.

Poultry Chicken: fried, roasted, barbecued, pies, soup, processed products, gravy, prepared dishes. Turkey: roast, pie, loaf, dressing, stews, stuffing, soup, gravy. Cornish hen, duck, goose liver paté, roast goose.

Dairy Foods Pasteurized, raw, canned and evaporated milk, milk shakes, egg nog, cream sauce, artificial cream, mousse, cream, butter, yogurt, cheese, ice cream.

Bakery Foods Pizza, cakes, pastries, pies and tarts, puddings, pasta products, bread and muffins, doughnuts, pancakes and crepes, cereal, tacos, pretzels, cookies, biscuits and crackers.

Eggs Omelettes, scrambled eggs, hollandaise sauce, deviled eggs, fried eggs, hard-cooked eggs, prepared products with eggs.

Infant Foods Canned formulas, formula (container not specified), cereal products, beef products in jars, fruit, vegetables.

Confectionery Chocolate candy, ''pop rocks,'' candy bars, licorice and jujubes, molasses and honey, chewing and bubble gum.

Vegetables and Fruits Canned and bottled low acid products, canned and bottled acid products, potatoes, mushrooms, wild mushrooms, soup, corn and corn products, beans, vegetable oil, greens (lettuce, broccoli, etc.), molasses, maple and corn syrup, canned tomato juice, other canned and bottled fruit juices, other fruit juices, bottled acid fruits, nuts and nut products, jams and marmalades, dried and preserved fruit.

Salad Potato, cole slaw, vegetable salads, chicken, seafood, ham, egg, fish, meat, macaroni, multiple ingredients.

Sandwiches Beef, ham or ham salad, luncheon meats, turkey or chicken, tuna or tuna salad, other fish or shrimp, cheeseburger, sandwich spreads, egg or egg salad, cream cheese, submarine sandwiches, other multiple ingredient sandwiches.

Beverages Bottled soft drinks, canned soft drinks, beer, cider, coffee, tea, spirits, wine, flavoring crystals.

Miscellaneous Margarine, fats and oils, chili sauce, sloppy joes, gravy, soups, seasoning mix, cider vinegar, fish and chips, macaroni and cheese, custard, other multiple foods, popsicles and slush, spaghetti and meatballs, Mexican food, snails and escargots, tube feeding formulas, dressings and dips, sauces and relishes.

in order to determine all variables in the process and how they might change, thus causing a hazard to develop. Prevention measures must be established in the form of control policies, procedures, and standards whereby hazards can be kept out of the food, hazards can be kept below a nonrisk level, and hazards can be reduced to a nonrisk level by some form of processing.

4. Establishment of procedures for employees to follow and use to monitor each process variable at each critical control point, thus ensuring that the process will continually meet safety control standards.

5. Establishment of corrective action(s) to be used by employees if there is a critical deviation beyond the set standards for a variable at each critical control point. Employees must be trained and

performance-certified to recognize and to control these critical variables.

6. Establishment of an effective record-keeping system (statistical process control) that documents the performance of the process and the HACCP program. This record-keeping system is the basis for the systematic improvement of the process by management over a period of time.

7. Establishment of procedures to verify that the HACCP process is working according to plan. This verification can be made by auditors or other designated personnel with the use of microbiological, physical, chemical, and sensory tests. When these procedures are used, government inspectors can review the records for compliance with operating policies, procedures, and standards to ensure that the process is stable and controlled.

Note that when a process is controlled under a correct HACCP program, the output has so few defects that it becomes statistically impossible to determine safety by sampling the output for hazardous contamination. The only way to have confidence that the output is safe is to verify that the personnel producing the food control the process at each step.

Degree of Hazard

The degree or seriousness of a hazard is dependent on the clientele or target population of consumers. There are two categories of clientele: (1) Normal, healthy people with strong immune systems due to exposure to pathogens when they were young and who maintain a good nutritional diet and (2) People at risk (those with an immunosuppressed system), which include babies, elderly people, people with allergies, people in a weakened physical state (malnourished), people with controlled illnesses (for instance, diabetes, high blood pressure), pregnant women, and hospital patients with a weakened system (that is, transplant patients).

Human Susceptibility and Resistance to Foodborne Illness Agents

Not all people who consume food known to cause illness become ill. Some individuals can become resistant to certain numbers of pathogenic bacteria in foods. This resistance is unpredictable. It is dependent on the degree of stomach acidity, which varies in individuals. The greater the degree of stomach acidity, the greater the probability of inactivating bacteria before they reach the intestinal tract. Competitive microorganisms exist within the intestinal tract and are a part of the "gut microflora," which actually aid in the digestion and assimilation of food. Some of these microorganisms also suppress the growth of pathogenic bacteria. When individuals are given certain antibiotics, the microflora of the gut is changed and these individuals can then become more susceptible to bacterial foodborne pathogens.

Individuals who have been previously exposed to certain bacterial and viral pathogens and have become ill as a result may develop an immunity and do not become ill again when exposed to these pathogens. Infants and young children have not yet developed this immunity and are more susceptible to low levels of pathogens in food.

Hence, the very young, the elderly, immune-compromised individuals, and those who have recently completed taking antibiotics are extremely susceptible to bacterial foodborne illness. As few as one *Salmonella typhi* per 25 grams of food can make a susceptible person ill. In persons who are debilitated by advanced age, underlying health problems, or alcoholism, the presence of enteric foodborne pathogens can be life threatening. The current FDA guidance (FDA/CDC 1989) is that these people must eat defensively. For example, they should eat only well-cooked food and must not eat food from salad bars and delicatessens.

Levels of Pathogens Necessary to Make Healthy People Ill

Some healthy persons can ingest as many as 100,000 viable cells of certain types of *Salmonella* per gram in a meal before becoming ill. Table 4 identifies some of the numbers or limits of pathogens and chemicals that cause illness in both healthy people and people at risk. Note in this table, the vegetative pathogen *Campylobacter jejuni*. In one case 500 microorganisms in a glass of milk of 180 milliliters made people ill. This is approximately 3 pathogens per milliliter. Since raw chicken can have upwards of 10,000 *C. jejuni* per gram, and because the public consumes large quantities of chicken, *C. jejuni* represents a serious cross-contamination hazard in a food production area that could have widespread effect. It is a much greater threat than *Salmonella* spp., which takes at least 10,000 or more microorganisms to cause illness.

On the other hand, the standard for removing feces from fingertips is based on *Shigella* spp. and human fecal pathogens. As few as 10 *Shigella dysenteriae* in a salad can make healthy people ill. Since feces will have approximately 10^9 per gram of this organism when excreted from the body, a tiny slip of the toilet paper can cause 10^7 (0.01 gram) to get under the fingernails. This is why it is critical to emphasize fingertip washing as the critical control procedure and to require a fingernail brush and a double hand wash.

Assessment of Hazards

Most raw food today is produced and sold by growers and processors who do not use HACCP. Consequently, the retail food industry and people preparing food at foodservice sites as well as in homes are the critical points for ensuring the safety of food products they prepare and serve. A number of different kinds of hazards must be controlled, as shown in Figure 2.

Microbiological hazards occur when the level of pathogens (disease- and illness-causing bacteria, molds, viruses, and parasites) in food approaches or exceeds the illness-causing level. At critical levels microorganisms cause illness (1) when living cells are ingested in sufficient numbers and survive within the body to cause illness and disease, or (2) when food containing toxins produced by the growth of a sufficiently large number of pathogens in the food is ingested.

Raw foods contain high levels of microorganisms (1,000 to greater than 10,000,000 per gram), most of which are not pathogenic. Nonpathogenic microorganisms, such as lactic acid bacteria in milk, cause foods to spoil (that is, deteriorate in flavor, texture, and odor). These nonpathogenic microorganisms also competitively inhibit the growth of pathogenic bacteria. When food is prepared or processed and stored, the goal is to inhibit or inactivate spoilage microorganisms in order to preserve food quality as long as possible, and at the same time to ensure the safety of the product by inactivating pathogens.

Bacteria that contaminate food can exist in two forms: vegetative cells and spores. Animal as well as human fecal material is the usual source of pathogenic bacteria. Pathogenic vegetative cells multiply over a temperature range of 32°F to 127.5°F (0°C to 48°C). These bacteria can multiply in most foods, in lettuce as well as in beef stew, and in water. The vegetative cells are

Fig. 2. Illness hazards and regulatory requirements in the food environment.

Microorganisms and Toxins

Bacteria: vegetative cells and spores
Molds
Viruses
Parasites

Toxic Substances

Intentional food additives (GRAS, generally recognized as safe)
Chemicals created by the process
Agricultural: pesticides, insecticides
Antibiotic and other drug residues in meat, poultry, and dairy
   products
Accidental addition during food handling
Equipment material leaching
Packaging material leaching
Industrial: from the environment

Adverse Food Reactions

Food allergies
Food intolerances
Food toxins
Metabolic disorders
Pharmacologial food reactions
Food idiosyncrasy
Food sensitivity

Nutrition

Overnutrition
Undernutrition
Antinutritional factors

Hard Foreign Objects

Objects large and hard enough to cause injury and choking

Fraud (Regulatory Requirements)

Filths
Misrepresentation
Inaccurate labeling

---

inactivated by ordinary heating and cooking (for example, 150°F for 1.2 minutes). Spore forms of some pathogenic bacteria (for example, *Clostridium botulinum*, *Bacillus cereus* and *C. perfringens*) are very heat resistant and can survive ordinary cooking procedures. Therefore, food must be maintained above 130°F or cooled to 40°F in less than 4 hours after cooking to prevent spore outgrowth within the food.

Molds are natural in the environment and are common indicators of spoilage in most food. Some molds produce toxic compounds (for example, aflatoxins) in food. These mold toxins are hazards and are difficult if not impossible to remove. Molds are ubiquitous. The best control of molds is to keep food surfaces moderately dry, below a humidity of 60 percent.

Viruses causing foodborne illness hazards normally come from the feces of people in the wholesale food system or from workers in retail food operations who do not wash their fingertips and under their fingernails. Viruses are hazardous at very low levels, for example as few as 10 per portion of food. To prevent transmission of viruses, the use of good fingertip washing methods by food workers is imperative.

Parasites include amoebas (*Giardia lamblia*) and worms (*Toxoplasma gondii*

Table 4. *Foodborne illness hazards: threshold and quality levels*

Agent	Estimated illness dose in healthy person (number of microorganisms)	HITM[a] suggested purchaser raw food quality standards (number of microorganisms)
Bacteria		
Bacillus cereus	3.4×10^4 to 9.5×10^8/g[4]	$< 10^2$/g
Campylobacter jejuni	5×10^2 in 180 ml milk [17]	< 1/g
Clostridium botulinum	3×10^3[10][b]	< 1/g[c]
Clostridium perfringens	10^6 to 10^7/g[5]	$< 10^2$/g
Escherichia coli	10^6 to $> 10^7$ (dose)[2]	
Salmonella spp.		
S. anatum	10^5 to $> 10^8$ (dose)[11][d]	< 10/g
S. bareilly	10^5 to $> 10^6$ (dose)[12][d]	< 10/g
S. derby	10^7 (dose)[12][d]	< 10/g
S. meleagridus	10^7 (dose)[11][d]	< 10/g
S. newport	10^5 (dose)[12][d]	< 10/g
S. pullorum	10^9 to $> 10^{10}$ (dose)[13][d]	< 10/g
S. typhi	10^4 to $> 10^8$ (dose)[7][d]	
Shigella spp.		
S. flexneri	10^2 to $> 10^9$ (dose)[1, 3, 18]	< 1/g
S. dysenteriae	10 to $> 10^4$ (dose)[9]	< 1/g
Staphylococcus aureus	10^5 to $> 10^6$/g [6,16][e]	$< 10^2$/g
Vibrio cholerae	10^3 (dose)[8]	< 1/g
Vibrio parahaemolyticus	10^6 to 10^9 (dose)[20]	< 10/g
Yersinia enterocolitica	3.9×10^7 (dose)[15][f]	$< 10^2$/g
Viruses		
Hepatitis A virus	?	< 1/g
Norwalk virus	?	< 1/g
Chemicals	(Amount in Food)	(Amount in Food)
Monosodium glutamate	0.5% (dose)[19]	$< 0.05\%$
Sodium nitrate	8–15 grams[14]	< 500 ppm
Sodium nitrite	?	< 200 ppm
Sulfites	> 0.7 mg/kg body weight/day[21]	< 10 ppm
Hard Foreign Objects	Unknown	

[a]HITM = Hospitality Institute of Technology and Management, St. Paul, Minnesota.
[b]Indicates the number of bacteria necessary to produce sufficient toxin for mouse LD_{50}.
[c]If a product is to be considered shelf-stable above 50°F, then it should be heat processed to reduce a spore population of *Clostridium botulinum* types A and B by 10^{12}, or have a water activity (a_w) < 0.86, or the pH of the product should be 4.1 or less, or a combination of processes should be used to control the growth of *Clostridium botulinum* types A and B and *Salmonella* spp.
[d]Results from feeding studies. Data from outbreaks indicate lower values.
[e]Indicates number of pathogenic bacteria necessary to produce sufficient amount of illness producing toxin.
[f]Probably lower.

1. DuPont, H. L., R. B. Hornick, A. T. Dawkins, M. J. Snyder, and S. B. Formal. 1969. The response of man to virulent *Shigella flexneri* 2a. *J. Infect. Dis.* 119:296–299.
2. DuPont, H. L., S. B. Formal, R. B. Hornick, M. J. Snyder, J. P. Libonati, D. G. Sheahan, E. H. LaBrec, and J. P. Kalas. 1971. Pathogenesis of *Escherichia coli* diarrhea. *N. Engl. J. Med.* 285:1–9.
3. DuPont, H. L., R. B. Hornick, M. J. Snyder, J. P. Libonati, S. B. Formal, and E. J. Ganarosa. 1972. Immunity in shigellosis. II. Protection induced by oral live vaccine or primary infection. *J. Infect. Dis.* 125:12–16.
4. Goepfert, J. M., W. M. Spira, and H. U. Kim. 1972. *Bacillus cereus:* Food poisoning organism. A review. *J. Milk Food Technol.* 35:213–227.
5. Hauschild, A. H. W. 1973. Food poisoning by *Clostridium perfringens.* Can. Inst. Food Sci. Technol. J. 6(2):106–110.

(continued)

6. Hobbs, B. C. 1960. Staphylococcal and *Clostridium welchi* food poisoning. *Roy. Soc. Health J.* 80:267–271.

7. Hornick, R. B., S. E., Greisman, T. E. Woodward, H. L. DuPont, A. T. Dawkins, and M. J. Snyder. 1970. Typhoid fever: Pathogenesis and immunologic control. *New Engl. J. Med.* 283:686–691.

8. Hornick, R. B., S. I. Music, R. Wenzel, R. Cash, J. P. Libonati, M. J. Snyder, and T. E. Woodward. 1971. The broad street pump revisited: Response of volunteer to ingested cholera vibrios. *Bull. N. Y. Acad. Med* (2)47:1181.

9. Levine, M. M., H. L. Dupont, S. B. Formal, R. B. Hornick, A. Takeuchi, E. J. Gangarosa, M. J. Snyder, and J. P. Libonati. 1973. Pathogenesis of *Shigella dysenteriae* I (Shiga) dysentery. *J. Infect. Dis.* 127:261–270.

10. Lubin, L. B., R. D. Morton, and D. T. Bernard. Toxin production in hard-cooked eggs experimentally inoculated with *Clostridium botulinum. J. Food Sci.* 50:969–970, 984.

11. McCullough, M. B., and C. W. Eisele. 1951. Experimental human salmonellosis. I. Pathogenicity of strains of *Salmonella meleagridis* and *Salmonella anatum* obtained from spray-dried whole egg. *J. Infect. Dis.* 88:278–279.

12. McCullough, M. B., and C. W. Eisele. 1951. Experimental human salmonellosis. III. Pathogenicity of strains of *Salmonella newport, Salmonella derby,* and *Salmonella bareilly* obtained from spray-dried whole egg. *J. Infect. Dis.* 89:209–213.

13. McCullough, M. B., and C. W. Eisele. 1951. Experimental human salmonellosis. IV. Pathogenicity of strains of *Salmonella pullorum* obtained from spray-dried whole egg. *J. Infect. Dis.* 89:259–265.

14. Magee, P. N. 1983. Nitrate. In *Environmental Aspects of Cancer. The Role of Macro and Micro Components of Foods.* Wynder, E. L., G. A. Leveille, J. H. Weisburger, and G. E. Livingston, eds., pp. 198–210. Westport, Conn.: Food and Nutrition Press.

15. Moustafa, M. K., A. A-H. Ahmed, and E. H. Marth. 1983. Behavior of virulent *Yersinia enterocolitica* during manufacture and storage of colby-like cheese. *J. Food Protect.* 46:318–320.

16. Newsome, R. L. 1988. *Staphylococcus aureus. Food Technol.* 42(4):194–195.

17. Robinson, D. A. 1981. Infective dose of *Campylobacter jejuni* in milk. *Brit. Med. J.* 282:1584.

18. Shaughnessy, H. J., R. C. Olsson, K. Bass, F. Friewer, and S. O. Levinson. 1946. Experimental human bacillary dysentery. *J. Am. Med. Assoc.* 132:362–368.

19. Snyder, O. P. 1985. Personal communication.

20. Stern, N. J. 1982. Foodborne pathogens of lesser notoriety: Viruses, *Vibrio, Yersinia,* and *Campylobacter.* In ABMPS Report No. 125, pp. 57–63. Washington, D.C.: National Academy of Science Press.

21. Taylor, S. L., and R. K. Bush. 1986. Sulfites as food ingredients. *Food Technol.* 40(6):47–52.

and *Trichinella spiralis*), their cysts and larvae. They are often found in animals and fish. Parasites may also be present on fruits and vegetables if these products have been fertilized with organic fertilizers. They can be added to foods by workers who do not wash fecal material from their fingertips and fingernails. The presence of parasites in food can be quite hazardous at very low levels, as few as 10 per portion of food. The critical controls are: washing all fruits and vegetables in cold water; proper hand and fingertip washing; correct cooking of meat (at least 140°F for 5.1 minutes).

Toxic substances include

- Overuse of approved food additives such as nitrites, MSG, sulfites, and Yellow #5
- Chemicals created by the process such as carcinogenic compounds formed on grilled foods
- Accidental addition of cleaning or sanitizing chemicals to food
- Equipment material leaching into food or beverages (such as copper from water pipes combining with CO_2 that has leaked from a carbonated beverage machine back into the copper water lines
- Package material leaching into food (for example, susceptors in microwave browning)
- Residues from agricultural chemicals, of which there are thousands

- From the environment (for instance, methyl-mercury in shark meat, PCBs (polychlorinated biphenyls) in fresh fish, and solanine in green potatoes)

Chemicals must be carefully controlled. Concentrated chemicals in food processing plants and food production areas can cause serious safety and food-borne illness problems when not used properly. Chemical supplies must be kept in separate locked storage units or areas (that is, separated from food). Only chemicals that have been diluted to nontoxic levels should be allowed in food production areas. Employees must be informed about each hazardous chemical used in the facility and must be trained to correctly measure and use all chemicals in the process area.

Adverse food reactions are serious concerns for sensitized individuals and hence, become concerns for food production units. A low percentage of the population has food allergies, food intolerances, metabolic food reactions, and food sensitivities. Ingestion of the offending food, even in a small amount, may be life threatening to this sensitized portion of the population. These individuals are usually aware that they are sensitive to certain ingredients or foods such as seafood, milk, eggs, and nuts, and know that they must avoid foods with these ingredients. Customers must be given accurate ingredient information for any food or menu item if they request it.

Nutrition is not currently considered a hazard. However, when one considers long-term birth-to-death hazard analysis, it is critical that we eat correctly. Far more illnesses and deaths are due to incorrect nutrition, which is a hazard, than any of the hazards listed above. This includes both overnutrition and undernutrition. Food is consumed to maintain and nourish the body. Nutrients can be preserved by not overcooking food and by avoiding holding the food for more than 30 minutes on a steam table or in a hot box.

Hard foreign objects are, as the description implies, pieces or particles of material(s) that should not be present in food when it is consumed. The presence of hard foreign objects in food is not only a hazard, it is also an indication of defective quality. Examples of hard foreign objects in food include pieces of glass, metal or plastic; whole spices or herbs such as bay leaves and whole peppercorns; and buttons or stones from jewelry settings. If consumers find these hazardous items in food and are injured by their presence, foodservice units and food production facilities are liable for any sustained injuries. The only controls for this hazard are employee training and awareness.

Fraud is a major concern for the FDA and the USDA. There are thousands of government recalls of wholesale food each year because of mis-branding of items including fish, canned goods, and so forth. Control is dependent on the honesty of the owner of the packaging operation.

Potential Pathogens in Food

In order to develop an overall strategy to control pathogenic microorganisms in food production units, pathogens can be categorized into two groups:

1. Vegetative pathogens that are assumed to be on the food coming into the process, unless otherwise certified by the supplier. They must be reduced to a sufficiently low level so that they will not multiply to hazardous levels during storage and distribution.
2. Pathogens that produce spores or toxins.

Table 5 lists important pathogens in foods. Infective pathogens are inactivated by pasteurization and most cooking methods. Uncooked fruits and

Table 5. *Important pathogens in food*

Food	Pathogens		
	Infective (inactivated by pasteurization)		Toxin and/or spore producers (not inactivated by pasteurization)
Meat, poultry, and eggs	*Salmonella* spp. *Campylobacter jejuni* *Escherichia coli* *Y. enterocolitica*	*L. monocytogenes* Foot and Mouth virus Hepatitis A virus *Trichinella spiralis* Tapeworms	*S. aureus* (toxin) *C. perfringens* *C. botulinum* *Bacillus cereus*
Fin fish	*Salmonella* spp. *Vibrio* spp. *Y. enterocolitica*	Hepatitis A virus *Anisakis* Tapeworms	*S. aureus* (toxin) *C. botulinum* Microbial by-products (Histamine poisoning)
Shellfish	*Salmonella* spp. *Vibrio* spp. *Shigella* spp. *Y. enterocolitica*	Hepatitis A virus Norwalk virus	*S. aureus* (toxin) *C. botulinum* Microbial by-products (Paralytic shellfish poisoning)
Vegetables	*Salmonella* spp. *L. monocytogenes* *Shigella* spp.	Hepatitis A virus Norwalk virus *Giardia lamblia*	*S. aureus* (toxin) *C. botulinum* *Bacillus cereus*
Cereals, grains, legumes, and nuts	*Salmonella* spp. Aflatoxins (mold) Hepatitis A virus Norwalk virus		*S. aureus* (toxin) *C. botulinum* *Bacillus cereus*
Spices	*Salmonella* spp.		*S. aureus* (toxin) *C. botulinum* *Bacillus cereus* *C. perfringens*
Milk and dairy products	*Salmonella* spp. *Y. enterocolitica* *L. monocytogenes* *E. coli*	*C. jejuni* *Shigella* spp. Hepatitis A virus Norwalk virus	*S. aureus* (toxin) *C. perfringens* *Bacillus cereus*

vegetables included in food items must be double washed in order to prevent foodborne illness in people who consume these items. The spore-forming pathogens (*C. botulinum*, *C. perfringens*, and *Bacillus cereus*) in their heat-resistant spore forms, and toxins produced by *Staphylococcus aureus*, *Bacillus cereus*, and *C. botulinum* are not normally inactivated at times and temperatures achieved when foods are pasteurized or cooked. The growth of toxin and/or spore producers must be controlled by other methods: pH (increasing the acidity of products to below 4.6); decreasing the water activity (a_w) to less than 0.86; or by maintaining the temperature of products above 130°F (54.4°C) or below 38°F (3.3°C).

D and Z Values   Although there are thousands of pathogens, only approximately 20 are responsible for most problems. Table 5 shows common microbiological toxin and biological poison contaminants of food. Each of these contaminants has a characteristic inactivation curve. The inactivation term is *D value* (length of time it will take to destroy 1 log cycle of a pathogen at a given temperature). This is the time it takes, at a specific temperature, to reduce the population of a microorganism or the strength of a toxin by a factor of 10. The *Z value* is the increase or decrease in temperature that will increase/decrease the inactivation by a factor of 10.

For most FDA and USDA pasteurization requirements (except milk, eggs, and pork), only pasteurization temperature, and not time, has been specified. The reason that no time was specified was simplicity. The temperatures are so high, that time is essentially instant for inactivation. Specified food standards for the USDA and FDA are given in Table 6. In commercial food processes whereby one product is handled at a time, the time and temperature can be uniquely specified for the product. Research to determine these times and temperatures can cost thousands of dollars for one item and is not practical in retail food operations.

Assume That All Raw Food Is Contaminated

In retail food operations, one wants to find the unique pathogens among the many that, when controlled, will assure control of all pathogens. This approach follows the basic assumption that unless raw ingredients are certified by suppliers as being safe to eat without processing, they are potentially hazardous. This means that if meat, fish, poultry, vegetables, and such are eaten raw without washing, a normally healthy person would be at risk from infective pathogens. In the case of spores, their numbers must be below a threshold that will cause a problem because they cannot be inactivated by normal food preparation procedures. Spores cannot be allowed to multiply to hazardous levels. In the case of toxins and biological poisons, which cause only a small number of illnesses and deaths each year, one must be able to rely on suppliers and the government for safety assurance.

Table 6. *USDA and FDA food temperature standards*

Item	USDA	FDA
Baked meatloaf	160°F 9CFR 317.8	None specified
Baked pork cut	170°F 9CFR 317.8	150°F FSSM 2-403
Pork (to destroy trichinae)	120°F to 144°F 9CFR 318.10	150°F FSSM 2-403
Cooked poultry rolls and other uncured poultry products	160°F 9CFR 381.150	165°F FSSM 2-403
Cooked duck, salted	155°F FSIS Policy Book	None specified
Jellied chicken loaf	160°F FSIS Policy Book	None specified
Partially cooked, comminuted products	151°F, 1 min 148°F, 2 min 146°F, 3 min 145°F, 4 min 144°F, 5 min FSIS Notice 92-85	None specified
All potentially hazardous food requiring cooking	None specified	140°F FSSM 2-403

Note: FSSM = *Food Service Sanitation Manual* (FDS Division of Retail Food Protection 1976).

Major Pathogen Control Data Summary

Low Temperature Control 32°F: Table 7 lists the major pathogenic organisms that must be considered in designing pasteurized food microbiological control processes. First, in terms of low temperature standards, two pathogens begin to multiply at 32°F: *Yersinia enterocolitica* and *Listeria monocytogenes*. Therefore, for raw foods to be safe, they must be held at temperatures below 32°F.

Table 7. *Food pathogen control data summary*

Microorganisms	Temperature range for growth	pH range and minimal a_w for growth	G = Growth or doubling time D = Death rate or 10:1 reduction time
Infective Microorganisms (inactivated by pasteurization)			
Yersinia enterocolitica	32°–111°F (0°–44°C)	4.6–9.0 pH	G (32°F [0°C]) = 2 days G (40°F [4.4°C]) = 13 hours D (145°F [62.8°C]) = 0.24–0.96 min
Listeria monocytogenes	32°–112°F (0°–44°C)	4.5–9.5 pH	G (32°F [0°C]) = 5 days G (40°F [4.4°C]) = 1 day D (140°F [60°C]) = 2.85 min
Vibrio parahaemolyticus	41°–109.4°F (5°–43°C)	4.5–11.0 pH 0.937 a_w	D (116°F [47°C]) = 0.8–48 min
Salmonella spp.	41.5°–114°F (5.5°–45.6°C)	4.1–9.0 pH 0.95 a_w	D (140°F [60°C]) = 1.7 min
Campylobacter jejuni	90°–113°F (30°–45°C)	4.9–8.0 pH	D (137°F [58.3°C]) = 12–21 sec
Toxin Producers and/or Spore-formers (not inactivated by pasteurization)			
Clostridium botulinum, Type E and other nonproteolytic strains	38°–113°F (3.3°–45°C)	5.0–9.0 pH 0.97 a_w	Spores D (180°F [82.2°C]) = 0.49–0.74 min Toxin destruction D (185°F [85°C]) = 5 min for any botulinal toxin
Staphylococcus aureus Toxin production	43.8°–122°F (6.5°–50°C) 50°–114.8°F (10°–46°C)	4.5–9.3 pH 0.83 a_w 5.15–9.0 pH 0.86 a_w	Vegetative cells D (140°F [60°C]) = 5.2–7.8 min Toxin destruction D (210°F [98.9°C]) = > 2 hr
Bacillus cereus	39.2°–122°F (4.0°–50°C)	4.3–9.0 pH 0.912 a_w	Vegetative cells D (140°F [60°C]) = 1 min Spores D (212°F [100°C]) = 2.7–3.1 min Toxin destruction Diarrheal: D (133°F [56.1°C]) = 5 min Emetic: Stable at (249.8°F [121°C])
Clostridium botulinum, Type A and Proteolytic B strains	50°–118°F (10°–47.8°C)	4.6–9.0 pH 0.94 a_w	Spores D (250°F [121.1°C]) = 0.3– 0.23 min Toxin destruction D (185°F [85°C]) = 5 min for any botulinal toxin
Clostridium perfringens	59°–127.5°F (15°–52.3°C)	5.0–9.0 pH 0.95 a_w	Vegetative cells G (105.8°F [41°C]) = 7.2 min D (138°F [59°C] = 7.2 min Spores D (210°F [98.9°C]) = 26–31 min

Source: Based on data from Snyder 1992b.

Note that yeasts and molds begin to grow at 14°F, and spoilage microorganisms begin to multiply at 23°F. Meat, poultry, fish, and most entrées thaw at 28.5°F. Therefore, it is best for foods to be kept at as close to 29°F as possible to minimize spoilage.

Nonetheless, when food is thawing, food is spoiling. During typical 40°F refrigeration thawing of a 35-lb. can of pasteurized whole eggs, there can be a 1:256 (9 generations) multiplication of spoilage microorganisms. Hence, when possible, thawing should be done in a rapid thaw box at 40°F with an air velocity of more than 500 feet per minute, so that it thaws in 12 hours. Thawing also can be done in a dielectric or microwave oven. *L. monocytogenes*, because of its probably low infective dose and lethal consequences with immune-compromised people, is the "organism of choice" for establishing a low temperature threshold.

Salad Dressings: *Salmonella* spp. does not begin to multiply until 41.5°F. However, *Salmonella* spp. will multiply in foods that have a pH as low as 4.1. Hence, when any shelf-stable salad dressing or acidified product that is to be held above 41.5°F is made with raw eggs and *Salmonella* contamination is possible, it must have a pH below 4.1 in order to ensure the control and eventual destruction of *Salmonella* spp. (Smittle 1977). Characteristically, this standard is used in the manufacture of dressings in which there is no pasteurization step, in order to ensure that the pathogens found on the spices and in egg ingredients are inactivated or controlled.

Infective Microorganisms Pasteurization: While *L. monocytogenes* is more difficult to inactivate at 140°F, with a D value of 2.85 minutes, than *Salmonella* spp. with a D value of 1.7 minutes, the USDA has declared that pasteurization means a reduction of 10^7 *Salmonella* spp., and 10^4 *L. monocytogenes* per gram of product (USDA-FSIS, January 31, 1990). Since much more is known about *Salmonella* spp. than *L. monocytogenes*, *Salmonella* spp. is used as the pasteurization control standard. Using the USDA time-temperature inactivation standard for chunked and formed beef and solid roasts, which has been used for more than 20 years to produce millions of pounds of safe cooked deli roast beef, the 7D time-temperatures given in Table 8 are prescribed.

Toxin Producers and/or Spore Formers: Once food is pasteurized and all pathogens are reduced to below 1 per 25 grams (the standard test for *Salmonella* spp.), the only organisms to survive will be spores.

Non-Proteolytic *Clostridium botulinum*: Unless the temperature is raised to above 180°F for approximately 10 minutes, one must assume that *C. botulinum* type E and other nonproteolytic strains of *C. botulinum* ($D_{180°F} = .74$ minute) will survive. Since nonproteolytic *C. botulinum* begins to multiply at 38°F, pasteurized food should be stored below 38°F in order to ensure safety from the multiplication of nonproteolytic *C. botulinum*.

Bacillus cereus: A very common contaminant of food, *B. cereus* begins to multiply at 39.2°F and is not effectively destroyed until it reaches 212°F for over 30 minutes. Therefore, if pasteurized food is to be stored for a period of more than 5 days, it must be stored at a temperature below 38°F.

Staphylococcus aureus: While it does not produce a toxin until the temperature is 50°F, *S. aureus* begins to multiply at 43.8°F. Since it is often expedient to mix large volumes of salads with hands in order to avoid damaging sensitive products such as potatoes, salads can be mixed safely with hands if the salad ingredients are kept at less than 50°F in order to prevent *S. aureus* toxin pro-

Table 8. *Salmonella spp. 7D with Z = 10°F*

Temperature	D (min)	7D (min)
130°F	17.29	121.0
135°F	5.47	38.26
140°F	1.729	12.1
145°F	0.547	3.826
150°F	0.1729	1.21
155°F	0.0547	0.3826
160°F	0.01729	0.121

duction. Note that it is not the *S. aureus* vegetative cell that causes illness; 1,000 *S. aureus* per gram is not a threat to people. Illness occurs when the cells multiply to 1,000,000 per gram, thereby producing enough toxin to cause illness.

Proteolytic *Clostridium botulinum:* A common contaminant of vegetables and fruits, proteolytic *C. botulinum,* which survives pasteurization, begins to multiply at 50°F. Therefore, 50°F is a critical temperature for fruit and vegetable storage. It is common practice today to buy pre-prepared vacuum-packed vegetables. All vegetables, if they are packed anaerobically (for example, vacuum packed, gas packed) must be stored below 50°F in order to prevent the multiplication of proteolytic *C. botulinum.*

Clostridium perfringens: The upper temperature for microbiological hazard control is defined by *C. perfringens,* which multiplies up to a temperature of 127.5°F.

32°F to 127.5°F Hazardous: Temperatures between 32°F and 127.5°F are hazardous. Shelf-stable foods that have not been pasteurized to destroy *Salmonella* spp. must have a pH of less than 4.1 so that the *Salmonella* spp. is prevented from multiplication and eventually is destroyed with acid. *Campylobacter jejuni* is easy to destroy, as shown by the table, but because it exists at such high levels in food, it must be considered to be a major source of cross-contamination in the kitchen.

Food Contact Surfaces: *Campylobacter jejuni:* Washing procedures on food contact surfaces must be designed to reduce pathogens to a safe level. It is also a very hazardous procedure to wash poultry in a kitchen sink because *C. jejuni* is likely to be spread to any other food washed in the sink unless the sink is meticulously washed, rinsed, and sanitized after the chicken has been in it.

Optimal Bacterial Growth Time-Temperatures

It is impossible, in a typical foodservice kitchen, to keep all food below 32°F or above 127.5°F. Therefore, time must be factored into the storage of raw food and food preparation. Hundreds of growth data values have been compiled in order to determine approximate growth rates for the pathogenic organisms over the range of less than 32°F to 127.5°F (see Table 9). This table of optimum growth rates for some microorganisms in food does not include lag times. In the temperature range of 38°F to 40°F, lag time is often 36 to 40 hours. These optimal multiplication times will all be reduced if any suboptimal pH, a_w, or other barriers are introduced.

Control of Time between 32°F and 127.5°F

If multiplication cannot be stopped, then it must be determined how much growth is allowed. Five generations, or a multiplication factor of 1:32, are designated as being acceptable for practical purposes. A multiplication factor of 1:1,000, or 10 generations, is unacceptable because for both infective organisms and spores, normal contaminants could multiply to a high enough level to cause a serious foodborne illness.

Cold Holding: 40°F, 5 Days Control. Considering 40°F as being a normal operating refrigerator temperature, *L. monocytogenes,* the most lethal of the low-temperature vegetative cells, will multiply at this temperature about once every day. Therefore, raw food held at this temperature must be used within

Table 9. *Optimal bacterial growth time-temperatures*

Temper-ature (°F)	Spoilage bacteria (1 G)	*Yersina entero-colitica* (1 G)	*Listeria monocyt-ogenes* (1 G)	*Salmonella* spp. (1 G)	*Clostridium perfringens* (1 G)
28	40.0 h	NG	NG	NG	NG
32	24.0 h	2.0 d	5.0 d	NG	NG
35	16.7 h	24.0 h	2.0 d	NG	NG
40	10.0 h	13.0 h	1.0 d	66.7 h (41°F)	NG
50	4.6 h	5.8 h	9.2 h	13.3 h	NG
60	2.3 h	2.8 h	4.2 h	6.0 h	10.0 h
70	1.3 h	1.6 h	2.1 h	3.0 h	2.3 h
80	50.0 m	1.0 h	1.3 h	1.5 h	42.0 m
90	37.0 m	40.0 m	46.0 m	54.0 m	15.0 m
95	36.0 m	?	38.0 m	40.0 m	10.0 m
100	?	?	40.0 m	32.0 m	7.2 m
				26 m (104°F)	
110	?	?	?	?	7.2 m
115	NG	NG	NG	NG	7.3 m
120	NG	NG	NG	NG	10.0 m
124	NG	NG	NG	NG	30.0 m
127.5	NG	NG	NG	NG	NG

Source: Based on data from Snyder 1992b.
G = doubling time; d = days; h = hours; NG = no growth; ? = data not sufficient to determine growth rate; m = minutes.

5 days in order to prevent multiplication of this organism 1:32, assuming that the food contains less than 10 *L. monocytogenes* microorganisms per gram.

Display Food: 50°F to 60°F, 1 Day Control. At 50°F to 60°F, which is a typical temperature range for food displays (for example, salad bars), *L. monocytogenes* multiplies one generation in approximately 4 to 5 hours. Considering the 5-generation standard, if leftover salad bar food were discarded at the end of the day, there would be no problem with *L. monocytogenes* causing a foodborne illness. There would be a hazard, however, if leftover salad bar ingredients were added to fresh ingredients the following day. Hence, a critical hazard control rule is: *add no old food to fresh.* Old food is always used or discarded.

At 80°F, pathogen multiplication is approximately 1 generation per hour. Critical temperatures, then, are approximately between 80°F and 120°F. At 104°F, *Salmonella* spp. can multiply about once every 26 minutes. At 115°F, *C. perfringens* multiples once every 7.3 minutes.

Food Heating: 40°F to 130°F within 6 Hours. Based on growth studies with *C. perfringens* (Shigahisa *et al.* 1985), I have determined that food will be safe if it is heated from 40°F to 130°F in less than 6 hours, because *C. perfringens* will not be able to multiply.

Food Cooling: 130°F to 40°F within 11 Hours. Remember, the USDA standard for cooling chunked and formed and solid roast beef from 120°F to 55°F has been 6 hours. This has been shown to be a safe cooling standard as graphically extrapolated from 130°F to 40°F, which results in a time of 11 hours.

Data from Shigahisa *et al.* (1985) show that if food is cooled from 130°F to 40°F in less than 11 hours, *C. perfringens* growth will be prevented, and the food will be safe to consume.

The FDA 4-hour cooling standard established in the 1976 model Food Service Sanitation Manual is not based on correct scientific reasoning. The FDA used three studies (Longree and White 1955; McDivitt and Hammer 1958; Miller and Smull 1955) on which to base its 4-hour standards. In these studies, live, rapidly multiplying cultures of *S. aureus* or *E. coli* were introduced into food at about 110°F. The data implies that actually, approximately 6 hours would be sufficient to control multiplication. Note that when one practices HACCP, live cultures will not be introduced into food, and only *C. perfringens* will be a potential hazard.

Clostridium perfringens, a Low Hazard

C. perfringens is considered by the National Research Council to be a low-hazard microorganism because it rarely causes death and only causes simple bouts of diarrhea. Hence, even if some multiplication of this organism occurred as a result of the above heating and cooling times being exceeded, the contaminated food would not be considered highly hazardous. Other spores multiply much slower than *C. perfringens* and will not be a problem unless there is gross abuse of the food, which would be prevented by a company's hazard control Policies, Procedures, and Standards Manual.

Integration of Pathogenic Microorganism Hazard Control Information

Figure 3 provides a list of the control rules for infective microorganisms and Figure 4 provides the control information for spore forming and exotoxin forming microorganisms.

HACCP Applied to the Foodservice Systems

Table 10 is an overview of HACCP applications in foodservice systems. HACCP begins at the *output*. The hazard threshold is determined by consumers of the food. Who is to be served? Do the consumers have normally functioning immune systems or are they immune-compromised? How much abuse of the food will there be once the consumer has possession of the food? Remember, spores will survive the cooking process and will multiply if the food temperature goes below 130°F. As pointed out earlier, healthy people can usually accept moderate levels of pathogens. They have normal stomach acidity, balanced intestinal microflora, and adequate immune cells. Some individuals can accept only low levels of pathogens. Once specifications are written for the output, then the emphasis shifts to the *input*, to buying food that has the lowest possible level of hazards. However, the input will include microorganisms, chemicals, and hard foreign objects on food from employees, air, water, and food contact surfaces. Finally HACCP deals with the *processes* that convert the ingredients to the output.

Preparation and processing methods (washing, peeling, cooking-pasteurization) must reduce the hazards to a safe level, and/or products must be obtained from suppliers who certify product safety. The products must be transported and stored in a manner that prevents them from becoming hazardous to consumers when consumed.

The Hazards of Foodservice Operations

In order to design a safe process, it must be assumed that the input food contains a maximum load of pathogens based on recognized microbiological measurements. Processing standards must be designed to decrease or maintain

Fig 3. Infective microorganisms control rules.
(Source: Adapted from O. P. Snyder, 1992, Developing a Total Quality Management-Based Food Safety Program for a Chilled Food System, St. Paul, Minn., Hospitality Institute of Technology and Management.)

Hazard

Low levels ($1-10^3$/g) are hazardous.

Control

Get supplier certification of safe pathogen levels in food products, if possible.

Heat makes food safe. (*Salmonella* spp. 7D pasteurization: 140°F [60°C] for 12.1 minutes; 150°F [65.6°C] for 1.21 minutes; or 160°F [71.1°C] for .121 minute)

1. *Shigella* spp., *Giardia lamblia,* Hepatitis A virus and Norwalk virus

   Hazard

   Very low levels (3 to 10 microorganisms/gram) in a food item can be dangerous. They will get onto food from hands or water contaminated with human or animal feces.

   Control

   Double washing of fresh fruits and vegetables removes surface contamination to a safe level.

   Double hand washing by employees with a fingernail brush in the first wash insures removal of fecal pathogens to a safe level.

   A "safe" water supply must be used in food preparation and production.

2. *Salmonella* spp., *Yersinia enterocolitica, Listeria monocytogenes, Vibrio* spp., *Escherichia coli,* etc.

   Hazard

   Expected contamination level is <10/g.

   L. monocytogenes begins to multiply at 32°F.

   Resistant person illness level is >1,000/g.

   Control

   Heat inactivation of pathogens during pasteurization.

   Control growth of these pathogens: five (5) generations (1:32) of multiplication are safe; 10 generations (1:1,024) of multiplication are dangerous.

   If food is stored at <32°F, it can be held until spoiled. If stored at 40°F, it should be used within <5 days.

3. *Campylobacter jejuni*

   Hazard

   Expected contamination level on pork and poultry is >1,000/g.

   Resistant person illness level is <5/g.

   Control

   Easily inactivated by *Salmonella* spp. pasteurization.

   Must reduce pathogen contamination on raw food contact surfaces >100,000:1 by correct washing in clean, hot solution of detergent or soap and water.

   Avoid cross-contamination by frequent cleaning ("clean-as-you-go").

---

the pathogenic population in the food at levels that will cause no risk to consumers. What pathogen levels in raw food should be considered high? Genigeorgis (1987) observed 1,400 *Salmonella*/100 gram of chicken skin. When muscle foods were tested for *L. monocytogenes*, raw fish was found to contain a maximum of 25–50 colony forming units (CFU)/gram (Anon. 1989). Johnson et al. (1990) tested core samples of muscle from 50 beef, 50 pork and 10 lamb roasts, purchased at retail outlets for the presence of *L. monocytogenes*. All lamb samples were negative, but 5 of the 100 beef and pork samples were positive. Two of these samples contained an estimated level of 10 CFU/gram.

Fig. 4. Spore-forming and exotoxin-forming microorganisms control rules.
(Source: Adapted from O. P. Snyder, 1992, Developing a Total Quality Management-Based Food Safety Program for a Chilled Food System, St. Paul, Minn., Hospitality Institute of Technology and Management.)

Hazard

Heat does not control the spore or toxin hazard.

Clostridium perfringens sets standards for heating and cooling rates because of its rapid multiplication rate of doubling every 7.2 minutes at 105.8°F (41°C).

Five (5) generations (1:32) of multiplication are safe, 10 generations of multiplication (1:1,024) are dangerous.

Must multiply to high levels (10^5–10^6/g) in food (normally in cooked food) to be hazardous.

Microorganism	Contamination Level/g	Hazard Level/g
Staphylococcus aureus	1,000	1,000,000
Clostridium botulinum	<1	10,000
Bacillus cereus	<100	100,000
Clostridium perfringens	<100	1,000,000

Control

Heat food from 40°F to 130°F in <6 hours control *C. perfringens*.

Cool food to 40°F in 4 hours (FDA standards)/11 hours (USDA regulations) to control *C. perfringens*.

Hold at <38°F if nonproteolytic *C. botulinum* spores were not inactivated by cooking to 180°F >10 min. Hold at <39°F if these are destroyed and *Bacillus cereus* is the hazard.

Chill ingredients for salad to 40°F and mix all chilled ingredients within a time that does not permit the temperature to rise above 50°F in order to inhibit the production of toxin by *Staphylococcus aureus*.

Isolation of *L. monocytogenes* in the other 3 samples was achieved by enrichment, suggesting that these samples contained less than 10 CFU/gram. The presence of *L. monocytogenes* in muscle cores is probably due to antemortem *Listeria* contamination. Table 11 provides the best estimate for expected numbers of pathogens in food coming into the retail food system today and an estimate of what people with normal immune systems can tolerate.

Hand Washing and Personal Hygiene

One in fifty employees who come to work each day is shedding pathogens, has had no symptoms, and no one knows who that one person might be. Therefore, it must be assumed that all employees are shedding pathogens in their feces and urine and from their noses and mouths. When an employee is ill, he or she will pass approximately 10^9 pathogens per gram of fecal material. If it is assumed that the toilet paper slips even a little, there will be 0.01 gram, or 10^7 pathogens on the user's fingertips after using the toilet. The double hand washing method using a fingernail brush, must be used by food handlers to ensure that viruses and other pathogenic bacteria that may be deposited on the hands and under fingernails are reduced to less than 10 on the fingertips in order to be below a hazardous level. Fingernails of employees must be kept short so that they can be kept clean and do not break gloves if gloves are worn.

When the double hand washing method is used, water at 110°F to 120°F (43.3°C to 48.9°C) flowing at 2 gallons per minute is used with a fingernail brush, with at least 2 ml of soap on the fingers and 2 ml of soap on the brush. The brush is used to clean fingertips and under the fingernails. The important critical control point in hand washing is the removal of fecal organisms from the fingertips and under the fingernails.

After the first wash, the hands and brush should be rinsed in the flowing

Table 10. *Application of HACCP to foodservice systems*

Input ──────→ Hazards	Process ──────→ Controls	Output

Material, supplies
  Water
  Meat, fish,
    poultry
  Fruits
  Vegetables
  Cereals and
    starches
  Legumes
  Fats and oils
  Flavoring
  Process aids
  Preservatives
  Packaging
  Cleaning supplies
Equipment
Employees
Environment
Facilities
Management
Consumers
 	
(All of these are a
  source of micro-
  organisms, chem-
  icals, and hard
  foreign objects)
	Methods
	Supplier certification that
	  products are below haz-
	  ard levels
	
	Control hazards by process-
	  ing products to levels be-
	  low the thresholds that
	  will make consumers ill:
	Wash off pathogens or use
	  pasteurization:
	    (cook, irradiate, acidify)
	    to inactivate/reduce 10^7
	    Salmonella spp or 10^4 *Lis-*
	    teria monocytogenes to 1
	    per gram.
	Lock up hazardous
	  chemicals.
	Measure all additives
	  precisely.
	Control toxic food contact
	  surfaces.
	Employees use hand wash-
	  ing methods that re-
	  duce pathogens on
	  fingertips from 10^5 to 1.
	Reduce pathogens on food
	  contact surfaces from
	  10^5 to 1.
	Do not mix old and fresh
	  food.
	Do not cross-contaminate
	  food items.
	Heat food in <6 hours
	  from 40°F to >130°F.
	Hold all hot food at
	  >140°F.
	Preserve nutrients by con-
	  suming food in <30
	  minutes.
	Cool food to 40°F in <4
	  hours.
	Use food in <5 days if
	  stored at 40°F to limit
	  L. monocytogenes less than
	  5 generations.
		*Safe food of maximum nutri-
		tional value and sensory
		quality for:*
		People who can accept
		  certain levels of path-
		  ogens:
		  Healthy individuals (1–
		    70 years old), with
		    normal stomach
		    acidity, balanced in-
		    testinal microflora,
		    and functioning im-
		    mune system.
		
		Immune-compromised
		  people who can accept
		  only very low levels of
		  pathogens:
		  Babies (0–5 years)
		  Pregnant women
		  Immune compromised
		  Frail, elderly
		This portion of the popu-
		  lation must eat defen-
		  sively, unless food is
		  prepared especially for
		  them.
		Hurdles are used to control
		  abuse during distribu-
		  tion and by consumers
		  Temperature
		  Time
		  Water activity (a_w)
		  Oxidation/reduction (E_h)
		  Chemical additives
		  Packaging
		  Customer consumption
		    and storage
		    information

Source: Based on data from Snyder 1992b.

water, and the hand washing is repeated using at least 2 ml of well-lathering soap. The fingernail brush is not used during the second wash. Hands and arms up to the shirt sleeves should be washed. Finally, hands should be rinsed and dried with a paper towel. Soaps and detergents containing bacteri-cidal chemicals should not be used. These types of soaps or detergents harm beneficial resident bacteria in the epidermal layer of the hands and may cause skin irritation.

Table 11. *Expected number of pathogenic cells per gram of food before processing and safe tolerance levels*

Pathogenic microorganisms	Expected	Safe tolerance
Spore-formers and/or Toxin Producers		
Clostridium botulinum	1/10 grams	1,000/gram
Clostridium perfringens	10/gram	1,000/gram
Bacillus cereus	100/gram	1,000/gram
Staphylococcus aureus	10/gram	1,000/gram
Infective Vegetative		
Salmonella spp.	10/gram	< 1/25 grams
Listeria monocytogenes	10/gram	< 10/gram
Viruses	10/gram	< 1/gram

Source: Based on data from Snyder 1992b.

Plastic gloves are no substitute for correct hand washing. They are dangerous because they can melt to the skin if the hands are subjected to high heat. Also, they get dirtier than hands because employees do not feel the dirt and hence, do not wash as often.

Foodservice Environmental Controls

Deep well city water systems are reasonably safe. Groundwater systems, however, have failures each year (Levine and Craun 1990). The amount of chlorine in water when the water arrives at the food processing plant varies because many pipes are old. Since some parasites (for example, *Giardia lamblia*) and viruses (for example, Norwalk virus) can survive in chlorinated water systems for a long time, it may be important for foodservice facilities to have a water filtration system as well as a chlorinator for the incoming water supply when the water system is unreliable.

The production area must be designed so that it can be easily cleaned and sanitized. There should be tile from floor to ceiling. Ceilings must be free of any overhanging obstructions and piping. Floors should be constructed of durable materials (for example, ceramic tile or brick), which are easy to foam, wash down, and sanitize each night or more often if necessary.

Lighting must be at least 80 foot-candles so that it is possible to see filth and dirt accumulating in corners and nooks, which should be removed during wash-downs throughout the process day. All finished food contact surfaces in operations should be stainless steel and should be sanitized regularly. (After sanitizing, there should be 10 organisms or less per cm^2 on these surfaces.) All equipment must be designed and constructed of materials to facilitate ease of cleaning and sanitizing. Only stainless steel cooking and storage container surfaces should contact wet food.

Cleaning and Sanitizing Food Contact Surfaces

Food contact surfaces must be washed and scrubbed with hot (120°F [48.9°C]) detergent water at least every 4 hours in order to minimize the growth of spoilage organisms. All surfaces, including all hard-to-reach corners and crevices, must be reached and then sanitized with 50 ppm chlorine or equivalent sanitizing solution.

There is a great overemphasis today on the use of sanitizers to keep food contact surfaces safe. It is not the sanitizer that assures safety; hot detergent and hot, clean rinse water are the critical variables.

In a typical food operation, the cook will cut up chicken, probably our most contaminated food, on a cutting board. The chicken will most likely have from 500,000 to 5,000,000 spoilage microorganisms per cm² of surface area. It does no good to wash the chicken. Washing forty times has been shown by Lillard (1988) to only reduce counts of, say, 500,000 to 100,000 CFU per cm² of chicken surface.

The cutting board, knife, and cook's hands immediately become contaminated with approximately the same contamination as the chicken. An average total count for the cutting board per cm² is:

1,000,000	Aerobic Plate Count (APC) microorganisms
10	*Salmonella* spp.
10	*Listeria* spp.
10,000	*C. jejuni*
200	*C. perfringens*

The author's studies have shown that at typical temperatures of 75°F (23.9°C) on the cutting board, the microorganisms really do not multiply in 4 hours. The cutting board is too cool and the water activity is not optimum (see Table 9). Further studies by the author have shown that if the cook wipes the cutting board with a clean, freshly wrung-out cleaning cloth in 100 ppm hypochlorite sanitizer, the greatest reduction of microorganism will only be 10 to 1, which is an insignificant reduction. The reason is simple. All sanitizers are very easily inactivated by food soil. In addition, the food soil has thickness, so that only the surface microorganisms are inactivated. The solution to reducing microorganisms to a safe level is detergent water and rinse water at 110°F to 120°F (43.3°C to 48.9°C).

The cutting board must be taken to a 4-compartment sink. In the first sink, which has a disposal, the cutting board is rinsed with hot water using a pressuring spray. If this is not done, the organic soil will get into the detergent water sink and cause the detergent to be consumed and wasted on excessive soil. This water flush will reduce counts about 100 to 1. Next, the cutting board is immersed in hot detergent water, 110°F to 120°F (43.3°C to 48.9°C). At this point, a stiff nylon scrub brush must be used with the detergent to get into the grooves in the cutting board to break the soil loose from the surface. The water in the sink must be changed often to keep microorganisms from building up in the water. Most detergents have no effect on microbiological multiplication. Some microorganisms can still multiply at 120°F (48.9°C). If the temperature drops to 100°F (37.9°C), this is optimum for most spoilage and pathogenic bacteria (see Table 7). The maximum count of microorganisms that should be in the wash water is 1,000/ml. The film of dirty, loose microorganisms and soil is then rinsed in the 110°F to 120°F (43.3°C to 48.9°C) rinse water. At this point, a maximum of approximately 10 to 100 microorganisms are still adhering to the cutting board. Since these microorganisms are no longer surrounded by food soil, they can be exposed in the final sink to a 50-ppm hypochlorite (bleach) solution, and the surface microorganisms are inactivated by the hypochlorite penetrating the outer membrane of the microorganism. The milk ordinance (U.S. Department of Health, Education, & Welfare 1989) states that a safe refillable milk bottle has 2 or fewer microorganisms per cm².

Since correct washing and rinsing of tabletops is an impractical procedure, it must be assumed that they are always contaminated with pathogens. Hence, all preparation must be done on good quality plastic or hard maple cutting boards.

Recipe and Serving System HACCP Thawing Methods

When raw food is thawed, some spoilage microorganisms begin to multiply slowly at temperatures as low as 23°F (−5.0°C). When food thaws, it also begins to deteriorate. Food should be thawed as rapidly as possible. Potentially hazardous food may be thawed according to the FDA Food Service Sanitation Manual (FDA Division of Retail Food Protection 1976) by one of several methods.

1. Potable (drinkable) running water may be used at 70°F (21.1°C) or less, with sufficient agitation and velocity to float loose food particles into the overflow. Note: No current research shows that this practice is safe. Thawing foods in this manner is thus product-temperature dependent. The temperature of the product must be maintained at 45°F (7.2°C) or less.

Sinks should be sanitized before the food is introduced. A clean, sanitized pot placed in the sink can be filled with running water and used to thaw food. Problems of sink contamination can be avoided by this practice. However, if the thawing product is allowed to thaw in nonflowing water, there is danger of microbial multiplication.

2. A refrigerator at 40°F (4.4°C) or below may be used. In a 40-feet-per-minute (fpm) air flow standard refrigeration unit, thawing of solid, 20- to 30-pound items will take about 3 days. There are special thawing refrigerators with high air velocity (500 fpm) that have heat coils that introduce sufficient heat to the refrigerator at 40°F (4.4°C) while the food is thawing at 28°F to 32°F (−2.2°C to 0°C). High velocity fans introduce air over the thawing food, reducing thawing time from 3 days to 12 hours.

3. A microwave oven may be used for thawing when the food will be immediately cooked in the microwave oven or in conventional cooking facilities. The requirement for uninterrupted cooking is due to the problem of uneven heat transfer in microwave-thawed food allowing for warm spots in which pathogenic bacteria can grow otherwise.

4. Cooking from the frozen state: Research for many years has shown that there is no difference in the sensory quality of meat cooked from the thawed or frozen state. Thinner items such as steak, chicken, and hamburger, as well as large cuts of meat can be cooked from the frozen state. Cooking from the frozen state eliminates the problem of microbial growth during thawing. Approximately 1/3 to 1/2 more time must be added to the cooking process to compensate for the initial thawing lag. Since the lag is somewhat unpredictable, the best HACCP procedure is to allow a safety margin of 1 to 2 hours, and when the meat is done, simply hold the meat hot at or above 130°F (54.4°C) to keep it safe.

The Seven Quality-Assured Recipe Processes

Millions of combinations of ingredients produce recipes with all varieties of flavors, appearances, textures, and aromas. However, each one is not a unique HACCP problem because all recipe processes fall into one of seven food processes or combinations thereof. Figure 5 shows these processes. It is necessary to be aware of potentially hazardous food. If a hazard analysis is conducted for each of the seven processes; if the critical control points for the microbiological, chemical, and the particulate hazards are determined;

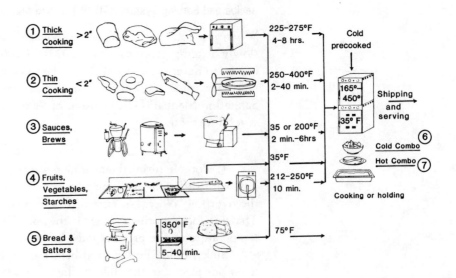

Fig. 5. The seven recipe processes.

and if quality-assured recipe procedures are specified, a safe process can be specified for any recipe. The seven basic recipe processes are as follows:

1. Thick, raw protein items, greater than 2 inches thick (1 inch center to surface). These items are solid and cannot be stirred. Internal contamination is minimal. These products are subject to slow heating and cooling by heat conduction. Examples include prime rib of beef, whole poached salmon, turkey, and a basket of crab. These foods must be cooked at lower temperatures [225°F to 275°F (107.2°C to 135.0°C)] for longer times (1 to 8 hours) to prevent surface burning, unnecessary shrinkage, and water loss before the center reaches required customer satisfaction and safety standards. Often after these products are cooked, they are not served immediately. If they are held for long periods of time before serving, there are hazards of spore outgrowth, particularly *C. perfringens*, associated with long holding at temperatures below 130°F (54.4°C).

There is also a problem with leftovers, which can be thick and difficult to cool and reheat later. Having leftover food should be avoided, if possible. If these thick items become leftovers, the leftover roasts and poultry should be cut into slices less than 2 inches thick and chilled to 40°F (4.4°C) in less than 4 hours.

The surface of the product will be exposed to pasteurization times and temperatures for a long enough period of time that there should be no surviving vegetative pathogens. On the other hand, there will be no spore destruction. Therefore, the food after cooking will be very sensitive to spore outgrowth, and the center must get hot enough to deactivate parasites. The basic rules for process hazard control are:

Pre-prep: Keep the temperature less than 50°F (10.0°C) and prep with 24 hours of use to minimize growth of *L. monocytogenes*.
Prep: Cook to less than 130°F (54.4°C) in less than 6 hours to prevent multiplication of *C. perfringens*. Pasteurize.
Cool: 130°F (54.4°C) to 40°F (4.4°C) in less than 11 hours.
Use: Less than 5 days if stored at 40°F (4.4°C). If stored below 32°F (0°C), the food can be held until spoiled.

2. Thin, raw protein items, less than 2 inches thick. These items can be solid or a mix of ingredients. They can be heated and cooled quickly because the center to surface distance is small. Examples include: small fish and fish fillets, chicken pieces, steaks, pans of casserole, pancakes, grilled sandwiches, and eggs.

These items are normally heated rapidly and are cooked at high temperatures (250°F to 400°F [121.1°C to 204.4°C]) for a brief time (2 to 40 minutes) to a desired internal temperature that meets both customer satisfaction and safety standards.

The key element to ensure safety of these products is heating them to an adequate center temperature for a sufficient period of time to achieve pasteurization. These thin items usually receive much handling and can be contaminated with many pathogenic microorganisms. If a food such as ground beef is to be served rare or raw, an ingredient certified as "low pathogen count" by the supplier should be used. This will avoid the possibility of making anyone ill, even if it is eaten raw. "Low pathogen count" means that the pathogenic microorganism count of the ground beef is less than 10 per gram and that the meat is safe to be served without cooking.

Chicken and turkey products, which may have very high pathogen counts, should reach a center temperature of 165°F (73.9°C) for more than 1 second. Most people cook dark meat to 185°F (85.0°C), but this is only for quality reasons.

Fish should be cooked to a center temperature of 160°F (71.1°C) for more than 1 second to make it safe. Otherwise, it should be certified by the supplier as having a safe pathogen and parasite count.

When raw pork is deep-fried, microwaved, or char-grilled, the FDA Food Service Sanitation Manual (FDA Division of Retail Food Protection 1976) states that the center temperature should reach 170°F (76.7°C) for 15 seconds. All other microwaved raw meat items (except beef steaks) should reach 165°F (73.9°C) for more than 1 second. Food being cooked in a microwave oven should be covered with an appropriate plastic film or glass cover to ensure even heat transfer.

In August 1990, the FDA classified shell eggs as a hazardous food because of the possible presence of *Salmonella enteriditis* within the white or yolk of eggs produced from diseased hens. Unless shell eggs used in foodservice operations are certified as being produced from *Salmonella*-free flocks of hens, eggs should be cooked to an internal temperature of 140°F (60.0°C) for 2.5 minutes. Pasteurized liquid or dried egg products are commonly used in foodservice operations because they are convenient and safe. Raw, unpasteurized eggs should never be used as an ingredient in the preparation of uncooked, ready-to-eat menu items that will receive no further heating or sufficient organic acid addition to inactivate *Salmonella* spp. Cracked or checked shell eggs must be discarded and should not be used in the preparation of food products. Remember, the outside of the shell is always contaminated with chicken fecal pathogens. One must be very careful about cross-contaminating food and equipment after touching eggs.

If meat is to be used in a casserole, it can be prepared and used hot, or, because it is thin, it can be cooled easily to less than 40°F (4.4°C) in less than 4 hours on a sheet pan in a refrigerator. Once cold, it can be incorporated into combination dishes. These thin food items should be held at temperatures above 130°F (54.4°C) for safety and above 150°F (65.6°C) for customer satisfaction, or eaten within 30 minutes. The FDA has an unwritten rule that allows 2 hours temperature abuse after cooking. This time should not be used in foodservice, but should be reserved for customer food abuse when customers take out food. Because thin foods can be cooked rapidly and can be prepared as needed, there should not be any problems with spore growth. If there are leftovers, they should be cooled to 40°F (4.4°C) in 4 hours.

3. Stocks, sauces and brews.   Hot examples include beef broth, gravies, soups, tomato sauce, stocks, jams, jellies, and custards; cold examples include icings, cold salad dressings, sauces, batters, egg nogs, ices, and ice cream. Hot items can be mixed and heated rapidly. Some products such as beef stock are subject to long cooking times for extraction. Once cooked or prepared, stocks, sauces, and brews normally are not served all at once but are often used over a period of many hours to support a meal service requirement. Since the spores have probably not been destroyed by boiling, they are subject to the hazards associated with long-term inadequate hot holding.

Soups and sauces should be held at a temperature of 150°F (65.6°C) or greater. The temperature needs to be uniform; a bain marie is the best piece of equipment to use. Soups and sauces should not be thickened until a few minutes before service. Thickened soups and sauces are much harder to maintain at a uniform temperature. Egg and heavy cream sauces, which do not tolerate continuous 150°F (65.6°C) holding, should be freshly prepared every 2 hours, unless a lab test indicates that the acidity of the sauce is less than pH 4.6. Leftover stew, stocks, soups, and sauces may be difficult to cool. The goal, then, must be to have a minimum of leftovers.

Cold sauces and dressing such as mayonnaise and salad dressings normally made with raw eggs should either be made with pasteurized eggs or should be acidified to below 4.1 pH and held at room temperature for 2 days after production for the acid to inactivate the *Salmonella* spp. and other vegetative pathogens. A pH of 4.1 will also assure that *C. botulinum* does not multiply (pH 4.6).

4. Fruits, vegetables, starches, seeds, nuts, and fungi.   Many of these foods are never cooked. To make them safe, these items require sorting and washing to remove dirt, particulates, chemicals, and many forms of microbiological contamination from the soil, irrigation water, and the hands of workers who cultivate, pick, and handle the products. Once cleaned, these items should be chilled for use in salads, fruit dishes, and such, or cooked. Most fruits are sufficiently acidic to prevent the survival and multiplication of most pathogenic microorganisms.

Low-acid vegetables and starches may be contaminated with the vegetative cells and spores of *C. botulinum* and *Bacillus cereus*. These items must be kept cold (less than 50°F [10.0°C]) or dry (below an a_w of 0.60) and packaged to allow air exchange before cooking. After cooking, all vegetables such as green beans, peas, corn, potatoes, and such, and cereals such as rice, may have activated spores and must be maintained at temperatures greater than 130°F (54.4°C) or cooled to less than 40°F (4.4°C) in 4 hours to ensure safety. Uncooked vegetables are nonhazardous, unless they are stored in airtight bags at temperatures above 50°F (10.0°C). At this temperature and above, proteolytic *C. botulinum* might multiply. Therefore vegetable bags and packages should be permeable to air or must have two 1/8-inch holes that allow air (oxygen) to enter the package.

Dry pasta, potatoes, and rice are nonhazardous because of their low water activity. When water is added to these products, they can become water activity. When water is added to these products, they can become potentially hazardous if not held at temperatures above 130°F (54.4°C) or cooled to below 40°F (4.4°C) in less than 4 hours.

Seeds and nuts are likely to contain shell particulates. Some seeds and nuts contain low levels of pesticides and mold aflatoxin that are hazardous. The shell particulates must be removed by hand inspection. The supplier must certify the items to be safe from pesticides and aflatoxins.

5. Doughs and batters. Unbaked doughs and batters can be hazardous if not handled properly. Infective microorganisms and spores are present in most of the ingredients. The growth of pathogens in doughs is controlled by the decreased amount of water in the mixture (low water activity) and by competitive inhibition of yeast (in bread dough). Batters contain more liquid (water) and support the growth of microorganisms, unless acidified. Batters (pancake batters, dipping batters) must be stored at less than 40°F (4.4°C) until used. Many of these items are made with raw eggs. Snacking on raw dough can be hazardous.

After baking, these products are nonhazardous because the temperature is hot enough to inactivate the infective vegetative cells. After baking the water activity is low enough, and there is no hazard. Baked products can become hazardous if too moist or when covered with contaminated icing. Bakers must wash the *Salmonella* from eggs and off of their hands, not work with infected cuts on their hands, and use the double hand (fingertip) wash to remove fecal pathogens. These foods must always be considered hazardous when combined with any filling such as egg custards, meringue, meat patés or other high a_w, high-quality protein components. Icing and protein (milk and egg) fillings should be cooled to less than 40°F (4.4°C) in 4 hours or less before combining them on or in baked products, such as filling an eclair shell.

When a hazardous topping such as an egg white meringue is baked or browned, the center temperature of the meringue and temperature at the interface of the pie and meringue must reach 160°F (71.1°C) for more than 1 second to inactivate any *Salmonella* spp. in the egg white. The pie and meringue must be cooled to less than 40°F (4.4°C) within 4 hours.

6. Hot combination dishes. Hot combination dishes are composed of mixtures of all of the ingredients previously discussed (meat, fish, sauce, starch, vegetables, and/or fruit). Examples of hot combination dishes are beef stew, chicken a la king, chili, meat pies, spaghetti sauce and meatballs, and oysters Rockefeller. When hot combination dishes are cooked or precooked, ingredients must be combined and heated to reach a center temperature of 165°F (73.9°C) for more than 1 second. Just as with the thick food previously discussed, the threat is from the outgrowth of *C. perfringens*. Casseroles, stews, and chili must be heated to above 130°F (54.4°C) within 6 hours for there to be hazard control.

Combination dishes are especially hazardous because they have all the potential problems of varied ingredients along with extended handling times at warm kitchen temperatures. Once prepared, hot combination dishes should be either kept above 130°F (54.4°C; 150°F [65.6°C] for customer satisfaction) and served and consumed within 2 hours so that there is a minimum amount of quality loss, or cooled to 40°F (4.4°C) or less within 4 hours. Since these products are already "leftovers," for quality reasons they should not be cooled to be reheated again. However, they can be handled safely if cooled to 40°F (4.4°C) within 4 hours and reheated in less than 6 hours to above 130°F (54.4°C). The final reheating temperature should be 165°F (73.9°C) as insurance against the possibility that there was vegetative pathogen contamination during preparation.

7. Cold combination dishes. Cold combination dishes are composed of meat, fish, poultry, sauce, starch, vegetables, and fruit. Examples of cold combination dishes include tuna salad, egg salad, macaroni and ham salad, and sandwiches made with meat, fish, poultry, eggs, and cheese. When cold combination dishes are prepared, all ingredients should be washed and prepared separately and kept at less than 40°F (4.4°C).

Any ingredients such as pasta, potatoes, or rice should be cooked separately and chilled to 40°F (4.4°C) before being added to cold salads or entrées. Flavorings and spices should be added to 40°F (4.4°C) sauces or salad dressings before mixing into other ingredients.

All ingredients should be prechilled to 40°F (4.4°C) and maintained at or below 50°F (10.0°C) during preparation. Avoid leftovers by preparing small batches. Use sanitized utensils and containers when preparing these products. Clean hands can be used to mix salads. If the temperature of the ingredients is kept below 50°F (10.0°C), the production of toxin from any *S. aureus* that might be introduced from the skin of the hands will be prevented.

Once prepared, cold combination dishes should be refrigerated at 40°F (4.4°C) and consumed as soon as possible. However, the more acid and spices are used, the longer the product will be acceptable. If products that are acidified to less than pH 4.6 (with the addition of vinegar, lemon juice, benzoates, and sorbates), these products can be stored for months at 40°F (4.4°C) or less. Deteriorative changes that take place in these stored products will result from oxidative and enzymatic reactions.

Writing an HACCP Recipe

Theories about time, temperature, acid, and water activity control are useless unless the person cooking the food makes practical use of the information. Figure 6 provides a practical application of the HACCP principles to kitchen operations. At the top of the recipe is information about the recipe: its name (BEEF STOCK); space for a number; the HACCP production style (SAUCES); space for portion size and number of portions; the final weight/volume, which is very critical in sizing of cooking and cooling equipment; space for prep time; and who is authorized/trained to prepare the recipe safely. There is also space for the author of the recipe and who certified it as being safe, as well as the date it was written.

The ingredients are listed next, in the order they are to be used in the recipe. There is one column for edible portion. More importantly, there is a column for weight percent. The weight percent is how the safety certifier verifies that controlled additives such as monosodium glutamate, nitrates, Yellow #5, and so forth are not used in excess. It is also the way that one can assure that there is enough meat in order for the recipe to comply with government standards of identity. Finally, there is a cross-reference column to a nutrition file number so that a computer can be used to produce a nutrition summary of all recipes.

At the bottom of the sheet is a template for writing the steps of the recipe so that all process hazards are controlled. The recipe should be divided into modules: pre-preparation, preparation, holding, cooling leftovers and reconstitution, served with, plating instructions, and ingredients that could produce possible allergic reactions. The key to a safe recipe depends on the

Recipe Name: BEEF STOCK
Recipe #:
Production style: Sauces

Portion size:
Number of portions:
Final weight: 4,000 oz: 125 qt.

Prep time:
To be prepared by:

Written by:　　　　　　　　Date:　　　　　　　SA/QA by:　　　　　　　Date:

Group Number	Ingredient Number	Ingredients and Specifications	Edible Portion Wt., Vol., Oz.	Weight Percent	Nutrition
1	1)	Beef bones for stock IMPS 134, cracked	1922.9	20.01	
2	2)	Water	4059.4	42.25	
	3)	Celery, US No. 2, rough cut	363.2	3.78	
	4)	Carrots, US No. 1, rough cut	363.2	3.78	
	5)	Onions, Granex, No. 2, rough cut	963.2	10.03	
	6)	Bay leaf	2.1	.02	
	7)	Thyme	2.1	.02	
	8)	Black pepper, fresh ground	2.1	.02	
	9)	Parsley	6.4	.07	
3	10)	Beef, Stew 3/4" dice, IMPS 135	1922.9	20.01	

Pre-preparation procedures:

1. Cut the bones (40°F) with meat saw or crack with a cleaver (wear eye protection) into 5" pieces (5 min., 45°F).
2. Rough cut the garnish (onions, carrots, and celery) (40°F) with a French knife into medium-size 1" pieces (45°F or less when finished).

Preparation procedures:

3. Place the bones in a large roast pan and brown thoroughly (35–40 min.) in a 400°F oven. Turn bones occasionally to brown evenly.
4. When the bones are brown, drain off any grease that may have accumulated in the pan. (Grease may be saved for one day at room temperatures for roux if desired.)
5. Add the rough garnish (45°F) and continue to roast approximately 10 min. until the garnish is slightly brown (170°F).
6. Remove the bones and garnish from the pan and add to a large stock pot or kettle with water as hot as possible from the tap (approx. 140°F) (10 min.).
7. Deglaze the roast pan with 1/4 of the water (70°F). (Deglazing is done by adding water to the hot pan to dissolve crusted juices.) Put the deglazing water (200°F) in the stock pot. (Deglazing with red wine will increase the safety of this recipe.)
8. Cover bones with remaining water (70°F). Cover and bring to a boil (212°F) in <30 min. Remove any scum that rises to the top.
9. Add all remaining ingredients (70°F). Reduce heat and simmer (195°F) overnight for 10 hr.
10. During the last hr. of stock simmering, brown stew beef (40°F) in the 400°F oven (120°F). Add stock from the pot (195°F) just to cover (160°F). Reheat and simmer (195°F) covered in a 300°F oven or on the range for 1 hr. (until the beef is tender). Remove beef for stew and combination dishes. Cool if appropriate to 40°F in <4 hr. Add the enriched meat stock back to the stock pot. Strain stock through a fine China cap into a clean 5-gal. stock pot.

Holding:

11. Hold hot (165°F) covered in a bain marie for <4 hr.

Cooling, leftovers:

12. To cool stock, pour it 2" deep into a 2 1/2"-deep steam table pan. Cover and place into blast chiller (35°F). Stock temperature will drop to 40°F or less in <4 hr. Maximum holding time is 5 days.

Reconstitution:

13. Reheat to 165°F or above in <2 hr. Do not save leftovers.

Served with:

Plating instructions:

Ingredients that could produce possible allergic reactions:

Hazard Control Process Date for Each Step	Start Fd. Ctr. Temp., °F	Thickest Fd. Dimension, Inches	Container Size H × W × L	Cover Yes/No	Temp. On/ Around Fd.	End Fd. Ctr. Temp. °F	Process Step Time, Hr./Min.

Fig. 6. Quality-assured recipe procedures (QARP).

times, temperatures, pH, and water activity that will control the pathogens. Each step is written with a beginning food temperature, step instruction, then a final food temperature and the time the step took.

To certify that a recipe is safe, one only needs to verify that food times and temperatures fall within the previously discussed guidelines for the control of vegetative pathogens and spores. A flow chart of this information is shown in Figure 7.

- Employee hand washing: *Shigella* spp. and Hepatitis A control by use of fingernail brush and double hand wash.
- Water: *Giardia* control by water supplier.
- Insects and rodents: Exclusion through cleanliness and construction.
- Food contact surfaces: Only use surfaces cleaned and sanitized to < 2 CFU/cm^2.

Expected Threat Level in raw food to be controlled.

Salmonella spp	<10/g
Listeria monocytogenes	<1/g
Staphylococcus aureus	<100/g
Clostridium perfringens	<100/g
Clostridium botulinum	<.01/g
Bacillus cereus	<100/g

- Control of hard foreign objects.
- If meat, fish, or poultry is to be eaten rare or raw, the supplier assures and certifies safe pathogen levels.
- The producers/suppliers provide standard plate count data that proves they have a stable, HACCP controlled process.
- Just-in-time delivery at <0°F (<−18°C) or 40°F (<4.4°C) maximizes freshness and minimizes pathogen multiplication. If food is maintained at <32°F (<0°C), there will be no *Listeria monocytogenes* multiplication.

Receiving. Some food and beverages will be contaminated and must be checked, sorted, trimmed

- Food must be stored before temperature reaches 46°F (8°C) or 5°F (−15°C).
- Damaged packages and cans of food are returned.
- Infested packages and products are returned.
- Moldy, spoiled foods are discarded.

Storage <40°F (<4.4°C) <4 days

- At 40°F (<4.4°C) and <4 days, *Listeria monocytogenes* will be controlled to an acceptable increase of <1:16 (4 generations).

Pre-preparation and Staging for production <24 hours before use. Cut, chop, wash fruits and vegetables. Weigh and measure. Keep temperatures <50°F (<10°C).

- Clean-as-you-go prevents pathogen cross-contamination.
- Control multiplication of *Listeria monocytogenes* to <1 additional generation. (Total *Listeria monocytogenes* multiplication is <1:32 (5 generations.)
- Fruits and vegetables are double washed to remove surface filth and reduce pathogens >100:1.

Cook <40° to 130°F (<4.4°C to >54.4°C) <6hr

Pasteurize
Reduce *Salmonella* spp 10^{-7}

Cool <130°F to 40°F (>54.4°C to 4.4°C) <11 hours

Mix Salads to maintain <50°F (<10°C)

- Heat from <40° to 130°F (4.4°C to >54.4°C) <6 hours to prevent multiplication of *Clostridium perfringens*
- Food pasteurization for 10,000,000:1 *Salmonella* spp reduction by temperature [130°F (54.4°C) for 121 min.; 140°F (60°C) for 12.1 min.; 150°F (65.6°C) for 1.21 min.; 160°F (71.1°C) for 0.121 min.) or by addition of sufficient organic acid to decrease the pH below 4.1 with a 2-day hold.
- Cool food from <130°F to 40°F (>54.4°C to 4.4°C) in <11 hours to control multiplication of *Clostridium perfringens*
- Prevent toxin production of *Staphylococcus aureus* in salads by precooling ingredients to 40°F (4.4°C) before mixing and then keeping the ingredients <50°F (<10°C) during mixing and use.

Finish Production.
Serve at 140°F (60°C) in <30 minutes, or **Package, Chill, and Distribute** at <40°F (<4.4°C).

- Retain nutrients at 140°F (60°C) by serving in <30 minutes.
- Prevent cross-contamination.
- Prevent customer abuse.

Food Holding and Leftovers.

- If stored at 32°F–40°F (0°C–4.4°C), use within 5 days of production to control possible post-processing *Listeria monocytogenes* contamination to <5 generations.
- If stored at 32°F (<0°C), food can be held until spoiled.
- Since postcooking contamination is controlled, reheating is not required as a critical control.

Fig. 7. Pasteurized-chilled food process hazard control flow diagram.

Chilled Food System

All of the HACCP principles that have been discussed apply directly to chilled food systems. Actually, any food process whereby food is prepared and held cold for later service can be called a chilled food system. Whether the food is in a covered, stainless steel pan, a sealed plastic bag, or a glass jar makes no difference. If food after preparation is held for less than 5 days at or below 40°F (4.4°C), pathogen growth will be restricted to a safe level of less than 5 generations (1:32 multiplication). If a longer time is desired, then the holding temperature should be at or below 32°F (0°C), or acid and additives should be used to ensure safety.

Those people who want to compete in the wholesale commercial chilled food market and sell food to food markets and other users should be very careful, since they will have no control over food times and temperatures once the food arrives at its next destinations through consumption. Food temperatures in food market displays often reach 50°F (10.0°C) or higher. Customers may time-temperature abuse the food in their refrigerators. The way to ensure safety in these environments is to do a study by inoculating food samples with selected pathogens such as *C. botulinum*, temperature abusing the food, and making sure it remains safe. Such a study can cost $10,000 to $20,000. So, one must be prepared for these laboratory testing costs. When care is taken in production, chilled food can have a long shelf life. Table 12 gives some examples.

Table 12. *Approximate shelf life[a]*

Food item	Days
Sous vide	21
Roasts	60–90
Stews and sauces	
low acid (>4.6 pH)	21
acid (<4.6 pH)	180
Roast cut packaged meat	42
Meat and sauce dinners	>21
Meat pies	>21
Sandwiches	<14
Salads (<4.6 pH)	30–180
Pizza	30–60
Uncured jellied meat	<7

Source: Based on data from Snyder 1992b.
[a]Storage at or below 30°F (−1.1°C)

Management of a HACCP Program

Who makes HACCP happen? Obviously the only people who can control the process to achieve zero defects are the employees on the line. They see/manipulate every particle of food produced and know whether it is being handled according to HACCP standards. For example, they are the ones who must have thermometers to make sure that food temperatures are correct. Additionally, if a food temperature is out of specification, they have the authority to take immediate corrective action. What, then, is the role of the supervisor? He or she must train and coach the employees to enable them to perform with zero defects. This is called *quality assurance. Quality improvement*, on the other hand, is management's responsibility. Management is responsible for ensuring that there is sufficient money for adequate cleaning and maintenance, and that every employee is continuously involved in helping to improve the performance of the process, especially keeping it simple.

Disciplined employee performance is at the heart of HACCP. Disciplined performance requires written rules for employees to follow for every task they perform, whether it is receiving boxes of raw chicken, the outside surfaces of which are contaminated with pathogens, or cooking pork to inactivate pathogens. The following is a listing of the major sections of a HACCP-based quality assurance manual that will provide the disciplined base for zero-defect production.

Foodservice HACCP-based QA Manual

Food Safety Quality Assurance Policy
Organization Chart of Food Safety Assurance
General Food Safety Procedures and Standards for All Personnel
    Personal Hygiene
    Sanitizing Surfaces
Food Preparation Persons Food Safety Procedures and Standards
    Pre-Preparation
    Preparation
    Storing Prepared Food
Service Persons Food Safety Procedures and Standards
Sanitation and Maintenance Persons Food Safety Procedures and Standards
Food Receiving and Storing Persons Food Safety Procedures and Standards
Operator or Manager Food Safety Procedures and Standards
Quality-Assured Recipe Procedures (QARP)
Foodborne Illness Prevention Training and Performance Improvement Program
    New Employee Training Record

Current Employee Performance Improvement Training Record
Cleaning and Sanitizing Schedule and Instructions
Pest Control Schedule and Instructions
Maintenance Schedule
Foodborne Illness Information Form
Retail Food Operation Food Hazard Control Checklist
    Food Safety Control Requirements
    Regulatory Control Requirements

Summary

It must be assumed that all of the raw food coming into a foodservice operation is contaminated with pathogens at a high enough level to make people sick. It must also be assumed that all employees handling food, while they feel fine, are shedding high levels of pathogens in their fecal material. The only answer to food safety is a highly disciplined hazard control program in which the employee on the line is trained and vested with the responsibility for zero defects in food safety. The rules for safety are common sense. Ultimately, the responsibility for the effectiveness of a HACCP program rests with top management, which makes it possible for the employee to perform with zero defects.

References

Anonymous. 1989. Hot dog processing "borderline" for *Listeria* destruction. *Newsogram* 13(1):9.

Bean, N. H., P. M. Griffin, J. S. Goulding, and C. B. Ivey. 1990. Foodborne disease outbreaks, 5 year summary, 1983–1987. *Morbidity Mortality Weekly Report* 39(SS-1):15–57.

Bennett, J. V., D. H. Scott, M. F. Rogers, and S. L. Solomon. 1987. Infectious and parasitic diseases. In *The Burden of Unnecessary Illness*, R. W. Amler and H. B. Dull, eds. New York: Oxford University Press.

Bourland, C. T., M. F. Fohey, R. M. Rapp, and R. L. Sauer. 1981. Space Shuttle food processing and packaging. *J. Food Protect.* 44:313–319.

Code of Federal Regulations (CFR 9). 1991. Part 318.17. Washington, D.C.: Office of the Federal Register. National Archives and Records Adm.

Code of Federal Regulations (CFR 21). 1991. Section 113. *Thermally Processed Low-acid Foods Packaged in Hermetically Sealed Containers.* Washington, D.C.: U.S. Government Printing Office.

FDA. 1990. Potentially Hazardous Food—Shell Eggs. Part 6—Inspection. Chapter 01. Section 04 - Interpretations by code section. Number 1-102q. Washington, D.C.: Retail Food Protection Program Information Manual.

FDA/CDC. 1989. *Eating defensively: Food Safety Advice for Persons with Aids.* TRT 14:30 (Video tape). Washington, D.C.: FDA Office of Public Affairs. Distributed by National AIDS Information Clearing House.

FDA Division of Retail Food Protection. 1976. *Food Service Sanitation Manual Including a Model Food Service Sanitation Ordinance.* DHEW Publ. No. (FDA) 78-2081. Washington, D.C.: U.S. Department of Health, Education, and Welfare (DHEW) Public Health Service.

Food Processors Institute. 1988. *Canned Foods, Principles of Thermal Process Control, Acidification and Container Closure Evaluation.* Washington, D.C.: The Food Processors Institute.

Genigeorgis, C. 1987. The risk of transmission of zoonotic and human diseases by meat and meat products. In *Elimination of Pathogen Organisms from Meat and Poultry.* F. J. M. Smulders, ed., pp. 111–147. New York: Elsevier Science Publishers.

Kletz, T. A. 1985. Eliminating potential process hazards. *Chemical Engineering* 92(7):48–68.

Johnson, J. L., M. P. Doyle, and R. G. Cassens. 1990. Incidence of *Listeria* spp. in retail meat roasts. *J. Food Sci.* 55(2):572, 574.

Levine, W. C. and G. F. Craun. 1990. Waterborne disease outbreaks, 1986–1988. *Morbidity Mortality Weekly Report* 39 (SS-1):1–13.

Lillard, H. S. 1988. Effect of surfactant or changes in ionic strength on the attachment of *Salmonella typhimurium* to poultry skin and muscle. *J. Food Sci.* 53:727–730.

Longree, K. and J. C. White, 1955. Cooling rates and bacterial growth in food prepared and stored in quantity. *J. Am. Diet. Assoc.* 31:124–132.

McDivitt, M. E., and M. L. Hammer. 1958. Cooling rate and bacterial growth in cornstarch pudding. *J. Am. Diet. Assoc.* 34:190–194.

Miller, W. A., and M. L. Smull. 1955. Efficiency of cooling practices in preventing growth of micrococci. *J. Am. Diet. Assoc.* 31:469–473.

Shigahisa, T., T. Nakagami, and S. Taji. 1985. Influences of heating and cooling rates on spore germination and growth of *Clostridium perfringens* in media and in roast beef. *Japan J. Vet. Sci.* 47(2):259–267.

Smittle, R. B. 1977. Microbiology of mayonnaise and salad dressing: A review. *J. Food Protect.* 40(6):415–422.

Snyder, O. P. 1992a. *Developing a Total Quality Management-Based Food Safety Program for a Chilled Food System.* St. Paul, Minn.: Hospitality Institute of Technology and Management.

Snyder, O. P. 1992b. *HACCP-Based Safety and Quality Assured Pasteurized-Chilled Food Systems.* St. Paul, Minn.: Hospitality Institute of Technology and Management.

Todd, E. C. D. 1985. Economic loss from foodborne disease outbreaks associated with foodservice establishments. *J. Food Protect.* 48(2):169–180.

Todd, E. C. D. 1989. Preliminary estimates of costs of foodborne disease in the United States. *J. Food Protect.* 52(8):595–601.

USDA-FSIS. 1990a. *The food safety and inspection service's Hazard Analysis and Critical Control Point (HACCP) implementation study.* Strategy Paper. Washington, D.C.: FSIS Information Office.

USDA-FSIS. 1990b. Recommendations of the National Advisory Committee on Microbiological Criteria for Foods for Refrigerated Foods Containing Cooked, Uncured Meat or Poultry Products that Are Packaged for Extended Refrigerated Shelf Life and That Are Ready-to-Eat or Prepared with Little or No Additional Heat Treatment. Washington, D.C.: USDA.

U.S. Department of Health, Education, and Welfare. 1989. *Grade "A" Pasteurized Milk Ordinance—1989 Revision.* (Recommendations of the Public Health Service) Public Health Service Publication No. 229. Washington, D.C.: U.S. Govt. Printing Office.

21

Human Resources

Harold Lane

Like a Polaroid picture that slowly emerges on paper, the vision of a human resources concept began to surface noticeably in the hospitality industry during the closing decades of the twentieth century.

In the past, it seemed as if all that mattered to management were financial or material resources. Insofar as employees were concerned, there was little in the literature to suggest that people in the workplace were to be treated with respect, dignity, and with recognition of their capacity to think for themselves and to manage their own work. Indeed, Frederick Winslow Taylor, who authored *The Principles of Scientific Management* in 1911 had asserted that the work of people in manufacturing plants could best be managed through tight controls, centralized top-down decision making, and carefully written job descriptions. History suggests that Taylor's ideas did not go unnoticed in the hotel and foodservice industry of those early days.

By the 1950s, however, scholars such as McGregor, Likert, and Argyris as well as Mayo, Roethlisberger, and Dickson, the three authors of the reknowned Hawthorne Studies at the Western Electric Company plant near Chicago, were focusing upon the negative effects that boring, repetitive jobs have upon employee motivation for turning out high quality work. Even so, employers generally could find no compelling reason for management practices to change. After all, as Professor Edward E. Lawler III of the University of Southern California observed, industry operations at that time were financially successful. And no one had proved that alternatives to traditional methods of managing lower level employees would produce superior results.

As a matter of fact, a midwest hotel-chain president of the fifties who was overheard laying down the law to a new front office employee declared "We hired you to come out here and just 'saw wood'. We do all the *thinking*. Your job is *not* to think. Just stick to *doing*."

In the 1970s, the management picture began to brighten, spurred on by at least two important developments. First, the United States Department of Health, Education and Welfare commissioned the preparation of a report, later published as a book under the title *Work in America* (1973). That book emphasized the costs to industry as well as to society of high employee turnover, chronic absenteeism, and poor work quality. In addition, the early 1970s saw the emergence of joint union-management *quality of work life* (QWL) experiments by General Motors. By 1977, these QWL experiments were being defined by the American Center for the Quality of Work Life in the following way:

> Any activity at every level of an organization which seeks greater organizational effectiveness through the enhancement of human dignity and growth . . . a process or approach through which the stakeholders in the organization (management, employees, and the union, if any) learn how to work together more effectively in order to determine *for themselves* what actions, changes, and improvements are desirable and workable in order to achieve the twin and simultaneous goals of improved quality of life at work for *all employees* of the organization and greater effectiveness of the organization itself.

As the 1990s began, it was clear that industry generally, including the hotel and foodservice industry, had found the idea of employee *participation* in management decision making an attractive way to obtain and maintain a cooperative, committed, and creative work force—if for no other reason than to maintain a competitive edge in the global marketplace. And so the term, *human resources*—best expressing the hope of forward-looking organizations intending to remain viable, adaptive, and dynamic in a rapidly changing world—came to embrace with high visibility and importance many of the functions formerly performed by a personnel department.

While current practices show wide variations in the range of responsibilities assigned to human resources executives in the hospitality industry, a description of some of the more outstanding ones will illustrate their dynamic character and the role played in the 1990s by specialists in human resources.

Recruitment

Faced with vacant positions, manager burnout, high turnover, and low employee morale, one hotel chain successfully instituted child care and flexible working hours to attract potential women employees, a group historically accounting for more than fifty percent of the industry's workforce. Its advertising stressed "our schedule fits yours" and "child care—we care."

With labor market analysts predicting increasing labor shortages, many hotel and restaurant employers who normally have not provided transportation for their employees are now doing so by chartered vans and buses.

In addition, at least one major U.S. resort hotel is claiming to provide "hassle-free" conditions for prospective employees in its on-site $14 million human resources building which houses

1. Employment offices with ample space and privacy for prospective employee interviews.
2. Training areas comprising four separate rooms large enough to accommodate alternative uses such as employee social functions, television, and motion pictures.
3. A day care center with playrooms for the children of working parents and with security furnished by the hotel.
4. An employees-only health club, open 24 hours a day, with saunas, whirlpools, and Nautilus exercise equipment.
5. A kitchenette with microwave, sink, refrigerator, and coffee-making facilities located on each floor of the building, for employee use.
6. An employee services office that is open 24 hours a day with staff to handle "anything and everything" (for example: broken fingernails; eyeglass problems; TV, telephone, or auto repairs; film devel-

oping; Ticketron and travel requests; company sports activities; operation of an employee store selling over-ordered food and/or beverage items; and issuance of VIP employee cards entitling employees to rent video tapes from the Employee Services library.

Effect of AIDS, Drugs, and Alcoholism upon Recruitment

While news reports suggest that some testing of job applicants for AIDS may be taking place generally in industry, there is no evidence as yet that such tests are prevalent in the hospitality industry.

Even though it believes the hospitality industry has its share of drug-using employees, the National Restaurant Association through its legal counsel neither recommends nor rejects drug-testing procedures for prospective employees.

It is known, however, that a number of hotel and foodservice organizations are coping with the AIDS, substance abuse, alcoholism, and related problems of the workplace through the establishment of an Employee Assistance Program (EAP). Such programs engage the services of professional counsellors to work an EAP hotline 24 hours a day answering whatever questions or problems may be posed by prospective employees, present employees, or managerial staff.

Honesty Tests

Passage of a federal law, the Employee Polygraph Protection Act of 1988, which made use of lie-detector tests illegal as an employment screening device, has spawned the emergence of paper-and-pencil honesty tests. Despite their apparent widespread use, scientific evidence of their validity and reliability has yet to be determined.

Equal Employment Opportunity

Statistics indicate that by the year 2000 nearly a third of all new entrants into the labor force will be minorities—twice as many as in the 1980s. Discovering that a major impediment to minority applicants being able to take full advantage of available job opportunities is the lack of basic skills, hotel and restaurant companies have inaugurated a variety of educational programs. Bakers who had trouble reading instructional manuals on how to make doughnuts are being taught how to read. English as a second language is being taught in a restaurant chain where 80 percent of the employees are Spanish speaking. Hotel chains are offering nationwide college scholarship plans aimed at attracting minority college students to the profession of hotel and restaurant management.

Women in Hospitality Management

Research undertaken at Michigan State University in 1978 revealed a surprising reluctance to employ women in the hospitality industry—the reason being given that women were not suited to perform work that demanded stamina in dealing with executive chefs or with aggressive purveyors. On the positive side, this research did discover a twenty-eight-year-old woman whose management of one restaurant in a nationwide chain was producing laudable results as a consequence of her initiative and talent.

Even so, the industry's image in closing the gender gap is scarcely a persuasive one today. Although women account for more than two-thirds of the workforce in the foodservice industry, only a small number of them ever make it up the ladder to executive or ownership positions. An American Hotel & Motel Association survey of persons listed in the 1988 *Who's Who in the Lodging Industry* disclosed that 23.5 percent of the general managers were women while more than 75 percent were men. On the other hand, the same survey revealed that 85 percent of the housekeepers were women while 14 percent were men. Nonetheless, as women vigorously demonstrate their drive, dedication and competence in the male-dominated world of hospitality management, it seems clear that the decade of the nineties holds unprecedented promise for the realization of women's managerial capabilities.

Training and Development

The high level of training capability possessed by today's successful hospitality organizations involves not only the customary orientation training and technical skills training but also the ability to tap the capabilities of the 15 million in the adult working-age population who have been identified as handicapped. To this end, at least one major university has incorporated in its foodservice management curriculum a three-credit course: "Working with the Handicapped in the Foodservice Industry."

Participative Management

The idea of giving employees a voice in management, while not a novel one, first came to light in the hospitality industry in 1987. At that time the official magazine of the American Hotel & Motel Association published an article about a hotel in Rockford, Illinois, featuring: "The Scanlon Plan: Hotel Pioneers in Bonus Plan Based on Labor Savings, with Motivation Tie-in Giving Employees a Voice in Management."

A year later saw the publication in the *Cornell Hotel & Restaurant Administration Quarterly* of a feature story about *quality circles,* a participative management plan for employees of Accor, a worldwide hotel chain headquartered in France. Quality circles—problem-solving groups traceable to the Japanese obsession with quality improvement—are today estimated to be in operation in more than two-thirds of the U.S. companies with over 25,000 employees. Accor reports that the opportunity to participate in management has increased employees' commitment to their jobs so dramatically that the concept of participative management is now an integral part of the Accor hotel management system.

Labor Unions and the Hospitality Industry

Like Banquo's ghost, the power of employees to bargain collectively with employers to protect themselves from unfair treatment has haunted both industry and government from ancient times down to the present day. During the 1980s membership generally in the 70,000 U.S. labor union organizations decreased significantly to the point where not more than twenty percent of the workforce belonged to a union. However, membership in the Hotel Employees & Restaurant Employees International Union, AFL-CIO dropped to approximately twelve percent of the workforce in the hotel and restaurant industry. Where unions do exist in this industry, they are generally to be found in the major cities. In 1986, the President's Commission on Organized Crime found that the Hotel and Restaurant Employees Union as well as three other international unions were allegedly engaged in flagrant practices tending to corrupt the marketplace. Such practices, the Commission alleged, enabled organized crime to gain a foothold in the overall market economy. Nonetheless, with nearly ninety percent of the workforce being nonunion in the hospitality industry, it is probable that this industry remains untainted by the threat of organized crime.

Bottom Line Benefits

While there is no research data establishing the link between human resource policies and financial gain for companies in the hospitality industry, surveys of such publicly held companies as IBM, General Mills, 3M, and Hospital Corporation of America do reflect a positive correlation between the degree of "progressiveness" of a company's human resource practices and its improved financial performance.

In sum, as one company president observed: "It is an organizational responsibility to provide the best working environment for our employees and to make sure they feel good about the company they work for." Flowing from that kind of commitment comes a body of forward-looking human resource practices most likely to yield enviable bottom line results.

Summary

While changes are inevitable in the many activities that affect human resources, few would disagree with the statement from *Megatrends 2000* that "the most exciting breakthroughs of the twenty-first century will occur not because of technology but because of an expanding concept of what it means to be human." Already involved in such breakthroughs as day care for children of working parents; flextime; free transporation to and from the work place; recruitment of minorities and of people with disabilities; employee assistance programs; and improving the quality of work-life through participative management, major segments of the hospitality industry are moving out of the pack into enviable leadership positions. Why? Because they effectively encourage the human beings in their employ to care more, know more, and do more.

References

American Hotel & Motel Association. 1987. The Scanlon Plan. *Lodging*, April.
Naisbit, J., and P. Aburdene. 1990. *Megatrends 2000*. New York: William Morrow and Company.
Orly, C. 1988. Quality circles in France: Accor's experiment in self-management. *Cornell Hotel and Restaurant Administration Quarterly* Nov.
Roethlisberger, F. J., and W. J. Dickson. 1939. *Management and the Worker*. Cambridge, Mass.: Harvard University Press.
Taylor, F. W. 1960. What is scientific management? In *Classics in Management*, H. F. Merril, ed. New York: American Management Association.
U.S. Department of Health, Education, and Welfare. 1973. *Work in America*. Cambridge, Mass. MIT Press.

Bibliography

Albrecht, K., and R. Zemke. 1985. *Service America*. Chicago: Dow Jones-Irwin.

Bowen, D. E., R. B. Chase, T. G. Cummings, and Associates. 1990. *Service Management Effectiveness*. San Francisco: Jossey-Bass.

Davidow, W. H., and B. Uttal. 1989. *Total Customer Service*. New York: Harper & Row.

Heskett, J. L. 1986. *Managing in the Service Economy*. Boston: Harvard Business School Press.

Heskett, J. L., W. E. Sasser, Jr., and C. W. L. Hart. 1990. *Service Breakthroughs*. New York: The Free Press.

Hudson Institute. 1988. *Opportunity 2000: Creative Affirmative Action Strategies for a Changing Workforce*. Washington, D.C.: Superintendent of Documents, U.S. Government Printing Office.

Kravetz, D. 1988. *The Human Resource Revolution: Implementing Progressive Management Practices for Bottom-Line Success*. San Francisco: Jossey-Bass.

Lawler, E. E., III. 1986. *High Involvement Management*. San Francisco: Jossey-Bass.

Sherman, A. W., G. W. Bohlander, and H. J. Chruden. 1988. *Managing Human Resources*, 8th ed. Cincinnati: Southwestern Publishing Company.

22

College and University Foodservice

Frederick J. DeMicco

Size and Scope of College and University Foodservice

Since colonial times in the United States, colleges and universities have provided meals for their students. Today in the United States there are approximately 3,000 colleges and universities. The operating philosophy of an institution's foodservice program and method for delivery relates directly to the objectives of the college or university. Of the approximately 3,000 foodservice programs, approximately two-thirds are self-operated (independent), with the remainder operated by contract foodservice management companies such as Marriott, ARA, or other contract company. College enrollment is at an all-time high, with 13.6 million students as the 1990s commence (U.S. Dept. of Education 1990). Campus enrollment is dependent on students in high school and elementary schools bringing up the ranks. For the past decade, high school enrollment has been down, but buoyed by the baby echo, (that is baby boomers having children), school enrollment at the lower grades is growing again. In addition, as more adult students return to campus, foodservice operators are aggressively targeting these customers. Both of these facts bode well for college/university foodservices.

College/university students today are more sophisticated consumers with a remote-control-like selection behavior when it comes to dining options. Students are responsive to choice and are more selective as to what they eat, when they eat, and in the type of delivery system they choose.

Today females make up over 50% of the student market. Student food habits have changed as a result of today's concern for physical fitness and weight control. Foodservice directors have attempted to meet this need through menu selections and nutrition education.

Other trends in residence hall dining are longer hours of service, fewer restrictions on the number of servings allowed, and greater flexibility in board plans, including a "pay as you eat" plan, rather than a set rate paid in advance (West et al. 1988).

In addition to residence hall dining, campus foodservices offer diverse dining options today. Student union buildings have, for example, set up creative and innovative units catering to students' changing food interests and demands. Commercial fast-food restaurants have been a major competitor for student food dollars. Some institutions have contracted with private enterprises or corporations to operate quick-service restaurants on campus. It is now also possible to obtain a franchise from one of the national fast-food chains.

Some college/university foodservices resemble the off-campus restaurants and fast-food outlets with which they increasingly compete. Food courts provide ethnic foods along with grills, fast foods, and pizza. Pizza deliveries to student dorms are rapidly expanding as well.

By effectively competing with the competition on the outside, college/university foodservices preserve their student customer base. They also create new marketing opportunities aimed at commuter students, faculty, staff, and others in the university community who were never reached by the traditional board plan cafeteria. Making the college/university foodservice internal environment more like that of the off-campus (external) environment helps to draw in these customers.

> Fast-food companies, hungry for new markets, have signed up to add their products to university menus nationwide. By-passing traditional sites on campus fringes, PepsiCo Inc.'s Pizza Hut unit, Dunkin' Donuts Inc., International Dairy Queen Inc. and others are setting up shop inside school cafeterias and dormitories instead.
>
> University officials . . . argue, however, that students want variety in their meal plans and would like students to think nutritionally and about issues of wellness. One strategy is to provide students with lots of choices. Among those are healthy choices.
>
> The branded concept . . . can pose problems for companies. Even students won't eat just pizza and doughnuts every day, as they have become more health-conscious than ever. . . . [F]ast-food outlets in college cafeterias in some cases have cannibalized sales of sites on campus peripheries. (Alexander 1990)

The Foodservice Operation

Foodservice should be considered an important component of the educational experience and it is the responsibility of the institution to determine the best way to have effective foodservice operations. Several methods are in use. Some institutions have one comprehensive foodservice department for all foodservice programs on the campus. Others have segmented the foodservice organization according to services performed, such as one department for residents, a separate department for cash operations, a catering department, and still another for foodservice facilities located in the college union (Barrett 1990).

Approximately nine out of ten college/university foodservice departments offer meal service seven days a week (Birchfield 1990). Once the form of the organization has been selected, it is necessary to determine how the services are to be managed. Most institutions employ a director to manage all or parts of their foodservice departments. The institution must decide to whom the director is to report. That could be Business Affairs, Student Affairs, Auxiliary Services, or combinations thereof. Figure 1 shows an organizational structure for a large college/university foodservice organization.

Some college/university institutions rely on contract foodservice management companies to manage the foodservice operation. In the case of contract management, the institution is relieved of obtaining its own managers

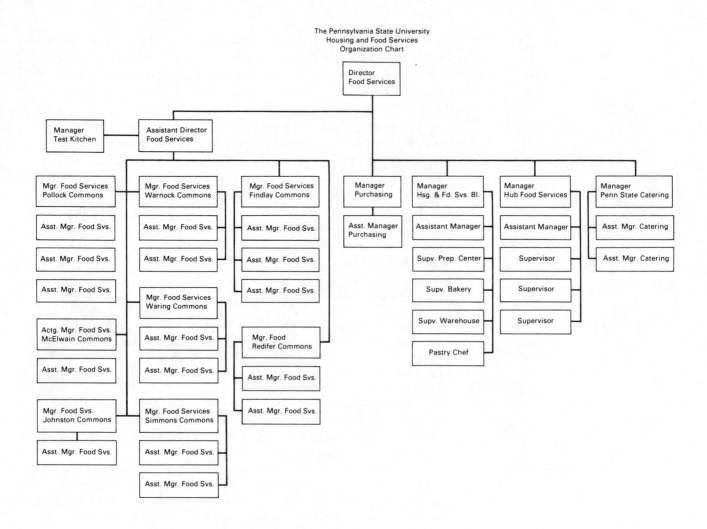

The Pennsylvania State University
Housing and Food Services
Organization Chart

Fig. 1. Sample organizational structure for college/university foodservice operation.

for that operation, purchasing food commodities, and paying the invoices for purchased goods. Monitoring responsibility, however, still rests with the institution, which also retains responsibility for student satisfaction (Barrett 1990).

Generally there are two distinct types of foodservice operations at an institution: (1) Foodservice provided for residence hall students through a board plan program, and (2) Cash operations, such as snack bars, campus restaurants, and specialty shops.

Students living on campus typically pay in advance for their meals; a choice of board plans helps to ensure student satisfaction through the school year. Various meal options can be offered at prices that differentiate between levels of service or number of meals. For example, a student may opt for 21 meals per week, 10 meals per week, or buy à la carte at a campus snack bar or fast-food outlet. An effective meal identification card system is necessary when multiple options exist. Such a system could use a punch card or a picture identification card with a magnetic strip on the back to be used in tandem with a computer system that depends on either a point system or dollar amount. Sophisticated computer systems give campus managers great flexibility in determining the specific features to be implemented while ensuring adequate controls (Barrett 1990). Control of any program is critical. The computerized access system utilizing a student ID card, for example, allows the great flexibility of student meal option plans by precisely counting and tracking allowable meals for the week.

As for the future, we are seeing new ideas now that will be commonplace by 2010. Students will routinely use their ID cards to buy not only meals and books but soft drinks in card-operated vending machines, pay for photocopies, FAX machine use, and other products and services. They will use their cards to access computers located off-campus for research projects. They will have their eligibility checked for using an ever greater variety of campus activities and facilities. Their ID card will come to represent the key to campus life and will become the glue that binds many of the campus operations that are now quite disparate into a more cohesive whole. (Lane 1990).

The College and University Foodservice Model

Figure 2 presents a model of the college and university foodservice operation. The *external environment* includes the environment outside the university domain that impacts the campus and ultimately the internal foodservice environment. The external environment includes the competitors for student food dollars (restaurants), the shifting demographics (leading to increases and decreases in enrollment), and the financial, political, employment, legal, technological, and environmental variables affecting the foodservice operation.

The next portion of the model refers to the *functional management areas* (Figure 3) within the foodservice operation. The four key functional areas of finance, operations, human resources, and marketing are typically staffed by assistant directors who report to the foodservice director and comprise the upper management team. These four functional management areas are keys for success in a competitive market environment. Typically these individuals have at least a four-year degree in hotel, restaurant, and institutional management (HRIM), management dietetics, business, or a related field. The director often comes up through the ranks starting as an assistant manager of a college or university foodservice unit (for example, the dining hall). The remaining part of the model is the *foodservice production core* (Figure 4) that in-

Fig. 2. College/university foodservice model.

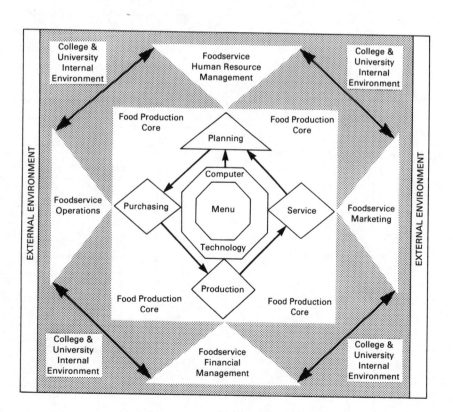

Fig. 3. The four functional areas of college/university foodservice management.

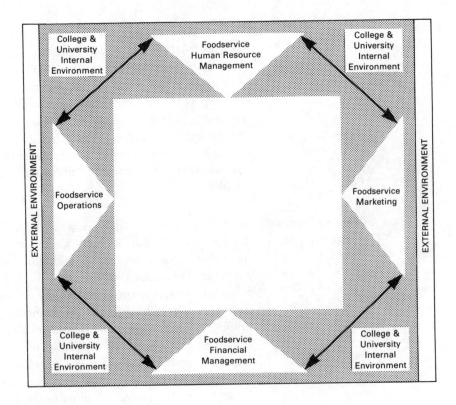

cludes menu planning and nutrition, purchasing, production, and service. The computer is integral to all of these foodservice functions within the core and is described following each function.

Finance In the functional area of financial management, the college and university foodservice operation differs in some respects from commercial operations. In comparing these two types of businesses, it is important to first examine the two in terms of market base, for this is what determines how each will engage in its own financial activities. In a commercial operation, there are always price parameters involved in financial decision making. Depending on the segment the business is trying to appeal to, there will be an effective price range that the market will bear. Many expenses are built into just opening the doors in a commercial operation, with a certain element of risk

Fig. 4. The food production core.

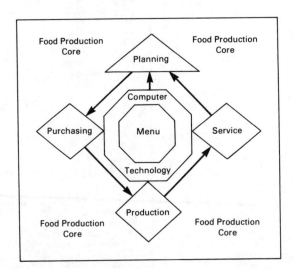

involved, and this risk can affect decisions made. This basic philosophy often differs from institutional foodservice operations in colleges and universities. For example, many institutions, such as healthcare facilities, hospitals, and schools have a captive audience. In other words, these institutional customers have little or no choice of eating locations. This may be true for some college/universities where students residing in the dorms for example, must eat in the campus resident halls. In financial terms, this means a built in revenue base for the operation. There is no imminent need to attract customers; the market is already there. Therefore in this case of captive audience, a college or university operation makes financial decisions based on an expense budget designed from the top down. An operator knows the costs per meal that he or she needs to recover, and a price parameter (or revenue) is developed based on the amount to cover. The challenge in working with this kind of system is that the number of meals to be served, within a strict percentage of deviation, needs to be known. Higher learning institutions generally use what is called a *daily rate* as the cornerstone of their financial plans.

The daily rate is defined as the amount of money required per day from each person to pay for the foodservice. It can be expressed in the following formula:

$$\text{Daily rate} = \frac{\text{Foodservice expenses (\$)} \div \text{Number of days}}{\text{Number of people entitled to eat}}$$

For example, if $1 million are used for foodservice expenses for 120 days in a foodservice operation where 1,000 students are entitled to eat, the daily rate will be

$$\frac{\$1,000,000 \div 120}{1,000} = \$8.33 \text{ per day}$$

As mentioned previously, expenses are built into the rate automatically so that costs will always be covered. In foodservice, these expenses include labor cost, food cost, operating expenses (overhead), and most interestingly, profit. The amount of profit desired is automatically translated (as is everything else) into terms of a per person, per meal amount, and then tacked onto the daily rate. The number of days is based upon how many days any particular eating site will be open during the school semester. The number of people entitled to eat is based on the amount of students and other customers who have prepaid their money for meal privileges for the upcoming semester. A skipped meal factor is also taken into account in financial planning. Generally, room and board payments, as well as tuition, are made by students well in advance of the next school period. These payments are usually made to a bursar's office, and a foodservice operation will draw its necessary operating expense budget from there on a monthly basis.

To accurately predict how many students will eat on any given day, an operation relies heavily on historical figures. From past attendance figures, a moving average will be developed, and this average will be updated each year, sometimes more often, with the use of computers. Even a foodservice operator on campus can recognize that prices and profit parameters must fall within reason or attendance and future sales may drop. To help gain a more accurate handle on how much should be charged for any given meal, an operator will develop a "food cost per meal." In other words, rather than just the cost for one entire day, an operator can determine the price of each meal—breakfast, lunch, and dinner. This, combined with an accurate prediction of customer attendance, can help save other nonfood costs. For instance, the labor budget is often closely linked to the daily rate and food cost per meal. Presently, food and labor costs account for approximately 74% of college/university foodservice revenue (food cost amounting to 34% and labor cost 40%, respectively) (Birchfield 1990). The number of meals to be served at any given meal, as well as the relative food cost of that particular meal helps to determine exactly how many employees are needed to efficiently produce and serve that meal. This is known as *position control*.

Profitability is probably just as important in college/university foodservices as it is in commercial operations. Therefore, the operation must exhibit frugal money management as well. Foodservice operations must plan strategically for the future, just like any business. Profit reserves or working capital are predicated on future projects, new purchases, maintenance and repairs, as well as potential problems such as growing inflation and equipment disasters.

College and university foodservice operations keep an eye on the future, because if they do poorly, they will become less competitive and lose revenue. So, most operations try to design a sound fact-based budget and financial buffers (profit saving) every year, so that if a budget is missed one year, the operation will be able to catch up the next.

Marketing The main competitors to any college and university foodservice operation are the off-campus, quick-service operations situated adjacent to the campus or within the "free delivery" zone. The number and types of restaurants providing delivery service to dormitories and campus offices have increased tremendously over the years.

A major "competitor" or challenge that campus foodservices face is its perceived image. This image is often that of a cafeteria with slow-moving lines, hastily prepared food that gets cold by the time one gets to one's seat and furniture and fixtures that are more functional and less attractive. With this in mind, college/university foodservice operators have adopted more aggressive marketing tactics to enhance their image.

At many college/universities today, the foodservice operation has a very sophisticated customer-input system, which provides very valuable information to management. A student advisory board keeps management abreast of trends in eating habits and other customer service needs. Because of the increase in the number of health-conscious and vegetarian diners, a vegetarian advisory board for example may be set up to make dietary recommendations. Taste tests are done regularly, especially when new menu items are being introduced. "Secret shoppers" also test service quality and give feedback on aspects such as time spent waiting in line, quality of food, dining room staff, and dining atmosphere.

The communications program at college/universities has become very assertive. Colorful posters and brochures are used to create awareness and redefine the image of college foodservice. Nutrition information booklets outline calorie counts, and fat and sodium content for example.

A communications manager may oversee a direct-mail program that targets students as well as faculty and staff. Students may receive a 30-day menu calendar with highlights of theme meals and other special events. Such events receive extra publicity with separate posters on bulletin boards and flyers in student mailboxes. Employees receive meal plan information and restaurant specials.

The physical environment of college dining services has also been altered dramatically to enhance its appeal. The drab, booth-filled dining rooms have been replaced with sun-filled rooms, colorful furniture, indoor plants, and platform arrangements creating the atmosphere of upscale, full service restaurants. At the same time, diners have easy access to different self-serve counters (salad and fruit, cereal and dairy, dessert, and juices) as part of the dining room layout. This feature cuts down on time spent waiting in line.

A new feature that has been introduced in the dining commons at some colleges/universities allows students to cook their own meals. For example, woks are provided and students have a wide choice of ingredients. This has proven to be very popular and has even had positive comments from some international students who often feel that dining services do not cater to their needs enough.

The convenience factor is one that students and staff take into consideration when selecting where to eat. Lunch time is often a rush and lines can be a problem when there is only one hour to spare. Penn State for example, has been able to overcome the problem because of its size. Its foodservice facilities range from the standard dormitory dining rooms, to quick-eat snack counters, to hot dog cart vendors, to full-service facilities. These are located all over the campus so that customers are within five minutes of any facility. Even after-hours, fast-food outlets situated adjacent to the dining rooms provide late night snacks to hungry students. During special events the catering service sets up its carts at strategic points on campus to reach customers.

Along with this, foodservice provides meal plan options that allow customers to buy points in advance and not have to worry about carrying cash. For Penn State on-campus residents, an "à la board" meal plan can be purchased at the beginning of the semester and customers can use points at anytime in any of the operations once they present their identification cards. For other customers a "diner's club" plan allows them to purchase points in blocks and use them in any of the campus facilities. A discount is built into the "diner's club" plans.

Thus, campus foodservice has come a long way over the years. Realizing that the campus foodservice can be a profit center and generate money for the university, on-going marketing programs seek to make it more attractive to the students and employees.

Human Resource Management

One of the biggest problems faced by human resource managers in college and university foodservices is that of finding qualified applicants for highly technical operations. Although the number of hospitality and foodservice management graduates has increased over the years, there is still a great shortage of workers in general. Also, institutional foodservice is often not seen as attractive as compared to other sectors of the industry and so it is often difficult to recruit graduates.

Many colleges rely heavily on part-time student labor to fill this gap. At the Pennsylvania State University, the largest college foodservice operation in the country, over 1,000 of the 1,750 workers at its main campus are students. One advantage of hiring students is that they can be paid lower wages and do not have to be provided with regular employee benefits. Another benefit is that they work on a flexible time schedule and so the university does not have to pay for "idle time" as it would other full-time workers.

However, off-campus foodservice facilities have become a major threat to this labor pool. These operations may pay higher wages and offer free meals even to hourly workers. In some cases, students can be offered permanent positions and receive fringe benefits.

In order to alleviate some of the problems and keep up with trends in service and production, some foodservice operations have had to be creative. In many facilities, self-service as opposed to over-the-counter service has become the norm. Students are able to select the food ingredients and do their own cooking in some of the newer facilities (for example using woks to create their own stir-fry).

Personnel directors have begun to highlight the very positive aspects of institutional foodservice as the industry becomes even more competitive. They stress the "normal, 40-hour work week" that workers enjoy as opposed to the longer hours in most other foodservice operations. College/university employees are given generous benefit packages, including free tuition and time off to attend classes. Supervisors can expect to receive management development training and promotions after successful completion of such training.

The job conditions of college and university foodservice workers have improved tremendously over the years, and human resource directors are aggressively pointing out these changes in order to attract more workers to this segment of the foodservice industry.

Operations Management

When examining the operations division of college and university foodservice, it is helpful to discuss the various types of operations. The most common type is the standard board plan cafeteria. This can be a traditional line style cafeteria or a food court with several different eateries, as found in modern shopping malls. This service is usually prepaid by the client and works off some sort of a meal plan (that is, full meal plan, à la carte eating, and punch or point plans). Other types of standard operation methods include retail sales, cash plans, and student union plans. These plans are most often competing more directly with local retail restaurants due to their cash basis and/or lack of prepaid contract. Another category of university foodservices is the delivery systems. These include concessions run for sporting and special events, catering for university functions, and operation of college vending machines. An additional, but not as large, division of foodservices is conferencing. Here, there is a combination of catering and regular cafeteria services for conferences or summer sports or music camps sponsored by the university.

Regardless of the type or types of operation used by a particular university, the common bond shared by all of these systems is that they are operations. In foodservice, operations is a line function, and the other functional areas such as personnel, marketing, and finance are staff functions whose main purpose is to support the execution of day-to-day operations. Often an assistant director in charge of operations is found on campus, (see Figures 2 and 3) which comprises operations management. The assistant director in charge of operations reports to the director of foodservices and, typically, is in charge of foodservice managers at the various campus units (that is, dining halls, snack bars, catering departments, and so forth). Operations performs important roles of the business, such as quality control and assurance, production, and sanitation and safety. Cost controls are also performed at this level. Within each of these roles several duties must be performed to help ensure smooth facilitation of operations. With respect to quality assurance, the design and development of acceptable and nutritionally oriented menus is expected. Standards for purchasing procedures are adopted. Distribution of foods from purchasing is maintained, and, most importantly, systems for production, the heart of an operation, are devised and enacted. Service, both style and policies, are also factors to be considered in quality assurance and control. In the area of sanitation and safety, attention is directed to personal sanitation, the offering of wholesome food, food handling practices, and the general safety and cleanliness of the property as well as the equipment. Other issues concern compliance with governmental or university standards and effectiveness of current safety/sanitation regulations. Cost controls are another important area falling under the supervision of operations management. An annual budget must be followed, operating statements must be produced, and dining room access and control must be developed and maintained. Other important areas of control include cash handling and the accountability of employees. Several other areas fall under the scope of the operations department, including, but not limited to, personnel administration, program development and support (for both customers as well as employees), and ultimately, as with any other business, satisfaction of the clients. All of these things help define the parameters of an operational division within a college or university foodservice operation. The most important factor common to all these numerous responsibilities is that operations must formulate and administer effective and efficient plans of action for all of these various systems, monitor their implementation, and provide continual updating of them in order to provide the smoothest flow of activities possible.

Core Foodservice

The food production core can be found at all food production/service units on the campus. Since Penn State has one of the largest and most diverse foodservice operations, it will serve as the focus of the following discussion.

The Menu—The Heart of the Operation

The menu is the heart of any foodservice operation, including those in a college/university setting (Figure 4). The menu is the means by which customers, in this case students, staff, and faculty, choose to dine in a university establishment or go elsewhere. With this fact in mind, the university must devise a menu that satisfies the majority of a diverse community. The menu also must be updated periodically to keep pace with changing customer trends and preferences.

The menu constantly changes, from month to month and year to year. The test kitchen manager, as part of his/her duties, finds new recipes and cooks one batch for a panel of six evaluators. The taste tests are conducted periodically for two main reasons: (1) to evaluate several brands of products to choose the best one, and (2) to iron out any problems with current menu items to ensure consistency throughout the university. If a new product is evaluated favorably the new product is added to the current menu.

Once a year, a menu committee is formed to evaluate current menu items. The menu committee consists of personnel from purchasing through service, in order to involve all areas that will be affected by menu changes.

Revisions on the menu also occur during the school year when the need arises. Certain groups who feel the menu is insufficient in some manner discuss the possibility of menu changes with the test kitchen manager and the assistant director of foodservices (operations functional area). If feasible solutions are presented, the changes are worked into the menu immediately. One group that frequently uses the process to better the menu are vegetarians. Their special diet requirements pose a challenge to all personnel in the foodservice operation.

Once the menu has undergone the necessary changes, it runs in a cycle. A cycle menu is a menu that repeats itself every so many weeks. Penn State has a 5-week cycle menu for example. To add variety to the menu, special dinners and entrée substitution occur.

A special dinner is an elaborate meal that focuses on a theme. For example for Bugs Bunny's 50th year anniversary, Penn State featured a "Hare's to you Bugs" theme. The food items served centered around the theme. For example, Tazmanian Tea, Porky's Pwime W-W-Wib, Elmer Fudd's Fwench Fwied Fantail Shwimp, Bug's Criss Cross Carrots, Thufferin' Thuccotash, and Tweeties Tweets were some of the items served during the meal.

Entrée substitution merely relies on substituting one entrée for another, in order to increase variety. For example, a chicken cosmo sandwich (deep fried breaded chicken patty on a roll) could be substituted for a grilled chicken sandwich.

Computer Applications and the Menu

The computer is a tremendous time-saving device. It forecasts customer count, based on average counts for that day and the previous year. With the forecasted count, the computer also forecasts the amount of each menu item to be served, based on an acceptability factor. The acceptability factor is based on how popular the item was over the past few years. With the forecasted patron count and menu item count, the dining hall manager is then able to determine how much of each ingredient needs to ordered.

Purchasing

Since each dining hall follows the standard menu and therefore needs the same ingredients, a central purchasing department was created. The purchasing department tallies the ingredients from each dining hall and places an order with the most economical supplier, or purveyor.

Purveyors, like the menu, often change. Penn State invites a variety of purveyors into its receiving location to test their products. The products are tested and evaluated for quality and price. The best product for the price is then chosen. Penn State then enters into a contract with the purveyor, in which quality needs and price are specified and agreed upon. A date is then set when the goods will be shipped and received. A purveyor evaluation is done periodically in order to purchase the best product at the best price.

The next step in the purchasing process is receiving the supplies. Large trucks unload the supplies at specific loading docks. Receiving goods is a crucial part of the purchasing process. Damaged or inferior products, once accepted, become the liability of the university. Unless the university has an agreement with the purveyor (regarding damaged goods), the goods are written off as a loss. All acceptable goods are then taken into storage areas.

The supplies are arranged in storage in a first in, first out (FIFO) sequence. The supplies stay in storage until they are ordered by a dining hall. At this point the supplies are shipped from the warehouse to each individual location. Each dining hall uses the FIFO sequence in order to use the oldest supplies first.

Not all supplies follow the steps just described. Some goods, for example produce and dairy products, are ordered by each dining hall directly from a vendor. Under these circumstances the purchasing department and warehouse are not used.

Computer Applications and Purchasing

The computer in the purchasing department has many functions. One function is to act as a liaison between the warehouse and each dining hall unit. The computer produces a list of supplies needed by each unit, which is then gathered and sent out (to the unit). It also helps with the clerical functions in the purchasing department. When purchase orders are input into the computer, it prints and files them for future use. The computer also sends the bill (purchase order) to the accounting office to pay for the supplies. As one can see, the computer once again is a valuable tool.

Production

Once the supplies are in the dining hall unit, they must be prepared and processed before they can be served to the consumers. The two main production areas in any of the university foodservice operations are the cooking, and salad preparation areas. Foodstuffs that are offered to consumers that do not come from the two production areas are usually pre-prepared products. The cook's production area comprises the majority of the prep and processing functions.

The cook's production area receives raw product and converts it into a finished product ready to be consumed. Some of the products come partially assembled or prepped. Quiche, for example, only requires the cook to assemble and combine the egg mixture. The pie crust is already made in pie tins. Soups during the week are homemade, but on the weekends many come from a can. These premade products cost a premium price but can be cost efficient in terms of labor.

The second production area is the salad area. Workers in this area convert raw products into a finished salad bar item. The typical products made in this area include cut vegetables, vegetable salads, fruit salads, and gelatin. Salad workers also receive finished products that only need to be portioned out. Most desserts are made in the central bakery, and only require to be cut and plated.

Two central departments, the bakery and the commissary, carry out the production process on a central level and then ship the product to the dining hall units. The bakery makes doughnuts, breads, and most desserts. In order to keep up with the demand for its products, the bakery has been forced to make products before they are needed and freeze them until required by the dining hall units. The bakery is beneficial because it provides fresh products (as opposed to purveyor bought products), at an economy of scale that is profitable for the foodservice operation.

The central commissary is another benefit for the dining hall units. The commissary cuts bulk cheeses and meats into slices. It also prepares meat salads, for example tuna salad, for each unit. Another responsibility of the commissary is to make sandwiches that are placed in the vending machines around campus. Like the bakery, the commissary provides a labor saving product/service (for each dining hall unit) and is profitable because of economies of scale.

Computer Applications and Production

The computer, on the dining hall level, prints out recipes and production methods (for the forecasted amounts), and uses a postcost printout to document actual quantities served. Once the quantities served are determined, these values are then input into the computer and are averaged with past values. Using historical data, food amounts are forecasted. At this point the computer cycle with regard to the menu has gone one complete revolution.

The computer performs many functions for the bakery and commissary. It tallies the needs from each of the dining hall units for each of its products every day. It uses these tallies to input the number of portions needed. The recipes and methods are then printed out with the total quantity. It also determines the food inventory on hand and projects the amount of ingredients that need to be ordered for the next production week.

Service

The next step after production is service. After the food is prepared, the dining hall must distribute its products efficiently. The university uses a serving line, similar to traditional cafeterias. The serving line consists of appetizers, entrées, vegetables, desserts, and hot beverages. A variety of self-service bars are in the dining room including salad, cereal, bread, fruit, condiment, cold beverages, and ice cream.

The customer has the choice of eating at the dining hall or at specialty operations run by the university. The main difference between the two is that the specialty operations are priced à la carte, whereas the dining hall relies on one price regardless of what is selected. The specialty operations offer a variety of products. These operations include deli, pizza, pastry shop, fast-food hamburger area, light dining, and casual lunch dining. Even though the specialty operations use the same production system as the dining halls, they are open all day long, as opposed to only during certain meal times.

Another service operated by the university are snack bars. These snack bars are located in each of the dining halls and operate a few hours each evening (excluding weekends). They offer sandwiches, subs, pizza, beverages, and snack items. This service grew out of a need for nighttime food for hungry customers who do not want to travel very far.

Computer Applications and Service

The computer is extremely important in the service aspect of the university foodservice operation. Consumers have the option of paying cash or using points when purchasing items. If the point system is chosen, the customer pays for an account with x amount of points (encoded into the university I.D.). Upon entering a dining hall or purchasing food from the specialty operations or snack bars, the consumers have points deducted from their account by scanning their card through the reader.

The computer system keeps a running balance for each customer and can make additions or deletions to any account. When a customer has a low balance, more points can be purchased by going through the proper channels. Sometimes a card is read incorrectly, so personnel must manually go into the system and deduct points from the appropriate account.

Sanitation and Clean-up

The last phase of the production system is sanitation. Employees should clean as the shift goes on, but when it is over sanitation is the main emphasis. Products must be taken back to their respective areas and either are thrown away or saved for another meal. Once the products are taken care of, a thorough cleaning is the next order of business. Equipment must be taken apart, washed, and sanitized. When the items dry, they must be replaced in their original locations. Lights are turned off and doors locked in anticipation of another service day to come. If the cleaning process is not done satisfactorily, serious problems can occur. Poisonings, accidents, and insect infestation are all problems caused by insufficient/careless sanitation. Even though it is the last task of the day, it is one of the most important.

Career Opportunities for Hotel, Restaurant, and Institutional Management Graduates

Management of college and university foodservices is usually under the direction of well-qualified foodservice managers and registered dietitians employed directly by the university or by a contract foodservice company.

The use of college and university dining facilities as laboratories for foodservice management students is a common practice. This, no doubt, has helped establish high requirements for foodservice directors on such campuses. Directing the students' laboratory experiences and the work of numerous part-time student employees used in most campus foodservices presents unique situations not common in other types of foodservice organizations (West et al. 1988).

Several career advantages exist in the college and university foodservice segment. Steady employment is combined with variety and life on a college campus. Relatively predictable and regular hours along with competitive salaries make this career path very attractive. Generally, there is freedom to try new ideas, with ample opportunities for experimentation. In addition, an opportunity exists for college and university foodservice managers to continue their educations (Minor and Cichy 1984).

Marketing Strategies and Trends in College and University Foodservices

Today's college/university market is ever changing, evolving around a demanding and sophisticated customer base. The following looks at how some operations across the United States are responding to this evolution.

Steak is out; Italian is in at the University of Maryland in College Park, Maryland. The University of Maryland Dining Services opened UMberto's this year. UMberto's, a 100-seat restaurant in the basement of the Student Union, features "casual country Italian cuisine." The restaurant replaced What's Your Beef?, a steak house whose sales had been declining. The menu features recipes handed down by the foodservice director's grandmother. It includes five different sauces, fresh-made lasagna, several veal and chicken dishes, sandwiches, salads, and desserts, including cannoli and cassata cake. In addition, UMberto's offers a menu item not usually found in Italian restaurants: Italian nachos, made with marinara sauce, melted mozzarella cheese, olives, and green peppers. The restaurant's motif features oak-topped tables, backlit stained glass windows and reproductions of Renaissance paintings.

The University of Virginia, Charlottesville, has spent more than $1.5 million on renovating the dining areas in the campus student center. Pavilion XI, a 225-seat facility, was gutted and a food court was installed, featuring contract company ARA Services' Del El Pollo Grande, Gretel's Bakery, Grille Works, and Itza Pizza concepts.

Bold and dramatic changes are in store at Virginia Tech, a university whose foodservice operation has been virtually unchanged for 30 years. Virginia Tech, long a traditional, cafeteria-based foodservice, has begun a four-phase program that will convert this department from one presently drawing virtually all its revenues from meal plans to one with 75% of its volume in retail sales. During the first phase, several dining halls will be remodeled into specialty restaurants specializing in one or two product lines, supplemented by gourmet-style salad bars. Next, will come a food court with five or six specialty shops. The third phase of the plan calls for opening a fine dining restaurant comanaged with the university's hotel, restaurant, and institutional management school. Finally, management envisions building an "all-you-can-eat" dining hall featuring exhibition cooking.

To cater to the takeout diner's needs and after noticing a marked increase in take-out sales among students, the foodservice staff at the University of Southern California in Los Angeles (UCLA) introduced the "Greens To Go" program. "Greens To Go," which comprises a variety of prepackaged salads, has been distinguished from other carryout items by a colorful printed logo. In addition, "Greens To Go," salads are packed with their own utensils and dressings. Salad varieties include tossed green, Caesar, seafood, steamed vegetables with brown rice, and broiled chicken breast salad.

These are just some of the innovative trends being marketed by foodservice departments on college and university campuses. If it is true that in today's market "the only constant is change," then today's foodservice directors are demonstrating this, as they constantly change to serve more variety driven consumers.

Summary

College and university foodservice has evolved through the years. To remain competitive and entice students demanding variety, foodservice operators are offering more options, ranging from quick-service branded concepts to remaining open 24 hours per day. To meet these challenges, successful college and university foodservice operations call upon the expertise of the functional areas of human resources, marketing, finance, operations, and computer foodservice management.

Acknowledgments. The author wishes to thank Clive Muir, Stan Suboleski, and Ann Spaeder of the School of Hotel, Restaurant and Institutional Management at Penn State for their research and efforts for this paper, as well as Tom Gibson, Lisa Wandel, and Sylvester Roy of Penn State Dining Services for their contributions.

References

Alexander, S. 1990. Hungry fast-food companies invade college eateries as nutritionists groan. *The Wall Street Journal,* November 27, 1990, p. B1.

Barrett, L. L. 1990. *College and University Food Service.* Personal Communication. Manuscript for College and University Business Administrators (CUBA). Personal Communication through the National Association of College and University Food Services (NACUFS).

Birchfield, J. 1990. Profit and loss study of college food services. *The Food Service Director,* September 15, 1990, p. 1.

Lane, B. R. 1990. 2010—The keyless/cashless world. *CBORD Systems Solutions,* Fall 1990, pp. 10–11.

Minor, L. J. and R. F. Cichy. 1984. *Foodservice Systems Management.* Westport, Conn.: AVI Publishing.

West, B. B., L. Wood, V. F. Harger, G. S. Shugart, J. P. Palacio. 1988. *Foodservice in Institutions,* 6th ed. New York: Macmillan.

23

Institutional Foodservice Management

Mickey Warner

"Institutional foodservice" is a term widely used, but defined differently by various areas of foodservice management, to describe the noncommercial segments of the foodservice industry.

The National Restaurant Association produces an annual survey of gross national foodservice sales, using three basic categories: I. Commercial, II. Institutional, and III. Military. The 1992 projection with classifications and sales dollars follows:

	1992 Sales
Commercial Foodservice	*(billion $)*
Eating places	$171
Drinking places	9
Foodservice contractors	16
Hotel/Motel restaurants	15
Retail, vending, recreation	21
	$232
Institutional Foodservice	
Businesses, schools, hospitals, nursing homes, and others that operate their own foodservice	$ 29
Military Foodservice	
Base exchange, Officers' and NCO club foodservice	$ 1
Total	$262

Restaurant Business magazine provides a similar annual report using the following categorical breakdowns: (1) Commercial/Contract (restaurants, bars, taverns, in-flight); (2) Institutional; (3) Military. No further breakdown is given for categories two and three.

Restaurant and Institutions magazine provides an annual summary of comparison sales and number of units between institutional and commercial segments of the foodservice industry. Table 1 is a summary of their 1990 report.

The academic community has its own definitions of "institutional" as it refers to curriculum regarding foodservice management. Some two- and four-year schools and colleges refer to themselves as Hotel, Restaurant, Institutional (HRI) Management Schools. Each school or college has its own view of what constitutes "institutional" foodservice as a management discipline.

The International Foodservice Manufacturers Association (IFMA) prepared an in-house study, "FOODSERVICE: A Segmented Industry" in 1987 (IFMA 1987). IFMA is a trade organization with a membership that includes all major food equipment and supplies companies, with an emphasis on marketing to the foodservice industry. They have identified twelve different segments as those that comprise the total foodservice industry. Following is a list of those segments taken from the table of contents of the above-named study. IFMA does not use the term "institutional" for any of their described segments.

1. Full service restaurants
2. Quick service restaurants
3. Healthcare foodservice
4. Elementary and secondary school foodservice
5. College and university foodservice
6. Hotel/Motel foodservice
7. Military and correctional foodservice
8. Transportation foodservice
9. Business and industry foodservice
10. Retail and convenience grocery foodservice
11. Recreational foodservice
12. Contract foodservice/vending

Table 1. *A comparison of institutional and commercial segments estimated sales and number of units*

Institutional segments	Estimated 1990 sales ($billions)	Estimated 1990 real growth (%)	Estimated 2000 real growth (%)	Units
Employee feeding	16.19	0.9	1.3	16,000
Schools	13.26	1.1	1.3	89,000
Hospitals	10.77	0.1	0.0	6,985
Colleges and universities	7.22	0.0	0.2	3,350
Military	5.57	0.1	0.2	3,320
Nursing homes	3.79	2.1	2.4	14,925
Transportation	3.15	1.7	1.3	155
Day Care	2.42	2.4	1.8	40,000
Elder care	0.94	2.7	3.0	4,075
Total	65.48 (28%)	0.9	1.0	187,810 (28%)
All commercial segments total	165.43 (72%)			476,297 (72%)

Source: Adapted from 1990 *Restaurants and Institutions,* January 10, p. 22.

As can be seen, the term "institutional foodservice" has been defined and evaluated in different ways, by different organizations and interested groups. Generally, institutional foodservices are located wtihin a business or facility whose primary mission is *not* foodservice. For purposes of this article the term "institutional" foodservice is used to describe all areas of the foodservice industry that are not primarily in the business of offering a public foodservice facility operated solely to make a profit from the foodservice. The major categories for this description are:

1. Business and industry foodservice
2. Primary and secondary school foodservice
3. College and university foodservice
4. Healthcare foodservice
5. Correctional institutions
6. Some areas of contract foodservice/vending

These are six of the twelve segments described by IFMA as comprising the total foodservice industry. Each of these segments is also contained in most other industry surveys, albeit they may be used under a different rubric. Regardless of the rubric used they contain the common descriptions used by all industry analysts as being "institutional."

The term *commercial* is herein defined as "having profit as an aim." The term *noncommercial* is defined as synonymous with "institutional." Although many contract foodservice companies are engaged in the management of various segments of the noncommercial foodservice area, and they do so for a profit, that profit is not usually derived from a commercial foodservice but from managing a noncommercial or institutional operation.

Business and Industry Foodservice

The genesis of business and industry (B & I) foodservice began in Scotland around 1800. Warner (1973) reports that Robert Owen, the operator of a mill, opened a large "eating room" for his employees, where employees could sit down and eat a lunch meal they had brought from home.

Stokes (1960) states that the cafeteria method of service, (which was to become prevalent in employee foodservice operations) was developed by the Ogontz Lunch Club for Women in Chicago. It was installed at the YWCA in Kansas City around 1891. Stokes further offers that the earliest known industrial (B & I) foodservice in the United States was in the Bowery Savings Bank in New York in 1834. Service was to all employees, sit-down, waitress style, and without cost to the employee.

What is believed to be the first employee cafeteria was installed at the Plymouth Cordage Company in Plymouth, Massachusetts. The company constructed a building that housed a kitchen, two cafeterias, and a recreational facility for its employees. Prior to this installation, lunch rooms and table service dining were the accepted methods of providing an employee foodservice.

Meakin (1905) prepared a survey that listed over fifty firms in the United States that were providing some form of employee foodservice at that time. Today the employee foodservice operation is common and the cafeteria is the most prevalent type.

The first known contract management company of employee foodservice operations (then called an industrial caterer) was N. W. Cease. He and his brother opened a cafeteria on the premises of the American Locomotive

Works, in Dunkirk, New York, with the permission of the company. Foodservice contract management companies are now giant national corporations.

Business and industry foodservice is a term commonly used by all of the national contract management foodservice companies. Harbingers to this term were "inplant foodservice" and "industrial foodservice." The definitions descriptive to this area are plants and factories, office buildings, and foodservice vending. These facilities provide services for employees, (usually as cafeterias), executive dining, and company guest dining. The latter two usually have sit-down, waitstaff service.

Service is on company premises, providing mid-shift meal service and coffee break service. The mid-shift meal is usually lunch but may be dinner or an overnight meal in a plant or factory. Many of the operations offer breakfast service to arriving personnel, particularly in urban areas and in three-shift factory operations. Coffee break service is often provided by vending machines strategically placed throughout the facility. Some locations still utilize portable carts for the coffee service. Full line foodservice vending is also used for remote areas and off shifts depending on the facility. Where it is used, it is usually part of the foodservice management responsibility.

B & I foodservices are managed by both the contract management companies and the business organization providing the service. The term used for the latter is *self-operators*. Contract management companies operate a major portion of this segment with an 80 percent market penetration in locations with over 500 employees. Self-operators manage the remainder.

Depending on which organization has prepared the survey, this segment is described as being 6 to 8 percent of the total foodservice industry. There are an estimated 16,000 individual unit locations. The *Restaurant and Institutions* survey (Table 1) indicates that 1990 sales for this segment were $16.19 billion, real growth is 0.9 percent and estimated year 2000 real growth rate will be 1.3 percent.

Primary and Secondary School Foodservice

Primary and secondary schools in the United States have a long history of providing foodservice to students. Serving food at school began with volunteer efforts of the Children's Aid Society of New York in 1853.

In the early 1900s lunch service in schools was primarily a volunteer effort. In 1921 the Chicago Board of Education claimed that it was serving lunch in all of its high schools and most of its elementary schools. Van Egmond Pannell (1990) reports that the first federal funding for school lunch programs came from the Reconstruction Finance Corporation in 1932 and 1933. Those funds paid labor costs for lunch preparation in several southwestern Missouri towns. By 1934 the program had expanded to thirty-nine of the then forty-eight states.

In 1935 the Works Progress Administration (WPA), a Roosevelt-era welfare-type program, assigned women in needy areas to the school lunch program and paid the labor costs. By 1941, the WPA had standardized menus, recipes, and procedures and was operating in all 48 states, the District of Columbia, and Puerto Rico. This encompassed over 23,000 schools serving over 2 million lunches daily, employing over 64,000 people.

In 1946, the National School Lunch Act was passed. It provided funding of $231 million to offer 4.5 million children lunch at school, with a subsidy. By 1979 over 27 million daily lunches were being served in over 94,300 schools and institutions.

The National School Lunch Program (NSLP) was enacted in 1946. Its purpose was stated in that law's introduction: ". . . as a measure of national security, to safeguard the health and well being of the Nation's children and to encourage the domestic consumption of nutritious agricultural commodities and other food. . . ." The catalyst to this law was a review of a study of malnutrition among World War II (WWII) draftees at their initial physical examination and a need to use the overproduction of flourishing farms developed during WWII. These farms were producing various agricultural commodities in excess and did not have a ready market.

Additional public funding was made for the School Lunch Program by the 1966 Child Welfare Act. This program helps provide a nutritious lunch to undernourished children, either free or at a reduced price. Lunches at a participating school are usually priced between 25 and 75 cents lower than at a nonparticipating school. Any nonprofit primary or secondary school is allowed to participate, providing their tuition is less than $2,000.

A participating school, agreeing to carry out federal regulations, may receive either a cash reimbursement or a commodity assistance for a nonprofit foodservice. This regulation is under the NSLP administered by the U.S. Department of Agriculture at the federal level and by the Department of Education at the state level. At this present writing payments and commodity rates are:

Paid	$0.1475
Free	1.5325
Reduced price	1.1325
Commodities	0.1325

Rates are increased annually based on the Consumer Price Index. The NSLP and some other programs are exempt from potential cuts under Gramm-Rudman legislation as entitlement laws. The paid program is not exempt.

Foodservice managers directing a school lunch program must be familiar with all subsidy and commodity programs. This industry segment requirement is not present in other foodservice industry segments. Commodity programs are very complex, requiring substantial administrative efforts.

Management companies (contract management) became active in the National School Lunch Program in 1969 when Congress amended the law to allow them to do so. Prior to that time a school district could not qualify for the NSLP funding if they allowed a management company to operate its program. During the White House Conference on Food, Nutrition and Health (1970) it was reported that some school districts were not meeting the nutritional needs of children at school. As a result Public Law 95-166 was passed allowing school districts to utilize an outside management company without losing their qualification rights for NSLP and commodity support.

Now, in 1990, management companies operate an estimated 8 to 10 percent of all school district programs. This figure is expected to double or triple over the next 10 to 15 years as school districts opt for a more painless way to operate the school lunch program under their responsibility. The contractors sell the idea that they can eliminate the operating loss that may now be occurring, eliminate personnel problems, assist in capital investment needs, eliminate complacency among school foodservice personnel, and provide trouble-free, no-hassle management.

The school lunch program has become a major potential market for the contract management companies, which is anticipated to continue.

College and University Foodservice

The Morrill Act, passed by Congress in 1862, granted public lands for the establishment of educational institutions. These institutions became known as land grant colleges. Each of the schools established contained a foodservice facility for both students and faculty.

In addition, numerous endowed institutions were formed by religious and private organizations. Kotschevar (1987) reports that by 1986 there were over 2,500 schools and colleges, each with a professionally managed foodservice.

The average foodservice in a modern school or college provides various types of service to its students, administrative employees, and faculty. Most schools with dormitories provide a meal plan for their occupants. This may be a 15-meal, 19-meal, or 21-meal plan, depending on the institution. Plans allow for full cafeteria service to resident students, depending on the plan selected.

Payment is usually made by the student as a "board rate" for the semester. This entitles the student (boarder) to eat at established locations within the constraints of the plan selected.

Many institutions also provide a faculty dining facility. Some also provide an administrative employee facility, similar to the employee cafeteria and executive dining room facilities provided in the B & I segment of the industry.

An additional foodservice found on many campuses is the Rathskeller, where beer is usually sold in addition to a small à la carte menu. Often this is part of a student union building that houses other student activities such as a book store, lounge areas, and so forth.

Catering can be an important part of the campus dining service. Most major campus operations, particularly those managed by a contract company, offer a catering service to both student and other groups present on the campus. This service can comprise up to 5 percent of total food sales of the location.

A comparatively new foodservice making its way to the campus is the various fast-food franchise operations. The pizza segment in particular has become increasingly popular. Some locations operated by the contract management companies have a fast-food franchise, also operated by the management company. Others offer a single product, (for example, pizza, donuts) from a brand name franchise. This trend is becoming popular. The contract management companies call this effort "branding."

In summary, campus dining offers board rate student cafeterias, administrative employee cafeterias, faculty dining rooms, rathskeller (student) services, catering, and some fast-food franchise menu items. The service may be operated by a contract management company or the institution itself.

Healthcare Foodservice

Stokes (1960) reports that crude hospitals were known in India and Egypt as early as six centuries before the Christian era. He further relates that the first hospital was established in England in 1004, and the first on the American continent in Mexico in 1524. It was not until the nineteenth century that modern standards of treatment and dietary management were formulated.

Present day health care foodservice may take place in a hospital, a nursing home or extended care facility, an elder care center, or a retirement home.

The advent of Medicare, and its control over allowable expenditures of hospitals (known as diagnostic related groups or DRGs) has had an effect on the management of a healthcare foodservice operation. Hospitals in particular are affected by this governmental control.

Hospitals   Hospitals fall into three basic categories: Voluntary, proprietary, and governmental. Voluntary hospitals are generally nonprofit institutions. Proprietary hospitals are operated for a profit the same as any other business. Governmental hospitals are operated by cities, counties, states, and the federal government. The Veterans Administration operates a complete chain of hospitals in all areas of the country.

A hospital foodservice operation may encompass a wide variety of foodservice facilities. Sullivan (1990) reports that hospitals have the following services:

- Patient foodservice (personalized diet room service)
- Cafeterias (employee and guest meals)
- Vending (contract or independent)
- Short order (coffee shop, snack bars)
- Table service (special luncheons and dinners)
- Banquet (special activities)
- Tea service (retirement, promotion parties)

Not reported by Sullivan, but existing in many hospitals, are special physician dining facilities. These provide a service to staff doctors much in the same manner as the executive dining room in a B & I location.

Hospital foodservice management is among the most complex of any area of institutional foodservice management. In some states the foodservice director must meet specific requirements. Sullivan reports that in Michigan the director of a medical foodservice must meet qualifications and guidelines established by the State Department of Health, federal guidelines for participation in Medicare and Medicaid programs, and standards for the Joint Commission on Accreditation of Hospitals (JCAH). Although these standards are stringent, they are rapidly becoming more common in this field.

Nursing Homes   Nursing homes and extended care facilities provide services similar to hospitals, but without their full range of medical services. Patients in a nursing home or extended care facility are usually there for a longer period of time to recover from a hospital confinement or to be treated for a long-term illness.

Elder Care Centers   These are similar to child care centers, but are for the elderly. Just as parents are responsible for the well-being of their children and often leave them at day-care centers while they are at work, some people have the responsibility to care for an older parent. These parents are often placed in an elder care center for care during the day. This method of caring for the aging population of America is becoming increasingly popular.

Retirement Homes   These locations are rapidly becoming a major segment of the healthcare foodservice industry. Residents are neither sick or in need of daily medical attention but do wish to receive daily meal service prepared by others and served in central dining facilities. Many retirement homes are operated by the various levels of governmental agencies. A wide variety of retirement homes are also operated for profit by real estate and/or hotel companies. Regardless of the management or ownership, these locations offer an institutional type service to a resident elderly population.

Correctional Foodservice

Correctional foodservice facilities are operated by various city, county, state, and federal agencies. Whereas the majority are operated by the responsible agency as a self-operated facility, many contract management companies are now active in this field. This is a relatively new market for the contractors.

When a correctional facility contracts out its foodservice, a Request For Proposal (RFP) is prepared by the responsible agency and bids are received from the contractors. The bidding process usually requires the bidders to present a proposal detailing their proposed method of operation, the professional staff they will provide, and the cost per meal they will charge for the service. The successful bidder is awarded a multiyear contract reflecting the terms of the RFP. In some cases the bidder also provides a capital investment to improve the foodservice facility. This is the case when an agency does not have sufficient capital funds for self-improvement and is often one of the reasons for them to utilize a management company.

A recent development that portends the future of contracting in this segment is the complete funding, construction, and management of the entire correctional facility by a contract management company. It remains to be seen how this new phenomena will progress.

Foodservice/Vending

Foodservice/vending is an integral part of almost all institutional foodservice operations. The use of vending machines to deliver foodservice to off shifts, remote locations, and other similar situations, is routine.

Vending is not a new phenomenon. It actually dates back to 215 B.C. Schreiber (1961) reports that Hero, a Greek, wrote in a book of that time titled *Pneumatika* of a machine that dispensed holy water when five drachmas were inserted.

Modern foodservice/vending originated about 1960. At that time the fresh brew coffee vending machine was invented. Around the same time the post mix soda machine, complete with flaked ice, came on the market. These two machines were the catalyst of today's combined contract foodservice and foodservice vending companies.

Prior to beverage vending, contract foodservice companies were basically regional in nature. Vending companies were mainly small family-owned businesses with some multiunit vending companies operating regionally. Coffee and soda machines, producing large amounts of cash flow, allowed the regional vending companies to make a number of both foodservice and vending acquisitions. In this manner they became national foodservice and vending organizations. Today, all the major contract management companies are actually foodservice and vending companies.

Institutional foodservice vending now provides many of the menu items available on the manual cafeteria menu. Hot and cold beverages, hot and cold meals, snack items, and more are all available through a vending machine. Modularly installed groups of machines (banks) are installed along with coin changers, microwave ovens, condiment stands, and tables and chairs. B & I cafeterias utilize vending machines to supplement their service and to provide a service for off shifts, coffee breaks, and other similar service. Both health-care and campus dining locations usually use vending as a supplementary foodservice for the same reasons.

Today institutional foodservice managers must have a working know-ledge of vending operations to be successful. They must be aware of the basic principles of vending machine operation and have a working knowledge of the economics of vending. Foodservice vending is an integral part of the aver-age institutional foodservice.

Institution Foodservice Contractors

The National Restaurant Association (1992) reports that the total foodservice industry has nine million employees. They project that the industry will employ 11.4 million by the year 2000. NRA estimates that about one-third, or 2.2 million, of the present employees are in the institutional foodservice sector.

Institutional foodservice contractors are estimated by some researchers to operate

> 80% of business and industry locations
> 40% of campus dining locations
> 15% of healthcare locations
> 15% of school locations
> 5% of correctional locations

Hard data accepted by all groups is difficult to obtain. Different re-searchers have arrived at different results. One fairly reliable source of infor-mation is the annual 400 issue of *Restaurant and Institution* magazine. Their survey is called the "Institutions 400." This lists the top 400 sales grossing foodservice companies in America. Among that group are all of the major and other institutional foodservice contract companies. An excerpt summary of contractors from this survey is shown as Table 2. It indicates that contrac-tors have approximately 15,719 locations with an annual sales estimate of $11.4 billion. This represents 5.01% of the NRA's total foodservice industry sales of $227.3 billion.

Contract management companies are a major force in the institutional foodservice segment. They are expected to continue as such and grow sub-stantially as more and more businesses and institutions contract out various services that are supplemental to their primary mission.

Summary

"Institutional foodservice" is a term generally used to describe the noncom-mercial segment of the foodservice industry. However, this term has been defined and evaluated in different ways, by different organizations and inter-ested groups. For purposes of this article, the term is used to describe all areas of the foodservice industry that are not primarily in the business of offering a public foodservice facility operated solely to make a profit from the foodservice. Different segments such as business and industry foodservice; primary and secondary school foodservice; college and university foodser-vice; healthcare foodservice; correctional institutions; and some areas of con-tract foodservice/vending are described in detail.

Table 2. *Summary of sales and number of units by contract foodservice companies*

Company	Gross sales ($ millions)	# Units
Marriott Food Service	3,950.0	2,390
ARA Services	2,500.0	2,600
Canteen Co.	1,369.9	1,972
Service America Corp.	1,100.0	1,500
Morrissons Custom Mge.	580.0	892
Seiler Corp.	376.1	487
Daka Food Service	270.0	283
Service Master Corp.	219.0	273
The Wood Co.	172.7	284
Trusthouse Forte Services	124.0	505
Greyhound Food Mge.	100.0	120
Professional Food Mge.	90.0	134
Food Dimensions Inc.	85.0	120
Valley Innovative Mge.	79.2	125
Sanese Services Inc.	65.0	62
Universal Services	60.0	134
Southern Foodservice Mge.	45.0	80
Sanos & Company	44.4	825
Nutrition Mge. Services	40.0	50
Lackmann Food Services	39.3	48
Corporate Food Service	36.9	50
CVI Service Group[a]	34.7	50
FLIK International	31.0	70
Blue Ribbon Services	30.0	65
Total	$11,393	15,719

Source: Restaurant & Institutions, July 25, 1990, p. 28
[a]A wholly owned subsidiary of the Marriott Corp.

References

IFMA. 1987. *Foodservice A Segmented Industry*. Chicago, IL: A proprietary document, International Foodservice Manufacturers Association.

Kotschevar, L. H. 1987. *Management by Menu*, 2d ed. Chicago, Ill.: National Institute for the Foodservice Industry.

Meakin, B. 1905. *Model Factories and Villages*. London: T. Fisher.

National Restaurant Association. 1992. *Foodservice Industry*. Pocket Factbook. Washington, D.C.: National Restaurant Association.

Schrieber, G. R. 1961. *A Concise History of Vending in the U.S.A.* Chicago, Ill.: Vend Magazine.

Stokes, J. 1960. *Food Service in Industry and Institutions*. Dubuque, Ia.: Wm. C. Brown and Co.

Sullivan, C. 1990. *Management of Medical Foodservice*, 2d ed. New York: Van Nostrand Reinhold.

Van Egmund Pannell, D. 1990. *School Foodservice Management*, 4th ed. New York: Van Nostrand Reinhold.

Warner, M. 1973. *Industrial Foodservice and Cafeteria Management*. Chicago, Ill.: Cahners Books.

White House Conference on Food, Nutrition and Health. 1970. Final Report. Washington, D.C.: U.S. Government Printing office.

24

Foodservice Franchising

Skip Swerdlow

The franchise is found in all types of businesses today, from restaurants to laundromats, from tax preparation services to auto parts stores. However, no franchise is more well-known than foodservice franchising. Mention the word "franchising" and images of the Golden Arches (McDonald's), Burger King, Kentucky Fried Chicken, Bob's Big Boy, Bonanza Family Restaurants, and Baskin Robbins Ice Cream Stores immediately come to mind. But franchising is much more than these popular images. Franchising is a very old concept that has become so popular in the United States that sales currently account for over 40 percent of total retail dollars (*Franchising in the Economy* 1988). A big portion of those sales is foodservice.

Definition

Franchising is a concept that describes one method in which goods and services reach the customer. A franchise relationship must be formed between two companies. The company that owns a trademark (such as McDonald's Golden Arches) and a method of doing business (how to make and sell hamburgers and other fast-food items the McDonald's way) is the *franchisor*. The company that buys from the franchisor the right to use its trademarks and to operate a business according to the franchisor's guidelines is the *franchisee*. The word *franchise* is sometimes defined as a right. Because that right is owned by the franchisor, the franchisee pays for it. Franchising, thus, is a way of doing business that benefits both the franchisor and franchisee.

The word *franchising* comes from an old French word that means "freedom from servitude." The idea underlying this word is that by owning a franchise, the franchisee is freed from the bondage of working for someone else as an employee. The franchisee becomes a business owner with much of the same self-reliant, decision-making ability as an independent businessperson who starts a firm from scratch. The primary difference, however, between a franchisee and an independent businessperson is that the franchisee has a legal, contractual relationship with a franchisor that requires him to do business as the franchisor instructs him. An old saying in franchising is "You're in business for yourself, but not *by* yourself. An independent makes all decisions independently."

The franchisor benefits from this relationship through the opportunity to expand the business at a much lower cost than otherwise. The franchisee invests much of the money for his or her store, but the franchisor controls the product, the service, and how the franchisee presents them to the customer.

This way of franchising is called the *business format franchise*, which is the way most foodservice franchises operate. A business format franchise is one in which the franchisor sells two essential rights to the franchisee: (1) the right to adopt the image or identity of the franchisor (this may be the official trademark of the company, such as the Wendy's girl, the Golden Arches, or the way the letters are shaped in Baskin-Robbins, or the color of a building.); (2) a fixed way of running the food service outlet. The franchisor will instruct the franchisee on all aspects of operating. In some instances, the franchisee must do it only one way. For example

1. How to make food. In Burger King, employees are told that to make a hamburger properly, exactly 1/3 of an ounce of ketchup and 1/9 of an ounce of mustard must be applied in a spiral from the outside of the meat patty to the inside—no exceptions.

2. Where to buy food and the equipment to make the food. Franchisors spend a great deal of time with the companies that sell to franchisees to ensure that what they ship to the franchisee meets very strict standards. Franchisees must purchase from these approved sellers.

In some instances, the franchisee may make decisions without asking the franchisor. Some examples include

1. How much to charge for menu items.
2. How much to pay employees.
3. Advertising purchased in the local market. While the franchisor buys television and radio advertising the franchisee may decide to hand out flyers or offer a special in a coupon book.

Thus, the business format franchise is different from independent operations. If a man named Skip decided to open a coffee shop as an independent businessperson, he could make all of the necessary decisions, including what kind of sign to put over the entrance door. If Skip instead decided to become a Village Inn Pancake House franchisee, he would have to make decisions the Village Inn Pancake House way, including using their highly recognizable sign over the door.

History of Franchising

General History of Franchising

Franchising can trace its origins to the Middle Ages when the Catholic Church and local governments granted tax collecting franchises. Tax collectors (franchisees) made their rounds, sending their revenues to the Church or government body (franchisor), but keeping a percentage for themselves. In 1562, the Council of Trent banned this form of taxation because it seemed to breed corruption. In the eighteenth and nineteenth centuries, the legislature and monarchy of England granted franchises to noblemen, giving them complete authority over large geographical areas to develop their personal wealth in exchange for their unwavering support.

In the United States, the first franchise businesses started in the mid-1800s. McCormick Harvesting Machine Company began franchising around 1850 (Justis and Judd 1989: 11). The Singer Sewing Machine Company started during the 1860s. Other companies to employ franchising were General Motors (1898), Coca Cola (1899), Rexall Drugs (1902), and Western Auto (1909).

Foodservice Franchising In 1925, Howard Johnson started an ice cream business. He used franchising to expand this business and a chain of restaurants throughout the East Coast. In 1940, his outlets were the first to be built on a freeway (then called a turnpike). His early efforts now boast over 200 restaurants nationwide.

In 1955 within about three months of each other McDonald's and Burger King began what was to become a revolution in foodservice franchising. McDonald's from southern California and Burger King from southern Florida have become international giants in the fast-food business. Also during the 1950s, Kentucky Fried Chicken and International House of Pancakes began their operations. Most of the growth in this field occurred in the 1970s and 1980s.

The history of foodservice franchising has demonstrated a pioneering influence on how all types of retail franchising are conducted. Foodservice is a competitive business. To remain successful, franchisors and franchisees have had to be innovative and creative. For example, Jack-in-the-Box in the 1960s was the first retail business to use computerized cash registers. Burger King was the first to use highly sophisticated, computer software and hardware for employee scheduling, inventory control, and other analyses. McDonald's was the first to install playgrounds. These are just a few examples. Each day, foodservice franchise participants continue to make history.

Types of Foodservice Franchises

Many types of operations come under the category of foodservice franchises. Some of the categories overlap, but the typical ones are

1. Fast-food restaurants. These are the most recognizable of the foodservice restaurants. They specialize in quick service and relatively limited menus. Examples are Burger King, McDonald's, Kentucky Fried Chicken, and Taco Bell.

2. Full service, family style, or coffee shop restaurants. These outlets specialize in a full menu, food cooked to order, table service, and they cater to family business. Many orient their menus to serve breakfast 24 hours a day. Examples are Denny's TGIFridays, and Ponderosa steak house.

3. Ice cream parlors. Baskin-Robbins made this category famous. Now, other companies, such as Dairy Queen and Swensen's, serve primarily ice cream and desserts.

4. Retail baked goods. These companies differentiate themselves by serving baked goods cooked fresh on the premises. Located in various size malls, companies such as Davids' Cookies and T. J. Cinnamons serve cookies and cinnamon rolls.

5. Retail food store. Hickory Farms is a well-known example of this type of foodservice operation. They sell traditional, specialty, and gift food items such as exotic cheeses, meats, and fruit preserves.

6. Doughnut shops. A type of fast-food operation, their menus are primarily for breakfast and snacks. Their "entrée" is a wide variety of doughnuts. Winchell's and Dunkin' Donuts are the most famous.

7. Other categories. Ethnic, limited and full menu, nutrition, and drive-in/drive-thru are just some of the other categories that usually overlap the previous six. For example, Benihana of Tokyo is a full service, ethnic (Japa-

nese) outlet, Rally's is a highly limited menu, fast-food hamburger restaurant, and Heidi's Frogen Yozurt is a nutritionally based, limited menu, fast-food operation.

Advantages and Disadvantages of Foodservice Franchises

Foodservice experiences the highest rate of failure of all retail businesses. Some statistics show (Justis and Judd 1989: 15) that 80–90 percent of restaurants are bankrupt within the first five years; other types of businesses have equally dismal prospects. Franchising helps brighten up these pessimistic numbers. In the mid-1980s, only 3.3 percent of all types of franchises were discontinued for any reason. The statistics seem to suggest that franchising a restaurant has important advantages that substantially increase the chance of success of the franchisee over an independent operator.

Advantages   Some of the most important advantages of franchising are

1. Recognized name and logo (for example, International House of Pancakes, Ronald McDonald).

2. A reputation. When we decide to eat at a particular franchise, we do so for many reasons, one of the most important of which is that we know what to expect (the quality of a Sizzler steak, seafood, or salad bar).

3. Technical assistance. An individual does not need any experience in foodservice to be a foodservice franchisee. In fact, some franchisors prefer minimal experience because novices go into the business without any preconceived notions about how to operate. The franchisors are the experts in their field, having done substantial research about what their customers want. They use this knowledge and their experience to give advice and provide operational manuals on how to do the simplest tasks (for example, how to mop a floor) and the most difficult challenges (for example, setting up a food inventory and a cost control system).

4. Lower costs. Franchisors train their franchisees to operate their foodservice outlets much more efficiently than that of an independent outlet. Franchisors have developed systems for everything, and that means saving money. The franchisor also sets up special buys with suppliers so that the cost of purchasing equipment and inventory are much lower.

5. Quality control standards. The standards for performance that the franchisor imposes on franchisees are beneficial because they ensure that consistency exists from restaurant to restaurant regardless of location or ownership. This consistency is good for business so that a customer who goes to a Ponderosa steak house in Las Vegas, Nevada, will visit the store in Blacksburg, Virginia.

6. Opportunities for expansion. Many franchisors grant territories so that franchisees can have more than one store. With their help and assistance, the franchisee can expand his or her success to multiple locations.

Disadvantages   Some of the most important disadvantages of franchising are

1. Restrictions on franchisee decision making. Some people have difficulty making decisions that are restricted by someone else (the franchisor). They do not want another person telling them what to do. Individuals are advised that franchising may not work for them. "Being in business for yourself, but not by yourself" is not for everyone.

2. Franchisor power issues. Franchisors are often perceived as being too

powerful and too involved in the franchisee's business. That perception may come from too many visits from their personnel, insensitivity to the differences in needs of franchisees in different locations (for example, not allowing ethnic items on the menu in an ethnically concentrated area, or requiring that buildings be protected from frost in desert locations), or disagreements over whether a termination of a franchise is really fair. This disadvantage may be nothing more than a difference of opinion between franchisor and franchisee, or it may be more serious. Disagreements always happen, even in the best relationships; honest and open discussion are the best solutions.

3. The perception that franchises are failure proof. They are not. Many franchisees believe that the reputation and the assistance of the franchisor is all that is necessary for success. Occasionally, the franchisor's literature is misleading concerning the amount of work required and the possibility for success. People need to be realistic. The foodservice business is one of the most difficult and time consuming, even in the best of all worlds. Prospective franchisees need to read all of the available literature and then visit locations and talk to franchisees in their restaurants about the requirements for a successful operation.

4. Inconsistency of standards. The larger the chain of foodservice outlets the more difficult are the efforts to ensure that the standards are the same at all stores. Customers often do not understand that different owners may operate differently; they have a reasonable expectation that their food, service, and cleanliness will always be the same.

Trends in Foodservice Franchising

Many of the innovations in retail business have come from the pioneering efforts of foodservice franchises. A few have already been identified. The following are some of the significant trends that appear to be forming today.

Nontraditional Franchising

The number of good locations is shrinking and their costs are rising. Competition is more intense and the price of effective advertising continues to grow. These factors have caused franchisors to look for places to build their restaurants that are different from their traditional, free-standing positions. Fast-food and limited menu outlets are now found in airports, malls, zoos, hospitals, train stations, gambling casinos, school campuses, and many other unusual places. Experts agree that these nontraditional places work well for several reasons: (1) The captive consumer is already there for a different reason and will want to eat; (2) Other competition is limited or nonexistent; and (3) Changes in how a city grows may be unlikely to affect sales.

International Expansion

As the economies of the world interact more and people of other countries want to try more Western goods and services, international foodservice franchises are becoming more popular. Most of the major fast-food and many of the other major foodservice franchise organizations have expanded to every continent except Antarctica. Recently, the McDonald's franchisee from Canada opened the first fast-food restaurant in Russia. Others are following. These foreign locations are among the busiest in the franchise chain. Look for the well-known signs in whatever country you travel for a familiar taste of home.

The Labor Shortage

Foodservice franchisees have traditionally hired teenagers to do most of their jobs. An ample number of them and other young people were always available because of the baby boom of World War II and the Korean War. In recent years the number of people under 21 years of age has been decreasing as the number of foodservice outlets have been increasing. In some areas, franchisees are running out of traditional young employees to hire. To solve this problem, franchisors and franchisees have been recruiting retired senior citizens, housewives, and college students. They are finding that these new employees work well with teenagers and provide a maturity and longevity to their work force. Some of McDonald's advertisements feature senior citizen workers. Another approach that franchise operators are taking to meet this challenge is to continue to automate their businesses. New equipment is being developed to reduce the number of employees that the franchise has to schedule.

Other Trends
Other trends and challenges that face foodservice franchise operators are

1. Limited menu versus expanded menu decision. Rally's Hamburgers, a relatively new franchise company, boasts a menu with only a few items so the quality is high. Other major chains add new menu items in the hopes of adding more customers.

2. Legal issues. In some states franchisors are being given more power to terminate their agreements with franchisees. In other states, the law is more franchisee-oriented. The laws also differ vastly in how much information the franchisor must offer to people who want to become franchisees. Overall, the legal issues are confusing and varied throughout the country.

Summary

Franchising is one of the most exciting forms of business in the world today. In no industry has franchising entered the consumers's mind more thoroughly than foodservice. It has provided opportunities for people from all walks of life and interests to get into the restaurant and food-related businesses. It has been an effective method of domestic and international expansion for foodservice franchisors. And it has helped bring comfort to customers looking for a meal that they know well regardless of the city, state, or country where they live or travel.

References

Franchising in the Economy. 1988. Washington, D.C.: 1988. U.S. Government Printing Office.

Justis, R., and R. Judd. 1989. *Franchising.* Cincinnati: South-Western Publishing Company, 670pp.

Bibliography

Axelrad, N. D., and L. G. Rudnick. 1987. *Franchising: A Planning and Sales Compliance Guide.* Chicago: Commerce Clearing House, Inc., 257pp.

Bard, R., and S. Henderson. 1987. *Own Your Own Franchise: Everything You Need to Know about the Best Opportunities in America.* Reading, Mass.: Addison Wesley, 455pp.

Kahn, M. A. 1992. *Restaurant Franchising.* New York: Van Nostrand Reinhold.

Kinch, J. E., with J. P. Hayes. 1986. *Franchising: The Inside Story: How to Start Your Own Business and Succeed!* New York: Harper & Row, 191pp.

Foster, D. L. 1988. *The Rating Guide to Franchises.* New York: Facts on File Publications, 298pp.

Siegel, W. L. 1983. *Franchising.* New York: John Wiley, 206pp.

Tarbutton, L. T. 1986. *Franchising: The How-To Book.* Englewood Cliffs, N.J.: Prentice-Hall, Inc., 226pp.

Webster, B. 1986. *The Insider's Guide to Franchising.* New York: American Management Association, 308pp.

25

Computers in the Foodservice Industry

Michael L. Kasavana

It has been said that the three most important success factors in the foodservice business are control, control, and control! Although computers are capable of altering the way a restaurant is planned, conducted, and analyzed, more importantly they provide unique advantages in the area of controls. Controls over such things as operations, marketing, menu, finance, accounting, labor, production, service, settlement, pricing, and inventory. Foodservice management has discovered that the best means to gain these controls is through computerization. Computers store large amounts of data and can provide accurate information in a timely fashion, as needed.

Just as the sophistication of restaurateurs has shifted from a fixation on menu planning toward bottom line profitability, so too have computer applications. No longer must an operator rely on haphazard forecasting, intuitive marketing research, seat-of-the-pants decision making, or indiscriminate data for strategic planning. Automated foodservice information systems are rapidly becoming part of the industry ambiance.

Computer-based restaurant management systems function through specific hardware components and a variety of applications software packages. Foodservice computer applications can be divided into service and management application areas. Service applications tend to be cash-register–based. Service area applications rely upon ECR/POS (electronic cash register/point-of-sale) technology to monitor front-of-the-house transactions. Major concerns associated with service area computerization focus on the coordination of production to service, data integrity, and vendor support. The term *management applications* refers to software used to process data related to back-of-the-house foodservice activities. The level of software integration is of extreme importance to efficient management applications processing.

Service-oriented Applications

Service-oriented applications of a computer-based restaurant management system rely upon ECR/POS technology to monitor service area transactions through cashier terminals, precheck terminals, remote work station printers and display screens, and network controllers.

Decisions in regard to foodservice automation may be different for different types of foodservice operations. For example, the presence of service personnel and guest check systems necessitate entirely different control mechanisms for table service operations than those appropriate for quick service restaurants. The identification and configuration of an electronic cash register (ECR) or point-of-sale (POS) system can be similarly affected.

From a hardware perspective computer-based restaurant management systems rely upon ECR and POS technology to monitor service area transactions through cashier terminals, precheck terminals, remote work station devices, and network controllers. Service-related applications software programs include prechecking, check tracking, sales analysis, and limited attendance (payroll) and inventory control packages.

ECR/POS system hardware components consist of user interfaces, display screens, various output devices, a network controller, and sometimes a cash drawer.

User Interfaces. User interfaces include traditional (reed style) keyboard designs, micromotion keyboard surfaces, touch screen units, hand-held order entry devices, and magnetic strip readers. The two primary types of keyboard surfaces are reed style and micromotion. The reed design contains wet-proof keys raised above the surface of the keyboard, while the micromotion design has a flat, wet-proof surface. More important than the physical design of the keyboard's surface is the number of hard and soft keys the keyboard provides. Hard keys are dedicated to specific functions programmed by the manufacturer. Alternatively, soft keys can be programmed by users to meet specific operational needs.

Both keyboard designs are usually capable of supporting interchangeable menu boards. A menu board overlays the keyboad surface and identifies the function performed by each key during a specific meal period. Menu boards, like soft keys, can be developed to meet the specific needs of individual properties. Menu boards identify a number of different types of keys. Key types may include preset keys, price look-up (PLU) keys, function keys, settlement keys, modifier keys, and numeric keypad. Servers enter orders by using preset keys and/or PLU keys. Modifier keys may be used in combination with preset and PLU keys to detail preparation instructions (such as rare, medium, well-done) for food production areas. Modifier keys may also be used to alter prices based on designated portion sizes (such as small, medium, and large). A numeric keypad is used to facilitate various data entry operations and to enable cashiers to ring items by price when prices for items are not identified by preset keys or PLU numbers. Function keys and settlement keys are used to correct and complete transactions.

Generally, management can determine the positioning of most keys on a keyboard overlay. By positioning keys for similar items and functions together and arranging groups into a logical order, management can improve system performance and enhance operational controls. Recently developed touch screen units, hand-held order entry devices, and magnetic strip (credit card) readers are used to complement and/or replace keyboard operations. Touch screen units enable the server to enter data without a keyboard. Orders are entered interactively by physically selecting items displayed on a predetermined series of screens. Hand-held terminals (HHT) allow the server to place an order table side. There is no need to walk to a centrally located terminal to enter orders. This user interface design requires that each server has his/her own data entry device.

Rather than employing a manual or external credit card authorization terminal, a magnetic strip reader can be directly interfaced to an ECR/POS device. Magnetic strip readers provide rapid entry of stored data, initial validation screening, and initiate transaction posting procedures. Some industry experts predict that touch screen units and hand-held terminals will replace traditional keyboard entry procedures; magnetic strip readers will play a crucial role in account settlement when electronic funds transfer system become operational. The area of transaction processing technology (TPT) holds great promise for the foodservice industry.

Display Screens. In addition to user interfaces, an ECR/POS device contains an operator display screen and may support a customer display unit as well. Important display screen concerns involve the size and function of displays. An operator display screen is generally a standard system component that enables the operator to review and edit transaction entries. The unit allows a server to monitor transactions in progress and also may serve as a prompt for various system procedures. The length and number of lines displayed is often an important consideration when selecting an ECR/POS device.

The design of customer display units include those that rest on top, inside, or alongside the ECR/POS device. Although customer display units are more restricted in size and scope than operator display screens, they permit a guest to observe the operator's entries. In many table service restaurants, settlement activities often take place outside the view of guests; therefore, a customer display unit may not be warranted. However, in those restaurants where guests can view settlement transactions, serious consideration should be given to the use of a customer display screen. Customer display units also permit management to spot check server/cashier activities.

Output Devices. ECR/POS output devices are sometimes described as either on-board or remote units. On-board units are normally located within six feet of the ECR/POS they serve. These devices include guest check (slip) printers and receipt printers. Remote units include work station printers/monitors and journal printers located more than six feet from the ECR/POS they support. Remote units almost always require separate cabling to operate.

1. *Guest check (slip) printers.* These on-board printing devices are sometimes referred to as slip printers. Most ECR/POS systems are capable of immediate check printing, delayed check printing, and/or retained check printing. Immediate check printing refers to the ability of the system to print items as they are input at an ECR/POS device; delayed check printing refers to the ability to print items at the end of a complete order entry; and retained check printing refers to the ability of the system to print the guest check at any time following order entry and prior to settlement. Sophisticated guest check printers may be equipped with an automatic form number reader (AFNR) and/or possess automatic slip feed (ASF) capabilities. An automatic form number reader facilitates order entry procedures. Instead of a server manually inputting a guest check's serial number to access the account, a bar code imprinted on the guest check presents the check's serial number in a machine readable format. A server simply slips the guest check into the terminal's AFNR unit, and the AFNR provides rapid access to the guest check account. An automatic slip feed capability prevents overprinting items and

amounts on guest checks. ECR/POS systems without ASF capability require a server to insert a guest check into the printer's slot and manually align the printer's ribbon with the next blank printing line on the guest check. This can be an awkward procedure for servers to follow during busy meal periods. If the alignment is not correct, the guest check appears disorganized and messy with items and amounts printed over one another or with large gaps between lines of print. A system with ASF capability retains the number of the last line printed for each open guest check. The server simply aligns the top edge of the printer's slot and the terminal automatically moves the check to the next available printing line and prints the order entry data. Since guest checks are placed within the printer's slot the same way every time, servers may spend less time manipulating machinery and more time meeting the needs of their guests. In addition, guests receive neatly printed, easy-to-read checks for settlement.

2. *Receipt printers.* These on-board printing devices produce hard copy on thin, narrow register tape. Although the usefulness of receipt printers is somewhat limited, these devices may help control the production of menu items that are not prepared at departments that receive orders through remote display or printing devices. For example, when servers prepare desserts for their guests and the pantry area is not equipped with a remote communication device, desserts could be served without ever being entered into the system. When this happens, it is also possible that desserts could be served without ever being posted to guest checks. This situation can be avoided by using a receipt printer. Servers preparing desserts can be required to deliver a receipt tape to the dessert pantry area as proof that the items are properly posted to guest checks for eventual settlement. This procedure ensures that every menu item served is printed somewhere in the system, thus enhancing management's internal control.

3. *Work station printers/monitors.* These remote devices are usually placed at kitchen preparation areas and service bars. As orders are entered at pre-check terminals, they are sent to a designated remote station device to initiate production. This communications system enables servers to spend more time meeting the needs of their guests while significantly reducing traffic in kitchen and bar areas. If the need for hard copy output in production areas is not critical to an operation's internal control system, video display units (also referred to as kitchen monitors) may be viable alternatives to work station printers. Since these units are able to display several orders on a single screen, kitchen employees do not have to handle numerous pieces of paper. An accompanying cursor control keypad enables kitchen employees to easily review previously submitted orders by scrolling full screens at a time.

4. *Journal printers.* These remote printing devices produce a continuous detailed record of all transactions entered anywhere in the system. Journal printers are usually located in a secure area remote from service and production areas. Hard copy is produced on thin, narrow register tape (usually 20 columns wide) and provides management with a thorough system audit. In addition to providing an audit trail, journal printers are also capable of printing a variety of management reports. Management should routinely review journal printouts to ensure the ECR/POS system is being used properly.

Network Controller. A network controller is used to direct and control output communications within an ECR/POS system. Network controllers represent one of the most important peripheral devices in an ECR/POS system that supports remote work station devices. A network controller coordinates communications between cashier or precheck terminals and work station printers or kitchen monitors, while ensuring that servers need only enter their orders once.

When several precheck terminals simultaneously send data to the same work station printer or kitchen monitor, the network controller processes data from one of the terminals immediately and temporarily stores (buffers) the other communications until the output device becomes available. As the remote printer or kitchen monitor outputs data sent from one terminal, the network controller communicates the next set of data, and so on, until all orders that have been entered at precheck terminals are printed or displayed. Since remote work station units are relatively efficient, the time delay between order entry and printout is minimal; even for those orders temporarily held by the network controller for eventual printing.

Without a network controller, a remote work station unit would only be able to receive and print one set of data at a time. When the remote printer is receiving data from one terminal, servers entering orders at other precheck terminals might receive a response similar to a telephone busy signal. Orders would have to be re-entered, since the original orders were not received or stored anywhere in the ECR/POS system.

Cash Drawers. While some foodservice operators and computer system vendors tend to use the terms *register* and *terminal* interchangeably, these terms actually connote different equipment functions. Typically the term register is used to refer to an ECR/POS device that is connected to a cash drawer. All other ECR/POS devices are referred to as terminals (for example, precheck terminal). A terminal without a cash drawer is commonly referred to as a precheck terminal. Precheck terminals are therefore limited in functionality to order entry and are incapable of supporting account settlement. An ECR/POS device with a cash drawer can normally support both prechecking and cashiering functions. Most ECR/POS systems enable the connection of several cash drawers to a single register device.

ECR/POS Hardware Configurations

Given the recent application of microcomputers (personal computers) to ECR/POS technology, four types of ECR/POS hardware designs are available to a restaurateur: stand-alone, master-slave, processor-based, and micro-based.

1. *Stand-alone configuration.* A stand-alone configuration creates self-sufficient work stations, each with a set of hardware components necessary for a complete computer system. A stand-alone configuration for a restaurant ECR/POS system is made up of a series of independent electronic cash registers. Each ECR/POS device possesses its own input unit (register keyboard), output unit (operator display screen and/or customer display screen), central processing unit, and internal storage capability. The presence of a network controller permits several ECR/POS devices to communicate with the same remote printers but may not enable them to communicate with each other. This is an important limitation of a stand-alone configuration. In order for management to receive reports that consolidate data collected by the independent devices, data from each ECR/POS must be manually transferred to report formats or re-input into a separate processing unit, such as a microcomputer. Recent technological advances can extend the basic capability of a stand-alone configuration by enabling the interface of individual units to a powerful microcomputer.

2. *Master-slave configuration.* In a master-slave design only one register contains all the necessary components of a complete computer system. This ECR/POS device functions as a master register by processing transactions entered through slave units, such as precheck or cashier terminals. Slave units are cabled to the master ECR/POS device. Although slave units are not equipped with their own central processing units, some may possess a limited internal memory capacity. The master-slave configuration places a heavy burden on the master unit. This device must not only process transactions communicated from slave units, but function as a cashier terminal and, in some cases, as a precheck terminal as well. The greatest danger associated with a master-slave configuration is that the entire system becomes inoperable should anything disrupt the master unit.

3. *Processor-based configuration.* This type of integrated configuration is similar to the master-slave system, except that the central processing unit and external storage capacity are significantly larger and placed in a location remote from actual restaurant operations. A processor-based configuration enables management to monitor a wide range of transactions from a central location. As with other ECR/POS configurations, a processor-based system depends upon a single central processing unit (CPU) and centralized storage capability. Should the CPU malfunction, the entire system could become inoperable and/or stored data could become permanently lost.

4. *Micro-based configuration.* The recent advent of a micro-based ECR/POS system is an attempt to avoid some of the expense associated with an ECR/POS network while, at the same time, capitalizing on the advantages of networking. With a micro-based system, a microcomputer is placed in an ECR/POS network to function as a file server and to process all system transactions. In a micro-based network, each terminal relays its transactions to the microcomputer for processing. Transactions are processed in the order in which they are received. Therefore, problems may arise when several terminals relay transactions at the same time.

ECR/POS Software Components

The hardware of any computer system does nothing by itself. For hardware components to operate, there must be a set of software programs directing the system what to do, how to do it, and when to do it. ECR/POS software programs not only direct internal system operations, but also maintain files and produce reports for use by management. Files that may be stored and maintained by sophisticated ECR/POS systems include menu item file, open check file, labor master file, and inventory files. Data maintained by these files (and others) can be accessed by ECR/POS terminals and formatted reports can be printed on narrow register tape. The following sections briefly examine the types of data stored by major ECR/POS files and the kind of information contained in some of the more significant reports they are capable of producing.

1. *Menu item file.* Menu item files usually contain data for all menu items sold in the restaurant. Records within this file may contain the following menu item data: identification number, descriptor, price, tax, applicable modifier keys, amount totals for inventory reporting, and printer routing code. This file is generally used to monitor menu keyboard operations. Management can control information about current menu items for various meal periods. Reports can be produced for each meal period identifying menu item descriptor, price, and applicable tax table. When menu items, prices, or tax tables need to be changed, the menu item file is accessed and appropriate

changes are entered according to procedures indicated in the user's manual provided by the system's vendor.

2. *Open check file.* The open check file maintains current data for all open guest checks. This file is accessed to monitor items on a particular guest check, add items to a guest check after initial order entry, and close a guest check at the time of settlement. For each open guest check, the open check file may contain the following data: terminal number where the check was opened, check number, server identification number, time check was opened, location of last printed line, descriptors of menu items ordered, prices of individual menu items ordered, and tax and total amount due. In some systems, settlement deletes the guest check from the open check file. When this is the case, the open check file will be empty at the end of each meal period.

Data contained in the open check file can usually be printed at any time. An open check report lists all checks that have not been settled. This report may also list items such as check number, server number, time check was opened, elapsed time since check was opened, number of guests, and table number. Before servers are permitted to use the time-clock feature of the register to clock-out, some systems require that individual server check-out reports be printed. This printout ensures that all checks assigned to servers have been closed. If not, the open check report can be used to produce a list of each server's open checks.

3. *Labor master file.* The labor master file contains one record for each employee and typically maintains the following data: employee name, employee number, social security number, authorized job codes, and corresponding hourly wage rates. This file may also contain data required to produce labor reports for management. Each record in the labor master file may accumulate hours worked, total hourly wages, declared wages, tips, credits for employee meals, number of guests served (if appropriate), and gross sales. Many ECR/POS systems are unable to compute net pay figures because of restricted processing ability and limited internal memory capacity. However, data accumulated by the labor master file can be accessed to produce a number of reports. Reports such as a labor master report and daily, weekly, and period labor reports may be printed at management's request.

A labor master report contains general data maintained by the labor master file. This report is commonly used to verify an employee's hourly rate(s), job code(s), or social security number. A daily labor report may list the names, employee numbers, hours worked, wages earned, and wages declared for each employee on a given workday. A weekly labor report contains similar information and may be useful for determining which employees are approaching overtime pay rates. A period labor report generally lists hour and wage information for each employee who worked during the period specified by management. Data stored in the labor master file may also be used to produce daily, weekly, and period employee meals reports which show amounts for meals provided to employees. Also, a weekly and period employee tips report may be printed showing the total tips reported by each employee.

4. *Inventory files.* The inventory files maintained by an ECR/POS system may not meet all the needs of some restaurant properties. Many registers are incapable of tracking the same item as it passes through the control points of receiving, storing/issuing, and production. Inventory data must be specific to each of these control points because purchase units (case, drum, etc.) commonly differ from storeroom inventory units (#10 can, gallon, etc.), which,

in turn, differ from standard recipe units (ounce, cup, etc.). Many systems are not able to support the number of conversion tables necessary to track menu items through ingredient purchase, storage, and use (standard recipe). Since restaurant operators do not purchase their inventory ingredients on a preportioned basis, they very often encounter significant problems when trying to implement a register-based inventory control system. In addition, the initial creation of an ingredient file and the subsequent file updates (daily, weekly, monthly) can be an overwhelming task for some foodservice operations. For example, a restaurant typically carries an average of 400 menu items and an inventory of 1,500 ingredients, and monitors at least 18 high-cost inventory items on a perpetual basis. ECR/POS systems may not be able to support the files necessary for effective register based inventory control.

Consolidated Reporting Functions

ECR/POS systems may access data contained in several files to produce consolidated reports for use by management. Such reports typically include daily revenue reports, sales analysis reports, summary activity reports, and productivity reports. A daily revenue report informs management of how menu items sales result in revenue. In addition, data contained in this report indicates sales trends, product needs, cash flow, and labor requirements. A sales analysis report enables management to measure the sales performance of individual menu items by department or product category within certain time intervals. Time intervals may vary in relation to the type of foodservice operation. Quick service restaurants may desire sales analysis reports segmented by 15-minute intervals, table service restaurants by the hour, and institutional foodservice operations by meal period. This report provides management with the ability to track individual item sales, analyze product acceptance, and monitor advertising and sales promotional efforts. This report typically contains unit price, quantity sold, extended dollar value, and percentage of sales by item. A summary sales report generally contains detailed sales and tax information by such categories as food items, beer, wine, and liquor. Labor and control totals may be also reported. Generally, totals for each category are printed for each meal period and totals for each meal period are shown in different sections of the report.

An activity report provides an in-depth analysis of sales transactions and employee timekeeping activity during selected time periods. This report may include number of customer transactions; number of servers, cashiers, and other employees on duty; average guest check amount; customer count; labor cost; and percentage of labor cost to net sales. Productivity reports typically detail sales activity for all assigned server sales records. Daily productivity reports may be generated for each server and cashier in terms of guest count, total sales, and average sales. In addition, a weekly productivity report may be generated, showing average sales amount per guest for each server.

ECR/POS Application Software Modules

Service-related applications software programs include prechecking, check tracking, sales analysis, time and attendance, and various inventory control packages.

Prechecking. Prechecking is a special type of order entry system used by foodservice operations to control activities linking service and production. Prechecking ensures that before any food items are removed from a production area they are recorded on guest checks. Prechecking, which predates computerized system technology, is a reliable means by which restaurants seek payment for all goods and services rendered. An integrated precheck system can provide a level of internal control and communications networking otherwise unavailable to the restaurateur. A precheck system is composed of order entry devices, network controllers, and remote printers. Orders entered through preset or price look-up (PLU) keys trigger an assortment of sales, service, productivity, inventory, and managerial reports. All subsequent precheck transactions use the same data from initial order entries. Such streamlining makes a strong case for integrated software in restaurants, but an even stronger case is made when precost systems are considered.

Check Tracking. Check tracking is primarily concerned with monitoring the activities spanning production to service and ensuring that all purchases are properly posted to guest checks for eventual settlement. Check tracking goes a step beyond prechecking in that check tracking divides guest checks into open checks, closed checks, and missing checks. An open guest check describes an account that has not been settled; hence, additional transactions can be posted to it. Settlement automatically changes a guest check's status from open to closed. Transactions can no longer be posted to closed guest checks. Guest checks that were opened but never closed are referred to as missing checks. Missing guest checks are problematic in that they represent products and services rendered for which no revenue was collected. Controlling checks has been an important aspect of foodservice automation.

Sales Analysis. A cash-register–based sales analysis report enables management to measure the sales performance of individual menu items by department or product category within certain time intervals. Time intervals typically vary in relation to the type of foodservice operation. Quick service restaurants may desire sales analysis reports on a very frequent basis (15 minute intervals), table service restaurants by the hour, and institutional food service operations by meal period. Sales analysis reports provide management with the ability to track individual item sales, analyze product acceptance, and monitor advertising and sales promotional efforts. This report typically contains unit price, quantity sold, extended dollar value, and percentage of sales by item. A summary sales report generally contains detailed sales and tax information by such categories as food items, beer, wine, and liquor. Labor and control totals may also be reported. Generally, totals for each category are printed for each meal period and totals for each meal period are shown in different sections of the report. Sales can also be analyzed, in relation to other variables, in the management area.

Attendance/Inventory Control. Service area labor management is achieved through time and attendance tracking. Cash register devices often are designed to serve as sign-in and sign-out devices for hourly labor. The replacement of a traditional time clock with a cash register device can be effective so long as it is eventually interfaced to a separate system for payroll processing.

Back-of-the-House-Applications

Restaurant management application process data related to back-of-the-house foodservice activities. Typical back-of-the-house applications include recipe management, precosting and postcosting, sales analysis, menu management, and back office accounting.

Recipe Management   The recipe management application maintains three of the most important files of an integrated restaurant management package: ingredient file, recipe file, and menu item file. Most other back office management applications must be able to access data contained within these files in order to effectively complete necessary processing functions.

Ingredient File.   An ingredient file contains important data on each purchased ingredient. Data may include ingredient code number, ingredient description, purchase unit, purchase unit cost, issue unit, issue unit cost, recipe unit, and recipe unit cost. The production of an ingredient cost listing, for example, is representative of output derived from data maintained by an ingredient file. An ingredient cost list report shows the current cost of each ingredient, the unit of measure by which each ingredient is purchased, the number of recipe portions by unit, and the recipe cost of each portion. This report is useful for verifying the accuracy of entered data, detailing unit expenditures at current costs, and monitoring relationships among various product units (such as purchase, issue, and recipe units of the same ingredient).

Some ingredient files may specify more than one recipe unit. For example, the recipe unit for bread used for french toast is by the slice; however the recipe unit for bread used for stuffing is by the ounce. In addition, most restaurant operations enter nonfood items into an ingredient file, thus ensuring that the ingredient file contains a complete list of all purchased products. This list becomes especially important if purchase orders are eventually generated for complete ingredient inventory. Additional data contained by the ingredient file may provide the basis for effective inventory control. Conversion tables can be maintained by which to track ingredients (by unit and by cost) as they pass through purchasing/receiving, storing/issuing, and production/service control points. In order to efficiently maintain a perpetual inventory record, the restaurant management system must be able to automatically convert purchase units into issue units and recipe units (also referred to as usable units).

For example, assume that an ingredient is purchased, issued, and used in different units. When a shipment of the ingredients arrives, it should be easy to update the inventory record by simply entering the purchase unit received. The computer system should then automatically convert this entry into issue units. Without this conversion capability, it would be necessary to manually calculate the number of units to be stored and increase the inventory record accordingly. Similarly, at the end of a meal period, the system should be capable of updating the inventory record by entering the standard recipe units that should have been used to prepare menu items. If the restaurant management system cannot convert issue units into recipe units, then these calculations may also have to be performed manually and the inventory record decreased accordingly.

Similarly, the system should also be able to track the costs associated with these various ingredient units. For example, assume that bottled ketchup is purchased by the case (24 twelve-ounce bottles), issued from the storeroom to the kitchen by the bottle, and used in recipes by the ounce. Given information regarding the purchase unit's net weight and cost, the system should be able to automatically extend costs for issue and recipe unit(s). If the purchase unit's net weight is 18 pounds and its purchase price is $20.40, then the system should be able to automatically compute issue unit cost at $0.85 and recipe unit cost at $0.07.

In order to arrive at the costs through manual calculations, an employee would first compute the price per ounce of the purchase unit. This is done by first converting 18 pounds to 288 ounces and then dividing $20.40 by 288 ounces to arrive at the recipe unit cost of $0.07 per ounce. Multiplying $0.07 by 12 ounces yields the issue unit cost of $0.85. Performing these calculations manually for every ingredient purchased can be a tedious, error-prone, time-consuming process. A restaurant management applications package can perform these calculations in fractions of a second. Care must be taken to ensure that the ingredient file contains the necessary data, conversions definitions, and algorithms.

Recipe File.   A standard recipe file must contain recipes for all menu items. Important data maintained by the standard recipe file may include recipe code number, recipe name, number of portions, portion size, recipe unit, recipe unit cost, menu selling price, and food cost percentage. A typical report generated within a standard recipe file module usually keys on up to ten ingredients for production with this specific application. A feature of this particular recipe record is the inclusion of a "high warning flag," which signals when the current food cost exceeds a predetermined level designated by management. Recipe records are instrumental to purchase order systems because stored recipes can indicate needed quantities prior to production and provide an index of perpetual inventory replenishment following production.

Some data contained in the standard recipe file overlap data within the ingredient file. This simplifies the creation and maintenance of recipe records because data should not have to be reentered. In addition, recipe management applications can access specific elements of data contained in ingredient and/or recipe files and format a number of different management reports. A summary recipe cost report can be especially useful in the menu planning process. Some recipe management applications provide space within standard recipe records for preparation instructions (also referred to as assembly instructions) which are typically found on standard recipe cards. Although this information is not accessed by other system management applications, it enables management to print recipes for production personnel. This can be a useful feature in relation to some menu items when batch sizes (number of portions yielded by a particular standard recipe) need to be expanded or contracted to accommodate forecasted needs.

For example, if a standard recipe is designed to yield 100 portions (batch size) but 530 portions are needed, it may be possible (depending on the particular menu item) to instruct the system to proportionately adjust the corresponding ingredient quantities. When batch size can be modified, unique recipes that include preparation information can be printed, thus providing a complete plan for recipe production. Few restaurants purchase all menu item ingredients in ready-to-use or preportioned form. Some ingredients are made on the premises. Therefore the ingredients within a standard recipe record may be either inventory items or references to other recipe files. Recipes that are included as ingredients with a standard recipe are called *sub-recipes.* Including sub-recipes as ingredients for a particular standard recipe is called *chaining recipes.* Chaining recipes enables the information system to maintain a record for a particular menu item that requires an unusually large number of ingredients. When ingredient costs change, computerized recipe management applications must be capable of automatically updating not only the costs of standard recipes, but also the cost of sub-recipes that are used as ingredients. Should this not be the case, new cost data would have to be separately entered into each sub-recipe record. This can be a time-consuming and error-prone process.

Menu Item File.   A menu item file contains data for all meal periods and menu items sold. Important data maintained by this file may include identification number, descriptor, recipe code number, selling price, ingredient quantities for inventory reporting, and sales totals. This file also stores historical information on the actual number of items sold. Generally, after a meal period, the actual number of menu items served is manually entered into the menu item file or automatically transferred from an ECR/POS system through an interface to the restaurant management system. These data can be accessed by management or by sophisticated forecasting programs to project future sales, determine the number of ingredient quantities to purchase, and schedule needed personnel. In addition, restaurant sales analysis applications access data contained in the menu item file in order to produce various sales analysis reports for management. When menu items, prices, or tax tables need to be changed, the menu item file is accessed and appropriate changes are entered according to procedures indicated in the user's manual provided by the system's vendor.

Precosting/Postcosting   Precosting is a special type of forecasting that compares forecasted guest counts with standard menu item costs to yield an index of expense prior to an actual meal period. Restaurant management system precosting applications can project costs on a portion, batch, or meal period basis. This projected cost of sales figure enables management to review and adjust operations before an actual service period begins. For example, if precosting finds projected costs to be outside an acceptable range, management may consider raising prices, decreasing portion sizes, altering accompaniments, or substituting menu items.

Although most nonautomated restaurants have access to the necessary data for precosting calculations, few actually perform the analysis because it can be time consuming. Computer-based precosting applications significantly streamline the analysis by accessing appropriate data from the ingredient file, recipe file, and menu item file and producing a precost menu plan within minutes.

Postcosting is a special type of sales analysis that multiplies the number of menu items sold by standard recipe costs to determine a potential food cost amount. When actual recipe costs are known, these figures are multiplied by the number of menu items sold to produce an actual cost figure.

Sales Analysis   Sophisticated ECR/POS systems typically capture important data regarding daily restaurant operations. When an ECR/POS system is interfaced to a restaurant management system, data maintained by ECR/POS system files can be accessed by the restaurant computer for management applications. Such an interface enables a merger of data from ECR/POS files with data from files maintained by a recipe management application. The sales analysis application can then process this combined data into numerous reports that help management direct daily operations in such specific areas as menu planning, sales forecasting, menu item pricing, ingredient purchasing, inventory control, labor scheduling, and payroll accounting.

The consolidated reports produced by an ECR/POS system can be supplemented by detailed information which the ECR/POS system may be unable to provide. In addition, management reports can be printed on paper larger than the narrow tape used by registers and journal printers. Although there are a wide variety of sales reports, four types of reports appear to be very popular. A daily sales report summarizes all sales revenue activity for a day. Revenue is normally itemized by the following categories: net sales, tax, number of guest checks, number of covers, dollars per check, dollars per cover, sales category, and day-part totals.

In addition, affected general ledger accounts may be included, and associated food cost and sales percentage statistics compiled. A weekly sales spreadsheet provides a weekly summary of all information reported by relevant daily sales reports. A sales category analysis report shows relationships between amounts sold by sales category and day-parts defined by management. This report enables management to view at a glance which menu items are selling and when they are selling. A marketing category report compiles weekly totals summarizing the revenue earned by food and beverage departments (or categories).

Menu Management While most computer-based restaurant management applications sort and index data into timely, factual reports for management, menu management applications help management answer such questions as

- What is the most profitable price to assign a menu item?
- At what price level and mix of sales does a foodservice operation maximize its profits?
- Which current menu items require repricing, retention, replacement, or repositioning on the menu?
- How should daily specials and new items be priced?
- How can the success of a menu change be evaluated?

Menu engineering is a menu management application that takes a deterministic approach in evaluating decisions regarding current and future menu pricing, design, and contents. This application requires that management focus on the number of dollars a menu contributes to profit and not simply monitor cost percentages.

Menu engineering begins with an interactive analysis of menu mix (MM) and contribution margin (CM) data. Competing menu items are categorized as either high or low. A menu item is categorized as high when its MM is greater than or equal to 70 percent of its equal menu share. When a menu item's MM is less than 70 percent of its equal menu share, it is categorized as low. The item's individual CM is similarly compared to the menu's average CM and categorized as either high or low. This analysis produces the following classifications:

Menu items high in both MM and CM are classified as stars (winners).
Menu items high in MM but low in CM are classified as plowhorses (marginal).
Menu items low in MM but high in CM are classified as puzzles (potential).
Menu items low in MM and low in CM are classified as dogs (losers).

The application goes a step further and identifies practical approaches by which to reengineer the next menu. For example, simple strategies include: retain stars; reprice plowhorses; reposition puzzles; and remove dogs. Data for analysis can be entered into the program's database manually, automatically (from an integrated system management applications package), or electronically (via an external ECR/POS system interface). A stand-alone version of menu engineering requires that the user input each menu item's product cost, selling price, and sales history. This minimal input is sufficient to generate a complete menu engineering analysis. Foodservice operators who employ recipe management applications to provide accurate product cost data can program a menu engineering application to read this data from a file, rather than rely upon user input. Other data, such as selling price and number of items sold, already collected by an ECR/POS system, can be electronically transmitted to the menu engineering application for processing. An establishment employing both a back-office computer and an ECR/POS system with interface capabilities will experience a minimal amount of data preparation and handling. Once the data requirements are fulfilled with preservice, postservice, or simulated information, program execution can begin.

Generally menu engineering output is composed of five reports: menu item analysis, menu mix analysis, menu engineering summary, four-box analysis, and menu engineering graph.

A menu item analysis report is an item-by-item listing of menu items accompanied by selling price, portion cost, contribution margin, and item count (number sold). The primary purpose of this report is to provide the user with a means by which to verify the data to be analyzed. This can be particularly helpful as a check on data input when data have been manually entered into the application.

A menu mix analysis contains an evaluation of each menu item's participation in the overall menu's performance. The percentage of menu mix (%MM) is based upon each item's count divided by the total number of covers sold. Each percentage is then ranked as high or low depending upon its comparison with the menu engineering rule for menu mix sufficiency. Each item's contribution margin is then ranked according to how it compares with the menu's weighted average contribution margin (ACM). A menu classification for each item is determined by considering its MM group rank and CM group rank together. Four menu classifications used in menu engineering analysis are determined according to the following table:

MM Rank	CM Rank	Classification
High	High	Star
High	Low	Plowhorse
Low	High	Puzzle
Low	Low	Dog

These classifications are not unique to menu engineering analysis.

A menu engineering summary report is probably the most informative report produced by the menu engineering application. This analysis presents important information in capsule form to enable a concise statement of operations. Such output as total menu revenue, average item selling price, lowest selling price, highest selling price, total menu costs, average item food cost, lowest cost item, and highest cost item are all important variables. In addition, total menu CM, average item CM, lowest item CM, highest item CM, total number of covers (sales per guest), average number of covers, lowest item count, and highest item count are also essential to a comprehensive analysis. Much of the information in the body of this report is used elsewhere in the overall menu engineering system.

The four box analysis restates the menu classifications developed in the menu mix analysis report. Since menu engineering leads to a series of decision strategies specific to each menu classification, this report provides the user with insight relative to the number of items found in each category. This type of evaluation process begins with the four-box matrix and continues through the menu engineering graph.

The menu engineering graph is a useful means by which to evaluate decision strategies. Since it indicates each competing menu item's relative position to all others, the menu engineering graph is considered the most powerful report produced by a menu engineering application. The vertical axis of the graph positions menu mix and the horizontal axis positions contribution margin. Each item is then graphed according to its CM and MM coordinates. It is especially important to note that not all items in the same classification possess identical characteristics. This technique, therefore, points out that a different menu engineering strategy may be appropriate for items even though they are similarly segmented. Prime rib, for example, presents a very different profile than fried shrimp. A foodservice operator is usually more willing to raise the price of prime rib (even if it means selling less), than the price of fried shrimp. Menu engineering strategies are concerned with trade-offs based upon elasticities of price and demand.

Menu engineering provides an objective way to develop strategies for menu improvement. It also supports the objective of menu planning, which is to increase contribution margin—not simply decrease food cost percentage.

Back Office Accounting   Restaurant management systems vary in the number of back office accounting applications they provide. The four major back office modules involve the fundamental accounting tasks within the areas of accounts receivable, accounts payable, payroll accounting, and financial reporting. Restaurant management applications address these same fundamental accounting tasks. Since the programs are only slightly modified to meet the particular needs of foodservice operations, their discussion in this section is limited to reviewing their functions and presenting sample reports specific to foodservice operations. Other modules warranting discussion are inventory, purchasing, budgeting, and fixed asset accounting. Restaurant management system inventory applications are generally more extensively developed for foodservice than those provided other industries. However, restaurant purchasing, budgeting, and fixed asset accounting applications function in much the same way as those applied to other industries.

The term *accounts receivable* refers to obligations owed to the property from sales made on credit. An accounts receivable system management application typically performs the following functions:

Maintains account balances
Processes billings
Monitors collection activities
Generates aging of accounts receivable reports
Produces an audit report indicating all accounts receivable transactions.

Since restaurants maintain few house accounts and accept a limited number of travel and entertainment or bank credit cards, they generally process fewer accounts receivable transactions than other industries. Therefore a restaurant management system may be responsible for creating and maintaining a relatively small customer master file. This file typically contains customer data and billing information such as the number of days elapsed between payments and the oldest invoice to which the last payment applied. Many accounts receivable applications maintain an accounts aging file, containing data that may be formatted into a variety of aging reports. An aging of accounts receivable schedule segments each account in the accounts aging file according to the date the charge originated. An important security function carried out by some restaurant computer systems is an audit report indicating all accounts receivable transactions. An audit report usually charts each account by account code, account name, invoice number(s) and amount(s), and the types of transactions processed for a specified time period.

The term *accounts payable* refers to liabilities incurred for merchandise, equipment, or other goods and services that have been purchased on account. An accounts payable restaurant management application maintains a vendor master file, an invoice register file, a check register file, and typically performs the following functions:

> Posts purveyor invoices
> Monitors vendor payment discount periods
> Determines amounts due
> Produces checks for payment
> Facilitates the reconciliation of cleared checks
> Generates numerous management reports

An important report produced by an accounts payable management application is the cash requirements report. This report lists all invoices selected for payment and the corresponding cash requirement totals. When this management application is part of an overall back office accounting package, it maintains current payables records through on-line, automatic posting of transactions to the financial reporting (or general ledger) management application. This process helps prevent duplicate entries of invoices and provides management with access to up-to-date information on invoices and vendors.

The labor-intensive nature of foodservice operations makes payroll accounting an important part of a restaurant computer package. This application streamlines recurrent payroll accounting tasks as it typically performs the following functions:

> Maintains an employee master file
> Calculates gross and net pay for salaried and hourly employees
> Produces paychecks
> Prepares payroll tax registers and reports
> Produces labor reports for use by management

A payroll accounting application is generally able to handle the complexities involved in properly processing time and attendance records, unique employee benefits, pay rates, withholdings, deductions, and required payroll reports. In restaurant operations, a single employee may work at different tasks over a number of workshifts, each of which may call for a separate pay rate. Therefore, an automated payroll application must be flexible enough to meet all the demands placed on the system with a minimum of actual programming changes. It must be capable of handling job codes, employee meals, uniform credits, tips, taxes, and other data that may affect the net pay of employees.

Since labor amounts to approximately one-third of all restaurant expenditures, management needs timely, accurate reports by which to monitor labor costs. In some properties, a computerized time-clock system or an electronic cash register records time-in and time-out for employees as they enter and leave the work area. Once the data have been transferred to the restaurant computer system, a payroll accounting application can produce a number of reports for management use.

The financial reporting application (also referred to as a general ledger application) is structured by the restaurant's chart of accounts, which lists financial statement accounts and their account numbers. The application maintains account balances, prepares trial balances, computes financial and operating ratios, and produces financial statements and a variety of reports for management's use.

Generally, the financial reporting application is capable of tracking accounts receivable, accounts payable, cash, and adjusting entries. However, in order to track these areas, the financial reporting application must have access to account balances maintained by other back office applications. With a fully integrated restaurant system, daily file updates ensure that the balances held in the financial reporting application are current.

From the point of view of restaurant managers, an inventory application is perhaps the most important part of a back office package. However, inventory applications tend to be the least uniform of all foodservice software. They vary widely in terms of file capacity and algorithmic design. The usefulness of inventory reports produced by the system will depend on the details within file records and the correctness of the formulas programmed into the design.

The initial creation of an ingredient file and the subsequent file updates (daily, weekly, monthly) can be an overwhelming task for some foodservice operations. Also, if errors are made when initially entering data, all subsequent processing will be unreliable and system reports will be relatively worthless. In addition, applications that do not support integrated files can be extremely cumbersome because users must re-input data from several files in order to run a particular program. Some inventory applications provide file space for more than one ingredient designation, such as item file code number, inventory sequence number, internal customer code, and so on. The ability to work with additional designations can increase the efficiency of the inventory control system, such as enabling a user to print ingredients on a physical inventory worksheet according to the order in which they are shelved.

Since many ECR/POS systems are incapable of tracking the same item as it passes through the control points of receiving, storing, issuing, and production, the data maintained by the inventory files of a back office restaurant package must be specific to each of these control points because most ingredients are purchased, stored, and used in different quantities. Computerized inventory applications should enable users to specify tables for converting purchase units, issue units, and recipe units for individual inventory items.

Another concern is how usage is charted by the inventory application—by unit, by cost, or by both unit and cost. A system that charts items by unit may be able to report changes in stock levels but may not be able to provide financial data necessary for food costing. On the other hand, a system that charts items primarily by product cost may not facilitate spot-checks of items in storage or maintain perpetual inventory data. The most effective inventory applications are those that track items in terms of both unit and cost.

Management should also clarify how basic foodservice concepts are defined within the inventory application design. For example, is an inventory item considered "used" (for costing purposes) at the time it is received, or when it is issued to the kitchen, or at the time of service? The point in time that is most desirable for a particular restaurant operation may not be the time frame that is built into the application's design. Methods of inventory valuation vary. Therefore management must be careful to clarify which methods a particular inventory package should support.

Multiunit Communications

When it comes to multiple restaurant communications, the shortest distance between store units and headquarters is a telephone line. The use of telecommunications to communicate unit level information to corporate headquarters is receiving an unprecedented amount of attention from multiunit foodservice companies and computer system vendors. Foodservice companies desirous of comprehensive, timely information are no longer interested in waiting for postal or carrier services to deliver store level data. Instead there is an increasing demand for improved electronic mail capability, remote cash register polling techniques, corporate reporting methodology, and facsimile (FAX) transmission technology. Collectively, these approaches are referred to as electronic multiunit communications.

Communications Technology   The development of enhanced communications technology has significantly extended multiunit foodservice information system capabilities. Communications technology enables the sharing of information across a large number of users with minimal data rehandling. In order to partake in electronic communications, users must possess some level of communications hardware and software. In order for computer communications to take place three required hardware components must be present at each participating location: a computer, a communications device, and a communications controller. The computer is used to collect and store the data files to be sent and/or received during communications. A communications device (called a 'modem') physically connects a computer to a telephone carrier. The communications controller (normally a computer circuit board) takes responsibility for sending/receiving data between source and destination computers once modems have established an open line for communications.

The software required to accomplish telecommunications is much more difficult to comprehend than is hardware. From a hardware perspective it is easy to place a phone call between two devices and establish a common line of communication. The problem is that creating the connection does not ensure that data will be transferred in a useable or compatible form. A person, for example, can dial a phone and make connection with a foreign country. Telephone system hardware enables the placement of such calls. Frustration may arise when the receiver and caller, speaking different languages, try to carry on a conversation. The productivity of such a session may be worthless. The same may be true for two computer devices or systems trying to send/receive incompatible file structures.

Two types of software are involved in communications. The more familiar is application software. Application software is the program the user is exercising to generate the data to be communicated. It is visible to the user. The second type of software is communication software which establishes the rules (protocol) governing data exchange. Protocol is concerned with the speed, format, and direction of data transmission. Similar to a translation dictionary, communication software ensures that data can be sent, received, and understood.

Long distances between users requires the establishment of a telephone connection for communications. In order to accomplish this, modems and public or private carrier phone lines are used. A modem is a device used to transform (MODulate) the store level (sender's) digital computer signals into analog telephone signals for transmission over phone lines. Modems also convert analog signals back to digital computer signals (DEModulate) at headquarter's (the receiver's) end. Hence, a modem is required on each end of a telephone line if data communication is to take place. In addition, modems can also be programmmed to place a call to a pre-specified phone number at an exact time (autodial) or can be left in a ready to receive (autoanswer) mode. In either case, human intervention at the time of call placement or reception is not necessary. This can be very beneficial to multiunit operations that have late closing times and/or multiunits located in different time zones. Autodial and autoanswer capabilities can enable unit data to be automatically transferred to a central computer during off hours. This methodology allows the company's central computer communications software to retrieve information from all of the units without having active user participation and at lower cost telephone charges.

Networking

A network is an interconnected system that includes both data processing and data communications components. In a telecommunication network each user operates a separate computer containing its own CPU. This design enables more effective file access, processing, and use of system memory. Multiunit restaurant managers, recognizing the versatility and productivity of telecommunications, are adopting networks at an unprecedented rate.

The primary reasons for developing a communications network are data, program, and device sharing. The commonality of need among a variety of users has led to a focus on data sharing. Regardless of whether raw data or processed information is disseminated, data sharing is an essential objective of telecommunication networking. Program sharing enables remote job execution under the control of a program stored elsewhere. In a multiunit operation, for example, individual stores may be required to forward their data to headquarters for processing even though they may receive their printed output at a local (in-store) site. Program sharing also provides a means for users not in possession of a particular program to benefit from its operation. From an economic perspective device sharing is perhaps the most important factor in networking. Expensive peripheral devices (high capacity storage devices, laser printers, and so forth) can become available to all users through the presence of a network. There simply may not be a need for management to purchase a specialty system component for each unit location.

Industry Telecommunication Applications

The movement of data from one computer to another, from one system to another, and from one location to another necessitates communications technology. Multiunit foodservice applications include remote cash register polling, centralized (corporate) reporting, and electronic mail.

Remote Cash Register Polling. A popular foodservice communication technique for many multiunit companies involves direct data capture from a unit level cash register system. Such an approach requires that the in-store register system support a data capture device that is accessible via telecommunications. Large multiunit foodservice companies have traditionally relied on remote polling to develop same day comprehensive managerial sales and statistical reports. The data from all store registers in a division or region may be collected and summarized and sent to headquarters for analysis. In turn, headquarters may evaluate the information and communicate aggregated reports back to divisional and store level managers as constructive feedback. Remote cash register polling continues to be more prevalent among quick service chain restaurants than other foodservice segments.

Centralized Corporate Reporting.   Corporate reporting normally involves a combination of the characteristics of several communication applications discussed in this article. Unit level reports are prepared for headquarters and can be directly communicated or stored for corporate accesss. In the first case, the unit decides when to communicate its required data report, and in the second case corporate management determines when to access the store's computer. The development of routine report preparation deadlines leads to the sending of documents from unit to central locations. Central polling of store level data is not as effective as store to headquarter reporting in most foodservice companies. In preparation for multiunit networking, restaurants typically install comprehensive store level computer systems and purchase modems.

Electronic Mail.   An alternative to direct modem communication to support corporate communications is the use of temporary computer storage files available through utility information service companies. In this case, the restaurant company basically leases storage space on another company's computer storage equipment. Unit level data files and documents prepared through an in-store computer can be sent from one location to another using electronic mail techniques (also referred to as E-Mail). Although there are several approaches to electronic mail the most practical involves communication to an electronic mailbox. To transmit a document to an electronic mailbox, the telephone number of the mailbox is dialed and the desired files and/ or documents transmitted. The received contents remain in electronic storage in the mailbox until the intended recipient calls the mailbox and accesses the file. Store level data files to be communicated include payroll, invoices received, sales and sales mix data, and projected monthly profit and loss information.

Historically, it was possible for multiunit operations to overload headquarter computer facilities with simultaneous or overlapping calls. In order to alleviate network contention problems, many companies establish a relationship with a large satellite computer service and direct company restaurants to send their data to the center on a prespecified day. In essence, each unit sends an electronic file to the satellite center where it is held until requested by headquarters. This use of electronic mailbox technology has led to more efficient multiunit communication capabilities for the company and has provided stores with more reporting flexibility.

Multiunit Communication Criteria   Assuming a store level restaurant's computer contains adequate memory to support a communications software package, the following factors should be evaluated: product documentation, hardware requirements, software requirements, transmission speed (baud rate), file transference methodology, conversational mode(s), error checking features, and modem features (such as autoanswer/autodial/autoredial capabilities).

Summary

Foodservice computer applications can be divided into service and management application areas. Service applications tend to be ECR/POS based. ECR/POS software programs not only direct internal system operations, but also maintain files and produce reports for use by management. Data maintained by ECR/POS files can be accessed and formatted into a variety of management reports.

The particular information needs of each type of foodservice establishment create unique automation demands. Service personnel and guest check systems of table service restaurants may require different ECR/POS mechanisms than those appropriate for quick service restaurants. ECR/POS system hardware components consist of user interfaces, display screens, various output devices, a network controller, and sometimes a cash drawer. There are four types of ECR/POS hardware designs: stand-alone, master-slave, processor-based, and micro-based. Careful analysis of a foodservice operation will help suggest which configuration would be most beneficial.

The hardware within any ECR/POS system does nothing by itself. In order for hardware components to operate, there must be a set of software programs directing the system. ECR/POS software programs not only direct internal system operations, but also maintain files and produce reports for management use. Files which may be stored and maintained by sophisticated ECR/POS systems include menu item file, open check file, labor master file, and inventory files. Data maintained by these files (and others) can be accessed by ECR/POS terminals and formatted reports can be printed.

Back office, management applications process data related to back-of-the-house foodservice activities. Applications include recipe management, precosting and postcosting, sales analysis, menu management, and back office accounting.

PART 2

Hotel Management

1

Strategic Management

Michael Olsen

The concept of strategic management has evolved from the ancient Greek word *strategia* meaning the art of the general. The practice of strategic management requires organization heads to allocate resources, establish policies and procedures, assign responsibilities, and give direction to the organization by employing a consistent pattern of decisions that reflect an overall mission and set of goals. The pattern of the decisions made in guiding the organization toward the successful completion of its goals is influenced by events occurring in the general and task environments of the organization. The strategic management process can be applied to all types of organizations and at all levels of those organizations. For example, it can be applied to individual hospitality firms, such as restaurants, or business units, such as a chain of hotels, or to entire corporations that have many business units. The purpose of the strategic management process at any organizational level is to assist the organization's leaders in helping their organization to adapt continually to its changing environment so that it can enjoy a strong, growing, and long-lasting life.

Three basic elements comprise strategic management: the process of formulating a strategy, deciding upon the strategy to follow, and implementing that strategy. Although each of these elements is often treated separately in the literature on strategy, it is important to recognize that a synergistic relationship exists among the organizational leaders that must develop all three elements for strategic management to be effective.

Strategy Formulation

An organization's strategy can be formulated in a variety of ways. The means used most often depend on the type of organization and the leadership within that organization. In general, the elements most often included in the process are

1. Environmental analysis: an assessment of the organization's specific competitive environment, as well as the activities taking place in the more general environment affecting all businesses in an industry. The purpose of this process is to identify the threats and opportunities that present themselves to the organization over the planning horizon under consideration.

2. Analysis of the organization's strengths and weaknesses: a thorough look at the internal resources (such as human, capital, and material) of the organization for the purpose of determining what the organization does well and what problems it needs to address.

3. Strategic gap analysis: a review of the organization's strengths and weaknesses in the context of the threats and opportunities presented by the general and task environment.

4. Mission statement development: the preparation of a statement defining what the organization is and where it is going. The mission statement identifies the target audience for which the organization will provide goods and services and clarifies how these will be provided and the standards by which they will be judged. This statement is the result of the analysis of the organization's environment, its strengths and weaknesses, and the strategic gap.

5. Strategic alternatives analysis: the identification of the types of possible strategies that can be used to achieve the mission of the organization.

6. Evaluation and selection of strategy: a thorough evaluation of the possible strategies available to the organization and the selection of the one(s) that will best fit its needs.

7. Monitoring and follow-up: the establishment of expectations and standards to control the process of strategy implementation and to determine the effectiveness of the chosen strategy.

Each of these elements in the strategy formulation process must be carefully studied and analyzed if an organization is to realize its full potential. To achieve the most effective strategy, those formulating strategy must believe that it will assist the organization in achieving a favorable coalignment with its environment (Hofer and Schendel 1978; Porter 1980; West and Olsen 1988; and Dev and Olsen 1989). They must believe that the potential exists for an optimal pattern or "fit" between the environment and the organization's strategy. Research evidence suggests that hospitality organizations that are active in environmental analysis and use that analysis to achieve a coalignment with their environment do perform better (Dev and Olsen 1989; West and Olsen 1988).

An organization that actively participates in environmental analysis must have established systems designed to monitor the dynamics and uncertainties that exist in the general and task environment in which it conducts its day-to-day business. The general environment consists of those broad forces affecting society, including trends in technology, politics, economics, and sociocultural activities. The task environment refers to those forces that affect an industry, such as changes in the supply of resources, shifts in competitor behaviors, specific industry legislation and regulation, and changes taking place in the organization's customer market (Porter 1980).

The most difficult part of environmental analysis involves assessing if and how events occurring in the environment will affect the firm and the probabilities associated with various impacts. To be successful, the organization must develop a network of reliable sources of information about the environment who have a history of making valid assessments of environmental impact. Even with the best of sources and probabilistic estimates, however, it is still impossible to predict how environmental events will exactly affect the organization. Those organizations that do a better job of meshing strategy with environment tend to perform better than those who do not.

Several models have been developed to guide the organizational leader through the various elements presented above. The model presented in Figure 1 was developed for use in the hospitality industry and serves as one example of the explicitness and complexity of the process. The degree of detail ultimately chosen to guide the organization through this process is totally dependent upon the organization's situation, its leader, its goals, and the time frame in which action must be taken.

Types of Strategies

The strategy formulation process guides the organization in developing a strategy that will result in organizational effectiveness. Once the process has been completed, the organization must then decide exactly what type of strategy it must choose to meet its goals and objectives. Since there are almost as many types of strategies as there are organizations, research in the field of strategic management has tended toward the development of classification systems that can be used by decision makers to understand types of strategies. This effort has been useful in grouping the many specific and similar strategies into a few broad generic categories. This classification effort has contributed in significant ways to the development of knowledge regarding the strategic process, enabling researchers to examine the relationship between the type of generic strategy a firm has chosen and many variables important to organizational success. These variables include organizational performance, organizational structure, and degree of environmental scanning performed by the firm (West and Olsen 1988, 1990; Tse and Olsen 1988; Dev and Olsen 1989). This enhanced knowledge of the relationships between the type of strategy and organizational variables has helped decision makers choose the strategy that is best for their organization.

While a great many classification schemes appear in the literature on strategic management, only a few appropriate to the hospitality industry have emerged. These schemes have been derived from the pioneering works of Miles and Snow (1978) and Porter (1980). Schaffer (1987), and West and Olsen (1988) have used these studies to develop two generic classification schemes of strategies used by hospitality firms which yield an increased understanding of those strategies. Schaffer postulated the following strategy types:

1. Do-it-all differentiators: attempts to build an excellent reputation within the industry; attempts to be an innovator in service processes; continually looks for new market opportunities; seeks high quality in service
2. Internalized resource conserver: strives to develop and refine existing products and services; aims to procure as much as possible in the raw material state
3. Narrow focused marketing innovator: has a narrow product focus; engages in environmental scanning activities
4. Efficiency/quality controller: relies upon experienced and trained personnel to provide quality service
5. Geographic focused price leader: seeks stability in operating environments; develops conservative capital structure policy; interested in price leadership, serves only specific geographic markets

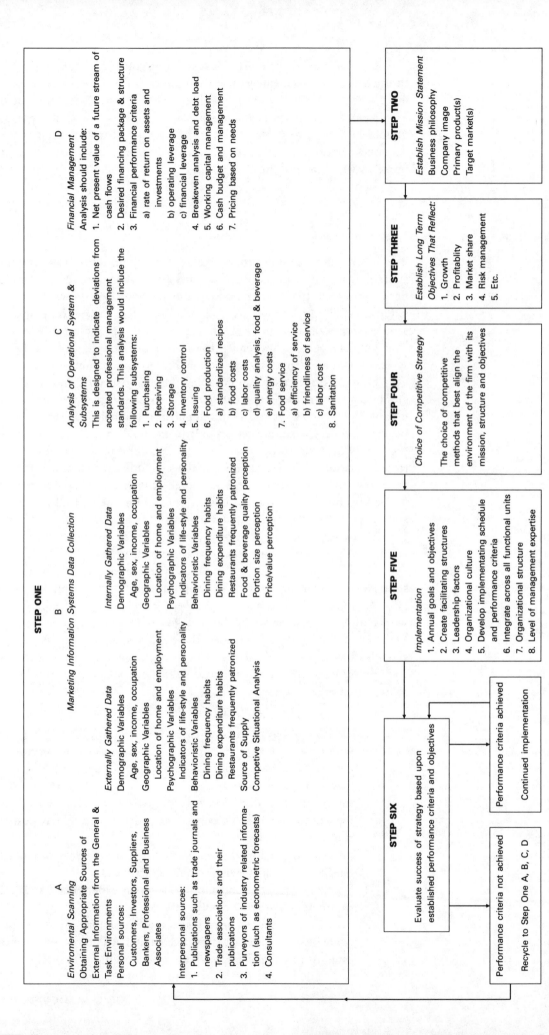

STEP ONE

A

Environmental Scanning

Obtaining Appropriate Sources of External Information from the General & Task Environments

Personal sources:
Customers, Investors, Suppliers, Bankers, Professional and Business Associates

Interpersonal sources:
1. Publications such as trade journals and newspapers
2. Trade associations and their publications
3. Purveyors of industry related information (such as econometric forecasts)
4. Consultants

B

Marketing Information Systems Data Collection

Externally Gathered Data
Demographic Variables
 Age, sex, income, occupation
Geographic Variables
 Location of home and employment
Psychographic Variables
 Indicators of life-style and personality
Behavioristic Variables
 Dining frequency habits
 Dining expenditure habits
 Restaurants frequently patronized
 Source of Supply
 Competive Situational Analysis

Internally Gathered Data
Demographic Variables
 Age, sex, income, occupation
Geographic Variables
 Location of home and employment
Psychographic Variables
 Indicators of life-style and personality
Behavioristic Variables
 Dining frequency habits
 Dining expenditure habits
 Restaurants frequently patronized
 Food & beverage quality perception
 Portion size perception
 Price/value perception

C

Analysis of Operational System & Subsystems

This is designed to indicate deviations from accepted professional management standards. This analysis would include the following subsystems:

1. Purchasing
2. Receiving
3. Storage
4. Inventory control
5. Issuing
6. Food production
 a) standardized recipes
 b) food costs
 c) labor costs
 d) quality analysis, food & beverage
 e) energy costs
7. Food service
 a) efficiency of service
 b) friendliness of service
 c) labor cost
8. Sanitation

D

Financial Management

Analysis should include:
1. Net present value of a future stream of cash flows
2. Desired financing package & structure
3. Financial performance criteria
 a) rate of return on assets and investments
 b) operating leverage
 c) financial leverage
4. Breakeven analysis and debt load
5. Working capital management
6. Cash budget and management
7. Pricing based on needs

STEP TWO

Establish Mission Statement

Business philosophy
Company image
Primary product(s)
Target market(s)

STEP THREE

Establish Long Term Objectives That Reflect:

1. Growth
2. Profitability
3. Market share
4. Risk management
5. Etc.

STEP FOUR

Choice of Competitive Strategy

The choice of competitive methods that best align the firm with its environment in the mission, structure and objectives

STEP FIVE

Implementation

1. Annual goals and objectives
2. Create facilitating structures
3. Leadership factors
4. Organizational culture
5. Develop implementating schedule and performance criteria
6. Integrate across all functional units
7. Organizational structure
8. Level of management expertise

STEP SIX

Evaluate success of strategy based upon established performance criteria and objectives

Performance criteria achieved

Continued implementation

Performance criteria not achieved

Recycle to Step One A, B, C, D

Fig. 1. The strategic management process model.
(Source: Robert Reid and Michael Olsen, A strategic planning model for independent foodservice operators, Journal of Hospitality Education 6(1):11–24, 1981.)

West's and Olsen's definition of strategy types consisted of the following categories:

1. Innovation and development: places major emphasis on innovation in menu design; develops new products and services; serves a specialized market and emphasizes efficiency
2. Focus: emphasizes service to a specialized market; strongly oriented toward efficiency and differentiation
3. Image management: emphasizes the use of advertising and innovative marketing promotions to achieve market share
4. No strategy: seeks to be everything to everybody with no strong orientation toward any area
5. Differentiation: emphasizes the offering of a unique product or service to a specialized market that is insensitive to price; strongly oriented toward the control of operations and market area
6. Control: attempts to exert strong control over operations; an internally oriented organization

As these schemes indicate, hospitality firms employ a wide variety of strategy types to accomplish their goals. The evidence suggests that hospitality organizations aim to be innovative, to differ from other firms, and to be efficient and focused in a particular market area. There are many variations of each of these strategy types and they are not mutually exclusive—an element of one strategy type may be included in another type. The choice of strategy type or combination of strategy types by the organization is decided after an analysis of how the organization can best meet the threats and opportunities that exist in its environment.

Strategy Implementation

The strategy formulation process leads to a decision regarding what type of strategy should be implemented. The process of successfully implementing that strategy type is essential if the organization is to enjoy long-term success. The framework for implementing strategy developed by Thompson and Strickland (1987), shown in Figure 2, illustrates the key elements necessary to ensure proper implementation of the organization's chosen strategy. The four major components of the implementation process are:

1. Successfully performing the recurring administrative tasks associated with strategy implementation
2. Creating a fit between the organization's internal processes and the requirements of a strategy
3. Making adjustments for the organization's overall situation in which implementation must take place
4. Choosing how to lead the implementation task

To perform the tasks in this framework, the organization must have in place systems designed to match the resources of the organization with its chosen strategy. This suggests that the structure of the organization, that is, its hierarchy and allocation and control of resources, must reflect the chosen strategy. It implies that a culture or set of shared values exists and its supportive of the strategy. Moreover, all of the organization's functional units must be performing at desired competency levels and a system of rewards must exist to facilitate the achievement of performance goals.

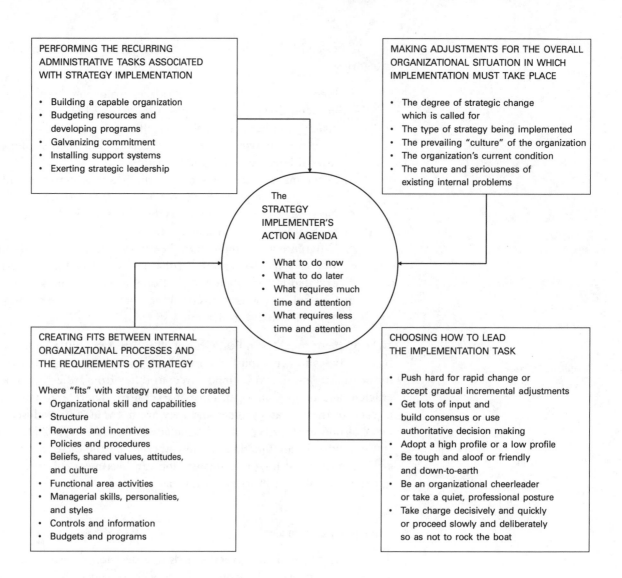

PERFORMING THE RECURRING
ADMINISTRATIVE TASKS ASSOCIATED
WITH STRATEGY IMPLEMENTATION

- Building a capable organization
- Budgeting resources and
  developing programs
- Galvanizing commitment
- Installing support systems
- Exerting strategic leadership

MAKING ADJUSTMENTS FOR THE OVERALL
ORGANIZATIONAL SITUATION IN WHICH
IMPLEMENTATION MUST TAKE PLACE

- The degree of strategic change
  which is called for
- The type of strategy being implemented
- The prevailing "culture" of the organization
- The organization's current condition
- The nature and seriousness of
  existing internal problems

The
STRATEGY
IMPLEMENTER'S
ACTION AGENDA

- What to do now
- What to do later
- What requires much
  time and attention
- What requires less
  time and attention

CREATING FITS BETWEEN INTERNAL
ORGANIZATIONAL PROCESSES AND
THE REQUIREMENTS OF STRATEGY

Where "fits" with strategy need to be created
- Organizational skill and capabilities
- Structure
- Rewards and incentives
- Policies and procedures
- Beliefs, shared values, attitudes,
  and culture
- Functional area activities
- Managerial skills, personalities,
  and styles
- Controls and information
- Budgets and programs

CHOOSING HOW TO LEAD
THE IMPLEMENTATION TASK

- Push hard for rapid change or
  accept gradual incremental adjustments
- Get lots of input and
  build consensus or use
  authoritative decision making
- Adopt a high profile or a low profile
- Be tough and aloof or friendly
  and down-to-earth
- Be an organizational cheerleader
  or take a quiet, professional posture
- Take charge decisively and quickly
  or proceed slowly and deliberately
  so as not to rock the boat

Fig. 2. A diagnostic framework for implementing strategy. *(Source: A. A. Thompson, Jr., and A. J. Strickland III, Strategic Management Concepts and Cases, 4th ed., Plano, Tex.: Business Publications, 1987, p. 206.)*

Leadership in Strategic Management

Leadership is an important but intangible ingredient in the successful implementation of strategy, and its role in this success is often difficult to determine. Leadership is contingent upon the situation, such as the threats and opportunities in the environment, upon the skills and competencies of the followers, those dependent upon the leader to accomplish the organization's goals and upon the leadership capabilities of the person responsible for the organization. An appropriate blending of these three elements is necessary if strategy is to be successfully implemented.

Summary

Strategic management is best defined as a pattern of decisions made in guiding an organization toward the successful completion of its goals. There are three basic concepts that influence this process. First, strategy formulation is a process that helps the organization decide which strategy to follow in the context of the threats and opportunities existing in the organization's environment. Second is the choice of the type of strategty that will allow the organization to omeet the threats, or take advantage of the opportunities, that exist in that environment. Last, strategy implementation is the process requiring the development of an organizational structure that will facilitate the allocation of all resources toward the type of strategy chosen. Strategic management is a dynamic process that requires constant review and evaluation if the organization is to succeed in a challenging, dynamic, and turbulent environment.

References

Dev, Chekitan, and Michael D. Olsen. 1989. Environmental uncertainty, business strategy and financial performance: An empirical study of the U.S. lodging industry. *Hospitality Education and Research Journal* 13(3):171–186.

Hofer, Charles W., and Dan Schendel. 1978. *Strategy Formulation: Analytical Concepts.* St. Paul, Minn.: West Publishing.

Miles, R. E., and C. C. Snow. 1978. *Organization Strategy, Structure and Process.* New York: McGraw-Hill.

Porter, M. E. 1980. *Competitive Strategy.* New York: Free Press.

Reid, Robert, and Michael Olsen. 1981. A strategic planning model for independent foodservice operators. *Journal of Hospitality Education* 6(1):11–24.

Schaffer, Jeffrey D. 1987. Competitive strategies in the lodging industry. *International Journal of Hospitality Management* 6(1):33–42.

Thompson, Arthur A., Jr., and A. J. Strickland III. 1987. *Strategic Management, Concepts and Cases,* 4th ed. Plano, Tex.: Business Publications.

Tse, Eliza, and Michael D. Olsen. 1988. The impact of strategy and structure on the organizational performance of restaurant firms. *Hospitality Education and Research Journal* 12(2):265–276.

West, Joseph J., and Michael D. Olsen. 1990. Grand strategy: Making your restaurant a winner. *Cornell Hotel Restaurant Administration Quarterly* 31(2):72–77.

West, Joseph J., and Michael D. Olsen. 1988. Environmental scanning and its effect upon firm performance: An exploratory study of the foodservice industry. *Hospitality Education and Research Journal* 12(2):127–136.

2

Financial Management

Francis A. Kwansa

The discipline of finance has the following subcategories all of which interact with each other: investments, money and capital markets, and financial management. Financial management is often confused with managerial accounting and financial accounting although the purposes of these branches of accounting and finance are different. Managerial accounting focuses on providing data for internal users, such as management. Such data include all information that management deems important, consequently, there is no requirement on the preparers to follow rules and guidelines set forth by the Financial Accounting Standards Board (FASB). Financial accounting targets external users, such as shareholders, governmental agencies, and creditors, thus this branch of accounting measures and reports the financial position of the firm according to formats and guidelines required by the FASB. Financial management, however, describes the process through which a firm makes financial decisions within the framework of the firm's goals by interpreting and analyzing financial data.

Two main responsibilities of the financial manager are to raise funds and to allocate funds. These responsibilities become clear when one analyzes the familiar accounting equation:

$$Assets = Liabilities + Owners' Equity$$

The left-hand side of the equation (assets) indicates all items of economic value owned by the firm, while the right-hand side shows that these items were obtained using funds provided by creditors and the owners of the firm. Numerous sources of funds, such as the stock market, commercial banks, loan sharks, and family and friends, are available to the firm, and each source has its own characteristics. The objective is to select the best mix of these sources without putting undue pressure on the firm's ability to meet its obligations, thereby risking the firm's survival. Having obtained these funds the financial manager becomes preoccupied with deciding, within the goals of the firm, what and how much of the funds should go to acquiring current assets versus fixed assets with the objective of maximizing the wealth of the firm's owners.

Due to the predominance of small-scale independent operators in the lodging and foodservice industries, in many cases, accountants have traditionally played the role of financial managers performing such activities as borrowing and investing funds (Geller et al. 1990).

There are several reasons why financial management is an important function in the hospitality industry. The location of a restaurant or a hotel has always been considered very important to the success of the business, consequently operators are constantly in search of prime locations. Although populations have relocated to the suburbs making many hitherto inaccessible areas viable locations, some operators believe that the best and most potentially profitable locations have all been taken. The cost of land has multiplied over the years and construction costs have also increased. The need for careful and prudent financial planning to minimize the impact of such costs has become more important today. Many industries, including the hospitality industry, are directly affected by changes in the economy. Much of consumer spending in the hospitality industry depends on the level of discretionary income available to the consumer, and the spending decisions are made by the consumer according to the economic cycles of expansion, recession, and recovery. The business consumer similarly makes travel plans based on the strength and direction of the economy. Thus the ability to anticipate changes in the economy, adjust revenue and profit forecasts, and make decisions regarding asset allocation and fundraising accordingly all become crucial. Yet another motivation to practice sound financial management arises from the threat of bankruptcy. The foodservice industry, for instance, has the highest incidence of business failures within the group of retail industries (Kwansa and Parsa 1990), and poor financial management has been the culprit in many cases.

Raising Funds

Funds, or capital, refers to all of the company's liabilities and owners equity, including short-term and long-term capital, preferred stock, common stock, and retained earnings. Short-term capital describes all debt due within a year, and there are two types. Spontaneous capital is a source of capital that arises simply from being in business. When a business is established vendors oblige the operator with the option to purchase supplies on credit and usually payable within sixty days. The terms of this credit offer an operator enough time to turn over inventory a few times before full payment is due thereby making the vendor the sole financier of the inventory. The other source of spontaneous credit arises from certain obligations that have accrued but will be paid at a later date, such as sales, income, and social security taxes collected by the business on behalf of federal and local governments. These are paid sometimes on a quarterly basis, so in the interim the business has a source of funds to use tax-free.

Negotiated credit is the other type of short-term capital and this requires formal or sometimes informal negotiations to obtain the funds. The need for such funds arises when a business has a temporary need for cash, such as to buy bargain inventory for which trade credit is unavailable or to pay employees during the slow season. Such credit is not intended to be held for too long, and sources may include friends and family, credit cards, loan sharks, financing agencies, and commercial banks. Commercial banks may offer a loan for several weeks or months, or they may also offer a line of credit. Line of credit is a facility negotiated for and made available by a commercial bank to a business, indicating a maximum amount of credit the bank is willing to extend to the business. Thus when the need arises for some funds the operator simply signs a promissory note to the bank for a specific time period and withdraws the money. The cost of short-term credit to the borrower is relatively less than the cost of long-term credit because short-term credit is held for less than a year.

Long-term capital are funds payable beyond one year and there are two basic types—long-term debt and equity. Long-term capital can be raised from several sources including commercial banks, the stock market, and through leases. Long-term capital is used for capital improvements of existing assets, purchasing new equipment, building new units, acquiring other businesses, marketing expenditures, and so on. Smaller and privately owned businesses usually seek such funds from commercial banks, but the banks' willingness to grant such funds have always depended on prevailing economic conditions.

A term loan is an example of a long-term debt instrument a commercial bank, insurance company, or pension fund is likely to offer. It is a contract under which the operator promises to make a series of interest and principal payments on specific dates to the lender. Term loans may be granted for periods ranging from two to thirty years but three- to fifteen-year ranges are typical. The interest rate on a term loan may be fixed or variable for the life of the loan. Fixed rates are set closely to rates charged on comparable bonds with similar risk while variable rates are set several percentage points over the prime rate (the interest rate large banks charge their most favored customers) or the Treasury bill rate.

Bonds are one of the more widely known forms of long-term debt used by most large companies. A bond, like a term loan, is a long-term IOU with a promise to pay back the principal and interest at specified dates to the bondholder. A bond issue, however, is advertised and offered for sale to the general public, thus the many investors across the country provide the funds for this endeavor. The service of an investment banker (for example Goldman Sachs, Merrill Lynch, or First Boston) is typically required to issue bonds and the investment banking firm charges a fee for providing advisory, marketing, and underwriting services to the issuer. When bonds are issued, they are generally priced at par ($1000), however, their resale price on the market may vary from par depending on the movement of the market interest rate at any time. Bond prices vary inversely with interest rate, that is, as the interest rate falls bond prices rise. The interest rate on the bond (also referred to as coupon rate) is generally fixed at the time of issue but other types of floating rate bonds have been available in recent years.

Some features of bonds are noteworthy. A trustee is usually appointed when a bond is issued and given the responsibility to protect the interest of bondholders as defined in the bond agreement. The trustee, usually an investment bank or legal firm, ensures that interest payments are made on time and also initiates legal action on behalf of bondholders in case of default or violation of any part of the bond agreement by the borrowing company. Bondholders must also receive their interest payments before other investors in the company are compensated. In case of liquidation, claims of bondholders are settled first before the claims of others.

Bonds may be secured, that is, specific assets are pledged as collateral. An example is a mortgage bond, which requires the pledging of specific real assets such as real estate. Bonds can also be unsecured in which case there is no lien against specific assets (for example, debenture). Bonds are rated at the request of issuing companies for a fee by financial services firms such as Standard and Poors and Moody's. This rating is based on factors such as integrity of the company, its financial strength, industry factors, assets of the firm, and size of market share. These factors together are used to estimate the creditworthiness of the company and the risk of default to the bondholder.

Bonds issued by the more creditworthy companies such as IBM are referred to as "investment grade" bonds. These bonds generally have low default risk and consequently their interest rate is relatively lower. As the financial, operational, and other circumstances of the company deteriorate the quality of its bonds are downgraded accordingly to reflect increased risk to the bondholder. *Junk bond* is a term describing speculative bonds issued by companies without a long record of sales and earnings or those with questionable credit strength. In the eighties these speculative bonds were popularized by the investment banking firm of Drexel Burnham Lambert and they provided funding for private and public companies that did not have access to the more traditional sources of financing because of their low credit rating. Junk bonds enabled many smaller companies to grow and expand and also participate in the merger wave of the eighties. Due to their relatively higher risk, interest rates on junk bonds are usually higher and risk-loving investors are generally attracted to them.

The other type of long-term capital is equity—funds provided by investors who are interested in owning a portion of the company. For the sole proprietor or partner in a partnership this represents all of their personal funds contributed to the business at the beginning and at other times during the life of the business. The corporation as a form of business organization is a legal entity that functions separately from its owners. That is, a management team manages the corporation on a day-to-day basis on behalf of the owners. Anyone can buy shares in a corporation and consequently own a portion of the business without necessarily being familiar with its operations. Such companies are termed public companies and their shares or stocks are sold on the stock market to raise funds for the corporation. Common and preferred stocks are the two main forms of equity financing.

Preferred stocks are similar to both common stocks and debt. They are similar to debt because they offer the promise of a fixed dividend forever but occasionally for a specified time period. Thus from the viewpoint of the company preferred stocks impose a fixed obligation on the business, therefore, it affects the firm's ability to borrow more funds in the future. Unlike debtholders, however, dividend payments to preferred stockholders are cumulative, that is, the obligation to pay can be postponed to a later date if the company lacks funds. Preferred stockholders commonly have no voting power.

Common stockholders represent the residual owners of the company. They collectively own the company and thus assume all risks of ownership. They are entitled to cash dividends only if the company's board of directors declares one, and they are entitled to vote in matters relating to the company. The ability of the company to raise funds through the sale of stocks in general depends on many factors such as economic conditions, the interest of investment bankers in the issue, the profitability and growth opportunities of the company, and many more.

Capital Structure   One of the decisions that must be made regards the kind of mix between debt and equity a company must have. Each source of capital has its advantages and disadvantages. For example, because their interest payments are a fixed obligation that cannot be postponed, debtholders have priority over equity-holders in the event of liquidation. As a result of their relatively lower risk debtholders charge relatively lower interest. In addition the federal tax laws are such that interest expenses paid on debt are tax deductible, thus making the use of debt even less expensive and very attractive. Consequently using debt improves a company's return on investment. There is a limit, however, to how much debt a company can assume because as more debt is assumed its cost begins to rise to compensate for the increased risk of default to lenders. Also, as the company uses more debt and the fixed payment obligation increases, the company becomes more vulnerable to bankruptcy if the economy slows down.

The use of equity, on the other hand, avoids the burden of fixed payments at specified dates and encourages the reinvestment of profits in the company. Yet, since common stockholders are residual owners and bear the risk of not knowing how much dividend they will receive periodically, and also since they are the last in order of priority in case of liquidation, their required compensation is higher. Also, as owners with a right to vote they exert influence on the running of the company unlike debtholders. Finance theorists believe that each company has an ideal (optimal) combination of debt and equity that will minimize the vulnerability of the company while maximizing its value. The financial manager then has the task of carefully balancing the use of debt and equity and determining a target mix of both sources that will be ideal for the company.

Allocation of Funds

The two main responsibilities of the financial manager are to raise funds and to allocate funds. The preceding section covered the two basic sources of funds, debt and equity, and their different types. Now that these funds have been raised, how should they be used? The balance sheet equation mentioned earlier shows that these funds are used by the company to obtain items of economic value (assets) to the firm. Some of the items, such as inventory, cash, and marketable securities are of a current nature, and they are meant to be used up within a year. The others are of a long-term nature meaning their useful life is expected to be beyond a year. The task of the financial manager is to allocate the available funds between current and long-term assets and to decide which of these investment choices will maximize the wealth of the owners of the firm.

Capital Budgeting

Capital budgeting is an analysis and selection of long-term projects to be included in the company's future plans. The emphasis here is on long-term assets and their careful analysis is important because these assets generally require the commitment of relatively large amounts of money and resources. Capital budgeting is also important because the kinds of investments involved have a long-term impact and are not reversible after resources have been committed to them. The following are some types of projects a company may undertake:

1. Equipment replacement expenditures (due to wear and tear, damage, obsolescence, refurbishment, and so forth)
2. Expenditures relating to new product development (for example, research and development, test marketing, and promotions)
3. Expenditures regarding expansion of existing markets, such as building new restaurant or hotel units, expanding existing physical facilities, marketing expenses to attract new customers, merger/ acquisition.
4. Mandatory investments such as projects required by federal or

municipal governments (for example, handicap access, smoking versus nonsmoking facilities, hotel sprinklers)

The decision process focuses on accepting or rejecting a proposed investment project based on some decision rules commonly used. These decision rules or investment evaluation techniques indicate how attractive a project is. If these techniques are used properly the ultimate decisions made will be consistent with the goal of maximizing the owners' wealth. The most common capital budgeting techniques used are the payback, net present value, internal rate of return, and the profitability index.

The payback technique determines how long a project will take to return the original investment. Most companies establish an internal standard payback period against which all other projects are evaluated. The decision rule is, if a project's payback is less than the company's payback period then accept the project, otherwise reject. This means a project that is able to recoup all of the investment that went into it in a relatively short time makes the investment capital available for other investment projects, thereby increasing the potential profitability of the company.

The net present value technique refines one of the deficiencies of the payback technique. Its underlying concept is that time has value so, if a project is expected to generate some cash flows, in the future those cash flows must be valued in today's terms in order to determine if the cash benefits from the project exceed the costs. This technique compares the present value of future cash flows from a project, discounted at an appropriate discount rate, to the cost of the investment. The decision rule here is, if the difference between the sum of the discounted cash flows and the cost of the investment (that is, the net present value) is greater than zero then the project is acceptable, otherwise it is unacceptable.

The internal rate of return is similar in concept to the net present value. It is the discount rate that equates the present value of all future cash flows to the cost of the project. Or, it is that interest rate that, used to discount the future cash flows, will make the net present value of the project equal to zero. The decision rule here is, if the internal rate of return is greater than the company's cost of capital then the project is acceptable, otherwise it should be rejected. Intuitively, a project that returns more to the company than the cost of the capital used to fund it will add more to the owners' wealth.

The profitability index is defined as the sum of the present value of future cash flows divided by the initial investment. This technique seeks to determine how much cash (in discounted terms) is attainable from a project per dollar's worth of investment. Projects must yield a profitability index greater than one to be acceptable, that is, they must yield more than a dollar in return for each dollar invested in the project.

These are the commonly used principles that guide the selection of investment projects in companies, and they are supported by the goal of maximizing the wealth of the company's owners. If unlimited funds are available then all projects that meet the decision rules can be undertaken. However, where there is a budget constraint then projects are chosen based on which offer the most additional wealth.

Current Asset Management   Current assets refer to those assets on the balance sheet that are used within a year or less. These are cash, accounts receivables, marketable securities, and inventory. In financial management, the more common terminology for these assets collectively is *working capital*. This term originated with the old yankee peddler who would load up his wagon with goods and go off to peddle. The goods represented what he sold or "turned over" to make a profit. Similarly in a company, these assets are traded daily to generate profits for the company.

Working capital policy focuses on a company's decisions regarding the target amounts of each current asset that must be held and specifically how these assets will be financed. The management of working capital is concerned with the administration of current assets and current liabilities within the framework of the company's stated goals. Current liabilities (short-term loans, trade credit, accruals) are included here because they are the sources used to finance current assets. The financial manager's objective is to ensure that these sources of financing are available to the company at the least possible cost and that the company can repay the obligations on time.

Cash management is one of the activities that must be accomplished in working capital management. John Maynard Keynes, the British economist, provided three motives why companies hold cash. The transactional motive refers to the company's need to hold cash to meet daily recurrent expenses such as setting up a petty cash fund, providing a change fund, and meeting current payroll. Also a company may experience unexpected large cash outlays or unanticipated delays in payments periodically and for these uncertainties cash must be set aside. This describes the precautionary motive. Finally, the speculative motive describes the company's need to carry cash to enable it to take advantage of bargain purchases that may arise from time to time.

The financial manager's goal is to maintain enough cash at all times to pay the company's bills when they are due, thereby minimizing the risk of insolvency. Yet, the manager must be careful not to have too much idle cash because the cost to the company will be the missed opportunity to invest such idle cash to generate some income for the company. This apparent conflict in objectives is referred to as the risk/return tradeoff, that is, holding large amounts of cash minimizes the company's risk of insolvency, yet it robs the firm of potential profits.

Marketable securities management is another activity under working capital management. These securities are financial instruments held by the company as current assets and they can be easily converted into cash when needed. They serve as a substitute for cash and also serve as temporary investment tools. Examples of marketable securities are U.S. Treasury bills, certificates of deposit (CDs), mutual funds, commercial paper, banker's acceptances, and federal agency securities. Each of these instruments have important characteristics that must be considered in order to assemble a proper mix of securities for the company.

United States Treasury bills (T-bills) are the most popular and best known of the marketable securities. These bills are issued by the Treasury Department and are backed by the full faith and credit of the government. Thus they are considered to be risk-free investments. They can be purchased only from the government (or through an authorized bank). T-bills are bought at a discount and when they mature the principal plus all the compounded interest is paid in a lump sum. If one needs to sell them before maturity then they are returned to the government (perhaps through the bank) in exchange for the principal and all accrued interest. They are sold in denominations of $10,000 and multiples of $5,000 thereafter.

For companies who have idle cash for temporary investment and cannot afford the relatively high denominations of T-bills, an alternative investment tool is a CD. This represents a specified amount of money placed in a bank that will receive a stated amount of interest after a specified time. If CDs are sold before maturity, usually a penalty is paid for early withdrawal. The denominations are as small as $1,000, therefore they are affordable to most companies, especially smaller ones.

Mutual funds also provide shares at smaller denominations such as $500. They are investment companies that pool funds from shareholders and invest them in diversified securities portfolios with a specified objective. These funds provide professional management and are always ready to sell new shares and redeem outstanding shares on a continuing basis. There are several types of mutual funds including growth funds, income funds, global funds, junk bond funds, municipal bond funds, money market funds, and many more.

The common feature of all marketable securities is their ability to be converted into cash when needed (liquidity), although some securities are more liquid than others. Indeed, one can invest in a mutual fund for a day or in a CD for thirty days depending on the flexibility desired, and in all cases some income will be earned. The objective of the financial manager is to select the proper mix of securities to generate maximum income while also considering the company's need for flexibility.

Another activity that comes under working capital management is inventory management. This refers to the control of assets being used in the production of goods and services for sale in the normal course of a company's business. Since absolute knowledge is unavailable about demand patterns, inventory must be held in order to meet demand whenever it occurs. Having proper inventory levels helps ensure better customer service, maintain uninterrupted flow of production and services, and reduces costs. The objective of the financial manager in inventory management is to maintain adequate levels of inventory to avoid delays in production and customer service delivery, while taking care not to have too much money tied up in inventory. Here again there is the risk/return tradeoff that arises because carrying large levels of inventory will prevent the possibility of being stocked out; yet carrying inventory results in storage and handling costs as well as the lost opportunity of temporarily investing the money tied up in inventory.

There are several other activities within financial management that are specialized topics such as, merger and acquisitions, divestitures, pension plan management, international finance, and financial analysis and planning. Generally, all the activities of financial management can be conceived as contributing to the performance of the two main responsibilities of a financial manager; raising funds and allocating funds.

Summary

The role of financial management has evolved from focusing on raising funds to include the efficient allocation of funds for maximizing shareholder wealth. Several sources of obtaining debt and equity funds abound, and the financial manager must carefully balance the risks and returns of each. Funds are allocated between current and capital assets using specific techniques that ensure the maximization of shareholder wealth.

References

Geller, Neal A., Charles Ilvento, and Raymond Schmidgall. 1990. The hotel controller revisited. *Cornell Quarterly*, (Nov.):1–7.

Kwansa, F., and H. G. Parsa. 1990. Business failure analysis: An events approach. *Hospitality Education and Research Journal*. 14(2):23–34.

3

Operations Budgeting

Raymond S. Schmidgall

An annual ritual virtually every business completes is preparing its annual operations budget. Only the smallest businesses avoid preparing a formal budget but even their owners/managers no doubt think through what they anticipate their sales and expenses to be for the coming year.

Budgets are simply written plans of business activity reduced to dollars (or some other monetary unit) for a period of time. For the operations budget the focus is sales and expenses, for the cash budget the focus is cash receipts and cash disbursements. Operations and cash budgets are prepared for periods as short as one month or less and as long as five years. All budgets, whether they are operations or cash, must be reduced to numbers so the plan can be easily communicated and more easily understood.

This article on budgeting focuses on the operations budget including benefits from preparing it, the budget process, the need for budget revisions, budgetary control, and budgeting by multiunit enterprises. For comparison purposes several types of budgets are first described.

Types of Budgets

An operations budget reflects forecasted revenues and expected expenses for the hospitality business for a period of time. When a hospitality executive announces the enterprise "exceeded the budget," almost always it is the operations budget that the executive is referencing. Most hospitality firms have set profits for the year as a prime and often the most important objective. The targeted profit is reflected in the operations budget; thus, this is the reason so much attention is focused on the operations budget.

The life blood of any business is cash. When a hospitality firm is out of cash it will very soon be out of business unless cash is quickly found. To monitor its cash flows, operators use cash budgets. The cash budget simply reflects expected cash receipts and cash disbursements for a period of time. Sources of cash, shown in the cash budget, include, but are not limited to, cash sales, collection of accounts receivable, interest received, dividends received, proceeds from sale of capital stock, proceeds from loans from financial institutions, and proceeds from bond sales. All sources of cash should be shown on the cash budget. Uses of cash, reflected on the cash budget, include all disbursements, such as payments for labor, payments for the purchase of food, beverages, utilities, and many other goods and services used by the hospitality enterprise. Uses also include disbursements for interest, dividends, and the repayment of borrowed funds. The cash budget often differs considerably from the operations budget in the area of disbursements as the cash budget reflects the outgo of cash while the operations budget shows the incurrence of expense. The cash disbursement related to the expense may have occurred years before, as in the case of depreciation expense, or the cash disbursement may occur after the expense is recorded, such as for utilities expense.

Still another type of budget is the capital budget. This budget's focus is on the acquisition of property and equipment. The capital budget includes the list of property and equipment to be obtained over the next several years.

The process of capital budgeting includes the evaluation of whether these items should be acquired. Various techniques for evaluating the feasibility of a capital item include payback, net present value, and internal rate of return (IRR). In summary, these techniques compare future cash flows from the investment to the cost of the investment. Schmidgall and Damitio (1990) found the IRR technique is currently used more often than any other approach by the lodging segment of the hospitality industry.

The operations, cash, and capital budgets are interrelated in several ways. One way includes the acquisition of property and equipment (capital budget), which requires financing, that is, cash must be used to finance the acquisitions. The sources of the cash and disbursements of cash for capital acquisitions are reflected in the cash budget. The acquisitions, when used in the ordinary conduct of the business, generate sales and incur expenses that must be included on the operations budget. Further, the capital acquisition is generally depreciated and the depreciation expense is also included as part of the operations budget.

Benefits of Budgeting for Operations

Budgeting is a time-consuming, tedious process during which many members of an enterprise's management team expend much energy. However, the benefits of budgeting generally exceed these costs. The major benefits of an operations budget are as follows:

- The budget provides a clearly understood plan for management to follow. It includes targeted prices to be charged, labor rates and expected hours, amounts to be spent on marketing and so on. The plan can be easily followed by managers, even those who join the hospitality enterprise in the middle of the year, when it is reduced to writing and clearly communicated.
- The budget process requires that managers be involved with its preparation in order to consider alternative courses of action. They must answer a multitude of questions, such as What prices should be charged? What services should be provided? What level of quality of these services should be provided? When the operations budget is adopted, management has decided on what it believes is the best of the many alternative plans.
- Budgeting requires management to examine just what measures are required to generate the desired results—most often a net profit. Certainly managers are dealing with the unknown since the budget

pertains to the future; however, they are faced with keeping projected expenses lower than forecasted sales.

- Budgeting provides a standard of comparison, that is, the budget is the basis for comparing the actual results of the accounting period. Any major differences should be carefully analyzed to determine the cause and appropriate action taken to correct the problem.
- Budgting allows management to look forward and prepare for the future. For example, if new equipment is required for a new menu item, then the equipment should be obtained in plenty of time to have it functioning properly when needed.
- When participative budgeting is used, that is, when those managers who are to be held responsible are involved in the budget process, then these managers feel they have ownership of their budgets and as a result they will be more motivated to expend energy to achieve their plans. Budgeted numbers forced on managers quite often results in managers blaming the budget preparers for poor budgeting rather than accepting responsibility.
- Finally, the budget process provides a channel of communication whereby the firm's objectives in numbers are communicated to all management levels. Further, as time passes the actual results are compared to the budget, both of which are furnished periodically to managers who are responsible for the actual results.

The Budget Preparation Process

The budget preparation process consists of five major steps:

1. Establishing financial objectives
2. Forecasting revenues
3. Estimating expenses
4. Determining forecasted net income
5. Reviewing and approving the budget

Establishing Financial Objectives

The board of directors of the hospitality organization must start the entire budget process by first establishing the enterprise's financial objectives. A major financial objective for many businesses is long-term profit maximization. The emphasis is on long-term as a firm may and generally should be willing to sacrifice short-term profitability in order to maximize long-term profits. Generally, a new hotel does not achieve profits until its second or third year of operations. A short-sighted firm may decide not to open a new hotel as short-term overall profits would be reduced, all other factors being equal.

In the mid-1980s, the major goal of Domino's Pizza, the current pizza delivery leader, was growth in units through the 1980s. Thus, for Domino's, short-term profits were sacrificed and even ignored in favor of expected long-term profits.

Other objectives set by hospitality enterprises have been (1) to provide high quality service, (2) to be the leading firm in its segment of the hospitality industry, (3) to be the fastest growing firm, and (4) to be recognized as having the best reputation.

The establishment of the objectives for the next budget year is essential and to be most effective they must be clearly communicated to all managers involved in the budget preparation process. For the majority of major hospitality enterprises this means the objectives must be communicated from the top levels in the organization down to the lowest managerial levels in the individual operating units.

Forecasting Revenues

In order for managers of profit centers, such as rooms and food and beverage departments of lodging operations, to be able to forecast revenues they must be provided information regarding the economic environment, detailed historical financial results of their departments, and in some cases, booked future reservations.

Information concerning the economic environment includes, but is certainly not limited to, the following:

- Economic trends of the country and region the establishment serves, for example, recession or growth
- Expected inflation for the budget year including an estimate of the operation's ability to increase its prices to cover inflation
- Expected changes in costs of specific purchases, including the expected changes in labor and related costs
- Changes in competitive conditions—new competition as well as changes in current competing operations
- Travel trends of all segments served

For lodging establishments using reservation systems, booked reservations for the upcoming budget year are most useful for forecasting room sales. For major convention hotels, many conventions are booked years in advance. Therefore, the booked reservations adjusted for expected changes by each group provides extremely reliable forecasts of room sales for this segment of the rooms revenue.

Many smaller hotels and operations in most other segments of the hospitality industry do not use reservation systems that provide reliable unit sales forecasts for several months in the future. Therefore, these operations resort to historical financial information. Even convention hotels use historical information to support their reservation information and to use as a basis to forecast revenues for the segments not adequately covered by the reservation system. For example, for some hotels, "business" reservations are made less than a week in advance of the guest's stay. Therefore, reservations information would yield little useful information for budgeting purposes for this segment for the upcoming budget year.

Historical financial information often serves as the base from which managers forecast future revenues. By examining the past, managers are able to project into the future. For example, if sales have increased at an annual rate of 10 percent for the past three years, then the manager may start by forecasting a 10 percent increase for the next year.

Figure 1 is an elementary illustration of using historical rooms information to forecast rooms revenue for the budget year. Historical information is from

Fig. 1. Forecast of rooms revenue.

Year	Rooms Sold	Average Room Rates	Room Revenues
19x1	25,000	$50	$1,250,000
19x2	27,500	51	1,402,500
19x3	30,250	52	1,573,000
19x4 (Budget Year)	33,275	53	1,763,575

the years of 19x1–19x3. The average rate has increased by $1 each year from 19x1–19x3, and analysis reveals rooms sold have increased by 10 percent each year. During 19x2 2,500 more rooms were sold than in 19x1 when 25,000 rooms were sold. The difference of 2,500 divided by the 25,000 rooms sold for 19x1 reveals a 10 percent increase in 19x2. Similar results occur in 19x3 compared to 19x2. Therefore, the initial forecast of rooms revenue for 19x4 of $1,763,575 is based on a 10 percent increase in rooms sold and a $1 increase in average room rate. The rooms manager should challenge this forecast based on the details of average room rate and rooms sales forecast in light of economic factors! If after this challenge, the initial forecast seems reasonable, then it will be used as the budgeted room revenue for 19x4.

This simplistic approach is only meant to illustrate a revenue-forecasting process. A more detailed and more meaningful approach would consider different types of rooms, rates by type of room for different guest classes, and seasonality including day of week and season of the year. Needless to say, the process in the real world is very complex and no mention has been made of other profit centers such as food and beverage, catering, telephone, and so on.

Estimating Expenses

The third step in the budgeting process is estimating expenses. Expenses are detailed by department by both profit centers and service centers (such as, marketing and maintenance). Expenses that change in relation to sales are variable while expenses that are constant regardless of the level of sales are fixed. Unfortunately, some expenses (mixed expenses) such as telephone expense have both variable and fixed components. Managers must be able to separate mixed expenses into their separate components for analytical purposes in order to properly forecast their expenses.

Before managers are able to forecast their variable expenses, they must obtain information regarding (1) expected cost increases for supplies, food, and other nonlabor expenses and (2) expected labor cost increases including wage rates and the cost of fringe benefits and payroll taxes.

Variable expenses are generally estimated in relation to sales. For example, if the cost of linen used in the rooms department operation was $.50 per room sales in the current year and is expected to increase by 5 percent, then $.525 would be multiplied by the forecasted number of rooms to be sold during the budget year to determine the budget year costs. Alternatively, cost of food sales may be budgeted at 30 percent of food sales for the year. For this expense then the forecast is simply to multiply the desired cost percentage by forecasted food sales.

Fixed expenses are projected on the basis of past experience and expected changes in the cost. These expenses are not a function of sales as variable expenses are as shown above. Assume the general manager's (GM) salary of a hypothetical hotel was $60,000 in 19x1 regardless of the amount of sales—this is clearly a fixed cost. Perhaps, the board has decided to increase his/her salary by $5,000 for the year; thus, the forecasted GM's salary for the budget year would be $65,000.

Fixed expenses for a lodging operation are part of the expenses of both profit centers and service centers. In addition, fixed charges of a hotel including depreciation, insurance on the building, interest expense, and rent expense are all generally considered to be fixed expenses. All of these expenses are forecasted on the basis of historical costs and any expected changes for the budget year. Let us consider budgeting interest expense. Figure 2 contains a schedule of our expected debt and the applicable interest rates during 19x2 the assumed budget year. A brief explanation of Figure 2 is as follows:

Fig. 2. Budget for interest expense for 19x2.

Debt		Principal	Annual Interest Rate	Period of Indebtedness	Estimated Interest Expense
Mortgage on hotel	1.	$5,000,000	10%	Jan. 1–June 30	$250,000
	2.	4,800,000	10%	July 1–Dec. 31	240,000
Notes payable		600,000	12%	Jan. 1– Dec. 31	72,000
Working capital loan		250,000	12.5%	May 1–August 31	10,531
				Total 13	$572,531

1. The mortgage note on the hotel requires semiannual payments including a reduction of principal of $200,000 on June 30. Therefore, two interest calculations are made. First, $250,000 of interest is calculated for the first six months and $240,000 of interest is calculated for the last six months.
2. The notes payable for $600,000 is outstanding for the entire year and the interest thereon is $72,000.
3. A working capital loan will be required to carry the business through the slow season. Therefore, the interest is calculated for the projected term of the debt, in this case 123 days, as follows:

interest expense = 250,000 × .125 × 123/365
interest expense = $10,531

The source of information and estimation of other fixed expenses is dependent on the expense. For example, the controller's office should be able to estimate the depreciation expense and a call to the firm's insurance agent should result in a reasonable estimate of the expected cost of insurance on the building for the budget year.

Determining Net Income

The next step is simply the determination of net income for the year. Simply put, revenues minus expenses equals net income. Of course, in a lodging enterprise, the operations budget should follow the format of the income statement so the basic format will be as follows:

Income from profit centers	+ $XXXX
Expenses from service centers	– XXX
Fixed charges	– XXX
Income taxes	– XXX
Net income	$ XX

Generally, the controller or personnel assigned by the controller coordinate this entire process. Still a final review must take place.

Reviewing and Approving the Budget

For the individual operation, the applicable committee, which is often the executive committee, reviews the entire budget to determine if the predetermined financial goals have been met. If the predetermined goals are met, then the budget can be forwarded with the appropriate comments to the board of directors for their approval. However, if the projected financial results fall short of the target, the budget will be reworked until a satisfactory bottom line has been budgeted. These changes may include price changes, promotion changes, and cost reductions, just to mention a few.

Flexible Budgets

The above discussion centers on having a budget targeted at one level of activity. However, no matter how sophisticated the budget process, it is unlikely the level of activity budgeted will be achieved. Therefore, differences will result simply because of a different volume of activity than anticipated. This potential problem can be resolved by using flexible budgets. Flexible budgeting includes a budget for each of several different levels of plan activities. For example, a hotel may produce a budget based on an average daily room occupancy of 75 percent, which may be the best estimate of the level of activity for the budget year. However, using flexible budgeting there would also be budgets for other occupancy levels such as ±1 and ±2 occupancy points. Thus, this hotel would have five budgets, one each for average daily room occupancy of 73, 74, 75, 76, and 77 percent. Then if the average daily occupancy for an accounting period is 74 percent figures in that budget would be compared. In a flexible budget, fixed expenses by definition remain constant across the various activity levels whereas variable expenses change directly with revenues; however, the variable expense percentages generally would remain constant.

Figure 3 contains flexible budgets for the hypothetical Example Restaurant at three revenue levels of $700,000, $1,000,000 and $1,300,000. The bottom line results are dramatic as this firm's budgets reflect losses of $12,000 when sales are $700,000; it makes $42,000 when sales are $1,000,000; and it makes $92,400 when sales are $1,300,000.

Elementary analysis of these flexible budgets reveals the following:

Labor costs (fixed)	$80,000
Cost of food sold (variable)	45% of revenue
Other operating expenses (variable)	8% of revenue
Fixed charges (fixed)	$100,000
Income taxes	30% of pretax income

Revising the Budget

Regardless of the sophistication in preparing budgets, many hospitality firms find they need to revise their operating budgets throughout the budget year. Budgets that are updated based on actual operating information for the prior

Fig. 3. Example Restaurant flexible operations budget for the year ended December 31, 19x3.

	$700,000	$1,000,000	$1,300,000
Revenue	$700,000	$1,000,000	$1,300,000
Cost of food sold	315,000	450,000	585,000
Labor:			
Variable	161,000	230,000	299,000
Fixed	80,000	80,000	80,000
Other operating expenses	56,000	80,000	104,000
Income before fixed charges	88,000	160,000	232,000
Fixed charges	100,000	100,000	100,000
Income before income taxes	(12,000)	60,000	132,000
Income taxes	–0–	18,000	39,600
Net income (loss)	$(12,000)	$ 42,000	$ 92,400

months of the budget year and revised expectations for future months allow subsequent comparisons of actual and revised budgets to be more meaningful. Schmidgall and Ninemeier (1987) found that 70 percent of the major lodging firms revise their budgets during the year. Several of these firms started budget revisions less than three months into the budget year. Generally, the budgets are revised on a monthly basis for the remainder of the year. Lodging firms revise their operations budgets to project year-end numbers, to measure performance, and to review pricing plans.

Budgetary Control

A major purpose for budgeting is that the budgets serve as a standard of comparison, that is, they provide a basis against which to compare at the end of each accounting period.

Budgetary control involves a five-step process:

1. Determine variances
2. Identify which variances are significant
3. Analyze significant variances
4. Determine problems
5. Take action to correct the problems

Variances are simply the difference between the budget and the actual results. Variances are significant when they are sufficiently large and require management's attention to investigate the cause of the variance. Criteria to determine if variances are significant generally are dollar differences and percentage differences. For example, assume a business budgeted $100,000 of sales for the month and had sales totaling $105,000. The dollar difference is $5,000 and the percentage difference of 5 percent is determined by dividing the dollar difference by the budgeted figure. There are no rules of thumb for dollar differences and percentage differences to determine when variances are significant, but each firm must consider the size of its revenues and expenses and the degree of control it has over each in establishing the significance criteria. Generally, the smaller the budgeted revenue or expense *and* the greater the control over the item, the smaller the significance criteria.

The analysis of variances involves determining how much of the variance relates to general causes. Determination of specific causes is step four of the control process. For revenues general causes include volume and price differences. Volume differences relate to more or fewer rooms being sold by a hotel than budgeted, or more or fewer meals being sold than budgeted by a foodservice operation. General causes differ by type of expense; however, several examples include

Expense	*General Causes*
Variable labor expense	Volume—difference in amount of work to be performed
	Rate—difference in pay rates
	Efficiency—difference in work performed per hour
Cost of food sold	Cost—difference in cost
	Usage—difference in amounts used

Next, specific causes are determined by investigating the reasons for the general cause. For example, assume a hotel paid its room attendants more than planned for a month. Further, assume that the general cause was wage rates, that is, the average rate paid per hour exceeded the budgeted average rate per hour. The subsequent investigation might reveal that several room attendants worked overtime, thus they were paid 150 percent of their regular wage for their overtime hours causing the variance.

Finally, management must take action to correct the problem. In the above example, it may require any overtime be approved six hours in advance. This rule requires managers to carefully consider alternatives and most likely will discourage supervisors having employees work overtime. In order for the control process to be successful, management must act. Steps 1–4 of the control process as described above can be used but if managers fail to act (Step 5) then the entire process is rendered somewhat useless.

Budgeting at Multiunit Hospitality Firms

Most of the literature regarding budgeting by businesses focuses on the single unit operation; however, both lodging and foodservice segments of the hospitality industry are dominated by major chains, many having over 1,000 properties.

Schmidgall and Ninemeier (1989) in their studies of the major lodging and foodservice chains found that 56 percent of these chains use a bottom-up approach, that is, budgets are developed at the unit level, and then they are "rolled up" through successively higher organizational layers to create the corporate budget. The primary reason a majority of these chains use this approach is the need for unit level managers to have the "feeling of ownership" in the budget. Increasing unit managers' involvement in the budget development process allows them to participate which, in turn, is believed to provide a motivating factor for budget attainment.

Alternative approaches to budgeting at chains is a top-down approach and an in-between approach where the budget is developed at a level between unit and corporate levels. The major reason top-down approaches are used is the belief that a bottom-up approach will not generate the firm's total profit requirement.

Finally, Schmidgall and Ninemeier (1989) found that executives from lodging and foodservice chains agreed on the major differences between budgeting practices of chains and single-unit firms. The major factors mentioned were

> More sophisticated procedures are used.
> Amount of information processed is greater.
> There is increased need for coordination.
> Greater amount of management attention is required.
> Amount of level time is greater.
> The process of cost allocation between unit and other organizational levels is unique.
> The budget process is governed by policies external to the unit.

Summary

The operations budget focuses on revenues and expenses; however it is interrelated to the cash budget and the capital budget. Major benefits of preparing an operations budget include managers having to plan and then having a standard of comparison they can use throughout the budget year. The budget preparation process includes (1) setting objectives, (2) forecasting revenues, (3) estimating expenses, (4) estimating net income, and (5) reviewing and approving the budget. Budgetary control includes a five-step process of (1) identifying variances, (2) determining significant variances, (3) analyzing the significant variances, (4) determining specific causes of variances and (5) acting to correct problems. Finally, budgeting at chains was discussed. The majority of lodging and foodservice chains use a bottom-up approach in order to give their unit managers the feeling of ownership in the numbers.

References

Schmidgall, Raymond S., and James Damitio. 1990. Current capital budgeting practices of major lodging chains. *The Real Estate Review* 29(3):40–45.

Schmidgall, Raymond S., and Jack Ninemeier. 1987. Budgeting in hotel chains: Coordination and control. *Cornell Hotel & Restaurant Administration Quarterly* 28(1):79–84.

Schmidgall, Raymond S., and Jack Ninemeier. 1989. Budgeting practices in lodging and food service chains: An analysis and comparison. *The International Journal of Hospitality Management* 8(1):35–41.

4

Organizational Management

Craig C. Lundberg

Imagine some task or activity that requires more than one pair of hands or more than one mind. The accomplishment of such a task requires that the two or more people involved act in some coordinated fashion. This situation requires organization and management. Organization is the term we use to mean that a group of people have come together under an identifiable label ("Westin Hotels and Resorts," "Hal's Delicatessen") to produce some service or product. For better or worse, we live in a society of organizations (Presthus 1962; Mintzberg 1989). We are born in, educated by, and work in organizations. Organizations supply us, govern us, protect us, bury us, and importantly, provide us with lodging, food, movement, and entertainment. All organizations, no matter how large or small, how simple or complicated, require management. Management is the process by which the people who are formally in charge of organizations or part of them, try to guide what members do and do not do. Organization management is important because there are so many organizations, because many organizations are getting larger and more complex, and because organizations touch nearly every aspect of our lives. Unless organizations are managed well, we all will suffer more or less.

Organizations of course have been around since before recorded history. History is full of examples of organizational accomplishments. Consider the great pyramids of Egypt, the Crusades, the settling of North America, the Panama Canal, automobile mass production, the discovery of medical cures, the European Common Market, and on and on. These major organizational products are paralleled by untold lesser ones. And always there have been organizations or parts of organizations to feed and sleep people. History also records famous managers, from Moses to Churchill, from Henry Ford to Martin Luther King, Jr., from Columbus to Lincoln, from Genghis Khan to Ray Kroc (McDonalds). But there have been millions of other managers who do not appear in history books or make headlines. The quality of management determines the success of organizations, and since organizations permeate our lives, managers therefore shape the quality of both our work and nonwork lives.

It is common to think that your organization or industry is somehow unique (for example, hospitality organizations are somehow different from manufacturing, educational, religious, military, agricultural, or social organizations), but all organizations resemble one another greatly. As Caplow (1983:4–5) reminds us,

> Every organization has a collective identity; a roster of members, friends, and antagonists; a program of activity and a time schedule to go with it; a table of organization; a set of formal rules partly contradicted by informal rules; procedures for adding and removing members; utilitarian objects used for organizational tasks; symbolic objects used in organizational rituals; a history; a special vocabulary; some elements of folklore; a territory; and a method of placing members within that territory according to their relative importance. Every organization has a division of labor that allocates specialized tasks to its members and a status order that awards them unequal shares of authority, honor, and influence.

Every organization, except the very smallest, is a cluster of suborganizations of varying sizes (which are organizations in their own right possessing all of the features noted above). It is important to remember that the goals of suborganizations are seldom completely compatible with the goals of the parent organization. Surprising to some people is that the issues of managing a small organization or suborganization are similar to those of managing a large organization.

All organizations have three general and fundamental tasks to accomplish if they are to prosper and survive (Lundberg 1989). First, they must continually make internal adjustments so things run smoothly: Part of a manager's job is to see that actual performance contributes to meeting goals. Second, all organizations must maintain their alignments to those parts of the environment that they are dependent upon: Part of the manager's job is to monitor markets and suppliers and regulators and then adapt the organization to them. The third fundamental task all organizations have is to anticipate the future: Part of the manager's job, therefore, is to try to understand what the organization will be faced with and to prepare the organization for those probable circumstances. Long ago, when the world had fewer and smaller changes, and organizations were mostly small and simple, management could concentrate on the first task. With stable organizational circumstances, managers could also rely on common sense and experience-based rules of thumb. Scholars of management even codified a number of universal principles or prescriptions and everyone believed that there was one best way to manage regardless of the type of organization or industry. As the world grew ever more changeful, managers and scholars alike found that universal principles and common sense just did not provide the guidance needed, especially as organizations themselves grew in size and complexity. While every organization had to exhibit the basic management functions (to succeed, an organization had to plan, to organize, to direct and coordinate, and to control operations), it became more and more necessary to carefully learn what the particular situation was both inside and outside a specific organization and then to define appropriate goals and design the structure and rules that would enable the accomplishment of those goals. The theory of organizations and their management shifted from a "one best way" in general to a situational one best way at a point in time, that is, a set of patterned practices that were contingent on the specifics of a particular situation and circumstances.

The environment of organizations runs from simple and stable at the one extreme, to complex and turbulent at the other extreme. Organizations with the former environment tend to be designed mechanistically, that is with carefully specified, routinized jobs, a lot of rules, a few clear goals, a well-defined hierarchy of authority levels, with decisions made at the top. Each part of the organization is much like the others. Managers in mechanistic organizations tend to emphasize efficiency of operations, and to keep things running smoothly through a combination of communication and control devices, for example, reports, quotas, budgets, and incentive systems. Since most problems are familiar ones, decision making is frequently programmed. Organizations in complex and changeable environments also reflect those environments internally. Here organizations are likely to be designed organically. Jobs are enlarged and more self-managed. There are fewer rules and there are multiple linkages between relatively dissimilar units. Information flows in every direction. Most decisions tend to be made by those directly involved. There are relatively few levels in the hierarchy and expertise is as important as positional authority. Teams are common. Managers in organic organizations have to be more innovative, more interpersonally skilled, and more flexible. Planning and organizing are less episodic and managers put more time into monitoring the environment, developing their subordinates, and linking their units to others. We should point out that the subunits of larger organizations will exhibit different degrees of mechanicalness or organicness—the more a subunit is involved with the environment, the more organic it is likely to be.

Many myths exist about managers. It is not uncommon to hear that an effective manager, like a good conductor, carefully orchestrates everything in advance, then sits back to enjoy the fruits of his or her efforts, responding occasionally to an unforeseen exception. This myth is paralleled by others such as, effective managers put a lot of time into reflective thinking and systematic planning; effective managers need aggregated information best supplied by a formal information system; management is quickly becoming a science. Studies about what effective managers actually do, however, contrast sharply with these myths (Mintzberg 1973; Kotter 1982). Managers actually work at an unrelenting pace, switching their attention swiftly from one thing to another, constantly interrupted, relying on and preferring first-hand verbal interactions about current matters over reports, yet performing a number of regular duties including rituals and ceremonies. How they do these things is mostly in their heads, not in scientific formulas or programs. Managers' jobs are enormously complicated and challenging; science has just started to scratch the surface of managerial work (Vaill 1989).

All managers must have three kinds of skills (Katz 1974): (1) technical skills—skills about the nitty-gritty of whatever the business or subunit does; (2) human skills—those skills involved in developing and maintaining relationships with and among people; and (3) conceptual skills—those useful for thinking about how things go together now and in the future. Each manager requires all three skills, but his or her position in the organization requires a different skill mix. Top management's responsibilities for overall direction of the organization, that is, strategic planning, objective setting, and policy formulation, mean they need a great deal of conceptual skill, somewhat less human skill, and little technical skill. First line supervisors, focused on getting the work out, need just the opposite skill mix from top management, that is, a great deal of technical skill, some human skill, and not very much conceptual skill. Middle managers, charged with seeing that those supervisors' units below them are in line with the overall thrust of the organization as given by top management, need a great deal of interpersonal skill and somewhat less of both conceptual and technical skill. These skill mixes are illustrated in Figure 1.

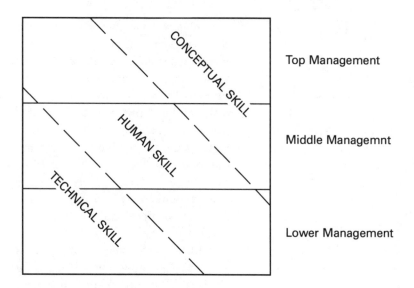

Fig. 1. The mix of management skills.

CONCEPTUAL SKILL

HUMAN SKILL

TECHNICAL SKILL

Top Management

Middle Managemnt

Lower Management

Recall that managers were defined as the persons in charge of an organization or one of its subunits. All are vested with formal authority from which comes status and which leads to various interpersonal relations, which in turn provide access to information upon which decisions and actions are based. Mixes of managerial skills vary not only by level in the hierarchy but also by their functional responsibility, that is, marketing, purchasing, food and beverage, engineering, and the like. Managers use these skills to perform those patterned sets of behavior we call roles (Mintzberg 1973). There are decisional roles such as resource allocator (deciding who will get what), negotiator (deciding formal and informal contracts and exchanges), disturbance handler (deciding how to handle conflicts and crises), and entrepreneur (deciding what new projects and ideas should be initiated). There are informational roles of monitor (soliciting all kinds of hard and soft data as well as receiving unsolicited information), disseminator (sharing information with associates) and spokesperson (sending information to people outside their units). There are interpersonal roles of being a figurehead (performing the ceremonies that are important to the smooth functioning of the organization), leader (influencing his or her subordinates to do the right things at the right times), and liaison (cultivating and using contacts with others outside his or her own chain of command). Having a managerial position and performing managerial roles not only requires a mix of skills but implies that the manager's relationships to others as individuals and to groups of others are critical (Bradford and Cohen 1988). It is in these relationships that information is acquired and shared, ideas created and clarified, and influence asserted. Managers are well advised therefore to periodically consider the number, scope, and quality of their relationships as well as invest in improving them on a continuous basis. While constrained by such things as authority, status, and self-interest, relationships ultimately reflect the exchanges between the people—the operative questions are what does the other want from the relationship that I am willing and able to provide, and what do I want that the other will or can provide? Careful observation and empathy are basic abilities as is some knowledge of interpersonal and small group dynamics.

Much of a manager's behavior is impacted by his or her basic assumptions about people and organizations (McGregor 1960). These assumptions (beliefs, attitudes, values) guide what managers see and hear and the meanings they give to what they perceive. Crucial sets of assumptions relate to the three fundamental tasks of organizations. One set is about managing internal affairs, especially the relationship between management and workers. Such assumptions are very often self-fulfilling. Managers, for example, might assume that workers only work for money, or to fulfill their social needs, or to feel useful and productive. Each of these assumptions would lead a manager to behave quite differently, for example, from highly directive to highly participative. A second set of assumptions has to do with how the organization relates to its environment. Managerial assumptions about what satisfies customers can range widely, for example, from cost to quality to timeliness—with consequent emphasis on the nature of the product or service offered. Assumptions here also determine an organization's stance to competitors, suppliers, and regulators. The third important set of assumptions always has to do with change—whether it is necessary or not, how easy it is, how best to accomplish it, how much effort is put into anticipating environmental changes. Managers' assumptions are also important to identify for other reasons. How does one manager's assumptions fit in with his or her associates? When they do, an organization's managers are likely to not only get along pretty well, to act in consort, but also to create a clear identity for their organization.

Managing, laid bare, boils down to having some intentions, using these intentions to pay attention to reality, comparing intentions to reality, and modifying either reality or intentions—on both a grand scale and a small scale—over and over as shown in Figure 2. Characterized thus, managing in essence appears simple indeed. It becomes more complex when we ask such questions as: Intentions about what? Attention to what? How do we compare? What should be modified, how much, and when?

There is an almost infinite number of things that a manager can attend to, that is, continuously acquire an understanding of. However, six general categories are worthy of every manager's ongoing attention. There are two that act as constraints on management's intentions and actions: (1) the *external context* the organization finds itself in, and (2) several major *internal circumstances* that also constrain managerial action. Then (3) there is the organization's leadership, *management* itself. Management's intentions are composed of three sets of things, (4) *organizational factors, people factors,* and the *processes and systems* that integrate them. In addition there are the consequences of intentions as (5) *emergent social/cultural factors* and (6) *organizational outcomes.* Let us examine each below.

The external context of organizations is usefully considered as two parts: a set of domains or sets of other organizations that have transactions with ours and the general environment that surrounds all organizations. There are input domains (those sets of organizations that supply resources—energy, money, materials, ideas, members, regulations), and output domains (those

Fig. 2. The cycle of managerial action.

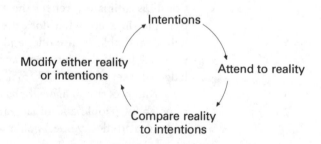

Intentions

Attend to reality

Compare reality to intentions

Modify either reality or intentions

sets of organizations that absorb the organization's products, services, wastes, and so on). Basic concerns about domain relations are two: (1) How easy or difficult is it to acquire resources and sell services and products? and (2) How easy or difficult is it to know about the domains? The first question reminds us that all organizations are dependent on their domains. The second question reminds us that we exist under conditions of more or less uncertainty. A situation of either scarce resources or high uncertainty makes organizational functioning problematic and the manager's job difficult indeed. Domains, in turn, are embedded in the general environment, those societal features such as the health of the economy, the prevailing political climate, the dominant values of society, shifts in population, and the like, that affect everybody.

A number of internal circumstances are worthy of managerial attention, too, because they also constrain what management can and cannot do. First, there is the organization's history, especially those notable events where the organization and its leaders were confronted with survival issues. How these issues were handled often serve as lessons as to how to handle similar future issues. Second, attention is usefully directed to where the organization is in its life cycle. Organizations begin, grow, mature, decline, and end much as humans do. Each stage has an impact on what can be done. It is usually much easier to manage a growing organization than either a stable or a declining one. A third internal circumstance to monitor is the organization's stakeholders—those parties with a vested interest in the success of the organization such as owners, suppliers, customers, members, unions, the local community, and so forth. The level of stakeholder satisfaction with the organization is ignored by managers with peril. The fourth constraining circumstance is so obvious that it is often underappreciated, namely, the tangible assets of the organization, that is, property, buildings, fixtures and equipment, cash, and so forth. Lastly, there is technology, defined as those processes for changing raw inputs into finished products or services. How easily is it understood? How much has to be invested in it? How easy is it to replace or change? There are the relevant questions.

Management itself deserves ongoing attention also. To our earlier discussion of managerial assumptions, appropriate skill mixes, and the quality of relationships, we add the management philosophy and vision of the dominant coalition. A dominant coalition is those members of management who share a basic philosophy (values, beliefs, and assumptions) and who, regardless of position, influence the organization according to their vision, including why the organization exists, what distinguishes it from others, and how it will be run (Nanus 1989). Sometimes this vision is written down as the organizational mission.

Management, as leaders of the organization, translates their philosophy and vision into three sets of designs or intentions. One is what the people should be like, second is what the organization itself should be like, and third is what sort of processes and systems are needed to integrate the people into the organization (Miles 1975). People who join an organization come with several important attributes: they come from a socioeconomic class, have a status in the community, possess certain capabilities or competencies and not others, hold certain attitudes and values, possess particular wants and needs, and differ demographically, that is, in terms of age, education, ethnicity, religion, and so forth. Managers intentionally recruit those people who are likely to contribute to the achievement of the organization's goals. Goals, along with strategies and policies, and structure are organizational factors that formalize management's intentions about purpose, guidelines, and arrangements respectively. Most organizational goals are in terms of outputs (that is, services and products) or major indices of performance (for example, market share, profitability, customer satisfaction). Strategies are those broad plans for how the organization intends to satisfy its stakeholders. Policies are guidelines for making day-to-day decisions consistent with strategies. Structure is how work tasks are arranged or grouped together (usually by product/ service, by business function, or by geography) and how these groupings are linked together vertically and horizontally through lines of authority, responsibility, communication, and control.

A third set of intentions represent management's choices about how the organization and people factors are integrated together through six critical processes and systems. Each process or system can be designed in several ways. Jobs can vary from a few simple, repetitive activities (job simplification) to many complex activities (job enlargement). Supervisory style can vary from constant monitoring and instructing subordinates (a close supervisory style) to encouraging both subordinate self-direction and inviting subordinate participation in job-related decisions (a consultative supervisory style). Reward systems can vary from those where an individual's monetary earnings depend on specific activity accomplishment to both monetary rewards, benefits and other forms of recognition by a whole group over a long period of time. Communication systems can vary from simple top-down, few topic formal ones to those where the information about everything flows in all directions formally and informally. Human resource systems (recruitment, selection, training and appraisal practices) can vary from hardly existent to highly elaborate. Decision-making and planning systems can vary from those only involving top management (centralized decision making) to those which involve everyone who is meaningfully engaged in any aspect of the problem or activity (decentralized decision making). Management's choices about each of these six systems and processes reflects their perception of members (how capable, motivated, and so forth) and the nature of the organization's goals, strategies, and structure. If, for example, the organization is in a high volume, limited service hotel where uniformity of product and swiftness of service is necessary, and the local labor pool is plentiful with young, inexperienced people, then a management is likely to design simple, repetitive jobs, supervise closely, not share decision making and planning, utilize highly standardized recruitment and training procedures, rely on formal, top-down communications, and pay modest wages to individuals for time worked or number of products served. If, in contrast, the organization's goals could only be accomplished by highly skilled professionals, we would probably find a more organic structure, enlarged jobs, decentralized decision making, free-flowing communications, well-developed development programs, and a consultative supervisory style.

Management's intentions, however, are just that, intentions. Since human organizations cannot be designed in every detail or anticipate everything, we can predict that some things will emerge that may not be intended. Several organizational features always emerge over time. Members who share similar self-interests sometimes band together to promote their interests, that is, they form cliques and coalitions. Coalitions and cliques in organizations may be temporary or relatively permanent. They may serve a variety of interests, from providing social satisfactions to preserving occupational prestige, from promoting a change to preventing a change, from forming a car pool to getting someone fired. Over time, widespread sentiments of various kinds also emerge about organizational practices. Members, for example, may gripe about lost benefits, get excited over a proposed merger, brag about their unit's reputation, and so forth—all such behaviors expressing a positive or negative sentiment. Organizational members also typically develop a psychological contract with the organization—an understanding of what constitutes a fair exchange between them and the organization. For example, in exchange for their time, productivity, and loyalty, they expect certain levels of reward and security and working conditions. Inevitably, a social structure emerges which may or may not be parallel to the formal hierarchy of jobs. Power and social status, for example, may be acquired or reduced beyond that which comes from one's formal authority and responsibility. Every organization or subpart also develops a unique personality or culture. A variety of things, events, and patterned practices take on meanings beyond that intended by management. Members invest symbolic meanings in elements of language, organizational stories, ritualistic practices, and particular artifacts, which serve to bind them together, clarify any ambiguities, and provide a common identity. Attention to these socio-cultural factors provide management with signs of whether their formal designs are perceived as just and functional by members.

Every organization is designed to produce certain outcomes. Individual members are to have a desired level of satisfaction with their jobs, supervision, and the organization, to achieve specified levels of performance in their jobs, and to more or less grow as persons through their employment. Similarly the groups of work related members are expected to accomplish some specified level of productivity, have some minimal level of morale, and more or less develop as a team. The organization as a whole likewise is expected to achieve certain desired levels of efficiency (the ratio of cost to output) and effectiveness (the degree of goal achievement), have a climate where members like coming to work, and are more or less open to change. These outcomes and all the other elements that managers need to pay attention to are outlined in Figure 3.

Fig. 3. A general model of organization management.

Constraints	Leadership	Design Features	Emergent Features	Outcomes
External Contexrs: General Environment, Input Domain, Output Domain		*Organization Factors* Goals, Strategies/Policies, Structure		
Internal Organizational Circumstances: History, Life Cycle, Stakeholders, Tangible Assets, Technology	*Management:* Assumptions, Skills, Relationships, Philosophy, Dominant Coalition, Vision/Mission	*Organizational Processes and Systems* Job Design, Supervisory Style, Reward Systems, Communication Systems, Human Resource Systems, Decision and Planning Systems	*Social-Cultural Factors:* Psychological Contract, Social Structure, Culture, Sentiments, Coalitions/Cliques	*Individual:* Satisfaction, Performance, Growth / *Work Unit:* Morale, Productivity, Development / *Organization:* Cilmate, Effectiveness/ Efficiency, Change
		People Factors: Demographics, Capabilities, Values/Attitudes, Needs/Wants, Class/Status		

If managers continually stay informed about all the elements of Figure 3, they can then compare what is actually occurring with what was intended to happen. If any of the actual and intended outcomes are not the same, then managers begin to systematically ask what else is out of line that causes the undesired outcome levels. Are the "constraints" (contexts and circumstances) accurately understood and taken into account? Does management hold appropriate assumptions and philosophy, have the right skill mix, and enough quality relationships to fulfill their responsibilities? Does management hold a viable vision for the organization? Is top management in fact the dominant coalition? Are the organization's goals, strategies and policies, and structure clear and reasonable given the context and circumstances? Are the right number of the right kinds of people employed? Are the organizational systems and process appropriate given who the members are and what they are expected to do? Are these systems and processes consistent with each other? Do the emergent socio-cultural factors help or hinder intended practices? When consistencies among design features are discovered, when design features do not reasonably reflect constraints, or when emergent features are nonsupportive to intentions, managerial action is called for. What managers can do is to modify one or more of those things under their control so that they are more internally consistent or lead to desired outcomes. Whatever aspects of the organization a manager selects to modify, every action taken should contribute toward the creation of a lasting, high-performance company (Schlesinger 1990). Thus, management actions, small and large, unique or repetitive, should contribute toward building a positive work climate, a clarified strategic direction, a just allocation of resources, an upgrading of the quality of management and other members, and the creation of excellence in operations and execution. Actions by managers thus are aimed at the fundamental tasks of all organizations—making major or minor internal adjustments, strategically realigning the organization to its domains, and preparing the organization for some anticipated future.

Summary

This chapter has outlined the essential skills, roles, and assumptions that hospitality managers need and utilize to accomplish organizational tasks. Organization management was characterized as a dynamic, cyclic process of attending, comparing, and acting. The arena for organizational management was explicated and exemplified in terms of internal and external constraints, leadership, intentional design features, emergent sociocultural features, and outcomes.

In recent years, hospitality management has become increasingly sophisticated as hospitality organizations have grown in complexity and size, competition has increased, and customers demand more and better service. We now find more and more kinds of professionally trained members—specialized experts and managers. Our society is experiencing far-reaching changes, reflected both in the service sector as a whole and in each organization. Change has become a way of life. Hospitality organizations are increasingly required to be simultaneously more strategic and more currently efficient and effective; simultaneously more innovative and more cost conscious; and simultaneously more member- and more customer-oriented. Organization management has undoubtedly become increasingly important and much more interesting, as well as much more challenging. It continues to be the arena for making those responsible contributions that make a positive difference in the lives of everyone: to the society as a whole, to organizational members, and to oneself. Organization managers should heed the words of Gandhi, "We must be the change we wish to see in the world."

References

Bradford, David L., and Allan R. Cohen. 1988. *Managing for Excellence: The Guide to Developing High Performance in Contemporary Organizations.* New York: John Wiley.

Caplow, Theodore. 1983. *Managing an Organization,* 2d ed. New York: Holt, Rinehart and Winston.

Katz, Robert L. 1974. Skills of an effective administrator. *Harvard Business Review* 52(Sept.-Oct.):90–102.

Kotter, John P. 1982. *The General Managers.* New York: The Free Press.

Lundberg, Craig. 1989. On organizational learning: Implications and opportunities for expanding organizational development. In *Research in Organizational Change and Development (Vol. 3),* ed. Richard W. Woodman and William Passmore, pp. 61–82. Greenwich, Conn.: JAI Press.

McGregor, Douglas. 1960. *The Human Side of Enterprise.* New York: McGraw-Hill.

Miles, Raymond E. 1975. *Theories of Management.* New York: McGraw-Hill.

Mintzberg, Henry. 1973. *The Nature of Managerial Work.* New York: Harper & Row.

Mintzberg, Henry. 1989. *Mintzberg on Management.* New York: The Free Press.

Nanus, Burt. 1989. *The Leader's Edge.* Chicago: Contemporary Books.

Presthus, Robert. 1962. *The Organizational Society.* New York: Alfred A. Knopf.

Schlesinger, Leonard. 1990. How to think like a manager: The art of managing for the long run. In *The Portable MBA,* ed. Eliza G. C. Collins and Mary Ann Devanna, pp. 1–18. New York: John Wiley.

Vaill, Peter. 1989. *Managing as a Performing Art.* San Francisco: Jossey-Bass.

5

Marketing in the Lodging Industry

Robert C. Lewis

For many, the term *marketing* conjures up images of selling and advertising. Because of this long-standing and common belief, selling and advertising are often called *traditional* marketing. Although they are important subsets of marketing, they are only subsets. All phases of marketing derive from the customer. This concept of marketing permeates both the traditional and *nontraditional* elements of marketing.

Today's lodging marketing executives and today's hotel managers should understand that their properties run as a system. Demand is balanced with the ability to produce. Marketing plans and strategies strike a balance between the needs of the marketing mix (product/service, price, distribution, communications) and the external needs, wants, and willingness to pay of the target markets.

The Two-Fold Purpose of Marketing

The only valid definition of business purpose is to create a customer.

> It is the customer who determines what a business is. For it is the customer, and he alone, who through being willing to pay for a good or for a service, converts economic resources into wealth, things into goods. What the business thinks it produces is not of first importance—especially not to the future of the business and to its success. What the customer thinks he is buying, what he considers 'value,' is decisive—it determines what a business is, what it produces and whether it will prosper (Drucker 1974:37–39).

Creating a customer does not mean simply making a sale. It means creating a relationship wherein a buyer wants your product before that of the competition. In addition to creating a customer, the purpose of both marketing and business is also to *keep* a customer once he or she has been created. A business' purpose and marketing's purpose, in fact, are really one and the same. Any definition of marketing must emphasize that the creation and keeping of customers is primary.

It should be clear then why marketing is defined as: Communicating to and giving the target market customers what they want, when they want it, where they want it, at a price they are willing and able to pay.

Any business that does this will fulfill its two-fold purpose of creating and keeping customers and, in turn, will produce revenue.

Solving Customers' Problems

There is a marketing premise that is even more basic than that already presented. Simply put, consumers do not buy something unless they have a problem to solve and believe that a purchase will provide the solution to the problem. It has been said that people do not buy quarter-inch drills, they buy quarter-inch holes. Another example, attributed to Charles Revson, founder of Revlon cosmetics, is, "In the factory we make cosmetics. In the store we sell hope."

In this sense, customers buy solutions, nothing else. If you think of goods and services that you want to sell in this sense only, you are a long way on the road to successful marketing. Thinking this way forces you to stand in the customer's shoes, to think like the customer thinks, and to understand what it is the customer wants, when, where, and at what price.

Consumers buy expectations at the same time that they buy solutions, both of which require a sacrifice. It then follows that the greater the sacrifice, the greater the risk, the greater the expectation, and the more demanding the customer is of the solution. To put it another way, if the solution meets the expectation and the value justifies the sacrifice, the risk becomes more justifiable, and a higher level of satisfaction becomes more likely. The result is a higher likelihood that a customer has been created.

Marketing, of course, does not create the needs or problems associated with the need to sleep in a hotel. However, it does identify the needs associated with *where to sleep*. Marketing differentiates the available solutions through the creation of expectations. On the other side of the equation, having created expectation, marketing needs to reduce perceived risk so that the prospective customer perceives the expectation as worth the risk.

Naturally, the solution to any problem rarely exists in a vacuum. That is why marketing becomes far more complex. If a solution to the problem of needing a night's sleep was only a room and a bed at the right price in the right place, then there would be little need for marketing. Solutions are not that simple and include many, many needs other than a simple bed in a simple room. The instant that one hotel provides something different than another hotel, competition is created and the mettle of marketing is tested. Instead of "here's a bed" (solution to problem), marketing creates "here's *this* bed," the *only* solution to *your* problem.

The goal for marketers is *to present the best solution to the problem as the lowest risk*. Marketing, however, does not stop there, especially in the lodging industry. The creation of expectations might be classified as traditional marketing. It is now operations management's job to ensure that those expectations are fulfilled. Although this is surely operations management's responsibility, it also means that operations management is totally involved in the marketing effort: traditional marketing only brings the customer to the door, it is up to nontraditional marketing to *create* and *keep* the customer.

The Marketing Concept

If a company adopts the marketing philosophy as its orientation, then the development and implementation of that philosophy is based on what has come to be known as the marketing concept. The marketing concept is based on the premise that the customer is king; the customer has a choice; the customer does not have to buy your product. Thus, the best way to earn a profit is to serve the customer better. According to the marketing concept, an organization should try to satisfy the needs of customers through activities that at the same time allow the organization to achieve its goals. To do this it must be determined what will satisfy its target customers. With this information, the business can create satisfying products. This concept is called the *product/service* element of the marketing mix.

In the lodging business, the business must then get customers to its product/service. This element of the marketing mix is called *distribution*. It includes location, travel agents, tour brokers, and other ways and means getting the customer to the hotel.

In attempting to satisfy customers, business must consider not only short-run, immediate tasks, but also broad, long-run desires. Thus a business must try to satisfy current needs in a manner that will not produce adverse long-run effects that will cause strong customer dissatisfaction in the future. To meet these short- and long-run needs and desires, all activities within a firm must be coordinated. Production, finance, accounting, personnel, and marketing departments must work together. This is part of the *pricing* element of the marketing mix.

Finally, the business must communicate all this to the customer whether by personal selling, advertising, word-of-mouth, promotions, or whatever other means. This element of the marketing mix is called *communications* or *promotion*.

Lack of coordination of all of these marketing mix elements may lessen customer satisfaction or even cause severe dissatisfaction. The marketing concept consists of a willingness to recognize and understand the consumer's needs and wants *and* a willingness to adjust any of the marketing mix elements to satisfy those needs and wants.

Practicing the marketing concept means putting yourself in the customer's shoes. It means selecting market segments that can be served profitably. This translates into profitable products and services that the company can produce, price, distribute. Practicing the marketing concept means positioning to those market segments in a way that creates an image, differentiates from the competition, and makes a promise to the customer.

Practicing the marketing concept means making the business do what suits the customer's interests. For management, it has implications of integrating and coordinating the research, planning, and systems approach of the firm. Practicing the marketing concept is a management approach to marketing that stresses problem-solving and decision-making responsibility to enhance the objectives of the entire firm.

Leadership   Many researchers have studied the qualities of effective leadership by observing the characteristics of men and women generally agreed to be successful leaders. Four major characteristics seem to be: A vision of the future, the ability to communicate that vision, an entrepreneurial spirit, and a constant quest for excellence.

These same characteristics can be applied to leadership in terms of the marketing concept. Marketing leadership accepts change as a constant. It not only recognizes needs and wants of the customer but it also recognizes that the customer changes; the customer is not in a static state and any successful company must change with, if not before, the customer. Marketing leadership envisions these changes through constant evaluation of the market.

Opportunity Great success stories in business almost always include tales of visionary leaders who saw and grasped opportunity. Howard Johnson, the founder, was certainly one of those. He saw the opportunity to give traveling Americans clean, inexpensive, dependable food and service from Maine to California. Kemmons Wilson, the founder of Holiday Inns, saw the opportunity to do the same with motel rooms.

Opportunities such as these are based on needs, wants, and problems of consumers that already exist. These men were visionaries with an entrepreneurial spirit. They did not create the needs, wants, or problems; they recognized them as opportunities. Practicing the marketing concept means constantly searching out opportunities. Very few opportunities are as grandiose as those above. To find the smaller ones, the marketing concept manager does not look for opportunities first; he looks for customer's problems because they are easier to identify.

Opportunity continues to be the lifeblood of successful marketing. It does not start with fancy drapery or upholstered walls. It starts with consumers' problems. Look for a problem, the real problem, and you will find an opportunity.

Planning The third element of practicing the marketing concept is planning. Planning is defining what has to be done and allocating the resources to do it. It means proacting rather than reacting. It means shaping destiny. One writer summarizes the accomplishments attributed to good planning, as follows:

1. It leads to a better position or standing for the organization.
2. It helps the organization progress in the ways that its management considers most suitable.
3. It helps every manager think, decide and act more effectively for progress in the desired direction.
4. It helps keep the organization flexible.
5. It stimulates a cooperative, integrated, enthusiastic approach to organizational problems.
6. It indicates to management how to evaluate and check up on progress toward the planned objectives.
7. It leads to socially and economically useful results. (Ewing 1968:9–14)

Planning in the marketing sense and in the sense of the marketing concept means planning with the customer in mind. While financial planning has become routine in many companies, marketing planning has yet to achieve that status. This seems strange if one accepts the premise that without customers there would be no finances to manage.

Control Control is the last element of the marketing system quartet, but it is also the glue that holds the other three together and makes them work. When control is lacking in lodging firms, leadership and planning founders.

Control is the sense of the marketing concept means something quite different than cost control, although certainly marketers must be aware of costs and their impact on the bottom line. Instead, control in the marketing sense means control of your destiny through leadership, planning, and opportunity by control of the customer, the market, and the product.

Control is the feedback loop of the system that tells if the system is working and provides information to management on who the market is, who the customer is, and what are the customers' problems, expectations, perceptions, and experiences. Control is knowing whether perceptions equal reality, why the customers come or do not come, how they use the product, how their complaints are handled, and whether they return. In short, control in marketing is knowing and serving the customer. Control is also knowing your employees for every employee is an integral part of the marketing effort in a lodging firm.

Control in marketing means a good management information system, an essential element of practicing the marketing concept.

Why the Marketing of Lodging is Different

Lodging services are *experienced*, rather than possessed. There is no passing of title when purchased. The buyer has nothing to be displayed, to be shown to friends or family, to put on the shelf, or ever to use again. In sum, the buyer goes away empty-handed. He does not, however, go away "empty-headed." He has an experience to remember and to talk about.

The intangibility of lodging has profound implications for the consumer, and thus for marketers. In the extreme, the buyer is not sure what he is buying or what he will get. Even if he has bought it before, he cannot go back and say. "I want one of the same" and show the seller what it is that he wants. The buyer cannot kick the tires, turn up the sound, choose the color, smell the aroma, measure the size, or taste the flavor.

The consumer: It is the experience that helps create expectations for future experiences. This point demonstrates why each experience in a service rendered is a marketing effort. It is the only true way the consumer has of *valuing* the purchase and determining if it is worth the *sacrifice*. Even then he is not sure if it will be repeated in an identical fashion. These factors, in turn, increase the *risk* for the customer. Buying "blind" is indeed the riskiest of purchases.

Suppose, as may more often be the case, that the prospective buyer has not previously had this exact same experience. In this case the buyer may have to rely on similar experiences. If there have been none of these, then he or she may choose to rely on the experiences of others, either with the same experience or with similar experiences. If this information is not available, the buyer may have only the advertising, the "promise," of the seller on which to rely. Without even this he or she is truly buying blind.

The marketer: The marketer's job is to solve consumer problems, to create and keep a customer, so the marketer's task in the case of intangibles relates directly to the problems of the consumer that were just discussed.

The marketer must convince the prospective buyer that he or she offers the right solution to the buyer's problem. The first step, then, is to develop the expectation. Traditional methods of doing this are through advertising, personal selling, and public relations. In many cases lodging companies use these methods but there are inherent problems: How do you advertise or sell an intangible service? You can use words but often these are as abstract as the service itself and serve only to compound the intangibility (for instance, "the finest," "the ultimate").

What marketers really do is make promises; the greater the intangibility, the greater the promise, and the greater the risk for the buyer commensurate with the sacrifice that has to be made. The customer has no choice but to believe us and take our word, or not believe us and go somewhere else where he or she will likely get the same promise and be faced with the same dilemma. Because of this quandary traditional marketing is only a small part of lodging marketing.

Simultaneity of Production and Consumption

The service characteristic of simultaneous production and consumption is probably the most unique of all service characteristics. It is also the strongest foundation for the premise that management *is* marketing in the lodging industry. This is so because in the case of simultaneous production and consumption, consumption depends on the participation of the seller, and the seller requires the participation of the buyer. The resultant effect is an interpersonal relationship between the buyer and seller that may supersede the service itself.

In lodging the customer is buying the service. One individual can totally personify the service of a particular establishment and cause a customer not to return. A friendly, smiling, call-you-by-your-name clerk is not enough. Each employee is literally part of the product because each employee is producing while the customer consumes.

Internal Marketing

Internal marketing means "applying the philosophies and practices of marketing to people who serve the external customers so that (1) the best possible people can be employed and retained and (2) they will do the best possible work" (Berry 1980:26). The emphasis of internal marketing is on the employee as the customer and the job as the product. Berry (1984:271-278) states: We can think of internal marketing as viewing employees as internal customers, viewing jobs as internal products, and then endeavoring to offer internal products that satisfy the needs and wants of those internal customers while addressing the objectives of the organization.

Careful perusal makes the case obvious: If the employees represent a major part of the hospitality product to the paying customer, then it is obvious that one of the first tasks of marketing and management is to have the employees believe in the product. Sasser and Arbeit (1976), in fact, suggest that "the successful service company must first sell the job to employees before it can sell its services to customers."

Viewed from this perspective, the job (or product) must satisfy the needs and wants and solve the problems of employees (the customers). If this is not the case, we will end up with dissatisfied customers (employees) who, in turn, will express, in one way or another, their dissatisfaction to the paying customers. Paying customers, in turn, find that their problems are not adequately solved so they go elsewhere. Clearly, this is not the way to create or keep customers.

What is practiced in the creation and keeping of customers of goods and services needs to also be practiced in the creation and keeping of employees. The elements of external marketing are just as appropriate and just as necessary in internal marketing. When we consider the tools of marketing such as segmentation, positioning, communication, product development, and research, we can see that they are just as essential to internal marketing as they are to external marketing.

As we separate customers according to needs and wants, so too should we choose employees. As we position a product to the marketplace, so too should we position the job to each employee. As we communicate with customers, so too must we communicate with employees. As we develop new products, so too must we develop new job methods, rewards, and satisfactions. And as we research consumers, so too must we survey our employees to determine needs, wants, and attitudes.

Successful internal marketing considerably eases the task of implementing the second element of nontraditional marketing, relationship marketing, the primary task of keeping customers.

Relationship Marketing Customers are assets, the most important assets a company can have. It is good management in business to protect your assets, but assets like buildings or a warehouse of goods, do not produce profits; the customer that buys the goods does.

Relationship marketing is defined as marketing to protect the customer base. It sees the customer as an asset. Its function is to attract, maintain, and enhance customer relationships.

Nowhere is relationship marketing more apropos than in the lodging industry. Relationship marketing is most applicable when

- There is an ongoing and periodic desire for service by the customer.
- The service customer controls the selection of the service supplier.
- There are alternate supplier choices.
- Customer loyalty is weak and switching is common and easy.
- Word-of-mouth is an especially potent form of communication about a product.

These conditions are obviously quite prevalent in the lodging industry. We do not sell one-time services and the consumer, especially today, has many choices. In an era of heavy hotel building, any hotel is especially vulnerable to new competition. Most everyone likes to try a new place. The question is, will they come back? Do we offer a competitive product on dimensions that are meaningful to customers, solve customer problems, and are difficult for competitors to duplicate? This is what relationship marketing is all about and when the above conditions pertain, the opportunities to practice it are abundant.

Customer Complaints If there is one place where internal marketing and relationship marketing come together it is in the handling of customer complaints. Customer complaints are a special case because they are one of the most misunderstood and mishandled areas of customer relations in the lodging industry. Customer complaints are

- Inevitable. Nothing is perfect. The diversity of the lodging customer and the heterogeneity of the hospitality product absolutely ensure that there will be complaints.
- Healthy. The old army expression is, "If the troops aren't griping look out for trouble." An absence of complaints may be the best indication management has that something is wrong. Hospitality customers are never totally satisfied, especially over a period of time. Probably, instead, they are simply not talking The communication process is not working. The relationship is deteriorating.
- Opportunities. Customer complaints are opportunities to learn of customers' problems, whether they are idiosyncratic or caused by the operation itself. It is an opportunity to make it better, to be creative, to develop new product, to learn new needs, and to keep old customers.
- Marketing tools. If marketing is giving customers what they want then the tool for doing that is to know what they want. All the customer surveys in the world will not tell you as much as customer complaints will tell you.
- Advertising. Negative, if you do not resolve the problems. There is nothing more devastating in the hospitality business than negative word-of-mouth. Positive, if you fix it. Research has shown that one of

the best and most loyal customers is the one who had a complaint that was satisfactorily resolved. He or she loves to tell others about it.

Practicing relationship marketing through consumer complaint handling is not the easiest task in the world. Many discontented customers will not take the trouble to complain, yet these may be some of the best opportunities. *Encouraging* complaints becomes the necessary objective.

Research has shown that people do not complain for three primary reasons: (1) It is not worth the time and effort; (2) They don't know where or how to complain; and (3) They believe that nothing will be done about it even if they do complain.

Marketing's task is to overcome these obstacles by making it easy to complain, making it known where and how to complain, and truly doing something about it when customers do complain. This means setting up specific procedures. Such action will also constitute internal marketing; when employees see management taking complaints seriously they will feel more inclined to do likewise.

The benefits are clear: long-term profit from loyal customers and more positive, and less negative, word-of-mouth advertising. There are other ancillary benefits such as new product ideas, new product information, improved image, better educated customers, and higher productivity and service. For line employees there are also the benefits of less customer conflict, better image and word-of-mouth about the company, and better respect for the company and the product.

All told, marketing in the lodging industry is a complex process albeit a most essential one, in all its components.

Summary

Marketing is defined as communicating to and giving the target market customers what they want, when they want it, where they want it, at a price they are willing and able to pay. In general, marketing is a function designed to solve customer needs. In carrying out this task, marketing personnel use the marketing concept. The marketing concept implies that the customers needs are met when management designs the appropriate *distribution systems, product/ service mix, and communications or promotion systems, and establishes an appropriate price.* These basic elements of the marketing concept are often referred to as the marketing mix. They must be blended together in appropriate proportions if a lodging facility is to be successful. This success will also depend on strong marketing leadership that will identify and seize appropriate opportunities and carefully plan, control, and implement both internal and external resources to create the correct marketing effort for a service industry-based firm such as a hotel. These efforts are designed to protect the customer base of a hotel by attracting, maintaining and enhancing customer relationships.

References

Berry, Leonard L. 1980. Service marketing is different. *Business*, May–June.
Berry, Leonard L. 1981. The employee as customer. *Journal of Retail Banking*, Reprinted in C. H. Lovelock, 1984, *Services Marketing*, pp. 271–278. Englewood Cliffs, N.J.: Prentice-Hall
Drucker, Peter F. 1974. *The Practice of Management*, New York: Harper & Row.
Ewing, David W. 1968. *The Practice of Planning*, New York: Harper & Row.
Sasser, W. E. and S. Arbeit. 1976. Selling jobs in the service sector. *Business Horizons*, June.

6

Marketing Management

Ken W. McCleary

Successful organizations exist because they perform a service or make a product that fulfills a need or a want. Those organizations that first seek to determine what the needs and wants of consumers are and then deliver product offerings that satisfy those needs and wants are following what is called the *marketing concept.* Firms that are truly marketing-oriented follow the marketing concept. Although this may seem obvious, many people confuse the process of marketing with the process of selling. In a classic article, Theodore Levitt distinguishes between selling and marketing: "Selling focuses on the needs of the seller, marketing on the needs of the buyer" (Levitt 1960). It is not uncommon in the hotel industry to find a person at a particular hotel who is called the marketing manager, but who really does little else than try to sell the hotel's services.

The American Marketing Association officially defines marketing as "the process of planning and executing the conception, pricing, promotion, and distribution of ideas, goods, and services to create exchanges that satisfy individual and organizational objectives" (AMA Board Approves New Definition 1985). Definitions of management typically include the functions of planning, organizing, leading, and controlling (Ivancevich et al. 1986). *Marketing management,* then, is defined as the planning, organizing, leading, and controlling of marketing activities.

All of the marketing functions in the definition of marketing (conception, pricing, promotion, and distribution) are performed in all organizations. If an exchange transaction is to take place, marketing functions cannot be eliminated. In the hospitality industry, many small lodging operations do not have a marketing manager. Nevertheless, marketing functions are performed even though they may not be planned and coordinated. The difference between an organization that uses marketing effectively and one that does not, lies in the fact that an overt effort is made to manage the marketing functions. This means that marketing activities have been planned ahead of time, organized carefully, and had their performance directed and their effectiveness measured through feedback so that changes might be made for future improvement. While there is no one single organization structure for managing marketing, Figure 1 depicts a typical organization chart for the marketing effort of a large convention hotel.

Fig. 1. Typical organization chart for the marketing effort of a large convention hotel.

The Role of the Marketing Manager

Marketing Mix

What does a marketing manager manage? In a truly marketing-oriented hospitality organization, the marketing manager manages activities that provide guest satisfaction at a profit. The way in which marketing activities are put together to accomplish the goal of satisfying guests reflects the unique skills of the marketing manager. This blending together of activities is called the *marketing mix*. The difference between a marketing manager who is competent and well trained and one who is not can be pointed out by comparing a master chef to a cook in a typical restaurant. They may both have the same ingredients to work with, but the master chef has the knowledge to create a unique and exciting dining experience. An untrained marketing manager has the same ingredients as the professional to work with, but unless they are mixed together properly, the results can be disastrous.

The marketing mix, then, is the unique blend of marketing activities used by hospitality firms to satisfy the needs and wants of their target customers. The activities that are traditionally considered a part of the marketing mix are often grouped under four broad functional headings: product (tangible goods and intangible services and ideas), communications, pricing, and distribution. This classification of marketing functions is easy to remember, but does not give a very detailed understanding of the specific activities performed by marketing managers. Table 1 provides a more detailed breakdown of the four functional areas of marketing.

A Hospitality Marketing Mix

Marketing theorists in the hospitality industry have attempted to modify the way in which the marketing mix is viewed in order to make it more specific for the hospitality marketer. Renaghan (1981) suggested that the hospitality marketing mix is made up of three submixes: (1) the product service mix, which is defined as a combination of products (tangibles) and services (intangibles), (2) the presentation mix, which includes all of those activities that a firm uses "to increase the tangibility of the product-service mix in the perception of the target market at the right place and time" (p. 32), and (3) the communications mix, which is basically the totality of communications between the firm and its target market. To these three submixes, Lewis and Chambers (1989) added the distribution mix, which they define as "all channels available between the firm and the target market that increase the probability of getting the customer to the product" (p. 302). This definition of distribution is different than the definition for tangible products. In marketing tangible products we are concerned with getting the product to the customers in their own homes. For most hospitality products we are more concerned with how to get customers to the hotel or restaurant so that they can consume our services.

Table 1. *Functions and activities of marketing management*

Product	Communications	Pricing	Distribution
Combining goods and services	Determine mix	Objectives	Objectives
Design	Set objectives	Discounts	Channels
Packaging	Advertising	Yield Management	Intermediaries
Branding	Select media	Negotiation	Location
Guarantees	Budget	Packages	Customer movement
Accessories	Copy thrust		Delivery time
	Campaigns		
	Themes		
	Internal		
	Publicity		
	Sales Management		
	Selection		
	Training		
	Recruitment		
	Territories		
	Motivation		
	Evaluation		
	Sales Promotion		
	Trade shows		
	Couponing		
	Contests		
	Games		
	Merchandising		

The marketing literature shows that there is some disagreement among hospitality marketing scholars as to whether there are great differences between how marketing management should be applied to goods versus services. Some of the disagreement is reflected in the terminology used, such as considering services something other than a product as in the marketing mix classification proposed by Renaghan (1981). The resolution of this disagreement can be found in examining goods and services from the consumer's perception. Levitt (1981) suggests that people are not really seeking to buy goods *or* services, rather they buy the *perceived benefits* derived from products. That is, people pay for the satisfaction of needs (benefits) whether the product is a tangible good or an intangible service. Put another way, goods are products and services are products. The former is tangible, the latter intangible, but no matter which the customer buys, that customer is really buying the benefit of need/want satisfaction.

With the idea that people buy benefits rather than tangibles or intangibles, the marketing mix can be considered in the same general manner whether it is being designed for goods, services, or ideas. The basic functions are the same whether used for tangibles or intangibles although, as with the conception of the hospitality distribution mix mentioned earlier, activities may be modified to fit the peculiar characteristics of how business is conducted in various industries. Therefore, hospitality marketing managers perform the same basic mixing function as in other industries: the combining of product-related, pricing, communications and distribution activities that best satisfy consumers. It would seem best, then, to use the same classification for the marketing mix for the hospitality industry as is used for marketing in general. This is the classification presented in Table 1. Even though some terminology is specific to the hospitality industry, and specific activities will be combined creatively to develop special "hospitality" mixes, the process is much the same for hospitality as for other industries. Having a special feel for their particular segment of the industry is what makes hospitality marketing managers able to find the right mixture of marketing activities necessary to satisfy their customers.

Selecting Target Markets Modern marketing is based on the marketing concept, which means that all of a company's marketing efforts will be aimed at satisfying customers at a profit (McCarthy and Perreault 1984). Until a hotel has defined who those customers are, it is impossible to match product offerings with specific consumer needs and wants. Therefore, the most important decision that a hospitality company makes is *who* it will market its products to. This decision guides the formulation of the marketing mix. The company decides who it would like to have as customers and this group is called its *target market*. This decision is made by top management but management should have major input from the marketing manager. Once the target market is chosen, all of the firm's efforts are aimed at satisfying the particular needs and wants of the people falling within the definition of the target.

Selecting a target market recognizes that in the total marketplace there are groups of people who have needs and wants that are unique. The process of identifying and grouping these people together is called *market segmentation*. Rather than simply designing a product that may have some broad appeal to everyone, greater customer satisfaction can be obtained if products are designed to more precisely meet the needs of smaller portions (segments) of the total market. Segmentation has become a dominant force in the hotel industry, with concepts being specially designed for business people, budget-minded customers, and those needing accommodations for extended stays, just to name a few.

Target market segments may be described in many ways. Often marketers use demographic descriptions, which include characteristics such as age, income, gender, occupation, and race. Perhaps of more use to the hospitality industry is basing segmentation strategy on the benefits sought by consumers (Lewis 1980). A marketing manager using this strategy would look for underlying reasons why potential customers seek a hotel or restaurant and then strive to provide benefits that appeal to those reasons. This is done through the development of an appropriate marketing mix, as mentioned earlier. For example, there may be a group of people who are seeking healthy food served in an elegant atmosphere. The marketing manager might match the product offering with the benefits sought by creating menu items which are attractively presented with a high level of service, but which are low in calories and prepared using little salt and low cholesterol cooking methods.

Geography is a segmentation base that is almost always used to define markets in the hospitality industry. Some hotel chains concentrate their efforts on the South or the Midwest, for example. Geographic segmentation helps to make decisions such as where to advertise. Markets can also be segmented based on meal occasion and psychographic characteristics. Typically, marketing managers use two or more bases of segmentation to help define their target market. Most firms have more than one target market, even though one may be the primary target.

Marketing Research One of the most important tasks of marketing management is to conduct research that will help the firm make better marketing decisions. Marketing research should be conducted on a regular basis to monitor such things as changes in consumer behavior and competitor strategies. It should also be designed to answer specific questions as they arise. Examples of specific research problems relating to the marketing mix include what price the firm should charge, where and how much to advertise, which site location is best, and what products the consumer desires.

Without research, the marketing manager is operating blindly. If research techniques are poor, results of the research may actually mislead decision makers. Therefore, part of the marketing manager's job is to make sure that research is thorough and sound. In the hospitality industry, there is more sophisticated research being reported in the marketing area than in any other functional area (Crawford-Welch and McCleary 1990).

Managing the Hospitality Marketing Mix

The Hospitality Product (Goods and Services) Mix

There is a large amount of intangibility associated with many hospitality products. Services like the benefits a guest receives from staying in a hotel room, flying in an airplane, or having a meal brought to the table in a restaurant cannot be touched or felt like a tangible product. Most hospitality products are not completely intangible. In fact, most services of all types have a tangible component to them so that it is common to have some combination of goods and services working together to make the total product offering. It is this special combination of goods and services that comprises the product mix.

The service component of the product requires some special understanding and skills on the part of the marketing manager because it is difficult to market something that cannot be felt or seen. Therefore, the hotel, restaurant, or travel marketer must devise ways to help the consumer visualize and understand what the product being offered is. The communications part of the marketing mix is a great aid in helping customers visualize the services offered by hospitality firms.

It is recommended that the marketing manager be an integral part of all product decisions, and all product decisions should be made with the customer in mind. Thus, a part of the marketing manager's job is to be knowledgeable of the needs and wants of hospitality consumers. Armed with an understanding of consumer behavior, the marketing manager provides expertise in selecting site locations, designing buildings, putting together menus, and deciding on service levels. Unless firms involve the marketing experts on their staffs, they are not being marketing-oriented. It is much easier for the marketing manager to put together a program to sell products designed with the customer in mind.

The Hospitality Communications Mix

Communications (also called promotion) consists of all the activities that a hospitality firm uses to get messages to the consumer regarding the product offering. Communications are often classified into four categories: advertising, sales promotion, publicity, and personal selling (Kotler 1988). Because of the highly visible nature of some communication activities, particularly advertising and personal selling, some think that communications is the only tool that marketing uses.

Advertising consists of nonpersonal presentations which are paid for by a hospitality firm and which identify that firm in the message. Major firms use virtually every medium available including network television, while smaller firms tend to rely heavily on less expensive, more direct advertising such as local newspapers, billboards, and brochures.

Sales promotion consists of miscellaneous activities that do not fit neatly in the other three categories. It is usually used in conjunction with other communications to strengthen the overall effort. Activities such as contests and couponing are widespread in the quick service sector of the restaurant industry but are usually accompanied by media advertising. Hotels and airlines use travel shows as a convenient means of sales promotion for selling space to tour wholesalers and packagers.

Publicity, like advertising, affects demand in a nonpersonal fashion because it is not paid for by an identified sponsor. Publicity consists of information which the general media conveys to the public regarding the hospitality firm and its products. The hospitality industry has the opportunity to use publicity very effectively because many newsworthy activities occur in hospitality firms. A good program of marketing management will have a carefully planned publicity strategy so that news releases are issued regularly and the media notified of important happenings at the hotel, restaurant, or travel firm.

Personal selling involves direct conversation with potential customers. The conversation may be through telemarketing (use of direct communication over the telephone) or face-to-face. In the hospitality business, all employees are potential salespeople and, therefore, should be made aware of all that the firm has to offer.

The design of the total communications mix is a major function of the marketing manager. Budgets must be set, media selected, advertising and sales promotions devised, publicity planned, and sales activities managed. In large hotels, restaurant chains, and travel companies there are likely to be several people assisting in communications management. For example, the position of sales manager can be found in most hotels of any size. Chains are likely to have specialists in generating publicity, making media buys and working with advertising agencies. In chain properties, the marketing manager may have lots of support, but he/she may have to perform all marketing communications functions single-handedly in smaller, independent operations.

Some specific communications methods are found in the hospitality industry that are not found in other fields. Elevator cards are advertisements placed in elevators which promote other parts of a hotel such as restaurants, lounges, and health clubs. Table tents, cards which are folded over so that they can stand by themselves on table tops in restaurants, are typically used to promote specials or beverages. The travel industry uses a variety of printed brochures and other materials called collateral, to distribute information to potential clients. At least three books list a wide variety of techniques available for hospitality industry communications (Coffman 1975; Gottlieb 1982, Powers 1990).

The Hospitality Pricing Mix

Setting prices for hospitality products is one of the most critical marketing mix functions. Prices are typically referred to as "rates" in the hotel industry and "fares" in the transportation sector. Prices convey an image of the product offering and set up consumer expectations of benefits to be derived. Price also is often used to segment markets as in the budget, midrange, and luxury hotel segments.

Sound pricing strategy must have clear objectives and be developed with the rest of the marketing mix in mind. Cost elements must be considered, but the marketing manager must remember that ultimately it is the customer who determines if prices are reasonable based on expectations and what is available at the competition.

The various sectors in the hospitality field have specific nuances in price setting. For example, the restaurant industry has several methods of setting menu prices (Kotschevar 1987) and both the airline and hotel industries work to maximize profits by using a flexible pricing strategy called yield management (Relihan 1989).

The Hospitality Distribution Mix   Distribution can be viewed as the bringing together of the product and the customer. In the pizza business this may entail both the rapid delivery of pizza to the customer's home or the movement of the customer to the restaurant. Traditionally, hospitality services were consumed at the provider's place of business and it was up to the consumer to overcome whatever obstacles necessary to get there. More and more, hospitality firms are realizing the advantages of making it easier for the consumer to get their products. Hotels have limousine services to pick people up at airports and other locations. Rental car agencies deliver people to their choice of airlines and moving walkways help travelers get to their airline gates. Even upscale restaurants are recognizing the value of home delivery.

The means by which customers and products are moved, the specific location of stores and outlets, and the intermediaries used are all distribution decisions. In marketing terms, the specific combinations of firms that are used to move products and people are called *channels of distribution*. For example, an airline might sell space on a flight to a tour operator who, in turn, offers a package tour through a travel agent who sells it to the ultimate consumer. The combination of the airline, tour operator, and travel agent constitutes the channel of distribution for that airline service.

Summary

An understanding of the customer is critical for success in the hospitality industry. The process of marketing management should be constantly monitoring the needs and wants of consumers and then designing products that meet those needs and wants at a price that consumers are willing to pay. That price must be set so that it is profitable for the firm. It is the job of the marketing manager to communicate with the customer about the firm's products and then be involved in making sure that the product is delivered in a manner that is consistent with customer expectations.

The firm that starts with the consumer and makes its decisions based on the consumer is a marketing-oriented firm. The planning, organizing, controlling, directing and staffing for the activities that lead to customer satisfaction is marketing management. Hospitality marketing management involves the knowledge of how marketing is conducted in the hospitality industry. That knowledge is then used to combine marketing activities to provide a unique offering that meets the specific needs and wants of the firm's target markets.

References

AMA Board Approves New Definition. 1985. *Marketing News,* March 1:1.
Coffman, C. DeWitt. 1975. *Marketing for a Full House.* Ithaca, N.Y.: Cornell University.
Crawford-Welch, Simon, and Ken W. McCleary. 1990. Hospitality Research: The State of the Art. Manuscript. Blacksburg, Va.: Virginia Polytechnic Institute and State University.
Gottlieb, Leon. 1982. *Foodservice/Hospitality Advertising and Promotion.* Indianapolis, Ind.: Bobbs-Merrill Company.

Ivancevich, John M., James H. Donnelly, Jr., and James C. Gibson. 1986. *Managing for Performance*, 3d ed. Plano, Tex.: Business Publications Inc.

Kotler, Philip. 1988. *Marketing Management: Analysis, Planning, Implementation, and Control*, 6th ed. Englewood Cliffs, N.J.: Prentice-Hall.

Kotschevar, Lendal H. 1987. Menu analysis: Review and evaluation. *FIU Hospitality Review* 5(2):19–25.

Levitt, Theodore. 1960. Marketing myopia. *Harvard Business Review* (July-August):45–56.

Levitt, Theodore. 1981. Marketing intangible products and product intangibles. *Harvard Business Review* 59:94–102.

Lewis, Robert C., and Richard E. Chambers. 1989. *Marketing Leadership in Hospitality*. New York: Van Nostrand Reinhold.

Lewis, Robert C. 1980. The science of target marketing. *Restaurant Business* (November 1):102,105,107,109,113.

Lovelock, Christopher H. 1984. *Services Marketing*. Englewood Cliffs, N.J.: Prentice-Hall.

McCarthy, E. Jerome, and William D. Perreault, Jr. 1984. *Basic Marketing*. Homewood, Ill.: Richard D. Irwin, Inc.

Powers, Tom. 1990. *Marketing Hospitality*. New York: Wiley.

Relihan, Walter J., III. 1989. The yield management approach to hotel-room pricing. *The Cornell Hotel and Restaurant Administration Quarterly* (May):40–45.

Renaghan, Leo M. 1981. A new marketing mix for the hospitality industry. *The Cornell Hotel and Restaurant Administration Quarterly* (August):31–35.

7

Hospitality Law

John E. H. Sherry

The place of law in business management is well recognized. Both undergraduate and graduate business schools offer at least one course dealing with the subject. This phenomenon is no less true of hospitality education. The latter curricula include law instruction either on the traditional business law model or utilize the emerging legal environment of business approach. In both cases appropriate inclusion of laws directly governing the industry are noted and reviewed. Recent emphasis is directed toward international law aspects and the interplay of law and ethics as a component of service industry management.

Historical Origins

Historically industry interest in hospitality law education focused on hospitality supplier liability to hospitality consumers. In keeping with early law developments, the security and safety of guest or patron property received primary attention. Unlike other hospitality suppliers, the law required innkeepers to insure guest property against loss or damage. Less concern was devoted to the physical needs of consumers. Why? Because economic and political power in ancient regimes was expressed in property rights, and human rights were accorded less value. It was not until middle class merchants became economically empowered that the innkeeper was held to a legal duty to admit all who sought admission and service for security from criminal elements irrespective of the owner's wish to pick and choose his or her customers.

An outgrowth of this later concern for physical safety was the early recognition that the right to travel would be rendered meaningless if certain classes of society were denied access and service in places of public accommodation. The constitutional right to travel and secure lodging and entertainment only protected persons against state and federal government refusals to admit. Likewise the common or decisional law governing innkeepers was limited in scope and could be overturned by state or local legislative enactments. The development of the legal right to access privately owned or operated public facilities was slow in coming. Not until 1964 did the federal government outlaw discrimination in public accommodations on the basis of race, creed, color, or national origin. Not until more recently did a majority of states enact laws outlawing such discrimination on the basis of sex.

Hospitality Business Law Relations

Supplier-Consumer Relations

From the afore-mentioned social and economic origins the law of hospitality supplier-customer relations evolved to encompass the protection of guests and their property from physical, emotional, and economic harm in four basic business areas.

1. *Contracts.* Legally enforceable agreements made by suppliers with customers involve the enforcement of promises to act or refrain from acting where each party has voluntarily undertaken rights and duties to the other. Such contracts involve reservations, private function, and convention contracts necessary for the operation of the business.

2. *Tort Law.* Certain legal duties flow by operation of law, not by contractual agreement. Legal wrongs arise when these laws are based upon the infliction of intentional harm: harm caused by negligent or careless acts or omissions and by laws that impose liability strictly, meaning *irrespective* of intent to harm others or carelessness. Examples of intentional legal wrongs are personal injuries arising out of deliberate or intentional physical harm inflicted by the owner or operator of a foodservice facility upon a customer or harm inflicted in reckless disregard for the consequences. Negligent harm arises out of failing to exercise reasonable care under the circumstances in the maintenance or supervision of the premises resulting in harm to a customer or other persons invited to use the premises. Strict liability for harm involves offering to a customer food or beverages unfit for human consumption that injure the customer.

3. *Agency Law.* Modern business could not function without the ability of owners and operators to delegate rights and responsibilities to others. The hospitality employer may hire agents to perform specific functions, such as providing feasibility studies, legal, architectural, building, engineering, or management services, where a task is assigned but the employer does not direct or supervise the doing of the work. In such cases any negligent or intentional harm inflicted upon a third person by the agent does not implicate the employer. But where the employer supervises and directs the work of the agent, then the employer is said to be vicariously responsible to the third party for his agent's acts or omissions, to the same degree that his or her employee would be responsible. It matters not that the employee disregarded his employer's instructions. The law, on the basis of public policy, makes the employer respond in damages. These issues are very important in the conduct of a labor intensive industry such as the typical hospitality enterprise.

4. *Regulatory Law.* Government regulatory agencies created to administer business operations have grown enormously and impact upon hospitality enterprises. Federal agencies administer occupational health and safety; national labor relations; all matter of environmental controls; and equal employment opportunity. State agencies license and regulate alcoholic beverage sales; foodservice health permits; worker, building, and fire safety; and land use. These are but a few of the areas subject to government oversight. Although agency decisions are subject to court review, their scope and authority to penalize offenders makes understanding and compliance a necessary part of hospitality management.

Commercial Relations In addition to recognizing and dealing with customer legal relations, the above analysis also applies to relations with advertising agencies, builders, financial institutions, insurance carriers, and suppliers of goods and service as well as the above-mentioned agencies. Management looks to these individuals or institutions to furnish the capital and raw materials with which to conduct business and attract patronage; and/or to secure permission needed to locate, build, and operate the facility in which the business will be housed. Understanding of the legal aspects of each of these transactions is essential to ensure the success of the hospitality enterprise. Otherwise a potentially successful operation may suffer loss or untimely termination.

Competitive Marketing Relations Another aspect of law that intrudes upon hospitality entrepreneurs is that of fair dealing with competitors. Here government regulates anticompetitive marketing activities that involve price fixing, group boycotts, and division of markets, among other problems, as well as monopoly power. These antitrust laws, originally intended to protect against unfair competitive practices, have now been expanded to protect consumers injured by such practices. If found guilty, business and individuals face heavy civil and criminal penalties, including treble damage remedies awarded to injured competitors or consumers under federal law. Ignorance of these legal requirements can be fatal.

International Relations Recent events worldwide, but particularly in Europe, which create opportunity for business expansion, make it necessary to note the growing role of international law in the hospitality marketplace. Economic unification by the European Economic Community (EEC), scheduled for 1992; free market developments in eastern Europe; and potential EEC laws and policies regulating tourism, travel, and hospitality enterprises, all require careful examination and negotiation where possible to provide fair and equitable application to U.S. interests. These activities may well cause Asian and African countries to establish economic unions and pattern their laws on the EEC model. Thus a global system of uniform laws may ultimately govern hospitality development. International law concerns are also underscored by heavy foreign investment in U.S. hospitality facilities. All these activities stress the need for legally aware and knowledgeable graduates who can operate competently and in both environments. This aptitude will be the hallmark of the future hospitality entrepreneur.

Law-Ethics Interplay Mention of the role of law and ethics in service industry management is needed. Although the traditional view of free enterprise asserts that profit is the sole responsibility of management, a more recent commentator suggests that social responsibility has its place in a market economy. Instead of total adherence to the lowest common denominator of gamesmanship in which any means justify the ends of business success and profitability, this commentator argues that:

> The competitive and strategic rationality that has for so long been the hallmark of managerial competence must be joined to a more disinterested community centered rationality. Gamesmanship must be supplemented with moral leadership. (Goodpaster 1984)

The point of these ethical considerations is to displace reliance upon law alone as the arbiter of what is permitted and what is forbidden in the exercise of management rights with a more enlightened approach. That approach is to accept legal commands as establishing minimum standards of conduct and to exercise moral leadership in seeking to raise those standards in the business community. Ideally, exposure to ethical aspects of business will define the subject, acquaint the student with various business ethical theories, ask whether ethics has a place in business, and evaluate case studies to raise ethical dilemmas but not pass judgment upon the outcomes. Coverage will include international problems and sensitivity to intercultural ethical differences in approach and solutions.

Hospitality Law Course Treatment

The above law and ethics curriculum cannot be uniform in all cases, since the mission of the teaching institution, the focus of its curriculum, and available resources must be taken into account. Moreover, the level of experience of the instructor may result in greater emphasis upon one or another topic, as well as the sequence and style of presentation. The ethics material may be included on a topic-by-topic basis or may be treated separately. A suggested objective of the course should be issue recognition, analytical reasoning, and preventive legal management, as well as knowledge of relevant law principles. Lawyers are trained in law schools to practice law; hospitality executives are trained in hospitality management schools to be conversant, competent, and familiar with global legal issues and lawyers so as to manage successfully the legal aspects of their various job responsibilities. Moreover, these executives should be sensitized to ethical issues that affect hospitality management so as to enhance their role in contributing to the welfare of the entire community. This challenge is the embodiment of the moral leadership to which contemporary hospitality management aspires and reflects self-development rather than reliance on legal norms as the sole arbiter of management behavior.

Reference

Goodpaster, Kenneth E. 1984. The concept of corporate responsibility. In *Just Business: New Introductory Essays in Business Ethics*, ed. Tom Regan, p. 319. New York: Random House.

Bibliography

Buchholz, Rogene A. 1989. *Fundamental Concepts and Problems in Business Ethics*. Englewood Cliffs, N. J.: Prentice-Hall.
Clarkson, Kenneth W., Roger Leroy Miller, Gaylord A. Jentz, and Frank B. Cross. 1989. *West's Business Law. Text, Cases, Legal Environment*. 4th ed. St. Paul Minn.: West Publishing.
Cournoyer, Norman G., and Anthony G. Marshall. 1988. *Hotel, Restaurant and Travel Law*. 3rd. ed. Albany, N. Y.: Delmar Publishers.
Dunfee, Thomas W. et al. 1986. *Ethics and the MBA Core Curriculum*. Philadelphia: The Wharton School.
Friedman, Milton. 1984. The social responsibility of business is to increase profits. In *Business Ethics, Readings and Cases in Corporate Morality*, eds. W. Michael Hoffman and Jennifer M. Moore, pp. 126–131. New York: McGraw Hill.
Goodpaster, Kenneth E., and Thomas R. Piper. 1989. *Managerial Decision Making and Ethical Values—Course Module*. Boston: Harvard Business School.
Gould, Rodney E., Thomas J. Ramsey, and John E. H. Sherry. 1980. The 1980 UNIDROIT draft convention on the hotelkeeper's contract: A major attempt to unify the law governing innkeeper-guest liability, *Cornell International Law Journal*. 13(1): 33–60.

Halbert, Terry, and Elaine Ingulli. 1990. *Law and Ethics in the Business Environment*. St. Paul, Minn.: West Publishing.

Kemp, Frederick G., Jr., Jeremy L. Weisen, and John W. Bagby. 1990. *Legal Aspects of the Management Process*. 4th ed. St. Paul, Minn.: West Publishing.

Paust, Jordan L., Robert D. Upp., and John E. H. Sherry. 1984. *Business Law*. 4th ed. St. Paul, Minn.: West Publishing.

Sherry, John E. H. 1981. *The Law of Innkeepers*, rev. ed. Ithaca and London: Cornell University Press.

Sherry, John E. H. 1984. *Legal Aspects of Foodservice Management*. Chicago: National Institute for the Foodservice Industry; and New York: Wiley.

Sherry, John E. H. 1985. *Supplement to The Law of Innkeepers*. Ithaca and London: Cornell University Press.

Sherry, John E. H. 1988. A uniform approach to legal aspects of travel and tourism abroad. *International Uniform Law in Practice*, pp. 506–508. Rome: UNIDROIT; and Dobbs Ferry, New York: Oceana Publications.

Woods, Robert H., and Florence Berger, 1989. Teaching Social Responsibility. *The Cornell Hotel and Restaurant Administration Quarterly*. 30(2): 61–63.

8

Lodging Operations

Peter Jones

This article considers lodging operations, that is, the provision of accommodation within specially designed properties. It begins by considering what is meant by an "operation" and proposes the idea of an operational "system." After looking at some operational problems typically associated with all service businesses, it considers the exact nature of providing lodging services to customers. The different types of lodging operation are identified along with the management issues related to them. The article concludes by considering the lodging operation managers' "key result areas"—those areas of the business that must be managed effectively in order to achieve success.

Lodging Operations as a System

A lodging operation can be defined as "an operation that provides accommodation and ancillary services to people away from home" (Lockwood and Jones 1989). Consumers stay away from home for a wide variety of reasons—on vacation, on business, due to illness, and so on. There are therefore a wide range of lodging operations to accommodate them; the principal being hotels, motels, hostels/dormatories, and hospitals. But even within these broad categories there is wide variation, reflecting how long customers may stay and how much they are prepared to pay.

An effective way to understand all these different lodging operations is to consider them as a system. A system can be modeled as in Figure 1. It

Fig. 1. Systems model of a service operation.

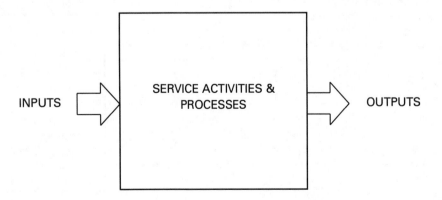

comprises "inputs"—all those resources needed to operate the system; "processes"—those activities carried out on these resources; and "outputs"—the results of adopting or changing the original inputs. In the case of the lodging industry, inputs would typically include buildings, furniture, a wide range of different types of staff, energy, and so on. There are then two main processes that are carried out relating to providing customers with rest or sleep and with sustenance or meals and drinks. And finally, the outputs of the lodging experience should be happy customers, satisfied workers, and profitable operating organizations.

The benefits the consumer purchases in terms of the lodging experience display many of the characteristics of typical services. These features have been identified (Sasser et al. 1978) as

Heterogeneity—each service experience is different

Perishability—if a service is not provided today that sale is lost forever

Intangibility—services, unlike products, cannot be sensed or measured easily

Simultaneity—the customer receives service at the same time as it is provided by the operator

These features make managing service operations so difficult. The ideal operation to manage has been described as one where "the market will absorb a single product at a continuous rate and as if the inputs flowed continuously at a steady rate and with specified quality" (Thompson 1967). In manufacturing, many of these features have been achieved through the introduction of mass production processes, automated technology, and large scale marketing. But a hotel, motel, or hospital meets few of these criteria, largely because of the characteristics of services identified above.

This can be explained by developing our systems model a little further. First, the processes and activities carried out in the operation can be thought of as "back-of-house" or "front-of-house." "Back-of-house" refers to all those parts of the operation not seen by the customer; "front-of-house" is all those areas that have a high degree of customer contact. As we have seen, in addition, lodging operations provide not just overnight accommodation, but also food and beverage services and products. This is illustrated in Figure 2.

The management structures of lodging operations tend to reflect this systems view. Reporting to the general manager (GM) there will typically be two operational managers: a food and beverage manager and a rooms manager. Other managers reporting directly to the GM may include functional specialists that support these two principal operating areas. Such specialists

Fig. 2. Systems model of a lodging operation.

	Back-of-House	Front-of-House
Accommodation	Linen room Housekeeping	Concierge Reception
Food & Beverage	Storage Kitchen	Bar Restaurant

INPUTS   OUTPUTS

Fig. 3. Management structure of a typical large hotel.

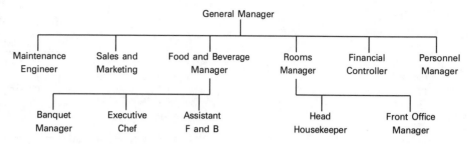

may include personnel, marketing, finance, maintenance, and security. Reporting to each of the operational managers will be assistant managers or department heads responsible for more specific areas of activity, such as the head chef, restaurant manager, executive housekeeper, front office manager and so on. This management structure is illustrated in Figure 3.

Since lodging operations are not one single operation but many, this means that the operations manager needs to understand some broad ideas about how to manage services in general, as well as some specific concepts about how to manage each part of the lodging operation in particular.

The Service Context

So far we have seen that providing a service has characteristics that cause operational problems and that the lodging operation is an extremely complex service. In order to understand its operation we need to examine the service context more fully. There are a range of approaches to examining service operations. One specific approach (Lockwood and Jones 1989) identifies specific features of lodging operations by comparing aspects of this service on two dimensional matrices (as proposed by Lovelock 1983).

The first question to consider is, what is the nature of the service act? Services can either be directed at people or at things. For instance, air transportation can move either passengers or freight. This provision can also be relatively tangible or not, on the basis that their effect on people is either physiological or psychological. A hotel therefore can be identified as a service that is directed at people in a reasonably tangible way, at least as far as providing rest during an overnight stay or meals in a restaurant. This is illustrated in Figure 4. Nonetheless evidence suggests (Nailon 1982) that intangible elements such as safety, security, and comfort are also significant in the

Fig. 4. Nature of the service act.

	Recipient of the Service	
	Person	Thing
Tangible	HOTEL	Laundry
Intangible	Theater	Banking

Level of Tangibility

Fig. 5. Customization and role of service personnel.

Level of Customization

	High	Low
High judgment	HOSPITAL Lawyer	?
Low judgment	HOTEL	BUDGET HOTEL Fast Food

Role of Service Personnel

lodging experience. These needs may vary quite considerably between a luxury hotel guest and a hospital patient.

Secondly, how standardized is the service act? If the ideal operation proposed by Thompson were the case, it would be totally standardized, with personnel engaged in entirely routine procedures. The reality is that the customer's participation in the service act enables a high degree of customization. The hotel customer, within the boundaries set by the operation, usually has a high degree of freedom over the sequence and nature of the individual events that make up the service experience. To this extent it is nonstandardized, particularly the more expensive and luxurious the operation is. At the same time the service personnel that deliver the service exercise little or no judgment in meeting customer needs. They are engaged in relatively routine operations, the timing of which is determined by the customer rather than by them. These two dimensions are illustrated in Figure 5.

Thirdly, what is the nature of the service operations relationship with the customer? This can be either continuous or discrete and can be directed at "members" or "nonmembers" as illustrated in Figure 6. As with the other analyses, placing lodging operations in this context is difficult. With regards to the time span, many transactions are clearly discrete, taking place at one specific moment in time, as for instance the chance guest staying over for one night. Other transactions are continuous however, as in the case of long-stay guests in hotels or patients in hospitals, or the relationship between a hotel and a corporate client. Similar difficulties occur when considering

Fig. 6. Relationship with customer.

Level of "membership"

	Member	Nonmember
Continuous	Patient plan	Radio station
Discrete	YMCA Frequent flyer	HOTEL

Time frame of transactions

"membership." Hotel guests are not members of the organization in the same way as you can become a member of a motoring organization or book club. But in many respects hotel guests feel and act as if they were members, particularly if they stay in the same property for any length of time. Indeed some hotel companies, such as Holiday Inn, have created membership schemes that offer customers special rates or facilities if they join the "frequent guest club." Also private patients create membership for those people who "lodge" in hospitals.

The final part of a lodging operations service context relates to the nature of demand and supply, as shown in Figure 7. Demand for accommodation is typically subject to many peaks and troughs, fluctuating widely over time according to the season, type of customers, and other factors. The physical infrastructure of the lodging operation means that its capacity, the number of rooms or beds, is fixed, so it is not always possible to cope with the peaks in demand.

Types of Lodging Operation

Many different types of property provide a lodging service. These range from five star, luxury hotels, through to motels, hostels, and hospitals. The issues identified previously impact in different ways on these types of operation.

Large hotels with a variety of facilities are potentially less affected by intangibility, heterogeneity, and perishability than highly focused smaller properties such as budget hotels, all-suite hotels, or motels. The latter are less flexible and attract a relatively narrow market. Whereas this may enable them to effectively develop a membership scheme, it does make them very vulnerable to market changes or competitive forces. The larger, more diversified property can adapt itself to changing circumstances by using its facilities to attract a broader spectrum of clientele. Typically, such hotels establish business with conference organizers, tour operators, the corporate travel market, individual tourists, and so on.

Likewise, lodging properties that are part of a chain face fewer problems than independently owned and operated units. By virtue of their geographic coverage, chain operators are much more likely to develop long-term corporate business and they can also generate referral business, that is, each hotel can promote and take reservations for all the other hotels in the chain. This spread of locations also has implications for the issues of membership, customization and management of demand. Chain hotels will find it very much

Fig. 7. Supply and demand.

Extent of Demand Fluctuations

	High	Low
Yes	Electricity	Insurance
Can peak demand be satisfied		
No	HOTEL	?

easier to foster a sense of "membership" among their clientele, even if they do not actively promote the concept as Holiday Inns have done. Also customization can be introduced by a chain offering a range of hotel types in a range of locations. Customers are not faced with a "take or leave it" choice that an independent hotelier has to offer.

Chains also manage demand in a very much more sophisticated way using the market intelligence available to them. They can create much higher levels of customer loyalty and repeat business; achieve economies of scale in marketing; afford to discount during slack periods while maintaining overall cash flow by maintaining tariffs in other hotel types within the chain; and they can transfer demand from one hotel to another, either through a central reservation system or even upon arrival if the hotel is overbooked.

For managers of operations in the institutional sector, hostels and hospitals, these issues and responses may appear to be less important. However, it has been demonstrated that commercial hotels and institutional lodging share many characteristics (Rice et al. 1981). These include a product that is an overnight stay; high investment cost; operating costs that are largely labor intensive; physical plant as a major focus of attention; reservations made through intermediaries; increasingly competitive markets; average size of units increasing; and relatively high occupancy rates. There is also a tendency to group together independent operators in all sectors, either through purchase by chains, merger, and takeover, or by creating and forming consortia. This trend derives from the advantages that a chain has over independents just discussed.

Operational Issues

By thinking of the lodging operation as a system and analyzing the service context in this way, it makes clear the extent to which management responses differ according to the type of lodging operation. It is possible to identify specific issues that the hotel manager must address. These issues are as follows: To what extent should hotel managers focus on the physical comfort and well-being of customers when compared with their psychological security? Attention clearly needs to be given to the intangible aspects of service, possibly by making them more tangible. This can be done operationally or through the marketing of the hotel. For instance, speed of service can be demonstrated by logging the time a guest makes orders and identifying when the request was acted upon, as in room service; and marketing material can have photographic illustrations of the property to show its style and comfort levels.

Second, there is a conflict between the customers' needs for customization and control over their service experience and the operational manager's desire for completely routine and standardized operations. This issue has been largely addressed by introducing technology to enable guests to receive service without the need for employees to deliver it. This includes self-dispense bars in rooms, guest checkout through in-room television, automatic telephone dialing, and so on.

Third, much of the marketing effort of hotels has been aimed at increasing guest "membership" either by following up guests to stimulate repeat business, developing corporate clients, or starting some sort of "club" scheme. This is greatly helped by the statutory requirement that guests register upon arrival, thereby providing the hotel with information about each guest that can be used for marketing purposes. Hotels often enhance the quality of this market intelligence by asking for additional information on the check-in form, for instance car registration or name of employing organization.

Finally, to respond to demand and supply characteristics operations managers attempt to make their physical infrastructure as flexible as possible, while marketing their property to maximize occupancy during slack periods.

Managing the Operations

For many years, the traditional approach to lodging operations was to focus on the process aspects of the system. Even today, many of the grading systems that categorize quality of hotels into five-star or four-star properties for instance, are based on measuring the inputs (size of room, equipment in the room, and so forth) and processes (floor service provision, coffee shop opening hours, and others). However, operations management theory argues that the most important focus should be on *outputs*. After all, it is the output of the operation that is purchased and experienced by the customer. In the final analysis, the operation will only be successful if customers continue to use the facility because it meets their needs.

One of the reasons for the lack of focus on outputs in lodging is that processes and outputs are mixed up. The customer becomes part of the process by entering the hotel and directly experiencing service there. Indeed, part of the service experience derives from the interaction customers have with each other. This comes back to the simultaneity characteristic of services.

If the operations manager should focus on outputs, what are these? Outputs have been described as *key result areas* (Lockwood and Jones 1989). Seven are relevant to the lodging industry, including

1. Protecting assets
2. Improving employee performance
3. Managing customer demand
4. Improving productivity
5. Ensuring customer service
6. Achieving satisfactory levels of return on investment
7. Managing quality

For each of these key result areas the operations manager sets specific objectives to be met. To meet these objectives the manager continually adjusts, develops, monitors, analyzes, and inspects those inputs and those processes designed to produce the desired outputs.

Protecting assets is clearly an important part of the operational management task. A lodging property is likely to be valued in millions of dollars with a wide range of assets, including the property itself, equipment and occupants, both employees and guests, and their belongings. These assets need to be protected from the normal wear and tear of day-to-day operation, as well as accidental threats such as fire, storm and other natural disasters, or deliberate threats such as pilferage, theft, arson, and explosion. Two distinct approaches are adopted to manage this key result area. Control procedures are carried out to monitor day-to-day problems and prohibit minor losses through negligence or deliberate acts. Such control includes things such as inspecting rooms, employing security staff, stocktaking, equipment repairs and so on. Such procedures and systems tend to put things right after the event rather than prevent the occurrence of the problem. Usually the operational managers and employees of the hotel are involved in these activities.

The second approach is an assurance strategy designed to prevent or minimize major threats. Measures adopted include smoke detectors, monthly systematic inspections, security responses to bomb threats and fire outbreaks, and so on. This type of activity is usually managed and carried out by the functional specialists, such as the property's maintenance engineers or security manager.

As well as managing the physical aspects of the operation, the manager also has to manage employees. Because lodging operations tend to be labor intensive and much of customer satisfaction is derived from interactions with employees, this key result area requires a high degree of people management skill. One approach to this suggests that managers should clarify the roles of employees, provide positive feedback, personalize the causes of successful performance, personalize pride in accomplishment, encourage personal goal clarification, match the job with personal motives, remove supervisory blocks and organizational blocks (Cook 1980). All of the above need to be carried out in an organization where there is a strong sense of shared values and common purpose. All managers need to take responsibility for this, irrespective of whether employees are working front-of-house or back-of-house.

We have already discussed the key result area of managing customer demand. The most important operational aspect is the effective utilization of space or capacity. Lodging operations have fixed capacity so that either demand will exceed capacity or capacity will be greater than demand. Operational responses to these two alternatives then require the manager to modify some aspect of the operation, usually in terms of its price, promotion, distribution channels, or product. Price can be modified for different groups of customers or for different time periods. For instance, center city hotels often offer price reductions of weekend break packages to customers. Second, promotions, such as press advertising or direct mail, can be increased or decreased according to the time of year or designed to appeal to specific types of guest. Third, the property can be marketed through a range of channels, such as central advanced reservations, tour operators, and so on. And, finally, the product can be modified by closing all or part of the hotel during the off season, using room space flexibly through sofa beds and suites, developing amenities, and building new space when justified. These changes are increasingly being managed in an integrated way through the application of computers and so-called yield management systems.

Yield management systems also contribute to achieving the key result area of increasing income. As many of the costs of hotel operations are fixed, managing income and profit is largely affected by prices. There are two stages to setting accommodation tariffs. First there is the setting of the standard rack rate or room rate. In the commercial sector there are a variety of methods for doing this: marginal pricing, market-oriented pricing, and the so-called Hubbart formula. The Hubbart formula is based on achieving a desired level of profitability in relation to the capital investment cost of the property. In the institutional sector, break-even analysis is often used for price setting. Once price has been established, the second stage is to alter this price as little as possible in order to maintain occupancy, encourage repeat business, and attract new customers. One way to do this is by developing a model called the Asset Revenue Generating Efficiency Index, so that income performance is judged on the extent to which actual performance compares with targeted performance. This target is not necessarily 100 percent occupancy at standard rack rate, but the index of this appropriate for that particular operating period. So during the high season the target index may be

100 percent occupancy and standard rack rate, during the low season it may be 80 percent occupancy at two-thirds standard rack rate. Attention also needs to be given to income and profits from ancillary departments, such as restaurants, shops, laundry, and so on. In most cases however, room rentals are by far the largest proportion of income in a lodging operation. Clearly the rooms manager is largely responsible for this key result area.

Managing service is the fifth key result area and, like managing employees, is highly complex. The customer and the service provider can be seen as playing out a series of roles that have identifiable scripts, as if on the stage. For instance, taking a customers' meal order in the restaurant or checking a guest in have specific items of information that need to be determined by both parties to the interaction. Both parties are subject to stress that will affect the success of the interaction. The manager can reduce stress and ease the interaction by developing scripts that employees can use and by designing the service point so as to help all participants. It is also extremely likely that service is greatly influenced by the management style and shared values of people within the organization. This is often referred to as organizational "culture."

At a time when there are labor shortages and increasing competition in the lodging industry, managing productivity is a major issue. The systems model helps to illustrate what is meant by productivity, since it is usually defined as the ratio of inputs and outputs. In the lodging sector, measuring and improving productivity is made difficult by the complexity and intangibility of both inputs and outputs as discussed previously. Looking at back-of-house separately from front-of-house is one way of reducing problems. Back-of-house offers many more opportunities for productivity gains as operations there are independent of the customer. It is therefore possible to change processes to match them more closely with the ideal proposed by Thompson. This has been done by developing central reservations systems, central food production facilities, the design of hotel buildings and rooms and so on.

Finally, the manager must manage quality. There has been a great deal of emphasis on this key result area among lodging organizations in the 1980s and 1990s. Many have instituted quality improvement programs of some kind. In doing so, these organizations found that they had to be very clear about what is meant by "quality." For many people quality is commonly thought of as being absolute, that is to say that a five-star hotel is of a higher quality than a budget hotel. This is the wrong way to think about quality, because it is not comparing like with like. It is rather like comparing apples with bananas; although they are both fruit, a comparison is meaningless. The correct way to think of quality is to think of the extent to which the product or service meets the needs of the customers or users. Therefore there may be high-quality and low-quality five-star hotels, and there may be high-quality and low-quality budget properties.

In many respects, quality is inherent in all of the other six key result areas. The effective management of service, income, employees, and so on should result in a high-quality operation. However there are distinct advantages of focusing managers' and employees' attention on this area in terms of making sure that customers' needs are truly met. Quality, as a key result area, therefore shares some approaches and techniques employed in other areas. For instance, control strategies tend to be adopted back-of-house, whereas assurance strategies prevail front-of-house, because if quality is mismanaged back-of-house there is the opportunity to correct it before the customer is affected. For instance, if a room attendant does not service a room correctly, inspection by the head housekeeper can ensure the faults are corrected before the room is let to a guest. Assurance techniques need to be adopted front-of-house because employees do not get a second chance to put things right. Front-of-house staff therefore receive much more training in social skills, guest relations, and so on than back-of-house employees.

Summary

Service industries, including lodging operations, have the distinctive characteristics of perishability, intangibility, heterogeneity, and simultaneity. These features create special characteristics of service businesses and present the operations with specific operational problems. These can be analyzed by looking in more detail at the nature of the service act, the level of customization and judgement of contact personnel, the organization's relationship with its customers, and the nature of demand and supply. Such analysis reveals that the lodging experience has some tangible elements but the main element of providing overnight rest is largely intangible; transactions are typically discrete for individual customers but continuous for corporate clients; customers are not subscribing members of the organization, although there is a trend to encourage this; customization is derived from the availability of the physical services within the hotel rather than from service personnel; and hotels have to chase demand to fill off-peak periods.

Different types of lodging operation share these features but are able to respond in different ways. Chain lodging operations have many more available strategies than independently owned and operated properties. Large, all-purpose hotels are more flexible than properties designed in specific ways for quite specific market segments. Hostels and hospitals have major similarities with some of these commercial lodging operations.

One approach to understanding what the operations manager does in order to respond to these challenges is to identify key result areas. Seven have been identified. Their relative importance will differ from one type of operation to another, but they all exist and interact with each other in any type of operation. Successful managers select from the range of systems, procedures, policies, and approaches that are available to ensure successful performance within each area, at the same time understanding the relationship between each area.

References

Cook, D. April 1980. Guidelines for managing motivation. *Business Horizons*, pp. 61–69.

Lockwood, A., and P. Jones. 1989. *The Management of Hotel Operations*, London: Cassell.

Lovelock, C. H. 1983. Classifying services to gain strategic marketing insights. *Journal of Marketing* 47:9–22.

Nailon, P. 1982. Theory in hospitality management. *International Journal of Hospitality Management* 1(3):135–142.

Rice, J. A., R. S. Slack, and P. A. Garside. 1981. Hospitals can learn valuable marketing strategies from hotels. *Hospitals* 55(22).

Sasser, W. E., R. P. Olsen, and D. D. Wycoff. 1978. *The Management of Service Operations*. Boston: Allyn and Bacon.

Thompson, J. D. 1967. *Organizations in Action*. New York: McGraw Hill.

9

Organization Structure in the Hospitality Industry

Eliza Ching-Yick Tse

All organizations have a structure that influences the flow of information and the nature of human interactions, be it formal or informal. In a formal setting, structure is defined as "the sum total of the ways in which (the organization) divides its labor into distinct tasks and then achieves coordination between them" (Mintzberg 1972). Structure reflects the design of organizations in which work roles are allocated and the clearly defined lines of authority and communication between the different positions. In other words, structure is the formal arrangement of roles and relationships among people for getting work done in fulfilling the mission of any organization (Perrow 1967; Wheelen and Hunger 1989).

Key Elements of Structure

There are two characteristics of organization structure: the structural elements and structuring elements (Campbell et al. 1974). The structural elements describe the physical characteristics of an organization, such as size, span of supervisory control, and flat/tall hierarchy. Structuring elements refer to policies and activities occurring within the organization that prescribe or restrict the behavior of organization members, such as the degree of internal structure as measured by centralization, complexity, and formalization.

Structural Elements The size of an organization can be measured by annual sales, number of corporate staff and operating employees, as well as the number of hotel properties or restaurant units that a company owns. Span of supervisory control refers to the number of employees for which a supervisor has the direct responsibility. Flat or tall hierarchy describes the chain of commands in the organization by specifying the number of layers of management: flat hierarchy has fewer management levels than tall hierarchy. Depending on the age, size, the number of units, technology (the process of converting inputs into outputs), and the diverse nature of businesses, different structural types can be selected in organizing the various activities in a company. These are simple, functional, divisional, strategic business unit, and matrix.

Fig. 1. Simple structure: The owner/manager makes most decisions regarding the day-to-day operation.

Owner-
Manager
|
Employees

Like many companies in the United States, a large proportion of hospitality firms start with a simple structure (Figure 1) where the owner/founder has the absolute power over all the decisions made in the company. The company is considered to be highly centralized. As the business becomes successful and grows, the company expands its volume either through size increase or in the case of hospitality firms, increases in the number of operating units, especially through chain operations. The entrepreneur finds that he or she no longer has the time and expertise to oversee all the functional activities necessary to keep the company running efficiently. The logical arrangement of the company is then functional structure. The activities of the company are organized by the six functions of management: finance, operations, marketing, human resources, administration, and research and development. Managers of specialized areas are recruited to be in charge of each of these functional activities. With this, the level of complexity increases. At the same time, the company is decentralized as the decision-making power is delegated to functional managers or staffs. With the introduction of rules and standard operating procedures of performing activities, the company becomes more formalized.

Functional structure (Figure 2) is appropriate for companies that operate in a stable and predictable environment. All of the activity in the firm is organized by the functional areas of management, with staff that have expertise in each function. However, when a company continues to grow, if it so desires, it branches into different regions of the countries or into different markets. The headquarters of the company no longer finds it feasible to monitor and control all the activities throughout the organization. Communication and information flows become difficult and time consuming between the corporate office and operating units all over the country. Firms with functional structure find it slow to respond and adapt to environmental changes that require coordination across departments. This structure becomes disadvantageous for, say, chain operators to compete favorably with independent owners on a local basis if the lead time for decision making and communication takes longer than necessary.

Thus, the alternate structural form would be the creation of divisions (see Figure 3). When a corporation is organized on the basis of divisions, one more layer of management, division heads, is added between the top management team and the functional managers. The functional areas are then designed around products, clients, or territories. The company becomes decentralized in that the authority to make some of the decisions is shifted to the division heads. The divisional structure is appropriate for a firm that

Fig. 2. Functional structure: All activities in the firm are organized by the functional areas of management and with staff that have expertise in each function.

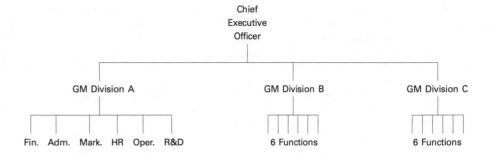

Fig. 3. Divisional structure: Appropriate when a firm diversifies its product/service lines, covers broad geographic areas, and serves different customer groups.

diversifies its product or service lines and serves many markets because it provides flexibility in decision making.

Throughout an organization's life cycle, some companies, such as McDonald's and Hilton, choose to remain in a single business. However, some companies diversify into either related or unrelated businesses by engaging in more than a single line of business or product or concept. For instance, in the 1970s Holiday Inn, in addition to its core hotel operations, diversified into over 30 different businesses. These different businesses generally are targeted for different markets so that different strategies are called for in order to gain competitive advantage. Marriott's nursing home group and contract foodservice require different sets of strategies than the lodging group in order to compete effectively. Thus, the appropriate structure for the company would be for each business to form a strategic business unit (SBU) (see Figure 4). For instance, General Mills was organized into consumer SBU, retail speciality SBU, and restaurant SBU. Each of these SBUs has its own customer base and target market. Each unit is run by a president and enjoys a good degree of autonomy and has its own set budget. Keeping the overall corporate mission and objectives in mind, the unit sets its own mission and strategies.

In matrix structures (Figure 5), functional and divisional areas are combined simultaneously at the same level of the corporation. Employees with a functional area expertise, such as marketing, are responsible to a functional manager (marketing VP) but at the same time are assigned to a divisional manager. Matrix structure is appropriate when the external environment is complex and ever-changing since it incorporates both the stability of the functional structure and the flexibility of the divisional structure. However, the disadvantage of this type of structure comes when conflicts arise with dual duties, authority, and resource allocation.

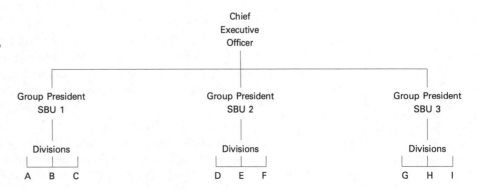

Fig. 4. Strategic business unit: In multibusiness companies, various divisions are grouped according to common strategic elements. Each SBU has a high degree of autonomy and its own budget.

Fig. 5. Matrix structure: Combines the characteristics of functional and product/project specialization and in large companies is used to control both skills and resources. It provides for dual channels of authority.

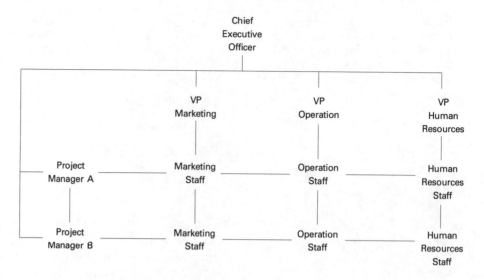

Structuring Elements

There are various measures to indicate the degree of structuring arrangements of an organization. The most common measures are centralization, complexity, and formalization. Centralization reflects how much of the decision-making authority is delegated to its employees throughout all levels of the organization (Hall 1977). It is the distribution of decision authority within the organization's hierarchy.

Centralization is measured by the lowest level in the organization with the authority to make decisions concerning operational and corporate levels of activities. Operational level decisions, such as number of unit production workers required, overtime to be worked at units, and hiring and firing of employees and managers, are generally delegated to unit management or the general manager. For decisions that concern multiunits, the multiunit managers, such as regional/district managers, have the authority to make decisions about the hiring and firing of unit managers. On the other hand, corporate level decisions—those decisions that involve the future course of the corporation or major resource allocation—are top management decisions. These include marketing expenditures and new advertising and promotion programs commonly made by the functional manager, such as the VP marketing, or VP operations. Issues such as expansion into new markets and allocation of resources are generally handled only by chief executive officers. A company is considered centralized if the power to make decisions is controlled by one or a few individuals. Decentralization occurs when employees of all levels have the opportunity to be involved in decision-making processes.

Complexity deals with the division of labor in a company and the degree of personal expertise within the organization, the distribution of official duties among a number of positions (Pugh et al. 1968). It is defined by the degree of specialization and task diversity. Organizational complexity is measured by a series of activities (functions) that are dealt with exclusively by at least one full-time individual. These activities include advertising or promotion, personnel hiring and training, purchasing and inventory control, financial resource management, operations and quality control, research and development, and administrative procedures.

Finally, formalization is the extent to which written rules, policies and procedures, and instructions exist and are used within an organization. The degree of formalization in a company is reflected by the presence of various documents such as employee handbooks, organization charts, a written mission statement, policy manuals, operating instructions and job descriptions and the extent to which these written manuals of procedures and rules are used throughout all company levels.

Mechanistic Versus Organic Structure

One of the factors that determines how a company is structured is technology. Technology is the process of transforming inputs (financial, human, and physical resources) into outputs (goods and services). The hospitality industry is a service-oriented industry in which customers become "partial employees" in that they are a part of the service delivery system. Thus, in every transaction the customers, being unique individuals, bring a certain degree of uncertainty to the process. Some researchers (Perrow 1967; Thompson 1967) have labeled service technology as knowledge technology, since the employee interacting with the customer carries the knowledge to solve the customer's problem (Chandrasekar and Dev 1989).

Burns and Stalker (1961) developed a continuum where the structure of an organization can be classified according to its technology: mechanistic versus organic. The "mechanistic" structure represents a high degree of specialization, division of labor, structured hierarchical control, vertical communication, centralized authority, and low autonomy. On the other hand, the "organic" structure allows less strict task differentiation, less clear hierarchy, more lateral communication, and a relatively higher degree of autonomy (Chandrasekar and Dev 1989). Different segments in the hospitality industry have different levels of technological requirements. Fast-food operations such as McDonald's, with routine technologies, are highly standardized in their operation procedures and more routine in their encounter with the customers so that the appropriate structure tends to be more mechanistic. This structure is compared to operations that experience more nonroutine technologies, such as white tablecloth theme restaurants where they provide highly differentiated services to the more demanding clientele. This type of operation would be better off with an organic structure. The technologies of most organizations tend to fall somewhere between these two extremes (Schaffer 1984).

Strategy, Structure, and Performance

As the hospitality industry enters the mature stage of its life cycle, the business environment in which the industry operates is more complex and competitive than ever. It requires firms in the industry to be adaptable to the external environment and select correct strategies for long-term survival and growth. The concept of strategy is generally believed to have effects on financial performance for a firm (Beard and Dess 1981). However, even though an organization may have a formulated strategy, this does not necessarily guarantee that the organization will achieve a desired performance. As Galbraith and Nathanson (1978) indicate, when implementing a chosen strategy, an organization has an array of structural forms and processes from which to choose. However, not all structural forms are equally effective in implementating a given strategy and the choice of structural forms has an impact on organizational performance. As an organization evolves through the different stages of its life cycle, strategy is generally believed to determine how it is structured (Chandler 1962). However, there also comes a time that the structure of a company contrains which strategy that it can espouse (Hall and Saias 1980). Whatever the circumstances may be, a match between strategy chosen and structural arrangement is essential for a company to gain positive performance. Thus, an organization's structural framework can be viewed as an important element relative to its overall strategy. This structural framework then becomes the vehicle through which all the resources (human, financial, as well as physical) are utilized to achieve the desired long-term objectives based on the mission of the organization (Chandler 1962).

With reference to the hospitality industry, Schaffer (1984, 1986) and Tse and Olsen (1988, 1990) have conducted empirical analyses to examine the relationship of strategy, structure, and performance. Focusing on the lodging industry, Schaffer indicated that the degree to which an organization is able to adapt not only its strategy, but also its structure to its situation affects its ultimate success. He used industry examples such as Hyatt, Holiday Inn, and Best Western to illustrate that strategy should be matched with appropriate structure in order to increase organizational effectiveness. Both Hyatt and Best Western were examples of successful cases in implementing strategies. Hyatt's strategy calls for developing unique hotels with differentiated high-quality services that cater to sophisticated affluent clientele in key market areas in the United States. The organization structure that Hyatt chose was a decentralized management system that provides management the needed flexibility to run each hotel. Best Western was organized as a "not-for-profit" association, that calls for an autonomous, decentralized structure to support the underlying strategy of the organization. The company's strategy was to enhance the individual operator's competitive position through centralized promotion and a national reservation system. On the other hand, structural considerations may have contributed to Holiday Inn's failure to achieve success when it diversified into over 30 businesses in the late 1970s. Holiday Inn's mission was then to move from a core hotel operation to become a travel business. However, this strategic move was not supported by any appropriate structural arrangements. The company failed to adapt from its relatively mechanistic organization to meet the needs of more diverse organizational acquisitions that operated in more dynamic environments. Thus, in the 1980s the company divested itself of most of its unrelated businesses and concentrated on its core brand again.

For the restaurant industry, Tse and Olsen surveyed 296 multiunit firms nationwide to examine the impact of strategy and structure upon performance. Restaurant firms varied in their strategy choices by the segment they were in, the geographic scope they covered, as well as the size of the company. Fast-food operations tend to pursue a strategy that emphasizes tight cost control and operational efficiency, whereas theme restaurants choose to compete by differentiating their products and services. Furthermore, it is generally found that those companies that match their strategies with the structures enjoy higher performances than those that do not. There were also significant differences in performance between companies in the sample with the various structural configurations. According to high and low formalization, high and low centralization, and high and low complexity. A company with a high degree of formalization, high degree of specialization, and low centralization enjoyed higher financial performances than companies of other structural configurations.

Summary

All organizations have structure. Structure refers to the properties internal to the organiztion such as locus of authority, levels of hierarchy, and line control of work flow. The two characteristics of structure: the structural and structuring were discussed. As a company evolves through the different stages of its life cycle, it can select the different structural types: simple, functional, divisional, strategic business unit, and matrix. The structural elements of an organization reflect the different degrees of centralization, complexity, and formalization of various activities. Depending on the different environmental conditions and internal processes (technology), a firm can have either a mechanistic or an organic structure. Finally, the relationship of strategy and structure upon performance was examined. A match of appropriate strategy and structure is essential for hospitality firms to survive in this competitive environment.

References

Beard, D. W., and G. G. Dess. 1981. Corporate-Level Strategy, Business-Level Strategy, and Firm Performance. *Academy of Management Journal* 24(4):663–688.

Burns, T., and G. Stalker. 1961. *The Management of Innovation.* Chicago: Quandrangle Books.

Campbell, J. P., D. A. Bownas, N. G. Peterson, and M. D. Dunnette. 1974. *The Measurement of Organizational Effectiveness: A Review of the Relevant Research and Opinion.* San Diego: Navy Personnel Research and Development Center.

Chandler, A. D. 1962. *Strategy and Structure.* Cambridge, Mass.: The MIT Press.

Chandrasekar, V., and C. S. Dev. 1989. *International Journal of Hospitality Management.* 8(3):237–245.

Galbraith, J. R., and D. A. Nathanson. 1978. *Strategy Implementation: The Role of Structure and Process.* St. Paul, Minn.: West Publishing Co.

Hall, R. H. 1977. *Organizations: Structure and Process.* Englewood Cliffs, N.J.: Prentice-Hall.

Hall, D. J., and M. A. Saias. 1980. Strategy follows structure! *Strategic Management Journal* 1:149–163.

Mintzberg, H. 1972. *The Structuring of Organizations.* Englewood Cliffs, N.J.: Prentice-Hall.

Perrow, C., 1967. A framework for the comparative analysis of organizations. *American Sociological Review* 32(2):194–208.

Pugh, D. S., D. F. Hickson, C. R. Hinings, and C. Turner. 1968. Dimensions of organization structure. *Administrative Science Quarterly.* 13(1):65–105.

Schaffer, J. D. 1984. Strategy, organization structure and success in the lodging industry, *International Journal of Hospitality Management* 3(4):159–165.

Schaffer, J. D. 1986. Competitive strategy, organization structure and performance in the lodging industry: an empirical assessment of Miles and Snow's (1978) perspective of organization, Unpublished Ph.D. dissertation, Virginia Polytechnic Institute and State University, Blacksburg, Va.

Thompson, J. D. 1967. *Organizations in Action.* New York: McGraw-Hill.

Tse, E. C., and M. D. Olsen. 1988. The impact of strategy and structure on the organizational performance of restaurant firms. *Hospitality Education and Research Journal* 12(2):265–276.

Tse, E. C., and M. D. Olsen. 1990. Business strategy and structure: a case of US restaurant firms. *Journal of Contemporary Hospitality Management* 2(3):17–23.

Wheelen, T. L., and J. D. Hunger. 1989. *Strategic Management and Business Policy,* 3d ed. Reading, Mass.: Addison-Wesley.

10

The Multinational Firm

Frank M. Go

The concept of the multinational firm dates from the early seventeenth century. In 1602 the East Indies Company was founded in Amsterdam in the United Provinces known today as the Netherlands. At the time it was the greatest "multinational trading" corporation in the world. However, it was many years after the ships of the East Indies company plied the oceans until the name "multinational" was introduced.

In April 1960, David E. Lilienthal, once head of the Tennessee Valley Authority, gave a paper at the Carnegie Institute of Technology entitled "Management and Corporations, 1985," published later that year as "the Multinational Corporation." In his work Lilienthal focused on the specific problems that directly involved managerial responsibility encountered by American corporations with operations abroad. He defined the multinational firm as "Such corporations—which have their home in one country but which operate and live under the laws and customs of other countries as well" (Fieldhouse 1986:9). In essence, the multinational firm is a company whose operations transcend national boundaries.

In the past 30 years multinational hotel, restaurant, and leisure time related firms have become more important. Much of the horizontal related expansion involving multinational firms has been driven by the emergence of new business centers around the world, foreign direct investment (FDI), and the growing volumes of leisure and corporate travelers.

A growing number of hospitality and travel firms are operating on a multinational scale. This change has forced a rethink of marketing goals, business strategy, and organizational structure in many organizations.

The terms international, transnational, and multinational are not well defined in general usage, even among business practitioners. For this purpose the term transnational corporation (TNC) has been used interchangeably with multinational corporation (MNC) or multinational enterprise (MNE). Typically MNC signifies a firm owned and managed in one country, whereas the TNC is usually owned and managed by nationals in different countries.

The role of transnational corporations and their relationship to international tourism was the focus of a United Nations study (1982). Since that study was released the transnational movement among companies has gained considerable strength. By the mid-1980s, 40 percent of the stock of foreign direct investment held worldwide by U.S., Japanese, Western, and a few Third World transnationals were in service industries, compared with 20 percent in the mid-1950s. And over half of the additional US $60-billion foreign investment that flows across borders each year is going into service industries (UNCTC 1988).

In 1980, services constituted over 60 percent of world gross domestic product (GDP), however, only 8 percent of these services were traded internationally. This may serve as a possible indication of the available potential for the expansion of transnational corporations in the service sector, including travel and tourism (UNCTAD 1984:4), a significant component of the TNC service sector. The picture is far from complete because services are not accounted for separately in the investment figures of some countries, and in fact there is not full agreement over what constitutes a service. With the growing interest in the service sector, there has been a proliferation of proposals of definitions and services typologies. It seems that to date there is no universally accepted theoretical and operational framework to distinguish services distinctively from other economic activities.

Some corporations are a mixture of manufacturing and service activities. Specialized service companies such as accounting firms have extended into other areas such as management consulting because of economics of scale advantages. Four main emerging clusters may be distinguished in the transnational service sector: (1) financial services, including banking and insurance; (2) data processing services, such as software services, telecommunications, information storage and retrieval services; (3) professional services, including accounting, management consulting, advertising, market research and public relations; (4) tourism and travel services, including hotels, airlines, tour operators, car rentals, air transportation, and global travel distribution systems (UNCTC 1988:404).

Rise of Multinational Firm

In the past 30 years tourism has perhaps been more affected and in its turn has had a profound effect on economic and social development internationally. Dicken (1986) suggests that foreign direct investment (FDI) is either market-oriented or supply (cost)-oriented. Much of the tourism related horizontal expansion across boundaries has been driven by demand derived from business and pleasure travel. The reasons for this demand have been earlier observed. But which specific determinants made possible multinational tourism activity?

The expansion of foreign travel and tourism TNCs was caused in particular by the following factors:

1. The emergence of new business centers throughout the world, in particular in the Middle and Far East, and the competition between the newly industrialized countries (NICs) to become the leading commercial and financial center resulted in a hotel construction boom and a big development opportunity for TNCs active in tourism.
2. The size of geographic location and of origin countries. The extent of foreign travel depends to a high degree on income levels, levels of education, and so forth, but is also heavily dependent on the size of the country of origin and its geographic location. For example, European travelers are much more likely to cross borders than

North American European travelers although the latter may travel a longer distance.

3. Government policy. Governments tend to play a significant role in either stimulating or restricting the growth of international tourism. A wide variety of barriers to travel may be found around the world: restraining the flow of persons; administrative delays that hinder licensing, for example to start the construction or operation of a hotel; and discrimination against national flag carriers. In contrast, government incentives can encourage many corporations involved in tourism to expand their activities to these newly industrialized countries. For instance the Spanish government's encouragement and support of tourism helped turn the country into one of the world's major mass-tourism destinations. Currently, the government of Turkey offers incentives to lure local and foreign investors to develop tourist facilities there (Baki 1990:61–62).

4. Multinational infrastructure. Most international business transactions in tourism, including the transfer of capital, technology, management know-how, and operations across national borders involve multinational or transnational corporations. Their travel infrastructure facilitates international tourism especially to and in developing countries (Ajami 1988; McQueen 1989:287). For example, the growth of air charters made possible rapid increases in traffic from North America to Europe, from northern Europe to the Mediterranean, and on a more limited scale from Europe to more distant locations such as Kenya, Thailand, and the Caribbean. Later, wide bodied jet aircraft increased both speed and comfort of air travel and led to a reduction of airfares. Hotel corporations and credit card companies offered "service networks" to international travelers sometimes following and in other instances leading customers (Heskett 1986).

The emergence of transnational corporations in tourism has contributed significantly to more effective operations, the efficient utilization of resources and the growing globalization of the economy in the 1990s. But the involvement of TNCs in tourism has also given rise to myriad challenges at the host nation level.

Character of the Multinational Firm

No matter what their country of origin, modern multinational firms share three common characteristics: (1) They appeared quite suddenly in the 1880s and 1890s in Western Europe, the United States, and somewhat later in Japan; (2) They were established and continued to grow in industries with similar technologies of production; (3) They expanded their activities in much the same manner (Chandler 1986:31).

The TNC is essentially a multiplant firm whose operations transcend national boundaries and may be defined as "an enterprise which owns and controls income generating assets in more than one country" (Fieldhouse 1986). The primary goal of TNCs has been to achieve long-term profits and one of the surest ways to attain and maintain this goal has been to reduce unit costs (Chandler 1986:31). TNCs share many common characteristics, but the following managerial features (Weekly and Aggarwal 1987:310–311) are particularly relevant to our discussion:

(1) A multinational corporation is an integrated worldwide business system. Such integration is evidenced through resource transfers, that is, movement of capital, technology, and managerial personnel between parent and affiliates and among affiliates themselves which allows the MNC to acquire materials and produce component parts wherever it is most advantageous to do so.
(2) MNCs are ultimately controlled by a single managerial authority (typically the top management group of the parent company) which makes the key, strategic decisions relating to the operations of the parent firm and all its affiliates. Such centralization of management is imperative for achieving and maintaining worldwide integration and for attaining the basic objective of profit maximization for the multinational enterprise as a whole;
(3) Managers of MNCs, especially the central management group, are presumed to possess a "global perspective." This means that the top managers regard the entire world as the relevant frame-of-reference for making the kinds of resource acquisition, focus of production, and market decisions.

The expansion of transnational corporations in tourism in the 1970s and 1980s may be explained by Dunning's paradigm (1981) whose model of international production asserts that the extent, pattern, and growth of value-added activities undertaken by multinational firms outside their national boundaries is dependent on the value of and interaction between three main variables: (1) ownership-specific advantages of multinational firms, (2) location-specific advantages of countries, (3) market internalization or coordinating advantages.

Ownership-Specific Advantages The concept of ownership advantage refers to the competitive advantage of multinational corporations over other firms (either domestic or foreign) in the country in which they are producing and typically arises from the MNC's ownership and ability to combine geographically dispersed activities.

Several factors in particular contribute to the competitive or ownership advantage of MNCs in the hospitality industry:

- The provision of high quality services, including such attributes as design, comfort, performance, efficiency, degree of professionalism, and attitude toward customers. The hospitality firm's trademark guarantees a certain desired quality level providing a significant competitive advantage on a firm, especially where customers are consuming the service in an unfamiliar environment.
- The ability of international hospitality chains to enter new markets faster and easier due to a set of intangible assets and logistical skills that it can provide to any newly associated hotel at a lower cost than (potential) new entries into the hotel business.
- Their managerial and organizational expertise allow for technically superior methods of production in the day-to-day production, control, and maintenance of hotels. Their ability to invest in training hotel staff allows for the recruitment and retaining of better staff by offering better promotional prospects over other firms (Dunning and McQueen 1982: 83–84).
- The availability of a global travel reservation system is generally also perceived by international travelers as beneficial and a means to facilitate the booking process (UNCTC 1988: 429).

In addition to economies of scale that may apply to tourism corporations, large multinational firms have other advantages. For instance, they may obtain supplies more cheaply than small firms because of available discounts. As a result of their bargaining power when implementing international advertising campaigns, they may be able to negotiate lower marketing costs. And because of their resources they may be able to attract and retain quality staff. International hotel chains for instance, tend to operate properties larger than their domestic rivals. Their size affords them the opportunity to profit from differential factor costs, the international specialization of value-adding activities, and the economies of management arising from their ability to move people between the different parts of the same organization.

The trend toward mega-organizations, events, and attractions in tourism to exploit scale economies and other benefits appears clear (Ritchie and Yangzhou 1987; Middleton 1988; Wheatcroft 1990; Go and Dev 1990; Holloway 1989:125–126). As this trend evolves, the involvement of multinational firms in mega-attractions and resorts will be inevitable because of the high levels of capital investment, expertise, and international marketing presence required in today's market. The themeparks by Disney Productions and Universal Studios provide evidence of this trend in the entertainment sector. And the mega-resorts developed by the Hyatt Corporation point toward potential polarization in the resort industry: mega-resorts on the one end of the continuum and boutique resorts on the other.

Technologies typical of service industries are primarily skill- and experience-oriented and intensive, requiring considerable organization and management capabilities (UNCTC, 1988:429). The "personality intensity" (Normann 1984:10) of tourism services is significant in that the quality supplied to customers is, in large measure, the result of how the host performs in a specific situation. Hence, tourism organizations are very dependent on social innovation to mobilize human energy and skills thereby enhancing quality and cost efficiency.

Multinational hotel and travel firms headquartered in the United States, Europe, and Japan enjoy a competitive advantage over their rivals in the host country because of their favored access to their domestic markets, their knowledge of what these respective customers want, and through collaboration with airlines and tour operators often based in the same locale. Consequently, TNCs active in tourism tend to attract a certain clientele and therefore influence the type of tourism in a particular destination (United Nations 1982:81).

Location-Specific Advantages

Hotel and tourism corporations that possess the competitive advantages described in the preceding section have a choice of where they engage their value-adding activities. Several variables determine whether the multinational hotel firm will become involved in a country by establishing a facility. They are broadly similar to those facing firms in other economic sectors, for example the size and growth of demand; the policy of the host government toward foreign enterprise; and the general political, social, and economic stability of the country (McQueen 1989:288; Go et al. 1990:299–300).

Last but not least location is critical in that it determines both the destination and the hotel's position within the destination. Typically, city center hotels cater to the business traveler and resorts tend to attract pleasure travelers. However, these distinctions are becoming increasingly blurred because resort hotels attract a growing number of conventions and meetings. And, on the other hand, city center hotels, which cater primarily to business-persons on weekdays attempt to appeal to the leisure market during weekends through discounted room rates (Witt et al. 1991:24).

The siting of hotels in resort areas depends to a great extent on the location of the scenery, climate, and amenities desired by visitors. In addition to these general reasons, several very specific factors (UNCTC 1988:423) influence the location of TNCs active in tourism services, such as:

1. Being close to markets of significant size or assured of convenient access at reasonable transportation fares.
2. Having the organizational capability to adapt products so that these coincide with the local infrastructure.
3. Being able to employ key human resources at reasonable wages.
4. Having access to suppliers who produce a wide variety of goods and services that are required for the operation of hotels.

Internalization Advantages   Since it is difficult in the diverse travel and tourism market to organize efficient intermediate product markets, there is a strong incentive for hotel firms to internalize these markets. Internalization is typically exercised through the acquiring of control over resources either through ownership of equity capital or through contracts (Dunning and McQueen 1982:83). Through the internalization process multinational firms create their own internal markets, which on the one hand increases their power and on the other hand increases their efficiency in the allocation of resources (Dunning and McQueen 1982:83; Litteljohn 1985).

The internalization of market transactions varies according to the type of service being exchanged and the market conditions in the host countries. In general however, the propensity to establish joint ventures or nonequity arrangements in the services sector has been greater than in the manufacturing sector. A major reason that the entry mode of TNCs in the hotel, restaurant, and car-rental industries has primarily involved joint ventures or nonequity agreements can be traced to the possibility of codifying and controlling the key competitive advantages of such service firms in a management contract or franchising agreement (UNCTC 1988:437).

Advantages that are especially relevant to explaining TNC internalization activities include (1) the sellers need to protect quality of intermediate or final products; (2) the reassurance of buyer uncertainty about the nature of the product sold through branding and; (3) the avoidance of negotiations costs and government intervention. Despite the significance of licensing and contracting in the services sector, foreign direct investment (FDI) is a concern.

Foreign Direct Investment

The economic development potential that TNCs may unleash should be a strong argument for developing countries to foster foreign direct investment (FDI). However, a major problem is that service industries and tourism in particular were up to recently not perceived by most authorities in industrialized and developing nations to make a positive contribution to the international balance of trade (Normann 1984:6).

Worldwide investment by transnational corporations has undergone dramatic change, spurred on by the revolution in communications and technology and the growing importance of the service industries in the economy. The growing significance of the service sector is attested to by negotiations on international trade in services that were held as part of the 100-nation Uruguay Round of trade talks, begun in 1986 and scheduled to adjourn by the end of 1990 (Segal 1988).

The conditions under which transnational service companies establish business affiliates around the world is central to the negotiations, as many developing countries are worried that their own infant service industries will be driven out of business by entering transnationals. This has been a strong argument for developing countries to build up their own service industries. Meanwhile, the newly democratized economies of Central and Eastern Europe have recognized that linkages between the service sector and other sectors of the economy, including manufacturing and agriculture, are desirable and that transnational corporations operating in tourism can play a vital role in the creation of employment, output growth, and development. Franck (1990), for example, examines how investments by transnational corporations are turning tourism into a services sector of growing importance in Central and Eastern European economies. Specifically, Franck makes reference to five important economic effects attributed to tourism, namely the balance of payments effects; the equalizing effect, that is, surpluses in tourism equalize deficits in the balance of payments and vice versa; the effect on employment; the multiplying effect; and the net product effect, which refers to the production of goods and services in the host country itself, leading eventually to a rise in national wealth (Franck 1990:333).

Tourism is a major factor in the generation of hard currency for many nation-states, and may be used by governments to reduce the national debt or the balance of payments without losing nonrenewable resources (Edgell 1985; Mathieson and Wall 1982). Multinational firms are heavily involved in transnational transactions that affect balance of payments and have frequently been linked to problems, such as causing or aggravating balance of payments deficits (Weekly and Aggarwall 1987:317).

Franck draws an important relationship between the balance of payments effects, the equalizing effect, and the multiplying effect. He points to the need for a coherent economic strategy and a massive input of capital to improve the neglected infrastructure and obsolete technology in Central and Eastern Europe (Go and Ritchie 1990).

Franck further suggests that the problem of financing in Central and Eastern Europe is augmented by existing debts incurred by the countries in this region. Hence financing in the tourism sector is likely to follow one or a combination of three possible scenarios, namely joint ventures, debt to equity swaps, and leasing.

Halfway around the world developed nations such as Australia have rather recently discovered the potential economic benefits of tourism. One of Australia's main tourist markets, Japan, is, as mentioned earlier, leading the change of direction in worldwide TNC investments. Foreign investment in services by Japanese companies rose from around 25 percent of their total outstanding FDI in 1975 to 57 percent in 1986. Bull (1990) attempted to investigate the net benefit of FDI in Australian tourism. He identified four main theories for foreign investors and suggests that Australia's main policy to guide tourism development, like those of most other countries, aims at earning substantial net foreign revenues.

Japan is often popularly considered as the leading investor in terms of total FDI. But a study of recent mergers, acquisitions, and foreign investments in Canada conducted by Desautels and Christensen (1990) reveals that, at least in Canada, "there seems to be no dominant country although the United States and Pacific Rim countries especially Japan and Hong Kong are the most prominent." For instance, construction in 1985 of the $110 million Pan Pacific Hotel owned by the Tokyo Group and the $42 million Mandarin hotel, originally owned by the Hong Kong Land Ltd., seem to have started the trend of accelerating off-shore tourism related investment in Canada.

A study by Murakami and Go (1990) focuses on how the "land of the rising sun" has become an international economic force to reckon with and it discusses how a growing number of Japanese corporations seem to be entering the tourism and leisure business as part of their diversification strategy. Finally it chronicles the dramatic internal transition Japan is going through and analyzes the implications of internationalization on Japanese TNCs and the country. However, the United States still ranks as top investor in services around the world. It accounts for 95 of the 246 transnational service companies, compared to Japan's 65, and nearly half of their affiliates, of which 5,200 are in developing countries (UNCTC 1988).

Strategic Orientation   The premise of strategic management is for the organization to adapt continuously to its changing environment so that it will survive, and better yet, succeed. This notion applies also to hospitality firms (Dev and Olsen 1989; West and Olsen 1989) and the multinational firm. The environment decision-makers select for their organization to operate in and the attitude or orientation toward the selected business environment results in five possible orientations to international business. Firms may or may not choose to go through a learning curve changing from one orientation to another over time. Each orientation suggests a particular corporate culture, organizational goals, strategies, and structure.

1. Little or no interests in operating abroad. The domestic market satisfies their expansion needs and foreign operations are often viewed as complicated and risky. Perlmutter (1967) identified four distinctive orientations associated with successive phases in the evolution of the internationalization process of firms.
2. Ethnocentrism or home-country orientation. Some firms view foreign operations as an "appendix" to domestic operations. A hospitality organization with this orientation tends to build its hotels or restaurants in foreign markets that are most like the home country. Usually, firms who fit in this category will not conduct extensive market research or adapt promotional activities to respond to foreign markets. Canada, a foreign country but near and similar to the United States remains a favorite international market for American multinational firms to expand to.
3. Polycentrism or host-country orientation. Some firms establish in each foreign or overseas market. Often these subsidiaries are managed by nationals and marketing activities are planned and administered on a country-by-country basis.
4. Regiocentrism or regional orientation. Certain firms gear their operations to a particular continental region, such as North America, which incorporates the United States and Canada, countries with similar economies and cultures. The regional orientation affords firms opportunities to pursue market segments that cross national boundaries and potential scale economies.
5. Geocentrism or global orientation. Some firms view the world market as their oyster. Levitt (1983) is a strong advocate of firms offering globally standardized products that are advanced, functional, reliable, and low-priced and is of the opinion that only companies that pursue this global approach will be successful in the long-term.

However, the global marketing approach as advocated by Levitt should be rejected as less desirable for tourism and hospitality marketing because of the societal and cultural differences between nations. It must be combined with a sensitivity for local customs and culture (Ziff-Levine 1990).

Transnational corporations have been subject to a lot of attention attributable to their size, power, and impact on the economic, social, cultural, and political environment of host societies around the world. Fieldhouse (1986:17) identified four central responses to the TNC phenomenon in the literature since the late 1960s: (1) those of popular alarmists; (2) theorists hostile to international capitalism; (3) applied economists, and (4) specialists in the theory of the firm. In surveying the aforementioned four central responses however, he found that one central theme seemed to emerge, namely "that while most early writers tended to accept the alleged universality of the MNC as a form of capitalism, many also asserting that its effects were harmful to both home and host countries, by the later 1970s both assumptions were in serious doubt."

Jafari (1988:289) observes a parallel development in the literature pertaining to TNCs especially as regards tourism in developing nations:

> First came those (Publications) which urge the developing countries to attract international tourism in order to expedite their process of development. Then came awareness of publications which hypothesized or attempted to document that tourism far from contributing, actually retards the process and also generates much unwanted socio-economic costs. Finally came those perspectives which acknowledged both the touristic prospects and problems and suggested ways to maximize the positive and minimize the negative.

Two issues seem relevant and significant to the potential involvement of transnational corporations in the tourism industry in a host society. First is the development role, if any, that these TNCs can play in the industry and host nation. The second corollary issue pertains to the way in which a particular nation views TNCs and the package of policy instruments it formulates to ensure that their participation is compatible with over-all goals of economic development (United Nations 1982:2). The latter process is heavily influenced by whether a nation is a net contributor or a net recipient of the resources that are being reallocated by the TNCs (Weekly and Aggarwall 1987:316).

Summary

The international travel and tourism industry is vast, diverse, and complex. Rather than analyzing it in an exhaustive manner an attempt has been made in this article to obtain a general understanding of the TNC phenomenon, its growth, and the issues confronting the various industry players, travelers, home and host governments.

The emergence of transnational corporations in tourism has contributed significantly to more effective operations and the efficient utilization of resources. The conduct of transnational corporations, often misunderstood, is influenced by their quest to conquer world markets by constantly exploiting industry and environmental changes.

Multinational firms attempt to exploit the advantages that flow from the paradigm of international production. Specifically they try to achieve their goal by

- Beating trade problems. Where to locate to attract desirable markets?
- Avoiding political problems. Which location offers a politically stable environment?
- Sidestepping regulatory hurdles. Who to merge with or join to avoid licensing and/or regulatory hassles?
- Balancing costs. Where to shift production to run operations at higher average capacity and keep capital costs down?
- Winning technology breakthrough. Being deployed globally helps to develop localized products at the lowest possible cost (Business Week 1990).

Several challenges have arisen as a result of the involvement of TNCs in tourism. In general TNCs have been subject to a lot of attention attributable to their size and impact on host nations around the world. Specifically, the conduct of transnational tourism corporations has given rise to serious problems, real or perceived, especially at the destination level causing local residents in developing nations for example, to leave traditional jobs in agriculture and manufacturing for work in TNC tourism facilities and in the process bring about labor shortages in traditional economic sectors (de Kadt 1979). TNCs must, in their own interest, become more sensitive to matters regarding the host environment in which they operate.

In the new era of the 1990s, few institutions have the potential to help make a contribution to solve humanity's problems like TNCs. A growing number of TNCs are providing evidence of this by their establishing of facilities in Central and Eastern Europe. This region's abandonment of the communist system has caused massive unemployment among workers who had been employed in traditional economic sectors. The "opening up" of Central and Eastern European borders has brought an onslaught of tourists and "hosts" totally unprepared for their new role. TNCs will play a pivotal part in transferring skills and expertise from West to East.

It is true that the imperatives of economies of scale, technology, and internationalization are leading to a greater convergence in tourism. Steps must be taken to ensure that convergence does not result in the type of standardization fashionable in the 1960s and 1970s for example in the hotel industry. Today's pluralistic travel market offers many opportunities for large and small scale enterprises alike to thrive in a chaotic business environment. In certain instances it will be possible and plausible to foster symbiotic relationships between small-scale entrepreneurial and large-scale tourism operations. In most cases closer cooperation between TNCs and host communities in tourism may lead to partnerships that help destinations on the local level celebrate their unique and cultural differences.

To be sure these are complex and challenging tasks but well worth responding to.

References

Ajami, Riad A. 1988. Strategies for tourism transnationals in Belize, *Annals of Tourism Research* 15(4):517–530.

Baki, A. 1990. Turkey: redeveloping tourism, *The Cornell H.R.A. Quarterly* 31(2):60–64.

Bull, Adrian. 1990. Foreign investment: the effects in Australian tourism, *Tourism Management,* 11(4):325–331 (December).

Business Week. 1990. The Stateless Corporation, May 14 (No. 3159):98–104.

Chandler, Alfred D., Jr. 1986. Technological and organizational underpinnings. In

Multinational Enterprise in Historical Perspective, ed. Alice Teichova, Maurice Levy-Leboyer, and Helga Nussbaum. Cambridge: Cambridge University Press.

de Kadt, Emanuel. 1979. *Tourism Passport to Development?* New York: Oxford University Press.

Desautels, Bob, and Julia Christensen. 1990. Hospitality trade development in Canada: mergers, acquisitions and foreign investment, *Tourism Management* 11(4):305–314.

Dev, Chekitan S., and M. D. Olsen 1989. Environmental uncertainty, business strategy, and financial performance: an empirical study of the U.S. lodging industry. *Hospitality Education & Research Journal* 13(3):172.

Dicken, Peter. 1986. *Global Shift, Industrial Change in a Turbulent World.* London: Harper & Row.

Dunning, John H. 1981. *International Production and the Multinational Enterprise.* London: Allen and Unwin.

Dunning, John H., and Matthew McQueen 1982. Multinational corporations in the international hotel industry, *Annals of Tourism Research* 9(1):69–90.

Edgell, David, L., Sr. 1985. *International Trade in Tourism: A Manual for Managers and Executives,* Washington, D.C. (October).

Fieldhouse, D. K. 1986. The Multinational: A Critique of a Concept. In *Multinational Enterprise in Historical Perspective*, ed. Alice Teichova, Maurice Levy-Leboyer, and Helga Nussbaum, pp. 9–29. Cambridge: Cambridge University Press.

Franck, Christian. 1990. Tourism investment in Central and Eastern Europe—preconditions and opportunities. *Tourism Management* 11(4):333–338.

Go, Frank M., and Chekita S. Dev. 1990. The Internationalisation of the Lodging Industry—New Realities of the Nineties. Unpublished manuscript.

Go, Frank M., and J. R. Brent Ritchie. 1990. Introduction (to a Special Issue on Transnationalism and Tourism). *Tourism Management* 11(4):287–290.

Go, Frank, Sung Soo Pyo, Muzaffer Uysal, and Brian J. Mihalik. 1990. Decision criteria for transnational hotel expansion, *Tourism Management* 11(4):297–304.

Heskett, James L. 1986. *Managing in the Service Economy.* Boston: Harvard Business School Press.

Holloway, J. Christopher. 1989. *The Business of Tourism,* 3d ed. London: Pitman.

Jafari, Jafar. 1988. Publications in review, tourism transnational corporations and cultural identities, *Annals of Tourism Research* 15(4):289.

Levitt, Theodore. 1983. The globalization of markets, *Harvard Business Review,* (May/June), pp. 92–102.

Litteljohn, David. 1985. Towards an economic analysis of trans/multinational hotel companies, *International Journal of Hospitality Management* 4(4):157–165.

McQueen, Matthew. 1989. Multinationals in tourism. In *Tourism Marketing and Management Handbook,* Eds. Stephen F. Witt and Luiz Moutinho pp. 285–289. New York: Prentice Hall.

Mathieson, Alister, and Geoffrey Wall. 1982. *Tourism economic, physical and social impacts.* Burnt Mill, Harlow Essex: Longman Scientific and Technical.

Middleton, Victor T. C. 1988. *Marketing in Travel & Tourism.* Oxford: Heinemann.

Murakami, Kazuo, and Frank Go. 1990. The Internationalization of Japan: Implications for Transnational Corporations, *Tourism Management* 11(4):348–353.

Normann, Richard. 1984. *Service Management Strategy and Leadership in Service Businesses.* Chichester: Wiley

Perlmutter, Howard J. 1967. Social architectural problems of the multinational firm. *Quarterly Journal of AIESEC International,* 3(3) (August).

Ritchie, J. R. Brent, and Ju Yangzhou. 1987. "The Role and Impact of Mega-Events and Attractions on National and Regional Tourism: A Conceptual and Methodological Overview," Vol 28 *Proceedings of the 37th AIEST Congress* held in Calgary, Canada (23–29 August), pp. 17–57. St. Gall, Switzerland: Association of Scientific Experts in Tourism.

Segal, Gerald. 1988. *The Stoddart Guide to the World Today.* Toronto: Stoddart Publishing.

UNCTAD. 1984. *Services and the Development Process,* United Nations Conference on Trade and Development, Twenty-ninth Session, 10 September, Geneva.

UNCTC. 1988. New York: United Nations Centre for Transnational Corporations World Bank (June 1972) *Tourism Sector Working Paper,* Washington D.C.: World Bank Group.

United Nations. 1982. *Transnational Corporations in International Tourism,* New York: United Nations Centre for Transnational Corporations (UNCTC).

Weekly, James K., and Raj Aggarwal. 1987. *International Business Operating in the Global Economy.* New York: The Dryden Press.

West, J. J., and M. D. Olsen. 1989. Competitive tactics in foodservice: are high performers different? *The Cornell HRA Quarterly* 30:68–71.

Wheatcroft, Stephen. 1990. Towards transnational airlines, *Tourism Management* 11(4):353–358.

Witt, Stepehn F., Michael Z. Brooke, and Peter J. Buckley. 1991. *The Management of International Tourism.* London: Unwin Hyman.

Ziff-Levine, William. 1990. The cultural logic gap—a Japanese tourism research experience, *Tourism Management* 11(2):105–110.

11

Franchising and the Lodging Industry

Joseph E. Lavin and Dallas S. Lunceford

The great American dream of becoming your own boss is alive and well these days, and in many cases franchising is opening the door to self-employment.

Franchising, as defined by the International Franchise Association (IFA), is simply a method of distributing products or services from various industries to consumers. Although we tend to think of fast-food restaurants such as McDonalds or Burger King when we think of franchising, many different types of businesses are franchised today, a reflection of our ever-changing society.

History of Franchising

The concept of franchising has been traced to the Middle Ages when the Catholic Church granted franchises to tax collectors, who retained a percentage of the revenue they collected for the church. In the mid-nineteenth century the Singer Company became the first U.S. corporation to use franchising as a distribution method for its products (Kinch and Hayes 1986).

As America grew and the Industrial Revolution took place, more and more manufacturers used franchising to sell their products. During this time most of the agreements between franchisors (those who lend their name, business systems, and products to franchisees for a price) and franchisees (those who pay a fee or royalty for doing business under the franchisor's name and system) dealt merely with the right of a franchisee to sell a particular manufacturer's product. This type of franchising is known as *product or tradename franchising*. Although tradename franchising was initially popular and involved such common businesses as car dealerships, gasoline service stations, and soft-drink bottlers, revenues from tradename franchising have steadily declined since the 1970s. A study of franchising trends put together for the IFA by The Naisbitt Group shows that annual growth rates by product and tradename franchisors has consistently slowed and is expected to level off or decline in the future.

While tradename franchising is slowing, another type of franchising, *business-format* franchising, is going strong. Business-format franchising describes operations like McDonalds, Choice Hotels International, Radio Shack and many other corporations where the relationship between the franchisor and franchisee involves not only the product and service of a franchisor, but also an entire business strategy including marketing, training, operations manuals, quality control, standards, and constant communication (IFA 1991; Naisbitt Group 1989).

Since 1972 the number of business-format franchises has risen steadily. According to a study published in 1990 by the U.S. Department of Commerce, sales of business-format franchisors increased from $192.4 billion in 1988 to an estimated $213.2 billion in 1990. The study, entitled *Franchising in the Economy: 1988–1990*, shows that business-format franchising is responsible for most of today's franchise growth with sales increasing by 155 percent over the last decade (Endoso 1990).

A third type of franchising, which can fall under business-format franchising, is called *conversion franchising*. Conversion franchising is an option for existing businesses to become a franchised outlet for a parent company. By doing so, the independent business will have access to the many extras a franchise organization can offer, such as greater marketing clout, constantly updated training sessions and the recognition factor that franchise outlets receive from consumers (IFA 1991; Naisbitt Group 1989).

In 1990, sales of goods and services by franchise outlets were estimated at $716.3 billion, 34 percent of all retail sales. It is estimated that by the year 2000 franchised businesses will account for half of all retail sales.

In recent years, franchising has grown at a rate outstripping the economy, with 1989's 7.9 percent growth in sales standing four times greater than the 2 percent growth in the gross national product (GNP) (Endoso 1990; IFA 1991; Naisbitt Group 1989).

According to the IFA 60 different industries use franchising as a means to deliver goods and services to consumers. Hardware stores, dry cleaning, real estate, printing and copying services, hospital care, and bookstores are but a few of the businesses that lend themselves to franchising. This broad range of categories has created nearly eight million jobs and has allowed 250 new companies to enter the franchising field annually (IFA 1991).

Franchising is often described as going into business *for* yourself, but not *by* yourself. It allows independent businesspeople to start a business based on a proven concept. With business-format franchises, a businessperson is literally able to have a complete business strategy, from marketing to products to operational concerns, mapped out before launching the business.

Franchising in the Lodging Industry

The lodging industry is one of the top industries to successfully incorporate franchising. Major hotel chains such as Hilton, Choice Hotels, Marriott, and Holiday Inns all franchise hotel brands and concepts to independent hoteliers who provide lodging to the public. Hotel chains franchise both new construction products and convert existing independent hotels to their franchised brands.

Just as there are different types of hotel products (economy, midpriced, upscale, and luxury) each hotel chain approaches franchising differently. Some well-known hotel brands, such as Best Western, are really not franchise organizations but are actually nonprofit referral groups made up of independent hoteliers. Such organizations provide a directory, common reservation system, and some national advertising, but the day to day operations and strategy of each hotel is determined by a property itself. Annual membership fees for such referral organizations may be less than franchise fees for some other hotel companies, but referral groups do not provide the depth or scope of services that are available to franchisees of full-service hotel franchisors.

It is also important to distinguish between a hotel franchisor and a management company. Many familiar lodging brands are not available as a franchise. These organizations offer their brand name only in conjunction with management services and/or some form of ownership in the hotel.

Examples of management companies in the luxury segment of the hotel industry include Hyatt, Four Seasons, and Westin Hotels. In contrast, the midpriced segment of the industry is dominated almost exclusively by franchised brands. The economy segment however, has a number of well-known brands that are exclusively owner-operator organizations. These include La Quinta, Red Roof Inns, and Motel 6.

Full-service lodging franchisors offer more than simply start-up services to franchisees. In addition to help with design, financing, and construction, hotel franchisors offer reservations services, public relations support, easily recognizable standardized signage, quality assurance standards, advertising campaigns, marketing programs, and other services that will help owners/operators in every aspect of their business.

Choosing a Franchisor

When choosing a lodging franchisor each entrepreneur should keep many considerations in mind. One of the first considerations is, of course, the product. If a market area is deluged with upscale, high-cost hotels, perhaps a more economy-minded hotel would do well. Target markets should be studied to determine where consumer demand exists and a product should then be found to meet that need. Independent hoteliers with an existing property looking to join a franchised chain should look toward brands that best fit the profile of their existing property.

The lodging industry offers a variety of lodging products to fit the different needs of today's travelers. Figure 1 summarizes the market position of a number of lodging's franchisable brands.

After selecting a product with the appropriate market, a prospective franchisee should then look for a lodging chain that offers a brand in that segment. Some chains carry only one product, such as Super 8, others, such as Marriott or Choice, offer a variety of hotel brands/products to fit different markets and needs. Prospective franchisees should begin their search by requesting franchise information from each group under consideration. These kits should be studied thoroughly and compared to one another to determine which hotel chain appears to offer the most services and is large enough to provide quality service. It may be wise to avoid some of the start-up mini-chains unless they are backed by a major franchise organization. These small chains may seem attractive at first because of low franchise fees and so forth, but they do not have the marketing clout of the larger chains.

Prospective franchisees should next inspect the franchisor in detail, and hotel franchise organizations will review prospective franchisees as well. Franchisees should study sample contracts and sales literature and study the company's disclosure document following talks with company representatives. Federal and state laws require franchise organizations to present a disclosure statement, containing the franchisor's history and method of operation, to all prospective franchisees at the first business meeting that discusses a fran-

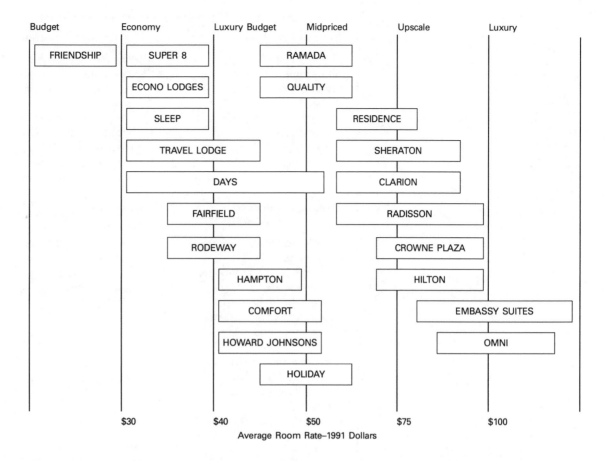

Fig. 1. Major lodging franchisors by market segment.

chise sale. Discloser statements include *nearly everything* that needs to be known about a franchisor including franchise fees, turnover rate (franchisees that have left the organization), litigation against the company, financial data, and other pertinent information. With this document in hand, a prospective franchisee should be able to get a good feel for the organization and how it works. One important task to remember is to ask questions. If anything seems to be interesting or unusual, whether positive or negative, the prospective franchisee should ask the corporate representative about it (Kinch and Hayes 1986; Arnold 1987; James 1987; Mandigo 1987; Kaplan 1987; Lowell and Kirsch 1991).

A good hotel franchise organization with a strong brand offering can be tremendously valuable to an owner/developer. A wealth of services and programs are available from the franchisor to enhance profitability (see typical services listed in Figure 2), however, a franchise is not a panacea. It can be worthless if the franchisee will not or cannot take advantage of what is offered. It would be unwise to build or buy a hotel without experienced lodging developers and/or operators as part of the team.

Lodging, even at its simplest levels, is a complicated, risky business, usually with high capital requirements. In these regards it is rather unlike many other franchise business opportunities.

If one acquires a lodging franchise and goes into business, he or she undertakes a number of responsibilities. For example, adherence to the chain's quality assurance standards is critical. Participation in mandatory marketing programs is another instance where the franchisee must operate the business in accordance with certain rules. Failure to comply with chain policy on such items endangers the owner's ability to retain the franchise and drags down the chain's overall public image, diminishing the value of the brand name.

Fig. 2. Typical lodging franchisor services.

Development Services

Site identification
Site acquisition assistance
Prototype plans and
  specifications
Architectural programming/
  plan reviews
Purchasing discounts
Interior design

**Sales and Marketing/
Marketing Support**

Worldwide network of sales
  locations
Domestic and international
  trade shows
Group sales department
Group and tour rate directories
Government and military
  rate directories
Corporate rate directories
Direct mail programs
Telemarketing and telesales
  programs
Preferred credit card
  discount rates

Advertising

National television and print
  advertising
Travel trade and meetings
  publications
Directory publication
  discounts
Cooperative advertising
  programs
Travel directory

Communications

Property public relations
  consultation
Assistance with press
  releases
Familiarization trips for trade
  and consumer press
Publicity with national
  charities and public
  interest groups
Internal/system publications

Quality Assurance

On-property operational consulting (profit improvement)
Standards inspections
Upgrading and refurbishing
  assistance and consultation

Training and Education

Managers and owners'
  orientation program
Housekeeping, front desk,
  maintenance, and super-
  vision training seminars
Marketing/sales seminars
Video instructional tapes
National and regional
  educational programs

Reservations

Monthly activity reports
Special package sales
Yield management
24-hour terminal
  maintenance

Graphic Design

Design and production of
  collateral materials
Specification for logos,
  brochures, stationery,
  billboards, rack cards
Planning and design of
  promotional programs

Corporate Identity

Design for all exterior signage
Specifications for all exterior
  signage
Coordination of approved
  signage at all locations

Fig. 3. U.S. hotel companies are taking franchising abroad with projects such as Choice Hotels International's Sleep Inn in New Minas, Nova Scotia.

Most good chains provide many services and programs to help the franchisee achieve profitability. But these services are worthless if the franchisee fails to use them.

Future of Hotel Franchising

There are three basic trends in the lodging industry that franchise companies will participate in and help shape.

The first is *consolidation.* Continued mergers, acquisitions, and alliances will shrink the number of major franchise lodging entries to less than five "mega chains" by the turn of the century. Each firm will represent an array of brands covering a broad spectrum. Small lodging franchise organizations, already near extinction, will disappear completely.

The second trend is *segmentation.* As part of our culture in every consumer product, segmentation will continue in the lodging industry. The difference will be that in the future, new hotel segments will be introduced by existing "mega chains" looking to capture the lion's share of a particular market segment.

The third and final trend in lodging is *globalization.* Franchising, especially in the lodging industry, has traditionally been a U.S. phenomenon. The practice is beginning to spread beyond U.S. borders, however (see Sleep Inn hotel in New Minas, Nova Scotia, Figure 3), as the world grows ever smaller.

References

Arnold, David E. 1987. Study your market's actual needs. *Lodging* 12(5):37–38.
Endoso, Joyce. 1990. New study predicts unsurpassed growth in franchising. *Franchising Opportunities* 1990(April):20–25.
International Franchise Association. 1991. Franchise Fact Sheet, Issued in press kit, 20 February 1991, Washington, D.C.
James, Robert M. 1987. Pinpoint your product segment. *Lodging* 12(5):40–41.
Kaplan, Dr. Atid. 1987. The franchisor-franchisee relationship: stronger partnership . . . greater growth. *Lodging* 12(5):47–48.

Kinch, John E., and John P. Hayes. 1986. *Franchising: The Inside Story.* Wilmington, Del.: TriMark Publishing Co.

Lowell, H. Bret, and Mark A. Kirsch. 1991. Growth by franchising: what both sides need to know. *Hotels* 14(2):50–52.

Mandigo, Theordore R. 1987. Gauge the franchisors' support systems. *Lodging* 12(5):43–44.

Naisbitt Group, The. 1989. *The Future of Franchising.* A Study for the International Franchise Association, Washington, D.C.

12

Conference Centers

Key-Sung Chon

The Meetings Industry

The meetings and conventions industry is one of the most rapidly growing industries in hospitality and tourism. In the United States, the meetings market has grown from an estimated $16.8 billion in 1979 to over an estimated $31.4 billion in 1986 (*Meetings & Conventions* 1989). Travel sales from meetings and conventions are so important to the economy that all levels of government have organized, advertised, and provided services specifically to attract these groups.

Meeting Demand Many businesses and organizations hold meetings for a variety of purposes. The demand for meetings can be largely divided into two major groups: association type meetings and corporate or company meetings. Associations include organized or structured groups of people who have an interest, activity, or purpose in common. These may involve professional and technical interests, religious, educational, fraternal, social, or interest activities that have a central issue for the purpose of enhancing or protecting that common interest for the membership of the association.

The American Society of Association Executives (ASAE), an organization of staff leaders of various volunteer association groups, reports over 6,000 member associations in North America alone and its total individual membership represents in excess of 55 million people (ASAE 1989). These associations hold meetings in a number of different types of facilities, usually dictated by the size and type of meeting. Often, major conventions are held in a downtown hotel facility or convention center, and smaller education seminars or board meetings may be held in more appropriately scaled facilities.

The corporate meeting segment is an important part of the meetings market although it is not as visible as the association market. It is common for a corporation or an association to have a designated meeting planner. These people plan meetings that range from intimate meetings of five people for product introductions to meetings for 1,000 or more people.

By definition, a meeting planner is the individual in an organization whose duties consist, in whole or in part, of planning the details attendant to meetings of various types and sizes (Rutherford 1990). According to a survey of professional meeting planners, the most important job skills required in the field of meeting planning include: (1) budgeting and accounting; (2) negotiating with meeting facilities; (3) establishing meeting design and standards; (4) planning with convention services staff; and (5) selecting sites and facilities (Chon and Feiertag 1990).

The growth of the meeting planning profession has resulted in the formation of professional associations in the field. These organizations are instrumental in promoting professionalism, establishing professional standards, and establishing a professional code of ethics. A few of the important professional organizations include Meeting Planners International (MPI), the Professional Convention Management Association (PCMA), and the Society of Government Meeting Planners (SGMP).

Historically, meetings and conventions have been serviced primarily by hotels and convention centers. However, there is an increasing trend toward using resort hotels and self-standing conference centers for educationally-oriented meetings and board meetings. At the same time, as a result of increased air travel, airport hotels have gained a significant amount of the meetings market share because in many instances attendees can fly in to an airport facility, hold a meeting, and fly out later that same day without having to spend a night at the meeting destination (Rutherford 1990).

Key Elements to Successful Meetings

Research conducted in the meetings industry is rather limited. Fortin and Ritchie (1976) conducted a study to determine the manner in which associations select their meetings and conventions site. The researchers sampled all associations that were known to have held their conventions in Canada over a five-year period. The study identified the relative importance of the following ten key variables that influence association meeting planners' site selection decisions: (1) hotel service level; (2) air accessibility; (3) hotel rooms availability; (4) conference rooms availability; (5) price levels; (6) hospitality in the city; (7) restaurant service and quality; (8) personal safety; (9) local interest; and (10) geographic location.

In the corporate meetings side, McClearly (1977) conducted a study on the decision-making process by corporate meeting planners. The researcher found that the decision process for selecting corporate meeting sites is similar to the process for purchasing other industrial products. Many factors influenced corporate site selection, but the most important factors were the meeting accommodations themselves, the supplier's staff, and location.
McClearly (1977) further identified the following as characteristics of the corporate meetings market as differentiated from the association market:

1. The majority of corporate meetings involve less than 50 persons, thus smaller lodging operators can capture a portion of this market.
2. Because corporate meetings are smaller, lodging facilities can take several groups simultaneously and may use small meetings to fill in around larger conventions.
3. Corporate groups tend to meet more frequently, are not tied to a north-south-east-west geographic pattern as are many associations, and tend to spread their meetings throughout the year. This allows the lodging operator to use the corporate market to fill shoulder periods (off-season periods).
4. Corporate meetings are generally better spenders, require fewer

price concessions, and tend to utilize the other profit centers of the hotels, including the restaurants, lounges, and recreation areas.

McClearly (1977) concludes that there are several unique aspects of marketing in meeting services as opposed to marketing in products:

1. Meeting services are purchased with an element of uncertainty since the benefits are not guaranteed owing to the intangibility aspect;
2. There is no transfer of ownership as with products;
3. Meeting services are produced and consumed simultaneously; and,
4. Uniform performance standards are difficult to attain.
5. A low price.

The specific demands of meeting planners vary according to the organization they represent and the purpose of the meeting. According to the trade literature, through the years there has been a trend that the emphasis of meeting planners has shifted from food and lodging requirements, which are now considered standard, to more emphasis on meeting room size, design, and equipment. Renaghan and Kay (1987) conducted a study to determine what factors are important to meeting planners when choosing a facility for their clients' meetings. Specifically, the researchers wanted to know what meeting planners expected in a facility, which of these attributes were most important, and which attributes they would give up to get something else. Using the conjoint-analysis approach, the researchers were then able to assess the relative importance weights of different attributes at the same time.

Meeting planners were asked to rate 16 combinations of these characteristics to determine their relative importance when choosing a meeting site. The findings resulted in the following conclusions:

- Meeting rooms that have the greatest ratio of space to people offer a competitive edge.
- Break-out rooms should be located close to the main meeting room whenever possible.
- Standard audio-visual equipment is preferable because meeting planners do not trust facility employees to operate complicated alternatives, and they are not willing to risk that something is likely to go wrong.
- Inside the meeting rooms, it is crucial that control of the climate and lighting be in the hands of the group instead of the staff.
- Price is not nearly as important as might be expected. Planners are willing to pay more to get quality, which ultimately translates into a successful meeting.

Further, Renaghan and Kay (1987) report that the top service concern to meeting planners is the competence of a facility staff. Other service related features meeting planners look for in site selection, depending on the size and type of meeting, include efficient registration procedures, instant communication with different areas within a hotel, maximum security for attendees, and quality food service.

The Conference Center Concept

By definition and design, a conference center is a specialized hospitality operation dedicated to facilitating and supporting conferences of small to medium size (20 to 50 people). The entire focus of the operation of a conference center is geared toward accommodating these conferences, from the design of the facility, to the professional support services, the specialized training staff, and the packaging of the product. The International Association of Conference Centers (IACC) in 1989 identified approximately 180 bona fide worldwide conference centers that meet the criteria established by the organization (IACC 1989).

IACC considers conference centers as a natural outgrowth of the age of specialization. Meetings have long been an integral part of the efforts of organizations to maintain internal and external communications, but the need to bring individuals together to communicate face to face in the "conference" format has increased dramatically in recent years. Historically, this conference demand has been serviced primarily by a number of different types of nonconference facilities, including hotels and resorts. Meeting planners have found that the characteristics of these facilities can often work against meeting efficiency because of distractions and poorly designed meeting rooms.

The Differences in Concept and Design

The key differences between the conference center concept and other hospitality operations that service meetings (for example, hotels or resorts) result from the specialized and focused approach of conference centers. The basic difference is the specialization in accommodating conference groups and the focus on providing the best possible environment for productive meetings. Among many differences between hotels/resorts and conference centers as identified by the IACC (1989), the following five areas represent the major differences:

1. Facility design. The orientation of a conference center, from the beginning, is focused on the primary purpose of the facility: accommodating conferences. The physical plant is organized so as to separate functions, minimize distractions, and provide convenience for the conferee. For example, conference rooms are separated from banquet rooms or other high traffic areas. In addition, conference centers are usually designed to incorporate informal gathering places for meeting attendees, sometimes referred to as dialogue centers or workshop suites, and it offers a good space ratio for interactive discussion or role playing.

2. Meeting furnishings and equipment. It offers state-of-the-art audiovisual equipment with staff to operate and service the equipment and offers comfortable swivel chairs on casters for long periods of sitting.

3. Food and beverage. Compared with hotel or resort operations, another major difference of conference centers is the orientation of the food and beverage department toward providing a product specifically designed to accommodate conference groups. The conference dining concept allows the meeting planner to plan the program without making decisions regarding banquet meals, preselected menus, and specific dining times. It allows the meeting planner to avoid numerous individual cost and budget decisions.

4. Personnel. Because of the market orientation, conference centers train their sales and marketing personnel to develop a sound understanding of their customers' organizational structures, group cultures, and goals, so that the conference center becomes an extension of each customer's normal working environment. Conference centers offer special services such as "conference concierge" services. The conference concierge service is usually provided in the form of a separate desk staffed by individuals with secretarial skills.

5. The "Complete Meeting Package". Another feature of the conference

center's orientation to groups is its unique system of billing, which aids the meeting planner in budgeting and payment. While hotels and resorts bill separately for sleeping rooms and add on charges for meals, meeting space, break refreshments, and other items, conference centers typically operate via a comprehensive billing package called a Complete Meeting Package (CMP).

Types of Conference Centers   The IACC (1989) categorizes conference centers into the following four types:

1. The traditional conference center. Among other criteria, a minimum of 70 percent of net area of meeting space must be dedicated single-purpose conference space and a minimum of 60 percent of occupied room nights must be generated by conferences.
2. The resort conference center. In addition to dedicated meetings facilities and other stringent requirements (up to and including the quality of meeting room seating), resort conference centers must have at least one major resort amenity—such as an 18-hole golf course—plus lesser recreational amenities such as racquet sports facilities or a swimming pool.
3. The nonresidential conference center. It is essentially the same as other conference centers, except that it does not offer sleeping accommodations.
4. The ancillary conference center. It meets the general criteria for conference centers but is also connected to or surrounded by a larger nonconference center entity—a conference center wing within a hotel or a conference center facility within a resort complex.

Summary

The demand for conference center facilities primarily comes from meetings of various types. An overview of the meetings and conventions industry was provided with a particular focus on two primary types of meetings, the association meetings and corporate meetings. Relatedly, the role of a meeting planner was discussed and the findings of research studies related to the meetings and conventions industry were discussed. Lastly, the concept of a "conference center" was discussed with an emphasis on the unique aspects of a conference center concept and the type of conference centers existing today.

References

American Society of Association Executives (ASAE). 1989. Membership Literature. Washington, D.C.: ASAE.
Chon, Kye-Sung and Howard Feiertag. 1990. The essence of meetings management. *The Cornell Hotel and Restaurant Administration Quarterly* 31(2)(August):95–97.
Fortin, Paul A., and J. R. Brent Ritchie. 1976. *A Study of the Decision Process of North American Associations Concerning the Choices of a Convention Site.* Quebec, Canada: Université Laval.
International Association of Conference Centers. 1989. *Understanding Conference Centers.* Fenton, Mo.: IACC.
McClearly, Ken W. 1977. Factors influencing the marketing of meeting facilities: an empirical study of the buying/selling relationship for corporate group meetings. Ph.D. diss., Michigan State University, East Lansing.
Meetings & Conventions. 1989. A guide to meeting planning courses, supplement to *Meeting & Conventions*, December, pp. 43–48.

Renaghan, Leo M., and Michael Z. Kay. 1987. What meeting planners want: the conjoint-analysis approach. *The Cornell Hotel and Restaurant Administration Quarterly* (May):67–76.

Rutherford, Denney G. 1990. *Introduction to the Conventions, Expositions, and Meetings Industry.* New York: Van Nostrand Reinhold.

13

Overview of the Conventions, Expositions, and Meetings Industry: A Major Hotel Market

Denney G. Rutherford

The conventions, expositions, and meetings industry (CEMI) is a broadly based, multifaceted collection of endeavors and functions that together orchestrate an economic machine of multibillion dollar proportions. The various people and organizations responsible for the activities of this industry are the focus of this article. An industry that is so decentralized as the CEMI does not lend itself to a singular or linear analysis. Each entity, however, has as a central part of its focus the concept and execution of a successful convention or meeting.

Webster's defines a *convention* as "An assembly, often periodical, of members or delegates, as of a political, social, professional or religious group" (*Webster's New World Dictionary*, 2nd ed). The word *meeting* is similarly defined as "A coming together of persons or things (or) an assembly; gathering of people, especially to discuss or decide on matters." These definitions would work for classifying such events to the layperson but for our purposes they need to be examined in a broader context in order that we might suggest a framework that can be used to investigate the major segments of the CEMI industry.

To more accurately define a modern meeting or convention, we must also pay attention to the fact that such assemblies may often

Occur at specific places called facilities
Involve food and beverage service
Provide for specialized technical support such as audio-visual equipment
Require transportation
Require housing
Involve exhibition of products
Require convention or meeting delegate entertainment

In a way, conventions and meetings may be compared to a theatrical or entertainment production wherein many details and specialists in their execution have to coordinate for the production to be a success. The remainder of this article examines CEMI productions by introducing the major actors in the CEMI.

Who Are the Actors?

The CEMI has been likened to a large wagon wheel, with the exposition or trade show manager at the hub and the various other specialists that service the production arranged around that professional (Figure 1 leaves the wheel hub blank, suggesting that at any given point during a specific production, one or more of the actors may assume a more central importance to the completion and success of the event. In Figure 1, delegates have also been arrayed on the circumference of the wheel, suggesting that in a greater or lesser way, each delegate's experience is influenced by each of the actors in the CEMI production.

Associations   Associations are defined as some organized or structured group of people who have a common interest, activity, or purpose. These may involve professional and technical interests, religious, fraternal, social, educational, avocational (or hobbyists) activities that have as a central issue, the purpose of enhancing or protecting that common interest for the membership of the association. The importance of associations to hotels and the CEMI is nested in the fact that virtually every association has regularly scheduled (and *ad hoc*) meetings and conventions designed to further their interests, exchange information, and promote membership activities. Additionally, according to Internal Revenue Service regulations, in order to maintain their tax-exempt status, associations must hold at least one board meeting and one general membership meeting (convention) each year.

The American Society of Association Executives (ASAE), an association of staff leaders of various volunteer association groups, reports over 8,000 member-associations whose total collective memberships represent in excess of 215 million people nationwide (ASAE 1990). The fact that many Americans have multiple association memberships suggests that we are a nation of association joiners. When these groups gather to meet in convention facilities and hotels, they generate an economic impact that in turn generates significant activity among the other actors in the CEMI.

A capsule description of this importance can be visualized by thinking of a typical convention delegate who purchases airline tickets, hotel rooms, food and beverage, local transportation, entertainment activities, and other services relative to his or her attendance at the meeting. Delegates also patronize retail establishments in those cities and may make purchasing decisions for their companies or groups at trade shows attendant to their convention. They may include their spouses, families, or friends in pre- and post-convention activities in the vicinity of the host city.

In 1988 a survey of the International Association of Convention and Visitors Bureaus reported that the associations industry spent US$22 billion at more than 194,000 meetings and conventions. These events attracted over 27 million attendees, emphasizing their economic importance (ASAE 1990). Couple the foregoing with the finding that over 90 percent of all conventions and meetings are still held in hotels, and not convention centers (M&C

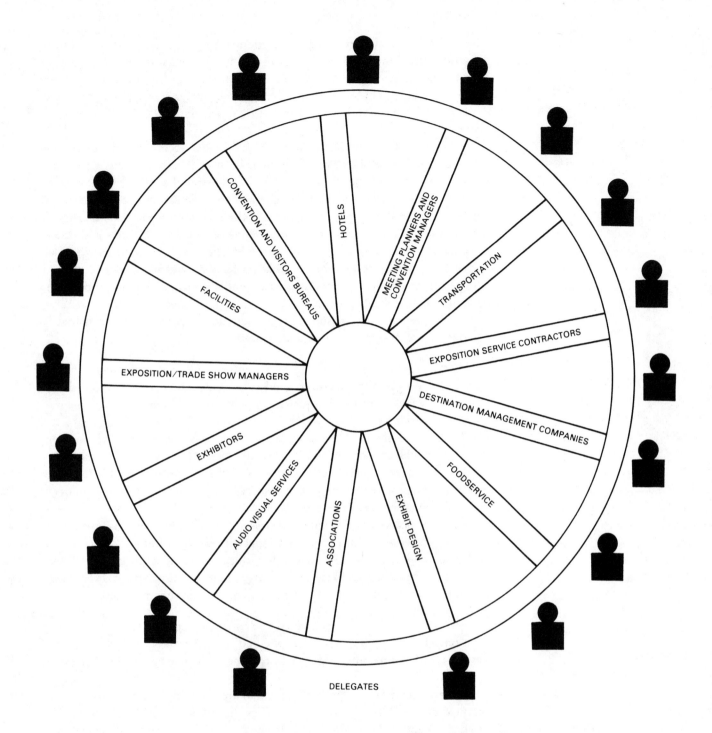

Labels in the wheel (clockwise from top):
HOTELS · MEETING PLANNERS AND CONVENTION MANAGERS · TRANSPORTATION · EXPOSITION SERVICE CONTRACTORS · DESTINATION MANAGEMENT COMPANIES · FOODSERVICE · EXHIBIT DESIGN · ASSOCIATIONS · AUDIO VISUAL SERVICES · EXHIBITORS · EXPOSITION/TRADE SHOW MANAGERS · FACILITIES · CONVENTION AND VISITORS BUREAUS

DELEGATES

Fig. 1. CEMI wheel.
(Source: Courtesy of Don Walter, National Association of Exposition Managers, 1989.)

1988), and a powerful case can be made for the importance of the CEMI to hotels and the communities in which they do business.

Economic data such as these underscore the importance of the meetings and convention delegates to communities, hotels, other facilities, and the affiliated components of the CEMI. It therefore should come as no surprise that communities encourage associations and similar groups to convene in their locale because such meetings are a major economic prize.

Trade Shows When the association that represents restaurateurs, foodservice executives, and other hospitality industry professionals across the United States has its annual convention, educational meetings, and trade exposition in Chicago in

May, the National Restaurant Association (NRA) attracts a vast number of manufacturers and vendors who make and sell products of special and particular interest to people in the foodservice industry. The resulting trade show is one of the biggest in the nation, utilizing nearly 600,000 square feet at McCormick Place exhibition halls and attracting in excess of 100,000 delegates and attendees.

The 1,800 exhibitors at the NRA trade show accomplish major portions of their marketing objectives by participation in this trade show, which in essence is a very carefully managed and orchestrated artificial marketplace for buyers and sellers to interact. The key to understanding the relationship between trade shows and conventions is the recognition that in gathering and convening such meetings, the memberships of those associations and other groups are congregating in a centralized location offering vendors who make their living selling to members of that profession or group a unique opportunity to interact with highly qualified potential customers. Trade shows then become a significant actor in the CEMI.

Tongren and Thompson (1981:31) identify three types of events that fall under the general category of trade show.

1. *Industrial Shows* are used by manufacturers to exhibit their products to other manufacturers, and to provide educational sessions describing new techniques in the industry and demonstrating new products.
2. *Trade Shows,* in the strict sense, are where sellers of goods and services contact all types of buyers (1981:31). Most of these shows are for members of the *trade,* as in the example of the National Restaurant Association. These shows may or may not be in conjunction with a convention or meeting.
3. *Professional or Scientific Exhibitions* are usually adjuncts to the annual meetings of professional or specialized organizations (1981:31). A convention of the American College of Cardiac Surgeons, for example, would likely attract large numbers of exhibitors who have specialized products or equipment used by heart surgeons.

The trade show events defined above are not open to the public at large but only to those who have a specific and demonstrable relationship to the event as either a member of the industry, the trade association, or professional society.

Large scale exhibit presentations that are open to the public are properly termed *consumer shows.* At these events, exhibitors who market products relative to a central theme display their goods to a wide variety of people who have a common consumer interest in (for instance) boats, automobiles, homes, or gardening. These shows are usually held annually in large stadiums or convention centers and typically charge a modest admission fee. Their impact differs from the other types of shows previously discussed in that they attract a local clientele, do not account for large numbers of hotel room-nights and only minimally impact local retailers and foodservice.

The National Association of Exposition Managers (NAEM) represents the professional people who manage the various intricate details of a modern trade show or exposition. NAEM reports over 3,000 members who are responsible annually for nearly 4,000 shows and expositions (Don Walter, pers. communic. 1989).

Facilities Because of the generally positive economic impact of conventions on host communities in the last 15–20 years, there has been a veritable explosion of building special-purpose facilities designed to make the planning and execution of conventions and trade shows convenient and attractive to their managers and attendees. This was not always the case.

Prior to 1970 very few buildings could be classified as comprehensive convention centers. In most instances, they were large public assembly facilities that did double or triple duty as auditoriums, basketball arenas, or hockey rinks. Many were cavernous, dark and noisy buildings in undesirable parts of town that were neither functional nor more than uni-dimensional in terms of use. According to Don Walter of NAEM (Hosansky et al. 1986:56), all that changed with the opening in the late 1960s of Detroit's Cobo Hall.

Cobo was designed to offer not only a large, divisible exhibit space, but also incorporated a second story for meeting rooms and a large corridor on the exhibit level that could be used for receptions, registration, or additional exhibit space.

The breadth of demand from meeting planners, trade show managers, exhibitors, and others is currently such that modern convention centers must be responsive to specialized needs. Communities or municipalities embarking on siting, design, construction, and management of such buildings are finding they have to pay attention to what these market segments are demanding, or they risk expending tax dollars for a facility that will be ignored or underused by its intended market. Robert Black (1986:11) cites a "conservative construction cost of US$125 a square foot" in discussing the economic dimensions of the capital cost of such buildings and notes that halls planned or under construction in 1986 represent a US$5 billion capital investment exclusive of land acquisition.

Taxpayers and their representatives need to be convinced that such capital outlays will repay their investment and generate the sort of economic activity the feasibility studies and promoters promise. It is no longer the case that such facilities can be *loss leaders*; they are under increasing pressure to be cost-effective at least to the break-even point. (Hosansky et al. 1986:57).

Meeting Planners and Convention Managers Conventions and meetings do not just happen. The myriad of details need to be carefully inventoried, assessed, and executed by an ever-increasingly professional group of people now referred to as meeting planners, convention, or event managers. According to Hosansky et al. (1986:65), "Of all aspects of the industry, the profession of meeting planning is, in a sense, the most bewildering." What he means is that as few as twenty years ago, the term "meeting planner" was not in common usage, and since then, a true profession has grown up that has many elements, operates in many venues, and has spurred technological advances in computer equipment, audio-visual equipment, and professional meeting management thought and inquiry.

Hotels No convention hosting out-of-town delegates would be successful without comfortable, safe, and modern lodging arrangements. Many hotels recognize the importance of the CEMI to their sales mix so that on any given day a significant portion of their rooms may be rented to people and groups who are gathered at meetings in conventions in the area. Hotels also are major providers of meeting facilities, either in conjunction or in competition with municipal convention centers. At first glance, however, most observers would say that the role hotels play in the CEMI is that of rooms provider. Upon reflection, many would also mention that hotels derive food, beverage, and banquet revenues from conventions and meetings. But their role is much larger than that. According to sources quoted by Hosansky and others (1986:54), as recently as 1966, group business was a relatively small percentage of hotel, motel, and resort sales activity. In recent years, the picture has changed dramatically and, for many hotels, ". . . group business may account for as much as 80 or 90 percent of bookings."

When 90 percent of the rooms in any given hotel are rented to members of a group or a collection of group meetings and conventions, the effects of these figures ripple throughout every department in the hotel.

These effects apply neither exclusively nor specifically to high-rise, urban mega-hotel properties. According to Dave Dorf, director of education and training for the Hotel Sales and Marketing Association International (HS-MAI), smaller hotels also vigorously market to group business (Hosansky et al. 1986:55). These properties may not qualify in terms of size and scope of facilities for the big conventions, but significant numbers of nonconvention meetings are held on hotel premises and the size of the meeting may in many ways dictate the size and location of the hotel chosen as host property.

Large hotels, however, are also recognizing the value of small group meetings. Whereas there is a limited or finite number of the types of conventions that are citywide or would fill up totally on a regular basis a 1,000- to 2,000-room hotel, the opportunities to fill hotels with numbers of small groups appear to be close to infinite. This recognizes that the corporate market can play a major role in filling rooms. Hotel marketing and operational activities are therefore significantly and broadly affected by the CEMI across all sizes and types of lodging facilities.

The ways in which hotel food and beverage departments have traditionally organized and operated themselves have also been significantly impacted by the demands of the diverse CEMI market. Separate facilities, staff, and policies dedicated to group events are becoming the norm. CEMI requirements for food events that are unique, memorable, refined, and sophisticated have focused increased attention on the management of all aspects of banquet and catering functions.

Hotels' meeting facilities have undergone a significant renaissance in response to demands from the CEMI market. Not only have the physical aspects of meetings rooms been changed and upgraded to be more flexible, but ballrooms and, in some instances, separate exhibit halls have emerged as a requirement of the CEMI market.

Convention and Visitors Bureaus

The primary purpose of a municipality's convention and visitors bureau (CVB) to the CEMI is to provide the hotels and convention facilities of that community with long-term marketing leads and contacts regarding potential convention and meetings business. To this end, CVBs are organized to employ sales staffs who are aware of the national conventions market, do research regarding that market, and generally serve as the initial contact regarding the capabilities of the host community to execute conventions and meetings.

CVBs are operated and funded under a wide variety of formulas, but most have some association with a taxing authority in addition to private sector funds generated through memberships.

Contrary to past practices, when many bureaus were staffed through political patronage with no clear mandate, CVBs have learned that the most successful such entities are staffed by professional marketing and hospitality people who know the market and command the effective marketing and sales strategies to "sell" their destination as a convention host community. This change was mandated when "communities began to recognize the economic benefits that tourism—as well as meeting and conventions—could bring" (Hosansky 1986:58).

CVBs may also offer a variety of services and functions that enhance the capabilities of groups and associations planning and executing details of their meetings.

Exhibitors and Exhibit Design

Exhibitors are those participants in trade shows who represent companies with goods, products, and services to sell to conventioneers, and meeting and trade show attendees. They represent those companies that have chosen trade shows and expositions as one of the major focuses of their marketing efforts. These are companies that have recognized the benefits of being able to market in a controlled environment to highly qualified potential buyers. Exhibitors, the exhibit staff, and the events they plan around trade show participation are also important to hotels. Exhibitors typically commit to hotel rooms not only for the period of the event, but also the move-in and move-out days. They may also rent hospitality suites and provide significant food and beverage revenues to hotels.

Exhibitors work very closely with exhibit design personnel to conceive, design, and even construct the exhibit chosen to demonstrate and display the exhibitor's or manufacturer's product. Exhibitors are represented by their own association, the International Exhibitors Association (IEA), and people who conceive and design exhibits are also represented by the Exhibit Designers and Producers Association (EDPA).

Transportation

At first glance one would assume that analyzing the role of a transportation company relative to the CEMI would be fairly simple. It is easy to recognize that airlines and car rental companies play a major role in assisting people in getting to and from conventions and meetings.

Since the final deregulation of domestic airlines in the early 1980s, the relationship between air carriers and the CEMI has changed substantially. Airline mergers, *hub-spoke* air terminals, lively competition, route expansion, frequent flyer programs, and a need for increasingly sophisticated and aggressive marketing efforts have combined to forge a new relationship between carriers and the CEMI, especially meeting planners.

Airlines now have account executives who specialize in the meetings and convention market. In a deregulated atmosphere, fare prices have been substantially reduced, and meeting planners and airlines can negotiate attractive rates for an airline to be the *designated* carrier for a given convention. Airlines may also provide complimentary fares for planners and association executives on site inspection and familiarization trips. Planners can also negotiate complimentary fares based on a designated number of paid convention fares. A typical arrangement may be one complimentary fare for every 40 to 50 convention fares. Planners may then use the complimentary tickets for speakers, VIPs, or association executives.

Other modes of transportation can also play major roles relative to the event. During the convention itself there is almost always a major requirement for ground transportation for large groups of convention attendees. The meeting planners and trade show managers may be responsible for arranging bus transportation between lodging and convention facilities. Similarly, delegates will require transportation from convention or lodging facilities to entertainment functions in other parts of the convention region.

A little-known element of the transportation industry also plays a major role in execution of a convention or meeting event that has associated with it a trade show or exhibition. The exhibitors have to arrange for transportation of their exhibits from trade show to trade show and region to region. Several transportation companies have dedicated divisions or parts of divisions that exclusively transport crated and packaged exhibits from one trade show to the next.

Exposition Service Contractors

Once called *general contractors*, the people and firms who provide special event services are now becoming more commonly known as *exposition service contractors*. These professionals provide services for the trade show, exhibitors, and meeting planners that help the event take place. Among these services may be drayage, booth and exhibit set-up and takedown, crating, erection of pipe and drape and other services under the general category of "decorating." These services may also include rental of furniture, logistics assistance, rental of floor coverings, booth cleaning, and labor planning and supervision.

This segment of the CEMI, through its professional association, the Exposition Service Contractors Association (ESCA), represents both national and local firms that provide these sorts of services.

Destination Management Companies

These suppliers of on-site meeting services, now known as *destination management companies (DMCs)*, have grown out of the companies who in the past arranged for buses and local transportation. They contract with meeting planners or associations to arrange for locally-oriented events and services that may include providing interface with transportation companies, planning and executing special parties, and assisting meeting planners and convention managers in making full use of the potential services of the host community.

Recently, it has become less possible to draw clear distinctions between some of the services the CEMI members may provide. For instance, DMCs may arrange for transportation or the meeting and convention planners may arrange for transportation themselves. Some DMCs may provide decorating services that traditionally have been the province of exposition service contractors. Audio-visual services may be either provided by a company that is dedicated specifically to those sorts of activities, or it may be a function of a DMC or a specialty service contractor. Increasingly, convention facilities may be absorbing some of these activities and renting them to meeting planners and convention managers as separate profit-making activities on behalf of the facility.

Foodservice

In the not-too-distant past, foodservice at convention sites often meant beer, popcorn, and hot dog-type concession food in the exhibit area and the infamous "rubber chicken" banquet food in the ballroom for convention delegates. Convention foodservices have become so critically important, however, that foodservice operators, hotels, and convention facilities have had to totally and completely rethink the management of this aspect of the CEMI. As reported by *Meetings and Conventions Magazine* in their 1987 study, "The Meetings Market '87," quality of foodservice was considered the most important factor by 80 percent of the corporate planners responding to the 1987 survey of all factors considered important in the selection of a facility or a hotel. Given this, foodservice companies, convention facilities, and hotel banquet and catering departments have had to respond with new levels of professionalism, creativity, food quality, and service. Because so many meeting and convention planning professionals network and interact within their professional associations, facilities and hotels that gain a reputation for mediocre or poor food and service quickly have those reputations spread throughout the meeting planners' grapevine.

Conclusion

The foregoing introduction of the major members of the CEMI strongly suggests that the definitions offered by *Webster's* are too simplistic for an industry that embodies the mix of capital, people and ideas that the CEMI does.

Summary

The overview presented here links the people and activities of the CEMI to demonstrate the potential monetary importance of the conventions and meetings industry to hotels. Understanding the dynamics of this vast market will assist the hotel operator in designing marketing programs to most effectively present the hotel's message.

Acknowledgment

This paper was adapted with permission from a recently published book on the CEMI (Rutherford, 1990). Additional, in-depth information about these functions of the CEMI can be obtained there, or membership information may be requested from industry organizations listed in the Appendix.

References

American Society of Association Executives (ASAE). 1990. *Membership Literature.* Washington, D.C.: ASAE.

Hosansky, Mel, et al. 1986. The Evolution of an Industry. *Meetings and Conventions Magazine* June:48–67.

M&C. 1988. *The Meetings Market '87.* Secaucus, N.J.: Meetings and Conventions Magazine.

Rutherford, D. G. 1990. *Introduction to the Conventions, Expositions and Meetings Industry.* New York: Van Nostrand Reinhold.

Tongren, Hale N., and James P. Thompson. 1981. The trade show in marketing education. *Journal of Marketing Education* Fall 3(2):28–35.

Appendix

Convention Industry Organizations

Air Transport Association of
  America (ATAA)
1709 New York Avenue, N.W.
Washington, D.C. 20006
(202)626-4000

American Hotel and Motel
  Association (AHMA)
888 Seventh Avenue
New York, NY 10019
(212)265-4506

American Society of Association
  Executives (ASAE)
1575 Eye Street, N.W.
Washington, D.C. 20005
(202)626-2723

Association of Conference and
  Events Directors - International
  (ACED)
Colorado State University
Rockwell Hall
Fort Collins, CO 80523

Association for Convention
  Operations Management (ACOM)
1819 Peachtree Street N.E., Suite 560
Atlanta, GA 30309
(404)351-3220

Association of Independent Meeting
  Planners (AIMP)
5103 Wigville Road
Thurmont, MD 21788
(301)271-4222

Convention Liaison Council (CLC)
1575 Eye Street, N.W.
Washington, D.C. 20005
(202)626-2764

Council of Engineering and
Scientific Society Executives
(CESSE)
2000 Florida Avenue, N.W.
Washington, D.C. 20009

Exhibit Designers and Producers
Association (EDPA)
611 E. Wells Street
Milwaukee, WI 53202
(414)276-3372

Exposition Service Contractors
Association (ESCA)
400 South Houston
Union Station, Suite 210
Dallas, TX 75202
(214)742-9217

Health Care Exhibitors Association
(HCEA)
5775 Peachtree-Dunwoody Road
Building D, Suite 500
Atlanta, GA 30342
(404)242-3663

Hotel Sales and Marketing
Association International
(HSMAI)
1400 K Street, N.W., Suite 810
Washington, D.C. 20005
(202)789-0089

Institute of Association Management
Companies (IAMC)
5820 Wilshire Boulevard, Suite 500
Los Angeles, CA 90036

Insurance Conference Planners
Association (ICPA)
8721 Indian Hills Drive
Omaha, NE 68114
(402)390-7300

International Association of
Auditorium Managers (IAAM)
4425 W. Airport Freeway, Suite 590
Irving, TX 75062
(214)255-8020

International Association of
Conference Centers (IACC)
362 Parsippany Road
Parsippany, NJ 07054
(201)887-3505

International Association of
Convention and Visitor Bureaus
(IACVB)
P.O. Box 758
Champaign, IL 61820
(217)359-8881

International Association of Fairs and
Expositions (IAFE)
P.O. Box 985
Springfield, MO 65801
(417)862-5771

International Communication
Industries Association (ICIA)
3150 Spring Street
Fairfax, VA 22031
(703)273-7200

International Exhibitors Association
(IEA)
5103-B Backlick Road
Annandale, VA 22003
(703)941-3725

Meeting Planners International (MPI)
1950 Stemmons Freeway
Dallas, TX 75207-3109
(214)746-5250

National Association of Exposition
Managers (NAEM)
710 Indiana Avenue
Indianapolis, IN 46202
(317)638-6236

Professional Convention
Management Association (PCMA)
100 Vestavia Office Park, Suite 220
Birmingham, AL 35216
(205)823-7262

Religious Conference Management
Association (RCMA)
One Hoosier Dome, Suite 120
Indianapolis, IN 46225
(317)632-1888

Society of Company Meeting
  Planners (SCMP)
2600 Garden Road, Suite 208
Monterey, CA 93940
(408)649-6544

Society of Government Meeting
  Planners (SGMP)
1213 Prince Street
Alexandria, VA 22314-9998

Society of Incentive Travel
  Executives (SITE)
271 Madison Avenue
New York, NY 10016
(212)889-9340

Travel Industry Association
  of America (TIAA)
2 Lafayette Center
1133 21st Street, N.W.
Washington, D.C. 20036
(202)293-1433

Trade Show Bureau
1660 Lincoln St., #2080
Denver, CO 80264
(303)860-7626

14

Branding in the Hospitality Industry

Simon Crawford-Welch

Definition of Relevant Terms

A brand is a name, term, symbol, or design, or a combination thereof intended to identify the goods or services of one seller or group of sellers and to differentiate them from those of competitors (Kotler 1980).

A brand name refers to that part of the brand that can be vocalized, for example, Hampton Inns, Courtyard by Marriott, Red Lobster restaurants, TGI Friday restaurants.

A brand mark refers to the part of the brand that cannot be vocalized, such as its symbol, design, or distinctive packaging, for example, the golden arches of McDonalds restaurants, the rounded "H" of Hilton Hotels. Brand marks, when given legal protection, become known as trademarks.

Branding is the process of developing, offering, and maintaining a product with a predetermined combination of unique goods and services. It involves the manipulation and positioning of both tangible (brand name and brand mark) and intangible (atmospherics) elements of the marketing mix to create a perceived image in the mind of the consumer.

Purpose of Branding

Organizations engage in branding to create consumer awareness of, purchase of, and loyalty toward their product. It is well documented that the hospitality industry is in the mature stage of its life cycle (Withiam 1985; West 1986; Dev 1989; Tse 1989; Crawford-Welch 1990). In order to survive in such an intensely competitive operating environment it is often necessary to develop a brand. The intention is that developing a strong brand will result in higher market share and increased profitability. Branding enables the company to develop a specific market position for its product, which is referred to as *product positioning*.

A brand that has been successfully positioned in the marketplace makes the consumer immediately aware of the product offering in terms of variables such as price, location, market level, size, or facilities, and allows the consumer to decide whether the brand is capable of meeting his/her particular needs and wants. The driving force behind the concept of branding is the creation of a standard product. The logic favoring the creation of a standard product is that the degree of risk experienced by the consumer in the product purchase decision will be significantly reduced if he/she is familiar with the total package of goods and services being offered for sale. Standardization of the product through the creation of a brand results in risk minimization for the consumer. In addition to reducing risk in the product purchase decision, the development of a brand has several benefits for the hospitality operator. These benefits include tighter operating procedures leading to reduced costs through economies of scale and increased control over the provision of the product itself.

Evolution of Branding in the Hospitality Industry

The development and operation of a single brand was almost exclusively pursued as an operating strategy throughout the 1950s and 1960s, for example, the single Holiday Inn brand. The 1980s saw the evolution of more complex branding strategies aimed at catering to the increasingly diversified needs of the marketplace. Withiam (1985) suggests that the proliferation of brands in the lodging industry is a response to the plurality of the marketplace. There has been a progression from the use of single brand strategies in the 1950s and 1960s to product line brand strategies in the 1980s and 1990s. Table 1 shows examples of the wide array of brands in the U.S. lodging industry. Today's hospitality consumers are more demanding than those of the 1960s and 1970s in that they hold very specific images of the services they want and the prices they are willing to pay for those services (Withiam 1985). This condition has led to the development by hospitality firms of new products geared toward the diverse price-value needs of multiple market segments.

Developing multiple brands is more widespread in the lodging industry than in the restaurant industry. However, some examples of restaurant firms developing and operating multiple brands include the Pepsico Corporation with their Kentucky Fried Chicken, Pizza Hut, and Taco Bell brands, and General Mills with their Olive Garden and Red Lobster brands.

Branding Strategies

There are four broad types of branding strategies. An *individual brand strategy* dictates a separate name for each product without reference to an integrated product line or to a corporate name. An example of an individual brand strategy in the hospitality industry was the Holiday Corporation when it had the Hampton Inn brand, the Crowne Plaza brand, and the Embassy Suites brand. Each brand stood individually and succeeded or failed by its own merits or faults. The restaurant industry almost exclusively follows an individual brand strategy. For example, although Kentucky Fried Chicken, Pizza Hut, and Taco Bell are all concepts owned by the Pepsico Corporation, each concept has a distinct operating name and strategy and each concept succeeds or fails on its own merits. One does not find Pizza Hut restaurants with a logo "Pizza Hut by Pepsico." No reference is made to the parent organization. Each concept exists as an operation in its own right.

A *product line brand strategy* applies a separate family brand to each product class or to each group of similar products. An example of product line brand-

Table 1. *Chain multi-tiered brand marketing strategies—brand names*

Economy/limited-service			Middle market	
Lower	Middle	Upper	Limited service	Full service
Motel 6	Red Roof Inn	Days Inn	Courtyard	Holiday Inn
Sleep Inn	Days Inn	Comfort Inn	Clubhouse Inn	Ramada Inn
Microtel Inn	Comfort Inn	Travelodge	Parksquare Inn	Sheraton
Regal 8	Travelodge	Econo-Lodge	Cresthil	Hilton
Sixpence Inn	Econo-Lodge	La Quinta		Quality Inn
Scottish Inn	Super 8 Motels	Hampton Inn		Radisson
Alistar Inn	Knights Inn	Rodeway Inn		Viscount
E-Z 8 Motels	Budgetel Inn	Drury Inn		Days Hotel
Thrift Lodge	Rodeway Inn	Suisse Chalet		Howard
	Shoneys Inn	Country		Johnson
	Fairfield Inn	Heath Inn		Lodge
	Exel Inn	Shilo Inn		Park Inn
	Arborgate Inn	Signature Inn		
	Best Inns	Cross Country		
	Luxury	Inn		
	Budget	Dillon Inn		
	Red Carpet	Country Hos-		
	Cricket Inn	pitality Inn		
	Envoy Inn	Lees Inn		
	Roadstar Inn	Cypress Inn		

(continued)

ing in the hospitality industry would be Choice (formerly Quality International) with their seven product lines of Quality, Clarion, Comfort, Sleep, Rodeway, EconoLodge, and Friendship. With the exception of the Sleep brand, all product lines contain two brands, for example, Quality Inns and Quality Suites, Clarion Inns and Clarion Suites, and Comfort Inns and Comfort Suites.

A *corporate brand name strategy* combines the corporate trademark with the individual product name. Examples in the lodging industry would include Best Western Hotels (a consortia), Westin Hotels, Days Inns, and EconoLodges. This type of brand strategy is sometimes referred to as a "singleton" strategy (Witham 1985).

The final type of brand strategy is a *family brand name strategy*, which involves placing a blanket or family brand name on all products. A corporation's entire product mix is marked under one family name. Individual brand names are not emphasized but, rather, products are identified by the corporate name and the product category. Examples in the lodging industry would include Hilton Hotels Corporation and their Hilton Hotels, Hilton Inns, Hilton Suites, and Hilton Plaza brands; and Trusthouse Forte Hotels (THF) with their THF Viscount, THF Little Chef, THF TraveLodges, THF Exclusive, and THF Post Houses.

Branding, Segmentation, and Differentiation

Branding is strongly related to market segmentation and product differentiation. Market segmentation is defined as the process by which an organization attempts to match a total marketing program to the unique manner in which one or more customer groups behave in the marketplace. It assumes a hetero-

First class	Luxury	All-suite		
Full service	Full service	Limited service	Full service	Extended stay
Marriott	Four Seasons	Comfort Suite	Embassy Suite	Residence Inns
Hyatt	Park Hyatt	Lexington Suite	Sheraton Suite	Hawthorne
Westin	Exclusive	AmeriSuite	Clarion Suite	Suite
Omni		Best Suite	Guest Quarters	Quality-
Registry		Imperial Suite	Radisson Suite	Residency
Doubletree		Sterling Suite	Pickett Suite	Woodfin
Royce		Manchester	Bristol Suite	Suite
Clarion		Suite	Ramada Suite	Homewood
Crowne Plaza		Woodfield Suite	Hilton Suite	Suite
Howard		Luxford Suite	Hyatt Suite	Neighborhood
Johnson		Days Suite	Park Suite	Inn
Plaza Hotel		Sunrise Suite	Marriott Suite	
Hilton		TraveLodge	Doubletree	
Sheraton		Suite	Suite	
Forte		Bradbury Suite	Howard	
			Johnson	
			Plaza Suite	
			Viscount Suite	

geneity of demand in the marketplace and a divergent demand. Brands are often designed to cater to the needs of a particular market segment. For example, Hilton Hotels with their slogans "America's business address" and "When American business hits the road, American business stops at Hilton" cater primarily to the business traveler.

Product differentiation (distinguishing a product from others in the marketplace) assumes a homogeneity of demand in the marketplace (Busch and Houston 1985; Lewis and Chambers 1989). Product differentiation separates product classes (for example, budget, mid-scale, and luxury hotels), and within those product classes it separates the competition (examples in the budget lodging segment would include Motel 6, EconoLodge, Super 8 Motels, Days Inn, TraveLodge, and Red Roof Inns). Product differentiation is thus often achieved through the creation of a brand.

Hospitality Branding—The State of the Art

Branding has become popular in the hospitality industry for three broad reasons (Olsen et al. 1989). First, conventional wisdom in financial management suggests firms should develop a portfolio of businesses to balance their earnings. In theory, the portfolio is designed so that the return to the shareholder will be stable over the life of the firm. Individual businesses are expected to complement each other such that when one business is experiencing a downturn, the other business will be up. Olsen and colleagues argue that it is in response to this type of portfolio thinking that hospitality firms have been so prolific in developing multiple brands (Olsen et al. 1989).

Second, while the diversity and maturity of the hospitality marketplace is often viewed as being the main reason for the development of multiple brands, there is an argument that the proliferation of brands in the hospitality industry is a result of the needs of the hospitality organizations themselves rather than the needs of the hospitality customers. Indeed, it has been argued that ". . . the strongest push for segmentation seems to be coming from the hotel companies and their potential franchisees and developers. . . ." (Withiam 1985:42) and that branding is a result of ". . . the need to maintain company growth in the face of a saturated market; the need to rationalize or unify an inconsistent existing chain; and the need to respond to developers' objectives by matching the hotel concept to the sites available" (Lee 1985:42).

A brand gives an organization a new vehicle for growth in a saturated market by becoming more focused in its attempts to cater to consumer needs and wants (Withiam 1985). Michael Leven (1985), ex-president of Days Inns, has been quoted as stating that much hotel branding is designed to meet the ego needs of developers.

The final reason for the popularity of branding is connected to the fact that it is often cheaper and financially wiser to build new concepts than it is to renovate existing hotel room inventory. In the United States, for example, it is estimated that over 50 percent of inventory in the lodging industry is old and tired. It is simply financially more rewarding to develop new properties and concepts rather than renovate the existing old inventory.

Hospitality organizations create their new brands in one of two ways. They either acquire a competitor's existing hotel chain, as Ladbroke's acquisition of Hilton International or Saison's acquisition of Westin, or they develop a new brand, as in the case of Holiday Corporation and Embassy Suites or the Marriott Corporation and their Courtyard by Marriott concept.

The practice of branding is so prolific in the lodging sector of the hospitality industry that a phenomenon known as inter-tier brand segmentation is occurring. An example of inter-tier brand segmentation would be the case of the all-suite segment (hotels comprised solely of suites as opposed to rooms) that has been divided into limited-service all-suites, full-service all-suites, and extended-stay all-suites. Within each of these respective subsegments lodging firms have attempted to develop distinct brands in the hope of creating perceived differentiation in the mind of the consumer. Unfortunately, differentiation may be moot when it occurs within the same product class such as the all-suite segment (Lewis and Chambers 1989). It may be that in the lodging industry, differentiation through the creation of multiple brands is being pursued to the extent that it only confuses the customer. It could be argued that creating differentiation through the development of a brand has become somewhat meaningless in the lodging industry since such differentiation may not clarify customer confusion and create brand awareness and loyalty, but rather only add to customer confusion. This customer confusion has arisen partly because firms pursuing a strategy of differentiation through branding have not developed a strong market positioning strategy.

However, not enough branding can also cause customer confusion. For example, Best Western members vary widely in terms of their market position. A Best Western hotel can be a luxury property, a budget property, or anything in between. The customer is confused because a consistent brand image has not been communicated. The brand name "Best Western" represent a whole array of products and services and the consumer has no practical means, based on brand name identification, of determining the type of property being marketed.

Positioning occurs after the market has been segmented on appropriate variables such as descriptive, psychological, psychographic, and behavioral variables (Crawford-Welch 1990). It is the process whereby a hospitality organization informs its target markets about its product attributes, both objective and subjective, and attempts to differentiate those product attributes from the attributes of its competition. There are three components of positioning: the creation of an image, the determination of benefits offered, and the differentiation of those benefits. Unfortunately, many lodging chains have experienced limited success in their attempts to position multiple brands. The success of a multiple brand strategy depends on creating and, more importantly, maintaining a clear differentiation in the consumer's mind (Yesawich 1985). Lodging organizations have often failed to create a strong positioning statement for each of their multiple brands in that each brand does not stand for a unique combination or package of goods and services. Yesawich states "With only few exceptions, the advertising and promotion that has been initiated on behalf of new product concepts has failed to communicate clearly or convincingly the basis of the differentiation. . . ." (1985:50).

Current attempts at branding in the lodging industry are both indicative of the product orientation of many hospitality organizations as well as of their preoccupation with descriptive criteria for segmentation purposes. Many attempts in the lodging industry to create brand loyalty and maximize brand switching costs have failed because of customer confusion brought about by a combination of a lack of clear positioning statements and poor segmentation strategies. Branding in the lodging industry has followed a product segmentation orientation as opposed to a market segmentation orientation.

Given the current state of the art of branding in the hospitality industry, hospitality organizations need to address several issues if branding in the hospitality industry is to achieve the success it has achieved in other industries such as the soft drink and automobile industries.

The Future of Branding in the Hospitality Industry

Branding assumes a heterogeneous marketplace that can be segmented into smaller homogeneous segments catered to by a specific combination of goods and services, that is, a brand. The evolution of branding in the lodging industry from a single brand strategy to complex multiple product line brand strategies geared toward catering to these smaller homogeneous segments poses some serious questions for the future of branding in the industry.

One such question concerns the issue of product standardization versus product customization. As noted, the operation of a brand is based on the premise that risk in the consumer purchase decision will be reduced through the provision of a standardized product. The 1980s, however, have seen the development and operation of brands that have become more and more customized toward catering to the needs and wants of very specific market segments, for example, the extended-stay all-suite segment. If this process of product customization were to reach its logical conclusion, then a situation would arise whereby each customer was catered to with an esoteric and unique combination of goods and services specifically designed to meet his/her needs and wants. This situation, albeit hypothetical, is clearly contradictory to the logic behind creating brands in the first place. Hospitality organizations need to determine at what point they cease to customize their products. At what point do they stop creating additional brands that have fewer and fewer differentiating characteristics and more and more similarities? This decision is a financial decision. Hospitality organizations need to determine at what point market segments become so small and esoteric that it is no longer financially feasible to cater to them with a unique brand.

A second issue hospitality organizations need to address in their branding strategies is the issue of differentiation. Historically, firms in the hospitality industry have tended to position their brands based largely on objective and functional attributes. Examples of such objective product attributes include providing in-house business facilities, in-room check-out facilities, or extra bathroom amenities. Little attention has been paid to the positioning of a brand through the manipulation of subjective product attributes such as "better" service or "friendlier" staff. As the industry becomes increasingly competitive, greater attention will need to be paid by marketing executives to differentiating and positioning their brands based on subjective product attributes such as the level of service. In the hospitality industry of the future, it is the efficient and effective positioning and differentiation of the brand along subjective attributes that will ensure long-term financial health and stability.

A third issue concerns the internationalization of the hospitality industry. There can be little doubt that the business of hospitality corporations is international. The industry is becoming increasingly global in its focus (Lewis and Chambers 1989; Crawford-Welch 1991). Hospitality organizations that operate internationally must determine whether there are adequate similarities between market segments in different countries to warrant the creation of a brand that is marketed similarly across borders. For example, can the needs and wants of business travelers in Singapore be met by providing the same brand that successfully meets the needs and wants of business travelers in Germany?

These three issues, by no means exhaustive, represent the type of concerns hospitality organizations operating in the 1990s need to address in relation to their branding strategies.

Summary

The concept and practice of branding has gained tremendous popularity and acceptance throughout the global hospitality industry. An attempt was made here to (1) precisely define the different elements of the branding process, (2) briefly describe the historical evolution of branding in the hospitality industry, (3) outline and discuss the nature of and the reasons for different branding strategies, (4) discuss the relationship between the practice of branding and the related practices of segmentation and differentiation, (5) outline the current state of the art of branding in the hospitality industry, and, finally (6) to offer some issues that hospitality corporations of the 1990s need to consider when pursuing a strategy of product branding.

References

Busch, P. S., and M. J. Houston. 1985. *Marketing: Strategic Foundations.* Homewood, Ill.: Irwin, Inc.

Crawford-Welch, S. 1990. An Empirical Investigation of Mature Service Environments: The Case of the Lodging and Restaurant Industries. Ph.D. diss. Department of Hotel, Restaurant and Institutional Management, Virginia Polytechnic Institute and State University, Blacksburg, Va.

Crawford-Welch, S. 1991. International marketing in the hospitality industry. In *Strategic Hospitality Management.* London: Cassell Publishing.

Dev, C. S. 1989. Environmental Uncertainty, Business Strategy and Financial Performance: A Study of the Lodging Industry. Ph.D. diss. Department of Hotel,

Restaurant and Institutional Management, Virginia Polythechnic Institute and State University, Blacksburg, Va.

Kotler, P. 1980. *Marketing Management: Analysis, Planning and Control.* New York: Prentice-Hall International.

Lee, D. 1985. In G. Withiam, Hotel companies aim for multiple markets. *The Cornell Hotel and Restaurant Administration Quarterly* (November):39–51.

Leven, M. 1985. In G. Withiam, Hotel companies aim for multiple markets. *The Cornell Hotel and Restaurant Administration Quarterly* (November):39–51.

Lewis, R. C., and R. Chambers 1989. *Marketing Leadership in Hospitality: Foundations and Practices.* New York: Van Nostrand Reinhold.

Olsen, M. D., T. Damonte, and G. A. Jackson. 1989. Segmentation in the lodging industry: Is it doomed to failure? *American Hotel and Motel Association Newsletter.*

Tse, E. C. Y. 1989. An Exploratory Study of the Impact of Strategy and Structure on the Organizational Performance of Restaurant Firms. Ph.D. diss. Department of Hotel, Restaurant and Institutional Management, Virginia Polytechnic Institute and State University, Blacksburg, Va.

West, J. J., and Michael D. Olsen. 1989. Environmental Scanning, Industry Structure and Strategy Making: Concepts and Research in the Hospitality Industry. *International Journal of Hospitality Management* 8(4):283–298.

Withiam, G. 1985. Hotel companies aim for multiple markets. *The Cornell Hotel and Restaurant Administration Quarterly* (November):39–51.

Yesawich, P. 1985. In G. Withiam, Hotel companies aim for multiple markets. *The Cornell Hotel and Restaurant Administration Quarterly* (November):39–51.

15

Service

Suzanne K. Murrmann and Cheri Becker Suttle

At its most basic level, service is defined as "the act of helpful activity." This definition, however, is somewhat ambiguous. Helpful activity takes many forms and even similar services can be implemented at different levels of intensity. Service is an elusive concept; the *Random House Unabridged Dictionary of the English Language* provides thirty-three separate definitions of service. It is no wonder that communication difficulties arise in discussions of what service is and what service should be. Contemporary views on service are in a state of flux. The only clear consensus on this issue is that service standards are on the decline. Before managers of hospitality firms or other service organizations can hope to improve the public perception of service and service quality, a full understanding of the evolution of the service concept and its multiple components is in order.

Since the 1970s the concept of service and its relative importance as a mangement concern has undergone dramatic changes. The traditional view of service organizations and service occupations as providing marginal contributions to the general economic well-being of society no longer holds. Today service industries generate more than 71 percent of the gross national product (GNP) in industrialized nations. In the 1980s the growth in service occupations accounted for approximately 93 percent of all new jobs created (Quinn 1988). Available data indicate such trends will continue into the next century; as a result services management has become a primary issue for both the traditional service organization and the general economy. The increased attention to services and service occupations has broadened the tradtional definition of service. Today service is viewed as a complex multidimensional concept. Recognizing the various elements involved in producing and delivering satisfying service experiences to customers is the first step in creating a successful service organization.

In the hospitality industry the concept of service has traditionally been confined to those duties performed by individuals who occupy positions as waitstaff or maids. To a large degree such definitions are still foremost in the minds of hospitality executives. This narrow focus limits the management perspective and the likelihood of successful service delivery in today's competitive service-based economy. An understanding of the broader perspective on services and the management of services requires a change in the primary orientation of the service manager; an orientation away from the view of service as an occupation (a kind of work) toward a perspective of service as a technology (a way work is done). As a technology, service work and service output can be differentiated from traditional manufacturing work and manufacturing products based on five major characteristics: intangibility, heterogeneity, inseparability, perishability, and customer participation. Each of these characteristics has serious implications for understanding and effectively managing both service organizations and service employees.

Service Characteristics

Intangibility   Because services include performances as well as products, much of the product-service mix cannot be seen, tasted, or felt in the same concrete manner that can be applied to pure products. Service is experienced by the customer psychologically as well as physically. The intangible nature of the service experience is an elusive element. Intangibility is the most difficult component of the service experience to measure. Unlike manufacturing output where the number of units per hour can be easily counted and the appearance of defects can be observed, the intangible elements of the service experience may be impossible to count. Because of the psychological nature of the service experience, the customer's perception plays a significant role in determining whether a service meets acceptable standards. Since there is often a discrepancy between managerial perception and customer perception, the most effective measurement tool available for service managers is to stay in touch with the customer on a regular basis. Customer feedback provides the only real source for evaluating the elusive, psychological elements of the service experience. Input from customers may be solicited through face-to-face exchanges or through the use of brief questionnaires or comment cards. The appropriate choice will be determined by the type of service being provided and the size of the operation.

     Although measurement has traditionally been viewed as the primary problem associated with service intangibility, a second problem of sizeable proportion is related to the use of marketing strategies and advertising copy that make unrealistic promises regarding the intangible benefits of the service experience. In product marketing the use of psychological appeals that promise increased sex appeal as a by-product to using a certain deodorant or a certain toothpaste has become fairly commonplace. Yet it is doubtful that such promises are taken too seriously by most consumers. Such is not the case in services where the experience itself may be paramount. In many services the promise of fun, romance, and excitement may be taken quite literally. Advertising promotions that focus on fulfilling intangible elements based upon the consumer's psychological needs may build up unrealistic expectations—expectations over which the service organization has no control. A promotional strategy that focuses on the concrete benefits associated with the service experience is a safer alternative for any service firm hoping to maximize customer satisfaction and long-term success.

Heterogeneity   Heterogeneity is concerned with the fact that no two service experiences are ever exactly alike. This absence of uniformity is unavoidable since service relies heavily on the input of people and people are unique individuals with different life experiences, different attitudes, and different personalities. Heterogeneity is experienced both at the individual level (in the exchange between customers and service employees) and also at the unit level. In this latter case differences associated with geographic location or individual leadership style may give one chain property a distinction that sets it apart from other affiliates of the same corporation. Although heterogeneity is not always negative, it is unpredictable and as a result it undermines the organization's ability to deliver a consistent service experience to the customer. Heterogeneity can never be completely controlled yet options do exist that minimize any negative impact it might create.

Standardized employee training with intermittent follow-up offers the most basic recourse to combat inconsistency in service production and service delivery. Training is appropriate regardless of the level of service or the type of service organization. The more intense or complex the level of service, the greater the training investment required.

When the type of service being provided is highly standardized, automation provides a solution because it reduces the organization's reliance on people. In large measure the success experienced by McDonald's can be attributed to a systems planning approach that substituted equipment for people and used hard technology to guarantee total product uniformity (Levitt 1972). Because the McDonald's approach greatly reduced the amount of contact time required for service, the influence of employee heterogeneity was also reduced. More recently the widespread success of automatic teller machines in banking has led to the adoption of similar machines in lodging firms where they provide automated check-in and checkout systems to expedite the transaction and eliminate the direct labor costs associated with these procedures.

Highly customized services are really not amenable to automation or rigid standardization policies. Organizations providing such services cannot always predict what kind of special service embellishments a customer might request. As a result it is impossible to provide employees with programmed responses appropriate for every possible situation they might encounter. For such firms the development of a service-oriented organizational climate is one strategy an operation can use to help overcome heterogeneity in employee behavior (Schneider 1980). Orientation of employees can be used to communicate important organizational values related to expected service standards. Over time as employees are subjected to the socialization process within the organization, these values become ingrained as part of the individual's own value system. Once a value preference has been established, employee behavior is generally more predictable and more likely to meet the standards desired by the organization (Mills et al. 1987).

Inseparability   Because services are first sold, then produced and consumed, the customer and the service provider are often engaged in close contact. In services management this close link between production and consumption, and service customer and service provider, is termed "inseparability." Inseparability creates a situation quite different from that encountered by the traditional manufacturing firm. In the traditional model products are manufactured and assembled in a factory, then sent to retail outlets for customer distribution. In service organizations, particularly those involved in producing and delivering hospitality, it is appropriate to visualize the customer as actually entering the factory and placing an order before the production process begins, then waiting around while the production takes place, and finally consuming the product before leaving the factory premises. The total service experience begins when the customer enters the facility and is not complete until the customer leaves. As a result the customer's evaluation of the service experience extends to factors such as decor and atmosphere, timeliness of service delivery, and any sounds, smells, or accompanying activity that may occur at any time the customer is on the premises. Special attention to these seemingly secondary elements in the product service mix is extremely important. Controlling these elements provides the service manager with an opportunity to make the service experience more tangible because these elements are experienced through the customer's sensory perceptions. When these elements are selected so that they fit together and create a cohesive organizational image, they reduce the impact of inconsistencies associated with uncontrollable heterogeneity.

Perishability   Perishability refers to the temporal nature of the service product, which can not be inventoried. Hotel rooms not occupied on Monday evening cannot be stored for later use. The same is true of seats on airlines and trains or in theaters and restaurants. For many service providers the effects of perishability are further exaggerated by fluctuating patterns of customer demand. In restaurant operations business peaks at normal mealtimes and dwindles away by mid-afternoon. City hotels may be filled to capacity during midweek when business travelers abound but virtually deserted during the weekend. Demand for tax services, beach resorts, and many types of transportation varies dramatically depending upon the season. Although total control over consumer demand is beyond the grasp of any service manager, strategies for leveling, or smoothing out, extreme fluctuations in demand can be effective.

Discounting is commonly used by service organizations to increase customer demand in nonpeak periods. For years AT&T has varied rates for telephone services to divert customer usage into less busy periods, seasonally affected resorts and transportation systems have commonly offered special off-season rates, and restaurants have used discounting by implementing early bird specials. The fast-food industry met the challenge of building demand in low use periods by expanding services to include breakfast. When fluctuations in consumer demand cannot be managed through smoothing strategies, forecasting provides an alternative. The forecasting of demand patterns provides information that can be used to vary employee schedules and adjust operating hours to correspond with anticipated usage.

Customer Participation   Most services require some level of customer participation. Operations such as cafeterias expect customers to perform self-service tasks. Banking organizations require that customers fill out standardized forms that expedite the service transaction. As services become more customized the amount of information required to produce the service expected and desired by the consumer increases. As the amount of customer participation increases, the service experience becomes more difficult for the service provider to control. One alternative that allows the service organization to maintain control is to limit customer participation by restricting the number and type of customer requests the operation will accept. Fast-food operations follow such a strategy by standardizing the menu items and limiting the available choices according to the specific meal period. At higher levels of service, interactions between customers and service employees are less structured and less predictable. Customers may make unusual nonstandard requests regarding their expectations for service output. One of the most effective means to maintain control over outlandish customer requests rests in the skills of the service employee. A well-trained service employee has the confidence "to seize the initiative in customer relations—to set the pattern for the relationship" (Whyte

1948:35). The most effective service employees are trained to communicate with courtesy and confidence while simultaneously maintaining control over the service interaction. Evidence suggests that customers react positively when this approach is used (Whyte 1948).

Service Delivery Models

Although the characteristics of service make the job of categorizing service virtually impossible, numerous models have been introduced into the literature on service delivery to help the researcher and service provider identify, in a logical and complete fashion, the most important variables or factors in the process. Although no one model, in and of itself, may be a sufficient framework for providing quality service in every service exchange situation, models do help in understanding the key components of service delivery.

One such model developed by Zeithaml et al. (1990) revolves around the view that the quality of service and service success is a function of the customer's perception of met expectations. Said differently, success in providing quality services is the ability of the service organization and provider to understand the expectations of the customer and to close the important service component "gaps" within the organization for the purpose of achieving expected service. Their model, presented in Figure 1 breaks down service delivery into basic components for individual analysis and identifies the most important gaps between those components that effect the overall mesh between expected service by the consumer and the perceived service they expe-

Fig. 1. Conceptual model of service quality.
(Source: From V. A. Zeithaml, A. Parasuraman, and L. L. Berry. 1990. Delivering Quality Service: Balancing Customer Perceptions and Expectations. New York: Free Press.)

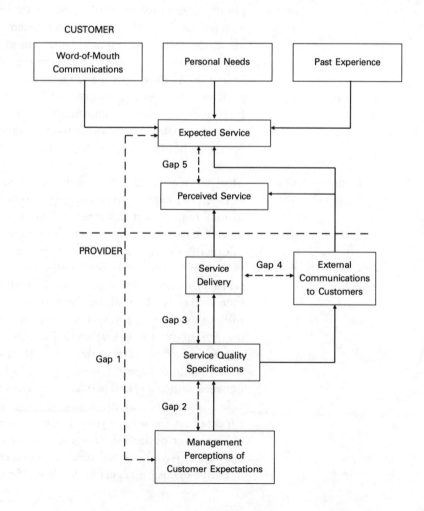

rience. In the model, Gap 1 refers to the discrepancy between customers' service expectations and management's perceptions of those expectations. Best described as "not knowing what customers expect," the gap is attributed primarily to a lack of marketing research or inadequate use of marketing research findings. Closing the gap requires increasing interaction between management and consumers through the use of focus groups, improving upward communication from contact personnel to management, or reducing the number of levels between these two groups.

The second gap identified within the model lies between management's perceptions of customer expectations and service quality specifications, that is, the setting of service quality standards. Thought to be wide in many organizations, the gap is caused primarily by an inadequate commitment to a standard of service quality, inadequate task standardization, and the absence of goal setting. Closing this second gap requires a commitment to quality service, the standardization of tasks, as far as it is feasible within the confines of the service provided through the use of technology, and taking on the task of setting service-quality goals.

The highly interactive, labor intensive nature of service provision often leads to Gap 3, the service-performance gap. Key factors contributing to this gap include the traditional human resource issues of employee role ambiguity and conflict, that is, what is expected of them from both the organization and the consumer of the service they are providing. It is further influenced by poor employee job fit and poor technology job fit, inappropriate supervisory control systems, and a lack of perceived control and teamwork. Good human resource practices including training, conflict management, performance appraisals, and teambuilding are key managment responsibilities necessary to close this gap.

Mention was made earlier to the problems encountered in the marketing of services due to its intangible nature. When promises do not match delivery, a major and often controllable gap occurs between service delivery and external communication to the customer. The key reasons for this occurrence include not only the propensity of the marketing department to overpromise what they cannot or are not delivering, but also inadequate horizontal communication among different functional groups within the organization. Closing this gap requires at the start an understanding and appreciation of the problem. This understanding is equally important in reducing all gaps identified in the model. In addition, there exists the need for opening the channels of communication between advertising and operations, sales and operations, and human resources, marketing, and operations. This can be done through providing opportunities for interaction, such as formal and informal meetings, and providing incentives to employees for engaging in such information exchange.

The gaps discussed previously can be thought of as key ingredients in a recipe for gaining a good understanding of service quality and its determinants. By breaking down the service delivery process into its basic components, the manager can then use the model to allocate or reallocate the organization's resources in specific areas of the process. By identifying the most significant deficiencies within the organization at these four basic points the gap between expected service and actual perceived service, Gap 5, can be narrowed.

Gap theory is representative of many models that provide a framework for identifying key problem points in the service delivery process. Others are designed to take a more microperspective approach to analyzing specific problems associated with the encounter between the service provider and the customer. The customer service transaction model developed by Barrington and Olsen (1987) provides an excellent example of such models. The service transaction, presented in Figure 2, is partitioned into a three-step process, beginning with anticipation of the experience of the service and culminating in residue. Prior to the actual service experience, customers develop an anticipated expectation of the service they will purchase. Expectation is affected by a variety of factors, the sum of which can be described as their reference bank. Included in this reference bank are their perceptions of the value of the service, past experience with the service (utility), motives for purchasing the service (occasion), their present emotional state, the amount of risk they are willing to assume, and the anticipated financial cost of the service. Anticipation within the service transaction model closely resembles customer perceptions of expected services within gap theory.

Their feelings about the actual service experience, the second phase of the process, are formulated by the anticipation they carry into the encounter and its congruity or fit with the actual experience. This encounter is made up of four components: service product components, service product char-

Fig. 2. Model of the hospitality service transaction.
(*Source: From M. N. Barrington and M. D. Olsen. 1987. Concept of service in the hospitality industry. International Journal of Hospitality Management 6(3):131–138.*)

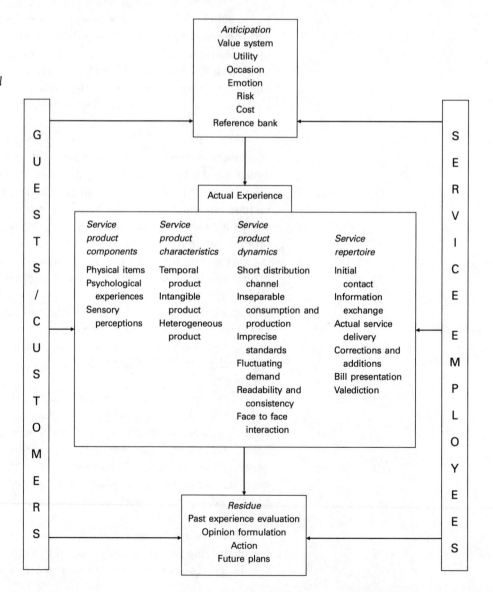

acteristics, service product dynamics, and the repertoire produced by the service provider, such as the waitstaff in a restaurant. Service product components are the physical items that surround the customer during this experience, such as lighting, decor, and cleanliness; sensory perceptions caused by these physical items as well as the interactions with service providers; and the psychological experience produced by such components. The encounter and its outcome is likewise a product of the characteristics of service described earlier. Service product dynamics reflect the volatile nature of service provision. Although it is difficult for the customer to consciously ascertain these dynamics as a separate component of the service they are experiencing, they are manifested in otherwise good service being provided in a poor manner, primarily because of the inability of management to anticipate or provide contingency plans for them. One example may be fluctuating demand, poorly anticipated in an organization's employee work scheduling, and culminating in extended waits for service. The fourth component of the service experience is service repertoire. The service repertoire is the framework in which service providers interface with the service consumer. The model assumes the provision of a quality service experience, and consequently, imparts consistency to the interface starting with initial contact and proceeding through to culmination of the service interaction.

Upon completion of the service experience, the final stage of the transaction is completed as the customer evaluates the total service package in relation to initial anticipation. Residue includes the use of this evaluation to formulate the customer's actions and future plans with regard to the service provided.

Such models become very useful for identifying the essential components of the service process. They can be used as a guide for directing organizational resources toward appropriate components, that is, the implementation of quality standards to control service dynamics and training directed at the service repertoire. They also provide a framework for identifying weaknesses in resource development or allocation, such as flawed marketing approaches to influencing anticipation, or lack of empowerment of service providers that can more efficiently affect positive residue.

Summary

This entry provides a basic overview of the important characteristics of services, as well as a discussion of service delivery models. Together they are useful in more clearly articulating the scope and nature of services provided by an organization. Though services differ from organization to organization, it is appropriate and essential to evaluate them in a systematic way, using the concepts discussed here.

References

Barrington, Melvin N., and Michael D. Olsen. 1987. Concept of service in the hospitality industry. *International Journal of Hospitality Management* 6(3):131–138.

Levitt, Theodore. 1972. Production-line approach to service. *Harvard Business Review.* 50(5): 41–52.

Quinn, James Brian. 1988. Technology in services: Past myths and future challenges. In *Technology in Services*, ed. B. Guiles and J. B. Quinn, pp. 16–46. Washington, D.C.: National Academy of Engineering.

Schneider, Benjamin. 1980. The service organization: Climate is crucial. *Organizational Dynamics* 9:52–65.

Whyte, William Foote. 1948. *Human Relations in the Restaurant Industry.* New York: McGraw-Hill.
Zeithaml, Valarie A., A. Parasuraman, and Leonard L. Berry. 1990. *Delivering Quality Service: Balancing Customer Perceptions and Expectations.* New York: Free Press.

Bibliography

Levitt, Theodore. 1976. The industrialization of service. *Harvard Business Review* 54:63–74.
Mills, Peter, Thomas Turk, and Newton Marguiles. 1987. Value structures, formal structures, and technology for lower participants in service organizations. *Human Relations* 40(4):177–198.
Quinn, James Brian, and Christopher E. Gagnon. 1986. Will services follow manufacturing into decline? *Harvard Business Review* 64:95–103.

16

Individual Unit Hotel Management

Eddystone C. Nebel III

Today, many hotels are individual operating units of larger hotel companies that are responsible for managing numerous hotels. While management at the corporate level is an important topic, it is not discussed here for four important reasons. (1) The vast majority of hotel executives spend their entire careers at the individual hotel level since there are fewer corporate level management positions than management positions at individual hotels. (2) Each individual hotel is a profit center of the larger company. If the individual hotels are profitable, the hotel company will be profitable. If the individual hotels are unprofitable, the hotel company will be unprofitable. While a hotel company can do much to help its individual hotels, the ultimate test of profitability will depend on how well each of the individual hotels is managed at the local level. (3) Any hotel, even if it is part of a larger company, can be thought of as an individual business unit responsible for its own profit or loss. A hotel earns revenues from the sale of various services; in turn, the hotel incurs costs in providing these services. The difference between the revenues a hotel earns and the costs it incurs represents its profit or loss from operations. It is in this sense that each individual hotel of a hotel company is referred to as a profit center. Thus, studying hotel management at the individual hotel level helps one understand what is involved in managing a *business* unit that is responsible for earning a profit. (4) Most young people who study hotel management at the undergraduate level begin their careers in individual hotels. They also must earn their promotion to higher executive positions by outstanding performance as operating executives of individual hotels.

Knowledge of what it takes to manage an individual hotel is one of the fundamental skills any aspiring hotel executive must learn. For this reason this article is limited exclusively to hotel management at the individual unit level.

An Overview of Hotel Management

Hotel management will be defined as the process of planning, organizing, directing, and controlling the activities of a hotel toward certain goals. This definition is an adaptation of the well-known *functional* approach to management (Aldag and Stearns 1987:11) that applies to many kinds of businesses and organizations in addition to hotels.

Defining hotel management as a *process* is meant to convey an ongoing or continuous endeavor in contrast to a one-time event. Building a hotel requires a variety of activities over a number of years, but these activities end upon completion of the physical facility. Managing a hotel does not end; it is an ongoing process that continues as long as the hotel is in operation. It takes place every hour of every day of every year.

The tasks of planning, organizing, directing, and controlling the activities of an organization are referred to as the four major *functions* of management. These four hotel management functions can be briefly described as follows:

- Planning: The process of setting a hotel's goals and objectives and developing the most appropriate strategies to achieve them.
- Organizing: Devising a structure that assigns specific tasks to individuals within the hotel, provides for coordination of activities between different groups, and sees to the hiring and training of a staff to carry out the assigned tasks.
- Directing: The process of leadership that motivates a hotel staff to perform the tasks necessary to achieve the hotel's goals and objectives.
- Controlling: The process of monitoring, evaluating, and providing corrective actions to the activities of the hotel in order to ensure that its overall goals and objectives are met.

Executives must manage the human, financial, and physical resources of a hotel. Thus, hotel management is concerned with *activities* that relate to employees (human resources), money (financial resources) and facilities (physical resources). Planning, organizing, directing, and controlling the activities of a hotel are accomplished with and through people. This statement may express the obvious, but it reinforces the importance of people in hotel management, which is reflected in the popular shorthand definition of management as "the act of getting things done through others."

The final concept in our definition is that hotel management is a *goal* driven activity. Thus, the activities of hotel executives and all the employees of a hotel need to be directed toward goal accomplishments. How well a hotel is managed is determined by its ability to accomplish its goals.

Two final points need to be made concerning this definition of hotel management. The first deals with the *interrelationships* between the planning, organizing, directing, and controlling functions of hotel management. Most management textbooks present these four functions as if they are performed independently of each other. In practice, there is a high degree of interrelationship between the four, as hotel executives continually make decisions and address functional problems while attempting to meet the hotel's goals. The second point is that hotels exist within an *environment* that affects many aspects of hotel management. The hotel environment includes *external factors* and *internal factors* that must be taken into account when managing a hotel. An example of an important external factor is the amount of competition in the hotel industry while an internal factor is the intangible nature of many of the services a hotel provides to its guests.

Figure 1 summarizes the points made in the definition of hotel management. The idea that management is an *ongoing, interrelated process* is depicted by the two-headed arrows connecting the major management functions of

Fig. 1. The management process.

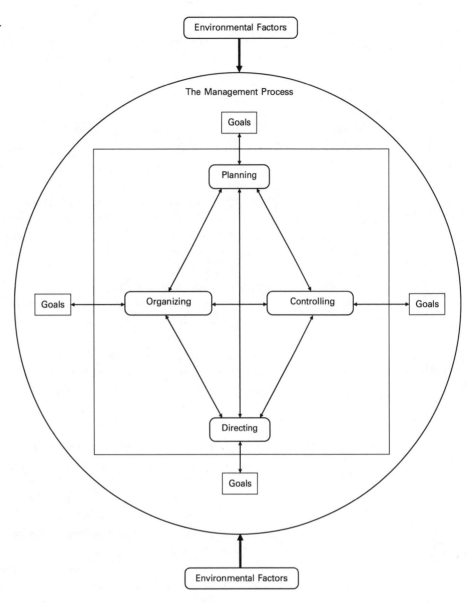

planning, *organizing, directing,* and *controlling.* That hotel management is a goal-directed activity is depicted by the two-headed arrows connecting a hotel's *goals* directly to the four management functions within the management process. Finally, the entire hotel management process takes place within a larger *environmental* framework. Various *environmental factors,* depicted as heavy arrows, impinge on the management process and influence how hotels should be managed.

Environmental Factors

Sixty-three senior level hotel executives, including general managers, food and beverage directors, rooms division managers, resident managers, controllers, chief engineers, sales and marketing managers, and human resource directors, were asked to describe the key characteristics of the hotel business that affect how they should be managed (Nebel 1991). Their answers follow.

Hotels Are Glamorous and Exciting   George Bernard Shaw said that "The great advantage of a hotel is that it's a refuge from home life." Important, dramatic, and sometimes historic events take place in hotels. Hotel executives take this into account in the way they manage. Many liken a hotel to a theatrical production and feel that a hotel "should work like magic for its guests." In other words, the hotel business is rather special with regard to the kinds of personal services that need to be provided, and successful hotel managers are "touched personally" by their efforts to provide these services.

The Pace and Scope of the Hotel Business

Hotels are open every hour of the day, each day of the year, a total of 8,760 hours per year. Few businesses approach this level of intensity. Hotels also experience great swings in their level of activity, with occupancy varying greatly between weekdays and weekends and between peak and slow seasons. Management must take this into account in its marketing and staffing strategies. Hotels are also quite diverse in the scope of their activities, some providing every possible personal service, including medical assistance, to guests. Because they provide a wide variety of services, hotels must continually be concerned about getting a great number of little things right. This requires constant vigilance and attention to detail.

Many of the problems that occur in hotels must be solved quickly or not at all. A delayed banquet or the lack of hot water in guest rooms are problems that require immediate resolution. In addition, there is a degree of unpredictability concerning many hotel problems. There is often little pattern, for example, to when guests get sick or cancel reservations. Hotels, therefore, must be able to respond quickly to unanticipated problems.

The Competitive Environment

Because there are few effective barriers to new competing hotels entering the market, the hotel business has long been characterized as extremely competitive. Some hotels may for a while enjoy a near monopoly position, but it is more typical to find intense competition in most hotel markets. There is often considerable similarity between the physical features of competing hotels so that few can claim a competitive advantage based on distinctive facilities. It is also difficult today to long maintain a competitive advantage because of a *uniquely* desirable location.

Hotels sell a perishable product, guest rooms. They cannot store unsold rooms one day when demand is low and sell them the next when demand exceeds the hotel's fixed supply of rooms. Faced with a fixed supply and variable demand for rooms, hotels must be very good at both forecasting demand and directing guests away from peak periods when occupancy is 100 percent and into slow periods when rooms are available.

The Importance of Service

Many hotel executives believe that guest service is the most important factor that differentiates one hotel from another in the minds of consumers. Because many of the services hotels provide guests are personal and intangible, one of management's greatest challenges is setting service standards and ensuring they are consistently maintained. Management must decide which services to provide and what level of quality is appropriate. These decisions are many and varied. They range from selecting the kinds of bath amenities to include in each room to determining the number of waitresses to staff in a restaurant. Many of the most important guest services are common, everyday things such as clean rooms, hot water for baths, properly prepared food, and accurate messages. Because these are seemingly "simple" services, guests often have little tolerance for mistakes or service breakdowns. A key challenge for management is to provide as close to an *error free* level of guest services as possible. This is particularly difficult because many services require an interaction between the guest and an employee, which introduces an inherent element of variability in the service provided.

People Serving People   A key characteristic of hotels is the sheer number of guests and employees that are involved. A 1,000-room hotel with 100 percent occupancy may have a staff of 900 serving nearly 2,000 guests. Because so many guests are being provided a wide variety of intangible and personal services, hotels must devise ways of staying *close to their customers* in order to ensure that guest service goals are being met (Peters and Waterman 1982:156–199). Management must recruit, train, coordinate, motivate, and control the activities of large numbers of employees who bear the major responsibility for guest service. This is all the more challenging because the competitiveness and labor intensiveness of hotels results in relatively low wage rates for many guest contact employees. Low pay forces hotels to employ many young, inexperienced, and unskilled workers, many of whom are first time entrants into the labor force. These are often the employees who interact most with guests, and ensuring that they perform properly is one of hotel management's major challenges.

This challenge and others place great demands on a hotel's lower- and middle-level managers. First- and second-level managers are responsible for directing the activities of a hotel's hourly employees. Their challenges include maintaining service standards and, at the same time, accomplishing financial goals such as meeting labor and food cost standards. In addition, they must contend with an extremely fast-paced business, problems requiring immediate solutions, long hours, and a significant number of unpredictable problems. These challenges explain why lower and midlevel management turnover in hotels is high and that a major concern of upper level hotel managers is the development of the hotel's junior management staff.

Service Versus Profits   Experienced hotel executives realize that long-run profitability is determined in large part by repeat business from satisfied guests and that guest satisfaction comes from outstanding guest service. Improving guest service, however, usually costs money which, in turn, reduces short-term hotel profits. On the other hand, owners of hotels are interested in both long-run and short-run profits. They therefore view decreases in short-term profits with legitimate concern. Thus, hotel management is a balancing act between service and profits. Without regard for costs, nearly any hotel executive can provide outstanding service. Conversely, without regard for service standards, it would be quite simple to cut costs. Learning to properly balance the two is one of hotel management's key challenges.

Learning how to make a profit (or minimize a loss) in both good times and bad is another important management challenge. The hotel industry has a tendency to exhibit cyclical swings. Hotel executives must therefore be adept at making as much profit as possible during good times when demand is strong. They must also be skilled at economizing and controlling costs when demand is weak.

Hotel Strategic Planning

A hotel's strategies are the plans it devises to win the competitive struggle. Its *strategic planning* can be defined as "the set of decisions and actions resulting in formulation and implementation of strategies designed to achieve the objectives of the organization" (Pearce and Robinson 1988:6). *Strategic decisions* impact a hotel's long-term profitability, often require the allocation of considerable resources, are future-oriented, often affect more than one department, and require consideration of the hotel's external environment. A number of strategic decisions have already been made for an existing hotel including its location, size, facilities and, to a certain degree, the types of guests it was built to serve. Still, strategic decisions are made at the individual hotel level that influence its ability to compete and to achieve its objectives. The larger and more complex a hotel, the more management will likely be faced with the need to plan strategically.

The hotel strategic planning process is shown in Figure 2. The process of setting goals and objectives and formulating a strategic plan involves a *two-way interaction* (indicated by the two-headed arrow connecting the first two boxes) as well as consideration of the hotel's external and internal environment. That is, a hotel must set realistic and attainable goals and objectives based on the environmental forces it faces and on the strategic choices available to it. Once management has properly aligned its goals with its strategies and the environment it faces, its task is to implement its strategic plans and then evaluate results by comparing them to goals and environmental conditions. Note that the arrow from the evaluation step in the process indicates information being returned to each of the three previous steps of the process. Strategic planning, therefore, is a continuing process and not a one time event.

Management can better organize its strategic thinking by engaging in an exercise called SWOT analysis. SWOT stands for a hotel's internal Strengths and Weaknesses and its external Opportunities and Threats. These four factors must be taken into consideration in order to clarify strategic choices (Pearce and Robinson 1988:252–253).

> *Internal strengths:* A resource, skill, or other advantage relative to a hotel's competitors and the needs of the markets it serves or anticipates serving. Examples would include a uniquely good location, a world famous chef, or large and flexible meeting spaces for conventions compared to competing hotels.
>
> *Internal weaknesses:* A limitation or deficiency of resources, skills, or capabilities that seriously impede effective performance. Examples would be an inexperienced sales staff, inadequate or insufficient meeting space, or outdated guest rooms.
>
> *External opportunities:* Major, favorable opportunities in a hotel's environment. Expansion of a nearby convention center or business, opening of a new tourist attraction in the area, or improved air service are examples.
>
> *External threats:* Major, unfavorable situations in a hotel's environment. Examples would include a major recession, construction of a number of new competing hotels in the area, or changes in travel patterns near a hotel's location.

Fig. 2. The strategic planning process in hotels.

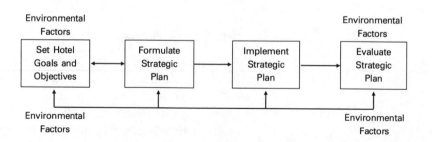

Discussion of external opportunities and threats helps clarify what a hotel is facing in the markets it serves and in the community in which it is located. Similarly, exploring internal strengths and weaknesses, in conjunction with scanning a hotel's external environment, helps bring into focus the strategic choices available to management. Hotels that face many external opportunities that also have internal strengths can afford to pursue aggressive strategies. For example, a hotel located near a convention center that will be expanded may choose to spend millions on an expansion of its rooms and meeting space. At the other extreme, a hotel could face a major external threat and serious internal weaknesses, such as might occur when an aging motel finds out about a plan to build a new super-highway in the area that will route traffic away from it. Such a weak situation might call for a strategy of cutting costs in order to survive. Numerous other possibilities exist, and it is management's task to sort out its options and choose the most appropriate strategy.

Strategic planning at the hotel level often revolves around (1) determining which markets to serve, (2) major capital improvement decisions, (3) setting service and quality standards, (4) human resource staffing and productivity goals, and (5) profitability goals.

Hotel Organization

The purpose of the organizing functions is to provide the necessary structure so that the work of a hotel is carried out in a way that ensures its goals and objectives are met.

Organizational Issues   Organizing a hotel goes far beyond preparing an organization chart. In giving *structure* to their organization, hotel managers must address the following issues:

Work Specialization.   Since there is more than one way to accomplish a task, conscious decisions regarding how to divide tasks among workers must be made. Up to a point, specialization can lead to increased worker efficiency. On the other hand, dividing jobs into ever smaller subunits increases the need for management coordination of workers and adds to employee boredom and dissatisfaction.

Departmentalization.   As organizations grow, managers are faced with the need to group certain jobs together for coordination and control reasons. Such groupings are called departments. In hotels, departmentalization usually takes place according to functions, meaning that workers who are performing similar tasks or functions are grouped together. As soon as departments are formed, patterns of supervision develop because departments are usually headed by managers, resources need to be allocated to the various departments, and departmental performance measures must be set to determine if resources are being used wisely.

Authority.   Management must decide how much decision-making authority should be granted to every job and department in a hotel. Centralized decision making keeps authority in the hands of a few top executives whereas decentralized decision making spreads authority widely throughout the organization. Thus, delegating responsibility for task completion and the authority to accomplish a task is a central issue all hotels must address.

Span of Control. As soon as departments are formed and supervisors assigned, management must decide on the most appropriate number of subordinates reporting to each superior. The fewer the subordinates per supervisor the better they can be supervised and coordinated, but the greater the expense for additional supervisory personnel. The more subordinates reporting to each supervisor, the lower the cost of supervision but the more difficult the task of supervision.

Coordination of Work. Methods of effective coordination differ depending on the tasks involved. When individuals or groups can perform their tasks with little interaction, the need for coordination is minimal. When the output of one task becomes the input of a second, detailed planning, scheduling, and standardization of procedures are necessary. An example in a hotel would be the need for standardization between front desk check-in procedures and the accounting department's guest billing procedures. The greatest degree of coordination occurs when two or more individuals or groups need to provide *each other* with input for task accomplishment. Considerable interaction between groups is required in this circumstance and this is only possible through *direct communication* and often *joint* decision making between groups. This kind of *reciprocal interdependence* is prevalent in hotels. Consider the sales, rooms, and reservations departments, all of which are involved in managing a hotel's unsold rooms. The output of each department, in the form of the number of rooms they separately book, is an informational input to each other department. These three departments must closely coordinate their activities or serious booking mistakes can be made.

Chain of Command. This concept holds that every employee in a hotel should have a supervisor to whom he or she is responsible. Each employee or manager, by tracing through an organizational chart, should be able to quickly determine for whom and to whom he or she is responsible. The chain of command in Figure 3 shows a front desk clerk in a hotel's rooms division reporting to the assistant front office manager who in turn reports to the front office manager, and so forth all the way up to the general manager. The chain of command results in a reporting principle within organizations to

Fig. 3. Chain of command.

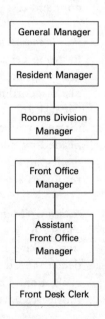

the effect that requests from subordinates and instructions from superiors should take place following the chain of command. At one time "following the chain of command" was a strictly enforced rule in many organizations. Today, many organizations and managers break this rule selectively when doing so fosters improved communications and organizational performance.

Unity of Command. This principle states that each employee is responsible to only one superior and is intended to decrease the inherent confusion of multiple bosses. While the desire to avoid organizational confusion is sound, the existence of various staff functions, such as personnel and accounting, within hotels often results in subordinates receiving instructions from more than one superior.

Organization Chart of a Midsize Hotel

Figure 4 depicts a typical organizational design for a midsize, 500 room hotel. The hotel is organized around five separate divisions based on the functions they perform, which are food and beverage, sales and marketing, rooms, accounting and control, and personnel. The executives in charge of these divisions report directly to the hotel's general manager. Reporting to each division head are the executives in charge of each separate department, for example, the room service manager who reports to the food and beverage director. In a functional organizational design, employees who perform similar tasks or who have similar skills are grouped together thus increasing efficiency within divisions, departments and subdepartments.

Functional specialization allows workers to learn quickly and decreases the need for coordination within functional units. A functional organization's greatest strength is the efficiency it fosters *within* functional units. This strength, however, is also its greatest weakness. Functional departments foster specialists within narrow skill categories. They do not develop employees with broadly based knowledge or perspective of other departments or the

Fig. 4. Organization of a midsize hotel.

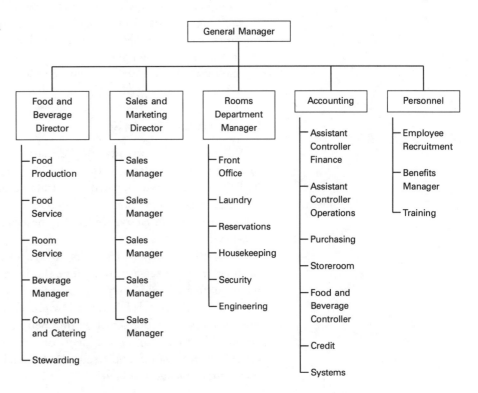

overall aspects of hotels. Many hotel tasks require close coordination and input from various departments, or reciprocal interdependence. Consider the challenge of ensuring that all of the services for a major convention take place smoothly in a hotel. This task requires the efforts, at a minimum, of nearly every department within the food and beverage division and, in addition, the rooms and accounting divisions of the hotel shown in Figure 4. In total, three different divisions and 19 separate operating departments could be involved. Management must find a way to organize and coordinate the activities of these diverse, specialized units in order to meet its overall goal of hosting a successful convention. Left to themselves, these 19 different departments may find it difficult or impossible to accomplish their common goal. Leadership from the general manager, who has hotelwide responsibility, is needed to effect close coordination between different departments. In addition, hotels develop specific *organizational responses* to remedy the problems that stem from lack of coordination. One response to the shortcomings of a hotel's functions organizational design is to use various committees to coordinate activities that involve various functional departments.

A Hotel's Committee Structure

In order to ensure that interdepartmental communication and coordination take place, many hotels have devised a meetings structure that is separate and distinct from their ordinary organizational charts. In many cases, these meetings are organized specifically to include representatives from different departments who are brought together at regular intervals to facilitate interdepartmental cooperation. For example, hotels that host numerous conventions often schedule weekly *convention coordination meetings* at which division and department heads coordinate their activities in advance of the week's conventions. Another example is bi-weekly sales forecasting meetings, attended by the hotel general manager, rooms manager, reservations manager, and sales manager. The purpose of these meetings is to ensure a coordinated reservations and pricing strategy during the upcoming weeks based on the specialized market knowledge of each participant. One major hotel regularly holds nine different kinds of meetings on a daily, weekly, or monthly schedule. Seven of these nine meeting types involve representatives from various departments of the hotel and are intended in part to foster interdepartmental communication, coordination, and cooperation.

Directing the Activities of a Hotel

J. Willard Marriott, founder of the Marriott hotel empire, said "I think that one of the big problems in the hotel industry . . . is indifferent employees." (O'Brien 1978:8). Neither brilliant strategic plans nor careful and exacting organizational design alone ensures outstanding hotel performance. Indifferent employees will *always* thwart the best laid plans or the most exacting organizational design.

To direct is to exert leadership that results in a staff motivated to perform the tasks necessary to achieve the hotel's goals and objectives. Management's ultimate goal is to have the entire staff willingly striving to accomplish the goals of the hotel. President Dwight D. Eisenhower is said to have defined leadership as the art of getting people to do what you want them to because they want to. Four aspects of directing are discussed in this section: (1) worker motivation and needs, (2) leadership styles, (3) leading organizations, and (4) leader behavior.

Worker Motivation and Needs   How employees are led depends in part on one's assumptions regarding their motivation toward work. McGregor (1960) made a classic distinction between two schools of thought about worker motivation by describing them as Theory X and Theory Y. According to the Theory X view of human behavior, the average person dislikes work, will avoid it if possible, is not particularly ambitious, wants no responsibility, is uninterested in the goals of the organization, and is looking primarily for security. If most workers behaved in this manner, management would have to closely control and direct their activities in order to meet the hotel's goals. In other words, an autocratic leadership style would be called for. McGregor rejected this view. Although workers sometimes exhibit this kind of behavior he felt that it was caused more by bad management than by human nature. His view, Theory Y, says that people are motivated by a variety of needs such as social affiliation, self-esteem, and self-fulfillment and that these needs can often be fulfilled through work. (See also Maslow 1954). To McGregor, most people have the capacity to assume a certain level of responsibility and, if *led properly*, will willingly work toward organizational goals. Under these circumstances, management should encourage worker involvement and participation in problem solving and decision making.

Another view of motivation is that workers are thought to be willing to exert *effort* to perform if their performance leads to rewards that they value (Porter and Lawler 1968). Management's job, then, is to increase the chances that effort results in improved performance, to ensure that improved performance results in rewards, and that these rewards are sufficiently valued by employees to motivate them to perform. Management must also set performance goals that are accepted by employees that also meet organizational goals.

Over the past few decades the positive assumptions about workers described in Theory Y have, on balance, predominated. A quote from the best-selling management book *In Search of Excellence* exemplifies this attitude: "The excellent companies treat the rank and file as the root source of quality and productivity gain" (Peters and Waterman 1982:14).

Leadership Styles   Two dimensions of how leaders behave are the amount of participation they foster in decision making and their concern for task accomplishment compared to their concern for subordinates as people. For simple, routine tasks, or when time pressures require quick decisions, it is often best for a leader to be authoritarian and make the decision alone. On the other hand, complex, ambiguous problems usually lead to greater subordinate participation in decision making. Participation also tends to increase subordinate commitment to a course of action and, therefore, may be the appropriate decision-making strategy when subordinate commitment is critical to implementing a decision. Leaders need to assess the circumstances they face in order to determine whether a particular decision should be made more democratically or more autocratically.

The second dimension of leader behavior relates to concern for *people* and concern for *task* completion. A strong people orientation is created through a leader's warmth, supportiveness, and concern for subordinate welfare. A strong task orientation is created when leaders assign tasks to subordinates, clarify expectations, schedule work, and generally set a tone that includes high performance and bottom line goals. A leader can have a genuine concern for subordinates and, at the same time, place a high priority on goal and task completion (Blake and Mouton 1985). In fact, relatively high scores on both dimensions are necessary for effective leadership. Conversely, extremely low scores on either dimension would, in most circumstances, result in ineffective leadership.

It is important to understand that leadership is part of nearly every aspect of the superior-subordinate relationship. In other words, the act of being a leader cannot be disassociated from the day-to-day issues and interactions between superiors and subordinates. Managers should consider most of their seemingly routine association with subordinates as an opportunity to exert leadership.

Leading Organizations

In addition to providing leadership to direct subordinates, management must shape the overall values, attitudes, and beliefs of the entire hotel staff. These shared values, attitudes, and beliefs are referred to as an organization's *culture*. Hotels, if they are to be truly excellent, need to foster a culture with which its employees can readily identify. This aspect of leadership strives to give people meaning in the organization for which they work. Meaning can often be expressed through what is called an organization *superordinate goals*. IBM's basic beliefs, for example, are (1) respect for the dignity and rights of each employee, (2) the need to provide the best customer service in the world and (3) the need to strive for excellence in everything the company does (Pascale and Athos 1981:256–257). From the very beginning McDonald's basic beliefs revolved around quality, service, cleanliness, and value. The superordinate goals of a hotel can relate to (1) the hotel itself, (2) its treatment of guests, (3) its employees, (4) the community at large, or some combination of the four. The goals must be framed in a manner that employees can relate to and accept. Examples for each of these categories would be (1) the hotel's maintenance of a five-star quality rating, (2) a no-excuses policy of guest satisfaction, (3) a commitment to employee development, job security, and promotion from within, and (4) a commitment to support the communities' artistic organizations. Whatever the superordinate goals, if they are accepted and shared by a hotel's staff, they can provide a powerful source of direction and purpose for every employee and manager.

Leader Behavior

Because leadership is so important in the hotel business, some of the behavioral patterns that characterize leaders are noted. Bennis and Nanus (1985: 26–27), in their book entitled *Leaders,* identify four leadership strategies: (1) attention through vision, (2) meaning through communication, (3) trust through positioning and (4) positive self-regard and response to failure. A clear, focused vision of what is important and where a hotel is going will draw the attention of all employees. Leaders pursue their vision with a single-minded intensity and have the ability to communicate this vision to all the hotel's employees. Leaders must be trusted if they are to lead effectively. Trust, say Bennis and Nanus (1985:44) is gained through the consistency and predictability of a leader's actions. Leaders are people who feel good about themselves. Their positive self-regard in turn makes the people around them also feel good about themselves. Leaders accept people as they are, do not hold grudges, and trust others, even in important things. Finally, according to Bennis and Nanus, leaders do not dwell on failures or worry about decisions once they are made. They regard failures as a way to learn or something that happens on the way to success. Leaders thus build positive self-esteem in others by admitting to the possibility of reasonable failure, which to them is a learning experience to build on for future successes.

Controlling the Activities of a Hotel

Management has the responsibility to ensure, through its control function, that the hotel's goals and objectives are met. Since the intent of control is to ensure goal compliance, it is a pro-active, forward-looking management activity. Through control, management intervenes in a hotel's activities in a timely manner to ensure that the future comes out as intended. An effectively managed hotel must devise strategies to control end results, specific employee actions, and employee skills and attitudes (Merchant 1982).

Controlling End Results   When the results of an activity can be measured along appropriate performance dimensions it is possible to develop controls based on *end results*. If precise, objective, and timely performance measures can be made, management can compare operating *results* with predetermined *goals*; it measures if, in fact, results are meeting goals. Suppose that a hotel sets a performance standard of 15 minutes for room service delivery. By measuring room service delivery time each day, management can determine if its 15-minute goal is being met. These daily comparisons give management *feedback* of results, which form the basis for *corrective action* when performance falls short of goals. Thus, if the 15-minute room service goal is not being met, management can either change its room service procedures, or add additional room service personnel, or some combination of the two as a response. This is an example of a *feedback control system* where output performance is measured, compared to pre-existing goals or standards, and corrective management action taken when performance is found wanting. Feedback control systems require activities that repeat themselves, such as the previously mentioned room service example, for corrective measures to be meaningful.

Many activities within hotels have characteristics that encourage the use of feedback control systems. Examples of activities that repeat themselves and whose output can be measured are the number of rooms cleaned by a room attendant, the speed (and accuracy) of guest check-in or checkout, the number of meals served in a hotel's dining room, the number of times a hotel overbooks, and the number of employee accidents each month. Because those activities repeat themselves and because their end results can be measured, feedback control is an appropriate strategy.

Well-managed hotels develop *annual business plans* in which they set a variety of measurable output goals relating to the businesses' performance. Examples of output goals include room occupancy, room revenue, food and beverage revenue, labor costs, food and beverage costs and, of course, profit goals. These annual business plans are subdivided into monthly, weekly, and daily plans. Goals are based on forecasts of future revenues and costs. If these business plans are used properly, they become a *results-oriented feedback control system* for the hotel. Suppose during November, when it is putting together its annual plan for the upcoming year, a hotel sets a 73 percent room occupancy goal for next September. As the year unfolds and September approaches, management continually updates its September occupancy forecast. These revised forecasts provide valuable feedback information regarding the likelihood of reaching the 73 percent occupancy goal. If in July it appears that September's occupancy goal will not be met, management may decide to institute a new marketing campaign or to change its reservations and pricing policies in an attempt to meet its predetermined goal for September. The hotel is trying to adjust its marketing strategy in order to control events and ensure at least a 73 percent occupancy in September.

Hotels also use detailed forecasts of occupancy and food and beverage volume to set staffing levels. They want to control the number of employees working at any time according to the volume of anticipated business. Too few employees result in poor service while too many result in cost overruns. Staffing at just the right level each day is a continuing management control challenge.

Specific Action Control

Experience often teaches us how best to do a variety of activities. In hotels, management often has very good knowledge of the best way to perform tasks and what kind of employee behavior is most beneficial to the hotel. In such cases management may institute control of the *specific actions* of employees as a strategy most likely to contribute to the hotel's overall goals. Specific action controls are appropriate in hotels in numerous instances. Many guest check-in procedures, especially when check-in is part of an automated front office system, include specific steps for employees to follow. Procedures for cleaning guest rooms, doing the hotel's laundry, reacting to an accident, or waiting on tables are other examples where management may prescribe specific employee actions.

Other specific action controls include many of a hotel's personnel policies, rules, and regulations. Absence procedures, dress and grooming codes, smoking prohibitions, rules regarding personal telephone calls, employee time card regulations, and key control of storage areas are examples of control over employee personal actions that hotels enforce.

Specific action controls extend beyond individual employees to include managers and groups of employees. For example, the procedures a manager must follow during the first months of a new worker's employment may leave little to the manager's discretion. Steps to follow in case of a guest complaint or accident may also be standardized. Even some rather complicated procedures entailing extensive interdepartmental cooperation may lend themselves to specific action control. An example would be the detailed plans and procedures to be followed by each hotel department in case of an emergency such as a fire or bomb threat.

Control of specific actions is also accomplished by *direct supervision,* since its objective is to direct the activities of subordinates in such a way as to ensure that events come out as the hotel wishes. Direct supervision is a future-oriented control strategy since its purpose is to *anticipate problems* and take corrective actions in order to control outcomes.

Controlling Employee Skills and Attitudes

Although control of end results and control of specific actions can go a long way, complex service organizations such as hotels must also rely on individual employees' own abilities to act in the best interest of the hotel. This is accomplished by controlling employee skills and attitudes or what Merchant (1982) refers to as *personnel control.* Consider the numerous employee-guest service encounters that take place in a hotel. It is possible for a guest to check in to a hotel and be provided with a wide variety of personal, often intangible services, by hourly employees completely out of the watchful eye of management. The *end results* of many of these activities cannot be easily measured (for example, just how friendly or helpful is a waiter?), and exact knowledge of the most appropriate *specific actions* of employees is limited (for example, how to best show empathy to an upset guest). This circumstance is the most difficult for a hotel or any organization to be in from a control standpoint because neither results nor specific action controls can be relied on to ensure that service goals are met. Faced with this situation, management is left with no choice but to rely on its employees to do *on their own* what is in the hotel's best interest. It is here that personnel control must be used.

Strategies of personnel control include (1) continually upgrading the capabilities of employees and managers through a variety of training and development programs, (2) effectively communicating the hotel's goals and objectives to the entire staff, and (3) fostering shared goals and values throughout all groups, that is, developing a strong culture within the organization. Outstanding hotels engage in a wide variety of training and development activities, employee relations programs (for instance, newsletters, employee sound-off programs, safety awards, good grooming contests, suggestion programs) and intense communication of goals and values in order to foster personnel control. The results of these programs are sometimes difficult to measure directly, but it is possible for management to gauge their overall effectiveness. Carefully designed questionnaires can measure employee morale and pinpoint problems; detailed analysis of employee turnover can sometimes discover when and where problems are developing; open-door grievance policies can keep management attuned to the concerns and needs of a hotel's staff. Carefully measuring guest satisfaction, a form of end results control, can and should also be used as an important measure of the ultimate effectiveness of a hotel's personnel control efforts. Finally, if all the managers of a hotel practice a hands-on, detail-oriented management style and keep attuned to what their employees are saying, they should be able to gauge, at least qualitatively, whether their efforts at personnel control are working.

Because hotels are complex and diverse organizations, their controls must accordingly be complex and diverse. Outstanding hotels do not rely only on one form of control. Rather, management devises a complex, interlocking series of all three control strategies to ensure that the varied activities of the hotel take place in a manner that leads to accomplishing its goals and objectives.

Summary

This article has dealt with management of individual hotels. Hotel management was defined as the process of planning, organizing, directing, and controlling the activities of a hotel toward certain goals. Furthermore, hotel management was described as an ongoing, interrelated process in which various environmental factors influence how hotels should be managed. Important environmental factors included the personal nature of the services provided guests, the fast pace of hotels, the extremely competitive nature of the industry, the importance of service and its relationship to profits, and the labor-intensive nature of the business.

Strategic planning was described as an interactive process in which a hotel sets realistic and attainable goals based on the environmental forces it faces and the strategic choices available to it. Strategic choices can be made by using a technique called SWOT analysis where a hotel analyzes its internal strengths and weaknesses and its external opportunities and threats.

Hotel organization provides the structure for the work of a hotel to be carried out. Hotel managers need to address a variety of organizational issues, including work specialization, departmentalization, authority, span of control, coordination of work, and chain and unity of command. The strengths and weaknesses of a typical hotel organization were discussed, as was the importance of a hotel's committee and meeting structure to ensure interdepartmental communication and coordination.

The third function of hotel management discussed was directing the activities of a hotel's employees and staff. Worker motivation and needs were discussed. Leadership style as it relates to decision making and concern for task completion and for people were reviewed. The need for managers to consider a hotel's culture through the use of superordinate goals was emphasized. This section concluded with a discussion of the distinguishing traits of leaders.

Control in hotels is intended to ensure goal compliance and is, therefore, a pro-active, forward-looking management activity. Through control, management intervenes in a hotel's activities in a timely manner to ensure that the future comes out as intended. Examples of how hotels devise strategies for controlling end results, specific employee actions, and employee skills and attitudes were discussed.

The final management function of control closes the planning, organizing, directing, and controlling loop. The article demonstrated how these management functions fit together into an intelligent and unified process of hotel management.

References

Aldag, Raymond J. and Timothy M. Stearns. 1987. *Management.* Cincinnati: South-Western Publishing Company.

Bennis, Warren, and Burt Nanus. 1985. *Leaders: The Strategies for Taking Charge.* New York: Harper & Row.

Blake, Robert R. and Jane S. Mouton. 1985. *The Management Grid III.* Houston: Gulf Publishing Company.

Maslow, Abraham. 1954. *Motivation and Personality.* New York: Harper and Brothers.

McGregor, Douglas M. 1960. *The Human Side of Enterprise.* New York: McGraw-Hill.

Merchant, Kenneth A. 1982. The control function of management. *Sloan Management Review* 23(4):43–55.

Nebel, Eddystone C., III. 1991. *Managing Hotels Effectively: Lessons from Outstanding General Managers.* New York: Van Nostrand Reinhold.

O'Brien, Robert. 1978. *Marriott: The J. Willard Marriott Story.* Salt Lake City, Ut.: Deseret Book Company.

Pascale, Richard T. and Anthony G. Athos. 1981. *The Art of Japanese Management: Applications for American Executives.* New York: Warner Books.

Pearce, John A., II, and Richard B. Robinson, Jr. 1988. *Strategic Management.* Homewood, Ill.: Richard D. Irwin, Inc.

Peters, Thomas J. and Robert H. Waterman, Jr. 1982. *In Search of Excellence: Lessons from America's Best-run Companies.* New York: Harper & Row.

Porter, Lyman W. and Edward E. Lawler. 1968. *Managerial Attitudes and Performance.* Homewood, Ill.: Richard D. Irwin, Inc.

17

Front Office Operations

Michael L. Kasavana

The front office is responsible for carrying out hotel front-of-the-house functions and serves as a liaison between management and guests (Fig. 1). The primary function of the front office is to sell guest rooms. Since guest rooms tend to generate the highest profit margin within the hotel, this function becomes crucial to hotel profitability. No other hotel department is held more accountable for a particular day's occupancy than the rooms department of the front office.

Related to room sales, the front office is also responsible for accepting

Fig. 1. Summary of front office functions.

1. Sell guest rooms
    Accept reservations
    Handle walkins
    Perform the registration process
    Assignment of the room
2. Provide information on hotel services
    Concerning internal hotel operations
    About external events and locations
3. Coordinate guest services
    Liaison between front- and back-of-the-house areas
    Handle guest problems and complaints
4. Chart room status reports
    Coordinate room sales and housekeeping: occupied status, on-change status, out-of-order status
5. Maintaining guest accounts
    Construction of folio and account
    Posting to folios (updating)
    Supervision of credit levels
    Documentation of guest's transactions
6. Settlement of guest accounts
    Preparation of guest statement
    Reconciliation of folio
    Perform the checkout procedure
7. Construct guest history file
    Record the guest's personal data for future references

reservations, handling walk-ins, and completing the registration procedure. The front office provides guest information, charts room status, coordinates guest services, and monitors guest accounts. Recently, many hotels have added the responsibility of creating and maintaining a reliable guest history file to the functions assigned to the front office.

The most visible area in a lodging property, with the greatest amount of guest contact, is the front office. The front desk itself is the focal point of activity in the front office because it is where the guest is registered, assigned a room, and checked out. Front office responsibilities may also include mail and information service, cashiering, and concierge services.

The mail and information section of the front office department was once a very prominent department. However, in recent years the responsibility for providing guests with mail, information, and messages has been divided among desk clerks, telephone switchboard operators, and front office cashiers.

Another recent development in the front offices of some hotels has been the establishment of concierge services. These services may include making theater reservations and obtaining tickets, organizing special functions, and arranging for secretarial, typing, or computer services for guests. In a sense, the concierge section is simply an extension of the front office that specializes in extended guest services.

Front and Back Office Areas

Back-of-the-house managerial responsibilities include planning, staffing, controlling, and supervising those areas of the lodging operation with which guests rarely have direct contact. The physical location at which back-of-the-house activities are coordinated is referred to as the back office. Front-of-the-house managerial responsibilities include service-related areas of the lodging operation with which guests normally have direct contact. The term *front office* refers to a specific department within the hotel and also to the physical location at which front-of-the-house activities are coordinated.

Guest Cycle

In order to effectively manage front-of-the-house activities, properties have adopted the notion of a guest cycle. The guest cycle identifies the physical contacts and financial exchanges that occur between guests and various revenue centers within a lodging operation. The traditional hotel guest cycle was based on interactions in terms of a sequence beginning with the arrival of a guest, continuing through the guest's occupancy, and ending with the guest's departure. Many properties have revised this traditional guest cycle into a sequence of phases beginning with presale events, continuing through point-of-sale activities, and concluding with postsale transactions. The primary reason for revising the traditional concept of the hotel guest cycle is the increasing need for improved coordination among various operating departments.

The presale phase of the hotel guest cycle involves all activities preceding the actual sale of a guest room. Important presale activities include processing reservations, recording advance deposits and prepayments, forecasting occupancy and revenue, and performing preregistration functions.

At the time of guest registration, the hotel guest cycle shifts into the point-of-sale phase. Rooms management, guest accounting, and auditing procedures are the primary areas of activity during this intermediate phase of the hotel guest cycle. Typical point-of-sale activities include registering guests, assigning rooms and rates, creating guest accounts (folios), and posting charged purchases to folios.

The final phase of the guest cycle begins at checkout. Typical postsale activities include reconciling guest accounts, transferring amounts to the city ledger, updating room status, and completing guest history records.

Front Office Resources

The front office, being the central artery of a lodging property, is the main channel of communication and information dissemination. The front office generates, processes, and audits large volumes of documents in its efforts to accurately monitor the guest cycle. Since the guest cycle involves a sequencing of hotel procedures accompanied by financial interactions, it is important that the front office develop adequate controls over such key areas as guest credit supervision, cashier reconciliation, and hotel guest receivables. The front office staff is responsible for establishing a sound data base of guest information and for coordinating guest services with back office operations in order to achieve maximum guest satisfaction.

The personnel typically found in a front office include reservationists, cashiers, front desk clerks, billing clerks, (night) auditors, switchboard operators, and bellhops. These persons are assigned specific tasks designed to assist the hotel in satisfying guest needs. Traditionally the front office has been organized along functional lines with different employees handling separate function areas in order to provide the hotel with better internal control over its operations. This separation of function may not be practical or feasible in a smaller hotel property.

The front office has evolved from a manually oriented operation to a machine-assisted environment to a computer-based information system. The guest cycles of the 1950s, 1960s, 1970s, and 1980s are differentiated by the design and implementation of forms and machinery and by the degree of data handling in the front office. The front office has shifted from a nonautomated labor-intensive work unit, to a semiautomated machine process, to a fully automated computerized environment. It is not uncommon to find hotels operating in any one of these three modes. As the impact of hotel computer systems becomes fully understood, all property sizes will likely participate in automation, thereby rendering the front office a more paperless environment.

Front Office Functions

The primary function of the front office is to sell guest rooms. On a long-range basis, reservations establish a commitment for a room at the hotel at some time in the future. In the short run (on any particular day), a front desk clerk is responsible for assigning unoccupied rooms to arriving guests and for verifying that the registration procedure is complete. A measurement of a desk clerk's performance is normally based on the number of rooms sold and the room rate (price) for which they are sold. Together the rate and the quantity of rooms sold determine room revenues. Room revenue is the total number of dollars collected for all rooms sold and is a critical component in the measurement of hotel profitability. The front office, striving to maximize room revenues, must require its desk clerks to select a proper room rate from a room rate range for every room sold.

A proper room rate is one that is appropriate for (1) the number of guests occupying the room, (2) the location of the room, and (3) the availability of services and furnishings in the room. Each guest room normally is assigned a range of rates depending on its ability to meet these criteria, and this gives the desk clerk some freedom in determining a proper rate for every room. A double bed in a small room without a television set, for example, will surely warrant a lower room rate than the same bed in a large room, poolside, with color television, VCR, and sauna. Although many hotels preassign rooms and rates, some front offices still allow the clerk to determine an appropriate rate and to complete the remainder of the rooming process. The rooming process consists of dealing with reservations; handling walk-in guests; carrying out the registration procedure; and assigning a room and rate to each guest.

The number of guests making hotel reservations has been steadily increasing, thereby enabling hotels to better forecast their business. Reservations enable the hotel to carry out many preregistration functions (such as room and rate assignment) and provide a sharing of the rooming process between the reservation department and the front desk. The guest with a reservation further simplifies the work of the desk clerk in that information usually collected at the time of check-in has already been recorded at the time of reservation. This data enables the desk clerk to verify the appropriateness of a room and rate assignment in a more efficient and less hurried manner than would be possible for a walk-in guest. Although the price and type of accommodation may be made in advance for a guest with a reservation, any changes in the original reservation requirements may void the predetermined assignments and create complex problems for the desk clerk.

A walk-in guest is one who comes to the hotel without a reservation. Walk-in guests offer the front office a more complicated situation than do guests with reservations. The guest who makes a reservation truly does the hotel a service in that the hotel can prearrange facilities to accommodate the guest. Also, because these requirements are known prior to arrival, the staffing, planning, and coordination of services are all simplified. The walk-in does not offer the front desk this luxury. The front desk clerk must spend more time with the walk-in (since little is known prior to the guest's arrival) and must follow the entire registration procedure to create a proper record of guest information. Since hotels know the least about walk-in guests, a lower credit limit is usually assigned to their folios and their rooms are assigned on a "next available" basis.

The registration procedure of the hotel is critical to the capturing of guest information and the initialization of the guest account. Almost all the paperwork in the guest cycle is based on the data that is recorded and verified at, or prior to, check-in. Although the hotel might require all guests to complete a registration card at check-in, the process is really not complete until a room and rate are assigned to the guest. Available rooms are found through an investigation of room status and the room's rate is selected from the room rate range. The acceptance of reservations, the handling of walk-in guests, the completion of the registration procedure, and the assignment of a room compose the room sales function. (See Figure 1 for a summary of front office functions.)

Front Desk

Regardless of how a hotel is constructed or organized, the front office is always an essential focal point. The front desk is the most obviously visible segment of the front office and is strategically located in the high traffic, lobby area. The front desk is where major decisions affecting the guest stay (room availability, room and rate assignment, and guest account supervision) are made. Since most front office departments are typically located away from the desk, they tend to serve the guest in a somewhat less direct manner. For this reason the desk is the major source of guest information and is responsible for the maintenance of guest records. Guest contacts with the front desk are usually the first (check-in) and last (checkout) activities experienced during a normal guest stay. Because of the guests' familiarity with the front desk, it serves as a sounding board for guest complaints and as coordinator of guest services. The front office, therefore, becomes the logical connecting link between the guest and the hotel.

Information Services

Because of its central location and because it becomes the major contact point for guests, the front office serves as the main source of information on hotel activities. In addition to its role in selling rooms, the front office must be prepared to provide marketing, instructional, and supportive information on internal and external operations and events to its guests. The suggestion of a restaurant, movie, or other events is a frequent informational request handled by the desk's staff. The desk clerk is truly responsible for the hotel's image and for promoting the hotel's resources. In addition to knowing about internal hotel opportunities and schedules, the desk must also maintain an in-house guest list and an information rack for operational purposes.

The switchboard and front desk areas both rely on up-to-date guest lists. Once the guest has checked into the hotel, phone calls, packages, visitors, and the like may follow. The use of a guest list (arranged alphabetically by the guest's last name or by room number) is very useful for tracking down the whereabouts of in-house guests. Large hotels usually maintain information racks, instead of lengthy guest lists, to enable a quicker response to a search for a guest's room assignment, because racks are easier to modify and update as guests check in and check out continually throughout the day.

Most front desks are required to furnish information and directions to establishments outside the hotel but within the surrounding community. Persons who stay in the hotel for more than one night, for example, may seek a change of eatery or scenery whereas a late night check-in might be more interested in what the hotel itself has to offer. In either case, the hotel is always best prepared for any situation when the front desk employees are well informed and courteous. Hence the most important hotel-guest support function of the front office is the disbursement of accurate information concerning the internal and external activities of and around the hotel.

Guest Services

Guests come to hotels to enjoy services they cannot get elsewhere. The front offices must serve as the liaison between the guest and the service departments of the hotel. The front-of-the-house areas of the hotel tend to be service centers, aimed at satisfying guest needs. The front desk, which represents the hotel to the guest, must interface the back-of-the-house support functions in such a manner that continuity and quality of services are maintained. The complaint that there is no heat in a room, for example, is received by the front desk and must be communicated to the engineering department for repair. Similarly, when a guest checks out the front office must notify the housekeeping staff that the previously occupied room must be cleaned. It is the front office's responsibility to develop and maintain the communication of guest requirements between the service and nonservice departments of the hotel. Once the front office becomes aware of any guest's dissatisfaction or unrest, corrective action should be initiated so that the guest's discomfort is reduced and the hotel stay becomes more enjoyable.

Room Status

Hotel room status can be viewed in the long run (more than a 24-hour horizon) as a reservation status and in the short run (within the next 24 hours) as a housekeeping status. Regardless of time frame, the purpose of charting room status is to enable the hotel to maximize the utilization of its most profitable commodity—its rooms.

The hotel depends on the front office to provide an accurate status of each room at any time. The front desk normally maintains a room rack, or its equivalent, for charting short-run guest room status. The room rack is composed of vertical file slots, one for each room, which hold housekeeping file cards and registration cards. Depending on a room's sell position (occupied or unoccupied) either a registration card or a housekeeping form will be in each file pocket. The room rack is considered to be the most important piece of front office equipment. The rack provides an up-to-the-minute inventory of rooms occupied, rooms being prepared for sale (on-change), rooms not to be sold (out-of-order), and rooms ready for sale (clean and vacant). Without an accurate knowledge of each room's status, the rooms department would have great difficulty assigning rooms and housekeeping would not know which rooms require service.

A room that appears to be occupied according to its rack status, but actually is vacant, causes an imbalance in the room status system. This discrepancy is commonly termed a sleeper, and the room will be assumed sold until the mistake is corrected (the status is changed to unoccupied). A guest who checks into the hotel and then leaves without paying is called a skipper and can be just as disruptive to an efficient room status system as the sleeper. A skipper is normally detected by comparing the housekeeping and rack statuses for a given room.

Although accurate, up-to-the-minute room status is a desirable goal, in reality few hotels enjoy this luxury. Unless the hotel has a rapid electronic communications relay between the housekeeper and the room rack, there is sure to be some time delay in room status at the front desk. Since the loss of room sales may hinge on effective room status reporting, hotels are striving to enhance their informational capabilities among operating departments. It is the responsibility of the front office to coordinate room sales and housekeeping and to try to provide a ready room for every guest.

Guest Accounting

A guest account can be initialized at the time of reservation (for posting advanced deposits and prepayments) or registration. The creation of an account begins the charting and monitoring of hotel-guest financial interactions within the confines of the guest cycle. The monitoring of guest accounts usually occurs in the front office and is later double-checked by the accounting department.

The outstanding balance of guest receivables (debits) must be properly recorded to the correct guest account record (folio) so that a complete payment (credit) in full can be requested of the guest. Charge purchases made during the occupancy phase of the guest cycle are posted to the guest's folio on the day they are incurred. Cash payments against these receivables are also posted to the folio to show a decrease in the account balance. Cash purchases made at various points of sale throughout the hotel (other than the front desk) will not appear on the folio as an entry. Hence, folio postings are performed only for charge purchases and deferred payments made against those purchases. Posting to folios updates the guest's outstanding balance and reflects the cash flow position of the hotel.

Although the front office is responsible for maintaining up-to-date guest accounts, it is also charged with the supervision of credit lines to guests. Credit limits vary from hotel to hotel, but in general the hotel has an established house limit and a floor limit. The house limit is a predetermined level of charges the hotel will allow the guest to accumulate prior to requesting a full or partial payment. Such a payment is used to reduce the outstanding folio balance to below the house credit limit. For example, a guest checks in and is assigned room 1019 but requests to defer paying for the room until checkout. The desk clerk approves and the guest leaves the lobby for the hotel's restaurant. There the guest runs up a bill of $29.50 that is charged to the room account (guest folio). Late in the evening the night auditor is reviewing this guest's folio and notices an outstanding (debit) balance of $69.50 for room, tax, restaurant, and telephone charges. Knowing the hotel has a house limit of $65.00, the auditor reports the status of this account to management. Management contacts the guest and requests a payment in full ($69.50) or part ($4.50) to bring the folio balance down to or below the house limit.

The hotel-guest transactional accounting cycle is completed when all the information in the system is compiled, summarized, and presented in guest statements, financial statements, and operating statistics. To complete the example, the final folio for room 1019 would show the restaurant charge for $7.90 and would alert the desk clerk to collect that receivable from the guest at the time of account settlement (checkout). The hotel front office becomes involved in processing numerous documents and large volumes of data. For this reason many hotels have begun to reevaluate their data handling procedures and are adopting automated data processing technology.

Account Settlement

Prior to a guest's departure from the hotel, the folio must be updated to show any outstanding balance remaining on the account. When the guest approaches the desk to check out, the folio is finalized and presented to the guest for review. Should the guest dispute any entry on the folio the front office, through its accounting system, should be able to produce supporting documentation to prove the folio balance. The ending folio balance reflects the tabulation of receivables (debits) and payments (credits) between the guest and the hotel. The guest can pay the folio balance in full, pay it in part and charge any outstanding balance to a credit card, or arrange a billing. Hotels usually require guests to present a credit card at check-in (to hedge against skippers) but will, of course, accept cash at checkout. Should the guest wish to have the balance transferred to his or her credit card account, this decision can be made at checkout. Problems arise in situations where hotels allow guests to transfer their folio balance to a "bill to" or a nonguest account without previous (prior to check-in) approval. Hotels are usually careful not to encourage this procedure but often it is unavoidable.

Hotels must emphasize accuracy and timeliness in the flow of their accounting information to eliminate late charges. A late charge is defined as a charge that reaches the front desk for posting after the guest has already checked out. The chance of collecting late charges balances is believed to be highly unlikely, since the guest may feel it is the hotel's problem that accurate account records were not maintained. Because the hotel is a 24-hour-a-day environment, guest accounting systems deserve a strong commitment to detail. The guest in room 1019 paid her balance in full at checkout and thereby zeroed out her account balance. Effective guest settlement procedures require that all account balances be brought to zero (debits equaling credits) at the time of checkout. Accounts can be brought to zero through payment in full or by transfer to a credit card or nonguest account.

Guest History

Since hotels collect so much data on their guests, it is only natural that the best source of guest information be the guest history file. The guest history file is created by assembling registration card information into an inactive guest file. This data serves as a valuable base of marketing information and can aid the hotel in developing strong personal relationships with its guests. The guest history file can answer many questions. Who were our guests? Where did they come from? How many rooms did they occupy? How many guests were in each party? How often does a particular guest stay in the hotel? What is the length of the average guest stay? The development of long-range marketing strategies and the enhancement of the hotel's knowledge about its clientele should enable the hotel to improve its market penetrations and thereby increase its room sales. Recall that the major purpose of the front office is to sell guest rooms and that an analysis of front office functions reveals a strong emphasis on this goal throughout. Although guest history data can be collected quite readily, some hotels have failed to make use of this potentially powerful data base.

Front Office Automation

Front office operations can be either nonautomated, semiautomated, or fully automated. The differentiating factors involve how data is collected, processed, and distributed. The physical equipment used to handle data processing functions is termed hardware. The arrangement of this hardware forms a configuration designed to accomplish the front office's information processing needs. Front office hardware requirements are not standardized and different operating modes require different types of equipment. A lodging property in which all transactions are recorded and maintained using manual processes requires the least hardware of any hotel operating mode. The type of hardware a hotel chooses is a function of its number of rooms, volume of business, and available resources. Hence, a small, nonautomated hotel would be able to operate with a minimum number of racks and storage files.

A medium-sized hotel would likely employ basic office and clerical machinery to support its processing operations. A posting machine, adding machine, cash register, typewriter, assorted racks, and the like typify a semiautomated hotel's hardware configuration. The fully automated establishment employs a computer system with electronic memory capabilities to control its operations. The computer-based hotel requires a central processing unit (CPU), memory unit, input device, and output device. These components are wired together for the purpose of communication and centralization of information. The fully automated hotel is the only type that has remote data entry (away from the front desk) capabilities.

Traditionally, hotels of fewer than 50 rooms have been nonautomated, hotels of 50–250 rooms have been semiautomated, and the larger properties (over 250 rooms) have been the first to become involved in fully automated procedures. It appears now that within the next decade all hotels, regardless of size, will employ some form of computerization in their operation.

While not all hotel property management systems (PMS) operate identically, there are four common front office software modules: reservations, rooms management, guest accounting, and general management. A reservations module enables a hotel to rapidly process room requests and to generate timely and accurate rooms, revenue, and forecasting reports. Reservations received at a central reservations site can be processed, confirmed, and communicated to the destination property before the reservationist finishes talking with the caller on the telephone. When the destination property uses a property management system, the reservations module receives data directly from the central reservation system, and in-house reservations records, files, and revenue forecasts are immediately updated. In addition, the reservations data received can be automatically reformatted into preregistration materials and an updated expected arrivals list can be generated.

A rooms management module maintains up-to-date information regarding the status of rooms, assists in the assignment of rooms during registration, and helps coordinate many guest services. Since this module replaces most traditional front office equipment, it often becomes a major determinant in the selection of one PMS over another. This module alerts front desk employees of each room's status just as room and information racks do in nonautomated environments. For example, with a room rack, an upside-down card without a folio covering it may signify that the previous night's guest has checked out but that the room has not yet been cleaned for resale. This status will remain unchanged until housekeeping notifies the front desk that the room is clean and ready for occupancy. In a computerized system, the front desk employee simply enters the room's number at a keyboard and the current status of the room appears immediately on a display screen. Once the room becomes clean and ready for occupancy, housekeeping changes the room's status through a terminal in housekeeping's work area and the information is immediately communicated to the front desk.

A guest accounting module increases the hotel's control over guest accounts and significantly modifies the night audit routine. Guest accounts are maintained electronically, thereby eliminating the need for folio cards, trays, or posting machinery. The guest accounting module monitors predetermined guest credit limits and provides flexibility through multiple folio formats. When revenue centers are connected to the PMS, remote electronic cash registers communicate to the front desk and guest charges are automatically posted to the appropriate folios. At checkout, outstanding account balances are transferred automatically to the city ledger (accounts receivable) for collection.

A general management module cannot operate independently of other front office modules. General management applications tend to be report-generating packages and, therefore, depend on data collected through reservations, rooms management, and guest accounting modules. For example, the general management module allows a front desk manager to generate a report showing the day's reservations (expected arrivals) and the number of rooms ready for occupancy. This information, stored in the PMS network, is a combination of reservations and room management module data. In addition to generating reports, the general management module is the central feature for linking front and back office applications of a property management system.

Summary

The front office is strategically located in the high traffic lobby area and represents the hotel and all its services to the guest. The front desk is the most visible part of the front office and most front office functions tend to be carried out at the desk. Because guests come in contact with the desk initially (at check-in) and as their last involvement with the hotel (at checkout), the desk serves as the liaison connecting the front- and back-of-the-house and it also tends to be a sounding board for guest complaints. The major functions performed by the front office are (1) to sell guest rooms, (2) to provide information on hotel services, (3) to coordinate all guest services, (4) to chart and report room status, (5) to maintain guest accounts, (6) to settle guest accounts, and (7) to construct a guest history file.

The guest cycle identifies the physical contacts and financial exchanges that occur between guests and various revenue centers within a lodging operation. The guest cycle is a sequence of phases that originates with presale events, continues through point-of-sale activities, and concludes with postsale transactions.

All guest services begin at the front desk and the information collected during registration provides the data base for hotel planning and operations. Hence, the selling of guest rooms, the establishment of registration, and the collection of account balances are the most important roles of the front office.

18

Hotel Sales

Howard Feiertag

There has been much confusion in the hospitality industry between the terms *marketing* and *sales*. The words have erroneously been used interchangeably, and in many cases where personnel are designated "marketing director" or "marketing manager," they actually perform the function of sales.

"Marketing" is a term that reflects the development and delivery of a product to a market. It encompasses research, advertising, public relations, merchandising, and sales promotion, as well as direct sales. Hotel sales is engaging the use of the product for a price. It is, therefore, a function of marketing. In the lodging business personnel are hired to do "sales" work. The sales representative, sales manager, or director of sales "engages the use of the property" for a price by making a "sale" to a user or customer. Therefore, we must think of "hotel sales" as a function of a person or department to bring in business by personal contact with prospects. A major responsibility of a sales department is to bring new accounts to a lodging facility. Along with that, there is a need to maintain account files, have a follow-up (trace) program, handle inquires, prospect, make sales calls, negotiate, and produce profitable sales.

Prospecting and Lead Development

To bring in new business, salespeople first need to develop leads. A lead is nothing more than a piece of information that could show the way to possible business. It may be the name of a person or the name of a company or organization. New business is also developed by the proper handling of inquiries. Inquiries are leads that come directly to the lodging property by mail, phone, or in person. Since the inquiry is considered a "hot" lead, it should be answered immediately. A good policy is to make sure the inquiry is directed to someone who can make the sale.

Leads need to be followed up to determine if the contacts could use a lodging facility for any reason. The process of making inquiries to determine if contacts can and will use a property is called prospecting. Prospecting is a key factor in developing new business. Sales personnel need to practice prospecting every day, by using existing leads and making calls (by phone or in person) on the lead contact. Prospecting is also accomplished by making "cold" calls, a process whereby a salesperson makes telephone or in-person inquiries unaware of whether the contact is a lead at all and gathers information to see if there is any possibility of business. Leads may be developed through

- Referrals of existing customers
- Items in newspapers or trade magazines
- Participation at trade shows
- Networking through local organizations
- Going door-to-door in a business complex or office buildings
- Vendors selling to the property
- In-house staff referrals
- Search of existing files

Actually, leads are literally endless. The act of selling comes once leads are qualified as prospects.

Sales Calls

Making sales calls is an interaction between a salesperson and a prospect for business. There are many techniques involved in making sales calls. Salespeople must learn how to analyze and respond to interactions between themselves and the prospective customer. Sales calls may come in different forms; however, a true "sales" call is one in which an attempt is made to bring a piece of business to a close. Other types of interactions may be generally referred to as being sales calls, but have purposes other than closing a piece of business. The different forms of interaction may involve

- the cold call (prospecting, gathering information to determine if there is a possibility of business)
- public relations call (good will, image building, responding to a complaint)
- appointment call (truly a sales call)
- in-house call (where an inquirer, or prospect, visits the property to check it out. This is also a good sales call.)

The Sales Blitz

The sales blitz is an opportunity for developing leads and locating prospects. It is a system of using a number of people to make a maximum number of cold calls in a small geographic area in a short time period. Property staff people may be used from different departments. Many blitz programs are conducted by students from nearby universities who are enrolled in a hospitality curriculum. Lodging operators have discovered that by conducting a sales blitz many prospects are uncovered that would not have otherwise been located. In many cases the development of new business more than pays for the time and expenses involved in a blitz program. It is not unusual for ten people conducting a sales blitz over a three-day period to make 1,000 contacts. Usually one third of the number of contacts would qualify as prospects, to some degree. Qualifying contacts is accomplished by asking a series of questions, the answers to which indicate if the contact is eligible or capable of providing business to the property. Proper planning is important to the success of the blitz. The use of a city directory and map saves time in locating business areas where calls are to be made. Participants need to be supplied with information sheets, property brochures, and a questionnaire, which is a single sheet of paper with specific questions to ask the contacts. The response to the questions help determine if the contact is a prospect for business. It also helps to provide briefings and role playing sessions for the participants.

HSMAI

The leading membership organization for hotel sales personnel is the Hotel Sales and Marketing Association International with headquarters in Washington, D.C. Membership is at 6,000, with members virtually from every country in the world. The organization was founded in 1927 by John C. Burg, vice president of Statler Hotels Company, who saw a need to educate hoteliers so that they not only could bring more guests into their properties but also do a better job of satisfying the needs of those guests. The first International Conference on Hotel Business Promotion, which was held in Chicago's Belmont Hotel in September 1927, dealt with those issues. Attendees at that meeting were general managers. Growth for the organization was slow at first, but in 1936, with the hotel business growing, membership began to grow. The first chapter charter was given to Atlantic City, New Jersey, in 1937.

Significant Changes

The hospitality business has undergone significant changes, not the least of which was the change from a sellers' to a buyers' market. New concepts in hotel building, advances in transportation, new emerging markets, new technology, increased leisure time, and various socio-economic facts have made it necessary for the hotel industry to reevaluate its promotional methods. The basic "selling" function has changed over a period of time. Instead of people being sold "features" (a room, a bed, meals, television, location), they had to be motivated to purchase "benefits" (relaxed atmosphere, attractive and tasty food, entertainment, security, privacy, comfortable bedding). Modern sales involves the realization that purchasers of hotel products are seeking both tangible and intangible benefits that are either completely different or more exotic than previously thought. Such intangibles include romance, allure, intrigue, glamor, adventure, novelty, and entertainment.

Cultural Diversity

Cultural diversity plays an important role in modern sales activities with the emergence of new market segments for business. These include ethnic groups, senior citizens, youth, women, foreign markets, blue collar workers, as well as the upscale CEO. Understanding these markets, how to approach them with respect to their specific needs, wants, desires, and interests is what is necessary to be successful in modern sales techniques.

Relationship to Marketing

All sales activities directly relate to marketing. Selling activities must be totally coordinated with and integrated into the total hotel marketing plan. Salespeople need to know what is being done in research and analysis, sales planning, advertising, public relations, publicity, and servicing the public.

Direct sales is an integral part of marketing and is a specialty of its own. Unfortunately, in many hotel companies the terms are confused and hotel salespeople often carry the title of marketing manager, but in effect have few or no marketing responsibilities other than direct sales. Today's hotel company officials recognize that a general manager accepts total responsibility for a property's marketing effort (including sales) and employs various people to implement programs to achieve sales goals.

Technology in Sales

Automation plays a large part in the successful administration of a sales program for a lodging property. The first automation for sales offices was seen in 1973, with the use of word processing equipment. It was not until 1983 that the industry began to use computers for maintaining files, tracing, and scheduling events in a hotel sales operation. In the late 1980s yield management systems started showing up in computer programs. These enhanced a manager's ability to control room rates depending on how busy the hotel was expected to be during certain days of the week or times of the year. Computers are expected to play an even more important role in sales management in the coming years. Facsimile (fax) machines and phone or voice mail were also innovations in the late 80s and early 90s that played an important role in improving sales office communications, internally as well as with accounts.

Central reservation systems play a most important role in the sales effort of hotel operations. All chain and membership type organizations provide computerized reservation systems tied into hardware located at a member or affiliated property. Prospective guests of a hotel call an 800 number to a central reservation office and a room is reserved almost instantaneously at a desired member or affiliated location. Improved technology in this area now allows certain travel agents and travel departments of corporations to directly tie into these systems so that they may also have access to reservations at particular locations for their clients and travelers. The latest technology in this area involves a system called JAGUAR SABRE VISION. Travel agents and others who buy into the hardware may now access not only copy information on selected hotels but are provided visuals of the properly on the computer screen. Hotel operations buy into the system, on a fee basis, and have the opportunity to provide a variety of photos of the hotel in addition to copy describing the property.

Third-Party Business Partners

Certain intermediaries play an important role in bringing sales to hotel properties. These are the third-party business partners on whom sales personnel make calls for the development of business. They include travel agents, travel wholesalers, tour operators, meeting planners, incentive travel houses, association executives, and corporate travel managers. All these "partners" control a certain amount of business that could be given to any number of hotels, motels, resorts, or conference centers. Salespeople work on developing relationships with key personnel in all these areas, in the interest of developing sales for their properties. Salespeople join associations to which these people belong and they attend conferences and conventions so that contacts with appropriate buyers may be made. Although these intermediaries have been around a long time it was not until the late 1960s that sales personnel realized the importance of making contact with these specialists. More and more business contacts are made through memberships in organizations such as Meeting Planners International, American Society of Association Executives, American Society of Travel Agents, National Business Travel Executives Association, Insurance Conference Planners, Society of Company Meeting Planners, National Association of Exhibit Managers, National Tour Association, and a wide variety of similar groups.

Summary

Although the hotel sales profession has been around for many years, only recently has it actually been recognized and accepted in the industry as an important integral part of hotel operations. In recent years industry leadership has been generated, more and more, from the sales ranks. Many of the major lodging companies have promoted people to senior executive status who had started in sales. With the help of technology sales has grown to a point that a great deal of training is necessary for one to compete in the lodging sales world today. A well-administered sales program in a hotel is necessary in today's highly competitive industry. There is a growing and unending need for people to join the ranks of the hospitality industry sales teams. And great rewards are available to those who work hard, study, train, are good at the job and strive for success.

Occupancy Rates in the Hospitality Industry

Giles Jackson

Occupancy rate is defined as the ratio of *potential* to *actual* capacity realized (in units of persons) over a given time period (*ceteris paribus*). It is expressed as a percentage.

Index of Industry Buoyancy

Occupancy rate is widely used as an index to compare relative industry buoyancy. For example, hotel occupancy rates in Japan averaged 85 percent in the first half of 1990. Compared to average occupancy rates in Australia of 53.7 percent, this appears to be high. However, compared to occupancy rates in Hong Kong of 92 percent in the same period, this appears to be low. Firms calculate their occupancy rates against industry averages and their own histories. For example, hotels might calculate occupancy rates for their room types (for example, single, double, suite) over given periods (day, week, month, season, year) and compare them to competitors. This method is used for accommodation and transportation alike.

Average percentages are useful for comparing different situations. However, they are a static measure. A more dynamic measure is the change in occupancies over a given period. This change in occupancies is a better indicator of the variability of occupancy rates. For example, following the pilot's strike in Australia, five-star occupancies dropped from 70 percent to 60 percent.

Potential Uses of Occupancy Rates

Occupancy rate is relatively straightforward to calculate in situations where the potential (that is, 100 percent) capacity limit is known (for example, in total number of beds or seats). It is difficult to calculate when this limit is not known. Yet, these situations may benefit greatly from such a measure. For example, one of the major problems facing resort communities and cities in the world today is "overcapacity due to too many tourists." It would be useful to establish an objective limit (carrying capacity) and find ways to compute occupancy rates for cities, resorts, and so forth over a given period. Different situations could then be monitored and compared over time to detect travel flows and vulnerable regions.

Relation of Occupancy Rates to Revenue

There is an indirect link between occupancy rate and revenue. For example, if an all-suite hotel with 100 double-occupancy rooms with one rate of $50 per person per night were full to capacity all year, annual revenue would be $3,650,000. However, if occupancy rates were halved the next year (for example, if half the number of couples came or if all rooms were filled at single occupancy) revenue would be $1,825,000. Hoteliers could take a number of actions to reduce this risk (discussed later in this article).

Occupancy rates are only partially related to revenue because an increase in occupancy rates will not always lead to a corresponding change in revenue. For example, if an airline raises its prices to cover fuel cost increases, the marginal decrease in revenue as a result of lower occupancy may be exceeded by the marginal increase in revenue from price rises. The net impact on profitability would depend on just how far occupancy decreased and on many other factors affecting profitability

Occupancy Rates and Profitability

Van Dyke (1985) hypothesized that the following 26 variables might have an impact on hotel profitability:

1. Room rate
2. Occupancy rate
3. Marketshare percent
4. Administrative/general expense
5. Labor cost for rooms
6. Rooms department advertising
7. Property tax
8. Restaurant total expense
9. Restaurant other revenue
10. Food cost
11. Beverage cost
12. Food and beverage (F&B) labor cost
13. F&B advertising
14. Room sales as percent consolidated sale
15. Depreciation
16. Interest expense
17. Unemployment percent
18. Chain affiliation
19. Location
20. Age of property
21. Whether renovated

Note: Other identified variables were combinations of the above.

Van Dyke found that occupancy was one of five variables having the most substantial influence on profitability. However, occupancy rate is influenced by combinations of many other variables, including the marketing variables (Monroe, 1979:6) of price, advertising, product development, sales promotion, distribution, and packaging. Since decisions in these areas are made by people, occupancy rates are ultimately determined by how well industry executives scan and interpret their environment. West (1988) studied the effects on performance of the extent to which managers scanned the environments of their firms and of the strategies that were implemented. The study found that these factors had a significant impact on return on assets and return on sales. The impact on occupancy rates is implied but not validated because publicly traded hospitality companies do not have to publish occupancy rates. Even rough estimates of occupancy rates are difficult to calculate with sales, room rate, and hotel capacity data because this data is not broken down by time or room type.

Practical Assessment Occupancy Rate Changes

A universal problem for hospitality businesses is that of deciding in advance what impact changes in the above marketing variables are likely to have on occupancy rates. Further, the impact of a given change may depend on the timing and context of the change. For example, it would be imprudent for senior management to assume that a change in price of a standardized global hotel brand would have the same impacts on occupancy rates regardless of location.

It would also be imprudent to assume that occupancy rates are subject to factors that can all be controlled by senior or unit managers of hospitality businesses. A simple hypothetical example can illustrate this important point.

Assume that an entrepreneur decides to launch a new ski resort in Eastern Europe after finding that Europe receives almost 65 percent of worldwide tourists. Having chosen a suitable location that satisfies access requirements, the entrepreneur negotiates with tour wholesalers and other organizations, works out projected demand, and builds the resort facility. The resort enjoys hotel occupancies of 80 percent by its fifth year of operation. In the following season occupancy rates drop to 72 percent. The entrepreneur concludes that the reason for the decline is increased competition. The chosen reaction is an increase in the intensity of promotions. The entrepreneur invests $150,000 in a new advertising campaign.

This may have been a fatal mistake, because occupancy falls are driven by a range of factors, many of which are beyond the entrepreneur's control. Some may seem of little importance to the entrepreneur, who, consumed by the importance of his venture, overlooks many other influencing factors. The decrease in occupancy to 72 percent might have been caused by remote political factors such as an escalation in social tensions in Russia. Consumer perceptions of Eastern Europe might well have been marred by events in Russia due to the possibility, however remote, of spillover effects into Eastern Europe.

The complexity of the many possible influences on consumer perceptions can be managed to some extent with strategies discussed elsewhere in this encyclopedia. But the above example does suggest that occupancy rates may be subject to factors with different levels of predictability and control. As technology connects more people in more places for more reasons and exposes the layman to an ever-wider range of global events and ideas, the range of possible factors influencing occupancies will continue to grow. These factors may also vary in their impact at different times. The range and rate of impact could also change as thousands of influences affect each other on a continuous basis.

Protecting Occupancy Levels

Trends in industry structure in the international hotel industry indicate that companies are attempting to buffer themselves from these complex uncontrollable factors by building a loyal customer base. The conventional wisdom is that this can be achieved by establishing a regional, pan-regional, or global presence and using aggressive marketing tactics. This is self-evident in an industry that is intrinsically international.

This conventional wisdom for aggressive strategies is supported by recent research on service industries using the Profit Impact on Market Share (PIMS) database. Allio and Patten (1991) studied the effects of varying the intensity of five variables on pre-tax return on investment. Figure 1 shows that, from a return on investment point of view, "more is better in everything but investment intensity."

Service firms that do not invest in strategies that increase market share, make productive use of assets, improve quality, and enhance value added will find their profitability eroded (Allio and Patten 1991). These firms will be forced to increase investment intensity in order to survive. In contrast, strategically focused firms will find the necessary investment funds to adapt as a consequence of their existing operations. They win by consistently delivering high-quality products (as defined by the markets they serve) to growth markets in which they own a high share.

While these conclusions are somewhat intuitive, the real challenge is to sustain a competitive position when a number of competitors decide to adopt a similar approach. Occupancy rate decreases are a first sign that the overall value of a strategy may be diluted when a large number of firms take the same approach. The effects of little differentiation are obvious in the budget sector, where companies have opted for cost advantages that limit the use of innovation as a competitive strategy.

This tendency of many firms in the hospitality industry to be guided by price and occupancy rates can be understood according to the workings of the market mechanism.

The Market Mechanism and Occupancy Rates

In the hospitality industry occupancy rates are a key source of information for determining *price levels*. Price changes are the means through which the competitive process determines the allocation of resources in the free market

Fig. 1. Key service industry findings. More is better in everything but investment intensity. *(Source: J. Allio and Joseph M. Patten, The market share/ excellence equation, Planning Review, September-October, pp. 15–45, 1991.)*

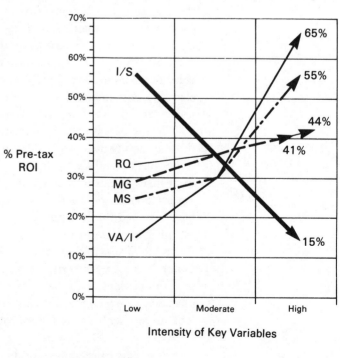

MS	Market Share	I/S	Investment/Sales
MG	Market Growth	RG	Relative Quality
VA/I	Value Added/Investment		

economy. This is done through the *price system* (Bannocle et al. 1977). The price system is not controlled by some central authority in the free market, although in special conditions the government may intervene to prevent price rises or price reductions. For example, the European Commission is now able to issue an injunction to block predatory pricing by larger airlines seeking control of routes at the expense of small airlines. In turbulent, newly deregulated markets, companies are finding ingenious ways to protect their positions against new entrants.

The pricing system relies on an "invisible hand," which is the effect of disparate decisions made by many independent suppliers. This mechanism makes airlines cut their fares in a recently deregulated market or slash fares to politically unstable countries. Occupancy rate trends indicate disturbances in demand, supply, and costs. When these disturbances occur, the prices of commodities change, because businesses must adjust their prices with the objective of maintaining required revenues to cover costs. (Note that it is also possible for occupancy levels to change when demand is constant, simply because supply levels change).

In the hospitality industry, this process of adjustment is continuous. *Market equilibrium*, the condition when one price settles for a commodity, is a relatively short-term phenomenon. Price theory explains this process of determining prices in individual markets. The *demand curve* (Figure 2) slopes downward from the left to the right, because according to price theory the higher the price of a commodity the lower the demand for it. The actual slope of the demand curve will depend on the response of demand to a change in price, known as *elasticity*. Commodities can be seen on a line with varying degrees of elasticity, from inelastic to elastic demand. In the case of inelastic demand, when a price increase occurs the quantity demanded will not fall as much, and so the total expenditure on the good will increase.

When demand is elastic, the quantity demanded falls more than the marginal price increase, and total expenditure decreases. It follows that in the case of inelastic demand we would expect occupancy rates to be more stable over time than in the case of elastic demand. The practicing manager in the hospitality industry develops a "feel" for how elastic or inelastic demand is. Thus, when occupancy rates in Singapore dropped below 80 percent, hoteliers increased their prices according to their perceptions of elasticity of demand. They viewed the change in occupancy levels as a temporary aberration in travel patterns.

In the past hoteliers instinctively adjusted their prices in relation to those of competitors when making such decisions. Increasingly, this easiest of options is proving insufficient. Very few markets exist that are impervious to changes in elasticity over time. A recent example is shown by the changing preferences of the Asian tourist markets in Australia. Australian hoteliers have assumed that wealthy Asian travelers will continue to demand the highest quality services and will pay a premium for them. Market research in Australia (Wada 1991) has shown that Japanese preferences are no longer uniform. A growing "product aware" minority are willing to forego luxury accommodations for a major portion of their stay, preferring to spend surplus income on high-profile activities that provide the experience they are looking for (such as excursions into sensitive microenvironments, and so forth).

It is time to examine closely standard market research formats that make assumptions about consumer tastes and needs on the basis of factors such as what car they drive. Clearly, more attention should be placed on purpose of

Fig. 2. The demand curve. (*Source: Adapted from K. Monroe, Pricing: Making Profitable Decisions, p. 26, 1979, New York: McGraw-Hill.*)

visit and psychographic factors (travel experience, cultural values, and so forth). An example of the more comprehensive approach is taken by the province of British Columbia in Canada. A standardized tourism data framework is applied which considers the role and importance of research, data collection methods, guidelines for questionnaires and interviews, sampling, data analysis and interpretation, and uses of an outside supplier of research skills (Ministry of Tourism, Recreation and Culture 1988).

Temporary Aberration or Fundamental Change?

A difficult question for hospitality executives is deciding when changes in occupancy rates are a temporary aberration in travel patterns and when they are a more fundamental change in market composition or market needs. Price levels can be changed at relatively short notice to cope with aberrations in travel patterns. However, dealing with fundamental changes in a more complicated matter. Hospitality products, especially those in geographically diverse, multiunit, standardized portfolios, require considerable time to change.

In many cases hoteliers prefer to work with price as much as possible. They are acutely aware of the risks involved in making system-wide changes when there are definite limits to predicting travel patterns. This use of price tends to reinforce a "growth with only marginal changes" approach. This approach has created problems for companies like Intercontinental Hotels, whose attempts to create a global service institution foundered on strategic and financial inflexibility.

Although inflexibility creates problems, there are limits to adaptation that may make price changes the only option for increasing occupancy rate. One of these limits is provided by a world recession. In the current recessionary climate of the United States and in Europe, discounting has become an accepted practice in three-, four-, and five-star (or equivalent) brands. When hotel chains have pledged to provide a given range of services, it is cheaper to keep them running at a reasonable occupancy and to try to increase the average spend of clients in-house than to let competitors take the business.

Protecting Occupancy Rates through Discounting

Average discounts from published room rates in Europe's major cities increased to 31 percent in 1990 from 27 percent in 1989. Amsterdam, Athens, and Dublin discounted most heavily in 1990 at about 40 percent, while Munich and Paris hotels discounted 20 percent. In Paris occupancy rates had fallen by 1.4 percent to 74.8 percent.

Although discounting may be a short-term option for maintaining occupancy levels, it is a futile one in the long term, because price level decreases may not lead to commensurate increases in occupancy. This is illustrated by what happened in the case of the U.S. convention center segment in the 1980s.

Convention center construction was driven by the belief that it would act as a catalyst for further economic growth in major and regional cities. Sensing this opportunity, many hoteliers entered the market expecting relatively inelastic conditions. In many cases the net effect was minimal or negative, because the large increases in room supply exceeded the marginal increases in demand. Also, demand increases themselves were a disappointment because cities did not consider the trade-offs clients made between convention facilities vis-à-vis other factors (climate, recreation, reputation, accessibility, and so forth). The result was that hotels had no option but to discount when there were definite limits on potential occupancy gains.

Another reason why discounting is a futile long-term strategy for protecting occupancy rates is its negative effects on cash flow. All hospitality businesses must, in spite of demand fluctuations, exceed a survival threshold known as the break-even point—the point at which sales revenue generates contributions equal to period fixed costs. When prices are discounted close to this threshold, an increase in period variable or fixed costs can cripple a company's ability to adapt.

A Pannel Kerr Forster (Travel Trade 1991) report in Australia found that pressure on occupancies was higher than the rest of the Asia-Pacific region due to increases in labor costs and labor-related taxes. Payroll as a percentage of total costs was 33 percent in Australia versus 16–18 percent in Asia. Competitive pressures forced hoteliers to discount with the result that average returns were the lowest in the Asian region. [*Note:* country payroll costs are not directly comparable because staff/guest ratios are higher in the rest of Asia.] Typically hoteliers rely on an appreciating asset base to bail them out, but with the collapse of the property market this luxury was eliminated. This collapse is particularly damaging for hospitality businesses, which unlike the agriculture and automobile industries, are not saved by the taxpayer. Nevertheless, as industry structure becomes more concentrated there will be more hospitality companies able to cut prices to the bone for long periods and emerge unscathed. Whether they can legally do this will depend on regulatory measures. One example of these measures is current attempts in Europe to distinguish between "vigorous price competition" and "predatory pricing" and to penalize those companies falling into the latter category (OECD 1989).

Occupancy Rates and "Demand-Curve Fixation"

In the hospitality industry occupancy is considered king. Unlike occupancy rates, profit and loss statements and balance sheets are not daily events. Hoteliers monitor each others' performance on the basis of occupancy rates. Hoteliers with a fixation on occupancy and other tangible indicators can become myopic in their approach to business problems. This myopia is illustrated by what happened in the U.K. hotel "short break" market in the mid-1980s.

Hoteliers (especially those positioned for business markets) had long been faced with low occupancies at weekends. Based on demand-curve thinking, they discounted until signs of increasing occupancy rates become evident. However, demand-curve thinking blinded hoteliers of the impacts discounting had on perceptions of their brands. Luxury properties—the epitomy of conspicuous consumption—were charging premium rates for meticulous hospitality on weekdays and slashing their rates at weekends. Clients became confused about what market these hotels were in. Hoteliers had assumed wrongly that they could break down their product mix into component parts and manipulate each part to satisfy their financial goals without affecting their overall positioning in the market. Clearly, strategies to increase occupancy rates in one area should consider the impact this might have on the overall positioning of the company.

One other important factor that should be considered regarding the protection of occupancy rates is that in today's hospitality industry these discounts cannot always be passed on to the consumer. Following the Gulf

War, the Asia-Pacific area saw tremendous declines in international passengers and freight, international tours, and occupancy rates in accommodation and cruising. The industry responded with heavy discounts. However, travel agents, some of whom now have tremendous bargaining power, started to charge higher service fees for postage/couriers, visa handling, traveler's checks, communications, amendments to original bookings, and cancellations. These higher fees diluted the effects of discounting for hoteliers and did little to improve occupancy rates.

Nonprice Competition

There are signs that hospitality organizations are pursuing different avenues to combat the declining occupancy problem by trying to compete on the basis of nonprice factors. Companies are trying to emphasize individuality. One example is the new Sydney Nikko, which is to have a prewar ocean liner theme (curved timber panelling and etched glass, and such). The question is whether these concepts can be adaptable. Nikko's argument would be that this concept is timeless. However, one result of massive product proliferation worldwide (in all industries) is a shortening of concept life-cycles, which have a life of months rather than years. This trend is especially true in the case of aggressive U.S. consumer markets, where few sectors of society have escaped commercialization of some form.

Many companies are aware that demand-curve fixation can damage product positioning in the long term. Companies have brought yield management techniques across from the airline industry in an attempt to curb the discounting mentality, or rather, to cope with it. Unfortunately, yield management, which sets room rates on the basis of short-term demand projections, does not guarantee increases in occupancy or revenue per se. It simply eliminates inefficiency in price determination by providing a formula based on occupancy levels. Companies that do not understand the limitations of yield management use yield management as an "autopilot." Their complacency can cost them their competitive position.

The Future: Declining Control over Occupancy Rates

Many companies will continue the fight for a "global network,"—the universal symbol of strength. They will take advantage of their bargaining power to develop hospitality products worldwide, unless discounting forces lower returns on invested capital. The industry leaders will be able to move up on price and move down on costs through technology and alliances. Many other companies are likely to attempt the same pattern and fail simply through bad implementation.

Unfortunately, increases in company bargaining power are being matched by increased customer bargaining power. Technology is empowering the individual consumer, effectively creating one giant "consumer corporation." Personal information services such as "Prodigy" in the United States give the consumer far more control over travel decisions. They have access to reservation systems such as SABRE and EAASY, giving them the ability to book seats on 300 airlines at the lowest fares, to make hotel and rental car reservations worldwide, to exchange ideas and get expert tips and recommendations through an on-line travel club. As the balance of power shifts more and more to the consumer, hospitality companies will have even less control over factors affecting occupancy rates.

Summary

Clearly, occupancy rates are intricately linked with many other decisions in the business enterprise. There is no tidy formula for locating the causes of occupancy patterns. But the major implications of this discussion are that, first, in the management of occupancy rates the "best practices" of the past may not be applicable in the future, and, second, managers should be scanning diverse sources of information to help reduce the possibility of error in their occupancy management decisions.

References

Allio R., and Joseph M. Patten. 1991. The market share/excellence equation, *Planning Review* (September/October), pp. 12–45.

Bannock, G., R. E. Baxter, and R. Rees. 1977. *The Penguin Dictionary of Economics.* Allen Lane: The Viking Press.

Ministry of Tourism, Recreation and Culture. 1988. *Standardized Tourism Data Framework.* March, British Columbia Subsidiary Agreement on Tourist Industry Development.

Monroe, K. 1979. *Pricing: Making Profitable Decisions,* McGraw-Hill Series on Marketing. New York: McGraw Hill.

OECD. 1989. *Predatory Pricing.* Paris, France: Organization for Economic Cooperation and Development Publications.

Travel Trade. 1991. Task force probes profitability decline, *Travel Trade* April 22, p. 12.

Wada, A. 1991. "Trends in the Budget Sector of the Lodging Industry," Unpublished monograph based on *The Australia/Asia-Pacific Trends Database,* Victoria University of Technology, Australia.

West, J. J. 1988. *Strategy, environmental scanning, and their effect upon firm performance: an exploratory study of the food service industry* Unpublished Ph.D. dissertation: Virginia Polytechnic Institute and State University, Blacksburg, Virginia.

Van Dyke, T. 1985. *An Exploratory Study of Key Variables Affecting Profitability in the Lodging Industry* Unpublished Ph.D. dissertation: Virginia Polytechnic Institute and State University, Blacksburg, Virginia.

20

Average Daily Rate

Bvsan Murthy and Chekitan S. Dev

Why Is ADR So Important?

Average daily rate (ADR), also referred to as average room rate (ARR) in many parts of the world, is one of the key statistics by which a hotel's performance is measured and monitored. Considering that rooms usually contribute the bulk of the operating profits of a hotel—no matter of what type and where it is located—ADR, together with percentage of occupancy, is considered to be a barometer of a hotel's performance.

How Is the ADR Calculated?

ADR is the result obtained by dividing total room sales by rooms occupied (also referred to as occupied roomnights). In other words, it is the weighted average room rate of all the rooms sold on a particular day. Table 1 illustrates the calculations for a 500-room hotel.

What Factors Affect the ADR?

Since ADR is so important to the overall profitability of a hotel, hotel managers the world over are constantly striving to achieve the best rate in the market vis-à-vis competition and improve upon it year after year. The ADR of a hotel can be affected by several macro- and microfactors. The former include conditions that affect the general business climate such as the economic and political situation of the destination. The latter are comprised of

Table 1. *Computation of ADR for a 500-Room Hotel (15,000 roomnights in a month)*

Type of business	Roomnights sold	Room rate	Room sales
Individual travelers	7,500	$100	$ 750,000
Tour groups	4,500	70	315,000
Total	12,000		$1,065,000
Average daily rate		$ 88.75	

such factors as destination attributes, type and location of a hotel, competition, and market mix.

Economic Conditions   Simply stated, economic conditions mean the level and health of the business and commerce of a destination. If a destination's economy is prosperous, more business travel to that destination results. General economic prosperity inevitably leads to greater investment in infrastructural development: better roads, airports, national parks, and hotels. Such developments facilitate more demand for hotel rooms.

Political Conditions   Political conditions affect the hotel industry in general and the ADRs in particular in three distinct ways. First, the attitude of and the importance given by the government to tourism in the larger context is a very important factor. If the government realizes the importance of tourism as an industry and supports its development, more developers will invest money in the industry and this increased participation of the industry further spurs the demand for rooms as visitor arrivals increase. Conversely, if the government is not inclined to support the development of the industry or even allows the existing infrastructure to decline, both visitor arrivals and, as a consequence, the developers' interest will decline.

Second, political strife can affect the hotel industry and its ADRs. This could take the form of either internal disturbances or external war.

Third, in some countries such as India and France, room rates are subject to scrutiny and varying control by the government. As a result, the ADRs are affected by such intervention.

Destination Attributes   Often, other things being equal, the destination itself significantly influences the general level of ADRs. Destinations can be classified either by geographic regions or by the purpose of the visit to the destination. There are definitely other ways of looking at differences in destinations, but for our current purpose, these two classifications have the most visible impact on ADRs.

Considering geographic differences, it is well known that hotel room rates (and consequently ADRs) are in general significantly higher in Europe and North America as compared with say, South East Asia. With labor costs being high in the industrial West, hotels there must charge more to remain profitable as compared to low-cost countries such as those in South East Asia.

ADRs also vary significantly between destinations as classified by the purpose of visit. Hotels in destinations that attract more business travelers need to provide more services such as business centers, concierge floors, and so on. Such additional services increase the costs and, consequently, the rate structure of the hotels.

Sometimes the class of the destination itself dictates the rates. Compare the room rates of hotels in Atlantic City and Monte Carlo for example. Though both are major gaming destinations, Monte Carlo's hotel rates are far higher because of the city's prestigious image.

Location and Type of Hotel   ADRs also vary with the classification of a hotel, as different classes of hotels—upscale, mid-price, and budget—have different published rates in keeping with their differences in facilities and services. Published rates, and consequently the ADRs, also vary with the location of a hotel. Location refers to both the broad area where a hotel is situated—city-center, suburban, highway/airport—as well as the specific location within that area. For example, in a beach resort destination, an oceanfront property can certainly charge more than a competing hotel four blocks away from the beach.

Competition

The room rates a hotel gets ultimately depend on the demand-supply equation. The higher the demand, the higher the rate. However, such high demand also leads to more new hotel development and the increased supply tends to depress the rates. The depressed rates act as a barrier to entry for other hotel developers and over a period of time the demand catches up with the static supply, raising the rates again and creating another business cycle. Of course, if some hotel companies go bankrupt in the process of waiting for better days or some new developments spur the demand unexpectedly, the cycle will be shortened.

Market Mix

Most, if not all, of the factors considered so far are not under the control of operating managers. Of course, if managers are involved in the investment decision itself, they may be responsible for or be able to influence the decision to build a hotel in a city rather than in a resort destination, downtown and not in the suburbs, and so on. But once the hotel is built, it becomes fait accompli to the operating manager and she or he must still get the best out of the property. Market mix is one factor that is very much within the control of the operating management and, given all other things, management can improve the ADR by striving to achieve the optimum market mix for the hotel. Market mix refers to the composition of the guests that a hotel attracts and caters to. Examples of market mix classification used by hotels are presented in Table 2.

Each of the above segments has a *rack rate* of its own. Rack rate is the maximum published rate applicable to the concerned segment as per the hotel's pricing strategy. The term *rack rate* has come into vogue because the appropriate rates used to be displayed on the "rack" inside and below the front desk for the benefit of the front desk personnel. However, with a plethora of rates currently in the market, particularly in some segments (for example, guaranteed company rate [GCR]) based on different contracted volumes, this is no longer true and the appropriate rates are now either on paper in the reservatons files or are resident in the computer memories. In today's world, except for the free individual traveler (FIT) rack rate—which is mostly applied to individual walk-ins—all other rates are negotiated separately

Table 2. *Examples of market mix classification*

Industry terminology	Description
Transient/FIT/Individual Commercial	Individual travelers
Corporate/GCR	Corporate rate
Tour/GIT	Group inclusive tourists
Conferences and conventions	Delegates
Crew	Airline/oceanline crews
Layover	Airline traffic (generally from delayed/ canceled flights)
Interline	Airline/Travel agency personnel
SMERF	Social, military, educational, religious, fraternal
Package	Special (promotional) packages

Table 3. *Market mix and computation of ADR (scenario I) for a 500-room hotel (15,000 roomnights in a month)*

Market mix	Roomnights sold	Weighted average rate	Room sales
Individual commercial	2250	$100	$225,000
Corporate	4500	85	382,500
Tour	3000	70	210,000
Conferences and conventions	1500	75	112,500
Interline	750	50	37,500
Total occupied roomnights	12000		
Occupancy	80%		
Total room sales			$967,500
ADR		$ 80.625	

with each generating source and thus each of these segments has a weighted average rate of its own depending upon the actual materialized roomnights at varying rates. Thus, the ADR is really a weighted averate rate of several weighted average rates of different segments of the market mix. A typical city hotel's market mix and the ADR may be worked out as shown in Table 3.

To appreciate how even a minor change in the market mix can have a serious impact on the ADR, consider a different scenario of the same hotel as shown in Table 4. It can be seen that the total occupied roomnights are still assumed to be 12,000 and only a shift of 750 roomnights from one segment to another is presumed. With a reduction of $1.88 per occupied roomnight in the ADR, and assuming the same percentage of occupancy for the entire year, the hotel will in this case lose $274,480! Considering that a typical hotel has around 40–45 percent of fixed and semifixed costs, most of this loss will be straight from the bottom line.

So, achieving an optimal market mix given the remainder of the factors is an extremely important objective of the operating management to realize a desired ADR, which is always forecast at the beginning of the year.

Table 4. *Market mix and computation of ADR (scenario II) for a 500-room hotel (15,000 roomnights a month)*

Market mix	Roomnights sold	Weighted average rate	Room sales
FIT rack rate	1500	$100	$150,000
Guaranteed company rate	4500	$ 85	382,500
Group inclusive tourists	3750	70	262,500
Conferences and conventions	1500	75	112,500
Other discounts	750	50	37,500
Total occupied roomnights	12000		
Occupancy	80%		
Total room sales			$945,000
ADR		$ 78.75	

Table 5. *ADR computation for two hotels*

Statistics	Hotel A	Hotel B
Number of rooms	500	500
Occupancy percentage	70	85
ADR	$ 90	$ 79

What Is the Limitation of ADR?

Although ADR is an extremely critical objective for all hotel managements, how the statistic is computed is sometimes misleading and may confuse the priorities. To illustrate, consider the two scenarios in Table 5.

Which hotel has performed better? In all likelihood, the manager of Hotel A will highlight the achievement of a higher ADR, whereas the manager of Hotel B will stress the better occupancy percentage. Which manager has achieved a better result overall? It is here that the inadequacy of ADR as a good barometer of performance and its limited utility as a control measure becomes clear.

Is There a Better Alternative?

The statistic yield per room (YPR) gives a more realistic picture because it is calculated by dividing room sales by the available roomnights instead of the occupied roomnights. Since percent of occupancy and ADR are somewhat inversely related in many situations, the YPR, which combines the effects of the two, is a better statistic to rely on for monitoring operational performance. Table 6, which shows the comparative computations, makes this clear.

Hotel B has, in fact, realized $62,250 more sales in the month. If the same ratios of room sales to sales of other services and GOP% are assumed, Hotel B will end up showing $261,450 more GOP than Hotel A, despite a lower ADR. Thus, ADR in isolation could be misleading and YPR is a preferable statistic to use. A simpler way to calculate YPR is to multiply the percentage of occupancy by the ADR. For Hotel A, it is 0.7 × 90 = $63.

Once the concept of YPR is accepted, the next step is to study how to improve the yield and that leads into the area of yield improvement programs (YIP), a concept popularized by the airline industry a decade ago. Yield improvement programs are aimed at maximizing revenues by the effective management of room inventory, forecast demand, and the rates charged.

Table 6. *ADR versus YPR*

Statistics	Hotel A	Hotel B
Number of rooms	500	500
Available roomnights in a month (30 days)	15,000	15,000
Occupancy percentage	70	85
Occupied roomnights	10,500	12,750
ADR	$90	$79
Room sales	$945,000	$1,007,250
YPR	$63.00	$67.15

Summary

The ADR is one of the key statistics used to evaluate the operational performance of a hotel. ADR is affected by market conditions (economic and political), destination attributes, type and location of the hotel, competition, and market mix. While most of these factors are beyond the control of the operating managers, market mix is one factor that is very much within management control. Even a minor change in the market mix can seriously impact the ADR and the profitability of a hotel. When occupancy percentage and ADR are inversely related, which is the case many times, an alternative statistic YPR is a better measure to evaluate and control a hotel's performance.

21

Hotel Pricing

Margaret Shaw

Hotelkeepers have been making room rate pricing decisions for years. From the small taverns and inns of Renaissance Europe to the 2,000-room mega fantasy resort hotels of the 1990s, someone has had the responsibility for making price decisions for travelers seeking lodging. The questions to be addressed include who are these travelers, what are their options, who are the price decision makers, and how do they go about it. As noted by Howard B. Meek (1938:2), a renowned and respected leader in the field of hospitality:

> The classical analysis explaining price in terms of supply and demand has passed through many examinations and revisions, but still stands in its essential idea as the most satisfactory, most generally acceptable explanation of the phenomena of price determination.

Key Elements of Pricing Decisions

Meek's statement of over 50 years ago is correct. All pricing decisions are based on the economic principles of supply and demand. More specifically, demand relative to available supply on any given day determines the price in the marketplace. This basic tenet of economic theory holds true for the sale of a hotel guest room, as it does for the purchase of a loaf of bread, a life insurance policy, a college education.

The essential elements of price theory include demand, competition, and cost. As graphically shown in Figure 1, these parameters offer a framework from which hotel room rate pricing decisions are made.

Demand   Demand determines the highest rate that can be charged, that is, "what the market will bear." Some business travelers to New York City are willing to pay a $200 daily room rate for first-class accommodations in mid-town Manhattan. Some families will pay up to $5000 a week for a family vacation at a fantasy resort in the Hawaiian Islands. College students going downhill skiing for a weekend may put their "ceiling" at $10 per night.

A key point here is the purpose of purchase, or for our industry, the purpose of the trip. All kinds of travelers are traveling for all kinds of reasons. "What the market will bear" will vary tremendously depending on the

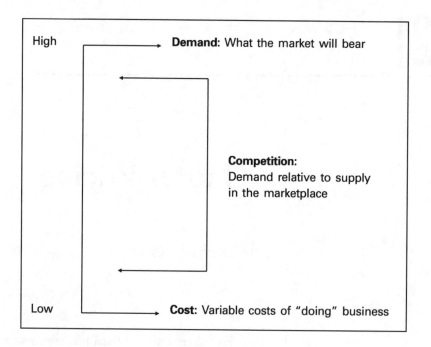

Fig. 1 Key elements of the pricing decision.

High → **Demand:** What the market will bear

Competition:
Demand relative to supply
in the marketplace

Low → **Cost:** Variable costs of "doing" business

market. Thus, the particular target market(s) of a hotel needs to be clearly defined when making a pricing decision for that target market.

Demand from any identified target market will fluctuate. Business travel tends to be heaviest in the fall and spring, and not surprisingly, hotel rates for this market peak during these time periods. Vacation travel of Canadians to Florida is particularly strong in the winter months. So are the rates they pay. Education associations like to meet during the summer months, when school is out of session. This market is also fairly price sensitive. Thus, hotels targeting to business travelers in the fall, winter, and spring, may target the education segment as a secondary market in the summer, at lower rates.

In short, demand determines the high end of a rate structure, depending on who the target market is and the price sensitivities of that market. Yet this is just a start. Competition in the marketplace and the costs incurred by hotels also have a major impact on final pricing decisions.

Competition   Competition can be viewed from both direct and indirect perspectives. Indirect competition refers to the broad range of alternatives available to travelers. Vacationers have the option of staying with friends and relatives, camping, or simply making day trips close to home. In other words, they have an option *not* to purchase a hotel room for overnight accommodations. The same holds true for business travelers. They, too, have the option of day trips only, or shortened trips of a 1–2 day duration. Indeed, the average night's stay for an individual business traveler is typically 1.3 nights. Faster jet travel, overnight couriers, fax machines, and the like have made the decision to even take a business trip in the first place a questioned business expense.

Direct competition are those hotels who compete for similar target markets. Sheraton, Marriott, and Hyatt Hotels, for example, all compete on a national level for the upscale business traveler including independent business travel, corporate business travel, and convention business travel. In many respects this market views these suppliers of hotel accommodations as close substitutes, or viable alternatives, when making a decision on where to book their room. Although the room price is only one of several factors in making the decision about where to stay, it is a salient and important factor. Suppliers who deviate from an acceptable relevant range will eventually lose potential customers to their competition.

Competition is a key element in putting a "cap" on or placing parameters on the relevant range of prices. When demand exceeds supply in the marketplace—known as peak demand periods—the relevant range is higher on the demand/competition/cost continuum. And conversely, when supply exceeds demand—known as off-peak periods or valley demand periods—the relevant range of prices is usually much lower. For example, in the Boston market first-class hotel convention rates can range from $125 to $150 during the September, October, May, and June peak periods. Yet, in the slower winter months, room rates offered to the convention market can fall much lower to the $75 to $95 range.

Experienced convention buyers are well aware of these price variations, or rather, the peak and valley fluctuations of the hotel business. Hotel price decision makers need to monitor the market closely, anticipate as best they can high and "soft" periods, and avoid the pitfalls of the "we don't discount" syndrome. This syndrome, especially when practiced in valley periods, can produce lost business, missed budgets, and unhappy owners.

Cost   As suggested by Rashkow (1981), there are essentially two kinds of costs for any business enterprise:

1. The inherent fixed costs associated with "being" in business, that is, those costs that remain the same regardless of business volume (depreciation, administrative salaries, and so forth).
2. The variable costs associated with "doing" business, that is, those costs that vary with business volume (materials, direct labor, and so forth).

Although there are a number of semivariable and semifixed costs associated with running a business, the purpose here is to distinguish between the short-run costs of doing business and the long-run costs of being in business.

The short-run, or variable, costs for hotel guest rooms are largely housekeeping labor, bathroom amenities, laundry, and the like. It is essentially the cost of an occupied room. Variable costs in the hotel industry are relatively low, ranging from $10–$50 depending on the service level of the hotel (budget, midtier, luxury), the location (metropolitan, suburban, resort), and the occupancy of the hotel (during high occupancy periods hotels often incur overtime labor costs). To give an example, variable costs for full-service hotels in metropolitan areas usually range from $25–$45.

In the short run, it is the variable costs that are relevant to the pricing decision. These costs of simply doing business need to be covered, and thus, are the minimum threshold for room rate pricing decisions. Any revenue exceeding these costs contributes something to overhead, which is better than no contribution at all. It makes no sense (both intuitively and financially) to sell a room for $25 if the variable cost to sell that room is $30.

Most hoteliers recognize that profit margins can and will be lower in the off-peak periods. Their focus is on contribution margins which are less during these slow periods, yet nonetheless contributing to the fixed costs of being in business. In the long run, cutting across both peak and off-peak demand periods, successful management realizes reasonable profits.

Pricing: A Marketing Decision

Marketing Objectives

Pricing is a marketing decision. And marketing's mandate is customer satisfaction. Indeed, charging the right price is clearly part of that mandate. As suggested by Lewis and Chambers (1989:9), marketing is "communicating to and giving the target market customers what they want, when they want it, where they want it, at a price they are willing to pay." This statement reinforces the notion that pricing is a marketing decision. The pricing decision needs to be made within the context of the consumer, and not in the confines of the accounting department. Through customer satisfaction long-run profit goals are realized.

Shaw and Heck (1989) raise the point that pricing is viewed in different ways by different constituencies. For example, liquidity issues concern hotel owners. To hotel managers, realities of the marketplace are of primary concern. Yet to the consumer, "pricing is the accepted, shopped for, or negotiated cost to get rooms" (p. 242).

The customer does not care about liquidity issues, financial statements, or returns on investment. Nor does the customer care about market share battles among suppliers in the marketplace. What the customer does care about is a hotel room for the night that is clean and secure, at a good price value as perceived by the buyer.

Market Positioning— The Final Key Element

Customer perception is what positioning is all about. There is much truth to the adage "perception is reality." If the customer thinks the price is too high, it is, regardless of what the owners and managers think. The same holds true if a price is perceived to be too low. Price is a signal of quality. Too low a price can signal poor quality whether the quality is there or not.

Positioning enters the demand/competition/cost continuum as both a minimum and maximum threshold for the hotel room rate pricing decision. If rates are perceived to be too high (within a product class such as the midtier hotel market), customers will go elsewhere. If rates are perceived to be too low, no one will come. In either case, of course, profits will not be realized.

Positioning decisions, made by senior level management, set the parameters for the relevant range of prices for a hotel. Actual price decisions, depending on the target market, will lie somewhere within the predetermined range. The term *rack rate* refers to the upper end of the range, often called "list price" in other industries. Deep discounts or special package rates are at the lower end of the range. If the rack rates are too high and/or discounts too low, the overall image or "positioning" of the hotel is in jeopardy.

A good example to demonstrate this point is the emergence of the weekend package. Now commonly referred to as the weekend package market, weekend package rates are largely directed to pleasure travelers and local residents to help boost weekend occupancies. Metropolitan hotels primarily cater to business travelers who are abundant during the week but absent on the weekends. Hotels needed a way to attract people during these "softer" periods at a price that would not fall below the variable costs. The strategy is essentially to reach out to a more price sensitive market with a lower price, but not so low as to compromise marketplace position. Hotels are not willing to risk their image as perceived by their primary target market, which in this case is the weekday business traveler.

Thus, the concept of the weekend package market was born. Local residents and/or pleasure travelers who cannot afford to stay at a hotel for $140 per night, can afford $75 a night when it is perceived as a good price value.

Just as importantly, the business traveler does not feel "squelched" or "ripped-off" when he or she hears of these special weekend package rates. In fact, a large portion of the weekend package market is the business person who is traveling for pleasure on the weekends. Hotel management realizes that individuals will surface in multiple target markets depending on the purpose of the trip. They also realize that the price sensitivities of these individuals will vary depending on the purpose of the trip as well.

Summary

Demand, competition, and cost all play an important role in the hotel room rate pricing decision. Demand sets the ceiling and costs set the floor. Competition, or supply relative to demand, helps determine more precisely how high or how low a price will be. Positioning, or marketplace perception, sets the upper and lower limits of the price range to be offered. Some hotels may have wider ranges than others, depending on the desired position to be achieved.

Most importantly, pricing is a marketing decision. This is not to imply that only the marketing department makes pricing decisions. Pricing decisions are made every day in the reservation and front office departments. What it does mean is that the customer is the one who really makes the decision. And it is the job of marketing-minded hoteliers to find out just what the customer really wants and what price they are willing and able to pay.

It is a tenet of marketing that the customer is always right. The hotel customer is always right, too.

References

Lewis, Robert C., and Richard E. Chambers. 1989. *Marketing Leadership in Hospitality.* New York: Van Nostrand Reinhold.

Meek, Howard B. 1938. *A Theory of Hotel Room Rates.* Ithaca, N.Y.: Cornell University.

Rashkow, Bertran. 1981. How to set the right price. *Inc.,* February.

Shaw, Margaret, and William H. Heck. 1989. Managing demand and adjusting inventory: pricing strategies in the hotel industry. In *The Pricing Decision: A Strategic Planner for Marketers,* ed. Daniel Seymour, Chicago: Probus Publishing.

22

Safety Management

Raymond C. Ellis, Jr.

OSHA: A Way of Life

Although safety would seem to be a logical management concern, the record of the business community at large was so poor, it led to government intervention in 1970. On December 29, 1970, Congress enacted the Occupational Safety and Health Act of 1970, more commonly called "OSHA." This act applied to most industries including the hospitality industry.

In the hospitality industry there had been a tendency to see safety as an insurance issue. Workers' Compensation would cover incidents where employees were involved and comprehensive general liability would cover incidents where a guest or the public was involved. Obviously, any manager paying attention to the bottom line would quickly recognize that a premium generated on industry and individual location or corporate experience could be controlled.

There are several elements in seeking a safer workplace; some are mandated by OSHA and others are a consequence of the mandates. All establishments must have on permanent display an OSHA poster that specifies the protections afforded each employee under the act. To support the employer in implementing the law, the employees are also advised of their responsibility to comply with all of the rules and regulations issued under the occupational safety and health act.

OSHA Recordkeeping

All establishments employing more than 10 employees must keep records. An OSHA log form No. 200 must be maintained for such an establishment. The reverse side of the form comprehensively defines those job-related injuries and job-related illnesses to be reported. Furthermore there must be a backup report, OSHA No. 101, or its equivalent for each log entry. The state workers' compensation report of injury or illness form will satisfy the OSHA requirements and reduce the necessity for repetitious filings.

Through compliance with the recordkeeping aspect, the establishment has the basis for initiating an effective safety program. Each entry on the log should automatically set the following actions in motion:

1. Inspect the area where the incident occurred.
   a. Obtain statements from any witnesses to the incident.
   b. Were mechanical, structural, or other physical (water on floor, for example,) factors involved?
   c. Through conversations with the victim, determine whether the individual, rather than a physical hazard, was a major factor. If so, does the individual need additional training? Did the individual fail to use personal protective equipment or machine guarding? Was the individual engaged in an activity on equipment or a procedure with which the employee was unfamiliar? Should the individual have requested assistance for an assignment requiring more than one individual to safely accomplish the work task?
   d. Note whether other individuals have had similar incidents in a given location. Look for physical hazards.
   e. Review whether the victim has had other recent incidents. If so, take appropriate training or supervisory action.

2. Develop a self-inspection form. To provide the most effective form, move beyond OSHA log entries to *ALL* incidents. Remember, the "near miss" this time could be a serious incident the next time.
   a. Consider work practices in addition to physical hazards.
   b. Include public and guest incidents also.
   c. Develop self-inspection form by departments, in addition to an overall document.
   d. And most important, USE the form on a regular basis. Be sure it doesn't become a checklist completed at a supervisor's or manager's desk.

3. Implement a safety-awareness training program. A major plus in the event of an OSHA compliance inspection is documentation. As in the inspection forms previously noted, a document exists for review if you carefully document all training programs. A growing number of training experiences are mandated by law, including
   Training in emergency evacuation procedures
   Training in use of portable fire extinguishers
   Training in hazard communication, that is, educating employees in the correct use of hazardous chemicals required for accomplishing work assignments
   Instruction in tag-out, lock-out procedures for electrical equipment
   Motor vehicle driver training for drivers of courtesy vehicles
   Heimlich maneuver, CPR, life saving for water facilities

Maintain a roster indicating the dates of training for each employee plus follow-up and retraining session dates. In addition, place a record of training, signed by both the trainer and employee, in each employee record folder.

Serious consideration should be given to providing training in American Red Cross First Aid. Available in an eight-hour multimedia presentation, this accomplishes two significant goals: Employees learn what to do in the event of an accident, and they learn the limitations of first aid and what NOT TO DO. This is particularly important in dealing with an injured guest or member of the public involved in an on-premise incident. For example, one does not urge the guest who has just fallen down a flight of stairs to "stand up and see if everything is OK." Rather, the trained staff member will keep the injured person in position until emergency medical service can respond. Of course, the staff will make the individual as comfortable as possible under the circumstances, responding to any immediate problems of severe bleeding or impaired breathing. The training of all employees fulfills the OSHA requirement for a currently certified first aider on each work shift for the establishment.

Every employee, new or old on the job, should be trained or retrained on a regularly scheduled basis.

Supervision

A cornerstone of an effective safety program is management support and supervisory implementation of that program. The degree of supervisory response to any program or emphasis on-the-job directly relates to the degree of management *concern!* Token support will be reflected in the application of safety standards and requirements. Safety occurs in spite of supervision or not at all.

In terms of ultimate bottom-line performance haphazard management concern is extremely short sighted. The hidden costs of the lack of safety are estimated in the range of from four to ten times the apparent costs. Insurance premiums are not the only safety-related costs. In the instance of lost time, staff replacement costs or less efficient operations because of spreading staff to cover the assignments of the absent employee is a major cost item. Time lost by staff during and immediately following the incident is another hidden cost.

The supervisor must be consistent in requiring safe performance from all employees. There can be no exceptions—no "looking the other way" when an employee is cutting corners or "cheating" on safety rules. To support this aspect of the program, rules should be in writing, thus eliminating the guesswork as to the standard procedure for every job assignment.

Immediate action must be taken by the supervisor when a safety violation occurs. The employee should be corrected in private concerning the safety violation. If a physical hazard is detected that cannot be corrected by an employee or the supervisor, warning signs or a barricade should be provided until the hazard has been eliminated. A supervisor must practice as well as preach safety as the most efficient and effective way of doing the job.

The Safety Committee

The smaller establishment may have only a three or four member safety committee. The owner-manager and two or three key employees may constitute the membership in larger operations, while the initial safety committee may be limited to a management supervision team. As the committee becomes an effective and integrated team, the membership may be extended to include line employees from each department. In large establishments there will frequently be supervisory and employee membership on the committee with safety as a regular agenda item on the executive committee's weekly meeting.

To provide a productive session, an agenda should be distributed several days in advance of the meeting. This permits members to determine whether initiatives of the prior meeting were implemented and whether safety hazards have been corrected and to prepare to intelligently address items on the agenda.

In order to avoid "having a meeting because it is nearing the time to do so," organizing an agenda will be a guide. If there is little to discuss, it is probably wiser to wait until later.

Frequency of meetings will be determined by need. Unless continuing and critical safety issues exist, it is generally possible to meet on a monthly basis. The meeting should be conducted according to Roberts Rules of Order and should be limited to a length of one hour.

A meeting will typically

1. Review recent safety incidents including employees, guests, the general public
2. Review inspection reports including correction of hazard and status of repair orders delayed because of unavailability of parts, cost of capital expenditures, and so forth.
3. Provide opportunity to review materials under consideration for distribution to all employees. This review may also include films or videotapes for use in employee meetings.
4. Include an "outside" speaker from local safety councils, the insurance company's loss control department, the local fire department, and others as appropriate.

The safety committee could be instrumental in the development and implementation of the aforementioned self-inspection lists. It is valuable to have safety committee members inspect areas other than their own. All too often, familiarity with a work area may lead to "not seeing" what another safety-oriented individual would immediately notice.

Hazard Alert Program

There is the need for ensuring response at the earliest possible time in an establishment. If a condition cannot immediately be corrected by an employee, a system should be devised that ensures an early correction. Some organizations have used a different color work order to alert the maintenance or engineering department of the need for correction of a hazardous condition or potential hazard.

The work order may have an overprint HAZARD ALERT to implement a quick response from repair and maintenance services. Consider the system that best meets the establishment's special needs.

HAZCOM Program

In 1988, the Hazard Communication (HAZCOM) Standard was extended from the chemical industry to include all industries. Consequently, the hospitality industry confronted new mandates for training employees. Again, the laws and regulations seek to provide a safer working environment for every employee. This program communicates to each employee the recommended exposure limits and safe procedures for handling chemicals and chemical compounds required in the satisfactory accomplishment of work assignments.

The program must be written and should contain material safety data sheets (MSDS) covering all hazardous chemical products in use. Generally a file should be established for each department and available on a 24-hour basis for quick review by the employees. In addition, a master file should be available at the front desk for referral to any agency responding to an emergency—fire, police, utilities, or others. An additional master file should be in the possession of the staff person in charge of the program—chief engineer, security director, or others. There must be a complete list of the hazardous chemicals known to be present. The list may be compiled for the workplace as a whole or for individual work areas. The manufacturer is responsible for providing the MSDS for each product provided to you.

The MSDS will warn of any potential hazards of products in use. It should also include recommendations for personal protective equipment, such as gloves, face and/or eye protection, respirator, or self-contained breathing apparatus, to be used by the employee while working with the specific product.

Labeling is critical to the success of the program. Each hazardous chemical product label must identify the hazardous chemical, provide warnings concerning the product's storage and use and the appropriate personal protective equipment recommended. Finally, the name and address plus emergency phone numbers of the supplier (manufacturer, wholesaler, or importer) must be indicated. When the product is being drawn from bulk, the organization must provide similar information on an in-house label. An employee should be designated to take charge of this program and be responsible for ensuring compliance by all departments and employees using the chemical product. While OSHA exempts the labeling requirement for employees drawing from bulk the quantity required for the single day's operation, it is recommended labels be used in spite of the exemption. The reality of the workplace is that a little more than is needed is drawn and after a period of time one has a collection of unlabeled containers containing a minimal quantity of unknown materials. Another caution is to absolutely prohibit use of any food container for a hazardous chemical product. Too many unfortunate incidents have occurred when chemicals have been mistaken as seasoning or a beverage because of the unlabeled container.

Although the law specifies labels in English, it makes good safety sense to also provide labels in the language of employees with another native language and limited ability to read English.

The training program must be detailed and in writing. Outline the staff member responsible, facilities to be used, frequency of sessions, review and follow-up systems, and the actual contents categorized by department for the presentation.

The nature and effectiveness of this training will establish compliance by the employees with use of personal protective equipment. This aspect of the program is one of the more difficult to administer and supervise as some employees resist using gloves or eye or face protection. One should refer to the section of the aforementioned OSHA poster that references employee compliance with all rules and regulations issued under the occupational safety and health act.

Critical to the successful implementation of the HAZCOM program is the employees' knowledge of the use and interpretation of the MSDS, the labels, and the safe use of all hazardous chemicals required for the job.

Emergency Evacuation

Under the original OSHA enactment, a section deals with "Means of Egress." At issue is the need for a written program indicating the role of each and every employee in an emergency evacuation. The program must be written and each employee must be fully aware of the appropriate action in such an evacuation. A few suggestions to assist in the development of the program include the following:

1. Assign by job title, rather than an employee's name.
2. Identify by job titles employees charged with evacuation of guests and the public, as well as those responsible for evacuation of other employees.
3. Determine a meeting point outside the establishment's physical structure for gathering of evacuees. This could save lives in a fire, when a rescuer enters the property under deteriorating conditions to attempt to save an individual who is safely out of the building but unaccounted for.
4. Review with local fire and police authorities for their input. Also, afford them a tour of all the property in order to be fully acquainted with the layout and nature of facilities and structure.

OSHA requires that all employees be trained in using a portable fire extinguisher. While there are exceptions, it is urged that such training be implemented.

If a trained fire team is on the premises, all employees need not be trained in use of the fire extinguisher. Unfortunately an untrained employee may discover the fire in a state in which it could be readily extinguished. By the time the trained employee is located and arrives, the fire may well exceed the capacity of the portable fire extinguisher to be effective. The alarm should always be sounded so the fire department may be immediately notified. Then, proceed with local action as long as the fire has not exceeded the capacity of the available portable fire extinguishers.

Some jurisdictions are considering eliminating portable fire extinguishers in fully sprinklered structures. This may, in fact, place a premise in violation of OSHA. It would certainly be unfortunate if use of the fire extinguisher could have prevented activation of a sprinkler head, which, by elimination of fire extinguishers, would be the only defense.

Tag-Out/Lock-Out Program

During 1990 OSHA mandated a tag-out, lock-out system to prevent injuries or fatalities to employees working on power-activated units. Frequently, such units have a power source that may be remote from the unit being serviced. There have been serious injuries and even fatalities where an employee has activated the power source when unaware another employee was working on the actual unit.

Again, a written program is required. The property as well as power-activated units should be identified by nature of unit, location, and power source. Employees by name and job title should be authorized to use a tag-out or lock-out procedure. Generally, power source units in the hospitality industry will not have a metal strip containing holes for holding individual employee's locks or tags on major electrical boards, hydraulic, steam, gas, air, or water pressure sources. However, the appropriate employees should be provided with a supply of tags or a lock where feasible. Such employees should be listed and instructed in the use of the tags and/or locks at the power control source.

In support of the program, all energy sources, such as switches or valves, should be surveyed and identified in relation to specific equipment. This survey and identification permits the establishment of an energy isolating system. If the machine or equipment to be maintained or repaired is operating it should be

1. Shut down by normal operating procedures
2. Isolated from its energy source with appropriate action
3. Adjusted so stored energy within the equipment may be dissipated (spring action, liquid or gas pressures)
4. Tagged-out or locked-out at the energy source
5. Verified by putting equipment in ON position to be sure power source is removed
6. Moved to neutral or OFF position in order to initiate the repair, maintenance, or cleaning

When more than one employee is involved with the tagged-out or locked-out unit, the employee should remove his or her tag or lock upon completion of assignment. The last employee to complete the assignment should activate the power source and verify satisfactory operation of the unit. At that point all tags or locks are removed and the unit is returned to regular operation.

Summary

In the review of safety management, it is noted that the Occupational Safety & Health Act of 1970 mandates the development of safety initiatives for each lodging establishment. A reporting requirement permits more effective management through knowledge of breakdowns in both the safety and health of the employees. Tools of safety management include the development of a self-inspection form. A continuing training program to effectively meet the growing body of safety regulation is essential. A cornerstone of the effective safety management program is management support fostered by concerned and involved supervision. Input from the employee is assured through use of a safety committee. Another support of safety that considers both the employee and the guest is a hazard alert form that focuses the engineering or maintenance staff attention on those conditions demanding immediate attention.

Recent expansion of hazardous chemical communication (HAZCOM) requirements to all industries sets information, self-protection, training, and labeling standards throughout the hospitality industry. Emergency evacuation, while focused upon the employee, becomes an excellent program for effective evacuation of guests and the general public, as well.

Finally, consideration is given to the lock-out, tag-out regulation which establishes a program to protect the employee during the cleaning, repair, or adjustment of power-actuated equipment.

23

Property Management Systems

James A. Bardi

Property management systems (PMS) is a term used to indicate the computer hardware and software that general managers and supervisors use to operate an efficient hotel. The word "efficient" is used because application of various software programs to the front office, food and beverage operations, marketing and sales, housekeeping, and security will improve guest satisfaction, employee performance, and profits for the hotel. The PMS is an extension of the management team in a lodging property because it forces managers to set measurable goals, to interpret results, and to apply insight into various operational directions. In today's competitive lodging market, the management team needs every possible edge over the competition to succeed.

Needs Analysis

A needs analysis is an essential step in the adoption of a PMS for a hotel property. After reviewing the uses and applications of hardware and software, the management team of a hotel may decide that implementation of such a system would be cumbersome and cost ineffective. Or it may determine how customer satisfaction and profits would improve if a PMS were installed. The needs analysis keeps management in control of technology— a critical concept in hospitality management where service and profits interact.

Figure 1 presents the structure for a needs analysis. It outlines the steps management should take prior to visiting a computer dealer. If this procedure is followed, it will ensure the management team of a PMS decision based on fact, not conjecture.

The team approach to determining the possibilities of application of technology to hospitality is essential not only to reviewing the tasks that can be performed with greater efficiency, but it allows those most familiar with daily use of the computer operations to have an opportunity to design the system. Hotel general managers who review computer needs and investigate hardware and software applications without the assistance of department managers, supervisors, and employees are headed for failure. Even the vast

Fig. 1. Procedure for preparing a computer needs analysis. *(Source: James A. Bardi, Hotel Front Office Management, p. 89, 1990. New York: Van Nostrand Reinhold.)*

1. Select a team to analyze needs.
2. Analyze the flow of the guest through the visit to the lodging property.
    Reservations
    Registration
    Guest accounting
    Checkout
    Night audit
    Guest history
3. Analyze the flow of information from other departments to the front office.
4. Analyze the administrative paperwork produced in other departments.
5. Review information in steps 2, 3, and 4.
6. Evaluate the needs that have been identified, such as control reports, communication, and administrative paperwork produced in other departments, in terms of importance.
7. Combine needs to determine desired applications.

experience a general manager brings to the computer adoption decision will not compensate for the front line supervisors' and employees' current experience in delivering hospitality to the guest. These front line staff are able to view the technology that will increase or decrease customer satisfaction though decreasing check-in and checkout lines, reviewing the variables in the data base that affect communication systems, reviewing the data needed to make a reservation decision, reevaluating the use of guest history in the marketing plan and so forth. Their involvement will make the final decision one that can be implemented. The "buy in" from the front line staff will assist in the often difficult and challenging transition period from manual front office operation to a PMS operated front office.

The second step in the computer needs analysis requires management to analyze the flow of the guest through the visit to the lodging property. This technique allows the "guest" to remain foremost in the interface of technology and hospitality. It also focuses on actual needs instead of conjectured solutions to perceived needs. Some of the questions to be considered include

1. The method used to process reservations (How is guest data collected, transcribed, stored, and retrieved?)
2. The routine for registration (How is the reservation retrieved? How are guest data collected? How are the room and room rate assigned? How is guest credit established? How is the room key issued? How are guest data transferred to telephone and room rack?)
3. The procedure for recording guest charges to accounts (How are room and tax, food and beverage, telephone, gift shop, fitness club, and paid outs posted?)
4. The process for checkout (How does the guest initiate the checkout procedure? How are charges verified by the guest? How are discrepancies in charges rectified? How is guest credit executed? How is guest data filed and retrieved for a usable guest history?)
5. The night audit procedure (Who and how long does it take to post room and tax charges? How are departmental income and charges

verified? How are paid outs and transfers verified, How are the outstanding balance of credit cards and accounts receivable tabulated?)

6. The use of guest history (Are guest registration data available for use in marketing and sales? What data are more usable than others?

These questions will form the basis of an efficient computer decision. They keep guest service in the forefront while applying technology to answer problems of efficiency.

The next step in the needs analysis is to review the flow of information from other departments to the front office. The front office is usually the communications and accounting hub of the hotel. Guests target the front desk as the place in a hotel where someone will help or have an answer to their problem. Will a central data bank of registered guests and scheduled functions assist in providing the guest with answers to their concerns? Departmental financial transactions must be balanced each day. Will the financial data required to complete the night audit be readily available from point-of-sale sources? Will the information produced from the night audit be readily available for departmental managers to guide in cost and quality control? The impact of technology at this point in the computer decision will usually have a positive influence.

The fourth concept requires departmental managers and front line staff to analyze the administrative paperwork produced. The word processing and desktop publishing documents in the form of formal reports, direct mail letters and fliers, memos, newsletters, and other items should be reviewed in terms of quantity, quality, cost, and time involved to produce the final document. Likewise the financial analysis application of an electronic spread sheet to inhouse produced profit and loss statements, budgets, purchase decisions, should be examined in terms of their help to managers in making daily decisions.

The next step requires management to review in an objective manner the data gathered in the previous steps. A clear statement of how procedures affect needs should be developed. Will technology assist in the delivery of hospitality and the building of a positive profit and loss statement?

As the needs analysis progresses to the sixth step, a hierarchy of needs should be established in which the importance of each need is clarified. This will certainly assist the buyer when presented with a variety of software applications.

The final step allows management to evaluate, in terms of cost effectiveness, all of the desired software applications. If a property management system not only streamlines reservations, registrations and checkouts, keeps guest charges in order, and produces daily reports for the manager while also assisting the marketing and sales department in producing more sales, it can be a very justifiable purchase. Also when word processing, desktop publishing, and electronic spread sheet needs can be combined, the purchase decision becomes more global.

Software Applications

A software application is the computer program selected to assist in processing information. Bardi (1990:92) lists the basic rudiments of software applications, as follows:

Reservations
  room availability
  confirmation
Front desk
  check in
  room status
  postings to guest accounts
  guest credit audit
  advance deposits
  cashier
Call accounting
  guest information
  call posting
Housekeeping
  room status
Maintenance
  work orders
Food and beverage
  point of sale
  menu profitability analysis
  inventory
  recipes

Marketing and sales
  client file
  direct mail
  guest history
  travel agent
Night audit
  room and tax posting
  various operational reports
Accounting
  accounts payable
  accounts receivable
  general ledger
  payroll
  profit and loss statement
  balance sheet
Human resource management
  personnel files
  time and attendance
Electronic mail
Security

Upon review of each of these applications, separate yet interrelated modules are seen to develop. The reservations module consists of subsystems that can receive individual guest or group data, check a guest's request against data banks of available rooms, and store this information (Bardi 1990:101). The registration module verifies the guest's request for room type, location, and rate with room inventory and room status (Bardi 1990:101–102). The room status module (which may share the same room data bank with reservations) provides very useful reports used by the housekeeper, front office manager and staff, maintenance engineer, night auditor, reservations clerk, and marketing and sales department (Bardi 1990:102). The posting module allows the posting to occur at the point of sale (restaurant, gift shop, spa, garage). Similarly, room and tax charges or telephone calls can be quickly posted to the electronic folio. The PMS call accounting feature retrieves data for time, charges, and service fee and then posts these charges to the electronic folio. Transfers and adjustments (with approval by management) to folios are easily made. Charges incurred on behalf of the guest can be posted to the electronic folio by entering room number, amount of charge, department, and transaction type (Bardi 1990:102–103). The checkout module prints out an accurate, neat, and complete guest folio within seconds. The desk clerk can retrieve a hard copy of the electronic folio and present it for review to the guest. The guest completes the checkout process by confirming the method of payment. Transfers to the city ledger are electronically made at this time. Cashier activity reports are monitored as well as other information about the day's checkouts (Bardi 1990:103–104). The call accounting module allows for the replacement of the information rack and the paperwork required to maintain it (Bardi 1990:103). In the housekeeping module the maid or houseman enters the room status immediately through a computer terminal on the guest floor instead of waiting to report a block of rooms to the floor supervisor. Personnel assignments for cleaning rooms can also be made very easily. Further labor analysis and the daily housekeeper's report are quickly generated.

Maintenance requests for guests rooms can be communicated through the PMS. If the maintenance department wants to take a room out of service for a few days to perform repairs, this information can be relayed to the housekeeping and front desk staff through this module (Bardi 1990:105–106). The maintenance module streamlines lists of repair orders by prioritizing incomplete work orders, and complete jobs are analyzed for cost. Inventories of equipment and parts can be maintained. The maintenance module is also used to track energy costs and areas of use. Heating and air conditioning in guest rooms can be activated at the front desk (Bardi 1990:106). The food and beverage module lessens the flow of paper (vouchers) and telephone calls to initiate guest charges from the restaurants and lounges to the front desk. It also facilitates the accounting process, verifying the integrity of the point-of-sale system. Menu profitability analysis, inventory, and recipes can also be a feature of this module (Bardi 1990:106). The marketing and sales module allows this department to retrieve guest history information from reservation and registration files. The source of the reservation (secretary, group, travel agent), type of accommodation requested, and zip code of business affiliation or personal domicile are only some of the data that can be obtained from the reservation files (Bardi 1990:106–107). Word processing and desktop publishing software can also be used to develop direct mail pieces inhouse. The night audit module allows management to balance guest accounts, update accounts receivable, and departmental activities of the day. The PMS simplifies the night audit by posting room and tax to the electronic folios and producing totals from departments and guest folios (Bardi 1990:104). The accounting module assists in the labor-intensive posting procedure of accounts payable, the transfer of accounts receivable from the guest ledger and city ledger, the payroll compilation and production, budget preparation, and the production of the profit and loss statement and balance sheet are simplified (Bardi 1990:105). The human resource module allows the personnel manager to keep track of employee information concerning job category, date of hire, record of orientation and training, rate of pay, and so forth (Bardi 1990:107). This module may also be used as a time clock for employees to enter time of arrival and departure. The electronic mail feature is very helpful in distributing current information on policies and procedures to a large staff. Staff members are able to check their electronic mail on the computer monitor (Bardi 1990:107). The security module allows for the enhancement of key control in a hotel. The guest receives a room for which no previous guest had keys, because the desk clerk changes the key configuration or combination for each guest. Blank key cards (pressed paper, plastic, or metal) can be coded at the front desk for each new guest. Fire alarm systems in guest rooms, public areas, and operational areas are kept under constant surveillance. Burglar alarms and security codes are also monitored through this module (Bardi 1990:106).

All of these modules may or may not be present on any one particular PMS in a hotel. If a proper needs analysis has been performed and matched with an existing budget, management will purchase the necessary modules. Additional modules may be added subsequently as needs become apparent and finances become available.

Hardware

Most available hardware, such as that provided by CARA Information Systems Inc., Computerized Lodging Systems, Inc., ECI/EECO Computer, Inc., Hotel Information Systems, and Lodgistix, Inc., is compatible with standard computer operating systems (Bardi 1990:93). This consideration is essential because most software programs are written to run on these standard operating systems. In short, you must choose your hardware based on its ability to handle the software.

The basic hardware requirements are organized around the various points of sale and customer service areas. Input terminals, cathode ray tubes (CRTs), disk drives, and printers constitute the basic user setup. The data manipulation and storage area is part of the mainframe, minicomputer, or personal computer. The interfacing among computer data bases (sharing or networking of information) is very important. As the application of computers becomes more sophisticated, sharing of data bases is essential.

Summary

Property Management Systems should be considered as a technical assistant to management. The options offered by a PMS should not overwhelm general managers. General managers who perform a needs analysis of their operation will find a vast array of PMS modules as options for use in organizing and streamling a lodging property. The guest must remain at the center of the PMS adoption and operation. Hospitality management organized and enhanced with the assistance of technology provides the basic plan to build a successful profit and loss statement.

Reference

Bardi, James A. 1990. *Hotel Front Office Management.* New York: Van Nostrand Reinhold.

24

Reservation Systems

Paul R. Gamble

The reservation system is the engine of a lodging property because in a sense it powers everything else along. If the reservation system is not working well then the hotel or motel will lose business or may even go out of business. Many hospitality companies are beginning to realize that their competitive survival may well depend on having a reservation system at least as good as their rivals.

The Tasks of a Reservation System

The problems that face the reservations manager in a busy hotel can be illustrated by reviewing the tasks that the reservation system must perform. The whole process of taking bookings, receiving guests, providing for their stay and billing them on departure is known as the guest cycle. The reservation system is therefore the start of the guest cycle, as indicated in Figure 1.

Receive Inquiry and Check Availability
A guest inquiry may arise from the hotel's sales department; directly from the guest by mail, telephone, facsimile, or telex; or from a sales agent such as a travel agent or airline reservation system. The inquiry may relate to one room or to many and to an arrival that may be tomorrow or a year away. The reservation system must help the clerk collect data in an efficient and orderly fashion. It is therefore important that the system operate rapidly and be easy to learn and use. Once the basic data are recorded, the system must then help the clerk decide whether the hotel is able to accommodate the sale. The available rooms and the price, or room rate, at which they might be sold must be displayed in a style that can be grasped at a glance. In this initial contact with the hotel, it is vital to give a good impression of sales efficiency.

The reservation system should link directly with the hotel's guest history file. This file is a record of previous guests, their organizational affiliations, and details of their hotel use. The ability to draw on previous data quickly can have a very positive impact. For individual guests it may appear to enhance personal service and for sales agents it saves time. However, this feature must be handled with some discretion to protect the privacy of visitors.

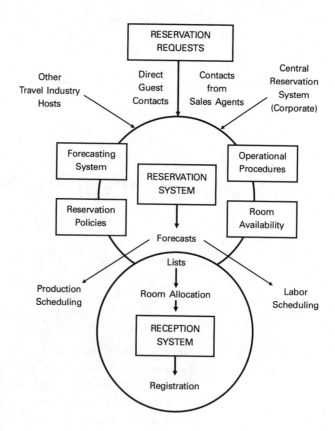

Fig. 1. Simplified diagram of a reservation system.

Make the Accept/Refuse Decision

A hotel that accepted every reservation inquiry it received would not be able to maximize its potential profitability. Deciding whether to accept or refuse a reservation is the most critical decision the reservation clerk makes, and it is not at all easy. The following factors should be taken into account:

Guest Status. A VIP, a frequent visitor, or the owner of a travel agency may be more important than a casual guest who is passing through the area, perhaps for one visit only.

Credit Status. There is not much point in selling rooms to people who do not pay their bills. The reservation system must be connected on-line to the city ledger, which keeps track of all revenues and credit charges. If the reservation system is on-line, the credit status records can be kept up to date all the time.

Occupancy Fluctuations. Unfortunately, hotel guests are not as reliable as hotels would like them to be. People have a habit of changing their plans. This causes short-term fluctuations in occupancy that must be predicted if the hotel is to maximize revenue. Factors that increase occupancy (the number of rooms sold) are walk-ins (sometimes called chance arrivals because the guest arrives with no prior reservation) and stay-ons, guests who extend their stay beyond their scheduled departure date.

These factors are offset by factors that decrease occupancy. Cancellations are relatively easy to manage since the hotel is given notice of the nonarrival but a no-show describes a guest who simply fails to turn up. This is not unusual for business executives whose travel plans often change. Extra departures are guests who leave before their planned departure date.

Some types of customers are more reliable than others. Vacation travelers tend to be fairly predictable whereas business travelers and convention delegates are less so.

Conversion Ratio. Particularly when large group bookings are concerned, the number of rooms that may actually result from an inquiry can be hard to judge. When negotiating for a rate, potential customers exaggerate the size of their group in order to get a lower rate. There is often a big difference between the number of provisional rooms sold and confirmed bookings. There may also be a reduction between the confirmed booking and the actual arrival. This ratio between the provisional booking and the arrival is known as the *conversion ratio* and it varies between types of customer.

Pressure of Business. The amount of business varies between day of week, month of year, and year to year. If the demand for rooms is stronger this year than last, the reservation manager would be well advised not to sell blocks of rooms to groups or conventions at a low rate well in advance. These early inquiries should be refused in the expectation of getting a better rate later on.

Effect on the Room Rate. Reservations will give the hotel a forecast of business, which is important to its cash flow. Since most of a hotel's revenue and most of its profit derives from room sales, it is important for the reservation system to manage the average rate, that is, the average price of all the rooms sold on a particular day. Some reservation systems, especially older systems, draw the manager's attention especially to occupancy, the volume of rooms sold. This can have the effect of increasing volume at the expense of rate since there is a temptation to sell rooms at a discount. Total revenue may actually fall with this approach.

A special aspect of this problem is multiple room occupancy. If twin rooms are sold too soon to individual guests, often at a lower rate, then potential spinoff business is lost in restaurants and bars because the number of people in the hotel is reduced.

Policy. The business plan also describes the long-term strategy of the hotel or the way in which the management team wishes to position the hotel in the market. Perhaps business from one source, although strong today, is expected to decline in the future. A sales effort to develop another market segment might be started and inquiries from this new segment would then receive higher priority.

Given all these issues, a hotel with say, 100 rooms, needs a reservation system that does more than simply count up to 100. Sometimes the hotel will sell 110 or perhaps even 120 rooms, overbooking in the expectation of no-shows or fall off from a provisional inquiry. Managing the level of over-booking is a difficult problem for a hotel. At other times the reservation manager will need to block rooms, which removes certain rooms from sale. Suppose a major trade show is held in the first week of September. Rooms may be blocked for release in say, August, when they can be sold for a high price. In addition, the hotel may have agreements with sales agents who are given a number of rooms to sell as they may wish. These agreements are known as freesale agreements. If the rooms are not sold by a certain time they revert to the hotel.

Once the reservation is accepted, it may need to be acknowledged. It may also be necessary to obtain advance deposits or credit card details. Good communications with the outside world and a facility with foreign languages are important in reservations. Sometimes, the reservation system may need to allocate a specific room for a guest when the booking is accepted, especially in small, resort hotels. More often, the actual room to be occupied is allocated on the morning of the day of arrival. The reservation system must closely support the receptionists who do this job by providing data in a convenient format. The arrivals list produced by the reservations system is of special interest to other operating departments in the hotel.

Links with Other Departments in the Hotel

The reservation system must have close contact with other hotel operating departments. It must collect instructions from the marketing and sales department about plans and targets and collect credit information from the accounting system. In turn it must provide information about future expected sales. Operationally, it must stay in touch with reception, housekeeping, the front hall staff, and even the banqueting and convention department. The reservation system must be fully informed about the operating plans and policies of the hotel. The annual maintenance schedule for redecorating blocks of rooms will be fixed in agreement with reservations. On a day-to-day basis, the reservation system must have direct access to the hotel's room status system. Not all hotel guests arrive and depart with plenty of advance notice. The reservation system also must cope with the daily fluctuations of unplanned arrivals and departures.

Types of Reservation System

Very small hotels may simply use a bookings diary. However, the most common manual system for hotels of any size is known as the Whitney System. This system was devised by the Whitney Paper Corporation of New York in the 1940s and it has been widely adopted worldwide. Each reservation is recorded on a small, multipart piece of paper mounted in a metal frame which, in turn, is filed in date and alphabetical order on a metal rack. The slips are usually color coded to denote the type of guest. Usually there is one rack for every day over say, the next three months, and fewer racks for future periods. Copies of the slips, also on racks, may be sent to other departments such as reception or telephones when the guest arrives. This system gave rise to the expression "rack rate," which is how hoteliers often refer to the price for rooms.

Whitney systems work very well but they do generate lots of paper. Clearly, organizing huge volumes of data is an ideal job for a computer. Unfortunately, in 1963 a large computer system to computerize the entire front office of the New York Hilton went disastrously wrong amid great publicity, discouraging both the hotel industry and the computer industry for some time. During the late 1960s and 1970s hotel companies installed reservation systems based on minicomputers. At this time well-known systems such as Holidex of Holiday Inns were started. So large and powerful was the computer system needed to run Holidex I in its day that it was designated as part of the strategic defensive reserve of the United States. However, large and powerful also means very expensive.

It was therefore not until the 1980s and the commercial success of the microcomputer that computerized reservation systems became commonplace in hotels as part of a property management system. Surveys conducted regularly for the American Hotel and Motel Association indicate that between 1980 and 1987, the number of microcomputer PMS installed in the United States grew from zero to 30,000 (Chervenak 1988).

In the 1990s, the power and performance of microcomputers is such that even hotel properties with very few rooms can use them cost effectively. Worldwide, nearly 200 different companies are offering PMS to the hotel industry. Essentially, a computerized reservation system undertakes the same sort of tasks as a Whitney System but the performance of the computer is exploited to organize data more efficiently (Kasavana and Cahill 1987).

Computers also provide for some augmentation of the product to enhance guest services. Preregistration is made easier by the computer, which means that all the guest has to do is sign a registration form on arrival. Indeed, available systems now allow registration from remote locations such as airports, using hand-held microwave transmitters. Self check-in is also available to guests so that they can avoid long lines at the reception desk. On departure, the system also provides for self checkout and this interfaces with the billing system.

Centralized Reservation Systems (CRS) Large hotel companies cannot maximize their profit potential, or even exploit the marketing advantages of sheer size, by managing their hotel chains on a piecemeal basis. A centralized reservation system allows a company to manage demand strategically, for entire regions or for large cities. This simplifies some aspects of the rooms inventory management problem when large groups or conventions can be switched between hotels. At the same time, customer convenience is improved. A single 800 number, which contacts a central point, enables a potential guest to make a convenient reservation at any property around the world. Almost all the major hotel groups now operate their own CRS. The competitive advantage of this service has even encouraged some cooperation between companies too small to warrant a CRS of their own.

The technology used to support these systems is quite sophisticated. Fast networks, fiber-optic cables, and satellite transmission are often used to transmit data between the CRS and the individual hotel. At the same time, even more service can be added for customer gain, including low-cost facsimile transmission and teleconferencing.

Links with Other Travel Industry Reservation Services The impetus for much of the development initiatives in hotel CRS has come from the airline industry. Powerful reservation systems such as SABRE owned by American Airlines, Apollo owned by United Airlines and System One owned by Texas Air have been particularly influential. Airline CRS do not confine their activities to selling airplane seats and their success in capturing more of the travel market by selling hotel rooms, renting cars, booking theater tickets, and even complete holidays has encouraged hotel companies to respond directly.

Techniques for Managing Reservations

The most important management science technique in a reservation system is that of forecasting. The reservations office works on two time horizons. There is a medium- to long-term period, which might extend anywhere from ten days to several months or even longer; very large conventions may wish to book hotel space two or more years ahead. From the reservations manager's point of view a four-month period probably covers the period over which critical decisions about hotel capacity have to be made. The short-term period includes the next five to ten days. The number of days between the reservation and the arrival is known as the *booking lead time*. In a commercial or business hotel the average booking lead time might be quite short, perhaps only a few days. It is not unusual for over half the hotel's entire business to be booked less than five days before arrival.

Reservation departments therefore produce regular forecasts for other departments of the hotel. Typically, these might include daily forecasts for the next ten days, weekly forecasts for up to two months out and two further monthly forecasts. These are extremely important. Most of the other hotel departments look at the forecasts closely and plan their labor scheduling, food production levels, and promotional activities based on the amount of business predicted by the reservations department.

Yield Management Systems Forecasting in any business can be difficult but is especially so in a service business like the lodging industry. Many factors have to be taken into account and many possible responses are available to the hotel or motel in marketing and sales terms.

Yield management systems are being incorporated into hotel reservation systems to try to help with these problems. The technique is actually the outcome of three marketing decisions. These are the strategic decisions as to which product to offer and in what quantity overall, the tactical decision to determine the configuration of the product on a particular day and, finally, the pricing decision to support that tactic. If it were to be relabeled more precisely yield management would probably be termed a pricing system (Relihan 1989). A yield management system actually seeks to maximize revenue, not yield.

The approach proceeds from known conditions to unknown conditions. Known conditions include the number of rooms available, demand as it is experienced by the hotel, and the range of prices that may be quoted. Unknown conditions include total demand in that market, the effect of short-term fluctuations such as cancellations and no-shows, the demand build up pattern in the current sales period, and competitor activity.

All of these elements are present in the decision process whether a hotel uses a yield management system or not. However, a yield management system tends to formalize both the data and the decision process with a view to increasing revenue by better price and marketing mix management. This increased revenue is achieved by more frequently adjusting the availability and price of rooms for different markets. It also aims to make the best of multiple night stays and reduce unnecessary discounting by prematurely releasing capacity.

Yield management systems are closely linked to the PMS from which they obtain data. However, they also need to obtain data to account for market conditions in the city or region. They then use a combination of statistical forecasts and rule-based procedures to identify the reservation status of the hotel. The statistical forecast uses conventional techniques for determining the trend of business and the way in which that will be affected by seasonal variations. The rule-based procedure uses techniques developed in the 1970s and 1980s to enable a computer to "reason" with the forecast, based on rules that have been programmed into it, in order to recommend appropriate actions.

It is expected that yield management systems will become as important and regular a feature of hotel reservation systems in the 1990s as they are in present day airline reservation systems.

Summary

An efficient reservation system is crucial if a lodging property is to meet its profit targets. However, the business of managing demand through the reservation system is complex. Many factors have to be taken into account and good operating systems are needed to track movements in the market. The basic procedures for receiving and recording bookings have not altered, but in today's business environment manual record systems can be too slow and expensive. Computerized systems help organize the vast volumes of data and allow for rapid, efficient communications with guests and with other hotel departments.

However, many of the problems with which a reservation manager has to struggle still depend on human judgment. Deciding whether to accept a booking right now or to refuse because there is an expectation of better business, or because the hotel is trying to cultivate a new market, is not easy. The procedures built into yield management systems are designed to help with parts of this problem.

The key concern for a hotel or chain of hotels is the reservation policy. Clearly policy is central to how the system is meant to work. If the management team decides that it will never walk (turn away from the hotel) a guest with a confirmed reservation, then overbooking must be managed very cautiously. If it decides to give priority to a travel agent in the high season because of promised business for the low season, then it must expect to refuse reservation inquiries at high room rates in some periods of the year.

As a result of these issues, the reservation system needs careful management attention. Both reservation policies and practice must be evaluated at regular intervals to ensure that the system is responding to the changing business environment of the hotel and allowing it to maximize profitability.

References

Chervenak, L. 1988. Hotel information processing 1988, *CKC Report* 5(1):3.

Kasavana, M. L., and J. Cahill. 1987. *Managing Computers in the Hospitality Industry.* East Lansing, Mich.: The Educational Institute of the AHMA.

Relihan, W. J. 1989. The yield management approach to hotel-room pricing, *Cornell Hotel Restaurant Administration Quarterly,* 30(1):40–44.

25

Guest Registration

Tom Van Dyke

Guest registration is one of the first and most lasting impressions on a hotel customer. Guest registration sets the tenor for the stay and is, therefore, a critical contact point. The front desk should promote the warmth and hospitality of the property. Guest registration is the point at which critical information is collected about the customer and his/her wishes. If a bottleneck develops in guest registration, customer complaints arise. As a result many front desk employees are particularly concerned with processing the needed information quickly and tend to neglect welcoming the customers. Hence, the warmth and hospitality the hotel would like to project is lost.

There are two types of guest registration systems, manual and computerized. When using a manual registration system, the front desk clerks and supervisors are the key elements to a successful operation. The front desk personnel process information on guests checking out and confirm the number and rooms of guests remaining. Once this has been determined, the front desk personnel assign reservations to vacant rooms. When a guest arrives seeking a room, the front desk clerk asks the guest if he/she has a reservation. If the answer is no, the front desk clerk checks to see if there is a room available. If there are rooms available, the clerk tells the guest what rooms are available and quotes the price for each type of room. When the guest does have an advance reservation, the clerk checks the registration information and asks the guest to confirm or complete the information on a registration card. At this point, the clerk may try to upsell the guest by offering upgraded accommodations at a slightly higher price. In this effort the hotel/motel tries to maximize its sales and simultaneously enhance the guest's satisfaction. Typical information on a registration card includes address, company represented, number of persons in the party, the length of stay, type of payment (cash or credit card and type of credit card) and information on the automobile (make, year, and license plate number). The credit card is then imprinted or cash payment is collected, and the clerk determines if an advanced assignment of a room is "ready to rent" or assigns a room that has been cleaned. The guest is issued a key or security key card providing access to his/her room. The front desk clerk will inform the guest of the location of the room, discuss the amenities of the hotel/motel and may call for a bellman to take the luggage to the room depending on the type of operation.

The front desk clerk then processes the information received. First, the clerk files the guest registration in the room rack, documenting for the other clerks that the room is occupied. The room rack is a vertical file with slots for each room in the hotel. This file system allows front desk clerks to visually check the status of all rooms in the hotel/motel. Different colored cards are frequently used in the room slots to signify if the room has been prepared, if the room needs repair, or if the room cannot be rented. The clerk also completes a slip with the customer's last name and room number and either files it in the directory for incoming calls or notifies the switchboard operator of the addition. The front desk clerk then verifies the credit card for the estimated amount of the room charge. The clerk then prepares a folio for each guest to record the nightly room charges and any additional charges the guest wishes to apply toward his/her room number. Once the folio has been completed, the clerk deposits the folio in an alphabetical/numerical filing system called the bucket. Once this action has been taken guest registration has been accomplished.

If the hotel/motel has computerized the front desk area, procedures for guest registration change. After the majority of guest checkout has been completed, the front desk personnel generate a computer printout of the number of customers remaining in the hotel/motel. Once the remaining guests have been confirmed, the front desk personnel generate another computer printout, indicating reservations for the coming evening. The front desk clerks then assign reservations to vacant rooms. Upon arrival the clerk asks if the guest(s) has a reservation. If the guest says no, the clerk checks availability of rooms. If rooms are available, the clerk states the room rates and describes the advantages of the more expensive rooms using upselling techniques. If the guest decides to stay, the clerk then asks the guest his/her address, the company represented, the number of persons in the party, the length of stay, the type of payment (cash or credit card and type of credit card) and information on the automobile (make, year, and license plate number). This information is then entered into the computer. If the guest has a reservation, the front desk clerk confirms the information and completes any missing information. At this point the clerk may try to upsell the guest. The clerk then either imprints the credit card or collects the cash payment and determines which room the guest has been assigned to or assigns a room that has been cleaned. The clerk then prints out a copy of the guest registration and gives the copy to the customer along with the key to the room. Depending on the type of hotel/motel, the front desk clerk informs the guest of the location of the room, gives the guest the key, discusses the amenities of the hotel/motel and if applicable calls for a bellman to take the luggage to the room. The clerk should wish the guest a pleasant stay and ask them to call if he/she can be of further assistance. When the front desk clerk completes the guest registration, the computer automatically updates the guest name and room number to its directory for incoming calls. Some properties will have the front desk clerk call the guest shortly after he or she registers to see if everything is suitable. The clerk may then post to the room the nightly room rental and any other charges the guest wishes to bill to his/her room.

A recent development in guest registration is using point of systems (POS) to hasten the check-in process (Bell, 1989). The POS systems lets the customer register at self-service terminals in the lobby or at self-service terminals in the airport van enroute to the hotel. Current innovations transform guest credit cards into room keys. The POS systems can eliminate the mind-numbing bottlenecks that develop during check-in times at hotels/motels, reduce management workload, and make hotels safer, friendlier, and more efficient places for guests. One popular check-in system asks the guest to insert his or her magnetic-stripe credit card into a check-in terminal which calls up the property's computerized reservations list filed by arrival date and last name. When the reservations match is found, the room selecting function of the hotel's property management system generates a room assignment and prints a check-in form. The guest removes the completed form, signs it and then is directed to the key pick-up area at or near the front desk. The Sheraton Meadowlands in New Jersey works with Avis Rent-A-Car so guests picking up cars at any of the New York area's three major airports can simultaneously check in to a room at the Sheraton.

Guests in four Kansas City area Marriotts can check in to their rooms at a special Marriott Marquis Club room at the airport. In Chicago guests of the O'Hare Marriott can check in while traveling to the property in the airport van.

Choice International and some other hotel companies take self check in a step further. Choice's new budget brand Sleep Inns employ a new keyless check in and guestroom entry system. Sleep Inn's guests present their credit cards at check in to obtain a room match. The guest then uses the credit card as his or her room key. Guests without a credit card receive a house card.

> David C. Elmore, Vice President of Development for Sleep Inns, believes the system is more than just a guest convenience, since in addition to the security of keyless entry it automatically alerts front desk of any unauthorized card insertion. For energy control, the system kicks-on the room's heating/cooling units when the guest is still at the front desk. Also, the room's sprinklers and smoke detectors alert the front desk in case of an emergency.
>
> "From a cost standpoint, time and money is saved in re-keying," adds Elmore. "Also, we're able to reduce our energy costs, and minimize losses from fire and theft." (Bell 1989:61)

To maximize guest satisfaction, certain hotels/motels are modifying check-in and checkout times. Typically a guest cannot check in until 3:00 P.M., unless the guest makes special arrangements. With flex check in and check out, the guests may rent the room on a 24-hour basis. For instance, if the guest checks in at 5:00 P.M., they may stay until 5:00 P.M. the next day. "Two of the most frequent responses expressed by the guests: they get more stay for their dollar and the hotel is accommodating the customer rather than the customer accommodating the hotel (Seeger 1990:74)." One of the few required changes for a hotel/motel using this system is scheduling a percentage of the maids to come in later in the day to clean and prepare rooms that check out later in the afternoon or evening.

Summary

Guest registration is a critical point for the hotel where vital information is collected on the guests and the guests gain their first impression of the hotel. Management is continually seeking ways to increase guest satisfaction. Guest registration is one area in which recent innovations have been devised to speed the registration process. Whether a hotel uses a manual or computerized registration system, the object is to make customer entry to the operation as simple and convenient as possible while trying to project warmth and friendliness.

References

Bell, Doreen. 1989. Speeding up check-in/out. *Lodging Hospitality* 45(1):59–61.
Seeger, Peggy. 1990. Breaking the old time rules. *Hotel & Resort Industry* 13(7):73–76.

26

Checkout

Melvin N. Barrington

A recent survey by an international hotel and resort chain revealed that two of the top ten peeves that business travelers had about their experiences involved the checkout process (Merrick 1990). Their complaints centered around the length of and inflexibility of checkout times. The checkout procedure is usually the last contact the guest will have with the property. This procedure is the final opportunity for the hotel to ensure the guest leaves with a positive memory or aftertaste of the service experience that was provided (Barrington and Olsen 1987). If the guest has had a particularly bad experience, checkout is the last chance to alter the guest's perception of the hotel by providing a positive experience in order to generate that all-essential repeat business. Conversely, if the guest had a good experience, there is a need to perpetuate it by ending his or her stay with a smooth easy checkout procedure. Bear in mind that people tend to remember their most recent experiences more vividly than those that occurred in the past.

Basically the checkout procedure consists of three elements: (1) the guest vacates the room, (2) the guest settles the bill, and (3) the guest departs the property.

Vacating the Room

Just when the guest decides to vacate the room may be governed by several factors: travel plans, checkout time, housekeeping pressure, bell staff availability, and/or post-checkout services provided by the property.

The chief factor that determines when guests decide to check out centers around their business or travel plans. Naturally they want to check out in ample time (but not too early) to keep their next appointment, whether it is driving to the next destination or catching a flight home. Probably the next most important factor governing departure is the formal checkout time, which often conflicts with the guest's travel plans.

The official checkout time is usually posted at the front desk, on the registration card, and on the inside of the guest room door (along with the room rate and emergency procedures). This time can range anywhere from 9:00 AM to 2:00 PM, but is normally around noon. In most cases, this time is established by the hotel for its purposes, not for guest convenience.

Although the hotel generally desires to accommodate the guest in any way possible, the rooms must be vacated in order for the housekeeping staff to have them ready by check-in time, which usually starts at about 3:00 PM. Most hotels will allow the guest to make arrangements for late checkout, depending on the volume of reservations that day. A few will attach a fee for late checkout (depending on policy or projected occupancy). When a hotel is projecting a sellout, upon check-in, guests are often required to sign a statement confirming their departure date. The law varies from state to state on the right of eviction of "stayovers" (guests who continue occupying a room beyond the anticipated checkout time).

Several properties are enhancing guest satisfaction by offering flexible check-in/out times (Seeger 1990). One hotel in Miami allows guests to check out up to 6:00 PM without an extra charge. The thinking is that since 80 percent of the guests check out by noon, the needs of the customer will be served with little problem to the hotel. A hotel in Dallas rents rooms on a 24-hour basis, similar to car rentals. With this system guests can check in and out at their convenience. This system was well received by the guests because they could make and receive phone calls, take a shower, change clothes, have a convenient and safe place to store their luggage, and their children could use the pool all afternoon while they were in meetings. Many hotels are extending late checkout options to their frequent-stay and weekend special guests. Basically they add extra hours to the weekend by extending the checkout to as late as 8:00 PM on Sunday. This presents little problem because the rooms are not scheduled to be cleaned until Monday morning when most of the housekeeping staff return to work. Finally these flexible checkout times eliminate bottlenecks created when too many people check out at the same time.

Other minor factors affecting the checkout time include

1. The availability of the bell staff. Experienced travelers plan their checkout time when they know the bellmen will not be busy.
2. Persistence of housekeeping. There are occasions when the guest does not hang a do-not-disturb sign on the door, and the house-keepers keep knocking until the guest feels compelled to leave and let them do their work.
3. Post-checkout services. If the hotel offers other services to the guests who are not leaving until many hours beyond the checkout time, such as complimentary baggage storage and a place to freshen up before departure, the guests will tend to take advantge of these services and opt for an early checkout.

Bill Settlement

The night auditor updates the guest folio between 11:00 PM and 7:00 AM in order for the hotel to be able to present the bill to guests when they are ready to check out. Depending on the property, the guest has several check-out procedures available.

The simplest and least troublesome method is to check in and out at the same time. With this system the guest pays cash in advance when check-ing in and simply leaves by the agreed upon time. Of course this method only works in a property where no other, except pay-as-you-go, services are provided. Such a system precludes any amenities including telephone service.

The regular checkout procedure is to go to the front desk at the end of the stay, request the bill, and satisfy the account. Although this method is personal and facilitates the handling of all problems on the spot, the major drawback is the extra time involved if the guest is unlucky enough to pick a busy time.

Many hotels offer an express checkout service allowing the guest to avoid the long lines at the front desk. The most popular method of express checkout is one in which the bill or folio is slipped under the guest's door by at least 5 AM on the morning of the scheduled departure date. If the bill is correct the guest gives tacit approval by doing nothing, simply departing by checkout time. Of course this system is only available to guests with prior credit approval.

For a number of years, selected Marriott hotels have offered a popular checkout procedure using the television. In this system the guest turns to the appropriate channel and simply follows the directions. Within minutes of completing the transaction, a printed statement is available to be picked up at the front desk. Not only are guests able to use the system for checkout, but they may also use it to review their folio at any time during their stay. As with most systems, this one is not infallible (Grimes 1991). It seems that in order to save time, a female traveler used her TV to check out at 6 AM and then went for her usual morning walk. When she returned her magnetic key would not open her door. By this time the hotel was very busy with heavy elevator use and long lines at the desk. When she finally got to tell someone of her problem, she was already late for an appointment. She discovered that the computer had changed the code for her door key and she had to be checked back in again. Luckily her bags were still in the room. Hopefully the consequences of the self-service checkout procedure will be explained to future guests.

Payment Options

As in most sales situations the hotel guest has a variety of options when paying the bill, such as cash, check, credit card, transfer to another guest account, or direct billing. Of course any hotel will take cash at the time of checkout, but cash in advance is another matter. A guest who pays cash in advance would not be allowed to make any other charges. This arrangement is more convenient in a facility where services are limited to sleeping rooms only. However, even the most basic property has a telephone and probably movie rentals in the room. In this case, the guest would be asked to pay for additional services when rendered.

Most hotels are reluctant to take a check for all the obvious reasons, not the least of which is the fact that most guests are writing checks on out-of-town banks. Normally, the only way a lodging facility will take a check is to use a check approval organization. Travelers' checks are different and, with proper identification, are treated the same as cash. Most properties have strict policies on handling checks and when followed there is seldom a problem. Be mindful, however, that just when the industry thinks it has the perfect system, along comes another scheme to defraud.

The most popular and widely accepted form of payment is by credit card. It is nearly impossible to rent a car without a credit card, and most hotels would like to move in the same direction. The credit card is so popular with businesses because the risk of extending credit is shifted from the hotel to the issuing institution. Normally when the guest checks in, his or her credit card is imprinted, and, by signing the guest registration card, the hotel has a "signature on file" thereby enabling the hotel to collect charges made by the guest even if he or she fails to sign the charge slip.

Another common method of satisfying a guest account is direct billing to a third party, which is transferred to the city ledger account. This method allows local companies who do frequent business with a hotel to set up an account for their clients or employees. These accounts are usually invoiced on a monthly billing cycle. An infrequent method of third party billing occurs when a guest's charges are transferred to another guest's account. Of course this method requires authorization from the account being charged, who must in turn adhere to the hotel's policies.

Settlement Problems When the guest checks out the bill is presented for verification of charges. Frequently there are discrepancies on the bill because many people are involved in reporting the charges, such as restaurants, lounge, gift shop, parking, telephone, and movies. These charges are then posted to the guest folio by the night auditor. Computers may be used to automatically post the charges at the point of sale but no system is foolproof and mistakes are made. Erroneous charges on the bill can be a real source of tension between the hotel and guest, especially telephone charges. Since deregulation many local and long distance telephone companies are vying for the lucrative hotel business. Each have varied rates and surcharges, which are not disclosed to the guest until he or she is shocked by the bill. For example, some companies automatically charge for a call after so many seconds. Therefore a guest may let a phone ring ten times with no answer and hang up, only to be surprised to be charged for a completed call. These and other phantom charges need to be resolved for guest satisfaction.

An increasingly popular method of dealing with guest satisfaction is called "empowerment," whereby lower level employees, such as desk clerks, have the authority and responsibility to solve problems without management intervention (Brymer 1991). If mistakes are made the desk clerks may adjust the bill, offer an upgrade on the next visit, or ask the customer what would satisfy him or her and try to act accordingly.

Departure

After the guests check out they are expected to make no more charges, surrender their room key, and leave the premises. These events do not always occur immediately, therefore checking out does not sever all guest-host relationships. Although no charges are allowed after checkout, a guest may have just charged breakfast to his or her room and those charges were not posted in time to present the complete bill. As a result of this problem, the clerk should always ask if there were any recent charges that do not appear on the bill. The hotel relies on guest honesty in this case but, if charges appear later, the hotel must go through the complicated process of collection. Point of sale computers that post charges immediately have all but eliminated this problem.

The guest is not expected to surrender the key immediately upon checkout. The time interval between checkout and departure seems to be a gray area that is not formally stated. The checkout procedure should trigger a signal to the housekeeping department that the room is ready for cleaning. The only delay in such cases may be when the guest retains the room key to do any last minute packing or to wait for a bellman. Guests can leave the key in the room, give it to the desk clerk, place it in a special key drop, or, if they forget completely, they can mail it back to the hotel. With disposable electronic cards gradually replacing keys, their return becomes moot.

Finally when the guest checks out a guest history card should be created listing all pertinent information about the guest. As one hotel executive once said, "It's amazing that I call for a pizza delivery, give my phone number, and they ask if I would like the large pepperoni like I got the last time." The hotel business has a lot of catching up to do (Greger and Withiam, 1991).

Summary

The checkout procedure from a lodging facility is extremely important to both the guest and the property. The guest is interested in completing this final transaction with the least amount of problems thereby completing the stay with a positive experience. The facility also wants the guest to have had a positive experience while ensuring that all charges will be paid in full.

References

Barrington, Melvin, and Michael Olsen. 1987. Concept of service in the hospitality industry. *International Journal of Hospitality Management* 6(3):131–138.

Brymer, Robert. 1991. Employee empowerment: A guest-driven leadership strategy. *The Cornell HRA Quarterly* 32:(1):58–68.

Greger, Kenneth, and Glen Withiam. 1991. A view from the helm: Hotel execs examine the industry. *The Cornell HRA Quarterly* 32(3):18–35.

Grimes, Paul, 1991. High tech: High touch or high anxiety? *The Cornell HRA Quarterly* 32(3):36–43.

Merrick, William. 1990. Creative concepts. *The Succesful Hotel Marketer* 3(23):2.

Seeger, Peggy. 1990. Breaking the old time rules. *Hotel & Resort Industry* 13(7):72–76.

27

Guest Services

Richard Teare and Martin Senior

Hotel Choice and Expectations of Guest Services

When a traveler seeks accommodation away from home, the type of hotel chosen will be determined by general factors such as personal values and preferences, prior experience, the perceived utility of the purchase, the nature of the occasion, financial circumstances, and anticipated risk (Barrington and Olsen 1987). Key product factors are likely to include

1. Location
2. Price
3. Range of services offered
4. Quality of guest services

In theory, they might best be considered in a logical and sequential way before deciding where to stay. However, it is more likely that the traveler subconsciously reviews them in random order and may assess aspects of two or more product factors at the same time.

Location has often been considered the most important factor in the commercial success of a hospitality unit. Travelers can and will lose interest in visiting an establishment if it is difficult to find. Visibility, easy access, and clear directional guidelines are therefore necessary to attract passing travelers and those who intend to use the establishment but have not done so before.

Price is not necessarily a fixed amount, but all travelers have an acceptable range in mind for the amenities and services they need and expect to use. This will be determined by several general factors such as ability to pay, prior experience, and personal perceptions as to whether the establishment offers value for money.

The range of services sought will be determined partly by the purpose of the trip and partly by the traveler's lifestyle. If it is a short overnight trip, the traveler may be content to use a simple economy-priced hotel. The expectation would be to find a clean, comfortable bedroom and, because of the low price, a limited range of guest services. In other circumstances such as the desire to rest, recuperate, or entertain, the traveler may seek a more expensive hotel, offering luxurious surroundings and guest services delivered by staff with extensive professional experience. Although the price will be higher, it should reflect the added value component of enhanced guest services and amenities, thereby providing equivalent overall value for money.

The quality of guest services refers to the subjective perceptions of the traveler. If the services are provided to the expected standard, the provider's service quality objectives have been achieved. The quality of guest services therefore relates to the degree of fit between the traveler's expectations and subsequent experience. For the most basic trip, the minimum requirements include a clean, comfortable and secure bedroom; in-room amenities such as a telephone, radio, and television; and facilities to dispense food and beverages. Depending on the nature of the trip, further desired services may include children's facilities for families, business services for business travelers, and leisure/entertainment for recreational purposes. The type of guest services provided should therefore be determined by the hotel's target market segment. The quality of the services should also meet and preferably exceed the minimum expectations of the market segment.

The range of guest services offered is sometimes referred to as the service package, the composition of which is determined by the requirements of the market segment. If all the elements of the service package meet or exceed the expectations of the guest, a quality service package has been provided. However, if one or more of the elements in the service package is inconsistent, then the guest may feel that the product has underperformed, which in turn affects perceptions of value for money and guest satisfaction.

All of these factors must be considered when defining the type, range, and style of guest services that constitute the service package. In this sense, amenities (which are a function of facilities design) and guest services (which are often intangible service offerings that require personalized delivery) should be viewed as complementary facets of the guest experience. This is how they are presented in most hotel guest service directories, which provide a framework against which guest perceptions of quality and value arising from the service experience can be evaluated. A typical directory of guest services for a midprice hotel is shown in Figure 1.

To summarize, the provision of guest services is dependent upon the range required by the market segment and the guest expectations of the service package.

Assessment of Guest Services

When using guest services, the traveler draws on preconceived expectations and assessment criteria to measure various aspects of product performance both during and after use. Research shows that the traveler is able to integrate many individual assessments which are used to calculate a moving average level of satisfaction with a hotel and the guest services it provides (Teare 1990).

By comparing perceived ideal product attribute ratings against prior experience, the traveler makes a mental cost-benefit analysis to assess "value for money" in relation to the guest services received. If expectations are experience-based, they will facilitate comparison against particular hotel reference standards, enabling the traveler to assess whether the current experience falls above or below the reference point standard.

The traveler may use an established routine to assess bedroom amenities and standards. For example, when families travel together, role specialization is commonplace and female assessment in particular can be rigorous, includ-

Fig. 1. A typical midprice hotel directory of guest services.

> **For added guest convenience:**
>
> **Air conditioning** in the bedroom that allows the guest to control the temperature; **baby sitting and facilities for children** that include rollaway beds and a children's menu available in the restaurant and from room service; a **business center** with photocopier, facsimile, PC, telephone, work station and full secretarial service available on weekdays; **car rental** that can be arranged by the hotel; the provision of **self-serve ice and drinks** (a range of spirits, beers, and soft drinks) via a guest room minibar and ice machines serving each floor of the hotel; a **room service** provision for snacks and meals; a **gift shop** providing newspapers, confectionery and tobacco; same day service **laundry and dry cleaning**; a **message service** with an electronic link between reception and the guest room
>
> **For guest entertainment:**
>
> Bar, restaurant, and lounge service of meals and drinks
>
> **To provide relaxation:**
>
> Health and leisure club equipment, which may include indoor gymnasium, swimming, spa bath, sauna, turkish bath and solarium facilities as well as outdoor sports facilities

ing checks for cleanliness and quality on bedding, fabrics, furnishings, and fittings. The most widely used reference point for gauging the acceptability of quality standards is the home. A common expectation is that the hotel should be able to provide all of the amenities enjoyed in the home and more. If this expectation is not met, the traveler may feel unwelcome because the environment is perceived to be inferior.

Reporting on a study of frequent travelers using economy, midprice and luxury hotels, Knutson (1988) found that they had clear expectations of bedroom amenities and the services they were likely to use in the hotel. Expectations varied according to the market segment. Key findings were as follows:

Economy hotels offered limited services and bedroom amenities although 12 percent of travelers expected to find personal-care items in their room other than the basic provision of a bar of soap and a towel. Although unexpected, 70 percent of travelers reported using personal-care products when they were provided and 80 percent used extra towels when they had been provided.

Midprice hotels offered a greater range of amenities and services. Travelers expected more and reported using most of what was available to them in this category of hotel.

Luxury hotels need to devote thought and attention to the amenities and services they provide, as travelers using this type of hotel have high expectations. For instance, 50 percent of the survey respondents expected to find 26 out of 29 itemized services. However, expectations do not reflect usage patterns. The survey indicated that 80 percent of respondents expected to find a shower cap or shoeshine cloth in their room, although only 40 percent said that they would definitely use these items. Findings would suggest that in this category of hotel, travelers are willing to pay for the convenience of having comprehensive guest services available to them even if they are not always required.

Guest Services in Economy Hotels

In the case of an economy hotel, the market segment it serves consists of travelers with low cost expectations who usually have limited time and choice options concerning location. It is therefore essentially a short stay, limited-service product.

To satisfy the needs of this market, an economy hotel usually has three common characteristics: (1) a convenient location, (2) a low tariff, and (3) limited services.

Convenient Location   Convenient location is a prerequisite for all travelers with a limited amount of time available. A passing traveler may have little or no time to plan ahead when selecting overnight accommodation and is unlikely to want to divert far from their planned route at the end of the day's travel. To facilitate easy arrivals and departures, economy hotels are therefore usually situated alongside major highways or close to an airport or railway station.

Low Tariff   As travelers are often constrained by choice or by budget to control their expenditure on overnight accommodation, guest services are more limited. Whereas full-service hotels tend to charge high tariffs, an economy hotel operates at minimum overhead cost and is therefore able to offer a low tariff structure.

Limited Services   As time and finances are restricted and therefore guest expectations more functional, an economy hotel offers only the core services essential to the passing traveler. These are likely to be clean, comfortable, and well maintained accommodation; professional service and friendly staff; and access to a reasonable product range refreshment facility.

Although these features appear self-evident, economy hotel operators commonly experience difficulty in providing convenient access to food and beverage facilities that offer a reasonable choice. Recruiting and retaining staff is also relatively difficult as economy hotels are not always as conveniently located for local employees as town and city center hotels. Secondly, as guest services are more restricted, the intrinsic level of satisfaction for staff in serving guests is not as high as in full-service hotels (Senior and Morphew 1990).

Guest Services in Midpriced and Luxury Hotels

Research undertaken by Wilesky and Buttle (1988) identified seven key product factors in hotel selection for midpriced and luxury hotels.

1. Opportunities for relaxation (leisure facilities)
2. Value for money (price-value relationship)
3. Standard of personal service (courtesy and efficiency)
4. Physical attractiveness (interior design quality)
5. Appealing image (hotel personality and reputation)
6. Standard of services (security, convenience, range)
7. Suitability for business guests (support services)

As expectations are more complex for these hotel categories, most travelers are likely to have interrelated needs. For example, business travelers may desire comfortable, modern surroundings, leisure facilities to relax, and access to advanced telecommunications equipment for business purposes. Consequently, hotel operators must provide a sophisticated service package in order to compete effectively in this marketplace. A typical development is the Business Center concept, designed to provide total support for business travelers. Services include

> *Secretarial*—dictation, photocopying, copy and audio typing of reports and letters;
> *Communication*—facsimile and telex (incoming and outgoing);
> *Information technology*—some hotel business centers now provide standard size and portable business computers for the use of business travelers who are able to send and receive computer data by telecommunication.

The Executive category bedroom is also designed to ensure that business travelers who are willing to pay higher than average prices receive extra guest services. Typically the service package includes a larger than average bedroom with high quality furnishings and decor equipped with a minibar, hairdryer and trouser press. The executive bathroom may be differentiated by a larger selection of complimentary toiletries, the inclusion of a bathrobe, extra towels, and other features such as telephone and radio extensions. Complimentary light refreshments are sometimes provided such as fresh fruit, chocolates, mineral waters, and fruit juices together with a daily newspaper.

All hotel operators providing Executive category bedrooms offer different variations on the enhanced guest service package in order to customize their product. The purpose of this is to create a superior brand image in order to achieve competitive advantage.

Delivering Guest Services in Midpriced Hotels

To illustrate the important role of staff in providing guest services, this section describes the duties typically undertaken by the hotel guest services departments in a midpriced hotel as depicted in Figure 2.

Hotel front hall staff are often the first people new guests meet on arrival so the initial impression of the hotel's service is closely related to the service interaction that takes place. Front office staff working in reception and reservations deal with room bookings, the administration arising from this work, and room allocations to guests. Administration also involves compiling up-to-date information on all the rooms in the hotel, which requires close cooperation with the housekeeping department so that guest room status can be verified. This involves checking on the number of rooms that are occupied,

Fig. 2. Delivering guest services: a typical organization chart for hotel accommodations departments.

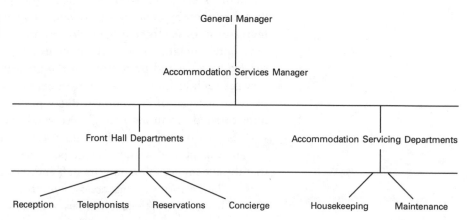

vacant, currently being serviced, or temporarily out of use so that maintenance or refurbishment can take place.

Front office staff also handle guest inquiries in conjunction with room service, housekeeping, and maintenance departments and may deal with incoming and outgoing guest telephone calls, requests for newspapers, and general hotel information. Front office staff also have the important task of handling complaints that may relate to any aspect of the guest's experience. This requires patience, tact, and the ability to respond quickly and effectively by dealing with the complaint or briefing management so that the appropriate action can be taken.

Front hall porters or concierge staff spend a considerable proportion of their time dealing with guest inquiries and providing personal service by carrying luggage, giving out room keys, and answering queries ranging from information about hotel services to advice on local excursions and shopping. In providing a comprehensive advice and booking service for hotel guests, it is necessary to be well informed about shops, theaters, restaurants, car rental services, and all local visitor attractions. Other duties usually involve organizing and ordering newspapers and taxis as well as assisting with other tasks such as sorting mail, servicing snacks, and transporting equipment around the hotel.

Accommodation staff care for the cleaning and maintenance of guest rooms and amenities. Housekeepers rely on a team of room attendants to clean bedrooms and bathrooms, replenish consumables such as toiletries and beverage items and service public areas. The supervision of this work involves ensuring that appropriate standards of cleanliness are achieved and that the fabric and fixtures of guest rooms and public areas are well maintained. To achieve this objective, supervisors must check to ensure that quality standards relating to cleanliness have been achieved, that all amenities are working properly and that the guest room inventory of consumable items has been replenished. Consistent standards can only be achieved if housekeeping, maintenance, and other accommodation services staff such as room service personnel and interior design specialists communicate effectively and coordinate their activities with front hall departments.

Guest Services and Competitive Advantage

The economy hotel guest expects a low tariff and limited services at a convenient location. This expectation actually provides hotel operators with the possibility of achieving competitive advantage over rival operators. Over supply in the full-service hotel categories is beginning to force hotel operators to consider defensive strategies for maintaining market share. In many cases, emphasis is being placed on enhancing the quality and range of guest services and thereby creating added value. However, this often necessitates tariff increases in order to cover additional costs incurred. In contrast, the economy hotel operator need only concentrate on three core elements of the service package and by improving the quality of accommodation, ancillary services such as food and beverage operations (where provided) and limited personal service, offer a competitively priced product that can be clearly differentiated for an increasingly crowded marketplace.

Service quality is broadly defined as the difference between what the guest initially expects and what he or she perceives has been received. This means that the accommodation unit, its staff and services will be judged according to how well it performs against assessment criteria derived from guest expectations. Therefore, strategic initiatives to enhance service quality and thereby achieve competitive advantage should incorporate a continuous review of the guest service provision and related support activities such as planned maintenance, refurbishment, and renewal programs. In some respects, technological innovation will also help to shape guest services of the future. Current technological applications identified by Kasavana (1987) include

Self check-in/checkout terminals
Guest information services
In-room movie systems
In-room beverage systems

These applications are likely to be extended in the future so that travelers can personalize the business information and entertainment they access through bedroom telecommunication systems.

In adding value to midpriced and luxury hotel operations, Knutson (1988) makes several recommendations that could provide the basis for a service quality program designed to ensure that guest services are delivered as effectively and competitively as possible. Such a program should focus on three aspects of guest services.

1. *Attention to detail* to enhance quality by systematically appraising and where necessary revising policies on cleaning, maintenance, and refurbishing. Thus, the service environment is cared for, and by encouraging staff to report and respond to minor variations in quality standards such as stained carpet or worn furniture, guests are more likely to make favorable comparisons with their home environment.

2. *Augmenting the product* by extending the service package content wherever possible. Many options can be considered. They include additions to the list of personal care items provided for guests (such as shampoo, shower caps, or an extra bath towel) or inclusive pricing for service package elements that are normally priced separately (such as a bedroom price tariff that includes breakfast). If it is important to ensure that travelers can readily perceive competitive advantage, hospitality managers will need to fully explore the packaging and pricing options available to them. Examples of innovative guest services implemented by ten luxury-priced hotels in different parts of the world are listed in Figure 3.

3. *Investment in service support* by regularly updating the technology, systems, and other resources used to deliver guest services. In some cases this may lead to a reduction in the element of personal service and an increase in the level of convenience to guests, for example a bedroom drinks dispenser augments or replaces room service.

Summary

All users of hospitality services expect to find that the quality and standard of the amenities supporting the provision of accommodation, beverages, and food are compatible with the price that is charged. By regularly appraising guest services and adopting low cost enhancement options such as an extension to the range of personal care items provided in hotel bedrooms, travelers are likely to perceive better value for money. As competition intensifies and hospitality design concepts become more sophisticated and expensive, guest services will assume greater importance in sustaining competitive advantage during the 1990s.

Fig. 3. Examples of innovative guest services from ten luxury-priced hotels around the world. *(Source: Adapted from a press release about "The Hotelier's Bible" from Innkeeping World, 1990, Seattle, Wash.)*

The Regent, Hong Kong: Dictaphone machines and typewriters may be used free of charge and are delivered to guest rooms on request.

Inn on the Park, London: Wives accompanying businessmen receive a letter from the hotel's public relations manager offering assistance with shopping and hairdressing.

The Ritz, Paris: Before guests arrive at their room escorted by an assistant manager, it is checked by an electrician, a plumber, a painter and varnisher, a housekeeper, and two assistant managers.

Hotel Vier Jahreszeiten, Hamburg: A thermometer is provided in every bathroom so that guests can check the precise temperature of their bath water.

Hotel Europe, Zurich: The lobby telephone booth is a 300 year old velvet-lined coach, which enables guests to relax in comfort during their telephone conversation.

Kowloon Hotel, Hong Kong: Multilingual video training courses on more than 200 modern management subjects are available on guest room televisions.

The Ritz-Carlton, New York City: Dimmer switches allow guests to adjust the brightness of their guest room lighting.

Four Seasons Biltmore, Santa Barbara: After children have been seated in the restaurant, they are immediately given a drink and a menu coloring book with washable crayons.

Mauna Lani Bay Hotel, Kohala, Hawaii: Guests celebrating their birthday during their stay are presented with an orchid and a birthday cake.

Imperial Hotel, Tokyo: Complimentary jogging wear—sweatshirt, shorts, warm-up clothes, socks and jogging shoes—are provided for fitness minded guests along with jogging maps.

References

Barrington, Melvin N., and Michael D. Olsen. 1987. Concept of service in the hospitality industry. *International Journal of Hospitality Management* 6(3):131–138.

Kasavana, Michael L. 1987. Hotel multiprocessor environments: guest and nonguest operated interfaces. *International Journal of Hospitality Management* 6(4):217–224.

Knutson, Bonnie J. 1988. Frequent travelers: making them happy and bringing them back. *Cornell Hotel Restaurant Administration Quarterly* May:83–87.

Senior, Martin, and Rod Morphew. 1990. Competitive strategies in the budget hotel sector: the potential of service quality. *International Journal of Contemporary Hospitality Management* 2(3):3–9.

Teare, Richard. 1990. An exploration of the consumer decision process for hospitality services. In *Managing and Marketing Services in the 1990s*, ed. Richard Teare with Luiz Moutinho and Neil Morgan, pp. 233–248. London: Cassell.

Wilesky, Lance, and Francis Buttle. 1988. A multivariate analysis of hotel benefit bundles and choice trade-offs. *International Journal of Hospitality Management* 7(1):29–41.

28

Amenities

Sue Baker

Many hotels spend a considerable amount of their annual expenditure budget on providing amenities, or guests' supplies. Amenities are normally personal-care products or services available in the hotel room to enhance the guest's comfort. Specific amenities may include

Bathroom

Soaps	Hair conditioner
Shampoo	Sewing kit
Toothpaste/toothbrush	Make-up tissues
Hand/body lotion	Washing line
Shower cap	Suntan lotion
Mouthwash	Scent/after shave
Bath/Shower gel	Hairdryer

Bedroom

Shoe shine kit	AM/FM radio
Shoehorn	Clothes hangers
Stationery	Direct company billing
In-room safe	Morning newspaper
Remote control	Selection of books and journals
Television/video recorder	

Food and Beverage Amenities

Minibar	Complimentary wine
Fruit basket	Water boiling facilities
Chocolates	Hot beverage supplies
Room service	

Lounge/Desk Area

Fax machine	Desk light
Personal computer	House directory
International direct dialing telephone	Mobile telephones
Desk pad	Stationery

Customers' Expectations

The introduction of amenities into guest rooms was initially a marketing strategy to encourage new and repeat business to the hotels. In many cases this strategy still works, but over the years the guests' expectations have changed. Many items that were originally amenities are now regarded as basic necessities (for example, soap, shampoo, stationery, and television) and therefore guests would be disappointed not to find them. For example, a British hotel provided an excellent room service facility for its guests but provided no tea- and coffee-making facilities in the guests' rooms. Numerous complaints caused the management to reassess its own perceived levels of services and thus tea and coffee facilities were introduced in the guests' rooms. The traditional bar of soap, the bottle of shampoo, the toweling robe, and the sewing kit are now an essential provision in the guest's room. Providing the welcome fruit basket, or welcome tea or good-night chocolate is common in many international as well as national and local hotels.

The Changing Environment

With sociological changes resulting in the desire for more leisure time and the increases in travel, guests' expectations in relation to amenities have continued to rise. Numerous other products and services have joined the list of extras the guest now expects to see in the hotel room. For example, in-room check-out, first-aid supplies, and umbrellas. Sheraton Corporation includes in all of their "Towers" brand rooms, bathrobes, designer toiletries, hair dryers, a luxurious complimentary continental breakfast in a private clublike lounge, daily complimentary hors d'oeuvres, a morning newspaper delivered to the door, and nightly turndown service.

Hotels services and facilities offered as well as guest expectations have changed over the years. Many large hotels now cater to the businessperson by offering separate executive floors. The executive floor has its own check-in/checkout desk, complimentary wine and beverages, restaurant services, and business center facilities, to name only a few. Also, some hotel rooms are prepared solely for a particular type of guest. For example, some hotels offer amenities and services solely for businesswomen.

Social changes have definitely had an impact on the amenities and services provided. An example is the general attitude against smoking that has become more prevalent in recent years. Hotels are now catering to the needs of nonsmokers by providing nonsmoking bedrooms or even whole nonsmoking floors: No smoking accessories such as ashtrays and matches are found in such areas.

Technology

In recent years technology has played an important part in the improvements and availability of amenities. For example, in-room computers, videotext, automated registration, and in-room checkout are becoming more common in hotels. The rental of computers, floppy discs and a printer to guest's rooms is a sign of today's modern technology. With such technology, business users can access their own files as well as keep in contact with their offices by using telephone modems. Also, automatic checkout through guestroom TV sets continues to grow as an option that is popular both with guests and management. Guests can review their folios at leisure in the privacy of their room and settle any disputed charges by telephone before checking out, either through the TV or at the front desk. This system is still being developed; in time it is hoped the guests will be able to enter a credit card number while still in the room, enabling them to leave without stopping at the front desk. Remote control televisions, clock radios and in-room safes are greatly appreciated by frequent guests. Many hotels provide 24-hour cable television and rent-free videos.

Cost Implications

Amenities are expensive to provide. Careful examination is needed to evaluate whether the cost incurred can be justified within the hotel's overall budget (thus affecting the hotel's operating profit). To keep up with competitors, new hotels, which are possibly working on a smaller and tighter budget, have to provide the expected basic amenities. These newer and smaller properties could find it difficult to absorb the increased costs with the rising expectations of guests. Despite the cost, most hotels still allow for the need of an amenities program. Different types of hotels can offer different amenities to their customers, which can have a bearing on the cost. To illustrate this point, Table 1 shows the amenities offered by two different types of hotels.

Many amenities provided by the hotel are normally free of charge and this forces hotels to raise their prices to cover the associated costs. Alternatively, many hotels actually charge the guest for use of particular services, an example being pay-television movie and rent-a-safe box.

Another approach introduced to control the use of amenities and thus save costs is providing the basic necessities in the guest room plus a place card inviting guests to call the front desk if they require any item on an extensive list of additional personal-care products. The advantage of this procedure is that the guests select whatever options make them feel most comfortable and the hotel is able to control the amenities being used.

Factors to Consider When Implementing an Amenities Program

Many factors must be considered when creating an amenities program. The ultimate influence must be how much money is available to spend. Other factors should include your competitors' current offerings and your hotel's current and future marketing strategy. The amenites are to a large extent dictated by the hotel's business market. Amenities available for the businesswoman would not necessarily be appropriate for a businessman or tourist. To determine the guests' amenity expectation level and their particular likes and dislikes, it is to the hotel's benefit to conduct market research to determine what the target guest is looking for. If the hotel's market is catering to the affluent businessperson, it would probably benefit the hotel to spend extra on amenities. Table 1, illustrating amenities typically available in deluxe and medium-class hotels, also indicates the service approach reflected by each type. For example, the medium-class hotel provides a fully stocked minibar and the guest serves himself. The nonprovision of a minibar in the deluxe hotel indicates the expectation of personal attention from room service, rather than self-service (unless this is more convenient in which case the guest can request the provision of a minibar).

Table 1. *Typical amenities*

600-Room deluxe class hotel, city center location, mainly business bookings	800-Room medium class hotel, suburban location, mainly group bookings

Entrance

Do Not Disturb card	Do Not Disturb card
	Breakfast menu
	Fire escape plan

Desk Top

Bible	Guest directory
Telephone directory	Guidebook
Fire escape plan	Tent card promotion
Typhoon safety regulations	Ashtray
IDD booklet	Match box
Guidebook	Folder with standard stationeries
Breakfast menu	
Sewing kit	
Ball pen	
Food and beverage information	

Desk-top Folder

Letter paper/envelopes	
Telex/Fax forms	
Thank you and postcards	
CNN movie guide	
Blotting paper	
Limosine service	
Health spa information	

Closet

Laundry bag and list	Laundry bag
Drycleaning bag and list	Shopping bag
Leather shoehorn	Wooden hangers
Leather clothes brush	
Shoe shine kit	
Shoe tree	
Hangers, male/female	

Minibar Service

Glasses and ice bucket	Ice bucket
Bottle opener	Opener
Water (mineral/distilled)	Glasses with coaster
Coasters	2 red wine glasses
Minibar on request	2 champagne glasses
	2 "304" glasses
	2 "306" glasses
	1 tumbler
	Napkins (2)
	Stirrers (2)
	Drink voucher
	Rattan basket with liquor

(continued)

Table 1. *Typical amenities (cont.)*

600-Room deluxe class hotel, city center location, mainly business bookings	800-Room medium class hotel, suburban location, mainly group bookings

Bedside Table

International direct dialing telephone	International direct dialing telephone
Control panel/switches	Control panel/switches
Radio channels	Radio channels
	Phone directory
	Bible
	Buddist book

Sitting Area

Television set	Television set
Remote conrol	Remote control
Magazines	Magazines/newspapers
Flowers	Luggage rack

Bathroom

Bath towels (2)	Bath towels (2)
Hand towels (2)	Hand towels (2)
Face towels (2)	Face towels (2)
Linen hand towels (2)	Tissue box and tissues
Bathrobes	Tumblers with coaster
Slippers	Soap dish with soap
Soap	Foam bath and shampoo
Gel	Rubbish bin
Glass jar and cotton buds	Sanitary bag
Bath salts	Shoe shine mitt
Bottle opener	Shaving socket
Tissue box and tissues	Plant
Vase (bud)	
Emery board	
Mild clothes detergent	
Sanitary bags	
Shower cap	
Hair dryer	
Tumblers	
Plastic rubbish bin	
Shaving socket	

Upon Request

Swimming goggles	Adaptors
Adaptors/transformers	Heaters
Heaters	Iron (with board)
Iron (with board)	Baby supplies/crib
Extension cord	
Baby supplies/crib	
Clothes rack	
Luggage rack	
Comb	
Disposable razor	
Shaving cream	

(continued)

Table 1. *Typical amenities (cont.)*

600-Room deluxe class hotel, city center location, mainly business bookings	800-Room medium class hotel, suburban location, mainly group bookings

Upon Request (cont.)

Table mirror
Curlers
Toothpaste/brush
Bandaids/plasters
Flask or freeze pad
Hot water bottle
Diapers
Bathroom scales
All types of stationery
Mousse, Aftershave

On Arrival

Fruit basket
Chinese tea

Food/Beverage Services

1 Qt. Scotch	All items on the F/B room service list
1 Qt. Gin	(24 hrs)
1 Qt. Vodka	
2 Soda	
3 Tonic	
1 Table Water (free)	
Assorted Mixed nuts	
1 Qt. Champagne	
1 tray of Homemade Chocolates	
Assorted French fruit bonbons	
1 Cheese Board (3 types)	
Celery and carrot sticks	
Crackers and breads	
Fruit basket (special)	
Deluxe fruit	
All other itms on the F/B room service list (24 hrs)	

Competitive Advantages

Providing amenities not available in competitor hotels could have positive results both for the hotel and the guest. Positive for the guest in that he or she would experience new amenities not available in other hotels. For example, all the rooms of a certain British hotel overlook a lake and, to allow guests to better enjoy the rural scene, all rooms are provided with binoculars.

The positive aspect for the hotel is that it could increase its business volume. Also, the amenities could influence the room rates quoted. Unique and better quality amenities provided could possibly command higher room rates, thus generating higher room sales and profit margins.

Managing Amenities

Managing amenities involves various people at different levels within the organization. Policy would dictate the initial range of amenities to be provided including the quality. Items such as brand names or the hotel's/company's own logo would normally be a top management decision. Individual hotels would develop local policies relating to individual items or specialties in their particular property. For example, an orchid left on the guest's pillow is common in Thailand. The decision of what amenities are found in guestrooms involves both financial and marketing input. How much can be spent and what marketing mix to target are two very important factors when considering an amenities program. The day-to-day administration of the amenities program requires the housekeeping manager to order, distribute, and control the amenities; the purchasing officer is responsible to order, store, and issue the amenities; and the Controller to report on how much has been spent.

Summary

The importance of an amenities program in any hotel, whether it be large or small, budget or deluxe, is that it should enhance the image and reputation of the hotel. A well-established and effective amenities program can provide guests with all the comforts of home, with the personal touch. Guests can enjoy the experience of staying at the hotel with all the necessary services and products available to facilitate and enhance that enjoyment. When establishing an amenities program the hotel must consider the characteristics of the hotel, the room rack rate it can command, the guests' needs and expectations in its marketing strategy and finally the costs necessary to implement an amenities program. The hotel's goal for any amenities program must be to improve the value, image, and reputation of the hotel, thus striving to increase room occupancy levels, average room rates, and operating profits.

29

Hotel Room Service

L. Taylor Damonte

Room service is a specialized form of foodservice that transforms hotel guest rooms into private dining rooms. The basic procedures in room service are the same as for any kind of table service. The guest places a food production order. Food is then delivered to the guest's table. Finally, the bill is presented to the guest after the food is served. But this is where the similarity ends.

Logistically there are several differences in guest room service versus dining room service. In room service, the order taker and the server are two different people. This division of labor necessitates a communications system, especially since the server usually does not have an easy opportunity for a second trip to the guest's table if some part of the order is inaccurately communicated. Finally, in dining room service, the food server or service assistant cleans and resets the table immediately after the guest leaves. In room service the server may or may not return within a short time. In many hotels the rule is for housekeeping department staff to place the equipment in the corridor outside the room. Although it may sit for some time just outside of the room, the dirty foodservice equipment is eventually retrieved either by the room service staff or the food and beverage steward.

Room service is also somewhat similar to home food delivery. For both of these types of service, food is delivered to remote settings for consumption. Consequently, time and food temperature become difficult service control factors. Also, both of these service systems utilize separate personnel to take the order and to serve it. However there are differences here as well. In guest room service, the flatware, silverware, all extra food items, and possibly even the table itself must be delivered, whereas in home delivery, customers are usually capable of providing some of these items themselves. Therefore, the preparation of the room service order requires a well-designed staging area. In addition, where home food deliverers usually use automobiles to transport the food to the customer's doorstep, hotel room service wait staff must transport all of the additional food and service equipment on foot and up, down, or across great expansive hotel complexes.

Segmentation of the hotel market has created a whole class of hotels with limited or no food and beverage service. Many hotels provide only breakfast for room service. Because of labor and equipment costs and the difficulty of forecasting sales, room service is typically the least profitable department in any hotel's food and beverage operation. Some hotels provide order forms for guests to complete before retiring. This gives the food and beverage department some advance notice as to production requirements for the next morning, which helps reduce labor cost. Other hotels with limited food service capability and no room service are now providing some form of buffet style breakfast in the hotel.

It is very probable that in the coming decade only the largest full-service facilities will provide any form of room service. We will therefore describe the organizational structure of a room service operation in a full-service hotel (Figure 1). Usually, at least in a property of one thousand rooms or more, the room service department operates with autonomy under the umbrella of the food and beverage department. The director is responsible for menu design as well as the appropriation of service equipment. He or she ultimately bears the responsibility for maximizing revenue and controlling expenses within the department. Operationally, the director is responsible for appropriation and control of all production and service equipment as well as human resources management and quality control within the department.

Human resources management may be the biggest factor affecting quality control and profitability. In a large hotel the room service department may operate a separate food preparation line. The operation may even run 24 hours per day. This requires staffing cooks, service personnel, and supervisors for three shifts. Room service technology is very labor intensive.

Although systems vary across hotels, most allow for one person to do nothing but take room service orders (Schmidt 1987). Another person is responsible for setting up the room-service cart with all utensils and service equipment. The room service waiter, or possibly in larger operations a set-up person, adds butter, condiments, salads, and all other required food items based on the food order. Lastly the hot entrée is added. For control purposes a room service captain expedites this final step.

Fig. 1. Organizational structure of a room service operation.

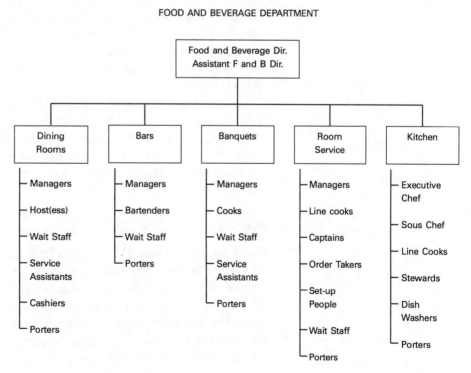

FOOD AND BEVERAGE DEPARTMENT

Pre-setting of carts adds speed to the service process and is possible whenever accurate demand forecasting can be done. For example, breakfast orders can be accurately forecast by allowing guests to order room service breakfast at night before retiring. In addition, many frequent-guests plans offer free continental breakfast as a perk. These orders can be forecast from front office records.

Room service forecasting is generally based on house count, the number of rooms in the hotel. For example, in some hotels room service for breakfast may be as high as 25 percent of the guest count. However, the market for room service can vary depending on the type of people in the hotel, check-in and checkout times, and the activities that the guests are engaged in. For example, when a hotel is filled with a group consisting of mostly women, even during dinner, room service use may be as high as 15 to 20 percent of the guest count. Other groups may have large numbers of late check-ins after the dining room closes. If room service operates after dining room hours, the service may be used. In addition, if businesspeople are required to do large amounts of work/entertaining in their rooms, room service demand can increase.

In-house service charges [note: some hotels deliver off premises] can be one to three dollars per cover. Yet, even with the extra revenue, it can be difficult to break even in the room service operation. The labor cost ratio can be higher than in banquets or the dining rooms. Also, room service requires extensive equipment. For example, a hotel that generates $4,000 to $5,000 in room service revenue per day may require over 300 portable room-service carts and coffee pots.

Loss of the smaller pieces of equipment through theft such as silverware, plates, and pitchers can be high. In an effort to reduce losses, some hotels send servers back to the room to pick up the equipment rather than waiting until housekeeping cleans the room the following day. This also helps in pest control. Nonetheless, it requires additional labor and training.

Delivery time varies with demand. For a complete meal during a peak period a guest may wait as long as 45 minutes. However, the market has come to expect faster service. Most hotels attempt to keep delivery times to less than 35 minutes. This can be more difficult than one might expect. Unlike most home delivery operations, menus are usually not limited to a few items. Having to transport more elaborate service equipment also strains delivery time.

Once room service was an expected part of the product/service mix at any midscale hotel. Now, it is becoming more the purview of full-service and luxury properties. Still, in those properties large enough to have a completely separate room service division, the food and the service can be as elaborate and as elegant as in the finest of dining facilities.

Summary

Room service is a specialized form of foodservice that is more labor and equipment intensive than dining room service. There are logistical differences in the preparation, transportation, and retrieval of the food and the foodservice equipment. Loss of equipment through theft can also be more problematic in room service operations than in dining room facilities. Segmentation of the hotel market has created limited and breakfast-only room service offerings. Many hotels provide only breakfast for room service. Today full scale room-service is fast becoming the purview of only the first class and luxury properties.

Reference

Schmidt, Arno, 1987. *Food and Beverage Management in Hotels.* New York: Van Nostrand Reinhold.

30

Hotel Food and Beverage

Nor K. Ishak

Food and beverage, as a component of the hospitality industry, refers to the sale of food and beverages in hotels, clubs, independent restaurant operations, catering services, institutional foodservices, and food and beverage operations on modes of transportation such as trains, airlines, and ships. Often, food and beverage operations have been classified either as profit-oriented or cost provision. The profit-oriented operations, such as independently operated restaurants and the restaurants in hotels, are those that provide food and beverage for financial gain. Those that operate as cost provisions, such as some institutional foodservices (military, nursing homes, schools and colleges, and penitentiaries), work within budgetary constraints, and the food and beverage is offered as a necessary adjunct to providing the main objective of public or social services. For the purpose of this article, food and beverage as a concept refers specifically to the operations and sale of food and beverage in hotels.

Importance of the Hotel's Food and Beverage Operations

The food and beverage (F/B) facilities in hotels started as a means of providing food and beverage services for the convenience of registered guests. However, this hotel unit is now considered as a major profit center. The hotel's division that oversees the planning and the effective and efficient operation of the F/B responsibility is often called the food and beverage department. In some instances, the hotel may opt to lease or contract out its F/B operation to other foodservice companies.

The F/B department provides food and beverages to registered guests, local customers, and, often, the hotel's employees as well. Food and beverages are sold in sales outlets such as restaurants, coffee- or snackshops, bars or cocktail lounges, and banquet and meeting rooms, as well as through off-premise catering including picnic meals. Food and beverages can also be served in guests' rooms as part of the room service offered. Often, the price of food and beverages served by room service will be higher than if served in its restaurants. The F/B outlets commonly differ on pricing and menu structures, type of services, table arrangement, atmosphere, restaurant decor, and operating hours. These differences are based on the type of customers expected, the time available for the meal, the turnover of customers expected, the type of menu presented, and the price range of the meals served.

As a profit center, the F/B department can maximize returns through controlling costs and optimizing its sales potentials. An important management function is to coordinate the demands for food and beverage with the availability of supplies such as raw materials for cooking, the availability of preparation and service employees, and the seats available. The hotel may also operate an employee dining area or staff cafeteria to provide food to its employees on a cost provision basis.

Variations of Food and Beverage Operation

Food and beverage operations vary to meet the requirements of the different types of customers and to provide variety in service. These differences can be classified into two categories: service type and menu. Basically, there are four different types of services offered:

1. Table service: the service to customers is provided with a laid cover at a table or a bar counter. Some variations of this type are the American service where customers are presented with preplated foods, and the French service where foods are presented to customers and the customers serve themselves.
2. Self-service: the customers queue and choose their own foods from the selection of foods provided. Cafeteria service and buffet are two examples of the self-service type.
3. Specialized service: customers are served in areas not primarily designated for service. Hotels offer room service for the convenience of their in-house guests and food is often also served in lounge areas.
4. Other services: these include take-away services, vending machines, and food courts. Customers are provided with the food and they consume it elsewhere.

The different outlets in the hotel, such as the coffee house, grill room, cocktail lounge, and the banquet room, may use one service type or they may combine two or more types. For example, the coffee house may offer table service as well as a buffet setting, and customers choose the service they desire.

Customers are also usually provided with choices of the food and beverage items they wish to order. The range of choices depends on the type of menu offered. There are two basic menu types, table d'hote and à la carte. The table d'hote menu is a set menu that offers limited choices within each course. The price is also fixed. Usually, the dishes are already prepared at a set time. The first course is often called the appetizer, followed by an entrée or main dish and the last course is the dessert and beverage. The à la carte menu list offers a wider selection of dishes. The dishes are only prepared on request by customers, therefore there will be a waiting time between placing the order and serving it. Each dish is priced separately and the dishes offered are often changed according to availability or season. A version of the à la carte menu is the carte du jour (menu of the day), sometimes referred to as the "specialty of the house," which is changed every day.

Organization of the Food and Beverage Department

The F/B department, as a profit center, is usually staffed by a department manager, with an executive chef in charge of the kitchen activities and a restaurant manager in each of the sales outlets. As a division of a hotel, the

F/B department needs to coordinate its activities with the other divisions of the hotel. Figure 1 gives an example of a hotel organization chart indicating the various other divisions that the F/B department liaises with and the internal structure of the F/B department.

The F/B department coordinates its functions closely with the personnel division because the personnel division oversees, among other things, the recruiting, selecting, and hiring of employees needed. The control or accounting division works with the F/B department in terms of cashiering, purchasing, and preparing the budgets, as well as authorizing payments to suppliers. Since food and beverage items need to be promoted, the F/B department coordinates its activities with the sales and marketing division especially in the promotion and planning of its banquet offerings. The front-of-house division, of which the front office and housekeeping are a part, update the F/B department with information on the in-house occupants, including expected conference and tour group arrivals. The housekeeping department supports the F/B department with the cleaning of public areas and the cleaning of linens and employee uniforms. This department must also work closely with the F/B department in providing room service.

Organization of Food and Beverage Service

The F/B manager, like the other department heads, reports directly to the hotel's assistant general manager or the general manager. His or her responsibilities include ensuring the attainment of targeted profit, developing menus and determining prices for the sales outlets, ensuring quality food and service, and determining training needs. Next in hierarchical rank are the restaurant managers. These managers have the overall responsibility for the successful administration of their particular outlets. Among their responsibilities are the setting of service standards, on-the-job training, and scheduling of employees. The headwaiter or the maitre d'hotel is responsible for seeing that the preparation for service is done according to requirements, and he or she is the team leader in the service delivery process who coordinates and assigns waiters their tables. The waiters' major role is to serve the customers, but their duties also include the preparation before service (termed mise-en-place) including setting tables and side tables. A team of waiters is usually

Fig. 1. Organization chart of a hotel.
(Source: Dennis R. Lillicrap and John A. Cousins, 1990, Food and Beverage Service, p. 12. Kent, U.K.: Hodder and Stoughton.)

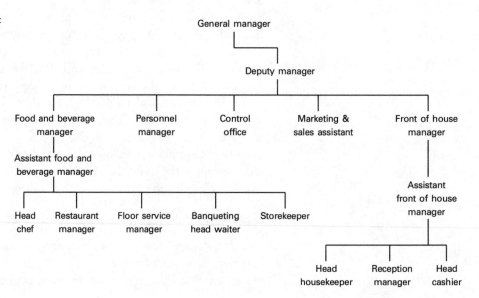

assigned to a number of tables and the head of the team is the station head-waiter. A waiter must be knowledgeable of the types of food and beverage offered and must have interpersonal skills. The floor waiters are responsible for serving food and beverage in guests' rooms. The cocktail bar waiter is responsible for the service of alcoholic beverages, and therefore must be knowledgeable on all the drink mixtures and wines available. The busboys mainly clear tables and may occasionally assist the waiters by serving water.

Food and beverage operations can be viewed as a service sequence, starting when the customers enter the outlet; followed by taking the customers' orders, serving their food, and presenting them with their bills; and ending with their exit from the outlet. There are set procedures established for each of the service sequences. For example, on entering, the customers should be greeted by the headwaiter, who checks the reservation list and leads them to their table. The station headwaiter unfolds each customer's napkin and places it on his/her lap, and gives the menu. The customers may also be presented with a wine list. Time is allowed for customers to make their selection and the station headwaiter can suggest and advise on the menu selection. He/she takes the order and changes or adjusts the cover as necessary. The meal is served course by course together with the accompaniments. If the outlet has a different menu for dessert, after the entrée the customers are presented with the dessert menu. The dessert order is taken and the waiter may change ashtrays and clear the unnecessary cutleries and plates. Dessert and beverage are then served. When the customers are ready to leave, or upon their request, the bill is presented. Upon payment, the station headwaiter sees guests out of the outlet. The buspersons clear the tables.

Food and Beverage Preparation

Personnel

The executive chef or head chef is in charge of the food and beverage preparation section in the kitchen. He or she reports either to the food and beverage manager or directly to the hotel's assistant manager. The head chef has the overall responsibility for the preparation of food, and duties include planning menus, having meetings with other department heads, and coordinating the kitchen activities. The chef assistant helps in the administrative functions such as deriving food costs and recipe development. Reporting directly to the executive chef is the sous-chef whose major responsibilities are the supervision of the cooks and training of new cooks. Figure 2 illustrates the organization of the kitchen staff.

Reporting to the sous-chef are the various chefs: sauce chef, restaurant chef, vegetable chef, pastry chef, garde-manager, relief chef, and duty chef. Reporting to the various chefs are their assistants. The sauce chef prepares fish, stews, hors d'oeuvre, hot entrées, and sauces. The vegetable cook prepares soups, vegetables, and pasta, and foods made of flour, eggs, and cheese. The pastry chef is in charge of making all basic desserts and pastries. The garde-manger cuts raw meat and prepares cold dishes and cold hors d'oeuvre, and the roast chef prepares all roasted and grilled items. The restaurant chef prepares à la carte dishes according to the customer's order. The relief chef and duty chef assume the work of a chef in the absence of any chef. In smaller hotels, the chefs are often called cooks.

Task Flow

The task flow for F/B preparation can be categorized according to when the tasks are performed: (1) tasks that are performed before the food and beverage items arrive at the kitchen, (2) tasks that are performed in the kitchen, and

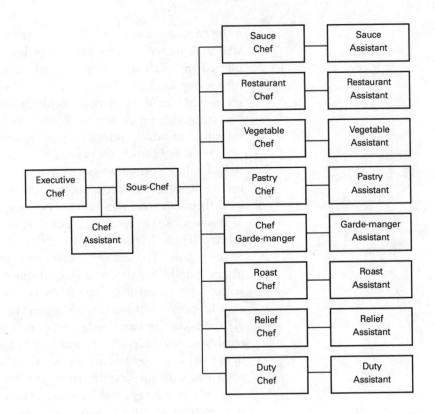

Fig. 2. Organization chart of a kitchen staff.
(Source: Eugen Pauli, 1989, Classical Cooking the Modern Way, p. 23. New York: Van Nostrand Reinhold.)

(3) tasks that are performed when the food and beverage items are sent out from the kitchen.

Tasks that are performed before the food and beverage items arrive at the kitchen include functions such as purchasing, receiving, storing, and issuing of food and beverage items. The task flow begins with the purchasing function. This function includes activities such as the preparation of purchase specifications. Every F/B item needed, as well as supplies for service such as napkins and condiments, must be described accordingly, for example, by their brand names, grade, chemical content, quality, and quantity. These specifications are recorded on the purchase order form sent to the respective suppliers. The process of selecting reliable suppliers is also important because F/B operations often have unpredictable demand and suppliers may be called on to deliver goods on short notice.

The determination of cost of food and beverages includes the purchase prices, transportation charges, and handling and administrative costs incurred such as the carrying, ordering, and processing costs. The receiving function ensures that the items received from the suppliers are as called for on the purchase specifications. Items received should be checked, if necessary, at random, and those that do not meet the specification standards should be returned for refund or replacement. The accepted items are sent either directly to the kitchen or to the dry storage or refrigeration area. The purchase invoice together with the receiving form should be sent to the accounting office where payments to the suppliers are initiated and certain inventory records maintained. Items delivered to the storeroom are recorded on the inventory and placed in their assigned storage area. Proper control of the storage room is required to prevent pilfering and deterioration of items. A minimum quantity of each item should be at hand so that the item is available when required. Proper issuing procedures for items leaving the store should be strictly enforced. The storage area should be restricted with entry permitted to a limited number of employees. The requisition forms used for issuing items contain information on the quantity, cost per unit, and the total cost. This information can be used for calculating the daily food costs for each menu item.

Food and beverage items used in the kitchen can be those that are issued from storage, those received directly from the receiving area, and those from the kitchen refrigerator (usually the leftovers from the previous day's preparation). Items needed each day should be well estimated to keep leftovers at minimum. The basis for estimating the daily raw food requirements is the sales budget, from which the menu is planned. Menu planning is the process of determining the nutritive balance, seasonal availability, and the color and taste of the combination of the items. The menu items offered should meet the needs and requirements of the potential or targeted customers.

Standard recipes are required for each menu item to ensure that the correct order quantity is made at varying quantity requirement levels. The quality of food and beverage items sold is maintained through a control procedure known as the scheme-of-work sheet. This sheet specifies the time, sequence of activities, and the method of cooking that should be used. When the items have been cooked and prepared, they should be portioned out according to the established amount, weight, and portion size. The portioned out food is arranged and garnished before being sent to the service area.

Food and Beverage Quality

Output quality depends on the quality of food and beverage items served as well as the quality of service provided by the employees in direct contact with the customers. The process of controlling the tangible product is continuous, extending from the purchasing to the delivery functions. The control is aimed at minimizing cost of sales or food and beverage cost. Standards and specifications have been well established for the tangible product. In an attempt to control quality of service, service (the intangible component) can be considered as having two elements: technical and behavioral. The technical elements include the flow, sequence, and time specifications. Manuals and operating procedures are available to delineate these procedures. For the behavioral elements, such as attitude requirements, attentiveness, and tact of service employees, standards are difficult to set and to regulate. These become increasingly difficult as the amount of contact time between the employees and the customers increases, as in a table service. The process of recruiting, selecting, and training of service employees is important to ensure service quality.

The tangible and intangible cues that provide an indication of product price and quality need to be consistent and synchronized. The tangible cues are provided by the combination of color schemes used, the quality of linens, tableware, uniforms, and menu cards, table arrangement, parking facilities, and the exterior design of the building. The intangible cues are indicated through the type of service provided, the menu items offered, and the pricing structure.

Food and Beverage Sales Maximization

The two ways to optimize profits are to minimize cost and to maximize sales. Sales can be increased through the proper determination of average selling price; the management of seating capacity, seat turnover, and operating periods; an increase in sales volume through price manipulation; and a change in sales mix.

To determine the average selling price per menu item, calculate the total sales required and divide it by the seating capacity, seat turnover, and the number of days the restaurant is opened. In calculating the sales required, all costs (including income tax and profits) need to be estimated. The average price derived from the calculation should be an estimated indicator of the range of menu prices to be offered. The menu should consist of a balance between high- and low-cost items in relation to their prices. Menu items can be changed through changing customers' expectations or by offering substitutes. Price changes should be carried out gradually, changing one item at a time and monitoring the customers' reactions at the same time.

Customers' expectations can be altered by changing table setting and arrangement, changing food garnishes, adding food accompaniments, or changing the design of waiters' uniforms. The number of seats available can also be a source of increasing sales if that number can be increased. However, the impact on the restaurant's atmosphere of adding more seats should be considered. If seating capacity is already at maximum, then sales increases could be accomplished by adding sales outlets such as carry-out and off-premise catering services. Sales can also be increased by expanding operating hours. All these options can be considered if the costs required for the additional outlets and the increase in operating hours are less than the potential sales to be derived. However, the efforts to increase sales must be supported by an additional increase in sales promotion budgets and sales effort. Sales increase should be made through increased customer counts rather than increased selling price.

An important factor to consider in maximizing profits through food and beverage is the need to synchronize the demand for food and beverage with the supply in terms of the availability of seats, employee requirements, and the raw materials. Demand can be controlled to a certain extent through such techniques as seat reservation requirements, providing comfortable waiting areas, and offering promotional discounts during slow periods. Capacity management is an important function of a food and beverage operation that, by nature, will not have the opportunity to function at full capacity all the time.

An efficiently organized F/B operation should fully utilize its facilities with minimum cost expenditure. Menu offerings should be reviewed every few months to accommodate the changing trends in customers' taste, and the facilities should be flexible enough to support the necessary menu change. A food and beverage operation should, therefore, be able to provide quality, palatable food at reasonable prices and at the same time provide profitable return on investments.

Summary

The food and beverage operations in hotels can have a significant impact on the overall profitability of the hotels. This article focuses on the food and beverage department's various job functions, task flow, and coordination of work required within and with other departments of the hotel. To ensure profitability, quality control of food and beverage service is important. This involves the proper management and synchronization of the intangible service component such as the service employees' attitude and service flow and timing; and the tangible cues, for example, the quality of tablecloth and menu cards. This article briefly discusses the factors that should be considered in maximizing food and beverage sales.

Bibliography

Brymer, Robert A. 1977. *Introduction to Hotel and Restaurant Management: A Book of Readings.* Dubuque, Iowa: Kendall/Hunt Publishing.

Coltman, Michael M. 1980. *Cost Control for the Hospitality Industry.* New York: Van Nostrand Reinhold.

Dukas, Peter. 1976. *Planning Profits in the Food and Lodging Industry.* Boston: Cahners Publishing.

Fuller, John. 1983. *Modern Restaurant Service: A Manual for Students and Practitioners.* London: Hutchinson and Co. (Publishers) Ltd.

Keister, Douglas C. 1973. *How to Increase Profits with Portion Control.* Chicago: National Restaurant Association Publications.

Kotas, Richard. 1980. *An Approach to Food Costing.* London: Hutchinson and Co. (Publishers) Ltd.

Lian, Mary. 1967. *Mary Lian's Manual for Hotel/Catering Service Personnel.* Singapore: Donald Moore Press Ltd.

Lillicrap, Dennis R., and John A. Cousins. 1990. *Food and Beverage Service.* Kent, U.K.: Hodder and Stoughton.

Pauli, Eugen. 1989. *Classical Cooking the Modern Way.* New York: Van Nostrand Reinhold.

Sutton, Donald F. 1979. *Financial Management in Hotel and Catering Operations.* London: William Heinemann Ltd.

31

Security for the Hospitality Industry

Robert J. Martin

The concept of "security" in hospitality operations is usually addressed in tandem with that of "safety" even though the general thrust of each term is somewhat different. The trend today is to use the term *safety* when discussing matters such as disasters, fire prevention, and protection; devices; and conditions that provide for freedom from injury and damage to property. Safeness is related to worker attitude about working cautiously, is measured through accident rates, and is controlled by both management and workers intent on operating a safe premise.

Security is used primarily to describe the need for freedom from fear, anxiety, and doubt involving ourselves, as well as to the protection and defense against the loss or theft of guest, employee, and company property. Both safety and security today, however, are recognized as only parts of a greater whole. There are new terms in the lexicon such as the protection and safeguarding of assets, threat analysis, security surveys, and risk management.

As a result of property owners and managers being accountable for the safety and protection of guests and employees, their property, and the assets of the company, the status of security has been elevated to the executive level in most hospitality operations.

Nature of the Security Function

Few facilities are more vulnerable to security hazards than hotels of any type. The nature of the business, which involves the presence of large numbers of people, most of whom are unknown to the innkeeper, pose an ever present threat to the security of the property and other guests. The risk of fire and natural disaster, riot, theft, embezzlement, civil disturbance, or bomb threats have increased in recent years, all of which can cause serious injury or loss of life, and loss or damage to property belonging to the guests, employees and/or the facility itself.

One might ask, is the security professional involved more with security, safety, loss prevention, or risk management? Today's answer is "all of the above." More succinctly, security has grown from the "night watchman-catch the burglar" image to a place where business is attempting to prevent or reduce losses through a systems approach in applying controls.

Additionally, heavy demands are being placed on public law enforcement agencies because of the continuous rise in drug traffic and a resultant increase in criminal activity. This demand has caused a diversion of attention and finite resources of public agencies away from their traditional efforts in the protection of private property, leaving the responsibility more and more to the innkeeper, and placing private security organizations in the position of playing an increasingly active role in many areas of crime and loss prevention.

Historically, the first security in America was private security. Then came the formation of public law enforcement organizations where municipal and county law enforcement bodies were the mainstay of public protection. During the past thirty years, the pendulum has reversed. Many organizations have assumed greater responsibility for their own protection, and private security agencies have grown to answer the public clamor for more protection.

The security function in the hospitality industry today is best described as that major preventive and proactive activity used to protect the assets of the organization. Assets, per se, are now recognized to include the guests, employees (and the property of both), supplies, equipment, and the facility itself. Add to this the cash-intensive nature of the hospitality and service industry and the challenge intensifies.

Security in a conceptual sense seems to imply a stable, predictable, and peaceful environment in which the individual or group might pursue its ends without harm or disruption and without fear of disturbance or injury. In the organizational sense those involved in security today must foresee (even predict) and assess threats, then make recommendations to operational management regarding appropriate action to safeguard both life and property. In addition, security department personnel must search out and alert operational management of the need to "prevent" unreasonable or imprudent activity that will increase the hotel's liability for incautious action and negligent behavior.

Surprisingly, because of the scope of the problem and the cost of adding (security) employees who are not directly associated with producing or servicing the product being sold, security organizations must enlist the support of all employees to become the eyes and ears of the security effort; hence the understanding that security as well as safety should be among the top priorities of all employees.

What Security Is Not
Security is not what was once seen to be—the plain-clothed "house detective" whose primary function was to keep the peace within the hotel and, on occasion, evict the noisy guest or those who did not have the means to pay a bill.

Even though private security officers may be uniformed, badged, and sometimes armed, persons involved in private security are not members of a legally constituted law enforcement body. Such legally constituted agencies are primarily involved in the detection of criminal activity, the apprehension of suspects, and the presentation of evidence designed to convict a guilty offender. Private security deals more with foreseeing and preventing crime, illegal activity, and negligent behavior in operations. The private security officer is also first and foremost an employee of the hotel staff who should put the welfare of people, both guests and employees, foremost in his or her thinking. The guest is the source of all income to the property and should be considered the most important person to ownership, management, and employees.

There are exceptional cases where law enforcement officers are contracted to perform private security operations when off duty. Should criminal laws be broken in the presence of a police officer, the off-duty contract officer immediately reverts to his or her primary status as a law enforcement official.

Another exception occurs when the security function is contracted out to a private security organization. Such security personnel are not hotel employees but the employees of the private security firm. Their allegiance to the hotel and its guests are once removed.

Persons involved in private security organizations possess no police powers; only the power of an ordinary citizen to perform a citizen's arrest and only if a crime is witnessed. It is not a prime objective of private hotel security to detect crime, apprehend suspects, or serve as accusers in regular courts of law in the prosecution of a suspect. If or when it is necessary for private security to detain a person for handing over to a legal law enforcement officer, failing to issue a Miranda Warning has no meaning and is not available to the suspect as a defense against self-incrimination.

The function of hospitality security organizations are strictly preventive in nature, foreseeing, predicting, and removing hazards and other causes of crime, injury, and unsafe practices.

Historical Perspective   Throughout history it is possible to trace the emerging concepts of security as a response to and a reflection of a changing society, mirroring not only its social structure but also its economic conditions, concept of law, perception of crime, and its morality. Nowhere is this more evident or more relevant in the development of modern security than in the passing of English common law into America as a basis for American criminal jurisprudence.

Law—A Framework for Security Operations

Laws provide part of the framework upon which businesses must regulate their operations. Although a number of laws apply to all businesses and individuals, many laws apply only to hotels, motels, restaurants, and other hospitality operations. Surprisingly, only five federal laws (or Codes) apply to hospitality operations. They are

> U.S. criminal laws (Title Thirteen U.S. Code)
> federal food and drug laws (FDA)
> occupational safety and health laws (OSHA)
> equal employment opportunity laws (EEOC)
> immigration laws (IRCA)

Other laws regulating the hospitality industry are found in state statutes, and county and local ordinances. Each state is somewhat different from the others but each has used common law precepts that have grown from historical law. Two of the most common are as follows:

1. The ultimate responsibility for assuring the legal and protective "security" attributes of a property rests with the owner of the property.
2. Matters regarding responsibility for "safety" of the guest and employees rest with the property management.

Where liability for negligence is an issue, it is case law (past precedents) that becomes significant. These actions are called civil actions and in such cases a jury decides the liability of an owner or operator for the purported negligent acts of the company and/or its employees.

The great majority of laws that security departments strive to uphold in their proactive endeavors are based on case law arising out of the innkeeper's responsibility to act prudently and wisely with due regard for reasonable care in day-to-day operations.

The innkeeper's responsibility to prevent the hotel and its employees from performing their duties in a negligent manner, and the need to foresee potential problems that could cause someone to become injured or killed is one of the reasons for the establishment of hotel security and protection departments. The balance of this concern is driven by the need to protect the assets of the corporation as described above. Whether federal, state, or local laws, or litigation brought about by claims of negligence, the security or protection departments of hospitality organizations are the watchdogs charged with the responsibilities that act to prevent violations from occurring. To this end the security function in hotels has grown from the "house detective" era of yesterday to a requirement for staffing at major department levels. Today we see even a further move into the future with consideration of tasks involving threat assessments, risk management, protection of assets, and substance abuse control. Security surveys now play a major role in helping organizations foresee problems before they happen, even to the point of predicting the probability of something happening.

The Elements of Security

Security authors have recently coined the acronym WAECUP as a multiloss orientation quite different from the traditional crime orientation of security. Loss control includes the prevention of waste, accident, error, crime, and unethical practice.

The tools available to those charged with managing the security function in the reduction or elimination of WAECUP may be simply stated as those elements that may be applied to the reduction of loss. They are people, hardware, and software. People, (the most expensive) are those who staff the security department. Hardware is the equipment used in communication, surveillance, and access control. Software (the least expensive and unrelated to computers) is the written policies and procedures for activity, direction, and control.

Policies and Procedures—The Software

Of major importance are the policies and procedures by which the security organization functions. The security department takes its cue from the executive and general policies established for the corporation or the hotel itself. Such policies are written and promulgated to all having a need to know within the hotel. Security departments then supplement basic policies and procedures with their own documentation of how the department will be administered and operated. Security or protection policies and procedures are usually augmented by simple restatements of those laws by which the hotel must abide and the house rules established by top management. Publications appropriate to a security department library would be

A good text on hotel law

Copies of the five federal laws to which all businesses are accountable

Copies of the state statutes regarding the operation of hotel establishments within the state

A security operations manual containing standard operating procedures (SOP) created for the uniqueness of the given property

A complete set of job descriptions for all members of the security department

In addition to the usual correspondence files, the department should maintain records of all investigations conducted of accidents and incidents occurring on the property and about its employees. The investigative report is one of the most important forms of documentation used by anyone in the security department. This type of report may later be used in the settlement of claims against the hotel, and for this reason must be timely, accurate, and complete. All accidents and unusual happenings that may later become the subject of litigation must be investigated thoroughly by a person qualified to conduct such an investigation.

When routine inspections are performed, there is usually a form to document the event and the outcome of the inspection. Such inspections are in the nature of threat assessments and security surveys, which can form the basis of risk management decisions. They should be routine in nature and are made to develop a history of events, status, and the outcomes of certain happenings.

Finally, there should be an Incident Journal that contains a chronological record of incidents and happenings appropriate to security concerns on the property. Most security departments utilize "logs" to keep a chronological account of happenings, assignments, location of certain specified personnel, and what they might be doing. Such a log is usually maintained by a watch captain or someone responsible for the operation of a particular work shift.

The essence of good security work is documentation of the current event to such a degree that no information is left for doubt. In most cases, documentation of events also serves to justify the costs and actual existence of security operations.

Security Equipment and Access Control—The Hardware

The most significant piece of control access equipment ever to be applied to the hotel industry is the keyless locking system used to gain entry to hotel guest rooms. A plastic card or device that might either be magnetized or have holes randomly punched into it that can be programmed to open a given door for a controlled period of time has literally allowed hotels to "throw away the key." Such devices have made the hard key obsolete and have revolutionized the methods whereby authorized persons may gain entrance to a specific space. It is estimated that more than seventy percent of guest room thefts have been denied to hotel thiefs at properties using such equipment.

Another piece of equipment that has improved the effectiveness of security operations and simultaneously reduced manpower costs is the closed circuit (CC) TV camera. One person can now figuratively do the work of ten by having a video monitoring station with a bank of TV monitors, each capable of accessing several cameras. One security person can actually grant access by remotely opening a door while monitoring the entrance being viewed on a TV screen.

Add to those the two-way radios or cellular phones that put the roving patrol in touch with a central station monitoring system instantaneously and constantly if necessary.

There are also microsensors that detect the heat of a human body and air movement. Such devices can monitor access to and inside of controlled warehouse storage and other sensitive spaces.

Even the above-mentioned equipment is sometimes dwarfed by the alarm, control, and sensing devices used to detect fire.

Expenditure for such devices although capitally intensive has resulted in saving the lives and property of numerous persons to the extent that cost benefit analysis can quickly prove the value of such investments.

Security Officers, Investigators, and Directors—The People

People provide the intelligence and the link that makes security happen. Although safety and security are the responsibility of all employees, it is through the efforts and professionalism of those specifically assigned to the security function that keep the awareness of the function alive and proactive within the industry.

Seen from the perspective of the late 1970s, security has become a major management function in hotel operations. There are now vice-presidents of loss prevention reporting directly to general managers of hotels and in some cases they are themselves members of corporate executive organizations. The perceived need for an integrated security function in the management of hotels can be anticipated as the norm for the future.

Risk Management and the Security Survey

Risk management includes more than security and safety. These two functions are, however, considered to be at the hub of most threat assessments and risk management programs. The objective of risk management is to manage risk effectively at the least possible cost. This cannot be done without reducing the total number of events that lead to losses. Before a risk can be reduced or eliminated it must be identified. One proven way of accomplishing this task is to conduct a "security survey," a critical, on-site examination and analysis of a facility to ascertain the present security status, identify deficiencies or excesses, determine the protection needed, and form the basis of recommendations to improve the overall security of a specific facility. Most times security surveys are arranged and/or conducted by security directors. After results of surveys are reported to top management, the responsibility for decision and action then rests at that executive level.

The latest available reports estimate that the cost of crime to American business is in excess of $40 billion per year and rising. The worst part of the problem is that most corporate managers do not even know if they have a problem. To counter this possibility, many organizations are now conducting security surveys, which also include a look into the administrative and financial areas of their facilities.

Assets Protection

The Protection Matrix—A System

After conducting the security survey of a specific property the next step would be to develop a set of alternatives and recommendations on how to best deal with the various risks that have been cataloged. A process by which this can be done is to develop a protection matrix (Figure 1; R. Oberholtzer, 1990, pers. comm.). The matrix suggests a process whereby assets (guests, employees, physical assets, and cash), are matched against the various threats that can impact these assets. The threats include crime, fire, natural disaster, and accidents. Included within a consideration of accidents would be the resultant possibility of injuries and illness. Twelve blocks are created by the matrix, each of which describe a concern that the security professional must address in a management way. First, the degree of risk associated within each block for a given operation must be analyzed, then alternatives must be established that can countermeasure a given risk at a certain price. Recommendations are then made to those in charge of operations regarding available alternatives. The degree of risk the company wishes to take in each case is established and is used to determine the justification to either expend funds in a given area, insure against the risk, or assume a self-insured posture.

For example: Assume that a security survey has been conducted in the area where unprepared meats and vegetables are stored in a kitchen area. In the matrix, the physical asset of food is being considered in relation to the threats that can most likely occur. The high threats might be crime (theft) and natural disaster (loss of refrigeration due to loss of power, the property being located in a high-risk area for hurricanes). A lower probable threat in this case might be fire and/or accident although both may be present to a degree. In each case an evaluation of the probabilities of such occurrences would be made. Records might also be reviewed to determine whether there is a history of past losses. Countermeasures at each level of threat would be established and recommendations made to operations management as to the

Fig. 1. The protection matrix.

ASSETS

	Guests	Employees	Physical Assets
Crime			
Fire			
Accidents Illness/Injury			
Natural Disaster			

THREATS

degree of risk that exists. The cost of several recommended countermeasures would then be identified.

Consider a high degree of risk of losing foodstuffs because of theft. Two possible countermeasures might be installing cameras that can observe the happenings within the refrigerator area and the back dock, or posting two guards, one at the refrigerator and one at the back dock. Although the latter is probably more effective, the overall long-range cost of TV cameras would be far less expensive and nearly as effective. With regard to natural disaster and the loss of power, the size (value) of the food inventory kept on hand and the frequency of hurricanes in the area might be weighed against the cost of an emergency generator. Another alternative would be to insure against the loss of food. Finally, after considering the risk, management might elect to become the insurer by doing nothing regarding the possible loss of food inventory. This is risk management and the function of the manager in charge of assets protection in a hotel.

Disaster Control and Emergency Action Plans

No emergency action program is complete without clearly stated and well-defined objectives, plans, and actions facing the possible threat of natural or human-made disasters, riot, civil disturbance, bomb threats, explosion, and most of all, fire. It is a top management responsibility to plan for such contingencies, but in most situations the director of security or the chief engineer will become the disaster control coordinator and will be responsible for carrying out the emergency action plan. Such plans should be in writing and should spell out in as detailed a manner as possible the steps to be taken in a given emergency and by whom.

A number of unique perils such as hurricane, tornado, or flood might be of particular concern in a given geographical location, but the threat of fire is universal.

Such planning is established to anticipate what might happen that could endanger people or damage property. In the case of fire, emergency plans are designed to anticipate the needs of personnel, training, and the appropriate hardware that will support prompt and effective action when a fire emergency does occur. Other types of emergencies might hinge on proper communications, but all emergencies require anticipation of the event itself. Proper training on how to deal with the situation in a logical way is vital in the planning function to ensure that people are protected and the possibility of panic reduced to a minimum.

The panic emotion is defined as that sudden and overpowering terror that takes control of a person when they find themselves lost, disoriented, or without the knowledge of what to do in an emergency situation. Panic is contagious and can cause people to act in bizarre ways. Panic itself can also cause people to kill. For this reason it is imperative that hotel staffs be trained and drilled as to what to do in different emergencies so they will be able to set the right kind of example for guests to follow in an actual emergency.

While the event of an emergency might be unforeseen and unpredictable, it is possible to make reasonable estimates of vulnerabilities for a given facility in a given geographical location. Continuity is essential in such planning. Provision should always be made for alternatives for each individual responsibility in the emergency plan. Since an emergency can occur at any hour of the day it becomes necessary that operation and direction for each shift be identified.

Another part of emergency action must include the provision for crisis communications. It is imperative that plans be published indicating who will become the sole spokesperson for the facility to the media should an emergency occur. Normally, such person will be the general manager. Whomever the person designated, this person must be known to all employees.

Professionalism and the Security Manager

The American Society of Industrial Security (ASIS) is an association of protection professionals who aspire to a management approach for the protection of assets. The association has been instrumental in upgrading the quality of management expertise of those who seek positions in the field of protection management.

More and more hotels today are placing a certified protection professional (CPP) at the directorship of security operations. This person ranks with other directors at the highest policy-making level of their organization. Vice-presidents of risk management or assets protection are titles becoming well known in major corporations, both in large properties and at the corporate level. Smaller hotels may, for some time to come, continue to observe the conventional title of security manager or director of security.

In areas where the need is apparent, physical security of the building and its assets, property surveillance, preemployment checks (background investigations), employee badge identification, and general investigations are also functions that occur under the umbrella of the protection of assets. Finally, the foot soldier of the security function remains the security guard and patrol—men and women well qualified to observe, detect, and prevent the unfortunate occurrence that can bring liability for negligence. The key words for staffing the security function will continue to be concern for people, integrity, alertness, curiosity, and service to others.

Summary

Security for the hospitality industry encompasses more than a consideration about safety or freedom from fear, anxiety, and doubt about ourselves and our property; there has been a modernizing of thought to include a total concern for the protection and safeguarding of all assets. Assets include our guests, employees (and the property of both), supplies, equipment, and the facility itself. Also included would be the reputation and good will enjoyed by the organization in the community.

Management must become proactively involved in those activities dealing with threat assessment and analysis, security surveys, and risk management. The security professional of today is responsible for searching out potential hazards and designing systems and procedures that will prevent incidents and accidents from happening, or at least minimize losses should an unfortunate event occur.

The elements available for the prevention of loss are people, hardware, and software. The people (the most expensive) are those who staff the security department. Hardware refers to the equipment used for communication, surveillance, and access control, and software pertains to the policies and procedures that regulate and govern security operations.

Although security personnel are often uniformed and give the appearance of legally constituted law officers, they possess no powers beyond that of a private citizen. It is imperative, therefore, that all personnel working in security understand the federal, state, and local laws, regulations, and ordinances that must be upheld by both ownership and property management. Of equal concern is the prevention of liability caused by negligence that can lead to *civil action*, in which case a jury will decide what the law will be in a given set of circumstances. The greatest efforts of all personnel working in the industry must be exercised to ensure that the responsibility to act prudently and wisely with due regard for a reasonable standard of care in day-to-day operations is attained and maintained through proactive direction and adequate supervision.

The essence of good security work is the proper and complete documentation of events under investigation and the regular journalizing of shift events. Such recordings may play an important role in identifying and preventing hazards not known to have existed.

Keyless locking systems for guestroom doors, closed circuit TV monitoring systems, and cellular communication equipment top the list of state-of-the-art equipment that have greatly reduced guestroom theft and manpower cost in asset protection. In addition, the safety aspects of alarm, control, and sensing devices used to detect smoke or fire provide the added safety needed when uncontrolled emergencies occur.

The hub of most threat assessment and risk management programs is the *security survey*. This is a critical on-site examination and analysis of a facility to ascertain the present security status of the operation. The examination also contains recommendations regarding risks observed. A *protection matrix* is often developed that displays type and degree of threats against the various assets being considered. Management may then make decisions regarding the application of resources to counter the identified threat.

Safety and security culminate with the development of a well-defined *emergency action plan*. This plan should indicate the possibilities of what might happen in a given circumstance (fire, flood, hurricane, and so on), and should be covered in all training activity to ensure that employees know what to do in the event of any given emergency. All training should provide the employee with knowledge of what to do and how to direct others in a way that the possibility of panic in emergency situations can be eliminated.

Regardless of title, the manager in charge of safety, security, and risk management should be a qualified industry professional. The American Society for Industrial Security (ASIS) provides continuing education for persons interested in the security profession and provides certification as a Certified Protection Professional (CPP) for those who wish to further their education and standing in the lodging and hospitality security field. Today, such professionals occupy positions at the highest levels of corporate management—a trend destined to continue for years to come.

Bibliography

Bottom, Norman R., Jr., and John Kostanoski. 1983. *Security and Loss Control.* New York: Macmillan.

Broder, James F., C.P.P. 1984. *Risk Analysis and the Security Survey.* Boston: Butterworth Publishers.

Buzby, Walter J., II., and David Paine. 1976. *Hotel & Motel Security Management.* Los Angeles: Security World Publishing Co.

Green, Gion. 1981. *Introduction to Security,* 3d ed. Boston: Butterworth Publishers.

Martin, Robert J., and Thomas J. A. Jones. 1992. *Professional Management of Housekeeping Operations.* New York: Wiley.

Sherry, John H. 1974. *The Laws Of Inkeepers.* Ithaca: Cornell University Press.

32

Maintenance and Engineering in the Hospitality Industry

Frank Borsenik

The hospitality industry provides services to the public or other clientele. For example, a lodging unit provides guest rooms and may offer or provide food, beverages, meeting space, retail shops, and recreation facilities (this list is not meant to be all inclusive). These services require facilities and a building to house such facilities. The facility may be simple, such as cabinets and shelves in a retail facility; complex, such as a restaurant; or very complex, for example a full-service hotel. Facilities are housed in a building, a complex network of structural components, interior arrangements of space, finishing materials, utilities, life safety systems, and electro-mechanical equipment to provide an environment, all of which are blended together to provide a unique atmosphere. In the hospitality industry buildings and facilities require a large capital investment and if these are not properly maintained, the owners may never fully recover their investment.

Building maintenance and engineering management is physical asset management. The physical assets are the building and its facilities. Management includes policy making, decision making, planning and organizing, control and communication, and human relations (workers and customers). This article reviews hospitality maintenance and engineering from its physical asset management role.

Hospitality Building and Facility Investment

Lodging investment per guest room (total facility investment divided by the number of guest rooms) has increased from $10,000 to over $300,000, and even over $750,000 for some recently purchased well-known hotels, during the past 35 years. Foodservice investment per customer seat has increased from $1,000 to over $10,000, and over $25,000 for selected foodservice units in recent years. Facilities cost for clubs have had similar percentage increases over the past two decades. If one considers a 500-guest-room hotel with an average cost of $100,000 per guest room, the total investment is $50 million. The owners would like to recover this investment and have the facility generate a fair profit. This is only possible if the facility is properly maintained and well managed.

Another way to look at facility cost is to review construction and furnishing costs per square foot of building area. Normal building construction costs vary from $50 to $200 per square foot. Furnishings, depending on the building type, can vary from $50 to $100 or more per square foot. Relating these costs back to the previous lodging guest room data generates similar total investment costs. For example, a hotel with a gross guest room floor area of 500 square feet (total building square feet divided by the number of guest rooms) and a total facility cost of $200 per square foot generates a guest room average cost of $100,000. Or, review foodservice cost per seat: If the total space per restaurant seat is 35 square feet, and if the average cost of $200 per square foot is used, the cost per seat is $7,000. Buildings and facilities require continuous maintenance so that they can continue to provide desirable products—a guest room that is desired by lodging customers, or a comfortable foodservice atmosphere and surroundings.

Maintenance Activities

The normal activities of a maintenance department are preventive, repair, corrective, and renovation maintenance.

Preventive maintenance includes inspections, standard comparisons, minor adjustments, replacement of low-cost components, and general lubrication, if required. A good preventive maintenance program starts with scheduled inspections of facilities and the entire building. Some items may require daily inspections; others may only require annual inspections. The purpose of an inspection is to find possible problems. A simple fan belt (the driving linkage between an electric motor and a ventilation fan) wears with use and deteriorates with age. As the belt wears either more energy is required to move a specified amount of ventilation air or less ventilation air is delivered to a section of the building or to a room. An inspection detects a loose, worn belt. The corrective procedure is to replace the belt or at least to tighten an idler pulley to increase system efficiency until a replacement belt can be installed. The primary purpose of preventive maintenance programs is to ensure the continuous operation of a system at efficient levels of performance and to minimize system breakdowns.

Repair maintenance is required when a system either stops or is not performing according to some acceptable standard. If an electric light bulb is not generating light, the simple repair maintenance procedure is to replace the light bulb. If a fluorescent light bulb is very dark at its ends and if it is only generating partial light, it is replaced, hence repair maintenance. Another example of repair maintenance is if there is a roof water leak, a section of the roof can be resealed to prevent that leak. Most hospitality industry maintenance is repair maintenance. Typical repair maintenance patterns are discussed later.

Corrective maintenance is frequently confused with preventive maintenance, hence the term may not be universally used in the hospitality industry. Corrective maintenance could be a change in the preventive maintenance routine; it could involve a slight redesign of a component that frequently fails or replacement of a component with an upgraded unit; or it could correct a continuing problem. If an electric motor is frequently replaced on a compressor, the corrective maintenance procedure could require a motor with a higher mechanical rating or a different type of motor. Another example is a guest room toilet (water closet) with a flush tank attachment that is not supplying water at adequate pressure to completely flush the toilet bowl. In this case corrective maintenance replaces the flush tank with a water pressure valve. If paint continually peels from a painted surface, corrective maintenance may be to remove the surface, install a moisture vapor barrier, and replace the surface. The purpose of corrective maintenance is to minimize repair maintenance through redesign or component change.

Renovation maintenance includes redesign, removal of items requiring continual maintenance, and the replacement of components with items that require less maintenance, reduce operating costs, or upgrade product or service standards. Replacing a roof on a building is renovation maintenance. Refurbishing guest room facilities on a schedule is an example of renovation maintenance. Replacing wood exterior siding that requires frequent painting with prepainted steel panels, aluminum siding, or vinyl exterior siding is renovation maintenance. Covering painted dry wall in guest rooms with a vinyl wall covering is renovation maintenance.

The maintenance department in a hospitality industry building is involved with preventive, repair, corrective, and renovation maintenance. The percentage of time spent in each activity depends on several factors, including business activity level, type of building construction, number and types of facilities, the age of the building and its facilities, the geographic location of the property, management standards, past maintenance activities and practices, customer expectations, and availability and cost of technology.

Engineering Activities

Engineering activities include energy management and building design and development criteria. Most maintenance departments are involved with energy management and some may be involved with the development of renovation design criteria. Very few departments have the on-staff expertise for engineering design.

Energy management in the hospitality industry can vary from a minimal requirement of verifying utility bill charges to the complete development, implementation, and monitoring of an energy management program for the entire building. At minimum, all energy charges should be verified by the maintenance department head. This usually involves reading electric, gas, and water meters and verifying purchased gallons (oil) or pounds (LPG or coal) of other energy sources. Energy meters should be read on a frequent schedule and compared to past records and business activity levels and any deviations must be investigated.

Some maintenance department heads may be required to suggest an energy management program for a property. The purpose of the program is to provide necessary energy for the successful operation of the property and to eliminate all energy waste, thereby reducing total energy consumption. For example, if a smaller wattage electric light bulb will provide adequate light for a necessary task, smaller bulbs should replace all larger wattage bulbs. Or perhaps guest bathroom hot water can be reduced from 140°F to 115°F. The department head should meet with the other department heads to develop the energy management program for the total property.

Current engineering design is frequently related to energy management programs in the hospitality industry. For example, it is known that incandescent lighting systems are seldom over 12 percent efficient (conversion of electric energy to light energy), so engineering design would develop a fluorescent lighting replacement system that would include lamp sizing to provide the necessary lighting level, required changes in the electrical system, the conversion cost, the estimated energy savings, changes in maintenance requirements, and the development of a payback period. Engineering design may also include determining the cost of alternate plans for periodic guest room renovation, evaluating service contracts versus on-premise cost of doing the same work, determining the cost of alternate energy resources (natural gas versus electrical or oil), and evaluating energy management control systems.

Energy Management Systems — Currently available technology can significantly reduce property energy consumption. In addition, if an appropriate energy management system (EMS) is selected for a property, system capabilities are such that life safety, building security, and many maintenance record-keeping procedures can be included with the basic EMS. Some EMS computer software programs are compatible with employee scheduling software and can be used to optimize employee activities.

The simplest EMS is a time clock. Time clocks can be connected to outside building and grounds lighting and some interior public space lighting. Normally lighting systems are activated 15 minutes before and 15 minutes after sunset and sunrise respectively. EMS load shedding is also available. Load shedding programs can control maximum energy consumption during a specified time period for any type of energy resource (electric, gas, water, or steam). All equipment utilizing a specific energy resource is connected to a control center that limits the maximum consumption during a specified time period. If a unit of equipment not currently in operation demands energy and if its energy requirement would exceed the maximum set energy level, this equipment is not activated until some of the currently operating equipment is shut off. Some systems automatically shut down some equipment if other equipment demands energy and has not been in operation for an extended time period.

Electric demand controllers only regulate maximum electric demand during a specified time period and operate very similar to load shedding systems. The current ultimate EMS is the computer-assisted system that can be used to replace the time clock, load shedding, and electric demand controllers. The computer-assisted system can also be connected to space occupancy sensors and hotel front office systems. Hotel guest rooms can be programmed for unsold-unoccupied status, sold-unoccupied status, or sold-occupied status with different room temperatures for each room status. Life safety, security, and employee staffing programs can frequently be included with these computer-assisted EMS programs. The maintenance head should be prepared to recommend an appropriate EMS for a property.

Maintenance and Engineering Management Functions

Maintenance and engineering management functions are policy making, decision making, planning and organizing, communication and control, and human relations.

Policy Making — Policy making as applied to the maintenance and engineering department is developing decision-making guidelines. Some policies are established by higher management, such as, the maintenance and engineering department head reports to the property general manager, property president, executive assistant manager, or property manager. Another management policy may define the customer market segment that is being attracted to the property. These customers are attracted because of room rates, property facilities, or standards of service. The maintenance department head cannot change these policies, but can recommend policy changes.

The department head establishes decision-making guidelines that reflect these policies. For example, if a work order (a request for maintenance department to do work) is received in the department, when should this work be done? As quickly as possible, of course. But what happens if two or more work orders are received at the same time? Or, if all workers are currently performing other activities, what activities are temporarily halted so that someone can be assigned to the new work request? A work order priority system that establishes department policy must be developed so that the correct decision can be made regarding work requests. Work orders are assigned one of three priorities: emergency, routine, or backlogged.

Emergency work orders have the first priority. An employee is immediately sent to handle a work request. In general, if guest or employee safety is affected, an emergency priority is assigned. Emergency examples include ice forming on the building entrance walks and roads, a leaking plumbing fixture flooding an area, or an activated fire alarm. The department head develops a list of emergency situations that serves as a general guideline for the immediate dispatching of workers. Examples of types of emergency work order requests are shown in Table 2.

Routine work orders—requests for work that does not require immediate action—have a second priority. These work requests are scheduled on a first-in first-out basis in many cases. A normal procedure is to accumulate all guest room work requests by selected categories (plumbing, electrical, by floor level, or building section) and to give the work requests to a single employee to handle within a 2- or 4-hour period. Hence, an employee may be given six guest room work requests that the employee can be expected to complete in a 4-hour period. The employee may be required to call the dispatcher after the completion of each task and notify the dispatcher which task will be completed next. Table 1 shows typical routine work order requests for three hotels. All data is given in work orders per 100 guest rooms per day.

The figures in Table 1 show the effects of three different property management policies. Hotel C was built over 30 years ago and management has established an excellent property renovation policy. The average age of guest rooms, dining rooms, and public space is 5 years and a high percentage of maintenance activities is for preventive maintenance. Hotel B was built 25 years ago and the average age of guest rooms, dining rooms, and public space is about 7.5 years and an average of one employee per 100 guest rooms

Table 1. *Work order requests per 100 guest rooms per day for three hotels*

Origin of request	Hotel A	Hotel B	Hotel C
Guest rooms	6.77	4.77	2.12
Food and beverage	4.47	2.29	1.00
Public and other	4.04	2.06	1.05
Total requests	15.28	9.12	4.17

Sources: F. D. Borsenick, "A Study of the Maintenance Department and Its Management at the XXX Hotel," unpublished, Howard Hughes Development Corporation, 1984; also extracts from various unpublished consulting studies conducted by F. D. Borsenick in 1972, 1975, and 1982.

is assigned to preventive maintenance activities. Hotel A was built about 30 years ago, but guest rooms are renovated only as they become excessively worn, dining rooms are renovated only when food sales decrease, and public space is renovated when money is available. Hotel A has about 550 guest rooms and only two employees are assigned preventive maintenance activities. Each work order request requires about 0.55 work hours for guest room repairs, 1.00 work-hours for food and beverage repairs, and 1.50 work-hours for public area repairs. The effects of these different property management policies are clear.

Table 2 compares the types of emergency work orders for the same three hotels. Data are expressed as a percentage of total emergency work requests for a 30-day period for the same three hotels. Hotel C has significantly lower lighting work requests because electric light bulbs are replaced on a set schedule based on estimated hours of operation in the three hotel areas. Hotel C still uses guest room keys, while Hotels A and B use plastic card computer controlled guest room door locks, hence the difference between Hotel C and the other two.

Backlogged work orders represent a request for work that cannot be completed at the time of request because either replacement parts or skilled employees are not available. Employees may not be available because of vacation time or sick leave. This could happen if a property had only one on-premise television repair employee who was either ill, on vacation, or not on scheduled duty. Backlogged work orders are scheduled as routine maintenance when the replacement part becomes available or the employee returns to work.

Management Inspections. Another example of a management policy function is establishing a maintenance inspection schedule. The normal maintenance inspection team includes the manager, maintenance department head, and executive housekeeper. During the property inspection the team establishes property and facility standards. *Property and facility standards* refer to facility performance levels or acceptable appearance levels. An acceptable appearance level is easy to see, for example, when the outside lawn is 4 inches high, it will be cut to 1.5 inches. However, a dirty interior corridor painted wall could be washed or repainted. Wall washing is generally a housekeeping task

Table 2. *Types and percentages of emergency repairs for three hotels*

Type of repair	Hotel A (%)	Hotel B (%)	Hotel C (%)
Environment (heat cooling)	14.1	7.7	11.6
Door and locks	5.7	5.5	14.6
Drapes and rods	2.3	7.1	3.0
Electrical (nonlighting)	1.4	2.4	2.8
Lighting	34.1	32.6	8.3
Plumbing	21.1	30.0	31.9
Smoke alarms	1.4	1.9	0.6
Television	10.8	4.3	7.0
Other	9.1	8.5	20.2
Total	100.0	100.0	100.0

Sources: F. D. Borsenick, "A Study of the Maintenance Department and Its Management at the XXX Hotel," unpublished, Howard Hughes Development Corporation, 1984; also extracts from various unpublished consulting studies conducted by F. D. Borsenick in 1972, 1975, and 1982.

and painting is a maintenance task. The inspection team will have to establish a policy regarding criteria for wall washing and criteria for wall painting.

Facility, and especially equipment, performance guidelines are usually easier to establish. For example, when the combustion efficiency of the hot-water boiler drops to 75 percent, the equipment and controls are adjusted to increase the efficiency to 80 percent. If the efficiency cannot be increased to 80 percent by normal adjustments, what is the proper action? Adjust the efficiency to the highest level above 75 percent by normal procedures? Renovate the equipment with appropriate components to increase efficiency to some level, 80 percent or higher? Or, replace the boiler with a new unit that has an efficiency of at least 80 percent? The development of these decision-making guidelines is policy making.

One of the primary purposes of management inspections is to develop standards of acceptable appearance and performance. A secondary purpose of inspection is to determine the general condition of the property and as a result of the inspection to revise procedures to improve the condition of the property.

As a general guideline, lodging guest rooms should be inspected by the management team at least once each year. This implies that 2 percent of the total number of guest rooms should be inspected each week. Public areas should be inspected by the management team every two weeks. The back-of-the-house areas and facilities should be inspected at least 10 times per year. An inspection form that lists items to be checked must be developed. If during the inspections, the team agrees that the general condition of the property is satisfactory or exceeds their established standards, the number of scheduled inspections can be reduced. If established standards are not being maintained, inspection frequency must be increased.

Decision Making

Decision making is selecting a single alternative from a list of two or more alternatives that could be used to solve a problem. Doing nothing is an alternative. Seeking assistance from higher management is also an alternative. The list of alternatives should minimize the "do nothing" and "seeking help" alternatives.

Policy establishes decision-making guidelines as indicated in the previous section. The maintenance head, usually in conjunction with his or her superior, has the responsibility of developing alternate courses of action for anticipated problems. For example, three alternatives were developed for dispatching a work order: emergency, routine, and backlog. When a work order is received in the maintenance department, it must be classified in one of these categories. The maintenance head can provide examples of emergency type work orders: These are decision-making guidelines. However, what should the dispatcher do when a work order is received that does not fit the developed guidelines? If nothing is done, a new alternative has been created, but this is not the desired decision-making action. Perhaps a fourth alternative, "seek assistance," should be developed for the decision maker.

The number and feasibility of alternatives is limited by management policy. For example, assume the maintenance head is asked to investigate new energy management control systems that could be used for the property. He or she calls a number of manufacturers and each develops a recommendation for the property. These recommendations (alternatives) are presented to management, all of which are rejected because they are too costly. The manager may now realize that a maximum cost for the system or other system parameters were not specified. Management executes its "do nothing" alternative by rejecting the other alternatives.

The decision-making concept as discussed above shows two important aspects of decision making: developing alternatives and responsibility. Decisions should be made at the lowest management or supervisory level. However, when this is done, management is still responsible for all decisions made at lower management levels, hence, the "seek assistance" alternative should always be present until appropriate decision-making guidelines are fully developed. Additional decision-making examples are shown in the following sections.

Planning and Organizing

Planning is applying management policy to decision making. Each maintenance head should be required to develop a weekly or, at minimum, a monthly work plan and present it to management for approval. The approval authorizes the maintenance head to carry out the work plan. The work plan itemizes estimated work orders by categories and lists special projects (such as the number of guest rooms to be renovated or other unusual work to be completed during the time period), estimated preventive maintenance activities (labor hours), scheduled management inspections, administrative activities, the cost of supplies for the period, and the projected hours of labor required for the time period. It may also list scheduled worker vacation time, and it usually includes a department budget update for completing this programmed work schedule and any comments. The work plan concept is recommended for all properties and allows the manager to thoroughly review proposed plans.

Organizing, in the context of the maintenance department, includes the development of the organizational structure; the development of work procedures; staffing the department with appropriate personnel; the development of a reporting network (including department forms to be used); the establishment of responsibilities; the development of a training program, if appropriate for the property; and the general allocation of work within the department.

The size and organization of the maintenance department is dependent on property size (number of guest rooms) and its facilities (foodservice operations, meeting and exhibition space, retail outlets, recreation facilities, outside space). Various general guidelines have been developed for lodging operations regarding organization and staffing. Smaller properties, for example 150 or fewer guest rooms, with limited facilities, for example one foodservice outlet and a very limited number of meeting rooms, may have a one-, two-, or three-person maintenance department with several maintenance service contracts. The department can handle normal emergency work orders and complete some routine repairs and may provide limited preventive maintenance. Such work as groundskeeping (grass cutting and landscaping upkeep, snow removal, and parking lot cleaning), television repairs, and building repairs (door locks, alarm systems, window replacement, refrigeration repairs, elevator maintenance and repair) are all contracted services. A significant percentage of the department head's time is spent on dispatching work requests to on-premise staff or the contract service and on the periodic evaluation of these contracts. This organization is utilized by most foodservice operations and many clubs.

As the property size increases (generally over 150 guest rooms for hotels with expanded services, two or more foodservice outlets, some recreational facilities, three or more meeting-banquet rooms, lounges), the number of maintenance service contracts is reduced and the number of maintenance personnel increases. In this case, the department will have a full staff of maintenance personnel that can handle most emergency work orders during the normal day shift, the preventive maintenance effort is increased, and most routine work orders are completed by the day shift or by a smaller second shift during the early evening hours. A very limited staff (one or two persons) are scheduled for the night shift to handle emergency work orders, complete simple routine work, and for very limited preventive maintenance (changing or cleaning air filters).

The complete on-premise 24-hour maintenance department is generally limited to very large properties of 300 guest rooms or more with complete facilities. These departments have a very limited number of maintenance service contracts (periodic elevator testing and certification is an example of a service contract for these larger properties). A partial organizational chart is shown in Figure 1.

A larger lodging property generally has from three to four maintenance persons per 100 guest rooms. Three persons are usually required for 100 available guest rooms, and four persons are required per 100 occupied guest rooms. Naturally, as the number of maintenance service contracts increase, the number of maintenance people must be decreased. Another factor affecting the department staff level is the meeting and exhibition space. The above 3–4 person per 100 guest room ratio applies to an average size property with two foodservice outlets, 1000 square feet of retail stores, and less than 5000 square feet of meeting space. Normally, maintenance is responsible for meeting room setups, although this could also be a housekeeping department function. Some managers provide a variable labor budget that depends on convention and meeting activities. Other managers project anticipated convention requirements and include these with the maintenance annual budget. Both techniques will increase the 3–4 person per 100 guest room ratio. If the property has an energy management program with energy monitors, this could increase staffing requirements by 5–10 percent. Other properties may have 10 percent of the guest rooms renovated per year, increasing staffing requirements by 10–20 percent. Several hotel additions during the past decade were finished with an on-premise staff, which completed interior wall construction, interior finishes, plumbing fixture installations, and finish flooring and installed cabinets and shelving.

Control and Communication Management

Control. Control includes establishing and meeting goals set by management. Control implies that a measurement system has been established for the property. A major control system is a budget. The budget can be expressed as dollars, man-hours, a percentage of revenue, a percentage of total property expenses, or by any other logical measurement peculiar to the property, department, or situation.

Fig. 1. Partial organization for a maintenance and engineering department for a larger hotel. R & M Engineer is the day shift engineer-supervisor in charge of emergency and routine work orders and preventive maintenance.

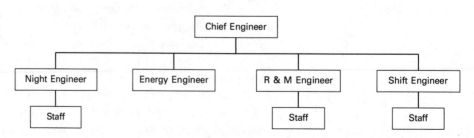

Table 3. *Property operation and maintenance expense subaccounts showing typical percentages, variance percentages, and actual percentages for an older hotel*

Subaccount item	Typical	Percent variance	Hotel A
Payroll and employee benefits	46	10	69.7
Building	8	2	1.6
Electrical and mechanical	10	6	15.3
Furniture	3	1	0.7
Grounds	3	1	0.9
Supplies	5	4	4.4
Painting and decorating	5	1	0.9
Removal of waste matter	4	2	2.7
Other	16	4	3.8
Total	100		100.0

Sources: various unpublished consulting studies conducted by F. D. Borsenick in 1972, 1975, and 1982.

Budgets are management guidelines and should allow for variances. In general, if the maintenance department is operating within established variances it should be considered as a well-run department. There are two primary department accounts established by the *Uniform System of Accounts for Hotels and Motels* (American Hotel and Motel Association, Washington, D.C.): Property Operation and Maintenance Expenses, and Energy Expenses. Each of these accounts has subaccounts. Table 3 shows Property Operation and Maintenance Expenses expressed as a percentage of the total account expenses. The subaccount item column is the subaccount as established by the *Uniform System.* The Typical column is the U.S. average percentage for each subaccount item. The variance column is a normal acceptable percentage variance for average lodging units. Hotel A is actual data from a hotel in Nevada.

Table 4 shows Energy Expenses expressed as a percentage of the total account expenses. The subaccount column is as established by the *Uniform System.* The Typical column is the U.S. national average percentage for each subaccount item; the Percent variance column is a normal acceptable percentage variance for average lodging units, and Hotel A is actual data from a hotel in Nevada.

The data indicate that "typical percentages" have been generated for the United States, but property deviations from the "typical" can be very large. It is important to develop historical property data and compare these data to

Table 4. *Energy expense subaccounts showing typical percentages, variance percentages, and actual percentages for an older hotel*

Subaccount item	Typical	Percent variance	Hotel A
Fuel (natural gas, oil)	23	8	33.6
Electricity	63	15	52.4
Water and sewage	9	4	14.0
Steam	5	5	0.0
Total	100		100.0

Sources: various unpublished consulting studies conducted by F. D. Borsenick in 1972, 1975, and 1982.

other very similar units in the same geographic area with comparable local costs.

Table 5 relates to budget and a possible control concept. Actual property and maintenance expenses and energy expenses are frequently compared to property income or to the number of property guest rooms. The figures indicate that the available U.S. average data may not be very appropriate for a specific property and that property budgets must be developed from past property expenses.

In addition to budget, control measures for the maintenance department management should include periodic evaluation of the department and the maintenance department head. The common department evaluation factors are budget, employee productivity, work order production, and a labor forecast. These factors must be correlated to building use or occupancy. Once again, past property data is critical for a fair evaluation.

Maintenance department head evaluation should be based on budget, management reports, guest and customer reactions, the general condition of the property, cooperation between the maintenance department and other property functional departments, and innovation and cost savings.

Each unit of equipment that has a value in excess of a specified amount and that requires maintenance should have an *inventory control card* and inventory number. The inventory control card lists all essential equipment information including required preventive maintenance routines and schedules. These are currently set up in computer software programs that will generate preventive maintenance schedules. In addition, the card (file) also includes any emergency or routine repairs for that equipment. Such items as type of repair, replacement parts, labor requirements, and repair cost are entered on the card. This data should be analyzed to determine if an appropriate replacement cycle can be developed for the unit. The purpose of the replacement cycle is to minimize future maintenance costs and minimize time loss in case of failure.

Communication. Communication involves the conveyance or transmission of information. Through communication managers can carry out their policies regarding the operation of the property. When communication fails, operations problems generally develop and employees may appear to be confused.

Table 5. *Property operation and maintenance and energy expenses shown as a percentage of income and in cost per guest room*

Ratio base item	Typical	Variance	Hotel A
Room sales	12%	8%	22.5%
Room, food and beverage income	6%	4%	9.3%
Occupied guest room/day	$7	$4	$14.17
Occupied guest room/year	$1700	$1700	$5170
Energy Expenses			
Room sales	10%	7%	18.5%
Room, food and beverage income	5%	3%	7.7%
Occupied guest room/day	$6	$4	$11.68
Occupied guest room/year	$1500	$1500	$4260

Sources: various unpublished consulting studies conducted by F. D. Borsenick in 1972, 1975, and 1982.

One of the most important communication tools available to management and the department head is the *management report*. The management report is a summary of maintenance activities during a time period, usually one month. It may also include energy consumption and comparison data, budget data, a proposed work plan for the next period, employee productivity data, and recommendations.

Training programs are prime examples of communication. In a training program, maintenance employees are taught how to respond in various situations. Thus management is able to control how various activities are to be performed. In larger properties the maintenance head has a training responsibility. Most maintenance training is some form of on-the-job training that allows for maximum employee motivation. Many maintenance skills are taught through an apprenticeship program, whereby both the employee and management become committed to a 6,000- to 8,000-hour program. Such a program allows for complete worker evaluation and results in low employee turnover rates in engineering related maintenance activities.

There are definite management-maintenance communication problem areas in the hospitality industry. Many maintenance department heads are never involved with the process of developing a budget, yet they are expected to meet a budget they may not understand. There have been hotel cases when the only time the manager met with the maintenance department head was once per month for 30 minutes or less. There was no communication between maintenance and management, yet management thought that maintenance was a big problem area. These are not isolated cases. Management must treat maintenance on an equal basis with other lodging departments. Managers who follow this simple rule do not have major maintenance problems.

Human Relations   The final management function is an application of the previous functions of management to the area of human relations (employees and guests). Leadership, simply put, is the manager's or supervisor's ability to get work done by employees working for him or her. Policies, planning, and organizing all define the work that must be done. Communication and control are necessary to direct the activities of the workers. The effective implementation of these principles and the successful completion of assigned work is one form of leadership. Through leadership a manager controls and directs departmental activities and motivates employees to their highest potential. Leadership is the ingredient that makes a good manager and department head.

Generally, if a property has managers that exhibit leadership qualities, this property will have satisfied customers. These managers know the wants and desires of their customers and will direct employee efforts toward satisfying these customer needs. The maintenance department head who is a leader is a valuable asset and normally has a well-run maintenance department.

Summary

This article presents an overall view of a property maintenance-engineering department. The department is essential for a property so that owners can realize the potential of their investment. An operational department is dependent on the successful application of the principles of management. These principles—policy making, decision making, organizing and planning, communication and control, and leadership—were all discussed and applied to maintenance-engineering. Various department controls and procedures were presented, which if fully utilized would assist in establishing, operating, and controlling the department. Energy management systems were discussed as the maintenance department head is frequently assigned an energy management responsibility.

Various U.S. average hotel data was presented so that property data can be compared to these average properties. Finally, it should be apparent, that the property (hotel) manager for a smaller property must personally direct the department and the personal direction is reduced with larger properties, and the role becomes a management function with less technical skills.

Bibliography

Borsenik, Frank D., and Alan T. Stutts. 1992. *The Management of Maintenance and Engineering Systems in the Hospitality Industry.* New York: Wiley.

Heyel, Bruce R. 1989. *The Encyclopedia of Management.* New York: Van Nostrand Reinhold.

Laventhol & Horwarth, CPA, (Annual ed.). 1988. *U.S. Lodging Industry.* Philadelphia: Laventhol & Horwarth.

Pannel, Kerr, Forster, CPA, (Annual ed.) 1988. *Trends in the Hotel/Motel Business.* New York: Pannel, Kerr, Forster.

Redlin, Michael H., and David M. Stipanuk. 1987. *Managing Hospitality Engineering Systems.* East Lansing, Mich.: Educational Institute of the American Hotel & Motel Association.

Stutts, Alan T., and Frank D. Borsenik. 1990. *Maintenance Handbook for Hotels, Motels, and Resorts.* New York: Van Nostrand Reinhold.

PART 3

Travel and Tourism

1

Defining Tourism and Related Concepts: Tourist, Market, Industry, and Tourism System

Neil Leiper

The twin descriptors *tourist* and *tourism* were devised two hundred years ago and subsequently grafted from English into many other languages. For most of the period their meanings have been significant only in relation to popular consciousness and everyday communication. More recently, specialized definitions have appeared. The following discussion describes popular meanings and examines how these have led to concepts defined in various ways by academic and professional researchers. One category of definitions has been basic to qualitative scholarship: "attempts to define tourism . . . have concerned researchers for decades. Such definitional explorations and articulations have indeed contributed to the understanding of tourism as a field of inquiry" (Jafari 1989:437). Another category of definitions has been necessary for quantitative research aimed at measuring tourism. The discussion to follow includes concepts associated with, but not synonymous with *tourism*: these are *tourist market, tourism industry, tourism system,* and *tourism studies.* They are included because often these items seem to be confused with tourism.

Tourist

"Tour" evolved from an ancient Greek word referring to a circular arrangement (*Webster's New International Dictionary, The Oxford English Dictionary*). However that etymology does not explain how "tour" came to mean particular types of trips among various types where itineraries are circular, beginning and ending at the same place. A possible explanation is that "tour" meaning a type of trip evolved from "tower" meaning castle, and originally referred to leisurely trips relaxing and sightseeing while going round the parapets of towers. Since seventeenth century writers used "tower" to mean a type of trip (cited in *The Oxford English Dictionary*: "towers round the world," "a tower of Italy") the alternative etymology seems plausible. Certainly by the early eighteenth century, "tour" in the modern sense of a temporary trip away from home for some pleasurable (leisure-related) purpose had become well established in

539

English: Defoe's (1720) best seller of the period, *A Tour through the Whole Island of Britain*, is evidence. By the middle of the eighteenth century the expression "Grand Tour" had come into use, referring to leisurely trips around Europe for cultural purposes.

Late in the eighteenth century Adam Smith, a Scottish professor whose writings dealt with a range of social and economic topics, worked for a period as a tutor accompanying a young aristocrat on a Grand Tour of Europe. His observations gave him the idea of tagging "tour" with "ist," coining a new expression. This idea seems to have stemmed from opinions he formed about a trend away from the cultural aims of the classic Grand Tour (educational and other creative leisure) and toward indulgence with frivolous recreation. But wanting the status available from "The Tour," many persons felt obliged to follow what became a ritual: visiting particular cities, sites, sights, and objects. Noticing how this ritual amounted to an ideology or "ism" of the tour, Smith coined "tourist" in the 1770s (Wykes 1973:130). Thus the original implication was pejorative: "tourist" was a mildly disparaging label in Adam Smith's mind. For many modern users, a disparaging connotation remains.

Three Sets of Meanings for "Tourist"

Adam Smith's idea has evolved into many subtle and shifting notions in modern popular consciousness. The emergence of research focusing on tourists has led to specialized meanings. One approach to analyzing this issue is to identify three sets: *popular notions, heuristic definitions,* and *technical definitions.* There are however additional perspectives (Smith 1990).

Popular Notions.   This set comprises meanings used in everyday communication and consciousness. Two examples are reported in *Webster's New International Dictionary:*

1. One that makes a tour, one that travels from place to place for pleasure or culture, one that stays overnight usually in an inn or motel;
2. Tourist class: a class of accommodation (as on a passenger ship) usually less expensive and less roomy than first or second or cabin class.

Often, popular notions of "tourist" refer to types of visitors. The latter is a broader expression, ignoring questions of trip format or purpose. Irrespective, popular notions of "tourist" are intrinsically subjective and tend to be highly variable, imprecise, or vague. As a result, dictionaries cannot represent everybody's perspectives and connotations about the idea. The second of the two meanings in the quotation above implies, in one sense at least, that tourists are an inferior type of traveler. Many popular notions of "tourist" contain variations on that, continuing Adam Smith's original sense. For instance Krippendorf (1987) listed several factors behind what he saw as "the much maligned tourist," often described, he remarked, as ridiculous, naive, organized, ugly, uncultured, rich, exploiting, or polluting. Fussell (1980:39) has described some underlying factors, claiming a distinction between explorers, travelers, and tourists: "All three make journeys, but the explorer seeks the undiscovered, the traveler that which has been discovered by the mind working in history, the tourist that which has been discovered by entrepreneurship and prepared for him by the arts of mass publicity."

Heuristic Definitions of Tourist.   An heuristic definition is one intended to clarify understanding. It may represent popular notions refined into academic concepts. Its function in this context is specifying a behavioral role (of tourists) to be studied or discussed. Ideally, whenever a formal study of tourists as a behavioral category is being prepared and presented, a clear statement should be made by the author showing what is meant by "tourist" in that study. Doing so has twin benefits. First, the exercise of formulating the definition concentrates the author's thinking. Second, a definition helps readers. Without it, different readers are likely to infer different meanings or connotations, because of the variety in popular notions. Heuristic definitions need not conform to official prescriptions, but may vary with the focus of each research project. Disparaging notions about "tourists" generally are avoided in heuristic definitions. Researchers should be aware of the disparagement issues, but while some researchers are specifically interested in them, none should be blinkered by them.

Often, heuristic definitions of "tourist" have at least three components. They state something about (1) distance covered in trips, (2) duration, and (3) purpose or motivation. Additional components that might be included include the class of facilities or services used and the type of travel arrangements: package versus independent, group versus individual. Two examples follow. The second example differs from the first in that it is not posed from the perspective of a place visited, and it is explicit about linking tourists with leisure:

1. Tourists are defined, in this section, as visitors in a region for at least one night and less than a year, whose main purpose of visit is other than earning money paid from within the region visited.
2. Tourists can be defined, in behavioral terms, as persons traveling away from their normal residential region for a temporary period, staying away at least one night but not permanently, to the extent that their behavior involves a search for leisure experiences from interaction with features or environmental characteristics of the places they choose to visit.

In the second example, the phrase "to the extent" allows a touristic role to be identified during trips made for purposes that are not popularly regarded as touristic. For instance people on business trips often spend part of their time in leisure-related pursuits and to that extent might be reasonably defined as tourists in a behavioral sense.

With an analytical anthropological approach, Jafari (1989) suggested a comprehensive general model of tourists as persons away from their usual habitat. Jafari's analysis identified seven components in the touristic process. These are corporation (entangled forms and forces of everyday ordinary life), emancipation (distancing oneself from the ordinary world), animation (experiences in nonordinary conditions), repatriation (leaving the spatial, temporal, and cultural zones of nonordinary conditions), and incorporation (getting back into ordinary existence). The seventh is omission (the ordinary current that flows in spite of the tourist's absence from home). While this model is a quite useful basis for understanding and researching tourists' behavior, it lacks a precise definition of "tourist."

Technical Definitions of Tourist. This category is most commonly applied in quantitative research. Besides statistical uses, it also has legal applications, such as with immigration administration. In either case, technical definitions of tourist are usually framed from the perspective of a region or country in the role of a destination or place visited by tourists in transit. Examples in this category usually have official status, but independent researchers can formulate their own. "Technical" refers to the definition's function, normally in statistics, of providing clear rules for interpreting any data under the heading "tourists." An unambiguous meaning is necessary if everyone responsible for collecting, analyzing, or interpreting the data is to understand what is included and what is excluded. Because popular notions about tourists vary, statistics, especially those emanating from official sources, cannot leave the issue for individuals' perceptions and opinions.

The first technical definition of tourist was framed in 1937. The League of Nations had a Statistical Committee responsible for recommendations to national governments on all kinds of international statistics. It concluded: "A foreign tourist is any person visiting a country, other than that in which he usually resides, for a period of at least twenty four hours" (OECD 1974:7). In the 1960s, several multinational organizations began refining the definition and other aspects of statistical systems dealing with tourists. Burkart and Medlik (1974) have described these events. In 1963 the United Nations conducted a Conference on Travel and Tourism, held in Rome. One of its recommendations to national governments was that the following definitions be used:

> For statistical purposes, the term "visitor" describes any person visiting a country other than that in which he has his usual place of residence, for any reason other than following an occupation remunerated from within the country visited. This definition covers:
>
> Tourists, i.e. temporary visitors staying at least twenty-four hours in the country visited whose purpose of journey can be classified under one of the following headings:
> (a) leisure (recreation, holiday, health, study, religion, sport);
> (b) business (family, mission, meeting);
> Excursionists, i.e. temporary visitors staying fewer than twenty-four hours in the country visited (including travelers on cruises).
>
> The statistics should not include travelers who, in the legal sense, do not enter the country (air travelers who do not leave an airport's transit area, and similar cases). (WTO 1983)

That set of definitions is now followed in many countries' official statistical reports, prepared by or for governmental organizations interested in monitoring inbound international tourists. They are used multinationally by the World Tourism Organization (WTO), the principal collator and publisher of global statistics on tourists' activities. However, not every country uses the standard WTO definition, which is why researchers interpreting and comparing data should check the definition applying in each case.

With regard to domestic tourists (those on trips within their country of residence) no standard technical definition has emerged. Quite different definitions are used in official statistics collected within different countries.

Note that the WTO definitions bisect international "visitors" into "tourists" and "excursionists," the latter being visitors in a country for day trips, less than twenty-four hours. In domestic contexts, a similar division is sometimes applied. This division is one basis for differentiating between "tourism" and "recreation." While that distinction may be useful in certain contexts, it should not be the basis for inferring that only day trippers, never tourists, have recreational experiences.

Which Category to Use?   The three sets of meanings for "tourist" previously discussed serve distinctive kinds of research. Popular notions are the focus when research aims to discover peoples' ideas about tourists. Heuristic definitions are used when researchers and scholarly commentators are expressing their opinions or findings relating to some aspect of tourists' behavior, in qualitative research. Technical definitions are used for statistical studies, in quantitative research. Inevitably there are differences. This need not be problematical, if the researcher is explicit and consistent with the definition used in each study. Unfortunately, many studies have been flawed by ignoring the distinction between heuristic and technical definitions. Searching the literature for a definition, researchers are more likely to find an official technical example. If such an example is adopted, quoted as "the" definition in an introduction, the report will be inconsistent and illogical if it then focuses on a narrower type of touristic behavior.

Why Are the Technical Definitions So Broad?

Technical definitions of "tourist" are usually much broader than popular notions. Thus, official statistics include persons on business trips for instance, not often regarded (by themselves or others!) as tourists. There may be two reasons for this.

The official technical definitions have been framed by persons representing organizations whose primary concerns are economic: how much money is spent by visitors, what it is spent on, what resources or facilities are needed, and so on. All visitors spending one or more nights in a place tend to be similar from that economic perspective. The fact that only some are "tourists" according to diverse popular notions is irrelevant and confusing in that context. So the conferences charged with deciding official technical definitions cast a very wide net, resulting in the inclusion of many kinds of visitors in their definition.

Another reason, which helps explain why "tourist" (rather than "visitor" for example) has been used in this technical context, seems to be that the organizations responsible for the official definitions usually have "tourist" or "tourism" in *their* titles. Their own bureaucratic interests are served by very broad definitions of "tourist." The policy means that official estimates of the economic value of "tourism" are maximized, which helps all the tourism organizations by making their role in the economy seem more important, useful when seeking support from governments. Evidence of this stratagem is discussed by Leiper (1990a:15).

Tourism

Popular Notions

In popular consciousness and language "tourist," coined in the late eighteenth century, naturally extended to "tourism." The latter expression, meaning the behavior of tourists, originated early in the nineteenth century (*The Oxford English Dictionary*). For a hundred and fifty years, dictionaries reported the popular meaning of "tourism" along lines such as "the theory and practice of touring; traveling for pleasure." Later, the expression acquired additional meanings. *Webster's* added "the guidance or management of tourists as a business or government function. . . ." The *Random House Dictionary* reported a third notion: "the promotion of tourist travel, especially for commercial purposes."

However a single word "tourism" used in reference to those newer meanings implies an extra qualifier; people often say "tourism" meaning "the tourism business/industry" in the same way that they say "plastics" to mean "the plastics business/industry." In everyday usage, the implication is usually apparent from the context, so that "he works in tourism" is interpreted as "he works in a business with tourists as customers" rather than "he works at being a tourist." Unfortunately, this semantic issue has carried over and clouded scholarly concepts, one of several problems discussed below.

Problems of Conceptual Definitions

Problems abound with conceptual definitions of "tourism," a point that writers of text books and other scholarly works usually agree on even though they seldom agree as to which definition is most appropriate! The first example was formulated in the 1940s by Hunziker and Krapf: "Tourism is the sum of the phenomena and relationships arising from the travel and stay of nonresidents, in so far as they do not lead to any permanent residence and are not connected with any earning activity" (cited by Burkart and Medlik 1974:40). Perhaps because it was pioneering, and perhaps because it appeals to those who for whom the study of tourism is a broad and amorphous theme, this definition has been widely quoted. Recent years have seen scholars from several disciplines frame new definitions. Many recent writers have defined tourism as an industry, a view expressed forcefully by Burkart (1981a, 1981b). However Kaul (1985) and others have argued that tourism is a market rather than an industry, while Jafari (1977) continued the tradition of Hunziker and Krapf but in a more descriptive manner, and defined tourism holistically as an academic subject. Leiper (1979) and Mill and Morrison (1985) also took the holistic view but defined it as a system. Meanwhile MacCannell (1976), Przeclawski (1986) and certain other social scientists have maintained the original popular sense of the term and have expressed the essence of tourism as the practice and theory of touring, the behavior of tourists.

Why are there so many different definitions? Stephen Smith (1990) points out that there can be no single, perfect, and widely accepted definition because of different perspectives. This is because different researchers have tended to define tourism in terms of their own discipline or personal perspective. Economists tend to see the economic issues and define tourism as an industry, marketers see markets as primary and therefore definitive, environmentalists focus on environmental impacts and see this as the essence, systems theorists try to express an integrated, holistic picture, social scientists may tend to see the human dimensions of tourists as the central factor, and so on. Perhaps these multiple views are understandable, and that tourism has so many definitions because there are so many uses for definitions. Or is this another case like the collection of blind men trying to describe an elephant, where some impressions lead away from the truth?

Behind the different uses of definitions, which may be relevant to some or other discipline and perceived in its terms, is the point that different writers have used a single word, "tourism," to represent substantially different things. This problem can be easily avoided. Professional and scholarly writings on tourism-related topics can and should differentiate *tourist, tourism, tourist market, tourism industry, tourism system,* and *tourism studies.* Each concept is distinct. Definitions for "tourist" have been discussed previously. The other concepts are dealt with next.

Tourism: A Fundamental Concept?

What, fundamentally, is tourism? Arguably, the most appropriate basis for a scholarly concept is the original meaning without any disparaging connotation. "Ism" denotes a collection of ideas, a set of theories put into practice by adherents, "ists." As idealism is the theory and practice of idealists, and socialism of socialists, so tourism is fundamentally linked to tourists. The following definition elaborates on the thinking of Przeclawski (1986) and others who have argued that tourism is, first of all, a form of human behavior: "Tourism is the set of ideas, the theories or ideologies for being a tourist, and it is the behavior of people in touristic roles, when the ideas are put into practice."

Jafari's (1989) model, outlined earlier, is useful for expanding on this definition. However, the definition must be accompanied by a sub-definition of "tourist" to become meaningful. For general studies, a relatively broad example from the heuristic set is desirable, because there is no single type of tourist, as Cohen (1979) emphasized, so there is no single type of tourism. Cohen pointed out the mistake (for researchers and scholars) of talking in general terms about "the" tourist, which leads to stereotyped inferences.

Tourist Markets
Tourism is usually (not always) associated with markets, by adding buyers to a huge range of existing general markets and by giving rise to opportunities for distinctly touristic markets. In either case, a market refers to an identifiable collection of persons who are willing and able to buy, consume, use, or experience some category of goods or services offered for exchange. But as Bain and Howell (1988) emphasize, clear property rights (to own goods or to use services and facilities) must be established for a market to exist. Thus if one accepts a definition of tourists that takes in behavior beyond dependency on goods and services exchanged via property rights then one recognizes that not all tourism is market-based. In the terminology of Gronhaug and Dholakia (1987) it is not all susceptible to "marketization"; some can be termed "nonmarket" tourism. This is another reason for rejecting the suggestion that "tourism" can be defined as "a market."

However most contemporary tourists seem dependent to some extent on a range of goods and services acquired in markets. Defining "tourist markets" or identifying tourists within broader markets depends on the perspectives and strategies of particular marketers, particular business organizations. An individual tourist might be very much part of a tourist market or market segment in the strategy of a business organization in the region where that individual is visiting, but the same tourist might be merely an incidental member of the general market for a department store in the same locality. For the store to treat tourists as a distinct market or market segment might be unfeasible.

Tourism Industry
The idea of a "tourism industry" is especially complex. Burkart (1981a, 1981b) and others have argued that the tourism industry is very large, comprising a very wide range of businesses and other organizations, touching virtually all areas of the economy. This perception begins with tourists, noting their consumption patterns. All the suppliers of all the goods and services tourists require are assumed to represent components of a tourism industry. While this leads to claims about a huge tourism industry, it also leads to perceptions of a highly fragmented industry.

A quite different opinion has been advanced by Kaiser and Helber (1978), de Kadt (1979) and Kaul (1985), who argued that there is no such thing as a tourism industry, and that what goes under that appellation is in reality a collection of separate industries with different sorts of links with tourists, some purposeful and others incidental.

An intermediate position has been proposed, using a different approach, by Leiper (1979, 1990a). Its foundation was asking "what is an industry?" which, drawing on the literature of industrial economics and strategic management, led to a proposition that a tourism industry comprises those organizations which (1) are in the business of providing goods or services to meet the distinctive needs of some identifiable collection of tourists, and (2) cooperate with one another, to some degree, in doing so. This position rejects the notion of "a fragmented industry" as a confusing contradiction in terms.

Thus certain types of organizations generally come within the scope of a tourism industry: travel agents, tour operators, airlines, and most hotels are in the business of serving identifiable sets of tourists and perform that function in a manner that is collaborative (nonfragmented) to a significant degree. But certain restaurants and general stores might be serving the same set of tourists without doing anything to meet their distinctively touristic attributes and without collaborating with other kinds of organization in the business of tourism. They are, accordingly, outside the tourism industry, even though they may be important, perhaps vital, to the region's role as a tourist destination.

This concept of an industry involves micro-economic and managerial concepts; it requires considering each business unit to determine whether, or to what extent, each is in the business and industry of tourism. It is a disaggregated approach. It tends to find a much smaller tourism industry than the wide-reaching concept proposed by Burkart.

Burkart's perception involves aggregated macro-economic concepts. It does not consider how particular businesses are managed in relation to tourists or in relation to one another; it assumes that tourists' expenditures reflect the existence and scale of a tourism industry. Possible advantages in this approach are firstly that it indicates a very large industry, a point both the boosters and critics of tourism development find appealing, and secondly, its indication of a very broadly-based industry, a potentially useful point for the boosters.

The advantage of the alternative approach proposed by Leiper might be that it better represents practical business matters, since it is directly linked to the strategic activities of each business organization. It leads to the concept that tourism tends to be partially industrialized, an idea with implications in business and interorganizational management, in government policy, and in tourism education (Leiper 1990a).

Tourism Systems

Cuervo (1967), Gunn (1972), Leiper (1979; 1990a), Mill and Morrison (1985) and Jafari (1989) have proposed models of tourism systems. Systems thinking has been applied in many fields of research, and as it is specifically useful for understanding complex subjects, it would seem particularly appropriate for the complexities apparent in attempting to study tourism in a comprehensive way. A system, in this formal context, can be defined as a set of elements interacting with one another; an open system is one where the elements, and the system as a whole, are also interacting with environments. Different models indicated above have proposed or implied different elements. In none of them is the systems approach developed to any great detail.

Leiper's (1990a) model of whole tourism systems is described in outline below, and represented in its simplest form, a system of tourism with a single destination region, in Figure 1. Among the others, Jafari's (1989) more detailed model may be most compatible with it. Leiper's model begins with a simple proposition, that tourists are elementary; without at least one person in that role, a tourism system has no empirical basis. The next elements are identified by considering the general pattern of tourists' itineraries. Every tourist's itinerary gives rise to three geographical elements, at least three places in three different roles that occur as a result of trips. The first is a traveler

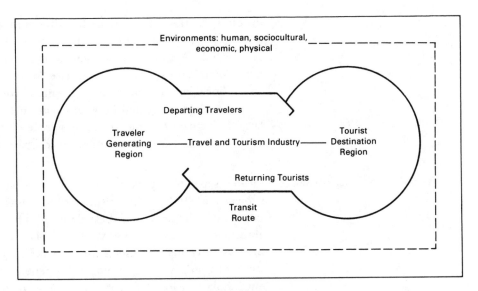

Fig. 1. A basic whole tourism system.

generating region, one per trip, the person's home region, where trips begin and end. It is where motivation forms, where resources to be spent on the trip are accumulated, and also where various sorts of pretrip arrangements are made. Next are places in roles as transit routes, paths along which each traveler must pass in order to reach the focus of each trip. The third geographical element is the most dramatic: in every touristic trip are one or more tourist destination regions, places where travelers are likely to be counted and popularly regarded as tourists, places they choose to visit in order to have touristic experiences of some sort, staying for at least a day before continuing along transit routes to another tourist destination or, finally, back home.

A travel and tourism industry is the remaining element in this model. It comprises organizations in the business and industry of tourism located along the itinerary, in all three geographical elements. Pretrip, in traveler generating regions, it normally includes agents and other travel retailers who help arrange logistics. Along transit routes it may include airlines and other public carriers, as well as transit accommodation. In tourist destinations, it includes accommodation, local tour operators, specialist retailers, restaurants, and entertainment aimed at tourist markets. This systemic approach to identifying a travel and tourism industry is geographically broader that the conventional notion of a tourism industry operating as a discrete unit within a tourist destination.

The primary marketplaces of the travel and tourism industry as a whole are not in tourist destinations, but in traveler generating regions. That is where people make key decisions about trips, so that is where the industry's most important market research is conducted and where its major promotional and distributive activities are staged.

Tourism systems are very open systems. Besides interacting with one another to form a system (tourists interacting with features and characteristics of places in the itinerary; industrial organizations interacting with tourists, and so forth) the system interacts with its environments, of many kinds.

In practice, tourism systems are created (or, more commonly, recreated) by tourists. When they set out, places assume the roles of generating regions, transit routes, and destinations. When they begin using services in tourist markets, the service-based components of the industry begin producing. This indicates an error in Leiper (1979) where "tourism" was defined as a system. A more precise view is to define tourism as the distinctive behavior of tourists, which gives rise to tourism systems.

Worldwide the number of empirical tourism systems is huge, for they are created or re-created by every trip. In terms of tourists' numbers, the largest international tourism systems recently have been those with Germany as the traveler generating country and Spain or Italy as tourist destinations.

Tourism Studies   Ideally, separate expressions refer to the object (tourism) and the academic subject that studies it (tourism studies). How are the objects, the subject matter, of tourism studies best defined? This depends on the perspectives, aims, and values of the individual scholar. The systems model described briefly above may be useful for indicating a comprehensive approach to the study of tourism. An advantage of a general systems approach is that different scholars, using different perspectives or disciplines, may be able to communicate via a general model.

"Tourism systems" has two meanings in that context, empirical and theoretical. The expression can refer to real systems, named by referring to their geographical extremities. Thus the Canada-U.S.A. tourism system has Canada as traveler generating country and the U.S.A. as tourist destination country. For systems with two or more destinations, the extra names are added. The expression's other meaning refers to theoretical systems, useful for abstract research. For example, hypotheses can be expressed in systemic terms, such as "tourists are motivated more by socio-cultural factors in traveler generating regions than by environmental features of tourist destination regions."

A fundamental concept of systems theory is the hierarchy, so that larger systems can be better understood in terms of their component subsystems. One example of this approach to tourism studies is with attraction systems, a subsystem found in all whole tourism systems (Leiper 1990a; 1990b).

The systemic model also allows an ecological approach to understanding the environmental impacts of tourism, for impacts on the environment affecting one element are reflected in opposite impacts affecting others (Jafari 1989; Leiper 1990a). Environmental questions are relevant to two broad themes in tourism studies. One is how environments affect tourism systems, the other is how tourism systems impact on their environments. The former is where the causes of tourism and tourism systems can be discovered; the latter is about effects.

Summary

This entry defines tourist and tourism. It also discusses some concepts that are associated with tourism, including tourist market, tourism industry, tourism system, and tourism studies.

Appendix: International Conference on Travel and Tourism Statistics (Ottawa, Canada, 24–28 June 1991), Conference Resolutions

A. INTRODUCTION

1. **Considering** that the environment for tourism has undergone rapid changes

since the last United Nations Conference on International Travel and Tourism held at Rome in 1963,

2. **Considering** that the development of statistical concepts and frameworks for tourism have not kept pace with this changing environment, and,

3. **Firmly convinced** that a stronger statistical base is essential for a deeper understanding by governments, industries, academia and the public of tourism's contribution to the social, cultural and economic development of all countries in the world,

4. **The World Tourism Organization** and the **Government of Canada** invited participants from the governments, business communities, industry associations, international organizations and academia from all countries to attend the International Conference on Travel and Tourism Statistics, Ottawa, Canada, June 24–28, 1991, to address and bring resolution to the many issues that have inhibited the development of internationally standardized statistics for tourism;

   The Conference,

5. **Convinced** that tourism has become not only a major force in world trade, but also a vital factor in each country's economic, cultural and social development,

6. **Recognizing** that the traditional measures of tourism are not keeping pace with the increasing economic interdependence of all countries and the reduction of political and economic barriers between them,

7. **Aware** that the limited resources for developing statistical programmes make cooperative arrangements between governments and between governments and industry in the gathering and sharing of statistics increasingly necessary,

8. **Considering** that this conference affords a unique opportunity for individual governments, international organizations, industries and industry associations to establish the groundwork for a harmonized statistical base for tourism,

9. **Decides to adopt** an agenda leading to the development of recommended principles and guidelines for the harmonized measurement of all tourism, both within and between countries, that includes adoption of common concepts, definitions and classifications for tourism supply and demand and the assessment of analytic tools such as economic accounts for tourism and performance measures for industry;

10. **Recommends also** the adoption of an Action Plan for implementing the recommendations supported by the Conference and for working towards resolution of those issues that remain outstanding.

B. CRITERIA FOR DEVELOPING COMMON MEASURES OF TOURISM

The Conference,

11. **Notes:**

    (a) that the present requirements for tourism statistics are exceptionally diverse;

    (b) that not only do the National Administrations of each country have requirements for specialized tourism data needs, but that the same holds true for many interest groups, such as industries, industry associations, local communities and academia;

    (c) that these interest groups each have specialized needs for data relating to a wide variety of issues such as market analysis, marketing effectiveness, industrial investment, human resource development, policy analysis, and issue-oriented advocacy;

12. **Notes also** that some countries and industries have already established a wide and diverse range of tourism data sources, with varying concepts and defini-

tions, to meet these diverse needs, while other countries have not yet developed significant statistical systems for tourism;

13. **Recognizes finally** that the development of a common language for tourism statistics in this environment represents a significant need;

14. **Endorses** the following principles for guiding discussions at the Conference and establishing priorities for implementation:

    (a) that the Conference will strive towards concurrence on the key concepts and common definitions that would fit the majority of situations, recognizing that there would be some cases that would require further analysis and study by the World Tourism Organization and other responsible agencies;

    (b) that the recommended definitions and classifications regarding the measurement of tourism should:

        i. be of world-wide practical application, in both the developed and developing countries;

        ii. emphasize simplicity and clarity;

        iii. be limited to strictly statistical purposes; and,

        iv. be consistent with current international standards and classifications in other related areas such as demography, transportation, business, international migration, the balance of payments, the system of national accounts, etc. to the maximum extent possible.

    (c) that the implementation of the Conference resolutions would focus on the evolutionary nature of data systems taking into account the specialized needs for data, the need to minimize respondent burden, the currently vested data infrastructure, and the resources available for further data development, as well as opportunities for cooperative programmes of data collection, shared methodologies and technological or training assistance;

15. **Recommends:**

    (a) that the proposed definitions and classifications be adopted by consensus;

    (b) that the text of these definitions and classifications be widely circulated to all interested parties;

    (c) that a consultation process be established by WTO to enable all interested parties to express their views on these definitions with a view to reaching agreement by the autumn of 1992, prior to their submission to the United Nations Statistical Commission in February 1993.

C. BASIC TOURISM CONCEPTS

The Conference,

16. **Recommends** that tourism be defined as the activities of a person travelling to a place outside his or her usual environment for less than a specified period of time and whose main purpose of travel is other than the exercise of an activity remunerated from within the place visited, where:

    (a) the term "usual environment" is intended to exclude trips within the place of residence (1) and routine trips (2);

    (b) the term "less than a specified period of time" is intended to exclude long-term migration; and

    (c) the term "exercise of an activity remunerated from within the place visited" (3) is intended to exclude only migration for temporary work;

17. **Considers** that this broad concept makes it possible to identify tourism between countries as well as within a country;

18. **Notes** that tourism between countries has been an internationally recognized and measured phenomenon for many decades;

19. **Also notes** that it is only relatively recently that many countries have recognized the importance of assessing tourism activity within a country's borders;

20. **Decides to adopt** a standardized terminology for the statistics used to describe and assess both aspects of tourism;

21. **Recognizes** that the initiating event that ultimately defines tourism is a demand-side concept; and

22. **Recommends** that in order to compare tourism activities with the economic activity of other industries, it is also important to define and develop the supply side of tourism statistics;

23. **Deeply conscious** that the term "domestic" ("intérieur" in French and "interior" in Spanish) to identify tourism within the country is in such prevalent common usage that changing the use of the term to a more economic orientation could cause *some* confusion,

24. **Recommends** that, in conformity with the economic accounting terms in general use, the following common terminology be adopted to describe the three basic categories of tourism:

   (a) *"domestic tourism"* which comprises "internal tourism" ("interne" in French and "interno" in Spanish) and "inbound tourism" ("récepteur" in French and "receptor" in Spanish), where "internal tourism" refers to residents of a country visiting their own country and "inbound tourism" refers to visits to a country by non-residents;

   (b) *"national tourism"* which comprises "internal tourism" and "outbound tourism" ("tourisme émetteur" in French and "turismo emisor" in Spanish), where "outbound tourism" refers to residents of a country visiting other countries; and,

   (c) *"international tourism"* which consists of "inbound tourism" and "outbound tourism";

25. **Also recommends** the collection of statistics from both the demand and supply sides by means of common classification systems for both these components of the tourism activity.

D. BREAKDOWN OF THE VARIOUS CATEGORIES OF DEMAND-SIDE TOURISM

The Conference,

26. **Noting** that consumption patterns for tourism are becoming more complex as the volume and variety of internal and international tourism rapidly increases,

27. **Noting also** that there are several factors leading to such increases: technological change in the travel industry is making travel more comfortable and affordable; the political and economic barriers to international travel are being reduced; increased personal incomes and more leisure time are making leisure travel more feasible on a wider scale; and the globalization of business is demanding a greater degree of business travel,

28. **Recommends** use of a common typology of tourism consumption that would serve both to make international comparisons and to assess the national contribution and impact of tourism;

29. **Recommends:**
   (a) that the World Tourism Organization submit the following basic definitions to the United Nations Statistical Commission for endorsement;
   (b) that the text of these definitions be annexed to the text of the recommendations; and
   (c) that National Administrations adopt these definitions as the core measurement for tourism demand;

TERMS	INTERNATIONAL (INBOUND AND OUTBOUND) TOURISM	INTERNAL TOURISM
Resident	A person is considered to be resident in a country if he has lived in that country for at least a year or twelve consecutive months prior to his arrival in another country for a period not exceeding one year.	A person is considered to be resident in a place if the person has lived in that place at least six consecutive months prior to his arrival at another place in the same country for a period not exceeding six months.
Visitor	A person who travels to a country other than that in which he has his usual residence and that is outside his usual environment, for a period not exceeding one year, and whose main purpose of visit is other than the exercise of an activity remunerated from within the country visited.	A person residing in a country, who travels to a place within the country, but outside his usual environment, for a period not exceeding six months, and whose main purpose of visit is other than the exercise of an activity remunerated from within the place visited.
Tourist	A visitor who travels to a country other than that in which he has his usual residence for at least one night but not more than one year, and whose main purpose of visit is other than the exercise of an activity remunerated from within the country visited.	A visitor residing in a country, who travels to a place within the country, but outside his usual environment, for at least one night but not more than six months, and whose main purpose of visit is other than the exercise of an activity remunerated from within the place visited.
Excursionist (Same-day visitor)	A visitor who travels to a country other than that in which he has his usual residence, and that is outside his usual environment, for less than 24 hours without spending the night in the country visited, and whose main purpose of visit is other than the exercise of an activity remunerated from within the country visited.	A visitor residing in a country who travels to a place within the country, but outside his usual environment, for less than 24 hours without spending the night in the place visited, and whose main purpose of visit is other than the exercise of an activity remunerated from within the place visited.

30. Feels that, owing to the importance of the phenomenon of short stays in developed countries, the "tourist" category should be classified more specifically, distinguishing for pleasure tourism (internal and international);

   (a) "holiday-maker", being a tourist who remains in a place for more than a certain number of nights or days; and

   (b) "short-term tourist", being a tourist who travels for a period of time not exceeding this limit but lasting more than 24 hours and involving at least one night's stay.

E. TRIP CLASSIFICATIONS

The Conference,

31. **Recommends** that the main purpose of visit be classified under the following three groups:

   (a) pleasure: leisure, culture, active sports, visits to relatives and friends, other;

   (b) professional: meeting, mission, business;

(c) other purposes: studies, health, transit, various;

32. **Also recommends** that national tourism statistical programmes progressively use classifications according to purpose of visit, length of stay or trip, origin and destination of trip, means of transport and type of accommodation, as modified by the Conference.

F. EXPENDITURE

The Conference,

33. **Recognizing** that the concept of expenditure is closely linked to that of tourism consumption, defined as the value of goods and services used for the direct satisfaction of visitors,

34. **Recommends** that tourism expenditure be defined as "any expenditure incurred by or for a visitor for his trip";

35. **Recommends** the following definitions for international tourism receipts and expenditure:

(a) International tourism receipts are defined as the receipts of a country resulting from the tourism expenditure of international visitors;

(b) International tourism expenditure is defined as tourism expenditure made by residents travelling abroad as visitors;

36. **Also recommends:**

(a) that receipts and expenditure generated by same-day visitors (excursionists) be classified separately;

(b) that tourism receipts and expenditure include payments for international transport of visitors; and

(c) that, for the sake of consistency with the balance of payments recommendations of the International Monetary Fund, international fare receipts and expenditure be classified separately.

G. GEOGRAPHICAL AGGREGATIONS

The Conference,

37. **Notes** that the standard practice of the United Nations is to publish geographical data with the following proviso: "Neither the designation employed, nor the presentation of material in this publication, implies any expression of opinion by the reporting organization regarding the legal status of country, territory or area, or of its authorities, or concerning the delimitation of its frontier or boundaries";

38. **Considers** that, with the advent of computers, it would be possible to report tourism data coded at the level of the reporting country or area and present it in that form to the World Tourism Organization. The various geographical aggregations can be derived depending on the analytic purpose.

H. DEFINITION OF SAME-DAY VISITS

The Conference,

39. **Notes** that, given the changing behaviour of consumers, the ever-improving technology for travel, which makes travelling over greater distances possible, and the increasing pressures of time, same-day visits are growing in importance as a part of tourism;

40. **Suggests** that the overall concept for same-day visits should be similar to that for tourism: that is, a non-routine break away from the usual environment;

41. **Recommends** that business trips of a non-routine nature be included in the concept of same-day visits and identified separately;

42. **Also recommends** that a distinction be made between the two main types of same-day travel:

(a) International same-day travel, which comprises the travel of those who have crossed an international frontier for activities of a non-routine nature;

(b) Internal same-day travel, which is more complex to define because of the lack of a delineating frontier. The use of thresholds regarding both duration and distance of travel would aid international comparability;

43. **Recognizes** the difficulty of developing effective and comparable measures for same-day visits, particularly within a country;

44. **Considers** that same-day visits would best be defined by a series of characteristics focused on the following criteria:

(a) Round trip
(b) Duration
(c) Distance;

45. **Recommends** that, for the sake of international comparison, minimum thresholds be established for round trip, distance and duration;

46. **Recognizing,** however, that the current inconsistency among countries needing and able to measure same-day visits makes effective international comparison difficult,

47. **Recommends** that data on this phenomenon be reported as a separate subset of tourism.

I. CLASSIFICATION OF TOURISM SUPPLY ACTIVITIES

The Conference,

48. **Convinced** that, while tourism cannot abandon the demand-based definition of its scope, it must seek to more clearly delineate a supply-based structure for its activities,

49. **Firmly convinced** that an internationally compatible standard activity classification system is essential to the proper and effective statistical representation of tourism,

50. **Recognizing** that any such classification system should be coordinated and integrated with the internationally-established systems, such as the Revised System of National Accounts and the Balance of Payments Manual,

51. **Also recognizing** that the WTO-developed Standard International Classification of Tourism Activities (SICTA) demonstrates that a supply-oriented activity structure, responsive to the needs of tourism as well as to the needs for consistency with other classification systems can, with suitable modifications, be constructed,

52. **Recommends:**

(a) that national tourism programmes seek to establish tourism-responsive activity classifications within their national statistical systems that are harmonious with ISIC;

(b) that any future development of tourism classification systems include classifications for functions, transactions and products as well as activities and that, in accordance with United Nations recommendations, the Central Product Classification System (CPC) be placed at the centre of the classification system;

(c) that the SICTA be modified to distinguish direct tourism consumption from the indirect effects of such consumption; and,

(d) that the SICTA code structure be modified to achieve comparability with

NACE (European Activity Nomenclature) before the classification is submitted to the United Nations for endorsement in 1993.

J. TOURISM SATELLITE ACCOUNTS

The Conference,

53. **Supports** the development of tourism Satellite Accounts in the framework of the System of National Accounts, deriving from it its main aggregates and basic concepts and allowing a better presentation of economic information;

54. **Recognizes** that the tourism Satellite Accounts will afford the following benefits:

    (a) reconciliation of the demand-side data with supply-side data within the Account brings greater coherence to definition of the industry;

    (b) use of a recognized accounting system bring enhanced credibility to the economic analysis of the industry;

    (c) use of an accounting framework can bring other important information into the analysis of tourism, such as data on value added, human resources development or financial flows;

    (d) the accounting framework would provide a useful guide to the development of primary data sources;

55. **Emphasizes** the extensive and innovative work by Canada in developing an overall tourism information system which incorporates a monetary account as well as other information on the volume and characteristics of the tourism industry;

56. **Recognizes** nevertheless the practical restrictions in implementing an accounting system, viz:

    (a) an initial base of reasonably reliable data from the supply side as well as from the demand side is necessary to make the investment in developing a Satellite Account worthwhile; and that

    (b) countries with an established System of National Accounts have an advantage in fostering the development of Satellite Accounts;

57. **Recommends:**

    (a) that the concept of a Satellite Accounting System be supported; and

    (b) that countries introduce the accounting systems into their analytic base for tourism data on an incremental basis as resources become available and the demand for this type of information is realized;

58. **Feels** that, for the implementation of the System, the OECD Manual could provide a useful and practical starting point.

K. MEASURING INDUSTRY PERFORMANCE

The Conference,

59. **Recommends** that a relatively small number of indicators be developed as soon as possible to permit comparative analysis of past performance, trends and forecasts of the industry worldwide;

60. **Recommends** that the range of performance indicators introduced by representatives of the transport, accommodation and attractions sectors of the industry provide the basis for further development, by an interdisciplinary group, before implementation.

L. WORK PROGRAMME FOR TOURISM MARKETING AND ECONOMIC STATISTICS

The Conference,

61. **Recognizing** that limited resources require countries to achieve efficiency in

expenditure on tourism marketing and on collection of marketing and economic impact statistics,

62. **Recommends** that a phased programme of improvements in tourism statistics be adopted by all countries;

63. **Feeling** that this programme should guide countries:

   (a) in maximizing the net economic contribution of tourism to the welfare of their citizens, recognizing that resources and stages of tourism product development vary from country to country,

   (b) in improving a nation's understanding of internal and international tourism markets,

   (c) in identifying target markets most likely to respond to its marketing efforts, and

   (d) in maximizing the positive net return on tourism marketing expenditure,

64. **Recommends** the adoption of the proposed phased programmes of tourism marketing and economic impact statistics and that:

   (a) developing countries adopt as a priority, the basic marketing statistics and economic impact statistics programmes and prepare to adopt the intermediate programmes,

   (b) developed countries adopt, as a priority the intermediate programmes and plan for adoption of the advanced programme as soon as resources permit,

   (c) all countries observe standard criteria for quality control in developing these data; and

   (d) all countries report their tourism statistics in a timely fashion to the World Tourism Organization and work to improve the Organization's bank of tourism statistics;

65. **Agrees** that work should soon commence on expanding this phased programme to include the development and implementation of standard measures of the environmental impact of tourism that can be applied in all countries.

M. ACTION PLAN

The Conference,

66. **Recognizing** that implementation of the recommendations would be the primary responsibility of the World Tourism Organization, in close cooperation with other competent international and regional organizations, as well as industries and international industry associations and, above all, individual countries,

67. **Recommends** that WTO:

   (a) submit to the United Nations Statistical Commission, for endorsement, a report developed in accordance with the appropriate procedures and format and setting forth:

      i. the broad concept of tourism, as developed by this Conference;

      ii. a classification system and definitions for the demand-side of tourism as outlined in the report;

      iii. the WTO-developed SICTA, with the modifications recommended in this report, as an appropriate provisional classification system for use by countries in incorporating tourism into the ISIC, given that a tourism-responsive International System of Industrial Classification (ISIC) is essential to the effective statistical description of the industry;

   (b) coordinate its activities with those of other international institutions, mainly regional, for the implementation of the Conference recommendations;

(c) publish and distribute the proceedings of the Conference, based on this report and with the modified Appendices for classification systems for the demand and supply sides of tourism;

(d) develop a series of technical manuals and guidelines to assist countries in the implementation of the recommendations;

(e) undertake a series of workshops and technical meetings at the regional level to assist countries direct in implementing the recommendations in accordance with their specific requirements;

(f) act as an adviser, clearing-house and coordinator to:

    i. further develop harmonized statistical bases for tourism and refine and implement the recommended classification systems and economic accounting frameworks for tourism; and

    ii. identify training needs of individual countries, and particularly those of the developing countries, for the implementation of the recommendations and encourage and foster cooperative assistance to those countries;

(g) institute a process of periodic review and refinement of the recommended classification systems to ensure responsiveness to changing needs and priorities;

68. **Recommends** further that the World Tourism Organization establish a committee composed of a small number of representatives of governments, international organizations and the tourism industry to carry out a concrete work programme leading to approval of the recommendations by the Untied Nations Statistical Office and implementation of the other recommendations of the Conference;

69. **Urges** countries to adopt the recommendations of the report, insofar as they are compatible with their own needs and possible within their available resources. . . .

Notes to items 16(a) and 16(b) on page 550:

(1) Relates to the area of usual residence.

(2) Relates to frequent and regular community trips between the domicile and the workplace and other community trips of a routine character.

(3) By an economic agent resident in the place.

References

Bain, Keith, and Peter Howell. 1988. *Understanding Markets: An Introduction to the Theory, Institutions and Practices of Markets*. London: Harvester-Wheatsheaf.

Burkart, A. J. 1981a. Tourism—a service industry? *Tourism Management* 2(1):2.

Burkart, A. J. 1981b. How far is tourism a trade or an industry? *Tourism Management* 2(2):146.

Burkart, A. J., and S. Medlik. 1974. *Tourism: Past, Present and future*. London: Heinemann.

Cohen, Eric. 1979. Rethinking the sociology of tourism. *Annals of Tourism Research* 6:18–35.

Cuervo, Raimondo. 1967. *Tourism as a Medium for Human Communication*. Itaxapalapa: Mexican Government Department of Tourism.

Defoe, Daniel, 1720. *A Tour Through The Whole Island of Britain*. (various modern editions).

de Kadt, Emmanuel, ed. 1979. *Tourism—Passport to Development?* Washington, D.C.: Oxford Univ. Press.

Fussell, Paul. 1980. *Abroad: British Literary Traveling Between the Wars*. New York: Oxford University Press.

Gunn, Clare. 1972. *Vacationscape: Designing Tourist Regions*. Austin: University of Texas.

Gronhaug, Kjell, and Nikhilesh Dholakia. 1987. Consumers, markets and supply systems: a perspective on marketization and its effects. In *Philosophical and Radical Thought in Marketing*, ed. A. Fuat Firat, Nikhilesh Dholakia, and Richard P. Bagozzi, pp. 3–14. Lexington, Mass.: Lexington Books.

Jafari, Jafar, 1977. Editorial. *Annals of Tourism Research* 5:6–11.

Jafari, Jafar. 1989. Structure of tourism. In *Tourism Marketing and Management Handbook*, ed. Stephen F. Witt and Luiz Moutinho, pp. 437–442. Englewood Cliffs, N.J.: Prentice-Hall.

Kaiser, Charles, Jr., and Larry E. Helber. 1978. *Tourism Planning and Development*. Boston: C.B.I.

Kaul, R. 1985. *Tourism, A Trilogy: Volume One—The Phenomenon*. New Delhi: Sterling.

Krippendorf, Jost, 1987. *The Holidaymakers: Understanding the Impacts of Leisure and Travel*. London: Heinemann (first pub. 1984, trans. from German by Vera Andrassy).

Leiper, Neil, 1979. The framework of tourism: towards a definition of tourism, tourist and the tourist industry. *Annals of Tourism Research* 6:390–407.

Leiper, Neil. 1990a. *Tourism Systems: An Interdisciplinary Perspective*. Palmerston North, New Zealand: Massey University.

Leiper, Neil. 1990b. Tourist attraction systems. *Annals of Tourism Research* 17:367–384.

MacCannell, Dean. 1976. *The Tourist: A New Theory of the Leisure Class*. New York: Schoken.

Mill, Robert Christie, and Alastair Morrison. 1985. *The Tourism System*. Englewood Cliffs, N.J.: Prentice-Hall.

OECD. 1974. *Tourism and Tourism Policy in Member Countries*. Paris: Organization for Economic Cooperation and Development.

Przeclawski, Krzysztof. 1986. *Humanistic Foundations of Tourism*. Warsaw: Institute of Tourism.

Smith, Stephen L. J. 1990. *Dictionary of Concepts in Recreation and Leisure Studies*. Westport: Greenwood Press.

World Tourism Organization. 1983 *Definitions Concerning Tourism Statistics*. Madrid: WTO.

Wykes, Alan. ed. 1973. *Abroad: A Miscellany of English Travel Writing 1700–1914*. London: MacDonald.

2

Leisure, Recreation, and Tourism

Laurel J. Reid, Robert W. McLellan, and Muzaffer Uysal

Lazarus Long, oldest member of the human race by virtue of a unique set of chromosomes, clonal and other rejuvenation techniques, has an inexhaustible zest for life (Heinlein 1978). His observations engendered over the thousands of years of his external existence chronicle his ironic appreciation of the successes and failures of human society. Lazarus Long has developed a finely tuned sense of rational self-interest from which his observations are honed.

Many of his observations are appropriate for introspection of our discipline of leisure, recreation, and tourism. We can use these as a springboard to contrast prevailing leisure philosophies and practices; to comment on the status of recreation and tourism as subdisciplines of leisure; and to make pedagogic conclusions regarding the mission of leisure recreation and tourism.

Two such observations follow:

> A human being should be able to change a diaper, plan an invasion, butcher a hog, conn a ship, design a building, write a sonnet, balance accounts, build a wall, set a bone, comfort the dying, take orders, give orders, cooperate, act along, solve equations, analyze a new problem, pitch manure, program a computer, cook a tasty meal, fight efficiently, die gallantly. Specialization is for insects. (Heinlein 1978:10)
>
> The difference between science and the fuzzy subjects is that science requires reasoning, while those other subjects merely require scholarship. (Heinlein 1978:13)

Two immediate questions arise: Are we more analogous to Long's "human beings" or "insects?" Is the overall profession of leisure, recreation, and tourism to be considered as a "science" or a "fuzzy subject?" Based on exploration of these questions, can we then move to a paradigm of leisure, recreation, and tourism; or can we decide if such a paradigm is necessary or desirable?

Leisure, recreation, and tourism students may initially feel dismay that these fields seem to have no true paradigm(s) of their own. This deficiency reflects the search for definitions, not only for recreation and tourism, but also their umbrella domain, leisure. Consequently, defining leisure becomes paramount in assessing its connection with recreation and tourism.

What Is Leisure?

There are essentially five different concepts of leisure. The first represents a work/nonwork dichotomy (Veblen 1899), with leisure constituting free, residual, or discretionary time—available after subsistence and other survival duties are accomplished (Clawson 1964, Weiss 1964, Brightbill 1960). This concept denotes an obvious relationship to "clock time" (Murphy 1975) and represents an objective framework by which leisure can be measured (Neulinger 1974). Although useful, this view is narrow, time-bound, and does not distinguish adequately between "work" and "job." The need exists for a more cyclical and personal focus involving the many dimensions of play, education, and work to give us both a more expanded and meaningful conceptualization and time reference.

Both de Grazia (1962) and Pieper (1952) embrace an Aristotelian perspective in the classical view, where leisure is a state of being (or mind). This orientation places high value on contemplative pursuits. Activity is performed for its own sake and own end. However, these notions make it difficult to clarify the concept; its evasive nature presents difficulties in deriving operational definitions.

A third orientation sees leisure as a social instrument. It is viewed as purposive; it serves to meet needs of the poor, ill, disabled, and deprived. This approach enables the latter groups to actualize social needs and develop self-help skills (Frye and Peters 1972, Kraus 1984). Albeit therapeutic, leisure in this context is narrowly defined since it ignores potential benefits to other populations.

The antiutilitarian concept views leisure as a state of mind, representing a worthy end in itself. This approach rejects the work ethic as the "only" source of value. There is no need to produce a useful end product as a result of energy expenditure. The only premise is that investment in self pursuits will yield an expression of self and seek joy, harmony, and pleasure (Gray 1973, Kerr 1962).

The holistic approach represents a synthesis of the above concepts. It is more encompassing and articulates leisure as a multidimensional construct (Bacon 1972) that embraces a complete range of self-determined activities and experiences. The concept is not simply activity-based, but includes time and attitudes toward activities relevant to both work and nonwork. Leisure thus incorporates choices that reflect individual and societal aspirations as well as lifestyles (Hendricks and Burdge 1972). The main consequence of fusing work and leisure is to improve each so that both are individually fulfilling (Murphy 1975).

Although the notion of discretionary time dominates scholarly approaches to leisure, the holistic notion is more self-deterministic and recognizes leisure as that time to be used at the individual's discretion, which encompasses both work and nonwork. Notwithstanding its subjective nature, the latter framework at least ascertains that leisure involves a sense of freedom, intrinsic motivation, enjoyment, and relaxation (Mannell and Iso-Ahola 1987).

Leisure: The Fit with Recreation and Tourism

To the individual, tourism and recreation represent experiences. If the holistic notion of leisure is extended to these subfields, both can be broadly defined. A holistic view of tourism incorporates the "study of [people] away from their usual habitats, of the industry which responds to their needs, and of the impacts that both people and the industry have on the host (sociocultural, economic, and physical) environments" (Jafari 1977:8). This concept encompasses attitudinal and behavioral components that fit within the leisure domain. Recreation can be viewed as a goal-directed human experience best understood from a perspective that shows "the interrelationships of the agency, the participant, the physical environment, and the social environment" (Murphy 1975). Murphy (1975) further states that recreation ingredients are exploratory, investigative, manipulative, and epistemic behaviors when the concept of leisure service functions to produce optimal arousal. The same can be said for tourism.

Although there is still no universally accepted definition or accepted rationale for either recreation or tourism, one can conclude that travelers often participate in recreation activities; in this sense, both travel and recreation are part of the satisfaction sought (Kelly 1987). While some characterize tourism as a component of recreation (Murphy 1985), this entry views both tourism and recreation as collateral areas falling into leisure's domain (see Figure 1). As depicted, recreation and tourism are cojoined. Much of recreation involves tourism in one form or another and vice versa. A major difference between the two is depicted where locally provided and patronized recreation falls outside tourism's realm. By the same token, business travel, under the auspices of tourism, can occur distinctly outside the tenets of recreation and leisure. Arguably, the time devoted to traveling for business reasons may serve to "re-create"; and elements of leisure and recreation are often incorporated into business trips. "For example, while the primary trip purpose may be attending a convention, . . . this may be integrated with pleasure activities" (Crompton 1990). However, travel undertaken strictly for business purposes is devoid of the primary leisure and recreation concerns or motivations.

The definitional problems with leisure, recreation, and tourism have "hindered many attempts at clarifying and specifying any theoretical relationships between the three concepts" (Fedler 1987:313). The vast amount of literature in the fields assumes overlap in the three areas and brings up a number of questions as to their interrelationships, but few answers are provided. As Harris et al. (1987) reiterated, there is currently little basis for building a theory that clarifies their linkages. Others argue the relevance of such distinctions and linkages are essential.

Traditionally, there has been a gulf between leisure and recreation on the one hand, tourism on the other. Tourism is viewed as more applied, connoting the "tourism industry" and involving essentially private commerce. Recreation, on the other hand, has focused on management situations and issues confronting the public sector (community and land management agencies) (Harris et al. 1987). The practice of providing "tourism" has often not

Fig. 1. Interrelationships between leisure, recreation, and tourism (Murphy 1985; Mieczkowski 1981).

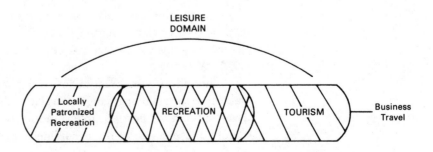

been integrated into studies by leisure and recreation scholars even though the fields share a common ground in their focus on management. One needs only to remember that the "great" theoreticians in the management field (for example, Fayol, Taylor, Babbage, Dupin) were in fact, practicing managers, not academicians.

The synthesis between common elements of the two subfields, however, cannot be denied. For example, it is commonly recognized that outdoor recreation attractions are a major purpose of leisure travel (Gunn 1979) and that natural settings and recreation opportunities they provide are often major tourist destinations (Rosenow and Pulsipher 1979). Moreover, the advances in defining leisure and recreation experiences can bring much added depth to understanding tourist experiences (Mannell and Iso-Ahola 1987). Similarly, developments in defining spatial configurations and economic transactions of the tourism industry would add substantially to the understanding of leisure and recreation (Jansen-Verbeke and Dietvorst 1987).

The battle for academic hegemony is even more pronounced by the fact that an understanding of the three areas requires the use and application of concepts, theories, practices, and analytical tools from a broad variety of disciplines, including anthropology, psychology, sociology, geography, history, economics, business management, and forestry.

Insects vs. Humans; Science vs. Fuzzy Subjects

The brief catalogue of disciplines contributing to the study of leisure, recreation, and tourism provides evidence of the interest in the subject area (see for example Perdue et al. 1988). Concerns about this area of study reflect a legitimate fear that the discipline is so all-pervasive that it cuts across any single disciplinary area; and thus does not and cannot have paradigms of its own. However, it is these very concerns that justify the subject being given separate attention and distinction as a field of inquiry. The multidisciplinary nature suggests the subject can be extremely broad in the areas from which it selects approaches, but virtuous in its content (the self-determined use of leisure for recreation and tourism).

Given both the strong connections between leisure, recreation, and tourism and the field's multidisciplinary nature, it is clear that a narrow view of the field is analogous with Lazarus's "insects." The need to be eclectic is obvious. Specialization not only limits initiative, it also chokes self-expression and requires that people use only a few of their abilities. As Adam Smith (1776) commented during the preindustrial era:

> The [individual] whose life is spent in performing a few simple operations . . . naturally loses the habit of (mental) exertion and generally becomes as stupid and ignorant as it is possible for a human creature to become . . . Dexterity at [one's] own particular trade seems . . . to be acquired at the expense of intellectual and social virtues. (Cited in Miller and Robinson, 1963:340)

This observation is equally true today. "The supreme specialist of an industrial era, both in work and leisure, has only marginal value in a postindustrial society, in which each element contributes to an organic whole" (Murphy 1975:196).

Individuals who practice in leisure, recreation, and tourism are, a priori, subject to the accompanying interrelationships. In order to be creative, innovative, and find the best possible solutions, we must be broadly acquainted with theory and practice of the disciplines from which we draw. This holistic orientation permits us to bring the paradigms and solutions from other fields and assess their usefulness in leisure, recreation, and tourism. Although specialization was well-placed during the industrial era, today's service and technological age demands knowledge from various fields. This feature indicates that the task of educating and training professionals must be broad in scope.

Leisure, recreation, and tourism is a complex and dynamic area of study. The definitional problems of a field still in its infancy make it difficult to assess which dimensions are crucial and which means of investigation are most useful. As McLellan (1980) stresses, leisure science should be regarded as a profession based on scientific reasoning, not merely a fuzzy subject. But the field's multidisciplinary nature often poses concern for those outside the field in designating leisure, recreation, and tourism as a "science."

Science requires reasoning and involves objective, systematic investigations into natural phenomena. Science is guided by theory; its basic aim is to understand relationships in order to establish theoretical frameworks. The relevance of many disciplines hinders acceptance of leisure, recreation, and tourism in the scientific arena. But the field's utilization of scientific approaches from other well-established disciplines in attempts to build theory, can be construed as "fuzzy" rather than "scientific."

A fuzzy subject is analogous to a fuzzy set. The latter are "classes where there are no clear-cut distinctions between membership and nonmembership" (VanDoorn 1982:151). However, one can specify a fuzzy set by breaking down the overall concept (for example, leisure) into its constituent elements. If one deletes all the nonapplicable elements from the set and validates a sufficient number of dimensions, the area's underlying foundations can be identified and its generative power enhanced (VanDoorn 1982, Cohen 1974). Given the eclectic nature of the field, such a task appears onerous, if not impossible.

The difficulty in categorizing the discipline as a science lies in the fact that while many other disciplines have boundaries, the scope of leisure, recreation, and tourism is still unknown. Unsure of the parameters of our object of inquiry, we apply familiar limits. We seek to identify, compartmentalize, and narrow the concepts. But this orientation, for the moment, may be misplaced. When parameters are ill-defined, complementary explanations drawn from other areas need synthesis; conflicts need resolution. Consequently, "the trend of subdividing a field may have to be reversed—at least for the moment—if we are to 'do science', if we are to produce coherent and plausible explanations" (Kelly 1987:iv).

We need to continue to explore the wide theoretical basis for leisure, recreation, and tourism. The superiority of any single paradigm cannot be presumed. The need to regard the discipline from various perspectives and identify interrelationships is critical. At the same time, if we are to build on theory, we must analyze and synthesize, manipulating and appreciating the work already conducted in other disciplines.

Pedagogic Concerns

Given the considerations raised above, can we adequately provide a leisure, recreation, and tourism framework? Can we look at ourselves as "human beings" as opposed to "insects?" The answer is yes, or at least, we can begin. How then, can an educational institution move from the status quo to ideal within the current missions of education, research, and public service? The following recommendations embrace the tenets previously presented.

Education Educators must systematically incorporate other relevant disciplines into the study of leisure, recreation, and tourism (LRT), offering such courses as the psychology of LRT, the sociology of LRT, geography of LRT, management of LRT, and so on. Undeniably, turf disputes will arise using this approach, but working with—not against—those in other areas will enable students to graduate with the knowledge to deal effectively in today's world. "Advanced" education connotes an education whereby a person has access to many disciplines, who can be deployed in a broad field, who can maintain liaisons, and who has an overview of the whole field (Bodewes 1981).

A commercial/economic or vocational emphasis on tourism tends to ignore its interdependency with leisure and recreation. However tourism cannot be taught purely as an abstract academic subject. There must be a combination and balance between conceptual learning and skill development (Jafari and Ritchie 1981) necessary to effectively perform on the job. Graduates need to be able to see parts of a situation, determine how these parts interact, and decide how to assemble these parts into a total framework.

From a pedagogical standpoint, leisure, recreation, and tourism is multidisciplinary. Consequently, teachers and students must have knowledge of the varied disciplines that contribute to solving a problem (Jafari and Ritchie 1981:24). This feature makes the subject difficult to teach since "professors and students must know not only problem solving techniques, but also where to search among the disciplines for contributions" (Meeth 1978:10). This implies that teachers must be resource persons, broadly acquainted with theory and practice in many fields. In some cases, this may mean teacher retooling in order to become acquainted with pertinent aspects of other disciplines.

Research Leisure and recreation research has proceeded in one direction, while tourism has proceeded in the other. This gulf must close so that each area can draw and learn from the others, build on past research, identify interrelationships, and delineate relevant frameworks.

The interrelationships between leisure, recreation, and tourism have been largely assumed, ignored, and/or unspecified given the associated definitional problems. Sound conceptual and theoretical development in future research will require an integration of research in these three areas. These challenges strongly prescribe the need to wend our way through the multidisciplinary labyrinth by providing focused and systematic research that specifies the interrelationships between tourism, leisure, and recreation, and builds on theories and approaches drawn from the numerous disciplines applicable to tourism, leisure, and recreation study.

Scholars and researchers can provide private and public tourism organizations with theoretical constructs relevant to practice. However, our ability to cut through the research maze depends on whether we build on past research efforts and how we develop and extend the body of knowledge in the leisure, recreation, and tourism field. We can indeed approach the status of "science" rather than investigating in the realm of "fuzziness."

Service The focus on providing leisure activities designed to fulfill expressed community needs and interests limits the goals of agencies. This view also restricts services to delivery of activity opportunities with little or no regard for the influence such activities have on the participants. Those planning recreation programs and tourist facilities must intimately know the cultures, wishes, social patterns, and life-styles of the people who use them so that programs and services fit the leisure needs of these publics. It is the job of scientists and educational institutions to disseminate information to both public and private sectors—to show the value of understanding patrons and provide planners/programmers with the framework and tools necessary to obtain this knowledge.

Summary

It is clear from the current ideology of leisure, recreation, and tourism that we need to strive toward a view that is both functional in today's world and serviceable from a pedagogical and scientific point of view. Given that the study of leisure, recreation, and tourism can only be properly addressed using a variety of disciplines, the field quite rightfully deserves special attention as a field of scholarly inquiry and professional activity. The initial dismay of leisure, recreation, and tourism students regarding the field's lack of paradigms should be somewhat subdued. They too are part of the demand for knowledge that links various disciplines and professions, in search for a holistic approach. The mastery of one discipline is not relevant in our field. The challenge is to merge the mastery of interrelated disciplines and the acquisition of the skills necessary to manage leisure, tourism, and recreation enterprises in the future.

The quest for a heuristically useful ideology of leisure, recreation, and tourism ultimately leads to some ideological questions about the field. No one solution suffices. We must examine our traditional opinions concerning the nature and interrelationships of leisure, tourism, and recreation. Whatever the outcome of these decisions, they too will be expressed in an ideology of leisure, recreation, and tourism and will require an ongoing, rational, and systematic reexamination—features that are essential to Lazarus Long's humanization and scientific concepts.

References

Bacon, A. W. 1972. Leisure and research: a critical review of the main concepts employed in contemporary research. *Society and Leisure* 4:83–92.

Bodewes, T. G. W. 1981. Development of advanced tourism studies in Holland. *Annals of Tourism Research* 8(1):35–51.

Brightbill, C. K. 1960. *The Challenge of Leisure.* Englewood Cliffs, N.J.: Prentice-Hall.

Clawson, M. 1964. How much leisure, now and in the future? *Leisure in America: Blessing or Curse?* ed. J. Charlesworth. Philadelphia, Pa.: American Academy of Political Science.

Cohen, E. 1974. Who is a tourist: a conceptual clarification. *The Sociological Review* 22:527–555.

Crompton, John L. 1990. Claiming our share of the tourism dollar. *Parks and Recreation Magazine* 25(3):41–88. Washington, D.C. National Recreation and Park Association.

de Grazia, S. 1962. *Of Time, Work and Leisure.* Hartford, Conn.: Connecticut Printers.

Fedler, A. J. 1987. Introduction: are leisure, recreation, and tourism interrelated. *Annals of Tourism Research* 14(3):311–313.

Frye, V., and M. Peters. 1972. *Therapeutic Recreation: Its Theory, Philosophy and Practice,* Harrisburg, Pa.: Stackpole Books.

Gray, D. 1973. This alien thing called leisure. In *Reflections of the Recreation and Park Movement,* eds. D. Gray and D. Peligrino. Dubuque, Iowa: Wm. C. Brown Publishers.

Gunn, C. A. 1979. *Tourism Planning.* New York: Crane, Russak and Co.

Harris, C., W. McLaughlin, and S. Ham. 1987. Integration of recreation and tourism in Idaho. *Annals of Tourism Research* 14(3):405–419.

Heinlein, Robert A. 1978. *The Notebooks of Lazarus Long.* New York: G. P. Putnam & Sons.

Hendricks, J., and R. J. Burdge. 1972. The nature of leisure research: a reflection and comment. *Journal of Leisure Research* 4:216.

Jafari, J. 1977. Editor's Page. *Annals of Tourism Research* 5:6–11.

Jafari, J., and J. R. Brent Ritchie. 1981. Toward a framework for tourism education: problems and prospects. *Annals of Tourism Research* 8(1):13–34.

Jansen-Verbeke, M., and A. Dietvorst. 1987. Leisure, recreation, tourism: a geographic view on integration. *Annals of Tourism Research* 14(3):361–375.

Kelly, J. R. 1987. *Freedom to Be: a New Sociology of Leisure.* New York: MacMillan.

Kerr, W. 1962. *The Decline of Pleasure.* New York: Simon and Schuster.

Kraus, R. 1984. *Recreation and Leisure in Modern Society,* 3rd ed. Illinois: Scott, Foresman and Company.

Mannell, R. C., and S. E. Iso-Ahola. 1987. Psychological nature of leisure and tourism experience. *Annals of Tourism Research* 14(3):314–331.

McLellan, R. 1980. . . . Research *Parks and Recreation* 15:7.

Meeth, L. R. 1978. Interdisciplinary studies: a matter of definition. *Change* 10 (August): 8–21.

Mieczkowski, Z. T. 1981. Some notes on the geography of tourism: a comment. *Canadian Geographer* 25:186–191.

Miller, N. P., and D. M. Robinson. 1963. *The Leisure Age.* Belmont, Calif.: Wadsworth Publishing Co.

Murphy, James F. 1975. *Recreation and Leisure Service: A Humanistic Perspective.* Dubuque, Iowa.: Wm. C. Brown Co. Publishers.

Murphy, P. E. 1985. *Tourism: A Community Approach.* New York: Methuen and Co.

Neulinger, J. 1974. *The Psychology of Leisure.* Springfield, Ill.: Charles C Thomas Publisher.

Perdue, Richard R., Ann S. Coughlin, and Laura Valerius. 1988. Tourism and commercial recreation: past, present and future use. In *Research About Leisure,* ed. Lynn A. Barnett, pp. 161–174. Champaign, Ill.: Sagamore Publishing.

Pieper, J. 1952. *Leisure: the Basis of Culture.* New York: Pantheon Books.

Rosenow, J. E., and G. L. Pulsipher. 1979. *Tourism: the Good, the Bad and the Ugly.* Lincoln, Neb.: Media Productions and Marketing, Inc.

VanDoorn, J. W. M. 1982. Can future research contribute to tourism policy. *Tourism Management* 3 (3, September):149–166.

Veblen, T. 1899. *The Theory of the Leisure Class.* New York: New York American Library (1953 reprint).

Weiss, P. 1964. A philosophical definition of leisure. *Leisure in America: Blessing or Curse?* ed. J. Charlesworth. Philadelphia, Pa.: American Academy of Political Science.

3

Travel and Tourism Law

Ronald A. Kaiser

The law is pervasive in the tourism industry because it permits, empowers, forbids, regulates, moderates, and promotes the activities of suppliers and travelers. It is a dynamic force in not only controlling the structure and operations of tourism businesses but also in maintaining order and ensuring safety for the traveler. While the legal principles of travel and hospitality law have been long recognized, only recently have specialized textbooks appeared[1] and formal university courses been offered in hotel, travel, and tourism law. Indeed, the vast majority of litigation over the past three decades clearly indicates that those providing services or preparing for a career in this industry must have an understanding of the laws that affect the traveler. This entry describes the legal obligations of selected service providers in the U.S. tourism industry. The reader may wish to consult more specialized texts for additional details on the intricacies of tourism law.

An orderly system of laws is crucial to the development of the U.S. travel and tourism industry. Tourism law functions like a social system of control over the conduct of service providers and consumers.[2] Its purposes range from outlining appropriate rules of conduct to giving expression to social and economic institutions—the so-called tourism infrastructure. In aggregate, tourism law incorporates "that body of rules derived from customs, usages and other legal authorities that are enforceable in courts."[3] At a minimum, tourism law creates and defines these basic concepts:

1. Travel is a legal right.
2. Reliable and safe transportation must be readily available.
3. Safe and adequate accommodations must await the traveler.
4. All travelers should have access to such accommodations.
5. Travel and accommodation costs must be reasonable.
6. Regulation of the travel and tourism industry may be necessary.
7. Redress for transgressions of rights and regulations is necessary.[4]

These concepts form the foundation for the various federal and state statutes and court decisions controlling and regulating the different segments of the U.S. tourism industry. Generally, tourism laws in the United States deal with (1) the legal obligations that travel and tourism businesses have to the traveler and (2) the business and tax regulations of a particular segment of the industry or a particular type of business within the industry. Since the tourism infrastructure is described in other articles of this book, this discussion focuses on the legal obligations of travel and tourism enterprises.

Sources and Classification of Tourism Law

Students of tourism should have a rudimentary understanding of the legal system before they can begin to comprehend the application of law to tourism services. While tourism law has long been recognized as a unique body of jurisprudence designed to control a specific industry, it is drawn from many of the same sources regulating all forms of businesses and services.

Historically, tourism laws evolved from court decisions involving English inns and taverns. A textbook author described it thus:

> the supply of food and shelter to a traveler was a matter of public concern, and the house which offered such food and shelter was (recognized to be) engaged in a public service. The law must make injustice to the individual traveler impossible: the caprice of the host could not be permitted to leave a subject of the king hungry and shelterless. In matter of such importance the public had an interest, and must see that, so far as was consistent with justice to the innkeeper, his inn was carried on for the benefit of the whole public, and so it became in an exact sense a public house.[5]

English tavern and innkeeper customs were recognized in English court decisions which in turn were adapted and adopted by American courts.

Sources of Tourism Law   Tourism law today is more complex and is drawn from a variety of sources beyond just "court made" law. In the United States, tourism law is derived from federal and state constitutions and statutes, decisions of federal and state courts, federal and state regulatory agency rules and from treaties negotiated between the United States and foreign nations (see Figure 1). Thus, tourism law comes from at least 51 different sources—the federal government and the 50 states.

Federal and State Constitutions.   A constitution is the "blueprint" creating the state or nation and outlining the authority for and structure of government. In our dual system of governance, the U.S. Constitution is the supreme law of

Fig. 1.   Sources of law affecting tourism enterprises and tavelers. *(Source: After J. Goodwin, Hotel Law, p. 319, 1987. Columbus, Ohio: Publishing Horizons Inc.)*

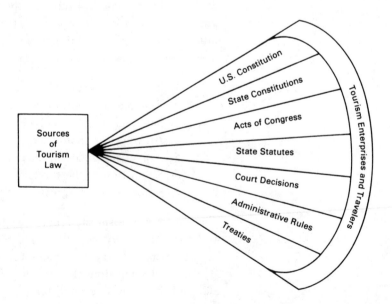

the land with each state constitution supreme in areas not reserved to the federal government. This supremacy concept has direct application to tourism, particularly in the regulation of foreign travel.

The primary authority for federal jurisdiction in tourism is based on the general welfare clause, the commerce clause, and the treaty clause of the U.S. Constitution.[6] Whereas the Constitution does not expressly mention tourism rights, Congress and the courts have recognized a right to travel based on an expansive reading of these Constitutional provisions. The United States Supreme Court has acknowledged that the right to travel has a constitutional basis in stating:

> The right to travel is a part of the 'liberty' of which the citizen cannot be deprived without due process of law under the Fifth Amendment. . . . Freedom of movement across frontiers in either direction, and inside frontiers as well, was a part of our heritage. Travel abroad, like travel within the country, may be necessary for a livelihood. It may be as close to the heart of the individual as choice of what he eats, or wears, or reads. Freedom of movement is basic in our scheme of values. . . . Freedom to travel is, indeed, an important aspect of the citizen's liberty. . . . [7]

By virtue of the Tenth Amendment of the U.S. Constitution the states have the plenary power to regulate resources, business, and human activity for the protection of public health, safety, and welfare of the citizens, but they cannot preclude a person from a right to travel.

Statutes. Rules of law enacted by law-making bodies (legislatures) are called statutes. The word encompasses acts of Congress, state legislatures, and ordinances passed by city councils. With 50 different state legislatures passing rules governing the tourism industry, the lack of uniformity in statutes between the states can sometimes present problems. Consider for example the problem faced by a motel corporation that has properties in many states. While an on-site manager may have to know the law in a particular state, the corporation must be familiar with the law in all the states in which it operates. In this instance, uniformity in regulations would provide a level of certainty sought by the corporation.

Common Law. The term *common law* refers to the law that has grown out of past court cases. Courts in common law jurisdictions either make the law from the beginning through case decisions alone, or they interpret the laws passed by legislative bodies, thereby giving the statutes actual content, meaning, and effect.[8] The concept of following past court decisions to resolve future disputes is often termed *stare decisis*, a Latin phrase meaning "the matter stands decided." It is also stated as *precedence*, a concept meaning that earlier cases establish rules that "precede" and govern future cases.

Not all states, nor countries, follow the common law system. The state of Louisiana and two-thirds of the countries of the world, including most of Europe, follow a civil law system incorporating an elaborate codification of written laws rather than a body of judicial decisions.

Administrative Law. In the highly regulated airline and bus components of the transportation industry the day-to-day impact exerted by administrative law is much greater than that of the courts.[9] Administrative law has been created in response to the evolution of the social, political, governmental, and economic structure of the United States. As a solution to these profound changes, Congress and state legislatures created "administrative agencies," popularly called bureaucracies, and gave them the power to manage and regulate human and business activity to ensure an orderly process of economic, political, and social change. Thus, administrative agencies became the fourth branch of government and an important source of law.[10]

Administrative agencies function by promulgating rules of procedure and conduct for a class of business activity to be regulated. These administrative rules have the full force and effect of law and must be observed. In addition to their ability to develop substantive rules regulating and controlling certain activity, administrative agencies also function like the executive and judicial branches of government by investigating, prosecuting, and adjudicating violations of their rules. Although administrative agencies and their rules have been challenged as an unconstitutional violation of the three-part separation of powers between the executive, legislative, and judicial branches, the courts have upheld this practice as an extension of the legislative power.

Administrative agencies at the federal and state levels of government directly impact many sectors of the tourism industry. At the federal level, the rules of the Federal Aviation Administration, the Department of Transportation, and the Interstate Commerce Commission directly affect airlines, bus companies, and railroads. State administrative agencies control the sale of alcohol through alcohol control commissions, restaurants and foodservice through public health departments, and transportation through highway departments.

Treaties. A treaty is basically an agreement or contract between two or more nations that creates rights, imposes duties and outlines rules of conduct governing a certain subject or activity. The U.S. Constitution specifically provides for the making of treaties by stating that the President "shall have power, by and with the advice and consent of the Senate, to make treaties, provided two thirds of the Senators present concur."[11] A treaty is the equivalent of an act of Congress and is binding on state and federal courts as the supreme law of the land.

Perhaps the most significant treaty that affects international travel and tourism is the Warsaw Convention.[12] This treaty outlines the duties and obligations of international airlines and provides monetary remedies up to a certain dollar limit for passengers suffering injury to persons or property at the hands of international airlines.[13] Most airlines incorporate the provision of this treaty in their "contracts of carriage" (airline ticket) and the passenger should refer to this when reading sections of their airline ticket.

Types of Tourism Law   The body of law affecting the tourism industry and traveler is large and complex. Once a law is created, regardless of its source, placing it in a subject category is necessary to understand where one law stands in relation to another. In order to study tourism law one must break it into meaningful parts before reassembling it into a subject matter classification.

Tourism law can be segmented into at least four major subject categories and a number of subcategories (see Figure 2). The four major categories are (1) substantive and procedural law; (2) public and private law; (3) criminal and civil law; and (4) contract and tort law. Each category can be distinguished by the interest and parties affected and by the remedies sought for invasion of the interests. The law in each of these categories deals, in great part, with the legal obligations imposed on individuals, businesses, and governments providing tourism services. A breach of a legal obligation often

Fig. 2. Types of law affecting tourism enterprises and travelers. *(Source: After J. Goodwin, Hotel Law, p. 319, 1987. Columbus, Ohio: Publishing Horizons Inc.)*

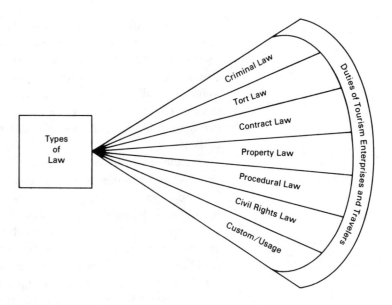

results in legal liability.[14] The responsibility for fulfilling the many legal obligations falls squarely on management. Thus a goal of good management is the minimization of legal liability.

Substantive versus Procedural Law. This distinction is based on the difference between the body of the law and on the process for enforcing the law. Substantive law includes all those rules defining, describing, and regulating conduct or creating some legal right or obligation. It is the law itself even though its origin may be in a state statute or in a common law precedent. For example, state laws that establish health regulations for restaurants or liability standards for innkeepers are examples of substantive law.

Procedural law is concerned with the methods and processes for enforcing rights, duties, and obligations imposed by substantive law. Typically, the filing of lawsuits, serving subpoenas on witnesses, collecting evidence, and controlling the conduct of a trial are governed by procedural law.

Public versus Private Law. This categorization is based on the relationship between persons and government. Public law governs the relationship between individuals and their government. Within this category are areas of law dealing with federal and state administrative agencies, constitutional protections, and crimes and criminal procedure. Administrative law is an example of public law that deals with the basic rights, obligations, and procedures that federal and state agencies must follow in regulating any tourism business. The authority for conducting foodservice and restaurant inspections by state and local public health departments is derived from state statutes that are within this public law classification.

Private law deals with the rights, obligations, and legal relationships that arise from "arms-length" transactions and agreements between individuals. This category includes contract law, property relationships, and torts. Thus, a traveler who sues a motel for failure to provide accommodations at a previously agreed upon price and time period is within the realm of private law.

Criminal versus Civil Law. The distinction between criminal and civil law is an important concept in our legal system that is reflected in the way lawsuits are filed and punishments assessed. Criminal law is concerned with establishing standards of conduct and for prosecuting offenses committed by an individual against the public at-large, even though there may be an individual victim. Since a crime is an act against society, the government, acting through a prosecuting or district attorney, brings the action against an individual who allegedly has committed a crime. A criminal proceeding is not concerned with compensating the victim but with protecting the public interest by punishing the offender through the imposition of a fine or imprisonment or both.

Rules of court and burdens of proof differ in criminal and civil law and proceedings. In order to find a person guilty of a crime, guilt must be proved beyond a reasonable doubt. The standard of proof required in a civil case is by a preponderance of the evidence—a much lower standard than beyond a reasonable doubt. Further when the same act gives rise to both a criminal and civil suit the actions are independent of each other. The constitutional prohibition against "double jeopardy"—a second prosecution after a first trial for the same offense—does not apply between civil and criminal trials.

Criminal law has direct application to many facets of tourism. One important area is in the accommodations sector of the tourism industry. Most states have enacted penal statutes making it a crime for a person to leave a hotel/motel with the intent to avoid payment for lodging.[15] These penal statutes relating to "skips" require that the guest leave the hotel/motel premises without paying in order to establish intent. Once established the "skipper" can be prosecuted for a crime.

Civil law deals with a breach of a legal duty created by a statute, common law, or contract. This area of law is concerned with defining conduct, rights, and obligations between individuals, or between individuals and their governments. It is akin to private law in that it dictates the conduct expected of individuals in business relationships. In a civil lawsuit, one party tries to make the other party comply with a duty of care or pay the damage caused by the failure to so comply. It should be noted that a wrongful act may result in both civil and criminal liability since different interests are protected in each category.

Contract versus Tort Law. The law of contracts and torts has evolved from common law origins and is a significant part of the law controlling travel and tourism. Both areas deal with standards of conduct and provide a means for imposing civil liability for wrongful acts or for the failure to act. The basis of liability is a violation of some duty owed to the injured party; such duty arises either by operation of law or by agreement of the parties. A contractual duty is voluntarily created by parties for their mutual benefit whereas tort law establishes standards of conduct that all citizens must meet.

Contract law regulates the creation and enforcement of agreements (contracts) between persons, corporations, or governments. A contract is a promissory agreement, voluntarily entered into between two or more parties that creates, modifies, or destroys a legal obligation. It is a deliberate engagement to do or refrain from doing some act. Since agreements almost always arise from the exchange of promises, the essence of contract law is the enforcement of promises voluntarily made by the parties.

Five elements are usually required to form a binding and enforceable contract. These elements are (1) an exchange of offers; (2) voluntary acceptance of the offer(s); (3) the exchange of consideration; (4) legal capacity of the parties to enter into contracts; and (5) legality of the contract subject matter. An offer is a proposal made by one person to another indicating what the offeror will give in return for a specific promise. If the person to whom the offer is made indicates consent to be bound by the terms of the offer this constitutes an act of acceptance. To change an agreement into a contract requires the element of consideration. Although the law does not equate consideration to money, most contracts express consideration in dollar values. The last two elements are capacity and legality. Capacity refers to the legal status of the parties that qualifies them as competent. For example, a minor child is presumed to lack the legal capacity to sign an enforceable contract. Thus the contract is not valid to bind the minor child to its terms. Legality means the contract subject matters fulfill a purpose subject to legal attainment. If a contract involves the conveyance of a product or service whose sale is illegal, the contract cannot be enforced against a person who breaches the contract.

The law of contracts is pervasive in the travel and tourism industry as it provides the underpinnings for (1) employment contracts and (2) for the sales of goods and services. Since the tourism industry is labor intensive, employment contracts are essential. These contracts set forth the terms of employment including salary and benefits, work responsibilities and obligations, and hours and length of employment. While employment contracts are agreements for service, many other types of agreements concerning a variety of services are provided by tourism enterprises. Transportation, hotel/motel accommodations, foodservice, and entertainment are services that fall within the regulatory purview of contract law.

Tort law is concerned with establishing standards of conduct to protect the public against unreasonable risks of harm. A tort is a civil wrong, other than a breach of contract, for which courts will provide a remedy in the form of an action for damages.[16] Derived from the Latin word *torquere*, which means twisted or wrong, tort law seeks to provide compensation to individuals who suffer losses because of dangerous or unreasonable conduct of others.

It is often argued that tort law encourages consumer protection and safety by allowing the injured party to sue the wrongdoer for dangerous conditions and practices. In that sense it is a means to deal with social injustices and to change behavior in a way that encourages safety.

Tort law is not static and limits to its application have not been firmly set. Indeed, new torts are often recognized by the courts where none previously existed. This practice is often justified in order to encourage safe conduct and to prevent social injustices. In spite of this apparent flexibility in recognizing new torts, three elements must be found in order to establish tort liability: (1) the existence of a legal duty of care, (2) the breach of the duty, and (3) damage as a proximate result of the breach. If these elements are present the injured party may seek damages for any resulting injury.

Categories of torts range from intentional acts, such as assault, battery, false imprisonment, slander, libel, and trespass to unintentional acts such as negligence, strict liability, and nuisance. These wrongs are unrelated and have little in common, except that they fall within the heading of tort and involve antisocial behavior for which the law provides a remedy. Of the various types of torts, liability based on negligence is pervasive in the travel and tourism industry.

Negligence means one thing to the layman and quite another to the lawyer or judge. In legal parlance negligence describes conduct that falls below the standard of care established by law for the protection of others against unreasonable risks of harm.[17] Under this definition, a tourist/traveler may recover damages only when there is actionable negligence consisting of

1. A legal duty imposed on the tourism service provider to act with the degree of care of a reasonable and prudent operator to prevent unreasonable risks of harm
2. A failure (breach) to conform to the standard required
3. A reasonably close causal connection (proximate cause) between the failure to meet the required standard and the resulting injury
4. Actual personal physical and mental injury or property loss[18]

This definition applies to actions against all services providers in the tourism industry in the United States. In negligence lawsuits, proof of these elements involve questions of law and fact. It is often said that the courts decide questions of law and the jury questions of fact. Thus the court decides if a motel has a legal obligation to inspect its premises to discover hidden hazards. If the court finds a legal duty, the jury must then decide, based on the facts (evidence), whether the motel adhered to the standard of conduct required to protect users against unreasonable risks of harm.

Tourism Law by Sectors of the Industry

To establish a foundation upon which to outline the parameters of tourism law it is necessary to describe in a general sense the components of the tourism industry. With apologies to Professor Gunn,[19] the travel and tourism industry consists of four basic sectors:

1. *Transportation.* Suppliers within this sector are often called "common carriers" and include airlines, bus companies, railroads, and cruise lines.
2. *Accommodations.* While not an exhaustive listing the vendors include hotels, motels, inns, lodges, resort condominiums, and spas.
3. *Travel Agents/Tour Operators.* This sector includes independent travel agents who promote the tours and services offered by the transportation and accommodations sectors as well as tour operators and wholesalers.
4. *Tourist/Traveler.* This sector is made up of the millions of consumers who use the services. Whereas some federal and state statutes and regulatory agencies are concerned with establishing, monitoring, and regulating business practices, the bulk of tourism law involves the obligations and liabilities of suppliers and sellers of tourism services to the traveling public.

This entry describes the obligations of the enterprises within the transportation and accommodation sectors of the tourism industry. With the exception of the transportation sector, there is almost a total absence of legislation directed toward the accommodations industry—it is largely unregulated and unlicensed and operates under the common law principles.

Transportation Law

One key factor in the growth of the tourism industry over the last thirty years has been the availability of relatively low cost public transportation furnished by "common carriers." Common carriers typically include commercial airlines, cruise lines, bus companies, railroads, and rental car agencies. An important part of tourism law is found in the rules and statutes that regulate and control the businesses providing public transportation. Although many of these laws originated in this century, the rules for cruise ships can be traced back for centuries to the common law. It should be noted that the law is in a state of transition, particularly in the airline industry, and that changes further deregulating the transportation sectors will continue.

Under the common law a common carrier has a contractual duty to transport passengers and their luggage, exercising the highest degree of vigilance and care for the passengers' comfort and safety.[20] Although the carrier is not the insurer of passengers comfort and safety the carrier is held to the highest standard just short of being an insurer. This duty of care applies to the employees and agents of the carrier. If an employee of a common carrier acting within the scope of employment harms a traveler, then damages are recoverable not only from the employee but also from the employer.

Airlines

Prior to 1978, nearly every aspect of the domestic airline industry was regulated by the federal government acting through the Civil Aeronautics Board (CAB). These federal regulations prohibited ticket pricing competition between airlines, imposed severe limitations on market entry for new airlines, and limited passenger ability to obtain compensation for flight delays and lost luggage.[21] Competition between airlines was basically limited to seat promotions, meals, movies, and free liquor.[22] Disputes between passengers and airlines were usually resolved according to federal regulatory rules despite efforts of passengers to convince the courts to apply state rules of law. According to one writer, without the stimulus of competition stifled by these federal regulations, airline safety was discouraged, management incompetency was encouraged, and competition between hotels, resorts, travel agents, and tour operators was stifled by the airlines.[23]

When Congress passed the Airlines Deregulation Act of 1978[24] they fundamentally changed the face of air travel in America. The act changed not only the manner in which domestic air transportation is marketed and delivered to the public but it also fundamentally changed the rules of law governing obligations and disputes between the airline and the passenger. Except for some minor federal regulations controlling smoking on flights and passenger overbooking, the basic legal document governing airline obligations to the passenger is the "contract of carriage." This means that airline/passenger disputes over (1) ticket purchases; (2) overbooking; (3) flight delays and cancellations; (4) lost, damaged, or stolen luggage; (5) personal injury liability; and (6) disclaimers of liability are governed, in part, by these contracts of carriage which in turn are enforced or interpreted according to state law. Many of these contracts contain one-sided language strongly favoring the airlines that, like adhesion contracts, may generate litigation over the reasonableness and conscionability of terms.[25]

Buses and Railroads

As contrasted with the airline industry, which is the transportation leader in sales revenue, the bus and railroad industry is the largest mass transporter of travelers.[26] In 1984, the bus industry carried 363 million passengers to 14,000 communities while the airlines carried 317 million passengers and provided service to 700 communities.[27] Since domestic railroads have fallen into such a sad state of physical, fiscal, and economic decay in recent years this discussion focuses on the bus industry.[28]

The bus is a very fuel efficient mode of travel and is likely to play an important role in the growth of the travel industry. There are two main segments of the bus industry in the United States. They are (1) intercity buses traveling along designated routes, and (2) escorted bus tours for recreation and sight-seeing. Greyhound and Trailways are the country's largest intercity carriers operating more than 10,000 buses over a route network of 150,000 miles and Gray Lines is the largest bus touring company offering more than 1,500 sight-seeing excursions annually.[29] The obligations of both types of carriers are not materially different and the following principles of law apply to both sectors.

As with airlines, the bus industry was highly regulated by the Interstate Commerce Commission (ICC) and by state agencies. These regulations often required federal and state approval when a new company tried to enter a market or when a current service company added or dropped a new line, or changed a route. In addition to these market control restrictions, federal and state regulations incorporated a tariff system establishing the terms and conditions for the contract of carriage. Not surprisingly the political tidal wave of deregulation that swept over the airline industry also flooded the bus industry and washed away many of the onerous market restrictive regulations.

In 1982, Congress passed the Bus Regulatory Reform Act, which deregulated the bus industry. This act eased exit and entry into the market and gave companies rate freedom. Since then about 1700 new bus companies have received ICC operating authority. Bus companies now may select the routes they travel, choose their pickup points, and set fares. About all that remains of the federal bus regulatory system are the tariffs limiting liability for lost or damaged baggage.

Cruise Ships As a segment of the travel industry, ship transportation is considered one of the oldest forms of travel, yet cruise ships are considered to be the "new kid on the travel block." In a real sense cruise ship companies are more in the entertainment business than in pure transportation. Whereas ships still provide "destination to destination" travel, cruise ships are veritable "floating hotels" featuring recreation and sports facilities, aerobic dance classes, and visits to ports of call.

Unlike travel cases involving domestic airlines and bus companies, disputes between passengers and cruise lines raise complex jurisdictional questions, namely what law to apply—foreign, federal, or state—and where to file the lawsuit—in a foreign, federal, or state court. These questions arise because maritime law (the law of the sea) often governs disputes with cruise ships. Under maritime law a vessel at sea is regarded as part of the territory of the country under which flag it flies and all on board are subject to the law of that foreign country.[30] Further, some cruise ship contracts contain jurisdiction classes that require that passenger disputes be resolved in the country where the ship is registered. In one case, a U.S. federal court upheld a contract provision that required that all disputes under the ticket be decided by Greek courts according to Greek law.[31]

Absent a forum selection clause in a cruise contract, passenger disputes could be brought in federal or state court using federal maritime law or state common law. Cruise ship litigation under federal maritime law is very complex. Because of this complexity and the expense of litigation, there is a strong incentive to settle disputes without resorting to litigation. According to one author, the most inequitable aspect of United States maritime law is the tendency of courts to strictly enforce cruise ship disclaimers of liability against passengers.[32] He argues that adherence to this rule is a vestige of antiquated protectionist practices that is not needed in today's market.

Tourism law is not static. Many areas of the law are in transition, particularly in the airline industry, and the tourism manager and student should stay alert to these changes.

Ticket Sales Form Contracts of Carriage.   In the transportation industry tickets to the public are sold through direct sales to the traveling public, retail travel agents who sell the tickets on behalf of the carrier, and sales contracts with wholesalers who resell the seats as package tours to the public. When a ticket is sold to a passenger, a "contract of carriage" arises between the carrier and the passenger requiring the performance of the specific conditions. The general terms of the contract are usually printed on the ticket with a notice that complete contract terms are available at the carrier's ticket counter or other office. Passengers would be well advised to periodically ask for a copy of the complete contract to be more informed of their rights.

Disclaimers of Liability—In General.   All common carriers in their contract of carriage include liability disclaimers as a device to limit their liability to a fixed monetary amount. These disclaimers are in derogation of the common law, which imposes higher standards on the carrier. Liability disclaimers are used to cover reservation dishonorment, overbooking, lost or damaged luggage claims, travel delays, and passenger injury or death claims. Their legal efficacy depends on several factors. First, in the absence of a state or federal statute that modifies the common law, carriers may only limit liability for breach of contract or negligence. Passenger injuries, travel delays or accidents caused by fraud, willful misconduct, or gross negligence on the part of the carrier or their employees cannot be disclaimed. Second, the disclaimers may be void due to lack of passenger notice of the existence of the disclaimer, readability, or unreasonableness. Third, if passengers are not given a choice of purchasing greater liability coverage at a higher fare rather than just accepting the disclaimer, the liability waiver is invalid. Lastly, some courts have invalidated the disclaimers because they violate public policy.

Failure to Honor Ticket Reservations (Overbooking).   One method that results in the failure to honor the reservation is the practice of overbooking. This practice arises where a common carrier deliberately sells more seats on a given trip than are actually available. Overbooking constitutes a breach of the contract of carriage in that the carrier knows that a seat will not be delivered when the passenger seeks to board the carriers.

Airlines: Under the Deregulation Act of 1978, the Civil Aeronautics Board abolished the tariff system as is related to flight delays but it retained regulations for overbooking. The federal regulations require that airlines use an "auction" procedure whereby "bumped" passengers may get a seat if other passengers voluntarily give up their seats. To encourage volunteers to give up their seats, airlines can offer incentives ranging from cash to free airline tickets. If an insufficient number of volunteers come forward, the airlines may deny boarding to other passengers in accordance with its boarding priority rules. The regulations require that passengers be given notice of their options and be furnished appropriate boarding compensation when denied a boarding pass because of overbooking.[33] The best way to understand the airlines' position on overbooking is to read the terms found on all U.S. airline tickets. Sample language governing overbooking is found in Figure 3.

If a passenger is denied a boarding pass on a domestic flight as a result

NOTICE—OVERBOOKING OF FLIGHTS

Airline flights may be overbooked, and there is a slight chance that a seat will not be available on a flight for which a person has a confirmed reservation. If the flight is overbooked, no one will be denied a seat until airline personnel first ask for volunteers willing to give up their reservation in exchange for a payment of the airline's choosing. If there are not enough volunteers the airline will deny boarding to other persons in accordance with its particular boarding priority. With few exceptions, persons denied boarding involuntarily are entitled to compensation. The complete rules for the payment of compensation and each airlines boarding priorities are available at all airport ticket counters and boarding locations.

of overbooking the airline shall immediately offer as compensation to the passenger an amount up to 200 percent of the remaining value of the ticket up to a $400.00 maximum. However, if the airline arranges for travel on another flight and the passenger arrives within two hours of the original flight, the compensation is one-half the amount of the ticket up to a $200.00 maximum.[34]

Buses: While the practice of overbooking is not as prevalent in the bus industry as in the airline and hotel industry, similar legal problems are created when a ticket is not honored. In such instances the traveler may seek to recover damages based on a breach of contract, or if it can be shown that the company knowingly overbooked then a cause of action alleging fraudulent misrepresentation may be successful. Where misrepresentation of facts can be shown punitive, or punishment, damages may be awarded.

Cruise lines: Overbooking is not generally a problem in the cruise line industry but ticket dishonoring does occur. As with airlines and buses, failure to honor a ticket creates liability risks for the cruise line company. When a ticket is not honored a passenger may be entitled to damages under a breach of contract, negligence, or fraudulent misrepresentation theory.

Travel Delays, Changes, and Cancellations. Timely transportation is the cornerstone of the contract of carriage. Any deviation from the date, time of departure, and return may constitute a breach of contract exposing the carrier to liability for passenger out of pocket expenses and damages resulting from passenger discomfort, annoyance, and inconvenience.[35]

Airlines: In the event that a flight is canceled the airline may be liable for passenger costs associated with alternative transportation, even when the alternative transportation is more expensive than that of the original airline ticket price. To avoid this liability, the airline will usually try to arrange transportation for the passenger on another airline. When this is not possible and the airline makes no other bona fide attempt to assist the passenger, filing a lawsuit against the airline for actual and consequential damages may be passengers' final resort to recovery.

Airlines may seek to limit some or all of their liability by disclaiming in the contract of carriage responsibility for the flight delay or cancellation or by offering a defense to the delay. Domestic airline ticket disclaimers are subject to attack on the grounds of readability, notice, reasonability, and unconscionability.[36] An airline is not limited to disclaiming liability in the contract of carriage but may offer other defense to fight delays or cancellations. Typically, these include bad weather and other acts of God, mechanical malfunctions, safety concerns, air traffic controller delays, misconnections, and improper scheduling by tour operators. These defenses can limit an airline's liability if there is a close causal connection between the delay or cancellation and events.[37]

Buses: Most bus and railroad tickets contain legally enforceable disclaimers that the carrier is not liable for delays and it is very difficult to overcome these provisions. If it can be shown that the delay was caused by equipment malfunction that could have been repaired in a timely fashion by the carrier or that carrier could not feasibly meet the advertised departure and arrival times then the disclaimer defense can be overcome. Where a passenger can overcome the disclaimer defense, recoverable damages could include lost business income and personal discomfort losses resulting from the delay.

Cruise lines: Most cruise line brochures advertise travel to a number of ports of call during a cruise. A common problem in the cruise line industry is a deviation from the scheduled departure and arrival times.[38] When a ship fails to arrive at scheduled ports of call at designated times passengers may be prevented from shopping or from participating in other activities that defeat the purpose of the cruise. If the passenger can show injury as a result of such itinerary changes they may, depending on the particular circumstances causing the delay, recover damages based on a breach of contract, negligence, or fraudulent misrepresentation theory.

As a way to protect themselves from liability from itinerary changes, cruise lines often insert disclaimers in their tickets (see Figure 4). These disclaimers have not been universally accepted by the courts particularly when the itinerary change was the result of equipment failure caused by negligent maintenance[39] or fraudulent misrepresentations by the cruise line.[40] Fraud occurs when a cruise line advertises and contracts for services they know they are not able to produce.

As an alternative to limiting liability a cruise line may seek to limit its damages for itinerary changes by using a damage disclaimer. In this type of disclaimer the cruise line seeks not to absolve itself from all liability but to limit liability to a specified amount of damages. Unless a court finds some public policy basis for striking down such a disclaimer it will probably be sustained.

Delayed, Damaged, or Lost Luggage. Delayed, damaged, or lost luggage is the bane of travelers and carriers. Baggage claims against common carriers number in the millions each year yet few passengers sue for lost, damaged, or delayed luggage. In spite of the paucity of lost luggage litigation, a common carrier is the insurer of a passenger's luggage and is generally liable for delayed, damaged, or lost luggage.[41]

Fig. 4. A typical liability disclaimer. (*Source: From Bloom v. Cunard Line, Ltd., 430 N.Y.S. 2d 607 (1980).*)

Neither the Company nor the ship . . . shall be or be held liable for . . . damage arising from . . . any defect or breakdown in the ship, machinery, gear or fittings whether existing before or at the time of sailing or otherwise or preventing or delaying the sailing . . . [or arising from] defaults or errors in navigation or in the management of ship.

Airlines: While airline responsibility and liability for lost, damaged, or stolen luggage is determined according to state common law rules,[42] monetary limits on airline liability for lost or damaged luggage is set by federal rules at $1,250 per customer.[43] Generally, these limits will be observed by the courts unless there are extenuating circumstances. In one case, for example, a passenger bought a golfing package featuring airfare, hotel accommodations, and all greens fees. The airline mishandled the passenger's luggage and golf clubs—he finally received them after the vacation was over—and he was required to purchase new clothes, toiletries, and golf clubs to enjoy his vacation. The passenger sued the airlines and recovered money damages for all of his out-of-pocket expenses plus an additional amount for the diminished value of the golf package.[44]

Buses: Liability under the common law and the tariff system depends on who has possession and control of the luggage. If the luggage is within the custody and control of the bus company then their liability for damaged or lost luggage under the common law is nearly absolute. When the passenger keeps the luggage the bus company's liability is based on a lower standard of negligence. Bus companies can change these liability rules by using disclaimer provisions in federal and state tariff systems and nearly all companies use this approach.

Interstate bus companies are regulated by the ICC and can use the federal tariff system to establish terms and conditions for their contract of carriage that changes the state common law rules on liability. This tariff system allows interstate bus companies to limit their liability for lost or damaged luggage to a fixed monetary amount. Thus, if a passenger entrusts to the bus company luggage worth $1,500 the company could limit its monetary liability for lost or damaged luggage to $500 by filing a disclaimer in its tariff application.

Courts will generally uphold these disclaimers if the following conditions are satisfied: (1) the tariff must have been filed with and approved by the ICC; (2) the passenger had notice of the disclaimer by statements printed on the tickets, baggage claim checks, and by signs posted on the station walls; (3) the passenger had an opportunity to pay a higher fee for more coverage; and (4) the passenger failed to declare a higher value for the luggage.[45] If the bus carrier fails to follow these conditions, the courts could ignore the disclaimer and follow common law liability standards.

Intrastate bus companies can use state tariff systems to limit their liability with the same results as with federal tariffs. In one reported case, a passenger watched her luggage as it was removed from the bus and placed outside the baggage room. When she returned a short time later her luggage was missing. She sued the bus company for losing her luggage and sought to recover damages for the full value of her luggage. The court found the bus company responsible but upheld the disclaimer lowering their liability even though the court found the carrier was grossly negligent.[46]

Cruise lines: Cruise lines have not been able to rely on a tariff system to limit liability and are often held to common law rules of near absolute liability for lost or damaged luggage. To overcome this high standard of care, cruise lines use ticket disclaimers to deny or limit their liability. Disclaimers of total liability for lost or damaged luggage have generally been struck down by the courts, however, disclaimers brought to the passengers attention that limit liability and damages to a reduced level have been upheld by the courts.[47] These disclaimers are always subject to attack based on lack of passenger notice, vague language, unreasonable terms, and contrary to public policy reasons. Passengers would be well advised to review their tickets for disclaimer terms.

Physical Injury/Death.   Travel is not risk-free. Accidents can and do happen, and a number of travelers are killed or injured each year. The law does not require that common carriers be the guarantor of passenger safety but it does impose on them a high standard of care to protect travelers from injury or death.

Airlines: The liability of an air carrier for passenger injury or death is based on negligence and common carrier law. As a general rule, an airline is liable for passenger injury or death caused by negligence in the maintenance and operation of the aircraft. Airlines must follow the maintenance and operation standards of care found in the rules of the Federal Aviation Administration, in operations manuals of the airlines and in the maintenance manuals of airline manufacturers. Failure to conform to these rules may establish the major elements of negligence.

Though not exhaustive, the following acts by the flight crew and airlines maintenance personnel illustrate some examples of negligence: low flying, flying into a storm or ignoring weather conditions such as wind shear, route deviation, aircraft overloading, incompetent or improperly trained crew, failure to maintain equipment, defective equipment, failure to provide safety equipment and safe passageways, failure to rescue, and error in judgment.

Disclaimers on domestic flights generally are not available to limit airline liability but disclaimers on international flights are recognized as a defense under provisions of the Warsaw Convention.

Buses: Bus companies may be liable for accidents causing passenger injury or death under a negligence or a breach of contract of safe passage theory and most disclaimer defenses have not been allowed.[48] As contrasted with the tariff system that allows bus carriers to limit liability for lost luggage, the courts have been reluctant to allow bus companies to disclaim liability for passenger injury or death.[49]

Cruise lines: Under the rules of law governing common carriers, cruise lines have a contractual duty to transport passengers to their destinations exercising the highest degree of care and vigilance for the passenger's safety.[50] This means that cruise ship companies are liable for passenger injury or death resulting from negligence in the maintenance and operation of the ship and its equipment. Further, liability can be imposed on the company for the negligence and willful misconduct of its employees acting within or even outside the scope of their employment.[51]

Disclaimers of cruise line liability for passenger injury or death are not enforceable. Congress passed a maritime law statute prohibiting cruise lines from disclaiming liability for physical injuries or death arising from the carrier's negligence.[52]

Accommodations Law

The accommodations/lodging sector of the tourism industry is highly fragmented with more than 50,000 establishments operating in the United States, ranging from small roadside motels to resort casinos with more than 3,000 rooms.[53] Included within the lodging industry are inns, hotels, motels, spas, taverns, restaurants, casinos, and resorts. Given this extreme diversity a brief explanation of the lodging industry is in order. For purposes of this section, the word *hotels* will be used to describe those facilities offering over-night accommodations to travelers.[54]

The Lodging Industry

Inns: The concept of the inn has been a part of recorded history since before the time of Christ. An inn basically describes a structure that is a place to stay for the traveler. Today, it is legally indistinguishable from a hotel or motel.

Hotels: The word *hotel* is derived from the French word *hostel* and the Latin word *hospes,* meaning the master of the house who entertains travelers or guests. The word first came into use in England in 1760 and first appeared in this country about 1797.[55] Prior to that time hotels were called inns and later taverns or coffee houses. The basic concept of the hotel is to provide accommodations, as well as food, drink, and entertainment to transient guests, as contrasted with the boarding house, which provides semipermanent housing to tenants.

Motels: Closely associated with the hotel is the motel. The word has been attributed to a merging of the words "motorist" and "hotel"[56] and has evolved so that any practical differences between the two providers is definitional fodder for lexicographers.

Taverns: Whereas inns and taverns share common origins they are legally different. An inn is an establishment designed to provide rest, nourishment, and entertainment for the traveler, whereas a tavern serves beverages and food to those who live in the immediate area and return to home each night.[57]

Travelers: The term is significant because travelers become guests at hotels and motels and thus are owed duties of care by the innkeeper. In a broad sense a traveler is one who passes from place to place whether for pleasure, instruction, business, or health. Undoubtedly, a person traveling from city to city fits the definition but so does a local who stays at a local hotel to attend a conference.

Guests: In determining if a person is a guest at a hotel or motel the courts will look to the intent of the parties. If a traveler manifests an intent to be accepted as a guest and is received as one by the innkeeper then a guest relationship arises.

Duties and Obligations of Innkeepers

In contrast with the transportation sector, there is almost a total absence of federal and state legislation directed toward the lodging industry. Except for common law rules, the hotel industry is largely unregulated, unlicensed, and operates under the principle of *caveat emptor.* As described in the travel section of the *New York Times,* June 7, 1981:

> The hotel industry is one of the most unregulated areas in the travel field. Some American states and municipalities and some foreign governments enforce fire safety and sanitation standards and antidiscrimination law in their hotels. Others require that current rates be posted prominently. In most places, however, hotels have virtual freedom to set and change their rates at will and establish their own policies on reservations (and overbooking), deposits, mode of payment, and minimum lengths of stay. Furthermore, there are no uniform standards in the United States by which hotels are rated, although some other countries have government-regulated ratings systems.[58]

In spite of this rather ominous critique the guest is not without any legal recourse in the event the innkeeper breaches one of the legal duties of care.

Common Law Duties—In General. Hotels and motels have a duty to provide accommodations without discrimination to all those who request them and to use reasonable care in the operation of the property to prevent unreasonable risks of harm to the guests and their property. The relationship between traveler (guest) and innkeeper has been consensual in nature and the common law duties arising from that relationship have their origin in contract and tort law.[59] Although these common law duties are old, having their origin in English law, they remain in effect unless muted by statute or case law.[60] Statutory changes that relax common law duties are carefully reviewed by the courts and any ambiguities are construed against the innkeeper and in the favor of the guest.

Today, a combination of common law and statutory duties are imposed on the innkeeper to protect the public, the traveler, and the guest. Generally, innkeepers have a duty to (1) receive and accommodate travelers; (2) provide safe accommodations; (3) protect guests from harm; (4) protect the property of guests; (5) provide food fit to eat; and (6) ensure privacy. It has long been recognized that an innkeeper assumes these duties upon holding out to the traveler hotel accommodations.

Duty to Receive and Accommodate. Since hotels are in the business of serving travelers, they have a common law duty to receive travelers as guests and to provide accommodations until the facility is at capacity. This obligation is a 24-hour a day, seven day a week duty and an innkeeper cannot refuse to accept a guest because of the lateness of the hour or the time of the week.[61] Nor is the duty to receive limited to guests who have the ability to contract for room services. The innkeeper is required to accept minor children, even though they are unaccompanied by their parents on the theory that they are in need of protection while on the journey. There is no requirement that the hotel furnish accommodations free of charge and a hotel has the right to determine if a minor can pay for the room or to collect from a minor's parents.

This nearly absolute common law duty to receive has been supported and strengthened by federal and state antidiscrimination statutes. The federal Civil Rights Act of 1964 prohibits places of public accommodation from discriminating against any person on the grounds of race, color, religion, or national origin.[62] The act specifically defines a "place of public accommodation" to include hotels, motels, inns, taverns, bars, roadhouses, restaurants, barbershops, beauty parlors as well as other types of service establishments.[63]

A number of states have supplemented the federal civil right law by enacting a state version of civil rights legislation that broadens the protected class of persons to include the physically and mentally handicapped. Some states have taken the duty to receive to very high levels by providing that an innkeeper who refuses to receive can be indicted or brought to a trial for a violation of the statute.[64]

While the duty to receive travelers and provide accommodations is nearly absolute there are limited circumstances under which an innkeeper can legally refuse services to a traveler. An innkeeper could refuse to receive a guest if

- The hotel is full and has no rooms available (a hotel is contractually obligated and may be liable to provide accommodations to a person with a valid reservation)

- The person seeking accommodations appears to be in an intoxicated or drug influenced condition
- The person is disorderly so as to pose a nuisance or is a threat to other guests
- The person has a communicable disease
- The person has no luggage, or has luggage or property, such as wild animals, snakes, firearms, or explosives, that may be dangerous to others
- There is a reasonable basis to believe the person will use the room to commit a criminal act
- The person is destitute, unwilling, or unable to pay[65]

Aside from these limited exceptions, the law imposes a strict duty on innkeepers to provide accommodations for the *bona-fide* traveler who seeks "a room at the inn." Selective discrimination for reasons other than those listed above may subject the innkeeper to criminal and civil liability.

Hotel reservations: In addition to a common law duty to receive, innkeepers may create contractual accommodations duties with travelers. Making a reservation may give rise to a binding contract between the hotel and the prospective guest. Actual registration is not the test for determining if a contractual relationship arises.

In order for a reservation to become a binding contract, it must include the material parts of the agreement such as dates and times of the reservation, the rate, the number of rooms, and the nature of the accommodation. A verbal or written confirmation of the reservation by the hotel constitutes their acceptance of the agreement. If either the hotel or prospective guest breaches this agreement, that party may be liable to the other for damages.

The minimum measure of damages if the hotel fails to furnish the accommodations agreed upon would be the difference between the contract price of the room and the cost to the guest for obtaining accommodations elsewhere. In addition the hotel could be liable for other damages and expenses to the guest, such as added travel costs, clothing cost, physical discomfort, emotional distress, loss of reputation, and inconvenience.[66] Correspondingly, if the guest fails to meet the terms of the contract, the guest may be liable for the rental rate of the room and other accommodations that were not used.[67]

Overbooking: When a hotel accepts more reservations on a given date than they have rooms available it engages in a practice of overbooking. While "economic necessity" may justify overbooking in the airlines industry, so long as alternative service is available, it is not clear that this justifies the practice in the accommodations industry.[68] Overbooking to compensate for "no-shows" hardly justifies the practice.

Overbooking constitutes a breach of the accommodations contract subjecting the hotel to compensatory damages to the guest. The damages could include the guest's out-of-pocket expenses plus an amount for physical discomfort, emotional distress, and loss of the pleasure of the trip. If the hotel overbooks, knowing in advance that it cannot honor the reservation, that is fraud for which punitive, or punishment, damages can be awarded. A variation of overbooking is the "bait and switch" practice where a guest is baited with a promise of a certain type of room and then upon arrival the switch is made to something less desirable. Again if the hotel knowingly engages in this practice it is fraud and the guest may seek punitive damages.[69]

Safe Accommodations. A hotel is not held to the standard of an insurer of the guest's safety but it has a duty to take reasonable precautions and care in protecting the guest from unreasonable risks of harm.[70] This duty is nondelegable, that is the duty cannot be given over to a third party or employee. The reported cases are full of examples of innkeepers breaching this duty of reasonable care.

Translating this rule into management practices means that the innkeeper must periodically inspect the facility to discover hidden or latent defects and then to remove or repair those defects. During the time prior to repair the innkeeper has a duty to warn the guests about the existence and location of the dangers. In a nutshell, inspections, repair, and warnings are the actions of a reasonable and prudent innkeeper.

At the very cornerstone of an innkeeper's duty is the obligation to provide a reasonably safe room. This safety duty extends not only to the furnishings of the room but also to safety from criminal actions of others. Hotels have been held liable for guest injuries where the guest was attacked by a third party while in the privacy of his or her room.[71] Illustrative is the case where entertainer Connie Francis was awarded $2.5 million from an alleged assault and rape that occurred while Miss Francis was staying at a Howard Johnson inn.[72] The rapist allegedly entered the room from an unsecured sliding glass door—the door gave the appearance of being locked but could not be secured.

Protecting Guests from Harm. It is well established that the innkeeper must follow the reasonable care rule in protecting the guests from injury. As previously stated, the hotel is not the insurer of guest safety but it must exercise the care of a reasonable and prudent operator in protecting the guest. This duty extends to an innkeepers obligation to protect guests from

- Negligent or deliberate acts of hotel employees
- Acts of other guests
- Acts by nonguests committed on the premises

Failure to conform to the reasonableness standard in these three areas provides a liability risk for the hotel.

Acts of employees: If an employee negligently or willfully injures a guest, tort liability falls not only on the employee but also on the hotel.[73] Under the doctrine of "respondeat superior" the acts of the employee become the acts of the employer subjecting the employer to liability. An important qualifier to the doctrine is that the misconduct of the employee must have been committed within the scope of employment to transfer legal risk to the employer.[74]

Acts of other guests: An innkeeper is a peacekeeper and must reasonably control the conduct of all persons on the premises, including guests. Illustrative of this duty is a case where a hotel was held liable for the cavorting of two members of a football team who were guests of the hotel when they ran through a revolving door and injured an elderly woman who was caught in the whirling dervish.[75]

Acts of third parties: Although the hotel is not an insurer of guest safety it has an obligation to protect its guests from assaults and criminal acts of third persons. This duty of control generally applies only to the property and is not imposed off premises. The primary issue in many of the cases involving assaults on guests is whether the hotel knew or should have known of the potential for criminal activity. If the answer to this query is yes, then the hotel can be held liable.

Protecting Guest Property.   Under the common law, a hotel was liable for the full value of lost or damaged luggage. All states have enacted statutes limiting a hotel's liability for loss or damage to a guest's property. Since each state statute is different, only general principles of law are discussed in this section. The student and hotel manager should review the statute in their state for particulars on the law.

Statutes limiting an innkeeper's liability for lost or damaged luggage are considered to be in derogation of the common law and will be strictly construed. This means that an innkeeper must strictly comply with the terms of the legislation, particularly the posting of Notice to the Guests of Limitations on Liability to receive the benefits of reduced liability. Once a hotel complies with the statute some of the risk of loss can be effectively transferred to the guest.

The statutes limiting liability generally divide the guest's property into three categories: (1) money and valuables, (2) losses from fire, and (3) property in transit.[76] As to money and valuables, hotels are required to maintain a safe for the valuables and to let guests know of the safe's availability. Failure to comply with this condition removes the hotel's limited liability and exposes them to liability for the full value of the guest's lost or damaged property.

Regarding property loss by fire, hotels have limited liability unless they were negligent in causing the fire. If negligence can be established, the hotel can be liable for the loss or damage to the full value of the guest's property. In New York, there is a statutory presumption that the hotel was negligent in causing the fire.[77] This puts the burden on the hotel to show a lack of negligence on their part. If the hotel cannot overcome this presumption, they are liable for the full value of loss.

As to goods in transit to and from the hotel, possession and control of the guest's property is the key in assigning liability. If the hotel is in possession of the luggage at the time of its loss or damage the hotel is responsible for the full value of the loss.

In addition to the statutory limitations on liability, a number of hotels use contractual disclaimers to absolve them of any liability or to drastically limit their monetary liability for guest property losses. As a general rule, courts have not looked with favor on these disclaimers and have willingly struck them down.[78]

Providing Safe Food.   This is the one area in which the hotel or its restaurant is held to the highest standard—that of an ensurer of food safety. Generally, restaurants are obligated to serve food that is fit to eat and are nearly always liable under a strict liability or breach of implied warranty theory. Hotels that operate a restaurant are bound by these very strict liability rules on food safety and fitness for human consumption.

Protecting Privacy.   As a general proposition, a guest has an expectation of privacy in his or her room and a hotel has an affirmative duty not to allow unregistered guests, unauthorized employees, and third parties to gain access to a guest's room.[79] This right of privacy is not absolute and it is understood that an innkeeper has a right to enter a room for cleaning, repair, and for *bona fide* emergency purposes.

A hotel guest has a constitutionally protected right against unreasonable searches and seizures of property from his or her room. The United States Supreme Court has held that hotel personnel cannot consent to allow a warrantless police search of a guest's room.[80] Obviously, this right ends when the guest-hotel relationship ends and at that time hotel personnel and the police may enter the room without a warrant.

Summary

The right to travel is a revered part of our culture and tradition that is embodied in our laws and legal system. A corollary principle in this right to travel is the right of travelers to receive the services contracted for and reasonably expected without undue risks of harm to their persons or property. Problems encountered by ancient travelers, namely safe transit, accommodations and food, are to a large extent the same encountered by modern travelers. Tourism law gives expressions to these basic rights while protecting the traveler by imposing obligations on the enterprises that supply travel and tourism services. In addition to establishing duties of care, tourism law provides a remedy to the traveler injured by the actions of a tourism enterprise.

Tourism laws have not remained static but have changed as the industry has grown. Deregulation of the airline industry, while opening up markets to new competitors, has created substantial traveler uncertainty over the duties of airline carriers. In resolving disputes between passengers and airlines the courts are not bound by the legal principles developed during the dark days of regulation but will use the tried and true common law principles in protecting passenger safety. The deregulation trend has spread to public bus companies as Congress has removed the yoke of regulation and allowed economic and market forces to guide development of new services. Aside from the trend to deregulate the transportation sector, the tourism industry remains to a large extent unregulated by federal and state agencies. This pattern will probably continue and principles of common law will, to a great extent, guide the right of travelers and obligations of enterprises in the tourism industry.

Notes

1. For a more detailed discussion on travel, tourism, and hotel law see Cournoyer, Norman and Tony Marshall. 1983. *Hotel, Restaurant and Travel Law.* North Scituate, Mass.: Breton Publishers.; Dickerson, Thomas. 1986. *Travel Law.* New York: Law Journal Seminars Press.; Goodwin, John. 1987. *Hotel Law: Principles and Cases.* Columbus, Ohio: Publishing Horizons Inc.; Jefferies, Jack. 1983. *Understanding Hotel/Motel Law.* East Lansing, Mich.: Educational Institute of the American Hotel & Motel Assoc.; Kalt, Nathan. 1971. *Legal Aspects of Hotel, Motel and Restaurant Operations.* Indianapolis: Bobbs-Merril Publishing Inc.; Miller, Jeffery. 1982. *Legal Aspects of Travel Agency Operation.* Wheaton, Ill.: Merton House Publishing Co.; Sherry, John. 1982. *The Law of Innkeepers,* 2d ed. Ithaca, N.Y.: Cornell University Press.
2. For a discourse on the role and nature of law in society see Harold, B. and William Greiner, 1980. *The Nature and Functions of Law,* 4th ed. Mineola, N.Y.: The Foundation Press.
3. See American Banana Co. v. United Fruit Co., 213 U.S. 347 (1909). In this case Justice Oliver Wendell Holmes defined law as ". . . a statement of the circumstances in which the public force will be brought to bear through the courts."
4. See Goodwin, John. 1987. *Hotel Law: Principles and Cases.* Columbus, Ohio: Publishing Horizons Inc., p. 5.
5. See Sherry, John, 1982. *The Law of Innkeepers,* 2d ed. Ithaca, N.Y.: Cornell University Press. p. 9.

6. Article 1, 8 of the U.S. Constitution provides that the Congress shall have power to . . . provide for the general welfare of the United States; . . . regulate commerce with foreign nations, and among the several states, and with Indian Tribes.

7. Kent v. Dulles, 357 U.S. 116, 78 S.Ct. 1113, 2 L.Ed.2d 1204 (1957).

8. See Cournoyer, Norman, 1978. *Hotel, Restaurant and Travel Law.* Belmont, Calif.: Wadsworth Publishing Co. p. 11.

9. Goodwin, John. 1987. *Hotel Law,* supra note 4, at 39.

10. Anon. 1991. American Jurisprudence, 2d., Administrative Law, 1, Rochester, N.Y.: Lawyers Cooperative Publishing Co., p. 806.

11. U.S. Constitution, Article 2, § 2.

12. This treaty was originally written in French in 1929 in Warsaw, Poland. Officially the treaty is known as The Convention for the Unification of Certain Rules Relating to International Transportation by Air. It has been adopted by most countries and governs air travel throughout the world.

13. For a more in-depth discussion of the Treaty see Lowenfield and Mendlesohm, 1967. The United States and the Warsaw Convention, 80 *Harvard Law Review* 497.

14. Legal liability is ". . . the state of being bound or obligated in law or justice to do, pay or make good something; the state of one who is bound in law or justice to do something which may be enforced by action." Fidelity v. Diamond, 34 N.E.2d 123 (Ill.).

15. See for example Cal. Penal Code 537 (West Supp. 1983); Fla. Stat. Ann. Supp. 509.151 (West 1983); Del. code Ann. Supp. Tit. 11 845 (1982).

16. For a more complete discussion of the etiology of tort law see Keeton, Page, and William Prosser. 1984. *Prosser and Keeton on the Law of Torts,* 5th ed., St. Paul, Minn.: West Publishing Co., pp. 1–32.

17. Restatement (Second) of Torts 382.

18. For the classic legal definition see Keeton, Page and William Prosser. 1984. *Prosser and Keeton on Torts,* supra note 16, at 164.

19. In his seminal text on tourism planning Professor Gunn describes the tourism system on a demand and supply side basis. His four components of the supply side include, transportation, attractions, services and information/promotion. See Gunn, Clare 1988. *Tourism Planning,* 2nd ed. New York: Taylor Francis, p. 67.

20. McManigal v. Chicago Motor Coach Company, 18 Ill. App.2d 183, 151 N.E.2d 410 (1958).

21. Deregulations First Two Years for Air Travelers, *N.Y. Times* Travel Section, pp. 1, 17. October 12, 1980 and CAB 78-8-87.

22. Dickerson, Thomas. 1990. *Travel Law,* New York: Law Journals Seminars Press, p. 2–8.

23. Ibid. at 2–9.

24. 92 Stat. 1705.

25. See Dickerson, supra note 22, at 2–20.

26. Ibid., at 3–9.

27. van Harssel, Jan. 1988. *Tourism: An Exploration,* 2nd ed. Elmsford, N.Y.: National Publishers. p. 54.

28. For a discussion of the sad condition of commuter railroads see Note, Availability of a New York Class Action for Railroad Commuters: David v. Goliath, 12 *Fordham Urban Law Journal* 841 (1984).

29. van Harsell, supra note 27, at p. 53.

30. Most of the discussion on law and cruise ships is adapted from Dickerson. See Dickerson Thomas. 1990. *Travel Law,* supra note 22, at 3–1 to 3–46.10.

31. Hollander v. K-Lines Hellenic Cruise, 670 F. Supp 563 (S.D.N.Y. 1987).

32. Ibid. p. 3–26.

33. See 14 CFR part 250-Oversales, 47 Fed. Reg. 52980, Jan 23, 1983 & 49 Fed. Reg. 43622, Nov 30, 1984.

34. 14 CFR 250.5.

35. Christensen v. Northwest Airlines, Inc., 455 F. Supp. 492 (D. Hawaii 1978) affd 633 F.2d 529 (9th Cir. 1980); Goranson v. Trans World Airlines, 121 Misc. 2d 68, 467 N.Y.S.2d 407 (1979).

36. See Dickerson, Thomas. 1990. *Travel Law,* supra note 22, at 2–58 citing a long line of state and federal cases striking down disclaimers.

37. See Klakis v. Nationwide Leisure Corp, New York Law Journal, November 30, 1978, p. 6, col 2 (N.Y. Supp. 1978); McMurray v. Capitol Internationals Airways Inc., 102 Misc.2d 720, 424 N.Y.S.2d 88 (1980); Zervigon v. Peidmont Aviation, Inc., 17 Aviation Cases 18,200 (S.D.N.Y. 1983) (passenger removed for safety reasons).

38. See Dickerson, Thomas. 1990. *Travel Law*, supra note 22, at 3–39.

39. Bloom v. Cunard Line, Ltd. 430 N.Y.S.2d 607 (1980).

40. Kornberg v. Carnival Cruise Lines, Inc., 741 F.2d 1332 (11th Cir. 1984).

41. See Dickerson, Thomas. 1990. *Travel Law*, supra note 22, at 2–91.

42. The federal Civil Aeronautics Board has adopted a rule applying state common law to issues involving airline mishandling of luggage. See C.A.B. Order 79-12-98 (December 17, 1979).

43. 14 C.F.R. Part 254-Domestic Baggage Liability (effective April, 1984).

44. See Seltzer v. American Airlines, Inc., reported in the *New York Law Journal*, June 1, 1979, p. 13, col. 6 (N.Y. Sup. 1979).

45. Patton v. Pennsylvania Greyhound Lines, 75 Ohio App. 100, 60 N.E.2d 945 (1944).

46. Margolis v. Greyhound, 335 N.Y.S.2d 899 (N.Y. 1972), affd 408 N.Y.S.2d 766 (1978).

47. Foster v. Cunard White Star, 121 F.2d 12 (2d Cir. 1941); Geller v. Holland-American Line, 201 F.Supp. 508 (S.D. N.Y. 1960), affd 298 F.2d 618 (2d Cir. 1961), cert. denied 370 U.S. 909 (1962).

48. Hudson v. Continental Bus System, Inc, 317 S.W.2d 584 (Tex. Civ. App. 1958); Casey v. Sanborns Inc of Texas, 478 S.W.2d 234 (Tex. Civ. App. 1972); Stevenson v. Four Winds, Inc., 462 F.2d 899 (5th Cir. 1972).

49. But see Dorkin v. American Express Co., 345 N.Y.S.2d 891 (1973), affd 351 N.Y.S.2d 190 (1974). This case has been criticized as harsh and unrealistic and is not generally followed.

50. Kermarec v. Compagnie Generale Transatlantique, 358 U.S. 625 (1958); Hall v. Seaboard Air Line Ry. Co., 84 Fla. 9, 93 So. 151 (1921).

51. Commodore Cruise Line Ltd., v. Kormendi, 344 So. 2d 896 (Fla. App. 1977).

52. See 46 U.S.C. 183c.

53. van Harsell, Jan. 1988. *Tourism*, supra note 27, at 53.

54. A more in-depth discussion on the principles of hotel/motel law can be found in three excellent books. See Goodwin, John. 1987. *Hotel Law*, supra note 4; Sherry, John. 1982. *Law of Innkeepers*, supra note 5, and Jefferies, Jack. 1983. *Understanding Hotel/Motel Law*. East Lansing, Mich.: The Educational Institute of the American Hotel & Motel Association.

55. Dickerson, Thomas. 1990. *Travel Law*, supra note 22, at 4–9.

56. Goodwin, John. 1987. *Hotel Law*, supra note 4, at 12.

57. Ibid., at 15.

58. Ibid. at 9–10.

59. As to the relationship between innkeeper and guest see Sherry, John. 1982. *Law of Innkeepers*, supra note 5, at 114.

60. For a discussion on the changes to common law rules see Zaldin v. Concord Hotel, 421 N.Y.S.2d 858, 397 N.E.2d 370 (1979).

61. For a landmark case on innkeeper liability for failure to receive see Rex v. Ivens, 7 Car. & P. 213, 173 Eng. Rep. 94 (1835).

62. 42 U.S.C. 2000a (a).

63. 42 U.S.C. 2000a (b).

64. Goodwin, John. 1987. *Hotel Law*, supra note 4, at 331 and Jefferies, Jack. 1983. *Hotel Law*, supra note 5, at 4.

65. Sherry, John. 1982. *Law of Innkeepers*, supra note 5, at 79–80, Goodwin, John. 1983 *Hotel Law*, supra note 4, at 328–333.

66. Scher v. Liberty Travel Services, 328 N.Y.S.2d 386 (2d. Dept. 1971).

67. Freeman v. Kiamesha Concord Inc., 351 N.Y.S.2d 541 (1974); Hotel Del Coronado v. Quip Systems, 186 NYLJ., July 16, 1981 at 13, Col 4. (NY Sup. Ct., Nassau Co. 1981).

68. Goodwin, John. 1987. *Hotel Law*, supra note 4, at 423.

69. Dold v. Outrigger Hotel, 501 P.2d 368 (S.Ct. Haw. 1972).

70. Alsup v. Saratoga Hotel, 229 P.2d 985.

71. Kiefel v. Las Vegas Hacienda, Inc., 404 F.2d 1163 (7th Cir. 1968); Orlando Executive Park, Inc. v. P.D.R., 402 So.2d 442 (Dist. Ct. of App., 5th Dist. 1981).
72. Garzilli v. Howard Johnsons Motor Lodges, Inc., 419 F. Supp. 1210 E.D. N.Y. 1976).
73. Tobin v. Slutsky, 506 F.2d. 1097 (2nd Cir. 1974).
74. In some jurisdictions the courts have extended the doctrine to cover acts of employees committed outside the scope of employment. See McKee v. Sherton-Russel Inc., 268 F.2d 669 (2nd Cir. 1959); Clancey v. Baker, 71 Neb. 83, 98 N.W. 440 (1904).
75. Schubert v. Hotel Astor, Inc., 5 N.Y.S.2d 203 (1938), affd 8 N.Y.S.2d 567 (1938).
76. Dickerson, Thomas. 1990. *Travel Law*, supra note 22, at 4–20.
77. Jefferies, Jack. 1983. *Understanding Hotel Law*, supra note 54, at 34.
78. Dallas Hotel Co. v. Richardson, 276 S.W. 765 (Tex. Civ. App. 1925); Oklahoma City Hotel v. Levine, 189 Okla. 331, 166 P.2d 997 (1941).
79. Campbell v. Womack, 35 So.2d 96 (La. App. 1977).
80. Stoner v. California, 376 U.S. 483 (1964).

4

The Anthropology of Tourism

Robert V. Kemper

Anthropology is the study of human societies and cultures around the world and throughout history. Anthropologists describe, analyze, and explain the range and variation in the human condition in diverse settings—from Australia's few remaining desert dwellers to India's sprawling urban slums to Florida's tourist destinations. As a discipline and profession, anthropology is barely a century old, yet its contributions to our understanding of the complex world around us are made manifest every day.

We read about the culture of corporations, we worry about ethnic and religious conflict, we are besieged by claims for the biodegradability of different packagings for our garbage, and we are thrilled at the "discovery" of a previously unknown hunter-gatherer population in the Philippines. We contemplate the ethical problems of returning American Indian artifacts and skeletal materials from the Smithsonian Institution for reburial in sacred grounds. We even reconsider the authenticity of our experiences as we deal with mass tourism in the late twentieth century. These are just a few of the ways in which anthropological perspectives inform, sometimes unconsciously, our pilgrimage to the future.

What distinguishes anthropology from the other "social" sciences—sociology, economics, geography, political science, and history? What are anthropology's distinctive features as a discipline and as a profession? And what does this mean for a uniquely anthropological perspective on tourism?

First, fieldwork is at the heart of the anthropological enterprise. Whatever one's specialization, anthropologists generally agree that first-hand, systematic study involving direct observation in natural settings provides the best basis for describing the wide range of human life. Although some other social scientists also do first-hand field research, many depend on secondary data sources (for example, government censuses, airport arrival-departure counts) to analyze contemporary tourism.

Second, anthropologists want to link their research in particular communities (for example, tribal, peasant, urban) with the broader regional and international systems in which particular peoples and places are embedded. This "holistic" perspective was a forerunner to systems approaches now popular with other social scientists. It also fits nicely with analyses of touristic encounters embedded in national and international political economies.

Third, anthropologists are convinced that "culture" and "cultural relativity" are critical to understanding different ways of life. The native's point of view (sometimes referred to as an "emic" perspective) can be fruitfully juxtaposed to the outsider's point of view (sometimes referred to as an "etic" perspective). Thus, when we appreciate the diversity of human cultures around the world, we also recognize that our own way of life is only one of thousands of cultures invented in human history. Of course, in touristic encounters, we must carefully define who is the "native." Depending upon one's analytical viewpoint, the tourists, the members of the host communities, and even the agents and operators within the touristic system might be seen as the natives whose culture is the subject of our fieldwork.

Fourth, anthropology is cross-cultural in its perspective. Although most anthropologists do research through a case study approach in specific communities, they strive to develop generalizations about diverse dimensions of the human experience. The net effect of thousands of case studies conducted throughout the world has been to provide the basis for understanding much of the range and variation of the human condition. For instance, the availability of a substantial number of anthropological case studies about the impact of tourism on island communities makes it possible to generate hypotheses about what will happen in future projects planned for similar settings.

The Four Fields of Anthropology

Unlike the other social sciences, only anthropology claims for itself the full span of the human experience. In America nearly all anthropologists are trained in the four-field approach to the study of human culture and societies. Thus, *physical anthropologists* are interested in human biology and human evolution; *archaeologists* are concerned with tracing changes in human societies through analysis of material remains; *anthropological linguists* study the development of languages, how languages are learned, and how languages are related to other domains of culture; and, finally, *social* and *cultural anthropologists* are concerned with human behavior in specific social settings, often with a focus on adaptation and cultural change. Even though individuals specialize in one of these subdisciplines they are trained to recognize the significance of other dimensions of a given research problem. This broad perspective also makes anthropologists good members of multidisciplinary teams created to examine large-scale tourist projects.

Despite the widespread commitment to a four-field approach in American anthropology, the study of tourism has become important only within social and cultural anthropology. Before turning our attention to this subdiscipline, we examine what little work has been done concerning tourism by physical anthropologists, archaeologists, and anthropological linguists.

Physical Anthropology and Tourism Our comprehensive, computer-based survey of the touristic literature revealed very little direct concern with tourism by physical anthropologists. The only research project directly related to tourism examined the "pathophysiological consequences of social change in Northern Sporades [Greek islands]" (Tsiakolos and Gilbert 1983). In addition, a primatologist studying monkeys in Nepal has written of his experiences of dealing with tourists in that exotic locale (Teas 1988).

Other physical anthropologists do work indirectly on projects related to travel and tourism. For instance, physical anthropologists collect body measurements used to design seats in automobiles and airplanes. A few specialists known as forensic anthropologists are responsible for assessing the consequences of disasters involving tourists, such as the destruction of Pan American flight 103 over Lockerbie, Scotland at Christmastime 1988. Physical anthropologists also gather data (mainly from blood samples) to monitor the spread of tourist-borne diseases from one region or nation to another. In fact, one of the greatest challenges facing physical anthropologists is the need to increase dramatically their research on the relationship of tourism to the spread of AIDS in Africa and other regions of the world (compare Cohen 1988a).

Archaeology and Tourism

Archaeologists have become concerned in recent years with how the results of their research and excavations may be tied to touristic development projects. For instance, in Mexico and Central America the reconstruction of a series of important Mayan sites has been followed by increased tourism in the region. Several archaeologists (Benavides 1980, for Yucatan; Lange 1980, for Costa Rica; Rosales 1980, for Quintana Roo) have expressed alarm about the possibly negative consequences of archaeological research for the communities surrounding their excavations. An important instance of this concern for "the Maya archaeologist as agent of change" is found in Freidel's (1990) work in the community of Yaxuna in the Yucatan. He finds himself (and his research project) caught between a desire to excavate an important site that might yield information on two millennia of Mayan history and the need to deal with village leaders who are ambivalent about the prospects for touristic developments that would follow in the wake of such excavations. On a regional and international level, the latest, and most promising, plan to resolve the problems facing Mayan archaeologists involves what is known as "The Maya Route" (Fonseca 1989), a multinational effort involving Mexico, Belize, Guatemala, Honduras, and El Salvador. This integrated scheme offers the possibility of blending archaeological research with ecologically sensitive tourism in environmentally fragile settings.

Governments and international conservation agencies are now alerted to the need to recover and preserve ancient monuments in culturally appropriate ways. By extension, archaeologists are involved in the decontextualized "packaging" of ancient cultures (for example, the Pharaohs of Egypt; the Bronze Age of China; the Gold of the Inca) for traveling museum exhibits seen by millions of people in the United States, Europe, and Japan (compare Trigger 1980). The temporary transfer of cultural properties represented by these exhibits has become a major touristic enterprise, but their very success suggests that the merchandising of archaeological materials (and the "Indiana Jones" stereotype of professional archaeologists) has not yet reached its peak.

Anthropological Linguistics and Tourism

Anthropological linguists have been slow to treat the encounter of tourists and natives as a promising context for the study of sociolinguistic change. Among the few studies of language and tourism, the only general treatment is provided by Cohen and Cooper (1986). They introduce the notion of *language brokerage* to parallel the older notion of cultural brokerage. In an interesting methodological study, Brougham and Butler (1981) use linguistic procedures to perform a segmentation analysis of resident attitudes to the social impact of tourism. A more traditional sociolinguistic analysis was carried out (White 1974) on the social impact of tourism on host communities among multilingual communities in Switzerland. A different approach—involving content analysis—was used in Moeran's 1983 investigation of the language of

Japanese tourism. In this case study, the author analyzed Japanese tourist brochures to see if the "keywords" used in domestic and international tourist advertising differed. He then examined how these keywords were related to certain ideological principles around which Japanese society is organized.

Perhaps it is not surprising that anthropological linguists have so far given limited attention to the language of tourism. Nonetheless, we may hope that linguists concerned with "meaning" (that is, semiotics) might follow the lead of the sociologist MacCannell (1976) in studying touristic encounters. A recent example of such a semiotic analysis is Urbain's (1989) analysis of "the tourist adventure and his images." At a time when English seems destined to replace French as the lingua franca of world travelers and CNN [Cable News Network] is broadcast to international-class hotels in more than 100 countries, the need for anthropological linguists to study the transformation of global communication could not be greater.

Social and Cultural Anthropology and Tourism

In the following discussion, we shall concentrate on the work of American-trained anthropologists since the 1960s. Other scholars, based in Europe, Israel, India, Latin America, and elsewhere have also contributed to the anthropological perspective on tourism. Nonetheless, examination of the substantial corpus of foreign scholarship would not, I believe, change the general thrust of our argument—that is, that the study of tourism by social and cultural anthropologists has followed the path of broad theoretical and methodological developments in the discipline, rather than making significant innovations that subsequently influenced theory and method in mainstream, traditional domains of anthropological inquiry.

Acculturation and Modernization Perspectives. The study of tourism by American-trained social and cultural anthropologists began in the early 1960s. In an article about "Weekendismo" in the Mexican village of Cajititlán, Jalisco, Nuñez (1963:347) suggested that "tourism may be studied and understood within the general framework of acculturation theory; for example, the urban tourists may be thought of as representing a 'donor' culture, while the host population may be viewed as a 'recipient' culture." He goes on to ask "What are some of the consequences of a weekending, urban leisure class in a Mexican peasant village?" In his conclusions, Nuñez argues that "tourism and its effects in a village society cannot be adequately understood without reference to the socioeconomic structure of the larger society of which it is a part" (1963:352). Finally, he hopes to have demonstrated (1) that tourism may bring about rapid and dramatic changes in the loci of authority, land-use patterns, value systems, and portions of an economy; (2) that it is a legitimate and necessary area of culture change research; and (3) that the study of tourism may provide another laboratory situation for the testing of acculturation theory (1963:352).

In many respects, Nuñez's article established the research agenda for the first generation of social and cultural anthropological research on tourism. Observe that he did fieldwork in a small, peasant village in a developing country; that he was concerned with the impact of tourists and tourism on the host population; and that he was interested in using the touristic setting to test the well-established theory of acculturation (Redfield et al. 1936). Also, it is no accident that a now classic study of Latin American acculturation— in which the Spanish conquistadores are the "donor" culture and the natives of the New World are the "host" culture—had just been published by Nuñez's mentor (Foster 1960).

Following the publication of Nuñez's article, the "first organized attempt by anthropologists to look at tourism was a symposium of the Central States Anthropological Society held in Milwaukee in 1964" (Bodine 1981:469). None of the papers presented at the symposium were published, although Nuñez himself gave a paper similar to what he had already published. During the 1960s and the early 1970s, social and cultural anthropologists in the United States continued to prospect in touristic fields, but no one struck the mother-lode that would create a rush of scholarly interest. Occasionally, mention would be made of tourism as a component of the broader process of modernization and regional economic development. Frankly, given the volume of tourism in certain areas, it would have been hard to ignore its role in cultural change (for example, Cole 1972, on the Eastern Alps; Dubisch 1977, on Spain; Friedl 1972, on the Swiss Alps; Greenwood 1970, 1972, 1976, and 1977 on the Basque region of Spain; McKean 1977, on Bali; K. Moore 1970, on the Canary Islands; Pi-Sunyer 1973, 1977 on Spain).

Political Economy, Dependency, and World Systems Approaches. By the mid-1970s, the acculturation and modernization paradigms on socioeconomic change were being replaced in anthropology and the other social sciences by new theories focused on political economy, dependency, and world systems. Since the initial wave of anthropological case studies of the impact of tourism on small-scale communities had suggested that its consequences were largely negative, these results seemed to fit better with the critical perspectives of (neo)-Marxist political economy theories, dependency theories, and world systems theories than with the more optimistic views of those who followed the acculturation and modernization paradigms.

The political-economic approach to the anthropology of tourism is most definitively illustrated by Nash's (1977) essay on "tourism as a form of imperialism" in the first edited volume devoted entirely to the anthropology of tourism (Smith 1977a). Subsequent analyses by Nash and other anthropologists have made this political-economic approach a consistent feature of social anthropological work on tourism, especially in Third World countries.

"Expressive Culture": From Arts and Crafts to Play and Ritual. In contrast to those interested in studying tourism as part of economic development and cultural change, by the 1970s a number of cultural anthropologists began to define tourism as "expressive culture," that is, as a symbolic system whose qualities could be contrasted with the ordinary, everyday, work-oriented world in which people in all societies found themselves and from which they sought escape in arts and crafts, play, and ritual.

Anthropologists have a well-established interest in ethnic arts and crafts. Fieldworkers had long been responsible for gathering collections of arts and crafts for museums in New York City, Chicago, Berkeley, Philadelphia, and elsewhere. Mass tourism in the post-World War II period made ethnic arts and crafts, as well as their touristic copies, significant collectibles or souvenirs for thousands of travelers to the developing countries of Africa, Asia, Oceania, and Latin America. Thus, it was a logical step from Boas's (1927) work on "primitive art" to Graburn's (1976a) edited volume on ethnic and tourist arts, treated as cultural expressions from the Fourth World (that is, the underdeveloped zones of indigenous populations located within Third World nations).

In the same vein, in 1975, anthropology students at Southern Methodist University received a National Science Foundation Student Originated Studies grant to study tourism in the well-known arts and crafts community of Taos, New Mexico. This study (Schouten and Osgood 1975) served as the baseline for additional summer fieldschools on tourism in the Taos region in 1976, 1977, and 1978.

A pioneer in the anthropological study of play was Roberts who, along with Sutton-Smith, emphasized the cross-cultural study of games and sports (Roberts and Sutton-Smith 1966). Although Roberts had published two articles (Roberts et al. 1956a; Roberts et al. 1956b) on "highway culture" in Nebraska several years before Nuñez wrote about "weekendismo" in Mexico, he did no more direct work on tourism until much later. His concern with tourism as a form of expressive culture was eventually given form in a collaborative study of tourism as a cultural domain in Taos, New Mexico, carried out through the aegis of the SMU summer fieldschool in the late 1970s (Kemper et al. 1983).

A related thread in the cultural anthropology of tourism was provided by the discipline's long-standing interest in ritual and religion. The work of Turner (1969) on the ritual process took up the theme of what van Gennep (1908) had called the "liminal phase" of *rites de passage* and what Durkheim (1912) had characterized as the "sacred" and the "profane" domains of human existence. By the mid-1970s, anthropologists concerned with the symbolic qualities of tourism were making good use of the ideas of Turner, van Gennep, and Durkheim to study civil festivals, religious rituals, and public performances. For example, Manning (1973) published a useful ethnography of the "play world" of Black clubs in Bermuda. Subsequently, he expanded his work to deal more directly with the impact of tourism on festivals in Bermuda (Manning 1979) and Antigua (Manning 1978). More recently, an excellent collection of essays on "the festival" has appeared (Falassi 1987). An internationally recognized form of festival—the World's Fair—has been brilliantly analyzed by Benedict (1983) through his essay prepared for a museum exhibit focused on San Francisco's Panama Pacific International Exposition of 1915.

Perhaps the most influential contribution to this "expressive culture" approach continues to be Graburn's (1977) description of tourism as "the sacred journey." As he says, "Our two lives, the sacred/nonordinary/touristic and the profane/workaday/stay-at-home, customarily alternate for ordinary people and are marked by rituals or ceremonies, as should the beginning and end of lives" (1977:26).

Theoretical Divergence and Ethnographic Florescence.   By the mid-1970s, social and cultural anthropologists were beginning to examine tourism in a more systematic fashion. The first doctoral dissertations appeared at this time (compare Jafari and Aaser 1988:412) and the first of a series of symposia were organized by Smith at the annual meetings of the American Anthropological Association. She edited the seminal volume, *Hosts and Guests: The Anthropology of Tourism,* (Smith 1977a) reissued with updated chapters in 1989, as well as two special issues of the journal *Studies of Third World Societies* devoted to anthropological studies of tourism (Smith 1978a, 1978b). This florescence of fieldwork-based publications really launched the anthropology of tourism in the United States.

Nash's (1981) essay on tourism as an anthropological subject in *Current Anthropology,* the leading international anthropology journal, and special issues of the *Annals of Tourism Research* devoted to tourism and development: anthropological perspectives (Smith 1980) and anthropology of tourism (Graburn 1983a) brought a number of other contributors to the scene. A steady flow of anthropological research on tourism was flowing into the *Annals* and articles began to appear with greater frequency in major anthropological and regional publications. As we move into the 1990s, the anthropological literature on tourism is substantial, with several hundred studies available on a wide range of societies and many topics.

The increasing number of contributions may be aligned into two broad groups. The divergence in theoretical perspectives on tourism is readily seen in the juxtaposition of Graburn's (1977) essay on tourism as a sacred journey with Nash's (1977) essay on tourism as a form of imperialism in *Hosts and Guests*. This symbolic-materialist division has continued in anthropological studies of tourism and in the discipline at large.

Geographical Dimensions of the Anthropology of Tourism

In the period since Nuñez's (1963) "first" anthropological study of tourism, the geographical distribution of fieldwork has reflected the general trends in the discipline. The continuing emphasis on native peoples and peasant communities has kept most research grounded in Latin America, Africa, Asia, and the Pacific, with relatively fewer studies conducted in Europe and in the United States and Canada. Far more attention has been given to the host side of the host and guest relationship than to the guest side. More than just emphasizing studies of tourism in the Third World, a number of anthropologists have followed Graburn's (1976a) lead in dealing with the impact of international tourism on the Fourth World.

Latin America   Latin America has always been an important region for fieldwork by American-trained social and cultural anthropologists. Scholars tend to specialize in a specific country or region (for example, Mexico or the Andes) so it is rare to find synthetic treatments of major social and economic issues on a continental level. A rare exception is the brief essay by Lee (1980), who discusses tourism in Latin America as "the commerce of underdevelopment" within a framework derived from neo-Marxist and dependency theories.

Mexico has been the site of the most anthropological studies of tourism within Latin America. Studies of large-scale beach resort tourism in Zihuatenejo-Ixtapa, Guerrero (Cowan 1987) and in Huatulco, Oaxaca (Long 1989); small-scale beach resorts in Chiapas (Passariello 1983); spontaneous tourism in Puerto Vallarta (Evans 1978, 1979); ethnic relations in the fishing port of San Felipe, Baja California (Brewer 1978); and elite control of tourism in Yucatan (Lee 1978) offer lowland alternatives to anthropological research carried out in the central highlands. Brandes (1988:88–109) addresses the role of the state in planning annual festivals in the village of Tzintzuntzan, Michoacán, whereas Kemper (1979a) offers a comparative analysis of tourism and regional development for the entire Lake Pátzcuaro region. He also investigated the role of migrants as tourists in the continuing development of festival tourism in Tzintzuntzan (Kemper 1991). Farther west, Talavera Salgado (1982) studied the American-dominated retirement community of Ajijic on the shores of Lake Chapala, Jalisco, as a counterpoint to Nuñez's (1963) seminal work across the lake in Cajititlán. The importance of arts and crafts in the Mexican touristic sector is reflected in Littlefield's (1980) study of Mayan artisans in the context of tourist development; Stromberg's (1976) work on *amate* bark-paper paintings of Xalitla, Guerrero; Ryerson's (1976) report on Seri ironwood carving; and Charlton's (1976) investigation of modern ceramics in the Teotihuacán Valley.

The Caribbean region has received considerable attention from anthropologists interested in tourism and regional development. Manning (1978 and 1979) examined the link between local festivals and tourism in Antigua and Bermuda, whereas Lett (1983) discussed the ludic and liminoid aspects of charter boat tourism in the British Virgin Islands. Freitag (1991) studied the enclave resorts in the Dominican Republic and Lerch and Levy (1990) examined the role of women in the tourist sector in Barbados. LaFlamme (1979) reported on the impact of tourism on a small, once isolated island community in the Bahamas, and Golberg (1983) explored relations between tourists and performers in Haitian voodoo shows. And Olwig (1980) examined national parks, tourism, and local development on the island of St. John, U.S. Virgin Islands. Her conclusions about tourism and development reflect those of many who have studied the Caribbean: "the most important role of the anthropologist in park planning and tourism would seem to be that of pointing out the inherent conflicts in projects which propose to preserve local resources in order to further tourism. Indigenous peoples, under present circumstances, are not likely to receive the greatest benefit of such development" (1980:29).

Other anthropological studies of tourism in mainland Latin America include Aspelin's (1977) report on the case of the Mamainde of Mato Grosso, Brazil; van den Berghe's (1980) case study of tourism as ethnic relations in Cuzco, Peru; and A. Moore's (1980a) analysis of touristic planning and development in the San Blas region of Panama. Swain's (1989) longitudinal study of the role of women in "indigenous tourism" through their production of *mola* cloth art among the Kuna people of this same region is only one of several studies of folk arts and tourism. Salvador (1976) wrote about the clothing arts of the San Blas Kuna, Boyer (1976) described how gourd decoration has become big business in highland Peru, and Lathrap (1976) analyzed the tourist arts of the Shipibo-Conibo people of the tropical forests of eastern Peru.

Africa   Anthropological studies of tourism in sub-Saharan Africa have emphasized the importance of ethnic and touristic arts, the special character of environmental/nature tourism, and the impact of foreign tourism on native populations. In Graburn's (1976a) edited volume on ethnic and tourist arts, Bascom (1976) discusses changing African art; Ben-Amos (1976) examines ebony-carving in Benin; Biebuyck (1976) considers the decline of Lega sculptural art in Zaire; and Sandelowsky (1976) reports on functional and tourist art along the Okavango River in South-West Africa. Subsequently, Richter (1978) offered an overview of the tourist art market as a factor and social change and Jules-Rosette (1984) examined the messages of tourist art through a cross-cultural semiotic analysis of selected contemporary African artists in the Ivory Coast, Zambia, and Kenya. The interaction of tourists and natives with African wildlife was described by Almagor (1985) and van den Berghe (1986) in terms of a "vision quest" by the foreign visitors. The impact of foreign tourism on indigenous enterprises and employment in the Gambia (Farver 1984), the connection between tourists and black markets in West Africa (Lehmann 1980), the development of Swahili stratification in the context of tourism in Kenya (Peake 1989), and the cultural and economic consequences of tourism among Kalahari San people in Botswana (Hitchcock 1991) demonstrate the widespread awareness of tourism among social and cultural anthropologists in contemporary Africa.

Oceania The Pacific islands have given anthropologists ample opportunity to study tourism in diverse settings. From the "staged authenticity" of the Polynesian Cultural Center in Hawaii (Stanton 1989; Brameld and Matsuyama 1978) to the firewalkers of Fiji (Brown 1984), fieldworkers have been concerned with the impact of foreign tourists on native cultures. Although Finney and Watson (1975) characterized tourism in the Pacific region as a "new kind of sugar," other observers have been more ambivalent about its effects on local economic development. The islands of Indonesia have, justifiably, received considerable attention. McKean (1989) examined economic dualism and cultural involution in Bali and Rodenburg (1980) discussed the effects of economic development on the same island. Crystal (1989) reported on the paradox of tourist development in Tana Toraja (Sulawesi), where 40,000 visitors a year have failed to dislodge traditionalists from their isolation. The dilemmas of tourism also concern aboriginal Australians (Altman 1989) and the natives of Tonga (Urbanowicz 1989).

The relation of folk arts to tourist development were discussed by Abramson (1976) for the Upper Sepik region of New Guinea, by Williams (1976) for Australian aborigines at Yirrkala, and by Mead (1976) for the Maori of New Zealand.

Two recent contributions from the Philippines (Dumont 1984) and Papua New Guinea (Errington and Gewertz 1989) raise important questions about the differences and similarities between tourists and anthropologists. In his conclusion, Dumont declares that the word "tourism" has "come to connote the very superficiality of interethnic encounters. . . . Of the tourist, too, it can be said that he looks but does not see, listens but does not hear. . . . he is to a greater or lesser extent impervious to the experience of otherness." (1984:149). He goes on to claim that "Not unlike the positivistic anthropologist, he operates backwards. Instead of letting things happen and interpreting their experience, both come to the field or to the tourist place with a set of ready-made hypotheses that hinder rather than enhance their perceptivity. . . . Ultimately, the positivist's confirmation of his hypothesis and the tourist's of his prejudices are . . . one and the same thing" (1984:149).

Awareness of such "interpretativist" postures (Crick 1985, 1989) and their own fieldwork experiences among the Chambri (Papua New Guinea) prompted Errington and Gewertz also to ponder tourism and anthropology in a postmodern world. Rather than focus their analysis on the natives, Errington and Gewertz concentrate on the tourists, especially the older, affluent foreigners who come to New Guinea on the small, luxurious cruise ship *Melanesian Explorer.* A detailed description and analysis of a Chambri ceremonial initiation, witnessed by tourists and anthropologists alike, leads them to conclude that "it enables us to talk knowledgeably about such interesting matters as the nature of the world political economy, the reasons that tourists come to Papua New Guinea and the effects on and the response of the Chambri—including their capacity to resist, adapt, transform. . . . For anthropologists to work toward reaching *and* conveying an understanding of such matters (even when specific events have a ludic form) strikes us as serious, but not as value-free, business" (1989:51). A final, unusual contribution to the anthropology of Pacific tourism involves a case study of a small South Seas cruise ship, the *Pacific Discoverer.* Foster (1986) describes the behavior of the aging, upper middle-class passengers, and the ways in which they relate to each other, in terms of the concepts of "short-lived societies," "cruise culture," and the ship as "environment." Foster's participant observation as a member of a short-lived cruise culture raises broader questions about the nature of "tourist culture" (compare Jafari 1987).

Asia   Anthropological studies of Asian tourism have been concentrated in Thailand, Japan, Hong Kong/China, and the Indian subcontinent.

Though a sociologist by training, Cohen has been conducting important ethnographic research on various aspects of Thai tourism, including the dynamics of relationships between Bangkok prostitutes and tourists (Cohen 1982a), bungalow tourism on the islands of southern Thailand (Cohen 1982b), hill tribe trekking in northern Thailand (Cohen 1989), and tourism and AIDS (Cohen 1988a).

Another central theorist in touristic studies, Graburn (1983b, 1987), carried out important studies of domestic tourism in Japan. He emphasized the cultural structure of Japanese tourism in "an attempt to display the basic grammar of Japanese tourism and particularly the relationship between the institutions of the home society, the tourist sites, and the tourist who goes back and forth and mediates between them" (1987:18). One of Graburn's students has also written about Ainu wood and stone carving in the context of tourism in northern Japan (Low 1976).

Schuchat (1979) and Guldin (1989) have analyzed the experiences of Western visitors who travel on guided tours to the People's Republic of China (PRC). The latter's experience is especially interesting because it involved leading a study tour group whose members were themselves being studied. Guldin concluded his report by suggesting that

> mutually beneficial cooperation between anthropologists, tourists and the industry is thus not only possible and pragmatic but good for the spread of anthropological values. On our study tours, for example, many tourists not only learned about the Chinese but learned from the Chinese about alternate human possibilities and patterns. . . . The anthropological responsibility lies in encouraging this type of tourism" (1989:133).

Changes in tourism policy between the PRC and the British colony of Hong Kong are discussed by Chow (1988), who notes that the rapid growth of tourism since the Open Policy of 1979 reflects the move from a centralized economy to a relatively decentralized, market-oriented economy in Guangdong Province.

In the Indian subcontinent, Smith (1981) briefly compared controlled and uncontrolled tourist development in the Himalayan nations of Bhutan and Nepal. At the other extreme, Maduro (1976) described the Brahmin painters of the pilgrimage center of Nathdwara, located in the Rajasthan desert. Another famous tourist site, the erotic sculptures at Khajuraho, Madhya Pradesh, was studied by Ichaporia (1983) from the dual perspective of domestic and international tourists. Continuing the theme of pilgrimage, so central to tourism in the subcontinent, Pfaffenberger's (1983) analysis of "serious pilgrims and frivolous tourists" highlights critical problems in the development of tourism in Sri Lanka. Finally, the "early effects" of tourism in the Seychelles Islands was analyzed by Wilson (1979). This well-documented examination of the role of tourism in local economic development concludes with the warning that "It remains to be seen how successfully the leaders of the new republic can . . . realize that vision of an Indian Ocean paradise cherished by Seychellois, tourist, and anthropologist alike" (1979:236).

The Middle East   Anthropological studies of tourism in the Middle East are scarce. Although Loeb (1977) wrote about Jewish merchants and touring coreligionists in prerevolutionary Iran, he has since remarked that "tourism came to a standstill" (1989:245) after the Shah was deposed in 1978–1979. Political and military conflicts have also destroyed the tourist industry that once flourished in Lebanon and other countries of the region. Moreover, the prosperity brought by OPEC and high oil prices has done more to send many Arabs abroad as tourists than to attract international tourists to the Middle East. In contrast, Israel has manifested a state policy to attract Diaspora Jews to the homeland (ideally, through *EL AL*, the Israeli national airline). Thus, the touristic image of Israel has been manifest in the metropolitan centers of Europe and the Americas, especially through brochures and guidebooks (Cohen 1974).

Europe and the Mediterranean Region

The increase of anthropological studies in Europe and in the Mediterranean region in the 1970s and 1980s was accompanied by recognition of the conflict between local economic development and cultural autonomy in the context of mass tourism.

Since Spain is the primary destination of European tourists, it is hardly surprising that social and cultural anthropologists encountered the consequences of mass tourism as they carried out their research in rural communities from the southern coasts to the northern Basque country. The best known of these studies are those of Greenwood (1970, 1972, 1976, 1977, 1989) whose ideas about the "commoditization of culture" emerged from his analysis of the *alarde* festival in Fuenterrabia. At first, he was quite negative about the impact of tourism on the local culture, but more recently Greenwood (1989:183) mused about what "authenticity mean[s] and why tourists seek it?"; argued that "tourist cultural performances provide an opportunity for a limited self-criticism of middle-class culture, a kind of pseudo-tragedy in which the affluence that makes touring possible is the very cause of the loss of cultural authenticity" (1989:184); and suggested that "those groups seeking to establish or expand political rights by the reinforcement of their cultural traditions and ethnic identity see tourism as a double-edged sword" (1989:184).

Other important anthropological studies of Spanish tourism include K. Moore's (1970) report on the role of Swedish tourists in transforming a Canary Island village; Dubisch's (1977) early study of emigration, tourism, and changing values; Pi-Sunyer's (1973, 1977, 1989) sympathetic treatment of his ancestral home, Cap Loc, which has become a significant Catalan resort town; Hermans's (1981) examination of the positive interaction of tourist development and agriculture in Cambrils, a village of the Costa Dorada; and Oliver-Smith et al.'s (1989) assessment of the struggle for local resource control in the hillside community of Mijas on the Costa del Sol. This last case "demonstrates that the local population is not totally bereft of options in the process of tourist development. But a decidedly activist stance dedicated to maintaining a balance between local and external resources control must be adopted by local governments" (Oliver-Smith et al. 1989:350).

France has also received considerable attention by anthropologists interested in tourism. Both Nash (1970) and Petit-Skinner (1977) wrote about Americans living permanently in France. Nash (1979) also described the historical development of "aristocratic" tourism in Nice from 1763 to 1936. French Alpine tourism has been examined on a comparative basis for the communes of La Roche (Basses-Alpes) and Mélèze (Hautes-Alpes) by Rosenberg et al. (1973). In contrasting the development model with the reality for villagers, the authors state that "tourism is found to benefit tourists and developers, but not to aid most villagers. Jobs available for locals in increasingly stratified resort communes are generally not attractive enough to prevent them from leaving the land" (1973:21).

Other European countries in which North American anthropologists have conducted fieldwork about tourism include: Portugal, where Mendonsa (1983) examined socioeconomic stratification in the fishing community of Nazaré; Switzerland, where Freidl (1972) and Cole (1972) dealt with the role of tourism in modernization of rural communities; Austria, where Gamper (1981) studied the influence of tourism on ethnic relations between two populations in southern Austria and where Pospisil (1979) conducted longitudinal research on the impact of tourism on the Tyrolean community of Obernberg; Italy, where van der Werff (1980) considered the polarizing implications of the tourist industry in the beach resort of Pescaia; and Malta, where Boissevain (1977, 1978) and Boissevain and Inglott (1979) assessed both negative and positive consequences of mass tourism. Perhaps because the Scandinavian countries generate more tourists than they receive, anthropologists have not reported on tourism in these lands, with the sole exception of Smith's related study of Greenland (1982).

North America Anthropologists have investigated tourism in the United States and Canada from Alaska to Florida and from California to Vermont. A major thrust of their research is the relationship of contemporary Native American peoples and visitors from beyond the reservations. Many studies of the changes in Native American arts and crafts as a result of tourism have been carried out (e.g., Graburn 1976b, on Canadian Inuit Eskimo; Kaufmann 1976, on the Canadian Haida; Brody 1976, Peck and Lepie 1977; Gill 1976, Deitch 1977 and 1989—all on Southwestern groups). Other anthropologists reported on the burlesqueing of tourists by Pueblo clowns (Sweet 1989); on Native American images of tourists among the Pueblo and Navajo silversmiths in New Mexico (Evans-Pritchard 1989); on touristic images of Native Americans as portrayed through historic post cards (Albers and James 1989); on the impact of tourism on "marginal men" among Alaskan Eskimos (Smith 1977b, 1989b); on the economic potential of reservation-based tourism among the Kaibab Paiute (Stoffle et al. 1979); and the neglected legacy of Indian cultural resources in California tourism (Evans 1986).

Perhaps in response to research opportunities mandated by U. S. environmental laws, anthropologists have been active in examining nature/recreational tourism. For instance, Miller (1987) reported on cooperative coastal tourism planning in Washington State; Rodriguez (1987) studied the impact of the ski industry on the Rio Hondo watershed in northern New Mexico; and Jordan (1980) discussed the effects of "the summer people" on a Vermont vacation village.

General treatments have been made of American vacations (Gottlieb 1982), group tours (Schuchat 1979, 1983), and the role of women as decision makers in vacations (Smith 1979). Other anthropologists focused their studies on specific tourist regions (e.g., Smith et al. 1986, on northeastern California; Boynton 1986, on the Amish of Pennsylvania; Hyland 1991, on tourism in the lower Mississippi delta; Peck and Lepie 1977, on North Carolina coastal communities; and Schouten and Osgood 1975; Kemper 1978, 1979a, 1979b; and Kemper et al. 1983—all on Taos, New Mexico). Specific cities have also been the scenes for anthropological inquiries into American tourism (e.g., Cameron 1991, on Bethlehem, Pennsylvania; Plotnicov 1990, on Pittsburgh; Greenbaum 1990, on Ybor City, Florida; and Sieber 1991, on Boston). Deserving special mention in this category of place-specific studies are two studies by A. Moore. His delightful analysis of Walt Disney World as a "bounded ritual space and pilgrimage center" (1980b) and his report on Japanese tourists in Southern California, "Rosanzerusu is Los Angeles" (1985), both employ a semiotic perspective to deal with the "sacred" qualities of touristic sites.

Themes in the Anthropology of Tourism

This global review of the literature demonstrates that anthropologists have a wide range of interests, often closely tied to their specific fieldwork setting. Nonetheless, this diversity may be evaluated within a set of central themes tied to the symbolic and materialist perspectives on tourism. On the one hand, in the symbolic domain, many anthropologists have focused on festivals, rituals, pilgrimages, performances, and arts and crafts. On the other, in the materialistic domain, emphasis has been placed on economic and regional development, class and social stratification, and macrolevel concerns for political and economic dependency within the world system. Certain themes, such as ethnicity and gender, serve to bridge the symbolic and materialistic domains in tourist studies because they constitute significant cultural categories and also have political economic potency. The continuing pursuit by anthropologists for "authenticity" and their preoccupation with "commoditization" is especially critical in situations where ethnicity and gender are critical to the touristic encounter (compare Cohen 1988b).

As we move through the 1990s, it is likely that anthropologists will address touristic problems beyond traditional anthropological research domains. Perhaps incipient efforts to develop an anthropology of industries and corporations can be focused on tourism as a global enterprise. The new concern for ecotourism sweeping through the affluent tourists of economically powerful nations opens up opportunities to link anthropology's ecological perspective with cultural conservation in the context of tourism (compare Chambers 1991). As Greenwood has suggested, tourism poses a profound research challenge for contemporary anthropologists and the broadest theoretical issues in the discipline: "culture as representation, cultural diversity, culture's dynamic properties, the importance of mythic authenticity, the character of intercultural interactions, and the links between political economy and systems of meaning" (1989:185).

Methodological Issues   The anthropology of tourism has shared in the methodological developments of recent decades. Although case studies of specific communities still predominate, and participant observation and other "traditional" ethnographic procedures remain significant, recent research has also included more sophisticated qualitative and quantitative approaches. Just as the other social sciences have learned the value of ethnographic techniques used by anthropologists, so anthropologists have begun to experiment with statistical and survey techniques from the social sciences and with textual and meta-analytical procedures from the humanities (compare Dann et al. 1988). The interplay between methodological sophistication and theoretical awareness remains a major challenge for all anthropologists, and those interested in tourism are no exception.

One promising avenue for the anthropology of tourism is the long-term study of a well-selected sample of communities and populations drawn from around the world. If we hope to go beyond the limitations of static, one-shot studies, we need to have systematic, longitudinal assessments of the impact of tourism on host societies and cultures. We also need to examine the touristic encounter to determine what are the long-term transformations in the tourists when they return to their sending societies. And we need to know how the tourist-generating areas are changing, so that the entire tourist system and its component processes can be more adequately comprehended. The possibility is that "increasingly sophisticated investigators . . . will gradually build up the same kind of cross-culturally applicable picture of the touristic process that already exists for other aspects of culture" (Nash and Smith 1991:20).

Anthropological Ambivalence about Tourism: From Theory to Application

We may now return to the questions raised earlier. What are anthropology's distinctive features? And what does this mean for a uniquely anthropological perspective on tourism? (Unfortunately, we cannot directly address the question of what distinguishes anthropology from the other social sciences since we have not done a systematic comparison of anthropological and nonanthropological analyses of tourism around the world).

Virtually all of the anthropological contributions reviewed here have been based on fieldwork in particular communities. Most of the investigators have also grounded their case studies within larger regional and international systems. Furthermore, most are concerned with the tension between "culture" and "political economy," that is, between what Lett (1989:276–277) has referred to as "the maintenance of human identity" and "the maintenance of human life." Lett goes on to clarify his position by arguing that, "Cross-culturally, the maintenance of human identity is most frequently accomplished through such activities as ritual, play, and art. . . . [whereas] the maintenance of human life is invariably accomplished . . . through learned and shared subsistence strategies" (Lett 1989:277). Without a doubt, anthropological studies of tourism emphasize ritual, play, and art, but they also give attention to subsistence strategies, that is, issues of economic development. The duality, or ambivalence, of the anthropological vision about the symbolic and materialist dimensions of the human experience is inherent in the fieldworker's effort to understand and translate the "other"—whether natives of Papua New Guinea or the tourists who have traveled thousands of miles to visit them.

From an early emphasis on acculturation and modernization theories to a more recent focus on political economy, dependency, and world systems theories, anthropologists have sought to deal with tourism as a component of the massive transformations of the world order in the late twentieth century. The special virtue of an anthropology of tourism is that it combines fieldwork on the local level with awareness of macroeconomic and macropolitical changes. Even when interpreting the "expressive culture" of tourism, anthropologists are sensitive to issues of wealth and power, local autonomy versus external control, and maintenance of tradition in the context of global change.

When applying their research on tourism, anthropologists are in the position to work with clients who may represent the tourist industry, governmental agencies, and the local host community. They can try to protect the interests of people with relatively little power, in accord with the ethical canons of the anthropological profession, at the same time that the tourist industry and the tourists themselves play culturally more appropriate roles in the touristic system. An important purpose of applied work is to reduce the tensions inherent in the cross-cultural, cross-class, cross-gender, and interethnic encounters so likely to be characteristic of global tourism in the twenty-first century. As Nash and Smith (1991:22) have argued, "ultimately, the anthropologist will have to ask (and answer) the supreme question: Will this particular research further the basic anthropological goal, which is to understand the human condition?" Anthropologists have already made important contributions to understanding tourism, especially as it affects local populations in developing countries, but much still remains to be done. We are still not close to achieving an adequate theoretical cross-cultural model of the global tourist system, much less knowing how tourism combines with other large scale forces to transform (or conserve) the cultures found among small populations in vulnerable environments.

Summary

Anthropology is the study of human societies and cultures around the world and throughout history. This article tries to show what distinguishes anthropology from the other social sciences. It also gives the distinctive features of anthropology as a discipline and as a profession. Finally, it discusses the anthropological perspective of tourism.

References

Abramson, J. A. 1976. Style change in an Upper Sepik contact situation. In *Ethnic and Tourist Arts*, ed. Nelson H. H. Graburn, pp. 249–265. Berkeley, Calif.: University of California Press.

Albers, Patricia C., and William R. James. 1989. Travel photography: A methodological approach. *Annals of Tourism Research* 15(1):134–158.

Almagor, Uri. 1985. A tourist's "vision quest" in an African game reserve. *Annals of Tourism Research* 12(1):31–47.

Altman, Jon. 1989. Tourism dilemmas for Aboriginal Australians. *Annals of Tourism Research* 16(4):456–476.

Aspelin, Paul L. 1977. The anthropological analysis of tourism: Indirect tourism and political economy in the case of Mamainde of Mato Grosso, Brazil. *Annals of Tourism Research* 4(3):135–160.

Bascom, William. 1976. Changing African art. In *Ethnic and Tourist Arts*, ed. Nelson H. H. Graburn, pp. 303–319. Berkeley, Calif.: University of California Press.

Benavides C., Antonio. 1980. Planificación regional y arqueología en Yucatán. In *Tourismo y Desarrollo*, ed. Antonio Benavides C., pp. 29–33. México, D. F.: SEP/INAH, Cuadernos de los Centros Regionales, Sureste.

Benedict, Burton. 1983. *The Anthropology of World's Fairs: San Francisco's Panama Pacific International Exposition of 1915*. London and Berkeley: Scolar Press.

Ben-Amos, Paula. 1975. "A la recherche du temps perdu": On being an ebony-carver in Benin. In *Ethnic and Tourist Arts*, ed. Nelson H. H. Graburn, pp. 320–333. Berkeley, Calif.: University of California Press.

Biebuyck, Daniel P. 1976. The decline of Lega sculptural art. In *Ethnic and Tourist Arts*, ed. Nelson H. H. Graburn, pp. 334–339. Berkeley, Calif.: University of California Press.

Boas, Franz. 1927. *Primitive Art*. Cambridge, Mass.: Harvard University Press.

Bodine, John J. 1981. Comment on "Tourism as an anthropological subject." *Current Anthropology* 22(5):469.

Boissevain, Jeremy. 1977. Tourism and development in Malta. *Development and Change* 8:523–538.

Boissevain, Jeremy. 1978. Tourism and development in Malta. In *Tourism and Economic Change, Studies in Third World Societies 6*, ed. Valene L. Smith, pp. 37–56. Williamsburg, Va.: College of William and Mary.

Boissevain, Jeremy, and Peter Serracino Inglott. 1979. Tourism in Malta. In *Tourism: Passport to Development?* ed. Emanuel de Kadt, pp. 265–284. New York: Oxford University Press.

Boyer, Ruth McDonald. 1976. Gourd decoration in highland Peru. In *Ethnic and Tourist Arts*, ed. Nelson H. H. Graburn, pp. 183–197. Berkeley, Calif.: University of California Press.

Boynton, Linda L. 1986. The effect of tourism on Amish quilting design. *Annals of Tourism Research* 13(3):451–465.

Brameld, Theodore, and Midori Matsuyama. 1978. *Tourism as cultural learning: Two controversial case studies in educational anthropology.* Washington, D. C.: University Press of America.

Brandes, Stanley. 1988. *Power and Persuasion: Fiestas and Social Control in Rural Mexico.* Philadelphia: University of Pennsylvania Press.

Brewer, Jeffrey D. 1978. Tourism, business, and ethnic categories in a Mexican town. In *Tourism and Behavior, Studies in Third World Societies 5*, ed. Valene L. Smith, pp. 83–100. Williamsburg, Va.: College of William and Mary.

Brody, J. J. 1976. The creative consumer: Survival, revival and invention in southwest Indian arts. In *Ethnic and Tourist Arts*, ed. Nelson H. H. Graburn, pp. 70–84. Berkeley, Calif.: University of California Press.

Brougham, J. E., and R. W. Butler, 1981. A segmentary analysis of resident attitudes to the social impact of tourism. *Annals of Tourism Research* 8(4):569–590.

Brown, Carolyn Henning. 1984. Tourism and ethnic competition in a ritual form: The firewalkers of Fiji. *Oceania* 54(3):223–244.

Cameron, Catherine. 1991. Questing gemeinschaft in post-industrial society. Paper read at 50th annual meeting of Society for Applied Anthropology, 13–17 March, 1991, at Charleston, S.C.

Chambers, Erve. 1991. International tourism and ethnic minorities in Thailand. Paper read at 50th annual meeting of Society for Applied Anthropology, 13–17 March, 1991, at Charleston, S.C.

Charlton, Thomas H. 1976. Modern ceramics in the Teotihuacán Valley. In *Ethnic and Tourist Arts*, ed. Nelson H. H. Graburn, pp. 137–148. Berkeley, Calif.: University of California Press.

Chow, W. S. 1988. Open policy and tourism between Guangdong and Hong Kong. *Annals of Tourism Research* 15(2):205–218.

Cohen, Erik. 1974. *The Touristic Image of Israel: An Analysis of Guide Books.* Tel Aviv: Tel Aviv University, Center for Urban and Regional Studies, Working Paper No. 21.

Cohen, Erik. 1982a. Thai girls and farang men: The edge of ambiguity. *Annals of Tourism Research* 9(3):403–428.

Cohen, Erik. 1982b. Marginal paradises. Bungalow tourism on the islands of Southern Thailand. *Annals of Tourism Research* 9(2):189–228.

Cohen, Erik. 1988a. Tourism and AIDS in Thailand. *Annals of Tourism Research* 15(4):467–486.

Cohen, Erik. 1988b. Authenticity and commodization in tourism. *Annals of Tourism Research* 15(3):371–386.

Cohen, Erik. 1989. "Primitive" and "remote": Hill tribe trekking in Thailand. *Annals of Tourism Research* 16(1):30–61.

Cohen, Erik, and Robert L. Cooper. 1986. Language and tourism. *Annals of Tourism Research* 13(4):533–563.

Cole, John W. 1972. Cultural adaptation in the eastern alps. *Anthropological Quarterly* 45(3):145–157.

Cowan, Ruth Anita. 1987. Tourism development in a Mexican coastal community. Ph.D. diss., Southern Methodist University, Dallas, Texas.

Crick, Malcolm. 1985. "Tracing" the anthropological self: Quizzical reflections on field work, tourism and the Ludic. *Social Analysis* 17:73–94.

Crick, Malcolm. 1989. Representations of international tourism in the social sciences: Sun, sex, sights, savings, and servility. *Annual Review of Anthropology* 18:307–344.

Crystal, Eric. 1989. Tourism in Toraja (Sulawesi, Indonesia). In *Hosts and Guests: The Anthropology of Tourism*, 2d ed, ed. Valene L. Smith, pp. 139–168. Philadelphia: University of Pennsylvania Press.

Dann, Graham, Dennison Nash, and Philip Pearce. 1988. Methodology in tourism research. *Annals of Tourism Research* 15(1):1–28.

Deitch, Lewis I. 1977. The impact of tourism upon the arts and crafts of the Indians of the southwestern United States. In *Hosts and Guests: The Anthropology of Tourism*, ed. Valene L. Smith, pp. 173–184. Philadelphia: University of Pennsylvania Press.

Deitch, Lewis I. 1989. The impact of tourism upon the arts and crafts of the Indians of the southwestern United States. In *Hosts and Guests: The Anthropology of Tourism*, 2d ed., ed. Valene L. Smith, pp. 223–235. Philadelphia: University of Pennsylvania Press.

Dubisch, Jill. 1977. Modernization in rural Spain: Emigration, tourism, and changing values. *Peasant Studies* 6(4):147–149.

Dumont, Jean-Paul. 1984. A matter of touristic "indifférance." *American Ethnologist* 11(1):139–151.

Durkheim, Emile. 1912. *Les formes élémentaires de la vie religieuse: le système totémique en Australie.* Paris: Alcan.

Errington, Frederick, and Deborah Gewertz. 1989. Tourism and anthropology in a post-modern world. *Oceania* 60:37–54.

Evans, Nancy H. 1978. Tourism and cross-cultural communication. In *Tourism and Behavior, Studies in Third World Societies 5*, ed. Valene L. Smith, pp. 41–53. Williamsburg, Va.: College of William and Mary.

Evans, Nancy H. 1979. The dynamics of tourist development in Puerto Vallarta. In *Tourism: Passport to Development?* ed. Emanuel de Kadt, pp. 305–320. New York: Oxford University Press.

Evans, Nancy H. 1986. The tourism of Indian California: A neglected legacy. *Annals of Tourism Research* 13(3):435–450.

Evans-Pritchard, Deirdre. 1989. How "they" see "us": Native American images of tourists. *Annals of Tourism Research* 16(1):89–105.

Falassi, Alessandro, ed. 1987. *Time Out of Time: Essays on the Festival.* Albuquerque: University of New Mexico Press.

Farver, JoAnn M. 1984. Tourism and employment in The Gambia. *Annals of Tourism Research* 11(2):249–265.

Finney, Ben R., and Karen Ann Watson, eds. 1975. *A New Kind of Sugar: Tourism in the Pacific.* Honolulu: East-West Center.

Fonseca, Julio Cesar. 1989. The Maya route. In *Travel Research: Globalization, The Pacific Rim and Beyond*, The Travel Research Association Twelfth Annual Conference Proceedings, pp. 233–234. Salt Lake City: University of Utah.

Foster, George M. 1960. *Culture and Conquest: America's Spanish Heritage.* New York: Wenner-Gren Foundation for Anthropological Research, Viking Fund Publications in Anthropology No. 27.

Foster, George M. 1986. South Sea cruise: A case study of a short-lived society. *Annals of Tourism Research* 13(2):215–238.

Freidel, David A. 1990. Lords of Yaxuna: Locating the archaeologist in the Maya field. Paper given at the 89th annual meeting of the American Anthropological Association, 28 November–2 December, New Orleans, La.

Freitag, Tilman G. 1991. "For whom the benefits roll": Enclave tourism and host community development in the Dominican Republic. Paper read at 50th annual meeting of Society for Applied Anthropology, 13–17 March, 1991, at Charleston, S.C.

Friedl, John. 1972. Changing economic emphasis in an Alpine village. *Anthropological Quarterly* 45(3):145–157.

Gamper, Josef A. 1981. Tourism in Austria: A case study of the influence of tourism on ethnic relations. *Annals of Tourism Research* 8(3):432–446.

Gill, Robert R. 1976. Ceramic arts and acculturation at Laguna. In *Ethnic and Tourist Arts*, ed. Nelson H. H. Graburn, pp. 102–113. Berkeley, Calif.: University of California Press.

Golberg, Alan. 1983. Identity and experience in Haitian voodoo shows. *Annals of Tourism Research* 10(4):479–495.

Gottlieb, Alma. 1982. Americans' vacations. *Annals of Tourism Research* 9(2):165–187.

Graburn, Nelson H. H., ed. 1976a. *Ethnic and Tourist Arts: Cultural Expressions from the Fourth World.* Berkeley, Calif.: University of California Press.

Graburn, Nelson H. H. 1976b. Eskimo art: The eastern Canadian Arctic. In *Ethnic and Tourist Arts*, ed. Nelson H. H. Graburn, pp. 39–55. Berkeley, Calif.: University of California Press.

Graburn, Nelson H. H. 1977. Tourism: the sacred journey. In *Hosts and Guests: The Anthropology of Tourism*, ed. Valene L. Smith, pp. 21–36. Philadelphia: University of Pennsylvania Press.

Graburn, Nelson H. H., ed. 1983a. The anthropology of tourism. *Annals of Tourism Research* 10(1):1–192.

Graburn, Nelson H. H. 1983b. *To Pray, Pay, and Play: The Cultural Structure of Japanese Domestic Tourism*. Aix-en-Provence: Université du droit, deconomie et des sciences, Centre des hautes études touristiques.

Graburn, Nelson H. H. 1987. Material symbols in Japanese domestic tourism. In *Mirror and Metaphor: Material and Social Constructions of Reality*, eds. Daniel W. Ingersoll, Jr., and Gordon Bronitsky, pp. 17–27. Lanham, Md.: University Press of America.

Greenbaum, Susan D. 1990. Marketing Ybor City: Race, ethnicity, and historical preservation in the Sunbelt. *City & Society* 4(1):58–76.

Greenwood, Davydd J. 1970. Agriculture, industrialization and tourism: The economics of modern Basque farming. Ph.D. diss. Ann Arbor, Mich.: University Microfilms.

Greenwood, Davydd J. 1972. Tourism as an agent of change: a Spanish Basque case. *Ethnology* 11(1):80–91.

Greenwood, Davydd J. 1976. Tourism as an agent of change. *Annals of Tourism Research* 3(3):128–142.

Greenwood, Davydd J. 1977. Culture by the pound: An anthropological perspective on tourism as cultural commoditization. In *Hosts and Guests: The Anthropology of Tourism*, ed. Valene L. Smith, pp. 129–138. Philadelphia: University of Pennsylvania Press.

Greenwood, Davydd J. 1989. Culture by the pound: An anthropological perspective on tourism as cultural commoditization. In *Hosts and Guests: The Anthropology of Tourism*, 2d ed., ed. Valene L. Smith, pp. 171–185. Philadelphia: University of Pennsylvania Press.

Guldin, Gregory Eliyu. 1989. The anthropology study tour in China: a call for cultural guides. *Human Organization* 48(2):126–134.

Hermans, Dymphna. 1981. The encounter of agriculture and tourism: A Catalan case. *Annals of Tourism Research* 8(3):462–479.

Hitchcock, Robert K. 1991. Cultural and economic impacts of tourism among Kalahari San. Paper read at 50th annual meeting of Society for Applied Anthropology, 13–17 March, 1991, at Charleston, S.C.

Hyland, Stanley. 1991. Tourism in the Lower Mississippi Delta: The struggle between proponents of economic growth and grassroots tourism organizations. Paper read at 50th annual meeting of Society for Applied Anthropology, 13–17 March, 1991, at Charleston, S.C.

Ichaporia, Niloufer. 1983. Tourism at Khajuraho: An Indian enigma? *Annals of Tourism Research* 10(1):75–92.

Jafari, Jafar. 1987. But the culture of the short-lived society lives on. *Annals of Tourism Research* 14(1):143–144.

Jafari, Jafar, and Dean Aaser. 1988. Tourism as the subject of doctoral dissertations. *Annals of Tourism Research* 15(3):407–429.

Jordan, James William. 1980. The summer people and the natives: Some effects of tourism in a Vermont vacation village. *Annals of Tourism Research* 7(1):34–55.

Jules-Rosette, Bennetta. 1984. *The Messages of Tourist Art: An African Semiotic System in Comparative Perspective*. New York: Plenum Press.

Kaufmann, Carole N. 1976. Functional aspects of Haida argillite carvings. In *Ethnic and Tourist Arts*, ed. Nelson H. H. Graburn, pp. 56–69. Berkeley, Calif.: University of California Press.

Kemper, Robert V. 1978. Tourism and regional development in Taos, New Mexico. In *Tourism and Economic Change, Studies in Third World Societies 6*, ed. Valene L. Smith, pp. 89–103. Williamsburg, Va.: College of William and Mary.

Kemper, Robert V. 1979a. Tourism in Taos and Pátzcuaro: A comparison of two approaches to regional development. *Annals of Tourism Research* 6(1):91–110.

Kemper, Robert V. 1979b. Tourism and the small community: dependence or development. In *A Decade of Achievement*, ed. Mary Lou Woods, Tenth Annual Conference Proceedings, pp. 176–178. Salt Lake City, Ut.: The Travel Research Association.

Kemper, Robert V. 1991. Migrants as tourists: The development of a touristic culture in a Mexican community. Paper read at 50th annual meeting of Society for Applied Anthropology, 13–17 March, 1991, at Charleston, S.C.

Kemper, Robert V., John M. Roberts, and R. Dwaine Goodwin. 1983. Tourism as a cultural domain: The case of Taos, New Mexico. *Annals of Tourism Research* 10(1):149–171.

Kent, Kate Peck. 1976. Pueblo and Navajo weaving traditions and the Western world. In *Ethnic and Tourist Arts*, ed. Nelson H. H. Graburn, pp. 85–101. Berkeley, Calif.: University of California Press.

LaFlamme, Alan G. 1979. The impact of tourism: A case from the Bahama Islands. *Annals of Tourism Research* 6(2):137–148.

Lange, Frederick W. 1980. The impact of tourism on cultural patrimony: A Costa Rican example. *Annals of Tourism Research* 7(1):56–68.

Lathrap, Donald W. 1976. Shipibo tourist art. In *Ethnic and Tourist Arts*, ed. Nelson H. H. Graburn, pp. 197–207. Berkeley, Calif.: University of California Press.

Lee, Rosemary. 1978. Who owns Boardwalk: The structure of control in the tourist industry of Yucatán. In *Tourism and Economic Change, Studies in Third World Societies* 6, ed. Valene L. Smith, pp. 19–35. Williamsburg, Va.: College of William and Mary.

Lee, Rosemary. 1980. El turismo en América Latina: el comercio del subdesarrollo. In *Turismo y Desarrollo*, ed. Antonio Benavides C., pp. 9–13. México, D. F.: SEP/INAH, Cuadernos de los Centros Regionales, Sureste.

Lehmann, Arthur C. 1980. Tourists, black markets and regional development in West Africa. *Annals of Tourism Research* 7(1):102–119.

Lerch, Patricia B., and Diane E. Levy. 1990. A solid foundation: Predicting success in Barbados' tourist industry. *Human Organization* 49(4):355–363.

Lett, James W. 1983. Ludic and liminoid aspects of charter yacht tourism in the Caribbean. *Annals of Tourism Research* 10(1):35–56.

Lett, James W. 1989. Epilogue to "Touristic studies in anthropological perspective." In *Hosts and Guests: The Anthropology of Tourism*, 2d ed, ed. Valene L. Smith, pp. 275–279. Philadelphia: University of Pennsylvania Press.

Littlefield, Alice. 1980. La especialización artesanl en el contexto del desarrollo regional: el caso de Yucatán. In *Turismo y Desarrollo*, ed. Antonio Benavides C., pp. 15–22. México, D. F.: SEP/INAH, Cuadernos de los Centros Regionales, Sureste.

Loeb, Laurence D. 1977. Creating antiques for fun and profit: Encounters between Iranian Jewish merchants and touring coreligionists. In *Hosts and Guests: The Anthropology of Tourism*, ed. Valene L. Smith, pp. 185–192. Philadelphia: University of Pennsylvania Press.

Loeb, Laurence D. 1989. Creating antiques for fun and profit: Encounters between Iranian Jewish merchants and touring coreligionists. In *Hosts and Guests: The Anthropology of Tourism*, 2d ed., ed. Valene L. Smith, pp. 237–245. Philadelphia: University of Pennsylvania Press.

Long, V. H. 1989. Social mitigation of tourism development impacts: Bahía de Huatulco, Oaxaca, Mexico. *Tourism Recreation Research* 14(1):5–14.

Low, Setha M. 1976. Contemporary Ainu wood and stone carving. In *Ethnic and Tourist Arts*, ed. Nelson H. H. Graburn, pp. 211–226. Berkeley, Calif.: University of California Press.

MacCannell, Dean. 1976. *The Tourist: A New Theory of the Leisure Class*. New York: Schocken Books.

Maduro, Renaldo. 1976. The Brahmin painters of Nathdwara, Rajasthan. In *Ethnic and Tourist Arts*, ed. Nelson H. H. Graburn, pp. 227–248. Berkeley, Calif.: University of California Press.

Manning, Frank E. 1973. *Black Clubs in Bermuda: Ethnography of a Play World*. Ithaca, N.Y.: Cornell University Press.

Manning, Frank E. 1978. Carnival in Antigua (Caribbean Sea): An indigenous festival in a tourist economy. *Anthropos* 73:191–204.

Manning, Frank E. 1979. Tourism and Bermuda's black clubs: A case of cultural revitalization. In *Tourism: Passport to Development?* ed. Emanuel de Kadt, pp. 157–176. New York: Oxford University Press.

McKean, Philip Frick. 1977. Towards a theoretical analysis of tourism: Economic dualism and cultural involution in Bali. In *Hosts and Guests: The Anthropology of Tourism*, ed. Valene L. Smith, pp. 93–107. Philadelphia: University of Pennsylvania Press.

McKean, Philip Frick. 1989. Towards a theoretical analysis of tourism: Economic dualism and cultural involution in Bali. In *Hosts and Guests: The Anthropology of Tourism*, 2d ed., ed. Valene L. Smith, pp. 119–138. Philadelphia: University of Pennsylvania Press.

Mead, Sidney M. 1976. The production of native art and craft objects in contemporary New Zealand society. In *Ethnic and Tourist Arts*, ed. Nelson H. H. Graburn, pp. 285–298. Berkeley, Calif.: University of California Press.

Mendosa, Eugene L. 1983. Tourism and income strategies in Nazaré, Portugal. *Annals of Tourism Research* 10(2):213–238.

Miller, Marc L. 1987. Tourism in Washington's coastal zone. *Annals of Tourism Research* 14(1):58–70.

Moeran, Brian. 1983. The language of Japanese tourism. *Annals of Tourism Research* 10(1):93–108.

Moore, Alexander. 1980a. Planificación y desarrollo en la Comarca de San Blas, Panama. In *Turismo y Desarrollo*, ed. Antonio Benavides C., pp. 55–65. México, D. F.: SEP/INAH, Cuadernos de los Centros Regionales, Sureste.

Moore, Alexander. 1980b. Walt Disney World: Bounded ritual space and the playful pilgrimage center. *Anthropological Quarterly* 53(4):207–218.

Moore, Alexander. 1985. Rosanzerusus is Los Angeles: An anthropological inquiry of Japanese tourists. *Annals of Tourism Research* 12(4):619–643.

Moore, Kent. 1970. Modernization in a Canary Island village: An indicator of social change in Spain. *Journal of the Steward Anthropological Society* 2(1):19–34.

Nash, Dennison. 1970 *A Community in Limbo: An Anthropological Study of an American Community Abroad*. Bloomington, Ind.: Indiana University Press.

Nash, Dennison. 1977. Tourism as a form of imperialism. In *Hosts and Guests: The Anthropology of Tourism*, ed. Valene L. Smith, pp. 37–52. Philadelphia: University of Pennsylvania Press.

Nash, Dennison. 1979. The rise and fall of an aristocratic tourist culture—Nice: 1763–1936. *Annals of Tourism Research* 6(1):61–75.

Nash, Dennison. 1981. Tourism as an anthropological subject. *Current Anthropology* 22(5):461–481.

Nash, Dennison, and Valene Smith. 1991. Anthropology and tourism. *Annals of Tourism Research* 18(1):12–25.

Nuñez, Theron A. 1963. Tourism, tradition, and acculturation: Weekendismo in a Mexican village. *Ethnology* 2(3):347–352.

Oliver-Smith, Anthony, Francisco Jurdao Arrones, and José Lisón Arcal. 1989. Tourist development and the struggle for local resource control. *Human Organization* 48(4):345–351.

Olwig, Karen Fog. 1980. National parks, tourism, and local development: A West Indian case. *Human Organization* 39(1):22–31.

Passariello, Phyllis. 1983. Never on Sunday? Mexican tourists at the beach. *Annals of Tourism Research* 10(1):109–122.

Peake, Robert. 1989. Swahili stratification and tourism in Malindi Old Town, Kenya. *Africa* 59(2):209–220.

Peck, John Gregory, and Alice Shear Lepie. 1977. Tourism and development in three North Carolina coastal towns. In *Hosts and Guests: The Anthropology of Tourism*, ed. Valene L. Smith, pp. 159–172. Philadelphia: University of Pennsylvania Press.

Petit-Skinner, Solange. 1977. *Americans in Paris*. Chicago: Aldine.

Pfaffenberger, Bryan. 1983. Serious pilgrims and frivolous tourists: The chimera of tourism in the pilgrimages of Sri Lanka. *Annals of Tourism Research* 10(1):57–74.

Pi-Sunyer, Oriol. 1973. Tourism and its discontents: The impact of a new industry on a Catalan community. *Studies in European Society* 1:1–20.

Pi-Sunyer, Oriol. 1977. Through native eyes: Tourists and tourism in a Catalan maritime community. In *Hosts and Guests: The Anthropology of Tourism*, ed. Valene L. Smith, pp. 149–155. Philadelphia: University of Pennsylvania Press.

Pi-Sunyer, Oriol. 1989. Changing perceptions of tourism and tourists in a Catalan resort town. In *Hosts and Guests: The Anthropology of Tourism*, 2d ed., ed. Valene L. Smith, pp. 187–202. Philadelphia: University of Pennsylvania Press.

Plotnicov, Leonard. 1990. Work and play: an urban lifestyle ideally portrayed. *City & Society* 4(1):3–19.

Pospisil, Leopold. 1979. The Tyrolean peasants of Obernberg: A study in long-term research. In *Long Term Field Research in Social Anthropology*, ed. George M. Foster, Elizabeth Colson, Thayer C. Scudder, and Robert V. Kemper, pp. 127–143. New York: Academic Press.

Redfield, Robert, Ralph Linton, and Melville Herskovits. 1936. Memorandum for the study of acculturation. *American Anthropologist* 38(1):129–152.

Richter, Dolores. 1978. The tourist art market as a factor in social change. *Annals of Tourism Research* 5(3):323–338.

Roberts, John M., and Brian Sutton-Smith. 1966. Cross-cultural correlates of games of chance. *Behavior Science Research* 1:131–144.

Roberts, John M., Robert M. Kozelka, and Malcom J. Arth. 1956a. Some highway culture patterns. *The Plains Anthropologist* 3:3–14.

Roberts, John M., Robert M. Kozelka, Mary L. Kiehl, and Thomas M. Newman. 1956b. The small highway business on U.S. 30 in Nebraska. *Economic Geography* 32(2):139–152.

Rodenburg, Eric E. 1980. The effects of scale in economic development: Tourism in Bali. *Annals of Tourism Research* 7(2):177–196.

Rodriguez, Sylvia. 1987. Impact of the ski industry on the Rio Hondo watershed. *Annals of Tourism Research* 14(1):88–103.

Rosales G., Margarita. 1980. Turismo, trabajos arqueológicos y desarrollo: el caso de Coba, Quintana Roo. In *Turismo y Desarrollo*, ed. Antonio Benavides C., pp. 23–27. México, D. F.: SEP/INAH, Cuadernos de los Centros Regionales, Sureste.

Rosenberg, Harriet, Randy Reiter, and Rayna R. Reiter. 1973. Rural workers in French Alpine tourism: Whose development? *Studies in European Society* 1:21–38.

Ryerson, Scott H. 1976. Seri ironwood carving: An economic view. In *Ethnic and Tourist Arts*, ed. Nelson H. H. Graburn, pp. 119–136. Berkeley, Calif.: University of California Press.

Salvador, Mari Lynn. 1976. The clothing arts of the Cuna of San Blas, Panama. In *Ethnic and Tourist Arts*, ed. Nelson H. H. Graburn, pp. 165–182. Berkeley, Calif.: University of California Press.

Sandelowsky, B. H. 1976. Functional and tourist art along the Okavango river. In *Ethnic and Tourist Arts*, ed. Nelson H. H. Graburn, pp. 350–365. Berkeley, Calif.: University of California Press.

Schouten, RoseMary, and Donna L. Osgood, eds. 1975. The impact of tourism on regional development: A case study of Taos, New Mexico. Dallas: Department of Anthropology, Southern Methodist University.

Schuchat, Molly G. 1979. State tourism in China and USA. *Annals of Tourism Research* 4(4):425–434.

Schuchat, Molly G. 1983. Comforts of group tours. *Annals of Tourism Research* 10(4):465–477.

Sieber, Timothy R. 1991. Urban tourism in revitalizing downtowns. Paper read at 50th annual meeting of Society for Applied Anthropology, 13–17 March, 1991, at Charleston, S.C.

Smith, Valene, ed. 1977a *Hosts and Guests: The Anthropology of Tourism*. Philadelphia: University of Pennsylvania Press.

Smith, Valene. 1977b Eskimo tourism: micro-models and marginal man. In *Hosts and Guests: The Anthropology of Tourism*, ed. Valene L. Smith, pp. 51–70. Philadelphia: University of Pennsylvania Press.

Smith, Valene, ed. 1978a. *Tourism and Behavior. Studies in Third World Societies 5*, Williamsburg, Va.: College of William and Mary.

Smith, Valene, ed. 1978b. *Tourism and Economic Change, Studies in Third World Societies 6*, Williamsburg, Va.: College of William and Mary.

Smith, Valene. 1979. Women: The taste-makers in tourism. *Annals of Tourism Research* 6(1):49–60.

Smith, Valene. 1980. Anthropology and tourism: A science-industry evaluation. *Annals of Tourism Research* 7(1):13–33.

Smith, Valene. 1981. Controlled versus uncontrolled tourism: Bhutan and Nepal. *RAIN* 40(October):4–6.

Smith, Valene. 1982. Tourism to Greenland: Renewed ethnicity? *Cultural Survival Quarterly* 6(3):26–27.

Smith, Valene, ed. 1989a. *Hosts and Guests: The Anthropology of Tourism*. 2d ed. Philadelphia: University of Pennsylvania Press.

Smith, Valene. 1989b. Eskimo tourism: Micro-models and marginal men. In *Hosts and Guests: The Anthropology of Tourism*, 2d ed., ed. Valene L. Smith, pp. 55–82. Philadelphia: University of Pennsylvania Press.

Smith, Valene, Arlene Herthington, and Martha D. D. Brumbaugh. 1986. California's Highway 89: A regional tourism model. *Annals of Tourism Research* 13(3):415–433.

Stanton, Max E. 1989. The Polynesian Cultural Center: A multi-ethnic model of seven Pacific cultures. In *Hosts and Guests: The Anthropology of Tourism*, 2d ed., ed. Valene L. Smith, pp. 247–262. Philadelphia: University of Pennsylvania Press.

Stoffle, Richard W., Cheryl A. Last, and Michael J. Evans. 1979. Reservation-based tourism: Implications of tourist attitudes for Native American economic development. *Human Organization* 38(3):300–306.

Stromberg, Gobi. 1976. The amate bark-paper paintings of Xalitla. In *Ethnic and Tourist Arts*, ed. Nelson H. H. Graburn, pp. 149–162. Berkeley, Calif.: University of California Press.

Swain, Margaret Byrne. 1989. Gender roles in indigenous tourism: Kuna Mola, Kuna Yala, and cultural survival. In *Hosts and Guests: The Anthropology of Tourism*, 2d ed., ed. Valene L. Smith, pp. 83–104. Philadelphia: University of Pennsylvania Press.

Sweet, Jill D. 1989. Burlesquing the other in Pueblo performance. *Annals of Tourism Research* 16(1):62–75.

Talavera Salgado, Francisco. 1982. *Lago Chapala: turismo residencial y campesinado*. México, D. F.: INAH, Centro Regional de Occidente. Colección Científica, Antropología Social, No. 105.

Teas, J. 1988. I'm studying monkeys: What do you do? Youth and travelers in Nepal. *Kroeber Anthropological Society Papers* 67/68.

Trigger, Bruce. 1980. Archaeology and the image of the American Indian. *American Antiquity* 45(4):662–676.

Tsiakolos, G., and K. Gilbert. 1983. Tourism as an environmental shock: Pathophysiological consequences of social change in Northern Sporades. *Journal of Human Evolution* 12(8):708.

Turner, Victor W. 1969. *The Ritual Process: Structure and Anti-Structure*. Chicago: Aldine Publishing Company.

Urbain, Jean-Didier. 1989. The tourist adventure and his images. *Annals of Tourism Research* 16(1):106–118.

Urbanowicz, Charles F. 1989. Tourism in Tonga revisited: Continued troubled times? In *Hosts and Guests: The Anthropology of Tourism*, 2d ed., ed. Valene L. Smith, pp. 105–117. Philadelphia: University of Pennsylvania Press.

van den Berghe, Pierre L. 1980. Tourism as ethnic relations: A case study of Cuzco, Peru. *Ethnic and Racial Studies* 3(4):375–392.

van den Berghe, Pierre L. 1986. Colonialism, culture and nature in African game reserves: Comment on Almagor. *Annals of Tourism Research* 13(1):101–107.

van der Werff, Peter E. 1980. Polarizing implications of the Pescaia tourist industry. *Annals of Tourism Research* 7(2):197–223.

van Gennep, Arnold. 1908. *Myths et légendes d'Australie*. Paris: E. Guilmote.

White, P. E. 1974. *The Social Impact of Tourism on Host Communities: A Study of Language Change in Switzerland*. Oxford: Oxford University Press.

Williams, Nancy. 1976. Australian Aboriginal art at Yirrkala: The introduction and development of marketing. In *Ethnic and Tourist Arts*, ed. Nelson H. H. Graburn, pp. 266–284. Berkeley, Calif.: University of California Press.

Wilson, David. 1979. The early effects of tourism in the Seychelles. In *Tourism: Passport to Development?*, ed. Emanuel de Kadt, pp. 205–236. New York: Oxford University Press.

5

Sociology of Tourism

Erik Cohen

From a sociological perspective a tourist is a temporary traveler and visitor, ordinarily using commercial travel and hospitality services, the principal reason of whose trip is the search for novelty and change at his or her destination. Contemporary tourist roles tend to become institutionalized, involving a set of culturally conditioned motivations, expectations, behaviors, and relationships. But tourism is often combined with other reasons for travel and with other traveling roles, and tourists frequently use other than specialized tourist services. The domain of tourism is thus not clearly separated from other social domains.

The sociology of tourism is a relatively new field of research, which has only in the late 1970s and the 1980s started to engage the attention of theoreticians and empirical researchers. However, a considerable amount of work has been produced in a relatively short period of time, making it possible to discern some principal theoretical trends and empirical generalizations emerging in the field.

Five major theoretical points of departure to the sociological study of tourism can be distinguished: the sociology of the stranger, of leisure, of hospitality, of travel, and of religion. The sociology of the stranger is a well-developed area, but researchers tended to emphasize permanent and semi-permanent strangers such as minorities, sojourners, and expatriates; only few attempts have been made to relate the insights gained in this work to the specific role of tourists as temporary strangers. The sociology of leisure is a highly developed area and served as the point of departure of the majority of tourism studies; however, the leisure perspective frequently limited the aims of the researchers to the more superficial facets of touristic phenomena. Hospitality has been extensively studied in simple and traditional societies; its commercialization in tourism poses some important problems relating to the contradictions between social exchange involved in hospitality and economic exchange involved in business transactions, which have not been fully explored. The sociology of travel is as yet a weakly developed area but constitutes an important framework for the study of tourists (as travelers on a "tour"). The sociology of religion, specifically of pilgrimage, has opened a new and unexpected perspective on tourism, to be discussed later.

Several general trends in the development of the sociology of tourism can be distinguished; these trends are interrelated but do not fully overlap.

1. From a critical attitude to tourism as a kind of aberration (e.g., Boorstin 1964; Turner and Ash 1975) to a more open-minded and neutral attitude, which approaches tourism as a "normal" social phenomenon worthy of dispassionate study (e.g., MacCannell 1973, 1976).

2. From the study of tourists as a product of (modern) society to the study of (modern) society through tourism: earlier authors (e.g., Boorstin 1964) sought to understand tourism as a consequence of changes that took place in modernity; recent authors (particularly MacCannell) see in "the tourist" an emblematic role through which modern society can be understood.

3. From an "etic" attitude, that is, one that approaches tourism from the outside, in terms of generic concepts and categories, to an "emic" attitude, or one which seeks to comprehend it from within, in terms of the tourists' and hosts' own concepts and categories (e.g., Gottlieb 1982).

4. From concern with the individual psychological motives for tourism to a growing preoccupation with tourism as expressing significant social symbols.

5. From an indiscriminate concept of *the* tourist and tourism, as general categories, to a growing awareness of the significant differences between a wide variety of types of tourists (Cohen 1972; Smith 1977) and touristic processes, and of their differential impacts on the hosts and their environment, economy, and society.

6. From serendipitous findings regarding tourism, emerging from studies that had originally been oriented to other objectives, to studies devoted specifically to the investigation of tourism as a field of inquiry in its own right.

These trends helped to turn the nascent sociology of tourism of the 1970s into a recognized target field of modern sociology, with a growing theoretical and methodological sophistication and an accummulation of research findings (Cohen 1984); however, the links between theory, method, and findings still remain precariously weak (Dann et al. 1988).

Modern tourism constitutes a complex international system of institutions, organizations, enterprises, and specialized roles, ranging from government ministries and trade associations, through airlines and hotel chains to souvenir shop owners, guides, waiters and "professional natives." This system is embedded in a wider context of economic, political, and cultural institutions (Leiper 1979). Tourists, as travelers and temporary visitors, flow through the system. Whereas the impact of each individual tourist on the system and its environment may be negligible, the flow of large numbers of tourists has a major transformational impact on both. Hence, tourism has also to be seen diachronically as a process, a perspective of particular significance for the examination of its impact on localities and countries with a growing tourist industry.

Tourism can be examined sociologically on several levels, as follows.

Individual. Most of the principal theoretical approaches to tourism previously mentioned focus on the individual tourist, and particularly on the nature of his or her motivations for travel and the quality of their experiences at the destination. The former focus links the study of tourism with some broader issues of the nature of modern society and the existential problems it generates: the alleged alienation of modern man and lack of meaning, inauthenticity, and boredom of modern life, which are generally considered to be the principal "push" factors that induce moderns to travel. Theoreticians differ, however, in their views regarding the exact nature of the prevailing motivation for tourism and of the experiences desired by tourists, and hence in their views regarding the factors that "pull" prospective visitors to a given destination. These differences hinge upon their diverging views of the relationship between modern society and the domain of tourism. The sociocritical approach of Boorstin, Turner and Ash, and some other early critics of tourism, saw in the tourist of reflection of the general shallowness, alienation, and inauthenticity of modern life; they hence postulated that tourists seek, or are at least satisfied with, unauthentic experiences. Tourism, according to this view, is just another institution. Indeed, as the number of tourists grows, a "tourist industry" necessarily develops, paradoxically forcing even those who seek to escape modernity to remain within the confines of a modern institutional framework.

MacCannell's sharp reaction to the sociocritical approach and his analysis of tourism as a form of (secular) pilgrimage, in quest of authentic experiences, put the theme of authenticity in the center of the sociological discourse on tourism. According to MacCannell's (1976) view, which is supported by Graburn's (1977) approach to tourism as a "sacred journey," there is a radical disjuncture between ordinary life and tourism. Modern tourists are said to seek authentic, rather than contrived, attractions. However, in well-developed touristic situations the locals, and the tourist establishment in general, "stages" the authenticity of attractions for the visitors, thus creating a spurious "tourist space." MacCannell's tourist is thus not an easily satisfied simpleton, but a serious seeker manipulated by the tourist establishment.

MacCannell's view of the tourist as a modern pilgrim has been reinterpreted through the application of V. Turner's (1969) "processual" approach to the domain of tourism. While the metaphoric view of the tourist as a "pilgrim" is preserved (e.g., Moore 1980), the nature of the tourist's motivation and desired experience is substantially reformulated: the tourist is said to seek an inversion of his daily experiences and the tourist world to constitute a reversal of the daily world, in which values and aspirations not realizable in the daily world are acted out in a "ludic" (playful) manner (Wagner 1977; Gottlieb 1982).

From the perspective of Turnerian processual theory, which emphasizes the quality of the tourist's experience, the question of the authenticity status of the context of that experience loses much of its saliency. Whereas each of these theoretical approaches is supported by some empirical findings, none can account for all the complex and heterogeneous phenomena of tourism. Although typologies of tourists have been proposed to qualify and integrate the theories (e.g., Cohen 1979), little empirical work has been done to determine their relative merits. Even less work exists on "tourist careers" or "travel biographies," that is, the changes that take place in an individual's motivations and travel style over his or her life span, and particularly the effects of earlier travel experiences on later travel behavior.

Interactional. The interaction of tourists with locals has received much less theoretical attention than the individual tourist. Central here is Sutton's (1967) insight that tourists typically meet locals in "encounters," the briefness of which precludes the development of a balanced social relationship. This is one of the principal forces transforming social into economic exchanges (Blau 1967) in tourism, and thus leads to the commercialization or "commoditization" (Greenwood 1972; Cohen 1988) of such areas as folk culture, (especially arts and crafts and cultural performances), religious festivals and rituals, and sex (i.e., as prostitution).

Different types of tourists, depending on the degree of their exposure to the strangeness of the destination, vary in the scope, variety, intensity, and continuity of their relations with locals. Whereas most mass tourists usually go only through short, highly structured encounters with the personnel of touristic establishments, nonroutine tourists, such as so-called world travelers or drifters, and some other alternative tourists frequently establish more durable and intimate relationships with ordinary locals.

Locals are often much attracted to the first tourists who penetrate their localities and are keen to establish personal relationships with them. As tourism expands, however, and novelty fades, impersonal and stereotypical attitudes to the visitors tend to develop. Such attitudes are reinforced by the emergence of professional intermediary roles—such as guides, taxi drivers, or hustlers—who interpose themselves between the tourists and the ordinary locals. Such intermediaries are frequently the agents who produce the "staged authenticity" of the tourist space (e.g., by living up to images of "friendly natives" or by misrepresenting local sights in a manner that corresponds to the tourists' preconceptions).

Destinational. Under the impact of tourism development, destinations undergo a series of transformations, ranging from the ecological and economic to the political, social, and cultural domains (Cohen 1984). These transformations tend to cause serious local dislocations, particularly at the early stages of tourism development, owing to the unbalanced growth of the service sector, which is usually not accompanied by concomitant developments in other sectors of the local economy and society.

The processes of change in destinations have been conceptualized in terms of "phases" or "stages" (Greenwood 1972; Noronha 1977), and of "cycles," such as the "resort cycle" (Butler 1980). The "stage" model postulates a gradual transfer of control over the tourism sector, as it grows into an "industry," from local to national and international enterprises and organizations, with an attendant loss of local autonomy and integration of the destination, often in a subordinate role, into wider, regional or even global, economic and political systems. Hence, it becomes increasingly vulnerable to forces over which it has no control, such as economic crises and changing fashions in touristic tastes.

The "cycle" model postulates a developmental trajectory for a destination, specifically a resort, in the course of which it is explored, it develops, consolidates, stagnates, and eventually declines under the impact of negatively evaluated transformations (brought about by the very development of tourism) and changing fashions. After this initial decline a new cycle may be started through efforts at a rejuvenation of the local tourist industry, usually in a new direction.

Historical. Together with a host of other factors, tourism itself is a factor in the progressive homogenization of the world, and in the growing threat of destruction and obliteration of those natural, ethnic, or cultural settings that constitute the principal attractions for modern authenticity-seeking tourists. However, whereas efforts at the preservation and, eventually, museumization of such settings will continue in the future, a gradual shift of emphasis in the culturally conditioned basic motivation for tourism can be detected, accompanying the transition of the modern into the so-called post-modern age. Significant changes already appear to be taking place in the nature of the touristic attractions, as well as in the touristic attitudes toward them. There is a growing trend toward the creation of new, artificial attractions, such as theme parks, living museums, historical or environmental reconstructions, as well as of large-scale entertainment centers of the Disney World type, whose popularity is constantly growing. Most of these either expressly simulate reality or create fantastic settings whose specific attractiveness lies precisely in the production of illusionary experiences not attainable in ordinary reality. The proliferation of these kinds of attractions is consonant with the growing predilection for the simulated and fantastic in "post-modern" popular culture; "post-modern" man is predisposed to accept attractions at their "surface value," as legitimate loci of experience, often of an "as if" or ludic quality, without too much concern for their "authenticity." This attitude, however, should not be confounded with mere superficiality in Boorstin's (1964) sense. Rather, it seems to be a consequence of a growing equalization or even interpenetration of the realms of reality, simulation and even fantasy in the "post-modern" consciousness. It can therefore be argued that, in broad, historical terms, the culturally prescribed prototype of the serious modern pilgrim-tourist in quest of authenticity, as portrayed by MacCannell (1973) is gradually transformed into a "post-modern" Turnerian ludic voyager, who seeks to be thrilled by experiences although, or even because, they are of a simulated or fantastic origin, beyond the limits of accessible reality. The growing strength of this broad historic trend will significantly transform the modern tourist system; the study of this trend represents a major challenge for tourism research in the future.

Summary

The sociology of tourism is a relatively new field of research. However, a considerable amount of work has been produced in a relatively short period of time, making it possible to discern some emerging principal theoretical trends and empirical generalizations.

References

Blau, P. 1967. *Exchange and Power in Social Life.* New York: Wiley.

Boorstin, D. J. 1964. *The Image: A Guide to Pseudo-Events in American Society.* New York: Harper & Row.

Butler, R. W. 1980. The concept of a tourist area cycle of evolution: Implications for management of resources. *Canadian Geographer* 24(1):5-12.

Cohen, E. 1972. Toward a sociology of international tourism. *Social Research* 39(1):164-182.

Cohen, E. 1979. A phenomenology of touristic experiences. *Sociology* 13:179-201.

Cohen, E. 1984. The sociology of tourism: Approaches, issues and findings. *Annual Rev. of Sociology* 10:373-392.

Cohen, E. 1988. Authenticity and commoditization. *Annals of Tourism Research* 15(3):371-386.

Dann, G., D. Nash, Ph. Pearce. 1988. Methodology in tourism research. *Annals of Tourism Research* 15(1):1-28.

Gottlieb, A. 1982. Americans' vacations. *Annals of Tourism Research* 9(2):165-187.

Graburn, N. H. H. 1977. Tourism: The sacred journey. In *Hosts and Guests,* ed. V. L. Smith, pp. 17-31. Philadelphia: University of Pennsylvania Press.

Greenwood, D. J. 1972. Tourism as an agent of change: A Spanish Basque case. *Ethnology* 11:80-91.

Leiper, N. 1979. The framework of tourism. *Annals of Tourism Research* 6(4):390-407.

MacCannell, D. 1973. Staged authenticity: Arrangements of social space in tourist settings. *American Journal of Sociology* 79(3):589-603.

MacCannell, D. 1976. *The Tourist: A New Theory of the Leisure Class.* New York: Schocken.

Moore, A. 1980. Walt Disney World: Bounded ritual space and the playful pilgrimage center. *Anthropological Quarterly* 53(4):207–218.

Noronha, R. 1977. *Social and Cultural Dimensions of Tourism: A Review of the Literature in English.* New York: World Bank.

Smith, V. L. 1977. Introduction. In *Hosts and Guests,* ed. V. L. Smith, pp. 1–14. Philadelphia: University of Pennsylvania Press.

Sutton, W. A. 1967. Travel and understanding: Notes on the social structure of touring. *International Journal of Comparative Sociology* 8(2):218–223.

Turner, L., and J. Ash. 1975. *The Golden Hordes: International Tourism and the Pleasure Periphery.* London: Constable.

Turner, V. 1969. *The Ritual Process.* Chicago: Aldine.

Wagner, U. 1977. Out of time and space: Mass tourism and charter trips. *Ethnos* 42 (1/2):38–52.

6

Cultural Impact of Tourism

Pierre L. van den Berghe

Definition of Tourism

Perhaps the simplest definition of tourism is traveling for pleasure. This definition implies four basic elements of tourism: transience, leisure, privilege, and what the French call *dépaysement* ("out-of-countryness"). By definition, tourists are not at home; indeed they often actively seek an exotic experience, a radical change of scenery, a flight from daily routine, a quest for the authentic "other" (MacCannell 1973, 1976). Tourists are thus inevitably passing strangers by choice. They are not at home, because they enjoy traveling and have the time and money to indulge in that form of leisure. Compared to their hosts who are at home and at work, tourists are privileged, transient, leisured, and out-of-place (Cohen 1974, 1979; de Kadt 1979; Graburn 1977, 1983; Nash 1977, 1981, 1984; Smith, 1977; Turner 1976).

If tourists are by definition not at home, they are strangers among strangers, and indeed, frequently savor that mutual otherness as a key ingredient of the tourism experience. Tourism inescapably involves contact between groups of people who might otherwise not meet, and who differ on one or more dimensions of social class, religion, language, ethnicity, or race. Tourism, thus, must be seen as a special form of culture contact, of race and ethnic relations, and of class relations, all phenomena of central interest to sociologists and anthropologists.

Properties of Tourist-Host Interactions

What are some of the properties of tourist-host interaction that make tourism a special case of social relations? At least seven such properties, if not unique to tourism, are at least salient in tourist-host interactions.

1. Tourist-host interactions are highly *asymmetrical* on two important dimensions that cut in opposite ways.

   - Tourists frequently have higher *status* than their hosts, if only because they can afford to *be* there. This is especially true of First World tourism in Third World countries, but it is also obvious in much internal tourism within rich countries. Even the seemingly "poor" counterculture tourist on a shoestring budget enjoys the enormous luxury of leisure. This is obviously not to say that all tourists are wealthier than all locals, but nearly all tourist-host interaction takes the form of an unequal relationship between consumers of sights, spectacles, and services, and those who provide these commodities either simply by being there, making a spectacle of themselves, or by making a living from tourism. Egalitarian interaction between tourist and host is rare.

- There is a great asymmetry of useful *knowledge* between tourists and hosts and one which cuts in the opposite direction to that of status. The host has the great advantage of being on home turf and, thus, knowledgeable of local conditions, prices, sights, services, and so on. That knowledge, pitched against tourist ignorance, can be turned to profit. The tourist, on the other hand, faces the option of either learning fast or being "taken." The burden on tourists of having to learn the local ropes fast is only imperfectly filled by guide books and is often aggravated by language barriers.

2. Tourist-host interactions are *ephemeral* and unlikely to be repeated, and, thus, especially open to mistrust, cheating, and broken contracts. Tourists so much expect to be "taken," that they frequently express surprise when they are *not* (e.g., when the swimming pool shown in a hotel brochure actually turns out to contain water). Conversely, natives are pleasantly surprised when they actually receive a print of the promised photograph of themselves. Both sides have limited expectations of each other where immediacy of the exchange is considered the best substitute for nonexisting trust.

3. Tourist-host interactions are *segmented* and *instrumental*, that is, they are entered into for specific, limited, and immediate purposes, and they are not expected to have far-reaching or long-lasting consequences. When they blossom into friendship, it is considered exceptional and atypical.

4. Tourist-host interactions are especially vulnerable to *faulty communication* and misunderstandings because they are often conducted across wide linguistic and cultural barriers and in the absence of mutually understood norms and expectations on such delicate matters as etiquette of politeness, standards of privacy, and the like.

5. Relative *cultural distance* between tourist and host (in such things as mutual linguistic intelligibility, overlap of food items considered edible, standards of privacy, familiarity with industrial technology, norms of sexual behavior, and so on) determines the degree of permeability of barriers to interaction.

6. Like other forms of relations between different class, ethnic, or racial groups, tourist-host interactions often take place within the framework of crude stereotypes that each side has of the other. In the absence of both the time and the incentive to develop more individualized, nuanced, and complex relationships, both sides find it expedient to draw caricatures of each other.

7. In spite of all these properties that would seem to doom tourist-host interaction to a perpetual state of friction and conflict, these interactions are typically found to be profitable and even enjoyable enough to be continued because mutual expectations are low and because the interactions are carefully *bracketed in both time and space*.

Neither side allows them to spill into "normal life," the tourist by removing himself from the situation whenever he chooses, the host by corralling tourists in narrow spatial enclaves. (Tourist hotels, restaurants, and sights typically contain 90 or more per cent of tourists within one per cent or less of the national territory.) Tourist segregation in gilded ghettos seems to be a mutually satisfying solution in many situations. Both tourists and hosts frequently keep each other at a carefully measured arm's length. (For example, tourist health phobias impede native friendship and hospitality, while native disapproval of public nudity, drinking, and love-making is accommodated by high walls around luxury hotels.) Mutual avoidance, except within well-defined situations motivated by curiosity (on the tourist side) and material interest (on the host side), is often a satisfactory *modus vivendi*.

The Impact of Tourism: Cautionary Remarks

The foregoing formulation is a mere sketch of the structural conditions within which cultural contact takes place. The cultural impact of tourism is a complex and varied topic because there are many different kinds of tourism and a great variety of host societies. About the only safe generalization is that tourism never leaves a host society and its culture *un*changed.

An objective assessment of the impact of tourism is rendered even more difficult by the intrusion of ideology into the evaluation. Broadly, there have been two polar views on the impact of tourism. The sanguine view, generally associated with government and private promoters and beneficiaries of tourism, stresses the positive aspects of tourism as a source of foreign exchange, a way to balance foreign trade, an "industry without chimneys," a source of international amity, peace, and understanding, a generator of internal wealth and employment, in short, manna from heaven. The opposite view emphasizes the negative impact of tourism as a form of cultural imperialism by rich capitalist countries over Third and Fourth World peoples, a destroyer and corrupter of indigenous cultures, a source of ecological destruction, an assault on people's privacy, dignity, and authenticity, a type of economic exploitation benefiting only the local bourgeoisie and foreign capitalism, in short, a symptom of inequality, dependency and domination linking the rich and the poor, both within and between nations. The critical perspective is more characteristic of the social science literature, especially in the 1970s (de Kadt 1979; Jafari 1979; MacCannell 1973, 1976; Nash 1977; Smith 1977; Turner and Ash 1976).

Clearly, reality reflects a complex blend of these two extreme views, as shown by a number of detailed case studies of the impact of tourism on specific communities (Graburn 1976; Keyes and van den Berghe 1984; Kottak 1983; van den Berghe 1980). Limiting ourselves to the *cultural* impact of tourism on *locals*, two further cautionary observations are in order.[1]

First, responses of locals to contact with tourists varies enormously. Some small-scale societies of nomadic or seminomadic hunters and gatherers, pastoralists or simple horticulturalists (such as Amazon Basin Indians) have been shattered by outside contact, but these fragile societies are generally destroyed by epidemics, habitat destruction, and land dispossession before tourists get to them. Usually missionaries, settlers, ranchers, miners, and road construction crews spell the doom of these microsocieties before tourism can have a significant impact. Larger societies, which have survived conquest, colonialism, epidemics, slavery, and other calamities, generally manage quite well to survive tourism, although their reactions range from aversion, withdrawal, and avoidance to enthusiastic exploitation of new economic opportunities and skillful adaptation to new conditions. The view of native peoples as passive victims of tourism is seldom if ever an accurate reflection of reality.

Doxey (1975) suggests that there is temporal sequence in the irritation index (Irridex) of locals towards tourists, progressing from euphoria, to apathy, to annoyance, to antagonism, as certain saturation points are reached. It is probably more accurate, however, to see that scale of irritation as reflecting different reactions of different people at a given time, dependent on involvement and interest in the tourist trade, rather than sequential shifts in the attitudes of entire communities.

Second, there is a widespread opinion, shared not least among tourists themselves, that tourism spoils, debases, and adulterates everything it touches. The great paradox of tourism, it is often alleged, is that it destroys the authenticity it seeks. The tourist's worst enemy is other tourists who spoil everything: prices, the behavior of natives, the quality of crafts, and so on. As Graburn (1976), MacCannell (1973, 1976), van den Berghe (1980) and others have shown, the tourist quest for authenticity[2] and the "touree's" response to that quest are highly complex phenomena not adequately captured by a simplistic notion of "spoilage." Value judgments as to quality or authenticity of cultural productions or artifacts are highly subjective and have no place in social science analysis. Furthermore, they are often based on an elusive notion that native cultures were once in a pristine state whereas, in fact, they have been typically bombarded by outside influences, often long before the impact of tourism.

With these cautionary remarks against oversimplifications out of the way, let us now look at the impact of tourism on specific cultural domains.

Tourism and Language Use

Tourist-host interaction is often inhibited by language barriers. Even when tourists and hosts ostensibly speak the "same" language, dialectical differences based on class, education, or regionalism almost inevitably set the two groups apart. It is also overwhelmingly the case that few tourists have either the time or the inclination to learn local speech, beyond perhaps half-a-dozen perfunctory greeting or courtesy forms (and frequently not even those). The reciprocal, however, is not true. Locals, insofar as they have an interest in associating with tourists, also have a powerful incentive in communicating effectively with them, and, therefore, in learning their language.

A wide range of sociolinguistic situations can arise, depending on whether the tourists come from single language groups or several; the local tongue is a dialect of a widespread national or international language such as English, French, or Spanish or a strictly restricted one; the local population is itself multilingual; and a host of other factors. Let us briefly examine a few recurrent situations.

A common situation of internal tourism is one in which most tourists speak a standard, dominant dialect of a language, and locals a regional dialect. Frequently in such cases, tourists are able to understand the local dialect but not to speak it, and locals are "diglossic," that is, they are able to shift back and forth between the standard and the regional (or class) dialect. In these situations, locals often subtly manipulate their diglossia in response to tourists. Where the local dialect is stigmatized as inferior, it will be avoided with tourists, but where tourists regard it as quaint (and yet comprehensible), it may be accentuated or even revived.

In international tourism, tourists often speak different languages, both from each other and from their hosts, and communications are through a lingua franca, often English, but also French, Spanish, Russian, German, or some other widespread language. Tourism is thus one of the forces that favors the spread of lingua franca. Indeed, many tourists confine their travels to the areas where they have some knowledge of the regional lingua franca. Some knowledge of English has become almost a prerequisite of international travel in most parts of the world. Whenever tourists unknown to one another and of uncertain nationality meet, they almost invariably try English first, and so do natives in addressing them, unless the region is dominated by another important world language, such as French in much of Africa or Spanish in Latin America.

A third situation is one in which not only the tourists come from different language groups but locals too are multilingual. An interesting special case of this situation occurs when the local urban elite speak the "national" language of the country but are surrounded by several groups (such as hill tribes in India or Thailand, or Indians in Mexico, Peru, and Guatemala) who speak strictly localized tongues. Often in these cases, the exotic aborigines are the principal tourist attraction and become what can be called *tourees*, that is, people who, quite literally, make a spectacle of themselves or are made a spectacle of. Yet interaction between tourists and tourees is extremely limited because of a lack of a common language. In such a situation, the local urban elite often interpose themselves as middlemen between tourists and tourees, capitalizing on their knowledge of English and the national language. The outcome is that tourism becomes one of the forces exposing the area to outside influences and to "modernization," and thereby indirectly contributes to the spread of the *national* language in the hitherto isolated areas (Spanish in the case of Mexico or Peru, Thai in Thailand, Hindi in India, and so on). Ironically, then, tourism can foster a "national" culture rather than undermine it (see White 1974 for the Romansch-speaking area of Switzerland, for example).

At the individual level, the acquisition of language skills by locals can open economic niches in the tourist trade, some of them quite specialized. Some locals achieve a smattering of several languages to reach the majority of tourists (like a Cuzco, Peru, beggar who greeted tourists in Spanish, French, English, and German, or a San Cristóbal, Mexico, restaurateur who already knew these languages and was learning Dutch). Others concentrate on becoming fluent in one language to escort guided tours (as one ex-teacher in San Cristóbal who specialized in French-speaking tourists). Tourism, then, clearly favors the spread of the major European tongues as second languages among the upper and middle classes of many host countries without threatening any of the "national" languages of these countries.

Tourism and the Arts

"Tourist" or "airport" art has a bad name and is often invoked as a paradigm of what happens to exotic cultures when exposed to the corroding influence of tourism. Artistic production becomes "commoditized," to use a fashionable phrase. To be sure, it does, and there are many examples of traditions becoming cruder under the pressure of commercialization. Craftsmanship becomes sloppier, materials cheaper, designs more stereotyped and repetitive,

techniques less sophisticated, and so on. It is sometimes hard to suspend negative value judgments when one has learned to love an artistic tradition and
is confronted with its mass-produced derivatives in the airport departure
lounge. However, suspend them one must if one is to understand how tourism
affects arts and crafts (Graburn 1976; Jules-Rosette 1984).

At least four considerations must be kept in mind. First, much tourist
art is *not* a "degenerate" version of a traditional form but something entirely
new. However low one's opinion might be of its esthetic merit, it has at least
some value, if only economic, and, far from displacing a higher art form, it
adds something that would not exist at all but for tourist demand. (A good
example is Kamba or Makonde ebony sculpture in East Africa—thoroughly
nontraditional art forms that may not compete with Yoruba or Bakongo mas-
terpieces but certainly do not detract from them either.)

Second, even when tourist art *is* a mass-produced derivative of a
"higher" tradition, it typically does not displace the higher tradition. Either
the high tradition continues to have a life of its own for an indigenous or
foreign connoisseur clientele, or it was already dead before the tourist influx
and has been revived, albeit in less complex form. (The mass production of
Pacific Northwest Coast Indian masks, totem poles, and so on is an example
of an art form revived by tourism from a moribund condition that had already
set in half-a-century before the advent of mass tourist demand.)

Third, whether neotraditional or altogether novel, art first created by
tourist demand can, and frequently does, take on a life of its own, become an
authentic new tradition, and meet the most demanding esthetic and technical
standards of quality. What may have begun as tourist art can, and not uncom-
monly does, acquire a kind of secondary authenticity by becoming reappropriated by its producers and can even serve as a basis for cultural revival.
Examples are hula dancing in Hawaii and many North American crafts such
as pottery, basket weaving, rug weaving, silversmithing, and wood carving, in
both the Pacific Northwest and the Southwest. Sometimes the exotic tradition of the touree can even "invade" the culture of the tourist, as when high-
quality "Indian" crafts are produced by non-Indian craftspersons, a common
occurrence in North America.

Finally, when art traditions do become defunct, tourism is seldom to
blame. The typical scenario for the demise of a tradition is not debasement
through the tourist trade, but failure to recruit new craftspersons because of
competing economic pressures and opportunities. For example, it is true that
fewer and fewer Indian women in Latin America are weaving their families'
clothing on home looms, but not primarily because they are now weaving
cheap imitations for tourists. Rather, they now have access to cheap secondhand Western clothing imported in huge bales from rich countries; they no
longer have the time or the land to cultivate the plants for the natural dyes
or to raise the sheep or alpacas for the wool; poverty compels wage employment away from the rural village; or trade or some other occupation is more
lucrative. Basic economic conditions affecting cost-benefit ratios for the productive use of labor are much more determining than tourism alone, although
tourism *can* be a part of that complex economic equation.

In conclusion, then, the impact of tourism on artistic production is best
examined without value-laden presuppositions. Tourism does have an enormous impact on all arts and crafts: the plastic arts, music, dancing, literature,
theatre. When lucre is the prime motivation the result may not be pleasing
to the esthete, but tourist patronage is not intrinsically any more debasing
than other sources of patronage. Quite the contrary, tourism can and frequently is a stimulus to creativity and inventiveness.

Tourism, Authenticity and Ethnic Consciousness

One of the more interesting ways in which tourism affects culture is in the redefinition of ethnic boundaries and ethnic consciousness. Since tourism is a form of what anthropologists call "culture contact" (that is, interaction between people coming from different traditions and belonging to different ethnic groups), tourism inevitably involves an ethnic "presentation of self" to use Goffman's (1959) famous concept. Governments and commercial promoters of tourism consciously try to project a picture of their culture to prospective customers. Tourists come with a set of preconceptions and expectations, often based on crude (albeit sometimes positive) stereotypes. Natives, in turn, willy-nilly "make a spectacle of themselves." Almost inevitably, they modify their behavior, consciously or unconsciously, in subtle and complex ways. Sometimes, they consciously attempt to behave in ways that will invalidate the tourist's stereotypes, as, for instance, when Latin Americans make special efforts to be more punctual with tourists than they would be with one another. Others, however, will try to humor tourists by making self-deprecatory remarks confirming the stereotype. Thus, Mexicans often jocularly refer to the *hora mexicana* ("Mexican time") when apologizing for their own or another Mexican's lack of punctuality. Along the same lines, a shop in a Yucatan resort displayed a straw effigy or a Mexican *bandito* with bandoleers and sombrero, next to a sign proclaiming, in English: "Broken English spoken perfectly."

In any case, tourees frequently have a sense of being "on show" in the presence of tourists and tend to be conscious that individual behavior reflects on the tourists' perception of their entire group. Many Third World governments launch "be-nice-to-tourists" campaigns and even create special tourist police forces to mediate tourist-host interactions and punish touree infractions (such as cheating by traders or petty street crime). Tourist presence clearly acts as a restraint on native behavior. At the same time, because it offers tempting new opportunities for gain, tourism also elicits forms of behavior that may be deplored by natives as projecting an undignified, negative image of themselves: pick-pocketing, begging, confidence tricks, short-changing, cheating at service stations, good-switching in stores and countless other scams to which tourists are especially vulnerable because of naïveté, guilt, bewilderment, or unfamiliarity.

In a Mexican town, San Cristóbal, Chiapas, with a recent massive growth in tourism, for instance, some Indian children have learned to approach tourists in a plaintive, whining voice to hawk their weavings. Indian adults, for the most part, find this behavior disgraceful and undignified and try to stop it. Children, however, have discovered that whining is an effective strategy to promote sales by playing on the sympathy of tourists who feel guilty about their own wealth in the midst of poverty. When the children are told to "cut it out" because the tourists would not respond, they immediately revert to normal, pretourist behavior and break into engaging smiles and bantering chatter (van den Berghe 1990).

Illustrations of hosts behaving "abnormally" in the presence of tourists could be multiplied. It is inherent in the nature of tourism that it is outside the boundaries of normalcy for both the tourist (who actively seeks an away-from-routine experience) and for the host (to whom the tourist is by definition an outsider). The abnormality of the situation necessarily calls forth abnormal and self-consciously guarded behavior on both sides. The abnormal behavior, in turn, inevitably modifies each side's perceptions and expectations of the other. Since, the situation is mutually defined in ethnic or quasi-ethnic "us-versus-them" terms, it follows that tourist-host interaction is a process of continuously moving, redefined and renegotiated *ethnic boundaries*. Tourism is a form of ethnic relations, and a uniquely unstable and dynamic one.

One of the most interesting aspects of this negotiation of ethnic boundaries is the tourist quest for authenticity. The paradox, of which most tourists are quite conscious, is that while tourists seek to see the exotic other in her pristine normalcy, their very presence destroys the authenticity they seek. Photography, perhaps the most blatant invasion of privacy that inevitably accompanies tourism, brings out the paradox in particularly sharp relief. Many tourists do not even want to see that which they cannot photograph (or *be* photographed with). Photography has become for many tourists the very validation of the tourist experience (MacCannell 1976). Obviously, photography involves a complex interaction and negotiation between tourist and touree. Many sophisticated tourist-photographers are only interested in "natural," unposed pictures of "real" natives doing "real" things. It usually does not take long for this new market for recorded authenticity to be responded to by tourees restricting and controlling the supply—themselves. They start demanding payment, or at least form of reciprocity. But, if payment is demanded, the photograph becomes posed, and, thus, less valuable.

The tourist retaliates with the telephoto lens, the right-angle objective, and other tricks of sneak photography. The touree responds with "staged authenticity" (McCannell 1973). Some will start "dressing up" in a more "traditional" way than they would otherwise. They might don ceremonial attire for everyday use, revive the use of articles of clothing or adornment that were becoming obsolete, "improve" the appearance of traditional dress or setting to make them more colorful and attractive to tourists, or even invent and create pseudotraditional items in response to their perception of the tourists' expectations of them (as when American Indians sport tepees and feather bonnets alien to their particular tradition).

In areas where the indigenous traditions have already been strongly eroded by westernization, missionary action, urbanization, and industrialization, such as in Hawaii, North America, New Zealand, and South Africa, staged authenticity usually blossoms into a cottage industry of made-for-tourists theatricals. Governments sponsor dance troupes to propagate local folklore (for example, the famous Ballet Folclórico de México). Private enterprise erects entire "native villages" complete with a cast of dressed-up "extras" who often do not even belong to the ethnic group they supposedly represent (for example, the Polynesian Cultural Center near Honolulu, Hawaii). Elaborate parks with scaled-down reproductions of monuments drawn from the entire country are found in places as diverse as the Netherlands and Thailand. Luxury hotels feature expensive dinner shows with "typical dances" and "voodoo ceremonies." At a "Zulu village" near Durban, South Africa, in 1989, I witnessed half-a-dozen black women peeling off T-shirts before performing a bare-breasted "maidens' dance" in front of an all-white audience, thus combining authenticity and erotic titillation.[3] Similarly, the National Ballet of Senegal looks like a swarthy version of the Lido show on the Champs Elysées.

Sophisticated tourists sneer at such staged authenticity, but sometimes such creations or recreations become the basis of a cultural revival, acquire over time a secondary authenticity of their own, and are reappropriated by their creators. This is likely to occur when staged events of this nature draw mixed audiences of both tourists and locals, as do, for instance, American Indian powwows in North America. Another example is the Inti Raymi, a reenactment of the Incan winter solstice festival, staged in Cuzco, Peru (van den Berghe 1980). What began as a chamber of commerce, sound-and-light spectacle to boost tourism and to coincide with the famous Catholic procession of Corpus Christi, soon drew a large local audience of both Indians and mestizos. It became a major cultural event involving tens of thousands of local spectators and hundreds of local participants, much as in the Bavarian Oberammergau passion play. The irony is that Corpus Christi had been introduced by the Catholic clergy four centuries earlier as a substitute for the "pagan" Inti Raymi. History has come full circle, and the two events now happily coexist.

Summary

In complex and unpredictable ways, tourism changes not only the behavior of hosts—their presentation of self—but their very definition of self. Far from destroying local cultures, tourism more commonly transforms and revives them. Of all forms of outside contact and modernization that affect isolated local cultures, tourism is probably the least destructive, precisely because it imparts a marketable value to cultural diversity. If the quest for authenticity sometimes initially seems to undermine and corrupt local culture, it can revive and reinvigorate traditions that were languishing under the assault of other modernizing forces such as industrialization, urbanization, Christianization, or Western-style schooling. Some of these neo- or pseudo-traditional products do indeed lack any authenticity, especially when sponsored by middlemen of tourism (hoteliers, travel agents, government officials, impressarios and the like), purely for commercial gain. Even then, locals often have the vitality to recapture their own heritage, the creativity to invent a new, redefined authenticity, and the resilience to resist the encroachments of the global village. To paraphrase Mark Twain, news of the death of Third and Fourth World cultures is greatly exaggerated. And, where cultures die tourism is seldom to blame.

Notes

1. Of course, tourism involves interaction, and thus has an impact on tourists as well as on locals. Much of the social science literature, however, has focused on the latter.
2. In the context of tourism, "authenticity" can be defined as the property of native behavior, sites, dress, cuisine, theater, dance, music, artifacts, and so on, of being unaffected by the presence of tourists. As the objective condition of authenticity self-destroys in the presence of tourists, the subjective perception of it by tourists is more important than the objective reality. "Staged authenticity" (MacCannell 1973) is the conscious attempt by hosts to modify their behavior, dress, artifacts and so on, so as to appear "real" to tourists. Tourists, in turn, may be "taken in" or not. Just as there are degrees of authenticity, there are degrees of audience gullibility. For example, many tourists take pictures of events they know to be staged, but which may be convincingly presented as authentic to a home audience. Thus, an event staged *in situ* may acquire recreated authenticity in a slide show or ethnographic film half a world away. Similarly, staged events, through repetition and if they acquire a native audience, may also acquire a secondary authenticity (van den Berghe 1980).
3. Public display of bare female breasts, incidentally, is a misdemeanor for whites in South Africa, but not for blacks, supposedly because for the latter, it was traditional. However, missionaries effectively repressed the custom at least three-quarters of a century ago.

References

Cohen, Erik. 1974. Who is a tourist? A conceptual classification, *Sociological Review* 22 (4):527–555.

Cohen, Erik. 1979. Rethinking the sociology of tourism, *Annals of Tourism Research* 6 (1):18–35.

de Kadt, Emanuel, ed. 1979. *Tourism: Passport to Development?* New York: Oxford University Press.

Doxey, George V. 1975. A causation theory of visitor-resident irritants, *The Impact of Tourism*, San Diego, Sixth Annual Conference Proceedings, The Travel Research Association.

Goffman, Erving. 1959. *The Presentation of Self in Everyday Life.* Garden City, N.Y.: Doubleday.

Graburn, Nelson H. H., ed. 1976. *Ethnic and Tourist Arts: Cultural Expression from the Fourth World.* Berkeley, Calif.: University of California Press.

Graburn, Nelson H. H. 1977. Tourism, the sacred journey. In *Hosts and Guests, The Anthropology of Tourism*, ed. Valene Smith, pp. 17–32. Philadelphia: University of Pennsylvania Press.

Graburn, Nelson H. H. 1983. The anthropology of tourism, *Annals of Tourism Research*, 10 (2):9–34.

Jules-Rosette, Bennetta. 1984. *The Messages of Tourist Art.* New York: Plenum Press.

Jafari, Jafar. 1979. Tourism and the social sciences, a bibliography: 1970–1978, *Annals of Tourism Research* 6 (2):149–194.

Keyes, Charles F., and Pierre L. van den Berghe. 1984. *Tourism and Ethnicity*, Special Issue of *Annals of Tourism Research* 11 (3):339–501.

Kottak, Conrad P. 1983. *Assault on Paradise, Social Change in a Brazilian Village.* New York: Random House.

MacCannell, Dean. 1973. Staged authenticity, *American Journal of Sociology* 79 (3):589–603.

MacCannell, Dean. 1976. *The Tourist: A New Theory of the Leisure Class.* New York: Schoken.

Nash, Dennison. 1977. Tourism as a form of imperialism. In *Hosts and Guests: The Anthropology of Tourism*, ed. Valene Smith, pp. 37–52. Philadelphia: University of Pennsylvania Press.

Nash, Dennison. 1981. Tourism as an anthropological subject, *Current Anthropology* 22 (5):461–468.

Nash, Dennison. 1984. The ritualization of tourism: Comment on Graburn's "The Anthropology of Tourism." *Annals of Tourism Research* 11(3):503–507.

Smith, Valene L. ed. 1977. *Hosts and Guests: The Anthropology of Tourism.* Philadelphia: University of Pennsylvania Press.

Turner, Louis, and John Ash. 1976. *The Golden Hordes: International Tourism and the Pleasure Periphery.* New York: St. Martin's Press.

van den Berghe, Pierre L. 1980. Tourism as ethnic relations, a case study of Cuzco, Peru. *Ethnic and Racial Studies* 3 (6):375–391.

van den Berghe, Pierre L. 1990. The quest for the other, ethnic tourism in San Cristóbal, Mexico. Unpublished manuscript.

White, P. E. 1974. The social impact of tourism on host communities: a study of language change in Switzerland. *Research Paper 9*, School of Geography, University of Oxford. Oxford, England.

7

Demonstration Effect

Valene L. Smith

Demonstration effect is the "tendency for a more economically primitive culture to imitate the behavior patterns of a more complex nature. Also, the human tendency to learn from another person or group and to incorporate the learned behavior into one's own lifestyle" (Metalka 1986:30) DeKadt (1979:65) suggests that when applied to the hospitality industry, the demonstration effect can bring about "changes in attitudes, values, or behavior which can result from merely observing tourists." These definitions imply that acculturation normally flows *from* a society of greater technological complexity *to* a less advanced society. Given the present outflow of tourism from industrialized nations to Third World countries, demonstration effect is more evident when tourist hosts borrow culture traits from their visiting guests. However, Western visitors also borrow culture traits from indigenous hosts.

Demonstration effect is therefore a visible immediate indicator of culture change induced by interpersonal contacts. Touristic encounters generate both positive and negative impacts on hosts as well as guests. The degree to which the demonstration effect can be directly attributed to tourism in contrast to other outside influences of modernization including the media and resident expatriates remains very unclear. Such correlations can probably be identified only on the local level and in individual contexts.

The Reality of Demonstration Effect

The concept of demonstration effect derives from economics, with locals' adoption of tourists' consumption preferences (Britton 1977). As a 1974 UNESCO study notes, tourists behavior involves a demonstration of financial superiority that is "seen as evidence of the superiority of behavior, hence to imitate the tourist is to ultimately ensure the same superiority not only in financial, but in intellectual and other spheres" (UNESCO 1976:93). Tourism is therefore credited with the introduction of new ideas that increase local aspirations for consumer goods and stimulate other economic and social changes. Further, DeKadt (1979:66) observes that

> tourists on vacation usually demonstrate a standard of living that is considerably higher than their average level of consumption at home during the rest of the

year. The image they project of their home society is thus distorted and further magnifies the great gap between their living standards and those of the majority of the host country's population.

Scholarly studies on the nature of tourism were first formalized in the mid-1970s, with the publication of *Annals of Tourism Research* (1974) and several major books (MacCannell 1973; Smith 1977; DeKadt 1979). Research during this period, now termed the Cautionary Platform research stage (Jafari 1989), tended to focus on the impacts of tourism and the demonstration effect was widely reported and discussed. However, research in the 1990s is now rooted in a Knowledge-based Platform (Jafari 1989) and directed toward understanding tourism as a *whole*, with its underlying structures and functions. Demonstration effect is now seldom mentioned because, as Nettekoven (1979) suggested, the true agents of the demonstration effect are the media (radio, motion pictures, and television) as they are produced both in the Western tourist-generating nations and in the host countries. Here, a brief historical review is fruitful.

Industrial societies developed and flourished in the urban centers of Western nations from the eighteenth century onward with minimal effect on many small closed societies. The geographical isolates included island states in the Pacific and Caribbean as well as remote inland locations in Africa and South America, which remained quite free from modernizing influences until World War II. Limited numbers of colonial administrators, traders, and missionaries had served as role models for a few local individuals but intensive culture change was not truly evident until the 1950s. Then, three items indicative of the Western emphasis on literacy, time, and transportation became the natives' first symbols of modernization: a ballpoint pen, a watch, and a bicycle (Vera Rubin, 1974 pers. commun.). For the most part, these were made available by storekeepers in response to customer demand and were not tourist-induced.

Most native aspirations for other consumer goods stem from post-World War II technological innovations, the first phase of which generated an expansion of shortwave radio networks. Then the booming Hollywood motion picture industry spawned small national clones, based in India, Japan, and Hong Kong, which produced Western-style films at much less cost. Isolated Third World and even Fifth World villages, serviced only by small diesel generators could show cheap B-category films at night in a school-classroom-turned-theater, and screen stars such as Mae West, John Wayne, Marilyn Monroe, and Clark Gable became symbols of Western lifestyles. By the mid-1950s in rural Europe and village Asia where only elite tourists ventured (Smith 1989a:12), youths who seldom saw tourists were emulating the mannerisms of leading Hollywood actors and openly discussing in detail the Asian-printed paperback versions of the Kinsey Reports (Kinsey 1948, Kinsey 1953) on the sexual behavior of American men and women (Smith 1954). Then television spread worldwide to gradually become the dominant entertainment and reinforced Western consumerism via serials and advertisements.

The first passenger jet flights in 1958 inaugurated mass tourism, and within a decade tourist demonstration effects were evident in the first communities to be accessible to significant influxes of visitors—Malta (Boissevain 1978), Bermuda (Manning 1979), and Cyprus (Andronicou 1979). The impacts from these and other case studies were a discussion topic at the 1974 Geneva meeting of the International Union of Tourist Organizations (IUOTO), now the World Tourism Organization (WTO). Throughout the tourists remained a rarity in many Third World communities but the media-generated Western influences expanded. Thus the *real* significance of demonstration effect is subject to question, as DeKadt (1979:98) states

> The demonstration effect of tourism, for example cannot be estimated or evaluated without an analysis of other aspects of openness. If the press, films, universities, and advertising are Western-oriented and there are 10,000 resident expatriates (equivalent in total contact to about 300,000 to 500,000 transient tourists), it is very doubtful that the problem—if so perceived—can be tackled primarily in the tourist context.

Impact of Demonstration Effect

Although the demonstration effect is described as imitative behavior especially among youths who are more susceptible to culture change, broader theoretical assessments are needed. Barth (1969), writing about the social organization of culture difference, describes ethnic units as culture-bearing entities with cohesive associations of identities and value standards maintained by social boundaries. Individuals who adopt new behaviors from external influences, including imitations of tourists, are breaking out of the traditional mold to identify with culture change. Thus the first of these innovators may become the "'marginal man' (an individual caught in the conflict of cultures, an individual who lives in two worlds, yet actually belongs to none)" (Jafari 1974:236; see also Smith 1989b). As Westernization progresses, they may ultimately be viewed as the front-runners or leaders, even the Pied Pipers. The visible hallmarks of this culture change frequently are personal status symbols: in Third World countries, some of the first observable traits in the 1960s were university class rings, Parker 51 pens, and Lettermen-style sweaters. In the early 1990s, especially in Eastern bloc countries and Third World capitals, heavily-zippered leather jackets, blue jeans, Seiko watches, and Nike shoes are prized status markers, together with large posters of favorite rock stars and audio cassettes.

The demonstration effect, however, is not restricted to members of the host culture. Individuals become tourists when they acquire sufficient discretionary leisure time and income to travel away from home, and when their societal peers sanction travel as an appropriate form of recreation. Major social changes at the end of World War II, and especially the changed work ethic, paralleled the aforementioned technological innovations to create the mass tourist industry. Further, as mass tourism mushroomed and the so-called global village with its homogenized culture displaced native villages and distinctive local traditions, foreign travelers and especially ethnic and recreational tourists tended to seek out ever more-distant targets and "unspoilt" destinations (Smith 1989a). Hall (1984:540) notes that for international tourism "destination countries represent a much wider spread than originating countries, reflecting a spatial diffusion of tourists from the developed world across the globe, with fastest growth in the more remote regions of the Third World."

For some individuals, to visit as many countries as possible has become a Western tourist status symbol, with the ultimate demonstration effect of conspicuous consumption being a membership in the exclusive Explorer's Club of New York or the lesser-valued Century Travel Club with its published list of approved nations. To talk knowingly of exotic destinations, customs and cuisine is also breaking out of ethnic boundaries, establishing identity with a targeted population. To wear souvenir T-shirts purchased abroad, ethnic clothing, and native jewelry is a form of demonstration effect as is the display of acquired art objects. By their choice of hotels and tour operators, tourists identify their social status and behavior (as "budget" or "upscale"), their interests and hobbies (in sports, music, art-and-culture, or adventure travel) or even identify with political causes (as eco-tourists or ecumenical travelers in small group home-stays). The demonstration effect in this instance may be domestic as well as international, influencing the travel behavior and consumerism of their peers and other local socioeconomic classes.

Negative Impacts
of Demonstration Effect

Numerous negative economic and/or socially disruptive impacts have been attributed to demonstration effect. Because young people in rural underdeveloped countries are most susceptible to social change, with heightened aspirations for the new consumer goods, they are usually the most ready to seek modernization and to identify with the lifestyle of arriving tourists. Vacationers become their role models of affluence and leisure, hedonism, and independence from traditional mores. The desire to acquire at least some of the tantalizing consumer goods that tourists carry and/or wear often leads to natives spending an unduly high percentage of their income for the purchase of imported clothing and gadgetry, with a proportionate decline in personal savings and loss of capital. If available employment with a poor pay scale cannot meet their consumer aspirations, juvenile delinquency and crime (theft or cheating the tourist) may become options as Bouhdiba (1976) noted for Tunisia. Social tensions and restlessness contribute to cultural malaise and may involve possible political or revolutionary activity. Alternately, young educated workers may seek jobs away from home, even out of their country, in order to acquire the perceived higher standard of living. Thus they contribute to an ongoing brain drain, often detrimental to a developing nation. Contrasts in aspirations between youths and older family members also widens the generation gap.

Tourist presence stimulates among locals the desire to travel abroad. Youths often seek this type of upward mobility by striking up friendships with "wealthy" tourists whom they hope will provide such a trip (possibly through marriage) and prostitution is often founded on this premise. Even if some natives have savings or can negotiate loans for foreign travel, when these tourees return home more Westernized from vacations or schooling abroad, they are often less able or willing to reenter both the local labor market and the social milieu. They may become "marginal men" and "start to criticize their society for its backwardness and hang-ups and the government for its negligence and incapability to handle and stimulate the economy. This naturally becomes a hot political issue that attracts multiplying listeners and sympathizers" (Jafari 1974:236).

Employee-tourist encounters frequently cast the native into the role of servant working as maid, busboy, waiter, or driver, not unlike that of a past Colonial era. Such disparities reinforce social distance, and may lead to the formation of local employee clubs as in Bermuda (Manning 1979). Changes in sexual morality are associated with tourism, especially in popular beach resorts such as Thailand (Cohen 1989), the Philippines (Smith 1990) and Goa (DeSousa 1989:20) where both male and female prostitution coexist with substance abuse. The consequent development of AIDS has to date been documented only in Thailand (Cohen 1988) but undoubtedly exists elsewhere in tourist enclaves.

The touristic requirement for on-going service, irrespective of sabbaths, local festivals, and holidays creates a negative impact (Johnson 1978). Service staff and vendors need the money but resent the tourist presence when they would prefer to be with families or at leisure to participate in festivities. In societies where modesty is a virtue, the presence of nude bathing and inappropriate attire on streets and in shrines is another source of irritation. Further, well-meaning tourists who give coins and candy to Third World children help to establish a pattern of begging around tourist centers. The children quickly master a few phrases in half-a-dozen languages, make their simulated poverty a ploy, and can often earn as much cash income in a day (away from school!) as their farming parents can earn in a month. Parents seek upward mobility for their children through education but instead they lose familial control (Blickwechsel nd).

Positive Impacts of the Demonstration Effect

The presence of tourists can and does promote bilingualism and language learning (Cohen 1988), and affords practice in idiom and pronunciation. Andronicou (1979) writing about Cyprus reports many positive benefits attributable to tourism, including the demonstration to older members of the community that incentives for change are consistent with traditional Cypriot values and that tourism fosters desirable acculturation. In Malta Boissevain (1978) describes tourism as a positive model for more local enjoyment of tourist-generated activities such as eating out (in restaurants) and sailing as well as more open social contacts among Maltese youths. Both Noronha (1979) and McKean (1989) point to tourist appreciation of Balinese art forms as a strong stimulus for their perpetuation and for expansion of festivals, classical dancing, puppet shows, and woodcarvings.

Summary

Demonstration effect clearly exists as a touristic phenomenon and its further study should be encouraged, especially as Theuns (1989:5) criticizes two recent studies (Kaplinski 1979; James 1987):

> the absence of any reference to tourists and tourism should induce tourism researchers to put statements on the impact of the demonstration effect in perspective by relating them to other possible agents of change such as the expatriate elite, the media and advertising, modern education and so on.

Indicative of demonstration effect are two contrasting quotations. Bouhdiba (1976) illustrates the potential negative aspects, writing about Tunisia with "a beach ball or a beach towel, a lipstick or a pair of sunglasses represent a temptation and an invitation to taste the indiscreet, but as yet forbidden charms of the consumer society." By contrast, MacNaught (1982:372) presents a strong case for its positive role in that "perhaps the best explanation of apparent demonstration effect is the simplest: tourism accelerates changes already under way."

References

Andronicou, A. 1979. Tourism in Cyprus. In Tourism: *Passport to Development?* ed. E. de Kadt, pp. 237–264. New York: Oxford University Press.

Barth, Fredrik, ed. 1969. *Ethnic Groups and Boundaries: The Social Organization of Cultural Difference.* Boston: Little Brown and Company.

Blickwechsel nd. *Turisten in Sri Lanka.* 16mm color film produced by Institut fur Film und Bild Wissenschaft Und Unterrecht. Stuttgart.

Boissevain, Jeremy. 1978. Tourism and development in Malta. In *Tourism and Economic Change*, ed. Valene L. Smith, pp. 37–56. Studies of Third World Societies No. 6. Williamsburg Va.: College of William and Mary.

Bouhdiba, Abdelwahab. 1976. The impact of tourism on traditional values and beliefs in Tunisia. Paper read at Joint UNESCO-World Bank Seminar on the Social and Cultural Impacts of Tourism, 8–10 December, Washington, D.C.

Britton, Robert A. 1977. Making tourism more supportive of small state development: the case of St. Vincent. *Annals of Tourism Research* 1V (5): 268–278.

Cohen, Erik. 1988. Language and tourism. *Annals of Tourism Research* 13 (4): 533–564.

Cohen, Erik. 1989. "Alternative tourism"—a critique. In *Towards Appropriate Tourism: The Case of the Developing Countries*, eds. Tej Vir Singh, Leo Theuns, and Frank M. Go., pp. 127–142. Frankfurt-am-Main: Peter Lang.

DeKadt, Emanuel, ed. 1979. *Tourism: Passport to Development?* New York: Oxford University Press.

DeSousa, Fr. D. 1989. Tourism as a religious issue. *Contours* 4 (1): 16–24.

Hall, Derek, 1984. Foreign tourism under stress: the Albanian "Stalinist" model. *Annals of Tourism Research* 11 (8): 539–556.

Jafari, Jafar, 1974. The social costs of tourism to the developing countries. *Annals of Tourism Research* 1: 227–262.

Jafari, Jafar, 1989. Sociocultural dimensions of tourism: an English language literature review. In *Tourism as a Factor of Change: A Sociocultural Study*, ed. Julian Bystrzanowski, pp. 17–60. Vienna: European Coordination Centre for Research and Documentation in Social Sciences (Vienna Center).

James, Jeffrey. 1987. Positional goods. Conspicuous consumption and the international demonstration effect reconsidered. *World Development* 15 (4): 449–462.

Johnson, R. Boyd. 1978. The role of tourism in Tongan culture. In *Tourism and Behavior* ed. V. L. Smith, pp. 55–68. Studies in Third World Societies No. 5. Williamsburg Va.: College of William and Mary.

Kaplinski, Raphael. 1979. Inappropriate products and techniques: breakfast food in Kenya. *Review of African Political Economy* 14: 90–96.

Kinsey, Alfred C. 1948. *Sexual Behavior in the Human Male*. Philadelphia: W. B. Saunders Co.

Kinsey, Alfred C. 1953. *Sexual Behavior in the Human Female*. Philadelphia: W. B. Saunders Co.

MacCannell, Dean. 1973. *The Tourist: A New Theory of the Leisure Class*. New York: Schocken Books.

MacNaught, Timothy J. 1982. Mass tourism and the dilemmas of modernization in Pacific island communities. *Annals of Tourism Research* 9 (3): 359–381.

Manning, Frank. 1979. Tourism and Bermuda's black clubs: a case of cultural revitalization. In *Tourism: Passport to Development?* ed. Emanuel DeKadt, pp. 157–166. New York: Oxford University Press.

McKean, Philip F. 1989. Towards a theoretical analysis of tourism: economic dualism and cultural involution in Bali. In *Hosts and Guests: The Anthropology of Tourism*. ed. V. L. Smith, pp. 119–138. Philadelphia: University of Pennsylvania Press.

Metalka, Charles R. 1986. *The Dictionary of Tourism* Wheaton, Ill.: Merton House.

Nettekoven, Lothar. 1979. Mechanisms of intercultural interaction. In *Tourism: Passport to Development?* ed. E. DeKadt, pp. 135–145. New York: Oxford University Press.

Noronha, Raymond. 1979. Paradise reviewed: Tourism in Bali. In *Tourism: Passport to Development?* ed. E. DeKadt, pp. 177–204. New York: Oxford University Press.

Smith, Valene L. 1954. Unpublished field notes.

Smith, Valene L. 1989a Introduction. In *Hosts and Guests: The Anthropology of Tourism*, 2nd ed., ed. V. L. Smith, pp. 1–17. Philadelphia: University of Pennsylvania Press.

Smith, Valene L. 1989b. Eskimo tourism: micro-models and marginal men. In *Hosts and Guests: The Anthropology of Tourism*, 2nd ed., ed. V. L. Smith, pp. 55–82. Philadelphia: University of Pennsylvania Press.

Smith, Valene L. 1990. Geographical implications of "drifter" tourism: Boracay, Philippines. *Tourism Recreation Research* 15 (1): 34–42.

Smith, Valene L., ed. 1977. *Hosts and Guests: The Anthropology of Tourism*. Philadelphia: University of Pennsylvania Press.

Theuns, H. Leo. 1989. Coping with tourism in Third World development: a plea for indigenization and de-massification. Paper prepared for the seminar on "Alternative" Tourism, sponsored by World Tourism Organization, 26–30 November. Algeria: Tamanrasset.

UNESCO, 1976. The Effects of Tourism on Socio-Cultural Values. *Annals of Tourism Research* 1V (2): 74–105.

8

Encounters in Tourism

Keith Hollinshead

One could argue that the quest to discover difference is the prime motivator for global travel. The discovery of difference and the encounters with "alien others" and with "novel environments" is certainly a first step toward enlightenment about the world. This article therefore looks at dissimilitude in the world not so much in the physical form of its geomorphic features, but in the divergences that characterize the way the world is seen by its variform humankind—particularly by those who shape or participate in the business of tourism. The article is thus a brief commentary on the cultural thought-ways—the reasons and the myths—that constitute the core of societies and nations and which play a platform role in the affairs of people. In investigating the host/tourist encounter it is one of two articles in this encyclopedia that focuses upon ethnocentrism—that perhaps inelegant term for the way individuals tend to view the world as "though the group to which one belongs is in the center of everything, all other groups being classified in relation to it" (Sachs 1976:5). While this article examines the relevance to tourism of an individual's "propensity to divide humanity into groups, identifying with some and rejecting others as alien and threatening" (Forbes 1985:2), the article entitled Ethnocentrism in Tourism details a number of important implications to which managers and researchers should pay attention in order to improve the level of servicing of host/tourist encounters. The two articles taken together consider the significance for the travel trade of the consequence of inherited or entrenched group attitudes, especially those that "value positively [their own] achievements and particular characteristics [whilst] adopting a projective type of behavior towards outgroups and [so] interpreting the out-group through the in-group's mode of thinking" (Preiswerk and Perrot 1978:14).

The Expansion of Tourism

As the world's traveling population becomes more pluralistic, so too does the market for tourist activities and travel pursuits (Fitzgibbon 1987). The predictability of market behavior is softening as travel options present themselves year round to an increasing number of tourists, and new, emergent and nontraditional consumer segments manifest themselves and hunt for novel locations as traditional drawcard areas are used up. The following long-term generalized trends appear to be crystallizing:

- Increasing differentiation of demand
- Appearance of new specialized markets
- A proportionate decrease in passive travel activities (whether they be essentially "physical" or "cultural" in style) relative to more active/participant/involved pursuits
- A rise in preference for modular vacations where individually-tailored experiences are packaged (Schwaninger 1987).

Thus critical components for the future expansion of travel across the globe are activities, experiences, participation, and learning (Martin and Mason 1987) as sophisticated marketing approaches (involving, for instance, psychographic segmentation) endeavor to identify new and workable typologies of tourists, which may run at a tangent to the established and previously predominant socioeconomic characteristics of age, sex, income, education, and occupation (Stabler 1988). Despite the developing richness of such new activity programs and the diversity of such special interest packages, Europe and North America remain the predominant international tourism originations (Bailie 1989) in an overall industrial structure, which in many senses consists of two incompatible systems—a generating universe of largely homogenous escapist and extraneously mobile people and a receiving macrocosm composed of essentially heterogenous host and residual populations (Jafari 1989).

Increase in Culture Contact

The sheer weight of European and North American animation in tourism gives the world's travel industry a heavily Europocentric profile where the business of tourism is dominated, like so many other spheres of activity have been, by Amero-European ways of thinking. Sachs considers Europocentrism to be, in many aspects, a highly pernicious force: "projected worldwide by colonialism and the expansion of capitalism, it casts contemporary culture in its own mold, placing blinders over the eyes of some and forcing itself on others by deculturation" (Sachs 1976:12). In tourism in the twentieth century, there has been a considerable increase not only in recreational tourism, but in a number of forms of tourism that involve a substantial degree of contact with given host populations, namely,

> Ethnic tourism—focusing on the customs of indigenous and exotic peoples
> Cultural tourism—emphasizing different lifestyles
> Historical tourism—stressing glories of the past
> Environmental tourism—largely in remote or alien locations (Smith 1989)

Accordingly today, increasingly specialized "human story" tour offerings are available, extending from sex tourism in Amsterdam to nostalgia trips to World War II battle sites in the South Pacific. In the travel pages of the Amero-European press one finds in close proximity large advertisements, for example

> "Encounter Overland". . . "meet the people of Asia, Africa and South America face to face"

"Transglobal". . . "imagine India and Nepal—overnighting in Royal Palaces"

"Explore Worldwide". . . [The fabled 'Golden Triangle: Hillside Treks']

"Hann Overland". . . "Longhaul Adventure Travel—Long Houses, Jungles plus Mulu Caves, et cetera" (Observer 1990)

Some industry analysts believe that it is the very existence of the ethnic boundary that creates the tourist attraction and that "cultural tourism" encounters share fundamental characteristics with other ethnic situations. Those characteristics include a superficial, segmentary, instrumental, effectively neutral, or aversive type of interaction; the formation of largely negative stereotypes arriving from these truncated interactions; and the relative absence of trust and prevalence of deceit and manipulation in contacts (Van Den Berghe and Keyes 1984:346–347).

Hence the tourism encounter is a distinct kind of ethnic situation in which

> The transience of the tourist enables both traveler and host to avoid social condemnation for many of the pitfalls of what in other circumstances would be aggressive/disrespectful behavior
> The tourist is a decidedly removed individual from the local citizenry usually in terms of his comparative wealth or his ignorance of local conditions
> The interface between the host population and the tourist in terms of materiality, display, and information is decidedly asymmetrical (Van Den Berghe and Keyes 1984:347)

In time, according to the view of many critics of such intimate tourism, the cultural/adventure travel industry "can turn exotic cultures into commodities and individuals into amusing 'objects' for tourism 'consumption' . . . [whereby] novel encounters become routine for both host and guest, and cultural 'presentations' become more and more removed from the reality of everyday life" (Klieger 1990:38). In Australia, for instance, the response of Aborigines to such colonizing processes via tourism encounters (and via other encroaching Euroaustralian activities) have ranged from resistance, through withdrawal from contact, accommodation, and a search for a functional relationship, to passivity and helplessness (Coombs et al. 1989). Elsewhere in the world, authorities in receiving nations have been decidedly more forceful in regulating the host-guest interface, notably in militaristic and fundamentalist states such as Pakistan where the laws of Islam dictate that women and children travel in separate railway accommodations (from men) and where Islamicization of local laws do not render it easy for non-Pakistani female travelers to eat, swim, or even walk alone (Richter 1989).

In many respects the sociopsychological map of the world may be thought of as being largely reducible to a cultural map. Moreover, in terms of the tourism product permitted to be seen and in terms of the selection and projection of authentic experiences, tourism is "a highly edited reality" (Daltabuit and Pi-Sunyer 1990:12). It is critical therefore that the perspectives of providers, visitors, trade intermediaries, and others are all decently and rigorously scrutinized in each given locale in order to spot the mobilization of bias, the favoring of certain symbolic activities, and the denial of unwanted behaviors. Such analysis ought to be the stuff of the monitoring of intercultural and intersocietal encounters in tourism.

Encounters Analyzed: Ethnocentrism Explained

The term *encounter* implies that two or more *different* populations/groups/individuals meet. An inspection of the distinct mindsets they bring to the encounter is called for. It is necessary to recognize that at each and every encounter the given hosts and travelers will have different ethnocentric viewpoints (i.e., group-loyal/interest-shaped "ways of seeing"). But ethnocentrism in the international political arena perhaps is one of those terms more readily defined than spotted. Booth (1979) proposes that the term has three chief uses:

1. *To describe feelings of group centrality and superiority.* This is W. G. Sumner's (1906) original meaning of the term, whereby an individual strongly identifies with his/her own group, regards that group as being the center of the universe and prefers his/her own culture over all others (*knowing* it to be the best and right way of acting!) and is routinely suspicious of the motives of all "foreigners."

2. *To describe, in technical terms, a faulty methodology in the social sciences.* Here Booth follows Roberts (1976:76) who maintains the ethnocentric view in human affairs is that which improperly utilizes the standards of one's own culture during analysis of another.

3. *To describe "culture-bound" individuals.* In this generalized sense Booth considers the term is used to represent the unsophisticated condition of an individual whose perceptions are ethnocentric. Such provincially minded and culturally narrow people are unable to empathize with externals and cannot conceive of the world from the outlook of those who belong to outsider societies or who uphold "alien" orientations.

Many early studies of ethnocentrism, in intersocietal or individual encounters, proffered a purely "psychological" explanation for the phenomenon, and the wider cultural, political, and economic parameters of the subject tended to be understated: researchers particularly failed to comprehend the role of social institutions in cultivating ethnocentric perspectives (Forbes 1985). More recently researchers have come to understand ethnocentrism as a somewhat panoramic ideological system that pertains to groups and to group relations—not just to an individual's inherited/set predilections. Thus a crucial characteristic of the ethnocentric person is his/her inclination to differentiate humankind into groups with which he/she either strongly connects or with which he/she strongly contraidentifies. Hence the group-bound ethnocentrist is a polarizer and is rarely neutral or indifferent on matters of debate. He/she has a propensity "to shift his/her ingroup-outgroup distinctions, depending upon the issue being discussed" (Forbes 1985) however, and once the cultural or societal context for an argument has been nominated he/she axiomatically discloses an insider-outsider demarcation. Consequently the ingroup may be distinguished in local, regional, national, religious, ethnic, racial, class, or other typology pertinent to the given discussion. And the ethnocentrism exhibited by that individual can be observed at various levels and to differing degrees over situations (Preiswerk and Perrot 1978).

By contrast, nonethnocentric people tend not to compulsively differentiate ingroup/outgroup societies, and humanitarian people (perhaps a democratic alternative for ethnocentrism) tend to be drawn toward or away from other individuals (rather than to groups, per se) because of specific encounters or singular circumstances. Consequently, while the apprehension of the ethnocentrist toward a newcomer or toward an unknown person is one of fear and hostility, the humanitarian is predisposed toward inquisitiveness and admission. These distinctions of style, exclusiveness, and emotional intensity of group loyalties (Forbes 1985) are, prima facie, of critical significance to the business of tourism, which fundamentally is an industry constructed around novel/different/refreshing encounters. Such views are particularly held by observers who deem ethnocentrism (rather than humanitarianism) to in fact be *"the natural condition of mind"* (Lewis 1976:13).

During the twentieth century another anthropological outlook has been identified which is conceivably a more direct opposite tendency to ethnocentrism than is humanitarianism. This important and controversial contribution to sociopolitical thought is the principle of cultural relativism, and it is built upon the premise that cultural phenomena and aesthetic criteria should be understandable in their own terms. This outlook necessarily dictates that the observer subdues his/her own preferences and, in a scientifically detached fashion, observes the actions of others from the procedural perspective of their own culture(s). In the early 1980s a pioneering behavioral segmentation of the Australian market for tourism was undertaken, and the cluster analysis procedures is deployed yielded a breakdown of the Australian travel/leisure market in terms of the prevailing attitudinal mindsets then in vogue in the marketplace. Figure 1 presents a rudimentary review of the findings of that immense study that involved 24 organizations—carriers, packagers, developers, travel agencies, financial institutions, and tourism commissions (The Banks Group 1984). This attitudinal analysis is a most rare and substantial attempt to determine the ethnocentrist/relativist makeup on the Australian market, although that insight into various sorts of travelers' predispositions toward novel or challenging encounters was, of course, only a by-product of the overall investigation.

As a body of social science interpretation, the theory of ethnocentrism has been conceivably more widely accepted and used than any other doctrine (Campbell and LeVine 1961). The main problem with the kind of ethnocentric stereotyping (as shown implicitly in Figure 1 for tourism) arises from "the terrifying primitivism" (Sachs 1976:74) individuals utilize in the derivation of the said stereotype. History and social relationships are unconsciously simplified, and within the resultant beliefs exists a power to pervert and to alienate. In studying tourism encounters in Baja California, and in particular the "ethnic" stereotypes that Baja Californian Mexicans held of tourists, Brewer (1984) found both general (vaguely attributed) and specific (contextually defined) stereotypes to exist regarding visitors from the United States. Given the ease and superficiality with which such stereotypes are produced in transient travel settings, he concludes that tourism may indeed lead to greater rather than lesser difficulties of understanding between peoples.

Having outlined in some detail the ethnocentric outlooks that tend to form the context for the tourism encounters of our age, a number of highly important issues which have a considerable bearing in the arena of travel encounters upon the theoretical relationship between tourism and ethnocentrism remain to be clarified.

Issue 1: Encounters and Nationalism

Misleadingly, ethnocentrism is often regarded as an omnibus or alternative term for "nationalism" (Forbes 1985). In fact both ethnocentrism and nationalism are representative forms of the more general phenomenon of sociocentrism where ethnocentrism is the valorization of a group, nationalism is the valorization of a nation, and (among other possible sociocentric perspectives),

Fig. 1. Ethnocentrism and the Australian holiday-maker—a segmentation study of attitudes via cluster analysis. *(Source: Adapted from The Banks Group, The Customer Connection: Travel '84—General Report on Market Segmentation, pp. 11–21, 1984. North Sydney, Australia: Product Development International.)*

Segment—16%: THE NEW ENTHUSIASTS . . . are young, fresh, eager, hungry for experience and challenge . . . they love to fantasize and to experiment. They want range, diversity and excitement. While inexperienced as travelers, they are very far from xenophobic. Different cultures fascinate them. They subscribe heavily to the ''immersion syndrome''—placing a high priority on absorbing a new place or culture.

Segment 2—18%: THE BIG SPENDERS . . . are almost the antithesis of New Enthusiasts—older, passive, nonphysical and the epitome of the old establishment. They are dedicated indulgers whose concept of bliss is the passive luxury of the first-class passenger on the QE II. Big Spenders are belongers and conformists. They do not enjoy difference or challenge. They prefer the mainstream of tourist haunts . . . are strongly DFY [done-for-you] . . . and they like [own] group travel.

Segment 3—18%: THE ANTI-TOURISTS . . . are essentially travelers (in the true sense of the word) rather than tourists and they reject what they see as tourist attitudes as behavior. They are egocentric, idiosyncratic and nonconformist. They are the most distinctively experiential of all the clusters, and are strongly DIY [do-it-yourself] to boot. They like diversity and newness and challenge. Where Segment 1 is enthusiastic, this cluster is interested. They have an insistence on authenticity: real food, real people, surroundings true to culture.

Segment 4—11%: THE STAY-AT-HOME TOURISTS . . . are best described by what they are *not* and what they *do not* like . . . They are intensely xenophobic, to the point of outright bigotry. They do not enjoy difference, reject cultures, want to be able to speak English, read the road signs, and boil the water. About the only things they do like are bus tours and familiarity. They are dependent, security-minded and passive. They want planning, but prefer to have it done for them. Given the long list of what they do not like, it is hard to see why these people travel at all.

Segment 5—14%: THE NEW INDULGERS . . . like Big Spenders they are strongly DFY, but they are experiential rather than acquisitive. They want the very best and are willing to pay or it. Traveling, for them, is the opportunity to be pampered and wrapped on all sides with luxury. Compromise is out; making do is not acceptable. They are almost narcissistic in their travel more with themselves as the absolute center. Because of their strong experiential bent, they are motivated by freedom, discovery, and difference. They are pacesetters, trendsetters. They will sample just about anything interesting, but if the food is no good they will never go back.

Segment 6—22%: THE DEDICATED AUSSIES . . . have some similarity to segment 4, but they are far more active and passionately DIY. They are the ultimate domestic traveler: pragmatic, independent, self-reliant. They are unashamedly nationalistic and believe that Australia [God's Own Country] has so much to offer that overseas travel is basically unnecessary. When they do travel overseas, they take their domestic mindset with them. . . . Dedicated Aussies do congregate, but only in small groups of their own making. They have not experimented with other cuisines and do not like foreign food. They do not like things too different and avoid trendy places.

class sociocentrism is the valorization of a social class (Preiswerk and Perrot 1978). Conceptual difficulties obviously arise between ethnocentrism and nationalism because of the partial concurrence of cultures and nations (Druckman 1968).

The problematic distinctions between "cultures" and "nations" frequently raise uncomfortable questions of ethnicity (Gathercole and Lowenthal 1990), particularly where travel encounters occur in new states torn between essentialist and epochalist strains where the tensions produced are occasioned by the manufacture of a nationalism not borne of intellectual passion but one charged with cultural disparity (Geertz 1973). Frequently in Africa this contentious arena can involve the abuse of history and prehistory by elites and/or governments to tally with new or preferred nationalist policies (Hall 1984). Similarly, in Sulawesi, the Toraja people claim to have long received mistreatment from the Javanese who control the Indonesian government. "In the eyes of some Toraja, an age-old rivalry is being played out on a new stage: whereas in the past those from neighboring kingdoms had come seeking highland coffee and slaves, today the coveted Toraja resources they seek are rich foreign tourists" (Adams 1990). The Torajan example is a quintessential insider/outsider conflict; its grave problems stem from conflicting cultural orientations—its interethnic and interelite competitivity places a cherished identity at stake. Yet the interface between such ethnonational stand-offs and tourism are far from rare. Elsewhere, for another example, tourism developers must acknowledge the resurgence of national and cultural pride in Fiji as has recently been highlighted by the Taukei (indigenous Melanesian "Sons-of-the-Soil" movement) mainly energized in response to fears of the increasing power that Indo-Fijians were accumulating over Melanesians in tourism and other spheres (Bayliss-Smith et al. 1988).

In the modern world, "nationalism" as a social force is becoming something of a bête noire in the battleground between communal and political loyalties. National unities are frequently being maintained "not by calls to blood and land but by a vague, intermittent and routine allegiance to a civil state, supplemented to a greater or lesser extent by governmental use of police powers and ideological exhortation" (Geertz 1973:260). The line between progressive nationalism and retrogressive nationalism is a difficult one to draw, and it is hard for each and every gelling regime to prevent the new nationalistic fervor it encourages from shifting toward chauvinism and racism (Sachs 1976). Tourism is often itself deliberately a chosen part of the nationalist platform, particularly where an ethnicity is ostentatiously reconstructed to constitute what MacCannell (1984:385) has deemed to be "staged authenticity." Such are the difficulties and uncertainties of a nationalistic approach to social facts (Fahim 1982). But though the role of the state can be quite critical in the projection of tourism (Swain 1990), often the host nation can receive severe unintended consequences. For instance, in China ethnic/adventure tourism has been an unexpectedly strong factor in sustaining the separatist Tibetan identity, providing "economic and ideological stimuli for the process of enclavement and serving as a bulwark [for the Tibetan people] against [full] assimilation [into China]" (Klieger 1990:41).

Thus "governments at all levels and of all types are becoming increasingly interested in controlling [the forms of] cultural production" incoming tourists encounter (MacCannell 1976:25). "[Approaches] based on cultural chauvinism or radical chic can warp interpretations no less than the self-aggrandizing views of aristocrats and power elites. Both biases alike universalize or sentimentalize history, to the detriment of us all" (Lowenthal 1990:312). Even among power-brokers nominally indifferent or otherwise ill-equipped to project ethnic plurality, the travel trade can serve to widen a given regime's interest in and animation of culture (Richter 1989). But these ethnocentric and/or nationalistic impulses are not always state contained. Quite commonly the sociocentric imperative will derive from a larger pan-ethnic calling. In late years virulent forms of Chinese and African macroethnocentrism have surfaced in response to the cultural strictures being metered out via the Western macroethnocentrism of recent centuries (Preiswerk and Perrot 1978). More often the sociocentric response is of a subnational/regional/local kind—reflecting the risen health of indigenous values in the last two decades.

Issue 2: Encountering "the Other"   Since tourism by definition involves some form of visitation away from home and normal circumstances it usually occasions an encounter of some kind with the "Other." Cohen (1988) believes that the fuller the experience craved by the vacationer, the more demanding will be this quest for difference and dissimilation, and for the unfamiliar and the unbeknown, in short, "The Other." Cohen (1979) calls those travelers (who maintain strict standards to gauge the authenticity of distant societies) "existential tourists," and while Berger and Luckman (1966) note the capacity of such travelers to temporarily adopt a whole new world, Blakeway (1980) concludes that they are the type who will take pains to journey farthest off common holiday route-ways—clearly the humanitarian Anti-Tourists of Figure 1. In comparison to these existential tourists, Cohen recognizes four other sorts of traveler, positioned on a scale of sought touristic experiences:

> *Experimental tourists* are one step along from "existentialists" and crave the opportunity to take on board novel lifestyle situations
>
> *Experiential tourists* only seek vicarious association with the culture of others
>
> *Recreational tourists* just demand personal enjoyment and refreshment from the time away, abroad or in foreign abodes
>
> *Diversionary tourists* (conceivably a fair proportion of Stay-at-Home-Tourists and Dedicated Aussies from Figure 1) who merely want diversion and remain in relative oblivion to the genuine societal rhythms of the peoples among whom they travel.

Thus Cohen's typology is a categorization of the differing propensity of tourists to search for and immerse themselves in "difference." Blakey (1990) maintains that one's relative preference for absorption within ones' own familial, ethnic, or national insider heritage (vis-à-vis one's quest for involvement with outsider entities) is broadly reflective of whom people think they are. He maintains that six major dichotomies channel the inherited Euro-American stereotype of themselves in comparison to the Euro-American perspective of "others"/"peoples-of-color."

Euro-American	*Other*
national	natural
American	ethnic (or tribal)
technological	artistic
intellectual	emotional
donor	recipient
powerful	passive

Blakey believes that such stereotypes are highly instrumental, for instance, in shaping the archaeological and museological exhibits that are revealed to tourists about the "Euro-American" and "Other" pasts.

Many travel commentators have in fact maintained that the Western world's inherited view of distant and alien places is strongly ingrained. Hence the cultures and lands of the South Pacific have been deemed to possess a rich paradisiac tradition which is not necessarily their "own," but one "projected upon them from afar, . . . an image . . . rooted in the Western imagination" (Cohen 1982:10). To Westerners the South Sea islands undoubtedly were and are prelapsarian places, free from want or sexual guilt (Smith 1984).

Such non-European "Others" were conceived during the age of exploration "on the horizon of Renaissance commerce and were constrained and imprisoned, essentially, within a commercial perception" (McCrane 1989:24). Such stereotypical notions have been inherited by the tourism industry of today which then perpetrates further false and partial images of distant destinations and their inhabitants (Telisman-Kosuta 1989). Contemporary advertising in the tourism industry readily translates such deeply set unconscious cultural values into consumer preferences (Assael 1987). The following 1980s schematic outline for an advertisement for a tourism site in the Cook Islands is in many ways the ultimate representation of the modern mass-market South Seas concept of Eden:

> [The vision is] of a small island; palm trees waving in the trade wind, with white coral, sandy beaches, a quiet island-studded lagoon and the surf pounding against the off-shore coral reef. Island hills, clothed in green vegetation rise to a deep blue sky. Inside the reef there is light green water, and outside it the deepest blue imaginable. Friendly people, who welcome strangers with dancing, singing and leis, complete the picture. . . . (A 1968 Air New Zealand script quoted in Cohen 1982:17)

The force of such vulgarized, paradisiac and stereotypical images for the South Seas may be judged from the fact that in Fiji there has been a progressive "pseudo-Polynesiation" of Melanesian-Fijian culture which in many aspects even indigenous Melanesian-Fijians themselves now act up to and adopt (Cohen 1982).

False destination images of this type are commonplace in the travel trade around the globe. Recently, researchers have condemned *National Geographic* for being particularly carefree in this regard. In constantly purveying the dominant political ideology of America, the glossy publication offers history purely in reference to the rise of Western civilization and constantly sustains a view of other "backward people" as "changeless" in relation to the implied meritorious advance of the West (Gero and Root 1990). The publication, it seems, continually stresses exploration in remote places, and "overemphasizes the findings of lost cultures, gaudy treasures and unusual cultish happenings." Thus, on its expensive pages and in its ornate style, the magazine romances the exotic "Other" for its readers and purveys, according to Gero and Root, nothing but an objectified and commoditized view of the world. Since there appears to be a positive correlation between destination images and visitation (Telisman-Kosuta 1989), the danger results that tourists' subsequent encounter experiences are largely reduced to the validation of such cliche and stereotypical apperceptions (Britton 1979).

Issue 3: Encounters with History

In the analysis of issue 2 it was inferred that there is commonly bias in historical awareness. The point warrants fuller delineation, since much of the travel trade is modeled as a response to perceived historical significance. To this end the chief problem appears to lie with the very ambiguity of the notion of civilization—a notion that so commonly fails to recognize the plurality of forms of civilizations (Preiswerk and Perrot 1978). Hence, the history on which the travel trade is structured is itself scarcely free of ethnocentric outlooks on human time. Gathercole and Lowenthal (1990) suggest that there are four predominant clusters of paregoric beliefs manifested in the historical Eurocentricity of Western hegemony:

> Eurocentricity as a Christian crusade
> Eurocentricity as chauvinism
> Eurocentricity as evolutionary superiority
> Eurocentricity as "The White Man's Burden"

Thus historical Europeanization implies the borrowing and solidification of European norms and behaviors as the model culture. Accordingly, it is ajudged that there was a profound *need* to propagate Christianity, a very *necessity* to "open-up" the extra-European world, and an empowering *mandatedness* to occupy land (Preiswerk and Perrot 1978). The history of Pax Romana, Pax Britannica, and other like realms upon which our tourists' storylines now tend to be established is replete with either copiously explained or otherwise assumed "legitimation."

The principal means by which our Eurocentric accounts are handed down are through the sins of commission or the crime of omission. Ethnocentrism by commission occurs from the conscious attempt to distort history (or from ignorance about the cognitive structure of the past) such as has occurred in Poland where school history books help manufacture an official fabrication concerning Polish uniformity by relating it to a past where it is claimed there were no Ukrainians, no Lithuanians, and no Jews—only Poles (Lowenthal 1990). Choice of illustration and layout are also a regular instrument of ethnocentrism by commission (Preiswerk and Perrot 1978).

In contrast ethnocentrism by omission generally concerns the exclusion of the history of "outsiders" whether it be consciously determined or not. The force of this omission is normally additive. Speakers claim a shortage of room and time, writers claim an absence of useable written records. Hence in the *National Geographic,* Central American archaeology is almost exclusively and restrictively focused upon the Maya (Gero and Root 1990). Sometimes historians are so fixated with the cultural backdrop of the "insiders" that their ethnocentric perspective denies even token consideration of outsider history. Thus the eminent British historian Lord Dacre (formerly Hugh Trevor-Roper) rejected undergraduate calls to learn African history by advising that "the history of the world, for the last five centuries, *in so far as it has significance,* has been European history" (quoted in Scarre 1990:17; added emphasis), and the distinguished Australian archaeologist Gordon Childe dismissed the Chinese and Indian civilizations as "placid and unchanging backwaters" in his landmark historical handbook *What Happened in History* (Scarre 1990:17). Certain topics and even continents do not rate, therefore in the predominant Eurocentric account of history, which the travel trade now necessarily feeds off. Program planners and site guides are just not sufficiently trained to spot such forms of perceptive selectivity or deliberate distortions at work in the fundamental historical narratives available to them. The problem, a subtle and enduring one, can never be completely overcome.

Thus the tourism industry remains somewhat dependent on the preconceptualization of historians on a globe where a Eurocentric legacy predominantly regulates the ways the past is judged. It seems, moreover, that not only is history written by the winners, to quote the old truism, but the designers of the great exhibitions and galleries of the tourist world are a similar self-explanatory and self-congratulatory lot. According to Horne (1984), museums—the paragon of tourist drawcards—represent "power" above all else. Museums conceivably mirror the approved, acknowledged, and asymmetrical power relationships that societies inherit. They affirm select versions of "authenticity," they demonstrate select features of "significance," they pay homage to the preferred ethnocentric illustriousness of their own establishment constituency. In history, and therefore concomitantly in tourism, the critical issue concerns not so much how the past is told, but whose past is being told.

In an increasing range of spheres over recent years, environmentalism appears to be "the flavor of the month." "Never have so many politicians seized so quickly on one idea" (Economist 1989). Environmentalism, it seems, evokes "a powerful rhetoric that is virtually identical to that of nationalism" (Daltabuit and Pi-Sunyer 1990:10). Accordingly, as with any large view of the world, environmentalism is not just the account of nature, it also constitutes a treatise on privilege and a discourse on patrimony. The land is held, ruled, or owned. And in revealing and displaying nature and the physical treasures of the earth, tourism necessarily must interpret those variform human rights in relation to Mother Nature and those environmental inheritances.

Under the ethnocentric Western perspectives of the culture-nature duality, man (unfortunately the sole right word, historically!) considers himself above nature with axiomatic property claims over the environment. With what Eliade calls "the strong imprint of Judaeo-Christianity" (quoted in McCrane 1989:77), the ethnocentrism of modern societies is reflected in a superior anthropocentric conceptualization. Whereas Westerners are therefore only truly connected with their own history, Eliade believes that many people of traditional societies tend to be indissolubly connected with the whole Cosmos and its more grand universal rhythms. The point is supported by Vecsey (1980) who maintains that these primal and indigenous societies which integrate humans, nature, and the supernatural in fact have "environmental religions." For a discussion on the degree to which Indian people in North America, for instance, see themselves as a functional and essential part of the natural environment in their traditional lands, see Hollinshead (1991:48–57).

Thus for Western society the environment is an entity that can be appropriated by people who are centrally significant in the universe: it remains "a commodity or experience [and] is no less a fantasy than any other industry elaborated by the leisure industry (Daltabuit and Pi-Sunyer 1990:11). Under this anthropocentric outlook, nature as a resource tends only to have exchange value (Knutson 1990:61). The brute force of utility rules. But for many traditional societies, mankind's relationship with the environment is a matter of reciprocity. Humankind in primal communities necessarily has what D. H. Lawrence termed a "revelationary, vivid and nourishing relation to the cosmos and the universe" (quoted in McCrane 1989:77).

The critical question for those who provide tourism opportunity and for those who promote new host/tourist encounters is therefore whether they themselves can decently and sensitively interpret the religiosity in nature of the societies they access. Collectively the travel trade has a responsibility not just to exploit nature and the cultures of the world dependent upon it, but to do its own part to help sustain those diverse cultures and to build understanding about those inherited and enervating relationships with the earth. In the interests of diversity and human responsibility, the tourism industry has a duty to help keep alive views of the world which are other than anthropocentric. There is mutual profit in this imperative of empathy and care. In Australia, where Black Australians have borne the weight of two hundred years of ethnocentric calumny, the situation is now particularly critical. Aboriginal identity emanates from the land, and people such as the Pitjantjatjara of Central Australia do not see the earth as separate from themselves: "they not only come from the land, but are the land" (Toyne and Vachon 1984:5). The restitution of access to and control over land is thus of rudimentary concern among Black Australians, and it will platform their exigencies during the twenty-first century. The travel industry, in presenting the awe and ordinariness of aboriginal society to tourists must, like other industries, take into account the ravages such a people have suffered as victims of the ethnocentrism toward nature: "any strategy [that aims to involve indigenous Australians] which is not based on greatly increased access [for Black Australians] to, and property rights in land, or which does not respect Aboriginal choices to live on their land, is almost certain to be ineffective" (Coombs et al. 1989:85).

Issue 5: The Service Encounter

Tourism may be viewed as, essentially, a service industry or rather set of service industries. The travel trade involves a considerable number of encounter situations where people receive, inform, direct, drive, look after, and entertain, other people. Much of this article has been orientated to the need to understand the ethnocentric space visitors and travelers occupy. But it is also important that the sociocentric milieux of the employee—the agents of service in tourism—are examined "the human family is converging not only at our front door, but at our employee entrance as well" (Shames and Glover 1989:29). And the travel trade and hospitality industries have long been recognized for their polyglot cultural makeup. One has only to conjure up common images of the oriental job market in the various Chinatowns of the world, the strong Philipino presence in Hawaii, or the constant round of youngsters from so many nations seeing Europe in peripatetic fashion as hotel staff.

The hospitality and travel sectors have been conceptualized however, as "a tired, generic pattern of reactive organizations regulated by a disjointed array of Western management principles borrowed from non-service industries" (Shames and Glover 1989:16)—in short, sectors within the industry are observed as being led in many parts of the world by rigid corporate styles and culturally insensitive management models that are hangovers from colonial, plantation, and agricultural eras. In so many instances cultural astigmatism is deep-rooted where these scenarios are somewhat common:

> Expatriate-native competition and conflict or social class gaps between organizational levels;
> Autocratic, insensitive managers;
> An orientation to efficiency at the expense of effectiveness in operations;
> One way (top to bottom) communication;
> Tendency to relieve the symptoms of problems rather than to solve them—or to ignore them altogether;
> Failure of managers to appreciate the relationship between satisfied employees and good service (Glover, Shames, and Friedman 1989:159).

If Glover and his co-writers are correct, the service components of tourism encounters are a fertile cultivation-ground for ethnocentrism. Cultural, ethnic, insider/outsider group biases will be rampant in the travel and hospitality sectors in so many areas of the globe. Social structures in the travel industry tend to have a heterogenous base: social networks embrace multivalent working populations.

Cultural difference is instrumental in helping influence who communicates comfortably with whom at all levels and spheres of the service encounter. Figure 2 lists typical faults that can readily arise out of this high potential for ethnocentric dysfunction. The echnocentric and other sociocentric impediments to internal management and service delivery, as suggested in Figure 2,

Fig. 2. Possible ethnocentric and related malignancies in hospitality, travel, and tourism service.

1. *Systemic Nature of Ethnocentric Expectations:* e.g., preponderance of expatriate managers working to adversarial expatriate values in time-positions in host nations

2. *Absence of Humanitarian or Emic Strategies:* e.g., failure of hotel or travel agency to objectify local flavor and feeling into its everyday operations

3. *Lack of Acknowledgement of Employee Diversity:* e.g., lack of skill among Western managers at bargaining skills in dealing with employees in give-and-take societies

4. *Language Constraints:* e.g., blocked communication arising from the lack of proficiency of transient/external managers with host state/nation languages

5. *Shortfall of Shared Decision Making:* e.g., denial of joint/aggregate processes in egalitarian societies and in those settlements that traditionally operate by communitywide decision mechanisms

6. *Unmatched Sense of Time:* e.g., expectancy that actions, decisions, and services can always be rendered at central-business-district/industro-metropolitan speeds

7. *Lack of Longitudinal Bonding:* e.g., in the Orient, the emphasis upon a singular sale or event, rather than upon the seeding required for long-term relationships beyond that particular transaction

8. *Absence of Consideration for Local Products:* e.g., failure to utilize items and material with which local staff are acquainted and proud

9. *Shortfall of Indigenous Training:* e.g., overlooking need for local service management schools and on the job tutelage for young talent

10. *Denial of Holist Outlooks of Life and Society:* e.g., programming of service in fragmentary episodes or via piecemeal activities which fail to capture the inclusive energy and universal rhythm of a given local community

point to a shortcoming of cultural synergy. Management systems based on standardized corporate models and unbending expatriate rationalities are destined to hamper compassibility. In an industry where ethnic and cultural multiformity permeates, imposed sameness should be avoided. Detached long-term corporate planning must be tempered with the kind of everyday emic flexibility that is promised in Figure 2 of the article on ethnocentrism.

In terms of ethnocentric orientations and perceptions of cultural difference, the tourism industry is conceivably still in "a twilight zone" of need recognition (Cullen 1981). Holistic and cross-cultural perspectives, which proactively shape the goodness-of-fit between corporate and indigenous values are not, the research literature suggests, endemic. If multicultural approaches are to become more common in hospitality and travel services to overcome the evident inwrought ethnocentrism of many aspects of the tourism system, management bodies must increasingly recognize that employees work and live in fond social systems. It is hard to produce efficacious service without sensitively perceiving and consonantly managing those "cultures." Such vision and such management effectiveness necessitate that whereas each manager ought to embrace and enfold the surrounding cultural diversity, each employee should be encouraged to internalize the given ideals of the corporate statement in terms of his/her own values (White and Kanahele 1989). And that ought not just be an abstract platitude. It should be a concrete and synergetic approach purposely designed to also enrich the vacation experience and embellish the allure of the host/traveler encounter.

Summary

This article has highlighted the importance of the comprehension of established group values in understanding the varied and various contexts in which tourism encounters occur. It first outlined the changes in tourism that increasingly bring new trickles and/or new hordes of visitors to novel, different, or previously unchartered parts of the globe. Following this exposition on the rise in scope and scale of intercultural contact in and via tourism, a more thorough critique of sociocentrism (i.e., of group loyalties and associative perspectives) was presented, and the contours of a number of critical ethnocentric issues were delineated in terms of their significance for travel encounters. In stressing the sociocentric dimensions of tourism encounters— notably the ethnocentric parameters—the article has introduced a "strong humanitarian" to "weak humanitarian" continuum that characterizes the actions and the expectations of each host and each guest participating in any given interface in modern global travel. This discussion of ethnocentrism in tourism provides a set of implications for both operators/developers and for researchers in the travel business, and serves as a dovetailing conclusion for this preliminary outline of travel industry meeting and service situation.

References

Adams, K. M. 1990. Cultural commoditization in Tana Toraja, Indonesia. *Cultural Survival Quarterly* 14(1):31–34.

Assael, H. 1987. *Consumer Behavior and Marketing Action.* Boston: Kent.

Bailie, J. G. 1989. International travel patterns. In *Tourism Marketing and Management Handbook,* ed. S. Witt and L. Moutinho, pp. 231–234. New York: Prentice-Hall.

Banks Group, The. 1984. *The Customer Connection: Travel '84—General Report on Market Segmentation.* North Sydney, Australia: Product Development International.

Bayliss-Smith, T. 1988. *Islands, Islanders and the World: The Colonial and Post-Colonial Experience of Eastern Fiji.* Cambridge: Cambridge University Press.

Berger, P., and T. Luckman. 1966. *The Social Construction of Reality.* Harmondsworth: Penguin.

Blakeway, M. 1980. The dilemmas of paradise. *PHP,* September, 73–84.

Blakey, M. 1990. American nationality and ethnicity in the depicted past. In *The Politics of the Past,* ed. P. Gathercole and D. Lowenthal, pp. 38–48.

Booth, K. 1979. *Strategy and Ethnocentrism.* New York: Holmes and Meier.

Brewer, J. 1984. Tourism and ethnic stereotypes: variations in a Mexican town. *Annals of Tourism Research* 11(3):487–501.

Britton, R. 1979. The image of the third world in tourism marketing. *Annals of Tourism Research* 6:318–329.

Campbell, D. T., and R. A. LeVine. 1961. A proposal for co-operative cross-cultural research on ethnocentrism. *Journal of Conflict Resolution* 5:82–108.

Cohen, E. 1979. A phenomenology of tourism experiences. *Sociology* 13:179–201.

Cohen, E. 1982. *The Pacific Islands from Utopian Myth to Consumer Product.* Aix-en-Provence: Centre des Hautes Etudes Touristiques: Universite de Droit, d'Economie et des Sciences.

Cohen, E. 1988. Authenticity and Commoditization in Tourism. *Annals of Tourism Research* 15(3):371–386.

Coombs, H. C., H. McCann, H. Ross, and N. M. Williams. 1989. *Land of Promises: Aborigines in the East Kimberley.* Canberra: Australian Institute of Aboriginal Studies.

Cullen, T. P. 1981. Global gamesmanship: how the expatriate manager copes with cultural differences. *Cornell Hotel and Restaurant Quarterly* 22(3) November:18–24.

Daltabuit, M., and O. Pi-Sunyer. 1990. Tourism development in Quintana Roo, Mexico. *Cultural Survival Quarterly* 14(1):9–13.

Druckman, D. 1968. Ethnocentrism in the inter-nation simulation. *Journal of Conflict Resolution* 12(March):45–68.

Economist, The. 1989. Costing the earth (special report), September, pp. 2–8.

Fahim, H. 1982. *Indigenous Anthropology in Non-Western Countries.* Durham, N. C.: Carolina Academic Press.

Fitzgibbon, J. R. 1987. Market segmentation research in tourism and travel. In *Travel, Tourism, and Hospitality Research*, ed. J. Ritchie and C. Goeldner, pp. 489–496. New York: Wiley.

Forbes, H. D. 1985. *Nationalism, Ethnocentrism and Personality.* Chicago: The University of Chicago Press.

Gathercole, P., and D. Lowenthal, 1990. *The Politics of the Past.* London: Unwin Hyman.

Geertz, C. 1973. *The Interpretation of Cultures.* New York: Basic Books.

Gero, J., and D. Root. 1990. Public presentations and private concerns: archaeology in the pages of National Geographic. In *The Politics of the Past*, ed. P. Gathercole and D. Lowenthal. 19–37. London: Unwin Hyman.

Glover, W. G., G. Shames, and H. Friedman. 1989. The service environment as a cultural meeting place. In *World Class Service*, ed. G. W. Shames and W. G. Glover, pp. 155–166. Yarmouth, Me.: Intercultural Press.

Hall, M. 1984. The burden of tribalism: the social context of South African iron age studies. *American Antiquity* 49:455–467.

Hollinshead, K. 1991. "White" gaze, "red" people—Shadow visions: The disidentification of "Indians" in cultural tourism. *Leisure Studies* 11(1):43–64.

Jafari, J. 1989. Structure of tourism. In *Tourism Marketing and Management Handbook*, ed. S. Witt and L. Moutinho, pp. 437–442. New York: Prentice-Hall.

Klieger, P. 1990. Close encounters: intimate tourism in Tibet, *Cultural Survival Quarterly* 14(2):38–42.

Knutson, P. 1990. Justifying injustice: law and "tradition" as moral argument? *Cultural Survival Quarterly* 14(2):59–63.

Lewis, I. M. 1976. *Social Anthropology in Perspective.* Harmondsworth, Middlesex: Penguin.

Lowenthal, D. 1990. Conclusion: Archaeologists and others. In *The Politics of the Past*, ed. P. Gathercole and D. Lowenthal, pp. 302–314. London: Unwin Hyman.

MacCannell, D. 1976. *The Tourist: A New Theory of the Leisure Class.* New York: Schocker.

MacCannell, D. 1984. Reconstructed ethnicity: tourism and cultural identity in third world communities. *Annals of Tourism Research* 11(3):375–391.

Martin, W. and S. Mason. 1987. Social trends and tourism future. *Tourism Management* 8(2):112.

McCrane, B. 1989. *Beyond Anthropology: Society and The Other.* New York: Columbia University Press.

Observer. 1990. Holidays and travel file. Sunday 19th August p. 36. (London)

Preiswerk, R., and D. Perrot. 1978. *Ethnocentrism and History.* New York: Nok.

Richter, L. K. 1989. *The Politics of Tourism in Asia.* Honolulu: University of Hawaii Press.

Roberts, G. K. 1976. *A Dictionary of Political Analysis.* London: Longman.

Sachs, I. 1976. *The Discovery of the Third World.* Cambridge, Mass.: M.I.T. Press.

Scarre, C. 1990. The Western World View in Archaeological Atlases. In *The Politics of the Past*, ed. P. Gathercole and D. Lowenthal, pp. 11–18. London: Unwin Hyman.

Schwaninger, M. 1987. A practical approach to strategy development. *Long Range Planning* 20(5):74–85.

Shames, G., and W. G. Glover, 1989. *World Class Service.* Yarmouth, Me.: Intercultural Press.

Smith, B. 1984. *European Vision and the South Pacific.* Sydney: Harper & Row.

Smith, V., ed. 1989. *Hosts and Guests: The Anthropology of Tourism.* Philadelphia: University of Pennsylvania Press.

Stabler, M. J. 1988. The image of destination regions. In *Marketing in the Tourism Industry.* ed. B. Goodall and G. Ashworth, pp. 133–161. London: Croom Helm.

Sumner, W. G. 1906. *Folkways.* Boston: Ginn.

Swain, M. 1990. Commoditizing ethnicity in S. W. China. *Cultural Survival Quarterly* 14(1):26–29.

Telisman-Kosuta, N. 1989. Tourist destination image. In *Tourism Marketing and Management Handbook*, eds. S. Witt and L. Moutinho, pp. 557–561. New York: Prentice-Hall.

Toyne, P., and D. Vachon, 1984. *Growing Up the Country: The Pitjantjatjara Struggle for Land.* Ringwood, Victoria: Penguin.

VanDenBerghe, P., and C. Keyes, 1984. Introduction: tourism and re-created ethnicity. *Annals of Tourism Research* 11(3):343–352.

Vecsey, C. 1980. American Indian religions. In *American Indian Environments*, eds. C. Vecsey and R. Venables, pp. 1–37. Syracuse, N.Y.: Syracuse University Press.

White, M., and G. S. Kanahele. 1989. Tourism: Keeper of the culture. In *World Class Service*, ed. G. Shames and W. G. Glover, pp. 51–59. Yarmouth, Me.: Intercultural Press.

9

Ethnocentrism in Tourism

Keith Hollinshead

This article should be read in concert with Encounters in Tourism and—in building upon it—serves as an action-oriented conclusion for the sociocentric and relativistic issues that underscore contemporary host/tourist encounters that were introduced there. Hence, as in that prior coverage of the enthnocentric/humanitarian continuum (upon which the beliefs and expectancies of each "host" and "every" traveler can be theoretically placed), ethnocentrism is regarded here as those forms of prejudice that may be positively or negatively adopted by an individual or group with regard to salient "insider" or "outsider" reference groups. The principal categories of those potential inter- and intragroup identifications and counteridentifications are highlighted in Figure 1. As that figure indicates, "ethnocentrism is based on a pervasive and rigid ingroup–outgroup distinction; it involves stereotyped, negative imagery and hostile attitudes regarding outgroups, stereotyped, positive imagery and submissive attitudes regarding ingroups, and an hierarchical authoritarian view of group interaction in which ingroups are rightly dominant [and] outgroups subordinate" (Horkheimer and Flowerman 1950).

Fig. 1. The essential duality of an ethnocentric perspective showing in-group exaltation and out-group contempt. *(Source: After R. Preiswerk and D. Perrot, Ethnocentrism and History, p. 21, 1978. New York: Nok.)*

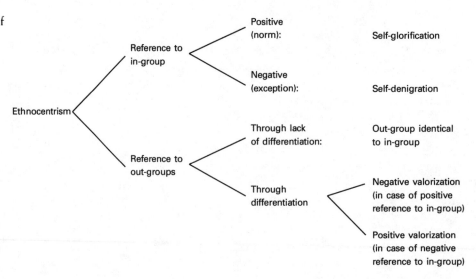

The subject is explored in the following paragraphs, via the provision of, first, a set of implications for the consideration of managers and developers within the industry, and, thereafter, a set of related implications for researchers who inquire of and into the travel trade.

Implications for the Tourism Industry: Ethnocentrism in Practice

Although cultural difference, ipso facto, is recognized to be a powerful generator of travel it ironically appears that, given the findings in Encounters in Tourism, the tourism industry is itself grounded in enthocentrism and that a large proportion of travel-trade planners and hospitality industry managers are themselves professional ethnocentrics, wittingly or unwittingly. In reflecting upon the subject of ethnocentrism for this article, it appears that, collectively, many of the movers and shakers within the industry have basically ignored the effects of ethnocentrism either because they were unaware it was a concern for them or because they have been under scant pressure from any given quarter to do anything about it. Indeed such industry catalysts have perhaps demonstrated a debilitating uninquisitiveness about the broad phenomenon of sociocentrism (of which ethnocentrism is but one valorization), nominally preferring to get on with the everyday doings of their trade, perhaps. But ethnocentric outlooks are prominent sources of pain and error in the practice of tourism. If such problems are to be reduced, management should place attention upon the following matters:

- *Cognition: An Untidy World.* Managers should realize that all cultures are hybrids (Murphy 1986), that societal adaptation is dynamic and continuous, and that individuals within each community will vary in the accepted or traditional purity of their worldview. The authenticity upon which so much tourism place and product is supposed to be conceived is thereby a negotiated order rather than an absolute condition (Cohen 1988). Such claims of tradition, purity and/or genuine originality depend for verification upon whose construction of reality is being applied.
- *Critical Care over Consultation.* Too frequently, because of the distant isolation of many foreign settlements, negotiations between projective bodies/corporations and indigenous groups have been conducted by individuals poorly fitted to undertake such sensibilities (Sachs 1976). Sterner guidelines are required to direct the contact between occidental agencies and local communities (Stoffle and Evans 1990), particularly with regard to whom (within the indigenous group) may be qualified to speak out on what topics to whom under which particular circumstances.
- *Training of Host Society Members.* The production of tourism development mission statements for local communities is insufficient in itself: Travel-trade relationships and service delivery arrangements must also be internalized by all involved group individuals. Intercultural training workshops on a regular/quarterly basis are crucial to this end, whether they be via in-house company schemes, outside consultant visits, supplementary management development programs, or otherwise (Shames 1990). But the required intercultural training must not be restrictively one-way. As Figure 2 suggests, managers themselves must spend considerable time and effort to ensure that they have a developed understanding of the societies among which they live and work and of the subcultures that are meaningful to their visitors and employees and intermediaries.

Fig. 2. Valuable intercultural competencies for the self-aware manager in intergroup service situations.
(Source: After G. W. Shames, Service quality and the multicultural manager, in World Class Service, ed. G. W. Shames and W. G. Glover, Yarmouth, Me.: Intercultural Press, 1989, p. 127.)

> *Self-awareness*—the recognition of one's own values, assumptions, needs, and limitations
> *Culture reading*—the ability to find and trace the inherent logic in each culture
> *Multiple perspective*—the ability to suspend judgment, remove one's cultural filters, and see through others' eyes
> *Intercultural communication skills*—the ability to send and interpret verbal and nonverbal messages accurately across cultures
> *Gear shifting*—the ability to readjust expectations, modify plans, try out new approaches, and rebound from setbacks
> *Culture shock savvy*—the ability to monitor and abet one's own progress through the cross-cultural adjustment process
> *Relationship-building skills*—the ability to relate and to inspire confidence in all kinds of people and to maintain a solid support system
> *Intercultural facilitation skills*—the ability to manage cultural differences and facilitate cultural synergy

- *Scale of Operations.* Worldwide travel industry corporations and professional tourism associations tend to favor large-scale enterprise and global marketing initiatives that pivot the consumer (visitor) as the significant clientele (Richter 1989). Such corporations and associations must also learn to orientate the scale of their thinking and the scope of their designs to also pay tribute to host community sensitivities.

- *Third World Tribulations.* If a travel-trade company operates in the emergent nations of the world, contemporary morality dictates that it has a responsibility to help emancipate the developing communities it comes into contact with (Sachs 1976). It should be particularly vigilant to the special problems of Third World societies, like the modern day breakup of indigenous kinship systems (Fahim 1982) that may be accelerated by tourism development.

- *Regional Culture Blocks.* Tourism corporations should recognize that "other" or indigenous peoples may live in identity blocks that may exist at levels greater or less than singular and commonly identified nation-states. Such travel trade operations ought to consider the mutual value to be gained from supporting umbrella indigenous development bodies for such ideological blocks, such as (for industry training and education) with the Organization of African Unity (Gathercole and Lowenthal 1990) and (for media and communications initiatives in tourism) with the emergent broadcast/air-space confederations of Latin America (Mattelart, Delcourt, and Mattelart 1984).

- *End of Eurocentric Certainty.* Management boards of government and private-sector bodies should recognize that Eurocentric geographic determinism (and the collateral distorted order of the international division of labor) ought no more be routinely manifest across the globe. Indigenous decision making, for instance, should no longer be axiomatically demanded by such agencies in other continents via unfamiliar Eurocentric instruments such as incorporated bodies, constitutions, and meeting procedures (Coombs et al. 1989). And where compensation and/or financial aid is due to such traditional communities, constraints upon block grants or other forms of development assistance should be tempered with reduction of or the remodeling of externally imposed bureaucratic criteria.

- *Rise of Indigenous Oversight.* Travel-trade corporations conducting business with microstates and with traditional peoples must expect an increase of host population scrutiny to occur over their orientations and their actions in the twenty-first century. The renewed Maori desire for Maori accountability over Maori culture in New Zealand is currently only one of the more confident illustrations of this rise of ethnic will against Eurocentric hegemony (O'Regan 1990).

• *Use of Inappropriate Technology.* Tourism corporations should recognize the ethnocentrism that is enwrapped within contemporary technology. In the so-called advanced societies there is a premium on the conveyance of decisions immediately from democratically positioned individuals in society and from hierarchically tethered representatives in given work settings. But the techniques and instruments of the Information Age *cannot* be axiomatically translocated invariably to each and every other society. Technological and information processes can clash outright with traditional bases of authority (Coombs 1989) and easily with lifestyle sensitivities (Shames and Glover 1989).

• *The Terminology of Tourism.* In the interpretation of historic events and cultural practices at visitor and interpretive centers, travel-trade copywriters must monitor their own output to check for value loaded terminology: even commonplace words such as "invasion," "attack," and "naturalize" must be used with extreme wariness (Preiswerk and Perrot 1978). Then the trade should be vigilant to the sensitivities involved with the spelling of sacred or strategic place names, such as in Australia where the anglicized "Mootwingee" reverted to "Mutawinttji" to placate Black Australian feeling (Creamer 1990).

• *The Vocabulary of Places.* Destination promoters can over time help reduce the likelihood that stereotypical conceptions of a given place will occur by presenting more balanced and rounded portrayals of the area they seek to popularize. Outsiders are inclined to couple cities with a few famous features: "Amsterdam *is* the canals, Pisa a leaning tower, Edinburgh a castle" (Goodall and Ashworth 1988:166), and no doubt for many the Swiss do little else but make clocks, Indians eat curry and New Zealanders farm sheep. Hence tourism bureau chiefs must monitor the need to offer corrective and more balanced vocabularies of their cities and regions.

• *Ownership of the Past.* The right to own or have access to relics of former ages is frequently a contentious matter. In Australia questions of largesse and privilege were raised by an envious Northern Territory government in 1983 when the federal government unexpectedly offered Uluru [Ayers Rock] National Park back to local Aboriginal people; many Territorians claimed the great rock to be a sacred site for *all* Australians and were highly disturbed by the action of the national government (Burger 1987). Planning and administrative bodies for tourism must be ever circumspect where precious and definitional matters of heritage are at stake. There were even complaints in the late 1980s that the wrong Aboriginal communities were accorded control of Uluru.

• *Expressed and Ulterior Motivations for Tourism.* Tourism agencies also need to be solicitous in their negotiations with "distant" and "alien" settlements over their involvement in the travel trade. The Warmun community in Western Australia, for instance, had apparently expressed an interest in tourism, per se, to government officials, yet closer scrutiny revealed they had, in fact, purchased the Turkey Creek roadhouse for social and cultural reasons—to prevent alcohol sales there, and to possibly deny a disliked East Kimberley tour operator from setting up a base to explore the Bungle Bungles there (Altman 1987).

• *Renegotiation of Contracts.* The greatest gains in involvement in international travel-trade developments often occur in the opening years of operation. Communities in peripheral nations (generally unaccustomed to business enterprise) may not readily understand the depreciation and other factors involved in such project life cycles given their own ethnocentric and principally present-tense focused world order. Thus they may need to be advised or encouraged to renegotiate the small print of their compacts after brief but preregulated time spans (Richter 1989).

• *Experimentation with Triage.* Studies of Indian people in North America indicate that many indigenous Americans tend not to have a wholesale negative ethnocentric reaction to development, per se (as is often touted) but channel their demands in accordance with who administers a given project and how that developer measures up to Indian preferences. Quite frequently, however, the lack of some Indian communities' association with development projects leaves them unsure how to state their case in safeguarding their precious resources and, in fact, which resources to protect first. In the United States some experimental work to help remedy such prioritization is currently being undertaken with cultural triage, that is, the forced choice scenario, where a cultural group or ethnic settlement seeks to minimize exogamous "upset" to its heritage by evaluating *in rank order* (in terms of their preciousness and indispensability) all of its significant cultural resources that could be affected by the given tourism or other construction (Stoffle and Evans 1990). It is imperative that similar pilot-testing of triage schemes occurs in other parts of the world wherever problems exist in the legal articulation of or the interpretation of indigenous feeling. Hopefully, in lieu of ethnocentric impasse, local populations can, through such improving triage mechanisms, help uncover matters of common concern with external developers, but can also more meaningfully determine when mitigation is likely to be a more productive instrument than litigation.

• *The Potent Symbols of Societies.* The tourism industry, collectively, has paid limited attention to the symbols societies utilize to arouse or reassure their citizens. Symbols are not only entities that are manipulable by political and religious leaders, they can be utilized or transgressed by tourism industry actors themselves. But in most instances managers and developers will not be able to learn the patterns of symbolic usage in a given world order overnight. The aggregate symbolic structure within states tends to be "a loose coupling of many themes and patterns, arrayed in an often untidy symbol system of shared understandings and common meanings" (Murphy 1986:31). But travel-trade entrepreneurs wishing to do business within removed societies ought not remain blind or dilatory in reference to such anomalous networks: Symbolic cues are always notabilia, by definition. Managers and developers need to work closely with anthropologists and sociologists to trace the cultural symbols of their targeted host populations.

• *The Indigenous Right for Contemporaneity.* A tendency exists in the industrial metropolitan world to stereotype remote, or indigenous, peoples into a fixed and invariable lifespace where their ancient traditions are deemed by outsiders to be immanent and unalienable. Ethnocentric expectancies can indeed cripple the perceived potentiality of such groups in this fashion. Too frequently indigenous groups are denied, by such mental straitjackets, the right to adapt to their changing environments. Hence the Basarwa of Botswana regularly complain of travelers who demand they remove their Western clothes in order that they can be filmed in "traditional" dress in line with the visitors' accepted conception of them (Hitchcock and Brandenburgh 1990). Tourism programmers and travel-trade publicists must guard against the maintenance of such exoticization: All receiving peoples should have their own freedom of choice to be contemporary.

- *Increasing Likelihood of Political Action.* Practitioners in the business of tourism today must become alert to the fact that local populations who oppose given developments may be more inclined than in the past to take political or violent actions to preserve what they perceive as their patrimony or matrimony under threat. Hawaii has seen a myriad of such conflagrations, such as in the 1975 Hui Alaloa (Group of the Long Trail) marches on West Moloka'i. In military fashion they assembled on private lands in order to force open access to the island's beaches (Spriggs 1990). Moreover, such groups closely examine the research findings of heritage-concerned professionals. Archaeologists, historians, and tourism programmers must now each acknowledge the political consequences of even their formerly believed most prosaic of activities.

- *Reconceptualization of World Making.* Macrolevel sociocentric differentiations based on major global value orientations are no longer as "reliable" (sic!) as they used to be. In past centuries, and for much of this one, individualized norms were generally associated with Western cultures, and collateral behaviors were generally regarded as being non-Western. But postwar anthropology has found substantial departures to these pragmatic laws of world making (Fahim 1982). No longer are the terms "Western" and "non-Western" readily communicable nomen; no longer is it proper to talk of the British "Empire," and in the 1990s the accepted (historical) barbarians of our past, as revealed in our school books, are much fewer than those of the 1950s. Our ethnocentric dictionaries and atlases "evolve" and the perspectives within our textbooks "mature."

- *Discovery of Universal Values.* But tourism itself has helped gradually conjoin or replace ethnocentric views with riper culturally relativist perspectives. It therefore behooves the tourism industry to monitor the changing values of its own globe-traveling flock as the unparalleled rate of geographic and leisuretime mobility in the late twentieth century leads increasing numbers of vacationers to various ways of conceiving the world (McCrane 1989). Travel can educate vacationers immediately; but there can be considerable lag before that same gain in perspective is recognized in any collective sense and conveyed back to mid and lower levels of the industry itself. The gaining of sophisticated levels of consciousness within the world's largest trade (or composite set of service spheres) has thereby been observed to be neither direct nor elegant.

Implications for Tourism Research

- *Action Research.* The study of tourism appears to be largely contained within the developmentalist paradigm (Browlett 1980). Here research has focused upon "the readily observable and the obviously spatial . . . and has been interpreted through the lens of apolitical, ahistorical social-science perspectives" (S. Britton in Britton and Clarke 1987:185). But tourism clearly needs more political analysis in proportion to this emphasis on the technical possibilities of the subject. If the sociocentric impulses (that have shaped "the uneven playing field" on which the business of tourism is conducted around the world) are to be measured with rigor and if the Eurocentric character of the contemporary travel trade is to be mapped with meticulousness, the subject must be afforded more action research. Thus, rather than continuing to offer technical and value-free analysis in the mold of positivist enquiry, tourism needs to have more social and cultural (or rather intersocietal and intercultural) enquiry as part of the political course of adaptation. Then tourism researchers are more likely to be able to gauge the shape and spread of the huge yet various ethnocentric shadows that blanket the world, and they can responsibly seek "to understand the processes of change and [thereby] promote a more equitable process of development by providing information which communities can use in order to [start to] take control of it" (Coombs et al. 1989:144).

• *A Wider Research Episteme.* It is not only the business of tourism that has an Amero-Eurocentrist bias, but tourism research itself does, too. If travel-trade analysis is to tap the macrolevel philosophical and sociopsychological currents that flow through it, a wider theoretical episteme is called for. Western study of societies "reifies transactive models of social relations based on the maximization of gains . . . and Western anthropological models [are favored which are] void of sentiment or emotion, [and] which . . . deny the humanity of local populations" (Fahim 1982:xvii). Thus if the science of humankind within tourism is ever going to lead to a fuller understanding of other peoples' points of view, the field must learn to capture different intellectual traditions. It is not, as was maintained in the well-known work of Geertz on Javanese religion, the unblemished account of ritual that matters, but the deep interpreted explanation of the home society's underlying values (Fahim 1982).

• *More Baseline Knowledge.* In order to facilitate future ethnocentric and other sociocentric studies and in order to make related and valid longitudinal cultural impact assessments of tourism developments, the field has a critical need for the publication of baseline studies of populations, particularly in those areas of the world under the threat of fast acting and potentially disruptive externally imposed change. Lonner and Berry (1986) have endeavored to draw out some general principles regarding the sampling required for such elementary cross-cultural research projects. Their recommendations on the issues and practicalities involved in the sampling of cultures, communities, individuals, and behaviors need to be read and digested in tourism research centers. Their work is particularly valuable in helping determine who counts in selecting individuals for a given sample in cross-cultural contexts.

• *Image Measurement.* A number of researchers are indirectly contributing to our understanding of the extent of various ethnocentric biases by evaluating destination images. Difficult questions arise, however, for images are tricky phenomena to measure being hard to express, highly subjective, and essentially subconscious; they are thus not readily quantifiable (Telisman-Kosuta 1989). Further work continues to be in demand to improve rank order research instruments, projective tests, and open-ended interviewing techniques. Yet in the 1990s and over the early years of the next century further experimentation with trade-off measures such as conjoint analysis (Claxton 1987) may prove to be the most rewarding zone of enquiry for the comprehension of such individual values and the mapping of preferences in relation to destination and cross-cultural images.

• *Interpretation of "The Other."* Research is also called for into the everyday pragmatics of the interpretation of external cultures. This will clearly be a long and ongoing effort, since each culture has its own narrative style, its own rhetorical rules, and its own symbolic behaviors that anthropologists and other lead agents must first inevitably become accustomed to before the precious revelationary stories of the given society can be translated for tourists. But even anthropologists' knowledge of those themes and tales will always tend to be secondhand and incomplete, that is, external and frequently ethnocentric in each instance, itself. "In their studies of the cultures of other people, even those anthropologists who sincerely love the people they study almost never think they are *learning something about the way the world really is*. Rather, they conceive of themselves as [merely] finding out what other people's *conceptions* of the world are" (Riesman 1972:14). They can never be *one* with a different cultural group, by definition. Tourist's perceptions of the other, it seems, will always necessarily be hampered since they rely so much upon the gatekeeper interpretations of anthropologists and like observers: "The Other," it seems, can rarely if ever occupy center stage!

● *The Burdens of Local/Indigenous Scholars.* The previous point noted the limitations faced by researchers working across cultures with data and insight with what is but "[one's] own constructions of other people's constructions of what they and their compatriots are up to" (Geertz 1973:9). The anthropological observations (which tourism interpretation is routinely dependent upon) are themselves only second and third order interpretations themselves. The field therefore needs, for instance, more Maori researchers and communicators of Maoritangi, yet there are few such non-Pakeha (non-white) graduates available in New Zealand (O'Regan 1990). Even when indigenous interpretors do appear, however, many problematic research difficulties will still survive. In Australia, if and when Aboriginal researchers emerge in numbers to project Black Australia, they will have to deal with the imposed limitations of the cultural logic of particular indigenous groups on the broadcast of knowledge. "[Euraustralians] encourage their children to ask questions about everything . . . culture curiosity is a virtue. [But this is] not so in Aboriginal society. Here [in Black Australia] cultural tradition safeguards knowledge, allowing it to be used only sparingly, restricted according to age, gender and status. Like a currency, knowledge bestows power and is not to be given away carelessly for fear of retribution" (Creamer 1990). Thus, by remaining necessarily moot in this fashion, Black Australians may actually continue to contribute to exogamous ethnocentric miscomprehensions about what is meaningful or important in their culture.

● *Tourism and Ethnographic Interpretation.* A trend has been observed in Western industrial metropolitan society for individuals to want enhanced opportunities for excitement, mystery, and variety in their world (particularly in terms of novelty, scientism, and antimaterialism [Yankelovich 1974]). If tourism is to be a vehicle for those opportunities, then that travel trade must investigate improved ways of revealing the cultural thinking of the societies they lead tourists to. Hence the travel-trade must research how to communicate what Geertz (1973) calls thick description about the significant values and norms of those societies. To Appadurai (1986:4, 6, 21) such significance lies in "regimes of value," in "the social potential" of products, and in various "tournaments [i.e., events] of value" which pertain to particular population groups. To Geertz (1973:7) himself, such deep exploration involves communication of the "twitches, winks, fake-winks, parodies [and the] rehearsals of parodies" that pertain to a given society. Thus, as the knowledge banks of ethnography and ethnoscience increase in response to the ongoing work of anthropologists and culture-brokers, a wider range of untapped story lines and arcane myths undoubtedly await revelation through tourism, providing of course that the weight of travel-trade entrepreneurs doing the programming of that interpretation and packaging is not going to remain just spatially concerned and culturally manqué. The industry's own tacticians need to be continually cultivated, themselves, to see beyond the scenery.

- *Measuring Ethnocentrism, Ipso Facto.* Forbes (1985:26–27) considers there are four underutilized ways that the ethnocentric-humanitarian continuum can be investigated—by asking questions about people's feelings of *belonging to* or *distance from* various groups; the respondent's most *salient ingroups;* the *characteristics* and intentions *of* important or salient *outgroups;* and *conflicts between groups* and the policies that should be followed by ingroups when dealing with outgroups. Preiswerk and Perrot (1978), however, have conceptualized a number of prototypes to facilitate richer theoretical study of ethnocentrism, namely,

self-defense	class antagonism
operationality	xenodefense
radical relativism	proselytism
legitimation	balance

Researchers in tourism could fruitfully apply either the Forbes or Preiswerk/Perrot schematic outline to the travel trade to overcome the paucity of intelligence on the sociocentrism of tourism. For example, following Forbes

1. Possible Research Area—The desire to explore Africa
2. Possible Research Hypothesis—Given individuals [*of which potential tourist groups?*] are humanitarian in their regard to the cultural diversity of Africa

or following Preiswerk/Perrot:

1. Possible Research Area—Legitimation: the reasons for the absence of interest in visiting Africa
2. Possible Research Hypothesis—African people are regarded as "strange," "backward," "unstable" [*by which potential tourist groups?*]

The ethnocentric travel world is in time going to be a rich research oyster for many tourism industry analysts.

Summary

It is hoped that this chapter will aid those who work or study tourism to increase their sensitivity to what ethnocentric bias is and where it might occur. Ethnocentrism has been understood in this article (and in Encounters in Tourism) to be concerned not so much with ethnicity as is so often erroneously thought elsewhere, but with the inclination of people to divide into groups—identifying with other people here, and rejecting other perceived collectives there. It amounts to the judgment of others in accordance with one's own inherited or chosen values. Although ethnocentric views can emanate from any type of psychological entity important to an individual—a nation, religion, race, vocational group, political party, class, and so forth—it has surprisingly not yet catalyzed into a major issue in the literature of tourism.

The existing tourism research literature implies, but does not yet make explicit, the pervasiveness of ethnocentric perspectives among travelers (and critically among nontravelers to given countries and destination regions) and among travel-trade practitioners. This is no doubt because sociopsychological states like Europocentrism are somewhat hidden phenomena as well as being virulent, endemic, and perhaps even in some senses natural ones. Thus, for illustration, a given insider living in the West may be found to accept the materiality of an outsider [non-Western] group (i.e., its canoes, its boomerangs, its pan pipes and/or its dances) but he or she may still not accept the people themselves.

During a period when the world is witnessing the rebirth of various forms of ideological and national sentiment and the reactivation of cultural individuality (Mattelart et al. 1984), it is incrementally important that the nuances of ethnocentric/sociocentric behavior are well charted. The ethnocentrism of group relations can be found at multifarious levels and to assorted degrees, but too frequently a lack of investigative rigor in research or an absence of sufficient thought in society fails to respectively develop theoretical or conversational concepts of ethnocentrism beyond national or racial clichés.

Moreover, tourism itself is rarely mere haphazard wonderment. Travelers have predispositions where they want to get to and whom they want to reach out to along the way. The crucial fact is not so much that travel can produce an awareness of difference, but that it in fact "presupposes an awareness of difference" on the part of the traveler in the first place (McCrane 1989:115). The problem is (in trying to solicit apposite research funds for more relevant, enhancing, or corrective management action) that there are just so many different possible group affiliations within given societies and so many differing patterns of cultural activity. The ethnocentrism research arena is obviously a huge one: informal groups and formal associations, to which one may belong or aspire, are everywhere. Furthermore, objectivity is so difficult to achieve, itself, in the quest for that insight given the impossibility of the complete suppression of the researcher's own upbringing, inclinations, preferences and his/her particular vocational biases. Can investigators always spot the existence of their own sociocentrist perspectives while examining subjects on the ethnocentric/humanitarian continuum?

Ethnocentric perspectives are fundamentally, then, stereotypes or rather failures in thinking on the part of members of particular groups or identifications (Booth 1979). Ethnocentrism research is very much, thereby, the study of thinking as a public activity (Geertz 1973). The critical endeavor in tourism is for researchers to know how to access and interpret the group thought within a given society. A useful goal in the call for further investigations of ethnocentrism is for researchers to be able to provide tour managers and travel programmers with insight that can be utilized to encourage tourists to be more aware not only of new cultures and groups, but of their own culture, affiliations, and unexamined partialities. That objective must necessarily be a subtle, collective, and cumulative one and, hopefully, not just empty rhetoric in lieu of a platitude. Hence, that goal implies a movement in and through tourism toward not only the liberty of the visited but the liberation of the visitor.

References

Altman, J. C. 1987. *The Economic Impact of Tourism on the Warmun (Turkey Creek) Community, East Kimberley.* Canberra: Australian National University.

Appadurai, A., ed. 1986. *The Social Life of Things: Commodities in Cultural Perspective.* Cambridge: Cambridge University Press.

Assael, H. 1987. *Consumer Behavior and Marketing Action.* Boston: Kent.

Booth, K. 1979. *Strategy and Ethnocentrism.* New York: Holmes and Meier.

Britton, S., and W. C. Clarke, 1987. *Ambiguous Alternative: Tourism in Developing Countries.* Suva, Fiji: University of the South Pacific.

Browlett, J. 1980. Development: The diffusionist paradigm and geography. *Progress in Human Geography* 4(1):57–80.

Burger, J. 1987. *Report from the Frontier: State of the World's Indigenous Peoples.* London: Zed Books.

Claxton, J. D. 1987. Conjoint analysis in travel research: A manager's guide. In *Travel, Tourism and Hospitality Research: A Handbook for Managers and Researchers*, ed. J. Ritchie and C. Goeldner, 459–469. New York: Wiley.

Cohen, E. 1988. Authenticity and commoditization in tourism. *Annals of Tourism Research* 15(3): 371–386.

Coombs, H. C., H. McCann, H. Ross, and N. M. Williams. 1989. *Land of Promises: Aborigines in the East Kimberley.* Canberra: Australian Institute of Aboriginal Studies.

Creamer, H. 1990. Aboriginal perceptions of the past. In *The Politics of the Past*, ed. P. Gathercole and D. Lowenthal, pp. 130–140. London: Unwin Hyman.

Fahim, H. 1982. *Indigenous Anthropology in Non-Western Countries.* Durham, N.C.: Carolina Academic Press.

Forbes, H. D. 1985. *Nationalism, Ethnocentrism and Personality.* Chicago: The University of Chicago Press.

Gathercole, P., and D. Lowenthal. 1990. *The Politics of the Past.* London: Unwin Hyman.

Geertz, C. 1973. *The Interpretation of Cultures.* New York: Basic Books.

Goodall, B., and G. Ashworth. 1988. *Marketing in the Tourism Industry.* London: Croom Hall.

Hitchcock, R. K., and R. I. Brandenburgh. 1990. Tourism, conservation, and culture in the Kolahan Desert, Botswana. *Cultural Survival Quarterly* 14(2):20–24.

Horkheimer, M., and S. H. Flowerman. 1950. *The Authoritarian Personality: Studies in Prejudice.* New York: Harper and Row.

Lonner, W., and J. Berry, eds. 1986. *Field Methods in Cross-Cultural Research.* Beverly Hills, Calif.: Sage.

Mattelart, A., X. Delcourt, and M. Mattelart. 1984. *International Image Markets: In Search of an Alternative* (trans. D. Buxton). London: Comedia. (First published in 1983 as *La Culture contre la Democratie?: L'audiovisuel a l'heure transnationale.* Paris: Editions la Decouverte.)

McCrane, B. 1989. *Beyond Anthropology: Society and the Other.* New York: Columbia University Press.

Murphy, R. 1986. *Cultural and Social Anthropology: An Overture.* New York: Prentice-Hall.

O'Regan, S. 1990. Maori control of Maori heritage. In *The Politics of the Past*, ed. P. Gathercole and D. Lowenthal, pp. 95–106. London: Unwin Hyman.

Preiswerk, R., and D. Perrot. 1978. *Ethnocentrism and History.* New York: Nok.

Riesman, P. 1972. The collaboration of two men and a plant. *New York Times Book Review*, October 22.

Richter, L. K. 1989. *The Politics of Tourism in Asia.* Honolulu: University of Hawaii Press.

Sachs, I. 1976. *The Discovery of the Third World.* Cambridge, Mass.: MIT Press.

Shames, G. W. 1989. Service quality and the multinational manager. In *World Class Service*, ed. G. W. Shames and W. G. Glover, pp. 124–131. Yarmouth, Me.: Intercultural Press.

Shames, G., and W. G. Glover, eds. 1989. *World Class Service.* Yarmouth, Me.: Intercultural Press.

Spriggs, M. 1990. God's police and damned whores: Images of archaeology in Hawaii. In *The Politics of the Past*, ed. P. Gathercole and D. Lowenthal, pp. 118–129. London: Unwin Hyman.

Stoffle, R. W., and M. J. Evans. 1990. Holistic conservation and cultural triage: American Indian perspectives on cultural resources. *Human Organization* 49(2):91–99.

Telisman-Kosuta, N. 1989. Tourist destination image. In *Tourism Marketing and Management Handbook*, ed. S. F. Witt and L. Martinho, pp. 557–561. New York: Prentice-Hall.

Yankelovich, D. 1974. *The Yankelovich Monitor.* New York: Daniel Yankelovich.

10

Input-Output Analysis: Applications to the Assessment of the Economic Impact of Tourism

Thomas W. Blaine

One of the most interesting and frequently asked questions about tourism concerns its contribution to the economic growth and development of a community or region. Perhaps the tool most commonly used to address this issue is input-output analysis (IOA). Developed by Wassily W. Leontief (1941) as a conceptual and empirical framework for estimating economic impacts, IOA is based upon the interdependency of industries (sectors) in the economy of a region. As any one industry produces output in order to satisfy demand, that same industry requires, or demands, output from other industries as inputs into its production process. Those industries, in turn, then require more inputs from the initial industry, and so on.

The consequence of IOA is that when a given amount of money is introduced into the economy of a region (an injection), the total impact or effect of the injection exceeds the amount of the initial expenditure (see Figure 1). Suppose, for example, that a tourist visits a resort in region Y and spends X dollars at a hotel. Then X is the *direct* effect of his expenditure. But the hotel, in turn, spends a portion of the initial expenditure on inputs necessary for its operation (electricity, maid service, and so forth). Some of the hotel's spending will be received outside of region Y. This portion of the expenditure is termed a *leakage*. However, the portion that the hotel spends within the region again contributes to the economy. This impact of the initial tourist expenditure is termed the *indirect* effect. Finally, those individuals or firms within region Y who received money through the indirect effect in turn spend money in the region. This final effect is termed the *induced* effect of the initial expenditure. The ratio of the three effects combined to the initial expenditure is labelled the *output multiplier* for that expenditure.

$$\text{Output Multiplier} = \frac{\text{Direct} + \text{Indirect} + \text{Induced Effects}}{\text{Initial Expenditure}}$$

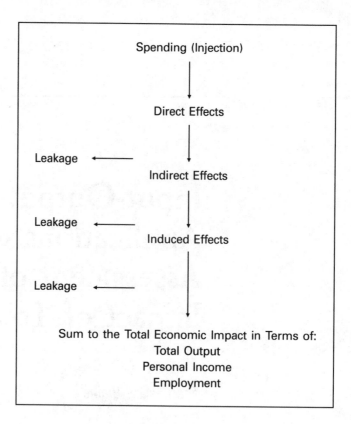

Fig. 1. The economic impact of spending on a given group of commodities in a given region.

Spending (Injection)

Direct Effects

Leakage ← Indirect Effects

Leakage ← Induced Effects

Leakage ←

Sum to the Total Economic Impact in Terms of:
Total Output
Personal Income
Employment

Thus, if every dollar spent at hotels in region Y creates a total impact upon the output of the economy of the region of $2.71, the hotel sector output multiplier in the region is 2.71. Magnitudes of multipliers vary greatly from region to region and sector to sector based upon the structure of the economy in the region, the size of the region, and specifically upon the extent of the leakages associated with the particular sector in the given region. Referring again to the example above, if we define as a study region a particular county, and the hotels in that county purchase their inputs from an adjacent county, then the leakages will be high and the resulting multiplier will be relatively low. However, if we redefine the study region as the two-county area, then what were considered leakages before now become indirect effects, and the multiplier will grow larger.

As in the case of output multipliers, properly constructed IO models, by taking into account the relationships between sectors within a region, make possible the calculation of *personal income multipliers, value added multipliers,* and *employment multipliers.*

The Mathematics of IOA

Suppose the economy were divided into n sectors; 1, 2, 3, . . . n. Each sector, in producing output for other sectors, requires input from other sectors which in turn, require input from that and other sectors. Following the notation of Chiang (1984), let **A** be the input-output table:

Output

	Input	1	2	3···	n	HH
$A =$	1	a_{11}	a_{12}	$a_{13}···$	a_{1n}	d_1
	2	a_{21}	a_{22}	$a_{23}···$	a_{2n}	d_2
	3	a_{31}	a_{32}	$a_{33}···$	a_{3n}	d_3

$$
\begin{array}{ccccccc}
\cdot & \cdot & \cdot & \cdot & \cdot & \cdot \\
\cdot & \cdot & \cdot & \cdot & \cdot & \cdot \\
\cdot & \cdot & \cdot & \cdot & \cdot & \cdot \\
n & a_{n1} & a_{n2} & a_{n3}\cdots & a_{nn} & d_n \\
\text{HH} & P_1 & P_2 & P_3\cdots & P_n & —
\end{array}
$$

Reading down the first column, a_{11} is the amount of input from industry 1, in dollar terms, necessary to produce one dollar's worth of output of item 1; a_{21} is the amount of industry 2's output necessary as an input for the production of \$1 worth of item 1, and so forth. Thus if sector one is electric power generation, and sector two is the water industry sector, then in order to produce one dollar's worth of electricity, a_{11} units of electricity itself are needed as an input, while a_{21} units of water are required and so on down the column. Each member, a_{ij}, of the table is an input coefficient and is interpreted as the amount of the ith commodity needed to produce one unit of the jth commodity. Reading across row one a_{11}, a_{12}, $a_{13} \ldots a_{1n}$, are, respectively, the amounts of electricity required as inputs into the production of one dollar's worth of electricity, water, and so on.

The letters HH stand for the household sector, which is considered distinct from all of the n production sectors. Reading down the HH column, d_i is the total household demand for commodity i (here viewed as an input into the household sector's operation). Reading across the HH row, P_j is the payment that industry j must make to households in order to acquire labor and capital for production. Thus industry j's total payments necessary for the production of one dollar's worth of output are:

$$
a_{1j} + a_{2j} + a_{3j} + \ldots a_{nj} + P_j = \sum_{i=1}^{n} a_{ij} + P_j
$$

This sum must be less than one, of course, in order for production to be feasible, since output is defined as "one dollar's worth," and to accommodate the notion that some payments are leakages and thus not received in the economy of the region.

Each industry desires to produce just enough of its output to satisfy the total demand for it, from all production sectors plus the household sector. Let x_i be the amount of output produced by the ith sector. Then the following equation must be satisfied:

$$
x_i = a_{i1} x_1 \ldots a_{ii} x_i + \ldots a_{in} x_n + d_i
$$

In order for the economy to be in equilibrium, this equation must hold simultaneously for all of the i sectors. The representative equation may be rearranged as follows:

$$
- a_{i1} x_1 - \ldots + (1 - a_{ii}) x_i - \ldots - a_{in} x_n = d_i
$$

This may be stated for all the equations in matrix form:

$$
\begin{bmatrix}
(1-a_{11}) & -a_{12}\cdots & -a_{1n} \\
-a_{21} & (1-a_{22})\cdots & -a_{2n} \\
\cdot & \cdot & \cdot \\
\cdot & \cdot & \cdot \\
\cdot & \cdot & \cdot \\
-a_{n1} & -a_{n2}\cdots & (1-a_{nn})
\end{bmatrix}
\begin{bmatrix}
x_1 \\
x_2 \\
\cdot \\
\cdot \\
\cdot \\
x_n
\end{bmatrix}
=
\begin{bmatrix}
d_1 \\
d_2 \\
\cdot \\
\cdot \\
\cdot \\
d_n
\end{bmatrix}
$$

In matrix notation, let the $n \times n$ matrix be denoted the technology matrix, $\mathbf{T}$ and express:

$$\mathbf{Tx} = \mathbf{d}$$

In order to get the solution to the problem of how much output each industry should produce, solve for $\mathbf{x}$

$$\mathbf{x} = \mathbf{T}^{-1} \mathbf{d},$$

where $\mathbf{T}^{-1}$ is the inverse of the technology matrix. Now, given any particular input-output relationship and the demand from the household sector, we can calculate the outputs x necessary to satisfy all demands.

As an example, let us consider a simple economy made up of three industrial sectors, electricity, water, and hotels, plus the household sector. Assume further that the input matrix $\mathbf{A}$ is as follows:

$$\mathbf{A} = \begin{bmatrix} .16 & .28 & .50 \\ .40 & .14 & .21 \\ .12 & .35 & .10 \end{bmatrix}$$

Recall the interpretation given previously—one dollar's worth of electricity generation required 16 cents worth of electricity, 40 cents worth of water and 12 cents worth of hotel use. The same procedure of reading down the second and third columns reveals the necessary requirements for producing a dollar's worth of water and hotel services respectively. For hotels, one dollar's worth of output requires 50 cents worth of electricity, 21 cents worth of water, and 10 cents worth of hotel accommodations itself. Note that for each industry, the sum of required inputs is less than one dollar. This is because leakages exist and households do not appear explicitly as a sector in this matrix. Household demands will appear in the $\mathbf{d}$ vector that follows. The technology matrix $\mathbf{T}$ is:

$$\mathbf{T} = \begin{bmatrix} .84 & -.28 & -.50 \\ -.40 & .86 & -.21 \\ -.12 & -.35 & .90 \end{bmatrix}$$

Recall that the final output matrix is the vector:

$$\begin{bmatrix} x_1 \\ x_2 \\ x_3 \end{bmatrix} = \mathbf{T}^{-1}\mathbf{d}$$

Thus the key to the solution is finding the inverse of the technology matrix. Inverting matrices is a very complicated mathematical procedure, even in the case of a simple three-sector model as we have here. Beyond three sectors, it is really infeasible to invert a matrix manually, and a computer must therefore be called upon.

Upon inversion of $\mathbf{T}$, the reader may verify that

$$\mathbf{T}^{-1} = \begin{bmatrix} 1.95 & 1.07 & 0.68 \\ 1.19 & 1.94 & 0.91 \\ 1.36 & 1.05 & 1.70 \end{bmatrix}$$

Thus, the final output equations read

$$x_1 = 1.95\, d_1 + 1.07\, d_2 + 0.68\, d_3$$
$$x_2 = 1.19\, d_1 + 1.94\, d_2 + 0.91\, d_3$$
$$x_3 = 1.36\, d_1 + 1.05\, d_2 + 1.70\, d_3$$

The final step in calculating the total output of the three industries is thus to ascertain the final, or household demands for each one. Inspection of the three equations reveals that the output multiplier for each of the three categories is equal to the vertical sum of the coefficients obtained from T^{-1}, respectively. For example, any additional dollar spent on hotels increases the total output of electricity by 68 cents, water by 91 cents, and hotels by $1.70. Thus in this example, the overall hotel multiplier is 3.29. For a more thorough mathematical treatment of IOA, see Chiang (1984) and Walsh (1986). For a more involved history of the conceptual development of IOA, in addition to mathematical analysis, see Blaug (1983).

The data collection tasks for calculating the economic impact of tourism in a region can thus be divided into two parts: (1) calculating the input-output coefficients in the input-output table and (2) obtaining tourist expenditures by relevant category (injections). Both of these requirements involve substantial commitments in terms of resources, but the development of the I-O model (input-output table) is an enormous task, even for relatively small regions.

In recent years in the United States, accounting standards and model development have facilitated the standardization of IOA through the development of standard industry classification (SIC) codes. The U.S. Department of Commerce currently classifies economic activity into 528 sectors. Of course, tourism, rather than occupying a single SIC code, cuts across numerous sectors, such as hotels, eating and drinking establishments, amusements, and so forth.

The U.S. Forest Service in the Department of Agriculture has developed an IO model that allows for disaggregation of study areas down to the county level for each of the fifty states. The IMPLAN model, as it is known, has been used extensively in the estimation of economic impacts in general and of recreation and tourism in particular. Perhaps the greatest advantage of the model is that it allows for aggregation of counties into a study region up to the state level for any state, while also allowing for any level of aggregation of the 528 sectors included in the model.

Empirical Results

In recent years, an increasing number of studies has emerged documenting the magnitudes of the economic impacts of recreation- and tourism-related spending upon regional and national economics. Walsh (1986) presented a review of studies of regional economic impacts of tourism and recreation in the United States. He noted that the regional output multipliers in these studies typically ranged from 1.5 to 2.6 and averaged approximately 2.0. Table 1 summarizes the studies he reported.

The analysis of the economic impact of international tourism upon various countries and regions of the world has developed into a major topic in the past two decades and has spawned alternatives to IOA as a method for calculating such impacts (Milne, 1987, Archer, 1976; Liu and Var, 1982). Fletcher (1989) presented a review of methods of calculating economic impacts, along with the strengths and weaknesses of each. In addition, he pre-

Table 1. *Regional output multipliers for expenditures on recreation tourism goods and services, United States*

Regions	Source	Type of development	Output multiplier
Teton County, Wyoming	Rajender et al. (1967)	Tourism	1.46
Southwest counties, Wyoming	Kite and Schultz (1967)	Fishing, Flaming Gorge	2.07
Sullivan County, Pennsylvania	Gamble (1965)	Summer homes	1.60
Itasca County, Minnesota	Hughes (1970)	Summer resorts	2.23
Ely County, Minnesota	Lichty and Steinnes (1982)	Boundary waters Canoe area, tourism	2.23
Wadsworth County, Wisconsin	Kalter and Lord (1968)	Tourism	1.87
Baldwin County, Alabama	Main (1971)	Tourism	2.58
Montana	Haroldson (1975)	Winter resorts	2.40
Grand County, Colorado	Rhody and Lovegrove (1970)	Hunting and fishing	2.00
Colorado	McKean and Nobe (1984)	Hunting and fishing Resident Nonresident	1.75 2.60
Yaquina Bay, Oregon	Stoevener et al. (1974)	Fishing	2.06
United States	National Marine Fisheries Services	Saltwater fishing	1.90

Source: Walsh (1986)

sented one of the most comprehensive lists of tourist personal income multipliers calculated by IO analysis for a wide array of travel destinations throughout the world. These results are presented in Table 2.

Note that the multipliers are presented in order of descending magnitudes and that this order corresponds fairly closely with the size of the region, as discussed previously. Here multipliers for entire countries are near the top, and those for counties and cities are near the bottom.

Summary

As an increasing number of communities, regions, and nations have begun to turn toward travel and tourism as vehicles for economic growth and development, input-output analysis has emerged as the primary method for assessing the resulting economic impacts. Although it is a very complicated mathematical procedure, IOA has become much more accessible in recent years as a result of better software programs used in the computation of multipliers. Less expensive computer hardware and more streamlined survey methods have also contributed to greater ease in performing IOA. In the future, IOA will almost certainly become an indispensable tool for planners interested in monitoring their region's success and potential for reaping the economic rewards from tourism.

Table 2. *Tourist income multipliers for selected countries, cities, and regions*

Destination	Personal income multiplier
Turkey	1.96
United Kingdom	1.73
Republic of Ireland	1.72
Egypt	1.23
Jamaica	1.23
Dominican Republic	1.20
Cyprus	1.14
Northern Ireland	1.10
Bermuda	1.09
Hong Kong	1.02
Mauritius	0.96
Antigua	0.88
Missouri State	0.88
Bahamas	0.79
Walworth County, Wisconsin, USA	0.78
Fiji	0.72
Cayman Islands	0.65
Iceland	0.64
Grand County, Colorado, USA	0.60
British Virgin Islands	0.58
Door County, Wisconsin, USA	0.55
Solomon Islands, Melanesia	0.52
Republic of Palau, Micronesia	0.50
Victoria Metropolitan Area, Canada	0.50
Sullivan County, Pennsylvania	0.44
City of Carlisle, Cumbria	0.40
Western Samoa, Polynesia	0.39
Gwynedd, North Wales, UK	0.37
East Anglia, UK	0.34
City of Winchester, UK	0.19

Source: Fletcher (1989)

References

Archer, B. H. 1976. The anatomy of a multiplier. *Regional Studies* 10(1):71–77.

Archer, B. H., and C. B. Owen. 1971. Towards a tourist regional multiplier. *Regional Studies* 5(4):289–294.

Blaug, M. 1983. *Economic Theory in Retrospect.* Cambridge: Cambridge University Press.

Chiang, A. C. 1984. *Fundamental Methods of Mathematical Economics.* New York: McGraw-Hill.

Fletcher, J. 1989. Input-output analysis and tourism impact studies. *Annals of Tourism Research* 16(4):514–529.

Gamble, H. B. 1965. Community income from outdoor recreation. Paper presented at the Maryland Governor's Recreation Conference, Ocean City, Maryland.

Haroldson, A. D. 1975. Economic Impact of Recreation Development at Big Sky, Montana. Research Report No. 75, Agricultural Experiment Station, Montana State University, Bozeman, Mont.

Hughes, J. M. 1970. *Forestry in Itasca County's Economy: An Input-output Analysis.* Miscellaneous Report No. 95, Forestry Series No. 4, Agricultural Experiment Station, University of Minnesota, St. Paul, Minn.

Kalter, R. J., and W. B. Lord. 1968. Measurement of the impact of recreation investments on a local economy. *American Journal of Agricultural Economics* 50(2):243–255.

Kite, R. C., and W. D. Schultz. 1967. *Economic Impact on Southwestern Wyoming of Recreationists Visiting Flaming Gorge Reservoir.* Research Report No. 11, Agricultural Experiment Station, University of Wyoming, Laramie, Wyo.

Leontief, W. W. 1941. *The Structure of the American Economy 1919-1939*. Fair Lawn, N.J.: Oxford University Press.

Lichty, R. W., and D. N. Steinnes. 1982. Ely, Minnesota: Measuring the impact of tourism on a small community. *Growth and Change* 13(2):36–39.

Liu, J., and T. Var. 1982. Differential multipliers for the accommodation sector. *International Journal of Tourism Management* 3(3):177–187.

Main, A. 1971. Impact of forestry and forest related industries on a local economy, Baldwin County, Alabama. Ph.D. diss., Auburn University.

McKean, J. R., and K. C. Nobe. 1984. Direct and indirect economic effects of hunting and fishing in Colorado, 1981. Technical Report No. 44, Colorado Water Resources Institute. Colorado State University, Fort Collins, Colo.

Milne, S. S. 1987. Differential multipliers. *Annals of Tourism Research* 14(4):499–515.

Rajender, G. R., F. K. Harston, and D. M. Blood. 1967. A study of the resources, and economy of Teton County, Wyoming. Division of Business and Economic Research, University of Wyoming, Laramie, Wyo.

Rhody, D. D., and R. E. Lovegrove. 1970. Economic impact of hunting and fishing expenditures in Grand County, Colorado, 1968. GS 916, Fort Collins: Colorado State University.

Stoevener, H. H., R. B. Retting, and S. D. Reiling. 1974. Economic impact of outdoor recreation: what have we learned? In *Water and Community Development: Social and Economic Perspectives*. eds. D. R. Field, J. C. Baron, and B. F. Long. Ann Arbor, Mich.: Ann Arbor Science Publishers.

Walsh, R. G. 1986. *Recreation Economic Decisions: Comparing Benefits to Costs*. State College, Pa.: Venture Publishing Company.

11

Elasticity of Tourism Demand

Golam Mohammad

Tourism can be viewed as an activity or experience that provides satisfaction to most contemporary households. Visits to tourist attraction sites, assessed as tourism demand, are largely due to often unique site attributes (e.g., visual aesthetics), characteristics (e.g., hydrosystem: water-based sports, forestry, wildlife), or services. Changes in the number of visits (i.e., quantity of tourism demanded) are in fact based on the quality of these site attributes/characteristics to the prices paid for the visits, among other factors. The degree of responsiveness to these changes is known as elasticity of tourism demand. Government planning and management decisions can modify or change the level and quality of the production of tourism related goods, services, attributes, or characteristics (Wilman 1984). This article identifies various factors that cause responses in the (quantity of) tourism demand (or number of visits) and provides different measures of (these responses—elasticities) along with their application to planning, policy, and management decisions.

Demand for Tourism-Related Products

Elasticity measures of tourism demand can only be derived if and when the relevant tourism demand function is identified for the specific site/region. It is well known from the basic principles of economics that an individual's demand for a commodity is driven by the (possible) satisfaction he or she gets from the consumption of the commodity. In this section, the terms goods, services, activities, commodities, characteristics, and attributes are used interchangeably. For example, one may visit Egypt to see the Pyramids, a site attribute; or go to Seoul, South Korea, just to watch the Olympics, a service; or go to Singapore for shopping, buying (cheaper) goods!

Following the law of demand, the demand for tourism services, defined as the quantity of tourism services that will be consumed/demanded at a given time period, is inversely related to the price of the tourism services, other things remaining the same. That is,

$$Q = f(P, \text{ other factors remaining unchanged})$$

and

$$\Delta Q / \Delta P < 0$$

Table 1. *Tourism demand schedule*

Quantity of tourism services demanded (Q)	Price per unit of tourism services ($) (P)
14	0
13	100
12	200
10	400
9	500
8	600
7	700
6	800
4	1,000
2	1,200
1	1,300

where Q = quantity of tourism services demanded, P = price of the corresponding tourism services, ΔQ = change in quantity demanded, and ΔP = change in price.

The inverse relationship between P and Q implies that the change in demand for tourism services (i.e., ΔQ) will be positive (negative) if the change in the corresponding price of the tourism services (i.e., ΔP) is negative (positive). The measures of Q may be number of visits, number of visitor days, or the number of arrivals, and P represents their corresponding prices. Furthermore, the estimates of quantity of tourism demand are observed for a particular period, such as per year, per month or per season. We know that in an imperfect world, everything affects everything else, but at different degrees. That is why other things are held constant in a demand model to allow P and Q to operate in their expected way. A hypothetical tourism demand schedule, representing a relationship between number of visits (quantity of demand for tourism services), Q, and corresponding price of a visit (price of tourism related services), P, is shown in Table 1.

The tourism demand curve generated from this demand schedule is shown in Figure 1. From Figure 1 we find that as price per visit to a tourist site increases, fewer visits are taken (consumed) by tourists, other things remaining the same. However, demand theory also suggests that in reality, other factors, such as income, price of substitute goods, price of complement goods, and taste and preference factors affect the demand for the commodity (e.g., a tourism service). Furthermore, some variables are important determining factors for domestic tourism demand, (e.g., cost of living index in various tourist destination sites) while some other factors (such as exchange rates between various countries) are critical in explaining the variability in international demand for tourism. For detailed discussions of domestic tourism demand, see Var et al., (1990b); and for international demand for tourism, see Var et al., (1990a) and Martin and Witt (1987).

The following sections show various responsivenesses (elasticities) of tourism demand as affected by the corresponding price of a trip, income [of tourists], and price of tourism-related substitute and complementary commodities.

Price Elasticity of Tourism Demand

Price elasticity of tourism demand measures the responsiveness of quantity demanded for tourism services to the changes in the corresponding price of the tourism service. It is thus defined as:

Fig. 1. Tourism demand curve and elasticity.

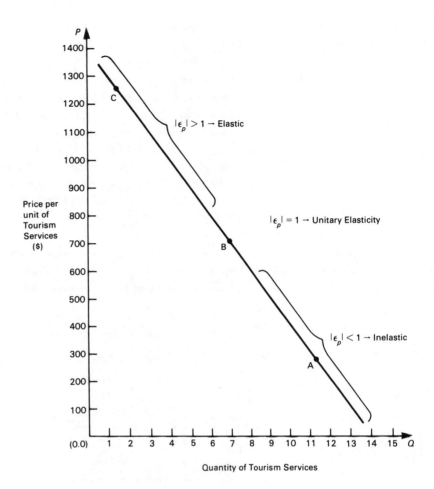

$$\epsilon_P = \frac{\% \text{ change in quantity demanded for tourism services}}{\% \text{ change in price of the tourism services}}$$

$$= \frac{\Delta Q / \overline{Q}}{\Delta P / \overline{P}}$$

where ϵ_P = price elasticity of tourism demand, ΔQ = change in quantity demanded for tourism services, ΔP = change in the price of tourism services, $\overline{Q}$ = average quantity of tourism services, and $\overline{P}$ = average price of the corresponding tourism service.

By referring to Figure 1, we can calculate price elasticity of tourism demand (ϵ_P) at various points on the tourism demand curve. We know that the movement along the tourism demand curve will only be caused by changes in the price for tourism services (other things remain unchanged). Consider a price change from $800 to $600 per trip to Florida. Such a change (decline) in prices will cause a response of an increase in the quantity demand for visits to Florida from 6 trips to 8 trips. This is why the price elasticity of [tourism] demand is always negative. However, for convenience, the absolute value of price elasticity, $|\epsilon_P|$, is used in interpreting the degree of responsiveness of the demand for tourism-related services from corresponding prices of tourism services. That is, when the percentage change in quantity demanded for tourism-related goods and services is greater than the percentage change in prices of corresponding tourism-related services, $|\epsilon_P|$ becomes greater than 1. If the numeric value of price elasticity is greater than one (i.e., $|\epsilon_P| > 1$), demand is known as elastic. Similarly, if the percentage change in tourism-related goods and services changes less than the percentage change in prices, $|\epsilon_P|$ becomes less than one, and demand is known to be inelastic. For most necessity goods and services, demand is found to be price inelastic (e.g., salt, shoes). On the other hand, for most luxury goods and services (e.g., automobiles, stereo systems, international tourism) demand tends to be elastic. Furthermore, we find that ϵ_P falls as we go down along a linear (tourism) demand curve (as shown in Figure 1 and Table 2). From Table 2, we find that the ϵ_P is greater at point C than at point B, and ϵ_P at point B is greater than at point A. The procedure to calculate ϵ_P at point A is shown in the next section, and the calculated values of ϵ_P at points B and C are reported in Table 2. (Interested readers may verify the values of ϵ_P at points B and C.)

Procedures to Calculate ϵ_P of Tourism Demand In order to measure the degree of responses to changes in the price of a trip on the number of visits to Florida, we first calculate the price elasticity of tourism demand (e.g., for point A):

$$\epsilon_P = \frac{\Delta Q / \overline{Q}}{\Delta P / \overline{P}} = \frac{(Q_1 - Q_2)/\overline{Q}}{(P_1 - P_2)/\overline{P}}$$

$$= \frac{(10 - 12)/11}{(400 - 200)/300}$$

$$= \frac{-2/11}{200/300} = \frac{-0.182}{0.667} = -0.273$$

Here

P_1 = original price of a trip = \$400
Q_1 = original quantity of trip taken = 10
P_2 = new [changed] price of a trip = \$200
Q_2 = new [changed] quantity of trip taken = 12
$\overline{P}$ = average price of a trip
   = $(P_1 + P_2)/2$
   = $(400 + 200)/2$
   = \$300/trip
$\overline{Q}$ = average quantity of trip taken
   = $(Q_1 + Q_2)/2$
   = $(10 + 12)/2$
   = 11 trips

An elasticity of -0.273 shows that if price were to decrease by 10 percent, the quantity of trips (tourism services) consumed (taken) would increase by 2.73 percent. Because the tourism demand curve is downward sloping, the price elasticity of demand will always be negative.

Elasticity of Tourism Demand and Changes in Total Revenue Consumer expenditures are the sources of business revenues. Whatever money tourists spend on tourism-related goods and services are receipts of the producers of tourism products. That is:

Total Expenditure by Tourists
= (Price per unit of tourism related goods and Services)
        ×(Quantity of tourism related services)
= $P \times Q$
= Total Revenue Generated by the Producers of Tourism Services

Table 2. *Estimates of price elasticities and revenues along a tourism demand curve*

Reference point on the tourism demand curve	Price elasticity of tourism demand	Numerical measure of price elasticity of tourism demand	Measure of revenue changes as price of tourism service declines
A	$\epsilon_p = -0.273$	$\|\epsilon_p\| = 0.273 < 1$ [inelastic]	$-\$1,600$
B	$\epsilon_p = -1.0$	$\|\epsilon_p\| = 1$ [unitary elasticity]	$\$0.0$
C	$\epsilon_p = -8.3$	$\|\epsilon_p\| = 8.3 > 1$ [elastic]	$+\$1,100$

Thus, it has become obvious that changes in total revenue will be responsive to the changes in prices of tourism services. Using the demand schedule depicted in Table 1, it is observed that when price per unit of a packaged trip is $400, number of trips (units) consumed (taken) is 10, generating a total revenue of $4,000 (=$400 × 10) to the producer of the packaged trip. Now, if the producer of the packaged trip cuts the price to $200, number of trips that would be taken will increase from 10 to 12, resulting in a total revenue of $2,400. The changes in total revenue will be −$1,600. (This corresponds to point A in Figure 1 and Table 2.) Alternatively, if price of the packaged trip were allowed to decline from $1,300 to $1,200, number of trips taken would increase from 1 to 2 with a change (increase) in revenue of +$1,100 (= $1,200 × 1 − $1,300 × 1). (This value corresponds to point C on Figure 1 and Table 2.) Interested readers may verify and find that the changes in revenue at point B remains unchanged due to changes in prices of tourism-related services.

From this simple example, we find that as prices of tourism-related services are reduced (say through a policy change) along the *inelastic* portion of the tourism demand curve, total revenue *increases* for the producer of the tourism services (i.e., from $1,300, to $2,400). Alternatively, if prices are reduced along the *elastic* portion of the tourism demand curve, total revenue for the producer of the tourism services (e.g., local government, businesses) *declines*. Thus, we find that tourism demand elasticities provide important measures to planners and policy makers in deciding their pricing strategy for tourism-related products.

Income Elasticity of Tourism Demand

Income elasticity of tourism demand measures the responsiveness of changes in quantity demanded for tourism services to changes in income. It is often stated as follows:

$$\epsilon_I = \frac{\% \text{ change in quantity demanded for tourism services}}{\% \text{ change in income}}$$

$$= \frac{\Delta Q / \overline{Q}}{\Delta I / \overline{I}}$$

where ϵ_I = income elasticity of tourism demand and I = a measure of income.

Whether there is a positive or negative relationship between income and quantity demanded for a commodity depends largely on the type of good or service under consideration. Such a commodity can be normal or inferior. If income elasticity (ϵ_I) is greater than 0 (i.e., positive) the commodity under consideration would be a normal good (commodity). On the other hand, if the value of the income elasticity (ϵ_I) is less than 0, (i.e., negative) then the commodity would be considered to be an inferior one.

Suppose a family who normally would purchase ground meat, but when its income increases, purchases less ground meat and more steak. Thus, ground meat would be considered an inferior good. Tourism, however, is considered to be a normal good, and therefore exemplifies a positive relationship between quantity of tourism services consumed (taken) and income. So with the increases in income, households' responsiveness to *income* would be expected to be positive. This means that if and when the income of households (personal income) or per capita income of a nation *increases*, the individuals/nations enjoying higher income will *demand* more tourism-related services. For example, Japanese are currently traveling more overseas, even vacationing or spending weekends in various resort cities of the western United States.

Cross-Elasticity of Tourism Demand

The responsiveness of tourism demand to changes in the prices of other commodities is known as cross-elasticity (or cross-price elasticity) of tourism demand. It is often stated as:

$$\epsilon_{XY} = \frac{\% \text{ change in quantity demanded of tourism services, } X}{\% \text{ change in the price of another commodity, } Y}$$

$$= \frac{\Delta Q_X / \overline{Q}_X}{\Delta P_Y / \overline{P}_Y}$$

where ϵ_{XY} = cross-price elasticity of tourism demand, Q_X = quantity demand for tourism services (X), and P_Y = price of another good (Y): a complement or a substitute.

In general, commodities can be either complements or substitutes. Complementary commodities are goods that are used/consumed jointly, and have negative cross-elasticities, that is, $\epsilon_{XY} < 0$. Suppose the price of airline passage to Bermuda (P_Y), a complementary good, increased dramatically. The demand for lodging in Bermuda [Q_X] would decline as people would vacation elsewhere to avoid the high cost of air transportation. Substitute commodities are similar goods that can easily replace one another and have positive cross-elasticities. Here, a large increase in the price of air transportation to Bermuda would lead to an increase in travel by cruise lines.

Private and Public Sector Influences on Tourism Elasticities

Demand for tourism services can be significantly influenced through provision of tourism products produced within the community. For example, because of its long beaches, Galveston, Texas, has been principally a tourist town but it served only a limited market of the Houston metropolitan area. However, the local government and private businesses worked together to renovate the Strand District, a historical street in Galveston, introducing a tourism package more appealing to tourists. Such provision of additional tourist attractions caused a recent increase (an outward shift) in demand for tourism in Galveston. A simple graphical exposition can be used to explain this scenario.

Suppose the initial tourism demand function facing Galveston before and after renovation of the historic Strand District is represented by the equations:

$$Q_d = 2.5 - 0.5P$$

and

$$Q_{dd} = 3.5 - 0.5P,$$

respectively. The second equation differs from the first by only the intercept term, meaning that there has been an increase in demand for tourism in Galveston at each existing price per unit of tourism services. For example, when $P = 3$, $Q_d = 1$ (before renovation) while $Q_{dd} = 2$ (after renovation) of the Strand District. Subsequently,

$$\epsilon_P = \frac{(\Delta Q)}{\Delta P}\frac{(P)}{Q}$$

$$= (-0.5)(3/1)$$

$$= -1.5 \quad \text{for point B, and}$$

$$\epsilon_P = \frac{(\Delta Q)}{\Delta P}\frac{(P)}{Q}$$

$$= (-0.5)(3/2)$$

$$= -0.75 \quad \text{for point A, Figure 2.}$$

We note two valuable and interesting observations here: (1) Tourism price remaining constant at \$3/unit, total revenue increased from \$3 (area OLBC)

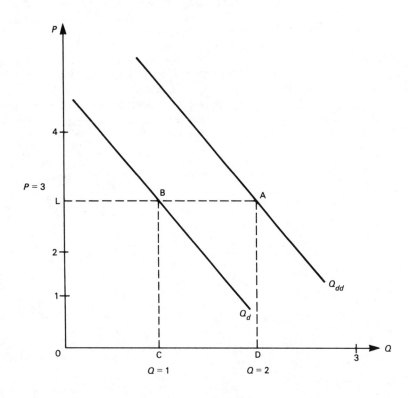

Fig. 2. Shift in tourism demand caused by private and public sector efforts.

to \$6 (area OLAD) following private and public efforts in renovating the Galveston tourist district, and (2) the elasticity value at point A (on the new tourism demand curve) is more inelastic than at point B (on the old demand curve) for the same price ($P = 3$), meaning that a small increase in the price of the provision of tourism services would, in fact, increase tourism revenues both to the public sector (in increased taxes) and to the private sector (in increased sales) now.

Summary

The objective of this article was to provide a conceptual understanding of elasticity of tourism demand along with various measures of tourism demand elasticities. Indeed, the responsiveness of various exogenous factors on the demand for tourism-related goods and services are important considerations to tourism-related decision makers, government and businesses alike.

Understanding the concepts and measures of elasticities of tourism demand helps allow management in the conscious creation of tourism-related opportunities in the country, region, or site under consideration. Various magnitudes of tourism elasticity measures provide various degree of tourism demand responsiveness, and thus affect the level of revenue that would be generated for the country or business (from the changed demand for tourism related goods and services). For example, if tourism demand (trips) for the Bahamas is price elastic, a reduction in the price of a trip (say air fare by an airline) would definitely increase revenue for the airline. Alternatively, exemption of taxes for tourist goods (e.g., duty-free shop) by the government of the Bahamas, a complementary good, would also increase tourist demand for the Bahamas. Thus, the concepts of tourism elasticity measures provide a guide in shaping the tourism planning and policy-making process.

References

Martin, C. A. and S. F. Witt. 1987. Tourism demand forecasting models: Choice of appropriate variable to represent tourists' cost of living, *Tourism Management* 8(3):233–246.

Var, T., G. Mohammad, and O. Icoz. 1990a. Factors affecting international tourism demand for Turkey, *Annals of Tourism Research* 17(4):606–610.

Var, T., G. Mohammad, and O. Icoz. 1990b. A tourism demand model, *Annals of Tourism Research* 17(4):622–626.

Wilman, E. A. 1984. Recreation benefits from public lands. In *Valuation of Wildland Resource Benefits*, ed. George L. Peterson and Alan Randall. Boulder, Colo.: Westview Press.

12

Tourism Forecasting: State-of-the-Art Techniques

Turgut Var and Choong-Ki Lee

Tourism today carries not only social and political significance but also provides considerable economic benefits. The international tourism trade has become the most important industry for some countries and is considered a highly desirable and feasible means of promoting economic development.

With the recognition that tourism plays a vital economic role, forecasting tourism demand has become increasingly important. To plan and operate tourism facilities successfully, investors, management, developers, governments, and other concerned groups need to know the volume of tourists to expect at a given future time. Forecasts, however, do not remain static; established trends can be altered by changes in the economy, technology, political circumstances, and tourism behavior. Thus, forecasts must be constantly revised to reflect these situations. Particularly when significant factors are in flux, forecasting can play an important role in maximizing tourism demand and utilizing resources, as well as in minimizing the risk of an oversupply of facilities.

Situations in which tourism demand forecasts are required vary, and the reliability depends on data availability, the forecasting environment, time horizons, and other factors. To predict tourism demand, a variety of forecasting techniques have been developed, which can be broadly classified into three approaches: quantitative, qualitative, and combined. The quantitative approaches that require historical data are further divided into two approaches, time series and causal methods. The causal methods include regression models, econometric models, and gravity and trip-generation models. The qualitative approaches, which involve experts or group opinions, also fall into two types: Delphi models and scenario-writing models. The combined approaches are of two types as well, those using weighting scheme techniques and those combining quantitative and qualitative techniques.

Quantitative Approaches

Quantitative approaches—those involving the measurement and analysis of the number of tourists—use historical data and are based on mathematical models of the patterns of demand or the relationships between variables that affect the volume of tourists and the actual volume. These methods can be used for forecasting when information about the past is available, when the information can be quantified (counted, or measured in some way), and when past patterns can be assumed to continue into the future (Makridakis and Wheelwright 1978). Two types of quantitative approaches are available, time series models and causal models.

Time Series Models
Time series models analyze historical data for the variable to be forecast to determine an underlying pattern. Once identified, this pattern is extrapolated into the future to yield forecasts. Time series methods are usually univariate, that is, they examine only a single variable and are concerned solely with the statistical analysis of past data related to that variable (Archer 1987).

Bar-On (1973, 1975a, 1975b, 1975c, 1984, 1989) used monthly series methods to analyze the nature, impact, and importance of seasonal factors on tourism. In several studies Bar-On (1972) described the use of the time series analysis program X-11, developed by Shiskin at the U.S. Bureau of the Census, to quantify the trend, seasonal, and cyclical components of several time series associated with the tourism industry in Israel, forecasting seasonal factors for the next 12 months. In particular he analyzed the following monthly series: (a) tourists arriving and departing by air; (b) total tourist arrivals; (c) foreign currency income from tourism; (d) residents departing; and (e) bed-nights in tourist hotels, total and broken down into visitors from abroad or Israelis. In his later studies (1973), these series were compared to those for 15 other countries. Furthermore, Bar-On also showed how the Israeli Ministry of Tourism uses the results of the analysis to determine the maximum annual utilization factor constrained by seasonality for specific years, which represents the percentage of peak-season facilities utilized over the entire year if the seasonality of demand is unchanged.

Probably the most sophisticated, complex time series method, known as the Box-Jenkins model, uses either univariate models or transfer-function models. Box-Jenkins model-building is a complex process involving highly complicated mathematical and statistical algorithms and utilizes subjective judgment on the part of the modeler. Experience can improve considerably the final models. Even though the transfer-model-building process is several times more difficult than the univariate process, the transfer model allows the forecaster to take into account discrete changes external to the system, for instance, a reduction in air fares that may affect the tourist arrivals series. One example of the Box-Jenkins technique is illustrated by Wandner and Van Erden (1980). In projecting tourism demand in Puerto Rico for 1977/1978, they developed two models of arrivals, the first, a simple univariate analysis, and the second, a transfer-function model. To compare the usefulness of the methodology, forecasts were made for 12 months. It was found that the transfer-function model outperformed the univariate model for the first six months, with average errors of 1.8 percent and 3 percent, respectively, but the univariate model was slightly better than the former over the full 12 months, with 5 percent versus 5.4 percent error.

Liepa and Chau (1977) used the Box-Jenkins model to investigate the possibility of forecasting quarterly tourist demand and international travel accounts for Canada. The results indicate that the eight models used in the Box-Jenkins method perform well, and the method is applicable to different series of tourist data. However, they caution that frequent updates should be made, since the predictions made using the Box-Jenkins method do not take into account such special circumstances as the Montreal Olympic Games.

Geurts and Ibrahim (1975) questioned whether the improved accuracy of the Box-Jenkins approach was worth the extra costs involved. They compared the performance of the Box-Jenkins approach in forecasting Hawaii's tourist demand with Brown's one-parameter exponential smoothing method. The exponential smoothing method assumes that the current forecast for one period ahead is a function of the forecast for the previous period and the actual current observation. The results showed that Brown's one-parameter exponential smoothing model and the Box-Jenkins method seem to perform equally well, leading them to suggest that Brown's one-parameter exponential smoothing model should be preferred, since it is cheaper to use and may be easier to apply. In his later study, Geurts (1982) demonstrated that the accuracy of the Hawaiian tourist market forecasting was greatly improved after the data were modified for atypical months and the forecasts were updated annually.

The traditional time series methodology has usually dealt with univariate analysis and this approach has been used for relatively short-term forecasting (see Table 1). While time series methods are highly preferred, the methods are sometimes criticized because they cannot take into account the impact of other independent variables on the dependent variable being examined.

Causal Models

Causal methods basically assume that the factor being forecast has a cause-and-effect relationship with one or more variables. For example, tourism demand (the factor being forecast), is a function of tourist income, population, cost of travel, exchange rate, and other variables. Therefore, a forecasting relationship can be hypothesized as a function of independent variables for which estimates over the span forecast are available. The objective of the causal models is to discover the form of the relationship between a dependent variable and independent variables and to predict future tourism demand.

Regression Models. A regression method is expressed as a function of a specified number of factors or variables that determine the outcome. Developing an explanatory or causal model facilitates a better understanding of the situation and allows experimentation with different combinations of inputs to investi-

Table 1. *Comparison of forecasting techniques by frequency of use and time horizon*

Technique	Frequency	Time horizon[a]
Quantitative		
Time series	High	Short term
Box-Jenkins	Medium	Short–medium term
Causal Methods	High	Short–medium term
Qualitative		
Delphi	Medium	Long term
Scenario writing	Medium	Long term
Combined		
Weighting scheme	Low	Medium
Quantitative and qualitative	Low	Long term

[a]Short term is less than three months; medium term is three months to two years; long term is greater than two years.

gate their effects on the forecasts. The multiple regression model, one of the most popular causal approaches, suggests that tourism demand for a particular tourism destination is a function of multiple variables, such as level of income of potential tourist, cost of travel, relative price, and exchange rate. Multiple regression models also permit the introduction of dummy variables to account for substantial trend shifts resulting from special circumstances, for example an oil crisis or hosting the Olympic Games. The most frequently used method is the multiple regression analysis using ordinary least squares (OLS). OLS is a statistical method that estimates an equation fitting the data best by minimizing the sum of squared errors between each observation and the fitted line (Bohrnstedt and Knoke 1982).

For example, Gray (1966) applied a regression model to forecast the demand for international travel and found that Canadian tourism was quite elastic with regard to both income and rate of exchange. Realizing that prices of goods and services at the destination were neglected in most tourism demand forecasting, Kwack (1972) attempted to insert that variable into a regression model. The results show that the real amount of money spent abroad depends positively on real income and negatively on the prices of the goods and services consumed abroad. Jud and Joseph (1974) used multiple regression to estimate the income, price, and travel cost elasticities of tourism demand in Latin American countries; the results indicated that reductions in travel costs do not generate a proportionate increase in tourism receipts of Latin American countries. Sunday (1978) estimated the parameter of prices on U.S. demand for foreign travel and tourism. Unlike the findings from Jud and Joseph, higher air fares appeared to generate fewer tourists but greater expenditure per tourist visit.

Kliman (1981) developed a pooled time-series cross-sectional regression model, which combines all time-series and cross-sectional data, to predict the number of visits per year by Canadian residents to 25 countries. Many explanatory variables were tested: an index of relative inflation in Canada and each of the destination countries, corrected for exchange rate changes; the economy air fare and the lowest discount air fare between Montreal and the gateway destination city; Canadian disposable income; the combined populations of Canada and each destination country; and a measure of ethnic attraction. The results show that a pooled model, applied to a data base, works quite well.

Quayson and Var (1982) developed the double-log regression model to examine the relative importance of existing determinants of tourism demand in the Okanagan in British Columbia. This study differed from earlier investigations in that it focused on the tourism industry in a particular region. Contrary to the assumed high-income elasticity of demand for tourism, the elasticities for some regions did not necessarily exceed unity, which means inelasticity, and the exchange rate and travel cost did not appear to be significant determinants of Okanagan tourism receipts.

Uysal and Crompton (1984) demonstrated by using multiple regression analysis that the variables of income, price, and exchange rate were important factors for tourism to Turkey from 1960 to 1980, but the impact of promotional expenditure was minimal. Steinnes (1988) analyzed the impact of oil price shocks on tourism demand and found that the coefficients for gasoline price and employment were elastic (-0.35, -2.44, respectively). Therefore, if gasoline prices are subject to considerable changes, the regression model will have an advantage because it can be used to estimate tourism for alternative future gasoline prices.

One of the disadvantages of using OLS in multiple regression is severe multicollinearity, which is a condition of high or near intercorrelation among the explanatory variables in a regression model. When multicollinearity exists, the standard errors associated with the regression coefficients are large so that estimates of true parameters become unstable and low t-values are produced. Furthermore, it is difficult for the analysts to separate the contribution of explanatory variables to a dependent variable. Multicollinearity can be diagnosed by inspecting the pairwise correlation matrix. A high correlation coefficient between two explanatory variables (close to 1) indicates a possible presence of collinearity. Belsley, Kuh, and Welsch (1980) proposed another diagnostic procedure with double conditions: (1) condition index greater than or equal to 30 or 100; and (2) at least two numbers in a variance proportion row greater than or equal to 0.5. In the presence of severe multicollinearity, ridge regression is used to circumvent the problem. The ridge regression method is designed to decrease overall mean square error by introducing a slight bias of k (diagonal matrix of non-negative constants) in the estimates at the expense of achieving efficiency (Hoerl and Kennard 1970). The appropriate value of k can be determined by using ridge-trace procedures in which the value of k gradually increases between 0 and 1 until the estimated coefficients become stable.

Because of multicollinearity, Gapinski and Tuckman (1976) used ridge regression to estimate their functions, which were designed to predict tourist demand to Florida. The variables of price, income, and a set of seasonal dummies were selected for the model. The results show that rapid price increases have little effect on the number of tourist trips taken, and gasoline availability appears far more consequential following the oil crisis of 1973–1974 than gasoline price. Since the ridge traces illustrate the stability patterns of the estimators and provide a graphic clue to the presence, source, and severity of collinearity, the results derived from ridge regression are satisfying. Furthermore, they suggest that ridge is simple to use and easily lends itself to those perplexing situations, often found, in which additional data cannot be collected or where extraneous estimates do not exist. As the average error of the ridge estimator is smaller than that of the OLS estimator, Fujii and Mak (1980) also used ridge regression estimates and demonstrated that ridge regression models yielded forecasts with significantly lower forecast error than OLS models when severe multicollinearity exists and the pattern of collinearity among regressors changes over time.

Econometric Models. Both multiple regression and econometric models are considered causal approaches, which attempt to measure the cause-and-effect relationship between dependent and independent variables. Strictly speaking, multiple regression models involve a single equation, whereas econometric models may include several simultaneous multiple regression equations (Makridakis and Wheelwright 1978).

Artus (1972) used an econometric model in an attempt to make a systematic analysis of the short-term determinants of international travel flows by specifying and estimating a complete world travel model. A travel structure was interpreted from the aggregate travel expenditures made by country i and the aggregate receipts from foreign visitors obtained by country j. Country i's aggregate travel expenditures were estimated separately, and relative prices were introduced as an explanatory variable in both the expenditure and receipt functions. Artus found the following results: (1) The best estimates of price elasticities may be those obtained from the estimation of the coefficients of the relative exchange rate variables; (2) travel flows between the United States and Canada are price elastic: -2.8 for U.S. spending in Canada and -2.47 for Canada's spending in the United States; (3) the estimated average price elasticity of market share for European countries is -2.89; and (4) in spite of the high multicollinearity between the income variables and simple trend factors, most international travel flows seem to be highly elastic with regard to income. Artus, however, recognized that the poor-quality data on foreign travel expenditures, receipts from foreign visitors, and prices of foreign travel services seriously limited the conclusions derived from the econometric analysis.

Loeb (1982), using the econometric model, evaluated the effects of income, exchange rates, and relative prices on U.S. exports of travel services to seven countries. The results show that the variables of income, exchange rates, and relative prices have a significant effect on the tourism demand to the United States, and the coefficients associated with the relative price variable appeared to be generally negative and significant.

Emphasizing the importance of seasonality and warning of the possible multicollinearity between exchange rates and relative prices, Chadee and Mieczkowski (1987) developed an econometric model to estimate the effects of the depreciation of the Canadian dollar on the Canadian tourist industry. Contrary to the conventional wisdom that the depreciation of the Canadian dollar via-à-vis the U.S. dollar results in substantial benefits to the Canadian tourism industry, the impact of the exchange rate on Canadian receipts from U.S. visitors in this study was found to be small. The two possible reasons are (1) as the Canadian dollar depreciated relative to the U.S. dollar, at the same time the currencies of major western European countries and Mexico depreciated even faster relative to the U.S. dollar, and (2) the relative prices in Canada are generally higher than in the United States because of the prices of gasoline, alcohol, and tobacco. These factors appeared to have directly or indirectly offset the advantages of a weaker Canadian dollar.

Witt and Martin (1987) developed a set of econometric models for forecasting international tourism demand, using the number of tourist visits from West Germany and the United Kingdom to their respective major destinations. The empirical results show that the estimated income elasticity is usually considerably higher for the United Kingdom than Germany, with the exception of the destination of Spain. Since no single model applies across all origin-destination pairs, the variables included in a particular model are chosen from a set of explanatory variables on the basis of empirical results. They suggest that experimentation is necessary to obtain an appropriate model, since economic theory does not give a clear indication of which factors are likely to be operative for particular origin-destination holiday-visit data sets.

Price as an explanatory variable is considered an important determinant in an econometric model. Consumer price index (CPI) has been frequently used for international tourism demand as a proxy for the cost of tourism in certain destination countries owing to difficulty in obtaining the appropriate data. Martin and Witt (1987), however, cast doubt on the reliability of the proxy variable (consumer price index) and thus attempted to find whether the consumer price index is acceptable in representing the cost of living for tourists. The three types of tourist-price variables were incorporated in the econometric model. The empirical results did not show clearly which was the best among those variables. A specific-cost-of-tourism variable was ranked first more frequently than either the consumer price index or the exchange rate, supporting the idea that the cost-of-tourism variable was a better indicator of the tourist-price variables than the others.

In a later study, Martin and Witt (1988) specified models of international tourism demand that allow for the impact of substitute prices, both substitute tourists' living costs and substitute transportation costs. The empirical results supported the hypothesis that substitute prices play an important role in determining the demand for international tourism. It was also found that the importance varied considerably according to the origin under consideration and the transport mode. Therefore, there is no single substitute price variable or set of applicable variables for all origin-destination pairs.

Because of multicollinearity between explanatory variables and possible incompleteness of the available statistical data, Smeral (1988) developed an econometric model by using simple estimation procedures. The decision process as described by Smeral is two-stage and separable. In the first stage, the volume of tourism goods and services, both domestic and foreign, is determined with reference to price and income. In the second stage, the country of destination is determined by taking prices of tourism goods and services into account in all possible countries of destination, given a certain available foreign-travel budget. Smeral indicated that future problems could arise out of the assumption that information on relevant values such as prices, exchange rates, and income should be perfect, and such misjudgment of these variables can result in an inaccurate estimation of real travel budgets, thus causing bias in the parameters of the models.

Although the econometric models explain well a dependent variable by employing a set of multiple regressions, they have some serious limitations. First, multicollinearity may exist among independent variables. Second, accurate and relevant data are difficult to collect, and misjudgment of the variables for the future will result in inaccurate tourism demand forecasts. Third, since no set of rules applies to all situations, once the models are developed, they cannot be applied easily to other situations. Therefore, they require much more cost and time. Many researchers have found that forecasts by econometric models are not necessarily more accurate than those by time series models.

Gravity and Trip-Generation Models. In searching for better ways to forecast tourist flows, gravity models have been developed from physical systems. The gravity models are somewhat similar in form except that they take more account of the effects of distance or journey time as a constraint imposed upon travel (Vanhove 1980). The gravity models are based on the laws of Newton in that they postulate that a specific and measurable relationship exists between the number of visitors to a destination from origin countries, specific markets, and a series of independent variables, namely *population* and *distance.* Ellis and Van Doren (1966) introduced a gravity model in an attempt to compare gravity and system theory models for statewide recreational traffic flows. The two models differ in that the gravity model is formulated with inherent parameters, whereas the system theory model involves a procedure for building a system analog. They expressed the basic gravity model as follows:

$$I_{ij} = G(P_i A_j)/TD_{ij} b$$

where I_{ij} = the interaction between originating subarea i and terminating subarea j; G = the gravitational constant; P_i = the population of origin i; A_j = the attraction index of destination j; TD_{ij} = the minimum time-distance on route ij; and b = exponent.

A similar gravity model was introduced by Armstrong (1972). The building of the model began with a simple relationship between the number of tourist arrivals generated to a destination from an origin and the latter's population; then a number of other independent variables were progressively introduced, such as per capita income and language similarity, in order to obtain the most satisfactory results. He also inserted in the model a time value to explain progressive changes over the period up to 1980 in such factors as population distribution, education level, and leisure time available. Malamud (1973) developed a gravity model to study tourist travel to Las Vegas. The results show that distance significantly discourages Las Vegas tourism in all cases examined; however, per capita income is more important than distance in explaining Las Vegas hotel tourism in May 1970. Both a population potential measure of alternative travel opportunities and a dummy variable indicating proximity to a competitive resort center were found to have significant effects on Las Vegas tourism.

Trip-generation and trip-distribution models are similar in form to gravity models, which are derived from analogies with various laws of physics and statistical mechanics. Trip-generation models usually estimate the allocation of such trips from a given area among competing destinations (Sheldon and Var 1985). Mansfield (1969) developed the trip-generation model to analyze weekend pleasure trips to the Lake District National Park. The principal objective of the study was to investigate how the demand for a pleasure journey is affected by changes such as a reduction in journey times because of the opening of a new road. The coefficients of the road variable were only significant at the 15 percent level or worse. However, he suggested it is possible to make some estimate of the effect of the road on the number of trips.

Cesario (1973) developed the trip-distribution model from a heuristic theory on the way people in the aggregate distribute their trips in a trip-making environment. He assumed that the number of trips made from any origin to any destination depends on certain origin characteristics, certain destination characteristics, and spatial separation costs. Initially it is useful to think of origin and destination effects as being independent in the statistical sense. Cesario referred to destination effects as "attractiveness" and to origin effects as "emissiveness." Whereas attractiveness refers to the trip-drawing power of a destination relative to others, emissiveness, in opposite, refers to the trip-generating power of an origin relative to others under *ceteris paribus* condition. As he assumed, the number of trips is proportional to the emissiveness of the origin, the attractiveness of the destination, and some function of spatial separation between origin and destination. Cesario applied this model to an outdoor recreation system located in northeastern Pennsylvania. Since the principal purpose of the model was to establish the principal sources of variation in trip-distribution data and, consequently, to establish some basic principles of mass behavior, little can be said about its predictive ability. Realizing the previous model yielded biased estimates of the parameters, Cesario, in his 1974 follow-up study, developed an alternative parameter estimation designed to alleviate the bias. The new method was superior to the old from the standpoint of the least-square criterion minimizing the sum of squared deviations from the mean.

Peterson et al. (1982) developed a trip-attraction model useful for single-site analysis and estimated six types of use, respectively (paddle canoeing, motor canoeing, motor boating, hiking, ski touring, snowmobiling) for campers. Since the parameters estimated from single-site analysis may not be applicable to other sites, they suggested building a multiple-site model for generalizability.

Although gravity models are useful in predicting travel flows, they have some limitations, as pointed out by Vanhove (1980): the absence of a sound theoretical understanding; a difficulty in defining origin zones; a danger of multicollinearity; and overestimation or underestimation resulting from the lack of available accurate data.

Qualitative Approaches

Qualitative techniques of forecasting do not require measurable data in the same manner as quantitative forecasting techniques do. Qualitative forecasting approaches depend on the accumulated experience of individual experts or groups of people assembled together to predict the likely occurrence and effects of future events. These approaches are most appropriate when data are insufficient or inadequate for processing or when changes of a previously unexperienced dimension make numerical analysis inappropriate. The qualitative forecasting techniques are particularly suitable for long-term forecasting when changes of a large and unprecedented nature may be expected (Archer 1987). Two types of qualitative approaches, the Delphi method and the scenario-writing method are, described.

Delphi Model   The Delphi method developed for long-term demand forecasting is a systematic approach combining the knowledge and experience of experts in many fields to obtain a group consensus of opinion about the likely outcome of specific events. The first step that should be taken in this approach is the assembly of a panel or panels of experts in many disciplines to give due weight to a long-term tourism demand. On the basis of the final round summaries, forecasts are prepared to show the most likely course of future events (Archer 1976). There are two underlying assumptions: first, with feedback and repeated estimates, the range of responses will decrease, with convergence toward the midrange of the distribution, and second, the total group's response or median will successively move toward the correct or true or the most likely answer (Kaynak and Macaulay 1984). The Delphi method overcomes the disadvantage associated with more conventional uses of experts, such as round-table discussion, by avoiding direct confrontation among panel members and thus eliminating pressure to conform to group opinion (Dalkey and Helmer 1963).

Gearing et al. (1976) developed the GSV technique, which has useful applications to tourism demand forecasting. The GSV technique consists of four steps: (1) determining the criteria for judging touristic attractiveness; (2) assigning numerical weights in accordance with the relative importance of these criteria; (3) employing the judgment of experts to evaluate each attraction using each criterion; and (4) determining the composite score of various areas. This approach is similar to the Delphi technique in that both methods rely on expert opinion, but the GSV does not need panel consensus.

A modified Delphi approach, referred to as Symposium-Delphi, was used by Robinson (1979). This approach includes three major departures from the traditional use of the Delphi method: use of Consensor (a microcomputer with video monitor) to tally votes instantaneously and display them by histogram; administration of the questionnaires in a face-to-face situation; and reduction of implementation time by the simultaneous administration of the questionnaire.

Another example of the Delphi technique was introduced by Kaynak and Macaulay (1984). This study was conducted in the context of Nova Scotia in Canada to gather data on tourism research, on future impacts of tourism, and to strengthen a regional data base. A panel of experts was selected for their knowledge of the subject to be studied. The experts did not interact with each other during the multiround process, to secure the widest possible range of ideas and opinions. The initial section of the questionnaire was designed to determine current tourist operator perceptions of how societal value changes in Nova Scotia may affect the development of tourism. The most significant events were those having a high probability of occurrence within the next decade and having a high impact on tourism—computer or technological change (check-ins) and training and development for employees. Although the possibility of little change in the structure of the tourism industry is foreseen, Kaynak and Macaulay noted that once it occurred, it would likely have a serious impact on tourism and hospitality development. They confirmed the assumption that the Delphi technique was suitable to use in dealing with uncertainty in an area of imperfect knowledge.

A slightly different Delphi approach from the previous studies was attempted by Var et al. (1986) and by Liu (1988) in Hawaii, involving two separate groups, tourist receivers and tourist senders. The panel of tourist receivers was selected from a list of local tourism experts, and the panel of tourist senders was chosen from experts primarily outside of Hawaii. The results show that the projections of Hawaiian tourism demand by the year 2000 made by both local and outside experts were generally consistent with state projections. Therefore, Liu suggested that the Delphi technique is useful for long-term tourism demand forecasting and assists decision makers by providing insights into the future of tourism.

Like other methods, the Delphi model also has some limitations (Vanhove 1980): the results can be affected by the manner in which the directors of the study interpret replies; particular events may be treated in isolation rather than as interdependent parts of a whole; and the nonresponse bias may be very high.

Scenario Writing   As the scenario-writing method is not yet well known in tourism demand forecasting, only a few applications have been attempted. Scenario writing provides an account of what could possibly occur rather than what will occur, given the known facts and trends. Van Doorn (1986:36) has provided a general definition, embracing the various aspects of the scenario technique: "A scenario gives a description of the present situation of one or more possible and/or desired situation(s) and of one or more sequence(s) of events, which can connect the present and future situation(s)." He also presented three minimum components from which a scenario is constructed: baseline analysis—a dynamic description and analysis of an existing situation as the starting point; future images—one or more eventual images of a desired and/or considered possible situation at a future moment; and future paths—one or more development processes containing a description of the development of an existing situation into an eventual image in the future. He recommended pursuing a modest approach, focusing on the development of miniscenarios with a limited scope and time span (for example, scenarios on the development of a ski area in a specific geographical region or the future of an already existing beach resort).

An earlier example of scenario writing was constructed by Bar-On (1979), who forecast international tourism to Thailand from 1975 to 1980.

Four of the most relevant fields related to tourism to Thailand were selected: political, economic, tourism development and promotion, and transport. Projections were made based on three assumptions—optimistic, intermediate, and pessimistic. Scenarios on the time needed for tourism by air to Israel (total and from France, Germany, the United Kingdom and the United States) to recover from the events in 1981–1982 were used to forecast these series from January 1983 to March 1984 (in Bar-On 1984a), with comparisons with actual monthly data. Bar-On (1989) presents the X-77 analysis of seasonality and trends for U.S. tourism by air to Israel for 1975 to 1986 with the ARIMA projection for January–December 1987 and forecasts for these 12 months using two basic levels and three forecasts of growth rate. The total for 1987 was 1 percent below the "optimistic" forecast but 30 percent above the automatic ARIMA forecast. Schwaninger (1984) developed the scenario technique to portray the probable trends in leisure time and tourism between the years 2000 and 2010 in the context of industrialized countries of Europe. The interaction of critical variables contributing to the scenario of future trends in leisure and tourism were presented: economic, political, technological, sociocultural, and ecological aspects. He recommended integral planning, calling for the incorporation of all aspects and components of knowledge in the process of analysis and design, long-term thinking based on large-scale and long-term relationships, and consistent action, putting the plans based on integral planning and long-term thinking into practice.

Van Doorn (1986) indicated special problems in using the scenario model: the quantitative analysis of the past and present of tourism systems is mostly inadequate; the theoretical basis for tourism is weak, making tourism modeling hazardous; and the exogenous development of alternative scenarios prior to major policy decisions is limited outside the tourism field and almost nonexistent within tourism.

Combined Approaches

Different forecasting methods, having their own limitations, may produce different forecasts for the same time periods. Combined approaches may therefore provide some useful information that is not conveyed by any single forecasting method. Although few studies have been tried in a tourism context, the empirical results prove that the use of combined forecasts produces more accurate forecasts. Two types of combined approaches are considered here. The first combines several quantitative models using a weighting scheme. The second combines quantitative and qualitative techniques. The first type, the combined model with a weighting scheme, has a basic form introduced by Bates and Granger (1969):

$$C_t = k_t f_{1,t} = (1 - k_t) f_{2,t}$$

where C_t = the combined forecast for time period t; k_t = weighted value for time period t; $f_{1,t}$ = the forecast at time t from the first set of forecasts; and $f_{2,t}$ = the forecast at time t from the second set of forecasts.

More weight is assigned to models that produce smaller error, and less weight to those with larger error, combining them into one forecast. On the basis of the formula, Bates and Granger combined two separate sets of forecasts of airline passenger data to form a composite set of forecasts, and they concluded that the combined forecasts could yield improvements, providing the sets of forecasts each contain some independent information.

Fritz et al. (1984) combined the Box-Jenkins stochastic time-series model with an econometric model to predict airline visitors to the state of Florida. Their results clearly show that the combined approaches improve the forecast accuracy and that a weighting scheme adjusted by variance outperforms an unadjusted weighting scheme. Calantone et al. (1987) demonstrated that combining time series with econometric methods allowed not only the use of multiple data series but also provided more accurate and more (managerially) useful forecasts than any one single method. It was noted that poor forecasts should not necessarily be discarded, since they may contain information valuable to the overall forecasts.

Today, socioeconomic, political, and technological changes proceed faster than in the past. Therefore, a forecaster can no longer rely solely on historical quantitative data to consider the likely occurrence of future events. Consequently, the second type of combined approach is highly recommended as the most appropriate in long-term projection (Archer 1980, 1987; Uysal and Crompton 1985).

Emphasizing that tourism systems for forecasting and planning must be comprehensive to consider a broad range of issues, Taylor (1976) developed a model for the Canadian Government Office of Tourism by combining the quantitative and qualitative techniques. The first step taken was to identify the major determinant variables of tourism demand for Canada and each of the provinces. These variables were changing population and demographic conditions and changing income and economic conditions. In the second step, a Delphi technique was used to provide the qualitative materials. The panels of experts were asked about four areas: demand, resources, impact, and general. Separate questionnaires were developed and separate panels were selected for each subject. The objective was to place the forecasts in a policy framework and to develop practical forecasts.

Indicating that existing forecasting models tend to ignore supply variables and are frequently static, Edgell and Seely (1980) recommended a combined technique to forecast tourist flows to states and regions with some characteristics: consideration of both demand and supply variables; development for short-term forecasts (1 to 2 years) to maintain viability; and use of both objective and subjective coefficients in the formulas developed.

Edgell et al. (1980) applied the combined approach to predict international tourist arrivals and receipts to the United States. To reflect constant changes in key variables affecting international tourism and to obtain an adequate amount of data, Edgell et al. decided to use regression analysis in the first stage and a Delphi-type technique in the second stage. The results show that the time-series model forecasted 43 million visitors with $27 billion receipts (current dollars) in the year 2000, while Delphi-type projections for the year 2000 were 55.8 million visitors with $33 billion receipts. The projections of visitors and receipts by the Delphi-type technique were larger than those by the linear regression model. The reason is that the panel of experts predicted that the purchasing power of other major currencies relative to the U.S. dollar would be a major factor in drawing increased volumes of travelers to the United States in the next few decades, along with increasing capacity of supply.

Criterion for Forecasting Models—Accuracy

Tourism planners and practitioners have many choices of forecasting models to use, ranging from naive ("no change") methods to highly sophisticated techniques. In comparing and selecting a tourism demand forecasting model, several factors should be considered: the pattern of the data to be forecast; the time horizon to be covered in forecasting; the cost of applying alternative methodologies; the ease of application; and the accuracy of forecasting models (Makridakis and Wheelwright 1978). Since the accuracy of forecasts affects the quality of management decisions (Archer 1987) and provides considerable benefits for the tourism planners and practitioners, accuracy may be the most important and overriding criterion in practical forecasting situations. However, very little attention has been paid to the accuracy in tourism forecasting methods. Van Doorn (1982:164) observed, "Despite the growing file of reports on tourism forecasting, surprisingly little attention is paid to the comparison of actual data with the corresponding forecasts."

The most frequently used measures for testing accuracy are mean square error, root mean square error, mean absolute percentage error, and Theil's U-statistic. The mean square error (MSE) is obtained by squaring each of the errors and computing the mean of those squared values. The objective is to select a model that minimizes MSE. The primary limitation of MSE is that it does not facilitate comparisons across different time series and for different time intervals, since it is an absolute measure (Makridakis, Wheelwright, and Victor 1983). The root mean square error (RMSE) is the square root of the average squared error. The greater the average absolute error of a set of forecasts, the greater the RMSE. However, this measure has less intuitive appeal (Ascher 1978). The mean absolute percentage error (MAPE) is obtained by computing the absolute error for each period, summing up the errors, dividing them by the number of values used, and multiplying by 100 percent. Since it is expressed as a percentage, this measure is relative and facilitates comparisons. For this reason it is often preferred to the mean square error (Wheelwright and Makridakis 1985). MAPE values are generally interpreted as highly accurate forecasting for less than 10 percent; good forecasting for 10 to 20 percent; reasonable forecasting for 20 to 50 percent; and inaccurate forecasting for greater than 50 percent (Lewis 1982). The U-statistic developed by Theil (1966) allows a relative comparison of the accuracy of a forecasting model with the naive approach, which merely uses the most recent actual value observed as a forecast. A U of less than 1 means that the forecasting technique being used is better than the naive, "no change" method, and a U greater than 1 indicates that it is worse than the naive method. A U of 0 signifies that it is perfect.

An earlier example in tourism flow was examined by Geurts and Ibrahim (1975), who compared the performance of Box-Jenkins and Brown's double smoothing method on the basis of Theil's U-statistic. The results show that both of them performed equally well, with a U of .102 for Box-Jenkins and .103 for Brown's double smoothing method. Geurts and Ibrahim, in their 1982 study, showed that the accuracy of forecasting was greatly improved, with U of .048. Fujii and Mak (1980) evaluated forecasts resulting from the two methods on the basis of root mean square error (RMSE) and Theil's U-statistic (model 1: RMSE = .132, U = 1.804 for OLS vs. RMSE = .069, U = .935 for ridge regression).

In an attempt to test accuracy, Van Doorn (1984) selected seven quantitative methods and three accuracy measures of MSE, Mean Percentage Error (MPE), and MAPE. Based on the combination of these three standards with 24 periods, the results show that Harrison's harmonic smoothing, Box-Jenkins, and generalized adaptive filtering are the most accurate.

Martin and Witt (1989) also tested the accuracy of econometric forecasts of tourism. In this study two measures of accuracy, MAPE and root mean square percentage error (RMSPE), were employed to compare the econometric model with other quantitative models. In general, the naive 1, the "no change" model, and the autoregressive model generated relatively accurate predictions and the econometric model was not more accurate than the time series models. These results are compatible with those observed by Van Doorn (1984), that the use of simple forecasting techniques proves, in general, more accurate than the use of more complex techniques. Makridakis and Hibon (1984:35) also observed the same result: "Surprisingly, the study shows that for these time series, simpler methods perform well in comparison to the more complex and statistically sophisticated ARIMA models." Since this result is contrary to expectations, Makridakis and Hibon insist that further researchers should shed light on the "mystery" of why, under certain circumstances, simple methods do as well or better than sophisticated techniques (see Table 2).

Since conventional measures of forecasting accuracy are tested on the basis of the magnitude of forecasting error, such measures pay attention to all large disturbances (errors), disregarding their association with turning-point errors, which exist when the signs of actual and forecast changes are different in two successive time periods (Cicarelli 1982). Challenging such conventional measures of forecasting accuracy, Witt and Witt (1989) used turning-point errors to examine the relative accuracy of forecasts predicted by seven quantitative forecasting models and then compared the results with their previous ones. Contrary to their previous results, this study shows that the econometric model appears to be the most accurate according to turning point error criterion, followed by exponential smoothing. Which criterion is more useful in measuring forecasting accuracy was not clarified and hence remains a future researcher's challenge.

Summary

Forecasting tourism demand is an essential ingredient in the decision making of tourism planners and managers. This article has presented the major forecasting techniques used for tourism demand, grouped into three broad categories, and their advantages and limitations have been also discussed.

Table 2. *Comparison of forecasting techniques in terms of accuracy*

Compared techniques	Findings
Qualitative techniques vs. Quantitative techniques	Qualitative (judgmental) forecasts do not necessarily perform better in terms of acuracy than quantitative when no major changes occur in the environment.
Single model vs. Combined models	Combined models tend to be more accurate than single or individual model.
Time series models vs. Econometric models	Time series models are not necessarily less accurate than econometric models.
Simple models vs. Sophisticated models	Statistically sophisticated models do not perform better than simple models in terms of postsample forecasting accuracy.

Source: Based on data from Spyros Makridakis, 1986, The art and science of forecasting: An assessment and future directions, *International Journal of Forecasting* 2 (1):18.

Pragmatically, choosing the most appropriate forecasting model depends heavily on the forecasting situation, such as data pattern, time horizon, cost, ease of application, and forecasting environment. In particular, where the time horizon to be covered requires a long-term projection, combining quantitative with qualitative techniques is recommended (Taylor 1976; Archer 1980, 1987; Edgell and Seely 1980; Edgell et al. 1980; Sheldon and Var 1985; Uysal and Crompton 1985).

Accurate forecasts are not only central to the successful implementation of policy, but they also provide the planner and practitioner with considerable benefits with regard to both profits and the quality of the policy decision. Contrary to the expectation that sophisticated methods produce superior results, many empirical studies show that large, complex, or statistically sophisticated methods do not necessarily lead to more accurate forecasts than smaller or relatively simple methods do (Makridakis 1986). As Ascher (1978:199) also observed, "The presumed advantages of sophisticated methodologies simply have not materialized." For this reason, Calantone et al. (1987) stressed that complex model building should not be undertaken for its own sake.

Van Doorn (1984) challenged the emphasis on such sophisticated efforts and suggested that, for policy makers, the criteria for evaluating the usefulness of tourism forecasting should be simplicity, cost, and accuracy. Van Doorn and Van Vught (1983:510) cited Van de Vall as observing, "The more that projects in the field of social policy research . . . satisfy the scientific requirement of methodological rigor, the less they tend to be used in organizational policy formation." In other words, administrators are particularly interested in relatively simple techniques that are readily intelligible and manageable.

For tourism planners and practitioners, the major challenge ahead is to find relatively simple pragmatic techniques that are intelligible, manageable, and least expensive, and to assess the likely accuracy of these techniques. To do this, it is necessary that they should better understand the limitations as well as the advantages of those forecasting methods to be employed, based on their specific forecasting situation.

References

Archer, Brian H. 1976. *Demand Forecasting in Tourism.* Bangor, U.K.: University of Wales Press.

Archer, Brian H. 1980. Forecasting demand: Quantitative and intuitive techniques. *International Journal of Tourism Management* 1(1):5–12.

Archer, Brian H. 1987. Demand forecasting and estimation. In *Travel, Tourism, and Hospitality Research,* ed. J. R. Brent Ritchie and Charles R. Goeldner, pp. 77–85. New York: Wiley.

Armstrong, C. W. G. 1972. International tourism: Coming or going—The methodological problems of forecasting. *Futures* 4(2):115–125.

Artus, J. E. 1972. An econometric analysis of international travel. *International Monetary Fund Staff Paper* 19(3):579–614.

Ascher, William. 1978. *Forecasting: An Appraisal for Policy-Makers and Planners.* Baltimore: Johns Hopkins University Press.

Bar-On, Raymond R. V. 1972. Seasonality in Tourism - Part I. *International Tourism Quarterly,* Special Article No. 6, pp. 40–57.

Bar-On, Raymond R. V. 1973. *Analysis of Seasonality and Trends in Statistical Series—Methodology and Applications in Israel,* vol. 3. Jerusalem, Israel: Central Bureau of Statistics.

Bar-On, Raymond R. V. 1975a. *Seasonality in Tourism—A Guide to the Analysis of Seasonality and Trends for Policy Making.* London: The Economist Intelligence Unit.

Bar-On, Raymond R. V. 1975b. "Forecasting of Tourism Flows" and "Forecasting Forum." In *IUOTO The Measurement of Tourism—A Guide Based on a Seminar Held at Haslemere* [England: September 1974]. London: British Tourist Authority.

Bar-On, Raymond R. V. 1975c. Forecasting of tourism to Thailand, Tourism Research Seminar (Bangkok, August 1975). Summarized in *Thailand Travel Talk*, Vol. 15, nos. 10 and 11. Bangkok: Tourist Organization of Thailand.

Bar-On, Raymond R. V. 1979. Forecasting tourism—Theory and practice. In *A Decade of Achievement*, The Travel Research Association 10th Annual Conference Proceedings (San Antonio, June 1979), The Travel Research Association, Salt Lake City. (Includes international tourism series and growth rates, with an international tourism diary for 1964–1978.)

Bar-On, Raymond R. V. 1984. Forecasting tourism and travel series over various time spans under specified scenarios, ISF 4—Fourth International Symposium on Forecasting, London, July 1984. Ministry of Tourism, Jerusalem, Mimeo.

Bar-On, Raymond R. V. 1989. *Travel and Tourism Data—A Comprehensive Research Handbook on the World Travel Industry*. London: Euromonitor.

Bates, J. M., and C. W. J. Granger. 1969. The combination of forecasts. *Operational Research Quarterly* 20(4):451–468.

Belsley, D. A., E. Kuh, and R. E. Welsch. 1980. *Regression Diagnostics, Identifying Influential Data and Sources of Collinearity*. New York: Wiley.

Bohrnstedt, George W., and David Knoke. 1982. *Statistics for Social Analysis*. Itasca, Ill.: F. E. Peacock.

Calantone, Roger J., Anthony Di Benedetto, and David Bojanic. 1987. A comprehensive review of the tourism forecasting literature. *Journal of Travel Research* 26(2):28–39.

Calantone, Roger J., Anthony Di Benedetto, and David Bojanic. 1988. Multimethod forecasts for tourism analysis. *Annals of Tourism Research* 15(3):387–406.

Cesario, Frank J. 1973. A generalized trip distribution mode. *Journal of Regional Science* 13(2):233–247.

Cesario, Frank J. 1974. More on the generalized trip generation model. *Journal of Regional Science* 14(3):387–397.

Chadee, D., and Z. Mieczkowski. 1987. An empirical analysis of the effects of the exchange rate on Canadian tourism. *Journal of Travel Research* 26(1):13–17.

Cicarelli, James. 1982. A new method of evaluating the accuracy of economic forecasts. *Journal of Macroeconomics* 4(4):469–475.

Dalkey, N., and O. Helmer. 1963. An experimental application of the Delphi method to the use of experts. *Management Science* 9(3):456–467.

Edgell, David, and Richard Seeley. 1980. A multi-stage model for the development of international tourism forecasts for states and regions. In *Tourism Planning and Development Issues*, ed. Donald E. Hawkins, Elwood L. Shafer, and James M. Rovelstad, pp. 407–410. Washington, D.C.: George Washington University.

Edgell, David, Richard Seely, and Harvey Iglarsh. 1980. Forecasts of international tourism in the USA. *International Journal of Tourism Management* 1(2):109–113.

Ellis, J. B., and C. S. Van Doren. 1966. A comparative evaluation of gravity and system theory models for statewide recreational traffic flows. *Journal of Regional Science* 6(2):57–70.

Fritz, Richard G., Charles Brandon, and James Xander. 1984. Combining time-series and econometric forecasts of tourism activity. *Annals of Tourism Research* 11(2):219–229.

Fujii, T. E., and J. Mak. 1980. Forecasting travel demand when the explanatory variables are highly correlated. *Journal of Travel Research* 18(4):31–34.

Gapinski, J. H., and H. P. Tuckman. 1976. Travel demand functions for Florida bound tourists. *Transportation Research* 10(4):267–274.

Gearing, C. E., W. W. Swart, and T. Var. 1976. *Planning for Tourism Development: Quantitative Approaches*. New York: Praeger.

Geurts, M. D., and I. B. Ibrahim. 1975. Comparing the Box-Jenkins approach with the exponentially smoothed forecasting model application to Hawaii tourists. *Journal of Marketing Research* 12(2):182–188.

Geurts, M. D., and I. B. Ibrahim. 1982. Forecasting the Hawaiian tourist market. *Journal of Travel Research* 21(1):18–21.

Gray, H. Peter. 1966. The demand for international travel by the United States and Canada. *International Economic Review* 7(1):83–92.

Hoerl, Arthur E., and Robert W. Kennard. 1970. Ridge regression: Applications to nonorthogonal problems. *Technometrics* 12(1):69–82.

Jud, G. D., and H. Joseph. 1974. International demand for Latin American tourism. *Growth and Change* 5(1):25–31.

Kaynak, E., and J. A. Macaulay. 1984. The Delphi technique in the measurement of tourism market potential. *Tourism Management* 5(2):87–101.

Kliman, M. L. 1981. A quantitative analysis of Canadian overseas tourism. *Transportation Research* 15A(6):487–497.

Kwack, Sung Y. 1972. Effects of income and prices on travel spending abroad, 1960 III–1967 IV. *International Economic Review* 13(2):24–56.

Lewis, C. D. 1982. *Industrial and Business Forecasting Methods.* London: Butterworth.

Liepa, R., and P. Chau. 1977. *Methodology for Short Term Forecasts of Tourism Flows.* Research Report No. 4, Economic Research Section, Policy Planning and Industry Relations Branch. Ottawa: Canada Government Office of Tourism.

Liu, Juanita C. 1988. Hawaii tourism to the year 2000: A Delphi forecast. *Tourism Management* 9(4):27–90.

Loeb, P. 1982. International travel to the United States: An economic evaluation. *Annals of Tourism Research* 9(1):7–20.

Makridakis, Spyros. 1986. The art and science of forecasting: An assessment and future directions. *International Journal of Forecasting* 2(1):15–39.

Makridakis, Spryos, and Michele Hibon. 1984. Accuracy of forecasting: An empirical investigation. In *The Forecasting Accuracy of Major Time Series Methods*, ed. S. Makridakis, A. Andersen, R. Carbone, R. Fildes, M. Hibon, and R. Lewandowsk, pp. 35–60. New York: Wiley.

Makridakis, Spyros, and Steven C. Wheelwright. 1978. *Forecasting: Methods and Applications.* New York: Wiley/Hamilton.

Makridakis, Spyros, S. C. Wheelwright, and E. Victor. 1983. *Forecasting: Methods and Applications*, 2d ed. New York: Wiley.

Malamud, Bernard. 1973. Gravity model calibration of tourist travel to Las Vegas. *Journal of Leisure Research* 5(4):23–33.

Mansfield, N. W. 1969. Recreational trip generation. *Journal of Transport Economic and Policy* 3(3):152–164.

Martin, Christine A., and Stephen F. Witt. 1987. Tourism demand forecasting models: Choice of an appropriate variable to represent tourists' cost of living. *Tourism Management* 8(3):233–246.

Martin, Christine A., and Stephen F. Witt. 1988. Substitute prices in models of tourism demand. *Annals of Tourism Research* 15(2):255–268.

Martin, Christine A., and Stephen F. Witt. 1989. Accuracy of econometric forecasts of tourism. *Annals of Tourism Research* 16(3):407–428.

Peterson, G. L., D. H. Anderson, and D. W. Lime. 1982. Multiple-use site demand analysis: An application to the boundary waters canoe area wilderness. *Journal of Leisure Research* 16(3):407–428.

Quayson, Jojo, and Turgut Var. 1982. A tourism demand function for the Okanagan, BC. *Tourism Management* 3(2):108–115.

Robinson, A. E. 1979. *Tourism and the Next Decade: A Look to the Future Through . . . "A Return to Delphi."* The Travel Research Association 10th Annual Conference Proceeding, Bureau of Economic and Business Research, College of Business. Salt Lake City: University of Utah.

Schwaninger, Markus. 1984. Forecasting leisure and tourism: Scenario projection for 2000–2010. *Tourism Management* 5(4):250–257.

Sheldon, Pauline, and Turgut Var. 1985. Tourism forecasting: A review of empirical research. *Journal of Forecasting* 4(2):183–195.

Smeral, Egon. 1988. Tourism demand, economic theory, and econometrics: An integrated approach. *Journal of Travel Research* 26(4):38–43.

Steinnes, Donald N. 1988. A statistical analysis of the impact of oil price shocks on tourism. *Journal of Travel Research* 26(2):39–42.

Sunday, Alexander A. 1978. Foreign travel and tourism prices and demand. *Annals of Tourism Research* 5(2):268–273.

Taylor, Gordon D. 1976. An approach to forecasting tourism future. In *Forecasting Leisure Issues*, ed. John Howarth and Stanley Parker. London: The Leisure Studies Association.

Theil, H. 1966. *Applied Economic Forecasting.* Amsterdam: North-Holland.

Uysal, Muzaffer, and John L. Crompton. 1984. Determinants of demand for international tourists flows to Turkey. *Tourism Management* 5(4):288–297.

Uysal, Muzaffer, and John L. Crompton. 1985. An overview of approaches used to forecast tourism demand. *Journal of Travel Research* 23(4):7–15.

Van Doorn, J. W. M. 1982. Can futures research contribute to tourism policy? *Tourism Management* 3(3):149–166.

Van Doorn, J. W. M. 1984. Tourism forecasting and the policymaker. *Tourism Management* 5(1):24–39.

Van Doorn, J. W. M. 1986. Scenario writing: A method for long-term tourism forecasting? *Tourism Management* 7(1):33–49.

Van Doorn, J. W. M. and F. A. Van Vught. 1983. Futures research in the Netherlands 1960–1980. *Futures* 15(6):504–516.

Vanhove, N. 1980. Forecasting in tourism. *Revue de Tourisme* 35(3):2–7.

Var, Turgut, C. Liu, and Stephanie Nagata. 1986. Future of Hawaiian tourism: Delphi Working Paper, Simon Fraser University, Burnaby, B.C.

Wandner, Stephen A., and James D. Van Erden. 1980. Estimating the demand for international tourism using time series analysis. In *Tourism Planning and Development Issues,* ed. Donald E. Hawkins, Elwood L. Shafer, and James M. Rovelstad, pp. 381–392. Washington, D.C.: George Washington University.

Wheelwright, Steven C., and Spyros Makridakis. 1985. *Forecasting Methods for Management,* 4th ed. New York: Wiley.

Witt, Christine A., and Stephen F. Witt. 1989. Measures of forecasting accuracy—Turning point error v-size error. *Tourism Management* 10(3):255–260.

Witt, Stephen F., and Christine A. Martin. 1987. Econometric models for forecasting international tourism demand. *Journal of Travel Research* 25(3):23–30.

13

Forecasting: The Econometric Approach

Stephen F. Witt

Since the early 1970s, the economic environment has experienced considerable turbulence, and within the context of such a changing and competitive business environment it has become increasingly necessary for companies in the hospitality and tourism industries to engage in more sophisticated planning. However, planning creates a substantial need for forecasts. It is therefore worthwhile setting up a forecasting system whenever the variables concerned are central to the main activities of the hospitality/tourism organization and the use of the forecasts is likely to provide significant benefits. For example, where the forecasts are of key variables relating to the organization's markets, such as tourist flows or expenditures, they are likely to justify the cost. Alternatively, the organization may be able to buy in appropriate forecasts from external sources at lower cost. Reliable forecasts of tourism demand are essential for efficient planning by airlines, shipping companies, railways, coach operators, hoteliers, tour operators, food and catering establishments, providers of entertainment facilities, manufacturers producing goods primarily for sale to tourists, and other industries connected with the hospitality and tourism markets. Such forecasts are also of great interest to governments in origin and destination countries and to national tourist organizations.

A broad range of techniques is available for demand forecasting in hospitality and tourism, and selection of an appropriate technique will depend upon the requirements of the forecaster. Forecasting techniques may be divided into causal and noncausal methods. Noncausal techniques assume that a variable may be forecast without reference to the factors that determine the level of the variable. They include quantitative techniques such as univariate time series models in which past history on the forecast variable is simply extrapolated (arithmetic moving average, exponential smoothing, trend curve analysis, decomposition methods, autoregression, univariate Box-Jenkins). Noncausal techniques also include qualitative approaches such as the Delphi technique, which aims to obtain information about the future through questionnaire surveys of a group of experts in the field; respondents provide their estimates of the probabilities of certain specified conditions or events occurring in the future and estimate when the events would be likely to occur. By contrast, causal techniques examine the factors that appear likely to influence the level of hospitality/tourism demand. The econometric approach to forecasting hospitality/tourism demand is a causal approach and involves specifying the demand function, that is the quantitative relationship between hospitality/tourism demand and the (mainly economic) variables that affect this demand. Multiple regression analysis is then used to estimate the demand function. The application of statistical methods in order to attempt to establish quantitative relationships between economic variables is termed *econometrics.* Estimation of the demand function is carried out using historic data on hospitality/tourism demand and the influencing variables. Forecasts of hospitality/tourism demand are then obtained by using forecasts of the determining forces in conjunction with the estimated relationship.

Other causal techniques include multivariate Box-Jenkins (or transfer function) forecasting; the model in this case incorporates autoregressive and moving-average terms as with univariate Box-Jenkins, but additionally allows causal factors to influence the forecast variable. Complex mathematical and statistical algorithms are involved, and experience is essential in order to apply the technique successfully.

Other multiple regression forecasting techniques exist. Gravity models represent a particular class of regression model that has been widely used in the past to forecast tourism demand. Gravity models are based on the gravity law of spatial interaction, which states (in the travel context) that the degree of interaction between two geographic areas varies directly with the degrees of concentration of persons in the two areas and inversely with the distance separating them. Whereas demand functions are derived from the theory of consumer behavior, the fundamental idea underlying gravity models was originally derived by analogy with Newton's gravitational law and evolved as part of the early work of social physicists who believed that social phenomena could be explained by physical laws. The most common form of travel gravity model is:

$$T_{ij} = a \, (P_i^{b_1} P_j^{b_2} / d_{ij}^{b_3}) \tag{1}$$

where T_{ij} denotes the number of trips taking place between node i and node j; P_i and P_j are the populations at nodes i and j respectively; and a, b_1, b_2, b_3 are constants.

The gravity law of spatial interaction has been popular as a tool of spatial analysis because of its empirical regularity, but it suffers from several drawbacks. One severe problem is that as an analogy it lacks a firm theoretical foundation, which means there is little theory to explain the values of the parameters in the model.

In this entry we are concerned with forecasting tourism demand, using econometrics, and, in particular, we shall concentrate on international tourism. Furthermore, the group of variables that influences international tourism demand will depend upon the purpose of visit under consideration. For example, the demand for business travel will depend upon where major business centers are located, whereas the demand for visits to friends and relatives will depend upon where close historical, cultural, or other ties exist that give rise to the location of friends/relatives in foreign countries. As by far the majority of international tourist trips take place for holiday purposes (approximately 70 percent), and it is only for holiday trips that individuals are completely free to choose the destination, transport mode, and so on, we shall focus on demand functions that explain the demand for international *holiday* tourism.

Tourism Demand Functions

Many authors have specified and estimated tourism demand functions (Artus 1972; Bond and Ladman 1972; Fuji and Mak 1980; Kliman 1981; Little 1980; Loeb 1982; Martin and Witt 1988; O'Hagan and Harrison 1984; Quayson and Var 1982; Stronge and Redman 1982; Witt 1980a, 1980b, 1983, 1990; Witt and Martin 1987b; Witt and Witt 1990). The holiday demand function takes the general form

$$Y = f(X_1, X_2, \ldots X_k) \qquad (2)$$

where Y is the demand for foreign holidays to a given destination from a particular origin; $X_1, \ldots, X_k$ are the influencing variables; and f denotes some function. Variables that may be included in the demand function are now considered.

Tourism Demand Tourism demand is measured in terms of tourist arrivals/departures or tourist receipts/expenditures. As the level of foreign tourism from a given origin is expected to depend on the origin country population, the demand variable is usually expressed in per capita form.

Income In general, income is included as an explanatory variable. Income usually enters the model (Eq. 2) as origin country real income per capita (corresponding to the specification of demand in per capita terms). For holiday visits the appropriate form of the variable is personal disposable income.

Own Price Price is usually included in demand functions. For international tourism there are two elements of price—those costs incurred in reaching the destination and those costs to be met while at the destination. Transport cost can be measured using representative air fares between the origin and destination for air travel and representative gasoline costs and/or ferry fares for surface travel. Transport cost should enter the model (Eq. 2) in real terms in origin country currency.

It may be possible to measure the cost of tourism in the destination by a specific tourists' cost of living variable if appropriate data are available. Otherwise the consumer price index in a country may be used to represent tourists' cost of living, and Martin and Witt (1987) have shown that this index is likely to be a reasonable proxy for the cost of tourism variable. Tourists' cost of living should be specified in real terms in origin currency. It is sometimes suggested that exchange rate should also appear as an explanatory variable influencing international tourism demand. Although exchange rates are already incorporated to some extent in the other price variables, in practice people may be more aware of exchange rates than relative costs of living for tourists in the origin and destination countries and thus pay considerable attention to this price indicator.

Substitute Prices Economic theory suggests that the prices of substitutes may be important determinants of demand. Potential tourists compare the price of a foreign holiday with the price of a domestic holiday in reaching their holiday decision. However, they also compare the costs of holidaying in a particular foreign destination with the costs involved in visiting other foreign countries. Thus substitute travel costs and substitute tourists' living costs may be important determinants of the demand for international tourism to a given destination from a particular origin (Martin and Witt 1988). Substitute prices can be accommodated in the model (Eq. 2) through the inclusion of a weighted average substitute transport cost variable and a weighted average substitute tourists' cost of living variable. The weights should reflect the relative attractiveness of the various destinations to residents of the origin under consideration and are often based on previous market shares (for a discussion of weighting systems in international tourism demand models see Witt and Martin 1987a).

Dummy Variables Dummy variables can be included in tourism demand functions to allow for the impact of "one off" events. These are specially constructed variables that take the value 1 when the event occurs and 0 otherwise. For example, the 1973 and 1979 oil crises are likely to have temporarily reduced international tourism demand because of the resultant uncertainties in the world economic situation (Martin and Witt 1988). Tourism flows to Greece were lower than expected in 1974 because of the heightened threat of war between Greece and Turkey as a result of the Turkish invasion of Cyprus (Papadopoulos and Witt 1985). When governments impose foreign currency restrictions on their residents, this is likely to reduce outward tourism, as was the case, for example, in the UK during the period late 1966 to late 1969. Foreign currency restrictions can also alter the *distribution* of foreign holidays (Witt 1980a, 1980b). Measurement of the impact of mega-events (such as the Olympic Games) on tourism flows through the use of dummy variables has been discussed by Witt and Martin (1987d).

Trend A trend term may be included in international tourism demand models. This mainly represents a steady change in the popularity of a destination country over the period considered as a result of changing tastes, but it also captures the time-dependent effects of all other explanatory variables not explicitly included in the equation, such as changes in air service frequencies and demographic changes in the origins.

Promotional Activity National tourist offices often spend considerable sums in foreign countries on promoting the particular country as a tourist destination, as do carriers, particularly airlines. Hence, promotional expenditure is expected to play a role in determining the level of international tourism demand and thus should appear as an explanatory variable in the demand function (Eq. 2). The appropriate form of the variable is promotional expenditure for the destination in the origin, expressed in origin country currency and real terms.

  A major problem regarding the inclusion of promotional variables as determinants of tourism demand relates to difficulties in obtaining the relevant data. A further problem concerns the form of the relationship; the impact of advertising on tourism demand may be distributed over time, so that advertising in a given period is likely to influence not only demand in that period but also in subsequent periods, although the effect will diminish with the passage of time. In addition the effectiveness of a given level of advertising expenditure in influencing the level of international tourism demand may vary across media. (A full review and discussion of the role of marketing variables in international tourism demand models is given in Witt and Martin 1987c.)

Lagged Dependent Variable   A lagged dependent variable (that is, the value of tourism demand in the previous period) is sometimes included in tourism demand functions to allow for habit persistence and supply rigidities (see Witt 1980a). Once people have been on holiday to a particular country and liked it, they tend to return to that destination. Furthermore, knowledge about the destination spreads as people talk about their holidays and show photographs, thereby reducing risk for potential visitors to that country. In fact, this word-of-mouth recommendation may well play a more important role in destination selection than does commercial advertising.

Supply constraints may take the form of shortages of hotel accommodation, passenger transportation capacity, and trained staff, and these often cannot be increased rapidly. Time is also required to build up contacts among tour operators, hotels, airlines, and travel agencies. Similarly, once the tourist industry to a country has become highly developed it is unlikely to dwindle rapidly. The hotel industry will have invested large sums of money in the country and tour operators will have established contacts there. If a partial adjustment process is postulated to allow for rigidities in supply, this results in the presence of a lagged dependent variable in the model (Eq. 2).

Estimation, Testing, and Forecasting

Having selected the variables expected to influence tourism demand, the econometric forecasting process proceeds as follows:

1. Specify the demand function in mathematical form (say, linear, or more commonly log-linear).
2. Assemble data relevant to the model.
3. Use the data to estimate by regression the quantitative effects of the influencing variables on demand in the past.
4. Carry out tests on the estimated model to see if it is sufficiently realistic.
5. If the tests show that the model is satisfactory then it can be used for forecasting.

When the tourism demand function (Eq. 2) is specified in log-linear form, a resulting characteristic is that the estimated coefficients of the income variable, price variables, and so on, may be interpreted directly as elasticities. It is necessary to evaluate the parameter estimates obtained in a regression model in terms of both sign and magnitude in order to determine whether these estimates are theoretically meaningful. Economic theory imposes restrictions on the signs and values of the parameters in demand functions, and the estimates need to be examined to see whether they satisfy these constraints. For example, foreign holidays are "superior" goods and thus a positive income elasticity is expected. In fact, most foreign holidays are regarded as "luxuries" and in such cases the magnitude of the income elasticity is expected to exceed unity. Similarly, the own-price elasticity of demand should be negative and cross-price elasticities for substitutes positive. Changes in consumer tastes may move toward or away from a particular holiday and therefore the trend variable could have a positive or negative coefficient. The promotional expenditure and lagged dependent variable coefficients are both expected to be positive. If an estimated parameter has an "incorrect" sign or does not satisfy the restrictions on magnitude it should be rejected, as it is theoretically implausible. In general, an unexpected parameter sign or size is the result of deficiencies in the model.

The empirical results may also be evaluated in terms of statistical measures of accuracy and significance of the forecasting equations. For example, the *t* test can be employed to examine the hypothesis that a particular explanatory variable coefficient is significantly different from zero or whether the estimated value may simply have been generated by chance. If the hypothesis that a coefficient is equal to zero is true, then the corresponding explanatory variable does not influence the dependent variable and should be excluded from the tourism demand function. However, when a parameter is not statistically significant (at, say, the five percent level), this does not prove that there is no relationship between the explanatory and dependent variables; the insignificance of the parameter may be a result of statistical problems. Prior belief plays a vital role in the decision regarding which explanatory variables should be retained in the equation in view of the statistical evidence. If there are strong theoretical grounds for expecting a particular explanatory variable to influence the dependent variable and a "correct" coefficient sign is estimated but the parameter is insignificant, the explanatory variable should not be eliminated from the equation, as weak support has been obtained for the hypothesis. If the "correct" sign is estimated for a coefficient and it is statistically significant, this provides strong support for the hypothesis that the variable has an impact on the dependent variable.

Once satisfactory empirical results have been obtained for the tourism demand function (Eq. 2), the estimated relationship may then be combined with forecasts of the explanatory variables to generate tourism demand forecasts.

Advantages and Disadvantages

A forecasting system cannot be expected to completely eliminate future uncertainty regarding tourism demand, but the less uncertainty present, the better organizations can plan. If forecasts of tourism demand are too high, then firms in related industries will suffer; for example, there may be empty seats on airplanes and coaches, empty rooms in hotels, unoccupied apartments, unused rental cars, and so on. It is likely that in general capital investment will be excessive, the labor force will be too big and excess stocks of goods normally sold directly to or used by tourists will be held. If, on the other hand, forecasts of demand are too low, then firms will lose opportunities; for example, there may be insufficient hotel accommodation or too few flights to cater for all those wishing to visit a certain area at a given time. Even if supply can be expanded to a limited extent at short notice, additional costs to firms are likely to be incurred as, say, less efficient aircraft are used and excessive overtime is worked.

Martin and Witt (1989a, 1989b) have carried out a comparison of the predictive accuracy of causal and noncausal quantitative approaches to forecasting international tourism demand. Specifically, they compared the econometric approach with six univariate time series methods: naive 1 (a "no change value" model in which the forecast value is set equal to the previous period's actual value); naive 2 (a "no change growth" model in which the forecast growth rate is set equal to the previous period's actual growth rate); exponential smoothing; trend curve analysis; Gompertz; and autoregression. The empirical results show that when accuracy is measured in terms of *error magnitude* (that is, the difference in size between the forecast and actual values), the econometric approach to forecasting is *not* particularly accurate—it lies approximately in the middle of the range of forecasting methods.

Further disadvantages associated with econometric models are that there may be situations in which they are inappropriate (for example because of incomplete knowledge regarding the causal structure), and generally they are more expensive to develop and maintain than noncausal models. In addition considerable user understanding is required in order to develop the correct relationships, and a major problem in attempting to generate accurate forecasts of tourism demand is the difficulty of obtaining accurate forecasts of the variables that influence demand—income, inflation, exchange rates, and so on.

When accuracy is measured in terms of forecasting the correct *direction of change* of tourism demand (that is whether there will be *more* or *fewer* tourist visits next year than this year), the ranking of forecasting techniques changes. Witt and Witt (1989) have shown that econometric models yield the most accurate results according to this criterion.

An additional major advantage with econometric forecasting models is that they explicitly take into account the impact on demand of changes in the determining forces, whereas forecasting by extrapolation presupposes that the factors that were the main cause of growth in the past will continue to be the main cause in the future, so any alteration in the trend is likely to generate poor forecasts. Furthermore, econometric models may be used for active ("what if") forecasting, that is to assess the consequences of possible changes in the causal factors, and they provide several statistical measures of the accuracy and significance of the forecasting equations.

Summary

Accurate forecasts of hospitality and tourism demand are essential for efficient planning by firms associated with these industries. Although more sophisticated forecasting methods provide no guarantee of greater forecasting accuracy, the econometric forecasting method provides considerable benefits over univariate time series methods, for example the former explicitly takes into account the impact on hospitality/tourism demand of changes in the determining forces, which permits a company to link its forecasting with tactical and strategic plans for the future.

The econometric forecasting process involves estimating the quantitative relationship between tourism demand and its determinants and then inserting forecasts of the influencing variables into the estimated relationship in order to generate the required forecasts.

References

Artus, J. R. 1972. An econometric analysis of international travel. *IMF Staff Papers* 19:579–614.

Bond, M. E., and J. R. Ladman. 1972. International tourism and economic development: A special case for Latin America. *Mississippi Valley Journal of Business and Economics* 8(Fall):43–55.

Fujii, E. T., and J. Mak. 1980. Forecasting travel demand when the explanatory variables are highly correlated. *Journal of Travel Research* 18(4):31–34.

Kliman, M. L. 1981. A quantitative analysis of Canadian overseas tourism. *Transportation Research* 15A(6):487–497.

Little, J. S. 1980. International travel in the US balance of payments. *New England Economic Review* (May/June):42–55.

Loeb, P. 1982. International travel to the United States: An econometric evaluation. *Annals of Tourism Research* 9(1):7–20.

Martin, C. A., and S. F. Witt. 1987. Tourism demand forecasting models: Choice of appropriate variable to represent tourists' cost of living. *Tourism Management* 8(3):233–246.

Martin, C. A., and S. F. Witt. 1988. Substitute prices in models of tourism demand. *Annals of Tourism Research* 15:255–268.

Martin, C. A., and S. F. Witt. 1989a. Accuracy of econometric forecasts of international tourism. *Annals of Tourism Research* 16(3):407–428.

Martin C. A., and S. F. Witt. 1989b. Forecasting tourism demand: A comparison of the accuracy of several quantitative methods. *International Journal of Forecasting* 5:1–13.

O'Hagan, J. W., and M. J. Harrison. 1984. Market shares of U.S. tourist expenditure in Europe: An econometric analysis. *Applied Economics* 16:919–931.

Papadopoulos, S. I., and S. F. Witt. 1985. A marketing analysis of foreign tourism in Greece. In *Proceedings of Second World Marketing Congress*, eds. S. Shaw, L. Sparks, and E. Kaynak, pp. 682–693. Stirling, U.K.: University of Stirling.

Quayson, J., and T. Var. 1982. A tourism demand function for the Okanagan, B.C. *Tourism Management* 3(2):108–115.

Stronge, G. B., and M. Redman. 1982. U.S. tourism in Mexico—an empirical analysis. *Annals of Tourism Research* 9(1):21–35.

Witt, S. F. 1980a. An abstract mode—abstract (destination) node model of foreign holiday demand. *Applied Economics* 12(2):163–180.

Witt, S. F. 1980b. An econometric comparison of UK and German foreign holiday behaviour. *Managerial and Decision Economics* 1(3):123–131.

Witt, S. F. 1983. A binary choice model of foreign holiday demand. *Journal of Economic Studies* 10(1):46–59.

Witt, S. F. 1990. Cash flow forecasting in the international tourism industry. In *Advances in Financial Planning and Forecasting, Volume 4, Part B: International Dimensions*, eds. R. Aggarwal and C. F. Lee, pp. 229–244. Greenwich: JAI Press.

Witt, S. F., and C. A. Martin. 1987a. Deriving a relative price index for inclusion in international tourism demand estimation models: Comment. *Journal of Travel Research* 25(3):38–40.

Witt, S. F., and C. A. Martin. 1987b. Econometric models for forecasting international tourism demand. *Journal of Travel Research* 25(3):23–30.

Witt, S. F., and C. A. Martin. 1987c. International tourism demand models—inclusion of marketing variables. *Tourism Management* 8(1):33–40.

Witt, S. F., and C. A. Martin. 1987d. Measuring the impacts of mega-events on tourism flows. In *The Role and Impact of Mega-Events and Attractions on Regional and National Tourism Development*, pp. 213–221. St. Gallen, Switzerland: AIEST.

Witt, C. A., and S. F. Witt. 1989. Measures of forecasting accuracy—turning point error v size of error. *Tourism Management* 10(3):255–260.

Witt, C. A., and S. F. Witt. 1990. Appraising an econometric forecasting model. *Journal of Travel Research* 28(3):30–34.

14

Seasonality

Raphael Raymond Bar-On

Causes of Seasonality

Seasonal variations are similar every year, but appreciable differences occur in the magnitude and timing of the climate in particular areas, for example, drought or storms, mountain snow for skiing.

Four main seasons are recognized in the Northern Hemisphere:

Spring, from March 21 (Equinox) to June 20
Summer, from June 21 (Summer Solstice) to September 22
Autumn or fall, from September 23 (Second Equinox) to December 21
    (Winter Solstice)
Winter, from December 22 to March 20

In the Southern Hemisphere Spring starts September 23, Summer December 22 and so on.

The festivals of the major religions are associated with the natural and agricultural seasons, with additional historical and theological significance, for example, the spring festival is Passover for Jews (the first ripe barley) and Easter for Christians; First Fruits is Pentecost; the harvest festival is called "Tabernacles" for Jews and for some Christians, Thanksgiving; and the Festival of Lights in midwinter is Christmas for Christians and Hanukah for Jews. The Jewish festivals are celebrated according to a calendar of 12 or 13 lunar months in a year, so that Passover can fall between March 26 and April 25. Easter was linked with Passover, but its date for Catholics and Protestants is set according to an ecclesiastic calendar, so that Easter Sunday varies between March 20 and April 23. For the Greek and Russian Orthodox churches and other denominations (Armenian, Syrian, Coptic) there are other variations. Moslem festivals are celebrated according to a 354-day year, so that they can fall in any Gregorian month. (For further details and references see Bar-On 1973; Smith 1970.)

Many religious festivals were associated with pilgrimages, for example, Jews to the Temple in Jerusalem three times a year. Rulers and the rich had summer and winter homes, and the hunting, legislative, and social seasons were set accordingly. Business travel was also seasonal. School and university years were set with a long vacation in July and August (in the Northern Hemisphere) to enable the pupils to help harvest the summer crops. Advances in technology and civilization made agricultural and other activities possible outside the traditional seasons. Other holidays were established, for example, New Year, Thanksgiving, Labor Day, Independence Days, Bank Holidays (in Britain). Christmas and New Year have fixed dates, but their day of the week varies, changing travel patterns over the extended holiday. Other holidays are on specific days, but at different dates (usually within a range of seven days). Other reasons for travel developed too, for example, visiting the ancestral home, health, and councils of scholars.

Vacation travel developed slowly until railways and steamships made it practicable in time and cost. The Industrial Revolution freed increasing numbers from being tied to endless farm work, with paid holidays and 5-day weeks widespread in this century. Vacation seasons developed in the summer, especially in the seaside or cooler mountain resorts, and in the winter away from the cold to warm resorts or for winter sports (especially in central and northern Europe). Spa holidays developed and business travel, then conferences, cultural and special-interest travel, incentive tours, and so forth. Individuals bought or rented holiday homes, at first for an extended vacation stay, then with the development of cars and other transport, for weekends throughout much of the year. Holiday resorts developed with hotels, boarding houses (pensions), and attractions, at first open only over the specific season, closing off season. Recent developments include apartment hotels and time-sharing schemes.

Tourism seasons therefore developed because of the climate at the origin and/or at the destination and because of nonclimatic attractions, including religious festivals, celebrations, and carnivals. In order to extend the tourism season, facilities were developed to be usable year-round, with reduced prices and other incentives to visit and stay over an extended season or year-round. Airlines and other transport facilities are also interested in balanced demand year-round. Most hospitality staff prefer year-round employment, with overtime during peak seasons: Students and others may be available only in the holiday seasons. Accommodations such as university campuses, residence halls, and school dormitories are available in the summer and other holidays, and may be used together with other facilities: lecturers and other staff may be willing to work then. Figure 1 shows the major causes of seasonality in tourism (in the Northern Hemisphere) as a clock, with January following December (based on Bar-On 1975).

National and religious holidays and local festivals may stimulate high demand on specific days or weeks, as may seasonal airline prices, inclusive tours, and so forth. Weekend demand may differ from weekday demand, with hotels and restaurants in business cities seeking clientele on weekends.

The Components of Time Series

Tourism, travel, and hospitality are measured daily by enterprises, and analysis is usually based on series for the 12 months in calendar years, often with cumulative series from January (or from the start of the summer and winter season). Monthly series can be regarded as the result of the combined operation of periodic, systematic, and other *components* in the time domain (refer to Figure 2 while reading the following three subsections).

Seasonality(s). Fluctuations recurring every year with similar timing and intensity, though they may change gradually over the years or even abruptly, due to changes in policies or regulations or different trends of subseries with

Fig. 1. The seasons in tourism. 1. Notation for the 12 calendar months. 2. In the Southern Hemisphere.

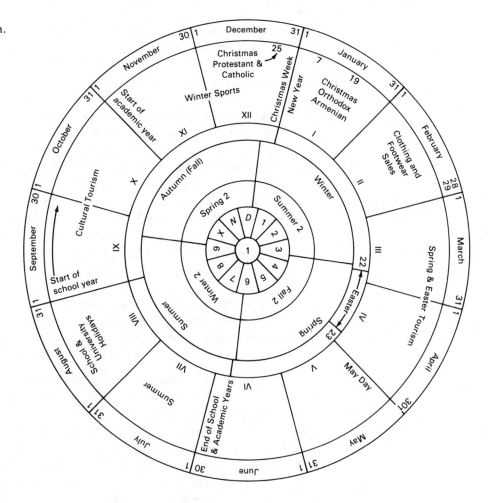

Fig. 2. The components of monthly series. Abbreviations: *Periodic:* S, seasonality. Other calendar effects due to variation of: F, festival dates; D, trading days. *Systematic:* C, trend-cycle; T, trend (secular); Cy, cycles; Cb, business cycles; G, multiannual events. *Irregular:* I, short-term effects. Unusual events related to other data: W, nonaverage weather; E, exchange rates; R, residual irregularities (noise).

Multiplicative Models for Monthly Series

Basic: $Y = C \times S \times I$;   S and I percentages, averaging 100% over each year.

Seasonally Adjusted Monthly Data: $M = Y / S = C \times I$ (deseasonalized), that is, Monthly Level = Trend-Cycle (monthly rate) perturbed by Irregularities.

Annualized Level: $A = 12 \times M$, $A = 12 \times Y / S$

More Comprehensive: $Y = T \times Cy \times S \times F \times D \times U \times R$;
$U = 1$ in regular periods
$M = Y/(S \times F \times D) = T \times Cy \times U \times R$

Short-Term Trend Level for month t is smoothed by a 3-month weighted moving average:
$B(t) = [B(t-1) + 2 \times B(t) + B(t+1)]/4$
For last month of series: $B'(t) = [B(t-1) + 2 \times B(t)]/3$.

different seasonal patterns (for example, tourists from specific countries, domestic tourists: See Tables 3 and 4). There are other calendar effects:

Festival date variations (F)—especially variations in the date of Easter, affecting relative travel in March and April.

Trading day variations (D)—Differential travel and use of accommodation over the seven days of each week, throughout the year or in specific seasons, for example, business trips mainly Monday to Friday, weekend trips, holiday tours starting and/or finishing on Saturday or Sunday. In any month other than February there may be four or five Saturdays, affecting the monthly total. Thus, in an extreme case where there is only one flight or ship a week from a particular source to a specific destination, with say 400 passengers, the monthly total may be 1,600 or 2,000, a difference of up to 25% between months with four or five arrivals. Leap year Februaries with 29 days may change travel levels in February (although they do not change monthly salaries), and can also be taken into account in the computer analysis.

Trend-cycles (C). Most tourism series show systematic increases (or decreases) over several years, due to population growth, disposable incomes, attractiveness of destinations, or changes in habits (travel abroad, second holidays), with variations in the rate of growth or of decline. These may comprise

> *Trends (T)*, long-term and medium-term, monotonically increasing (or decreasing) over three or more years.
> *Cycles (Cy)*, especially
>> *Business Cycles (Cb)*, which can be studied by macroeconomic indicators
>> *Multiannual Events (G)*, for example, biennial expositions or festivals, sports (the Olympic Games are held every four years, but at different destinations).

Irregularity (or irregularities) (I). Comprised of

> *Short-term effects of unusual events (U)*, for example, strikes (of transport, air controllers), terrorism (see Bar-On 1990), natural disasters (earthquakes, floods, epidemics), Expos, Olympics at a particular destination
> *Exchange Rates (E)*—devaluation at origin or destination, unexpected changes in fares or other prices
> *Nonaverage Weather (W)*, for example, snow suitable for skiing relative to the average for that month.

These irregularities may affect more than one month (even before an anticipated event and following it) and also cause changes in seasonality and/or trend-cycles for months or years following. Items *E* and *W* can be quantified for the months in which they occur, as related variables *Z*, and a functional relationship may enable adjustment and reduction of *I* (as for *F* and *D*).

Residual Irregularities (R) unexplained by any of the above (that is, "noise," or unwanted disturbances, masking the "signals" of the underlying seasonality and trends).

Analysis of Monthly Series into Seasonality and Trends

The most common study of trends is by analysis of annual data (which balance out most seasonal effects of constant seasonality). Table 1 and Figure 3 show an artificial example of a monthly series in which the trend-cycle *C* was

Table 1. *A seasonal series with a cyclical increase and decrease*

Symbol:	Seasonal factors S	Trend-cycle[b] monthly level C			Monthly data Y = C × S			% Change on corresponding month (period) last year[c]		% Change in trend-cycle on previous month	
Year:	1988–90[a]	1988	1989	1990	1988	1989	1990	1989[a]	1990	1989[a]	1990
Column:	(1)	(2)	(3)	(4)	(5) (1)×(2)	(6) (1)×(3)	(7) (1)×(4)	(8) (6)/(5)	(9) (7)/(6)	(10)	(11)
Month					**Tourists**						
1 Jan.	50% T	1,000	1,000	1,200 H	500 T	500 T	600 t	0	+20	0	0.2
2 Feb.	60%	1,000	1,026	1,198	600	616	719	+3	+17	2.6	−0.2
3 Mar.	80%	1,000	1,052	1,194	800	842	955	+5	+14	2.5	−0.3
4 Apr.	110% P	1,000	1,076	1,185	1,100 p	1,184 p	1,304 p	+8	+10	2.3	−0.8
5 May	80% t	1,000	1,100	1,173	800 t	880 t	938 t	+10	+7	2.2	−1.0
6 June	120%	1,000	1,122	1,159	1,200	1,346	1,391	+12	+3	2.0	−1.2
7 July	200% P	1,000	1,141	1,141	2,000 P	2,282 P	2,282 P	+14	0	1.7	−1.6
8 Aug.	180%	1,000	1,159	1,122	1,800	2,086	2,020	+16	−3	1.6	−1.7
9 Sep.	100%	1,000	1,173	1,100	1,000	1,173	1,100	+17	−6	1.2	−2.0
X Oct.	80%	1,000	1,185	1,076	800	948	861	+18	−9	1.0	−2.2
N Nov.	50% T	1,000	1,194	1,052	500 T	597 t	526 T	+19	−12	0.8	−2.2
D Dec.	90% r	1,000	1,198	1,026 L	900 r	1,078 r	923 r	+20	−14	0.3	−2.5
Annual total	1200%	12,000	13,426	13,626	12,000	13,532	13,619			Jan to Dec	19.8–14.5
Average per month	100%	1,000	1,119	1,136	1,000	1,128	1,135	+13	+0.6		1.5[d]–1.3
Totals by season:											
High: 6,7,8	500%	3,000	3,422	3,422	5,000	5,715	5,692	+14	−0.4		
Shoulder: 3,4,5; 9,X	450%	5,000	5,586	5,728	4,500	5,026	5,158	+12	+3		
Low: 1,2; N	160%	3,000	3,220	3,450	1,600	1,713	1,845	+7	+8		
Relative peak: D	90%	1,000	1,198	1,026	900	1,078	923	+20	−14		
Cumulative: Jan. to June					5,000	5,368	5,907	+7	+10	Jan. to June	12.2–3.4
Seasonal Range[e] P − T	150%				1,500	1,782	1,756	+19	−1.5		
Seasonal Ratio[e] P / T	4.00				4.0	4.6	4.3	+14	−5		

Note: *Seasonality*: P, peak; p, secondary peak ($S' \geq 105\%$); T, trough; t, secondary trough; r, relative peak ($S' \leq 100\%$). In some Tables also: q, other high month ($100\% < S' < 105\%$, noncontiguous). Trend-cycle: H, High; L Low.

[a]An artificial example of S for complete months (see Figure 3). Changes in S over the years; D, F and I and ignored (for simplicity).

[b]A sinusoidal curve. C can also be expressed as annual levels A, for example, for Jan. 1988 to Jan. 1989 12,000 per annum (the right-hand scales in Figure 3a and 3d).

[c]Percent change of both C and Y on the corresponding month of the previous year are equal in this example. The annual totals of C are not used; they and their percent change from year to year differ from those of Y (because the weights S differ over the months).

[d]The arithmetic average of d: for strong changes the geometric average should be used for average rate of growth.

[e]January and July have 31 days. If the length of month of the P and T months differ, LM factors should be taken into account.

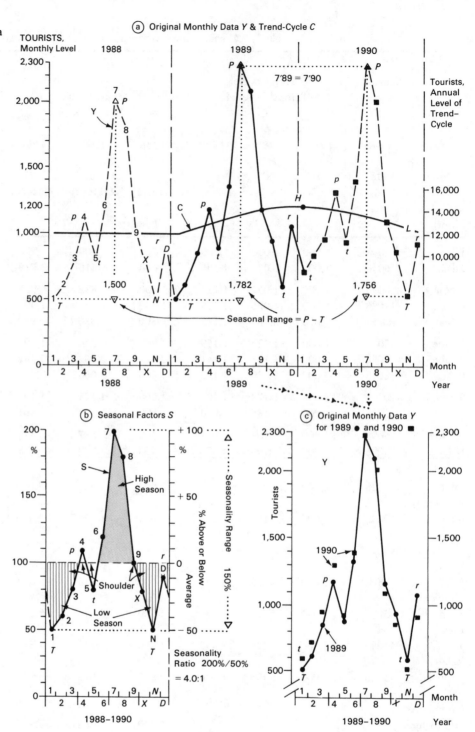

Fig. 3. A seasonal series with a cyclical increase and decrease. For P, p, q, r, T, t, see Table 1.

stable during 1988 at 1,000 tourists per month, totalling 12,000 for the year, then increased from January 1989 by 20% to January 1990, followed by a decrease of 15% to December 1990. The annual total for 1989 was 13,426, a 13% increase over the year 1988, with a further increase to 13,626 in 1990, 1.5% more than 1989 despite the decrease in C in every month from February 1990!

For most tourism, travel, and economic series with strong trends and seasonality, the magnitude of the seasonal effects depends on the level of the trend-cycle (C), which is expressed in the same units as the *original monthly data* (Y), for example, tourists. If the trend-cycle was steady at the level of (say) $C = 1,000$ tourists per month for a specific series and year (say 1988:

Fig. 3 *(continued).*

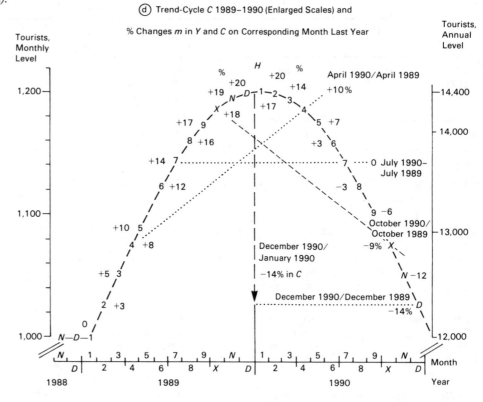

(d) Trend-Cycle *C* 1989–1990 (Enlarged Scales) and

% Changes *m* in *Y* and *C* on Corresponding Month Last Year

column 2 of Table 1 and Figure 3a) and the *irregularities* (*I*) and other components were negligible, then the original data for each month (column 3) would be related to the trend-cycle by twelve *seasonal factors* (*S*) (expressed as percentages), whose average over the year is 100% (column 1: in the other tables each month has a column). For each month this relative seasonal factor would continue more or less constant over the years while the trend-cycle grew or declined, or the seasonal factors might change comparatively slowly, usually because of assignable causes. This is called *multiplicative seasonality* and is expressed algebraically as $Y = C \times S$ (or $Y = C \times S \times I$, if irregularities are taken into account), and implies similar rates of growth in all the seasons (that is, of both high-season and off-season tourists).

As an example, we assume the following seasonal pattern for the 12 months of each year, shown in these tables and graphs by 1, . . . , 9 for January through September, using *X, N, D* for October, November, and December; the data are presented at the midpoints of each month and have a summer peak (Figure 3b). The effects of variations in the number of days of each month should be taken into account for intrinsic seasonal factors *S'* if the activity in each month is affected by its length (Table 2):

- A seasonal trough (indicated by *T*) in January at half the average level, that is, the seasonal factor was 50% (column 1) and the number of tourists was 50% of 1,000 = 500 tourists in January 1988 (column 3), 4.2% of all the tourists in 1988 (the average per month was 8.3%).
- Continuation of the off-season in February with a higher factor of 60% (40% below average), or 600 tourists.
- Increased spring tourism (shoulder): in March *S* 80%, 800 tourists; in April, 1,100 tourists, a secondary peak factor of 110%, 10% above average (indicated *p*); followed by

Table 2. *Analysis of seasonality and trends, X-11 ARIMA program*[a]

Year month	Jan. 1	Feb. 2	Mar. 3	Apr. 4	May 5	June 6	Jul. 7	Aug. 8	Sep. 9	Oct. X	Nov. N	Dec. D	Total year

1. Original data Y (Unadjusted Data, in thousands: A1)[b]

Total year: ΣY

Year	Jan.	Feb.	Mar.	Apr.	May	June	Jul.	Aug.	Sep.	Oct.	Nov.	Dec.	Total
1975	21.8	27.2	49.3	39.9	40.0	40.4	65.3	51.4	41.9	50.9	29.7	51.9	509.7
⋮													
1984	44.3	52.0	74.2	109.6	84.9	79.0	99.6	83.1	75.0	95.4	63.6	75.2	935.9
1985	58.9	75.9	112.0	122.1	96.6	94.5	114.8	89.1	77.2	92.0	67.5	78.7	1,079.3
1986	56.4	64.6	97.6	91.6	72.2	66.5	93.7	76.3	75.9	78.7	71.8	84.3	929.5
⋮													
1989	62.1	71.1	103.4	96.0	93.0	90.0	100.5	84.7	73.9	95.3	78.3	85.1	1,033.4

2. Average per day Y/LM (thousands)[c]

Year	T		P	p		p			t	p		r	Average
1989	2.00	2.54	3.34	3.20	3.00	3.00	3.24	2.73	2.46	3.07	2.61	2.75	2.83

3. Seasonal indices SX (annual average per day = 100)[d]

Seasonal Ratio 1.67

Year	Jan.	Feb.	Mar.	Apr.	May	June	Jul.	Aug.	Sep.	Oct.	Nov.	Dec.	Total
1989	71	90	118	113	106	106	115	97	87	109	92	97	100

4. Current Monthly data Y (thousands)

G (above Aug.); Total

Year	Jan.	Feb.	Mar.	Apr.	May	June	Jul.	Aug.	Sep.	Oct.	Nov.	Dec.	Total
1990	67.8	84.7	109.0	130.2	92.2	82.8	106.3	84.4	51.5	48.5	31.1	44.6	933.1

Conventional comparisons with past data:

5. % change each month on corresponding month of previous year (m)

Year on previous year

Year	Jan.	Feb.	Mar.	Apr.	May	June	Jul.	Aug.	Sep.	Oct.	Nov.	Dec.	Total
1985	33%	46%	51%	11%	14%	20%	15%	7%	3%	−4%	6%	5%	15%
1986	−4%	−15%	−13%	−25%	−25%	−30%	−18%	−14%	−2%	−14%	6%	7%	−14%
⋮													
1989	−12%	−18%	−11%	9%	25%	29%	6%	8%	12%	9%	9%	13%	6%
1990	9%	19%	5%	36%	−1%	−8%	6%	0%G	−30%	−49%	−60%	−48%	−10%

6. Cumulative data, from January of each year (thousands, rounded)

Year	Jan.	Feb.	Mar.	Apr.	May	June	Jul.	Aug.	Sep.	Oct.	Nov.	Dec.	Total
1984	44	96	171	280	365	444	544	627	702	797	861	936	10%
1985	59	135	247	369	466	560	675	764	841	933	1,001	1,079	15%
1986	56	121	219	310	382	449	543	619	695	773	845	930	−14%
⋮													
1989	62	133	237	333	426	516	616	701	775	870	948	1,033	6%
1990	68	153	262	392	484	567	673	757	809	857	889	933	−10%

7. % change of each cumulative on corresponding cumulative of previous year (c)

Year	Jan.	Feb.	Mar.	Apr.	May	June	Jul.	Aug.	Sep.	Oct.	Nov.	Dec.
1985	33%	40%	45%	32%	28%	26%	24%	22%	20%	17%	16%	15%
1986	−4%	−10%	−11%	−16%	−18%	−20%	−20%	−19%	−17%	−17%	−16%	−14%
⋮												
1989	−12%	−15%	−14%	−8%	−2%	2%	3%	3%	4%	5%	5%	6%
1990	9%	14%	11%	18%	14%	10%	9%	8%	4%	−1%	−6%	−10%

8. Festival date adjustments F % (A2)[e]

Year	Jan.	Feb.	Mar.	Apr.	May	June	Jul.	Aug.	Sep.	Oct.	Nov.	Dec.
1985			101.9	95.5						99.0	101.8	
⋮												
1989			104.5	91.7						102.7	94.8	
1990			97.4	106.6						100.1	99.8	

Seasonality

9. Seasonal factors S % (for calendar months: average = 100%: D10)

Average

Year	Jan.	Feb.	Mar.	Apr.	May	June	Jul.	Aug.	Sep.	Oct.	Nov.	Dec.	Average
1975	60.3	76.2	124.6	128.8	99.5	91.4	145.6	113.1	89.4	105.6	73.8	91.0	99.9%
⋮													
1985	66.7	81.9	123.3	132.4	103.8	99.7	125.3	100.8	90.5	105.5	80.2	92.2	100.2%
⋮													
1988	70.5	86.7	123.2	122.9	102.3	97.6	117.6	98.6	86.5	105.7	92.0	97.4	100.1%
1989	70.8	87.1	123.2	121.6	102.4	97.4	116.9	98.8	86.2	105.8	92.1	97.6	100.0%

10. Projections (automatic) of seasonal factors for next year Sf (D10A, %)

Year	Jan.	Feb.	Mar.	Apr.	May	June	Jul.	Aug.	Sep.	Oct.	Nov.	Dec.	Average
1990	71.0	87.3	123.2	120.9	102.4	97.4	116.5	98.8	86.1	105.9	92.2	97.8	100.0%

11. Intrinsic seasonal factors S' % (adjusted for length of month: ave. = 100%)

Seasonality ratio

Year	T		p	p		t	P		t	q		r	ratio
1975	59.2	82.1	122.3	130.6	97.7	92.7	143.0	111.1	90.7	103.7	74.9	89.4	2.41

(continued)

Table 2 *(continued).*

Year month	Jan. 1	Feb. 2	Mar. 3	Apr. 4	May 5	June 6	Jul. 7	Aug. 8	Sep. 9	Oct. X	Nov. N	Dec. D	Total year

11. Intrinsic seasonal factors S' % (cont.)

⋮	T		P	P			p		t	q		r	ratio
1989	69.5	93.8	121.0	123.4	100.5	98.9	114.7	97.0	87.5	103.9	93.5	95.9	1.77
	T 69.5			P 123.4	Seasonality range 53.9%								−26%

12. Changes in seasonality from 1975 to 1989, for each month

	+10.3	+11.7	−1.3	−7.3	+2.9	+6.1	−28.2	−14.1	−3.3	+0.2	+18.5	+6.5	

13. Seasonality relative to average month, S'−100% (rounded)

1989	−30%	−6%	+21%	+23%	+1%	−1%	15%	−3%	−13%	+4%	−7%	−4%	

Seasonally adjusted data and trend (thousands) — Original data, avg. per month

14. Monthly levels, seasonally adjusted: $M = Y / (S \times F) = C \times I$ (D11)[f]

1985	88.4	92.7	89.2	96.6	93.0	94.8	91.6	88.4	86.2	85.6	84.2	85.3	89.9

15. Levels, annualized seasonally adjusted data: $A = 12 \times M$[g] — Original annual totals

Historic				H		H							
1985	1,060	1,113	1,070	1,159	1,116	1,138	1,099	1,061	1,034	1,028	1,010	1,024	1,079
						L							
1986	990	925	935	866	842	805	919	923	991	965	1,004	1,069	930
⋮			L										
1989	1,052	980	964	1,033	1,090	1,108	1,032	1,029	1,002	1,140	1,020	1,046	1,033
Current				H					G		L		
1990	1,146	1,164	1,090	1,212	1,080	1,021	1,095	1,025	717	551	405	547	933

16. Short-term trend: $B = [1,2,1]\, A$[h]

Historic					H								
1985	1,060	1,089	1,103	1,126	1,132	1,123	1,099	1,064	1,039	1,025	1,018	1,012	1,079
					L	L							
1986	982	944	915	877	839	843	891	939	967	981	1,010	1,043	930
⋮			L										
1989	1,002	994	985	1,030	1,080	1,085	1,050	1,023	1,043	1,075	1,056	1,064	1,033
Current				H					G		L	$B'=[1,2]A$	
1990	1,126	1,141	1,139	1,148	1,098	1,054	1,059	965	753	556	477	500	933

17. Monitoring of changes in level A from month to month a (E6: %)[b] — Drop H to L in B −26%

				H		H							
1985	5%	5%	−4%	8%	−4%	2%	−3%	−4%	−2%	−1%	−2%	1%	
						L							
1986	−3%	−7%	1%	−7%	−3%	−4%	14%	0%	7%	−3%	4%	6%	
⋮			L			p				p			
1989	14%	−7%	−2%	7%	6%	2%	−7%	0%	−3%	14%	−11%	3%	
Current				H					G		L		
1990	10%	2%	−6%	11%	−11%	−6%	7%	−6%	−30%	−23%	−26%	[34%]	−58%

18. Relative contributions to variance from month to month (F2, %)

1979–89	S 92.7%,		F 2.2%,		C 0.6%,		I 4.5%						

[a] Example: Tourist arrivals by air in Israel, January 1975–December 1990 (selected years).

[b] Sometimes abbreviated O, or called Raw Data. Tables of the Basic X-11 ARIMA printout are numbered A1, A2 . . . as indicated. Other Tables, see Bar-On 1989 and Fisher 1991.

[c] P, Peak; T, Trough; p, t, secondary peak, trough; r, relative peak.

[d] First approximation to Seasonality (used in Table 4): differ slightly from S' (subtable 11).

Festival	Dates:	Easter	Passover	Jewish New Year	Tabernacles
	1985	Apr 7	Apr 6	Sep 16	Sep 30
	1989	Mar 26	Apr 20	Sep 30	Oct 14
	1990	Apr 15	Apr 10	Sep 20	Oct 4
Highest F	1984	Apr 22	Apr 17 : 117% for April		
Lowest F	1975	Mar 27	Mar 30 : 81% for April	(See Pfefferman and Fisher 1982).	

Other Prior Adjustments possible, for example, for trading-day variation D (Dagum 1990).

[f] The changes comprise changes in the trend-cycle C together with irregularities I and inaccuracies in adjusting for regular seasonality S and F: H, High of trend-cycle over the months; L, Low of trend-cycle over the months; G, Gulf crisis.

[g] The total for the 12 months from the current month if C would remain at about the present level and S approximately as forecast.

[h] Weighted 3-term moving average of A, to smooth irregularities I and inaccuracies: 0.5 weight for the current month, 0.25 for the preceding and subsequent months (Figure 4). For the last month 0.67 weight and 0.33 for the preceding month. X-11 provides a 15-month weighted average C for the trend-cycle (D12) after imputing M for months affected by unusual events U.

- Reduced tourism in May (800), a shoulder trough (indicated t) with S 80%.
- The summer season starting in June ($S = 120\%$, 1,200 tourists), peaking in July P to 2,000 tourists (that is, double the annual average, 16.7% of the annual total) with seasonal factor of 200%, indicated S (P), then decreasing by one-tenth to 180% in August (1,800 tourists). This 3-month peak (or high) season had 5,000 tourists, 41.7% of the annual total.
- September with 1,000 tourists, the average per month in that year. $S = 100\%$ (another shoulder season), decreasing in the late autumn (fall) to 80% (800 tourists) in October.
- Decrease to 50% in November (500 tourists, a trough T as deep as in January).
- Increased tourism in December because of Christmas and other holidays, say 900 tourists, that is $S = 90\%$ (10% less than average), a relative peak (r) compared with November and the following January.

The twelve monthly seasonal factors total 1,200%, that is their average is 100% per month (column 1). The original monthly data of 1988 total 12,000 tourists (column 5), as do the corresponding 12 "levels" of the stable trend-cycle (column 2).

The *seasonality ratio* between the peak month's factor (August, 200%), and the trough (both January and November, 50%) was 4.0 to 1, and in this year was identical to the seasonal ratio between the number of tourists in the peak month of the year (2,000) and in each trough month (500), since the trend was assumed stable.

The *seasonality range* is the difference between the peak and the trough seasonal factors, $200\% - 50\% = 150\%$. The *seasonal range* for the original data was $2,000 - 500 = 1,500$ tourists.

The month-to-month changes in the original monthly data Y of 1988 are the same as the month-to-month changes in the seasonal factors S in this example (because of the stable trend), varying from

+80% for December over November
and +67% for July over June, to
−44% for September relative to August
and for January (1989) relative to December (1988)

The Effects of an Increase and a Cyclical Change in the Trend-Cycle

We now assume that the trend-cycle C of this series increased from January 1989 by 20% to 1,200 tourists per month over the 12 months up to January 1990, followed by a symmetric decrease back to 1,000 tourists per month in January 1991 (possibly as the result of a 4-year sinusoidal cycle—columns 3 and 4 in Table 1 and Figure 3a, c, d). We assume that the multiplicative seasonal factors S (column 1) stayed unchanged over this period, and we neglect irregularities and other factors (for simplicity).

January was the trough month in 1989 too, with 500 tourists (as in January 1988). By February 1989 the trend-cycle C increased by 2.6% to 1,026 tourists (columns 3 and 9), raising the original data $Y = C \times S$ to $1,026 \times 60\% = 616$ tourists (column 6), 2.6% above February 1988 (the corresponding month of the previous year, column 8).

In March 1989 $C = 1,052$, so $Y = 1,052 \times 80\% = 842$, 5.2% above March 1988. In April 1989 $C = 1,076$, $Y = 1,184$ (a secondary peak, as in 1988), in May 1989 $Y = 880$, and in June 1989 $Y = 1,346$.

In July 1989 C reached 1,141 tourists (14% above July 1988), so $Y =$

1,141 × 200% = 2,282, the peak month of 1989. The trend-cycle continued to increase in August through November 1989, while the seasonal factors decreased vis-à-vis July (column 1). In November 1989 $Y = 1,194 \times 50\% = 597$, a secondary trough t (19% above the trough of January 1989, but below May 1989, the shoulder trough).

By December 1989 $C = 1,198$ tourists, nearly 20% above December 1988, but only 0.3% above C for November 1989, as the trend-cycle nears its turning point in January 1990; December is a relative peak (1,078 tourists) as in 1988.

In January 1990 $C = 1,200$ (indicated H for the high point of the trend-cycle) so $Y = 1,200 \times 50\% = 600$, 20% above January 1989 and a secondary trough in 1990 (14% above the trough of 526 tourists in November 1990).

As the trend-cycle dropped, the seasonality continued its role in determining the monthly data. February 1990 had $1,198 \times 60\% = 719$ tourists, 17% above February 1989, and March 1990 had 955. April 1990 was again the secondary peak, with $1,185 \times 110\% = 1,304$ tourists, 10% above the corresponding month in the preceding year (April 1989), despite C having decreased by over 1% in the three months from January 1990.

Similarly, July 1990 was the peak month with 2,282 tourists, the same number as in July 1989 (that is, no change over the corresponding month), while C had dropped by 5% over the six months from the turning point.

August 1990 (with $1,122 \times 180\% = 2,020$ tourists) was the first month to show a decrease on the corresponding month in the previous year, being only 3.2% less than August 1989, while C had decreased by 6.5% in the seven months from January 1990.

By October 1990 we see a decrease of 9% over the corresponding month (October 1989), while C had dropped by 10% in the nine months from the turning point (January 1990). November 1990 was the trough month of 1990 (526 tourists), 12% below November 1989; C had also dropped 12% from January 1990. December 1990 had 923 tourists, 14% less than December 1989 (a similar drop to that in C from January 1990).

The magnitude of the seasonal effects increased as the trend-cycle increased (and vice versa). In this example the seasonal range was $2,000 - 500 = 1,500$ in 1988 (between July and January). In 1989 it increased to $2,282 - 500 = 1,782$, and in 1990 was 1,756 tourists (between August and November). The seasonal ratio also increased from 4.0 in 1988 to $2,282 / 500 = 4.6$ in 1989, and to 4.3 in 1990 (because of the changes in the trend-cycle).

For some series the seasonal differences are constant, for example, each January would have 500 tourists less than the annual average per month and each July 1,000 tourists more than the average. The seasonal range would then remain constant at $2,000 - 500 = 1,500$ tourists, but the seasonal ratio would fluctuate according to changes in the trend-cycle. This is called *additive seasonality* and is expressed algebraically as $Y = C + S + I$, where S and I are in the same units as Y (positive or negative, not in %), totaling 0 each year.

For many series the seasonal factors alter to some extent over the years, as a result of changes in conditions and/or in policies (of the organization concerned and/or of supplementary and competing organizations), causing differential growth among the seasons and/or changes in the relative importance of subseries with different seasonality (for example, by market segments, see Table 3 and Bar-On 1973, 1975, 1978, 1984).

Computer analysis can identify and measure changes in multiplicative S (Tables 2 and 3) or in additive seasonality.

Table 3. *Intrinsic seasonal factors and ratios for tourism series and subseries[a]*

Series	Month 1 Jan.	2 Feb.	3 Mar. F	4 Apr. F	5 May	6 June	7 July	8 Aug.	9 Sep. F	X Oct. P[b]	N Nov.	D Dec.	1975 Peak: trough months, seasonal factors	Seasonality ratio S(P)/S(T)[c] 1989	1975	MUS 1989	Annual 1975, % 1989 change 1989/1975 (thousands)		Volume subseries as % of total 1989	1975
																				Intrinsic seasonal factors S' 1989

A. Tourist arrivals by air[d]

Series	Jan	Feb	Mar	Apr	May	June	July	Aug	Sep	Oct	Nov	Dec	1975 P:T	S(P)/S(T) 1989	1975	MUS 1989	Annual (thousands)	1989 change	Vol % 1989	1975
	T		P	P			þ		q		r		7 m 1				508 (×2.0)			100%
Total	70	94	121	123	101	99	115	97	87	104	93	96	143 + 59 +	1.77	2.41	81%	1,033	103%	100%	
	T					P	P		q		r		7 m 1				144			28.3%
From: U.S.A.	71	78	94	91	95	156	146	105	86	102	82	91	141 + 59 +	2.21	2.39	64%	238	66%	23.1%	
	T			þ		t	P	P			r		8 1				66			13.0%
France	62	98	115	142	97	70	164	157	65	72	76	80	229 + 44 +	2.63	5.16	61%	129	94%	12.5%	
	T			P		T	r	r	1 þ	q			7 m 1				46 (×2.7)			9.1%
U.K.	72	94	123	131	106	71	97	96	87	118	101	105	149 + 59 +	1.83	2.53	76%	126	173%	12.2%	
	t		P				T		þ				3 1 m				36 (×3.1)			7.1%
Germany F.R.	66	106	197	143	106	66	66	54	72	126	113	84	192 − 45 +	3.67	4.29	51%	113	212%	10.9%	
Nordic			P		t			T			þ		3 8				28 (×2.5)			5.4%
Countries	92	136	175	151	58	71	51	47	77	112	123	112	186 + 51 −	3.75	3.63	57%	68	146%	6.6%	
Central and	þ		t			þ	t	P		T			1 m N				25			4.9%
South America	118	77	73	106	116	99	119	84	141	99	66	100	186 + 50 +	2.12	3.70	71%	35	40%	3.4%	
Australia and	T		þ	þ			t		þ		t	P D	2				10			2.0%
New Zealand	111	63	89	123	121	102	73	77	111	95	81	150	162 + 68 −	2.38	2.39	67%	14	43%	1.4%	
																Total 7 Countries			70%	70%

B. Person-nights in tourist hotels[e]

Series	Jan	Feb	Mar	Apr	May	June	July	Aug	Sep	Oct	Nov	Dec	1975 P:T	S(P)/S(T) 1989	1975	MUS 1989	Annual (thousands)	1989 change	Vol % 1989	1975
	t			P		t	r	r	T	þ	þ		4 1 m				3,944		1989% of TNH TourN	
Tourists-Total	86	95	120	135	110	81	97	97	73	110	109	88	141 − 68 +	1.84	2.08	74%	6,565	66%	100%	56%
	T			þ			r	r	t	þ			4 m 1				1,200		of Resort	
Jerusalem	75	86	117	129	112	90	97	95	86	130	102	78	141 − 68 +	1.73	2.08	77%	1,826	52%	27.8%	79%
	T			P			P		t	þ			4 1				1,167			
Tel Aviv-Yafo	79	80	93	122	115	102	113	124	85	108	94	83	130 − 77	1.56	1.68	82%	1,500	29%	22.8%	77%
	P					T			T	þ			3 m 6				235 (×4.3)			
Elat	172	176	162	126	53	28	33	36	27	63	170	160	160 + 38 −	6.44	4.17	57%	1,017	333%	15.5%	43%
					þ			P	t	þ	T		8 1 m				274			
Netanya	62	79	86	114	136	100	124	147	93	118	86	54	172 − 39 +	2.72	4.39	68%	423	54%	6.4%	61%
	T			P					t	þ			4 1				159 (×2.5)			
Tiberias	60	102	141	173	119	70	92	80	71	127	102	65	174 − 55 +	2.89	3.18	58%	402	153%	6.1%	31%
	T			P				t	þ				4 7 m				45 (×6.3)			
Dead Sea	54	72	139	172	147	89	78	70	83	119	112	65	171 56 −	3.19	3.06	58%	283	534%	4.3%	46%
Total, by Grade[f]																Total 6 Resorts			83%	
	T			P			þ	t	þ				4 1				1,139			
Five star	72	75	97	132	115	98	112	114	80	125	95	83	136 + 62 −	1.84	2.18	76%	2,179	91%	33.2%	
	T			þ			þ	t	P				8 m N m				118 (×2.8)			
Holiday Villages	67	89	131	129	107	82	115	81	90	97	138	79	265 + 33 +	2.06	8.14	73%	325	176%	4.9%	
	T						P			t	r		8 1				2,401 (×2.2)		1989% of INH +SFN	
Israelis-Total[g]	62	67	69	90	88	114	154	201	117	99	65	70	215 + 58 +	3.23	3.73	50%	5,163	115%	100%	44%
	r				T			P		T	r		8 1 m				245		of Resort	
Jerusalem	82	78	80	84	72	98	128	232	109	81	71	82	262 + 67 +	3.29	3.92	43%	484	98%	9.4%	21%
				t	t			P		T	r		8 4 m				194 (x2.3)			
Tel Aviv-Yafo	88	93	90	82	82	102	116	171	114	87	81	91	139 − 81	2.12	1.73	58%	454	134%	8.8%	23%
	T	T					P						8 1				461 (×3.0)			
Elat	40	40	54	97	112	129	183	205	124	117	50	46	184 − 53 −	5.13	3.47	49%	1,372	198%	26.6%	57%
	t			q	t	P	P			T	r		8 11				179			
Netanya	61	63	77	104	66	118	186	190	124	82	56	70	268 + 32 +	3.37	8.27	53%	273	52%	5.3%	39%
	r							P		r	T		2 m 6 m				207 (×4.2)			
Tiberias	85	90	85	89	80	109	148	191	83	92	67	78	172 − 59 −	2.86	2.93	52%	879	325%	17.0%	69%
	t	r	T					P	t	þ			X m 1 m				181			
Dead Sea	92	100	73	85	98	114	112	124	92	118	97	97	142 + 68 +	1.71	2.10	80%	338	87%	6.6%	54%
																Total 6 Resorts			74%	
Tourists and Israelis	T			þ		t			P	t	þ						6,345			
Total	76	84	100	114	101	96	123	141	92	104	88	80	136 + 68 +	1.41	2.02	71%	11,728	85%		

Abbreviations: Seasonality: *P*, peak; *p* secondary peak (S', 105%); *q*, other high month (100% < S' < 105%, noncontiguous); *T*, trough; *t*, secondary trough; *r*, relative peak (S < 100%); *F*, affected by festival dates. Changes in seasonal peaks and troughs from 1975 to 1989: +, improved significantly; −, worsened; *m*, moved to another month (indicated).
[a]Examples: Arrivals by air (by origin) and nights at hotels (origin and destination) for Israel.
[b]X-11 ARIMA analysis 1975–1989: adjusted for length of month and festival dates: average S' each year = 100%.
[c]Maximal utilization constrained by seasonality = 1/S'(P) (see Bar-On 1975a).
[d]Principal countries of residence, in order of arrivals 1989.
[e]Principal resorts, in order of tourists' nights TNH 1989.
[f]For 1987: re-graded in 1988–1989.
[g]INH: mainly domestic tourism: includes routine business, etc.

Comparisons of each month's original data with the *corresponding month of the preceding year* are widely used, since they eliminate the effects of multiplicative seasonality (unless there has been a considerable change in the seasonal pattern since the preceding year) and are useful when the trend is increasing (or decreasing) at a more or less constant rate over two or more years (exponential or "compound interest" growth or decline). The comparison with the corresponding month of the preceding year (sometimes called the "same month last year") does not eliminate significant festival-date F or trading-day effects D or high irregularities I, especially if one (or both) of the months compared is affected by an unusual event U. In some cases comparisons are also made with the corresponding month two (or more) years ago, especially with previous high (or low) months.

The preceding example and Table 2 show that these comparisons may provide very misleading measures of the changes in the trend-cycle over the previous few months, especially in the vicinity of a turning point, when it is most vital to carefully monitor changes in C.

In order to minimize seasonal, irregular, and other effects, comparisons are often made of the *cumulative* from January of each year to that of the preceding year (or from the start of a summer or winter season). For the example in Table 1, in January to June 1989 there were 5,368 tourists, 7% above the corresponding six months of 1988, while C had risen by over 12% from January to June 1989. Similarly, in January to June 1990 there were 5,907 tourists, 10% above January to June 1989, despite the trend-cycle's *decrease* from January 1990. After the peak month, July, the 1990 cumulative was still 7% above that for 1989, despite the drop of C for six months (3.4%). Even by November 1990, after the 10 months' drop of C by 12% from January 1990, the 1990 cumulative was 2% above that of 1989. By the end of 1990 the cumulative was 13,619 tourists, identical to the annual total and still 0.6% above that for 1989, despite the trend-cycle's drop of 14% to December 1990.

The simplest presentation of trend-cycle and of the seasonality of the original monthly series around it is by use of a 12-month moving average. This average cannot be calculated for the last six months (usually of greatest interest) or for the first six months, and can mislead as to the timing and magnitude of cyclical and unusual changes (Bar-On 1973).

Computer Analysis of Monthly Series

Computer programs have been developed over the last 35 years to analyze monthly (and quarterly) series into the previously given components, taking into account changes in the seasonal pattern over the years. The best known is X-11, developed at the U.S. Bureau of the Census (by Julius Shiskin and others, see Shiskin et al. 1969), which uses reiterated moving averages and ratios and identifies extreme months.

In the frequency domain the original monthly data Y may be regarded as the combined effects of sinusoidal cycles whose periods are 12 months, together with cycles of shorter periods (2, 2.4, 3, 4, and 6 months, which correspond to the seasonal frequencies) and longer cycles for the trend-cycle (especially 18, 24, 36, and 72 months), which are studied by spectral analysis, which is similar to the analysis of light and of chemicals that show power at specific wavelengths. Random irregularity should show a spectrum of equal power at all frequencies, called *white noise* (analogous to radio signals: white light is a mixture of all spectral frequencies). The interrelationship of seasonality in two series can be studied by cross-spectral analysis, including leads or lags (Bar-On 1973a: Chapter II.7 gives further details, illustrated by an example of Tourist Arrivals by Air in Israel, 1956–1970, for which a detailed X-11 analysis is shown).

Another approach is to analyze the correlations between data 12 months apart (and possibly 24 or 6 months apart) and those of successive months (and possibly 13 months apart) for seasonality and trend-cycles. Auto-Regressive Integrated Moving Average techniques (ARIMA, sometimes called Box-Jenkins techniques) are used. A powerful program X-11 ARIMA developed by Statistics Canada combines the advantages of both techniques and provides ARIMA forecasts of the monthly data for the next 12 months. The latest version X11 ARIMA/88 Seasonal Adjustment Method is available from Statistics Canada for personal computers (see Dagum 1990). Detailed definitions and explanations are presented in Bar-On 1978, comparing X-11 techniques with ARIMA (with a month-by-month analysis of tourist arrivals by air in Israel for 1956 to 1976), and Bar-On 1989 contains an example of analysis covering 1975 to 1986 and forecasting tourist arrivals from the United States in Israel for 1987. Improvements have been introduced by Praedicta, especially for use with data banks of original monthly series, for festival date adjustments and short-term trends and for forecasting under different assumptions (Fisher and Bar-On 1991).

Breaking a monthly series down into its components should be carried out in conjunction with appropriate sub- and related series plus a diary of events that might have affected the series. This enables

1. The measurement of the seasonal pattern (S) for each month of each year and its relationship with other series and changes over the years analyzed
2. Month-by-month analysis of the historic trend-cycles (C), which can be studied in relation to the policies and events that affected growth and other changes
3. Forecasting of the seasonal factors for one or more years in advance. The program projects S for the last 12 months ahead (for the next 12 months) by adding half of the change calculated from the corresponding S of the year before (Table 2). Other forecasts are possible, for example, when policies and tactics are planned that should decrease seasonal peaks or raise troughs, or affect the relative importance of subseries with different seasonality (for example, an increase of golden-age tourists, see Table 4).
4. Speedy analysis each month of the current level of the trend-cycle for each series (usually based on the in-depth analysis once a year, to December).
5. Forecasting of the trend-cycle (C) and of the monthly data Y for each series, for at least 12 months ahead (Var and Lee 1991)

Table 2 presents an example of the X-11 analysis of a seasonal monthly series, tourist arrivals by air in Israel from 1975 to 1989, followed an analysis for 1990. This series has been analyzed every year since 1962 (Bar-On 1963, 1969, 1971, 1973a, 1975a, 1978, 1984), together with the subseries for the 12 principal countries and regions of origin (Table 3). The subtables show

1. Original (unadjusted) data (Y), for the 12 months of each year, with annual totals. We present in this subtable data for 1975, 1984–1986, and 1989 only (for simplicity), and in Figure 4 for 1985–1986 (with "flags" added manually for the seasonal peaks and troughs).

Table 4. *Seasonal indices and ratios for selected series, 1989[a]*

Month / Series	1 Jan.	2 Feb.	3 Mar.	4 Apr.	5 May	6 June	7 July	8 Aug.	9 Sep.	X Oct.	N Nov.	D Dec.	SX(P)/ SX(T)	MUS[c]	Number of peak seasons[d]
						Seasonal indices SX 1989[b]									
A. Tourist Arrivals in Israel: Selected Age Groups															
(markers)	t			þ	t		P		r	T		þ			
15–19	52	64	94	110	68	133	214	152	60	84	45	118	4.7	47%	3
(markers)	T		P												
30–44	80	91	113	106	101	109	109	98	86	105	100	101	1.4	88%	2
(markers)	T			P			t	t		þ					
65 and over	61	89	130	163	136	87	63	64	103	130	105	68	2.7	61%	2
(markers)	T		P	P			þ		t	þ					
Total (all ages) foreign tourist arrivals	72	89	116	114	105	104	113	100	89	109	92	95	1.6	86%	3
B. For Selected Countries, by Continent[e]															
Africa — Egypt															
(markers)	T		q		t		P	P							
Foreign visitor arrivals	76	81	103	85	79	85	125	122	105	123	103	110	1.6	80%	1
Americas — Bermuda															
(markers)	T					P									
Visitor arrivals	26	50	89	107	130	144	134	139	115	117	90	54	5.5	69%	1
Jamaica															
(markers)			þ		t		þ		T			P			
Tourist arrivals	94	114	121	97	87	100	113	107	71	75	96	125	1.8	80%	3
U.S.A.															
(markers)	T	T	q		t		P								
Tourist arrivals	72	73	101	94	91	96	154	148	109	94	83	84	2.1	65%	1
Canada															
(markers)	T						P								
TF 1988	38	50	48	64	100	145	223	201	137	79	55	55	5.9	45%	1
Asia — Hong Hong															
(markers)		t		P			T			þ					
Visitor arrivals	95	91	113	126	117	87	83	89	94	105	100	99	1.5	80%	2
Japan															
(markers)	T		q			t	þ			P					
Foreign visitor arrivals	76	89	93	104	99	94	115	108	106	125	104	85	1.6	80%	1+
Singapore															
(markers)	t		r		T			þ				P			
Foreign visitor arrivals	93	96	99	95	89	92	106	108	102	103	107	110	1.2	91%	1
Thailand															
(markers)		þ				T		r	t			þ			
Foreign tourist arrivals	91	117	101	94	87	85	101	104	87	96	114	123	1.4	82%	2
Europe — Austria															
(markers)	þ			t			P	P		T					
TN, Accom. Reporting	145	103	150	37	55	81	194	199	109	42	16	63	12.1	50%	2
Greece															
(markers)	T	T						P							
Foreign tourist arrivals	15	17	43	82	141	161	214	222	163	87	29	19	14.5	45%	1
Italy															
(markers)	T						P	P							
Foreign visitor arrivals	56	62	83	80	109	107	163	169	122	100	72	73	3.0	59%	1
(markers)	t						P		þ			T			
Nights in hotels — Tourists	36	51	86	80	133	144	177	146	164	106	42	32	5.5	56%	1+
(markers)	T							P				T			
Italians	58	62	78	79	69	115	180	249	128	67	52	58	4.3	40%	1
Spain															
(markers)	T	T						P			t	r			
Foreign visitor arrivals	56	56	70	73	93	103	185	215	128	88	58	69	3.8	47%	1

(continued)

Table 4 *(continued).*

Month Series	1 Jan.	2 Feb.	3 Mar.	4 Apr.	5 May	6 June	7 July	8 Aug.	9 Sep.	X Oct.	N Nov.	D Dec.	Seasonal ratio $SX(P)/SX(T)$	MUS[c]	Number of peak seasons[d]
					Seasonal indices SX 1989[b]										

B. For Selected Countries, by Continent[e] (cont.)

Europe (cont.)

Series	1 Jan.	2 Feb.	3 Mar.	4 Apr.	5 May	6 June	7 July	8 Aug.	9 Sep.	X Oct.	N Nov.	D Dec.	$SX(P)/SX(T)$	MUS	peak seasons
Switzerland		*q*	*t*				*P*			*T*					
TN at hotels	79	102	72	86	108	148	163	126	80	42	66	64	3.8	61%	1
U.K.															
Visitors from		*T*	*r*					*P*							
overseas	78	66	92	89	92	107	141	154	115	99	84	79	2.0	65%	1
	T							*P*				*T*			
Visits abroad	66	69	79	84	92	125	128	168	153	115	65	54	3.1	60%	1
Oceania															
Australia															
Visitor arrivals		*p*			*T*		*p*					*P*			
1988	84	105	97	87	82	89	106	103	97	109	113	129	1.2	94%	1

Abbreviations. Seasonality: *P,* peak; *p,* secondary peak, *SX* > 105; *q,* other high month (100 < *SX* < 105, not adjacent); *r,* relative peak (*SX* < 100); *T,* trough; *t,* secondary trough.

[a]Tourists to Israel by age group, international tourism to 16 countries.

[b]Adjusted for length of month, average = 100%. Approximation for intrinsic seasonal factors *S'*, but may be affected by trend-cycle, festival dates, and irregularities. Easter Sunday March 26, 1989 (April 15, 1990).

[c]Maximal utilization constrained by seasonality: MUS = 1 / *SX(P)*.

[d]1 + seasons: single high season, but *p* not adjacent to *P*: adjacent peak month indicated only if *SX* is approximately *SX(P)*.

[e]*TF,* tourist arrivals at frontiers; *TN,* tourist nights (from abroad); *V,* visitor arrivals (at frontiers).

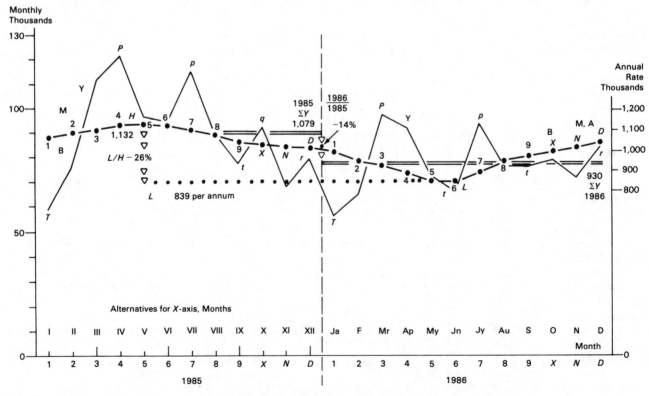

Fig.4. Original monthly data, seasonally adjusted levels, and short-term trend:
Tourist arrivals by air in Israel, 1985–1986. Abbreviations: *Y,* original monthly data;
ΣY, annual total. Seasonally adjusted data each month: *M,* monthly level;
A, annualized level (rate per annum); *B,* short-term trend; *H,* high; *L,* low.
For *P, p, q, r, T, t,* see Table 1.

The total for 1985 ΣY was 935,900 (averaging 89,900 per month, Y) and for 1986 1,079,300 (77,500 per month, Y).

2. Average per day (Y/LM) for 1989, adjusted for the length of each month (28, 30, or 31 days), to illustrate seasonal and other differences in 1989. Trading day factors could be used as a "prior adjustment" (Dagum 1990).

3. Seasonal indexes (SX) for 1989, where the average per day over the year—2,831 tourists—is set at 100. These indexes (and subtable 2) show a trough T 71 in January, a peak P 118 in March, with April slightly lower (113), and secondary peaks p in July and October (115 and 109, respectively), with a secondary trough t in September (87), and a relative peak r in December (less than 100, but higher than November and January). The seasonal ratio P/T was 3.34/2.00 = 118/71 = 1.67. The magnitudes of P, p, T, t, and r in each year are affected by the trend-cycle (C), festival-date effects (F), and irregularities (I).

4. The monthly data (Y) for 1990, affected especially from August by the Gulf crisis.

Conventional Comparisons
with Past Data

5. Percent change each month compared with the corresponding month of the previous year m. March 1985 was 51% above March 1984 (due partly to the differences in the dates of Easter and Passover), continuing positive until September 1985 (+3%), although the trend-cycle dropped after June 1985 because of international terrorism in the Spring of 1985 (subtable 15). The last column shows that the total for the year 1985 was 15% above 1984's total, followed by a decrease of 14% in the total for 1986.

6. Cumulative data from January of each year.

7. Percent change of each cumulative compared with the corresponding cumulative of the preceding year c. In 1985 these cumulatives vary from +45% in March to +15% in December, despite the decrease in the trend.

8. Festival-date adjustments F for the effects of the changes in the dates of Easter (which affect many tourism series throughout the world), Passover, and the Jewish Festivals in September–October (Pfefferman and Fisher 1982): the maximum for these adjustments was 117%.

Seasonality

9. Seasonal factors (S) for each month are calculated by smoothing $S \times I = Y / (C \times F)$ in a complex series of iterations to estimate and adjust for the changes in trend-cycle (C) and irregularities (I), identifying the data for the months with the most and the least, and excluding them from the sliding averages used to estimate S for each month over the years in question. For 1989 the lowest was 70.8% for January and the highest 123.2% for March: their average over each year was limited to 100%.

10. Projections (Sf) for the next year (1990), calculated as S (1989) + half the change from S (1988), for example, for January 1990 70.8 + (70.8 − 70.5)/2 = 71.0%.

11. Intrinsic seasonal factors $S' = S/LM$, which takes into account the length of each month (using 28.25 days for each February. More precise trading-day factors D can be used, which will also distinguish

leap-year Februaries with 29 days). These are shown here only for 1975 and 1989, followed by the next two items.

12. Changes in S' from 1975 to 1989.
13. Seasonality relative to the average month, $S' - 100\%$. Stages 5 to 7 and 11 to 13 are additions to the Canadian X11 ARIMA/88 Program (Fisher and Bar-On 1991).

We see trough T, which was 59% in January 1975, improving to nearly 70% by 1989 (but still 30% below average in 1989); a peak P of 143% in July 1975 decreasing to 115% in July 1989, when the peak was 123% in April (less than the secondary peak p of 131% in April 1975) and 121% in March (slightly less than in 1975, when it was 122%).

Secondary troughs t of 93% in June 1975 improved to 99% in 1989, and those of 91% in September deepened to 88% in 1989. May (100.5%) and June form a shoulder season. October showed an S' of 104% in both 1975 and 1989, which is not continuous with the summer high season (we call such months with $100\% < S' < 105\%$ "another high month" q), forming the fall shoulder season, which is affected by festival dates, with September.

December's S' was 89% in 1975, improving to 96% in 1989 due to the increase in winter tourism: relative peaks r in comparison with November (94% in 1989, improved from 75% in 1975) and the following January, due partly to Christmas arrivals (see Figure 5), though still under the average (by 4% in 1989).

The *seasonality ratio* (S.R.) between S' (P) and S' (T) was 2.41 in 1975, improving to 1.77 in 1989 because of the changes just mentioned. Also, the

Fig. 5. Microseasonality: Weekly sliding averages of daily data for multiperiodic series—tourist arrivals and departures by air at Tel Aviv Airport, 1986. Ratios of highest to lowest week: Arrivals $h/l = 27.7/8.8$ thousand $= 3.15$; departures $H/L = 30.8/7.8$ thousand $= 3.95$. Abbreviations: Festivals: Arrivals high before: C, Christmas; P, Passover; A, Day of Atonement. Departures after: E, Easter; T, Tabernacles; N, New Year. Summer peaks: s, arrivals; S, departures.

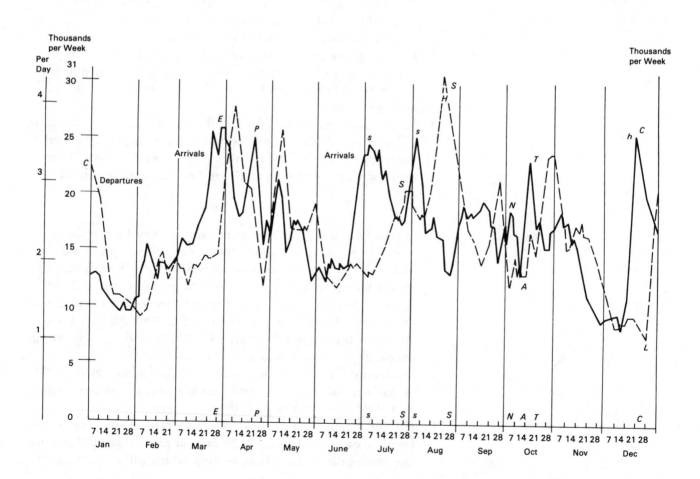

seasonality range (Sr) decreased from 84% in 1975 to 54% in 1989. The absolute seasonal range between the peak and trough months' original data decreased from 43,500 in 1975 to 41,300 in 1989, despite the doubling of the annual total.

Another useful measure is the *maximal utilization constrained by seasonality* (MUS or M.U.S.), calculated as $1 / S' (P)$, that is, 0.81 or 81% for 1989, which is the maximal use of the year-round supply needed for the peak month when demand varies according to the previously discussed seasonal pattern. Actual use of MUS will depend on the possibilities of spreading supply over the months and occupancy during the peak month (affected by peak days, Stage 5). Its complement is called the *seasonal underutilization factor* (SUF), $100 - 81 = 19\%$ in this example (Bar-On 1975).

Seasonal adjustment of the original data provides

14. Monthly deseasonalized data $M = Y / (S \times F) = C \times I$, that is, the trend-cycle level for each month as perturbed by irregularities (I). For January 1985, for example, $M = 58,900/66.7\% = 88,400$ tourists (in Figure 4 the left-hand scale is for the monthly data and the right-hand scale is for annual data and rates: the months of each year are indicated by $1, \ldots, 9, X, N, D$).

15. For activity series that accumulate over the months, it is often better to present annualized seasonally–adjusted "Levels" $A = 12 \times M$, or $12 \times 88,400 = 1,060$ thousand (1.06 million) for January 1985, the annual total that would have resulted if the trend had continued stable at this level for the following 11 months (up to December 1985) with the above seasonality, and so on: In unusual periods this should be regarded only as a guide to changes. This subtable and Figure 4 present A for 1985–1986. The decreases were mainly due to the effects of international terrorism against tourists (especially from the United States) from spring 1985 (Bar-On 1990 presents a detailed monthly analysis for tourism from the United States and Canada to Israel, with comparisons with travel from North America to thirty European and Mediterranean countries, and to other destinations during 1985 to 1987). Similarly for the effects of the Gulf crisis from August 1990. The highest level in 1989–1990 was 1.21 million in April 1990, dropping to about 410,000 by November, with some recovery in December 1990.

16. In the X-11 program one uses the Henderson weighted 15-term sliding average, after assigning M for extreme months, to smooth seasonally adjusted data for successive months to show the underlying trend-cycle C. For short-term trends the average number of *months for cyclical dominance* (MCD) is calculated (from 1 for very regular series up to 6 months), then a uniformly weighted sliding average of M over this span (up to MCD/2 months from the last month analyzed) is determined. In subtable 16 we use instead a centered 3-month sliding average of A, with weights [1, 2, 1] to smooth most of the irregularities in the seasonally adjusted levels; we call this the *short-term trend* (B) (Bar-On 1973a, 1978). The highest levels H of A were in April 1985 (about 1,159 thousand per annum, after adjusting for festival dates) and in June 1985 (1,138 thousand per annum), while the lowest level L was 805 thousand per annum in June 1986 (Figure 4 shows this curve, with points for A, subtable 15). The conventional comparisons with the corresponding month

of the previous year (subtable 5) continued to show increases over 1984 up to September 1985, and decreases from 1985 up to December 1986. For the last month analyzed we use the [1,2] average of the last two months as a preliminary measure B', unless it shows a considerable unusual change.

17. The monitoring of changes in the level A from month to month a%. These were positive for January, February, and April 1985 (the decrease in March 1985 may be due to inaccuracies in adjusting for the complex festival effects; see Figure 5). May was 4% below April, with a 2% increase to June 1985, followed by decreases through June 1986 (apart from small increases in December 1985 and March 1986, which are smoothed by B). The changes in B from month to month are not calculated, since consecutive B's are correlated. Changes in B over longer periods are useful measures of changes in C and U, for example, the 26% drop in B from a high H of 1,132 thousand in May 1985 (averaging A for April–June 1985) to a low L of 839 thousand in May 1986 (calculated from A for April–June). This drop is shown in Figure 4 and in the last column of this subtable. It was mainly due to international terrorism and was followed by a rapid recovery to 1,043 thousand in December 1986 (24% up on L, but still 8% less than H) and throughout 1987 (not shown). The annual total for 1986 was 14% less than for 1985, since both annual totals comprise levels higher and lower than these turning points. Similarly, there was a 58% drop from May to November 1990 (the Gulf crisis), while the total for 1990 was only 10% less than for 1989.

18. Summary measures. X-11 calculates many statistical measures for the series, especially the relative contributions of the components to the variance of month-to-month changes—seasonality 92.7%, festival-date factors 2.2% (both calendar effects that can be adjusted by X-11 nearly 95%), trend-cycle 0.6% from month to month (the considerable changes in C outweigh S and I over longer spans), and irregularities 4.5% (much higher for specific months).

Daily Series and Microseasonality

Most travel series and most hospitality series are collected on a daily basis (usually from midnight, to link with the calendar date), although monthly summaries may only be reported to management and to the Tourism Statistics System (some countries require the daily hotel data to be submitted together with the monthly totals, UNSO 1978).

Daily data Y can easily be analyzed and plotted by a computer.

Calculation of a seven-day moving total V, that is, the sum of the data for January 1 to January 7, followed by January 2 to 8, and so on.

Calculation of the corresponding weekly sliding average (W), that is, one seventh of the sliding total (V): W for January 1 to 7 should be displayed in a table or chart at the midpoint Jan 4, and so on.

These calculations smooth out the *trading day factors* (D) relating to the differential activity on Sunday, Monday, and succeeding days and much of the *irregularity* (I) in daily series. The average W can be presented for each series in a graph whose horizontal scale is 365 days, by month (366 in leap years): for January 1 to 3, data for the end of the previous year should be used to complete the graph (and similarly December 29 to 31 data for the succeeding January 1–3).

An example of tourist arrivals by air at Tel Aviv airport 1986 is presented in Figure 5, showing the microseasonality. A strong peak is seen at the end of March before Easter (*E*) and in mid-April before Passover (*P*). In the summer season there were two peaks of *W*, one at the end of June through early July, and the other at the beginning of August (both indicated *s*). There is a sharp peak before Christmas (*C*), and small peaks before the Jewish New Year and Tabernacles festivals (*N, T*). The week with the highest number was December 21 to 27 with 27,660 arrivals, 3.15 times the week with the lowest number, December 6 to 12 with 8,801 arrivals (only 15 days before), while the ratio of the highest month, July (93,465 arrivals), to January (46,923) was 1.99 to 1. Table 2 includes arrivals at Elat airport (mainly for the winter sun) and at Jerusalem. The day with the highest number was the Sunday before Christmas (December 21), with 6,565 arrivals, 12.5 times the day with the lowest number, Saturday January 25, with 524 arrivals (IMT/CBS 1987). Such days can also be indicated on the chart.

The graph also shows tourist departures by air at Tel Aviv for the same year. The seasonality of departures shows a very high peak *S* at the end of August, when most of the summer tourists depart, including many who arrived in July: the peak *S* at the end of July is lower. Other peaks can be seen following the festivals, for example, in January (departures of Christmas tourists), and following *E, P, N*, and *T*. On the Day of Atonement (*A*) the airport is closed and El Al flights restricted before and after, showing a dip between *N* and *T* for both series.

Daily activity ratios (DAR) can be calculated as *Y/W* for each day and tabulated and plotted separately for each day of the week. *Trading day ratios* (TDR) can then be calculated for each season, excluding unusual days (for example, those close to the festivals or that are affected by a large conference or other unusual event). In this example Sundays average 1.71 times the average over all regular days, and Saturdays 0.43 times the average, with variations over the seasons (IMT/CBS 1987). These averages can be used to improve the X11 analysis [see Bar-On 1973 and 1989, pp. 66–70, from which the graph is copied (with thanks to Euromonitor, London), and which provides the detailed data and calculations].

The demand on peak days may be considerably higher than the average for that month, even if it is the peak month. For example, on the eve of Passover April 9, 1990 (which was in the Holy Week for Catholics and Protestants, with Easter Sunday April 15) the room occupancy in tourist hotels in Israel was 81% (national average), which was 14% above the average over all of April 1990, which was 72%. In Netanya 91% (because of Passover rather than Easter), 38% above all of April's 66%; in Tiberias 86% (28% above April's overall 68%), and in Jerusalem 75% (6% above April's total of 71%). These are all explainable by the characteristics of international and domestic tourists' stay. On the other hand, occupancy in Elat on April 9 was 83%, 5% less than the average for April 1990.

Seasonality in Tourism and Hospitality Series

Table 3 presents the seasonal pattern and summary measures for some Israel series, showing that almost every month is a peak month for some series and the considerable differences in seasonality.

The peak months for tourist arrivals from the United States were June and July (1989 intrinsic seasonal factors P were 156% and 146%), with October slightly above average (with a q of 102%) and a relative peak in December (r of 91%), compared with November's 82% and the trough (T) in January of 71%. For 1975 the peak was in July (141%), while the trough in January was a much deeper 59%. Thus the seasonality ratio improved from 2.39 in 1975 to 2.21 in 1989. The peaks from France were higher, that is, 164% in July and 157% in August (similar peaks are seen in French arrivals in other countries as well as in domestic tourism), with a secondary peak in the spring (April's 164%). The trough in January (62%) was deeper than from the United States, as was December r. For August 1975 P was 229% and T 44%, so the seasonality ratio decreased from 5.16 to 2.63. Tourists from the United Kingdom had spring peaks, with July and August slightly under 100% and December 105%, producing the lowest SR of these series (1.83). German tourists and those from the Nordic countries (Scandinavia and Finland) had higher spring peaks and lower summer tourism. Tourists from Central and South America had their peak in September, with secondary peaks in January (their summer vacations), May, and July. Australia and New Zealand showed similar peaks in December and January, April and May, and September.

Tourists' Hotel Nights: The total number of nights spent in hotels by tourists peaked in March and April (135%) and in October and November (110%), which corollates with the arrivals by air analyzed previously (but with some lag, since the average stay for hotel tourists was 10 nights: also, March, April, and October are affected by festival dates). In July and August the peaks are less than 100% (many summer tourists do not stay in hotels). In Jerusalem the pattern was similar, with peaks for the festivals, while in Tel Aviv–Yafo there were also peaks in July and August (124%), and the seasonality ratio was only 1.56 (due partly to conference and other business tourists). Elat (on the Red Sea) showed peaks from November through April caused by winter charter programs, with troughs in June and September of 27%, giving a seasonality ratio of 6.44. Netanya (on the Mediterranean) had peaks in spring, summer, and October. Tiberias (on the Sea of Galilee) peaked in the spring and fall, as did tourists' nights at the Dead Sea (including psoriasis patients for sun therapy).

Tourists' nights in five-star hotels peaked in spring, summer, and fall: They formed 80% of all nights in this category. April's peak of 132% caused the MUS for tourists to be 76% (individual hotels had higher or lower MUS). In holiday villages the peaks were in November, spring, and July.

Israelis' Hotel Nights: The number of nights spent in hotels by Israelis showed a stronger peak summer season, 154% in July and 201% in August, with a peak in Jerusalem of 232% and in Tel Aviv of 171%, and troughs in November of 71% and 81%, respectively (both have considerable business tourism). In Elat the season was mainly in the summer, providing the balance needed to offset the foreign tourists' pattern. There were summer peaks in Netanya, Tiberias, and the Dead Sea, too. The weeks of Passover and of Tabernacles are peak periods for domestic tourism, reflected only partly in the factors for the months March, April, September, and October [which need festival date adjustments (F)].

The different seasonal patterns of foreign and domestic tourists reduced the seasonality of total demand at each resort. There were considerable changes in the relative weights of these patterns over the 14 years analyzed. The seasonal adjustment of total hotel nights in Israel and in the different resorts is therefore performed by the seasonal adjustment of the appropriate foreign tourist and Israeli series for each month (historic and current) and totaling their levels, $A[T] + A[I]$, rather than by using seasonal factors from the analysis of the total series. We illustrate the factors for hotel nights by giving the total for 1989, for comparison: the seasonality ratio was 1.41, lower than for tourists (1.84) and for domestic nights (3.23).

By Age Groups (Table 4) (C)   All tourist arrivals in Israel (including those by land and sea) had peaks in March and April (seasonal indices were about 115 in 1989), 113 in July and 109 in October, while August was an average month ($SX = 100$) and there was a trough of 72 in January. Youth aged 15 to 19 peaked more sharply in July (214) and August (152), with a deep trough of 45 in November, followed by a secondary peak of 118 in December (tourists from the Southern Hemisphere) and in April. Tourists aged 30 to 44 showed a moderate peak of 113 in March and 109 in June and July, with a peak in October of 105 and a moderate trough of 80 in January. Golden-age tourists 65 and over avoided the hot summer, but peaked in April (163) (mainly due to Passover and Easter) and in October (130) (similar to the indexes for March and May), while the troughs were in January, July, and August.

Other Countries (Table 4) (D)   Most of the series analyzed showed one main high season (seasonal indexes for 1989, as approximations to S', and rounded off here). The highest peak indexes SX for international tourism studied were 223 for tourist arrivals in Canada (1988), corresponding to MUS = 45%, followed by 200 in August, and 222 for foreign tourist arrivals in Greece in August with a July total of 214. For foreign visitor arrivals in Spain, SX was 215 in August (MUS 47%) and 185 in July: Many of the Balearic and Canary Islands have winter-sun seasons. Austria had seasonal indexes of 195 and 200 in July and August for tourist nights at accommodation reporting, while winter sports caused a secondary peak of 145 in January and 150 in March [February (103)]. In Italy foreign visitor arrivals peaked at 163 and 170 in July and August, respectively, while their nights in hotels reporting peaked at 177 in July, followed by 164 in September and 146 in August. Domestic tourism nights had a higher peak (as in Israel) of 250 in August and 180 in July. Switzerland showed a peak of 165 for tourist nights at hotels reporting in July, with 150 in June and 125 in August. The Winter season caused a relative peak r of 102 in February, with many resorts having strong peaks in the winter. In the United Kingdom visitor arrivals from overseas peaked at SX 155 in August (140 in July), while U.K. visits abroad reached 170 in August (return to U.K., many having departed in July) and 155 in September. Tourist arrivals in the United States peaked at about 155 in July and 150 in August, with troughs of 72 in January and February.

The lowest summer peak was 104 for Thailand in August [July (100)], while its cooler winter showed peaks of 125 in December, 117 in February, and 114 in November (but 90 in January). Similarly Singapore had a peak of 108 in August, which rose to 110 in December. In Hong Kong the peaks were 113 and 126 in March and April, respectively, with a trough of 83 in July, while for Japan the peaks were 125 in October and 115 in July. Visitors to Egypt peaked in July (125) and August (122), with October (123) and December (110) also registering peaks.

The number of visitors to Bermuda peaked during the months of June–August (133 to 144), with the season extending from April to October. January had a very low index of 26 in 1989. Jamaica's peaks were in December

(125) and March (121), with a July peak of 113. Australia's visitor arrivals peaked in December with 129 (their summer), with a season extending from July [August (103), September (97)] and reached another peak of 105 in February. A detailed analysis of the seasonality and trends of tourism series of 16 countries and six IATA (International Air Transport Association) series (passengers over the North Atlantic) up to 1973 was published in Bar-On 1975a.

Improving the Seasonal Pattern of Tourism

International and domestic tourism have developed along four main lines:

1. Summer tourism seeking sunshine and bathing in sea or lakes. The summer tourism season is comparatively short in July and August in the more northern European countries, but is longer further south, with a corresponding summer season in January and February in the Southern Hemisphere.
2. Cultural tourism (museums, cathedrals, and other sights: Wiener 1980) and pilgrimages. This line of tourism can take place throughout the year, but will peak around specific cultural or religious festivals, as well as around the vacation seasons of the tourism-generating countries. The volume of this type of tourism may be low, however, when the weather at the destination is poor (unless special measures are taken to attract tourists then, also).
3. Winter sports. This line of tourism is frequently associated with a second holiday, which may, on the other hand, be a sun-seeking holiday (for example in the Caribbean).
4. Business and conference tourism. To a large extent this category takes place outside the usual vacation seasons, although academic conferences and those associated with holiday making are often timed for the vacation season.

The principal vacation for the majority of the working population is in the summer months, largely because school and college holidays in the Northern Hemisphere are usually in July and August, even though the historic reason for this time frame (the need for children's help in agricultural work) is no longer valid for the majority of the population of developed countries.

Tourism is therefore characterized by a single main season in many regions and in some entire countries, with the hotels and other facilities closed or operating at reduced potential during the remainder of the year. The staff employed in the tourist season may have to find other employment in the slow months, or even remain unemployed or move to other areas for the remainder of the year, causing many social and economic problems.

The rapid expansion of tourism up to 1990 has to a large extent been associated with an increase in tourism in the summer season. The increase was often based on charter flights and package tours, which brought international tourism within the reach of millions of people for whom it was an impossible dream 20 or more years ago.

The growth of peak-season tourism has necessitated vast investments in accommodation, transport, and other tourist facilities, which are utilized for only a fraction of the year, and also great increases in the need for staff to serve the tourists—with all the problems of lower standards of service in the peak months, as well as overcrowding at the airports and on the roads and trains. There are therefore many "seasonal losses"—economic, social, and personal.

It is therefore very important to consider methods to spread the seasonality of tourism *demand* and/or to introduce some seasonality into the *supply* in order to reduce the seasonal losses. It may be possible to provide marginal resources for the peak season (or seasons), for example the chartering of additional planes or the renting by hotels of additional guest space in private homes, without wasting basic investments over the rest of the year. The cost of these rentals may be higher than the average cost per week of permanent facilities, but the economic advantages of using marginal resources are great. It may also be possible to use some buildings for tourism purposes in the main season (such as student hostels), and similarly to employ students and even teachers for the peak seasons as guides or lecturers or in hotels and other branches of the tourist industry. Seasonality could also be introduced into the supply-side of year-round tourism facilities, for example, by opening new hotels or reopening older hotels after improvements just before the start of the main season. All these methods have some effect on alleviating seasonal losses, but it is generally more important to consider plans to change the demand for tourism services.

Table 5 indicates a number of scenarios relating to the seasonal patterns

Table 5. *Seasonal patterns for various scenarios: From short high season to balanced utilization[a]*

Example	Jan. 1	Feb. 2	Mar. 3	Apr. 4	May 5	June 6	July 7	Aug. 8 R(P)	Sep. 9	Oct. X	Nov. N	Dec. D	Total year ΣR	Average per month R^b	Annual occupancy rate	Peak seasonal factor S(P)	MUS = 100/ S(P)	SUF = 100 − MUS	Seasonal ratio S(P)/ S(T)
Thousand Rooms Occupied															RO %	%	%	%	
1. Short high summer season	T	T	T					P			T	r							
	1	1	1	2	2	4	7	9	4	2	1	2	36	3.0	30	300	33	67	9.0
2. Stretching the summer season	T	T						P											
	1	1	2	2	4	6	8	9	7	4	2	2	48	4.0	40	225	44	56	9.0
3. Filling high season	T	T						P											
	1	1	2	2	4	7	9	10	8	4	2	2	52	4.3	43	231	43	57	10.0
4. Adding spring season	T			p	t			P											
	1	2	4	7	4	7	9	10	8	4	2	2	60	5.0	50	200	50	50	10.0
5. Improving between seasons	T			p				P											
	1	2	4	7	6	8	9	10	8	4	2	2	63	5.3	53	190	53	48	10.0
6. Improving shoulders	T			p				P											
	1	3	5	7	6	8	9	10	8	6	3	2	68	5.7	57	176	57	43	10.0
Adding short winter season:																			
7. to (3)		T						P				r							
	3	1	2	2	4	7	9	10	8	4	2	4	56	4.7	47	214	47	53	10.0
8. to (4)		T		p	t			P			t	r							
	3	2	4	7	4	7	9	10	8	4	3	5	66	5.5	55	182	55	45	5.0
9. Adding off-season attractions to (8)	T	T	T	p				P			T	r							
	4	4	4	7	5	7	9	10	8	5	4	5	72	6.0	60	167	60	40	2.5
10. Year-round attractions		T	T	p			P	P			T	r							
	7	6	6	8	7	9	10	10	8	7	6	8	92	7.7	77	130	77	23	1.7
11. (10) + extra peak accommodation		T	T	p	t		P	P			T	r							
	7	6	6	8	7	9	12	12	8	7	6	8	96	8.0	77[c]	150	67	33	2.0
12. Balanced year-round demand	T	T		P			P	P			T	r							
	8	8	9	10	9	9	10	10	9	9	8	9	108	9.0	90	111	90	10	1.3

Source: Figure 6: based on Bar-On 1975, by kind permission of the Economist Intelligence Unit.
For abbreviations, see Table 1. Also, see Figure 6.
[a]Rooms occupied R (daily average) out of 10,000 hotel rooms, by month.
[b]The arithmetic average of the 12 R, for simplicity. Taking into account the length of each month gives a total of 1,102 thousand rooms occupied over the year, averaging 3.02 thousand per month.
[c]The average occupancy of the 10,000 year-round rooms was 77% (as in scenario 10) and that of the 2,500 extra rooms in July and August assumed to be 80% (2,000 R per month), resulting in the average of 96/125 = 77% for the rooms supplied (open) over the year, but 96/150 = 67% for all rooms (including those closed off-season).

of the occupancy of hotel rooms. It also shows the average annual occupancy, the MUS, and SUF. The eight principal examples are also illustrated in Figure 6, and refer to a "tourism economy," for example, a resort area with 10,000 hotel rooms, indicating for each month of the year the average occupancy of these rooms.

Example 1 is of a *short high summer season* with peak occupancies in July of 7,000 rooms (per night) and in August of 9,000 rooms. June and September were assumed to have above-average occupancy, too—4,000 rooms. The average occupancy over the whole year ($\overline{R}$) was assumed to be 3,000, so that the annual room-occupancy rate (RO) was 30%. The maximum seasonal factor $S(P)$ was 9,000/3,000 in August, that is, 300%, and the maximal utilization factor limited by seasonality (MUS) was therefore 100/300, or 33%, and its complement, the seasonal underutilization factor (SUF), was 67%. Since occupancy in the peak month was assumed incomplete at 90% (possibly 100% on some days), the annual average occupancy was 90% of 33%, or 30%. The trough months (January to March and November) were assumed to have

Fig. 6. Examples of seasonal patterns of various scenarios, from short high season to balanced utilization. Thousands of rooms occupied *R* out of 10,000 hotel rooms: daily average for each month and for the year. Eight scenarios selected, see Table 5. See Table 1 for abbreviations for *P, p, q, r, T, t.*
(*Source: R. Bar-On, Seasonality in Tourism—A Guide to the Analysis of Seasonality and Trends for Policy Making, London: The Economic Intelligence Unit, 1975.*)

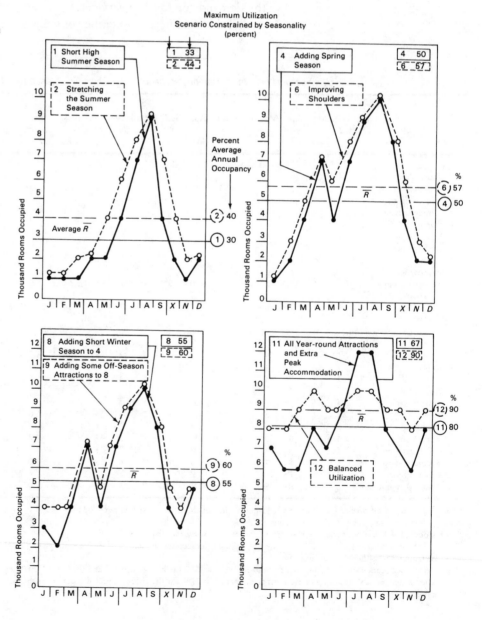

10% occupancy, so the seasonal ratio (peak-to-trough months) was 9:1; December was assumed to have 20% occupancy.

Example 2 shows the result of *stretching the summer season* by increasing demand over May to July and in September and October, by augmenting demand in March and November, and by increasing the annual occupancy to 40% and the MUS to 44%.

Example 3 shows the result of *full occupancy* in the peak month and of increasing occupancy in June, July, and September, thereby causing the annual occupancy to increase to 43% (which is also the MUS in this case). The peak/trough ratio worsens to 10:1.

A *spring season* is added in example 4—March 40% occupancy and April 70% (with February also rising to 20%), raising the annual occupancy and MUS to 50%. A slight improvement to 52% occupancy is obtained by adding *between-season* occupancy in Example 5 in May and June. The *improvement of the shoulder seasons* (March, October, and November) brings annual occupancy up to 57% in Example 6.

The effects of adding a *short winter season* to Examples 3 and 4 are presented in Examples 7 and 8, with annual occupancies of 47% and 55%, respectively.

Example 9 shows an improvement in occupancy to 60% as a result of adding some *off-season activities* in the period November to February, which brought the occupancy in the trough months (January–March and November) to 4,000 rooms and reduced the peak/trough ratio to 2.2:1.

Providing more *attractions all the year round* in Example 10 plus full occupancy in July raised the annual occupancy to 77%.

Example 11 indicates the results of providing *extra peak accommodation* of 2,000 rooms, thus enabling the utilization of 12,000 rooms in July and August (or 2,500 extra rooms with 80% occupancy). The average annual occupancy of the basic 10,000 rooms, however, was still 77%.

The *balanced use* of the 10,000 rooms and the relevant staff is indicated in Example 12 (full occupancy in April and July–August, 80% in January to February and November). The peak/trough seasonal ratio is only 1.2 and the average occupancy is 90%.

We may summarize the alternatives as follows: *If there is a single season,*

- Extending the season
- Introducing a secondary season in the spring, autumn, or winter, and possibly a third season in accordance with the climatic, cultural, and religious possibilities of the country
- Providing activities that are not dependent on the weather, such as conferences or festivals that can be timed outside the main season, or spa and health tourism
- Encouraging tourism only outside the high season.

If there is already more than one main season of tourist demand, it may be possible to fill in the periods between the seasons or build up the "shoulder periods" adjacent to the main seasons, for example, in June or September.

Off-season tourism may be attracted by means of favorable price policies and nonmonetary inducements. Similarly, disincentives may be used to persuade some of the present or potential high-season tourists to come at other times. The problems of pricing tourism services are more complex than those of pricing industrial products and services, for which the economic theory of marginal prices and various operations research techniques have been applied. It is, however, possible to quote different prices for hotels, air fares, and package tours according to different seasons of the year (Bjorkman 1982). Seasonal price variations in seven air fares and for hotels in nine countries were detailed in Bar-On 1975.

In many cases, more services can be offered off-season for the same money, for example, extra hotel nights at a certain destination (ensuring an economically minimum number of nights for each guest) or special free tours and other attractions (as offered by national tourist administrations, airlines, and municipalities in many tourist countries). Most of these prices must be quoted in advance in order to market the tour, and it is possible to provide appropriate discounts if the tour is booked sufficiently in advance (advanced booking systems for airlines, for example), and "remaindering" for tours, hotels, or flights not fully booked.

The majority of potential tourists can take a vacation outside the main season if there is sufficient incentive to do so, especially in regard to the second holiday, the importance of which is growing in most industrialized countries.

There are, of course, some dangers in stressing off-season tourism: some travelers may be disappointed as a result of poor weather, insufficient entertainment, or inadequate food and service in the hotels as a result of cost-cutting. Experiments have been made to insure holiday makers against bad weather, for example, Ashqelon (Israel's southern Mediterranean resort) offers "rain insurance." Guests staying three or more full days between October and March receive a Rain Check for a day's accommodation (bed and breakfast, for continuation of their stay or another stay) for each "rainy day"—more than 5 mm between 8:00 A.M. and 5:00 P.M. It is not difficult to calculate the risk of too much rain or cold weather at a beach resort (or too little snow at a ski resort), and by applying actuarial theory and cost-benefit research to offer the holiday under money-back terms, that is, complete or partial refund by the resort and/or travel agent. The off-season discounted prices may cover the marginal cost of operations and attract tourists who otherwise would not have come. On the other hand, they may be insufficient to cover the true costs of the appropriate level of service, or may transfer tourists who would have been prepared to pay higher prices at other dates without causing seasonal overload ("dilution" of the year-round income from tourists).

In the marketing of perishable goods (such as fruit, vegetables, or fashions) there may be a very wide range of prices over the seasons, and it is possible to rapidly adjust prices to changes in supply and demand. It is desirable to regard empty airplane seats and hotel rooms as highly perishable commodities, too, and to make a greater effort to fill them. Computer booking systems that indicate the extent of advance bookings and cancellations and the prevailing booking trends should be used to offer a wide range of alternative destinations and prices to those seeking specific types of holidays, in order to facilitate speedy use of available resources. Airlines and some tour operators use a standby system with greatly reduced prices to match this kind of demand and fill seats.

The Tourism Committee of the Organization for Economic Cooperation and Development (OECD) includes a section on Staggering of Holidays in its annual reports. A number of experiments and conferences have been aimed at spreading seasonality more evenly (BTA Operation Off Peak, 1990; CEU 1983; ETAG 1983; ETC 1984; Snepenger et al. 1990; Soesilo and Mings 1987; WTO 1983). It would be desirable to study further the attitude of the public and of employers and institutions, especially the school and university systems, to measures to spread seasonality. In order to set optimal marketing policies, market studies should also be undertaken to quantify the different levels of demand for selected tours in different seasons with possible price differentials.

The benefits of more evenly spread seasonality are many:

- More enjoyable holidays for larger numbers of people, without the overcrowding so common in the peak seasons
- Optimal utilization of tourism facilities—hotels, aircraft and other transport, beaches, and entertainment; it will then not be necessary to build so many hotels for a particular number of tourists each year, with ecological as well as economic advantages
- More even employment of hotel and other tourist staff, aiding their careers and improving the service offered
- Reduced average prices and/or increased profitability.

Other Periodicities The discussion so far has referred to seasonality over the months of the year. There are also peaks and troughs over the *days of the week* (and even over the *hours of the day*, for example, in regard to transport (Bar-On 1971), shops, museums, and other cultural facilities. In these respects, too, the existence of peaks and troughs brings crowding and other economic or personal losses. It should be possible to smooth these differences and obtain better use of the facilities by appropriate planning and incentives. Some price differentials and restrictions are used in regard to air travel on particular days or during specific hours, for example.

Summary

This entry deals with the problem of seasonality that almost every tourist business and organization is faced with throughout the calendar year. It also gives certain techniques to eliminate the impact of seasonality on statistical data in order to have a better understanding of year-to-year movements.

References

Bar-On, R. 1963. *Seasonality in Israel—Seasonal Analysis and Adjustment of Selected Time Series.* Jerusalem: Central Bureau of Statistics.

Bar-On, R. 1969. *Seasonality and Trends in Israel Tourism.* Jerusalem: Central Bureau of Statistics.

Bar-On, R. 1971. Models for analyzing multi-periodic transport series [ORSIS—ORSA Conference (Operations Research Societies of Israel and America), Tel-Aviv, 1969]. In *Developments in Operations Research*, vol. 2, ed. B. Avi-Itzhak, pp. 389–415. London: Gordon and Breach.

Bar-On, R. 1973. *Analysis of Seasonality and Trends in Statistical Series—Methodology and Applications in Israel*, 3 vol. Jerusalem: Central Bureau of Statistics.

Bar-On, R. 1975. *Seasonality in Tourism—A Guide to the Analysis of Seasonality and Trends for Policy Making.* London: The Economist Intelligence Unit (based on articles in *International Tourism Quarterly* No. 4, 1972 and No. 1, 1973).

Bar-On, R. 1978. The analysis of single and related time series into components: Proposals for improving X-11. In NBER (National Bureau of Economic Research)/US Bureau of the Census Conference, Arlington, September 1976, *Seasonal Analysis of Economic Time Series*, pp. 107–158. Washington D.C.: Bureau of the Census.

Bar-On, R. 1984. Forecasting Tourism and Travel Series over Various Time Spans under Specified Scenarios. Paper read at ISF 4—Fourth International Symposium on Forecasting, July 1984, London.

Bar-On, R. 1989. *Travel & Tourism Data—A Comprehensive Research Handbook on the World Travel Industry.* London: Euromonitor, and Phoenix: Oryx.

Bar-On, R. 1990. The effects of terrorism on international tourism. In *Terror in the Skies—Aviation Security,* The Proceedings of the First International Seminar on Aviation Security, February 1989, pp. 83–103. Jerusalem: Government of Israel, Ministry of Tourism.

Bjorkman, B. 1982. The effect of traffic stimulating measures on the travel market, *ITA (Institut du Transport Aerien) Monthly Bulletin,* June 1982.

BTA, *Operation Off Peak.* 1990 (occasional from 1985). London: British Tourist Authority.

BTA, 1990. Working for a brighter weekend. *Horizons* 1:13.

CEU, 1983. *Staggering of Tourism,* Madrid: World Tourism Organisation Commission for Europe.

Dagum, E. B. 1990. *The X11 ARIMA/88 Seasonal Adjustment Method—Foundations and Users Manual,* Ottawa: Statistics Canada.

ETAG, 1983. *Action to Combat the Effects of Seasonality In Europe.* Dublin: European Travel Commission for European Tourism Action Group.

ETC, 1984. *Staggering of Tourism,* Report of a Conference (Cyprus). Dublin: European Travel Commission.

Fisher, J., and R. Bar-On, 1991. *X11 ARIMA/88 with Improvements,* Jerusalem: Praedicta.

Gal-Or, G. and R. Bar-On. 1978. The Development of Year-round Convention Tourism under Varied Conditions—The Israel Model. Paper read at INCOM *International Convention Organizers Meeting,* Cannes, Nov. 1978.

IMT/CBS, 1987. *Tourism 1985-1986* (in biennial series of detailed statistics). Jerusalem: Central Bureau of Statistics with Israel Ministry of Tourism.

OECD, *Tourism Policy and International Tourism in OECD Member Countries* (annual). Paris: Organisation for Economic Cooperation and Development.

Pfefferman, D., and J. M. Fisher. 1982. Festival and working days prior adjustments to economic time series. *International Statistical Review* 50:113–124.

Shiskin, J., J. C. Musgrave and M. Somer. 1969. *X-11—Information for the User,* Seminar on Seasonal Adjustments. Washington D.C.: U.S. National Association of Business Economics and U.S. Bureau of the Census.

Smith, A. 1970. *The Seasons.* London: Weidenfeld and Nicolson.

Snepenger, D., B. Houser, and M. Snepenger. 1990. Seasonality of demand. *Annals of Tourism Research* 17(4):628–630.

Soesilo, J. A. and R. C. Mings. 1987. Assessing the seasonality of tourism. *Visions in Leisure and Business* 6(2):25–38.

UNSO, 1978. *Provisional Guidelines on Statistics of International Tourism.* New York: U.N. Statistical Office.

Var, T., and Choong-Ki Lee. 1992. Tourism forecasting: State of the art techniques. In *VNR's Encyclopedia of Hospitality and Tourism,* ed. M. A. Khan, M. Olsen, and T. Var. New York: Van Nostrand Reinhold.

Wiener, L. W. 1980. Cultural Resources: An old asset—A new market for tourism. In *Tourism Marketing and Management Issues,* pp. 187–192. Washington D.C.: George Washington University.

WTO. 1983. Risks of saturation or tourist carrying capacity overload in holiday destinations. In *Reports to the 5th General Assembly* (New Delhi, October 1983) PG IV (B.4.2.2). Madrid: World Tourism Organization.

15

Statistical Measurements in Tourism

William B. Stronge

Virtually every country in the world today produces statistics on tourists and tourism. These statistics provide basic information on this important and growing industry, and there is a large technical literature on the appropriate procedures for the collection and analysis of statistical measurements of tourism.

Purpose

Three main purposes have been identified for the production of statistics of tourism (Burkart and Medlik 1974.) First, there is a need to assess the impact of tourism on the tourist destination. Tourists make expenditures that provide employment and incomes to residents of the tourist destination. The recipients of these incomes make expenditures that lead to further employment and income at the destination. Additionally, tourists pay taxes and support cultural and recreational activities at the destination that may not be economically feasible without tourist demand. Information on the magnitude of tourism is needed to determine the contribution of tourists to the economy and lifestyle at the tourist destination.

A second purpose of tourism statistics is to assist in the planning for and development of tourist-oriented facilities. Included are the public infrastructure needs of tourists including airport and highway capacity and the capacity of businesses to meet the needs of tourists. These businesses include accommodation facilities, such as hotels and campgrounds, restaurant facilities, and cultural and recreational facilities that appeal to tourists.

The third purpose in collecting tourism information is to facilitate tourism promotion and market research. Most major contemporary tourist destinations engage in tourism marketing and promotion. Information on the geographical origin of tourists as well as on the social and economic characteristics can assist in the selection of target markets and effective advertising media.

Statistical Definition of a Tourist

The dictionary defines a tourist as "one who makes a tour or a pleasure trip" (Funk and Wagnalls 1978). Although conceptually clear, this definition does not correspond to the commonly employed statistical definitions of tourists.

The traditional notion that a tourist is making a tour probably has its origins in the undertaking by English and German notables of a Grand Tour of Europe in the eighteenth and nineteenth centuries. Today, the only "tour" that is required of a tourist is that the tourist must make a circular trip, that is, he or she must make a trip that returns them to their starting point.

The idea that tourists travel for pleasure has also been modified in statistical measures of tourism. Travelers on business are included in most measures of tourism. Many business travelers combine the leisure or cultural activities engaged in by pleasure travelers with their business activity so that their impact on the tourist destination is similar to the impact of pleasure travelers.

The standardization of the definition of tourists for the purposes of statistical measurement began in the 1930s, particularly as it related to international tourism (Chadwick 1987, Gee et al. 1984, Hudman 1980, Kaul 1985). In 1937, the League of Nations established a Technical Committee of Experts to develop standard definitions of tourists. A number of conferences introduced modifications of the 1937 definitions, which culminated in the adoption of standard definitions by the United Nations in 1963.

The first distinction underlying standard definitions is between resident and nonresident travelers, with tourists constituting a subset of *nonresident travelers*. Note that a resident of a country does not have to be a citizen of the country, so that not all foreigners entering a country are nonresidents.

A second distinction arises between migrants and visitors. Migrants constitute people arriving in a country (or domestic tourist destination) who intend to become residents of that country. A tourist is defined as a visitor who is *temporarily visiting* a country or destination with the intention of leaving after a limited period of time. Operationally, this requirement of a tourist is frequently implemented by requiring the length of stay of a tourist to be no more than one year.

Finally, a tourist *does not travel to seek remuneration*, although a tourist may be remunerated for the travel undertaken. This requirement excludes commuters and "guest workers." On the other hand, business travelers are included in tourism statistics. The distinction between business travelers, commuters, and guest workers is that business travelers receive their normal employment compensation from employers based outside the tourist destination, whereas commuters and "guest workers" receive their normal compensation from employers at the tourist destination.

Commuters are frequently excluded from tourism statistics by requiring that the *distance* traveled to the tourist destination be a *minimum length* (e.g., 100 miles one way in the United States or 50 miles one way in Canada.) This requirement, however, can exclude travelers for the purpose of shopping (where taxes are lower on one side of an international border than on the other), or minivacation travel, such as a weekend trip to a ski resort or beach that is less than 100 miles from an urban area. As a result, the minimum distance requirement for a tourist is usually applied to tourism between states (as opposed to local tourism) and where travel by day visitors is relatively small.

Tourist Arrivals Versus Tourist Persons

The previous discussion is in terms of tourist persons. However, most tourism volume statistics refer to tourist arrivals rather than persons. If a destination reports that there were two million tourists who visited it during the course of a year, the figure normally refers to arrivals not individuals. If a single individual visited the destination on five different occasions during the year, he would account for five arrivals. If the average visitor to the destination made five visits during the course of the year, the two million tourist arrivals would represent four hundred thousand individual tourists.

Length of Stay and Tourist Definitions

Tourists are usually defined as visitors to a destination who are staying less than one year. At the other extreme, some visitors may spend no more than a few hours at a tourist destination. One group of visitors who spend very little time at a tourist destination are transit passengers who are awaiting connecting flights at the airport. Such visitors are normally excluded from tourism statistics.

Another group of short term visitors are *excursionists* or *day visitors*. Such individuals display many of the characteristics of tourists who spend at least one night, but they are distinguished by the fact that they do not use accommodations at the tourist destination. Included in this category are cruise passengers, shoppers who travel more than one hundred miles each way to the destination, and visitors on a day trip to an attraction or shopping facilities at a tourist destination. Because of their similarity to tourists who spend one night, most tourism statistics include day visitors, but they are usually reported in a separate category from those spending at least one night.

Some statistical agencies distinguish another category of tourists as *vacationers* or *holidaymakers*, consisting of tourists who spend a minimum of four nights at the tourist destination. The purpose of this distinction is to identify tourists on traditional family vacations. The distinction excludes people who travel for weekends (spending Friday, Saturday, and Sunday nights, and even one additional night on a "long" weekend).

In many destinations, the vacationer-holidaymaker categorization is of limited usefulness. Length of stay at a tourist destination tends to be positively related to the distance traveled to the destination, so that the vacationer category includes many business travelers, for example, who have traveled relatively long distances such as transatlantic. Moreover, the distinction is of limited use even in terms of economic impact. The vacationer traveler defined in this way will include owners of second homes whose economic impact may be relatively low relative to their stay.

Finally, there is a category of seasonal residents or visitors. This category of individuals is characterized by lengthy stays, and many individuals are either retired or they can engage in their occupations from their place of residence (such as trading on financial or commodity markets via computer and telephone.)

A characteristic of seasonal visitors is that they tend to behave much like residents. They will often have second homes or live in an apartment rather than a hotel; their average daily use of tourist facilities or visits to attractions is less frequent than those who stay at the destination for a shorter period of time.

The World Tourism Organization defines a "standard tourist" as tourist who stays more than one night and less than ninety nights at a tourist destination. This definition is somewhat arbitrary. In a winter tourist destination such as Florida, for example, there is a well-defined "winter season" that exceeds ninety nights, and winter residents are commonly expected to stay at least 120 nights.

Unusual Visitors

A number of visitors to tourist destinations fall into unusual categories. Included are airline and other crews, diplomats, and students. Crews are usually included in tourism statistics (unless they are in transit at an airport) since they display the economic characteristics of other tourists. In international statistics, diplomats are excluded because they are similar to to resident expatriates. In international statistics, students are reported as tourists, although this not so for domestic tourism.

Methods of Collecting Tourism Volume Data

Tourism data are collected in a variety of ways from a variety of sources. A basic distinction lies between collecting information on tourism volume, namely, the number of tourists arriving at a destination, and tourist characteristics, such as the geographic origin and spending patterns of tourists.

Tourism Volume   Traditionally, data on the volume of international tourism have been more readily available than have data on domestic tourism because of national frontier controls that require the determination of the immigration status of travelers at national points of entry. These data may become less available in Western Europe as border controls are reduced or eliminated in the 1990s.

Domestic tourism information is also often collected at points of entry. However, the quality of the information is closely linked to the mode of travel. In general, information collected at terminals such as airports, docks, and railroad stations is of much higher quality than is information collected on automobile traffic through highway points of entry.

A number of domestic tourist destinations collect information at airports. For some destinations, such as Hawaii or Puerto Rico, highly accurate measures of the flow of tourist arrivals can be obtained from airport deplanement statistics because the overwhelming majority of tourists arrive by air. The only task is to develop procedures for distinguishing travel by local residents on incoming air flights.

In other domestic destinations, the portion of the tourism market accounted for by air travelers can be determined accurately at airports, although a large number of tourists arrive by automobile. Florida, for example, collects information on incoming air tourists by sampling incoming flights and estimating the fraction of travelers who are tourists. Using deplanement statistics, the sampling fraction is extrapolated to the entire population of travelers.

When a significant number of tourists arrive in automobiles along highways, the situation becomes more difficult. Counts of vehicles are available for selected highways, but not all point of entry highways have their traffic counted at reasonably frequent intervals. There is also extensive use of highways by residents of tourist destinations.

One approach to distinguishing automobile tourists from residents is by means of license plate surveys. This is undertaken in Florida. One problem is the difficulty in distinguishing tourists from migrants, a sizeable group of incoming travelers in the state. An attempt to adjust for inward migration can be made by subtracting estimates of inward migration obtained from other sources from the total number of incoming automobile passengers in out-of-state licensed cars as estimated from the license plate survey.

Another problem with license plate surveys is the assumption that all passengers in all cars with out-of-state license plates are nonresidents and that all passengers in cars with in-state license plates are residents of the state. For example, elderly seasonal residents may employ Florida residents to drive their cars to Florida while they fly.

The biggest problem with license plate surveys arises where there are a multiplicity of incoming highways, however. Few tourism statistical agencies have the resources to count cars on all point of entry highways on a frequent basis. Further, changes in traffic conditions or tourist-oriented events can result in significant short-term changes in the distribution of tourist traffic across the various port of entry highways.

Statistics from Accommodations

Many tourist destinations collect information on the volume of tourists from hotels, campgrounds, and other registered accommodations. In many countries, hotels record information on international tourists.

Even at domestic tourism destinations, most hotels keep records of occupancy, including person nights and room nights. Surveys of registered accommodations can be extrapolated to the population of all registered accommodations using lists available from the registering government agency (Redman 1990).

The lists of registered accommodations are not always current because of the entry and exit of firms into the industry and, even more important, because of fluctuations in the inventory of rooms due to the seasonal shutdown of certain facilities and portions thereof and renovations and alterations to existing facilities.

It can also be difficult to obtain cooperation from registered accommodations. Response rates from smaller facilities are usually lower than from larger facilities, and some firms refuse to participate in order to prevent information about their business going to competitors. There are also the usual concerns about information going to taxing authorities.

Even when information can be gathered from registered accommodations, the result is a partial view of tourist volume. Many tourists stay with friends and relatives and are, therefore, missed by estimates of tourism based on occupancy of registered accommodations. Other tourists stay in second homes owned, but not concurrently occupied, by nonresident friends and relatives. Still other tourists stay at paid lodging which is unregistered and which will not be reported for tax reasons.

Statistics from Attractions

An even more unsatisfactory method of collecting information on tourist volume is to collect information on attendance at tourist attractions. There are, of course, the usual problems in distinguishing resident from tourist use. In addition, however, there is the assumption that all tourists visit the attraction during their stay at the destination. Few attractions meet this requirement, although a beach at a beach resort might come close. Additionally, allowances must be made for multiple visits to the attraction during a single visit.

Statistics from Bank Records

A commonly used method of obtaining data on tourist expenditures is by means of bank records that record the flow of funds into and out of a tourist destination. The total flow of expenditures is a measure of the spending of tourists, but not of the number of tourists. In some countries, foreign exchange controls provide detailed information that can be used to estimate tourist expenditures.

Other Sources of Volume Data

Two other sources of volume data may be mentioned: surveys of people who inquire about tourist destinations and household surveys at tourist origins. These surveys are usually undertaken to obtain information about tourist characteristics, but they may yield volume information on a portion of the volume of tourism at tourism destinations.

Some tourist destinations advertise the availability of tourist information and receive requests for the information. Conversion studies are undertaken to determine the success rate of converting these information requests into actual tourist arrivals. Projections of total arrivals from this subpopulation of potential tourists can be made on the basis of the survey. Of course, this method does not provide total coverage of tourist volume and, additionally, response rates to the survey can be unsatisfactorily low (Shaw et al. 1990).

Another potential source of information on tourist volume consists of household surveys at tourist origins (U.S. Department of Commerce, Travel and Tourism Administration 1989). Such surveys are undertaken to provide marketing information and they have the same problem of incomplete coverage as do conversion studies. Additionally, the sample size is often too small to provide a basis for measuring tourist volume at a particular destination with sufficient accuracy.

Indicators of Tourism Volume

Because of the difficulty of measuring total tourism volume, particularly for domestic tourism, many tourism statistics consist of indicators rather than estimates of tourism volume. Included will be airport enplanements or deplanements, highway counts or toll road receipts, hotel occupancy, attraction attendance, and sales at tourist-oriented establishments, or tourist-related tax receipts.

International Tourism Volume

Table 1 presents estimates of the volume of tourist arrivals for the top five international tourist destinations in 1985. The largest destination in terms of tourists who stayed at least one night was France, followed by Italy, Germany, Spain, and the United States. Data on "excursionists" who stayed less than a night are also provided. Germany and the United States accounted for the bulk of the "excursionists."

The average length of stay of tourists ranged from a low of four nights in Germany to eleven in the United States. Multiplication of the average length of stay by the number of tourist arrivals gives tourist nights, a volume of tourism measure that is widely used. By this measure the greatest volume of tourism is in Spain, closely followed by the United States.

Methods of Collecting Data on Tourist Characteristics

Aside from measuring the volume of tourism, information is required on the characteristics of tourists. Such information is usually obtained from surveys of tourists (Shaw et al. 1990).

Tourist surveys can be distinguished by the different times that they are administered: front-end surveys, surveys administered while the tourist is at

Table 1. *Tourist volume in five largest international tourist destinations*

Country of destination	Tourist arrivals (millions of persons)	Excursionists (millions of persons)	Average stay (nights)	Tourist nights (millions of person nights)
France	36.7	22.0	9.0	331
Italy	28.0	28.6	7.0	196
Germany F.R.	28.0	100.0	4.0	112
Spain	27.5	15.8	10.5	289
U.S.A.	25.4	93.0	11.0	279

Source: R. Bar-On, *Travel and Tourism Data*, Phoenix, Ariz.: Oryx Press, 1989.

the tourist destination, and surveys at the end of the tourist trip or after the tourist has left the tourist destination.

Front-End Surveys

Front-end tourist surveys are useful for determining tourist characteristics that will not change as a result of the trip to the destination. Included are characteristics such as geographic origin, mode of travel, and main destination, as well as party size and composition, length of stay, and lodging if predetermined.

Front-end tourist surveys are usually reasonably brief, particularly because they can result in delays for tourist arrivals. Front-end tourist surveys are inappropriate methods of collecting information on tourist characteristics that are subject to change during the visit. For example, anticipated tourist expenditures may be an inadequate guide to actual tourist expenditures, and anticipated activities at the destination (including travel to secondary destinations and recreational activities) may also differ from the actual experience.

Surveys During a Tourist Visit

Surveys during a tourist visit may be administered at tourist attractions, or they may be left in the sleeping quarters at registered places of accommodation. The information collected is often a mixture of tourist characteristics that could have been collected at the point of entry and projections of expenditures and local travel and activities whose accuracy depends on how close in time the survey is administered to the end of the tourist visit.

Additional problems arise when these during-visit surveys are extrapolated to the tourist population. First, as discussed previously, the survey coverage may be incomplete. Not all tourists visit the attractions, and not all tourists stay in hotels. Second, the response rate for these surveys can be low, particularly if they are not administered in person but are left on counters or in hotel rooms.

Nevertheless, during-visit surveys are widely used because they are cheap to administer and because they meet the needs of segments of the tourism industry (such as particular attractions or the hotel industry).

These during-visit surveys should be distinguished from diary surveys, which consist of daily records each day during a tourist's stay that are returned at the end of the stay. Such records, when properly administered, are highly accurate. However, the response rate to such surveys is very low and there is reason to believe that the respondents are significantly different in their tourism behavior from the nonrespondents.

Exit Surveys

Exit surveys are widely used to obtain information on tourist characteristics. These surveys are particularly effective in departure lounges or even during return flights to tourist origins. Exit surveys have two advantages. First, they are often administered in departure lounges when tourists have available time to cooperate with the survey. Second, they are administered at a time when tourists can be presumed to have maximum recall of their expenditures and activities during their stay.

Tourist characteristics are sometimes collected after tourists have returned to their origins. One example is the use of conversion surveys consisting of follow-ups of individuals who have requested information and have later visited the destination. The usual problems of nonresponse are encountered with these surveys. Additionally, however, there are problems of recall because of the time elapsed since the tourist made the visit.

Table 2. *Geographic origin basis for selected tourist profile characteristics of air visitors to Florida January through March 1990*

Geographic origin	Percent	Visit purpose	Percent	Activities on trip	Percent
New York	14.5	Vacation	39.1	Shopping and restaurants	17.5
New Jersey	7.7	Friends or relatives	28.9	Rest and relaxation	16.7
Massachusetts	7.2	Business	22.5	Climate	16.4
Pennsylvania	6.3	Other	9.4	Beaches	12.2
Illinois	5.4	Total	100.0		

Source: Florida Department of Commerce, Division of Tourism, Office of Marketing Research. Unpublished.

Nonparticipant Surveys

Information is sometimes collected by observation of tourists, either by researchers or by electronic means. Time budget studies can be obtained by observing tourists over the course of a visit. Such surveys are expensive, difficult to extrapolate to the population, and may antagonize the tourists being observed. They are not widely used by tourism agencies.

Data Collected on Tourist Characteristics

Information collected in surveys of tourists falls into three categories, namely, visitor profiles, trip activities and expenditures, and tourist attitudes.

Visitor Profiles

Visitor profiles include mode of travel, geographic origin, purpose of trip, age, education, family income. Tables 2 and 3 present information on the profile of air visitors to Florida in the first three months of 1990, the peak tourist season in the state. During 1989, total tourist arrivals on all modes of transportation amounted to 38.7 million, making Florida as a tourist destination larger than the top five destinations for international tourists as reported in Table 1.

The information provided in Tables 2 and 3 is typical of the profile information collected in surveys of tourist characteristics. Geographic origin information identifies the states of New York, New Jersey, Massachusetts, Pennsylvania, and Illinois as the major markets for Florida tourism. Almost 40 percent came for vacation, but more than one in four came to Florida to visit friends or relatives. Business travel is less than 25 percent. The dom-

Table 3. *Age basis for selected tourist profile characteristics of air visitors to Florida January through March 1990*

Age	Percent of males	Percent of females	Family income	Percent
Under 18	10.6	11.9	Under $30,000	16.1
18–25	8.9	11.4	$30,000–59,999	35.4
26–55	58.3	66.2	$60,000–89,999	22.6
Over 55	22.3	21.9	$90,000+	26.0
	100.0	100.0		100.0

Source: Florida Department of Commerce, Division of Tourism, Office of Marketing Research. Unpublished.

inance of pleasure travel also shows up in activities enjoyed with restaurants, rest and relaxation, climate, and beaches listed as the most enjoyable part of the tourist trips. Although most visitors to Florida are in the middle years from 25 to 55, more than one in five tourists is older than 55 (Table 3). Family incomes of Florida tourists are relatively high, with the median family income of close to $60,000.

Tourist surveys often focus on marketing information including when the trip was planned and the role of travel agencies. In addition, tourist surveys collect information on expenditures. Usually, expenditures for the tourist traveling party are collected from the questionnaires, and party size as well as length of stay information is used to derive spending per person and spending per person day.

A sample of information for Florida winter air travelers is provided in Table 4. The average tourist party visiting Florida in the first quarter of 1990 contained 1.94 persons, spent 8.57 nights and spent $935.24. The largest category of expenditures was lodging (although many tourists stayed with friends, relatives, or in second homes), followed by food, transportation, and entertainment. Transportation included expenses on rental cars and tours at the destination, rather than the cost of travel to the state.

Given an estimate of the volume of tourists, such as the number of arrivals, total tourist expenditures can be calculated. In the first quarter of 1990, Florida estimated that air tourist arrivals were 6.4 million. This number times average spending per tourist in Table 3 yields a total estimate of tourist expenditures equal to $3.1 billion.

In market analysis, expenditures per person per day is a key variable. Average expenditures per person per day amounted to $56.25. This number is reduced for the population of tourists as a whole, since over 38 percent stayed with friends or relatives and 5 percent stayed in lodging that they owned. When tourists are classified by lodging type, expenditures per person per day tend to be very highly related to income.

The Tourist Industry

Technically speaking, there is no such industry as a tourist industry, because the term tourist describes a particular customer of a number of industries, rather than a group of firms producing a particular range of products. Nevertheless, the popular use of the term *tourist industry* refers to firms for whom

Table 4. *Expenditures ($ US) of Florida air tourists, winter 1990*

Category	Per party	Per person	Per person/day
Lodging	317.80	163.81	19.11
Food Restaurant	222.95	114.92	13.41
Food Grocery	47.24	24.35	2.84
Entertainment	99.69	51.39	6.00
Gifts	68.51	35.31	4.12
Transportation	100.99	52.06	6.07
Gasoline	21.08	10.87	1.27
Other	56.98	29.37	3.43
Total	935.24	482.08	56.25

Source: Florida Department of Commerce, Division of Tourism, Office of Marketing Research. Unpublished.

Notes: Average party size was 1.94 persons. Average length of stay was 8.57 nights.

tourists constitute a major part of their customer base and, perhaps, some firms that are important to tourists even if tourists are a relatively small part of their customers.

The data in Table 3 can be used to identify members of the tourist industry defined in this way. Included in the industry are hotels and other lodging places, attractions and recreational facilities used by tourists, firms in transportation including car rentals, bus tour firms and so on, and certain retail stores particularly those selling souvenirs and gifts. Restaurants and bars are important to tourists but in many places residents outnumber tourists as customers. The same is true of gasoline stations.

The following list from the *Florida Statistical Abstract 1989* (p. 465; Fla. Dept. Labor and Employment Security) shows employment in tourist-related industries in Florida in 1988, excluding restaurants and other eating and drinking places.

Industry	Employees
Bus transportation	1,949
Water transportation	451
Air transportation	45,979
Arrangement of transportation	12,162
Total transportation	60,541
Gift shops	11,494
Hotels and lodging places	131,059
Car rental	12,867
Motion pictures	12,510
Amusements and recreation	93,346

Another view of the tourist industry can be provided by tourist-related sales data. In Florida, tourist-related sales amounted to almost $30 billion in 1988, according to the following data from the *Florida Statistical Abstract 1989*:

Business	Sales (in million $)
Restaurants	$ 10,518.1
Bars	1,713.7
Hotels	6,192.1
Gifts and Novelties	1,806.9
Newsstands	162.1
Admissions	1,956.9
Seasonal Vendors	7.3
Auto and Gas	5,836.0
	$ 28,193.1

Source: State of Florida, Department of Labor and Employment Security. Published in *Florida Statistical Abstract 1989*, page 463.

Once again, the sales in the list above include the expenditure of local residents as well as tourists, but they exclude certain tourist expenditures, particularly expenditures on personal services such as hairdressing and even medical services.

Summary

This entry provides a general overview of statistical measurements in tourism. It gives statistical definitions of a tourist, arrival, length of stay, and other related terms. It also stresses the ways and methods of how statistical information is collected.

References

Bar-On, R. 1989. *Travel and Tourism Data*. Phoenix, Ariz.: Oryx Press.

Burkart, A. J., and S. Medlik. 1974. *Tourism*. London: Heinemann.

Chadwick, R. A. 1987. Concepts, definitions and measures used in tourism and travel research. In *Travel, Tourism and Hospitality Research*, ed. J. B. Ritchie and C. R. Goeldner, pp. 47–61. New York: John Wiley.

Funk and Wagnalls. 1978. *New Comprehensive International Dictionary of the English Language*, Encyclopedic Edition. New York: Publishers Guild Press.

Gee, C., D. J. L. Choy, and J. C. Makems. 1984. *The Travel Industry*. Westport, Conn.: AVI Publishing Co.

Hudman, L. E. 1980. *Tourism: A Shrinking World*, Columbus, Ohio: Grid Publishing Co.

Kaul, R. N. 1985. *Dynamics of Tourism*, 3 vols. New Delhi: India Sterling Publishers.

Redman, M. B. 1990. Method for Estimating Tourist Expenditures in a Local Area. Paper presented at the ORSA-TIMS Annual Meeting, Las Vegas, Nevada.

Shaw, G., A. Williams, and J. Greenwood. 1990. "U.K. Visitor Survey" *Tourism Management* pp. 247–251.

Stronge, W. B. 1987. *Florida Tourism Models*, Report Submitted to the Florida Department of Commerce, Division of Economic Development.

United States Department of Commerce, Travel and Tourism Administration. 1989. *Pleasure Travel Market to North America: Australia*. Washington, D.C.: Government Printing Office.

16

Government's Role in Strategic Planning for Tourism

Salah E. A. Wahab

Irrespective of the existing diversification in the economic and political institutions of various countries, government intervention in tourism has been found necessary. The nature and scope of such intervention undoubtedly differ from one country to another but one common denominator is that tourism cannot be left entirely to the initiative of the private sector at least in the area of national image promotion. Even in countries with an essentially free economy system, need has arisen to create governmental bodies that are receptive to the professional sectors but have been given minimum functions. In 1989, about 180 official tourist bodies, governmental or semi-governmental, existed in countries and autonomous territories and were members of the World Tourism Organization.

Such government involvement in tourism has been noted by the United Nations Conference on International Travel and Tourism held in Rome in 1963 where it was made clear that in order to ensure the smooth running of tourist activities, it is important to entrust to governments the overall policy and control of tourism.

As modern tourism is a by-product of the post–Second World War period, government activities in tourism in various countries at large and in Europe in particular, showed three fairly distinct phases. A first phase was in the aftermath of World War II, in the late forties and early fifties, when there was a need to ease and dismantle the many regulatory measures in police, currency, health and customs that were the remnants of a world war. Thus, governments were active in tourism facilitation, that is, the simplification of border formalities.

A second phase of government concern in tourism started when some countries, developed and developing, realized the existence of the "dollar gap" and thus the pressing need to increase their earnings of dollars and any other hard currency. It was felt that tourism could be a useful tool for enhancing the country's foreign exchange. Therefore, foreign tourists had to be encouraged to visit destinations through various national promotional efforts exerted by governments in the United States and other major tourist-generating markets devoting substantial budgets for such promotion at a macro level.

During this period, the growth of international tourism became a landmark, and tourism started to gain repute as a phenomenon of social mobility in large numbers involving various segments and stratas of the traveling public in various countries. It was then recognized that tourism was not only dynamic but was also a growth industry whose future seemed bright, as predicted by scientific long-term forecasting techniques led by the International Union of Official Travel Organizations (IUOTO) at that time (the forerunner of World Tourism Organization).

But whereas government involvement was felt growing and accepted by public opinion, to varying degrees in various developed and developing countries, the encouragement of the private sector was made a basic tenet of the government policy in various Western countries and to a lesser extent in developing countries. In Eastern Europe, the role played by governments in tourism, as in other sectors of their economies, became preponderant.

The growth of tourism within the "social dimension" of the 1960s marked a change in the prevalence of tourism from urban centers with sufficient accommodation capacity and amenities to receive the expanding tourist flows to new holiday centers at coastal and mountain area resorts for vacationers of diversified spending powers. Thus, the world witnessed a revolutionary upsurge in international and domestic tourism in the 1970s particularly with the devaluation of the dollar. The capacities of the then existing centers became less and less sufficient to accommodate the continued growth of tourism with the result that bottlenecks increased, the quality of services fell, and the price level rose noticeably, especially at certain times of the year.

A third phase became apparent when, in the seventies and early eighties, tourism entered a new dimension, which may be labeled the "dimension of tourism diversification." Various tourism typologies were emphasized such as the vacation active tourism, green tourism, and surprise tours. New forms of investment policies, such as secondary home condominiums and timesharing, succeeded in invading the tourism field. Moreover, governments started to implement price controls to protect both the consumer and the international competitive position of their respective countries.

In addition, government policy took on new dimensions characterized by earnest measures for the security and legal protection of tourists as well as enhancing international cooperation in tourism. Governments also became more involved in developing depressed regions touristically, in land use, manpower development policy, environmental conservation, and directive rather than prohibitive control of private enterprise.

In sum, international competition, national interest, and the complex nature of the tourist industry are all specific factors that make government intervention in strategic planning for tourism a matter of varying necessity in countries of the contemporary world. Another facet for such intervention is the challenging gradual change in emphasis from quantity to quality in tourism, which is a real shift for decision makers in developed as well as developing countries.

Beneficial and Detrimental Impacts

Although tourism has witnessed more than forty years of steady growth, its development is still considered precarious. It is a phenomenon that is sensitively susceptible to political, economic, social, health, and environmental factors, as well as to terrorist acts. Such an image is hardly conducive to expanding investments in tourism development by public and private sectors unless governments encourage such investments through various incentives that lead to the growth of tourism. This encouragement requires nonprotectionist measures that embody certain liberal principles in national priorities to formulate a tourism national policy that would translate these priorities into practical applications.

In contrast to the undeniable economic benefits that could accrue to the receiving country, tourism also exacts a price from the receiving country. Such a price is represented by investments in tourism infrastructures and superstructures, in the cost in foreign exchange of required imports, and in other aspects such as the invasion of the national value system, vandalism, congestion, increased crime, and the possible change or sacrifice of the national architectural heritage and natural beauty.

In developing countries with good tourism potential, tourism may be adopted as an economic activity that could rationalize its economic policy especially through balanced growth brought about by new or additional business production cycles caused by tourism expansion. Thus, tourism can become the cause and the effect of rationalizing economic development along with the economic production sectors of agriculture and industry.

General Framework for Strategic Planning for Tourism

Tourism expansion in developed countries, although a semireliable source of economic prosperity, must be planned in order to mitigate its negative impacts and make its remedial measures more effective. As illustrated by Mathieson and Wall, "the continued expansion of tourism at its present rate and in its existing form is not a desirable phenomenon in most destination areas (Mathieson and Wall 1982). In fact, tourism is a complex activity that usually gives rise to differing and sometimes contradictory effects. Thus, the rationalization of tourism growth through sound scientific planning measures is a must. This could be labeled strategic planning for tourism. It is a higher level of planning than the operational level and lower than the normative level where plans are kinetic. It is the type of planning that puts up a descriptive and analytical strategy for tourism development at the national or regional levels in the host country (Wahab 1988).

Accordingly, such strategic planning is or should be the main preoccupation of governments in every destination, whether developed or developing, at least in an indicative manner. Even when strategic planning is conducted in a certain region or area by private enterprise, it should be deemed master planning rather than strategic planning. Strategic planning envelops the policy making determinants of the country at large or of a whole region. The value judgments that underlie the various policy alternatives must be based on criteria that have been previously chosen by the component government authority. This presupposes specialized expertise since tourism policy in this case must be coordinated with other productive and services sectors policies in the country.

Although governments must manage a sector they barely understand, a strategic plan of tourism development must tailor make, where possible, its tourism traffic to make it more responsive to the needs of the country's population, which is and should be the ultimate beneficiary of tourism development. Thus, one of the basic tenets of strategic planning is to ascertain how much tourism is enough. Therefore, governments need to have longer-term scenarios for future development in tourism that require a reliable statistical system on which forecasts can be based. Moreover, the increasing multiplicity of tourism concerns, the growing trend in various countries toward decentralization and, to a varying degree, privatization will also increase the need for coordination as a basic government function.

The protection and security of tourists need special government attention. Such a function is growing in importance and becoming a major concern of governments as part of an overall security policy.

Environmental conservation is gaining ground as a goal of government policy on pollution control. Protecting the environment is to save a heritage and well manage a national common resource. More and more voices are now pleading for effective international cooperation shared by various countries to safeguard and protect the environment. The Environmental Program for the Mediterranean Workshop held in Paris on December 1989 and sponsored by the World Bank and the European Investment Bank is the most recent international meeting of government representatives to provide a plan of action to stop environmental degradation.

Scope of Government Action on Tourism

The scope of government action on tourism varies according to the importance that the state attaches to tourism and on the conditions prevailing in the country (politico-economic-constitutional system, socioeconomic development, degree of tourism development, and degree of private enterprise maturity and financial capabilities).

In free market economies where the basic premise was the minor role played by the government in tourism, it is now increasingly felt that its intervention in the field of tourism is bound to grow, with the prime aim of conceptualizing and planning tourism growth and achieving the priority objectives of the national tourist policy. In socialist countries where the economy is centrally planned, the question of the scope of government action does not arise, since the government is the sole or main planner, executor, and manager of various economic programs including tourist programs.

In various types of economies, when the government actively intervenes in tourism, it normally pursues overall national profitability sought from large or small individual projects by private entrepreneurs. Of course, it should also consider the economic return, in relation to other economic sectors, of its tourist policy, but its main objectives should be the benefit to the economy as a whole or the development of a certain region necessary for national equilibrium rather than immediate profitability from one or more specific projects.

Furthermore, tourist expansion also depends on the policy of frontier formalities related to tourists, which is conventionally a government monopoly. Providing a friendly tourist facilitation climate is a necessary prelude to any government interest in tourism development.

Tourist Legislation

The complexity of the tourist industry requires sound legislative policy in order to bring about an orderly, regulated rate of tourist growth, to determine the respective shares of domestic and foreign capital, and to prepare a suitable climate for stimulating investment in the tourist sector.

Moreover tourist legislation and regulations should deal with the operation and management of tourist enterprises (hotels, various other lodging establishments, travel agencies), including financial and fiscal incentives; organization of tourism inside the country; the use of land and other natural resources for tourism development; generation of tourism demand (holiday legislation); businesses of ancillary interest to tourism; and so on.

Some of the natural, historical, and cultural attractions of the country will be in the hands of various departments of the central and local government, and the government should coordinate efforts to use these in both the national and tourist interest.

Another important government tourism function is to exercise, through the National Tourism Agency (NTA) as well as other government departments, a certain degree of control over the quality and standard of tourist services. This function is part of the duty of the government to see that the tourist image of the country is enhanced. The extent of such control as part of the national tourist policy should be spelled out in legislative enactments in order that public, private, and foreign tourist concerns may see clearly where they stand and develop their management policies accordingly.

A moderate, steady, and well-defined control policy is desirable in all tourist countries irrespective of their varying economic and political systems, since tourism is a sensitive international movement, which if put under too much pressure in one country moves to another.

Pricing Policy

Prices should not be included in the control function. The market mechanism, when reasonably sufficient, should be able to set prices of tourist services at an acceptable level within the country's standard of living and in relation to other countries' comparable tourist services.

The governments of some developing countries, believe it necessary to control the prices, because if prices are left in the hands of tour operators and hoteliers, the country might be "priced out of the market." This argument is false as tourism is a highly competitive "product" where, if prices are below average the ought-to-happen increase in tourism to that particular country should result in an increase in prices and vice versa. Only certain regulatory measures should be practiced by the government in the case of abuse or exploitation on the part of foreign tour operators. In brief, the law of supply and demand is the best safety valve insofar as tourist prices are concerned, provided that the service standards remain highly satisfactory.

The overall responsibility for education and training in all sectors of the tourist industry may be another important government concern in some countries. As training of tourism personnel at all levels is an indispensable tool to help raise productivity, the government might like to take the lead by providing all necessary facilities in order that such training be effectively undertaken in cooperation with the established tourist concerns. This is practiced not only in socialist countries but also in some free-market countries such as Italy and France. In the United States this function is the responsibility of professional associations and large companies rather than the government. Expenditures on tourist education and training should be regarded as investments equally as important as those investments in tourist infrastructure, superstructure, and promotion.

Taxes levied on tourists and tourist concerns by governments and local authorities to recoup the costs incurred in financing tourist infrastructure and superstructure should be carefully reviewed. There is no need to argue about the rationality of such tax policy, nor should we ask the governments to reconsider these taxes as possible hindrances to tourism development, because the idea of users paying for the facilities used by them is gaining widespread acceptance. The only reservation we have about these taxes is that a convenient and economical tax collection method should be developed that avoids discrimination and channels all yields toward the expansion and amelioration of tourist conditions and facilities in the country. The best way is to establish a National Tourist Development Fund which would receive these yields and be entrusted to use them, according to a certain plan, in the development of the country's most important tourist attractions and creating proper amenities.

The Special Case of Government Aids and Incentives in Tourism

In supporting the tourist industry, governments may take different measures ranging from ensuring a suitable climate for private investments through regulations that guarantee economic stability to actively providing investors in tourism with considerable subsidies. It is advisable that government aids to tourism be specified in legislation after a careful study of the economic conditions.

Economic stability is a basic requirement for stimulating investment in tourism. The preparation of a tourist development plan is a good indication of the government's readiness to assist and support the tourist industry. The government should urge local private investors to invest in tourist projects in general and tourist accommodation in particular because if left alone they might be reluctant. The reason for such reluctance is that tourist and hotel projects in general do not yield more than 10 to 15 percent as net return on capital invested. This yield may not be sufficient for investors who expect larger profit margins.

Government aid to the tourist industry may be either financial or administrative and technical.

Financial Aid   Financial aid varies from one country to another according to its tourist policy and political and economic conditions. Financial aid includes subsidies—sums of money payable by the government to private investors to help them in launching tourist projects and amenities in economically developing areas. These subsidies represent a fixed percentage of the total cost of the project in order to stimulate maximum participation by the investor. Among the countries where government subsidies to the hotel sector exist are Belgium, Cameroon, Egypt, France, Hungary, Ireland, Japan, Lebanon, Malta, Morocco, the Netherlands, Panama, Portugal, and Tunisia.

Some countries give aid in kind such as granting land plots in certain remote areas of particular tourist significance or giving such land on concessional terms, or under favorable conditions with purchase options where the land is expensive. Examples of in-kind aid are found in Argentina, Cameroon, Sri Lanka, Egypt, Morocco, Nepal, Peru, Tunisia, Turkey, Lebanon, and India.

Other examples of government aid include

Exemption from payment of customs duties: In most cases governments grant exemptions from custom duties on the importation of material and equipment required for the construction or management of tourism amenities.

Long-term loans at reduced interest: Governments in several countries provide investors with long-term loans at low interest rates to encourage tourism investments. These loans are usually afforded through normal banking channels or by certain governmental development agencies. Loans for construction are provided for about 20 to 25 years and for modernization and renovation for 8 to 12 years. A grace period before the start of repayment is usually afforded. Interest ranges from 7 to 9 percent on such loans. Examples of this type of government aid exist in Algeria, Belgium, Ceylon, Colombia, Cyprus, Czechoslovakia, Egypt, France, Gabon, Germany, Greece, Hungary, India, Iran, Ireland, Italy, Lebanon, Mexico, Morocco, Nepal, the Netherlands, New Zealand, Norway, Pakistan, Peru, Portugal, Spain, Sweden, Switzerland, Trinidad, Tunisia, Turkey, United Kingdom, and the United States.

Guarantees for credits: Some governments provide full financial guarantees without fee for national and international credits obtainable through normal banking and financial arrangements. Examples are Algeria, Austria, Belgium, Canada, Germany, India, Ireland, Italy, Mexico, the Netherlands, New Zealand, Norway, Panama, Portugal, Sweden, Switzerland, and Tunisia.

Exemptions from income and real estate taxes: Governments sometimes grant exemptions on income and real estate taxes. This procedure constitutes a real incentive for private investment. Income tax exemption is usually granted for five years with partial exemption for the following 10 to 15 years. Examples are Algeria, Argentina, The Bahamas, Belgium, Bolivia, Brazil, Cambodia, Cyprus, Egypt, France, Gabon, India, Iran, Italy, Japan, Jordan, Lebanon, Libya, Malta, Morocco, Nepal, New Zealand, Nigeria, Pakistan, Panama, Senegal, Trinidad, Tunisia, and Turkey.

Deduction of capital expenditure: This allows for the possibility of claiming that capital expenditure incurred in the construction or renovation of hotels and purchase of equipment and fittings be deducted from profits over a certain number of years.

Favorable public utilities charges: Reductions are often accorded to the hotel industry on light, power, heating, and telephone charges.

Special rate of exchange for tourists: To allow a better exchange rate than the official rate (IMF) is most encouraging to international tourism.

Technical Aid and Favorable Regulations

Some governments extend their technical assistance to private investors in tourism by helping them prepare feasibility studies and advising them on their implementation. Moreover, governments usually issue regulations intended to win the confidence of investors. These regulations grant relaxed requirements as to licenses, building permits, construction conditions, and so on.

Attracting Foreign Investments in Developing Countries

Since local capital in developing countries is scarce and the aid that international development agencies can provide is limited, governments can attract foreign capital by several means. First and foremost is to create a suitable climate, that is, to establish economic and political stability. Moreover, there should be no discrimination against foreign investments. Foreign interests should be safeguarded against expropriation without compensation. Clear statutory provisions should be made for transfer of profits, amortization, and a low rate of profit tax. Finally, no undue restrictions should be applied in respect of labor permits for foreign staff.

Summary

This entry discusses government's involvement in strategic planning for tourism. In most cases governments are involved in providing tourist-friendly climates through parks, monuments, and other attractions. Governments regulate the tourist industry to be responsive to the needs of their citizens, the ultimate beneficiaries of tourism development, and supply infrastructure such as roads, ports, airports, communication systems, sewage, electricity, and health and security services.

References

Mathieson, Alister, and Geoffrey Wall. 1982. *Tourism: Economic, Physical and Social Impacts.* New York: Wiley.

Wahab, Salah E. A. 1988. *Planning of Tourism Resources* (in Arabic). Cairo.

17

Tourism Infrastructure and Development

Clare A. Gunn

Nations, states, provinces, and communities increasingly consider tourism development as a significant form of economic development. But, because it is a relatively new form and is very complicated as compared to other industrial development, it requires understanding of its interrelated functions, the importance of destinations, and the roles of the sectors involved in creating new and improved physical plant. Such development is often described as being made up of two parts. The term *superstructure* usually refers to the buildings and land developments used directly by travelers, such as hotels, restaurants, resorts, attractions, and campgrounds. *Infrastructure* is a term applied to necessary support development, such as roads, airports, water supply, waste disposal, police, and fire protection. Both superstructure and infrastructure require considerable capital investment at destinations. They are characterized by their fixed location and vulnerability to market changes, demanding careful consideration of planning and management.

Unlike an industry that is relatively cohesive and directed toward a product, the physical development of tourism is made up of a great diversity of business, government, and nonprofit components. Gee et al. (1984) have placed the business aspects of tourism into three categories. The direct providers include airlines, hotels, ground transportation, travel agencies, restaurants, and retail shops. The support services encompass tour organizers, travel and trade publications, management, and research firms. A third category, developmental organizations, includes planners, government agencies, real estate developers, and educational and financial institutions.

Another approach to the developmental side of tourism is to view it as it functions for the traveler. For example, a cross section of the entire travel route from home and return might be diagrammed as in Figure 1. A variety of transportation modes might be utilized along the journey, including automobile, RV, taxi, bus, or airline. These require streets, highways, automobile service stations, signage, and airports. Critical to the travel would be its objectives—parks, zoos, scenic roads, museums, battlefields, shrines, forests, mountains, beaches, convention centers, sports arenas, industries, and trade centers. Necessary services would include lodging accommodations of many

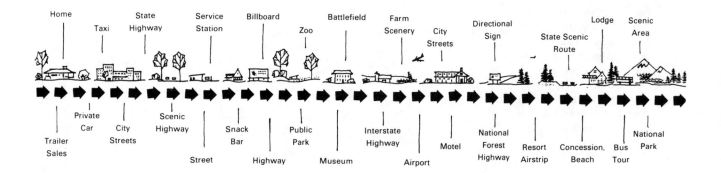

Fig. 1. Tourism functional flow. Diagram illustrating the great number and diversity of elements of tourism development. (*Source: From C. A. Gunn, 1988, Vacationscape: Designing Tourism Regions, 2d ed., New York: Van Nostrand Reinhold, p. 10.*)

kinds, foodservices, and several forms of travel assistance. All of these occur on the land and utilize various assets of the landscape. Thus, when tourism is viewed in a holistic functional way, the immense mass of development becomes almost incomprehensible.

The Functioning Tourism System

One way to help understand tourism's complexities is to conceive of it as being driven by two main forces—*demand* (markets) and *supply* (development). Each intimately relates to the other (Figure 2). What people seek as objectives of their travel is composed not only of what they wish but also of what is available to them. What is developed on the supply side is not only related to travelers' desires at distant locations but also to the land and its geographic characteristics. Tourism is an extremely dynamic system, always in a very delicate balance. It is subject to change from both forces. Over time, societies and travel market segments, the "push" side of tourism (Dann 1977), undergo changes in their travel interests and preferences. At the same time, innovative developers create new uses and interpretations of land resources, the "pull" side. This fundamental—dynamic balance—forces constant monitoring of both the demand and supply sides in order to maintain proper equilibrium.

Taylor (1980:58) calls this balance the "market-plant match." Figure 3 illustrates his model of a process whereby macro and micro matching could be assessed. Within the Canadian federal tourism office, he was able to initiate this concept, first by surveying market segments in prime Canadian market sources. For example, he found that Canada could supply plant for only one of six segments of Swedish travelers. Of all segments from (then) West Germany, Canada could match two with its tourism development. The U.S. market segments could be supplied entirely with what Canada had to offer. A guide for tourism development in Western Australia (Western Australian Tourism Commission 1985:14) suggests that areas can study their markets and development to determine "gaps" between the two.

From a tourism development perspective, the market-plant match problem is quite different from manufactured goods. Manufactured products are distributed to market areas whereas tourists (markets) are distributed to products (destinations). The location of a manufacturing plant is of no consequence to the purchaser of goods but the location of travel development at

Fig. 2. Driving forces of tourism: demand and supply factors. Development should strive for balance.

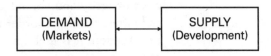

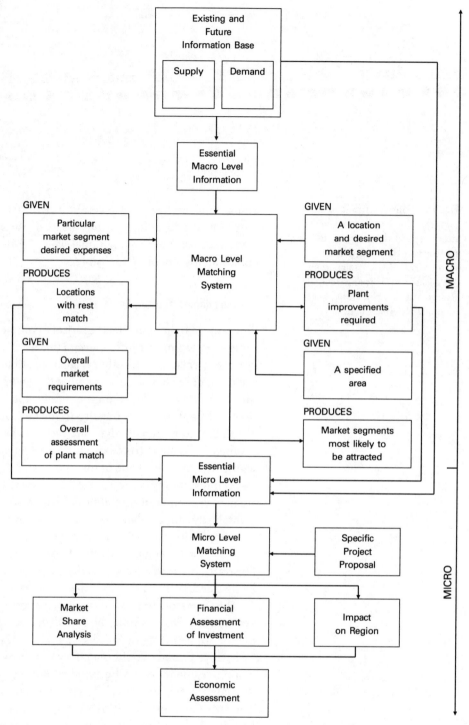

Fig. 3. Market-plant match. Shown is a systems model for guiding a balance between market and plant for tourism development. *(Source: After G. D. Taylor, 1980, How to match plant with demand: A matrix for marketing, Tourism Management 1(1):58.)*

destinations is of great significance to travelers. This fundamental exposes the need for developers of tourism to recognize the importance, and vulnerability, of tourism development locations—the many factors of land and place.

Of particular interest to tourism development and developers is the great diversity and volume of physical development—both superstructure and infrastructure. In order to clarify this huge mass of land modification and construction, it is useful to identify the supply side as made up of five major components (Figure 4). These could be labeled *attractions, transportation, services,*

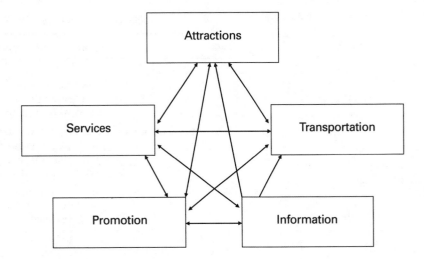

Fig. 4. Components of tourism supply. For best tourism development, all supply components should be kept in balance and in accord with market demand.

information, and *promotion.* Land development for tourism is concerned primarily with the first three of these because information and promotion deal mostly with activities and programs rather than physical construction.

If one were to identify the most powerful force of the supply side of tourism, it would have to be *attractions.* Attractions are here defined as all those things for visitors to see and do—for business and pleasure. They not only draw tourists to a distant location; they also contain all the design, development, and managerial factors that make the visit worthwhile.

Attractions are predominantly based on natural and cultural resources. Even though great growth in popularity of human-made attractions, such as theme parks, has occurred, it has not been at the expense of attractions based on resources. For example, visits to the U.S. national parks have increased over one-third in the last decade (National Park Service 1989). In 1989, there were approximately 96.5 million visits to cultural areas administered by the U.S. National Park Service.

Very important is the interaction between all these components. Any change in one affects the others. Lodging and foodservices must have high quality internal products and management but are even more dependent upon access and attractions. Or, an attraction may have little patronage because descriptive information was not available and promotion did not call attention to it.

This basic functioning system of tourism is influenced by several external factors (Figure 5). *Natural resources* provide the foundation for a great amount

Fig. 5. Influences on the tourism system. The tourism system does not function in isolation as it is influenced by several external factors.
(Source: After C. A. Gunn, 1988, Tourism Planning, 2d ed., New York: Taylor & Francis, p. 73.)

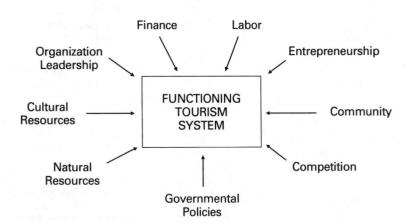

Table 1. *Key natural resource factors for tourism development*

Factor	Significance for tourism
Water, Waterlife	Suitability for resorts, campgrounds, parks, vacation homes, cruising, boating, fishing, hunting, historic redevelopment, photography, nature appreciation, organization camping; high water quality; adaptability at all seasons.
Vegetative Cover	Suitability for scenic enjoyment, nature trails, photography, parks, campgrounds, resorts, hunting, organization camping, vacation homes, habitat for wildlife; usefulness at all seasons (spring wildflowers, autumn leaf colors).
Wildlife	Suitability for hunting, nature appreciation, photo safaris, wildlife resorts, wildlife museums and interpretation centers; seasonality of potential.
Topography, Soils, Geology	Suitability for snow skiing, mountain climbing, hang gliding, scenic overlooks, scenic roads, photography; suitable for building construction, landscape development; freedom from erosion; geological study interest.
Climate, Atmosphere	Freedom from severe storms, fog, excessive humidity, cloudiness, intense heat or cold, pollution; impact of high altitude; unusually heavy precipitation.

of tourism development preferred by tourists. In recent years *cultural resources* have become increasingly important for attraction development of historic, ethnic, craft, and entertainment interests of travelers. Tables 1 and 2 illustrate the key natural and cultural resource factors and their relationship to several kinds of tourism development. The extent of entrepreneurship in a region has much to do with development of tourism. This factor is traditional in market economies but may have to be nurtured in developing countries. Essential to all development is availability of finance. Neither public nor private development will take place without adequate financial support. All hospitality and travel businesses as well as public tourism development requires an adequate supply of labor at all levels. A study of the competition should be made before an area launches an extensive tourism development program. How well the community accepts and is willing to support tourism is a major influence on the smooth functioning of tourism. Certainly, in all

Table 2. *Key cultural resource factors for tourism development*

Factor	Significance for tourism
Prehistory, Archeology	Suitability for developing visitor interpretation centers, outdoor dramas, displays, exhibits depicting ancient peoples at sites and areas.
Historic Eras	Suitability for restoring, protecting historic buildings and sites for visitor enrichment and interpretation; historic reuse; docudramas; exhibits, displays, dioramas; living history sites; reenactments of historic events.
Ethnic, National	Suitability for pilgrimages, interpretive visitor centers, ethnic displays, artifacts, crafts, music, art, foods; opportunities for dance, drama; ethnic and national events, shrines, monuments.
Economic Development	Suitability for plant tours; visiting human-made inventions, achievements; scientific laboratories; agriculture, manufacturing, processing; conferences, meetings, sports gatherings; trade and business attractions.

regions, the many governmental policies have important bearing on how tourism will be developed. Finally, tourism development depends greatly on the leadership and organizational support it is given.

Concept of Destination Zone

The interrelation between the physical components of supply is well illustrated by the concept of *destination zone*. All travel is directed toward destinations, whether the trip is for business or pleasure. In order for a receiving area to function for tourism, it must be developed as a total destination zone.

The diagram in Figure 6 illustrates the relationship of destination zones to a region. A region, nation, state, or province can be considered as containing

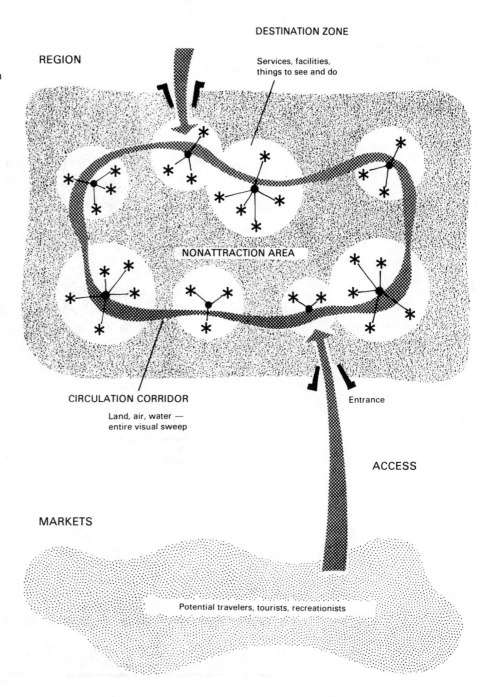

Fig. 6. Destination zones in a region. Tourism development focuses on destination zones, linked to markets through a main access and circulation corridor. *(Source: From C. A. Gunn, 1988, Vacationscape: Designing Tourism Regions, 2d ed., New York: Van Nostrand Reinhold, p. 71.)*

REGION

DESTINATION ZONE

Services, facilities, things to see and do

NONATTRACTION AREA

CIRCULATION CORRIDOR

Land, air, water — entire visual sweep

Entrance

ACCESS

MARKETS

Potential travelers, tourists, recreationists

destination zones, a *circulation corridor*, and a remaining *nonattraction area*. Important also is the region's relationship to the several travel market sources.

An enlargement of the destination zone is presented in Figure 7. In order for a destination zone to fulfill its functions, it must be developed to contain four essential parts. *Attraction clusters*, either within a community or within a reasonable radius, provide the pulling power. The logical location for most travel services is in one or several *communities*. Communities contain basic infrastructure, such as water supply, waste disposal, police, fire protection, and a diversity of shops and services. Nearly all travel service businesses rely upon residential as well as travel markets. Critical to both attraction complexes and communities are the *linkage corridors* and *main access corridors* (Gunn,

Fig. 7. Destination zone. A conceptual diagram illustrates the key components of destination zones for tourism development. *(Source: From C. A. Gunn, 1988, Vacationscape: Designing Tourism Regions, 2d ed., New York: Van Nostrand Reinhold, p. 57.)*

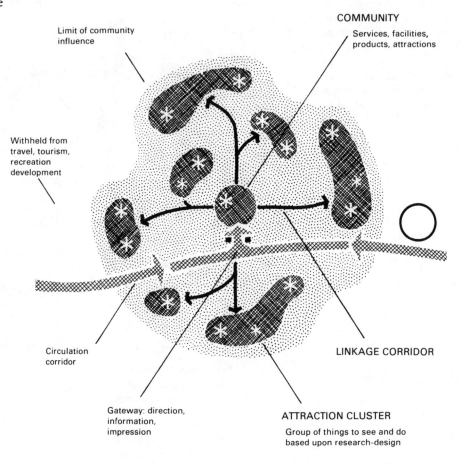

RADIAL DESTINATION ZONE

COMMUNITY
Services, facilities, products, attractions

Limit of community influence

Withheld from travel, tourism, recreation development

LINKAGE CORRIDOR

Circulation corridor

Gateway: direction, information, impression

ATTRACTION CLUSTER
Group of things to see and do based upon research-design

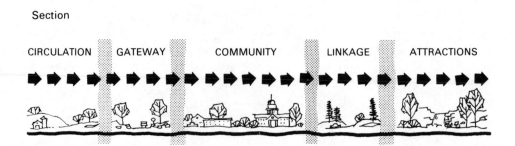

Section

CIRCULATION   GATEWAY   COMMUNITY   LINKAGE   ATTRACTIONS

1986b). Developers of tourism must plan for all these elements and make sure that at all times they are functioning together as a whole.

Most attractions seem to function best when they are clustered. Modern transportation does not allow attraction features to be strewn along travel ways as in the past. Most national parks are examples of clustered attractions, often including scenic beauty, wildlife, opportunities for nature study and photography, hiking, horseback riding, fishing and other outdoor recreation, and visiting historic sites and buildings. A cluster of attractions fosters each unit to contribute to a larger theme, resulting in greater visitor appeal and easier promotion. Larger clusters are more easily managed and serviced. Utilities, such as water, waste, and power, are more efficiently supplied.

Linkage corridors between communities and attraction complexes (and between complexes) require special examination and development for tourism. The landscapes and developments that travelers pass through provide important visual impressions. If these are littered, trashy, and ugly, they detract from the quality experience of the attraction cluster upon arrival. Not only must these linkage corridors be designed for anticipated volume but also for stimulating appropriate and compatible impressions upon the traveler.

Communities present special planning and development problems (Gunn 1988a: 241). Historically, most communities were developed on an economy other than tourism—agriculture, forestry, mining, manufacturing. As a consequence, tourism is an adaptation. This adaptation is compatible if the local society adjusts to the acceptance of a host role. In other instances, the adjustment is difficult and divisive (Blank 1989:5a). The community, when planned and developed to do so, can provide many tourist services and amenities. But, the community must be willing to make the social, economic, and environmental adjustments needed to accept tourism.

Essential to a destination zone is how well it is linked with main travel arteries. Highway access is desirable. But, volumes of traffic passing through do not necessarily foster tourism. Nearness to major thoroughfares, airports, and even harbors can be an asset provided visitors have excellent intermodal access to the community. Essential to visitor enjoyment and participation of activities in communities as elsewhere is adequate pedestrian access.

Variants of the destination zone concept are illustrated in Figure 8. Figure 8A illustrates a very important destination zone, the city. Several travel market segments seek urban attractions for both business and pleasure. Cities contain businesses, industries, technical centers, and research institutions important to business travel. They often contain parks, zoos, historic sites, entertainment, arenas, and shopping opportunities. Developers of tourism must make sure all parts of the urban destination zone are in place and functioning well.

Perhaps the most popular variant is the radial destination zone, Figure 8B. This zone includes not only urban attractions but also those of the surrounding region. Short trips can provide access to nearby attractions, focusing most travel services on the community where they can serve both resident and travel markets. A modification includes such special cases as resorts, hunting lodges, and farm vacations where most services would be located on the same site as the attraction. Even so, the larger mass and greater diversity of services would be located in the nearest community.

Another pattern, popular with long-distance air travel, is illustrated in Figure 8C. Here, the traveler may or may not use the attractions of the major city at the end of the primary access flight. Then, travel continues by a secondary flight or land tour to the final destination zone.

Fig. 8. Three kinds of destination zones. Analysis and development varies depending on whether it is for an urban, radial, or extended type of destination zone. *(Source: From C. A. Gunn, 1988, Tourism Planning, 2d ed., New York: Taylor & Francis, p. 194.)*

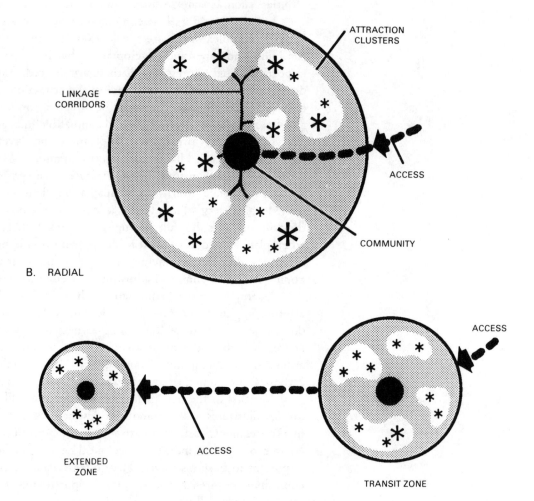

A. URBAN

B. RADIAL

C. EXTENDED

Throughout all destination zone development, the strong interdependencies between the major parts are fundamental to success. This implies the need for coordinated design, planning, and management.

Regional Analysis for Potential Zones

If tourism functions are centered on destination zones, the question arises regarding how zones with future potential can be found. An early attempt to do this was made in Michigan (Blank et al. 1966). A review and graphic mapping of key resources resulted in identifying nine zones with tourism-recreation potential in Michigan's Upper Peninsula. Refinements in this process have been made in recent years, utilizing computer graphic overlays (Gunn and Larsen 1988). Getz (1986) has summarized several techniques and approaches to planning for tourism development.

Fundamentally, tourism will thrive best where key factors converge in greatest amount and quality. If a regional search is made to identify the general areas where these occur, zones of potential can be delineated (Gunn 1988a:224). Briefly, the process of identifying potential zones includes the following seven steps.

1. *Generalizing market demand.* For determining potential zones, today's markets can be generalized into two major classes. Most pleasure travel markets are seeking development based on natural resource characteristics. A second major class including pleasure and business travel markets seek development based on cultural resources.

2. *Researching key factors.* A region can be studied for the purpose of summarizing and mapping the basic factors. The natural resource factors to be studied are

> water, waterlife
> vegetation, wildlife
> topography, soils, geology
> existing natural resource development

The cultural resource factors include

> prehistory, archeology
> history, ethnicity
> economic development
> existing cultural resource development

In addition, transportation and cities are studied, especially for their geographic distribution and degree of access.

3. *Preparing generalized factor maps.* For each factor, a generalized map is prepared showing the location of the area of its influence. For example, an interstate highway may be shown as a ribbon ten miles in width to indicate its influence in future development. These maps show three levels of quantity and quality—best, good, fair.

4. *Converting maps to computer overlays.* Modern computer programs, such as ARC/INFO (trademark Environmental Systems Research Institute), can be utilized to digitize the hand factor maps to a desired uniform scale.

5. *Weighting the factors.* Because all factors are not equal in their importance for future tourism development, they can be weighted. Weighting is subjective and may best be done by a panel of experts in tourism development.

6. *Aggregating the factors.* By computer, the two sets of map overlays can be aggregated, producing two composite maps, one showing areas of high, medium, and low values for the natural resource foundation, and another with similar value plots for the cultural resource base (Figure 9).

7. *Generalizing potential zones.* Using the research information together with the two composite maps, one can then generalize potential destination zones.

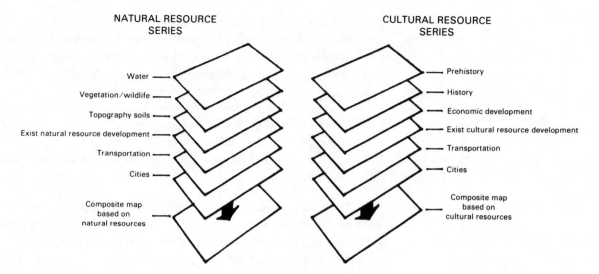

NATURAL RESOURCE
SERIES

Water
Vegetation/wildlife
Topography soils
Exist natural resource development
Transportation
Cities

Composite map
based on
natural resources

CULTURAL RESOURCE
SERIES

Prehistory
History
Economic development
Exist cultural resource development
Transportation
Cities

Composite map
based on
cultural resources

Fig. 9. Overlay mapping by computer. Using a GIS program, two series of map overlays can produce two composite maps showing areas of greatest resource support for tourism development.

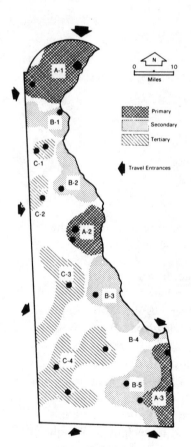

0   N   10
Miles

Primary
Secondary
Tertiary

Travel Entrances

Fig. 10. Potential destination zones for Delaware from an interpretation based on analysis of several natural resource factors.
(Source: From C. A. Gunn, 1990, Delaware's Natural Resources Potential for Tourism, prepared for Price Waterhouse and Delaware Tourism Office, College Station, TX: C. A. Gunn, p. 25.)

This process has been applied to several state tourism plans, including Oklahoma, Washington, and Delaware. In the Delaware case, only the potential based on natural resources was examined. The final step, the composite map of zones of potential based on natural resources, is illustrated in Figure 10 (Gunn 1990). Figure 11 illustrates the comparative support from each factor for each suggested zone.

This process has several implications. It identifies areas with the best resource base—areas that developers from all sectors (government, non-profit organization, private enterprise) should further study and analyze. It is in these areas that expanded and new attractions have adequate foundations. The identification of potential zones suggests also that the tourism leaders have the opportunity of cooperating on joint efforts toward future development, especially enlarging and adding attractions. Equally important is to analyze each zone in greater depth to determine its degree of saturation; can it be expanded without environmental and social damage? The process does not identify areas now ready to be promoted. Rather it assists in guiding future development where it is most logical.

Rural and Small Town Tourism Development

Government programs of special assistance to rural areas to bolster weakening economies often include tourism. At a rural tourism conference in Portugal, Edwards (1989:73) summarized governmental initiatives in several countries as well as Portugal where rural area tourism development is included in the National Plan for Tourism. Emphasis is placed on a scheme called *Tourismo Habitacao* to stimulate lodging in larger, privately owned country homes. France has a special program supporting rural tourism. In 1989, the U.S. Congress mandated a study of rural tourism to be carried out through the United States Travel and Tourism Administration. The consulting firm of Economic Research Associates held hearings throughout the country identifying tourism development needs in rural areas (U.S. Travel and Tourism Administration 1989).

Some governments are assisting rural tourism development through ed-

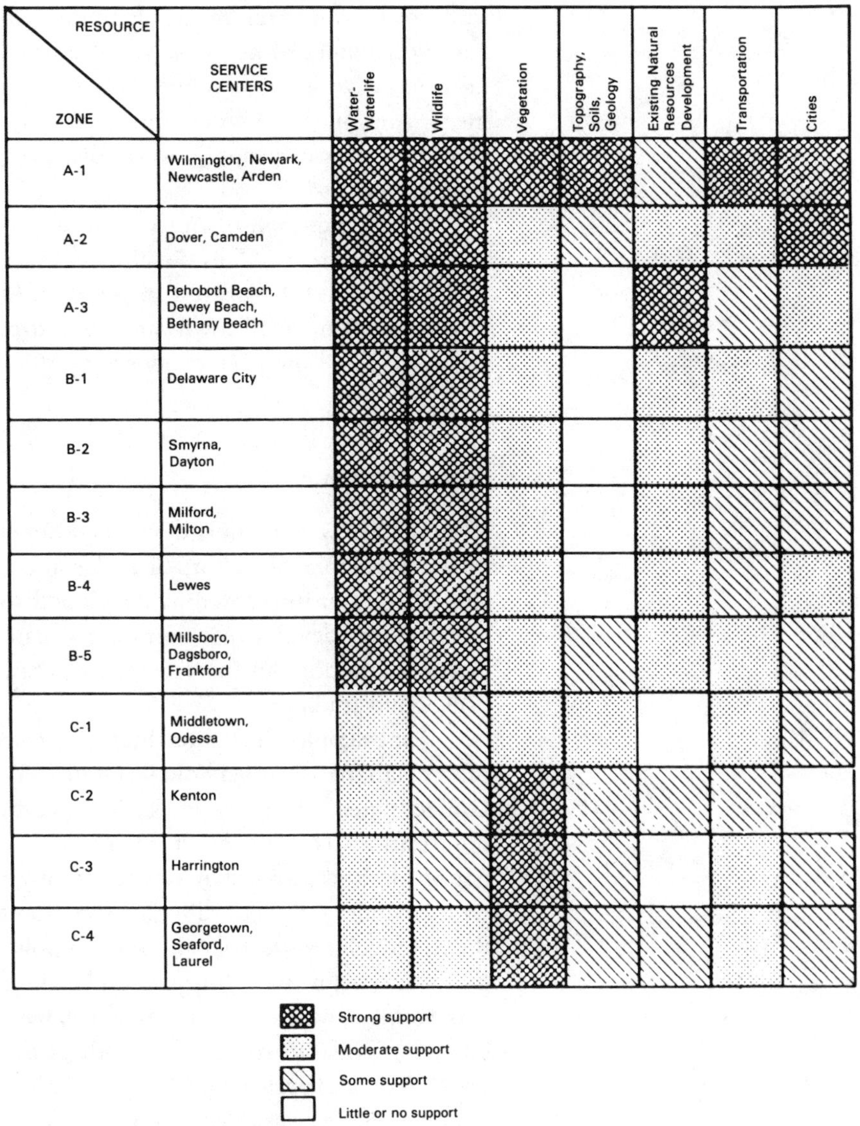

Fig. 11. Comparative resource support shown in a matrix illustrating the relative importance of support of resource factors. *(Source: From C. A. Gunn, 1990, Delaware's Natural Resources Potential for Tourism, prepared for Price Waterhouse and Delaware Tourism Office, College Station, TX: C. A. Gunn, p. 25.)*

ucational programs. Alberta Tourism, the provincial tourism governmental agency, issues numerous bulletins directed toward guidance for small community tourism development. Extension programs in the United States often focus on educational assistance for small town tourism development. Minnesota, for example, has published a rural and community guide, *So Your Community Wants Travel/Tourism?* (Simonson 1988). Increasingly, researchers and policy makers are studying the potential of outlying areas for tourism development such as Hunt's (1989) discussion of the significance of wildlands in tourism.

But, rural and small town tourism development poses some special issues. Wall (1979) has identified several negative social, environmental, and economic impacts of tourism in rural areas. Ironside (1971) cited disturbance of stock, erosion of trails, erosion of riverbanks, damage to crops, loss of vegetation, and disturbance of wildlife as potential threats of tourism to rural areas. Frequently, these areas have limited human and financial resources. Because much of the potential for tourism will lie in surrounding resources, old jurisdictional rivalries (between city and county, nearby cities) will need to be overcome. Preference for traditional lifestyles may be a barrier to accepting volumes of new visitors. Leaders of rural tourism development will need to be very much concerned with conservation and sustainable development. And, many small communities may already have reached maximum capacities of water supply, waste disposal, police, fire protection, and other public services.

Rural and small town tourism development can be diagrammed as shown in Figure 12. This development implies strong cooperation between small towns and the nearest major city. And as a basic principle, tourism development of small towns and rural areas is best accomplished at a small scale and at a slow pace (Rodenburg 1980:177).

Developing Tourism

What and how tourism is developed depends upon the policies and practices of the development sectors of each nation. Throughout the world the supply side of the tourism system is developed by three categories of sectors—governments (as developers), nonprofit organizations, and commercial enterprise. In addition, all three sectors operate within the framework of national policy and tradition.

For example, the United States had no firm policy on tourism until passage of the National Tourism Policy Act of 1981. This act replaced the former United States Travel Service with the United States Travel and Tourism Administration. The mission of this agency is to carry out travel policies of the nation. The act also called for the establishment of a Tourism Policy Council with an interagency coordinating function and a Travel and Tourism Advisory Board (Edgell 1990). In Japan, tourism policies are formulated and administered by the Department of Tourism, under the Bureau of International Transport and Tourism, Ministry of Transport (Japan National Tourism Organization 1986:48). The tourism agency has three divisions: planning, travel agency, and development. Tourism development policies vary from nation to nation depending on the political structure and functions ascribed to governments.

Governmental Role in Tourism Development   A major role in tourism by virtually all governments is that of *promotion*. Tourism promotion encompasses four main functions. Advertising is the dominant

Fig. 12. Rural destination zones. Rural tourism potential is closely related to development of a nearby larger city.
(*Source: From C. A. Gunn, 1988, Tourism Planning, 2d ed., New York: Taylor & Francis, p. 249.*)

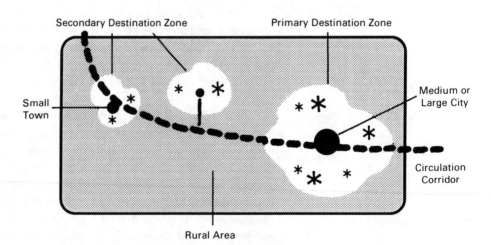

form of promotion and is believed to perform a major role in stimulating travel to destinations. Most nations, states, and provinces engage in publicity by means of journalism, familiarization tours, participating in travel shows, and disseminating literature about destinations. Public relations is a more subtle form of promotion and includes appearances at travel and tourism conferences, sponsorship of films and events, and sending performers into market areas. A final function, incentives, is used by businesses in the form of discounts, gifts, prizes, and specially priced packages.

In most countries, governments provide basic *infrastructure* for tourism development. Local governments usually provide the roads, airports, water supply, waste disposal, police, fire protection, streets, lighting, and power supply. In new development locations, not so serviced, often the developer must share the costs of installing new infrastructure.

Many nations engage in *direct intervention* or *subsidy*, obtaining land, building facilities, and sometimes supplying management. In Korea, the Law of Tourism Promotional Development Fund provides for direct building of hotels, transportation, shopping facilities, as well as construction and repairs of infrastructure (Ministry of Transportation and Korea National Tourism Corporation 1985: 120). Although most of Western Australia's physical plant has been developed by commercial enterprise, the Western Australian Tourism Commission often purchases land and develops facilities for future purchase by the private sector (Western Australia Tourism Commission 1986). Finland provides considerable financial aid, up to one-third the cost, to large scale projects such as family holiday complexes, water activity development, and skiing facilities (Kelley 1986:210).

Perhaps the largest governmental role for tourism in the United States is that performed by many land agencies at the federal and state levels. Extensive *natural and cultural resource lands*—approximately 755 million acres—are owned and managed by federal agencies such as the USDA Forest Service, U.S. Army Corps of Engineers, USDI National Park Service, Bureau of Indian Affairs, Bureau of Land Management, Fisheries and Wildlife Service, and Bureau of Reclamation. These federal lands represent 33 percent of the U.S. land bases (Cordell and Hendee 1982). These agencies supply the bulk of outdoor recreation attractions for travelers: areas for hunting, fishing, water sports, skiing, and nature appreciation. To this must be added state, county, and municipal parks. Another important governmental contribution to tourism is provision of highways and air traffic control.

In recent years, both federal and state agencies have increasingly purchased, restored, and operated historic sites and structures for visitor enrichment. These governmental operations are directly linked to tourism business success by providing much of the attraction for travel. In Texas, for example, outdoor recreational travel had an economic impact of $9.3 billion in 1983 (Texas Parks and Wildlife Department 1984).

Nonprofit Role in Tourism Development

Worldwide, the nonprofit sector is increasingly involved in tourism development. Health, religious, conservation, historic, ethnic, archeological, and youth organizations frequently own, develop, and manage land and facilities that involve travel. Most of the historic sites in the United States are sponsored by nonprofit, voluntary groups. Examples include Williamsburg, the Alamo, Mt. Vernon, and the Polynesian Culture Center. Virtually all festivals and events are sponsored by nonprofit groups who see value in promoting historic, ethnic, or other special events and celebrations, such as the Mardi Gras and Gasparillo Invasion. A great many private hunting, fishing, and ski clubs lease land from federal and state agencies for the development of slopes, trails, camping and other facilities. Fairs and festivals often spark other tourism development in communities. Nostalgiafest, a week-long festival in Petersburg, Virginia, includes over 20 concerts by local and state performers and attracts more than 75,000 people each year. Consequently, the city has been revitalized, the historic district has been developed, power lines have been placed underground, and parks have been beautified (Department of Housing and Urban Development 1981:9).

Commercial Enterprise The greatest volume of construction and development of tourist facilities and services is provided by the commercial enterprise sector. Most lodging, food services, car services, travel services, and shops are developed by this sector. In carrying out its profitmaking role, this sector is more responsive to shifts in travel market trends than any other. Its major characteristic is its innovative and creative development that often stimulates new travel market activity.

This sector depends wholly on the free market system whereby decisions of what to produce, where, how much, and at what price is decided not by a central power but by the market. The dominant characteristics of free enterprise have been identified by Allen et al. (1979).

1. *Private property.* Essential to free enterprise is individual ownership and control of property. This is based on the premise that individuals know best how to develop and manage their lands. The owner has the right to transfer use and enjoy income and other benefits from ownership.

2. *Economic freedom.* Rather than an outside force, the individual owner protects freedom of choice for the consumer. The owner has the right to start or discontinue business, purchase resources, use technology, and invest in any way.

3. *Economic incentives.* Workers receive incentives through wages and other rewards for providing goods and services that meet market needs. More productive operations become more profitable. Conversely, poor service and poor production are equally rewarded by failure or business loss. These economic incentives direct scarce resources to the production of goods and services that the market values the most.

4. *Competitive markets.* Each individual strives for his market share by doing the best job possible at a competitive price. This fosters efficiency and lower prices. When a business exhibits capacity sales, it stimulates competitors who strive for their market share.

5. *Limited role of government.* The system of market choice and free enterprise is upset by any interference in the system. Certain rules and regulations are necessary for environmental and consumer protection. But, too much intervention by government in ways that upset the relationship between sale price and productive effort destroys the free and competitive value of the system.

The development of primary tourist services—hotels, restaurants, carriers—is done by individual business enterprise at the site scale. The decision to establish a business is predicated on its *feasibility.* Studies of feasibility may be performed by the company making the proposal or by a consulting firm. The usual steps in a feasibility study are

1. Identification of a potential market: the people who can be expected to patronize the proposed hotel, resort, or restaurant.

2. Quantification of the market: how many people can be expected to patronize the hotel, resort, or restaurant if a particular facility is built.

3. Identification of the kind of facility that will appeal to the market.

4. Estimation of the size of the facility needed for the market.

5. Estimation of the cost of the facility that will serve the market.

6. Estimation of the income and expense of operating the facility, itemized by department.

7. Estimation of profit as a percentage of sales and as a percentage of investment. (Lundberg 1979:79)

Perhaps the most difficult aspect of tourist business feasibility is estimating the potential market. One basic principle is to evaluate the relationship between attractions of the area and relative success of existing travel businesses. If existing attractions are expanding and becoming more popular, the demand for services will increase. This premise has both qualitative and quantitative dimensions. Statistics of room occupancy of existing lodging may provide a major clue to an existing oversupply or deficiency. However, such total statistics do not reveal differences in market segment demand. It may be that even though statistics suggest an oversupply, there may be a deficiency in a special market segment.

The Tourism Product

The complexity of tourism makes it difficult to identify the tourism "product" as compared to a manufactured product. Roughly, the tourism product could be defined as the traveler's experience(s) en route and at a destination. The primary causal element of this experience is the attraction. Service businesses are facilitators.

This intimate functional relationship between attractions and travel services influences business success in many ways. Establishing new attractions such as parks, historic sites, or convention centers can increase business because of greater travel flows. Conversely, closing a major attraction or establishing a new one in a competitive location could erode service business activity. Even though services and attractions are developed by separate entities, their interdependency suggests the need for strong cooperation. Because most attractions are not profitmaking within themselves, there may be need for subsidy from the businesses who do profit.

Promoters of tourism products recognize the need for all components to function properly. It is unfortunate when travelers are attracted to a location only to discover that the attraction features are not as promised, that service businesses are not catering to their market segment, and that the time and money invested in the trip are out of proportion to the significance of the attraction features. The tourism product, because of its complexity, demands close integration of the government, nonprofit, and commercial sectors in order to meet expectations of travelers and to provide the best business success.

Development Issues

The future of tourism development faces several important issues. First, new mechanisms need to be found in order to produce greater integration of the many components of tourism. New competition, greater growth, and heightened costs of development require more efficient operation. The many businesses, trade groups, governmental agencies, and nonprofit organizations will discover greater success for each when greater understanding and cooperation replace segregation and fragmentation of tourism development. Cordell and Hendee concluded from their study of federal outdoor recreation in the United States: "There is a critical need to better define, implement, and coordinate desirable roles by the private sector and by local, state, and federal governments." (Cordell and Hendee 1982:84)

Second, the great growth of tourism is pushing the limits of capacity in many regions. Community tourism growth demands expansion of basic infrastructure. Rural tourism growth requires more careful planning and protection of natural and cultural resources. Quality water, air, forests, wildlife, and soil are the basic elements upon which tourism depends. All tourism sectors can gain by a strong proactive stand against all threats to resources and resource quality.

Third, when tourism is recklessly developed it can exact great stress upon the social and economic stability of an area. Host-guest relations require measures that protect the integrity of local life-styles and quality of life. Areas must be willing to accept the changes that tourism development demands, including economic as well as social costs if they wish to develop tourism. Although major development is sometimes needed to identify new and emerging destinations, a more amenable type of development is slow-paced small-scale indigenous development.

Fourth, in nearly all regions, seasonality of tourism has hindered commercial success of much development. Increasingly, this seasonality is being overcome from two sides. A greater number of market segments today are able to travel at all seasons. And, developers are increasing all-weather and all-season attractions. These factors are contributing to much greater stability of tourism businesses.

Fifth, all developers of tourism must work toward assuring greater traveler safety—freedom from sickness, crime, terrorism, accidents (Edgell 1990:48). No matter how appealing the attractions may be, travelers will not seek those destinations that cannot be enjoyed freely. Especially important is sensitivity to the special needs of foreign visitors.

Finally, the complicated nature and great growth and competitiveness of tourism demand much greater understanding of the scientific, technical, political, and managerial aspects of tourism. This requires massive increases in educational programs at all levels. Children need to be taught how to gain the most from travel experiences and to comprehend the many career opportunities associated with tourism. Higher level educational programs need to stress the interdisciplinary nature of tourism. Much higher competence will be demanded from all leaders and actors in tourism development in the future. Educational programs, seminars, conferences, and workshops are being directed toward greater cooperation among the many sectors. The first conference between national parks and tourism in the United States was held in Biloxi, Mississippi, in 1988. More technical, scientific, and policy articles on the relationship between parks and tourism are appearing regularly, such as "Tourism and the National Parks," by Priscilla Baker of the National Park Service (Baker 1986:50).

Summary

This entry discusses the relation between infrastructure and tourism development and shows the role of the nonprofit sector in the overall tourism system. It also discusses the concept of destination zone and regional analysis for potential zones including rural and small towns. Finally, the issues of tourism development are discussed in light of the tourism system.

References

Allen, John W., David G. Armstrong, and Lawrence C. Wolken. 1979. *The Foundations of Free Enterprise*. Center for Education and Research in Free Enterprise. College Station, TX: Texas A & M University.

Baker, Priscilla. 1986. Tourism and the National Parks. *Parks & Recreation*, October, 51+.

Blank, Uel. 1989. *The Community Tourism Industry Imperative: The Necessity, the Opportunities, Its Potential*. State College, Pa.: Venture Publishing.

Blank, Uel, Clare A. Gunn, and Johnson, Johnson & Roy, Inc. 1966. *Guidelines for Tourism-Recreation in Michigan's Upper Peninsula*. Cooperative Extension Service. East Lansing, Mich.: Michigan State University.

Cordell, H. Ken, and John C. Hendee. 1982. *Renewable Resources Recreation in the United States: Supply, Demand, and Critical Policy Issues*. Prepared for the National Conference on Renewable Natural Resources. Washington, D.C.: The American Forestry Association.

Dann, G. 1977. Anomie, ego-enhancement and tourism. *Annals of Tourism Research* 4:184–194.

Department of Housing and Urban Development. 1981. *The Urban Fair: How Cities Celebrate Themselves*. HUD-PA-661. Prepared by Porter, Novell & Associates, Washington, D.C.: Department of Housing and Urban Development.

Edgell, David L. 1990. *Charting a Course for International Tourism in the Nineties*. Washington, D.C.: U.S. Travel and Tourism Administration.

Edwards, Jonathan. 1989. Tourism in rural areas. *Tourism Management* March, pp. 73–74.

Gee, Chuck, Y., Dexter J. L. Choy, and James C. Makens. 1984. *The Travel Industry*. Westport, Conn.: AVI.

Getz, Donald. 1986. Models in Tourism Planning. *Tourism Management* March, pp. 21–32.

Gunn, Clare A. 1988a. *Tourism Planning*. 2nd ed. New York: Taylor & Francis.

Gunn, Clare A. 1988b. *Vacationscape: Designing Tourism Regions*. 2nd ed. New York: Van Nostrand Reinhold.

Gunn, Clare A. 1990. *Delaware's Natural Resources Potential for Tourism*. Prepared for Price Waterhouse and Delaware Tourism Office. College Station, TX: C. A. Gunn.

Gunn, Clare A., and Terry R. Larsen. 1988. *Tourism Potential—Aided by Computer Cartography*. Serie C, No.116. Aix-en-Provence, France: Centre des Hautes Etudes Touristiques.

Hunt, John D. 1989. The significance of wildlands in tourism and trends affecting their future. Presentation at the Alaska Interagency Wildlands Management Workshop, Geophysical Institute, March 16, 1989. Fairbanks: Univ. of Alaska.

Ironside, R. G. 1971. Agricultural and recreational land use in Canada. *Canadian Journal of Agricultural Economics* 19(2):1–12.

Japan National Tourism Organization. 1986. *Tourism in Japan 1986*. Tokyo: Japan National Tourism Organization.

Kelley, Edward M., ed. 1986. Marketing strategy. In *Perspectives: Leisure Travel and Tourism*, pp. 206–212. Wellesley, Mass.: Institute of Certified Agents.

Lundberg, Donald E. 1979. *The Hotel and Restaurant Business*. Boston: CBI Publishing.

Ministry of Transportation and Korea National Tourism Corporation. 1985. *Korean Tourism Annual Report 1984*. Seoul: Ministry of Transportation and Korean National Tourism Corporation.

National Park Service. 1989. *NPS Statistical Abstract 1989*. Statistical Office. Washington, D.C.: National Park Service.

Rodenburg, Eric E. 1980. The effects of scale in economic development—tourism in Bali. *Annals of Tourism Research* 7(2):177–196.

Sessa, Alberto. 1983. *Elements of Tourism Economics*. Rome, Italy: Catal.

Simonson, Lawrence R. et al. 1988. *So Your Community Wants Travel/Tourism?* Minnesota Extension Service, CD BV-3443. St. Paul, Minn.: University of Minnesota.

Taylor, Gordon D. 1980. How to match plant with demand: a matrix for marketing. *Tourism Management* 1(1):56–60.

Texas Parks and Wildlife Department. 1984. *1983 Outdoor Recreation Trips, Expenditures in Texas.* Austin: Texas Parks and Wildlife Department.

U.S. Travel and Tourism Administration. 1989. *National Policy Study on Rural Tourism and Small Business.* Prepared for U.S. Travel and Tourism Administration by Economics Research Associates. Washington, D.C.: U.S. Travel and Tourism Administration.

Wall, G. 1979. The nature of outdoor recreation. In *Recreation Land Use in Southern Ontario,* ed. G. Wall, pp. 3–13. Waterloo: University of Waterloo.

Western Australia Tourism Commission. 1985. *Tourism Research for Non-Researchers.* Perth: Western Australia Tourism Commission.

Western Australia Tourism Commission. 1986. *Western Australian Tourism Profile.* Perth: Western Australia Tourism Commission.

18

Elements of Community Tourism Development Planning Process

Leland L. Nicholls

In the past one hundred years the populations of many countries, including the United States, have migrated to great commercial and industrial cities. Many of these urban clusters have drawn irresistibly into themselves, both the products of the countryside and the people and talents of the countryside communities. New evidence indicates a movement back to the suburbs and beyond into smaller communities. As inner cities become more desolate, filthy, ugly, dangerous, and constipated, many people are seeking a more appealing setting.

People are beginning to seek good communities based upon trust, good faith, good will, and mutual help. Communities are based upon the ancient rule of neighborliness, by the love of precious things, and by the wish to be at home or to enjoy a sense of place (Barry 1990).

There is an apparent return to and quest for livable communities with a new civic spirit. In a study at Rutgers University only 10 percent of those people surveyed rated their interest in living in a city as "very desirable." Percentages for new suburbs, old suburbs, small towns, and rural areas were 22, 38, 50, and 34, respectively (Williams 1991).

Since about 1970 many communities have incorporated the discovery, revitalization, and maintenance of special places. The joy of experiencing special places often includes tourism. Uniqueness is a popular attraction in today's mobile society. Many communities, however, remain vulnerable to the character loss created by change while often also being the most in need of the elements of change, economic progress, and increased social and cultural opportunity. This problem has often resulted in an over balance or distorted definition of "progress" and the absence of an understanding of the total range of "quality of life" costs to the local population (Garnham 1985).

Many communities have goals that include the development of tourism. Community leaders recognize the social and economic benefits of tourism. Management of a community tourism product, however, is based upon the integration of several complex and interlocking parts. This article examines and identifies the components of a tourism-based planning and management scheme.

The Beginning

Community planners must recognize at the onset that tourism, like other types of economic development, impacts the entire population. Planning efforts must include the input of all representative groups in the community. A divided community will thwart positive planning efforts. Secondly, planners must identify, focus, and trust the planning, promotion, and development efforts to preferably one organization or a small tourism planning team.

Inventory and Profile

Once a community decides to pursue tourism, planners must analyze the site and situation of the community. Community resources, tourism markets, competition, and intervening opportunities must be identified, assessed, and evaluated by planners. An inventory may include the following:

Resources

New and unusual opportunities for tourism investors	Tours
	Food specialties of the community
Existing tourist attractions and recreation facilities	Theatrical activities
	Interesting institutions
Special events	Flora and fauna
Natural attractions and scenic views	Homes of celebrities
	Camping facilities
Musical and art activities	Hotel and resort lodging accommodations
Historical and archaeological sites	
Scientific attractions	Convention and meeting facilities
Shopping opportunities	Recreation/real estate developments
Local sports events	
Hunting and fishing areas	

Additional Resources Needed

Transportation (volume, projections, existing network and services)	State government and taxes (including structure, condition, and attitudes)
Labor (labor force, wage rates, unions, legislation, recruiting)	Financing (mechanism available, business conditions, and special inducements to tourism)
Materials and services	Climate
Power and fuel	Community facilities
Water and waste disposal	Planning and zoning
Local government and taxes (including civic attitudes toward tourism)	Federal activities in the community
	Individual sites

Market Analysis

Define market	Consumer characteristics
Location	Retail sales trends

Population trends   Competition
Income trends   International factors

The Master Plan

After an inventory of the community site and situation, a more detailed plan is developed by the tourism planners. A few short- and long-term goals should be identified for one- to five-year periods. These goals and objectives are best achieved when they are quantifiable. Master plans also include the who, what, where, and when questions of the implementation of the plan. Examples of tourism goals, objectives, and related local tourism policies include those listed in Table 1.

Table 1. *Objectives, and related local tourism policies*

Goals	Objectives	Policies
1. To stabilize or increase the population	Halt out-migration Accommodate immigrants Attract families	Provide land and service for development Attract investment Supply housing
2. To create employment	New jobs in tourism Reduce unemployment Attain diversity Jobs for target groups (skilled or skill-giving)	Economic development Attract year-round tourism Encourage local investments; cooperatives Establish training programs
3. To increase incomes	Raise personal, household and community income/revenue Minimize inflation Benefit target groups	Taxation/incentives Local ownership fostered Preferential use of local labor and services
4. To enhance community viability	Use existing resources efficiently Provide services for future growth Promote self-sufficiency and local leadership Satisfy local aspirations regarding change	Foster local organizations and cooperation Request public input for policies Request public involvement in development changes Provide political leadership and control
5. To foster social welfare and integration	Minimize crime and social problems Provide adequate health and social services equitably Socially integrate newcomers and visitors	Develop health, police, social work, and welfare policies Discourage transient tourism labor
6. To strengthen local culture	Promote traditions Provide necessary facilities/leadership Encourage local events Avoid commercialization Satisfy local aspirations	Parks and recreations: events arts/cultural programs Grants/aid to groups Controls on entertainment or types of development Themed promotion of indigenous cultural attractions
7. To increase local leisure opportunities	Obtain new/improved facilities at low cost Give priority to local needs	Agreements with developers Control of entertainment and liquor; resource use
8. To assist conservation	Preserve heritage and natural resource base	Environmental controls Conservation programs
9. To enhance local amenity	Avoid crowding, loss of privacy, noise Develop high standards of design, open spaces, facilities	Parks and recreation beautification Architectural and site design controls

Source: Donald Getz, A Research Agenda for Municipal and Community Based Tourism in Canada, paper read at the Travel and Tourism Research Association Conference at Banff, June 1983.

Measuring the Results

Once the plan is in place, planners must create a system for measuring the results. These measures include a constant and consistent quantification of tourism data. Annual plans should be revised each year and the community profile should be reviewed and revised every two years. Documentation of completed activities should also occur every two years (Wisconsin Department of Development 1986).

Management of a community product provides many options. By placing tourism in a community perspective it becomes only one of several functions and opportunities for a community. It must, however, be planned in accordance with its relative importance and contribution (Murphy 1985:38).

Major Tourism Components

Four prime areas are usually considered for community tourism development:

1. Environmental and accessibility
2. Business and economic
3. Social and cultural
4. Management and planning

Successful planning efforts include a humanistic and community-oriented approach. Tourism products must be in harmony with each consideration and issue. Table 2 highlights some examples of the prime considerations associated with tourism development.

A Case Study

The citizens of LaCrosse, Wisconsin, recently completed a Tourism Facility and Attraction Master Plan. The project and procedure included the following components (LaCrosse Area Convention and Visitors Bureau 1989):

1. Form special task force with members of diversified interests.
2. Identify scope, scale, and purpose of project.
3. Qualify trend studies and research gathered for reference library, identify level of impact on travel, customer profile and demographics, entertainment, and recreational preference.
4. Assess assets based on past experience and research gathered.
5. Identify liabilities experienced from past studies and research identifying future trends.
6. Develop preliminary report based on committee's findings.
7. Initiate sample survey to civic clubs, organizations, and individuals the committee felt would be responsive to providing further input and concerns; i.e., Economic Development Corporation, arts, transportation, city planning.
8. Establish public speaking engagements addressing Master Plan and again reemphasize the overall concern for feedback from the community at large.
9. Reassess all input received and reexamine preliminary Master Plan based on community-wide concerns for preparation of final draft.
10. Produce models to further understanding of plan and catalogue research by individual project or development.

Table 2. *Examples of prime considerations associated with tourism development*

Development issues	Examples
Environmental and accessibility	Resource integrity in national parks (Great Smoky Mountains, Yosemite, Grand Canyon (U.S.), Banff (Canada), Peak District and Snowdonia parks (U.K.)
	Congested coasts (Costa Brava, Spain and South Florida and California, U.S.)
	Congested waterways (Norfolk Broads, U.K.; Okanagan Valley, British Columbia, Canada; Northern Mediterranean; St. Croix Scenic Waterway, U.S.)
	Image conflicts (canoeists vs. auto campers; waterskiers vs. fishermen; cross-country skiers vs. snowmobilers; older-family campers vs. young-singles campers; hunters vs. nonhunters
	Resource allocation (North American wilderness parks)
	Physical access (Nepal)
	Travel patterns (Chicago O'Hare Airport)
	Intervening opportunities (Orlando, FL)
	Zoning (Parks Canada)
	Carrying capacity (Banff, Canada; French Alps)
	Multiple use (Tennessee Valley, U.S.)
Business and economics	Short-term development issues (ski season)
	Medium-term development issue (Hurricane Hugo and its impact on tourism)
	Long-term cycles (Atlantic City, NJ)
	Economic benefits (Las Vegas, NV)
	Employment opportunities (Orlando, FL)
	Farm tourism (Austria)
	Second homes (Florida, U.S.)
Social and cultural	Community attitudes (Carmel, CA)
	Resident-visitor relations (Jamaica)
	Authenticity (Williamsburg, VA)
	Acculturation (Hawaii)
	Social carrying capacity (Bahamas)
	Concentration (Baltimore Harbor)
	Dispersion (Los Angeles, CA)
	Pace of change (Hilton Head, SC)
Management and planning	Ecological approach (Walt Disney World, FL)
	Public participation (Wisconsin; Dorset, England)

11. Establish completion deadlines for project based on priority identification.
12. Prepare market plan to publicize and implement plan.
13. Plan to look for investors from outside immediate community as primary objective to include local investment may not get the job done.

Numerous local, regional, and national sources of data were incorporated into identifying preferences, resources, and needed developments. The lists of priorities included

A. Leading Recreation Preferences
   1. Boating
   2. Fishing/Hunting
   3. Camping

4. Gold panning
5. Bicycling
6. Skiing—Cross country/downhill
7. Hiking/Jogging
8. Swimming
9. Bowling
10. Snowmobiling
11. Fitness/Spa Complex

B. Leading Entertainment Preferences
1. Sightseeing/Attractions
2. Dining
3. Shopping
4. Festivals
5. Spectator Sports
6. Arts
7. Night Life
8. Amusement Park

C. Current Resources
1. Mississippi River
2. Scenic beauty/Four seasons
3. Businesses, i.e., Medical Facilities/Corporate Influence/Education Institute
4. Attractions, i.e., Brewery Tour/Two Excursion Boats/LaCrosse Center
5. Shopping
6. Boating
7. Festivals/Special Events
8. Fishing, i.e., tournaments and general
9. Hotels/Motels
10. Ski Slope
11. Arts and Culture
12. Bike Trails

D. Needed Developments
1. Major Attraction Anchor—Dog Track
2. Lodging Alternatives, i.e., Major Convention Facility, Resort Complex
3. Bowling Facility to Host Tournaments
4. River Boardwalk
5. Improvement of Present Resources, i.e., Attractions, Facilities, etc.
6. Better Access and Further Development of Trails, i.e., Bike, Snowmobile, Cross Country
7. Transient Access to River for Overnight Dockage
8. Dinner Theater
9. Cheese Factory
10. Development of Canoe Trails
11. Public Fitness/Spa Complex
12. Dining Alternatives
13. Revitalization/Beautification Campaign—Traveling Public's First Impression

The Master Plan included complete integration of numerous community individuals and interest groups. The Plan and a Restoration and Land Use

Model were unveiled simultaneously at a special banquet attended by five hundred people. Adoption and development are scheduled between 1988 and 1993. The plan is being developed and implemented on schedule.

Summary

Communities are built by people. Today, many communities destined for decay are bursting with new life. This life comes from individuals—some in government, some in corporations, some in professional capacities, some volunteers from the communities themselves—who saw the good in their particular "place" and worked to save it. Not all the problems can be solved. Many communities, however, will successfully implement development schemes based heavily upon the opportunities afforded by tourism. Some of these communities have already been extremely successful in balancing the planning components.

Again, public participation in tourism planning has increased rapidly the past 15 years. While tourism's economic impacts are generally welcomed, many of the social and ecological consequences of tourism development are perceived as negative. The negative implications of tourism often result in deteriorating and hostile resident attitudes about tourism and tourists. When this happens everybody loses: residents, visitors, and tourism. Community involvement in tourism planning can assume a number of different forms and serve several purposes, but a basic aim of any planning effort should be to provide concerned citizens with accurate information (Keogh 1990:450–451).

In conclusion, Blank recently recognized the following characteristics of tourism (Blank, 1989):

1. Every U.S. community has a tourism industry;
2. Nearly every business providing goods or services at retail is a part of the tourism industry;
3. Tourism produces jobs, profits, rents, and taxes just as do other economic activities;
4. Over a wide range, tourism and most other industries are complements; and
5. Everyone (almost) is a tourist.

Prior planning for tourism usually prevents poor community performance. An absence of community planning control, however, can often result in numerous and well-known negative impacts of tourism.

References

Barry, Wendell. 1990. *What Are People For?* San Francisco, Calif.: North Point Press.

Blank, Uel. 1989. Tourism: The Cinderella stepchild of economic development, in *The Community Tourism Industry Imperative*. State College, Pa.: Venture Publishing, Inc.

Garnham, Harry Lance. 1985. *Maintaining The Spirit of Place*, Mesa, Ariz.: PDA Publishers Corporation.

Getz, Donald. 1983. A Research Agenda for Municipal and Community Based Tourism in Canada. Paper read at the Travel and Tourism Research Association Conference at Banff, June 1983.

Keogh, Brian. 1990. Public participation in community tourism planning. *Annals of Tourism Research* 17(3):449–465.

LaCrosse Area Convention and Visitor Bureau, 1989. *Tourism Facility & Attraction Master Plan*, LaCrosse, Wisc.: LaCrosse Area Convention and Visitor Bureau.

McNulty, Robert H., et al. 1986. *The Return to the Livable City,* Washington, D.C.: Acropolis Books, Ltd.

Murphy, P. E. 1985. *Tourism: A Community Approach.* London: Methuen.

Williams, Harold S. 1991. Of settlements and subdivisions. *Small Town* 21(5):10–22.

Wisconsin Department of Development, 1986. *Wisconsin Community Preparedness Manual.* Madison, Wisc.: Wisconsin Department of Development.

19

Sustainable Tourism Development

James R. MacGregor

Principles of Sustainable Development

The concept of sustainability and its contemporary label, "sustainable development," has been expressed in traditional cultures for hundreds of generations. It does not, as many suggest, have its origins in the landmark report, "Our Common Future," published in 1987 by the World Commission on Environment and Development.

In fact, the origin of creating an economy that is sustainable, and consequently protected for all generations, could have been found in the villages of India thousands of years ago or in the speeches of North America's aboriginal people as they tried, with futility, to warn their European visitors of the folly of relentless environmental abuse.

In his enlightening book, *The Compassionate Universe*, Eknath Easwaran recalls the role of the traditional head of an Indian village, who when calling family representatives together to make an important decision would remind them, "there is only one consideration to take into account. Don't look at this matter from your own point of view. And don't look at this matter from the way those living in the village now will be affected. Look at it from the point of view of our grandchildren" (p. 53).

Similarly, a Haida elder from the Pacific Northwest Coast of Canada, recalling the wisdom of a hundred generations, has said; "We do not inherit from our ancestors, we borrow from our children" (p. 54).

In more current terms, the 1980 World Conservation Strategy advanced the idea of integrating development and long term environmental protection: *"Development and conservation are equally necessary for our survival for the discharge of our responsibilities as trustees of natural resources for the generations to come"* (Berkmuller and Monroe 1986). This definition however, does not necessarily satisfy the needs of a sector such as travel and tourism. The strategy did not ask how an industry could meet its immediate economic requirements without compromising the opportunity of future generations to have an equally viable and prosperous life.

The Bruntland Commission advanced the feasibility of economic development and the potential to ensure that future generations inherit a technological, capital, and environmental wealth that is greater than the one inherited by the present generation. The Commission stated: "Humanity has the ability to make development sustainable—to ensure that it meets the needs of the present without compromising the ability of future generations to meet their own needs." (World Commission on Environment and Development 1987: 8).

The significance of this idea for the travel industry is potentially dramatic. If accepted by the industry, it fundamentally proclaims that future generations of travel industry operators, suppliers, influencers "should either inherit a resource and capital base that is as good or better than today's generation or they should be compensated for reductions in the endowments of resources brought about by the actions of present generations" (Pearce, Markandya, and Barbiet 1989:3).

Much has been written on the link between tourism and the environment, but the dimensions of "intergenerational equity" and the value of the environment as part of a wider agenda that embraces opportunity and quality of life for all humans (intragenerational equity) has never been addressed. The first international attempt to deal with tourism and the travel industry within the framework of sustainable development occurred at the Globe '90 Conference (Tourism Stream) held in Vancouver, Canada, in March 1990. During that conference, a select group of delegates with diverse professional (nongovernmental organizations, government, industry, university), and geographic (Switzerland, New Zealand, Scotland and eastern, central and western Canada) backgrounds met to prepare a short, but focused, report called "An Action Strategy for Sustainable Tourism Development." That document has subsequently become a policy for the Canadian government and its federal agency, Tourism Canada as well as a background policy statement for several other countries (MacGregor 1990).

The first Canadian application of sustainable tourism development planning was undertaken by the British Columbia's Ministry of Regional and Economic Development. In early 1991 they commissioned "The Clayoquot Sound Sustainable Development Strategy," a comprehensive planning exercise for the west coast of Vancouver Island that included seven sectors including tourism, fisheries, biodiversity and life support, forestry and timber, community lifestyle, native issues, and mining (MRED 1992). The Tourism Sector Study, prepared by SNC-Lavalin (1992), addressed the intergenerational needs of the marine/coastal and old forest based tourism as well as the involvement of aboriginal communities.

The Tourism Sector Study was guided by the same seven principles that shaped the overall strategy developed with strategy manager, Robert Prescott-Allan. They include

Principle 1. Limit human impact on the planet (global) and on the region (local) to a level that is within its carrying capacity.

In terms of the travel industry, this regional impact reflects the number of people or visitors multiplied by how much energy and raw material each individual uses or wastes. For instance, an excessive impact would be caused by many tourists individually consuming a little or by a few people consuming much of the resource. For the purposes of this study, carrying capacity was defined as the ability of the various watersheds and marine ecosystems that either renew themselves or absorb impacts and waste, whichever is less. Impacts on carrying capacity were considered negligible if they could be minimized by careful management or technology. For instance the region's important migrating whale population could be protected by either managing the distance between viewers and the whale pods as well as lowering noise levels of the marine vessels. Also, floating resorts proved to be an excellent way of minimizing impact on the land system and, with improved onboard waste management systems, there would be minimal impact on the marine environment.

Principle 2. Maintain the stock of biological wealth in the region.

This principle was also expressed as "conserve the conditions of life" or "preserve, protect and enhance the environment." Several activities enable tourism to minimize impact on the biological wealth of Clayoquot Sound. They include

• Conserving life support services. Life support services are those ecological processes that allow the land, air, water, and life to be productive, to adapt to tourist volumes, and to renew themselves. In order for these ecological processes to continually support tourism, chemical balances must be maintained, nutrients must be recycled, the air and water must remain pollution free, and water flows must remain constant. Any impact of tourist volumes or actions taken by the travel industry that interferes with these processes decreases the opportunity for a sustainable tourism economy.

• Conserving the diversity of nature. North Americans, and particularly Canadians, consistently rate environmental protection as the most important issue facing society. Generally, they are prepared to pay increased taxes for protection, to support strong environmental legislation, and in recent elections have voted for more responsible politicians. Growth of ecotourism and soft adventure travel also seems to support this. In order for a region or a country to have a long-term resource base that attracts these, it must conserve the variety of different species of plants, animals, and other organisms. It must also be aware of the different genetic stocks within each species as well as a variety of different ecosystems that are to be protected.

• Ensuring that all resource impacts are sustainable. The travel industry must assume the responsibility of ensuring that its impacts on the soil, wilderness, and ecosystems in general ensures their sustainability.

Principle 3. Minimize the depletion of nonrenewable resources.

The travel industry is a major user of nonrenewable resources. Use of metals, plastics, fossil fuels, and others may appear to be more obvious in large urban center tourism facilities but even the most wilderness-based tourism operation must rely on some nonrenewable resources. For instance, although a wilderness destination resort may be entirely built of local materials, it nonetheless requires fuel for transportation, plastics for food preservation, and metals for everything from boats and motors to cooking utensils. In order to respect this principle, tourism operations should do whatever is possible to extend the life of these nonrenewable resources by both recycling and by using as little of the nonrenewable resources base product as possible.

Principle 4. Promote long-term economic development that increases the benefits from a given stock of resources and maintains natural wealth.

The travel industry is in a position to maintain natural wealth in a number of ways. These practices apply equally at the regional, national, and global levels. They may include

Promoting technologies such as solar power and high efficiency engines that use resources more efficiently.

Ensuring that the tourists pay the full costs to society for the use of a particular resource, which may include, among others, green taxes, a surcharge on tour package prices to support conservation, or other economic instruments.

Ensuring that the components of the travel industry pay for the cost of any environmental damage or changes to the natural resource stock. For instance, anglers could be assessed a particular charge on the removal of fish stocks, which would be used to support fisheries' enhancement.

Expanding value-added tourism especially in those areas where the natural and cultural resources are unique and still relatively intact. This can be accomplished by improving and diversifying product lines as well as improving service levels and information. In a region such as Clayoquot Sound where its natural and cultural resource base is one of the most varied and pristine in the Pacific Northwest the opportunity for value-added tours is very high. Since so many of the unique features of the area are accessible by marine transportation there is ample opportunity for creating packages that include wildlife viewing, native heritage, hiking and coastal rainforest, sportfishing, and visits to native villages.

The sustainable development process ensures that all those who could be potentially affected by any decision that involved or informed. This process was long and very difficult in the Clayoquot Sound Sustainable Development Strategy but it contributed to all participants, anticipating and hopefully preventing future problems.

Principle 5. Provide for an equitable distribution of the benefits and costs of resource use and environmental management.

The benefits and costs of resource use and environmental protection have not always been shared equitably among the various communities, industries, and interest groups. Within the Clayoquot Sound area there are both large international corporations, mostly in the forestry sector, and small independent operators, particularly in the tourism sector. Residents range from those who live in the larger communities to those dwelling in small isolated locations with little access to the decision-making process. There are native bands with land claims and multinational forest companies with tree farm licenses. Finally there are those who would anticipate maximum utilization of the resource base within the next few years as well as those who would prefer to see part or most of it intact for future generations.

This mix of attitudes and values has made the planning process tumultuous and obviously the transition to sustainable economy is more difficult for some groups than for others. Tourism in particular has created difficulties for those who support the more traditional industry sectors including logging. As in many regions, tourism is a relatively new phenomenon and job opportunities are growing quickly, whereas jobs are being lost in the logging sector.

Sustainable tourism planning must accept change but also manage it in order to limit the negative disruptions it may have on the communities. In time locals will accept change but government and the various industry sectors must ensure a smooth shift away from unsustainable activity but still supply adequate support for sustainable development options.

The mechanisms for ensuring job and business stability in the more traditional industries, such as forestry, commercial fishing, and mining must be put in place to facilitate a smooth transition and the opportunity for those most affected to have the time to integrate into the new sustainable industry sectors. For instance unions, government agencies (Ministry of Education, Advanced Education, etc.), and the private sector must work to ensure that adequate tourism training is available regionally to assist those wishing to reposition themselves in the emerging travel industry. Equal opportunity should be afforded to native and nonnative communities and, as much as possible, training should be provided at the local level to ensure equal access for the entire region.

Principle 6. Provide for effective participation of communities and interest groups in the decisions that most affect them.

Sustainable development begins with a commitment by all the industry sectors, communities, special interest groups (environmentalists, Chamber of Commerce, unions, etc.) and individuals making a commitment to taking part in a sustainable development planning process. The tourist industry in particular must become familiar with all aspects of sustainable development in order to make a serious contribution to the planning process. It should be able to articulate its understanding of sustainability and its participation in contributing to sustainable development.

Principle 7. Promote the values that encourage others to achieve sustainability.

In a sustainable development strategy tourism is uniquely positioned to assume a leadership role. Because the success of the travel industry product is so closely linked to the preservation of the environment, tourism delegates to a planning process play a very important and influential role to be able to express and demonstrate their commitment to sustainability. Each individual member of the tourism industry must help foster those values that are compatible with promoting tourism as a sustainable economy. The travel industry should carefully try to eliminate all those practices and activities that do not support sustainability.

The study also demonstrated how competing resource users could coexist in a socially and ecologically responsible manner.

Tourism and Sustainable Development

Both the Globe 90 Tourism Sustainable Development Strategy and its application in the preparation of the Clayoquot Sound Strategy emphasize the irrevocable relationship between tourism and the natural, cultural, and heritage environment. They address the real challenge of sustainable development, which is to protect and enhance the environment, while meeting basic human needs, promoting current equity among all socioeconomic groups, improving the quality of life, and ensuring intergenerational equity. As well, the Clayoquot Sound Study provided mechanisms that give equal weight to tourism and its economic development options while still reflecting the needs of other resource users such as forestry and commercial fisheries.

The report, more than any other document, substantiates the implications of establishing policy that supports sustainable economic development and respects the role that tourism can play in that development.

Several goals of sustainable tourism development directly affect the future of the travel industry. They include

• Opportunities for an improved quality of life. There is a shift away from the growth vs. development argument toward opportunities to create employment, income, and an improved local quality of life and well-being. Tourism jobs, although not as high paying as some other sectors, tend to be longer than nonsustainable sectors and reflect certain lifestyle needs and qualities.

• Full value of the environment. Economic growth is adequately measured to reflect the full value of the natural and cultural environment including the costs of protecting, revitalizing, or renaturalizing and recycling not only in the present but in the future. Tourism can make a substantial contribution.

• Compensation for loss of wealth and capital. Tourism development involving any loss of existing natural or cultural wealth or environmental capital will increasingly indicate how future generations will be compensated. Also the loss of natural stock and cultural assets cannot simply be substituted for by the creation of industry-generated capital wealth.

• Intergenerational equity. Sustainable tourism development must provide for intergenerational equity. To be fair to future generations of tourists and travel industry workers, they must be left with a resource base no less than the present generation inherited. Each generation of tourism developers, planners, and operators are obliged to look after the generations that follow.

• Avoidance of irreversible actions. Sustainable tourist development must avoid all actions that are *irreversible*. Some natural and cultural resources can be replaced, but old-growth forests, endangered wildlife species, and sacred spaces, once lost, can never be enjoyed by future generations. Ancient monuments, historic urban areas, and distinct landscapes are also irreplaceable.

• Equality for the poor and disadvantaged. Development that causes changes in the environment usually has a greater impact on the poor than on the rich. In the cases of relatively poor or developing regions, the preservation of sustainable livelihoods must be taken into account. This is apparent where there is dependence upon fish stocks, wildlife, water supply, and other resources upon which tourism can have an impact.

• Trans-border impacts. Tourism development in one region or country clearly can have positive or negative effects on other regions or countries. Therefore countries should work together to ensure that tourism is integrated into the overall planning and management of the environment. Cooperation in establishing and attaining economic, social, and environmental goals in regard to tourism is necessary.

Role of Governments and Their Policy Initiatives

For sustainable tourism development to become an accepted activity it must be driven by government policy at the national, regional, and local levels. Sustainable tourism development is concerned with economic growth, increases in real per capita income, access to and production of natural/cultural resources, research and planning, and an equitably distributed level of economic well-being. It is therefore a responsibility of governments to establish policies that promote sustainable tourism development. In particular national and regional levels of government should become active and

- Develop and implement new economic indicators that define well-being in the sustainable development sense.
- Prepare tourism economic models that define appropriate levels and types of sustainable activities for natural and urban areas. This includes creating local environmental accounting systems specifically for the tourism industry.
- Prepare, in conjunction with the travel industry, standards and regulations for the environmental/cultural impact assessment, monitoring, and auditing of tourism projects. Specific emphasis should be placed on establishing guidelines for the use of heritage sites, ancient monuments, sacred landscapes, and such, where change can be irreversible.
- Establish guidelines that define carrying capacities that reflect sustainable development as well as prepare regulations that control indiscriminate and uncontrolled travel to environmentally sensitive regions and sites.
- Ensure that tourism is an integral part of all land use planning and that design and construction guidelines are available to ensure environmentally sensitive and culturally sympathetic development.
- Establish the mechanisms to ensure that all cultural, ethnic, indigenous, and disadvantaged groups have equal access to participation in the benefits of tourism.
- Design education and training seminars, provide public consultation workshops, and create tourism advisory boards that teach the concepts of sustainable tourism development.
- Ensure that all departments within the various levels of government are familiar with and supportive of sustainable tourism development, that tourism is well represented at caucus or inner circle government strategic planning sessions, and that national and regional tourism agreements stress sustainability.

The Role of the Travel Industry

Although government may undertake the research and establish the policy for sustainable tourism development, it must eventually be accepted and implemented by the travel industry. More frequently some tourism, in particular adventure/alternative and ecotourism, is regarded as being benign and may improve the environment. But the impacts of mass tourism are still considered significant and not within the framework of sustainable development.

A number of actions can readily be adopted by the industry that can eventually lead to a balanced use of resources and a protection of its environmental and cultural base. They may include

- Minimizing and eliminating pollution and all forms of environmental/cultural degradation, especially irreversible change. By focusing on the sustainable management of the resources, and using them while still protecting and conserving them, it ensures they will be available for future generations of operators and tourists.

• Ensuring that all the economic values are a part of business planning, product development, and pricing. If a particular tourism package "uses up" the environment, it is the responsibility of the operator to include the costs of restoration in the price. This is generally known as *green consumerism* and is a concept that has been embraced more eagerly by the clients than the travel trade. Tourists, for instance, tend to pay more for an environment that is intact and preserved. They have also contributed to its protection and preservation.

• Reflecting a new environmental sensitivity through *green marketing* and promoting the minimal environmental and cultural impacts of particular travel products. This approach also includes providing complete and credible information to the tourists on all possible adverse implications as well as the long-term benefits of benign or soft tourism.

• Undertaking regular environmental audits to assess the environmental performance of the business operation. This may include everything from the evaluation of recycling/reuse programs to impacts on carrying capacity, landscape aesthetics, local lifestyles and values, and water quality.

• Making environmental management a priority within the company and ensuring that it is an integral part of all aspects of corporate management including policies, programs, and practices.

• Evaluating the environmental practices of the suppliers of all goods and services to ensure that each supplier demonstrates an environmental responsibility and is an efficient consumer of natural resources.

• Establishing the necessary educational or training programs for management and staff with the focus on motivating all members of the corporation to act in an environmentally sensitive manner.

The potential for the travel industry to have a significant impact on environmental protection is considerable. With over 120 million employees worldwide, it is one of the world's largest employers. The employees' knowledge of sustainability and their participation in environmentally appropriate tourism development and operations can make a significant contribution.

Summary

Tourism, as the world's largest nonmilitary industry, has a major social and ecological impact on the planet. Collectively its small- and medium-size operations contribute to air-borne emissions, toxic waste, and loss of our forest resources. As an example, a medium-size hotel generates 100,000 empty liquor bottles annually and collectively the $30 billion travel industry advertising expenditures (very little of which is on recycled paper) contribute to the loss of thousands of acres of forest lands annually.

The travel industry will increasingly be held liable for these impacts and if their related businesses do not change, political forces and regulations will force them to contribute to society's shift to sustainability. Some companies have moved quickly to embrace a green strategy. Canadian Pacific Hotels and Resorts, following a survey of their 10,000 employees, immediately adopted a green plan that has put them in the forefront of sustainability. In August of 1991 they created an Environmental Affairs Office that reports directly to the CEO.

Increasingly, the travel industry will realize that sustainability is good for business. Consumers will also increasingly expect blue boxes for recycling in their room, energy efficient lighting, and promotional material printed on recycled paper. They will question tourism operators who do not reduce waste and contribute positively to the environment.

Companies such as Canadian Pacific Hotels and Resorts, Ramada Renaissance, and certain individual properties will find they have an edge on the competition because they have adopted policies and practices that promote environmental protection.

Environmental responsibility can become a common goal that reflects all participants in the travel industry (clients, managers, investors, shareholders, employees, policy makers). This will result in a sustainable resource base that will remain intact for future generations of tourists and travel industry operators, as well as an improved bottom line for individual businesses.

References

Easwaran, Eknath. 1989. *The Compassionate Universe*. Petaluma, Calif.: Nilgiri Press.

Berkmuller, K., and M. C. Monroe, eds. 1986. *World Conservation Strategy*. Gland, Switzerland: International Union for Conservation of Nature and Natural Resources.

MacGregor, James R., ed. 1990. *A Sustainable Tourism Development Action Strategy*. Vancouver, B.C.: Globe 90 and Tourism Canada.

MRED. 1992. *A Sustainable Development Strategy for Clayoquot Sound*. Victoria, B.C.: Ministry of Regional and Economic Development.

Pearce, David, Anil Markandya, and Edward B. Barbiet. 1989. *Blueprint for a Green Economy*. London: Earthscan Publications.

SNC-Lavalin. 1992. *A Sustainable Tourism Development Strategy for Clayoquot Sound*. Vancouver, B.C.

World Commission on Environment and Development. 1987. *Our Common Future*. New York: Oxford University Press.

20

Urban Tourism

Peter E. Murphy

Urban tourism is a simple concept at first glance, signifying tourism that takes place in urban areas. However, closer examination reveals it to be a complex and significant factor that is becoming more important to the tourism portfolio. When the term *urban tourism* is examined in detail, it not only resurrects the debate over tourism and tourist types (discussed elsewhere in this encyclopedia) but adds the additional variable of an urban setting. Although there is no consensus regarding what constitutes urban areas, it is agreed that they provide the most dynamic and complex of socioeconomic systems, where tourism is but one part. However, as more European and North American cities enter the postindustrial era, this aspect of urban life is becoming more significant and beginning to receive more attention.

Size and Significance

It has been estimated that 76 percent of the western Europe population and 74 percent of the North American population live in urban areas (Northam 1979: 67–68). This proportion depends on how one defines urban. "Unfortunately there is no universally accepted definition of urban places, and considerable variation exists from country to country" (Yeates 1990:29). What is certain is that there is an urban hierarchy and interlinked system of trade areas. One of the commercial activities taking place throughout this urban system is tourism, whether it be in the small villages of peripheral mountain areas (Christaller 1964) or in major metropolitan regions like Los Angeles (Palomba and Barbier 1986).

Despite the fact that much tourism takes place in an urban context most of the literature has ignored this setting and its implications for urban policy. In one of the few references to this situation, Ashworth (1989:33) maintains there has been a "double neglect." He contends that not only has tourism neglected the urban context, but that urban studies have also failed to observe the importance of tourism activity to the life of the city. Possible reasons for this he suggests are that tourism activity is more difficult to isolate in most urban economies, the exception being resort towns. This is because tourist facilities serve both visitors and residents, and that visitors come with such a variety of motives they may function as tourists one moment and business persons or students the next. As he says "In 60 years of urban spatial modelling tourism is ignored, rendered invisible by its very ubiquity" (Ashworth 1989:34).

Although Ashworth's comments are still pertinent there is growing evidence that researchers and administrations are beginning to appreciate the significance and size of this ubiquitous urban activity. In 1985, the International Geographical Union held a seminal conference on Big City Tourism in Berlin, the proceedings of which have been edited by Vetter (1986), and a chapter on urban tourism was included in the Travel and Tourism Research Associations' 1987 Handbook, (Ritchie and Goeldner 1987). In this chapter, Blank and Petkovich (1987:165) claim "urban tourism is almost certainly among the most misunderstood and underestimated of all tourism types", but that is starting to change thanks to the evidence of recent surveys.

A Canadian survey of its United States market in 1985 found that the traditional image of Canada as a mecca for outdoor vacation and wilderness experiences had undergone a transformation. The largest United States vacation type to Canada was now a touring holiday, followed by visits to friends and relatives, outdoor trips and city trips. Within these travel segments the influence of urban centers is undeniable. Not only were urban areas the prime objective in city trips, they were also important locational magnets within the friends and relatives market, and important staging and accommodation nodes on the tour routes throughout the regions of Canada. Such evidence has led Tourism Canada to pursue a new marketing strategy that emphasizes Canada's cultural and urban attractions, as well as its scenic beauty and outdoor recreation opportunities (Dybka 1986).

A similar pattern is emerging in overseas perceptions of, and travel within, North America as a whole. A 1989 survey of the United Kingdom, French, West German, and Japanese overseas traveler market revealed the majority of these travelers possessed a strong awareness of, and interest in, North American cities. Six of the eight most frequently mentioned locations in Canada were cities and in the United States, nine of the twelve. In addition, many of those surveyed had visited cities during their previous visits to North America (Market Facts of Canada 1989).

In Europe, with its longer urban history and higher population densities there has been an even greater interest in urban trips. Pearce (1989:58) cites a European survey that "showed that 52 percent of the respondents had spent holidays during 1985 at the seaside, 25 percent in the countryside, 23 percent in the mountains and 19 percent in towns (multiple responses were given)." Such statistics are likely to underestimate the contribution of urban places to the vacation experience, especially since the touring component is not captured in these figures and use of the word *town* may have led some to discount seaside resorts and countryside villages that are part of the urban milieu.

The significance of this urban tourism goes beyond actual numbers to opening up new opportunities for the tourism industry and urban destinations. The traditional symbol of urban tourism—the hotel— is changing to accommodate a greater variety of tourist needs and incomes, ranging from all-inclusive resort-style luxury to basic self-catering accommodation. More private accommodation is being drawn into the industry as bed and breakfast options continue to grow in popularity and more residents take advantage of this opportunity. Urban areas are noting the dual purpose function of more facilities and functions that can be used by residents and tourists alike (Jafari 1983).

This wide range of accommodation and activity options reflects the growing demand for special interest tourism. Special interest tourism has grown dramatically during the 1980s as predicted by Read (1980) and found a natural breeding ground in our cities where there is such a variety of activities and opportunities. Among these one could cite cultural tourism (Hall and Zeppel 1990), heritage tourism (Peterson 1990), educational visits (Andressen and Murphy 1987), sporting events, (Bale 1988), conferences and trade shows (Murphy 1985). These growing market segments are leading more tourists to our urban centers and forcing urban governments to recognize and plan for this growing service sector. Consequently, we find more urban areas spending funds to promote their destination, to build facilities such as conference centers, and to monitor their tourism business.

This interest and commitment, in turn, is leading more urban areas to change in appearance and style. We are witnessing a renewed interest in the waterfront (Baltimore, Miami), in heritage restoration (Lowell, Massachusetts, and Covent Garden, London), in urban renewal involving a tourism component (London's Dockland), and in major sports centers (Sky Dome, Toronto). All of which reflects the growing significance of tourism to the modern urban economy and relates to the changing urban landscape.

Urban Tourism Landscape

One approach to urban tourism analysis has been to study the location of facilities and land use patterns in this industry within the urban landscape. There have been several case studies of hotel location, involving Toronto (Wall et al. 1985); Christchurch, New Zealand (Pearce 1987); Nuremberg (Ritter 1986); and attempts to draw comparative studies of several cities (Burtenshaw et al. 1981; Kulinat 1986). These studies have generally shown spatial concentration around gateway locations (railway stations and airports) or close to major attractions (town center, conference center, or beach). The beach is the main attraction in resort towns and due to its elongated nature it has helped to create a distinctive T-shaped resort morphology. Hotels and other tourist facilities stretch along the shoreline cap of the T, supported by a stem of commercial development leading away to a commercial core that often includes the main railroad and intercity bus station (Barrett 1958; Lavery 1971).

A similar morphological and functional model that can be applied to a wider range of tourism oriented cities has been described by Stansfield and Rickert (1970). They recognize that in many urban areas the tourism function must coexist with other economic activities and that in certain cities a Recreational Business District (RBD) has developed to serve tourist needs alongside the Central Business District (CBD) which primarily serves local residents. While the CBD emphasizes the higher order goods and services expected in an urban area of that size, the RBD focuses on tourist accommodation, attractions, entertainment, and support facilities. The two are often contiguous because of the appeal of the central city (location and heritage) and the mutual benefit from a synergistic transfer of services, with tourists shopping in the CBD while residents use the nightclubs and restaurants of the RBD.

Studies of urban tourism landscapes have revealed how closely linked the central city has become to tourism, especially in Europe and eastern North America where the older districts retain so much of the heritage and many of the public institutions (museums, galleries, theater, center of commerce and government) that are major tourist magnets. Jansen-Verbeke (1986:80) maintains that inner-city tourism has become "a part of the general leisure and recreation function of the urban environment" and requires multi-disciplinary research and integrated planning. She suggests the inner city can be viewed as an "activity place" and treated as a single product in tourism development. Within the product will be the primary elements of its historical setting and morphological characteristics, but it is important these be supplemented with support elements such as accommodation, restaurants, and shopping facilities, and coordinated through the provision of adequate accessibility, parking, and information services. Many of these points are supported in Murphy's (1980) examination of the link between land use planning and tourism management in the city of Victoria, British Columbia. He shows how that central city is attempting to build upon the success of its Inner Harbour tourist area (RBD) by drawing visitors into the adjacent and under-used heritage area of Old Town, using many of the components identified by Jansen-Verbeke.

In some cases, the central city has become too successful in drawing visitors and must now examine ways to spread tourism to the suburbs or outlying areas. This is happening as part of the normal city growth and diffusion process, with hotels clustering around airports and the freeway intersections of beltways (Kulinat 1986). It is a response also to some reactive planning restrictions imposed by certain inner-city jurisdictions, as in the case of Westminster, London (Murphy 1982), and the pull of suburban tourism developments such as Disney World outside of Orlando.

In many cases it is not proving easy to divert tourists from busy prime central attractions to underutilized resources elsewhere in the urban area (Murphy 1980; Murphy 1985). To direct or channel visitors requires a greater understanding of the urban tourist. If a city is to maximize its resource opportunities and to satisfy the visitor, while maintaining its multifunctional role, it must ascertain what a visitor is expecting and how best to fulfil those needs within the context of its overall responsibilities.

Understanding the Urban Tourist

In his review of tourism research Pearce (1987:21) states the "area of motivation and demand has been one of the least researched areas of tourism to date," and while this is still true, one area in which it is beginning to change is with regard to the urban tourist. Interest in the urban tourist stems from the very competitive market in this form of tourism, especially with regard to resorts and conferences, and from a growing desire to convince tourists to stay longer and visit new attractions—in other words, to spend more money. When there are so many resort areas that basically offer the same product (surf and sun) backed up by the same facilities (hotels, restaurants, and entertainment), how can they differentiate their particular product and position it in the minds of a prospective tourist? When an urban area has succeeded in attracting tourists, how can it facilitate their visit and encourage them to stay longer and visit new attractions? The first question has been addressed through image research, the second through consumer behavior research.

An image may be defined "as the sum of beliefs, ideas and impressions that a person has of a destination" (Crompton 1979:18) and can be equated to the geographical concept of a "sense of place," used to identify and distinguish between different locations. A study by Goodrich (1977) has shown how popular resort areas for the North American market have similar image dimensions (entertainment and culture/lifestyle), but within this framework they tend to form clusters and attempt to differentiate themselves to some degree in the tourists' eyes. He suggests such clustering can be used to guide advertising themes and used to emphasize a destination's image strengths or to improve on its image weakness. It is in the latter regard that Brown (1988) reports on the efforts of some traditional U.K. seaside resorts to update and change their image. Also in the United Kingdom, Middleton (1989) has noted that managed visitor attractions will need to address their image in an increasingly competitive sector, needing to focus "on the development and enhancement of products which provide satisfaction and repeat visits for a more demanding public" (Middleton 1989:232).

This interest in image has been brought to the fore in a new book entitled *Marketing Tourism Places* (Ashworth and Goodall 1990). "The theme of this book is that tourist destinations as place products have to be sold like any other product to potential customers, the holidaymakers" (Goodall 1990:259). The relevance to urban tourism is demonstrated in Ashworth's chapter concerning the historic city of Groningen (Ashworth 1990:138–155). He states the past can be "exploited" as a resource, but how it is exploited will be determined by the different images various groups have of "historic Groningen." Ashworth identifies four different image groups, including urban tourists. In his opinion, any attempts to sell historic city to the tourist will necessitate synchronizing these different images into the city's marketing and development strategies.

Convincing visitors to stay longer and to try new attractions or activities involves image, but draws the urban tourism agency (private or public) more deeply into consumer research. Mayo and Jarvis (1981) helped to pioneer this aspect of tourism research and development and many of their observations are pertinent to urban tourism marketing. Their perception factor has been applied by Stabler (1988) with regard to the activity profiles portrayed by the brochures from different resorts in the Languedoc-Roussillon area. Ashworth (1987) relates how the City of Norwich is attempting to sell its historic city after "defining" its customer, including such characteristics as motive and attitudes. Murphy and Rosenblood (1974) examined the learning process of first time visitors to Victoria and tried unsuccessfully to influence their travel pattern with various oral and financial inducements (Murphy 1973). Uysal and O'Leary (1989:172) have examined the influence of race (culture and subculture) on city trips and conclude "black and white travellers are likely to be responsive to different travel experiences during a city trip."

The combined impact of image and consumer behavior modification can be seen at work in the numerous attempts to use tourism as an agent of change for some urban redevelopment schemes. Buckley and Witt (1985) provide an analysis of such developments in what they describe as "difficult" U.K. areas. There has been a similar study of Harlem in New York, where it is felt the district could promote its unique "cluster of cultural amenities," including its gospel music, if it could overcome its security image (Highet and Johnson 1984).

Issues in Urban Tourism

Several issues are emerging in urban tourism. First, this topic is finally emerging as a subfield within tourism, worthy of separate consideration and analysis. Reasons for this include recognition of its size and its potential to assist cities experiencing severe postindustrial adjustment. We can expect to see greater consideration given to tourism resources and potential in future urban planning, even to the extent of developing separate planning portfolios in the major tourist destinations.

Second, urban areas and the tourist industry will see more synergistic opportunities in multiple use facilities and events that can serve both residents and visitors. The cost of maintaining the heritage and cultural fabric of urban areas will be spread over a larger base, with the tourism component offering a commercial source of revenue. However, as Middleton (1989) has pointed out, few managed visitor attractions are likely to be self-sustaining, so some form of partnership seems desirable.

Third, serving dual or more market segments means urban tourism will become more involved in consumer research as it attempts to reach and satisfy various needs (Ashworth 1989). Urban tourism has much to learn from retail marketing (Murphy 1980) and the modern concept of marketing that combines sales with other agency mandates (Kotler and Armstrong 1989:10).

Fourth, and most important for urban tourism, is to operate within a sustainable development philosophy. One of the key mandates of an urban area is to maintain or enhance the quality of life for its residents. While tourism can definitely enhance the aesthetics and facilities of an urban area, it can also overload the ecological system of an urban area in the same way it has done in some natural environments. Consequently, physical and social carrying capacities need to be established and respected within the urban environment if the benefits of this activity are to be maintained. Venice is one place where this is already underway, according to Moulin (1990:6), which "limits its tourist capacity to 40,000 people each summer day."

Summary

Urban tourism may be one of the least understood areas of tourism, but that situation is about to change. Tourism is now such an important part of many urban economies its employment and tax benefits cannot be ignored. It is so interrelated with other urban functions such as health, education, heritage, and culture that it is becoming a viable partner in more aspects of urban life. As more urban areas consider their environment, heritage, and quality of life, they will be creating "sense of place or product" that is appealing not only to their own residents but to various tourist segments around the world. After all, cities are meant to be people places, and, in a global economy, that includes people of the world.

References

Andressen, B. and P.E. Murphy. 1987. A Report on the Travel Behaviour and Economic Impacts of Japanese Students in Summer English Language Programs. Department of Geography, University of Victoria, B.C.

Ashworth, G. 1987. Marketing the historic city: The selling of Norwich. In *Urban Conservation: International Contrasts*, ed. R. C. Riley, pp. 51–67. Department of Geography, Portsmouth Polytechnic, Occasional Paper No. 7.

Ashworth, G. J. 1989. Urban tourism: An imbalance in attention: In *Progress in Tourism, Recreation and Hospitality Management*, Vol. 1, ed. C. Cooper, pp. 33–54. London: Belhaven.

Ashworth, G. 1990. The Historic Cities of Groningen: Which is Sold to Whom? In *Marketing Tourism Places*, ed. G. Ashworth and B. Goodall, pp. 138–155. London: Routledge.

Ashworth, G. and B. Goodall. 1990. *Marketing Tourism Places*. London: Routledge.

Bale, J. 1988. The place of "place" in cultural studies of sports. *Progress in Human Geography* 12(4):507–524.

Barrett, J. A. 1958. The seaside resort towns of England and Wales. Ph.D. dissertation, University of London.

Blank, U. and M. D. Petkovich. 1987. Research on urban tourism destinations, In *Travel, Tourism, and Hospitality Research,* ed. J. R. B. Ritchie and C. R. Goeldner, pp. 165–177. New York: Wiley.

Brown, B. J. H. 1988. Developments in the promotion of major seaside resorts: How to effect a transition by really making an effort. In *Marketing in the Tourism Industry,* ed. B. Goodall and G. Ashworth, pp. 176–186. London: Croom Helm.

Buckley, P. J. and W. Witt, S.F. 1985. Tourism in difficult areas, case studies in Bradford, Bristol, Glasgow and Hamm. *Tourism Management* 6(3):205–213.

Burtenshaw, D., M. Bateman, and G. J. Ashworth. 1981. *The City in West Europe.* Chichester: Wiley.

Christaller, W. 1964. Some considerations of tourism location in Europe. *Papers and Proceedings of Regional Science Association* 12:95–105.

Crompton, J. L. 1979. An assessment of the image of Mexico as a vacation destination and the influence of geographic location upon that image. *Journal of Travel Research* 17(4):18–23.

Dybka, J. M. 1986. Attracting U.S. tourists to Canada. *Tourism Management* 7(3):202–204.

Goodall, B. 1990. The dynamics of tourism place marketing. In *Marketing Tourism Places,* ed. G. Ashworth and B. Goodall, pp. 259–279. London: Routledge.

Goodrich, J. N. 1977. Differences in perceived similarity of tourism regions: A spatial analysis. *Journal of Travel Research* 14(1):10–13.

Hall, M. and H. Zeppel. 1990. Cultural and heritage tourism: The new grand tour. *Historic Environment* 7(3/4):86–98.

Highet, B. P. and W. H. Johnson. 1984. Harlem—Tourist Market—Assessment and Potential. *Tourism Management* 5(2):142–148.

Jafari, J. 1983. Anatomy of the Travel Industry. *Cornell Quarterly* 24(1):71–77.

Jansen-Verbeke, M. 1986. Inner-city tourism: Resources, tourists, and promoters. *Annals of Tourism Research* 13(1):79–100.

Kotler, P. and G. Armstrong. 1989. *Principles of Marketing,* 4th ed. Englewood Cliffs, N.J.: Prentice-Hall.

Kulinat, K. 1986. Hotel Tourism and Hotel Locations in the Cities of Frieburg, Heidelberg, Heilbronn, Karlsruhe, Mannheim, Pforzheim, Stuttgart—Urban Tourism in Baden Wortt. In *Big City Tourism,* ed. F. Vetter, pp. 267–280. Berlin: Dietrich Reimer Verlag.

Lavery, P. 1971. *Recreational Geography.* Newton Abbot, U.K.: David and Charles.

Market Facts of Canada. 1989. *Pleasure Travel Markets to North America: United Kingdom, France, West Germany and Japan Highlights Report.* Ottawa: Tourism Canada.

Mayo, E. J. and L. P. Jarvis. 1981. *The Psychology of Leisure Travel.* Boston: CBI.

Middleton, V. T. C. 1989. Marketing implications for attractions. *Tourism Management* 10(3):229–232.

Moulin, C. 1990. Cultural heritage and tourism evolution. *Historic Environment* 7(3/4):3–9.

Murphy, P. E. 1973. The potential and problems of experiments in geography: A case study. *B.C. Geographical Series* 17:7–12.

Murphy, P. E. 1980. Tourism management using land use planning and landscape design: The Victoria experience. *The Canadian Geographer* 24(1):60–71.

Murphy, P. E. 1982. Tourism planning in London: An exercise in spatial and seasonal management. *The Tourist Review* (1):19–23.

Murphy, P. E. 1985. *Tourism: A Community Approach.* London: Methuen.

Murphy, P. E., and L. Rosenblood. 1974. Tourism: An exercise in spatial search. *The Canadian Geographer* 18(3):201–210.

Northam, R. M. 1979. *Urban Geography,* 2nd ed. New York: Wiley.

Palomba, M. C. and B. Barbier. 1986. Background Information on Tourism in Los Angeles, California. In *Big City Tourism,* ed. F. Vetter, pp. 325–338. Berlin: Dietrich Reimer Verlag.

Pearce, D. 1987. Motel location and choice in Christchurch. *New Zealand Geographer* 43(1):10–17.

Pearce, D. 1989. *Tourism Today: A Geographical Analysis.* Harlow, U.K.: Longman.

Peterson, K. I. 1990. The heritage resource as seen by the tourist: the heritage connection. In *The Tourism Connection: Linking Research and Marketing*, Proceedings of Travel and Tourism Research Association's 21st Annual Conference, pp. 209–215. Salt Lake City, Utah: TTRA.

Read, S. E. 1980. A prime force in the expansion of tourism in the next decade: Special interest travel. In *Tourism Marketing and Management Issues*, eds. D. E. Hawkins, E. L. Shafer and J. M. Rovelstad, pp. 193–202. Washington D.C.: George Washington University.

Ritchie, J. R. B. and C. R. Goeldner. 1987. *Travel, Tourism, and Hospitality Research: A Handbook for Managers and Researchers*. New York: Wiley.

Ritter, W. 1986. Hotel locations in big cities. In *Big City Tourism*, ed. F. Vetter, pp. 355–364.

Stabler, M. J. 1988. The image of destination regions: Theoretical and empirical aspects. In *Marketing in the Tourism Industry*, eds. B. Goodall and G. Ashworth, pp. 133–161. London: Croom Helm.

Stansfield, C. A. and E. J. Rickert. 1970. The recreational business district. *Journal of Leisure Research* 2(4):213–225.

Uysal, M. and J. T. O'Leary. 1989. Ethnic marketing—city trip. *Tourism Management* 10(2):169–173.

Vetter, F., ed. 1986. *Big City Tourism*. Berlin: Dietrich Reimer Verlag.

Wall, G., D. Dudycha, and J. Hutchinson. 1985. Point pattern analysis of accommodation in Toronto. *Annals of Tourism Research* 12(4):603–618.

Yeates, M. 1990. *The North American City*, 4th ed. New York: Harper & Row.

21

Motivation of Pleasure Travel and Tourism

Muzaffer Uysal and Lee Anne R. Hagan

In the field of travel and tourism, researchers, marketers, and practitioners are interested in knowing why people travel and why they choose their specific destination. To explain travel behavior, one must first examine the motivators to travel. Understanding what motivates people to travel or participate in recreation activities allows us to better define the value of tourism behavior, and ultimately researchers and practitioners can predict or influence future travel patterns (Schreyer 1986; Pearce 1987). Iso-Ahola (1980, 1982) has stated that motivation is one of the most important determinants of recreation travel. How does one examine motivations for pleasure travel? To answer this important question, we must begin with a definition of motivation. The term *motive* has been used to refer to internal forces and external goals and incentives that guide, direct, and integrate a person's behavior, for future, potential satisfaction (Murray 1964; Atkinson and Raynor 1975; Iso-Ahola 1982; Hoyenga and Hoyenga 1984; Pyo and Uysal 1990). Therefore, motivation is an interpersonal phenomenon. This fact has led theorists and researchers to examine pleasure and recreation travel as a psychological experience (Driver and Knopf 1977; Dann 1977, 1981; Crompton 1979; Knopf et al. 1983; Schreyer 1986; Tinsley 1986; Williams 1986; Chon 1989).

Leisure travel reflects inner needs, which are often difficult for the individual and researcher to identify and describe. Van Doren (1983) pointed out that the urge to travel for pleasure depends on individual motivations and cultural conditioning. Examining motivators to travel is a difficult task because of conceptual and methodological issues. Behavioral scientists have not agreed on a conclusive explanation of the concept of motivation; different theorists have given the "same" motivational concepts very different operational definitions (Hoyenga and Hoyenga 1984). There are many competing theories of pleasure travel motivations and often travelers themselves have a difficult time describing their motivations and may not even be aware of them. This article is an overview of some travel motivational theories and studies.

Historically, motivations for travel have included economic gain, migration, war, survival, spiritual values, education, health, self-indulgence, relaxation, and escape. Some of these motivations are still determinants for modern travelers. Yet, how are these motivations described, categorized, or determined? One concept deals with motivation being related to the individual's needs. The individual can be aware of some of these needs and the needs may also be subconscious. Travel motivation may be the result of the intention of satisfying a known need. Iso-Ahola (1980, 1982, 1989) has developed a travel motivational theory which deals with this concept and is based on physiological and psychological motivators.

Social/Psychological Tourist Motivations

When an individual travels he or she is seeking to satisfy a set of needs that can be influenced by physiological or psychological motives. Physiological motives are the result of biological and physical needs. In the past some of the physiological motives of travel were food, shelter, security/safety, and health. Modern physiological motives include culture, climate, education, health, and fitness. Psychological motives are influenced by the individual's needs that are created by his or her environment.

Travel is rarely the result of a single motive; rather, it is a complex form of behavior in which the individual is striving to satisfy multiple needs (McIntosh and Goeldner 1990). Desiring something and needing something are two different things. Desires are recognized needs and the difference between needs and desires is awareness. Therefore, motivation occurs when an individual intends to satisfy a known need (Mill and Morrison 1985). Iso-Ahola (1980, 1982) classified motivational forces, for optimal stimulation and arousal (equilibrium), into approach (seeking) and avoidance (escaping). Many of the motivation factors mentioned are brought together by his proposed model of social psychological theory of tourism motivation. He indicated that, depending on the daily mundane stimulation and arousal level, people pursue leisure activities for feelings of mastery and competence or to leave the routine environment. Iso-Ahola (1980, 1982) presented the idea that after awareness for satisfaction has developed there are two motivational forces that become determinants of tourism behavior:

1. The desire to leave the everyday environment behind—escaping personal and/or interpersonal environments
2. The desire to obtain psychological or intrinsic rewards through travel in a contrasting environment—seeking personal and/or interpersonal intrinsic rewards

Not all vacations and trips can be classified on the 50-50 principle of escaping and seeking. For example, one family may be interested in traveling to Myrtle Beach, South Carolina, to "get away" from the hectic work-school-after-school schedule whereas another family may travel to Kenya, East Africa, to "seek" out a new environment and culture. Also, a traveler may visit family and friends on one vacation and then may take a cruise to the Bahamas, to escape from everyone, on his or her next vacation. All the individual motives can be incorporated in Iso-Ahola's (1989) Seeking and Escaping Dimensions model, shown in Figure 1, to explain his theory of social/psychological tourist motivation.

According to the model, a tourist can be placed in any one of the four quadrants at a given time and under certain conditions.

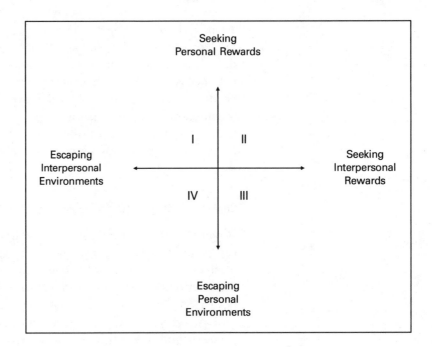

Fig. 1. The seeking and escaping dimensions of leisure motivation (Iso-Ahola 1984:111; Iso-Ahola 1989:262).

Seeking
Personal Rewards

I   II

Escaping
Interpersonal
Environments

Seeking
Interpersonal
Rewards

IV   III

Escaping
Personal
Environments

Quadrant I: Need to escape interpersonal environment
                (e.g., family or group situations)
Quadrant I: Desire to seek personal rewards
                (e.g., rest and relaxation)
Quadrant II: Desire to seek intrinsic rewards
Quadrant III: Need to escape personal environment
                (e.g., personal problems and difficulties)
Quandrant III: Desire to seek interpersonal rewards
                (e.g., cultural or group activities)
Quandrant IV: Desire to get away from everyday environment

The model represents two dimensions as motivational forces rather than separate or independent motives. Iso-Ahola (1989) suggests that each quadrant condition in itself or together with other quadrants are the driving forces for travel. The model further suggests that it is possible to locate any tourist or group in any given quadrant at any given time, and for any particular tourist or set of tourists the quadrant may change during the course of a trip or from one trip to another.

Other researchers who studied why people participate in leisure and recreation activities, suggest that the reasons and motivations for vacation travel may be similar to the reasons for participation in leisure and recreation activities. For example, Leiper (1984) distinguishes between recreational leisure, which restores, and creative leisure, which produces something new. He discusses three functions of recreation: (1) rest (recovery from physical or mental fatigue), (2) relaxation (recovery from tension), and (3) entertainment (recovery from boredom).

Push/Pull Model of Tourist Motivations

Another look at travel motivations from a two-dimensional or forces approach is the concept of "push" and "pull." This concept involves the theory that people travel because they are pushed and pulled to do so by "forces."

These forces or motivational factors describe how individuals are pushed by motivational variables into making a travel decision and how they are pulled or attracted by the destination area. Travel patterns can be distinguished by the push and pull factors influencing vacation decisions.

The literature on tourist motivation indicates that the examination of motivations based on the concept of push and pull factors has been generally accepted (Dann 1977; Crompton 1979; Epperson 1983; Pearce and Caltabiano 1983; Pyo et al. 1989; Brayley 1990; Yuan and McDonald 1990). Push factors are considered to be those sociopsychological constructs of the tourists and their environments that predispose the individual to travel and help explain the desire to travel. They are origin-related factors that motivate or create a desire to satisfy a need to travel. Most of the push factors are intangible desires of the individual traveler (Lundberg 1990). Some of the psychological motivations acting as push factors may include escape, rest and relaxation, prestige, health and fitness, adventure, and social interaction.

Mill and Morrison (1985) reported that travel motivation occurs when an individual wants or desires to satisfy a need. Pizam et al. (1979) suggested that tourist motivation refers to the set of needs that influence (or push) a person to travel and participate in travel-related activities. Maslow's (1954) hierarchy of needs has been suggested by Hudman (1980) as a basis for push factors of travel. The six levels of needs that are related to the push factors of travel motivation are

> Need for self-actualization
> Need for self-esteem
> Need for recognition/status
> Need for belonging
> Need for safety/security
> Need for physiological requirements

Push factors can also be identified by socioeconomic variables; demographic variables; and attitudes, interests, and opinions (AIO) that the traveler possesses, along with knowledge about the market. This information would include age, gender, income, education, family structure and size, race/ethnic group, occupation, and other personal variables that influence the traveler's decision to travel (Smith 1983).

Understanding what pushes the traveler can be effectively used by destination areas in their marketing strategies. Knowing the objective and perceptions of the traveler helps the destination area to develop opportunities favorable to meeting the desired needs of the individual. Brayley (1990) pointed out that the attitude of a tourist toward a vacation destination may be a measure of that destination's ability to pull or attract the tourist. Thus, pull factors are those that emerge as a result of the "attractiveness" of a destination and are thought to help establish the actual destination choice (Bello and Etzel 1985a, 1985b).

Pull factors are, therefore, destination attributes that respond to and reinforce push factors of motivations. They are the attractiveness or "drawing power" of the destination as perceived by the traveler. In order for a destination attribute to meaningfully respond to or reinforce the motivation to travel, it must be perceived and valued by the tourists (Brayley 1990). Destination attributes can either be tangible resources or the perceptions and expectations of the traveler (Smith 1983). Examples of pull factors would include the following:

Tangible Resources

Beaches
Snow
Historical sites
Recreation facilities
Scenic beauty

Travelers' Perceptions and Expectations

Novelty
Benefit expectation
Marketed image of destination

The push and pull theory of travel motivation can be used in explaining travel patterns and behavior. Figure 2 shows examples of push and pull factors that motivate the individual to travel. Understanding the implications of push and pull factors can be an advantage for marketers and researchers of tourist destination areas. Destination promotion activities could reflect both motives and destination attitudes. For example, Pyo et al. (1989) attempted to delineate the nature and extent of the relationship between two sets of factors, motives (push) and destination attributes (pull), by utilizing canonical correlation analysis. They demonstrated that it is possible to combine attraction attributes with motives. One of their four variates for the U.S. touring trip market indicated that tours to museums and galleries should appeal to intellectual needs. Destinations with attributes of outdoor recreation, nightlife activities, and amusement parks should attempt to cater to social and stimulation motives.

Cultural and Social Influences on Tourist Motivations

Cultural-Social-Psychological Disequilibrium Continuum

Crompton (1979) suggested that motives can be conceptualized as being located along a cultural-social-psychological disequilibrium continuum. All of

Fig. 2. Push and pull model of tourism motivations. Factors are examples, not an exhaustive list.

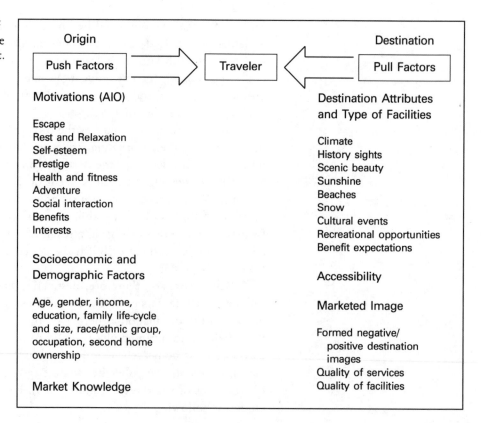

the social-psychological motives for every individual are often not expressed explicitly but Crompton has specifically identified seven social-psychological motives for travel, as follows:

1. Escape from a perceived mundane environment
2. Exploration and evaluation of self
3. Relaxation
4. Prestige
5. Regression
6. Enhancement of kinship relationships
7. Facilitation of social interaction

The idea behind Crompton's theory is that before the travel experience or the long-awaited vacation, there is disequilibrium in the individual's cultural-social-psychological needs. Then after traveling or during the vacation equilibrium of those needs is established. On the other hand, Maslow (1954) pointed out that an unsatisfied (disequilibrium) need, not the gratified (equilibrium) need, energizes and directs human actions. A sense of internal damage or depletion (disequilibrium) can be changed to enriched and recharged feelings (equilibrium) because of vacation experience (Hill 1965). Well-adjusted people need a mixture of consistency and complexity in their lives, and this need is usually fulfilled (equilibrium) by seeking consistency of certain experiences and complexity of others (Mayo and Jarvis 1981).

Cultural Conditioning as a Function of Motivation

Dann (1981) identified seven approaches toward motivation in terms of individuals and their cultural conditioning. The first approach, travel as a response to what is lacking (disequilibrium) yet desired (equilibrium), can be extended further and may be used to explain the other six approaches: destinational pull in response to motivational push; motivation as fantasy; motivation as classified purpose; motivational typologies; motivation and tourist experiences; and motivation as auto-definition and meaning.

Travel as a response to what is lacking yet desired refers to the situation when the environment inadequately meets the needs of the individual, who therefore tries to satisfy such needs by traveling to a different environment. For example Smith (1979) found from examining the motivations of a middle-class California sample that getting away from their current environment to travel to a different atmosphere that was perceived as being more relaxed and offered opportunities for prestigious attachments was a common reason for taking a vacation. She reported that the peer pressure of "keeping up with the Joneses" was an important motivator for travel. Cohen (1972) revealed that modern man has a strong desire for obtaining and experiencing something different. There is an interest in novelty and variety mainly because they are different from the accustomed environment.

Destination "pull" in response to motivational "push" refers to the concept that there are specific attributes that attract the individual or group to a specific destination once the decision to travel has been made. This concept is discussed in greater detail earlier in the article.

Motivation as fantasy may actually be a subset of the first two approaches because they both encompass culturally "normal" desires as well as fantasy desires. Travel to a different area may permit one to behave or encounter experiences that would "normally" be considered "taboo" or "deviant" in their current environment. Fantasies may be "played out" or experienced in the destination environment. Fantasy desires may be in the form of any of the following (as classified by Dann [1976]): name, color, noise, sexual, political, religious, educational, familial, sporting, and economic.

Motivation as classified purpose refers to the classification of the purpose or goal of the trip or vacation. The "purpose" can be further distinguished between the "general" purpose, "specific" purpose, and the "rationalized" purpose. For example, the high-pressured, corporate business executive may take a vacation to Jamaica for a general purpose of pleasure. Her specific purpose may be to escape or for a change of environment. The rationalized purposes could be that she plans to travel to Jamaica to improve her health and become more culturally educated.

Motivational typologies imply motivation in the use of ideal types or mental construct that can be used or compared with one or more ideal types. Motivational typologies provide a way to take a complex phenomenon, tourism, and classify people on the bases of their personal traits and behavior to explain their travel motivation. This concept looks more at the tourists' roles, such as vacationer, business traveler, excursionist.

Motivation and tourist experiences is an extension of typology analysis of people yet focuses on the individual's travel experience more than on his or her "role" as a tourist.

Motivation as auto-definition and meaning relates to the concept that how tourists define situations provides a greater understanding of their actions than simply examining their behavior.

Psychocentrism/Allocentrism Approach

Psychographic types of people are also used to examine travel behavior and motivation. One such popular psychographic model was developed by Plog (1974), who classified the U.S. population along a psychographic continuum delineating personality types, ranging from the psychocentric at one extreme to the allocentric at the other. He pointed out that an individual character and personality could indicate with some consistency preferred recreation and tourism experiences. It was found (Plog 1990) that the psychocentric type demonstrated a shared set of characteristics: territory boundness, generalized anxieties, and a sense of powerlessness. Psychocentrics seem to display a stronger than normal sense of insecurity and a feeling that they have little control over what happens to themselves. They tend to prefer familiar destinations, including areas that promote relaxation and low-level activities. Allocentrics on the other hand, seem to be almost the "opposite" of the psychocentrics. They tend to be self-confident and enjoy discovery, new experiences, and new areas, and they like to travel to different or even exotic destinations. (Recently Plog's psychocentrism/allocentrism has been debated by Smith [1990] and Plog [1990].)

Social Influences on Travel Motivation

One of the strongest influences on travel motivation and behavior is the effect that other people have on the traveler's decisions (Moutinho 1987). The forces that other people exert are called social influences. Social influence has been a stronger predictor of human behavior and can also be used in understanding and predicting travel behavior. Figure 3 shows that social influence can be grouped into four major areas: (1) role and family influences, (2) reference groups, (3) social classes, and (4) culture and subculture. Social influence has a tremendous impact on motivating an individual to travel. Therefore, understanding this influence on travel decision behavior and travel motivation is extremely important in understanding the overall tourist industry. Krippendorf (1987) argues that the motivation of the individual to travel is produced not so much by an innate impulse, but develops primarily

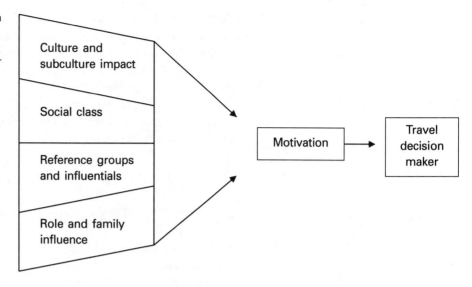

Fig. 3. Social influences on travel motivation. *(Source: Adapted from L. Moutinho, Consumer behavior in tourism, European Journal of Marketing 21(10):5–44.)*

under the influence of the social environment, from which every individual draws his norms.

Travel and Tourism Motivation Studies

A growing interest in examining travel motivation has resulted in several studies and models being developed to examine the possible factors that give rise to travel motivation. Some of these studies introduce possible categorizing techniques to help classify individual motivations.

McIntosh and Goeldner's Four Categories of Travel Motivations

McIntosh and Goeldner (1990) suggest that traveler's motivations can be classified into four basic categories: physical, cultural, interpersonal, and status and prestige.

The physical motivations category represents such needs as physical rest, recreation, participation in sport activities, and health and fitness. Medical purposes or doctors' recommendations for rest and relaxation, stress and tension reduction, or physical exercise for health reasons would also be classified in this category. Cultural motivations are related to the need of wanting to find out more about certain cultures, environments, societies, countries, and overall the desire to satisfy curiosity. The intrigue may stem from wanting to know specifically about folklore, religion, art, music, food, life-style, and the like. Interpersonal motivations include the desire to strengthen relationships, meet new people, visit friends and relatives, and escape. The desire to build and develop one's self-esteem and the need to strengthen personal development are both examples of the status and prestige category of travel motivation. Travel for business, conventions, and educational pursuits would be included in this category.

From their research project examining the travel motivations of travelers traveling to and from Germany, Card and Kestel (1988) found three categories of motivation rather than the four suggested by McIntosh and Goeldner. The three categories that emerged from their research were (1) curiosity, (2) social interaction, and (3) rejuvenation. They found that McIntosh and Goeldner's status and prestige motivation was an underlying influence in each of the other categories and did not emerge as a separate entity or category.

Gray (1970) discussed two basic reasons for pleasure travel: "wanderlust" and "sunlust." Wanderlust refers to the idea that basic traits in human nature cause some individuals to want to leave things with which they are familiar and to go see firsthand different exciting cultures and places. Sunlust, on the other hand, depends on the existence elsewhere of different or better amenities for a specific purpose than they are available locally. Wanderlust and Sunlust are *distinct* categories of reasons for pleasure travel, as seen in the following list of their attributes (Gray 1970:14):

Wanderlust	*Sunlust*
May visit several countries	Usually visit only one country at a time
Seek different culture, institutions, and cuisine	Seek domestic amenities and accommodations
Interested in special physical attributes likely to be artificial; climate less important	Interested in special natural attributes (especially climate)
Travel is an important ingredient throughout the visit	Travel is a minor consideration after arriving at destination
Usually interested in educational experiences	Interested in either rest and relaxation or being very active
More interested in international travel	More interested in domestic travel

Travel motivation studies have also looked at the types of motivations related to segmentation. One such type of segmentation is the life cycle. The life cycle involves grouping people based on their stages in life, rather than simply classifying them by their chronological age. For example, a 34-year-old women may be married with three children or she could be single with no children. The stage of the life cycle she is in may affect her behavior. Hill et al. (1990) studied the motivations that led to a resort vacation and examined how the motivations differed among four life cycle stages: (1) single-no children, (2) married-no children, (3) single with children, and (4) married with children. They found no significant differences between life cycles for the relaxation and escape motivation and the novelty, education, and prestige motivations. Relaxation and escape motivations are most important to every life cycle. Novelty, education, and prestige are relatively unimportant to all life cycles. However, the motivation of enhancement of kinship relationships is more important to those who are married than those who are single. Health and social motivations are more important to single vacationers than married vacationers. A similar finding was also reported by Uysal et al. (1990), who studied motivation and activity differences between married and single resort visitors who were 50 years of age and older. For both populations "having fun and being entertained" reflected a major impetus for visiting a resort, as was "escaping the pressures and responsibilities of daily life." Rest and relaxation was ranked number one for both populations. Married people assigned more importance to "spending time with someone special" and "family togetherness" than they placed on "having fun" and "being entertained." On the other hand, single visitors tended to place a greater significance on "fun and entertainment."

Tourists' Expectations

When people travel to a destination they usually have certain expectations not only about the logistics of the trip but also about the possible benefits that they are likely to derive from that trip, as directed by destination attributes or activities offered by destinations (Goodrich 1978; Schewe and Calantone 1978; Calantone et al. 1980; Calantone and Johar 1984; Backman et al. 1986). The intensity and level of such benefits and travel experience are a function of several interrelated forces of sociodemographic, psychological, cultural, and physical factors (Gitelson and Kerstetter 1990; Kerstetter and Gitelson 1990). Tourism has been viewed as a psychological experience derived from the interaction between the tourist and the environment (Pearce 1982). Situational variables such as season and time of the year more specifically than destination attributes influence one's propensity to travel and travel experience (Belk 1974, 1975; Calantone and Johar 1984; Bonn et al. 1990).

One of the reasons that people travel to destinations that are different from their home environment is that the destination area offers something that they cannot obtain from their home environment. The travel experience involves the relationship between the attributes that the traveler desires and the attributes that the destination area actually offers or provides. Evidence suggests that the choice of a vacation destination is the result of comparing the attributes of the destination area with the individual's set of preferred attributes. When choosing a vacation destination area, travelers will more than likely choose an area that offers the type of accommodations, activities, transportation, adventure and experience that they desire. This fact can be related to the idea that if a traveler's perception of the destination area is higher than what he or she actually experiences at the destination area, then it is likely to result in "dissatisfaction" of the travel or vacation experience. Conversely, if the vacation experience exceeds the traveler's expectations of the destination, the vacation is likely to result in "satisfaction" (Plog 1974; Pizam et al. 1979; Crompton 1983).

Summary

Travel behavior is a phenomenon that has led to several theories and models all trying to explain and describe travel patterns. Motivation is one of the variables that helps explain this phenomenon, and through most of the research motivation has commonly been conceptualized as goal-directed behavior. Crompton (1979) and Pearce (1982) suggest that motivation should be seen as only one of the many variables that contribute to explaining and predicting tourist behavior. They also believe that travel decisions are the result of several or multi-motives. Understanding that travelers are motivated by several variables is important to destination areas in that they should be able to provide a broad range of activities, attractions, and services to fulfill the particular psychological needs of each individual traveler. Individuals have desired needs and perceptions that help determine their travel decisions and destination choice.

Although several different types of needs and motives have been categorized to help explain the push or psychological motivations for travel, Pearce (1982) argues that no single theory of travel motivation can completely explain the tourist behavior. He suggests that a travel motivation theory should consider long-term goals, the perspective of the observer, multi-motive causes of behavior, measurement issues, and the qualitatively different nondeterministic nature of intrinsically motivated behaviors. Future research on travel and tourism motivation should rely more on inferences of travel motivations from travelers' experiences (Dann 1981; Pearce and Caltabiano 1983; Snepenger 1987) rather than attitude measurement scales. Tourist motivation should be viewed in a long-term behavioral context, not a simple short-term process assessed by measuring the immediate satisfaction and causes of tourist behavior. Epperson (1983:32) argues that "as the pressures in a complex society continue to produce more and more stress at work, at home and in social environment, the intrinsic motivations for travel will surely increase."

Although, we are far from completely understanding tourist behavior, there has been significant progress in determining the relationships of motivation and travel behavior in travel and tourism.

References

Atkinson, J. W., and J. O. Raynor. 1975. *Motivation and Achievement.* Washington, D.C.: Winston.

Backman, J. S., R. B. Ditton, R. Kaiser, and J. Fletcher. 1986. An investigation of benefits sought at Texas beaches. In *Tourism Services Marketing: Advances in Theory and Practice,* ed. W. B. Joseph, L. Moutinho, and I. R. Vernon, vol. 2, pp. 53–62. Cleveland, Ohio: Academy of Marketing Science, Cleveland State University.

Belk, R. W. 1974. An exploratory assessment of situational effects in buyer behavior. *Journal of Marketing Research* 11(May):156–163.

Belk, R. W. 1975. Situational variables and consumer behavior. *Journal of Consumer Research* 2(December):157–164.

Bello, D. C., and M. J. Etzel. 1985a. The role of novelty in pleasure travel experiences. *Journal of Travel Research* 24:24–26.

Bello, D. C., and M. J. Etzel. 1985b. The role of novelty in the pleasure vacation. *Annals of Tourism Research* 6(4):408–424.

Bonn, M., M. Uysal, and L. Furr. 1990. A segmentation analysis of peak season and shoulder season resort visitors. In *The Tourism Connection: Linking Research and Marketing,* pp. 61–79, 21st TTRA Annual Proceedings, New Orleans, Louisiana.

Brayley, E. R. 1990. The quantification of vacation attractiveness and its implications for tourism marketing. Paper presented at the Tourism and Commercial Recreation Session, 1990, NRPA Symposium on Leisure Research, October 12–15, Phoenix, Arizona.

Calantone, R. L., and J. S. Johar. 1984. Seasonal segmentation of the tourist market using a benefit segmentation framework. *Journal of Travel Research* 23(2):14–24.

Calantone, R. L., C. S. Schewe, and C. Allen. 1980. Targeting specific advertising messages at tourist segments. In *Tourism Marketing and Management Issues,* ed. D. Hawkins, E. Shafer, and J. Rovelstad, pp. 149–160. Washington, D.C.: George Washington University.

Card, J. A., and C. Kestel. 1988. Motivational factors and demographic characteristics of travelers to and from Germany. *Society and Leisure* 11(1):49–58.

Cohen, E. 1972. Toward a sociology of international tourism. *Social Research* 39(1):164–182.

Chon, K. S. 1989. Understanding recreational traveler's motivation, attitude and satisfaction. *Revue de Tourisme* 44(1):3–6.

Crompton, J. L. 1979. Motivations of pleasure vacation. *Annals of Tourism Research* 6(4):408–424.

Crompton, J. L. 1983. The tourist experience: Satisfaction and dissatisfaction. *Journal of Physical Education, Recreation and Dance—Leisure Today* 54(4):50–52.

Dann, G. 1976. The holiday was simply fantastic. *The Tourist Review* 31(3):19–23.

Dann, G. 1977. Anomie, ego-enhancement and tourism. *Annals of Tourism Research* 4(4):184–194.

Dann, G. 1981. Tourism motivation: An appraisal. *Annals of Tourism Research* 8(2):187–219.

Driver, B. L., and R. C. Knopf. 1977. Personality, outdoor recreation and expected consequences. *Environment and Behavior* 9:109–193.

Epperson, A. 1983. Why people travel. *Journal of Physical Education, Recreation and Dance—Leisure Today* 54(4):53–54.

Gitelson, R., and D. Kerstetter. 1990. The relationship between sociodemographic variables, benefits sought and subsequent vacation behavior: A case study. *Journal of Travel Research* 28(3):24–29.

Goodrich, J. N. 1978. The relationship between preferences for and the perceptions of vacation destinations: Application of a choice model. *Journal of Travel Research* 17(2):8–13.

Gray, P. 1970. *International Travel—International Trade.* Lexington, Mass.: Lexington Books.

Hill, J. B., C. D. McDonald, and M. Uysal. 1990. Resort motivations for different life cycle stages. *Visions in Leisure and Business* 8(4):18–27.

Hill, J. M. M. 1965. *The Holiday.* London: The Tavistock Institute of Human Relations.

Hoyenga, K. B., and K. T. Hoyenga. 1984. *Motivational Explanations of Behavior,* pp. 3–20. Belmont, Calif.: Brooks/Cole Publishing.

Hudman, E. L. 1980. *Tourism. A Shrinking World.* Columbus, Ohio: Grid Inc.

Iso-Ahola, S. E. 1980. *The Social Psychology of Leisure and Recreation* Dubuque, Ia.: Wm. C. Brown Company.

Iso-Ahola, S. E. 1982. Toward a social psychological theory of tourism motivation: A rejoinder. *Annals of Tourism Research* 9(2):256–262.

Iso-Ahola, S. E. 1989. Motivation for leisure. In *Mapping the Past, Charting the Future,* ed. E. L. Jackson and T. L. Burton, pp. 247–279. Venture Publishing.

Jaun, S., and C. D. McDonald. 1990. Motivational determinates of international pleasure time. *Journal of Travel Research* 29(1):42–44.

Kerstetter, D., and R. Gitelson. 1990. An exploratory study of the relationship between benefit profiles of college-educated older adults and travel behavior characteristics. In *The Tourism Connection: Linking Research and Marketing,* pp. 175–187, 21st TTRA Annual Proceedings, New Orleans, Louisiana.

Knopf, R. C., G. Peterson and E. Leatherberry. 1983. Motives for recreation river floating: Relative consistency across settings. *Leisure Sciences* 5:231–255.

Kripendorf, J. 1987. *The Holiday Makers: Understanding the Impact of Leisure and Travel.* Trowbridge, Wildshire, England: Heinemann Professional Publishing, Redwood Burn, Ltd.

Leiper, N. 1984. Tourism and leisure: The significance of tourism in the leisure spectrum. In *Proceedings of 12th New Zealand Geography Conference,* pp. 249–253, N.A., Geographic Society Christchurch.

Lundberg, D. E. 1990. Why tourists travel. In *The Tourist Business.* New York: Van Nostrand Reinhold.

Maslow, A. H. 1954. *Motivation and Personality.* New York: Harper & Row.

Mayo, E. J., Jr. and L. P. Jarvis. 1981. *The Psychology of Leisure Travel.* Boston: CBI Publishing Company.

McIntosh, W. R., and C. R. Goeldner. 1990. *Tourism: Principles, Practices, Philosophies,* 6th ed. New York: Wiley.

Mill, R. C., and A. M. Morrison. 1985. *The Tourism System.* Englewood Cliffs, N.J.: Prentice-Hall.

Murray, E. J. 1964. *Motivation and Emotion.* Englewood Cliffs, N.J.: Prentice-Hall.

Moutinho, L. 1987. Consumer behavior in tourism. *European Journal of Marketing* 21(10):5–44.

Pearce, D. 1987. *Tourism Today: A Geographical Analysis,* ch. 4, pp. 21–25. Longman Scientific and Technical.

Pearce, P. L. 1982. *The Social Psychology of Tourist Behavior.* Oxford: Pergamon Press.

Pearce, P. L., and M. L. Caltabiano. 1983. Inferring travel motivation from traveler's experiences. *Journal of Travel Research* 22(2):16–20.

Pizam, A., Y. Neumann, and A. Reichel. 1979. Tourist satisfaction. *Annals of Tourism Research* 6(2):195–197.

Plog, S. C. 1974. Why destination areas rise and fall in popularity. *The Cornell Hotel and Restaurant Administration Quarterly* 14(4):55–58.

Plog, S. C. 1990. A carpenter's tools: An answer to Stephen L. J. Smith's review of psychocentrism/allocentrism. *Journal of Travel Research* 28(4):40–45.

Pyo, S., and M. Uysal. 1990. Regional implications in tourism motivation. Unpublished manuscript, Department of Parks, Recreation and Tourism Management, Clemson University, Clemson, S.C.

Pyo, S., B. Mihalik, and M. Uysal. 1989. Attraction attributes and motivations: A canonical correlation analysis. *Annals of Tourism Research* 16(2):277–282.

Schewe, C. D., and R. J. Calantone. 1978. Psychographic segmentation of tourists. *Journal of Travel Research* 16(Winter):14–20.

Schreyer, R. 1986. Motivation for participation in outdoor recreation and barriers to that participation: A commentary on salient issues. In *A Literature Review: The President's Commission on Americans Outdoors*, pp. 1–9. December, Motivations.

Smith, L. J. S. 1983. *Recreation Geography.* London and New York: Longman.

Smith, L. J. S. 1990. A test of Plog's allocentric/psychocentric model: Evidence from seven nations. *Journal of Travel Research* 28(4):43–45.

Smith, V. 1979. Women: The taste-makers in tourism. *Annals of Tourism Research* 6(1):49–60.

Snepenger, J. D. 1987. Segmenting the vacation market by novelty-seeking role. *Journal of Travel Research* 26(2):8–14.

Tinsley, E. A. H. 1986. Motivations to participate in recreation: Their identification and measurement. In *A Literature Review: The President's Commission on Americans Outdoors*, pp. 9–16. December, Motivations.

Uysal, M., P. Zimmerer, and M. Bonn. 1990. Marketing resorts to the "gray" traveler. *Leisure Information Quarterly* 16(4):4–7.

Van Doren, S. C. 1983. The future of tourism. *Journal of Physical Education, Recreation and Dance—Leisure Today* 54(4):27–29.

Williams, R. D. 1986. Psychological perspectives on the environment–experience relationship: Implications for recreation resource management. In *A Literature Review: The President's Commission on Americans Outdoors*, pp. 17–31. December, Motivations.

Yuan, S., and C. D. McDonald. 1990. Motivational determinates of international pleasure time. *Journal of Travel Research* 29(1):42–44.

22

Pleasure Travel Destination Choice

Seoho Um

Consumer behavior is an output of consumer decision making. The process by which a consumer makes choice decisions must be reviewed in order to understand consumer behavior. Consumer decision making in tourism refers to all the choice decisions related to the process of taking a pleasure trip, including destination choice, travel mode choice, travel date choice, travel party choice, and so on. Among these sorts of decision making, the destination choice decision has been regarded as the most important in developing marketing strategies for tourism promotion. This article explains the process of pleasure travel destination choice decision, suggesting some destination marketing implications.

Image, Attitude, and Destination Choice

Tybout and Hauser (1981) suggested that the decision-making process can be thought of as following three distinct tasks and may be represented by the following equations (Figure 1).

$$Y = f1 \, (X) \tag{1}$$

$$A = f2 \, (Y) \tag{2}$$

$$C = f3 \, (A) \tag{3}$$

The first equation states that for each of the opportunities in a choice set there are observable and objectively measurable features (X), which when perceived by decision makers yield perceptions (Y) of the attributes present at the respective opportunities. According to this perspective, a physical attribute such as travel distance to an alternative destination forms the basis for an individual's perception of accessibility.

A physical attribute need not lead to a unique perception; it may contribute to several perceptions in different ways. For instance, travel distance may be negatively correlated with perception of accessibility and positively correlated with perception of the travel cost or the inconvenience of a long

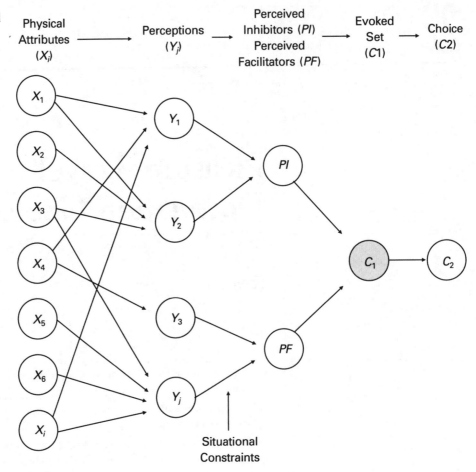

Fig 1. Pleasure travel destination choice.

Physical Attributes (X_i) → Perceptions (Y_j) → Perceived Inhibitors (PI) Perceived Facilitators (PF) → Evoked Set ($C1$) → Choice ($C2$)

Situational Constraints

drive. Indeed, any single physical attribute is likely to be an imperfect indicator of a particular perception.

The second equation indicates that decision makers integrate their perceptions of each attribute into attitude toward an alternative (A). Attitude is viewed as the aggregation or combination of perceptions (Y) not physical attributes (X), and this is represented in Fishbein (1963) and Rosenberg (1956) models. This aggregation process may be described in a variety of forms including linear compensatory, conjunctive, disjunctive, or lexicographic models.

Equation 3 states that choice of an alternative destination is a function of attitude toward the alternatives. Here, attitude can be regarded as a psychological expression of image, which has been noted as one of the major issues in tourism literature; however, attitude is different from image in that it is more likely to be connected with destination choice decision than image.

Lancaster (1966) suggests that consumers do not choose goods themselves, but rather the attributes possessed by the goods, and that they use perceptions of attributes as input factors to assess utility. Potential travelers generally have limited knowledge about the attributes of a destination they have not previously visited. For this reason the image of a place as a travel destination is likely to be a critical element in the destination choice process, irrespective of whether the image is a true representation of what that place has to offer.

Most studies of pleasure travel destination choice have been concerned with exploring the relationship between image of a place and destination choice (Goodrich 1978; Mayo 1973; Matejka 1973; Scott et al. 1978). Hunt (1971, 1975) regarded destination image as one of the major factors in choice decision making along with access, population concentration, physical facilities, and intervening opportunities. Mayo (1973) reported that the average auto vacationer considered scenery, a general lack of congestion, and a pleasant climate to be the most important image attributes of an ideal destination.

Several multiattribute models have been developed that measure images and attempt to relate images to behavior. Goodrich (1978) using Fishbein's multiattribute model, reported a relationship between tourists' images of destinations and their perceptions of those destinations' attributes. That is, images of tourist destinations were enhanced by favorable perceptions that tourists held about those destination attributes. Therefore, the more favorable the images of a vacation destination, the greater the likelihood of that destination being selected over less favorably perceived destinations.

While most image studies have been concerned with identifying critical positive image attributes (Hunt, 1971, 1975; Anderson and Colberg 1973; Riley and Palmer 1976), McLellan and Foushee (1983) focused on identifying the major problems perceived by potential travelers to the United States. Respondents answered that personal safety and cost were their primary concerns. The study also reported that anticipated problems were greater than those actually experienced by visitors to the United States. McLellan and Foushee (1983) concluded that promotional efforts should be focused on alleviating fears of perceived problems as well as enhancing the positive aspects of tourist-attracting resources.

Many tourism studies concerned with the role of image in travel destination choice have focused on the first and second equations. They have been much concerned with the relationship between positive image of a place and preference for the place as a destination. However, they have not paid much attention to actual choice behavior (the third equation). On the other hand, some studies of recreation site choice are concerned with the relationship between physical attributes and site choice without considering any of the mediating steps described above. This trend might be described as follows, using the same notation as above:

$$C = \int 4\ (X) \qquad\qquad (4)$$

For instance, travel distance, the most important variable in recreation site choice, has been calibrated into models as the number of miles from an origin to a destination (Ewing 1980; Fesenmaier 1986; Peterson et al. 1983). However, the same travel distance might be perceived differently by those who have reliable low-mileage cars and those who have unreliable high-mileage vehicles. In addition, site attributes calibrated into the models were those identified by the researcher rather than those perceived by the decision makers (visitors). These problems might reduce the ability of models to accurately predict or describe recreation choice behavior.

Hansen (1976:118) suggested a general framework for reviewing psychological approaches to consumer choice:

> The conflict situation (for choice) is analyzed as a system; where the input factors are (1) predispositions inherent in the individual prior to the conflict, and (2) situational influences acting on the individual at the time of the conflict. As a result of interaction among those variables, a certain number of perceptions, values, beliefs, or whatever one's theory labels them, will become activated, and only those activated or salient will influence the response selection.

Many researchers in consumer behavior have been concerned with the relationship between the input factors mentioned above and outputs. Among the individual dispositional variables, attitudes have been used most frequently to predict consumer behavior (Bass and Talarzyk 1971).

Day and Deutscher (1982) reported that awareness and attitudes toward major appliance brands were only weakly related to subsequent brand choice because such attitudes were susceptible to change during the period of active information search prior to the purchase decision. Belk (1975), Rockeach and Kliejunas (1972), and Sheth (1974) have suggested that explicit recognition of situational variables can enhance the ability to explain and understand consumer behavior. Belk (1975) suggested there were five groups of situational factors: physical surroundings, social surroundings, temporal perspective, task definition, and antecedent states. Sharpe and Granzin (1974) clustered their subjects on the basis of consumption situation and were able to improve predictions of choice based on attitudes. Multiattribute models that ignore this component are unlikely to accurately reflect consumers' choice processes.

In the context of tourism, Crompton (1979) suggested that destination choice should be conceptualized as being a function of the interaction between pragmatic constraints such as time, money, and skills, and destination images. Destination images were prioritized but the ranking was amended by the impact of perceived pragmatic constraints. In his empirical study, Crompton found that there were no significant differences between the image of respondents' dream vacation destinations and the image of their selected destination. Crompton (1977) concluded that neither images nor perceived constraints were sufficient by themselves to explain differences in vacation or destination selection behavior.

For that reason Tybout and Hansen's three-step decision process was extended to Equation 5, which implies that choice is a function of interaction between attitudes and situational constraints. Equation 5 shows that attitude is decomposed into both perceived facilitators (PF) and perceived inhibitors (PI) by the influence of situational constraints.

$$C = f5 \ (PF, PI) \tag{5}$$

Some efforts have been made to describe destination choice based on the concept of evoked set (Woodside and Sherrell 1977; Woodside et al. 1977; Thompson and Cooper 1979). Howard (1963) originally defined evoked set as "the collection of brands the buyer actually considers in his or her purchase decision process." More recently, Woodside and Lysonski (1989) developed and empirically tested a general model of traveler destination choice, focusing on potential traveler's mental categorization process. In their study, traveler's mental categorization process included formation of consideration set, unavailable/aware set, inert set, and inept set in relation to destination awareness. These types of studies identified the existence of evoked set in destination choice process and the role of attitude toward each alternative in mental categorization of destination awareness, based upon a hypothetical destination choice rather than an actual destination choice. The distinction is important because significant differences have been reported between the factors considered in making an actual decision and those involved in a hypothetical decision (Beaulieu and Schreyer 1985).

A Model of Pleasure Travel Destination Choice

Um and Crompton (1990) formulated a cognitive model of pleasure travel destination choice to describe an individual's decision-making process related to actual destination choice with special reference to the role of attitudes.

The pleasure travel destination choice model (Figure 2) that was developed identifies and integrates five sets of processes: (1) the perceptions (belief formation) of destination attributes in the awareness set, through passive information catching; (2) a decision to undertake a pleasure trip (initiation of a destination choice process); (3) evolution of an evoked set from the awareness set of destinations; (4) the perceptions (belief formation) of the destination attributes of each alternative in the evoked set of destinations, through active solicitation of information; and (5) selection of a specific travel destination (or destinations). The model also identifies three constructs that evolve from these five processes. They are awareness set, evoked set, and travel destination selection.

Description of Concepts Used in the Model

External Input. External inputs can be viewed as the sum of social interactions and marketing communications to which a potential pleasure traveler is exposed. They can be classified into significative stimuli, symbolic stimuli, and social stimuli (Howard and Sheth 1969:63). Significative stimuli are those which emanate from actually visiting the destination, that is, from being physically exposed to the travel destination. Symbolic stimuli are the words, sentences, and pictures disseminated as promotional material through the media by the travel industry. Social stimuli emanate from other people in face-to-face interactions. They include other people communicating their direct or indirect travel experiences.

Gitelson and Crompton (1983) reported that 74 percent of all respondents that they had received travel information from friends and relatives (social stimuli), whereas 20 percent of the respondents had received travel information from print media (symbolic stimuli) such as newspapers, general magazines, and travel magazines. Nolan (1976) and Walter and Tong (1977) reported that the most influential source of information for destination choice was interpersonal relationships with family, friends, and relatives. Similarly, Crompton (1981) reported that social groups exerted a normative influence on choice of destinations.

Internal Inputs. Internal inputs derive from the socio-psychological set of a potential traveler, which includes personal characteristics (sociodemographics, life-style, personality, and situational factors), motives, values, and attitudes (Assael 1984). Beliefs about destination attributes are formed by being exposed to the external stimuli display, but the nature of those beliefs will vary

Fig. 2 A model of the pleasure travel destination choice.

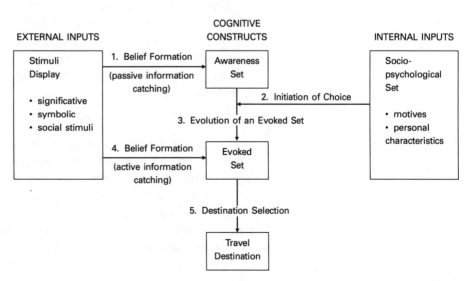

according to a potential traveler's sociopsychological set. In this context, motives are perceived to be the most important internal input since they play a central role in regulating the selective perception of external information (Howard and Sheth 1969).

Motives perform two functions. First, they are the impetus for behavior (Osgood et al. 1957). That is, motives arouse the need to travel and lead to an intention to select a travel destination. Second, through the evaluation of perceptions of destination attributes, they also direct potential travelers to select specific travel destinations.

Cognitive Constructs. Cognitive constructs represent an integration of the internal and external inputs, into the awareness set of destinations and the evoked set of destinations.

The awareness set includes all travel locations that people might consider as potential destinations before any decision process about their trip has been initiated. That is, it refers to "all the preferred destinations of your dreams" (Crompton 1977). In deriving the awareness set, people are likely to include everywhere they desire to travel, without being inhibited by such situational constraints as money or time.

The evoked set includes all the travel destinations that potential travelers might consider to be reasonable alternatives in selecting a specific destination(s). In this stage, people are likely to consider their situational constraints as well as their preferences for alternative destinations. It is assumed that an evoked set is developed simultaneously or after a fundamental decision is made on whether or not to take a pleasure trip. Thus, evolution of an evoked set is an intermediate stage between the awareness set and the final choice.

The Interaction of Attitudes and Situational Constraints. Attitudes have been shown to be a useful predictor of overall preferences but their success in predicting behavior has been less definitive (Assael 1984). In this model, situational variables were considered together with attitudes toward a destination. Perceptions of destination attributes were evaluated as either perceived facilitators or perceived inhibitors in terms of accommodating situational constraints as well as satisfying specific motives for pleasure travel. The perceived inhibitors and the perceived facilitators were recognized to be input factors that impact utility (Mercer 1971). The maximization of utility over all alternatives is the most common choice decision rule (Corstjens and Gautschi 1983; Peterson et al. 1985).

In the context of the destination choice model (Figure 2), attitudes toward alternatives are formulated at both the evoked set and destination selection stages. At both stages, attitudes were operationalized in terms of their perceived utility, which was defined as the difference between the magnitude of perceived facilitators (PF) and the magnitude of perceived inhibitors (PI) (Peter and Tarpey 1975).

$$\text{Attitude} = \text{perceived utility} = PF - PI$$

The perceptions of alternative destinations in the awareness set, which are formed through passive information catching, are susceptible to change during the period of active solicitation of information stimulated by an intention to select a travel destination (Bettman 1979; Park and Lutz 1982). Therefore, perceived inhibitors and perceived facilitators measured at the evoked set stage after active solicitation of information were symbolized as PF' and PI' to differentiate then from PF and PI.

Travel Destination Choice.   Travel destination choice is conceptualized as a two-stage process. The first stage is the evolution of an evoked set of destinations from an awareness set. The second stage is to select a destination from the evoked set. At the first stage, all alternative destinations in the awareness set are evaluated in terms of magnitude of the perceived utility of each alternative $(PF - PI)$. Alternative destinations judged to be unsatisfactory in terms of magnitude of their perceived utility are eliminated from further consideration. At the second stage, a travel destination (or destinations) is selected from the alternative destinations in the evoked set based on magnitude of the perceived utility associated with actually traveling to each alternative $(PF' - PI')$. The alternative likely to provide the highest utility is selected as the travel destination (Corstjens and Gautschi 1983; Edward 1954; Lawler 1973).

Description of the Model's Flows   The model begins with an assumption that potential travelers already possess an awareness set of pleasure travel destinations. Perceptions (belief formation) of destination attributes in the awareness set are mostly formed through passive selective perception based on prior beliefs (flow 1). Selective perception suggests that individuals are more likely to retain supportive information and to avoid information contradictory to what they already know. That is, perceptions of destination attributes in the awareness set are formed through information being chosen that is consistent with prior beliefs about those places (Assael 1984).

Attitudes toward possible destinations in the awareness set are formed with the emergence of an intention to select a specific travel destination (or destinations), which is caused by a decision to undertake a pleasure trip (flow 2). Active decision making begins with a decision to go on a trip and the flows prior to this decision are a preparatory stage (Stynes 1983). Evaluation of destination attributes is influenced by potential travelers' internal inputs. These include their motives for traveling and the situational constraints that influence their ability to travel. That is, perceptions of destination attributes might be evaluated as either potential facilitators or potential inhibitors in terms of satisfying decision makers' motives or accommodating their situational constraints to traveling.

The evoked set is determined by the magnitude of perceived utility derived from the difference between inhibitors and facilitators associated with each alternative in the awareness set (flow 3). For instance, the following perceptions might be evaluated as facilitators and inhibitors: "I know that there are a lot of things to see in Mexico" and "I know that I cannot speak any Spanish."

After formulating the evoked set, an intention to select a destination (or destinations) stimulates active solicitation of information about destination attributes. These are evaluated either as potential inhibitors or as potential facilitators (flow 4). The prior perceptions obtained through passive selective perception without any decision to go on a trip are susceptible to change during the period of active information search (Day and Deutscher 1982; Park and Lutz 1982). In this case, "active information search" refers to a mechanism for reducing the degree of uncertainty about destination attributes in the evoked set (Bennett and Harrell 1975). As a result, a set of beliefs about the possible outcomes of traveling to an alternative in the evoked set are formed and evaluated as either potential facilitators or potential inhibitors. Perceived utility of traveling to the alternative is a function of those beliefs and their relative strength as either facilitators or inhibitors. Flow 5, travel destination choice, is concerned with selecting a destination or a set of destinations from the alternatives in the evoked set based on the magnitude of perceived utility about the action of traveling to each alternative. Here, "perceived utility" reflects a judgment about the relative efficiency in satisfying specific motives and the ability to accommodate constraints. It is the product of perceived facilitators minus perceived inhibitors. The alternative likely to lead to the highest utility is selected as the vacation destination (Corstjens and Gautshi 1983; Edward 1954).

Empirical Findings   Um and Crompton (1990a) tested a part of this conceptualization empirically based on the longitudinal survey. In early February, 1987, a field survey was administered to a judgment sample ($n = 359$) to identify potential travelers' awareness sets of their potential summer vacation destinations and to measure perceived inhibitors and perceived facilitators of alternative destinations in the awareness set. In May, a second survey was administered to these respondents who indicated that they were likely to take vacation trips in the first survey ($n = 204$). Their final destination selection as well as their evoked set were identified in the second survey, but only 102 met the conditions needed to be included in the data analysis to test the following hypotheses.

1. The mean score of the perceived utility among alternative destinations selected in an evoked set is greater than that among the alternatives not selected in the evoked set.
2. The mean score of the perceived utility of the alternative(s) selected as a travel destination(s) from the evoked set is greater than that among the alternatives not selected as travel destinations from the evoked set.
3. The average number of alternative destinations in the awareness set is greater than the average number of alternative destinations in the evoked set (Um 1988).

The first and the second hypotheses were developed and accepted to confirm the roles of attitudes in the travel destination choice process. The third hypothesis was developed and accepted to test the utility of the evoked set concept in the context of travel destination choice behavior.

In this study, perceived inhibitors and perceived facilitators were measured by the multi-item scale which were developed to incorporate three personal and situational dimensions consistently reported in the literature as impacting travel decisions (Um and Crompton 1990b). They were need satisfaction, social agreement, and travelability. The need satisfaction dimension incorporated a set of motivations for travel, which included novelty, challenge, relaxation, learning, and curiosity. The social agreement dimension reflected travelers' inclinations to act in accordance with their social groups' opinions. The travelability dimension described an individuals' capability to travel to a place in terms of such variables as money, time, skill, and health.

Um (1989) also found that whereas at the early stage of selecting a destination, the magnitude of perceived facilitators was a significant indicator in predicting which destinations evolved to an evoked set from an awareness set; at the later stage this changed and it was magnitude of perceived inhibitors that was the significant indicator of destination selection. The sample used to test the hypotheses was a judgment sample and for this reason, the findings are not generalizable. Nevertheless, they do provide some tentative evidence to suggest that inhibiting and facilitating factors considered by potential pleasure travelers in evaluating alternative destinations may be different at different stages of the choice process.

Summary

This entry deals with consumer behavior in selecting destinations to visit. It attempts to apply utility theory in consumer travel decision making. Finally, empirical findings of research dealing with consumer choice mechanism are presented.

Reference

Anderssen, P., and R. T. Colberg. 1973. Multivariate analysis in travel research: A tool for travel package design and market segmentation. In *Proceedings of the Fourth Annual Conference*, pp. 225–240. *Travel Research Association*.

Assael, H. 1984. *Consumer Behavior and Marketing Action*. Boston: Kent Publishing.

Bass, F. M., and W. W. Talarzyk. 1971. Using attitude to predict individual preference. *Advertising* 4:63–72.

Beaulieu, J. T., and R. Schreyer. 1985. Choices of wilderness environment differences between real and hypothetical choice situation. In *Proceedings Symposium on Recreation Choice Behavior*, in USDA Forest Service General Technical Report (INT-184), pp. 38–45, Missoula, Montana.

Belk, R. W. 1975. Situational variables and consumer behavior. *Journal of Consumer Research* 2:157–164.

Bennett, P. D., and G. D. Harrell. 1975. The role of confidence in understanding and predicting buyer's attitudes and purchase intention. *Journal of Consumer Research* 2:110–117.

Bettman, J. R. 1979. *An Information Processing Theory of Consumer Choice*. Reading, Mass.: Addison-Wesley.

Corstjens, M. L., and D. A. Gautschi. 1983. Formal Choice Models in Marketing. *Marketing Science* 2:19–56.

Crompton, J. L. 1977. A systems model of the tourist's destination selection decision process with particular reference to the role of image and perceived constraints. Ph. D. diss., Texas A&M University.

Crompton, J. L. 1979. Motivations for pleasure vacation. *Annals of Tourism Research* 6:408–424.

Crompton, J. L. 1981. Dimensions of the social group role in pleasure vacations. *Annals of Tourism Research* 8:550–568.

Day, G. S., and T. Deutscher. 1982. Attitudinal predictions of choices of major appliance brands. *Journal of Marketing Research* 19:192–198.

Edward, W. 1954. The theory of decision making. *Psychological Bulletin* 51:380–417.

Ewing, G. O. 1980. Progress and problems in the development of recreation trip generation and trip distribution models. *Leisure Science* 13:1–23.

Fesenmaier, D. R. 1986. Integrating activity experience into destination choice model. Unpublished Paper. Texas A&M University.

Fishbein, M. 1963. An investigation of the relationships between beliefs about an object and the attitudes towards that object. *Human Relations* 16:233–239.

Gitelson, R. J., and J. L. Crompton. 1983. The planning horizons and sources of information used by pleasure traveler. *Journal of Travel Research* 21:2–7.

Goodrich, J. N. 1978. The relationship between preferences for and perceptions of vacation destinations: Application of a choice model. *Journal of Travel Research* 17:8–13.

Hansen, F. 1976. Psychological theories of consumer choice. *Journal of Consumer Research* 3:117–142.

Howard, J. A. 1963. *Marketing Management*. Homewood, Illinois: Irwin Publishing Company.

Howard, J. A., and J. L. Sheth. 1969. *The Theory of Buyer Behavior*. New York: Wiley.

Hunt, J. D. 1971. Image a factor in tourism. Unpublished Ph. D. diss., Colorado State University.

Hunt, J. D. 1975. Image as a factor in tourism development. *Journal of Travel Research* 13:18–23.

Lancaster, K. J. 1966. A new approach to consumer theory. *Journal of Political Economy* 74:132–157.

Lawler, E. E. 1973. *Motivations in Work Organizations*. Monterey, Calif.: Brooks/Cole Publishing Co.

McLellan, R. W., and K. D. Foushee. 1983. Negative images of the United States as expressed by tour operators from other countries. *Journal of Travel Research* 22:2–5.

Matejka, J. K. 1973. Critical factors in vacation area selection. *Arkansas Business and Economic Review.* 6:17–19.

Mayo, E. J. 1973. Regional images and regional travel destination. In *Proceedings of the Fourth Annual Conference*, pp. 211–217. Travel Research Association.

Mercer, D. 1971. The role of perception in the recreation experience: A review and discussion. *Journal of Leisure Research* 3:261–276.

Nolan, S. D. 1976. Tourists use and evaluation of travel information sources: Summary and conclusions. *Journal of Travel Research* 14:6–8.

Osgood, C.E., G. T. Suci, and P. H. Tannenbaum. 1957. *The Measurement of Meaning*. Urbana: University of Illinois Press.

Park, C. W., and R. J. Lutz. 1982. Decision plans and consumer choice dynamics. *Journal of Marketing Research* 19:108–115.

Peter, J. P., and L. X. Tarpey. 1975. A comparative analysis of three consumer decision strategies. *Journal of Consumer Research* 2:29–37.

Peterson, G. L., J. F. Dwyer, and A. J. Darragh. 1983. A behavioral urban recreation site choice model. *Leisure Science* 6:61–81.

Peterson, G. L., D. J. Stynes, D. H. Rosenthal, and J. F. Dwyer, 1985. Substitution Recreation Choice Behavior. In *Proceedings Symposium on Recreation Choice Behavior*, USDA Forest Service General Technical Report (INT-184), pp. 19–30. Missoula, Montana.

Riley, S., and J. Palmer. 1976. Of attitudes and latitudes: A repertory grid study of perceptions of seaside resorts. In *Exploration of Interpersonal Space*, ed. P. Slater. London: Wiley.

Rockeach, M., and P. Kliejunas. 1972. Behavior as a function of attitude-toward-object and attitude-toward-situation. *Journal of Personality and Social Psychology* 22:194–201.

Rosenberg, M. J. 1956. Cognitive structure and attitudinal affect. *Journal of Abnormal and Social Psychology* 53:367–372.

Scott, D., C. D. Schewe, and D. G. Frederick. 1978. A multi-brand/multiattribute model of tourist state choice. *Journal of Travel Research* 17:23–29.

Sharpe, L. K., and K. L. Granzin. 1974. Brand attributes that determine purchase. *Journal of Advertising Research* 14:39–42.

Sheth, J. N. 1974. A field study of attitude structure and attitude-behavior relationship. In *Models of Buyer Behavior*, ed. J. Sheth, pp. 242–268. New York: Harper and Row.

Stynes, D. J. 1983. Times series and structural models for forecasting recreation participation. In *Recreation Planning and Management*, eds. S. R. Lieber and D. R. Fesenmaier, pp. 105–119. State College, Pa.: Venture Publishing.

Thompson, J. R., and P. D. Cooper. 1979. Attitudinal evidence on the limited size of evoked set of travel destinations. *Journal of Travel Research* 17:23–25.

Tybout, A. M., and J. R. Hauser. 1981. A marketing audit using a conceptual model of consumer behavior: Application and evaluation. *Journal of Marketing* 45:82–101.

Um, Seoho. 1988. Evoked set in the vacation destination choice process. *Korean Journal of Leisure and Recreation* 5:62–70.

Um, Seoho. 1989. The roles of perceived inhibitors and perceived facilitators in the pleasure travel destination choice process. In *Proceedings of 20th Annual Conference*, pp. 249–254. Travel and Tourism Research Association.

Um, Seoho, and J. L. Crompton. 1990a. Attitude determinants in tourism destination choice. *Annals of Tourism Research* 17(3):432–448.

Um, Seoho, and J. L. Crompton. 1990b. Development and verification of attitude dimensions relating to pleasure travel destination choice decision. *Annals of Tourism Research.* Forthcoming.

Walter, C. K., and Hsin-Min Tong. 1977. A local study of consumer vacation decisions. *Journal of Travel Research* 15:30–34.

Woodside, A. G., and S. Lysonski. 1989. A general model of traveler destination
choice. *Journal of Travel Research* 27:8–14.

Woodside, A. G., and D. Sherrell. 1977. Traveler evoked set, inept set, and inert
sets of vacation destinations. *Journal of Travel Research* 16:14–18.

Woodside, A.G., I. A. Ronkainen, and D. M. Reid. 1977. Measurement and utilization of the evoked sets as a travel marketing variable. In *Proceedings of Eight
Annual Conference*, pp. 123–130. Travel Research Association.

23

Religious Tourism

Kadir H. Din

Religious tourism is a category of travel primarily or partly motivated by religious considerations. Although such journeys may be regarded as sacred by the travelers concerned, they differ from the more inclusive concept of tourism as a sacred journey as used by social scientists in discussions on tourism as a form of "non-ordinary" activity (Graburn 1977; Jafari 1987; Allcock 1988). Within the field of tourism studies the religious element is frequently mentioned in discussions on tourist motivation and tourist attraction. From the demand side, religious-motivated tourism includes travel for performing pilgrimages, attending religious meetings, conferences, staged dramas and musical productions, and visiting religious headquarters and historical sites (Hudman and Hawkins 1989:41). The nature of such travels, and the spatial forms manifested, differ between these categories and within them. From the supply side, religious destinations are usually categorized as centers of historic and cultural attractions in association with one or more religious identities.

Religious tourism is estimated to have contributed over 130 million tourists or about 9 percent of the total tourism market in 1987 (Jackowski 1987:37). The magnitude of religious travel varies among countries and among ethnic groups in each country, owing to the different degrees of spiritual significance attached to these forms of travel and the different sizes of the population base. Cities such as Mecca, Jerusalem, and Benares, being the centers of the major world religions, receive heavy concentrations of visitors, especially during pilgrimage seasons. Mecca received over three million pilgrims per year in the late 1980s, as compared to some 4.6 million arrivals in Lourdes (1979), and over half a million religious visitors to Israel in 1984 (Rinschede 1986:23; Ben-Sahar et al. 1989:258). In the case of Allahabad (India), some 30 million Hindus gathered at the confluence of the Ganges and the Yamuna rivers in February 1989 for a religious festival, Jumbh Mela, which occurs every twelve years (Waters 1990:122; Heiderer 1990:106). A conservative estimate of visitors to some 150 major holy places in India suggests an annual average of twenty million arrivals (Eliade 1987:353). Across the border in Pakistan, over 26 million visitors were estimated to have visited the various sacred grounds including the 84 main Muslim and Sikh shrines (Government of Pakistan 1987).

The above pattern of concentrations can be explained by the location of elective religious centers such as Mecca and Jerusalem, and the large population in India (800 million) and Pakistan (110 million). Beside these world order centers, there are also a hierarchy of other subcenters and spiritual centers for other religions. With the exception of the lowest order neighborhood subcenters, a visit to the higher echelon centers would generally require an overnight stay, thus qualifying visitors to temples and shrines as tourists (Demars 1988). Based on the Encyclopedia Britannica 1989 Book of the Year estimate, over 83 percent of the 5.2 billion world population subscribe to a religion and most of the religions, including the newly-found religions, have a hierarchy of spiritual centers. This suggests that, although there has been no serious attempt to estimate the volume of religious-motivated travel, such travels form an important segment of the world tourism market. Its magnitude is clearly reflected in the number of religious groupings and the number of religious shrines in most areas of the world. In the United States alone there are over 1,200 different religious groups (Melton 1978), and in Europe there are 6,150 active pilgrimage shrines (Nolan 1986:14). These figures seem to indicate that the magnitude of religious travel has so far been underestimated, or to some degree overshadowed by other more secular, and perhaps more marketable forms of travel.

More often than not, the decision to travel is prompted by more than just one motivation, however. The fact that between 75 to 80 percent of the American tourists arriving in Israel are Jews (Landau 1989:59), suggests that in certain regions of the world, religious affinity can be an important factor, in a combination of factors, which motivates people to travel. In a study of the propensity to travel among Greek-Americans, for example, Constantinou and Walle (1988) conclude that a significant component of overseas travel is made up of pilgrimage to ancestral lands of ethnic groups. Visiting sacred grounds, however, does not necessarily mean that the visitor must subscribe to a particular faith, although to be sure, it is still the spiritual significance of a place that attracts even the nonbeliever or adherents of other religions.

Personal curiosity and attractions to aesthetic and ethnic features may also provide equally strong motivations to travel to such sites. Indeed, surveys conducted in India, Pakistan, and France, show that religious sites usually welcome all visitors irrespective of their religious backgrounds (Unisa et al. 1989; Bharati 1963; Government of Pakistan 1987; Schweyer 1984).

General Characteristics

As in other categories of tourism, there are wide variations in the practice of religious tourism. Within the precepts of each religion there are also a range of religious travels, some more significant and rewarding (spiritually) than others (Eickelman and Piscatori 1990). A side visit to a Muslim shrine, for example, is certainly of a lower order and less meritorious when compared to an off-season visit to Mecca (*umrah*), or the annual Hajj. Despite these differences there are at least three discernible elements in all religious-motivated travel: a purpose, a structure, and a process.

The Purpose Religious travel by definition is spiritually purposive. Subject to specific tenets as enjoined for various forms of spiritual journeys, the purpose is to attain at least one of the following goals:

1. *To fulfill a pilgrimage as an act of worship.* Most religions enjoin pilgrimage as an act of worship and salvation, but only Muslims and Jews regard pilgrimage as conditionally obligatory. The Hajj is a religious duty for every adult Muslim who is healthy and financially capable of undertaking the journey. Among the Jews, pilgrimage tradition commits all males to visit the temple in Jerusalem during the three annual festivals: Passover, Pentecost, and Feast of Tabernacles (Eliade 1987:346).

2. *To perform a vow, express gratitude, confess sins, and convey petitions.* When faced with a crisis in life that cannot be resolved through worldly means, most believers turn to divine help. A visit to a sacred site is partly meant to facilitate communication with the apparitional custodian of the sites for such help. Here believers confess sins, repent, make vows, and declare new resolutions for a more blessed life in the future.

3. *To attain social and spiritual elevation.* Socially, taking a religious trip is a mark of piety which is virtuous in most societies. Among Hindus a visit to holy places is one of the means for accumulating religious merit, whereas Buddhists regard pilgrimage as an important preliminary step along the path to enlightenment. In many religious groups, for example Muslims, Jews, Hindus, and Buddhists, it is common to find older members performing pilgrimage as a stage of "retiring" from the secular life in preparation for final departure from this world.

4. *To commemorate certain religious events.* Every religion has myths and rituals associated with certain events that are regarded as sacred among the believers. The birth of a prophet or the death of an apparitional figure, or certain journeys undertaken by them, are carefully documented in mythologies or tenets. Such events are reenacted during religious festivities to commemorate the lives and deeds of mythical figures.

5. *To be in communion with coreligionists.* This applies to most religious meetings, which can be missionary meetings or pilgrimages. Indeed, in many religions one of the expressed purposes of pilgrimage is to provide an occasion for a social gathering of fellow believers.

6. *To spread the gospel.* Most religions support missionary activities, either for the purpose of indoctrinating the believers with the true teachings of the faith or for purposes of proselytization. In new religious movements and some of the established religions, instructional camps are held in retreats or ashrams (Melton 1986; Morreale 1988). One such example is the Hare Krishna Temple in West Virginia (Prorok 1986).

7. *To organize conference and clerical meetings.* Like other secular organizations, religious groups require efficient management of their affairs. This is achieved through periodic meetings to review progress and to educate and help members pursue their spiritual goals more effectively.

Clearly, a great deal of travel is required to accomplish the above religious pursuits. Some of these travels are sponsored by the organizer but most religious tourism is comprised of individually initiated trips, either in fulfillment of a religious obligation, a side trip during a vacation, or a journey in support of a virtuous cause.

The Structure   The literature on religious travel highlights two structural dimensions, one experiential and the other spatiotemporal. Whereas the experiential dimension refers to emotion and behavior of individual travelers, the spatiotemporal dimension represents the physical and geographic manifestations of travel on the tourist landscape. A description of this structure serves to distinguish religious travel as a distinct category from other secular forms of travel.

The Experiential Dimension.   Religious tourism, as in any other form of tourism, proceeds in three stages from the stage of separation, through the liminal stage, to the stage of reaggregation (for further differentiation see Jafari 1987). The journey usually begins with the intending traveler making preparations and bidding farewell to friends and relatives before leaving the ordinary day-to-day situation to enter the stage of sojourn. During sojourn the traveler is theoretically free from all clutches of social norms, sanctions, and obligations which he is expected to observe in the home community. The religious tourist is also drawn to a purposeful destination, or a "center out there" which he would want to cover and in so doing engages the sentiment of *communitas*, a special kind of bonding and fraternity with other travelers who mostly visit the same destinations with a common purpose. Once the goal or purpose is accomplished, the traveler returns home to be reaggregated into the fold of his community of origin.

The itinerary may be straightforward and singular, as in the case of Muslim pilgrims visiting Mecca for the Hajj. It may also be fairly peripatetic such as the circuitous wanderings of Buddhist monks in search of the virtues of Lord Buddha. In the same vein, visitors to religious shrines abroad may include side trips to visit distant friends and relatives, do shopping, and perhaps spend a part of the journey touring the ordinary tourist route. Despite these expected variations in purpose and itineraries, the religious traveler cannot avoid experiencing the above three-stage transformations. Indeed, the entire cycle of sojourn-separation-reaggregation itself is ideally expected to enrich the believer with a deep spiritual experience, including certain ascetic abstinences from a variety of temptations. The nature of experience, however, becomes more complicated if the journey is taken with the intention of realizing both religious and secular goals, such as a vacation tour of Europe after a business meeting in Amsterdam, plus a subsequent visit to the Temple in Jerusalem.

The Spatiotemporal Dimension.   Space and time are essential elements of all human activities, including travel. Most forms of religious travel, however, are bounded by a greater degree of specificity with regard to these two elements. The standard approach in the spatial analysis of religious travel focuses attention on the *center*, tributary and circulation *fields* which are laced with *routes* studded with landscape *features* associated with the phenomenon. As in the case of the experiential dimension, the spatial and temporal dimensions can also be traced in cycles. Among the pilgrims to Mecca, for example, intending pilgrims must begin their rites from a number of designated embarkation gateways (al-miqat) to the holy land where they must don the purity garb (ihram), before proceeding for the next rite. From there the pilgrim follows a strict sequence of procedures over a period of six days, which involves prescribed rites and stops along some 25 miles of circular route that extends eastward from the center of the holy city.

To each pilgrimage field (of regional scale), is a focal point usually associated with the most sacred site (Jackson and Henrie 1990:106). For Mecca, it is the Kaabah, which is a square monument of roughly the same size and shape as the inner Holy of Holies of the Jerusalem Temple. The focal center in Jerusalem is a four-cornered multireligious core consisting of the Western

Wall, the Dome of the Rock, the Al-Aqsa Mosque, and the Church of the Holy Sepulchre; for Lourdes it is the Domain of the Gratto.

The tributary field for all these sacred sites is the world, although in practice pilgrimage visits are obviously influenced by the cost of travel and hence a center tends to draw patronage in a distance-decay pattern, that is, most visitors tend to originate from adjacent areas. Because the pilgrimage centers of the major world religions are located in the Middle East, there is a preponderance of West Asian and European visitors at the congregations. In prescribed pilgrimages such as the Hajj, the influence of distance on arrival may be offset by doctrinal precepts. Whereas for Muslims there is one obligatory center, for Christians there is no such definitive center (Lewis 1989:389). This explains why Fulani tribesmen would spend an average of eight years of travel on foot covering over 2,500 miles to Mecca (Birks 1977:47).

One universal characteristic of pilgrimage landscapes is that they are associated with features that Ritter (1975:57) calls "tourism of the dead" (compare the Japanese pilgrimage island of Shikoku meaning "lands of the dead"). Not only do the sites attract predominantly old groups for whom the visit might be the last journey before retiring from this world, the sites also contain antiquities, tombs, and monuments set up in memory of the dead. Many of the spectacular historical and architectural heritage characteristics of such centers were built in memory of prophets, martyrs, and sages. Pilgrims of many religions, such as Islam, Hinduism, and Shintoism, wear attires that closely resemble the dress for the dead. It is ironic that in most religions the austere and ascetic existence as reflected in the manner of dressing contrasts with the tendency to be overly lavish in the construction of buildings and monuments.

Even in newly established sites such as the Hare Krishna Palace of Gold, the architectural form derives from ancient religious motifs, in this case the traditional Indian temple structure. The temple was intended to be "an international place of pilgrimage for Krishna-conscious people" (Prorok 1986:137). In choosing the site for the temple, the founder, like the ancient temple planners, paid careful attention to ensure that the site has a mountain and running water, sanctified by the mystery and wonder associated with remoteness. It is perhaps for the same reason that Shikoku Island has evolved to become the "center out there" among adherents of the Shinto religion. The island is mountainous and the 750-mile pilgrim route, which links 88 temples on the island, runs through some of the most rustic areas of the Japanese outback.

The Process and Trends | Process here refers to the genesis, evolution, and institutionalization of religious travels and not the ritual procedures that are part of the spatiotemporal structure. All forms of religious travel have their historical roots and are subject to change; the nature of change varies from one form to the other. A sacred place may derive its origin either from divine revelation, acts of consecration, or from mythological sources.

The earliest historical reference to pilgrimage undertaken with a religious motive appeared in the edict of the Buddhist emperor Asoka who erected sacred places for pilgrims in the third century before the present era (Hastings 1974:15). Similarly, the Japanese places of worship and pilgrimage were consecrated by Buddhist missionaries in the eighth century. By the end of the seventeenth century, the pilgrimage route around the island of Shikoku was already established with 88 designated temples along the way.

According to Reader (1987:135), the conduct of pilgrimage to Shikoku has since evolved from an unstructured journey to a more structured tour which in many respects resembles the modern package tour.

A similar trend is also observable in the case of religious travels to Mecca (hajj and *umrah*), which have evolved from individualized and disorganized forms of travel to highly orchestrated travel packages. The ritual procedures remain, but the organizational aspects involving the entire industry, which cater to pilgrim needs, from medical and immigration requirements to ritual rehearsals prior to departure to the Holy Land, have been carefully programmed by pilgrimage authorities to ensure that intending pilgrims will be fully prepared for embarkation to Mecca.

The evolution of tourist movements worldwide is to a large degree reflected in the trends in religious travel. In absolute terms religious tourism has grown exponentially over the decades, and this growth is mainly attributable to the growing number of believers who can afford to undertake the journeys and to the improvements in transportation, especially the air transport technology. This trend is likely to continue in the foreseeable future, not only because of the above income and technological factors, but also because of other changes occurring in modern society. While modernization has generally brought prosperity along with secularization of values, this post–World War II trend has also resulted in problems of alienation and spiritual poverty, making revitalization of spiritual values a necessity especially among the younger generation in the 1970s.

With the waning of influence from socialism and communism in the 1990s, the importance of religious values is likely to be reinstituted in both the metropolitan and satellite socialist societies, thereby permitting more religious travel among the people of the world. The general trend in the tourism market shows a gradual shift in consumer preferences from the more hedonistic pursuits to a more spiritually fulfilling travel. Whereas some may visit similar types of destinations as they did during their previous trips, they have now become less easily impressed by gimmickries of the upmarket services, but are at the same time becoming more sensitive to the spiritual aspects of the journey. Travelers may now opt for travel that leads them to be in communion with nature, or they may opt for the adventure tourism which leads them to greater appreciation of culture and history. Religious destinations, with their own congeries of cultural and historic attractions, would be appealing even to the nonbelievers.

Thus, while the growing trend in travel implies a corresponding growth in religious tourism, this growth is likely to be augmented further by the shift in consumer tastes in favor of spiritual pursuit. In the long run, however, religious tourism, like other segments of travel, is more likely to assume cyclical growth patterns, with alternating peaks and troughs. But the significance of this segment of the total market is likely to continue to assume a greater prominence than the previous situation. One other factor that supports such optimism is that it is only within the last decade or so that the religious authorities worldwide have begun to preach on the spiritual virtues of travel.

In the meantime religious tourism has gradually evolved from its stoic and ascetic character in the past to become a partially hedonistic pursuit. The lifetime endurance among the Fulani pilgrims mentioned earlier, who slept in makeshift tents and trekked on foot across the Sahel, is a far cry from the typical mass pilgrim to Mecca or Jerusalem who can now arrive in the jetliner and opt to stay in star-rated air-conditioned rooms. With few exceptions, changes in the experience of pilgrimage runs parallel with changes in the host-guest relationship. Although most religious traditions, including Islam and Judaism, encourage hospitable treatment of pilgrims through offering shelter and other forms of assistance, the nature of modern encounter situation tends to assume the euphoria-antagonism cycle of attitudinal changes of the host community as the sacred sites become increasingly swarmed by pilgrims. It is not uncommon nowadays for politicians of all creeds to take a pilgrimage trip partly as a means of redeeming their loss of popularity before the onset of the election season. At the same time custodial states are becoming more conscious of the political significance of sacred sites so much so that the institution of pilgrimage has now assumed a greater role in the world community.

The above scenario suggests a number of implications. It points to the needs for tourism planners, marketers, and entrepreneurs to assume a more proactive position with regard to catering for the needs of religious travelers. In Jerusalem for example, the most successful hotel operations are those that pay attention to the peculiar aversions and preferences of pilgrims from different religious backgrounds (Gruber 1988:37). So far the initiatives toward satisfying religious consumers have come mostly from religious authorities; it behooves decision makers in the industry to begin to address the needs of the pilgrim more than they have given in the past, both for the benefit of business and for spiritual gains.

Summary

Religious tourism is one of the least researched areas of tourism phenomena. However, religious tourism in the form of pilgrimages contributes both economically and culturally to the countries and communities where holy sites are located.

References

Allcock, John B. 1988. Tourism as a sacred journey. *Society and Leisure* 11(1):33–48.

Ben-Shahar, H., G. Fichelson, and S. Hirsch. 1989. *Economic Cooperation and Middle East Peace.* London: Weidenfeld and Nicolson.

Bharati, Agehananda. 1963. Pilgrimage in the Indian tradition. *History of Religions* 3(1):135–168.

Birks, J. S. 1977. The Mecca pilgrimage by West African pastoral nomads. *Journal of Modern African Studies* 15(1):47–59.

Clark, Janet. 1988. Pakistan. *EIU International Tourism Report.* No. 3, pp. 23–44.

Constantinou, S., and A. H. Walle. 1988. Ethnicity and its relevance to marketing: the case of tourism. *Journal of Travel Research* 26(3):11–14.

Demars, Stanford E. 1988. Worship by the sea; Camp-meetings and seaside resorts in 19th century America. *Focus* 38(4):15–21.

Eickelman, D. F., and J. Piscatori. 1990. *Muslim Travellers.* Berkeley: University of California Press.

Eliade, Mircea, ed. 1987. *The Encyclopedia of Religions.* Vol. 11, pp. 327–355. New York: Collier McMillan.

Government of Pakistan. 1987. Religious tourism in Pakistan: A Survey Report. Islamabad.

Graburn, Nelson H. 1977. Tourism: the sacred journey. *In Hosts and Guests: The Anthropology of Tourism,* ed. Valene Smith, pp. 17–31. Philadelphia: University of Pennsylvania Press.

Gruber, Kenneth J. 1988. The hotels of Israel: Pressure and Promise. *The Cornell H.R.A. Quarterly* 28(4):37–43.

Hastings, James, ed. 1974. *The Encyclopedia of Religion and Ethics,* Vol. 10, pp. 10–28. New York: T. & T. Clark.

Heiderer, Tony. 1990. India's Maha Kumbh Mela draws millions: Sacred space, sacred time. *National Geographic* 177(5):106–117.

Hudman, Lloyd E. and Donald E. Hawkins. 1989. *Tourism in Contemporary Society: An Introductory Text.* Englewood Cliffs, N.J.: Prentice-Hall.

Jackowski, A. 1987. Tourism and religious pilgrimages. *Problemy Turystyki* 10(1):37–53.

Jackson, Richard H. and Roger Henrie. 1990. Perception of sacred space. *Journal of Cultural Geography* 11(2):94–107.

Jafari, Jafar. 1987. Tourism models: The sociocultural aspects. *Tourism Management* 8(2):151–159.

Landau, Phillip. 1989. Israel. *EIU International Tourism Report,* no. 4, 49–69.

Lewis, Christopher. 1989. On going to sacred places. *Theology* 92(749):388–394.

Melton, J. G. 1978. *The Encyclopedia of American Religions.* Wilmington: McGrath.

Melton, J. G. 1986. *The Encyclopedia Handbook of Cults in America.* New York: Garland.

Morreale, D., ed. 1988. *Buddhist America: Centers, Retreats, Practices.* Sante Fe: John Muir.

Nolan, Mary Lee. 1986. Pilgrimage traditions and the nature of mystique in western European culture. *Journal of Cultural Geography* 7(1):5–20.

Prorok, Carolyn V. 1986. The Hare Krishna transformation of space in West Virginia. *Journal of Cultural Geography* 7(1):129–140.

Rinschede, Gisbert. 1986. The pilgrimage town of Lourdes. *Journal of Cultural Geography* 7(1):23–24.

Reader, Ian. 1987. From asceticism to the package tour: The pilgrim's progress in Japan. *Religion* 17:133–148.

Ritter, Wigand. 1975. Recreation and tourism in Islamic countries. *Ekistics* 236:56–59.

Schweyer, F. 1984. Who goes on pilgrimages? A study of statistics (Fr.) *Haltes* 33:7–11.

Unisa, S., U. V. Somayajulu, N. C. Das, A. Kumar, and P. Ramachandran. 1989. Profile of visitors to places of worship. *Social Action* (New Delhi) 40(1):57–70.

Waters, Somerset R., ed. 1990. *The Big Picture,* Travel Industry World Yearbook, Vol. 34. New York: Child & Waters.

24

Information Search
by Pleasure Travelers

David Snepenger and Mary Snepenger

For many vacationers, gathering, processing, and evaluating information is an integral part of the travel experience. Information search activities help to fulfill vacation motives such as achievement, social affiliation, cultural experiences, pampering, escape from the everyday environment, relaxation, and novelty seeking (Crompton 1979; Plog 1974). In addition, an information search is often required for deciding among alternative destinations, attractions, activities, transportation modes, and lodging choices.

Both public and private sector tourism providers endeavor to understand information search behaviors by pleasure travelers. Supplier promotion is facilitated by knowing what and how much information should be provided, in what form the information should be provided, and how consumers use the information. As Gunn (1988:171) writes

> Communications of all types are becoming more and more important to link the consumer to the product. Simply, if tourists do not know about travelways, attractions, services, and facilities, and do not know how to get to them, tourism can be less than satisfactory for both consumers and suppliers. Certainly, the planning for tourism must include understanding of the essential component of promotion/information.

Vacation Decision Making and Information Search

The type of vacation experience desired influences the level and type of information search employed. Vacation experiences range from routine trips to visit family to exotic vacations to new destinations. Routine vacations have little or no information search, whereas exotic vacations incorporate considerable information search. Marketers have classified decision-making behaviors into three broad categories, and this classification applies to vacation decision making as well. The three processes involve different types and amounts of information search and are labeled routine, limited, and extensive decision making (Howard and Sheth 1969).

Involving the most elaborate purchasing process, extensive decision making is associated with vacations that have high financial, social, and/or psychological risk. For example, a lengthy vacation to a novel destination to explore indigenous cultures and habitat would involve an extensive decision-making process.

For the extensive decision making, marketers have identified a five-stage model consisting of problem recognition, information search, evaluation of alternatives, purchase, and postpurchase evaluation. In the problem recognition stage, one or more members of the vacation group becomes aware that there is a difference between a desired state and the actual condition. For example, someone recognizes the need for a novel experience. During the information search stage, members of the vacation party search for information about products or services that will help resolve the problem or satisfy the need. Extensive decision making employs an information search strategy that has both internal and external components. Internal information search entails recalling information to which members of the vacation group have been exposed in the past. In contrast, external information search represents a conscious effort to seek out new information through communication with others, from media, or from commercial brochures or guidebooks. As Gitelson and Crompton (1983) observed, vacationers are likely to turn to external sources in order to learn about the number of alternative destinations that may fulfill their motives, the characteristics and attributes of those destinations, and their relative desirability.

The next stage in extensive decision making involves evaluation of alternatives. The vacationers establish criteria for evaluating destinations or experiences while on vacation. At this stage vacationers identify those experiences that are most likely to meet their financial, temporal, and other constraints. Research indicates that most consumers making vacation plans "actively consider" only about four vacation destinations (Woodside and Carr 1988). In the purchase stage the vacationer selects the product or service to be bought. The selection is based on the analysis in the previous stage. The last stage is the postpurchase evaluation. After the purchase and the vacation experience, members of the vacation group evaluate the trip to ascertain if the vacation met the expected requirements of the experience. The outcome of this stage is either satisfaction or dissatisfaction with the vacation experience. These feelings often influence whether the visitors will purchase the same or similar vacation experiences again. Furthermore, word-of-mouth communication about the experience tends to be greatest when the vacationers are either extremely satisfied or dissatisfied with the experience (Garfein 1988). The whole extensive decision-making process from problem recognition through postpurchase evaluation may take a year or more to complete.

At the other extreme, routine decision making incorporates much less effort and time and involves decisions made on a regular basis. Examples of routine vacations include repeat visits to family and friends or trips made to the same destination each year. For routine decisions problem recognition tends to be more specific in nature. For instance, a family may decide it is time to visit the grandparents. Information search is limited to the group's past experiences, with little or no external information search involved. Besides having little or no information search there is essentially no evaluation of alternatives. After the vacation there is usually little or no postpurchase evaluation except in cases where the vacationers were dissatisfied with the experience.

Limited decision making lies somewhere in between extensive and routine decision making. It tends to involve a problem recognition stage; an information search stage, which has an internal search component and limited external component; an evaluation of alternatives that involves few alternatives and simple decision rules; and a limited postpurchase evaluation. Side trips to new attractions and alternative routing of an otherwise routine trip are examples of limited vacation decision making.

The travel literature has examined what sources of information travelers use when planning their trips, when they plan, how they use the information, and who uses what types of information. These findings seem to support the notions of information search associated with the three purchasing decision-making modes. However, no one has as yet examined information search in the context of routine, limited, and extensive decision making. Future research in the area of information search for travel should formulate the research questions in terms of this theoretical construct.

Information Source Usage

The Five Types of Information Sources

Travelers tend to use five broad categories of information when planning their trips. These categories consist of family and friends, prior visits, destination specific literature, media, and travel consultants. The use of these different types of information depends greatly on the type of trip, distance to be traveled, and expense (Gitelson and Crompton 1983). Those taking routine trips, visiting family and friends or a favorite destination, often utilize only past experience and family and friends. Perhaps as much as half of all vacations incorporate routine decision making and thus, little or no information search.

Information search increases when more variety becomes important. Even when taking a routine trip to family or friends some variety might be desirable through a change in route or some side trips. Information for these types of decisions often comes from destination specific literature (Perdue 1985). Destination specific literature consists of maps, brochures, and travel guides. This information is available by requesting information from commercial providers of tourism services or through state and local tourism agencies. Many states also provide this information at welcome centers strategically positioned on major routes into their state (Gitelson and Perdue 1987; Fesenmaier and Vogt 1991).

Past visits to a site also influence use of destination specific literature. It seems to take two visits to a site to become informed to the extent that additional information is less likely to be requested (Etzel and Wahlers 1985). Furthermore, destination specific literature does not appear to influence destination decisions. Rather it is requested after the decision to travel to a particular destination has occurred (Perdue 1985). It is used in route selection and in planning stops and side trips.

To inform potential travelers about their attractions and the availability of information many private tourism enterprises and most public tourism organizations advertise in magazines, newspapers, television, and radio. The advertisements contain information on how to receive free additional information. States and travel locations also invite travel writers to visit them so that the author can write about their particular destination or attraction. These articles in magazines and newspapers can attract people to a destination. Media coverage of major events also attracts people to a destination. For instance, the major fires at Yellowstone National Park in 1988 brought the park much media attention, which resulted in increased visitation to the park (Snepenger et al. in press).

Overall only about 20 percent of all travelers utilize travel agents, motor clubs, and tour operators to help plan their trips (Woodside and Ronkainen 1980). The use of travel consultants, especially travel agents and tour operators, increases sharply with longer trips, trips requiring air transportation, first time trips to a destination, and overseas travel (Woodside and Ronkainen 1980; Sheldon and Mak 1987). These types of trips require extensive decision making. Travel consultants simplify the information search process for many travelers. Many travelers further simplify the decision-making process for these types of trips by taking packaged tours. Approximately one-third of all U.S. travel abroad utilizes package tours. People purchase package tours because of convenience, price, unfamiliarity with the destination, or because they think they will see and do more (Sheldon and Mak 1987).

Information Search Strategies

The combination of information sources used by a vacation group can be viewed as an information search strategy. Two studies have examined information search strategies. Woodside and Ronkainen (1980) found that travelers to South Carolina utilized three information search strategies: (1) used a motor club (19 percent), (2) used a travel agent (4 percent), and (3) did self-planning (77 percent). Snepenger et al. (1990) classified first-time vacationers to Alaska who were not visiting friends or relatives as being destination naive. These vacationers employed three distinct information search strategies: (1) used a travel agent only, (2) used a travel agent and other sources of information, and (3) used sources other than a travel agent. An examination of destination naive tourists to Alaska revealed that the largest segment utilized the travel agent only strategy. Travelers utilizing this strategy usually used tour operators, visited many destinations in Alaska, and took shorter vacations. In contrast, those utilizing a travel agent and other sources often spent more money and time on their trips and engaged in more activities. They also frequently utilized tour packages. Those who did not use a travel agent also did not usually use tour operators. They stayed the longest at the destination but spent the least. Exploring the area on their own they often engaged in outdoor recreation activities.

Timing of Information Search

Research on information search has not only examined what types of information travelers use, but also when they obtain and use information. For routine trips external information may not be collected or used. A study by Fesenmaier and Vogt (1991) on the use of information at state welcome centers suggests that a majority of travelers stopping at the center had not collected information prior to their trip. However, many of these travelers did collect information during their trip. Gitelson and Crompton (1983) found that those taking a trip for excitement and those wanting a well-planned trip planned more in advance than those just wanting to relax. This agrees with Snepenger's (1987) findings that travelers to faraway, novel destinations gathered information and planned their trips many months in advance.

Influences on Information Search

The degree of vacation novelty, the culture of the travelers, the demographics of the vacationers, and family decision-making styles all influence information search behavior.

Novelty Seeking Influence. The use of travel agents and other sources of information frequently corresponds to the degree of novelty desired on the trip (Gitelson and Crompton 1983; Snepenger 1987). Whereas novelty is often a major motivation for travel to unknown destinations, travelers can control the degree of novelty experienced by utilizing various levels of service infrastructure as a buffer to the host community (Cohen 1984; Snepenger 1987). Those travelers who want to travel to different locations but also want the security and comforts of home often utilize travel agents and tour operators. Those travelers who like exploring new destinations on their own utilize tour brochures, guidebooks, and other media, relying less on travel agents.

Cultural Influence. Most of the studies on information search behavior of travelers have focused on U.S. travelers, but there have been a few studies on the information search behavior of those living in other countries who travel to the United States (Schul and Crompton 1983; Uysal et al. 1990). Uysal and co-workers (Uysal et al. 1990) found that travelers in different countries utilize different types of information with varying frequency. Travelers from the United Kingdom tend to use travel agents, then family and friends, brochures and pamphlets, and magazine and newspaper articles the most. West German travelers utilize family and friends, then travel agents, brochures and pamphlets, and books and library material. French tourists consult family and friends, then travel agents, brochures and pamphlets, airlines, and articles in magazines and newspapers. Japanese travelers are more likely to use books and other library material first, then brochures and pamphlets, family and friends, and travel agents.

Demographic Influence. Demographics have been correlated with information search behavior in studies on the elderly (Capella and Greco 1987), studies examining the use of destination specific literature (Etzel and Wahlers 1985), and car travelers (Gitelson and Crompton 1983). The most important sources of information for the elderly were family and past experiences (Capella and Greco 1987). Both Etzel and Wahlers (1985) and Gitelson and Crompton (1983) found that those with more education and income tend to seek more information. However, both studies revealed that factors other than demographics tended to have a stronger impact upon vacationers' information search activities. Etzel and Wahlers (1985) observed that experienced travelers, those taking more pleasure trips, were significantly more likely to request information. These types of travelers would not be taking as many routine trips. Similarly, Gitelson and Crompton (1983) found that motive for the trip—seeking excitement, relaxation, and desiring a well-planned trip—influenced information search more than demographics.

Family Decision-Making Influence. Decision making modes vary among family vacationers with joint decision making between husband and wife being the most prevalent followed by either wife dominant or husband dominant decision making. In a study on family vacationers to Alaska, Nichols and Snepenger (1988) observed that the planning horizon, the number of information sources consulted, and the use of specific sources varied across the three family decision-making modes. Joint decision makers tended to spend the most time seeking information and also consulted the most sources. Husband dominant travel parties tended to have a slightly shorter time horizon and used fewer sources of information than did the wife dominant travel parties. All three family decision-making modes were most likely to use destination specific advertisements, brochures and guidebooks, and friends and relatives.

Summary

Information search behaviors make up an important part of extensive decision-making vacations, a moderate component for the limited decision-making vacation, and little or no contribution to routine vacations. The amount of information search depends upon the financial, social, and psychological risks associated with the vacation. Often vacationers combine information sources into a search strategy. Dominating search strategies is the use or nonuse of travel agents. Several factors shape information-gathering efforts by pleasure travelers and include novelty-seeking, culture, social group dynamics, and demographics. Travel marketers will continue to be keenly interested in understanding information search behaviors of vacationers in an effort to efficiently develop satisfying vacation opportunities.

References

Capella, Louis M., and Alan J. Greco. 1987. Information sources of elderly for vacation decisions. *Annals of Tourism Research* 14(1):148–151.

Cohen, Erik. 1984. The sociology of tourism: approaches, issues, and findings. *Annual Review of Sociology* 10:373–392.

Crompton, John L. 1979. Motivations for pleasure vacation. *Annals of Tourism Research* 6:408–424.

Gunn, Clare A. 1988. *Tourism Planning*, 2nd ed. New York: Taylor & Francis.

Etzel, Michael J., and Russel G. Wahlers. 1985. The use of requested promotional material by pleasure travelers. *Journal of Travel Research* 23(4):2–6.

Fesenmaier, Daniel R., and Christine A. Vogt. 1991. Exploratory analysis of information use at Indiana state welcome centers. Paper read at 22nd Annual Travel and Tourism Research Association Conference, June 1991, Long Beach, California.

Garfein, Richard. 1988. Guiding principles for improving customer service. *Journal of Services Marketing* 2(2):37–41.

Gitelson, Richard J., and John L. Crompton. 1983. The planning horizons and sources of information used by pleasure vacationers. *Journal of Travel Research* 21(3):2–7.

Gitelson, Richard J., and Richard R. Perdue. 1987. Evaluating the role of state welcome centers in disseminating travel related information in North Carolina. *Journal of Travel Research* 25(4):15–19.

Howard, John A., and Jagdish Sheth. 1969. *The Theory of Buyer Behavior.* New York: Wiley.

Nichols, Catherine M., and David J. Snepenger. 1988. Family decision making and tourism behavior and attitudes. *Journal of Travel Research* 26(4):2–6.

Perdue, Richard R. 1985. Segmenting state travel information inquiries by timing of the destination decision and previous experience. *Journal of Travel Research* 23(3):6–11.

Plog, Stanley C. 1974. Why destination areas rise and fall in popularity. *The Cornell H.R.A. Quarterly* 14(4):55–58.

Schul, Patrick, and John L. Crompton. 1983. Search behavior of international vacationers: travel-specific lifestyle and sociodemographic variables. *Journal of Travel Research* 22(2):25–30.

Sheldon, Pauline J., and James Mak. 1987. The demand for package tours: a mode choice model. *Journal of Travel Research* 25(3):13–17.

Snepenger, David J. 1987. Segmenting the vacation market by novelty-seeking role. *Journal of Travel Research* 26(2):8–14.

Snepenger, David J., William Collins, and Mary Snepenger. In press. Media viewing behavior by the public regarding the 1988 fires in Yellowstone National Park. *Annals of Tourism Research.*

Snepenger, David J., Kelli Meged, Mary Snelling, and Kelly Worrall. 1990. Information search strategies by destination-naive tourists. *Journal of Travel Research* 29(1):13–16.

Uysal, Muzaffer, Cary D. McDonald, and Laurel J. Reid. 1990. Sources of information used by international visitors to U.S. parks and natural areas. *Journal of Park and Recreation Administration* 8(1):51–59.

Woodside, Arch G., and Jeffrey A. Carr. 1988. Consumer decision making and competitive marketing strategies: applications for tourism planning. *Journal of Travel Research* 26(3):2–7.

Woodside, Arch G., and Ilkka A. Ronkainen. 1980. Vacation travel planning segments: self-planning vs. users of motor club and travel agents. *Annals of Tourism Research* 7(3):385–394.

25

International Tourism

Robert Christie Mill

Most people agree that international tourism is important but there is disagreement as to what it actually entails. This survey of international tourism begins by following the evolution of the various definitions of *international tourist* and *international tourism.*

Because international tourism involves people from one country traveling to another there are many implications for both host and guest country. There are economic effects on the respective balance of payments; sociocultural effects as people from different societies meet; and political effects as countries show their pleasure or displeasure with others by encouraging or discouraging travel by its citizens.

International tourism does not occur evenly throughout the world. It is heavily concentrated in Europe and the Americas. Nevertheless, it is growing fastest in Asia and the Far East and can be more important, relatively speaking, to developing countries than to industrialized nations.

A variety of factors influence the demand for international tourism. They range from the demographics of citizens in the countries of origin and the effect of exchange rates between countries to changes in technology and communications and the level of promotion of a destination country.

Forecasts indicate that, with the support of a variety of organizations that seek to facilitate international tourism, the number of people traveling between countries will continue to grow.

Definitions

International Tourist

To properly define international tourism it is necessary to begin with a definition of what constitutes an "international tourist." It is instructive to see how the definition of "international tourist" has undergone various transformations through the years.

In 1937, the League of Nations defined a "foreign tourist" as "any person visiting a country other than that in which he usually resides for a period of at least 24 hours."

The following persons were considered tourists:

Persons traveling for pleasure, for family reasons, for health
Persons traveling to meetings or in a representative capacity of any kind

> (scientific, administrative, diplomatic, religious, athletic, and so
> forth)
>
> Persons arriving in the course of a sea cruise, even when they stay less
> than 24 hours (The latter should be regarded in a separate group,
> disregarding if necessary their usual place of residence.)

The following were not regarded as tourists:

> Persons arriving, with or without a contract of work, to take up an
> occupation or engage in any business activity within that country
> Other persons arriving to establish a residence in that country
> Students and other persons in boarding establishments or schools
> Residents in a foreign zone and persons domiciled in one country and
> working in an adjoining country
> Travelers passing through a country without stopping, even if the jour-
> ney takes more than 24 hours (OECD 1980)

In the foregoing definition the major deciding factor was one of time—
staying in the country for more than 24 hours. Exceptions were made for
those on a sea cruise. The defined motivations for travel were rather loose.
People were "tourists" whether traveling for business or for pleasure as long
as they were not students nor were arriving to take a job.

In 1950 the International Union of Official Travel Organization
(IUOTO), the official worldwide organization representing the interests of
tourism (later replaced by the World Tourism Organization [WTO]), suggested two changes to the foregoing definition. It recommended that "Students and young persons in boarding establishments or schools" be regarded
as tourists. IUOTO also felt that the term "excursionists" should be used for
someone traveling for pleasure in a country in which the person did not
normally reside for less than 24 hours if the person was not there to work.
IUOTO coined the term "transit traveler" to refer to "any person traversing
a country even for a period of more than 24 hours, without stopping, or a
person traversing a country during a period of less than 24 hours, provided
that the stops made are of short duration and other than for tourism purposes"
(WTO 1981).

The United Nations Conference on International Travel and Tourism,
held in Rome in 1963, adopted the following definitions of "international
visitor" and "international tourist" on the recommendation of the International
Union of Official Travel Organizations. An international visitor is

> any person who travels to a country other than that in which he has his usual
> residence, the main purpose of whose visit is other than the exercise of an activ-
> ity remunerated from within the country visited, and who is staying for a pe-
> riod of one year or less.

The purpose of the visit can be leisure (recreation, holiday, health,
study, religion) or business (family, mission, meeting).

An international visitor is classified as an international tourist if the stay
is at least one night. Visitors from abroad are termed *excursionists* if they are
cruise passengers who visit the country but return to their ship at night, or
if they are other day visitors.

In 1968 the United Nations Statistical Commission accepted this definition but recommended that member-nations decide for themselves whether
to use the term *excursionist* or *day visitor*. The important consideration was to
distinguish between those who stayed or did not stay overnight.

In 1978 the Department of Economic and Social Affairs of the United Nations defined an *international visitor* as one who visited a given country from abroad (inbound tourist) and one who went abroad on visits from a given country (outbound tourist). The maximum time a person could spend in a country and still be called a visitor would be one year.

Most countries at the national level accept the United Nations definition. Basically, an international tourist is someone who spends at least one night, but less than a year, in a country other than his or her own. The visit can be for a variety of reasons but not for pay from the country being visited. People who meet the above criteria but who do not stay overnight are called *excursionists*.

International Tourism

How one defines "international tourism" will determine the size, scope, and importance of this entity. The WTO recommends the following definitions:

International tourism receipts:

> The receipts of a country resulting from consumption expenditures, i.e. payments for goods and services, made by visitors out of foreign currency. They should, however, exclude all forms of remuneration resulting from employment, as well as international fare receipts.

International tourism expenditure:

> Consumption expenditures, i.e, payment for goods and services, made by residents of a country visiting abroad. They should, however, exclude all forms of remuneration resulting from employment, as well as international fare payments. (OECD 1989)

The Organization for Economic Cooperation and Development's (OECD) definition of "travel" in its balance of payments accounts follows that of the WTO and excludes passenger fares.

In most countries data are collected by the central bank using a method called the *bank reporting method*. When currency is purchased either before or after a trip abroad the transaction is recorded by the bank. Data are broken down according to currency used and not according to the traveler's country of origin or destination. The *estimation method*, based on sample surveys, gives data broken down by tourists' country of origin and destination. Few countries use the *mixed method*, a combination of the two previous methods which allows the statistics reported by the bank reporting method to be adjusted.

Because these figures represent net balances and not gross volumes, international tourism receipts and expenditures tend to be understated (OECD 1989).

International tourism, in the United States balance of trade account, is defined as "travel and transportation" and is included as a "business service." It is defined as

> Travel: Services provided to U.S. citizens traveling abroad (U.S. imports) and to foreigners visiting the United States (U.S. exports).
>
> Passenger Transportation: Transportation provided by foreign carriers to U.S. residents for transportation abroad (U.S. imports) and by U.S. carriers to foreign residents (U.S. exports). (Edgell 1990)

Size and Scope of International Tourism

Economics

The World Tourism Organization estimated worldwide international tourism arrivals in 1989 to be over 400 million, with receipts of more than $200 billion (excluding expenditures on transportation). In 1986 14 percent of international passenger arrivals were traveling for business or to attend conventions. The proportion ranged from a low of eight percent for Southern Europe to a high of 23 percent for Northern Europe and the Middle East. Seventeen percent of arrivals in both Africa and the Americas were on business or attending a convention while the corresponding number for Asia was 19 percent (The WEFA Group 1989).

Expenditures for worldwide domestic and international tourism were estimated at more than $2 trillion. While the number of domestic tourists is many times greater than the number of international tourists, the latter spend much more per visit. For example, the foreign visitor to the United States spends almost six times as much on tourist services as the domestic tourist (Edgell 1990).

The WTO forecasts that by the year 2000 there will be 532 million international tourist arrivals spending, in 1990 (constant) dollars, $304.3 billion. The U.S. Department of Commerce estimates that, in the year 2000, the United States will capture 13 percent of foreign visitor arrivals (67 million people) and 21 percent of worldwide international tourism receipts ($63.9 billion in 1990 [constant] dollars).

As an international export tourism accounts for almost seven percent of total world exports and about 26 percent of international trade in services. These figures place tourism among the three largest items in international trade (Edgell 1990).

In developing countries tourism is even more important, representing about one third of the trade in services. Tourism is particularly important in countries such as the Dominican Republic, Jamaica, and the Bahamas where it represents about 70 percent of foreign exchange earnings. In Mexico it varies from being the second or third most important earner of foreign receipts.

Industrialized countries account for 70 to 75 percent of all international travel. Industrialized countries usually have a deficit in their travel accounts and developing countries usually have a surplus.

According to Sessa (1983), the ideal national tourism balance would include on the debit side

> Tourism expenditures (outlays of national citizens abroad)
> Importation of commodities (chiefly foodstuffs and instrumental goods)
> Transportation (share of international travel by national citizens)
> Tourism investments abroad
> Interest payments on foreign investments and refund of capital
> Repatriation of income paid to foreign tourism workers
> Publicity and advertising, spent outside the country.

Against this the following credits would be set:

> Tourism receipts (expenditures of foreign tourists)
> Exportation (goods, durables or semidurables, handicraft products)
> Transportation (share of international travel by nonnationals)
> Foreign tourism investments within the nations
> Income from tourism investments made abroad
> Repatriation of income paid to national tourism workers residing abroad
> Publicity and advertising spent in the country

A destination can maximize the foreign exchange potential of tourism by reducing items on the debit side of the account. The greatest potential comes from reducing the propensity to import goods, services, and workers and to encourage backward linkages to other sectors of the national economy.

Sociocultural   International tourism involves the movement of, and contact between, people across international boundaries, which inevitably means that there are sociocultural effects. This includes social relations between people who would not normally meet, the confrontation of different cultures, ethnic groups, and life-styles, the behavior of people released from many of the social and economic constraints of life and the reconciliation on the part of the host population of potential economic gain and benefits with the cost of living with strangers.

The effects of this interaction between hosts and guests can be felt in many ways. Local people often seek to emulate the behavior of their visitors. Termed the *demonstration effect,* this effect can lead to stereotyping by both sides. Tourists tend to behave differently on vacation than they do at home. Locals may be exposed to a standard of living and a standard of behavior that they seek to emulate. This situation can cause problems, particularly in conservative societies where the gap in values between the tourist and the local is great. The result can be good if it is used as a spur to improve; bad if it results in discontent.

In an attempt to reap some of the economic benefits of tourism, locals have often migrated from rural to urban areas, or even from one country to another. This migration can lead to problems for the nation in keeping enough people on the farms to harvest the crops. The entrance of women and younger people into service industries can be particularly disruptive to rigidly structured societies.

A marketing orientation seeks to identify the needs and wants of the tourists and to develop goods and services to satisfy these needs and wants. The difficulty for a country is attempting to satisfy the needs and wants of the market and still maintain its own sense of identity. British tourists are notorious for wanting "chips (french fries) with everything," cups of tea and British ale served warm. Can a country provide for these needs without losing its own national cuisine?

Acculturation is the process by which cultures borrow from each other when they come into contact. Generally, when a strong culture comes into contact with a weak culture, it is the weaker culture that is likely to change. To the extent that travelers from strong, Westernized nations visit poorer, lesser-developed countries, it is the latter that will change the most.

Tourism has been accused of encouraging cultural involution wherein the modernization of an area and a people can be halted because of the demand for "the old ways."

A 1976 seminar held jointly by UNESCO and the World Bank recognized the potential for problems and recommended the following to take advantage of social and cultural contacts while limiting the potential damage to the host society by these contacts (de Kadt 1979, Ascher 1985):

Involve the local population as much as possible
Avoid too uneven a distribution of the earnings from tourism
Preserve public ownership of tourist resources and ensure that they remain accessible to their own nationals
Ensure that domestic demands for leisure are met
Implement cultural policies designed to preserve and develop national

and regional peculiarities; provide information for tourists and train local staff

Coordinate local resources to strengthen their position vis-à-vis national and international groups.

Tourism seems to act as a medium for social change rather than as the cause itself. It is not the major element of culture change in most societies (Smith 1989).

Politics   Because international tourism involves travel over international boundaries, political aspects must be taken into consideration. Tourist flows can be a crude measure of international relations between tourist-generating and tourist-receiving countries (Richter:1989).

It has been suggested that tourism flows may be predictors of military and economic aid. Aid tends to flow disproportionately to countries with high tourist arrivals compared to others of similar size and political importance (Richter 1989).

In some countries inbound tourism is encouraged to showcase the achievements of the government as well as to increase understanding of government policies. By the same token other countries sponsor outbound tourism, involving such things as cultural exchanges and lecture programs, with a view to increasing the world's awareness of a country's heritage, culture, and way of life.

At the same time countries that seek the economic benefits of tourism (largely foreign exchange earnings) can become dependent on the tourist-generating countries. This in itself can influence foreign policy towards these tourist-generating countries.

Tourism has also been used as a political weapon as in the United States showing its opposition to policies in Cuba and the People's Republic of China by forbidding travel by U.S. citizens to these countries for many years.

On the positive side, since 1978 the United States has negotiated tourism agreements with Mexico, Venezuela, Egypt, The Philippines, Hungary, Poland, and Morocco. In the cases of Mexico and Venezuela the agreements acknowledge tourism promotion personnel as members of a diplomatic mission or consular post, thereby giving tourism promotion a status similar to other government activities abroad.

There are those who see tourism as a catalyst for peace (D'Amore 1988). They argue that it can help bridge the psychological, cultural, and economic gaps between the peoples of the world and can help foster the need to live in harmony with others in other countries.

Regional Importance

Regions   The vast majority of international travel occurs in developed countries (Mill 1990). This situation has changed very little in recent years. Europe receives over two-thirds of all international arrivals and approximately 60 percent of all receipts. The Americas receive approximately 18 percent of all international arrivals and over 20 percent of all receipts. East Asia and the Pacific, which account for 10 percent of arrivals and receipts, are the regions of the world showing the greatest growth.

International tourist demand in Europe is dominated by five large markets that make up more than half of the total nights spent in all means of accommodations (OECD). In 1987 these were Germany (27 percent), the

United Kingdom (14 percent), the United States (eight percent), France (five percent), and Italy (five percent).

Countries Which is the top tourism country? It depends upon the definition of "top." The top two generators of international tourism expenditures are the United States and West Germany. They are followed at some distance by the United Kingdom, Japan, France, Canada, and the Netherlands.

The United States also receives most international tourism receipts followed by the European countries—Spain, Italy, France, the United Kingdom, and West Germany. However, in terms of international arrivals, France is followed by Spain, Italy, the United States, Canada, and Austria (Travel & Leisure: 1988/1989).

The vast majority of international travel occurs between neighboring countries. For Italy, the largest number of arrivals come from Switzerland, West Germany, and France. For Spain, the main generating countries are France, the United Kingdom, and West Germany. For the United States, Canada and Mexico send most tourists (see Figure 1).

As stated earlier, on a worldwide basis domestic tourism far exceeds international tourism. Approximately 90 percent of all trips are domestic. Some individual countries, however, have more international or abroad tourism than domestic tourism (Boniface and Cooper 1987). While the proportion of international to domestic tourism is relatively small in Spain, Portugal, Italy, France, the United Kingdom, and the United States, it is at par in Sweden, the Netherlands, and Switzerland and greater in Austria. West Germany, and Belgium. In some of the European countries this can be explained by the small size of the countries and the easy access to other countries. The wealth in West Germany helps encourage international travel while the size of the United States and the variety of high quality tourism resources there

Fig. 1. Major tourist flows.

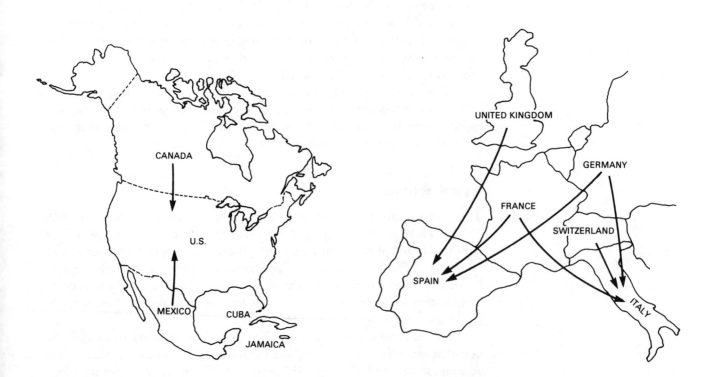

help assure a high volume of domestic tourism compared to international departures.

United States The United States accounts for approximately eight percent of world tourist arrivals and just over 10 percent of world tourism receipts (Child & Waters Inc. 1990). In 1989 the United States earned about $43 billion (including expenditures on transportation) from sales of both goods and services to 38 million international visitors, making it the most important business services export for the United States (Edgell 1990).

About 40 percent of foreign arrivals to the United States are from Canada. While the number of Canadians visiting the United States has increased slightly over recent years, their share of the market has dropped considerably from the 1970s when they accounted for almost three-quarters of all international arrivals (see Figure 2).

Mexico's share of international arrivals to the United States has increased from nine percent in 1970 to 24 percent in 1990. In that year Europe sent 15 percent of all arrivals; Asia 11 percent and South/Central America 4 percent. The largest individual generators of foreign visitors to the United States, after Canada and Mexico, are Japan (eight percent), the United Kingdom (six percent), and West Germany (three percent). Almost half of all visi-

Fig. 2. Person-trips of one night or more between Canada and the U.S. travel regions in 1986 (in thousands).
(Source: Statistics Canada, Touriscope: Tourism in Canada, pp. 53, 73, 1988. Ottawa, Ont.)

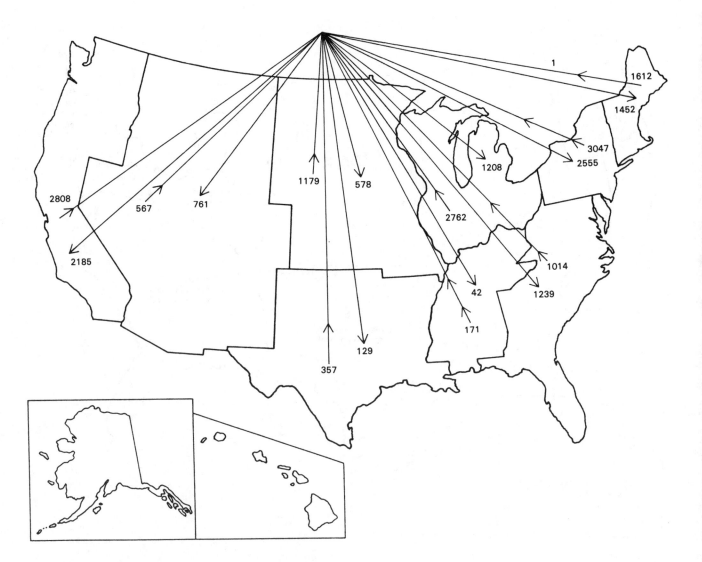

tors (business and pleasure) confined their visit to one state. Almost one-third visited three or more states (see Figure 3).

The outbound U.S. market has been called a "mini mass-market" in that, while substantial in size, it represents only a fraction of the U.S. population. About 10 percent of vacation trips taken by U.S. residents are outside the contiguous United States.

In 1990 the United States Travel and Tourism Administration projected that 43.8 million Americans travel internationally. About two-thirds of all U.S. departures to foreign countries are fairly evenly split between Mexico and Canada. However, in recent years, travel to Canada has leveled out while that to Mexico has increased.

Europe accounts for an additional 17 percent of the total. In 1948 200,000 U.S. nationals traveled to Europe and 70 percent of them went by ship. In 1989 over 6.5 million Americans traveled to Europe, all but a few thousand traveling by plane. The major destinations in Europe are the United Kingdom, Germany, France, Switzerland, and Italy. Over 70 percent of U.S. travelers overseas visit only one country; one in eight visit three or more countries.

In recent years, the traveler gap—the difference between the number of Americans traveling abroad and the number of foreigners visiting the United States—has closed. In 1985 the gap was almost 10 million; in 1991 it

Fig. 3. Distribution of foreign visitors to U.S regions.

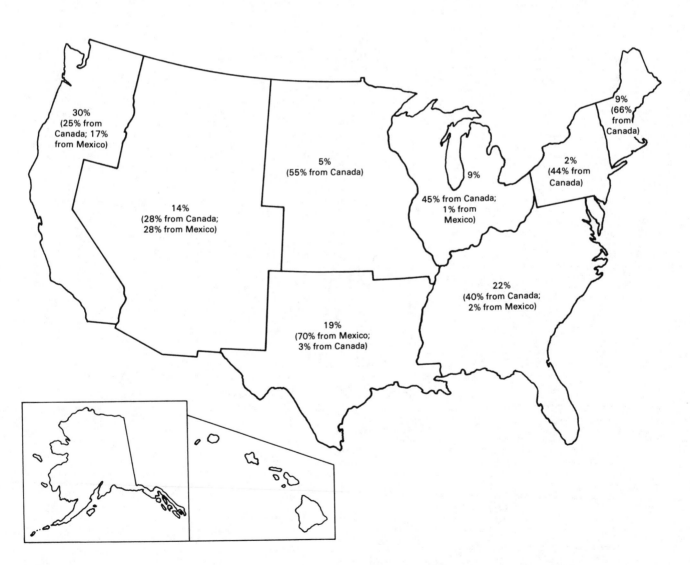

Fig. 4. The U.S. traveler gap. *(Source: United States Travel and Tourism Administration.)*

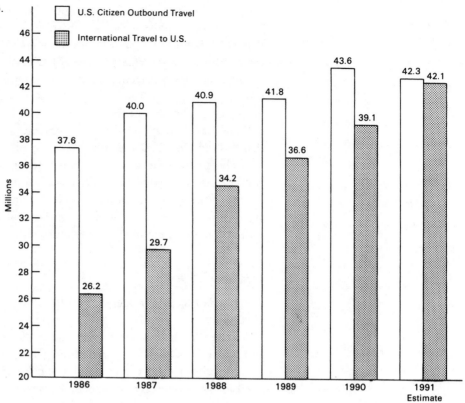

was less than 200,000. The travel gap—the difference between the amount Americans spend abroad and the amount foreigners spend in the United States—has also closed. In 1985 Americans spent $9.8 billion more than foreign visitors spent in the United States. However, in 1989 there was a projected $1.2 billion surplus in the travel account, and an $11.9 billion surplus was projected for 1992 (see Figures 4 and 5).

Main Destination Ratio   Leiper (1990) has pointed out the difficulties involved in developing meaningful analyses of who travels where. Official data about international tourist movements is rather superficial, recording simple raw data in each country. Data is not readily available on multidestination or circuit tourism. Leiper

Fig. 5. The U.S. travel gap. *(Source: United States Travel and Tourism Administration.)*

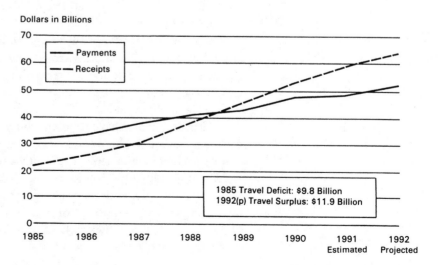

proposes the Main Destination Ratio (MDR) to remedy that. The MDR is "the percentage of arrivals by tourists or visitors in a given place for whom that place is the main or sole destination in the current trip, to the total arrivals in that place" (Leiper 1990: 105). MDR draws upon data collected at two points—a generating point where trips begin and a destination where tourists visit.

The application of this technique can add greatly to knowledge of international travel flows. For example, while more Australians visited Italy in 1984 than visited New Zealand, the MDR for New Zealand was 95 percent while for Italy it was 14 percent. Italy was a secondary destination for most Australian visitors. The MDR also has marketing implications for the national tourist offices of the countries being visited. Neighboring countries that are secondary destinations for a particular international market might better cooperate rather than compete in their marketing effort.

Influencing Factors

A variety of factors influence the demand for international tourism (Leiper 1990).

The population is one such factor. Other things being equal, regions and countries with large populations generate larger volumes of travelers.

Another factor, the disposable income of a nation, is positively correlated to the propensity of its people to travel. In the early 1980s the real incomes of many New Zealanders decreased. The figures for overseas holiday travel dropped accordingly from 255,000 travelers in 1981 to 193,000 in 1986.

Of particular importance is the distribution of income among the population. Countries with a large middle class, in terms of disposable income, have a larger number of people with the money to travel.

The major contributor to the amount of time available to people is the annual leave entitlement—the number of paid days off work to which workers are entitled each year. Countries where the minimum annual leave entitlement is relatively large generate more tourism. In many European countries workers can earn five weeks annual holiday. The minimum in Australia is four weeks, in New Zealand and Canada three and in the United States two.

The effect of the amount of paid leave can be seen in Australia (Leiper 1990). In 1984 the Australian Council of Trade Unions won a court decision that gave all paid employees in the country an extra week of paid annual leave. Between 1984 and 1986 the number of departures for overseas trips increased 49 percent.

Since the 1970s Germany has generated more international travel than any other country. In addition to having a large and prosperous population the demographics encourage international travel. The large percentage of middle-aged people in the country have a higher propensity for travel than younger and older adults.

Certain peoples have a greater interest in travel than others. This fact can be measured as the net departure rate (OECD 1989) or net travel propensity (Schmidhauser 1973) of residents in a country. The net departure rate is defined by OECD as the ratio of population having traveled to the total population. In Italy, with a population of 57 million people, the net departure rate is 46 percent, 10 percent of which is to foreign destinations. By contrast Norway, Sweden, and Switzerland have net departure rates exceeding 80 percent.

More than one hundred countries impose some kind of currency restrictions on their residents when traveling abroad. Residents of the former Yugoslavia were allowed to take with them the equivalent of $250 in foreign currency when leaving the country. The effect of such restrictions was seen in 1983 when France instituted restrictions on the number of trips and the amount of money that French citizens could take abroad. The tourist earnings of other countries normally reliant on French tourists suffered greatly.

Another example of an attempt by a government to deter people from traveling abroad can be seen in the actions of the British government in 1966. The government imposed a £50 travel allowance in an attempt to curtail travel abroad. This strategy actually backfired as it encouraged tour operators to put together creative packages to maximize value within the travel allowance. In 1967 18 percent more British travelers visited the United States than in the previous year (Mill and Morrison 1991).

By contrast, the United States has a pilot program in place whereby the Secretary of State is authorized to waive the visa requirements for up to eight countries that qualify under the law. If this is made permanent and even expanded it will facilitate foreign travel into the United States.

Research is underway to develop a plane capable of flying from the United States to Japan in two hours. The introduction of such a plane would increase the amount of traffic between these countries by making the trip shorter and more enjoyable.

The demand for pleasure travel is price elastic. The demand for pleasure travel changes proportionately more than changes in price. A relatively small increase in the cost of international travel will have a relatively larger (reducing) effect on demand.

The exchange rate between countries is a major factor in influencing international travel flows. For example, depreciation of the dollar in the latter half of the 1980s made it more expensive for Americans to travel abroad and less expensive for foreigners to visit the United States. The net result by 1989 was a surplus in the tourism account of the United States.

Promotion is used to inform people about destinations, to persuade them to travel to a particular country and to remind them of a destination previously visited. Properly designed promotions can help shape the demand for particular destinations.

Role of International Organizations

Helsinki Accord A number of international conferences have dealt with tourism as part of their agendas. The 1975 Helsinki Accord is primarily known for the section detailing the rights of people to migrate freely. The tourism section of that accord indicated that "freer tourism is essential to the development of cooperation amongst nations" (Edgell 1990). The 35 nations who signed this agreement indicated an intention to

> Encourage increased tourism on both group and individual basis
> Conduct detailed studies on tourism
> Endeavor, where possible, to ensure that the development of tourism does not injure the artistic, historic, and cultural heritage in their respective countries
> Facilitate wider travel by their citizens for personal and professional reasons

Endeavor gradually to lower, where necessary, the fees for visas and
official travel documents

Increase, on the basis of appropriate agreements or arrangements, cooperation in the development of tourism, in particular, by considering bilaterally, possible ways to increase information relating to
travel to other questions of mutual interest

Promote visits to their respective countries

World Tourism Organization

The World Tourism Organization (WTO) is the only worldwide tourism organization. Headquartered in Madrid, it had 109 member countries in 1989.
It was established in 1975 as a world clearinghouse for the collection, analysis,
and distribution of information on tourism. As an agency of the United Nations the WTO works to ease foreign travel globally.

Organization of American States

The Organization of American States (OAS) first met in 1939. A tourism
development program was formed in 1970 with the objectives of helping
members develop and promote tourism in their respective countries; supporting efforts to increase tourist visits to the region; providing broad policy
advice on tourism and coordinating with other international organizations on
tourism concerns. Recently tourism programs have been merged into the
Department of Regional Development.[1]

International Civil Aviation Organization

The ICAO, formed in 1944, is made up of 80 governments. As a specialized
agency of the United Nations it seeks to promote efficient, safe, and economical civil aviation worldwide.

International Air Transport Association

The International Air Transport Association (IATA) is the global organization
for almost all international air carriers. It aims to facilitate the movement of
persons and goods throughout the worldwide air network. A single ticket
bought for one price in any currency is valid anywhere for the same amount
and quality of service. Tickets, waybills, baggage checks, and similar documents are standardized through the various traffic conferences—Western
Hemisphere, Europe, Africa and the Middle East, and Asia and Australia—of
IATA.

After governments decide bilaterally on the exchange of rights and individually what air carriers will serve its area, IATA serves as a forum for member
airlines to agree on rates.

To be a member of IATA an airline must hold a certificate for scheduled
air carriage from a government that is eligible for membership in the International Civil Aviation Organization (ICAO) (McIntosh and Goeldner 1990).

Regional International Organizations

A variety of international organizations exist which cover particular countries
or regions of the world.

The Organization for Economic Cooperation and Development
(OECD), headquartered in Paris, conducts studies and negotiations to resolve problems related to trade and to coordinate policies regarding international negotiations. The Tourism Committee, which came into being when

---

[1]The Organization of American States, headquartered in Washington D.C., is made up of Antigua and
Bermuda, Argentina, the Bahamas, Barbados, Bolivia, Brazil, Canada, Chile, Colombia, Costa Rica, Cuba,
Dominican Republic, Ecuador, El Salvador, Grenada, Guatemala, Haiti, Honduras, Jamaica, Mexico, Nica-
ragua, Panama, Paraguay, Peru, St. Kitts and Nevis, Saint Lucia, Saint Vincent and the Grenadines,
Surinam, Trinidad and Tobago, United States, Uruguay, and Venezuela.

the OECD was formed in 1960, publishes annual statistics and policy changes.[2]

The Pacific Area Travel Association (PATA) represents 34 countries in the Pacific region and Asia. The objective is to encourage the growth of tourism in the Pacific area through joint marketing efforts, development, and research.

A variety of regional organizations, such as the Caribbean Tourism Association and the European Travel Commission, have been set up to promote tourism to their respective regions.

Trends for the Future

It is projected that, in 1999, there will be 909.7 million international trips accounting for 5.251 billion nights abroad and expenditures (excluding fares, at constant relative prices, expressed in 1985 dollars and exchange rates) of $196.2 billion (Edwards 1988).

It is forecast that, between 1986 and 1999, the number of international trips will more than double for Germany, Denmark, and Norway; almost triple for the United Kingdom, Spain, and Japan; and more than quadruple for Sweden. The number of international trips taken by U.S. residents is forecast to decline by 17 percent (Edwards 1988).

Travel to neighboring countries is expected to grow at a rate less than the average while other trips of short to medium distance are projected to increase at a faster than average rate. Long-haul travel (over 1,500 miles or 2,400 kilometers) would decline initially then rise.

These projections are based on two major assumptions: (1) the U.S. dollar will continue to be soft and real private consumption will slow, and (2) the oil exporting countries will experience economic standstill accompanied by sharp declining currency values in real terms.

If these forecasts hold, by 1999 the leading countries, in terms of international trips taken, will be Germany (268.3 million), the United Kingdom (77.9 million), the United States (51.2 million), Switzerland (40.3 million), and Austria (33.9 million).

In terms of nights abroad the top countries will be Germany (1.018 billion), the United Kingdom (863 million), France (271 million), the United States (234 million), and Sweden (210 million).

The countries whose citizens are projected to spend the most abroad (excluding fares, at constant relative prices, expressed in 1985 dollars and exchange rates) are Germany ($28.9 billion), the United Kingdom (21.6 billion), the United States (15.8 billion), Japan (15.5 billion), and Sweden (10.3 billion) (Edwards 1988).

Summary

International tourism is very important, not only as an item of international trade, but also as a medium for change in a society, as a way of showing political support for another country, and perhaps even as a vehicle for world peace.

---

[2]The Organization for Economic Cooperation and Development, headquartered in Paris, is made up of Australia, Austria, Belgium, Canada, Denmark, Finland, France, Germany, Greece, Iceland, Ireland, Italy, Japan, Luxembourg, Netherlands, New Zealand, Norway, Portugal, Sweden, Switzerland, Turkey, United Kingdom, United States, and Yugoslavia.

Whereas most international tourism occurs in Europe and the Americas, it is growing fastest in Asia and the Far East.

A consideration of the factors that influence demand suggest that, with the support of various international bodies and organizations, international tourism will continue to grow.

References

Ascher, Francois. 1985. *Transnational Corporations and Cultural Identities*. Paris: UNESCO.

Boniface, Brian G., and Christopher P. Cooper. 1987. *The Geography of Travel and Tourism*. London, England: Heinemann Publishing.

Child & Waters, Inc. 1990. *Travel Industry World Yearbook: The Big Picture*, annual. New York: Child & Waters.

D'Amore, Louis J. 1988. Tourism—The world's peace industry, *Business Quarterly* reprint, 8 pp.

Edgell, David L., Sr. 1990. *Charting a Course for International Tourism in the Nineties*, Occasional Paper. Washington, D.C.: U.S. Department of Commerce.

Edwards, Anthony. 1988. *International Tourism Forecasts to 1999*. London, England: The Economist Intelligence Unit.

de Kadt, Emanuel. 1979. *Tourism: Passport to Development?* New York: Oxford University Press.

Leiper, Neil. 1990. *Tourism Systems: An Interdisciplinary Perspective*. Occasional Papers Number 2. Palmerston North, New Zealand: Massey University.

McIntosh, Robert W., and Charles R. Goeldner. 1990. *Tourism: Principles, Practices, Philosophies*. New York: Wiley.

Mill, Robert Christie. 1990. *Tourism: The International Business*. Englewood Cliffs, N.J.: Prentice-Hall.

Mill, Robert Christie, and Alastair M. Morrison. 1991. *The Tourism System: An Introductory Text*. 2d ed. Englewood Cliffs, N.J.: Prentice-Hall.

OECD. 1980. *Tourism Policy and International Tourism in Member Countries*. Paris: Organization for Economic Cooperation and Development.

OECD. 1989. *Tourism Policy and International Tourism in Member Countries*. Paris: Organization for Economic Cooperation and Development.

Richter, Linda K. 1989. *The Politics of Tourism in Asia*. Honolulu: University of Hawaii Press.

Sessa, Alberto. 1983. *Elements of Tourism Economics*. Rome: Catal.

Schmidhauser, H. 1973. Travel propensity and travel frequency. In *Management and Tourism*, ed. A. J. Burkhart and S. Medlik. London: Heinemann.

Smith, Valene L. 1989. *Hosts and Guests: The Anthropology of Tourism*, 2d ed. Philadelphia: University of Pennsylvania Press.

WTO. 1981. *Technical Handbook on the Collection and Presentation of Domestic and International Tourism Statistics, Introduction*. Madrid: World Tourism Organization.

Travel & Leisure's World Travel Overview, 1988/1989, annual. New York: Travel & Leisure.

The WEFA Group. 1989. *The Contribution of the World Travel & Tourism Industry to the Global Economy*. New York: American Express Travel Related Services.

26

International Airlines and Tourism: Opportunities and Challenges

Kevin B. Boberg and Linda A. Riley

Most international travelers are carried by surface modes of transportation. For example, the largest outbound destinations from the United States are Canada and Mexico, both dominated by rail and automobile as the primary means of transportation. Much the same conclusion can be drawn about intra-European travel.

Long-haul travel is, however, dominated by airlines. Europe and the Caribbean are the favored overseas destinations of the overseas market from the United States. Although the international cruise market has rebounded in recent years, airlines are the dominant mode of overseas travel measured by both volume and dollars. Therefore, tourism planners and practitioners must be cognizant of current trends in the international airline industry and their implications for tourism.

This article examines the relationship between the international travel and airline industries. For the most part, this relationship is examined from the perspective of the U.S. outbound market, particularly travel to destinations in the Pacific Basin. However, many of the observations regarding this particular market are equally applicable to other international market situations.

Trying to distinguish between the international travel and airline industries is a difficult and somewhat self-deluding task. One could not exist without the other. Therefore, the relationship must be examined from many perspectives. In this article, the relationship is explored via: (1) an analysis of the international airline industry and the impact of regulation thereon, and (2) a profile of the U.S. outbound market and its implications for the international airline industry.

An Analysis of the International Airline Industry

The Pacific Basin, including Asia and Oceania, air travel market is the most rapidly growing in the world. Total two-way passenger travel volume between the United States and Asia/Middle East was 12,123,622; between the

United States and Oceania bilateral travel amounted to 2,438,402 travelers in 1989 (U.S. Department of Commerce 1990). With an expected growth rate of 10.5 percent per annum, which in 1989 translated into an increase of 1.2 million trips, compared to a worldwide average of 7 percent, little wonder the Pacific Basin is among the most intensely competitive airline markets in the world. Raw numbers by themselves, however, tell only part of the story.

On a global basis, U.S. carriers maintain a majority share of the market for international travel entering and leaving the country. U.S. carriers have a 51.1 percent market share, leaving 48.9 percent for foreign-flag carriers. This is not consistently true in the Pacific Basin, however. In the U.S.–Asia/Middle East market, U.S. carriers captured a 47.6 percent market share and foreign carriers 52.3 percent. In the U.S.–Oceania market, U.S. carriers attained a 57.1 percent share while foreign carriers had 42.9 percent. Presently, then, the market split favors foreign-flag carriers in the Pacific.

Long-term prospects may not bode as well for foreign-flag carriers. The United Nations protocol, as followed by the U.S. Travel and Tourism Administration (USTTA) is to divide the world into eight regions. U.S.-flag carriers gained market share in only three of the eight markets during 1989. U.S.-flag carriers enjoyed their greatest resurgence in the Asia/Middle East market, experiencing an 18.3 percent increase compared to a 4.5 percent increase for foreign-flag carriers. The second largest gains were made in the Oceania market, where U.S. carriers experienced a 15.3 percent increase at the same time foreign-flag volume dropped by 9.1 percent.

At first glance it is difficult to explain these figures. Traditional wisdom has held that U.S. carriers find it difficult to compete with foreign-flag carriers. Labor wages, unionization, the cost of capital, and service orientation have been held to favor overseas carriers. The phenomenal growth of Singapore Airlines and Thai International Airlines are often linked to their advantages in these areas. The USTTA figures cited above suggest other factors may be important.

Total passenger traffic to and from the United States increased by 68 percent from 1980 to 1989. At the start of the decade, foreign travelers held a slight majority in terms of total traffic. By the end of the decade, U.S. travelers exceeded foreign travelers on routes to and from the United States by seven million passengers.

As with many nationalities, U.S. citizens prefer to fly on their own carriers. In fact, 1988 was a high point for U.S.-flag carriers, when they captured nearly 60 percent of the total U.S. citizen overseas travel market.

What does this mean for international airlines and the destinations they serve? To the extent that carriers and destinations are linked, they are faced with a perplexing dilemma. Increasing outbound travel from the United States will help the international tourism industry in general. These gains will not necessarily be translated into gains for the flag carrier of a particular destination or country. To the contrary, historical evidence suggests that as the percent of total route traffic represented by U.S. citizens increases, the share of total route volume captured by foreign-flag carriers decreases. Technological changes may reinforce this trend.

Technology will continue to shape the future of the airline, and therefore, tourism industry. Some carriers in the region already are planning for the introduction of hypersonic transport. Northwest in particular is preparing today for a plane, appropriately named the Pacific Clipper, with block speeds of between mach 5 and 12 to be in use around the year 2000. If travelers are able to travel from, say, Los Angeles to Tokyo in two hours, the face of Pacific Basin tourism will change dramatically. U.S. enterprises in particular are at the forefront of developing hypersonic transport, the HST. Even short of some future technology yet to be developed, derivatives of today's aircraft will reshape the future of tomorrow's tourism industry.

Between now and the year 2000, perhaps no plane will have as great an influence as the Boeing 747-400, often referred to as Asia's plane, and a comparable aircraft promised by Airbus Industrie. A glimpse of the future was clearly demonstrated when Boeing was unable to meet delivery dates for several carriers in the region in the later part of the 1980s. Because of the late delivery dates, carriers and tourism industry officials alike were forced to alter their strategic and marketing plans.

The 747-400 promises to alter air routes and tourism markets. West Coast gateways have been the norm for several reasons. In the past, bilateral aviation agreements tended to restrict carriers to coastal gateways. Not insignificantly, the U.S. West Coast is the largest single market for both Asian and European destinations. Finally, carrier load and lift capacities meant that carriers practically were restricted to serving U.S. coastal rather than inland markets. These factors were mutually reinforcing. Technology and law worked to make the West Coast the most viable market for airlines and destinations.

These "rules" may no longer be applicable. The 747-400 will open new markets for nonstop service to and from mid-continent airports. Phoenix, the tenth largest metropolitan statistical area in the country, will be open to nonstop service. Dallas/Fort Worth likewise will become viable for increased service. Denver, with its new international airport scheduled to open in 1992, becomes an immediate possibility for nonstop international travel and tourism.

U.S. and non-U.S. flag carriers must be prepared to exploit these opportunities. The total market will increase as more direct and convenient service is available to a larger percentage of the U.S. population. Competition will intensify as more carriers, U.S. and foreign flag, gain technological access to the U.S. market. Finally, competition will move inland from the West Coast to important but heretofore relatively inaccessible markets.

Complementing technological evolution are changes in the regulatory arena. With passage of the International Airline Competition Act of 1979, the U.S. signaled its intention to press its deregulation agenda on the rest of the world. Multiple designation of carriers, new gateways, and more liberal negotiated bilateral aviation agreements between countries were to become the order of the day. While results to date are far from clear, deregulation has had some impact on the international airline industry.

New gateways have in fact been opened. Mid-continent gateways especially have been opened to direct service. Some traditional gateways are losing their importance as a result. For example, Seattle-Tacoma International Airport is declining in relative importance compared to other West Coast gateways and to mid-continent and East Coast gateways.

More carriers have accompanied the growth in air traffic and new gateways. In 1987 only four U.S.-flag carriers and nine foreign-flag carriers were identified as important in the U.S. market. Today, some twenty-two carriers are operating in the Pacific Basin. Thirteen of the carriers are flagged in Asia or Oceania. Five U.S. carriers operate across the Pacific. Four carriers flagged in neither the U.S. nor Asia/Oceania provide trans-Pacific services.

In spite of the growth in the number of carriers serving the Basin, it is generally recognized that there is a shortage of capacity across the Pacific. In one sense, decidedly short run, this is advantageous for the carriers. Load factors and yields are unusually high as compared to trans-Atlantic routes. In the long term, the situation could prove detrimental to tourism.

Deregulation should provide relief on several fronts. Tokyo has been the traditional hub for trans-Pacific flights. Thus, even as more nations and carriers are given the opportunity to offer service, Tokyo's Narita International Airport has acted as a bottleneck to actual growth. Given its intransigence on deregulating airline service until recently, Japan was hindering tourism growth in the area.

More recently, Japan has agreed to at least modest reforms in the bilateral agreement governing airline service. The latest U.S.-Japan bilateral agreement provides for three new routes from any point in the U.S. and Japan, plus three routes from any point in Japan other than Tokyo or Osaka. All told, eleven different U.S.-flag carriers have applied for more than a dozen different U.S.-Japan routes (*Travel Weekly* 1990a).

As Japan opens to more services, it will enhance its role as the predominant hub for trans-Pacific services. Cathay Pacific has clearly demonstrated its intention to position Hong Kong as a major hub airport. United has looked to Taipei as the emerging hub in the area. Regardless of which airport comes out on top in this battle, the opening of a new hub will greatly enhance the additional services envisioned by airline deregulation.

Self-regulation has always been an important part of the international airline industry. Unarguably, the International Airline Transportation Association (the IATA) has been the most important organization in this regard. From the conclusion of World War II until the late 1970s, IATA tightly controlled provision of airline services. Actions taken by the Civil Aeronautics Board (CAB) in 1978 and 1979 acted to significantly weaken the power of the IATA.

Asia always seemed to be the last bastion of free market competition in the airline industry. While most U.S. and European carriers studiously adhered to IATA regulations until forced to do otherwise by the CAB, most carriers in the Pacific Basin avoided cooperating with IATA. Restrictions on service, pricing, and travel sales distribution proved anathema to Asian carriers, who welcomed the opportunity to compete in a free market environment.

Deregulation has witnessed many changes in IATA. Gone are the days when the organization could enforce its cartel-like powers over services and fares. IATA is becoming more of a clearinghouse for regulatory affairs and less of a rate-making body. IATA was coming to Asian carriers, rather than the opposite.

Curiously, the situation was reversed in June, 1990 (Lockwood 1990). Cathay Pacific, Singapore Airlines, Malaysian Airline Systems, Thai International, and Royal Brunei announced that they will join IATA as trade association members. These carriers will have the right to participate in IATA discussions and research efforts, although they will not be able to vote on rate or service matters. Most importantly, trade association members are not bound by restrictions on travel sales distribution systems. Sales through bucket shops (selling less than published fares) can continue in full force.

Delta and Northwest are the only major holdouts from IATA in the Pacific Basin. It is difficult to explain the reluctance of these carriers to join IATA even as trade association members. Their cost structures, among the highest on an available seat mile basis, would suggest, a priori, a desire if not a need to join a rate-setting cartel.

Pacific carriers must prepare for a more orderly, if not rigorously controlled, marketplace. IATA no longer effectively controls pricing and distribution of services. Rather, the association has turned into an international body concerned with infrastructure issues. In this sense, the IATA has joined the International Civil Aviation Organization (the ICAO) in dealing with some of the most pressing issues confronting the growth of international tourism.

Deregulation is not without its critics, however. Thailand signed one of the most liberal bilateral agreements with the United States. In fact, the bilaterals with Singapore and Thailand frequently are counted as among the most liberal bilaterals by U.S. policy makers. Apparently, deregulation is not satisfactory to all parties, as Thailand has refused to extend the agreement.

It was noted earlier that U.S. citizens prefer to fly U.S.-flag carriers. Deregulation has made for more competitive rates and services in the U.S.-Thai market. At least to some extent, this has resulted in greater travel by U.S. citizens to Thailand. With multiple carrier designations, the primary beneficiaries, according to the government of Thailand, have been U.S. carriers. Again there seems to be a paradox between national tourism interests and those of a particular carrier.

Recent machinations over route sales to Europe lend further insight into the problem. Seeking to raise capital, Pan Am and TWA proposed to sell valuable European routes to stronger U.S. carriers. Eventually, the British and U.S. governments agreed on the route transfer. The transfer, though, was made contingent on several important revisions to the existing bilateral agreements.

From the U.S. perspective, relatively weak carriers are to be replaced by financially stronger carriers; United and American in lieu of TWA and Pan Am. Perhaps most importantly, new entrants will be allowed to operate through Heathrow. Furthermore, the agreement provides for expanded service to the United Kingdom and eventually more extensive beyond rights to the rest of Europe, so-called fifth freedom rights.

The United Kingdom also gained significant advantages. One new entrant on the routes was permitted, Virgin Atlantic. In addition, U.K.-carriers were given long-sought beyond rights (the right to extend flights into another country's territory) to Canada and Asia. Surely, every party "won" in this situation. That is, everyone except for British Air.

British Air has enjoyed its position as the preeminent carrier on North Atlantic routes. Facing financially strapped U.S. carriers and no other U.K.-flagged carriers, BA has dominated the market through Heathrow. Now, the carrier will be forced to compete with mega-carriers from the United States and a new U.K.-flag carrier. The alleged quid pro quo—that is, the promise of beyond rights—is little consolation. Beyond rights are not automatic, but instead must be negotiated with and approved by the so-called beyond countries. Tourism between the United States and United Kingdom may increase, but this will not necessarily help British Air. More liberal aviation agreements and the attendant increased travel will have impacts beyond carrier concerns.

Airline infrastructure barely is able to meet existing travel demands, let alone keep pace with future needs. Asian destinations have announced plans for more than $30 billion of airport expansion and construction projects in the next decade (Stier 1990). Without this expansion, Pacific Basin airline travel will choke on its own success.

Many factors point to a mutually reinforcing growth of international tourism and airline service. The demand for tourism creates the demand for increased international airline services. Technology and deregulation are spurring the demand for increased international tourism. Infrastructure, capital, and political instability currently seem the only significant brakes on this development. This international service is reflected in the current nature of the U.S. outbound market.

The U.S. Outbound Market and International Tourism

Many research houses, both publicly and privately-funded, profile and study the U.S. outbound travel market. Among the most often cited studies are the Lou Harris U.S. Travel Agency Survey (*Travel Weekly* 1990b), the Menlo Consulting Group, Inc. study of Americans as international travelers (Menlo Consulting Group 1989), and various studies conducted by the USTTA. Other studies undertaken by Simmons Shulman Yankelovich and American Express specifically study certain components of the U.S. outbound travel market from an aggregate, or macro level.

The Menlo Consulting Group, Inc. study, TravelStyles, surveyed 2200 leisure/pleasure international travelers from a national sample frame of American households. The study reports, "nearly a half (48.8 percent) [of respondents] have taken four or more trips outside the contiguous U.S. in the past 10 years (Menlo Consulting Group 1990:2). The study also reported that approximately 70 percent of international pleasure travelers prefer to travel independently as opposed to on packages or in tour groups (Menlo Consulting Group 1990:2). From the Menlo study, California is reported as the single greatest revenue generator for Asian pleasure travel with 27.7 percent of revenue generation for retail travel agencies.

The Lou Harris study of U.S. travel agencies makes an important contribution to the study of the U.S. outbound travel market in that it views both the pleasure and business travel markets. The Harris study recognizes the divergent characteristics and motivations for the business versus the pleasure travel client. Among the major findings of the Harris study are

1. Leisure travel continues to represent a smaller proportion of overall revenues for travel agencies, declining from 50 percent to 48 percent of the agencies' revenues.
2. Business revenues for travel agencies have risen 28 percent between 1987 and 1989 moving corporate revenue to 41 billion dollars. (*Travel Weekly* 1990b:1)

Although a number of privately supported studies are documented through the popular press, the most comprehensive and statistically valid study of the U.S. outbound market continues to be the United States Department of Commerce, United States Travel and Tourism Administration survey of International Air Travel to and from the United States on U.S./Foreign Flag Carriers. The study is a yearly effort that comprehensively measures the travel demographics, psychographics, and trends of international travelers. The USTTA publishes a number of reports documenting the trends among U.S. travelers from the Survey of International Air Travelers Departing the United States. The following list highlights the profile of the U.S. outbound market as advanced by the USTTA (U.S. Department of Commerce 1990):

- In 1989, the total volume of air passenger traffic between the United States and other countries (excluding Canada) was up 5.9 percent from 1988.

- For the second consecutive year, the greatest growth rate in traffic occurred between the United States and Asia/Middle East. The greatest passenger volume growth occurred between the United States and Europe, gaining 1.8 million travelers in 1989.
- Foreign-flag carriers increased their passenger volume by 7.4 percent in 1989. U.S. carriers increased their passenger volume 4.4 percent from 1988.
- Foreign-flag carriers achieved a 48.9 percent share of the total market, up slightly from 48.2 percent in 1988. For the second straight year, U.S. carriers captured over 50 percent of the air market, although their share fell from 51.8 percent in 1988 to 51.1 percent in 1989.
- The number of U.S. citizens traveling internationally in 1989 was up by 2.7 percent; U.S. carriers transported 1.7 percent more U.S. citizens, while foreign carriers' volume of U.S. citizens rose by 4.0 percent from 1988.
- U.S. citizens flew on U.S. carriers on 56.7 percent of their trips.
- Travel to Asia/Middle East specifically by U.S. citizens had an increase of 18.3 percent for 1989 on U.S. carriers, while foreign-flag carriers expanded by 4.5%.
- U.S.-flag carriers saw a 15.3 percent growth in the Oceania market, while foreign carriers' volume decreased by 9.1 percent in 1989.
- For all carriers, the routes with the greatest growth rate came from Asia/Middle East with a 10.7 percent growth rate in 1989 over 1988.

It is apparent that the U.S. outbound market continued its expansion in 1989. Total traffic increased by nearly 6 percent over 1988 traffic volume. The greatest volume growth came on routes between the United States and Europe. However, the greatest percentage gains were registered on routes between the United States and Asia/Middle East, up 10.7 percent over 1988 traffic volumes.

Maintaining a pattern first evident in 1986, U.S.-flag carriers maintained a slim majority of the total U.S. outbound market, 51.1 percent in 1989. Foreign-flag carriers made further inroads into the U.S. market, capturing a 48.9 percent share, up from 48.2 percent in 1988.

U.S.-flag carriers registered significant gains in market share in the Asia/Middle East and Oceania trades, specifically among U.S. citizens. On the former routes, U.S. carriers registered an 18.9 percent increase of U.S. citizen traffic over 1988, while foreign-flag carriers only realized increases of 4.5 percent. The disparity was even greater in Oceania, where U.S. flag carriers increased their volume by 15.3 percent versus the 9.1 percent decrease suffered by foreign-flag carriers operating in the region.

U.S. citizens prefer to fly on U.S.-flag carriers. In 1989, 56.7 percent of U.S. citizens traveling abroad did so on U.S. carriers. An absolute increase in traffic on a given route, therefore, will not necessarily be translated into an absolute increase for a specific carrier nor will it necessarily translate into an increase in market share. This is particularly true for foreign flag carriers.

The USTTA also breaks out the international travel market by specific demographic and psychographic characteristics of the market. Table 1 presents an overview of the U.S. outbound travel market.

The majority of overseas trips, 56 percent, are taken for holiday or vacation purposes. Business travel represents the next largest single segment, comprising 33 percent of the market. Surprisingly, the combined visiting friends and visiting relatives segments nearly equal business travel, at 31 percent of the total outbound market.

U.S. travelers abroad tend to be experienced international travelers. For only 10 percent of the total market was the trip in 1989 their first foreign trip experience. The balance, 90 percent, were taking at least their second foreign trip in 1989. For USTTA purposes, these travelers are considered "repeat visitors." It is important to note that the term is not used to denote repeat visitors to a particular destination, but merely a means of identifying travelers making other than their first trip abroad.

Travel agents are a critical element in the travel sales distribution system. Retail agents are the primary source of information for the international traveler and are responsible for booking more than two-thirds of international travel. Although consulting agents for information and reservations, U.S. citizens do not tend to buy package tours from agents. Nearly ninety percent of the outbound market traveled independently.

Outbound travel tends to reflect business patterns in the United States. More than half of all travelers are male, although forty percent of the market is comprised of adult females. Few children, only four percent of the market, take long-haul vacations. As a result, the average party size for the U.S. outbound market is less than two.

Professionals, executives and managers account for nearly two-thirds of the market. Homemakers, retirees, clerical staff, and students combined represent a smaller percent of total outbound traffic than do professionals. Consistently, the average household income of outbound travelers is $57,175.

U.S. citizens are traveling to Europe and the Caribbean in record num-

Table 1. *Demographic and psychographic analysis of U.S. outbound passengers*

Percent of Travelers from U.S. Regions	New England	8%
	Middle Atlantic	17%
	East North Central	9%
	West North Central	4%
	South Atlantic	19%
	East South Central	3%
	West South Central	12%
	Mountain	5%
	Pacific	22%
	Pacific Islands	2%
	Atlantic Islands	1%
Purpose of Trip	Vacation, Holiday	56%
(multiple responses allowed)	Business	33%
	Visit Relatives	20%
	Visit Friends	11%
	Attend Convention	5%
Foreign Trip Experience	First Time Visitors	10%
	Repeat Visitors	90%
Information Sources	Travel Agency	62%
(multiple responses allowed)	Friends, Relatives	25%
	Airline	23%
	Published Sources	15%
	Company Travel Dept.	11%
	Newspaper, Magazines	10%
	Government Sources	7%
Advance Trip Decision	Mean Number of Days	13.6
	Median	48.0

(continued)

Table 1 *(Continued).*

Type of Airline Ticket	Economy, Tourist	71%
	Executive, Business	16%
	First Class	8%
	Other	4%
Means of Booking Air Travel	Travel Agent	68%
	Self	16%
	Company Travel Dept.	9%
	Other	7%
Advance Airline Reservations	Mean number of days	9.1
	Median	25
Use of Prepaid Package/Inclusive Tour	Yes, on package	20%
	No, independent	88%
Type and Size of Traveling Party	Family Group	42%
	Traveling Alone	38%
	Business Group	9%
	Mixed Business, Family	13%
	Average Party Size	1.6
Sex and Age of Travelers	Male Adults	56%
	Female Adults	40%
	Children Under 18	4%
	Average Age of Traveler	43
Occupation of Travelers	Professional, Technical	34%
	Manager, Executive	27%
	Homemaker	9%
	Retired	8%
	Clerical, Sales	7%
	Student	6%
	Government, Military	5%
	Craftsman, Mechanic	3%
Average Annual Family Income	Average	$57,175

Source: In-flight survey of International Air Travelers, Profile of U.S. Residents Traveling to Overseas Destinations, January–December 1988, United States Department of Commerce, Travel and Tourism Administration, Washington, D.C., October, 1989.

bers, capturing nearly three-quarters of the total outbound market. Asia is a distant third, attracting fifteen percent of the total market. Once in a region, U.S. citizens tend to spend their time in a single country, on average visiting 1.6 countries per trip.

Perhaps not the largest spenders in the world, a title now generally conceded to the Japanese, the U.S. outbound market still is quite lucrative. The typical travel party spends a total of $3,820 for an overseas trip. More than half of this amount is spent outside the United States, that is, at the destination(s). The question becomes one of balancing the interests of carriers and destinations involved with international tourism.

Summary

Lest we forget, international overseas airline travel is barely sixty years of age, with trans-Pacific travel a modest fifty years old. Given today's technology and travel patterns, it is difficult to imagine that the first trans-Pacific airline routing went from Los Angeles to Honolulu to Midway to Wake to Guam and then to Manila. After much negotiation, the flight eventually continued on to Hong Kong. Technology and regulation certainly have changed the face of international tourism.

Today's international traveler is well-educated, well-traveled, and well-heeled. He or she travels for business purposes, most often alone or at most with a spouse. Few overseas travels are family-oriented. The business traveler ventures overseas independently, booking through retail travel agents or corporate business travel departments. Therefore, tourism planners must be cognizant of current trends in the international airline industry and their implications for tourism.

References

Lockwood, Chris. 1990. Five Asian carriers poised to join IATA after organization relaxes membership rules. *Travel Agent Magazine,* July 2, p. 4.

Menlo Consulting Group, Inc. Palo Alto, California, November 1989. As reported in *Tourism Management,* "US Traveller Profile," December, 1989.

Stier, Kenneth J. 1990. Aviation growth In Asia-Pacific held inadequate. *Journal of Commerce,* July, p. 5B.

Travel Weekly. 1990a. DOT staff unit favors American for Chicago–Tokyo. *Travel Weekly,* July, p. 2.

Travel Weekly. 1990b. Vol. 49, No. 52, June 28.

United States Department of Commerce. 1990. *Analysis of International Air Travel to and from the United States on U.S./Foreign Flag Carriers During 1989.* Washington, D.C.: U.S. Dept of Commerce, Travel and Tourism Administration.

27

How to Generate
and Evaluate Ideas
in Tourism: A Guide
to Brainstorming

John L. Crompton

Ideas, not money, are the most valuable currency of the future, particularly in the recreation, park, and tourism field. Creative ideas will have to be used to accommodate the growing demands for leisure opportunities, since available tax dollars are unlikely to be adequate. Given this scenario, where are the ideas to come from? They can be sought from five sources: (1) existing service users; (2) citizens who do not currently use services; (3) the literature; (4) suppliers of recreation and tourism services and products in other public agencies or in the private sector; and (5) agency personnel.

This article is concerned with generating ideas from an organization's own personnel. Several techniques have been developed over the years to help individuals and groups develop better ideas. Generally, it has been found that groups generate higher quality, more diverse, and a greater number of ideas than individuals acting independently. That is, the ideas generated by groups exceed the sum of the individual contributions. In addition, the involvement of a group arouses greater interest in the problem to be solved and increases acceptance, understanding and, therefore, implementation of solutions.

This article focuses on brainstorming, one of the two group techniques that have emerged as the most successful approaches for soliciting ideas for groups. The other technique, nominal group technique (NGT) is discussed elsewhere in this book. These techniques can be used by any manager at any agency level and will work equally well in large and small departments.

In brainstorming, individuals generate ideas orally in a face-to-face setting. In NGT, a collection of individuals generate ideas alone in writing without any oral interaction and ideas are then pooled. Some research comparing the two techniques concludes that NGT appears to produce more ideas than brainstorming. However, the evidence is not conclusive because other studies conclude the reverse. Until more studies are conducted, any conclusions about the superiority of one procedure over another must be tentative at best.

It is important to emphasize that the purpose of these techniques is limited to generating ideas. All ideas that emerge will not be solutions. These techniques are *not* a way to solve problems but are methods for generating ideas that are *potential* solutions to problems. Ideas are raw material; solutions are the final product. Perhaps the best way to view ideas is as diamonds in the rough with the potential to be refined and combined to produce workable problem solutions. Every idea does not have to be a polished gem when it is first proposed. Just proposing an idea is a significant contribution to problem solving, because all ideas have the potential to spark solutions.

The basic principles of brainstorming were developed in the 1950s by Alex Osborn (Osborn 1963). Unfortunately, the term has been frequently misused to refer to a group of people sitting around a table and throwing out ideas. This is nothing more than a bull session, resulting usually in a small number of not very good ideas (Rawlinson 1981). Brainstorming, in fact, is a carefully structured technique that is governed by a set of rules.

Group Size and Advance Preparation

A group of seven to ten people is an optimum size for a brainstorming session. This group should include people from outside the agency or division, both experts and nonexperts, since outsiders bring a different perspective and may be more likely to generate unconventional ideas.

Group members should be acquainted with the topic area in advance of the session and have some opportunity to think about it. The problem statement should encourage a range of different ideas (e.g., "In what ways can we . . ."). Efforts should also be made to make the problem definition fairly specific so the ideas will be relatively focused.

A session should be open-ended, without a stated finish time. It stops when ideas have dried up. Most brainstorming time periods do not exceed 40 minutes since groups tend to become fatigued or bored after this period, but there are exceptions. Given the need for initial orientation and warm-up drills participants should be instructed to "allow about an hour and a half" or "Don't fix anything for after the session. We may run on." Even groups who are inexperienced in using brainstorming are likely to produce 80–100 ideas in this time. A sample memorandum inviting participants to a session is shown in Figure 1.

Setting the Environment: Psychological and Physical

The goal is to create an environment in which participants feel psychologically safe and nonthreatened. The major barrier to a successful brainstorming session is likely to be the desire of participants not to appear foolish. If this barrier is not discussed and removed it will prevent wild ideas from emerging and inhibit creative suggestions. Warm-up exercises are designed to surmount this concern of being laughed at and to facilitate the joyful experience of being laughed with.

The existence of this "looking foolish" barrier suggests that the group should consist of people who are substantially of the same rank. If ranks are mixed, junior managers may be inhibited by thinking "what will my supervisors think of that suggestion?" whereas senior managers may be discouraged from freewheeling creativity by thinking, "what will the junior staff think of

Fig. 1. Sample of an invitation to a brainstorming session.

(Source: Adapted from Joseph J. Bannon, 1981, Problem Solving in Recreation and Parks, 2d ed. Englewood Cliffs, N.J.: Prentice-Hall, p. 81; with permission from Sagamore Publishing Co., Inc.)

To: Name of participant

From: Name of coordinator

                    Date _____

You are invited to a brainstorming session on *Wednesday, July 7,* at 10 a.m. in the conference room, to discuss the problem of increasing attendance at the Arcola Recreation Center.

The lack of attendance at the center has been seen as a symptom of a much larger problem—the lack of involvement in the center by the neighborhood residents. Thus, we have formulated our problem for this session as: *How can the people in the Arcola neighborhood become more involved in the programs at the Arcola Recreation Center?*

There is currently little involvement by residents in the center's programs. The attendance of the center has dropped during the past few years. The advisory board seemed to be apathetic toward the center's programs and policies. It is felt that more involvement by the residents from this generally low-income area should increase our ability to understand and deal with the concerns of the community and thereby increase attendance. The purpose of this brainstorming session is to generate ideas that might be used as solutions for meeting that objective.

Remember the brainstorming rules we shall be following:
1. No criticism of ideas is allowed.
2. Free-wheeling is welcomed.
3. Quantity of ideas is wanted.
4. Listen and improvise on other people's ideas.

The session is likely to last about an hour but we may run on, so don't fix anything for immediately after it.

that idea?" For the same reason, nonparticipant observers should not be permitted at sessions for their presence may inhibit the participants.

When the session convenes, participants should be seated in a U configuration to encourage cross-fertilization, with the facilitator and recording sheets at the open end of the U. The group facilitator is responsible for creating the right atmosphere. The brainstorming session should be fun, generating a good deal of laughter, enjoyment, noise, and a sense of taking part in solving a problem.

Laughter is an excellent catalyst for it encourages wild ideas and creativity. The session that is totally quiet apart from the ideas that are being put forward, will quickly lose steam and die.

Getting Started

At the start of the session, the group leader explains the procedures that will be used, reviews the rules, and conducts warm-up exercises. The fundamental principle upon which brainstorming depends is the postponement of judgment. The leader emphasizes, "Remember we want as many ideas as possible, the wilder the better, and no evaluation." "Wild ideas" are encouraged so that chains of habit are broken and ideas flow freely without being condemned by previous experience. The goal is to create an environment in which participants feel psychologically safe and nonthreatened.

Before focusing on the problem, a series of two-minute warm-up exercises are recommended to illustrate the brainstorming technique. Even if the group is experienced in brainstorming, a warm-up should be included in order to raise the level of arousal and to facilitate the transition from the judgmental approach which characterizes daily thinking, into a nonevaluative mode of thinking. I have successfully used one or two selections from the following list as three minute warm-up drills:

> "How many other uses can we think of for—a dining room table; a cigarette box; an ash tray; a paper clip; a pair of rubber gum boots; a brick; a toothbrush; a lump of sugar?"
>
> "If you woke up tomorrow and were twice (or half) the size you are now, what would you do?"

When the brainstorming session starts, one member of the group should be designated to write the ideas on a chalkboard or flip chart where they are clearly visible to all participants. Displaying the ideas is important, so a tape recorder should never be used. The flip chart pages should be torn off as they are filled and hung on the wall for display. Each idea should be numbered to facilitate easy cross-referencing and to reinforce the success a group is having with the total number of ideas being generated. As ideas emerge, one idea sparks another and everyone participating is encouraged to build on other people's ideas.

Rules of Brainstorming

Four brainstorming rules must be observed. They should be reviewed at the start of the session and referred to whenever any of them is violated during the session. The rules, together with the problem statements, should be posted prominently so they are on view to all throughout the session.

Rule 1: No Criticism of Ideas Is Allowed.   Adverse judgment of ideas must be withheld until later. The following types of reactions are prohibited:

"We tried that before and it didn't work"	"The boss won't like it"
"We've never done it that way"	"That's ridiculous"
"It's too radical"	"No one will accept it"
"It's against policy"	"You'll be laughed out of town"

Creativity is so delicate a flower that praise tends to make it bloom, while discouragement often nips it in the bud. Any of us will put out more and better ideas if our efforts are appreciated. Unfriendliness can make us stop trying. Wisecracks can be poison . . . Every idea should elicit receptivity, if not praise. (Osborn 1963:50)

Rule 2: Free-Wheeling Is Welcomed.   The wilder the idea, the better; it is easier to tone down than to think up. A far out and impractical suggestion may spur another creative and practical idea by someone else.

Rule 3: Quantity Is Wanted.   The brainstorming principle is "Quantity Leads to Quality." The greater the number of ideas, the more likelihood of useful proposals.

Rule 4: Combinations and Improvement Are Sought. "Hitchhiking" is encouraged. In addition to contributing ideas of their own, participants are urged to suggest how ideas of others and their own can be turned into better ideas, or how two or more previous ideas can be joined into still another idea. Brainstorming takes advantage of the power of association. "This" suggests "that" and "that" leads to something else.

Procedures in Soliciting Ideas

There are three alternative ways for a group leader to manage the process. First, ideas can be called out by group members immediately as they think of them. Second, if this proves to be unmanageable or causes confusion, the leader can request members to raise a hand. If their idea builds on a previous idea, then members snap their fingers so they receive priority attention.

The third approach is called sequential solicitation. This is a more structured approach and most appropriate in situations where a few group members tend to dominate the discussion or some of them appear to be inhibited. The method involves going in sequence to each group member and giving him or her a chance to suggest an idea. A member who does not have an idea to offer simply says "Pass" and works on developing an idea for the next turn. This process promotes greater involvement and it also discourages members from developing one "good" idea and dropping out, with the thought in the back of their mind that the problem has been solved. However, there is a danger that this approach may cause embarrassment to an individual who feels inadequate or humiliated from frequently having to pass when he or she cannot think of another idea.

Fig. 2. The brainstorming cycle.

Keeping the Session Flowing

Frequently, a brainstorming session starts with a flood of ideas but this is followed by a slackening off. This pattern is shown graphically in Figure 2. There is a tendency to give up too easily or too early. When this slackening-off occurs, the leader should work hard at persuading the group to think of ways of modifying the ideas. If the group perseveres through this first lull, the flow will often increase after participants have had time to think beyond their initial ideas. Indeed, early ideas are not usually the best because they tend to be the most obvious and superficial. It has been observed that "quantity of ideas breeds quality. In case after case, the last 50 ideas produced at a brainstorming session have averaged higher in quality than the first 50" (Osborn 1963:167).

This second effort can be structured, if it cannot be brought forth spontaneously, by using the second effort technique (Lyles 1982:117). This involves having the entire group sit or mill about the room in absolute silence for three full minutes, reviewing and studying all the alternatives, or the alternatives on the list nearest them, that have been suggested so far. No talking is allowed. The group is instructed to think of ways they can spin off from previous ideas. The leader then goes around the room soliciting at least one additional idea from each person. Quite often the very best ideas are generated during this reflective incubation period because people have been bombarded with all the other ideas, which act as a stimulus is inspire higher quality thinking when members are forced to "change gear" in their thought processes.

Session Follow-up

When the brainstorming session is completed the ideas should be classified into logical categories—usually between five and ten such categories emerge. The typed list is then circulated to all participants within 24 hours of the session with plenty of blank spaces for additional ideas to be inserted. After this short incubation period, more ideas may have occurred to the group members, supplementing their original efforts.

Personnel at all levels of the organization can use brainstorming effectively. Better results are not necessarily related to high levels of education or seniority in the agency. Indeed, Osborn (1963:159–160) suggests that new ideas tend to contract as knowledge and judgment expand:

> Probably the most difficult panel members are executives who have been over-trained in the usual kind of non-creative conference . . . Executives traditionally rate each other on the basis of judgment . . . "We are far more apt to look up to the other fellow if he makes no mistakes than if he suggests lots of ideas."

As education and experience increase, individuals may develop inhibitions which rigidize thinking and make it more difficult to engage in "free-wheeling" thinking.

It is sometimes valuable to engage in *reverse brainstorming* as a prelude to a brainstorming session. This encourages critical comment. The process involves listing all the things wrong with an agency's existing efforts. The group then reverts to brainstorming and brainstorms each negative feature to determine ways of improving it.

Evaluation

When all of the fragile original ideas have been allowed to live for a brief period (because nobody was permitted to critique or eliminate them), judgments must be made on which to discard and which to investigate further. The usefulness of the tentative ideas depends on what is done with them—how effectively they are evaluated. Most of the ideas will not be useful and the evaluation has to be carefully structured to identify the few good, among the many inappropriate ideas: "A pile of dross has to be discarded before the nugget is found. Looking for a needle in the proverbial haystack can be easy, compared to finding the good ideas in the typed lists from a brainstorming session" (Rawlinson 1981:70).

There are two objectives in the evaluation process. The first is to identify the few good ideas and implement them. The second is to demonstrate to the participants that action is being taken. If action does not follow within a day or two after the brainstorming session, enthusiasm wanes and participants will be reluctant to take part in further brainstorming sessions.

The evaluation process has three stages. They are: (1) to establish criteria against which the usefulness of ideas will be measured; (2) to reduce the large number of ideas down to a more manageable set; and (3) to examine in more detail the usefulness of this smaller set of ideas.

The first stage of evaluation is to establish criteria against which to measure the usefulness of ideas. The question to be answered for each idea is, "Does it have the potential to measure up to the criteria?" or "Can it meet at least the most important of them?" Often what happens is that ideas are selected without there being any conscious awareness of what criteria are being used to guide the selections. Thus, it is possible that different members of the group intuitively use different criteria when assessing each idea, resulting in suboptimum selections.

In developing criteria, the group should try to generate as many criteria as possible without regard to their initial value or relevance. The more criteria the group generates, the less likely it is that a relevant criterion will be overlooked. Again the deferred judgment principle should be enforced until all criteria possibilities have been offered. After the group has generated a list of criteria, it must select those to be used in evaluating the ideas. The criteria may include such items as:

- To what degree is the idea compatible with the agency's mission and its objectives?
- Is the need served a high priority for the agency?
- What is the size of the potential target market?
- Are existing opportunities provided by other suppliers?
- Is it technically feasible; for example, are the necessary facilities available?
- What present and potential personnel knowledge and skills are needed?
- Are monetary and personnel resources available?

The second stage in evaluation is to reduce the large number of ideas down to a manageable set. The two most important criteria should be selected by the group and placed at the top of a typed list of all the ideas which is given to each of the participants. Each participant is asked to examine the list of ideas privately and without discussion with the other participants and to select about 15 percent of the ideas he or she considers to be useful, worthy of further and more detailed examination (Rawlinson 1981:75).

The number 15 percent is not significant and each participant may select more or less. The participants are asked to return the selected ideas to the leader within the next two or three days. The leader tallies the responses and those that receive most support form the basis of the more detailed evaluation, which constitutes stage 3. An alternative procedure is to give each member a certain number of votes. For example, if there are 100 ideas, each member could be given 15 votes (15 percent of the idea pool) to allocate as desired. Thus, all of one member's votes may be allocated to one idea, one vote may be allocated to one idea, half the votes may be allocated to one idea and the other half on another idea, and so forth.

In Stage 2, ideas are evaluated against only the two most important criteria to reduce the complexity of the task and to make it less time consuming. The group should discuss each of the ideas in turn in an effort to elaborate on the terse phrases, increase awareness of their potential, and clarify their meaning and implications. After a thorough discussion of all the ideas, a final quantitative effort is made to prioritize them. Now that the large set of ideas has been filtered to a relatively small number, more criteria can be introduced if they are considered to be important. This final stage is conducted through the use of a matrix which is shown in Figure 3.

Each idea should be rated against each of the criteria as "very good," "good," "fair," or "poor," and scored with the 3, 2, or 1 point, respectively. (A high number should always indicate a more favorable rating.) If the criteria

Fig. 3. A matrix for assessing the usefulness of each idea against its selected criteria.

	Criterion #1	Criterion #2	Criterion #3	Criterion #4	Criterion #5	Criterion #6	Criterion #7	TOTAL
Weighting	3	3	2	2	2	1	1	
Idea #1	3	2	2	1	4	3	1	29
Idea #2	2	4	3	1	4	2	3	35
Idea #3	4	3	2	0	1	3	1	28
Idea #4	2	0	1	2	0	2	2	16
Idea #5	1	2	3	0	3	4	2	24
Idea #6	3	3	2	1	0	4	3	31
Idea #7	3	4	2	3	1	4	4	40

are considered to be of varying importance, then they can be weighted. Thus, if idea 1 when measured against criterion 2 is considered to be "fair," it receives 2 points. Since criterion 2 is weighted by a factor of 3, when the totals are added idea 1 against criterion 2 scores a total of 6.

These ratings should be done independently to enable each participant to record his or her opinion without being influenced by the views of other members. After the matrix results compiled independently by each member have been tabulated and displayed, the group discusses them. If one receiving a high score does not "feel" right to the group members, the reasons for that need to be identified and perhaps its status reviewed. A particular danger at this stage is that some older members of the group may point out that an idea was tried in the past and failed. This should not necessarily exclude it being introduced again:

> Younger executives come to me with what they think are good ideas. Out of my experience I could tell them why their ideas will not succeed. Instead of talking them out of their ideas, I have suggested that they be tried out in test areas in order to minimize losses. The joke of it is that half the time these youthful ideas which I might have nipped in the bud, turn out either to be successful or lead to other ideas that are successful. The point I overlooked was that while the idea was not new, the conditions under which the idea was to be carved out were materially different. (Osborn 1963:278)

The evaluation phase of brainstorming is time consuming and it requires some drive and persistence on the part of the leader to ensure that it is completed.

Summary

A great deal of evidence suggests that many efforts to produce new ideas to meet client needs are "incestuous." That is, there is a tendency to reach for prior experience, prior approaches, or modest distortions of old answers, as opposed to really searching for new ideas. We become victimized by habit. Brainstorming offers a mechanism for transcending the habit of restricting new ideas to the limits of past experience.

References

Lyles, Richard I. 1982. *Practical Management Problem Solving and Decision Making.* New York: Van Nostrand Reinhold.

Osborn, Alex F. 1963. *Applied Imagination,* 3d ed. New York: Charles Scribner's Sons.

Rawlinson, J. Geoffrey. 1981. *Creative Thinking and Brainstorming.* New York: John Wiley.

28

The Nominal Group Technique for Generating and Evaluating Ideas

Carson E. Watt

The nominal group technique (NGT) was developed by Andre Delbecq and Andrew Van De Ven in the late 1960s. (Delbecq et al. 1975). Although this technique provides some opportunity for group discussion, its primary idea-generation component requires silent, written generation of ideas. In addition, NGT incorporates a procedure for idea evaluation and selection, so that group members can leave an NGT meeting with a sense of closure on the problem.

NGT was developed from studies that examined the character of communication between two different groups: (1) a "nominal group," that is, one in which members indicated ideas through written communication, and (2) the interacting group, where members exchanged ideas through spontaneous verbal communication (Gill and Delbecq 1982). Research showed that groups that wrote prior to verbal interaction generated a higher number of ideas on a given problem, a greater quality of ideas, as determined by external judges, and a set of ideas that were more inclusive than those that were generated by spontaneoulsy interacting groups. However, interacting groups were better at the evaluation tasks of weighing alternatives and selecting alternatives when they were able to clarify through interaction.

NGT has three main advantages compared to brainstorming. First, it better enables individuals of different ranks to participate since the fear of sounding foolish to subordinates or supervisors is largely removed by initially writing down ideas. Second, it ensures that each person participates equally in the process and makes it more difficult for a few individuals to dominate. Third, it usually requires less time than brainstorming to generate and evaluate ideas. The major disadvantage of NGT compared to brainstorming is the reduced emphasis on camaraderie, socialization, and sharing of ideas, which may inhibit the generation of wilder, "way out," unconventional ideas. The NGT process occurs through four basic steps.

Step 1: Silent Generation of Ideas in Writing.   The question or issue is written on a flip chart for all to see. The phrasing of the question is perhaps the most important step in the whole NGT process. It must be pretested and carefully written or else the subsequent effort is wasted. The group members are requested to write down their ideas without engaging in any discussion with other group members. Seven or eight minutes are allotted for this activity. The ideas should be written in short, brief phrases, not long sentences, because they must all be recorded by the group leader in Step 2.

Step 2: Round-Robin Recording. Each group member is asked to read aloud one of his or her ideas, in turn. As each idea is read, it is numbered and recorded on a flip chart visible to all group members. Similar and even duplicate ideas are recorded. No discussion of the ideas is permitted at this stage, but participants are encouraged to "hitchhike," that is, to continue writing down ideas, if those recorded on the flip chart spark new thoughts. This step is likely to take 20 to 30 minutes to complete.

Step 3: Elimination of Duplicates and Combining of Similarities. This is the first opportunity that individuals in the group have to discuss their ideas. The purpose of this step is to eliminate duplication and combine similar phrases that have been previously recorded. Logistically, statements should be reviewed in pairs, that is, limit discussion to not more than two items at a time. Group members are encouraged to ask questions or make comments about each idea's importance, clarity, meaning, or underlying logic. Illustrations expanding on the idea from all members of the group are often helpful. Individuals who suggested an idea need not comment on it if they do not wish to do so. A key role of the facilitator is to avoid heated debate of an idea's merit. At the end of this step, remaining phrases should communicate the ideas clearly and should be as discrete or mutually exclusive as possible. Typically, this third step of discussing each item in order takes approximately 20 to 30 minutes to complete.

Step 4: Vote and Ranking. In this stage, a subset of priority items are selected from the total common list by each individual. Each group member is given seven 3" × 5" cards and requested to write down the best seven ideas, one per card. (The group leader should determine the number of ideas to be chosen. A number between five and nine usually works well.) The idea number from the master list should be recorded in the upper left-hand corner of each card.

Next, after all participants have silently recorded the seven ideas, they are requested to rank each one by assigning a 7 (assuming only seven ideas were selected) to the most important one, a 6 to the next most important idea, and so forth, until all have been ranked. The ranks for each idea should be recorded on the lower right-hand corner of each card. At the conclusion of the ranking, the cards are passed to the next person and then to another person who is responsible for reading them aloud. The intent is to provide anonymity to each individual's ranking.

The leader goes down the master list, reads out each item, writes down each member's ranking for it, and records the total score. The ideas with the highest scores are those perceived by the group to be the most useful. If there are clear-cut idea winners at this point, the process can be terminated; if there are not enough clear-cut winners or there are inconsistencies in voting, two additional steps may be added to the process.

First, peculiar voting patterns are examined (e.g., if an idea receives five 7 votes and four 1 votes). The group then discusses the idea in question to clarify meaning and logic, but they should not be permitted to try to influence the vote of others.

Second, after the clarifying discussion has ended, group members are asked to vote on the ideas again, using the ranking procedure described for the preliminary vote.

Variations of the basic NGT process have been developed and applied in recent years in tourism and other fields (Bartanek and Murninghan 1984; Ritchie 1987; Watt et al. 1988) Because of its highly structured procedure, NGT is used in a variety of settings and is useful in homogeneous or heterogeneous groups.

NGT requires careful planning and a qualified facilitator. Pre-meeting preparations require

- Formulating and testing for NGT questions based on desired outcomes.
- Identifying target audience and carefully selecting participants to avoid bias in representation.
- Assembling supplies (flip chart sheets, markers, masking tape, 3 × 5 cards, name tags).
- Securing and preparing the meeting room. Walls must be suitable for flip chart sheets to be attached with masking tape. Paper (2 sheets to avoid bleeding of markers on wall) should be placed on wall to record ideas generated.
- Training of facilitators if appropriate. Necessary if more than one group is used (multiple groups produce comparative results).

Summary

NGT has been used effectively to resolve conflict as well as to initiate planning processes. In a time of strategic planning and quality management systems, NGT is a valuable process tool for tourism planning. As an open, nonthreatening process, NGT sets the stage for focused planning. Professionals should learn to use this valuable tool.

References

Bartanek, J. M. and J. K. Murninghan. 1984. The nominal group technique: Expanding the basic procedure and underlying assumptions. *Group and Organization Studies,* 9(3) September.

Delbecq, A. L., A. H. Van de Ven, and D. H. Gustafson. 1975. *Group Techniques for Program Planning: A Guide to Nominal Group and Delphi Processes.* Glenview, Ill.: Scott-Foresman.

Gill, S. L., and A. L. Delbecq. 1982. Nominal Group Technique NGT. In *Group Planning and Problem-Solving Methods in Engineering Management,* ed. Shirley A. Olsen. New York: Wiley.

Ritchie, J. R. Brent. 1987. The nominal group technique—Applications in tourism research. In *Travel, Tourism and Hospitality Research* ed. J. R. Brent Ritchie and Charles R. Goeldner. New York: Wiley.

Watt, C., J. Stribling, and T. Var. 1988. Use of nominal group technique in tourism information needs assessment. In *Tourism Research: Expanding Boundaries,* 1988 Conference Proceedings. Travel and Tourism Research Association, Montreal, Quebec.

29

The Psychology of Tourism

Philip L. Pearce

The psychology of tourism may be likened to a recently discovered natural landscape where the overall perspective is one of a slightly undulating plain. In the foreground some interesting well-vegetated hills command initial attention and additional exploration. On the horizons some further peaks contain recently discovered pathways to other landscapes and disciplines. Regrettably there is a good deal of flat deserted terrain where few explorers have ventured. Nevertheless the total view is appealing and the area has vast potential for academic and applied settlement. This article attempts to guide the reader through the key features of this new landscape.

Research in social psychology is one of the first key landmarks. Tourism itself is essentially a social psychological phenomenon. Other levels of psychological analysis deal with processes that may contribute to the tourist experience, such as motion sickness, map-reading, or one's motivational state. But social psychology research relates to the heart of travel for many people since this study area tackles the analysis of people's experiences in new settings in the company of others.

Attitudes, long a traditional social psychological topic area, are prominent in this research. Much existing tourism consumer research has been cast within a loose attitudinal framework, as have studies relating to the recreational use of natural environments (e.g., Stankey 1972; Zube 1980; Absher and McEvoy 1985). Several studies of tourists' posttravel attitude changes have been reported (Pearce 1982; Steinkalk and Taft 1979; Cort and King 1979). In these studies group package tourists were shown to change their attitudes and perceptions as a consequence of their travels. When favorable holidays took place and initial pretravel attitudes were positive, even more positive attitudes were acquired. Less satisfactory holiday experiences and moderate pretravel attitudes resulted in some negative attitudes to host cultures.

Another plateau in the social psychology region is represented by a number of studies on tourist guides. Taft (1977) suggested that the best local tourist guides are talented and exceptional members of their cultures. Gatto (1977) viewed guides as parental figures distributing local insights to their "dependent children." The functionality of the guided tour group was underlined by Schmidt (1979). In her account she noted that guided tours provide both information and ready solutions as to what to see. Guided tours also help members relate to the out-group, or host culture, thus diminishing the impacts of culture shock (Furnham and Bochner 1986). The observation by Lopez (1980) that communication difficulties or an inappropriately authoritarian style of leadership on the part of a guide can seriously undermine the quality of a tour suggests considerable scope for studies of tour group satisfaction and guide education.

The importance of social dynamics within tour parties was noted by Gorman (1979). In particular, he observed that tourist groups develop roles for their members. The comic, the informed expert, and the critic are frequent roles tourists fill in extended bus tours. At the individual level, "shifting environmental contingencies meant that virtually every group member had a turn at controlling crucial resources and performing indispensable functions" (p. 483). Schuchat (1983) remarks on the satisfaction to be derived from being a member of a like-minded tour group, as well as the more general rewards of sociability and safety. More specifically, she suggested that tour groups may provide a defined and delimited field for the resolution of such crises as divorce or bereavement; and that couples may use other group members to mediate their own interaction difficulties.

Many of the influences on people's tourism behavior derive from primary or secondary groups to which they belong. One example is given by Kelly's (1985) analysis of the museum visit as a new status symbol which serves to separate the cultured "us" from the uncultured "them." He contends that many visitors are motivated to attain a state of "having been" to a museum rather than to enjoy "being there." In such a case, group pressures are given priority over more individually based satisfactions. Anecdotal evidence would suggest that there are many more examples of tourism behavior under conditions of conformity with social status implications for the participants.

Behavior, at whatever level it is conceived, occurs in time and space. While the historical location of behavior has been given relatively little attention by social psychologists (cf. Gergen 1973), environmental psychology has grown in the past two decades to become an accepted part of the discipline (Darley and Gilbert 1985). The individual brings to social interaction certain requirements for personal space, an understanding of the social meaning of interpersonal distance, and cognitive processes necessary for representing the natural and built environment.

Two representative concepts from environmental psychology that have been applied in tourism studies are "image" and "crowding." (A broader review of the field can be found in Fridgen 1984 and Stringer 1984). Images are publicly held and consensual schemata, usually with a visual component (Uzzell 1984), and constructed rather than "realistic." Environmental images are sociospatial schemata (Lee 1968) in which both people and place form an essential part. For example, Riley and Palmer (1976) used the repertory grid technique to examine the images that people have of seaside resorts. The study revealed a strong split between domestic and international destinations with a further division occurring along a high class, with style, versus low class, less-style, dimension. Most image studies report this dimension of the social standing or social value of a destination (Pearce 1988) and this theme relates to the central point made earlier that tourism is a very social and socially conscious human process.

Crowding, too, has been of interest to environmental psychologists primarily because of its association with increasing urbanization and the possible resulting stress to urban residents. In tourism settings, crowding is seen rather as a stress upon the environment itself (Pigram 1980) or as a constraint upon desired tourist experience (Schreyer and Roggenbuck 1978; Womble and Studebaker 1981; West 1982). It is particularly when tourists are aiming for solitude or "escape" that they are likely to be most sensitive to crowding (Gramann and Burdge 1984; Hamitt et al. 1984); while those whose goal is excitement and action, or social interaction, even in a wilderness setting, are less likely to interpret the presence of others as crowding (Schreyer and Roggenbuck 1978). Graefe and Vaske (1987) place crowding within a more general framework of the impacts of tourism on the quality of the tourists' experience. These include impacts on the environment, such as littering, and conflicts arising from different use requirements (e.g. mechanized vs. nonmechanized). The authors describe a tourist management approach that systematically takes into account the observations from empirical studies of impact. Projected national increases in tourism growth rates, which in many cases suggest a doubling of visitors in the next decade, will keep such issues at the forefront of universal attention.

Another notable feature of the tourism psychology landscape is the work with a strong cognitive perspective. The vast area of contemporary psychology broadly referred to as cognitive studies deals with such topics as memory, information processing, decision making, attention, thinking, problem solving, and language acquisition. Regrettably the considerable resources of cognitive psychology have not been widely applied in the tourism landscape. Three illustrations of this kind of work will be discussed but such applications need to be prefaced by the remark that the studies cited are merely the leading edge of a potentially influential mountain of tourism studies from a cognitive perspective.

One study employing the cognitive construct of a schema was conducted by Lee and Uzzell (1980). Schema is a construct with a long history in psychological inquiry dating back to physiological work on the mental organization of reflexes, to studies in memory and maze learning and child development through to recent applications in environmental perception (Bartlett 1932; Tolman 1948; Lee 1968; Piaget 1954: Canter 1977). The concept can be interpreted as a unit of storage with a specific content or theme. Thus there are schema for environmental referents such as one's neighborhood or for the kings and queens of England as well as for specific bodily and motor processes such as learning to bowl a cricket ball or to perform a backward somersault.

Lee and Uzzell studied visitors to farm open days in Britain and compared the contents and structure of people's beliefs about modern farming before and after their short visit. The use of multivariate statistical procedures such as factor analysis and multidimensional scaling is useful in this kind of work to provide a "map" of the relationships between concepts and the evaluation of those concepts by visitors. Lee and Uzzell demonstrated that the schema of farm visitors did change as a result of the visits, with many visitors shifting their perceptions toward the view that modern farming is a highly technical, industrial activity with little of the romance of the countryside as is sometimes depicted. They also discovered that for some visitors this change in the organization of their schema and the information they received about farms through their visits actually left them with a more negative overall perception. This work on the schema or mental organization of people's images can be connected to marketing studies such as the work on the demand for farm tourism (Pearce 1990). In one particular study of farm tourism in New Zealand it was shown that many visitors were attracted to farms because of the chance to meet the farmers and relax in a pleasant physical setting. If the farmers did not appreciate this mental set of the visitors they often felt frustrated with them when they showed little interest in the specifics of farm work.

An active area of cognitive psychology with specific relevance to tourists and tourism is that concerned with the processing of maps and map information. Several researchers have recognized the need for visitors to be well oriented to enhance their on-site experiences (cf. Screven 1986; Pearce 1988). The disoriented visitor is confused, anxious, and likely to use so much mental effort in negotiating the labyrinths of such settings as museums that they have little capacity for attending to the exhibits. Winkel et al. (1976), for example, report that disoriented museum visitors frequently missed exhibits they wanted to see and spent time in parts of the museum which were of lesser interest.

To summarize this work it can be proposed that a map is easy to read when it contains the least number of cognitive steps for the user. A cognitive step can be defined as a mental transformation of information from the language of the map to the reality that the viewer can be expected to encounter. For example, any map drawn in two dimensions is a cognitive step away from the three-dimensional world confronting the individual. Other examples of cognitive steps include black and white versus color, a rotated map versus a map oriented in the same direction as the viewer, and an indexed system as opposed to names on the map. Other cognitive steps include any schemes for color-coded routes, as well as variations in text type and symbolic representation. The evidence seems to be consistent with the view that such cognitive steps take longer to process and are harder to remember (Cooper 1975, 1976; Pearce and Black, 1984).

Where possible, three-dimensional, image-based maps with the labels of the objects on the map itself and with the map orientation corresponding to the environment as the user sees it are important in making maps more effective. Gallagher (1983) in a study of visitors to gardens and historic sites notes that

> The map is the most frequently consulted item in a guide book. They vary enormously in legibility and style. Colour plans tend to be most legible but black and white plans can equally well portray the extent and main features of the garden. Aerial oblique ("birds-eye") views tend to give a clearer overview that flat diagrammatic forms. (p. 6)

As a third illustration of the potential power of cognitive psychology concepts in the field of tourist psychology, the mindfulness-mindlessness distinction deserves attention particularly as some studies in museums and visitor centers have already pursued and demonstrated its usefulness (Moscardo and Pearce 1986; Moscardo 1988). Langer and her colleagues first identified the mindfulness-mindlessness distinction in a series of laboratory and field experimental studies (Chanowitz and Langer 1981; Langer and Newman 1979). Langer (1989:5) summarizes her working definition of mindfulness as: "active information processing in which the individual is fully engaged in creating categories and drawing distinctions."

On the other hand mindlessness is conceived as the use of routines to guide behavior with minimal processing of available information. Langer's formulation does much to integrate the work on cognitive "minimising." Her work has elevated this line of research to addressing large-scale social behaviors, which makes it applicable to a range of settings. In her own studies Langer has demonstrated relationships between mindlessness and poor health, susceptibility to burglary and criminal assault, and poor social skills (Langer 1989). Mindlessness can result from either repeated exposure to the same phenomenon or set of circumstances or a single exposure to new information not perceived as personally relevant. Mindfulness, however, is the product of novelty, surprise, variety, the unexpected, and situations requiring effort from the individual. Recent experimental work by Langer and Piper (1987) suggests that mindlessness can be prevented by adopting a "conditional" view of the world when learning new information. For example, if a tourist receives information on Bermuda and forms the perception of Bermuda as a "rich man's destination," the commitment to this view will influence subsequent perceptions and behaviors. But if the tourist takes the stance that Bermuda might be a destination for the rich but could also be for other people then there will be less stereotypic, mindlessly enacted behaviors.

The scenario presented above will stimulate many of the psychology readers of this article to connect Langer's concepts with other approaches. For example, it is clear that mindless tourists will use stereotypes to fit existing categories, that self-fulfilling prophecies will operate to confirm the content of categories and that the information search of such a visitor will be biased (cf. Rosenthal and Jacobson 1968). There is also a direct link with the work of Schank and Abelson (1977) on scripts. This concept refers to sequential routines of behavior appropriate to a social situation such as eating at a restaurant. Most scripts, once initiated, are enacted mindlessly. It is only when something unusual happens that we mindfully process the situation (such as when the waiter asks for a tip before serving a meal).

Many tourist behaviors are scripted, particularly on guided tours where a planned pattern of the day's activities is given to visitors. It is highly likely that many tourists attend to the outline of the day's events and then experience much of the trip mindlessly. If this view is correct then there will be little information recalled about the journey since mindlessly processed information is not remembered. Tourists will become mindful only when something unusual, dramatic, or novel takes place. Low levels of recall by tourists of places they have visited or countryside they have driven through are consistent with the mindlessness formulation. A cognitive mapping study of caravan travelers in Northern Australia found that many tourists remember only four or five features in a 200-mile (320 kilometer) trip (Pearce 1981).

Other landscape features deserve attention in our exploration. The area of motivation connects the psychology of tourism to many other aspects of tourism study, notably marketing and tourism development. Most of the work labeled motivational studies that the student encounters in library indexes of tourism studies is in fact mislabeled. It should be titled an assessment of attitudes toward destinations. Motives and motivational studies are better conceived as being concerned with more enduring, long-lasting determinants of behavior that are likely to apply across situations. Thus, an individual with a high level of affiliative or social motivation will be likely, in a consistent manner, to seek the company of others, to prefer group tours and to be attracted to the excitement of more densely populated city centers

Any motivational theory to understand tourist behavior needs to consider the fact that tourists have long-term goals, the notion that there can be multiple causes of behavior, that it is difficult to measure people's needs, and that some behaviors reflect what people would like to be rather than what they now are (Pearce 1982). Whereas no single prevailing theory of motivation fits all these requirements, a combination of Maslow's hierarchy model and some features of attribution theory and achievement motivation can serve as an interlocking set of ideas that can be applied effectively to tourist motivation. These kinds of adaptations of the Maslow hierarchy of motives have been successfully employed in studying tourist theme parks, visitors to outback towns, day trippers to a marine environment (Pearce 1988), downhill skiers (Mills 1985) and wilderness users (Young and Crandall 1984). The danger in motivational studies is to see the motivation of tourists as fixed rather than changing during their life cycle. Additionally, motivation must be seen as a joint social and biological process, which makes it susceptible both to social change and influence as well as linking us to our physical needs.

Of the lesser explored areas in the psychology of tourists the simple issue of how tourists spend their time offers much fertile ground. Only a small number of research studies have concentrated on tourists' time budgets which, in turn, can be related to how satisfied people are on holiday. In addition, a study of tourist time budgets can assist vacationers to plan and enjoy their holidays more. The first finding from these time diary studies— the technique of collecting information here is one of asking vacationers to fill in a detailed diary of all their holiday activities—is that the obvious does not always emerge. For example, in looking at tourists to Spanish coastal resorts one might expect that vacationers would spend a lot of their waking time on the beaches. In fact only 26 percent of waking time was spent at the beach itself, which prompts the question what are the visitors doing? (D. Pearce 1988)

The research revealed that vacationers were spending 30 percent of their total waking time in and around their accommodation, 22 percent of their time on the streets (especially using the sidewalk cafes) and 14 percent in places of entertainment. If these figures for staying in and around the hotel appear high, it is likely that they are common rather than atypical in many seaside settings. In the South Pacific D. Pearce's study of visitors' time and activity schedules in Vanuatu revealed similar findings; visitors spent nearly 60 percent of their time in and around their resort hotel with the direct activities of the holiday being drinking and diving and swimming/ sunbathing.

An analysis of vacationer's time and behavior patterns in Singapore provides another perspective on tourists' activities (Lew 1987). Sometimes tourists are doing things they do not really want to do. Singapore, one of the most modern centers in Asia with its huge international airport and a thriving tourist industry, can be considered as a prototypically well-organized tourist destination. Five categories of visitors to this small island nation can be identified: tourists from English-speaking countries (Australia, New Zealand, United Kingdom, United States), from Continental European countries (notably France and Germany), from Japan, from neighboring countries (Indonesia and Malaysia), and from other Asian countries (Hong Kong, India, Taiwan, Thailand). The continental European visitors are frequent visitors to the ethnic attractions of the island whereas English-speaking visitors and Japanese have high visitation rates to the gardens and some ethnic attractions. Asian visitors, with the exception of the Japanese, attend the more commercial and modern attractions of the city.

There is, however, a distinction between actual visitor rates and what tourists really want to do. While many studies of visitor behavior might make the mistake of assuming that attendance reflects interest in a linear fashion, Lew's diary style study revealed that many sites were over-visited. For example, only 48 percent of visitors expressed an interest in modern shopping centers but 83 percent actually visited such locations. This kind of discrepancy also applied to bargain shopping centers (expressed interest 51 percent: visitor rate 65 percent), Tiger Balm Gardens (expressed interest 28 percent: visitor rate 44 percent) and modern business and industry (expressed interest 23 percent: visitor rate 38 percent). The discrepancy in these figures attests to the organization of guided tours where the itineraries are directed toward percentages and commissions on tourist purchases at commercial establishments. There were also attractions where the expressed interest was greater than the actual visitor rate. This occurred for rural communities (49 percent interest; 23 percent visitor rate), natural and rural scenery (50 percent interest; 29 percent visitor rate), cultural performances (53 percent interest; 32 percent visitor rate); and other Southern islands (29 percent interest; 9 percent visitor rate). English-speaking visitors in particular were dissatisfied at their inability to explore the rural areas of the country, which is so poorly promoted and serviced that a visitor could be forgiven for believing that there is no rural scenery or village life on the island. Here, the research reveals an entrepreneurial opportunity, since it is apparent that some visitors to Singapore are not able to organize visits to areas in which they are interested.

This work on detailing visitor activities and relating them to visitor preferences represents one important direction for the psychology of tourism. There are a host of international tourism settings, whether they be city guided walks, rainforest tours or Sunday drives where the pattern of visitor activity could be monitored. Rather like cataloguing the botanical and physical resources of a new landscape, the activity of systematically noting and recording tourist behavior is a building block for the psychology of tourism of the future since such activity provides the basic data where models of motivation, cognition, social interaction, and personality may be profitably constructed.

On the horizon of the tourist-psychology landscape there are links to other areas of tourism analysis. The health of tourists and the effects ill health can have on their moods and general holiday satisfaction is one such bridge between medical work and psychology. In one Caribbean study it was estimated that over 60 percent of nearly 2,000 tourists at a resort club suffered from diarrhea. It was shown that being young, eating hamburgers, being North American, and having an ill roommate were excellent predictors of individual illness (Spika et al. 1987). The authors argued that isolated resorts pose problems in disease control similar to those of cruise ships since there are many visitors with limited exposure to local pathogens, and many food handlers in whom the pathogens can persist between groups of visitors. Improvements in food handling and preparation as well as surveillance of the problem would result in marked improvements in visitor health and well-being.

The topic of human stress is also an area of joint psychological and medical interest with important implications for tourists and tourism. The process of traveling imposes certain physical stresses on the human body. For example, in international flights we may cross several time zones thus disrupting our circadian or daily rhythms. Reason (1974) reports that it can take 21 days to adapt fully to a change of time following trans-Atlantic travel. Sleep-wakefulness cycles may also be disrupted by North-South travel with longer daylight times being experienced closer to the poles in the summer months. Since the human body only adapts gradually to increasing daylight in its production of hormones such as melatonin (the so-called summer hormone), stress and tiredness are likely to follow such travel patterns (Winfree 1982).

Many contemporary modes of transport also fool our human sensory receptors, particularly those concerned with balance and orientation. These sensory systems in the inner ear were designed to detect rapid angular displacement rather than slow regular displacement (such as the slow roll of a ship at sea or a car winding through hills). Motion sickness, the consequence of our systems not processing the body's movements accurately, has been a curse for many travelers, including the early Apollo astronauts. A series of studies have produced and researched the effectiveness of slow-release drugs to anesthetize the feedback from the inner ear to the brain and mind. The products resulting from these studies are now available in oral form or in patches to be worn behind the ear (Oosterveld 1987). Some travelers would undoubtedly claim this patch is one of the real contributions of psychophysiological research to the well-being of travelers.

As this exploration of the tourism psychology landscape comes to the end of its journey, some observations on future topics for study are warranted. One underexplored hidden valley in the psychology of tourism scene is that of consumer reaction to technological changes and products of the future. Moscardo (1989) observed that the use of computers in tourism settings is not a universal panacea for information delivery and customer satisfaction. In her review of the psychology of computer use Moscardo notes that anxiety remains a key factor inhibiting people from using airport computer check-in and ticketing facilities. She argues that computer anxiety may be seen as falling into three categories: being fearful of using computers, negative attitudes toward computers, and beliefs that computers will not be helpful. From her analysis of computer exhibits in various Australian museums, Moscardo recommends giving visitors high levels of control and personal relevance in the computer data bases (questions are easy to ask, material relates to personal needs, menus are clear, flexibility is high). Additionally, adopting a "games and flashy graphics" approach will deter many visitors who appear to take such exhibits less seriously. Age and gender were unrelated to computer use in the study.

The psychology of responding to changing technologies in a tourism context is a wider issue than merely dealing with computers. Shafer and Divine (1988) review the potential impacts of innovations in science and technology on tourists. They observe that sensavision TV (multisensory programs), simulators, and large film quality home entertainment centers with well-stocked film libraries, will alter the demand for being in natural settings. Such facilities will undoubtedly also affect destination choice and the preferred activities at the destination. Transport innovations (vertical take-off and landing domestic vehicles, new design helicopters, super-fast trains and high-speed cruise ships) will have impacts on accessibility to tourist environments. Advances in robotics and medicine will see people living longer with less menial work and a greater focus on experiencing the world in their leisure time. The public acceptance of such innovations will be determined by many of the psychological issues already reviewed.

Summary

The first settlers of the tourist-psychology landscape have had to cope with some problematic issues including the appropriateness of traditional concepts, colleague respect, and funding. The strong hypothetico-deductive system of empirically based psychology research has many virtues, including experimental and design rigour and analytic acumen, but its practitioners have not readily transferred their skills to the non-laboratory, inherently social- and context-dependent phenomenon of tourism. As can be seen in the references cited here, there have been only a few pioneers willing to stay in the area and work at adapting and modifying psychological practices and concepts to the tourism phenomenon. The social, cognitive, and motivational psychology areas, in particular, are key nodes in the tourist-psychology landscape that need to be settled more thoroughly in the near future, both for a better understanding of tourism and to extend the breadth of understanding of human conduct within psychology.

References

Absher, J. D., and L. H. McEvoy. 1985. *Wilderness Values in de facto Wilderness: Management Policy Perceptions of Managers and Commercial Users.* Fort Collins, Colo.: National Wilderness Research Conference.

Bartlett, F. C. 1932. *Remembering.* Cambridge: Cambridge University Press.

Canter, D. 1977. *The Psychology of Place.* London: The Architectural Press Ltd.

Chanowitz, B., and E. Langer. 1981. Knowing more (or less) than you can show; Understanding control through the mindfulness-mindlessness distinction. In *Human Helplessness,* eds. M. Seligman and J. Barber, pp. 97–129. New York: Academic Press.

Cooper, L. 1975. Mental transformations of random two-dimensional shapes. *Cognitive Psychology* 7:20–43.

Cooper, L. 1976. Mental transformations and visual comparison processes: Effects of complexity and similarity. *Journal of Experimental Psychology: Human Perception and Performance* 2:503–514.

Cort, D., and M. King. 1979. Some correlates of culture shock among American tourists in Africa. *International Journal of Intercultural Behaviour* 3(2):211–226.

Darley, J. M., and D. T. Gilbert. 1985. Social psychological aspects of environmental psychology. In *Handbook of Social Psychology,* eds. G. Lindzey and E. Aronson, pp. 949–992. New York: Random House.

Fridgen, J. D. 1984. Environmental psychology and tourism. *Annals of Tourism Research* 11(1):19–40.

Furnham, A., and S. Bochner. 1986. *Culture Shock.* London: Methuen.

Gallagher, J. 1983. *Visiting Historic Gardens.* Leeds, U.K.: School of Planning and Environmental Studies, Leeds Polytechnic.

Gatto, J. 1977. An overview of TA (Transactional Analysis). *Eighth Annual Conference Proceedings. The Travel Research Association.* Salt Lake City, Utah.

Gergen, K. 1973. Social psychology as history. *Journal of Personality and Social Psychology* 26:309–320.

Gorman, B. 1979. Seven days, five countries. *Urban Life* 7(4):469–491.

Graefe, A. R., and J. J. Vaske. 1987. A framework for managing quality in the tourist experience. *Annals of Tourism Research* 14(3):390–404.

Gramann, J. H., and R. Burdge. 1984. Crowding perception determinants at intensively developed outdoor recreation sites. *Leisure Sciences* 6:167–186.

Hammitt, W. E., C. D. McDonald, and F. P. Noe. 1984. Use level and encounters: Important variables of perceived crowding among nonspecialized recreationists. *Journal of Leisure Research* 16:1–8.

Kelly, R. F. 1985. Museums as Status Symbols II: Attaining a state of having been. In *Advances in Non-Profit Marketing,* ed. R. Belt. Greenwich, Conn.: JAI Press.

Langer, Ellen J. 1989. *Mindfulness.* Reading, Mass.: Addison-Wesley.

Langer, E., and A. T. Piper. 1987. The prevention of mindlessness. *Journal of Personality and Social Psychology* 53:280–287.

Langer, E., and H. Newman. 1979. The role of mindlessness in the typical social psychology experiment. *Personality and Social Psychology Bulletin* 5:295–299.

Lee, T. 1968. Urban neighbourhood as a socio-spatial scheme. *Human Relations* 21:241–267.

Lee, T., and O. Uzzell. 1980. *The Educational Effectiveness of the Farm Open Day.* Perth, Scotland: Countryside Commission for Scotland.

Lew, A. 1987. English speaking tourists and the attractions of Singapore. *Singapore Journal of Tropical Geography* 8:44–59.

Lopez, E. M. 1980. The effect of leadership style on satisfaction—Levels of tour quality. *Journal of Travel Research* 18(4):20–23.

Mills, A. S. 1985. Participation motivations for outdoor recreation: A test of Maslow's theory. *Journal of Leisure Research* 17:184–199.

Moscardo, G. 1988. Towards a cognitive model of visitor responses in interpretive centres. *Journal of Environmental Education* 20:29–38.

Moscardo, G. 1989. *Why Johnny Won't Use the Computer.* Museum Education Association of Australia Conference, Adelaide, September.

Moscardo, G., and P. Pearce. 1986. Visitor centres and environmental interpretation: An exploration of the relationships among visitor enjoyment, understanding and mindfulness. *Journal of Environmental Psychology* 6:89–108.

Oosterveld, W. 1987. The combined effect of Cizzarizine and Domperidome on vestibular susceptibility. *Aviation, Space and Environmental Medicine* 58:218–223.

Pearce, D. 1988. Tourist time-budgets. *Annals of Tourism Research* 15:106–121.

Pearce, P. L. 1981. Route maps: A study of travellers' perception of a section of countryside. *Journal of Environment Psychology* 1:141–155.

Pearce, P. L. 1982. *The Social Psychology of Tourist Behaviour.* Oxford: Pergamon.

Pearce, P. L. 1988. *The Ulysses Factor. Evaluating visitors in tourist settings.* New York: Springer-Verlag.

Pearce, P. L. 1990. Farm tourism in New Zealand. *Annals of Tourism Research* 17(3):337–352.

Pearce, P. L., and N. Black. 1984. Dimensions of National Park maps: A psychological evaluation. *Cartography* 13:189–203.

Piaget, J. 1954. *The Construction of Reality in the Child.* New York: Basic Books.

Pigram, J. J. 1980. Environmental implications of tourism development. *Annals of Tourism Research* 7:555–583.

Reason, J. 1974. *Man in Motion.* London: Weidenfeld and Nicolson.

Riley, S., and J. Palmer. 1976. Of attitudes and latitudes: A repertory grid study of perceptions of seaside resorts. In *Explorations of Intrapersonal Space,* vol. 1, ed. P. Slater, pp. 153–165. London: Wiley.

Rosenthal, R., and L. Jacobson. 1968. *Pygmalion in the Classroom.* New York: Holt, Rinehart and Winston.

Schank, R. C., and R. P. Abelson. 1977. *Scripts, Plans, Goals and Understanding.* Hillsdale, N.J.: Lawrence Erlbaum.

Schmidt, C. J. 1979. The guided tour. *Urban Life* 7(4):441–467.

Schreyer, R., and J. W. Roggenbuck. 1978. The influence of experience expectations on crowding perceptions and social-psychological carrying capacities. *Leisure Sciences* 1:373–394.

Schuchat, M. G. 1983. Comforts of group tours. *Annals of Tourism Research* 10(4):465–477.

Screven, C. G. 1986. Exhibitions and information centres: Principles and approaches. *Curator* 29:109–137.

Shafer, E., and H. Divine. 1988. *Here's the Action in Science and Technology,* Pacific Area Travel Association Conference, Singapore, July 1988.

Spika, J. S., F. Dabis, N. Hargrett-Bean, J. Salcedo, S. Viellard, and P. A. Blake. 1987. Shigellosis at a Caribbean resort. *American Journal of Epidemiology* 126:1173–1180.

Stankey, G. H. 1972. A strategy for the definition and management of wilderness quality. In *Natural Environments: Studies in Theoretical and Applied Analysis,* ed. J. V. Krutilla, pp. 88–114. Baltimore: John Hopkins University Press.

Steinkalk, E., and R. Taft. 1979. The effect of a planned intercultural experience on the attitudes and behavior of participants. *International Journal of Intercultural Relations* 3(2):187–198.

Stringer, P. 1984. Studies in the socio-environmental psychology of tourism. *Annals of Tourism Research* 11(1):147–166.

Taft, R. 1977. Coping with unfamiliar cultures. In *Studies in Cross-Cultural Psychology,* vol. 1, ed. N. Warren, pp. 121–153. London: Academic Press.

Tolman, E. C. 1948. Cognitive maps in rats and men. *Psychological Review* 55:189–208.

Uzzell, D. 1984. An alternative structuralist approach to the psychology of tourism marketing. *Annals of Tourism Research* 11(1):79–100.

West, P. C. 1982. Effects of user behaviour on the perception of crowding in recreation settings. An urban case-study. *Leisure Sciences* 9:87–99.

Winfree, A. 1982. Human body clocks and the timing of sleep. *Nature* 297:23–27.

Winkel, G., R. Olsen, F. Wheeler, and M. Cohen. 1976. *The Museum Visitor and Orientation Media: An Experimental Comparison of Different Approaches in the Smithsonian Institution and National Museum of History and Technology.* New York: City University of New York, Center for Environment and Behavior.

Womble, P., and S. Studebaker. 1981. Crowding in a national park campground. *Environment and Behaviour* 13:557–573.

Young, R. A., and R. Crandall. 1984. Wilderness use and self-actualisation. *Journal of Leisure Research* 16:149–160.

Zube, E. 1980. *Environmental Evaluation.* Monterey, Calif.: Brooks/Cole.

30

The Tourism
Promotional Mix

John Bowen

The promotional mix is one of the most dynamic areas of tourism marketing. Markets are becoming more segmented, requiring our promotion to be more targeted and direct. Competition for the travel is increasing, both in the domestic and international markets. State tourist organizations are developing campaigns to attract the interstate customer, while at the same time trying to persuade their own residents to experience the state's attractions. Nations are realizing the importance of tourism as a means of bringing in foreign currency. In addition individual tourist businesses, such as airlines, hotels, resorts, and wholesalers are promoting their operations. As a result of this promotion the leisure traveler, the business traveler, and the meeting planner are being bombarded with promotional material. To be effective a promotional campaign must cut through the clutter of the competitors' promotions and have a positive impact on the customer. A promotional campaign that is ill-conceived or poorly executed will mean a lost opportunity in today's marketplace.

Promotion is communication. To be more precise promotion is communication that organizations use to pursue their marketing objectives. The term *promotional mix* refers to the total marketing communications program. When developing a communication program, the question is not if one should communicate but with whom to communicate, what are the objectives of the communication, what media to use, what should be the message, and how much to spend (Kotler and Armstrong 1989). The objectives of the promotion are linked to the marketing objectives. Thus, the promotional mix is used in accordance with the marketing plan and is an integral part of that plan. A list of common uses of a promotional plan includes

> Establishes an image
> Creates awareness for new products
> Maintains demand for existing products
> Creates additional demand during slow periods
> Gains access to scarce resources
> Maintains relations with channels members, travel agents, and wholesalers

Facilitates the buying process
Closes sales
Provides customer follow-up
Provides responses to customers' questions
Turns features into benefits (Evans and Berman 1990: 455)

Elements of the Promotional Mix

Advertising Advertising is a paid form of nonpersonal communication about an organization and/or its products that is transmitted to a target audience through a mass medium (Pride and Ferrell 1989). Advertising allows one to develop a message and direct it to a target audience. Advertising also allows one to control the intensity, media, and timing of the campaign. In addition to having the benefit of control, advertising is also an efficient way to reach large numbers of a target market.

The following examples illustrate how tourist organizations target markets through the planning and placement of advertising. American Airlines placed a two-page spread on the inside cover in the August 1989 issue of *Modern Maturity*. The advertisement is for a special promotion that American Airlines was offering to the members of the American Association of Retired Persons (AARP) and their spouses. The ad communicates a sales promotion, $40 to $50 off the lowest discounted fare available on any flight in the contiguous United States with Florida as its destination. This price discount is an example of price discrimination, giving a price advantage to a price-sensitive group without lowering the price for the entire market. *Modern Maturity* has the largest circulation of any magazine in the United States, because all members of AARP receive a subscription to the magazine. The retired members are able to fly on a short notice. The ad was targeted at the leisure traveler who is more price sensitive than the business traveler. It was aimed at a specific market (the senior citizen) and was trying to create immediate sales by selling unsold space over the next two months at a discount.

The Greek National Tourist organization placed a four-page removable insert in the November 1989 issue of *Successful Meetings*. The readership of *Successful Meetings* includes incentive travel planners, the target of the advertisement. The ad was in color and contained two postpaid reply cards for the reader wanting to receive more information. The advertisement was being used to identify prospects for a direct marketing campaign. The following is an excerpt from the advertisement:

> A Greek incentive program is easy and fast to put together. Our on-site support organizations have a grasp of both U.S. incentive requirements and of the possibilities offered by destination—they'll help make your incentive program an unqualified success.
>
> Greece is a dream to promote. Just take a look at the next page. Whoever doesn't already harbor a strong longing to visit Greece will be easily swayed by photos of incredibly beautiful Aegean vistas, ancient ruins that stand proud and majestic against the sky, friendly, lively, people and fabulously colorful Greek cuisine.

Note how the ad communicates specific benefits to the incentive meeting planner, experience and professionalism in handling their meeting, and a destination that will be a dream to everyone. The Greek National Tourist Organization also realizes that it cannot provide all the information needed by an incentive travel planner in an advertisement. The full package of information is provided to those who show enough interest to mail the reply card.

The preceding advertisements illustrate some of the key principles of advertising. First, determine the purpose and objectives of the advertising. These objectives should be linked to and flow from the organization's overall marketing strategy. The platform, or basic issues, of the campaign should now be developed. The issues should state benefits to the target market. In the case of the American Airlines' ad the issues were discounted flights to Florida, available exclusively for AARP members. Next, select media for the advertisement. The media plan for a large campaign can be complex as it involves the specific media, frequency, and size of advertisements. Some campaigns may involve television, radio, and print media. The issues communicated in each medium will be the same but the copy will vary between the media. Often the advertising is tested before the advertisements are placed. Then the advertising campaign is executed and evaluated.

Public Relations

Public relations is being given an increasingly important role in the promotional mix. A key area of public relations is publicity or the free use of media. The consumer realizes that anything can be promised in advertisements, but that does not mean that it will always be delivered. The customer often views tourism products as being risky, since they are intangible. The purchaser does not know exactly what he will receive until after he has received the product. For example, pictures of a hotel in a brochure may have been taken six years ago when the room was new, or the staff may not be as friendly and proficient as promised in the brochure. This uncertainty makes personal sources of information important to those who are purchasing tourism products (Zeithaml and Baysinger 1981). The personal source might be a travel agent, a friend, or an editorial in a magazine or a newspaper. The editorial is an example of publicity. Many tourism organizations are now realizing the importance of the credibility that publicity offers and are shifting more emphasis to this area of the promotional mix. Gladwell and Wolff (1989:49) illustrate the effectiveness of publicity with the following example. In January, 1985, the New York Times published a three-page article on Wilmington, North Carolina. The Wilmington Chamber of Commerce was deluged with requests for information for the next month. It would be both difficult and expensive to achieve these same results through advertising.

Many people view publicity as being free, a gift from the media. Occasionally it is possible to receive a favorable article with no prior contact, but most of the time an editorial is the result of hard work. Publicity, as well as the other areas of public relations, has to be managed. Every public relations campaign should have an objective. A press release should be designed for a specific target audience, with a message that will create interest and action within that market. It must be remembered that media organizations also follow the marketing concept. The editors must publish or broadcast items that will be of interest to their customers. Successful attempts to gain publicity must be relevant and newsworthy to a media's audience. Press releases with a standard message distributed to media aimed at different audiences will not be as successful as those with a customized message for each medium.

Another use of public relations is to enhance the image of the organization with its publics. These publics include investors, employees, suppliers, governmental agencies, and the community. A country wishing to promote tourism should be concerned with the tourism image of both its own residents and those organizations that are required to support its tourism efforts.

Lewis and Beggs (1988) report the disastrous effects of a tourism promotion that was not supported by the local tourist businesses and their employees. The "Rendezvous Time" promotion was developed by the department of tourism of an island nation. The objective of the promotion was to increase the number of visitors during the off season. It developed special events for this period and promoted the event as a time when the island was relaxed, uncrowded, and friendly. Employees thought that it was futile to try to attract tourists during the low season—why put forth all that effort now when during the high season we get more people that we can handle with little effort. Hotel management saw this period as a time when hotels lost money due to low occupancy. They cut their staff to a minimum, closing many outlets. The advertisements promoted this as a time to enjoy all of the island's amenities. The guests expectations were not met, since many of the amenities they were looking forward to enjoying were closed. The staff of the tourist-oriented business were indifferent, and sometimes less than friendly. What had been promised to the tourist through promotional material had not been delivered. Customer expectations were not met. Many tourists who came during this period had no desire to return to the island. When they returned home these travelers had little positive to say about their vacation to their friends. The result was that during a six-year period from 1976 to 1982 hotel occupancies dropped by almost fifty percent during "Rendezvous Time." The nation's tourist office was able to provide a successful concept, promote it well, and get tourists to the island. But, they failed to get internal support for the project. The campaign lacked an effective public relations program. Thus, an organization should look beyond its customers and develop public relations campaigns for all those constituencies that can impact its future.

Personal Selling

Personal selling is persuasive communication carried out through personal communication. Making a sales call is expensive. It can involve preparation, travel, entertainment, and providing the clients with brochures and other material. The cost of an average outside sales call can reach $250, and in many instances it requires more than one sales call to close a deal. Although personal selling is the most expensive method of contacting potential business, the expense can be justified when face-to-face contact and interpersonal communication is needed to establish a relationship and close a deal. Personal selling can be effective when customers meet any of the following criteria: geographically concentrated, purchase in large volumes, or purchase products that are expensive and/or complex (Evans and Berman 1990). Obtaining tourist groups or contracts from associations, businesses, social or fraternal organizations, political organizations, and members of the distribution channel such as wholesalers often requires the use of effective salespersons.

The sales activities of a tourist organization are not limited to making face-to-face sales calls. The telephone is being used to increase the effectiveness of the sales team. Telemarketing has the benefit of allowing direct communication between the salesperson and the customer. One of the reasons for the increasing popularity of telemarketing is the cost of face-to-face sales calls. Telemarketing is particularly useful as a tool to locate and qualify potential customers and to improve communication with existing customers.

Personal selling is not limited to the sales department. General managers and politicians need to support the tourism sales effort by making calls on key clients. Travel missions provide an example of getting everyone involved in the sales effort. Members of the mission include politicians, hotel general managers, representatives of the convention and tourist bureaus, and managers of other tourist-related businesses. The mission typically targets a key tourist source such as Germany or Japan. The members of the delegation travel to the target market and make sales calls on potential generators of tourist business. Even heads of state make sales calls. In 1990 Melbourne was trying to land the 1996 Olympic Games. The Prime Minister of Australia, Bob Hawke, made a personal visit to the Olympic Selection Committee, trying to persuade them to choose Melbourne. It is useful for anyone involved in management to have some sales experience. Those readers who are presently enrolled in a college program are encouraged to take part in a sales blitz, should the opportunity present itself. Those who are managers with little or no sales experience should make sales calls with the organization's best sales people. This will impress the clients and provide the manager with some insights into making a sales call.

Management of the sales effort is essential. Objectives must be set for the sales staff, managers, and those providing prospective clients with information. The sales skills and support needed by each of these groups will vary. Those making sales calls will need to have the ability to find and qualify prospective clients, develop a sales presentation, gain access to decision makers, deliver effective presentations, overcome objections, close the sale, and follow up with the client. They will need promotional materials to take on sales calls, expense accounts for travel and entertaining, and a compensation package that will provide them with an incentive to close the sale. Those occupying information desks are also part of the sales force. These persons will need different skills and support. The organization must determine its needs in the area of personal selling, hire the right type of employee, and provide appropriate support to achieve its objectives.

Sales Promotion

Sales promotion is an activity or material that acts as a direct inducement to consumers, salespersons, or travel agents. It can take the form of coupon books used to attract tourists, familiarization trips, free hotel nights, and price discounts. Sales promotions are designed to promote immediate sales. Promotions are particularly advantageous in tourism products, as they can be used to fill periods of low demand. One caution with the use of sales promotions is that they should not be used to prop up sales because the rest of the marketing mix is not sound. When organizations continually offer discounts, customers often feel cheated when they have to pay full price.

Sales promotions are very rarely used alone; they are usually combined with some other element of the promotional mix. For example, the offer of the promotion is often carried to the target market through advertising. In the American Airlines ad referred to earlier, the promotion of $40 to $50 off was communicated through an advertisement. Sales promotions can be used solely for short-term promotions to fill excess capacity, but they have their greatest impact when they create new customers that are likely to return.

Packaging

The final area of the promotional mix is packaging. One purpose of packaging is to provide physical evidence that promotes the image of the tourist product. Marketers must try to tangibilize the product for the guest. This is often done by providing brochures with pictures of tourist facilities and attractions. The effort that goes into making these facilities as attractive as possible is a function of packaging. Whether the tourist is staying at a campground or an expensive resort, they expect clean, well-kept facilities. The city of Houston spent many weeks preparing the city physically for the 1990 Economic Summit. Trash was cleaned up from the streets and vacant lots, thousands of plants were added to the city's landscape, buildings were cleaned or painted. The purpose of these efforts was to provide tangible evidence that would enhance the image of the city. The citizens of Houston realized that the event would attract thousands to the city and hundreds of thousands more would watch portions of the event on television. These persons would have the ability to plan meetings in Houston or speak positively of the city to others.

Packaging can also include putting together the right package of goods to offer the client. Wholesalers offer packages that include all or some of the following items: accommodation, airfare, ground transfers, rental cars, golf, fishing, diving, and other forms of entertainment. The combination of products in a package are designed to attract a specific target market. The package often offers an attractive price and also saves customers the time and trouble of trying to put together their own vacations. In summary, the two purposes of packaging are to provide tangible evidence to customers and to put together an attractive bundle of products that will encourage them to buy.

Components of Successful Tourism Promotions

The elements of the promotional mix should not be used alone; they should be integrated with each other to create synergy. For example, Delta's "We Love To Fly," campaign included not only advertising, but also each of the other elements of the marketing mix. The advertisements were filmed using Delta employees. A few employees actually got to make a commercial, but even those who did not had a positive feeling when they saw the advertisements with fellow employees instead of actors. To further stimulate a team spirit Delta created a film on the making of the advertisements. The film featured the selection of the Delta employees and the actual production of the ads. This film was shown to the Delta employees. It was an internal marketing tactic that helped to create customer orientation with Delta's employees and had a positive impact on the sales staff when they were dealing with customers over the phone or in person. In addition to being used for internal public relations the film was also distributed externally to college professors. Thus, Delta was creating goodwill with marketing instructors and creating a positive image with students, their potential employees. Sales promotion material in the form of bumper stickers and other items with the "We Love to Fly" motto was distributed. Finally, the packaging element was represented by the appearance of the employees, Delta's airport facilities, and the planes. Delta did not create an advertisement, they created a well-planned promotional event.

Producing a promotional event that includes all areas of the promotional mix takes planning. Not only do the areas of the promotional mix have to be integrated, but the promotion has to fit into the organization's overall marketing plan. In the case of Delta's campaign it was designed to differentiate Delta from its competition and emphasize its excellent service record. Delta had suffered a number of pilot errors and near accidents. In July 1987, a Delta pilot inadvertently shut off the plane's engines; another pilot landed in the wrong city; still another pilot landed on the wrong runway; and a Delta plane had a near miss with another airborne jet (Pride and Ferrell 1989). They wanted to create a positive image of Delta, an airline that had previously had an excellent safety record. Delta also wanted to create a point of differentiation from the other airlines and give the customers a reason for choosing

Delta. All airlines have similar schedules, equipment, and fares. Delta wanted the customer to perceive that there was a difference in flying, created by friendly and professional customer service.

Another requirement of promotional campaigns, pointed out in the Delta example, is that they should flow from the marketing plan. The promotional campaign is a series of well-planned tactics that should help to achieve the strategies of the marketing plan. Promotions that are done as a knee jerk reaction to increase sales can have disastrous effects. The promotional plan has to communicate benefits to a target audience. This requires knowledge of the important or salient benefits for that target market and the media that will reach the target market. Research is required to gain this information. Promoting a poor quality product, one that does not provide the features the guest is looking for, or is perceived to be over priced could actually damage business. Such promotion will create customers who will be dissatisfied and spread negative word-of-mouth. It is essential to understand the market and how one's product is perceived by the market before starting a major promotional campaign.

Current Issues in Tourism Promotion

Direct Marketing

Direct marketing is defined by the Direct Marketing Association as "an interactive system of marketing which uses one or more advertising media to effect a measurable response and/or transaction at any location." An interactive system means that there is a chance for interaction between the seller and the buyer. It is not simply one-way communication. This interaction could come in the form of a request for more information (as in the case of the Greek National Tourist advertisement discussed earlier), a reservation, or a sale. Since the customer can respond to a direct marketing offer, the response rate and actual sales from the campaign are measurable. Another benefit of direct marketing is that the customer does not have to come to the location of the tourist agency. National tourist offices that have just one office in a foreign country can gain access to that market through the mails and toll-free phone lines. Direct marketing campaigns require the use of one or more of the elements of the promotional mix to communicate with the target market.

Direct marketing is increasing in popularity for a number of reasons. First, as a result of increased competition product offers are being designed to meet the needs of specific target markets. Thus, the marketing of tourism products has evolved into a microsegment approach. Distinct promotions are developed for different markets. Direct marketing allows efficient access to specialized markets. The Greek National Tourist ad was aimed at the incentive market. They realized that not all the readers of the magazine would be interested in foreign destinations. Through direct marketing, they let those who were interested communicate this interest and provided these potential customers with detailed information. Direct marketing eliminates the expense of wasted distribution and also creates a data base of potential customers for future use. The popularity is evidenced by the fact that almost two-thirds of the tourism advertising budget for Texas is allocated to direct marketing (Burke and Lindblom 1989). Further evidence is provided by a recent issue of *Conde Nast Traveler*, which had direct marketing advertisements from four national tourist offices, two cruise lines and two tour operators. The advertisements typically contained both a coupon and a toll-free number which the reader could use to respond to offers of more information. Direct marketing is efficient, measurable, and allows one to develop a relationship with one's customers. For these reasons direct marketing will have a significant impact on the promotions of tomorrow.

Technology Technology is responsible for the growth of direct marketing. The development of data base software that can be easily run on personal computers, coupled with the affordability of personal computers, has given most tourist organizations the ability to develop their own data bases. These software programs will print individualized letters, address labels, sort data bases by customer segment, and keep a customer profile indicating who has responded to certain promotions in the past. Another impact of technology is the interactive computer data bases, such as Prodigy, which will allow consumers to seek information on tourist destinations and make their reservations using the computers. The electronic dissemination of information will also be used by travel agents and meeting planners. Electronic catalogs in the form of CD ROMs will contain information as well as pictures of tourist destinations. These catalogs will be targeted at the corporate meeting planner, incentive, association, and travel agent markets, allowing them to have volumes of information. For example, if a tourist wants to go to Belize the travel agent can access the on-line catalog, show the customer pictures, provide information about each hotel listed in the catalog, and provide general tourist information about the area. Electronic catalogs will make it easier and less expensive to disseminate information about tourist attractions.

Technology has also created the ability to produce inexpensive video tapes. One benefit of video is that it is perceived to be more credible than brochures because it is more detailed and complete. Video is being used by airlines, cruises, national tourism offices, and travel agencies. Air France determined that about twenty percent of the 25,000 persons per year who obtained their videos purchased tickets. American Express distributes videos on various destinations at its travel agencies. Royal Viking found that those who ordered videos were twice as likely to purchase tickets as those who received brochures. Royal Viking sells its videos for $9.95 to $14.95 and loans them free of charge to travel agents (First 1988). Technology will continue to create new opportunities and means for using the promotional mix, making this area of marketing both exciting and challenging.

Alliances Alliances come in many forms, and once they are made can serve as a barrier to markets for those organizations who are not part of the alliances. An airline, hotel company, and rental car company may link up to provide packages promoted through the airline. A wholesaler may select three hotels that will represent his offering for a destination. The customer who walks into a travel agent, asking to go to that destination, is handed the wholesaler catalog. Those hotels not in the catalog have been eliminated from the guest's choices of accommodation. Alliances can be developed with state and national tourism organizations. Northwest Airlines pitched in three dollars for every dollar Minnesota spent on tourism media. The Great Lakes states of Illinois, Indiana, Michigan, Minnesota, Ohio, and Wisconsin have formed an alliance to promote their states to European travelers (Strazewski 1989). As the tourist market becomes more competitive those who can create a competitive advantage will join forces. The advantage of combining the resources of two or more organizations to achieve a mutual goal creates a powerful force.

Summary

The promotional mix provides communication that tourist organizations use to pursue their marketing objectives. It involves much more than just advertising or selling. A well-developed marketing plan involves all elements of the marketing mix: advertising, personal selling, packaging, public relations, and sales promotion. The promotional mix is used to achieve the marketing strategies and objectives of the organization and should be an integral part of the marketing plan. The tourist promotional mix is receiving increased attention from tourist marketers and is changing very rapidly as a result of the increased attention, technology, and other environmental forces.

References

Burke, James F., and Lisa A. Lindblom. 1989. Strategies for evaluating direct response tourism marketing. *Journal of Travel Research* 28(2):233–237.

Evans, Joel R., and Berry Berman. 1990. *Marketing.* New York: Macmillan.

First, Sharon Efroymson. 1988. Videos' lure proves seeing is believing. *Advertising Age* 59(18):523–524.

Gladwell, Nancy J., and Robert M. Wolff. 1989. An assessment of the effectiveness of press kits as a tourism promotion tool. *Journal of Travel Research* 27(4):49–51.

Kotler, Philip, and Gary Armstrong. 1989. *Principles of Marketing.* Englewood Cliffs, N.J.: Prentice-Hall.

Lewis, Robert C., and Thomas J. Beggs. 1988. Selling Bermuda in the off-season. In *The Complete Travel and Marketing Handbook,* ed. Andrew Vladimir, pp. 101–108. Lincolnwood, Ill.: NTC Business Books.

Pride, William M., and O. C. Ferrell. 1989. *Marketing: Concepts and Strategies.* Boston: Houghton Mifflin.

Strazewski, Len. 1989. Destination: U.S. *Advertising Age* 60(4):S1–S2.

Zeithmal, Carl P., and Barry D. Baysinger. 1981. *Barriers to Corporate Growth.* Lexington, Mass.: Lexington Books.

31

Advertising in Tourism and Travel: Tourism Brochures

Graham M. S. Dann

The promotion of tourist destinations assumes a variety of forms. McIntosh and Goeldner (1984), for instance, identify several types of advertising in magazines and Sunday supplements, on radio, television and billboards, and via direct mail. In addition, there is sales promotion at travel shows, publicity through documentaries and special features, an abundance of sales literature comprising guidebooks, posters, and maps, and campaigns ranging from bumper stickers to personal telephone calls. According to these authors, the aim of such promotion is to elicit further inquiries about a destination area and to project its appropriate image. Generally, a two-stage process is also envisaged: arousing sufficient interest in the target group (passive phase) and following up with more detailed material once that interest has sparked a request for additional information (active phase).

However, a far more ubiquitous device used by tour operators attempts to collapse the procedure into one active stage, namely the tourist brochure (Buck 1977). Now, in one or more glossy volumes, potential tourists (who have already taken the step of procuring the material themselves), can exercise their choice with respect to competing destinations and from a variety of resorts within the selected destination. The need for further information is reduced by pictorial content and associated commentary, but can be supplemented if necessary at the point of sale—the travel agent. Since brochures are so widespread and effective, and given that they attempt to woo, seduce, inform, project, and sell in one operation, they undoubtedly represent tourism advertising par excellence. For this reason they constitute the principal focus of this brief presentation.

Advertising Tourism and Other Products

If, for the sake of argument, tourism is considered purchasable like any other commodity, then certain similarities can be seen to occur with respect to the advertising of a product (Dann, 1988b). First, the language of the appeal is in the future perfect tense. The targeted persons, while gazing at the pictures and reading the accompanying blurb, project themselves into the future

893

and, on reflection, envision themselves as already having participated in the various associated activities. The plate of untasted delicious lobster, the tempting crystal blue ocean and waving palm trees, the beckoning dusky maiden, pull the voyeurs into the picture and end up selling to them their newly identified selves (Williamson 1983). In this respect, travel advertising is no different from the creation of a new person through the power of beauty cream, deodorants or a sports car. The *projection* into the future becomes transformed into a personal *project* or plan.

Second, at the stage of reflection, individuals measure this intended course of action by reference to the past. If on other occasions they have found, either directly or vicariously, similar situations to be rewarding, this is usually sufficient reason to repeat such "approach behavior." This will be so whether one is purchasing a tropical island vacation or a silk dress. Memory is thus brought into play, complete with its array of collective representations, as a checking device for what remains unsampled. Hence the future becomes added to the past and the tense of the advertisement blends into the future perfect.

Third, the above situation is further achieved by elimination of the present. Here the attractiveness of the product is enhanced with the realization that current circumstances are inherently dissatisfying and that they can be ameliorated. The "once I was . . . , but now thanks to . . ." formula can be just as easily applied to the attractions of an exotic destination replacing the tedium of everyday existence as to the beneficial effects of a diet improving the flabby condition of an overweight individual. Hence the typical example of comparative temperature charts in many cold climate brochures featuring sunny destinations.

However, tourism is not just a product, not even a complex array of products. Unlike a commodity, tourism cannot be evaluated by the senses prior to purchase. Nor does it simply represent a series of services formed into a chainlike system. Tourism is something extra. It is more in the nature of manifold experiences, several of which are intangible, corresponding to a set of motives, many of which are deep-lying and difficult to articulate. The language of tourism advertising deals not so much with place but with the selected images of a destination. It speaks less of the filtered attractions of the resort than to those personality characteristics that correspond with them. Finally, tourism is a people to people phenomenon. It has to do with encounters, which, seen in their most optimistic light, can lead to greater international understanding, certainly a far cry from product advertising.

Brochures and Authenticity

One debate that has figured prominently in the academic treatment of tourism is that focusing on the authenticity of touristic experiences. Without tracing the development of this intellectual cut and thrust, one can nevertheless pinpoint three basic positions. The first, articulated by Boorstin (1961) and his followers, adopts a critical stance toward tourism, to the extent that it portrays the tourist as a cultural dope, a purveyor of inauthentic experiences provided by a cynical tourism establishment. The second, by way of reaction, advocates a neo-Durkheimian viewpoint. It argues that tourism is a quasi-religious quest of modern secular man as pilgrim in the search for his identity through (w)holy authentic experiences in the Other (see, for example Graburn 1989; MacCannell 1976). The third assumes a midway position, arguing that there are essentially four possibilities generated from the nature of the experience (authentic or otherwise) and how it is perceived (authentic or otherwise) (see, for example Cohen 1979b). Generally speaking, the further one moves away from mass tourism and the familiar toward existential tourism and strangeness, the more likely it will be phenomenologically to encounter the authentic (Cohen 1979a).

The foregoing standpoints can be related to travel brochures. A number of commentators stress the inauthenticity of such material. Britton (1979), for instance, maintains that it provides distorted images of developing countries when it refers to them in such terms as "paradise" or "unspoilt." Adams (1984) further believes that the industry, by concentrating on select cultural markers (for example, funeral celebrations and buffalo sacrifices in Sulawesi, Indonesia), is in fact supplying ethnic stereotypes as indices of authenticity, a mental grid through which tourists are persuaded to filter their own perceptions. Even though these rarely depict the true life of a host society, nevertheless they are perceived on arrival as authentic by tourists thus prepared by the operator. Weightman (1987), in relation to package tours of India, reckons that these are artificial since they isolate tourists from reality, they only show one section of the country, and they emphasize monuments to the dead rather than concentrate on everyday life.

Buck (1977), on the other hand, while agreeing that brochures highlight front-stage events with a veneer of authenticity ("genuine," "real," "natural," "historical"), claims that they actually protect the back-stage regions (Goffman 1959) of the inhabitants from the prying eyes of visitors. Thus tourism among the Amish of Pennsylvania, for instance, can be seen as a blessing, so long as tourists are content to view representations of reality rather than seeking to penetrate reality itself.

Urbain (1989), in a more reflective vein, argues that it would be a mistake to conclude that tourism advertising simply treats its prospective clients as nitwits merely reacting to stimuli of basic needs without any choice. Rather its language is based on the narrating consciousness of the leisure traveler, (itself authentic), and this discourse is turned into action. In this sense, the language of promotion originates in the tourist, wherein enunciation overcomes self-confessed deficiency.

Push and Pull Factors

Due to the nature of competition, particularly with respect to developing countries vying for a slice of the tourism cake, there is often a perceived need by the destination authorities to highlight their attractions and to minimize their failures. In the hands of the tour operator a glossy brochure is produced that relies on the bliss formula of Eden images and pastoral myths. At the same time, it downplays poverty, foreigness, and the local people (Britton 1979, Dann 1988a, Dann 1988b, Mohamed 1988). Consequently, the emphasis is placed on the destination and the various sights and experiences it has to offer, that is, the pull factors of tourism. The potential tourist, in perusing the brochure and the various alternatives supplied therein, thus weighs the rival offerings and selects the one with the greatest pull.

However, many argue that this is only half the story. More specifically, they maintain that psychological push factors (without which there would be no travel at all), are both temporally and logically prior to pull factors (Dann 1977). Tourists are therefore not so much motivated by a given destination. Rather the destination is seen as a means towards the evocation or reinforcement of personal needs (Uzzell 1984), such as escape from a perceived mundane environment, exploration and evaluation of self, relaxation, prestige, regression, enhancement of kinship relationships and facilitation of social interaction (Crompton 1979). Under this perspective, the discourse of advertising relates primarily to the inner world of personality and seeks to match and call forth its features rather than accentuating those of a given place (Mayo and Jarvis 1981). Perhaps for this reason some argue that tourism can occur anywhere, so long as it takes people away from the home environment. After all, tourism is capable of transcending both time and space (Thurot and Thurot 1983).

Tourist Motivation

From the notion of push factors it is but a small step to the concept of motivation, that set of meanings and values which underpins and explains human behavior. Yet ironically, the study of motivation is one of the most under-researched areas in tourism studies. In attempting to fill the intellectual void, Pearce (1982) argues that, in order to reach a satisfactory basis for the analysis of tourist motivation, it is necessary to combine the elements of self-actualization, attribution, and achievement theories. Only in this way will it be possible to devise an explanatory scheme that both caters to a Maslowian need hierarchy and is capable of differentiating between short- and long-term goals. At the same time, it is important to identify the source of explanation and to decide whether this resides in the subject or the analyst.

A typical example of motivational analysis can be found in Moeran (1983). He maintains that, whereas Japanese tourists formerly seemed quite content to travel in groups and to take in various sights, today the accent is much more on the individual and on "skin participation." Coterminously, there has been a parallel switch in the discourse of brochure advertising and an emphasis on nature, ethnicity, self-discovery, and the status of long-haul travel, corresponding to a reordering of Japanese values.

Yet this example fulfils only the first of Pearce's (1982) criteria, since it simply addresses the Maslowian self-actualization component, without examining attribution or achievement. As a matter of fact, the analysis begins and ends with the brochure and researcher, overlooking the targets of the discourse and their "definitions of the situation." For a complete picture of motivation, argues Chalfen (1985), one needs to investigate the way brochures are put together and how they are understood, that is, through an "ethnographic semiotic approach" it is necessary to explore the cognitive processes of all participants.

Mayo and Jarvis (1981) make the same point somewhat differently. They believe that a person's mental picture is what affects destination choice. This in turn is based on selective perception or how individuals make sense of the world. The latter is derived from interpretation of stimulus, and that itself is grounded in personality, experiences, needs, motives, and mood. Thus, in order to obtain a complete understanding of this complex scenario, it is necessary to examine the combination of this last set of factors. At the same time, it should be noted that, whereas psychologists distinguish them as separate components, sociologists tend to merge them under the single concept of motivation.

Themes and Images

Britton (1979) accepts Gunn's (1972) distinction that images of a place can be said to be "organic" or "induced." While the latter evolves from the conscious effort of promotion, advertising, and publicity, the former is derived from more traditional sources, such as books and newspapers. Since so much of induced imagery, particularly in relation to Third World destinations, is replete with stereotype, and given that a great deal of organic imagery is frequently based on biased colonial accounts, many developing countries pursuing tourism as a path to development become aware of the need to set the record straight by mounting countercampaigns of their own. In the Caribbean, for example, there is often quite a real danger that violence, disregard for human rights, or even the effects of a hurricane on one island may come to be associated through the media with the entire region. The tourism authorities in both offending and nonoffending territories thus find themselves fighting a battle for survival and engaging in a costly image correction exercise.

What is clear to both parties, however, is that images and impressions are, in many senses, far more important than reality itself. An image is carefully compiled by selectively constructing those features of a destination that have the power to strike a resonant chord in the personalities of the target audience. A factual recital of everyday life in the host society would scarcely evoke the same response.

In assembling the image, several themes are employed to call forth the appropriate response in the potential tourist. Urbain (1989), for example, points out that two universal and complementary brochure themes are those of quest and escape. The former is often elaborated in terms of archetype and the appeal to basic needs. Thus the "eat, drink and be merry" formula of Club Med (Thurot and Thurot 1983) is issued as a moral imperative to escape the society of daily crisis and enter the destination of abandon.

Sometimes the appeal is addressed in a "back to nature" format. Here the imagery of grandiose mountains is often presented. In pursuing the cult of nature and conquest this can be attractive to the puritan ethic (according to which everything but hard work is sinful (Barthes 1984). Alternatively, a more hedonistic sexual connotation can be introduced by contrasting the majestic peaks with fertile valleys, an imagery which is frequently extended to encompass the host architecture of towers, domes, and even hotels (Dann 1989).

One of the most interesting themes, however, has been highlighted by Gottlieb (1982). According to her, since the principal characteristic of a vacation is inversion of everyday life, one can expect to find this differentially associated with social class. Hence the attraction for an upper or upper middle class traveler to be a peasant for a day and for one from the lower social echelons to be a king or a queen for a day.

Techniques of Persuasion

Uzzell (1984), basing himself on Barthes (1984), outlines six principal methods whereby advertisers use photographs and other pictorial representations to create the desired effects in their subjects. In the *trick effect* technique, the picture is altered in some way, often by superimposing one image on another, so as to bestow an additional meaning on the original. Through *pose*, the designer of brochures can present pictures in such a way as to evoke similarities between them and well-known works of art. The message now assumes an air of affluence and status enhancement for those who make the connection (Berger 1972). The symbolism can be further extended to include stereotypical expressions of male activity and "having" and of female passivity and "being" through representations of sexual power and games of mock assault (Goffman 1979). By means of *objects*, local inhabitants and their surrounding paraphernalia (for example, archimandrites, peasants in folk costume) can be introduced as stage props to add a touch of authenticity to the portrayed scene (Dann 1988b). In *photogenia*—photographic technology or the use of filters, lighting, and such—the connoted message is the image itself; in *aestheticism*, the artistic treatment signifies beauty and desirability; whereas in *syntax*, a collage of pictures is brought together to create a story or theme.

Williamson (1983) elaborates on the differential treatment of men and women in advertising. She maintains that, whereas in the portrayal of males the viewer is invited to *look with* the subject, where females are depicted they are to be *gazed at*. For this reason the latter normally stare out of the picture, and, although there may be various clues as to a male presence, the man himself is invisible. It thus becomes fairly simple for the male purveyor of brochures to identify with the invisible man and so become drawn into the scene. From this technique it is but a stone's throw to the presentation of a personless picture. The interior shot of an empty seat on the luxurious Orient Express, with a copy of the London Times, a pair of dark glasses and a pack of "pure gold" on the table, and an open carriage window leading out to a Venetian canalscape, has a similar effect of bringing the viewer in and then taking him out toward mystery and adventure.

Mayo and Jarvis (1981) allude to three other pervasive techniques. Under *comparison*, they provide the example of two competing airlines, Allegheny and Pan Am, the former in the picture nosing out the latter, with the caption "Did you know Allegheny is 2 million passengers bigger than Pan Am?" They claim the message is particularly effective since many Americans might have mistakenly believed that the U.S. flag carrier was much bigger than a national rival. With *perceptual omission*, they give the instance of "If you haven't seen Rhode Island, you haven't seen New England" to illustrate the usefulness of pointing out the deficiencies in the traveler's mental picture, and at the same time offering a solution to its completion. Finally, the authors highlight the technique of *inconsistency*. Here the advertiser places seemingly incongruous elements side by side (for example, a riding saddle and tennis balls), while providing the answer to the problem: "Saddle up for a super tennis clinic"—The Wickenburg Inn, Tennis and Guest Ranch.

Mohamed (1988) shows that there are additional verbal techniques that can be found in the commentary surrounding brochure pictures. In particular he highlights the strategy of "key wording." In relation to Morocco, for instance, certain expressions are played up which are estimated to be attractive to the potential visitor, for example, "Imperial Cities," "Souk," "Casbah," while others relating to the lives of the inhabitants are significantly omitted. Similarly, the country is portrayed as being green and thick with forests, conveniently forgetting that a substantial area is covered by the Sahara Desert.

The Discourse of Advertising

In order for advertisers to make their clients dissatisfied with their current circumstances and to seduce them with alternatives, it is first necessary to change the values from one system to another (Barthes 1984, Uzzell 1984). This is achieved principally through the language of signs. Here one encounters a *signifier*, the *signified*, and a *sign*, which combines the first two elements. The sign in turn can become a new signifier, leading to a different signified and a further sign (Williamson 1983). For instance, the bikini-clad girl clutching a bottle of wine (signifier) can signify the good life, and the combination yielding the sign of good lifeness. The latter in due course becomes signified in a holiday maker, but more specifically in a Medina holidaymaker (Uzzell 1984). However, it is important to realize that the meaning is supplied by the viewer and that there may well be more than one definition of the situation. In the above example, the wine, for instance, can represent a relaxing of inhibitions and the girl may be interpreted in terms of sexual arousal. The skillful operator will be able to gauge the range of interpretations and to match these with various market segments. In this sense, Williamson (1983:14) is surely correct when she argues that, since advertisements have no subject, we become listener and speaker, subject and object; we fill the gap.

Alternately stated, Weightman (1987:230) maintains that the advertisement becomes a self-fulfilling prophecy, (or tautology, Buck 1977), since the brochure directs expectations and influences perceptions, thereby providing a preconceived landscape for the tourist "to discover".

One of the ways that the discourse of advertising shapes and molds the target's definition of the situation is by the use of superlatives. Another is by asterisking various sights, monuments, routes, and restaurants which the traveler *must* see and experience (Gritti 1967).

Thurot and Thurot (1983) believe that the signs portrayed in the discourse are ideologically grounded, just as Veblen (1899) had shown that conspicuous consumption was itself a sign of social status. Travel now becomes something more than the fulfillment of a need—it has social signification. According to them, it is therefore most important to discover who produces the code for the interpretation of these signified messages. In answer to this rhetorical question they provide a number of models that essentially involve center-periphery communication from aristocratic and intellectual elites whom would-be travelers, consciously or unwittingly, try to emulate. Naturally this is a difficult task since the elites dictate the pace. Moreover, through their affluence and connections, they can decide which resorts are fashionable, what is in and what is out, how long a destination should last, and to whom they will permit entry.

Finally, and by way of corollary to the previous position, there are those who emphasize that the discourse of advertising is also a language of social control (Dann 1989). Now it is the operator who holds the aces and who very much determines the terms under which destinations are to be promoted and exactly whom to target for maximum profit. Since controlling the host society is a relatively simple task, especially Third World destinations dependent on tourism (Britton 1979), the operator can now direct attention more fully toward the visitor. One very effective way of achieving this goal is to treat the tourist as a child, with the simple realization that "many of the primary motivations for pleasure travel are clearly motivations which reside in the child ego state" (Mayo and Jarvis 1981:136). Indeed, an application of transactional analysis to brochures (Dann 1989) reveals that much of the discourse of promotional literature can be related to various stages of the socialization process (protection and security, satisfaction of biological needs, learning to walk, learning to talk, play and games).

Summary

Although tourism advertising assumes many forms, the brochure is one of the most pervasive and efficient means of advertising at the tour operator's disposal.

Through the brochure it is not so much a product that is promoted as a set of images, which in turn portray those selected features of a destination that correspond to the personality characteristics of the target audience.

Although many of the projected images are distorted, stereotypical, and inauthentic, they very much depend for their success in paralleling touristic definitions of situations. In some senses also, the staged attractions can actually protect a host community from visitor penetration.

For travel advertisements to be truly effective they must deal with push factors and deep seated touristic motivation, rather than simply describing the offerings of a given resort. Furthermore, analysis of the motivational appeal is all the more complex with the appreciation that its vocabulary is often difficult to articulate.

Various themes and images were outlined, as well as examples of techniques of persuasion and types of promotional discourse.

In many ways, throughout this article the brochure creator comes across as someone rather unpleasant, as a person who attempts to "mystify the mundane, amplify the exotic, minimize the misery, rationalize the disquietude and romanticize the strange" (Weightman 1987:229). His master, the tourism industry, "produces information that too often depicts places as unreal and demeans their inhabitants . . . (information which) is not simply harmless propaganda, but adversely affects the tourist receiving society and the quality of the travel experience" (Britton 1979:319). Advertisers thus appear as grand conspirators, as exploiters, as molders of hapless tourist motivation and peddlers of fantasy.

But is this the whole story, and can the scenario be changed? The answer to this double-barrelled question is surely both no and yes respectively. Just as the cure for alcoholism resides in an admission of the failing, so too should the "unhooking" of a tourist become easier to tackle once there is an appreciation of the various forces at work. It has been the purpose of this essay to present a familiarization of these forces. At the same time, it should be fairly apparent that, if authorities in destination areas wish to rectify false images of their lands and peoples, they should see to it that they produce their own promotional material.

References

Adams, K. 1984. Come to Tana Toraja, 'Land of the heavenly kings'. Travel agents as brokers in ethnicity. *Annals of Tourism Research* 11:469–485.

Barthes, R. 1984. *Mythologies*. London: Paladin.

Berger, J. 1972. *Ways of Seeing*. Harmondsworth: Penguin.

Boorstin, D. 1961. *The Image. A Guide to Pseudo Events in America*. New York: Harper & Row.

Britton, R. 1979. The image of Third World tourism in marketing. *Annals of Tourism Research* 6:318–329.

Buck, R. 1977. The ubiquitous tourist brochure: explorations in its intended and unintended use. *Annals of Tourism Research* 4:195–207.

Chalfen, R. 1985. An alternative to an alternative: comment on Uzzell. *Annals of Tourism Research* 12:103–106.

Cohen, E. 1979a. A phenomenology of tourist experiences. *Sociology* 13:179–201.

Cohen, E. 1979b. Rethinking the sociology of tourism. *Annals of Tourism Research* 6:18–35.

Crompton, J. 1979. Motivations for pleasure vacation. *Annals of Tourism Research* 6:408–424.

Dann, G. 1977. Anomie, ego-enhancement and tourism. *Annals of Tourism Research* 4:184–194.

Dann, G. 1988a. The people of tourist brochures. Paper read at First Global Conference, Tourism a Vital Force for Peace, 23–27 October 1988, at Vancouver Trade and Convention Centre, Vancouver, B.C.

Dann, G. 1988b. Images of Cyprus projected by tour operators. *Problems of Tourism* 11:43–71.

Dann, G. 1989. The tourist as child : some reflections. *Cahiers du Tourisme* série C, no. 135.

Goffman, E. 1959. *The Presentation of Self in Everyday Life*. Garden City: Doubleday.

Goffman, E. 1979. *Gender Advertisements*. London: Macmillan.

Gottlieb, A. 1982. American's vacations. *Annals of Tourism Research* 9:165–187.

Graburn, N. 1989. Tourism the sacred journey. In *Hosts and Guests. The Anthropology of Tourism*, ed. V. Smith, pp. 21–36. Philadelphia: University of Pennsylvania Press.

Gritti, J. 1967. Les contenus culturels du Guide Bleu : monuments et sites à voir. *Communications* 10:51–64.

Gunn, C. 1972. *Vacationscape*. Austin: Bureau of Business Research, University of Texas.

McIntosh, R., and C. Goeldner. 1984. *Tourism: Principles, Practices, Philosophies*. Columbus, Ohio: Grid Publ.

MacCannell, D. 1976. *The Tourist. A New Theory of the Leisure Class*. New York: Schocken.

Mayo, E., and L. Jarvis. 1981. *The Psychology of Leisure Travel. Effective Marketing and Selling of Travel Services*. Boston: CBI.

Moeran, B. 1983. The language of Japanese tourism. *Annuals of Tourism Research* 10:93–108.

Mohamed, M. 1988. Moroccan tourism image in France. *Annals of Tourism Research* 15:588–561.

Pearce, P. 1982. *The Social Psychology of Tourist Behaviour*. Oxford: Pergamon.

Thurot, J., and G. Thurot. 1983. The ideology of class and tourism: confronting the discourse of advertising. *Annals of Tourism Research* 10:173–189.

Urbain, J. 1989. The tourist adventure and his images. *Annals of Tourism Research* 16:106–118.

Uzzell, D. 1984. An alternative structuralist approach to the psychology of tourism marketing. *Annals of Tourism Research* 11:79–99.

Veblen, T. 1899. *Theory of the Leisure Class*. New York: Macmillan.

Weightman, B. 1987. Third World tour landscapes. *Annals of Tourism Research* 14:227–239.

Williamson, J. 1983. *Decoding Advertisements*. New York: Marion Boyars.

32

Psychographic Segmentation

Russell E. Brayley

The success of the tourism and hospitality industry depends on its ability to appropriately respond to consumer needs and wants. Obviously, the industry must become aware of those needs and wants in order to satisfy them. Such an awareness is an important part of the broader responsibility that providers of touristic experiences have with respect to understanding their markets. In addition to being aware of tourist needs and wants, tourism and hospitality service providers must understand the opportunities and constraints that impinge on consumption as well as recognize the many lifestyle and other differences that exist between specific groups of consumers.

Where significant differences are identified between measurable, accessible, and meaningful groups of consumers in the population, there is potential for market segmentation. Market segmentation involves defining groups of individuals by using a variety of key descriptors. Thus defined, these groups are generally referred to as "target markets." Crompton (1983:8) defines a target market as "a relatively homogeneous group of people having relatively similar service preferences, with whom an agency seeks to exchange." The descriptors that have been used to define tourism and hospitality market segments include personal demographics (Woodside and Pitts 1976, Graham and Wall 1978, Gentry and Doering 1979), distance between destination and origin (Etzel and Woodside 1982), trip destination (Scott et al. 1978), search behavior (Darden and Perreault 1975, Schul and Crompton 1983), means of travel (Hawes 1978), and psychographics (Plog 1974, Perreault et al. 1977, New South Wales Tourism Commission 1984, van Raaij and Francken 1984, Brayley 1990, Gladwell 1990). There is no apparent consensus in the tourism and hospitality literature on the most appropriate of effective way to segment the modern travel market. In practice, each of the approaches discussed in the literature finds application and a degree of acceptance.

By far, the most common segmentation criterion in use is demographics. Demographic descriptors include such characteristics as sex, age, income, education, occupation, ethnic origin, and household size. Market segments identified using demographic characteristics are easy to measure and are generally accessible, but their description lacks richness (that is, no insight is offered with respect to values, motivation, activity, interests, or lifestyle variations). For example, a young, single, well-educated male market segment may be easy to identify but we do not necessarily know what these consumers want and need, nor do we know what will get this population to consume a particular tourism product. Demographics do not tell the tourism and hospitality marketer if the target segment is thrifty, gregarious, adventurous, or independent. Knowing these characteristics would greatly assist the marketer in designing, pricing, scheduling, and promoting touristic experiences. Many tourism and hospitality researchers and marketers have recognized the need for richer information about their study populations and have taken an interest in psychographics as a basis for market segmentation and comparison in their research.

Psychographics is the measurement and description of motivation, lifestyle, and personality dimensions that relate to consumer behavior. It reveals the face behind the demographic mask or, as pioneering psychographics researcher Stanley Plog (1987) suggests, it provides the "inside the skin" look at travelers that enables us to understand why they do what they do and what they want from managers and providers of the touristic experience. Whereas demographics tells us what the market looks like, psychographics tells us what we need to know to appeal to the market and be successful in winning the opportunity to satisfy its needs and wants. It tells us about consumers' activities (how they spend their time), interests (what is important to them), opinions (their view of themselves with respect to the world around them), and some basic characteristics that relate directly to consumer behavior (age, income, residence location, family life stage, etc.) (Schewe and Calantone 1978).

The researcher and marketer do not have to choose one set of consumer information over the other. Both demographics and psychographics offer useful views of the market. In fact, when combined with demographic data, psychographic data provide a substantially richer profile of more appropriately segmented groups of tourists (Tigert et al. 1971).

How Psychographic Information Is Used

Because psychographic segmentation identifies groups of individuals with similar motivations, values, and attitudes, tourism and hospitality marketers can make decisions about product features, pricing, distribution, and promotion with those motivations, values, and attitudes in mind. The marketer is thereby well equipped to recognize and attempt to satisfy the target market needs and respond to its consumption preferences.

For example, in developing the tourism or hospitality product psychographics can be used to create an experience that is appropriately positioned within the consumer's frame of positive reference. In promoting that well-designed product, the advertising manager can use the information gained from psychographic profiling to ensure that the message and its style, setting, mood, and language are consistent with the interests and tastes of the intended audience.

How Psychographic Segments Are Defined

Psychographic profiles are developed using data gathered through a questionnaire instrument. The questionnaire usually provides for response to a large number of statements about activities, interests, and opinions (AIOs) and is ideally administered to geographically dispersed samples of 1,000 subjects or more. Numerous psychographic batteries exist, but few are in the public domain because they were developed for use in proprietary research. Some of the instruments that are in the public domain enjoy more widespread use than others, but there is currently no psychographic measurement instrument recognized as the standard in tourism and hospitality research.

The data collected through such questionnaires are then subjected to factor analysis. Factor analysis is a statistical procedure designed to reduce and summarize data and to identify a set of dimensions that are not easily observed (Hair et al. 1984). The procedure helps to collapse the large number of AIO statements into a few related groups (primary factors) which are then labeled by the researcher. There are no formal protocols for labeling and the researcher is free to use his or her creativity in this endeavor. These labeled factors are referred to as psychographic classes. Other statistical procedures (mostly cluster analysis and multiple discriminant analysis) are then used to define the points at which an individual is classified in one psychographic group or another. Cluster analysis identifies groups of individuals who exhibit a high degree of internal homogeneity and a high degree of external heterogeneity with respect to their psychographic classification. Multiple discriminant analysis is a statistical procedure that can also be used to identify significantly different clusters of individuals. It is particularly useful for determining which psychographic dimensions account for the greatest difference between clusters of individuals (Hair et al. 1984). Table 1 illustrates some of the many ways in which psychographic segments have been defined and labeled in published tourism and hospitality research.

Examples of Applied Psychographic Segmentation

The tourism and hospitality literature makes reference to numerous research efforts in which psychographic segmentation has been attempted. Several have been identified in Table 1 and referenced at the end of this entry. In order to promote a greater understanding of the nature and potential use of psychographics in market segmentation, three interesting projects (two of which are very specific to tourism and hospitality) are described here.

Plog's Allocentric/Psychocentric Model Perhaps the best known research in tourism and hospitality that uses psychographics as the basis of market segmentation is that of Stanley Plog. In 1974 Plog described a personality dimension called centrism (meaning personal focus or interest) and suggested that the traveling population could be classified along a continuum with allocentrics at one extreme and psychocentrics at the other.

Allocentrics are described as individuals who have a wide range of interests and activities. Allocentrics are more adventurous, outgoing, and self-confident, and they are motivated to travel by a desire to experience novelty, challenge, power, and learning. Only about 3 percent of the American population is purely allocentric.

Psychocentrics are at the other end of the centrism continuum and they too represent about 3 percent of the population. By definition, a psychocentric is an individual who focuses on his or her own narrow range of interests and activities, is self-inhibited, nervous, and nonadventuresome. Psychocentrics are motivated to travel by status and conformity, and are most likely to choose destinations and hospitality services that are familiar, socially acceptable, and safe.

Most individuals would, according to Plog, be classified as near-allocentrics, mid-centrics, or near-psychocentrics. As illustrated in Figure 1,

Table 1. *Psychographic segments identified in selected tourism and marketing research*

Researcher(s)	Psychographic segments	
Ziff 1971	Self-indulgents Contented cows Worriers	Outgoing optimists Conscientious vigilantes Apathetic indifferents
Plog 1974	Allocentrics Near-allocentrics Mid-centrics	Near-psychocentrics Psychocentrics
SRI 1978 (VALS)	Survivors Sustainers Belongers Emulators Achievers	I-am-me's Experientials Socially conscious Integrateds
SRI 1988 (VALS 2)	Actualizers Fulfilleds Believers Achievers	Strivers Experiencers Makers Strugglers
Lastovicka and Bonfield 1979	Positivism–self-confidence Liberalism-cosmopolitanism Frustration Home-family orientation Community involvement	
Goldberg 1981	Health concerned Swingers Social responsibility Conservatives Independent leaders	Cosmopolitan sophisticates Passive sports enthusiasts Outdoors enthusiasts Constant feeders Drinkers
NSW Tourism Commission 1984	New enthusiasts Anti tourist Dedicated Aussies	Stay at home Big spenders New indulgers
Mazanec 1984	Versatile comfort seekers Water and sun lovers Walking tourists	
Perrault et al. 1977	Budgeters Adventurers Home bodies Vacationers Moderates	
Gladwell 1990	Knowledgeable travelers Budget-conscious travelers Travel planners	

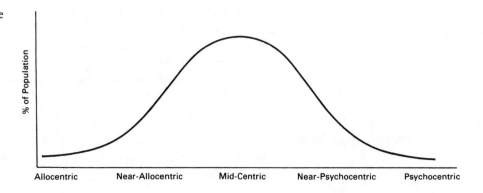

Fig. 1. Distribution of the U.S. population along the centrism continuum. *(Source: S. Plog, 1974, Why destination areas rise and fall in popularity, The Cornell Hotel and Restaurant Administration Quarterly 14(4):55–58.)*

the U.S. population is thought to be normally distributed along the centrism continuum.

Plog developed a simple five-item questionnaire that provides all the necessary data to indicate an individual's position along the centrism continuum. Repeated use of the instrument has established its statistical reliability, but some questions concerning validity remain (Plog 1987, Smith 1990). Regardless, the model continues to be used in segmentation activities and is widely cited in tourism and hospitality textbooks (Mathieson and Wall 1982; Gee et al. 1984; Murphy 1985; Mill and Morrison 1985; McIntosh and Goeldner 1986; Gunn 1988; Ritchie and Goeldner 1987).

VALS

A different psychographic segmentation scheme that is very popular in other industries and also has relevance to tourism and hospitality is Values and Lifestyles (VALS) (Shih 1986). VALS was developed in 1978 by SRI International (Mitchell 1981). In its original form, VALS classified consumers according to cultural values and identified those individuals who were (1) need-driven, (2) outer-directed, (3) inner-directed, and (4) combined outer-inner directed. Accordingly, nine psychographic segments or lifestyle types were differentiated and used to describe expected consumer behaviors. Need-driven individuals were classified as having either a survivor or sustainer lifestyle, outer-directed individuals were belongers, emulators, or achievers, and inner-directed individuals lived what were called I-am-me, experiential, or societally conscious lifestyles. The integrated lifestyle applied to the combined inner- and outer-directed group of individuals.

In 1989 VALS was revisited by SRI International researchers and important changes to the system were made. VALS 2 (as the new system is called) suggests that people are either principle-oriented (guided in their choices by beliefs or principles), status-oriented (heavily influenced by the actions, approval, and opinions of others), or action-oriented (guided by a desire for social or physical activity, variety, and risk taking). In consideration of the resources (education, income, self-confidence, health, eagerness to buy, intelligence, energy level) that these types of consumers might draw upon, VALS 2 identifies eight market segments and labels them Fulfilleds, Believers, Actualizers, Achievers, Strivers, Strugglers, Experiencers, and Makers.

As consumers of touristic experiences and hospitality services, Actualizers, Strivers, and Experiencers are more interested in variety, novelty, "upscaleness," excitement, and risk. Their respective abilities to support these interests vary due to resource limitations that are different for each segment. Their motivations, values, and attitudes, however, are very similar. Fullfilleds, Believers, Achievers, Makers, and Strugglers share an interest in predictability, stability, and security. Their travel and recreation choices are likely to be conservative and practical, and they are more likely to use domestic (American) products.

Both VALS and VALS 2 have been used extensively by marketers in a variety of industries. Because of the insights that VALS 2 offers about its psychographic segments, this segmentation approach can be valuable to tourism and hospitality marketers in catering and appealing to groups with specific interests, service expectations, and purchasing power.

Gladwell's Indiana State Park Study

A more recent study that employed psychographic analysis was conducted by Nancy Gladwell (1990). To understand users of state park inns, Gladwell modified a questionnaire developed by Perrault et al. (1977) and generated profiles of three distinct travel market segments. She labeled them Knowledgeable Travelers, Budget-Conscious Travelers, and Travel Planners.

The profiles described activity preferences, interests, and opinions (based on responses to 87 AIOs), general predisposition lifestyle characteristics (also based on responses to AIOs), and socio-demographic features of the segments. To better appreciate the richness of the information provided by the combination of psychographic and demographic analysis, consider Gladwell's description of the Budget-Conscious Traveler:

> Psychographic profile: Representing 32.46% of the total sample, these people were concerned about the cost of their vacation travel. They demonstrated no interest in educational, historical or tour travel. Little or no interest was shown for camping of any type, sports participation, or sports spectating as part of their vacations. The people in this group were not gregarious about their travel but did possess a moderate interest in vacation travel.
>
> Socio-demographic and general predisposition lifestyle characteristics: The budget-conscious travelers had lower income and educational levels than the other two groups. They also had the fewest individuals employed in professional/administrative jobs. In addition, these individuals had less interest in the arts and in widening their horizons. They were also lowest in their predisposition to use credit. These findings seem to be consistent with an economic orientation in their vacation activities. (Gladwell 1990:17)

Armed with such detailed information about potential customers and guests, marketers in tourism and hospitality are more able to make sound decisions and to properly direct their creative efforts toward the satisfaction of consumer needs and the realization of corporate objectives.

Limitations of Psychographics

Although psychographics offer the developer and marketer richer information than is available from more traditional approaches to market segmentation, there are some limitations to keep in mind. The two most important concerns are discussed here.

Accessibility A major limitation of psychographics lies in the problem of accessibility of the psychographically defined target markets. To illustrate this limitation, consider a target market that is defined by some demographic feature such as age. There are numerous ways to identify different age groups within a population and there are numerous ways to isolate them for marketing purposes. Now consider a target market that is defined by a psychographic feature such as centrism. Without applying a measurement instrument (questionnaire) to each individual in the population, it is practically impossible to separate allocentrics from psychocentrics and to concentrate marketing efforts for either group. This limitation can, however, be minimized by the combination of demographics and psychographics in segment profiling and by the inclusion of relevant behavioral variables (such as print media preference) in psychographic batteries.

Stability Another limitation of psychographics as a segmentation approach is the potential instability of the segments. While demographic characteristics either do not change (females are always going to be females) or change relatively slow (it takes a while for a middle-age person to become a senior citizen), motivations, values, and attitudes (as expressed through questionnaires) may change dramatically according to situations and within shorter periods of time (MacIntosh and Goeldner 1986). The solution to this problem lies in the development and use of good questionnaires that measure primary motivations and underlying values and attitudes rather than temperamental predilections and emotional dispositions. In other words, the instrument used in psychographic measurement must be both valid and reliable.

Summary

If the tourism and hospitality marketer wishes to influence consumer behavior, concerted effort must be applied to the understanding of those personality dimensions, motivations, and lifestyle characteristics that are directly related to the travel choices and activities of specific market segments. Psychographics offers rich data that contribute to this understanding. It provides a view of "what makes a person tick" and facilitates the orientation of products, services, and promotion efforts towards satisfaction of consumer wants and needs. While some refinement of the psychographics approach to market segmentation is warranted, the approach nonetheless contributes to advanced understanding and improved marketing effectiveness.

References

Brayley, R. E. 1990. *An Analysis of Destination Attractiveness and the Use of Psychographics and Demographics in Segmentation of the Within-State Tourism Market.* Unpublished Ph. D. dissertation. College Station, Texas: Texas A&M University.

Crompton, J. L. 1983. Selecting target markets—a key to effective marketing. *Journal of Parks and Recreation Administration* 1(1):7–27.

Darden, W. R., and W. D. Perrault, Jr. 1975. A multivariate analysis of media exposure and vacation behavior with life style covariates. *Journal of Consumer Research* 2(2):93–103.

Etzel, M. J., and A. G. Woodside. 1982. Segmenting vacation markets: the case of the distant and near-home travelers. *Journal of Travel Research* 20(4):10–14.

Gee, C. Y., D. J. Choy, and J. C. Mackens. 1984. *The Travel Industry.* Westport, Conn.:AVI.

Gentry, J., and M. Doering. 1979. Sex role orientation and leisure. *Journal of Leisure Research* 11:102–111.

Gladwell, N. 1990. A psychographic and sociodemographic analysis of state park inn users. *Journal of Travel Research* 28(4):15–20.

Goldberg, S. M. 1981. An empirical study of lifestyle correlates to brand loyal behavior. *Advances in Consumer Research* 9:456–460.

Graham, J., and G. Wall. 1978. American visitors to Canada: a study in market segmentation. *Journal of Travel Research* 16:21–24.

Gunn, C. A. 1988. *Tourism Planning,* 2nd ed. New York: Taylor and Francis.

Hair, J. F., R. E. Anderson, and R. L. Tatham. 1984. *Multivariate Data Analysis,* 2nd ed. New York: Macmillan.

Hawes, D. 1978. Empirically profiling four recreational vehicle market segments. *Journal of Travel Research* 16:13–20.

Lastovicka, J. L., and E. H. Bonfield. 1979. Exploring the nomological validity of lifestyle types. *Advances in Consumer Research* 7:466–472.

McIntosh, R. W., and C. R. Goeldner. 1986. *Tourism: Principles, Practices and Philosophies,* 5th ed. New York: Wiley.

Mathieson, A., and G. Wall. 1982. *Tourism: Economic, Physical and Social Impacts.* New York: Longman Scientific.

Mazanec, J. A. 1984. How to detect travel market segments: A clustering approach. *Journal of Travel Research* 23(1):17–20

Mill, R. C., and A. M. Morrison. 1985. *The Tourism System.* Englewood Cliffs, N.J.: Prentice-Hall.

Mitchell, A. 1981. *Changing Values and Lifestyles.* Menlo Park, Calif.: SRI International.

Murphy, P. E. 1985. *Tourism: A Community Approach.* New York: Methuen.

New South Wales Tourism Commission. 1984. *The Customer Connection: Travel '84 General Report on Market Segmentation.* Sydney: New South Wales Tourism Commission.

Perreault, W. D., D. K. Darden, and W. R. Darden. 1977. A psychographic classification of vacation life styles. *Journal of Leisure Research* 9(3):208–224.

Plog, S. 1974. Why destination areas rise and fall in popularity. *The Cornell Hotel and Restaurant Administration Quarterly* 14(4):55–58.

Plog, S. 1987. Understanding psychographics in tourism research. In *Travel, Tourism and Hospitality Research: A Handbook for Managers and Researchers,* ed. J. Ritchie and C. R. Goeldner, pp. 203–213. New York: Wiley.

Ritchie, J. and C. R. Goeldner, 1987. *Travel, Tourism and Hospitality Research: A Handbook for Managers and Researchers,* New York: Wiley.

Schewe, C. and R. Calantone. 1978. Psychographic segmentation of tourists. *Journal of Travel Research* 16(4):14–20

Schul, P. and J. L. Crompton. 1983. Search behavior of international vacationers: travel specific lifestyle and sociodemographic variables. *Journal of Travel Research* 22(2):25–30.

Scott, D. R., C. D. Schewe, and D. G. Frederick. 1978. A multi-brand/multi-attribute model of tourist state choice. *Journal of Travel Research* 17:23–29.

Shih, D. 1986 VALS as a tool of tourism market research: the Pennsylvania experience. *Journal of Travel Research* 24(3):2–11.

Smith, S. 1990. A test of Plog's allocentric/psychocentric model: evidence from seven nations. *Journal of Travel Research* 28(4):40–42.

SRI. 1978. The Values and Lifestyle Program. Described in A. Mitchell, 1983, *The Nine American Lifestyles.* New York: Macmillan.

SRI. 1988. The Values and Lifestyle Program. Described in J. Graham, 1989, New VALS 2 takes psychological route, *Advertising Age* (Feb. 13):22.

Tigert, D. J., R. Lathrope, and M. Bleeg. 1971. The fast food franchise: psychographic and demographic segmentation analysis. *Journal of Retailing* 47(1):81–90.

van Raaij, W. F. and D. A. Francken. 1984. Vacation decisions, activities and satisfactions. *Annals of Tourism Research* 11(2):101–112.

Woodside, A. G. and R. E. Pitts, 1976. Effects of consumer life styles, demographics and travel activities on foreign and domestic travel behavior. *Journal of Travel Research* 14(Winter):13–15.

Ziff, R. 1971. Psychographics for market segmentation. *Journal of Advertising Research* 11(April):3–10.

33

Linkages Between Agriculture and Tourism

Morton Fox and Linda J. Cox

An early perception of the linkage between agriculture and tourism in a tourism-based economy was one of two independent industries competing for scarce resources. Land, labor, and capital resources were seen as being diverted away from agriculture to the expanding visitor industry. At the 1974 West Indies Agricultural Economics Conference that examined the linkages between tourism and agriculture, several participants (Alleyne 1974, Brown 1974, Bryden 1974) reinforced this theory by presenting evidence that tourism had diverted labor from agriculture or had resulted in increased food imports.

More recently, it has been recognized that when tourism arrives at a primarily agrarian destination, numerous positive linkages can develop (Latimer 1985, Bowen, Cox, and Fox 1990). Tourism initially takes advantage of the roads, airports, utilities, and retail outlets that were developed to support agriculture. Then as tourism begins to flourish, it builds on the existing infrastructure and provides enhancements that benefit agriculture.

Agriculture, in support of the tourism industry, turns to new, higher-valued crops. The enhanced transportation capabilities provided to support tourism also improve the marketing options for agriculture. Agriculture services, such as landscaping, are expanded to meet the needs of the tourist industry. Agriculturally based leisure attractions such as farm tourism provide additional sources of income for farmers and alternative activities for visitors. The symbiotic relationship that develops between tourism and agriculture is best exemplified by the open spaces and attractive landscapes provided by agriculture and enjoyed by tourists.

Economic Linkages

Figure 1 is a simple diagram of the market linkages between agriculture and tourism. The initial competition between the agricultural sector and the visitor industry for resources is illustrated at the bottom of the diagram. As agriculture adjusts to the economic changes brought by the increasing flow of visitors from and back to the external economy, three important market link-

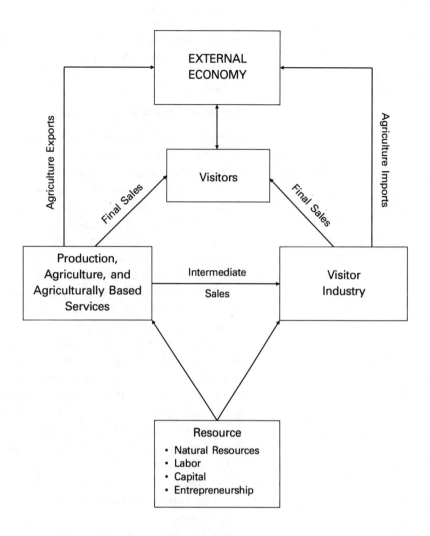

Fig. 1. Agriculture-tourism market linkages. *(Source: Richard L. Bowen, Linda J. Cox, and Morton Fox, Linkages between Agriculture and Tourism, 1990. Unpublished manuscript.)*

ages develop between the agricultural sector and the visitor industry: the flows of agricultural goods and services to the visitor industry, directly to visitors, and to the external economy.

Tourists are responsible for generating both direct and indirect demands for agricultural products and services. The types of commodities, processed products, and services generated by the agricultural sector will adjust to reflect the demands of visitors. For example, farmers may sell their goods directly to tourists at roadside stands where the products are packed for export or provide services such as nursery tours or trail rides to visitors.

Large quantities of agricultural goods and services are sold indirectly to visitors through the hotels, restaurants, and other service establishments that are part of the visitor industry. Food and beverage products are sold to the visitor industry through wholesalers or directly by food processors, although large farmers or farmer cooperatives may deal directly with hotels and restaurants. Flowers and landscaping services are used by the visitor industry to beautify the visitor infrastructure and to enhance the tourists' vacation experience.

Leakage of tourists' dollars out of the visitor destination's economy is experienced by many resort areas due to the large import of agricultural goods. The local agriculture industry may not be able to meet all the demands of the visitor industry for a consistent supply of quality products at competitive prices (Fox and Cox 1990). However, as farmers learn about modern agribusiness practices and the needs of the visitor industry, they will be able to compete more effectively with imports (Belisle 1983).

Agricultural Production and Tourism

Hermans (1981) discusses much of the early research examining the influence of tourism development on agriculture along the shores of the Mediterranean in the 1970s. Labor shortages and high land prices were perceived to be the consequences of tourism bringing at best problems and at worst disaster for agriculture. Research done over the same time period in the Caribbean also shows the decline in agriculture as a direct result of competition for land and labor brought about by tourism development (Belisle 1983). However, both Hermans and Belisle conclude that the relationship between tourism and agriculture is poorly understood and worthy of further study.

The decline of traditional crops in tourist destinations has been documented by a number of researchers (Valarche 1984, Tyrakowski 1986, Bowen et al. 1990), although Latimer (1985) and Bowen (1988) suggest that increased competition from other producers of these crops worldwide would have eventually brought about the same result. While foreign competition might have played a role in decreasing the production of traditional crops, farmers have adjusted to tourism-induced demand increases by producing more high valued specialty products. Bowen, Cox, and Fox (1990) report the increasing value of fresh pineapple, macadamia nuts, floriculture and nursery products, papayas, coffee, and guavas in the Hawaiian agricultural sector, and Hermans (1981) found an increase of the production of fruits and vegetables by farmers in Cambril, Spain.

As tourists consume the agricultural products during vacations, they may acquire new tastes. Studies by Scott and co-workers (Scott and Shehata 1980, Scott and Dik 1981, Scott et al. 1983, Scott and Sisson 1985, Scott et al. 1986) and Valarche (1984) indicate that the preferences of visitors were influenced by their trips and their consumption of products from the tourist destination increased after they returned home. In addition, the family and friends of the visitor might be exposed to these products. Consequently, the external economy presents a potential export market based on the visitors' exposure to the area's agriculture products.

Complementing this new export market is the fact that as a tourist destination's transportation system expands to support the travel industry, the capability to export agricultural goods improves. In addition to better service, tourist carriers may offer lower back haul rates for agricultural products. Garrod et al. (1982) found that exporters of agricultural products in Hawaii only paid the variable cost of transportation because the fixed costs are recovered from passengers and in-shipments.

Research indicates that the initial effects of tourism development will be demonstrated by the changing face of agricultural production. Higher value commodities will be produced as farmers find economic solutions to higher land and labor costs. However, this adjustment process may be difficult. Belisle (1983) and Thaman (1978) discuss adjustment problems stemming from the efficiency of the agricultural distribution system in the Caribbean and Fiji, respectively. Foodservice requires a consistent supply of high quality products, which small farmers experienced in commodity marketing rather than product merchandising, may have problems supplying. Belisle et al. (1982) report that in some cases problems with the marketing system may be large enough to prevent agriculture from responding to tourism demand. Other factors also affecting the relationship between production agriculture and tourism include natural conditions, the ability to produce the commodities desired by tourists, availability and price of imports, government policy, and the willingness of resource owners to take advantage of opportunities afforded agriculture by tourism (de Kadt 1979).

Agricultural Services and Tourism

Agriculture services in support of tourism are an important source of employment and income in tourism-based economies. With the notable exception of farm tourism, researchers have largely neglected this area. This neglect may be due to the traditional view of agricultural services as including only production activities or it may be because production activities are generally the first to respond to tourism development. Regardless, landscape services and agriculturally based leisure attractions are two types of agriculturally based services that can be directly linked to tourism.

Landscape Services — Landscape services are used to beautify the infrastructure of the visitor industry and represent an intermediate service, sold indirectly to tourists. Articles in the popular press and various trade journals indicate that enjoying landscapes is becoming an increasingly important leisure activity (Glass 1985; Doyle 1988; Gibbs 1988). This trend is expected to increase the demand for landscape services in areas heavily frequented by individuals, such as tourists, who have large amounts of leisure time.

There is no general consensus on what constitutes landscape services. The Horticultural Research Institute and the National Gardening Association (NGA) define them as the planning, construction, and planting of landscapes (Waldrop 1989). The U.S. Standard Industrial Classification (SIC) System broadens the NGA definition of landscape service to include maintenance and recognizes firms marketing these services as an agricultural industry group. Furthermore, the U.S. Department of Labor Statistics recognizes the provision of landscape services as an agricultural occupation.

The visitor industry may purchase landscape services from an agricultural service firm or landscape service professionals may be employed by members of the visitor industry. For example, large hotels and resorts often employ a staff to supply the landscape maintenance activities needed by the business rather than contracting the work out. The in-house employment of landscape service workers by the visitor industry represents a sizable linkage generally overlooked because the jobs are generated by nonagricultural firms.

Very little data are available on the market value of landscape service to the visitor industries throughout the world. Census data on the U.S. employment of the landscape service industry group are available over time, but nothing is available on in-house spending or employment for landscape services. The only data on gross receipts for the industry group in the United States were produced on a one-time basis and they indicate that the gross receipts of the group are the largest of the six agricultural service industry groups in the United States (U.S. Department of Commerce 1980).

In addition to the market linkages just discussed, landscape services also provide benefits to the visitor industry that cannot be measured in financial terms. Roberts and Roberts (1988) discussed the use of landscape services to provide a recreation area to make clients feel better, claiming that these services may be worth more to the visitor, in nonmarket terms, than previously estimated. No quantitative research has been done on the nonmarket values resulting from the use of landscape services.

Agriculturally Based Leisure Attractions

A workshop, held in May 1989, in Minneapolis entitled "Using Tourism and Travel as a Community and Rural Revitalization Strategy," recognized that a sizable portion of U.S. tourism revenues were due to the attractions of vast and beautiful natural resources, much of it accessed through many small rural communities. Honadle (1989) expounded on the opportunities that agriculture and natural resources provide tourists, such as free hunting, pick-your-own farms, camping, wildlife photography, whitewater rafting, and backpacking. Moyer (1989) discussed a set of successful business and community events in Wisconsin that were relatively unorganized but clearly involved agriculture and tourism. These included vacation farms, farmstead bed and breakfast operations, sales of produce to tourists at roadside stands, community festivals based on agricultural products, county fairs, and the international World Dairy Exposition.

The proceedings of the National Extension Workshop in the United States indicate many successful businesses and events are based in agriculture and attract tourists. The term "agriculturally based leisure attraction" was coined by Cox and Fox (1990) and defined as an enterprise that produces and/or processes plants or animals that also strives to attract visitors to enjoy the agricultural attributes of the operation and its site and/or purchase agricultural products produced or obtained by the enterprise. This definition encompasses a variety of operations.

It includes all enterprises that give tours of production and/or processing facilities and provide retail areas so that visitors can purchase products. A cut flower nursery and a coffee processing plant that provide informational tours and gift shops are examples of these types of attractions. The revenues generated by these operations are closely associated with a specific agricultural commodity. Other attractions provide tours of production or processing facilities that are no longer in operation; these attractions interest visitors because of their historical connection with agricultural commodities.

Farmers who invite visitors to stay at their farms for a fee also have the dual objectives of agricultural production and visitor attraction, which make the farms agriculturally based leisure attractions. In addition to farm tourism, many farms and ranches in the United States allow visitors to fish, hunt, or camp on their land for a fee. Much of the research on farm tourism has been done in Europe (Dernoi 1983; Frater 1983; Reisegg 1982), where this activity has developed rapidly over the past two decades.

In 1982 a five-day symposium on "Agriculture and Tourism" in Finland highlighted farm tourism as a promising possibility for integrating tourism and agriculture for the benefit of farmers and tourists and the development of rural areas. The symposium participants identified the positive aspects of farm tourism as (Report of the Symposium on Agriculture and Tourism 1982)

Additional employment and income for farmers

The use of vacant premises on farms

Increased possibilities for contacts with other groups and segments of the population and an improved understanding of agriculture and its problems by those people

The provision of facilities and comfort for tourists in the farmers' homes that results in improved standards of living for the farmers' families

It is difficult to establish a definitive point at which one attraction is based in agriculture and another is not. Stables and zoos do not produce or process agricultural commodities, but they do engage in animal production primarily to provide services to visitors. Some people may feel that zoos raise wild animals rather than domestic animals, but as zoos become involved in breeding programs, this distinction fades.

Other attractions covered by the definition by Cox and Fox include those that provide visitors with the opportunity to enjoy a landscape. Cox and Hollyer (1988) argue that because the design, installation, and/or maintenance of landscapes is an agricultural service that facilitates plant production, attractions that provide natural or artificial landscapes are agriculturally based. These attractions would include botanical gardens and parks, which are popular leisure spots throughout the world. Many private parks that provide access to natural and cultivated scenery also feature visitor activities that replicate integral parts of early agrarian cultures. In Hawaii, for example, a private park on the island of Oahu gives visitors the opportunity to string leis (necklaces made of various materials such as flowers, seeds, nuts, feathers, and so forth) and to see demonstrations of coconut harvesting and poi pounding (processing of taro root). Parks such as these would be defined as agriculturally based because scenic plants are maintained and because other agricultural commodities are produced for use in the attraction.

While agriculturally based leisure attractions offer potential to help develop favorable economic situations in rural regions, one of the main challenges is the need to adjust tourism and agriculture to ensure that the assets of each are not spoiled. Honadle (1989) noted also that some of agriculture's actions, such as cutting down scenic trees or spraying vegetation with noxious chemicals had a negative influence on visitors' destination decisions. The following negative aspects of farm tourism, identified at the Finland symposium, tended to grow in importance as tourism developed (Report of the Symposium on Agriculture and Tourism 1982):

There is competition for the land and labor resources such that agriculture degenerates.

The natural environment often is rather fragile in remote regions and does not tolerate heavy touristic activities without problems.

The peaks of the touristic season and the seasonable labor peaks in agriculture coincide.

Sometimes touristic activities on farms add mainly to the workload of the wives who are already overburdened.

The constant contact with tourists can lead to a loss of cultural traditions in rural regions.

As agriculturally based leisure attractions develop in rural areas, attention will need to be given to the potentially negative aspects of this relationship.

Common to all of these agriculturally based leisure attractions is the desire of the visitor to learn more about or experience aesthetic pleasure from agriculture. Many visitors are genuinely interested in the lifestyles and environments of the rural areas they are visiting. Agricultural activities in these areas may influence the visitor to stay longer or spend more and thereby play a role in meeting the economic objectives of the tourist destination areas.

Summary

The linkages between agriculture and tourism are more intricate than previously identified in literature. The tourist industry initially took advantage of the resources and infrastructure existing in a primarily agrarian location, and as it developed it enhanced the infrastructure and provided many additional resources for the agriculture industry to use. In addition, as a symbiotic relationship developed between agriculture and tourism, the visitor industry provided additional employment and income to farmers.

Encouraged to meet the requirements of the visitor industry, agriculture in tourist destinations changed from lower-valued plantation crops to higher-valued, fruits, vegetables and exotic crops resulting in greater income for farmers and an expanded export market. Agriculture continues to provide the open space and attractive landscapes vital to tourism.

An important new source of economic growth is found in the provision of agricultural services in support of tourism. Landscape services are required by large hotels and resorts to provide the beautiful ambience desired by tourists. Agriculturally based leisure attractions have been developed by farmers and large agribusinesses to offer more diverse activities for the visitors. Activities such as farm tourism allow farmers to earn extra income by fully utilizing their existing facilities and tourists, primarily from the city, are able to see farming up close.

An in-depth look at the linkages between agriculture and tourism has just begun. More comprehensive research on tourism-agriculture linkages in various tourist destination areas is needed to help clarify the overall relationship between the two industries.

References

Alleyne, F. A. 1974. The expansion of tourism and its concomitant unrealized potential for agricultural development in the Barbadian economy. In *Proceedings of the 9th West Indies Agricultural Economics Conference.* Nassau, Bahamas: University of the West Indies.

Belisle, Francois J. 1983. Tourism and food production in the Caribbean. *Annals of Tourism Research* 10:497–513.

Belisle, Francois J., S. B. Seward, and B. K. Spinard. 1982. Summary and conclusions. In *Tourism in the Caribbean; The Economic Impact,* eds. S. B. Seward and B. K. Spinard, pp. 151–163. Ottawa, Canada: International Development Research Centre.

Bowen, Richard L. 1988. The linkage between the agriculture and visitor industries: a new perspective on an old issue. In *Alternative Agricultural Enterprises For the Caribbean and Pacific Basins.* Miami: Institute of Food and Agricultural Science. University of Florida.

Bowen, Richard L., Linda J. Cox, and Morton Fox. 1990. Linkages Between Agriculture and Tourism. Unpublished manuscript.

Brown, Headley. 1974. The competition for resources and the market for food production in Jamaica. In *Proceedings of the 9th West Indies Agricultural Economics Conference.* Nassau, Bahamas: University of the West Indies.

Bryden, J. M. 1974. The competition for resources and food demand aspects. In *Proceedings of the 9th West Indies Agricultural Economics Conference.* Nassau, Bahamas: University of the West Indies.

Cox, Linda J., and James R. Hollyer. 1988. What is landscaping? *Hawaii Landscape Industry News* 2(5):18–19.

Cox, Linda J., and Morton Fox. 1990. Agriculturally Based Leisure Attractions. Unpublished manuscript.

de Kadt, Emmanuel. 1979. *Tourism—Passport to Development?* Oxford.

Dernoi, Louis A. 1983. Farm Tourism in Europe. *Tourism Management* 4(3):155–166.

Doyle, Margaret. 1988. Resort development boosts lodging. *Building Design & Construction.* 4(29):56–65.

Fox, Morton, and Linda J. Cox. 1990. Why Tourists' Dollars Leak Out of Hawaii's Economy (mimeo). Honolulu: University of Hawaii, School of Travel Industry Management.

Frater, Julia M. 1983. Farm tourism in England—Planning, funding, promotion and some lessons from Europe. *Tourism Management* 4(3):167–179.

Garrod, Peter, John Roecklein, Margarita Macario, and Walter Miklius. 1982. *Transportation Costs of Agricultural Products in Hawaii: 1980.* Hawaii Institute of Tropical Agriculture and Human Resources Information Text Series 003, p. 71. University of Hawaii.

Gibbs, Nancy. 1988. Paradise found. *Time* 131(25):62–81.

Glass, Joel. 1985. Designing hotels on a human scale. *Hotel & Resort Industry* 8(11):18–36.

Hermans, Dymphina. 1981. The encounter of agriculture and tourism: A Catalan case. *Annals of Tourism Research* 8(3):462–479.

Honadle, Beth Walter. 1989. Cooperative extension and tourism development. In *Proceedings of the National Extension Workshop,* pp. 45–50. Minneapolis, Minn.

Latimer, Hugh. 1985. Developing island economies—Tourism vs. agriculture. *Tourism Management* 6(1):32–42.

Moyer, Harriett. 1989. Ag-tourism—how to get it started in your state: Using tourism and travel as a community and rural revitalization strategy. *Proceedings of the National Extension Workshop,* pp. 116–119. Minneapolis, Minn.

Reisegg, F. 1982. Farm tourism in Norway. In *Proceedings of the Symposium on Agriculture and Tourism,* pp. 184–201. Mariehamn, Finland.

Report of the Symposium of Agriculture and Tourism. 1982. *Proceedings of the Symposium on Agriculture and Tourism,* pp. 2–11. Mariehamn, Finland.

Roberts, Eliot C., and Beverly C. Roberts. 1988. Lawn and Sport Turf Benefits. Pleasant Hill, Tenn.: The Lawn Institute.

Scott, Frank, Jr., and Ibrahim E. Dik. 1981. *Characteristics of Consumer Demand for Papaya Nectar in Portland, Oregon.* Hawaii Institute of Tropical Agriculture & Human Resources (HITAHR) Research Series 221. University of Hawaii.

Scott, Frank, Jr., and Sabry Shehata. 1980. *Characteristics of Consumer Demand for Fresh Pineapple.* HITAHR Research Series 243. University of Hawaii.

Scott, Frank, Jr. and John S. Sisson. 1985. Comparative Consumer Demand for Macadamia Nut Products in Honolulu and Los Angeles. In *Annual Proceedings of the Hawaii Macadamia Nut Association,* pp. 5–26. HITAHR. University of Hawaii.

Scott, Frank, Jr., Gorlal Osman, and Maurice Kanda. 1983. *Characteristics of Consumer Demand for Chocolate-Covered Macadamia Nuts.* HITAHR Research Series 024. University of Hawaii.

Scott, Frank, Jr., Margarita Marcario-Weidman, and John S. Sisson. 1986. *Characteristics of Consumer Demand for Fresh Papayas in Los Angeles and Orange Counties.* HITAHR Research Series 024. University of Hawaii.

Thaman, Randolph R. 1978. *Tourism and Agriculture in the Pacific Islands: Conflict or Symbiosis.* Draft. School of Social and Economic Development, University of the South Pacific, Suva, Fiji.

Tyrakowski, Konrad. 1986. The role of tourism in land utilization on the Spanish Mediterranean coast. *Geojournal* 13(1):19–26.

U.S. Department of Commerce. 1980. *1978 Census of Agriculture: Agricultural Services.*

Valarche, J. 1984. Agriculture and tourism, conflict and complementarity: the Swiss example. In *Agriculture and the Management of Natural Resource: Proceedings of the Eighth Symposium of the European Association of Agricultural Economics.* Milan, Italy: European Association of Agricultural Economics.

Waldrop, Judith. 1989. The color green. *American Demographics* 4(5):8.

34

Development of Seaside Resorts

Charles A. Stansfield, Jr.

The world ocean, covering nearly two-thirds of the planet's surface, clearly is a mammoth leisure and tourism resource. The edge of the sea, where land and salt water meet, is the focus of a great variety of recreational activities. The most intense recreational use of the seashore is in the vicinity of nearby metropolitan centers. Seashore resorts developed within a framework of both historical and geographical contexts, and seashore resorts represent a unique form of urban development and structure. The nature of tourism has helped to create "landscapes of leisure" along attractive beaches the world over.

Historical Geography of Seaside Tourism

Aristocratic Beginnings

Leisure time must be accompanied by surplus income in order to produce a tourist. Seaside tourism can trace its roots at least to imperial Rome but then only the wealthy few could participate. The caesars who vacationed on Capri inaugurated a long tradition of seashore resorts being founded by the leisured and monied elite.

Prior to the Industrial Revolution, resorts were relatively small centers, based as they were on the patronage of the relatively small leisured classes. These pre-Industrial Age ancestral resorts in Europe usually were inland towns based on the shrewdly exploited natural resource of a mineral spring. The supposedly curative waters were drunk and often bathed in as well. People went to the mineral spring resorts, or spas, for recreational purposes in addition to seeking relief from ailments; the spas provided socialization among the leisure classes and featured music and entertainment. Some have suggested that the medicinal aspects of such spas mostly were an excuse for having a good time in societies that then frowned on travel for pleasure alone.

The Shift to the Sea

Inland spas were supplanted by seashore resorts through the late eighteenth and early nineteenth centuries. The seashore, once an exposed front line of defense, vulnerable to attack, became a relatively safe environment at the close of the Napoleonic era in Europe and following the War of 1812 in America. Secondly, a great revolution was sweeping through the United Kingdom and the United States—the two countries that produced the world's first large seashore resorts. Early examples include Brighton and Margate in England and Long Branch and Cape May in the United States. The Industrial Revolution was both a social and a technological revolution. Any form of tourism obviously involves transportation because tourism requires movement across space. The Industrial Revolution produced two great innovations in transport, the steamboat and the steam train, both of which greatly reduced the time and money required to travel any given distance. It became easier, faster, and cheaper to travel for pleasure, so that a day by the sea came within the financial reach of a great many people.

The inland spas, tightly focused on a mineral spring, were not readily expandable to host the increasing hoards of tourists. The curiously Puritan pretension that one was traveling for medical treatment rather than just for fun did not long persist into the age of mass tourism. Although doctors of the time did prescribe sea-bathing and even drinking salt water as having curative effects, it became clear that treats rather than treatments motivated most seashore visitors.

Industrialization not only provided faster transportation to link growing industrial urban populations with the seaside, but also generated the rising incomes that enabled the majority to become tourists, at least for a day. As England led the world into the Industrial Revolution, it also led in the development of seaside resorts of mass appeal.

English Antecendents

As British social historians have noted, "The story of the English seaside is the story of a social revolution" (Stokes 1947:1); and, "The development of our coast resorts was due first to the aristocracy . . . then to the middle classes, and lastly to the patronage of the working people. The annual hegira widened, ever widened . . . ." (Cruikshank 1946:50). This progressively broadening participation in the trek to the sea for recreation occurred in the middle decades of the nineteenth century due to the coincidence in time of technological and social changes. "Many [English] seaside watering places, including Brighton, began their existence as resorts during the eighteenth century, but it was not until about the middle of the nineteenth that they gained real significance in the life of the nation as a whole" (Gilbert 1954:1). Railroads had placed the means of recreation within reach of most classes of society, satisfying the demand for recreation of an increasingly "enlarging sector of society, provided with increased leisure and the wherewithal to enjoy it" (Smailes 1953:29).

Thus, Brighton, on the English Channel coast of England and due south from London, was transformed from a sleepy little fishing village to one of the 30 largest cities in England by the early twentieth century. The slavish imitation of royalty that characterized the period meant that courtiers and would-be courtiers followed the Prince of Wales, afterward King George IV, to Brighton beginning in 1783. Physicians' advocacy of sea water cures doubtless enhanced the popularity of Brighton and other similar resorts. Brighton contained about 3,500 inhabitants at the time of the Prince's first visit; by 1841, when the railroad from London reached Brighton, its population already was over 40,000 and it doubled that by 1865 (Gilbert 1954). Many other

British seaside resorts likewise trace their period of lusty growth to the era of rapid expansion of railways.

American Beginnings

New Englanders locate America's earliest seaside resorts in the neighborhoods of Boston or Providence; New Jersey partisans argue whether Cape May or Long Branch qualifies for first honors. At any rate, the historical record indicates that Americans' interest in leisured recreation by the sea was contemporaneous with British development of seaside resorts (Demars 1979). Just as in the case of Brighton, the appearance of the first American seashore resorts predated the railroad. It was these resorts' period of rapid and intense development that was fostered by the shining rails, not necessarily their origins in every case.

Cape May's claim to be the earliest seashore resort is based partly on an advertisement placed in the *Pennsylvania Gazette* in 1776 offering for sale a Cape May plantation ". . . within one mile and a half of the Sea Shore, where a number resort for health and bathing in the water" (Cunningham 1958:113). By 1792, a hotel and bathing houses had been erected at Long Branch; when that property was sold in 1806, the hotel was enlarged to accommodate 250 guests, a stupendous figure for the time (Nelson 1902).

The Key Role of Transportation

Geographers speak of the "friction of space," that is, the costs, in time and money, of overcoming distance. Where transport technology is relatively primitive, the friction of space is high; if one must rely on sailing ship or stagecoach, the costs of overcoming distance (or space) will be considerable in both time and money. As transport technologies advance, the time and money costs of travel are diminished. People, including would-be tourists, consider both time-distance and cost-distance, even if they don't use those terms. Resorts may be advertised, for example, as an "hour away" from a given city, and airlines boast of placing distant attractions within reasonable cost-distance.

As the development of transport technology and systems reduces time and cost-distances, progressively lower income groups will be enabled to patronize any particular resorts. For example, a small, socially exclusive seaside resort near New York City gradually was transformed into the epitome of a mass-appeal resort through advances in "lubricating the friction of space" through the increasing efficiency of transportation. When it embarked on its career as a seashore resort, Coney Island "catered almost exclusively to excursionists wealthy enough to own carriages" (Pilot and Ranson 1941:15). By 1847, a steam boat connected Manhattan with Coney Island, bringing more middle-class passengers. During the Civil War era, horse-cars brought Manhattan closer to the beach in terms of time and cost; electric trolleys followed, further diminishing time and cost distance. The extension of New York City's subway system to Coney Island completed the process of transforming that resort into one accessible to virtually the entire population of the metropolitan area. The socioeconomic orientation of any particular seaside resort often is thus tied directly to its relative accessibility, in both contemporary and historical contexts. The specific technology changes, but the relationship of increased accessibility and decreased time and cost-distances with socioeconomic traits of tourists continues in evidence. Each form of transport has helped to boom development of an array of resorts. Just as the railroad "created" Atlantic City, the auto and the jet plane were instrumental in the further development of such resorts as Disney World, Las Vegas, Cancun, and Hawaii.

Form and Function

Seafront Characteristics

Seaside resorts around the world exhibit one salient morphological feature. The part of town that proclaims its social and economic nature and, at the same time, marks its common identity as a seaside resort, is the character of development of the seafront. Since the origins of the popular seaside resort, the edge of the sea has been the linear focus of visitor interests and activities. The seafront is the basic economic zone of the seaside resort. The primary economic functions of the resort are carried out in this linear aggregation of transport terminals, hotels, eating establishments, entertainment facilities, and specialized vacationer-oriented retail shops. Here, as elsewhere, form and function interact.

The social qualities of the resort are reflected in its "face"—the seafront facade. Middle-class summer cottage communities may present a sedate, small-town appearance, while upper-income resorts would be typified by a complex of luxury hotels, expensive restaurants, and, perhaps, exclusive casinos. In resorts of working-class appeal, the seafront commonly will be developed very intensively. Inexpensive food and souvenir stalls stand side by side with mechanical amusements, candy and novelty shops, and amusements piers.

The permanent alignment of visitor interest and activities along the seafront can be traced to the earliest phase of seashore resort development. Brighton, England, for example, in common with other fledgling resorts, had earlier witnessed a major divergence from the pattern established in the older, inland spas. The promenade, shops, libraries, and even the Prince Regent's summer palace, had been grouped about a low, open valley perpendicular to the sea. By the early nineteenth century, however, visitor interest clearly had shifted to the seafront in common with the other seaside resorts of the day. Retailers and amusement facilities proved alert to the singificance of the shift in visitor interest to the seafront. Commercial activity along the beach itself was typical by the mid-Victorian period. In 1880, the scene on Brighton beach included "the town band, a French string band, other bands of minstrels, performing canaries, ponies and monkeys, sellers of brandy balls and pincushions, a conjurer, fruit stands, gingerbeermen and newsboys" (Gilbert 1954:184–186).

The Recreational Business District

The characteristic blend of retail establishments and their distribution among retail districts may serve as a measure of resort status and degree of dominance of resort functions. Most sizeable towns possess a central business district (CBD), shopping thoroughfares or "strings," major subcenters or neighborhood shopping districts, minor centers and isolated retail nodes. Each of these characteristic districts is composed of, and may be identified by, a typical set of retail establishments that varies little from city to city. Neighborhood shopping centers, for example, usually include food stores, drug stores, dry cleaners and laundromats, barbers and beauty shops, and automobile service stations. These are "convenience" retailers and services, frequently visited, close to the purchaser's home, and featuring relatively low unit prices. In contrast, "downtowns" or CBDs exhibit a quite different array of establishments, typified by "shopping" and specialty goods and services—those purchased less frequently and commonly featuring relatively high unit prices and characterized by a great variety in style and quality. CBDs must draw customers from a large hinterland, as each customer will make only infrequent visits there in contrast to regular visits to neighborhood centers. To this long-recognized array of urban retail trade districts must be added the recreational business district or RBD (Stansfield 1965). This area is the seasonally busy linear complex of restaurants, specialty food stands, candy stores and an array of novelty and souvenir shops that cater to tourists' leisurely shopping and entertainment requirements. Tourists and seasonal residents provide, in varying degree, business for most of a resort's retailers; the RBD, however, exists almost entirely on the proceeds of tourist patronage. The almost complete seasonal closing of RBD establishments in the "off season" attests to this specific tourist orientation.

The RBD in seaside resorts commonly lies along the seafront, as in the "boardwalks" of American seashore resorts and the seafront promenades of European seaside towns. The scenic attraction of the seashore, the stimulation of fresh air, and the lack of any apparent necessity to shop—all seemingly combine to encourage the tourist to pass considerable time in the most casual sort of shopping. The RBD is a social phenomenon as well as an economic one. It provides a means of entertaining, as a unit, family members who may not otherwise participate jointly in various forms of amusement or shop with each other in an atmosphere of relaxation. To the prevalent, if often unexpressed, desire to take home visible evidence of visits to a resort must be added the social activity of casual shopping and shopping for resort clothing and decorative items. The inclination of vacationers is to spend a considerable portion of their leisure, particularly in the evenings, shopping for such goods, resulting in a concentration of gift stores and variety stores in the RBDs.

Other contrasts of RBDs with CBDs and other standard urban retail districts include a predominance of food and beverage, gift-novelty-variety, and candy establishments, commercial amusements and theaters, clothing stores, and a comparatively small number of barber and beauty shops, gas stations, financial services, grocery stores, and auto and accesssory sales. The relative dominance of luxury goods shopping versus commercial amusements and inexpensive fast foods within various RBDs can be a measure of the social status of different resorts (Stansfield 1971).

The Resort Cycle   Several geographers have noted the process of evolution of resorts or tourism regions (Christaller 1963, Stansfield 1978, Butler 1980, Meyer-Arendt 1985). Seashore resorts provide several notable case studies of this life-cycle phenomenon (Debbage 1990).

As developed by Richard Butler (Butler 1980), the resort cycle of evolution begins with an *exploration* stage in which a few adventurous tourists "discover" the resort potential of an area not yet equipped with visitor service facilities. In the *involvement* stage, there is a growing perception that tourism is a desireable, logical, and likely profitable use of local physical environmental resources, as in an ocean beach for example. Basic recreational facilities and visitor accommodations are created. If the involvement phase is the "take-off" of the area's career as a resort, then the third stage, *development,* is the period of accelerating investment in expansion. Typically in development, outsiders come to control the tourist trade through large-scale investments and provision of more experienced management. The tourist hinterland or customer supply area is expanded through better transportation access and advertising. By the *consolidation* stage, tourism has triumphed as the major (sometimes, only) industry, but growth rates have begun to level off from the hectic expansion of development. Some older facilities now are viewed as obsolete and of inferior quality. The fifth stage is *stagnation*, in which peak numbers of visitors are reached. This stage is a crisis stage for the seaside resort, or any resort, as the resort is losing its appeal. No longer fashionable, the resort no longer attracts consistent reinvestment in modernizing existing visitor-service infrastructure, much less new facilities.

Pioneer recreation geographer Roy Wolfe characterized the situation in which the original physical amenities of the site are supplanted by the built and shaped cultural environment as the "divorce from the geographic environment" (Wolfe 1952). An example of this "divorce from the (physical) geographic environment" can be seen in the case of Atlantic City's attempted revitalization through legalized casino gambling. This famous seaside resort had reached stagnation by the 1940s. Most of the resplendent seafront hotels had been built by 1930; few new ones were built until after casinos were authorized in 1976 (Stansfield 1983). Decline through the 1960s and early 1970s can be documented in the city's loss of 3,500 hotel rooms between 1964 and 1969 alone (40 percent of the total), and a population decline that cost the city nearly a fifth of its citizenry between 1960 and 1970. Clearly, the intended revitalization of the aging resort was based on a political advantage (the only legal casino location in the United States outside Nevada) rather than on the physical environmental resource of the beach and ocean.

Leisureopolis Seaside resorts, like all resorts, are the product of the spatial coincidence of environmental resources and accessibility relative to market. The physical qualities of site must be evaluated in the context of situation, which is *relative* location, relative to the recreational hinterland or source of tourists.

The nature of seaside tourism, based as it is on ocean shorelines, tends to create strongly linear resort zones. When these attractive ocean shores are highly accessible to nearby urban industrial centers with high average incomes that facilitate leisure and recreation away from home, an intensely developed strip of resorts may follow. Such seashore resort strips may be termed a leisureopolis. Examples of leisureopolis can be found on the New Jersey shore, Cape Cod, portions of Long Island, the southeast coast of England and the French and Italian Rivieras (Zimolzak and Stansfield 1983). A leisurepolis also exhibits the characteristic in-filling of development between older urban centers, which forms a continuous urbanized region. This phenomenon of old cities embedded in a matrix of newer, suburban-style development was first observed in Megalopolis (Gottmann 1961).

Summary

Seashore resorts are more than just a major aspect of modern tourism; they rank among both the earliest forms and sites of tourism. Studies of seashore resorts provide a variety of perceptions on the nature of tourism and the interrelationships apparent among tourism, geographic site and situation, accessibility factors including transport technology, and the interaction of form and function in seashore resorts. The cultural landscapes shaped by seaside tourism offer profound insights into the motivations and effects of contemporary and historical social and economic forces in society. In novelist Paul Theroux's words, ". . . a country tended to seep to its coast; it was concentrated there, deposited against its beaches like the tide-wrack from the seas" (Theroux 1983:17). A nation's seashore resorts are, literally, its face to the sea, its outward image of leisure, recreation, and sport.

References

Butler, Richard. 1980. The concept of a tourist area cycle of evolution: implications for management of resources. *Canadian Geographer* 24(1):5–12.

Christaller, Walter. 1963. Some considerations of tourism location in Europe: The peripheral regions—underdeveloped countries—recreation areas. *Regional Science Association Papers 12.*

Cruikshank, R. J. 1946. *Roaring Century.* London: Hamish Hamilton.

Cunningham, J. T. 1958. *The New Jersey Shore.* New Brunswick, N.J.: Rutgers University Press.

Debbage, Keith. 1990. Oligopoly and the resort cycle in the Bahamas. *Annals of Tourism Research* 17(4):513–527.

Demars, Stanford. 1979. British contributions to American seaside resorts. *Annals of Tourism Research* 6(3):285–293.

Gilbert, Edmund. 1954. *Brighton: Old Ocean's Bauble,* London: Methuen and Co.

Gottmann, Jean. 1961. *Megalopolis: The Urbanization of the Northeastern Seaboard of the United States.* New York: The Twentieth Century Fund.

Meyer-Arendt, Klaus. 1985. The Grand Isle, Louisiana resort cycle. *Annals of Tourism Research* 12(3):449–465.

Nelson, W., ed. 1902. *New Jersey Coast in Three Centuries,* 3 vols. New York: Lewis Historical Publishing Co.

Pilot, C., and J. Ranson. 1941. *Sodom by the Sea: An Affectionate History of Coney Island.* Garden City, N.Y.: Doubleday, Doran and Company.

Smailes, Arthur. 1953. *The Geography of Towns.* London: Hutchinson.

Stansfield, Charles. 1965. An analysis of retail trade districts within selected British and American seaside resorts. Ph. D. diss., University of Pittsburgh, Pittsburgh.

Stansfield, Charles. 1971. The nature of seafront development and social status of seaside resorts. *Society and Leisure* 4:117–148.

Stansfield, Charles. 1978. Atlantic City and the resort cycle: background to the legalization of gambling. *Annals of Tourism Research* 5(2):238–251.

Stansfield, Charles. 1983. *New Jersey: A Geography.* Boulder, Colo.: Westview Press.

Stokes, H. G. 1947. *The English Seaside.* London: Sylvan Press.

Theroux, Paul. 1983. *The Kingdom by the Sea.* Harmondsworth, Middlesex, England: Penguin Books.

Wolfe, Roy. 1952. Wasaga Beach—the divorce from the geographic environment. *Canadian Geographer* 2(1):57–66.

Zimolzak, Chester, and Charles Stansfield. 1983. *The Human Landscape: Geography and Culture.* Columbus, Oh.: Charles Merrill.

Bibliography

Boorstin, Daniel. 1962. *The Image.* Harmondsworth, Middlesex, England: Penguin Books.

Clay, Grady. 1973. *Close-Up: How to Read the American City.* New York: Praeger.

Cosgrove, Isobel, and Richard Jackson. 1972. *The Geography of Recreation and Leisure.* London: Hutchinson.

Funnell, Charles. 1975. *By the Beautiful Sea: The Rise and High Times of That Great American Resort, Atlantic City.* New York: Alfred Knopf.

Jakle, John. 1985. *The Tourist: Travel in Twentieth-Century North America,* Lincoln, Nebr.: University of Nebraska Press.

Kaufman, Wallace, and Orrin Pilkey. 1983. *The Beaches Are Moving,* Durham, N.C.: Duke University Press.

Matheson, Alister, and Geoffrey Wall. 1982. *Tourism: Economic, Physical and Social Impacts.* London: Longman.

McIntosh, Robert, and Charles Goeldner. 1986. *Tourism: Principles, Practices, Philosophies.* New York: Wiley.

Meinig, Donald, ed. 1979. *The Interpretation of Ordinary Landscapes: Geographical Essays.* New York: Oxford University Press.

Pearce, Douglas. 1981. *Tourist Development.* London: Longman.

Rosenow, John, and Gerreld Pulsipher. 1979. *Tourism: The Good, and Bad and the Ugly.* Lincoln, Nebr.: Century Three Press.

Smith, Stephen. 1983. *Recreation Geography.* London: Longman.

Stansfield, Charles, and John Rickert. 1970. The recreational business district. *Journal of Leisure Research* 2(4):213–225.

Wall, Geoffrey. 1975. Form and function in British seaside resorts. *Society and Leisure* 7:217–226.

35

The Evolution of the Ski Industry

Peter Williams

The history of winter-based sports as tourism activities seems timeless. Sagas, legends, paintings, verse, and script all allude to a broad range of snow-based sporting activities providing the impetus for sport and travel throughout northern Europe as far back as neolithic times (Flower 1986). Indeed the evolution of skating, sledding, curling, and tobogganing from primitive pursuits for a select few into leisure endeavors for the masses is well documented in the northern portions of both Europe and North America. Perhaps most significant from a tourism perspective has been the growth of skiing as a sport and tourism business.

Development Evolution

Unlike its other winter counterparts, skiing's early history was primarily linked to utilitarian functions associated with transport in hunting, mining, and military endeavors. Reference is made to skiing's role in facilitating the movement of people and goods for industrial purposes from the Stone Age through the Middle Ages and well into the late 1800s (Flower 1986).

Documentation of skiing's earliest emergence as a leisure pastime associated with tourism dates to the mid nineteenth century in Europe. Reference alludes to Norwegians traveling on skis from Telemark to Christiania (now Oslo) in Norway in 1868, primarily for social purposes. Almost two decades later (1890), recreational skiing emerged in western North America (Scharff 1974). Not long after these dates, socially focused ski clubs began to develop across Europe and North America. The first decade of the twentieth century heralded the creation of several ski clubs on both continents. These organizations not only fostered travel between them for socially focused competitions but also facilitated the creation of more and better ski facilities (Batchelor et al. 1937).

During these early years, North American and European ski clubs fed upon each other for ski development concepts. For instance, it was not unusual for highly organized ski meets to be arranged between American and Canadian ski clubs to not only provide a basis for friendly competition, but also to stimulate information exchanges concerning new and improved techniques for skiing as well as methods for enhancing ski trails and equipment. Notwithstanding these development issues, the primary motive behind these meets was still the improvement of the activity from social perspectives. Little interest was expressed in commercial dimensions of the activity.

The roots of a more tourism-oriented approach to skiing were slow in surfacing, but appear to have been seeded in 1905 when the Olympic committee for the III Olympic Winter Games settled on Lake Placid, New York, for its site (Scharff 1974). While skiing was not then a recognized Olympic event, the developers of the Lake Placid venue for the event included skiing in their program of activities. This inclusion was in response to not only a growing interest in skiing as a participant sport, but also a desire on the part of the destination's managers and developers to keep the site operational for the entire winter season. In the process of developing this strategy, the concept of a broader set of physical facilities and a more sustainable market base for skiing development is believed to have originated. However, skiing on the North American and European continents remained relatively primitive from a tourism industry perspective until the late 1920s. An impetus was needed to make it viable as a tourism product. That push eventually came from the development of uphill lift technology and Olympic recognition.

Few skiing centers had any skier-specific uphill transport capability until the 1930s. Railways, ratchet trains, and buses provided the early means of uphill transportation. These were used primarily for summer visitors and a few skiers in such European areas as Davos, Zermatt, Wengen and Adelboden. In 1929, the first mechanically propelled uphill lift designed specifically for skiers was installed on slopes in the Canadian Laurentian mountains (Lewis 1967). Although primitive, it was to the ski industry what Henry Ford's Model T was to the car industry. Its concept offered skiers cheap and reliable uphill transportation. Within a few years, most ski slopes of any significance in North America and Europe had one or more improved versions of it in place. Demand for ski area facility usage exploded.

This demand was further enhanced as a result of the higher profile that skiing was receiving in potential travel markets. In 1924, skiing was introduced as a formal event at the Olympics in Chamonix, France. It was highlighted again in the 1932 Olympic Winter Games in Lake Placid. These two occurrences helped to place skiing in the forefront of winter recreational activity on both continents and gave a further push to its development as a major contributor to winter-based tourism travel (Liebers 1963).

Sno-trains transporting thousands of skiers to the slopes became common sights throughout eastern North America in the 1930s. In response to their popularity, Union Pacific stunned the North American ski industry in 1936 by conceiving and developing the first tourism-oriented ski resort in Sun Valley, Idaho (Scharff 1974). This project became the prototype for world-class ski areas in North America. In Europe, traditional summer alpine vacation destinations were beginning to recognize the potential of skiing as a source of winter tourists. By the end of the 1930s, many of the major resorts were investing in uphill lift facilities and associated lodging facilities designed specifically for skiers in an emerging winter tourism market.

It was not until after World War II that skiing in a mass tourism context began to emerge. Pushed by the military role skiing played in northern combat areas, its introduction to thousands of returning troops as a form of winter recreation, rapid improvements in safer and more comfortable ski equipment, better access to ski destinations brought on by the development of family automobiles, and rising standards of living, skiing demand mushroomed during the postwar period (Smith 1974).

By the mid 1960s, skiing had woven its way into the leisure and travel patterns of a strong core of North American and European residents. Skiers began seeking opportunities for longer stay visits to ski destinations. Along with the availability of on-slope activities for skiing, off-slope amenities for après-skiing became apparent. Ski facilities and services associated with lodging, food and beverages, and entertainment became important components of the ski vacation experience (Tanler 1966). This trend intensified throughout the 1960s and 1970s. In Europe it led to the creation of a new generation of fully integrated ski stations, particularly in such destinations as Switzerland, Austria, and France (Pearce 1989). In North America, larger resorts in New England, Colorado, California, the Canadian Rockies, and eastern townships of Quebec emerged to meet the growing demand for winter vacations. Each new ski destination sought to provide a greater and more varied array of opportunities for the skier markets that they were cultivating. Each included as an integral part of their management strategy, the development of facilities and services for not only short-stay resident skiers but also longer haul and longer stay ski vacationers (Short 1988).

While the 1970s were a period of massive market and product expansion, the 1980s presented a decade characterized by industry consolidation and product management. Influenced by changing demographic realities, skiing markets began to mature at unprecedented rates. The increase in the incidence of downhill skiing in households began to decline and traditional markets grew at considerably slower rates than in previous decades (Williams 1986). By the mid 1980s ski facility supply had in many regions outstripped demand, and many less well-managed ski destinations were experiencing financial difficulties (Kottke 1990). In response, many ski centers were forced to address both product and market issues in a more businesslike fashion. Larger ski centers with tourism rather than primarily resident ski markets continued to grow, while many smaller centers faltered. Consequently, the number of ski areas in North America dropped 18 percent between 1980 and 1990. Counteracting this trend, ski area lift capacity expanded by approximately 51 percent during the same period (Kottke 1990). In some instances, more efficiently managed ski areas purchased smaller ski centers and incorporated them into their management systems. These acquisitions resulted in a more business-based approach to the skiing development in many regional and national ski destinations. It also set the stage for a more tourism-focused approach to ski area development. While the full impact of ski area consolidation is unclear, if other industries offer a guide, it is likely to lead to greater profitability and higher levels of capital investment in the ski industry (Gogel 1990).

Several key management challenges face ski destinations in the 1990s. These issues relate to product development, marketing, and planning concerns. Each brings a need for a more sophisticated approach to ski industry management.

Product Development

In order to attract and retain skier markets, ski destinations are increasing efforts to enhance the quality of the ski vacation product. Research clearly suggests that a growing number of skiers are taking relaxed, eclectic, and even hedonistic views of what encompasses the winter ski vacation experience

(Spring 1989). Well-designed runs, good grooming, and fast lifts represent the focus of product development attention for on-slope activities. Recent improvements in lift technology, notably the proliferation of high speed, four passenger chairlifts, make it possible to get in a lot more runs in a day than formerly. Similarly, high-tech snow cannons and hill grooming equipment provide a capability to offer consistently high-quality snow conditions. In combination, these technologies heighten the probability of a good skiing product. What is now in demand is an alpine lifestyle, which, in addition to skiing, offers upscale shopping and dining, health club and spa facilities, and includes a choice of low-impact winter sports activities such as cross-country skiing, skating, tobogganing, and sledding.

Demographics and technology are both factors pushing this trend. Skiing's target markets are getting older and generally ski more conservatively and less often (Williams 1990). Many of them are now in their 40s and are moving into their peak earning years. They are now able to take long-haul family winter vacations at ski destinations. Although still fitness-minded, they are no longer able to ski as long on a daily or weekly basis. Consequently, they seek opportunities for off-slope activities to help compensate for their inability to stay on-slope (Witchel 1990). Technology has increased this trend by making it possible for skiers to fulfill their physical needs from skiing in a shorter period of time than previously required. As a result, traditional all-day skiers are leaving the slopes well before the lifts close and are seeking other forms of entertainment to fill the remainder of their day (Beaudry 1990). From a ski vacation perspective, those who ski usually spend less time on the slope than was the case a decade ago. They ski fewer hours in the day and fewer days of a ski package. Augmenting their off-slope demand are additional visitors traveling with ski party groups who do not ski at all. In many ski centers between 20 and 30 percent of all accommodation is occupied by nonskiers (Williams and Dossa 1990).

In combination, these shifts in skier behavior have caused many ski destinations to begin selling an alpine tourism product rather than solely a ski experience. From a product development perspective, it has necessitated many ski centers to make significant capital investment in retrofitting and expanding activities (Rowan 1989). Product development initiatives include ski slope and ski lift upgrades, lodging facility renovation programs, and après-ski expansions in the form of shopping, dining, entertainment, and fitness facilities. Under such circumstances, it is not surprising that a minor percentage of what is spent by ski vacationers is actually allocated to on-slope activities.

Marketing

Given the capital investments associated with building a winter tourism product capable of consistently drawing ski enthusiasts to ski destinations, many ski centers are expanding their operations to attract tourists on a year-round basis. Numerous single season ski resorts of the 1970s and 1980s are now positioning themselves to push into the multiseason resort marketplace of the 1990s (Lewis 1990). Catering to a growing demand for quality environments, several ski destinations have already introduced facilities and programs for summer-based outdoor sports and entertainment. Utilizing infrastructure and superstructure initially developed for skiing markets and enhancing it with summer-based facilities such as hiking and biking trails (Blumenthal 1989), beaches, tennis courts, and golf courses (Barnhart 1989), cultural facilities and sightseeing programs, ski destinations across North America have begun marketing themselves as year-round destination resorts catering to both regional and long-haul markets.

Considerable research suggests that the traditional markets for skiing have flattened in recent years (Ruston/Tomany and Associates 1990). Skier markets are getting older, and although they continue to participate in winter ski vacations, ski destinations need new markets to ensure their future growth. Even with substantial product improvements, it is not necessarily evident that skier vacations will increase in the future. Traditional skier markets have been waning for some time, and evidence suggests that there is a need to broaden the appeal of skiing within other current nonskier markets. Skiing has historically catered to white-collar professionals and the more affluent. Initiatives to "democratize the ski slopes" are required (Waldron 1989). In particular, targeted marketing designed to overcome skiing's barriers to participation for people who have never skied or have stopped skiing represents a significant challenge for the 1990s. Research suggests that a general lack of awareness exists among nonskiers concerning the sport's social and psychological benefits, health benefits, physical accessibility, risks, and costs (McKinsey and Company 1989). To stimulate market growth, major industrywide marketing programs focused on correcting misinformation concerning skiing's perceived impediments to participation are emerging. Simultaneously, coordinated intersectoral programs established to communicate the benefits of skiing in clear and consistent terms are occurring. As never before, all ski industry sectors (for example, manufacturers, wholesalers, retailers, ski area operators) have begun working together to develop a strong and consistent image of skiing's benefits (Rowan 1990).

Complementing domestically focused communication and promotional efforts, large ski destinations are beginning to look beyond traditional geographic market boundaries for greater market extension. A significant portion of their potential new skier demand will be derived from international sources (Norden 1990). Global improvements in communication and transportation have enabled travelers to access foreign ski destinations more easily and cost effectively. It is estimated that approximately 60.6 million skiers exist worldwide. About 34 percent of that market is located in the Americas, 43 percent in Europe and 20 percent in Asia (Table 1). The influx of foreign visitors to international ski destinations has increased dramatically in recent years. Over 288,000 overseas visitors skied in the United States in 1988 (Table 2), a 24 percent increase over 1987 levels. More than half of all Japanese skiing outside of Japan occurred in Canada in 1988 (Rowan 1990). With the influx of foreign visitors to resort destinations will come a need for cultural adaptions on the part of ski destinations and travelers. Key ingredients associated with the globalization of skiing from a ski destination perspective will include the incorporation of signage and ski instruction delivery in foreign languages as well as culturally sensitive customer service and entertainment programs (Castle 1990).

Planning

While large and impressive ski developments provided the attraction for skiing's growth in the 1980s, they also raised distinct planning and environmental management concerns. In many alpine jurisdictions, growth and development have increasingly been perceived as environmentally dangerous. As small-scale operations have evolved into larger forms of development, they

Table 1. *World inventory of skiers*

Country	No. of skiers (in thousands)	Percent of world skiers
Americas	[20,585]	[34.0]
Canada	5,100	8.4
Mexico	2,905	4.8
U.S.A.	12,390	20.4
Argentina	80	a
Chile	60	a
Other S. America	50	a
Europe	[25,900]	[42.7]
W. Germany	5,500	9.1
France	4,700	7.8
Austria	3,000	4.9
Italy	3,000	4.9
Norway	2,500	4.1
Switzerland	2,000	3.3
Netherlands	1,300	2.1
U.K.	900	1.5
Other Europe	3,000	4.9
Asia	[12,000]	[19.8]
Japan	12,000	19.8
Others Asia	a	a
Oceania	[1,128]	[1.9]
Australia	888	1.5
N. Zealand	240	
Others (incl. Russia, E. Eur.)	[1,000]	[1.6]
TOTAL	60,613	100

Source: Ski Area Management 29(1):27, 1990.
Note: Figures in brackets represent totals.
[a]Less than 1%

Table 2. *Visitors to the United States who skied—1988*

Country	No. of visitors (in thousands)	Percent who skied	No. who skied
Total	12,518	2.3	288,000
Japan	2,562	2.5	63,600
U.K.	1,828	3.1	56,700
W. Germany	1,153	3.9	65,000
Mexico[a]	1,055	2.6	27,400
Australia	337	4.8	16,200
France	619	2.0	12,400
Italy	356	0.9	3,200
Brazil	299	3.1	9,300
Other S. America	714	0.8	5,900
Scandinavia	447	2.7	12,100
Belgium	114	2.4	2,700
Other Far East	828	1.9	15,700
Other overseas	2,226	0.8	17,800

Source: Ski Area Management 29(1):26, 1990.
[a]Does not include those arriving overland.

have destroyed many environmental qualities that first attracted visitors to the mountains. For many ski destinations in the 1990s, a significant issue will be how to address increasing tourism pressures brought on by the multiseason use of finite and fragile mountain resources. Not surprisingly many ski destinations in North America are confronted with the challenge of meeting skier demands for further development, while still maintaining their ability to give visitors and residents a unique mountain experience (Lawrence 1990). Ski destinations in the 1990s will have to be designed using sound environmental principles if they are to continue to draw tourists on a sustainable basis. Consequently, they will be challenged to focus more attention on balancing facility expansion and development programs with such fundamental concerns as sustaining water rights, wetlands, and wildlife habitat (Branch 1990).

Summary

Over skiing's history, it has evolved from essentially a small socially-focused recreational pursuit, into a family focused cottage industry, to a large and multidimensional tourism attraction business, drawing literally millions of skiing enthusiasts and other mountain visitors on a regular basis. As its markets have grown and matured, and as its products have expanded and improved, so has the need for careful planning and management increased. To compete in a rapidly globalized marketplace the ski industry will require a management approach capable of understanding and balancing such diverse demands as product development, highly targeted marketing, financial viability, and long-term environmental sustainability.

References

Barnhart, T. R. 1989. Putting golf on a mountain. *Ski Area Management* 28(1):79–82, 100.

Batchelor, D. E., F. Brewster, A. N. Carscallen, H. P. Douglas, F. A. Hall, A. A. McCorbey, and C. E. Mortureux. 1937. Skiing in Canada. *Canadian Geographical Journal* 14(2):57.

Beaudry, C. W. 1990. Towards a successful 21st century mountain resort. *Ski Area Management*, November, pp. 51–52, 74–77.

Blumenthal, T. 1989. Mountain bikes take off. *Ski Area Management* 28(1):68–69, 97.

Branch, J. 1990. Gut thoughts about the 90's. *Ski Area Management* 29(1):61–62, 92–93.

Castle, K. 1990. Reshaping the ski industry Japanese style. *Ski Area Management* 29(3):65–66, 94.

Flower, R. 1986. *The Story of Skiing and Other Winter Sports.* London: Angus Robertson.

Gogel, D. J. 1990. A coming of age. *Ski Area Management* 29(1):70, 93.

Kottke, M. 1990. Growth trends: Going both ways at one. *Ski Area Management* 29(1):63–65, 96–97.

Lawrence, A. M. 1990. Seeking the optimum point. *Ski Area Management* 29(1):75.

Lewis, C. R. 1990. Forecasting the ski resort economy. *Ski Area Management* 29(1):66, 104–106.

Lewis, J. E. 1967. An analysis of the spatial distribution and location of ski resorts in Southern Ontario. Master's thesis, Waterloo Lutheran University, Waterloo, Ontario.

Liebers, A. 1963. *The Complete Book of Winter Sports.* New York: Coward-McCann.

Longwoods International. 1989. *Colorado's Opportunities in the U.S. Ski Vacation Market,* Colorado Tourism Board, Denver, September.

McKinsey and Company. 1989. *Building Ski Industry Demand.* Denver: National Ski Industries Association and Ski Industries America.

Norden, D. 1990. Japan's trendy ski boom. *Ski Area Management* 29(3):67–69.

Pearce, D. 1989. *Tourist Development,* 2d ed. Essex: Longman Scientific and Technical.

Rowan, D. 1989. Lifts 1988. *Ski Area Management* 28(1):74–76.

Rowan, D. 1990a. Attracting new skiers. *Ski Area Management* 28(1):103.

Rowan, D. 1990b. The cosmopolitan future of America's ski resorts. *Ski Area Management* 29(1):76–77.

Ruston/Tomany and Associates. 1990. *The 1990 Ontario Ski Study*, Toronto: The Ontario Ski Resorts Association.

Scharff, R., ed. 1974. *Ski Magazine's Encyclopedia of Skiing*. New York: Universal.

Short, D. E. 1988. Tourism in France: recent trends in winter sports, *Geography*, 17:359–363.

Smith, K. E. 1974. Location analysis of high volume skiing in the Western United States. Ph.D. dissertation. University of Minnesota, Minneapolis.

Spring, J. 1989. Survey suggests undeveloped ski vacation potential, *Ski Area Management* 28(4):51–52, 75.

Tanler, B. 1966. A decade of growth, *Ski Area Management*, Summer, pp. 10–14.

Tanler, B. 1989. Reinventing mountain tourism, *Ski Area Management* 28(3):48, 50.

Waldron, J. 1989. Where will new customers come from? *Ski Area Management*, March, pp. 72–73, 94.

Williams, P. 1990. *Canadian Ski Industry: Market Trends Study*. Ottawa: Industry, Science and Technology Canada and National Ski Industries Association.

Williams, P., and K. Dossa. 1990. *British Columbia Downhill Skier Survey 1989–90*, B.C. Ministry of Tourism, The Centre for Tourism Policy and Research, Simon Fraser University, and Canada West Ski Areas Association.

Williams, P. W. 1986. *Where Do The Trails Lead? A Focus on the Canadian Ski Market*. Ottawa: National Ski Industries Association, The Canadian Ski Council, Tourism Canada.

Witchel, D. B. 1990. The seniors are coming, *Ski Area Management* 28(4):54, 55, 78.

36

Theme Parks and Attractions

Ady Milman

Sightseeing and visiting attractions have always been major activities for tourists. Since the early days of tourism and travel, people have traveled to particular locations to experience natural or human-made attractions that provided a pulling power and motivation to visit.

Theme parks are a relatively new concept of tourist attractions and aim to create an atmosphere of another place or time, and usually concentrate on one dominant theme, around which architecture, landscaping, costumed personnel, rides, shows, foodservices, and merchandise are coordinated.

The themes are used to unify the structure and organization of the park through constant visual statements. Consequently, many theme parks attempt to incorporate the visitor experience into almost any aspect of the parks' operation. For example, visitors to Walt Disney World's Magic Kingdom in Florida can experience the Mickey Mouse motif through life-size roaming characters, ice cream bars, local currency, telephone directories, and mailboxes.

Theme parks are designed mainly to cater to the family as a visiting unit, and are considered a form of leisure activity because they provide an opportunity for enjoyment during the individual's discretionary free time (Milman 1991).

In most theme parks, a single admission is charged at the gate, and all rides, shows, and attractions are inclusive of this price. This widely accepted policy is different from traditional amusement parks where admission is charged only for the particular rides that were used.

Classification of theme parks and attractions may be a complicated task. Theme parks may be classified according to their theme: historical, cultural, geographical, and so forth. While some theme parks and attractions concentrate on a single theme or motif (like the marine zoological Sea World parks or the Dark Continent of Busch Gardens in Tampa, Florida), others concentrate on a variety of themes located in distinguished geographical areas of the park. Kings Island in Ohio, for example, is a family entertainment center divided into six theme areas: International Street, Octoberfest, River-town, Hanna Barbera Land, Coney Mall, and Wild Animal Habitat (*American Automobile Association: 1991/1992 Illinois/Indiana/Ohio Tour Book*). Likewise, Great America in California, is a 100-acre family entertainment center that evokes North America's past in five themes: Hometown Square, Yukon Territory, Yankee

Harbor, Country Fair, and Orleans Place (*American Automobile Association: 1991/ 1992 California/Nevada Tour Book*).

Theme parks may also be classified according to their size expressed in terms of attendance, acreage, annual revenue, or the number of rides, shows, retail outlets, and restaurants offered. Walt Disney theme parks both in Florida and California may be considered the largest in the world in terms of the above attributes.

Some parks may spread over a large area like Darien Lake in New York, a 1200-acre family entertainment complex offering over 100 rides, attractions, and shows, or the Six Flags Great Adventure in Jackson, New Jersey, which stretches over 350 acres (*American Automobile Association: 1991/1992 New York and New Jersey/Pennsylvania Tour Books*). On the other hand, Xanadu in Kissimmee, Florida, is an energy efficient computer monitored house built of polyurethane insulation—an example of a small attraction of less than 5,000 square feet featuring the "home of the future" theme.

In addition, theme parks may be classified according to their geographical location, capacity, or resources used to create the theme. For example, Cypress Gardens in Winter Haven, Florida, is a natural park offering shelter to over 8000 varieties of plants and flowers (*American Automobile Association: 1991/1992 Florida Tour Book*).

Some distinctions were made between core and supporting attractions. According to Mill (1990), a core attraction forms a theme for the area and it is the principal reason for tourists to visit the destination. It may be a natural attraction such as the Grand Canyon or a human-made attraction like Disney World. Supporting attractions are those built around the theme like museums, restaurants, souvenir shops, and so on (Mill 1990:191–197).

The concept of product life cycle is also relevant to the attraction and theme park industry. Many theme parks and attractions go through a life cycle and experience phases like discovery, development, stagnation, decline, and rejuvenation (Haywood 1986). Coney Island, for example, has gone through all product life stages and was phased out for other attractions because of changes in visitors' demographic characteristics, consumers' tastes and preferences, increased propensity to travel, and competition from other attractions.

Some theme parks, however, have remained in the development stage for many years. Careful initial planning by Disney's EPCOT Center allowed the park to add additional features and rides on parcels of land originally designated for future expansion.

Other parks tackle stagnation by adopting unique strategies to modify and add features to their total theme product. Sea World of Florida, for example, has modified many of its ski shows almost on an annual basis to stimulate repeat visits. Throughout the years the park has also successfully added new features that committed high investments like a Penguin encounter or an ocean reef exhibit that houses dangerous fish.

Attraction and theme park management has become an integral part of tourism and travel literature and consequently, many text books have adopted sections on this developing industry (Hudman and Hawkins 1990; McIntosh and Goeldner 1990; Mill 1990; and Walsh-Heron and Stevens 1990).

History

The original amusement parks dated back to seventeenth century England and France. These "pleasure gardens" offered balloon ascensions, fireworks displays, or parachute drops. Some of the most famous amusement parks in the last century included Jone's Wood, which bordered New York's East River, Sealine Park at Coney Island, Ruggieri Gardens in Paris, and the Pratter in Vienna.

In 1893, the Chicago's World Fair became a milestone in amusement history. One of its features was a 250-foot wheel with thirty glass cabs suspended from its girders, each carrying sixty people. This was the first "ride" to become a regular feature at fairs, carnivals, amusement parks, and theme parks.

World's fairs have proven to be a hit and have been located around the world to enable a great range of people to participate in the experience.

Modern theme park development was pioneered in the mid fifties with the development of Disneyland in Anaheim, California. Further, the development of the interstate highway system coupled with the introduction of the jet aircraft created new markets for theme parks throughout the United States.

Entrepreneurial operations like the Knott's Berry Market which originally opened in 1920 in Buena Park, California, or the Anheuser Busch Beer Gardens opened in Tampa, Florida, in 1959, are good examples of leisure parks that evolved into theme parks by adopting one or more themes. Other pioneering parks include California's Sea Lion Park, opened in 1954, New York's Freedomland U.S.A. in the Bronx, which was opened in 1960, and Six Flags over Texas that was opened 1961.

Scope

The International Association of Amusement Parks and Attractions (IAAPA) is the world's largest amusement industry association. The nonprofit association serves the industry through a system of committees that provide direction in preparing educational programs, video training materials, and publications about the industry. IAAPA also monitors closely U.S. federal legislation that affects attraction and theme park operations. The association has over 2500 members in fifty countries, including parks of all sizes, their suppliers, and amusement industry consultants.

According to IAAPA, there are between 600 and 700 amusement facilities in the United States, many of which are family owned and operated. Some facilities, however, are owned and operated by large corporations like Busch Entertainment Corporation, International Broadcasting, MCA Universal Studios, Six Flags Great Adventure Inc, S P Parks Inc, and the Walt Disney Company (Lyon 1987).

The U.S. Census Bureau also provides data on amusement and recreation operation through the *Census of Selected Services*. The group includes establishments primarily engaged in providing amusement, recreation, or entertainment on payment of fee or admission charge, including motion pictures (McIntosh and Goeldner 1990:113).

The industry is composed of forty major North American theme parks that draw over one million visitors annually. The 1990 attendance at these North American theme parks and attractions was estimated at 123.7 million visitors, a one percent increase from 1989 (O'Brien 1990b:84–86).

Although Florida's Walt Disney World and California's Disneyland were North America's leading parks in terms of attendance in 1990 (28.5 and 12.9 million visitors, respectively), other large theme parks drawing more than three million visitors annually include: California's Knott's Berry Farm, Universal Studios, Sea World, and Six Flag Magic Mountain, as well as Florida's

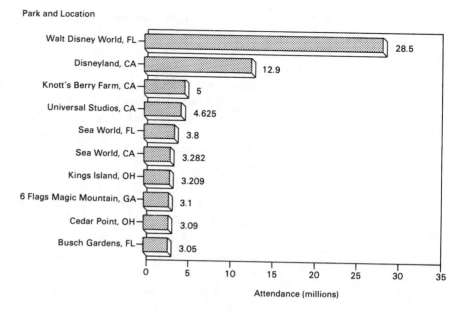

Park and Location

Walt Disney World, FL — 28.5
Disneyland, CA — 12.9
Knott's Berry Farm, CA — 5
Universal Studios, CA — 4.625
Sea World, FL — 3.8
Sea World, CA — 3.282
Kings Island, OH — 3.209
6 Flags Magic Mountain, GA — 3.1
Cedar Point, OH — 3.09
Busch Gardens, FL — 3.05

Attendance (millions)

Sea World and Busch Gardens. Ohio's King's Island and Cedar Point are also part of this top theme park list (O'Brien 1990b:84).

The largest theme parks are located in California and Florida, with a large concentration in the Northeast, Midwest, Southwest U.S., and Canada.

In the international arena, European theme parks have grown in the last two decades. The growth in popularity was attributed to the increase in car ownership and disposable income (Brown and Church 1987:37). West Germany traditionally has been the park center of Europe, however, other Northern European countries such as Belgium, the United Kingdom, the Netherlands, France, Denmark, and Sweden have also developed theme parks.

The reason for theme park dominance in certain countries may well be historical and social: Populations are denser in northern European countries, and in some southern European countries, particularly Italy, the traveling fair is still a major attraction (Brown and Church 1987:38).

Unlike the United States, the majority of European theme parks and attractions are family owned and operated (Brown and Church 1987). Euro

Fig. 2. Top North American amusement/theme parks by geographical location (1989). (*Source: Editorial, Amusement Business, December 30, 1989.*)

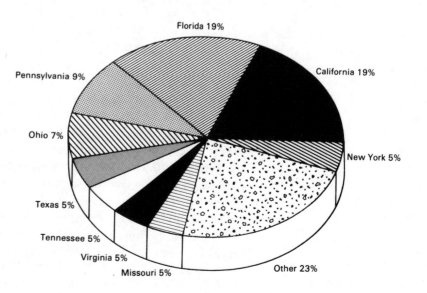

Florida 19%
California 19%
Pennsylvania 9%
New York 5%
Ohio 7%
Texas 5%
Tennessee 5%
Virginia 5%
Missouri 5%
Other 23%

Disneyland, a $4.2 billion project opened in 1992, is the first major U.S. investment in Europe. The attraction, twenty miles east of Paris, features a theme park with 29 attractions, six hotels, a campground, and a golf course. Disney's future plans for the attraction include building a convention center, a second golf course, and several more hotels (Rudolf 1991).

The largest European theme park in terms of visitor attendance is De Efteling at Kaastsheuvel in the Netherlands. The park, opened in 1951, is primarily a fantasy based park that features fairy tale themes such as the Sleeping Beauty, Little Red Riding Hood, and Hansel and Gretel (Brown and Church 1987).

Although France has been one of the most active European countries in theme park development, it has also suffered one of the highest mortality rates. Some of the new theme parks developed in the 1980s have already declared bankruptcy due to miscalculated market research studies and projections that were based on parks in the United States, Britain, and Germany (O'Brien 1991a:24).

Although heritage centers and theme experiences have boomed in Britain in the past few years, Britain does not have large theme parks with the exception of Alton Towers and Thorpe Park, which are Britain's major operating attractions (Editorial, *Economist* 1986:86). Britain's theme park industry has suffered from operational drawbacks regarding site development, finance, and management. The British weather also discouraged most of foreign theme park entrepreneurs (Editorial, *Economist* 1986b:86).

Spain has exhibited a rapid growth of theme parks. The Rioleon Super Park, founded in 1971, is a combination of an amusement park, a water park, and a zoo (O'Brien 1991a:24).

Prior to the establishment of Tokyo Disneyland 1983, the concept of theme parks was almost unknown in Japan. However, recent theme park developments are comparable to parks in North America, and consequently their design and operation is adopted from American or European firms. For example, Sesame Japan is patterned after Sesame Place in Langhorne, Pennsylvania (O'Brien 1991b:38).

Some Japanese theme parks have modified the traditional activities of the North American parks and substituted rides and shows with visual images of extensive landscaping. For example, Nagasaki's Oranda-mura's (Holland Village) major goal is to simulate the experience of walking through the streets of a foreign country (Makanae 1991:22–24).

Although the Japanese government is encouraging new emphasis in the development of leisure attractions (Paris 1988), the steep cost of acquiring land is the biggest obstacle for building theme parks there (Nemoto 1990, Makanae 1991).

A different modification of the Northern American theme park is also found in Seoul, South Korea. The indoor Lotte World opened in 1988 and is considered the largest indoor facility in the world. The park includes major rides like a looping roller coaster and a log flume (O'Brien 1991a:27). Other recent theme park developments took place in Australia. The $95 million Warner Bros. Movie World was opened in 1990 in Queensland, Australia. A sample of major international parks is summarized in Table 1.

The internationalization of the theme park industry has caused some cross-cultural areas of concern. For example, although in Tokyo Disneyland, only one of the thirty restaurants serves Japanese food, the French government has been trying to maintain the indigenous culture as much as possible in its parks (Rudolph 1991).

Table 1. *International theme parks at a glance*

Theme park	Projected 1991 attendance (millions)
Lotte World, Seoul, South Korea	4.6
Tivoli Gardens, Copenhagen, Denmark	4.1
Lisberg, Gothenburg, Sweden	3.0
De Efteling, The Netherlands	2.5
Alton Towers, Stratfordshire, Britain	2.5
Expoland, Osaka, Japan	1.6
Parc Asterix, Plailly, France	1.5
Grona Lund, Stockholm, Sweden	1.3
Bellewaerde Park, Leper, Belgium	1.0
Dreamworld, Queensland, Australia	0.9
Rioleon Super Park, El Vendrell, Spain	0.5
Warner Bros. Movie World, Queensland, Australia[a]	0.7

Source: Tim O'Brien, 1991, '91 season: Park officials worldwide positive, but on guard. *Amusement Business,* April 22–28, p. 24.

[a] A 1991 new park.

Park Features

Many theme parks offer thrill rides, which are slightly disguised to fit the respective theme. The most popular rides are the roller coaster, the flume or log ride, race cars, and carousels.

Ride manufacturers from around the world invest heavily in research and development to create original rides for the competitive market. Technological advancement has resulted in a new generation of roller coasters which are faster, higher, and more thrill-oriented. The recently developed coasters are constructed with tubular steel, which lends itself to loops and corkscrew twists. Technology has also improved safety; some coasters, for example, require two operators, pushing separate buttons to dispatch a train (Woodbury 1990).

Many new theme park rides incorporate visual and audio effects. The new simulators employ fancy visuals and moving theaters that allow visitors to experience sensations like flat-out acceleration, zero-gravity free falls, and high impact crashes (Lubove 1991:110).

Some new rides on the drawing boards include solar driven carousels and three-dimensional theater ride simulators. Other new theme park features include the adoption of technology in landscaping, buildings, games, live shows, circus acts, and food and beverage facilities.

Major corporations try to enhance images by sponsoring attractions at theme parks. In exchange for annual fees, corporate sponsors are given signs and displays that put their name and product in front of millions of visitors.

Visitor Profile

Offering a "fun" atmosphere along with food and drink seems to appeal to all age groups. According to the U.S. Travel Data Center, Americans took about 220 million trips to amusement parks and attractions during the peak season of March to September 1987. About 86 million trips were part of a summer vacation trip (United States Travel Data Center 1987).

A 1987 study commissioned by the International Association of Amusement Parks and Attractions (IAAPA) indicates that 82 percent of those who visited theme parks while on vacation knew about the park before leaving home, and 60 percent said that the attraction was an important factor in their choice of a vacation destination. The study also showed that of the summer vacationers who visited theme parks, 49 percent had children in their household, and 42 percent came from households with two wage earners (TTRA Florida chapter, *Florida Sun News*, 1987).

Theme parks both in the United States and worldwide, appear to attract a higher proportion of visitors between optimum earning ages. International theme parks tend to attract younger clientele than U.S. theme parks. A recent survey of theme parks' international marketing managers reported quite a uniform distribution around the United States, Europe, and other international locations. The largest age group that attended theme parks was between the ages of 22 and 55 (Editorial, *Funworld* 1990:42).

While a specific breakdown of the origins of theme park visitors is not available to the public, it is estimated that about 75 percent of their attendance is likely to be derived from residents living within 150 miles of the park (Lyon 1987). On the other hand, some theme parks located in major tourist destinations such as California, Florida, or Texas rely more heavily on out-of-town tourists. For example, a spokesman for Walt Disney World estimated that 90 percent of its visitors originate outside Florida (Lyon 1987).

Attendance Predictors

One of the major critical issues facing the theme park industry is predicting attendance. This type of forecasting is risky because a number of external factors can negatively affect attendance, such as a solid week of rain or high temperatures. These conditions may reverse dramatically a preseason predicted trend based on the "classical" socio-economic characteristics or vacation travel behavior.

The factors determining theme park attendance can be divided into two major groups: location factors and design factors. Location factors include the local market residing within a certain geographical range, as well as the number of tourists and their accessibility convenience (airport, major highway) to the park. Other location factors may include weather, value of local currency (attractiveness to foreign tourists), landscape, other competing attract-

Fig. 3. U.S. and international amusement park visitors by age.
(*Source: IAAPA Abstract, 1989.*)

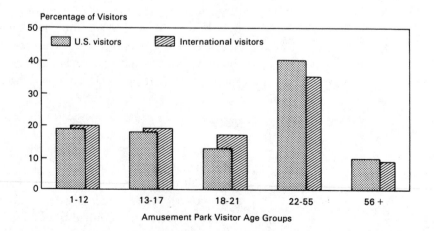

ions, and tourist-supporting facilities such as hotels, restaurants, and other attractions.

Design factors refer to the overall attractiveness of the park and its market positioning compared to competing parks. Design factors include (1) number and type of exhibits like shows and rides, (2) architectural design and landscaping, (3) internal logistics such as capacity, length of lines, rest areas, and foodservices, and (4) pricing.

Many theme parks attempt to capture market share by using sophisticated promotional campaigns. Inaugurating the 1990 season, Six Flags Over Texas introduced its 143-foot tall roller coaster and claimed it was the tallest in the world. Six Flags Magic Mountain made similar claims by spotlighting the debut of its "world's tallest looping steel roller coaster" (Wyatt 1989). In 1991, Cedar Point premiered its new $7.5 million wooden coaster, which has a lift and drop of 160 feet (O'Brien 1990a).

When locational factors are identical, design factors may enhance or detract from potential attendance figures.

Operating Expenses

Data on the operating expenses and revenues of parks is sparse due to the proprietary nature of such information. However, some information collected by IAAPA indicated that theme parks and attractions allocate the lion's share of their resources to employees salaries (full-time and part-time), followed by food and beverage services, marketing, maintenance, utilities, and other expenditures.

A 1989 survey conducted by the IAAPA revealed that U.S. parks spend their budget differently than international counterparts. U.S. parks spend higher proportion of their budget on part-time employees, marketing, food and beverage services, maintenance, and utilities than do international parks. This may be explained by the fact that most larger parks in the United States are located in metropolitan areas (Orlando, San Diego, Los Angeles, New York), and consequently have higher labor and media costs (IAAPA 1990).

Fig. 4. Attractions operating budgets by expense categories. *(Source: IAAPA Abstract, 1989.)*

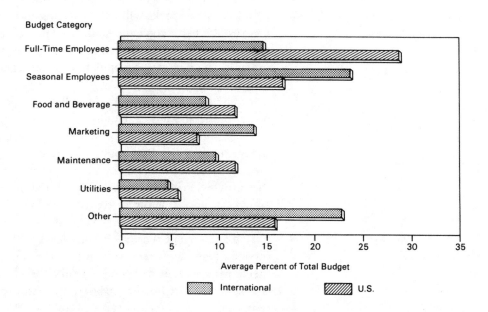

Personnel

The theme park work force is composed of the following broad categories: ride operators, entertainers, foodservice workers, administrators, maintenance workers, and other service employees. In water theme parks, a major category of the work force include lifeguards who often operate rides as well.

The seasonal work force is an important component of theme parks and attractions, especially in the Northern Hemisphere countries and in particular in the United States. For example, teens between the ages of 14 and 19 make up to 72 percent of the seasonal work force in the United States, but the same age bracket accounts for only about 45 percent internationally (IAAPA 1990).

Future Indicators

In 1990, the theme park and attraction industry reported 28 openings of new attractions, major construction of at least five more, and more than 20 plans are on the drawing board for ground breaking in the near future (Editorial, *Amusement Business* 1990a). For example, Opryland USA has announced an agreement in principle with United States Automobile Association to build a multi-million-dollar theme park in San Antonio. Waterparks, Inc. announced plans for a $10 million water attraction in Kenner, Louisiana, and plans were also unveiled for North Star Depot, a $15–20 million theme park designed to reflect historic ties to the railroad (Editorial, *Amusement Business* 1990).

It appears that in order to compete successfully in the existing theme park industry, owners and operators would have to sustain their parks in the life cycle's development phase as long as possible. To meet this goal, some existing theme parks, in an attempt to increase market share, must add additional features and upgrade their rides and facilities. With a major capital expenditure, the 1990 season opened with the premiere of 17 new roller coasters (Wyatt, April 30, 1989). Furthermore, a recent survey conducted by IAAPA revealed that promotional campaigns of theme parks and attractions were normally tied to capital investment in new adult rides and entertainment projects, followed by new water rides (Editorial 1990c; 42–43).

Theme parks will also carefully monitor changes in consumer demographics. Many parks will keep catering to families and will add conveniences like baby changing stations. The population's age composition may also result in a change in the product mix offered by many theme parks. For example, the decreasing population of teenagers may result in modification of thrill rides.

The future of theme parks will also experience more integration with other tourist and leisure facilities (Lawson and Baud Bovy 1977). In addition to rides, shows, shops, and restaurants, future theme parks will also offer supporting facilities like hotels and transportation services near by. Development of informal themed restaurants with limited menus or speciality shops that provide entertainment through browsing experience begin to emerge as an indication of this future trend. In the same context, Gee (1981) projected an incremental development of theme parks to true resorts, that is, sophisticated amusement-recreation complexes with accommodation and foodservices, along with recreational facilities not associated directly with the theme park. Recent developments like the Hyatt Regency Waikoloa, Hawaii, is a 62-acre resort hotel that offers themed experiences in a self-contained resort.

Furthermore, it appears that current trends of the U.S. and international theme parks and attraction industry call for additional investment in water parks and entertainment facilities. It is not unusual to find that many traditional theme parks add special events where celebrities fill in the entertainment demand of visitors. Some theme parks in the United States added water park facilities as an annex to their parks coupled with sophisticated marketing campaigns that promote both facilities. For example, California's Disneyland opened Splash Mountain in 1989, which may be the most high-tech, high-thrill, fastest, longest, tallest log-flume ride in the world.

Other future trends of the theme park and attraction industry are the indoor family entertainment centers. These indoor facilities are often built in shopping malls, such as West Edmonton Mall in Edmonton and Mall of America in Minneapolis, and often offer rides and attractions such as miniature golf, artificial beach and wave pools, small amusement rides, vaudeville theater, multimedia performances, night clubs, and so forth.

Summary

This entry looked at the growing theme park and attraction industry. Originated in the seventeenth century, theme parks and attractions have especially proliferated in North America, Europe, and the Far East in the last few decades. Park features, visitor profile, attendance predictors, and operation issues such as budget and personnel were discussed. The entry concluded with a view for the future role of theme parks in today's society.

References

Brown, John, and Ann Church. 1987. Theme parks in Europe. *Travel and Tourism Analyst* February, pp. 35–46.

Editorial, 1986a. The American dream and the great escape. *The Economist* 298:83–84.

Editorial, 1986b. Nice idea, shame about the weather. *The Economist* 298:86.

Editorial, 1987. Theme parks prominent in vacation plans. *Florida Sun News*, p. 2.

Editorial, 1989. The top 40 amusement/theme parks. *Amusement Business* 102, December 30:91.

Editorial, 1990a. Growth of parks and attractions industry held steady in 1989. *Amusement Business* 102, January 8:21–22.

Editorial, 1990b. The top 40 amusement/theme parks. *Amusement Business* 103, December 24:84.

Editorial, 1990c. International marketing managers survey. *Funworld* 4(10):42–43.

Gee, C. Y. 1981. *Resort Development and Management.* East Lansing, Mich.: Educational Institute of the American Hotel and Motel Association.

Haywood, Michael K. 1986. Can the tourist-area life cycle be made operational? *Tourism Management,* September.

Hudman, Lloyd E., and Donald E. Hawkins. 1990. *Tourism in Contemporary Society.* Englewood Cliffs, N.J.: Prentice-Hall.

Lawson, F. R., and Baud Bovy, Manuel. 1977. *Tourism and Recreational Development.* London: Architectural Press.

Lubove, Seth. 1991. Fooling the inner ear. *Forbes* 147:110.

Lyon, Richard. 1987. Theme Parks in the United States. *Travel and Tourism Analyst,* January, pp. 31–43.

Makanae, Masa. 1991. The Status of Theme Parks in Japan. *Funworld* 5(3):22–24.

McIntosh, Robert W., and Charles R. Goeldner. 1990. *Tourism: Principles, Practices, Philosophies.* New York: Wiley.

Mill, Robert C. 1990. *Tourism: The International Business.* Englewood Cliffs, N.J.: Prentice-Hall.

Milman, Ady. 1991. The Role of Theme Parks as a Leisure Activity for Local Communities. *Journal of Travel Research* 29(3):11–16.

Nemoto, Yuuji. 1990. Japanese Theme Parks Come of Age, *Funworld* 4(10):16–17.

O'Brien, Tim. 1990a. Cedar Point's tenth coaster will be world's tallest. *Amusement Business* 102, September 10:23.

O'Brien, Tim. 1990b. Top 40 parks draw more than 123.7 million. *Amusement Business* 103, December 24:84–85.

O'Brien, Tim. 1991a. '91 Season: Park officials worldwide positive, but on guard. *Amusement Business* 103, April 22–28:1.

O'Brien, Tim. 1991b. New Sesame Japan themer a hit with Tokyo youth. *Amusement Business* 103, February 25:38.

Paris, Ellen. 1988. A yen for fun, *Forbes* 142:38–39.

Rudolph, Barbara. 1991. Monsieur Mickey, *Time Magazine*, March 25, pp. 48–49.

United States Travel Data Center. 1987. Outlook for attractions and parks. In *1988 Outlook for Travel and Tourism: Proceedings of the Thirteenth Annual Forum.* Washington, D.C.: United States Travel Data Center, pp, 128–134.

Walsh-Heron, John, and Terry Stevens. 1990. *The Management of Visitor Attractions and Events.* Englewood Cliffs, N.J.: Prentice-Hall.

Bibliography

Bates, Patricia. 1991. Ripley's attractions to open in England, Korea, and Mexico. *Amusement Business* 103:46, 49.

Editorial, 1987. Mickey Mouse Money? *The Economist* 303, April 25:64.

Editorial, 1989. A dance to the music of theme. *The Economist* 313, October 21:68.

Editorial, 1991. Thorp park lauded for customer service, staff training program. *Amusement Business,* February 11:18.

IAAAP. 1990. *1989 Amusement Industry Abstracts*, Alexandria, Va.: International Association of Attractions and Amusement Parks.

Kyriazi, Gary. 1976. *The Great American Amusement Parks.* Secaucus, N.J.: Citadel Press.

Mannix, Daniel Prat. 1951. *Step Right Up.* New York: Harper.

Milman, Ady. 1988. Market identification of a new theme park. *Journal of Travel Research* 26(4):7–11.

Norris, John, and Joann Norris. 1986. *Amusement Parks: An American Guidebook*, Jefferson, N.J.: McFarland and Company.

O'Brien, Tim. 1991. Desert Storm stirs booming business for Saudi Arabian amusement parks. *Amusement Business* 103, March 18–24:17, 19.

Roddewig, R. J., S. P. Schiltz, and G. Papke. 1986. Appraising theme parks, *The Appraisal Journal* 54(1):85–108.

United States Travel Data Center. 1986. Outlook for theme parks. In *1987 Outlook for Travel and Tourism: Proceedings of the Twelfth Annual Forum*, Washington, D.C.: United States Travel Data Center pp. 131–133.

Woodbury, Richard. 1990. Eeeeeyyooowiiii: A new generation of roller coasters is scarier but safer than ever. *Time Magazine*, August 6, pp. 60–62.

Wyatt, Mark. 1989. A Report on New Rides and Attractions at U.S. parks, *Amusement Business* 101, April 29:24–25.

37

Festivals and Special Events

Donald Getz

Festivals, together with an ever-increasing variety of other special events, have important roles to play in tourism development and marketing. From the largest events, such as the Olympics and World's Fairs, to the smallest of community festivals, each has potential to generate tourism demand. Collectively, special events also provide important activity and spending outlets and build or enhance a destination's image.

Events can also be considered as short-term hospitality services, with the emphasis placed on creating a festive ambience and providing high-quality service under unique conditions. Developing a customer orientation among volunteers and staff is one of the most important challenges facing event managers.

Although data on events have not been systematically collected in most countries, recent growth in numbers, diversity, and popularity of festivals and special events has been enormous. The International Events Group Inc. (1990) estimated there were 6,000 annual events in North America, while Long and Perdue (1990) estimated there were 2,000 in only two American states.

The major reason for this growth and the parallel increase in professional event management is the general rise in disposable incomes and leisure demand in industrialized countries. More specifically, there has been an explosion of special-interest recreation and travel demand, which has led to events oriented to all types of target markets. Aging and better educated populations have generated greater interest in cultural and heritage events, including a strong element of nostalgia. Governments have encouraged the trend by financially assisting cultural and ethnic events, whereas corporations have sponsored events by supplying money and promotion as an integral part of corporate communication strategies. Numerous communities are actively developing events as leisure and cultural pursuits for residents, as well as for their economic and community development benefits (Getz and Frisby 1990). In a tourism context, events have become attractive to those seeking unique and authentic experiences, especially close to home and for short breaks. They have also added considerably to the attractiveness of a resort vacation.

Definitions

Festival Festivals are themed, public celebrations. Many are traditional, having important and often multiple religious and cultural meanings for the host community. The majority, especially in North America, are more recent in origin and have been created for a variety of reasons: as leisure and cultural opportunities for residents; to foster community development; for profit; as fundraisers for nonprofit organizations; as tourist attractions and activity outlets; as political or civic symbols; as public relations tools and image-makers.

Special Event Other special events, of which sports are clearly the largest category, often incorporate a festive element to their program. Any event can be "special" from the point of view of its organizers (that is, one-time or infrequently occurring and outside the normal program of activities) and from the perspective of customers (that is, opportunities for leisure, social, and cultural experiences outside the normal range of choices or beyond everyday experience).

Specialness Some festivals and events are more "special," or attractive, than others. The quality of specialness resists precise definition, but it appears that the attractiveness of an event is heightened to the extent that the following criteria are met:

> A multiplicity of roles linked to tourism, conservation, heritage, arts, leisure, community development, and other social or cultural goals are fostered.
>
> A festive spirit is created, especially through the celebration of shared values.
>
> Basic human needs are satisfied, including physical, interpersonal/social, and psychological.
>
> Uniqueness is emphasized through infrequency, having appeal to special interests, and quality.
>
> Authenticity is created or preserved, so that the event is culturally important to the host community and does not seek to exploit visitors.
>
> Tradition is fostered, giving the event community roots and a sense of mystique. In this context "hallmark events" can be defined as those that have a strong enough tradition to indelibly link the event with the image of the host community.
>
> Flexibility regarding site, schedule, program, and markets is maintained.
>
> Hospitality makes every visitor feel an honored guest.
>
> Tangibility brings destination themes alive.
>
> Theming is achieved through coherent programming, promotions and packaging.
>
> Symbolism links the event to ideals and values.
>
> Affordability enables everyone to attend (although not necessarily to the exclusion of merchandizing and profit making).
>
> Convenience and easy accessibility encourages spontaneous attendance and repeat tourist trade.

Mega-Event This term occurs frequently in the literature, but it can be only imprecisely defined. Marris (1987) noted that mega-events can be measured by reference to volume of visits, capital cost, or psychological appeal. In terms of tourism impacts, mega-events are those which generate the most tourist demand or contribute most to creating a positive destination image.

The Tourism Roles of Events

Attractions Festivals and special events can generate substantial tourist demand, with related benefits being the overcoming of seasonality and disbursement of tourists geographically. Events have advantages in attaining these goals, as they can capitalize on whatever natural appeal the off-season presents and can be developed in almost any community regardless of other attractions and facilities. For example, Ritchie and Beliveau (1974) documented the success of Quebec's Winter Carnival in turning a traditional low period of tourist demand into a peak season.

Vanhove and Witt (1987) concluded that mega-events can reduce tourist outflow from a country by as much as half and increase inflow by a similar proportion. Canada experienced a major upsurge in foreign arrivals during Vancouver's Expo '86 (Lee 1987), along with a substantial internal shifting of travel, but it proved to be a one-year anomaly in relation to a continuing decline in visitation from the United States. Smaller events have also been shown to generate travel demand, as in Gartner and Holecek's (1983) study of the Greater Michigan Boat and Fishing Show. Other research has shown that events can attract longer stays and higher levels of visitor spending than the average tourist in an area (see for example, Nova Scotia Department of Tourism 1987, regarding the Antigonish Highland Games; Vaughan 1979, on the Edinburgh Festival). Longer events naturally have a greater potential for attracting overnight visits and maximizing visitor spending.

However, research has proven most events, even the biggest, to be dependent upon local and regional markets. This fact should strongly influence their planning and marketing.

Animators   A related role of events is the animation of static facilities and attractions, to enhance their appeal and encourage repeat visits. Ski resorts such as Aspen and Telluride in Colorado have launched popular festival programs in the summer season (Special Events Report 1982). Theme parks employ entertainment and other special events to keep the vital local market interested (Kelly 1985). Research has shown that special events are high points in attendance at some Canadian historic sites (Dewar 1989), and Thorburn (1986) reported how European cultural heritage sites are made more attractive to foreigners through festivals and events. Similar potential exists for convention centers, museums and galleries, and shopping areas. The growth of "festival markets," along with downtown and waterfront festival parks and plazas, shows the important connection of events in animating urban settings (Benson 1985; McNulty 1986).

Image-makers   As a means to create or enhance a tourist image for communities and destinations, festivals and events have tremendous potential. Competition for mega-events is intense, partly because of the so-called halo effect, which encourages tourist visitation for some time afterwards. Sparrow (1989) observed this positive effect in Western Australia following the 1987 America's Cup Challenge in Perth/Fremantle. A sequence or cluster of globally publicized mega-events can maximize the effect.

On a smaller scale, research has found that multiple festivals in Canada's National Capital Region create a positive image of the area, giving the impression that there is always something for the visitor to experience (Coopers and Lybrand Consulting Group 1988; EKOS Research Associates Inc. 1985). Cameron (1989) documented the efforts of residents in Pennsylvania's Lehigh Valley to use cultural events to overcome negative local attitudes and encourage more positive tourist images.

Catalysts   Major events are often partly justified as catalysts for urban renewal and development, such as Knoxville's World's Fair (Mendell et al. 1983), and for infrastructure improvements and general economic development, as in the case of Vancouver's Expo '86 (Anderson and Wachtel 1986). Many expositions and Olympics have generated legacies of facilities and infrastructure (Dungan 1984; Ueberroth 1985), whereas some events, such as Calgary's 1988 Winter Olympics, have created financial legacies for subsequent investment in sport.

Alternative Tourism Festivals and special events have unique value in the context of alternative tourism. Small events have the advantage of requiring minimal capital development and taking advantage of existing infrastructure. They are generally volunteer intensive, are locally controlled, and can generate substantial returns on small financial investment. To the extent that festivals are authentic cultural expressions and supported by the host community, they can be considered culturally appropriate and are sustainable through community dedication. Some events have potential to assist directly in nature conservation and to foster friendly host-guest relations. Events are also an excellent way to foster a community-based approach to tourism planning, as they inherently require considerable community support and involvement, which leads to consideration of tourism development issues.

Event Tourism Planning and Marketing

Policy Event tourism as a policy field has only recently emerged, with most governments providing minimal levels of support and being generally preoccupied with attracting or creating mega-events. New Zealand has pioneered event tourism policy, with goals of enhancing the country's image abroad, attracting foreign tourists, and spreading demand for tourism throughout the country. Like many governments, New Zealand capitalized on an anniversary celebration (its sesquicentennial in 1990) to launch a major event-related marketing campaign, including hosting the Commonwealth Games.

In destination planning and marketing, product development is the biggest challenge. Event products must be conceptualized and fostered in a manner quite different from other attractions and services. For the individual event, adopting a marketing and customer orientation is the principal task. The key elements of planning and marketing in event tourism are described below.

Market Research Despite the growth and popularity of events, tourist organizations have been very slow in directing research toward a better measurement of the significance of event tourism or an understanding of motivations for attending events. Most of the published research has concerned economic impacts, whereas some event organizers have determined customer characteristics.

A few major travel research projects have shed light on this field. Tourism Canada's (1986) study of the U.S. pleasure travel market revealed that from 35 to 54 percent of American respondents in five trip types indicated that ethnic festivals were important in trip planning. Examination of overseas market potential for pleasure travel to North America by Tourism Canada and The U.S. Travel and Tourism Administration found that 9 percent of West German respondents and 18 percent of Japanese thought local festivals were important in selecting a travel destination. However, 47 percent of West Germans actually participated in local festivals while abroad, whereas only 16 percent of Japanese did so (Tourism Canada 1987). Segmentation of respondents in these studies was undertaken so that the characteristics of persons most interested in festivals and events could be discerned. For example, in the U.S. City Segment, 18 percent rated festivals and events as an important tourism product.

Although an increasing number of event organizers have conducted visitor studies to determine impacts and evaluate markets, little can be concluded about general event-goer characteristics. It appears that females favor arts festivals, whereas sports events attract a preponderance of males. Racial and ethnic differences occur, either by design or through perceptions of what the event offers. Loyal, repeat visitors are important to many events, with word of mouth often the most important way in which people learn of events. Festivals in general are social occasions but not just for families. More research on this aspect of public celebration is required.

Determining Market Potential

Segmentation studies are important, but estimating market potential and demand for events is much more difficult. Recurring events can show trends, but many organizers do not pay adequate attention to their markets and some do not even worry about attendance levels. Managers of one-time events cannot assume that similar events in different locations will be a useful predictor of attendance, although comparisons are a starting point. Mega-events can justify employment of waves of market area surveys, starting well in advance of the event, to measure trends in awareness and intent; data can be converted to estimates of attendance using probability functions. Advance surveys of this type were conducted for the Calgary Winter Olympics (Ritchie and Lyons 1987), and a modified survey has been suggested by Louviere and Hensher (1983) in which choice theory is employed. Another technique showing promise is the use of linear regression analysis, with one study (Blackorby et al. 1986) demonstrating that attendance at world's fairs varied mostly according to average price, size of site, and number of foreign pavilions.

Themes and Image-Making

Events can be used to create or enhance destination themes and create positive images. Themes should be supported by residents and authentically reflect the area's character. Strategies can include

> Promoting the area as having a variety of events to experience all year round
> Using mega-events to attract media attention
> Developing events to make an established theme come alive
> Fostering a hallmark event that forever links the destination and event images
> Focusing on many events of one type, or of many different types, to attract target markets

Cooperative promotion among events is vital to implement these strategies.

For events, themes are employed to coherently integrate all aspects of the production (that is, activities, specialties, setting, costumes, merchandise) and its marketing (name, logo, promotions).

Organizational Development

Tourist organizations can take a lead role in event tourism planning, one element of which should be the fostering of organizational development so that events can be created and improved. One-time mega-events require enormous planning and management efforts and are often won through an elaborate bidding process, whereas numerous volunteer-run festivals can be fostered with far smaller levels of assistance. A sound destination strategy might be to develop a geographically diffused hierarchy of permanent events of local, regional, and international appeal. Occasional anniversaries can become the basis for destination-wide celebrations and events, many of which could be encouraged to become permanent.

Getz and Frisby (1990) found that municipalities have a key role to play in developing festivals and special events, but that in the province of Ontario, Canada, few communities had explicit policies in this field. Event organizers indicated what they most wanted from their municipalities: predictable funding; tangible help with staff, facilities, or equipment; advice and coordination.

Packages and Tours

The bus tour is a mainstay of event markets, but apparently little has been done to package event tours at the destination level. Festivals and events can be packaged on their own or in conjunction with other attractions. Event-based packages and tours could be based on themes, season, circuits, or the "piggybacking" of small events with concurrent mega-events.

Adopting a Customer Orientation

Even for nonprofit, community-oriented events, the adoption of a customer orientation is essential to ensure success. Careful attention to visitor benefits is the base for tourism marketing. Figure 1 illustrates a model of the event product from the visitor's perspective, and this can be used to help shape the theme, program, setting, promotions, and interactions with customers.

All festivals and events should first provide essential services (food, safety, communications) to a high standard, then consider the generic benefits sought by consumers of festivals and special events. Research and theory (Falassi 1987; MacAloon 1984) suggest that most events are social occasions and have cultural meanings, so fostering a sense of belonging and sharing is vital. Elements of ritual, if only opening and closing ceremonies, are important, and this might be closely related to providing an authentic cultural

Fig. 1. Festival and event products from the visitor's perspective.

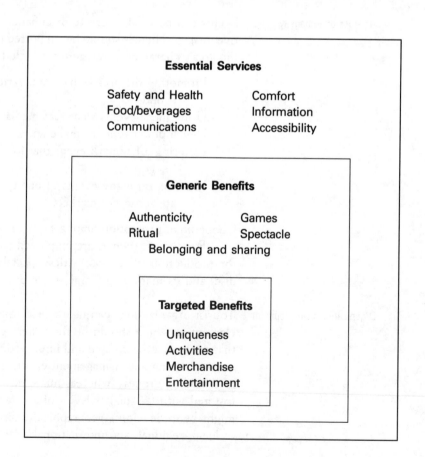

Essential Services

Safety and Health   Comfort
Food/beverages   Information
Communications   Accessibility

Generic Benefits

Authenticity   Games
Ritual   Spectacle
Belonging and sharing

Targeted Benefits

Uniqueness
Activities
Merchandise
Entertainment

experience. Games (including competitions, risk-taking, and humor) and spectacle (larger-than-life displays) are usually prominent features of events. Research is needed to link this concept of generic benefits more closely to leisure and play theory and to demonstrate the roles of each element in motivating and satisfying event-goers.

Most important from a tourism marketing point of view is the creation and promotion of targeted benefits, as these are most likely to attract interest groups, tours, and longer-distance travelers. Any element of the program (entertainment, merchandise, or activities) can be targeted, such as the case of craft, jazz, and ethnic food festivals. Also, uniqueness of the theme, infrequency, or promotion of the exotic can generate interest.

Product Life-Cycle   Just as individual events tend to go through stages of growth, maturity, and decline, so too can the destination area's themes and tourism products. To prevent decline, a number of strategies can be pursued. One is to initiate new events with different themes, or to shift images away from static attractions to action-oriented events. At some point an area might become saturated with regard to event potential, but there has been little research (see Janiskee 1985) on this point.

Organizers of recurring events can extend the life cycle by adopting a number of strategies. Market penetration involves attracting more users through a more competitive marketing mix. Sometimes the product itself should be reformulated to stimulate new and repeat visits, without necessarily attracting new market segments. Or new markets can be developed through more extensive product changes or diversification with other events. When an event goes bad and attracts undesirable patrons or negative publicity, choices range from shifting themes, program, and setting, to complete termination of the event or its management.

Promotions   Tourist organizations commonly publish calendars of events, but many are unimaginative listings that do little to inform or to attract tourists to events. Only occasional mega-events seem to receive sophisticated and sustained promotional efforts. To overcome this problem, events and tourist agencies must cooperate in joint promotions that feature the special color, action, and atmosphere of events in the context of destination themes and other attractions.

One of the greatest challenges facing the event organizer is that of corporate sponsorship. Sponsors look for opportunities to reach target markets, sell products, and enhance their image through events, while organizers seek financial or technical support, enhanced promotion and growth. It is important to achieve a match between the event mandate and theme on one hand and the sponsor's image and priorities on the other, so as to avoid negative effects. Tourist attractiveness can be heightened through association with well-known sponsors.

The Setting   Festivals and events occur in four types of setting: places of assembly (for example, theatres, parks, plazas) where an audience is oriented to a stage or performance; along streets or rivers to view parades; activity places, such as playing fields or stadia; and exhibition/consumption settings in which people move among displays or booths to view or sample. Each type of setting requires different operational approaches, but there are generic considerations as well. All festivals settings should strive for authentic relationship with the theme and for maximization—through design and decoration—of a festive atmosphere. Elements of spectacle, games, ritual, and belonging/sharing have to be accommodated.

Tourists require special design and site management consideration, since they will lack familiarity with the setting. They should be treated as honored guests in the host community. In particular, access, information, communications, sanitation, comfort, and catering must be oriented to the visitors' needs. Events held in center-cities and established tourist areas have the advantage of being able to use existing services and are places where tourists expect attractions and activity.

Impact Evaluation

Economic Effects   Most research on events has been for the purposes of assisting marketing efforts and demonstrating economic effects. It is in this latter area that theoretical and methodological progress is most needed.

There are major problems in securing reliable estimates of attendance and visitor spending at events, particularly where entrance and ticketing controls are absent. A variety of techniques can be used to estimate attendance and to sample visitors systematically, including a postevent, random telephone survey within the event's market area. However, once average spending is estimated, determining the true economic impact and worth of the event is quite another problem.

There are problems of theory, particularly in determining the validity of many assumptions commonly employed in economic impact assessments. A common mistake is failure to distinguish between gross economic activity (that is, all spending associated with the event, including that of all visitors) and true tourism impact. In the context of tourism only "incremental income" or "new money" (that is, the amount that tourists bring into an area because of the event) can be considered (Archer 1982). To estimate this impact requires "attribution," that is, the determination of what proportion of tourists' expenditures can be attributed to the event in question. This can be done through visitor surveys which ask tourists to indicate their travel motivations and specify the degree to which the event actually generated the trip. For example, in an assessment of the impacts of eight festivals in Canada's National Capital Region the researchers (Coopers and Lybrand Consulting Group 1988) found that Winterlude, a festival in February, attracted the highest proportion of true tourists (75 percent) whereas the Festival of Arts, held in the summer, attracted a very low 8 percent.

"Attribution" is fraught with validity problems. First, some amount of tourist travel and related event expenditure is likely to be a mere switching from one time to another, as events can disrupt normal travel patterns (Burns et al. 1986). Some planned visits to an area might actually be canceled because of fears of crowding or cost inflation associated with mega-events. These two possibilities should somehow be entered into the calculations.

Then there is the question of whether events might encourage tourists to stay longer and spend more in an area, even if they were not motivated to travel because of the events. And events can add to the positive image of an area, given an incentive to travel there, regardless of any particular event. These benefits should also be considered.

Income multipliers are typically applied to estimates of incremental income on the assumption that new money circulates through the local economy generating a cumulative effect greater than the initial expenditure. Archer (1982) has exposed the many risks in using multipliers this way, not the least of which is the problem of using the wrong type of multiplier and borrowing it from a completely inappropriate source (most are calculated for states or countries, not cities). Furthermore, there is little research evidence to prove that expenditures from a single event can, in fact, be converted through surplus capacity in the local economy into increased production—an assumption that must be made when using the income multiplier. Also, multipliers cannot be used to estimate long-term impacts of incremental expenditure, and they do not take into account opportunity costs, such as the possible diversion of productivity from other sectors into tourism services.

Since many events create little or no permanent jobs, and since many events are simply one of many potential spending outlets for tourists, using a multiplier might very well exaggerate economic impacts on the basis of faulty assumptions. The study of eight festivals in Canada's National Capital Region (Coopers and Lybrand Consulting Group 1988) used an econometric model more sensitive to the actual state of the economy and found that a mere 10 percent of estimated economic impacts were secondary (that is, due to the multiplier effect). A simple estimation of an event's role in attracting tourists and of related direct tourist expenditure will undoubtedly reveal most of the economic benefits.

Evaluating Costs and Benefits There are many theoretical and methodological problems associated with estimating the economic impact of events. Furthermore, the typical assessment of economic impacts is far too narrow to answer important questions about the costs and benefits of hosting festivals and special events. Few evaluations of the economic impacts of events have addressed the three most important questions, namely, (1) What is the return on investment? (2) Was it a worthwhile investment, given all costs and benefits? and (3) Who exactly gained or lost because of the event?

A pioneering study to assess the costs and benefits of a mega-event was undertaken for the first Australian Grand Prix car race (Burns et al. 1986). Although theoretical and methodological problems were encountered, that study ambitiously measured tangible and intangible costs and benefits (sorting out, for example, the question of whether grants are costs or benefits), calculating tangible benefit-to-cost ratios, and evaluating the intangibles. That study also explored the important issue of determining the distribution of effects among levels of government and individuals.

Future progress on this vital research area will require new field-research methods, more rigor in measuring effects, and debate among scholars and practitioners as to the inherent value of different approaches to quantifiable impact assessment and more subjective evaluation of costs and benefits.

Summary

Festivals, together with special events, have important roles to play in tourism development and marketing. Events and festivals collectively provide important activity and spending outlets and build or improve a destination's image. This article emphasizes the various definitions used as they relate to special events and festivals. It also discusses the role of special events and festivals in tourism development and marketing.

References

Anderson, R., and E. Wachtel, eds. 1986. *The Expo Story.* Madeira Park, Vancouver, B.C.: Harbour Publishing.

Archer, B. 1982. The value of multipliers and their policy implications. *Tourism Management* 3(4):236–241.

Benson, J. 1985. Mall marketing. In *Banking on Leisure Transcripts*, ed. L. Ukman, pp. 45–49. Chicago: International Events Group.

Blackorby, C., R. Ricard, and M. Slade. 1986. The macroeconomic consequences of Expo '86. In *The Expo Story*, ed. R. Anderson and E. Wachtel. Madeira Park, Vancouver, B.C.: Harbour Publishing.

Burns, J., J. Hatch, and T. Mules, eds. 1986. *The Adelaide Grand Prix: The Impact of a Special Event*. Adelaide: Centre for South Australian Economic Studies.

Cameron, C. 1989. Cultural tourism and urban revitalization. *Tourism Recreation Research* 14(1):23–32.

Coopers and Lybrand Consulting Group. 1988. *National Capital Region 1988 Festivals Study Final Report*. Report for the Ottawa-Carelton Board of Trade. Ottawa.

Dewar, K. 1989. Interpretation as attraction. *Recreation Research Review* 14(4):45–49.

Dungan, T. 1984. How cities plan special events. *The Cornell H.R.A. Quarterly* (May):83–89.

EKOS Research Associates Inc. 1985. *EKOS Report on Winterlude: Executive Summary*. Report for the National Capital Commission. Ottawa.

Falassi, A., ed. 1987. *Time Out of Time: Essays on the Festival*. Albuquerque: University of New Mexico Press.

Gartner, W., and D. Holecek. 1983. Economic impact of an annual tourism industry exposition. *Annals of Tourism Research* 10:199–212.

Getz, Donald. 1990. *Festivals, Special Events, and Tourism*. New York: Van Nostrand Reinhold.

Getz, D., and W. Frisby. 1990. *The Role of Municipalities in Developing Festivals and Special Events*. Occasional Paper No. 16, Department of Recreation and Leisure Studies, University of Waterloo.

International Events Group Inc. 1990. *The Official 1990 Directory of Festivals, Sports and Special Events*. Chicago.

Janiskee, B. 1985. Community-sponsored rural festivals in South Carolina: a decade of growth and change. Paper presented to the Association of American Geographers, Detroit.

Kelly, J. 1985. *Recreation Business*. New York: Macmillan.

Lee, J. 1987. The impact of Expo '86 on British Columbia markets. In *Tourism: Where Is the Client*, ed. P. Williams, J. Hall, and M. Hunter. Conference Papers of the Travel and Tourism Research Association, Canada Chapter. Ryerson University, Toronto, Canada.

Long, P., and R. Perdue. 1990. The economic impact of rural festivals and special events: Assessing the spatial distribution of expenditures. *Journal of Travel Research* 28(4):10–14.

Louviere, J., and D. Hensher. 1983. Using discrete choice models with experimental data to forecast consumer demand for a unique event. *Journal of Consumer Research* 10(3):348–361.

MacAloon, J. 1984. Olympic Games and the theory of spectacle in modern societies. In *Rite, Drama, Festival, Spectacle: Rehearsals Towards a Theory of Cultural Performance*, ed. J. MacAloon, 241–280. Philadelphia: Institute for the Study of Human Issues.

McNulty, R., ed. 1986. *The Return of the Livable City: Learning from America's Best*. Washington: Acropolis Books and Partners for Livable Places.

Marris, T. 1987. The role and impact of mega-events and attractions on regional and national tourism development: Resolutions of the 37th Congress of the AIEST, Calgary. *Revue de Tourisme* (4):3–12.

Mendell, R., J. MacBeth, and A. Solomon. 1983. The 1982 world's fair—a synopsis. *Leisure Today, Journal of Physical Education, Recreation and Dance* (April):48–49.

Nova Scotia Department of Tourism. 1987. *1986/87 Highland Heart Evaluation: Antigonish Highland Games*. Halifax.

Ritchie, J., and D. Beliveau. 1974. Hallmark events: An evaluation of a strategic response to seasonality in the travel market. *Journal of Travel Research* 13(2):14–20.

Ritchie, J., and M. Lyons. 1987. Olympulse iii/olympulse iv: A mid-term report on resident attitudes concerning the XV Olympic Winter Games. *Journal of Travel Research* 26(1):18–26.

Sparrow, M. 1989. Quoted in D. Getz, 1990, *Festivals, Special Events and Tourism*. New York: Van Nostrand Reinhold.

Special Events Report. December 6, 1982. *Telluride, Colorado . . . How One Town has Profited from Festivals*. Chicago, Ill.: International Events Group.

Thorburn, A. 1986. Marketing cultural heritage. *Travel & Tourism Analyst* (Dec.):39–48.

Tourism Canada. 1986. *The U.S. Pleasure Travel Market Study, Canadian Potential Highlights Report*. Ottawa.

Tourism Canada. 1987. *Pleasure travel markets to North America: Japan, United Kingdom, West Germany, France, Highlights Report*. Ottawa.

Ueberroth, P. 1985. *Made in America, His Own Story*. New York: William Morrow.

Vanhove, D., and S. Witt. 1987. Report of the English-speaking group on the conference theme. *Revue de Tourisme* 4:10–12.

Vaughan, R. 1979. *Does a Festival Pay? A Case Study of the Edinburgh Festival in 1976.* Tourism Recreation Research Unit, Working Paper 5, University of Edinburgh.

38

State Welcome Centers: An Important Part of the Visitor Information System

Daniel R. Fesenmaier, Christine A. Vogt, and William P. Stewart

> Warm welcomes await you at Iowa's 18 Welcome Centers. Iowa's Welcome Centers are diverse as the state's many attractions—one thing you'll always find is helpful, friendly people ready to answer your travel questions. Pick up free brochures and maps about Iowa while you refresh and relax in settings that range from picnic parks to historic landmarks. Sample the diversity of Iowa's Welcome Centers, and discover Iowa's treasures. (Iowa Division of Tourism 1991:4)

Welcome centers are an important ingredient in the overall effort of a state to encourage visitors to stay and sightsee within the state. In 1986, approximately 440 welcome centers were operating in 46 states and were servicing millions of visitors each year (U.S. Travel Data Center 1987). Located primarily at entry points to states, welcome centers provide the opportunity for travelers to rest and relax and to obtain various types of information ranging from highway maps to brochures that feature attractions, accommodations, and recreation activities. An additional function of welcome centers, which is often overlooked, is that of establishing expectations (that is, "setting the stage") of visitors to an area. Welcome centers are a communications tool for exposing visitors to a state's tourism resources. Experienced travelers may use the information as a reminder of what a state offers or to learn about new attractions, whereas an inexperienced traveler may be learning about an area for the first time. Regardless of the level of experience with a destination, the hope is that visitors will regard the tourism offerings in a state positively and enthusiastically.

Information Products at Welcome Centers

The ultimate purpose behind the information products offered at a welcome center is to influence a travel group by creating attention and interest in state destinations and attractions. A variety of information products exist within welcome centers to affect demand for tourism within a state. The most common product is brochures produced by local businesses, tourism agencies, and state tourism offices. Another information product at welcome centers is staff; that is, many welcome centers are staffed to provide travel suggestions to travelers or to assist travelers with the execution of their itineraries. Some welcome centers also offer reservation services whereby travelers can request hotel rooms. Less obvious information products found at welcome centers are the visuals found on walls and display cases. These visuals include state maps, photographs, diagrams, and crafts produced in the state. Additionally, some welcome centers feature state tourism attractions in short movies or videos, in which the traveler can see other people having a good time.

Uses and Users of Welcome Centers

A number of studies have been conducted to identify and evaluate the reasons why people stop at welcome centers (Perdue 1986; Gitelson and Perdue 1987; Tierney and Haas 1988; Fesenmaier 1991). The results of these studies generally show that the use of restroom facilities is the primary reason travelers stop at welcome centers. Beyond this, however, it appears that travelers stop at welcome centers to obtain information in the form of highway maps and sightseeing and accommodation brochures. Additionally, travelers use welcome center facilities to stretch and sleep, exercise pets, purchase refreshments, and picnic. Mason (1975) found information centers with full services were perceived as more beneficial to travelers than rest areas.

Considerable research has also focused attention on comparisons between travelers who stop at welcome centers and those who do not stop (Muha 1977; Cadez and Hunt 1978; Gitelson and Perdue 1987; Howard and Gitelson 1989; Stewart, Lue, and Anderson 1991). These studies employed a variety of methods which, in part, may explain the mixed results. Howard and Gitelson (1989), for example, indicated that no significant differences exist between out-of-state travelers who used welcome centers and those that did not in terms of both demographic and trip characteristics. Muha (1977, see also Cadez and Hunt 1978), however, reported that welcome center visitors, compared to the highway traveling public were associated with higher income, larger party size, and more likely to be on a pleasure trip.

More recently, Stewart, Lue, and Anderson (1991) found that the characteristics of the general population of highway travelers were not accurately represented by assessing the characteristics of welcome center visitors. Specifically it was found that travelers who were residents of adjacent states tended to be substantially underrepresented within the ranks of welcome center visitors which, in turn, influenced the magnitude and direction of differences on several variables including age, trip length, trip planning horizon, and expenditure patterns. Stewart and colleagues (1991) found that approximately 40 percent of travelers who stopped at the Texas welcome centers were from the immediately adjacent state, whereas approximately 70 percent of travelers who did not stop at the Texas welcome centers were from an adjacent state. In this study, distance from point-of-origin was associated with visitors' expenditure patterns. For example, non-Oklahomans spent at least twice as much per party on food and room than did Oklahomans. Interestingly, Oklahomans were three times more likely to report the shortest trip planning time horizon (for example, "less than one week") than were non-Oklahomans. A similar pattern of responses was associated with the welcome center along the Texas-Louisiana border. Welcome center visitors represent a substantial underestimation of the proportion of highway travelers from the neighboring state, which in turn influences response patterns on several other auto visitor characteristics.

Measuring the Effectiveness of Welcome Centers

Of the studies dealing with welcome centers, Gitelson and Perdue (1987) and Tierney and Haas (1988) focused attention specifically on the influence of information obtained at state welcome centers. The results of these two studies indicate that information obtained by visitors may influence the places visited and the amount of time and money expended as well as the likelihood of using the information to plan future trips. Importantly, the findings of Tierney and Haas (1988) suggest the marginal economic impact of information obtained at state welcome centers appears to be substantial, accounting for a 25 percent increase in visitors' average daily expenditures.

More recently, the Indiana Department of Commerce commissioned a study to better understand the role of information in impacting travel behaviors. As part of the study, a series of four questions were used to measure the extent to which welcome center visitors were "influenced" by the tourist information obtained at the center. These questions asked respondents whether the information obtained at a welcome center influenced the length of time spent in Indiana, the places visited in Indiana, the amount of money expended, and the future use of information to plan other trips in the state. The responses to these questions were summed to create an overall measure of influence ranging from "no influence" to a "high level of influence."

The results of the Indiana study show that almost all travelers were influenced to some extent by the information obtained at welcome centers (see Table 1). Ninety-two percent of the respondents indicated they were influenced to some extent by the information they obtained at the Indiana welcome center; that is, 49 percent ($n = 171$) indicated they were slightly influenced (having scored 1 on the five-point scale), 17 percent ($n = 58$) scored two, while 14 percent ($n = 48$) and 12 percent ($n = 42$) scored three and four, respectively. Detailed analysis of this scale suggests that the strength of various types of influence varies. As shown in Table 1, almost all welcome center visitors reported that they would use the information obtained at the center to plan future trips, whereas relatively few travelers reported being influenced to visit new destinations or increase the length of their stay in Indiana.

Table 1. *Reported influence of travel information[a]*

	Levels of influence				
	0 (Low)	1	2	3	4 (High)
Reported influence of welcome center information	$n = 25$	$n = 171$	$n = 58$	$n = 48$	$n = 42$
Increased length of stay in Indiana	0.0	0.0	15.5	52.1	100.0
Visited additional places in Indiana	0.0	0.0	41.4	75.0	100.0
Increased expenditures in Indiana	0.0	2.9	46.6	79.2	100.0
Will use information to plan future trips to Indiana	0.0	97.1	96.5	93.7	100.0

Source: 1990 Indiana Welcome Center Study, Leisure Research Institute, Bloomington, Ind.
[a]Values represent the percent of respondents who modified their travel patterns.

A second phase of the study sought to investigate relationships between the extent to which visitors were influenced by welcome center information and trip characteristics such as trip purpose, travel route as it related to Indiana, information search strategies before, during, and after the trip, and the perceived importance of welcome center services. Further analyses were performed to investigate relationships between levels of influence and the sociodemographic characteristics of travelers.

A series of analyses were conducted to evaluate the role that information obtained at welcome centers plays in influencing travel through Indiana. As shown in Table 2, travelers on a "close-to-home leisure trip," a "touring trip," or an "outdoor recreation trip" were much more likely to be influenced by the information obtained at a welcome center. Travelers on other types of trips such as "visits to family or friends," "business trips," "city trips," "resort trips," "theme park or special event trips," or "personal/family-related trips," on the other hand, were less likely to be highly influenced by welcome center services.

The stage of a traveler's trip had a bearing on whether information was likely to influence travel. Travelers who indicated that Indiana was their primary destination were more likely to be influenced by the information obtained at a welcome center (see Table 3) than travelers who were en route between states. Indiana residents returning home were unlikely to be influenced, in any way, by Indiana travel information. Interestingly, out-of-state travelers passing through Indiana to another state were likely to use information collected at an Indiana welcome center on a future trip to the state.

A third phase of the study was to investigate possible relationships between trip planning, perceived importance of information services at welcome centers, and the extent to which respondents were influenced by visitor information. As one would expect (see Table 4), highly influenced travelers were more likely to have read and collected travel information before and during their trip. As shown in Table 5, travelers who perceived "picking up the state map," "picking up tourist brochures," and "talking to welcome center staff" as very important services of welcome centers were more likely to be influenced by these services.

Table 2. *Reported influence of travel information by trip type[a]*

| Trip types[b] | Levels of influence | | | | | Chi-square value |
	0 (Low)	1	2	3	4 (High)	
Visit to friends or family	57.7	43.3	44.8	37.5	33.3	4.56
Business	7.7	14.6	6.9	6.3	9.5	4.77
Close-to-home leisure	7.7	4.7	8.6	20.8	14.3	13.62**
Touring	15.4	25.2	20.7	39.6	38.1	9.66*
City	11.5	4.1	10.3	6.3	9.5	4.64
Outdoor recreation	7.7	3.5	8.6	14.6	14.3	10.25*
Resort	0.0	2.9	3.5	4.2	2.4	1.15
Theme park/special event	0.0	5.9	8.6	4.2	2.4	3.72
Personal/family	23.1	15.2	12.1	4.2	7.1	7.81

Source: 1990 Indiana Welcome Center Study, Leisure Research Institute, Bloomington, Ind.
[a]Values represent the percent of respondents taking each particular type of vacation trip.
[b]Respondents were allowed to check all the trip types that described this summer trip.
*significant at alpha < .05
**significant at alpha < .01

Table 3. *Reported influence of travel information by travel patterns of summer motorists[a]*

| Travel patterns through Indiana[b] | Levels of influence | | | | | Chi-square value |
	0 (Low)	1	2	3	4 (High)	
Indiana was their destination	11.5	26.3	37.9	43.8	35.7	11.79*
Resident of Indiana returning home	30.8	8.2	12.1	6.3	14.3	13.38*
En route *to* another state	57.7	59.1	39.7	41.7	57.1	9.67*
En route *from* another state	50.0	49.1	32.8	43.8	52.4	5.72

Source: 1990 Indiana Welcome Center Study, Leisure Research Institute, Bloomington, Ind.
[a]Values represent the percent of respondents taking a particular type of trip through Indiana.
[b]Respondents were allowed to check all answers that applied to this summer trip.
*significant at alpha < .05

Table 4. *Reported influence of travel information by information search strategy[a]*

| Information search strategies | Levels of influence | | | | | Chi-square value |
	0 (Low)	1	2	3	4 (High)	
Before trip	11.5	23.1	29.3	55.3	57.1	35.40*
During trip	40.0	68.4	81.0	93.6	100.0	44.95*

Source: 1990 Indiana Welcome Center Study, Leisure Research Institute, Bloomington, Ind.
[a]Values represent the percent of respondents searching for travel information prior and during trip.
[b]Respondents were allowed to check all answers that described this summer trip.
*significant at alpha < .01

Table 5. *Reported influence of travel information by welcome services rated very important[a]*

| Welcome center services | Levels of influence | | | | | Chi-square value |
	0 (Low)	1	2	3	4 (High)	
Stretch/exercise/sleep	16.0	17.8	19.2	15.6	14.6	18.56
Use picnic area	4.2	1.3	2.0	4.7	0.0	21.23
Pick up state map	8.0	9.7	21.6	26.1	14.3	39.26*
Use rest rooms	80.0	73.1	84.6	67.4	63.4	18.59
Pick up tourist brochures	0.0	3.8	4.0	17.4	9.5	41.41*
Purchase refreshments	8.7	1.3	2.0	2.4	2.4	33.26
Talk to welcome center staff	0.0	2.5	2.0	2.3	10.0	62.65**

Source: 1990 Indiana Welcome Center Study, Leisure Research Institute, Bloomington, Ind.
[a]Values reflect the percent of respondents considering the service very important.
*significant at alpha < .05
**significant at alpha < .01

Lastly, sociodemographic variables were analyzed to ascertain whether individuals differ in their characteristics with respect to levels of influence. The results indicate that with the exception of income levels, no significant differences in sociodemographic characteristics were found across the respective levels of influence. Moderately influenced travelers (identified with scores of 1 or 2) tended to be in low-income brackets (under $20,000); "highly influenced" travelers (as identified with scores of 3 or 4), on the other hand, tended to have midrange income levels ($30,000 to $40,000); travelers "not influenced" by the travel information tended to have annual income levels of $20,000 to $30,000 or over $60,000 (see Table 6).

Discussion

The interest of consumers to gather information to assist in their decision making and the role of service providers to facilitate the consumption of products and services suggests a dynamic system of supply and demand. Tourism promoters appear to satisfy this demand for travel information at various stages of the travel consumption process. Fulfilling requests from 1-800 calls, for example, provides information before departure; welcome centers and local visitor centers, on the other hand, are information distribution sites accessed during a trip. However, the question from a promoter's point of view is whether the high investment in this network actually results in increased visitor expenditures.

The results of the Indiana study (Fesenmaier 1991) suggest that information does influence travel behaviors. Travelers indicated that they were highly likely to use the information obtained at welcome centers to plan future trips, suggesting that information is often collected and then stored for future use. Influencing travelers to stay longer in a state appears to be the most difficult type of influence to achieve. Increasing expenditures and altering those places visited in a state are somewhat easier to influence than extending stays. Additionally, the findings suggest that certain types of trips are more likely to be altered by information collected during a trip. These trips types (that is, close-to-home, touring, outdoor), by their own nature, are trips that we would associate as having a purpose but a rough itinerary that is further developed during the trip.

Only those travelers who made Indiana their primary destination were highly influenced during their current trip. En route travelers on their way

Table 6. *Reported influence of travel information by sociodemographic characteristics of respondents[a]*

| Sociodemographic variable | Levels of influence | | | | | Chi-square value |
	0 (Low)	1	2	3	4 (High)	
Percent married	80.8	84.7	75.9	87.5	85.4	3.42
Percent with children	60.0	38.8	44.2	36.4	55.9	6.92
Age of household head						
18–29 yrs. old	4.0	10.8	7.3	4.46	2.4	
30–44 yrs. old	11.5	4.1	10.3	6.3	9.5	
45–64 yrs. old	7.7	3.5	8.6	14.6	14.3	
65 and older	0.0	2.9	3.5	4.2	2.4	15.58
Total annual household income						
$9,999 and below	0.0	3.0	7.6	0.0	0.0	
$10,000–$19,999	13.0	10.2	20.8	6.4	5.0	
$20,000–$29,999	17.4	14.5	9.4	19.2	12.5	
$30,000–$39,999	8.7	29.5	22.6	14.9	32.5	
$40,000–$49,999	34.8	16.3	17.6	19.2	20.0	
$50,000–$59,999	0.0	16.3	13.2	12.8	12.5	
$60,000 and over	26.1	10.2	7.4	27.7	17.5	41.96**

Source: 1990 Indiana Welcome Center Study, Leisure Research Institute, Bloomington, Ind.
[a]Values reflect the percent of respondents in a particular sociodemographic segment.
**significant at alpha < .01

to another state indicated they would use the information on a future trip. These findings encourage states to provide information to two types of travelers—those who come to the state to stay and those who pass through but are considering places for future trips. Additionally, travelers who are influenced by information are those individuals who collect travel information both before and during a vacation. Importantly, welcome centers serve an important function of distributing the information that they need (that is, state map, tourist brochures, travel guidance by staff members).

There are several important managerial implications of these findings. First, these results indicate promotional material provided at welcome centers should be oriented toward those types of trips (close-to-home, touring, and outdoor recreation) in which people appear to be more likely to be influenced. Second, promotional efforts by local and state agencies should target those regional areas that "generate" visitors that tend to take close-to-home, touring, and outdoor vacation trips. In addition, this promotional effort should target potential visitors who are more likely to consider a specific state as their primary destination. Third, the results indicate that those individuals most influenced by the information obtained at the welcome centers were relatively active in searching for information prior to their trip. This finding suggests it is important that promotion agencies continue (or enhance) efforts to get travel information to prospective visitors prior to their trip. Finally, the finding that almost all welcome center visitors actively seek information during their trip emphasizes the importance of a well-developed and promoted information distribution system within a state.

A word of caution needs to be provided concerning the interpretation of the research results when evaluating the relative merits of welcome centers as opposed to alternative locations for providing travel information to state visitors. The results of these studies clearly indicate that information obtained en route may influence one's travel patterns through an area. However, none of these studies has evaluated the importance of other facilities (hotel/motel, gas station, local visitor centers, or state-owned welcome centers) in influencing travel behavior. Therefore, although it appears that welcome centers attract a certain segment of the traveling population and the information provided influences the nature of the trip through an area, the welcome center, per se, may or may not be an effective way to encourage visitors to stay longer and spend more money at attractions within the state.

Summary

Visitors to welcome centers appear to be a distinct segment of the general highway traveler. They are influenced by the information obtained at the center, but the ability of this information to influence behavior is contingent upon several factors as described in this article.

References

Cadez, G., and John Hunt. 1978. *A Comparison Between Port-of-Entry Visitor Center Users and Nonusers.* Logan, Utah: Utah State University, Institute for the Study of Outdoor Recreation and Tourism.

Fesenmaier, Daniel. 1991. *Exploratory Analysis of Information Use at Welcome Centers.* Bloomington, In.: Indiana University, Leisure Research Institute.

Gitelson, Richard, and Richard Perdue. 1987. Evaluating the role of state welcome centers in disseminating travel related information in North Carolina. *Journal of Travel Research* 25(Spring):15–29.

Howard, Dennis, and Richard Gitelson. 1989. An analysis of the differences between state welcome center users and nonusers: A profile of Oregon vacationers. *Journal of Travel Research* 28(Spring):38–40.

Iowa Division of Tourism, Department of Economic Development. 1991. *Iowa: Visitor Guide and Calendar of Events.* Des Moines, Ia.

Mason, Joseph. 1975. The motorist traveler and the interstate highway system: An exploratory analysis. *Journal of Travel Research* 13(Winter):11–14.

Muha, Steven. 1977. Who uses highway welcome centers? *Journal of Travel Research* 15:1–4.

Perdue, Richard. 1986. The influence of unplanned attraction visits on expenditures by travel-through visitors. *Journal of Travel Research* 25(Summer):14–19.

Stewart, William, C. C. Lue, and B. S. Anderson. 1991. A preliminary validity study of the Texas auto visitor profile. Research Report 1299–1F. College Station, Tex.: Texas Transportation Institute.

Tierney, Patrick, and Glenn Haas. 1988. *Colorado Welcome Centers: Their Users and Influence on Length of Stay and Expenditures.* Ft. Collins, Co.: Colorado State University, Department of Recreation Resources and Landscape Architecture.

U.S. Travel Data Center. 1987. Survey of State Travel Offices: 1985–1986. Washington, D.C.: U.S. Travel Data Center.

39

Global Information Technologies in the Airlines Tourism Business

Monika Echtermeyer

To manage a business well is to manage its future; and to manage its future is to manage information.

(Kotler 1989)

In nature, the sophistication of communication systems directly correlates to the evolutionary stage of a species. Moreover, a species organized in a group needs a more highly developed communication system than individuals do. Dolphins for example fulfill both criteria: Over time they have developed a complicated sonar-echo-system, which allows them not only to communicate with one another but also to "see" their environment acoustically and thus define exactly their "fish of the day." In a similar fashion, people in the tourism business can communicate with one another and define their "customer of today (and tomorrow)" with computer-aided Information and Reservation Systems (IRS).

Until the 1950s, tourism management focused on material, natural financial and human potentials without realizing the importance of information as a sector of economic value.

Information has now become one of the most important links between producers and consumers of tourism services. Receiving and/or giving the right information at the right place or time is a key factor for success in general, not only in the tourism industry. Since you cannot store tourist attractions and actually show them at point of sale, exact visual, oral, and written information about the product is the only way for the customer to mentally get in touch with the product desired.

International tourism connects the integration, activation, and coordination of many companies, which all give their contribution to the preparation, shaping, and realization of a travel product. Customers with different travel motives, income structures, social backgrounds, and origins are awaiting that product. In order to skillfully find the right links between the individual customer's needs and the multidimensional products offered in a rapidly changing market, information technology (IT) gives us a valuable and flexible tool for serving both sides. For these reasons, what IT has done for the tourism industry can be compared to what the gasoline engine did for the transportation industry.

American, European, and Asian IRS are aiming to spin their own global information net and, therefore, are leading aggressive fights for market share. The result is a confusing variety of IRS and other compatible and noncompatible IT on the world market.

Development and Presentation of Major Commercial Information and Reservation Systems

The first Information and Reservation Systems were developed during the mid 1970s in the United States in order to respond to the need for an efficient distribution mechanism for a rapidly growing industry. It soon became obvious that the control of computer reservation systems (CRS) represented a big advantage in the airline industry. In addition to creating a higher rate of occupancy, CRSs also generated substantial fees from travel agents who used the systems to book airline, car rental, hotel, and other reservations.

In the late 1970s European and Asian airlines also realized the importance of new IT, especially for marketing. They, therefore, developed their own CRS which were further developed into IRS.

Airlines use IRS to improve efficiency, productivity, and capacity as well as strengthen their market position. Tourism offices use IRS to be effective in customer services and to improve their general efficiency (back office and front office functions and productivity). Tour operators and other tourism service providers through one IRS connection only try to find new markets and achieve a growing number of markets and international offers.

European IRS In 1987 two European IRS systems were developed: AMADEUS was developed by Lufthansa, Air France, Iberia, and Scandinavian Airline System (SAS); and GALILEO was developed by British Airways, KLM, Swissair, and COVIA, a United Airlines subsidiary.

AMADEUS, the market leader in European IRS, was founded as AMADEUS-Holding in Madrid (AMADEUS 1989). Three companies are affiliated:

- AMADEUS-Development in Nice; their main duty is the development of software together with System-One (a basic software developed in the United States)
- AMADEUS-Operations in Munich; their main duty is data processing
- AMADEUS-Marketing Company in Madrid and Frankfurt; their main duty is giving information, training travel counsellors as well as developing concepts and strategies for communication and marketing

On the German market all main central and decentral offers of AMADEUS (e. g., airline, train, touristic side offers, administration) are presented to tourism offices by the installation and use of START Personal Computers.

Until 1990 one billion German marks had been invested. In that year 16,000 airline ticket office terminals worldwide and 65 percent of all European automated travel offices with 19,000 terminals were connected to AMADEUS. Up to one thousand bookings per second were possible at that point. In addition to its four founding airlines, 17 airline companies worldwide have become partners of the AMADEUS group. For the first time in a computerized IRS, two railway networks have become partners in AMADEUS: Deutsche Bundesbahn (Germany) and SNCF (France) (AMADEUS 1990).

The main aims of AMADEUS are to become one of the most established IRS in Europe and in other parts of the world, to achieve at least 70 percent of the European market share, to stay competitive with functionality, price, capacity, and productivity, and to attain the best connection of airlines and other providers of tourism services.

GALILEO, the second largest European IRS and a company still in its built-up phase, was founded in 1987 by a group of airlines with the purpose to provide global CRS functions (Eisele 1990). It is now a joint venture of many airlines. United Airlines' Automation Vendor COVIA brings Apollo, a functional IRS with the full coverage of the United States to GALILEO. Alitalia, British Airways, KLM, and Swissair also have an ownership in COVIA Partnership. COVIA has an ownership in GEMINI, the Canadian IRS. Both embrace 100,000 terminals worldwide. GALILEO's system is primarily based on COVIA's Apollo software with several additions from the various partners.

GALILEO was established in Swindon, England, where most of its employees are located. The local distribution and support is provided through national distribution companies (NDCs) either provided by the partners (i.e., Sigma Travel Systems in Italy, GALILEO United Kingdom, GALILEO Netherland B.V., TIMAS in Ireland, TRAVISWISS, TRAVIAUSTRIA, GALILEO Hellas in Greece, GALILEO Belgium, TAP Air Portugal), by affiliates (Southern Cross in Australia) or by GALILEO owned NDCs in nonpartner markets (i.e., GALILEO España SA, GALILEO France, GALILEO Deutschland GmbH, GALILEO Nordiska).

Providing an outstanding product to air vendors is GALILEO's number one priority. On the supply side, vendors have been eager to sign up. By the end of 1991 over 380 airlines had signed the GALILEO Airline Participation agreement (GALILEO 1991).

In addition, the NDCs currently provide access to various nonair vendors such as hotels, cars, rails, ferries, leisure/tours and so forth on a national basis. Moreover GALILEO's sales team has been signing key multinational accounts.

Current subscribers receive services through the existing partners' systems of GALILEO or through Apollo in nonpartner markets or countries.

GALILEO accesses other service providers such as SITA for credit card authorization services, message switching and transmission services to communicate with air vendors and with some of the subscribers (Eisele 1990).

So far 200 million British pounds has been invested. GALILEO invoices vendors for the sum of 5.5 million British pounds each month. By 1990 the message capability was about 500–700 messages per second and the capability of the systems environment is several thousand messages per second. Seven thousand travel agencies with about 20,000 workstations were connected to GALILEO in 1990 (GALILEO 1991).

GALILEO's targets are to provide a top airline flight schedule and availability of products to the agencies and airline sales offices and to provide airline services to airlines, serving them with their specific transfer-connection-building functions, eliminating the need for the airlines to run their own schedule and availability function. Hence, a carrier specific display of a carrier X, having the necessary service agreement with GALILEO, will be generated by GALILEO both to agencies connected to GALILEO as well as to those connected to other IRS. (Eisele 1990)

American IRS
American IRS represent strong competitors worldwide, not only because of their capacity of international offers, but also because of their dominating market size. SABRE, the biggest American IRS, had 64,000 terminals connected on the U.S. market in 1989 (Fremdenverkehrswirtschaft International, 1989).

In comparison, the biggest European IRS had 19,000 terminals connected. Moreover, efforts to penetrate in the European market resulted in a market share for SABRE of 12 percent by 1991, with 2,200 subscriber locations in Europe (Fremdenverkehrswirtschaft International 1991: *Travel Weekly* 1991a).

The economic success of major American IRS is obvious. In 1986 American Airlines achieved a higher profit from their system SABRE than from their normal flight operations.

Other American IRS in addition to SABRE are

- SYSTEM-ONE founded by Texas Air (31,200 terminals in 1989) and the System One Corporation with 7,120 retail locations in the USA, 9 in Canada
- WORLDSPAN which grew out of a merger between PARS (27,314 terminals in 1989) and DATAS II (16,040 terminals in 1989) and is owned by three major airlines (Delta, Northwest, and TWA) with 8,500 retail locations in the USA, 25 in Canada; presently WORLD-SPAN and SYSTEM-ONE are discussing a merger
- GEMINI from The Gemini Group, based in Canada, with more than 3,500 retail locations (*Travel Weekly* 1991a: 29–34; Fremdenverkehrswirtschaft International 1989).

Asian/Pacific IRS and Their Connections to U.S. and European IRS
At the end of 1970 airlines in the Asian/Pacific area also developed their own IRS.

- ABACUS is based on software technology of the American system PARS and was founded by Singapore Airlines, Cathay Pacific Airways, China Airlines and Royal Brunei Airlines (ABACUS 1990)
- FANTASIA was developed by Japan Airlines and Qantas.
- In 1990 All Nippon Airways joined ABACUS, the Singapore-based IRS, in forming a new company called INFINI, to serve Japanese agencies. The INFINI IRS is an upgrade of All Nippon Airways own reservation system, ABLE. Through INFINI agents can access their local system. Because of a 5 percent cross-equity arrangement with Atlanta-based WORLDSPAN, INFINI-subscribers can also access the PARS system. (*Travel Weekly* 1991b: 37–38)

Asian/Pacific IRS render similar services as their European or American competitors but have less market share worldwide.

Nowadays overseas IRSs have come into the Asia/Pacific as friendly partners. The only major player in the region without a U.S. partner is Japan Airlines, which in mid-1988 launched a four-year $1 billion project to replace its old system, JALCOM, with a technologically superior choice called AXESS.

ABACUS is not the largest IRS in the Asia/Pacific area, but it is the most widely distributed. It has interlocking relationships with a Japanese system and with WORLDSPAN in the United States (*Travel Weekly* 1991c: 49–51).

Shareholders of ABACUS in addition to the previously mentioned founder airlines are Malaysian Airline and Philippine Airlines. About 1,600 locations use ABACUS, which is a system based on the PARS core and housed in a separate partition of the PARS mainframe in Kansas City. WORLD-SPAN and ABACUS each owns a 5 percent share of the other. All Nippon Airways's new INFINI system is now in about 1,500 locations, all in Japan. ABACUS owns 40 percent of INFINI, which means WORLDSPAN indirectly also participates as an INFINI owner with 2 percent.

The U.S. vendor is acting as a technical consultant, providing software for specific features like direct access, seat maps, seat assignments, and others. The intent of WORLDSPAN is to bring ABACUS, INFINI, and WORLD-SPAN closer together and to see sharing of information in data bases. Similarly, special Asian data bases on hotels, cruises, and so forth would be accessible to WORLDSPAN.

It is through the Swindon, England-based GALILEO that APOLLO is marketed throughout the Pacific except in Australia. GALILEO's four founder carriers are shareholders in the APOLLO operation. The GALILEO partners in Europe agreed that APOLLO would retain Japan as its Asian territory while the rest of the Asia/Pacific would be GALILEO's. However, GALILEO has only one distribution company in the area—Southern Cross in Australia, owned by Ansett and Australian Airlines—and has authorized COVIA to undertake the CRS business by installing APOLLO sets elsewhere in the Pacific on GALILEO's behalf.

COVIA counts 1,900 APOLLO sites in the Pacific, 900 in Japan (even offering laptops with kanji characters) and the remainder in China, Hong Kong, Malaysia, New Zealand, the Philippines, Singapore, and Taiwan. APOLLO is the system second after ABACUS in all its markets and second to JAL's AXESS.

SABRE is marketed in the Pacific exclusively through joint ventures whereby local interests acquire the rights to market SABRE. American Airlines does not own shares or plan to be a partner in the local marketing businesses; the vendor, which does not market directly in the area, said it will seek other such relationship instead. SABRE is accessible in 2,000 Asia/Pacific agencies (in 1991). Quantas Distribution Services markets products in Australia under the FANTASIA name, including SABRE. In Japan, SABRE has been installed through joint ventures with two large agencies, Japan Travel Bureau and Nippon Travel Agency. Finally, SABRE users anywhere in the world have the same capabilities of domestic SABRE locations—that of giving other agents access to passenger name records (PNRs) to serve one another's clients or to transmit information.

So far System One has worked solo in the Asia/Pacific area. Its two hundred locations (in 1991) include about 60 in Australia/New Zealand, while the remainder are in mid-Pacific spots (*Travel Weekly* 1991d: 51).

Conquering the Japanese market is a tough job for IRS companies because the use of airline IRS by agents to book business travel is not widespread in Japan, despite sophisticated internal computer reservation systems. A reservation center is unheard of in Japan. As in other segments of the

Japanese market, customer service is clearly a priority. It is common for agents to visit clients at their offices, take their travel requests, and hand deliver tickets. So airline systems have been thought of in Japan more as ticketing machines than time-saving information and reservation devices.

Also in the European and American market, IRS's high tech should be combined with the necessary "high touch" (service industry), which represents another key factor of success, especially in public service industries, creating a lasting link between the customer and the producer of travel services.

The IRS's world is changing very rapidly. Old connections break, new ones are being built up, functionality rises and with it complexity rises while the education has to keep pace for those who work with the education software.

Latest Developments on the Information Technology Market

In terms of using computers it has been since about the mid 1950s that these machines have begun to move heavily into our organizational and daily lives. In terms of IRS for tourism a comparable effect started in the mid 1970s. Many new generations of hardware and software have been developed since then. Changes in configurations and in the way in which hardware, software, and people are connected to one another still keep taking place. But the sense of communication remains the same: Communication can be defined as a transfer of information produced from data with the purpose of increasing the knowledge level of its recipient.

Whereas Integrated Touroperating Digital Network Services (ITDNS) are due to explore their markets, Compact Disc Read Only Memory (CD-ROM) has already penetrated it. Once the necessary infrastructure exists on each side, with these new IT communication between producers, sales agents, and clients can be handled much more attractively, effectively and cheaply in the long run.

Integrated Touroperating Digital Network Services (ITDNS) This project sponsored by the European Community is making use of personal computers (PC) already existing in travel offices. Through specially installed ITDNS cables travel packages and all kinds of touristic offers can be electronically transferred, or teleordered, between each party of the itinerant trade. After being transferred, the data will be filed in a data bank of a PC in order to be available when needed.

The advantages of ITDNS are clear to see if you compare them with catalogs. A change in demand can be met much quicker by updating special offers or teleordering brand new offers from producers of tourism services. In comparison, a catalog cannot be changed quickly because it is printed twice a year only. In addition, ITDNS opens up new prospects for effective marketing, especially in direct selling, because pictures of the desired vacation destinations, cruise ships, hotels, and such can be displayed right in front of the customer on the screen of a PC. Even picture displays along with local music sounds are presented.

Another advantage of ITDNS is the easy way to handle it. Most of the system can be applied by using graphic variables, which means that no specific computer language has to be learned.

The major problems of ITDNS are that the system needs a long time to be developed, costs are high, and a longer period of amortization follows. An appropriate technological base must be installed (e.g., cables) in the offices of the information recipients. Only a widespread net of ITDNS-connections can provide the promised advantages and efficiency. Therefore a cross-border acceptance of the system is required (Fremdenverkehrswirtschaft International 1990).

Compact-Disk Read Only Memory (CD-ROM)

Technically CD-ROM has similar functions as a normal music CD except that it does not memorize music but instead 300,000 DIN A four pages of text on one CD-ROM only. This is equivalent to the capacity of about 2,000 normal floppy disks (Fremdenverkehrswirtschaft International 1990: 26). By means of CD-ROM all kind of destination criteria that can be interesting to know for a customer are listed: description of an area or town, climate, water temperature, sporting activities, and location, service, availability of rooms, and price of hotels. Thus it can produce an individual travel-product fit for the customer.

Touristic information about 4,400 towns and 36,000 hotels in Germany are listed on a CD-ROM called "Travels in Germany," which is already widespread on the German travel market. Its information is based on a data bank called Tour Base. The costs are 980 German marks for one CD-ROM and the same price has to be paid yearly for the updates because a CD-ROM can not be overwritten. The frequency of updates varies depending on the subject and is performed by the same company that produces the CD-ROM.

The only precondition for travel offices in order to use CD-ROM as a new marketing tool is to have a PC equipped with a special CD-ROM drive.

Since 1990 the capacity of a CD-ROM has risen to 715 megabyte. In 1988 a similar disk with further developed functions had entered the market called WORM (write once read many). It is a plate rather than a CD, produced in a magneto-optical-process that can be updated once. But development continues and the producer already promises more sophisticated "WORMs" (write often read many) in the future.

The advantages of CD-ROM are high memory capacity, high picture memory potential, and high processing velocity. In comparison to ITDNS, initial investments and cost patterns are lower. Moreover a PC equipped with a CD-ROM drive that also has a link to a reservation system makes direct bookings of individual product choices possible.

A disadvantage that has been stated from the travel office (practical) point of view is the fact that CD-ROMs have exceeded the consulting time enormously, which caused lower productivity.

In addition to the never-ending development of IT, a growing number of mergers and cooperations are taking place with the result being a growing number of products offered by a diminishing number of IRSs. This development is not only a result of rising costs but also of the trend toward globalization of IT networks.

Mergers and Cooperations between IRS and Joined Development of New IT Products

With a cooperation agreement between IRSs, both new partners always try to benefit on the technical side and in marketing. Through a merger or cooperation they try to achieve a strong reinforcement of their competitiveness worldwide. Also users of the new (merged) system will benefit because products of both (compatible made) systems are then available on the same terminal. Besides common marketing and technological transfers, the exchange of customer data (passenger name records, customer profiles, addresses, credit card numbers, etc.) is included.

Just like the two American IRS, PARS and DATAS II, joined together in 1990 to create a new system called WORLDSPAN with 100 percent compatibility to the Asian system ABACUS, similar processes are taking place in other parts of the world. Several new IT products have already been released since the merger, for example WORLDSPAN has released a new product called Commercial World for corporate clients. New enhancements in Commercial World include improved flight availability, automatic file downloading, seat maps, seat assignments, destination information, show and entertainment information, waitlisting, faster check-in and much more. This service carries a one-time charge of $100 for the software and a monthly fee of $119 charged to the host agency for access to the product (*Travel Weekly* 1991: 54).

WORLD IRIS, another new development of WORLDSPAN, is an integrated reservations imaging system which is both a global reservation workstation and a persuasive audio/visual tool, all in one PC. A keystroke matches client requests with soundtracks plus still and motion pictures of cruises, hotels, tours, rental cars, and destinations. Thus hotel facilities for a business convention or cruise ship cabins can be compared. It is also possible to hardcopy from the system's mapping features, showing hotel proximity to points of interest in hundreds of cities nationwide (*Travel Weekly* 1991f: 55).

SABREVISION, a product from SABRE, offers similar possibilities utilizing a 5-inch CD-ROM disk that is updated quarterly. Thus it serves as a sales and productivity tool for agents (*Travel Weekly* 1991g: 3). Moreover subscribers now have direct access to the Travel Document Systems Data Base. The enhancement provides information on entry and visa requirements for more than 200 countries, as well as information on health and customs regulations. (*Travel Weekly* 1991h: 36)

And the mergers go on. In 1991 Continental Airlines Holdings, owner of SYSTEM ONE and WORLDSPAN planned to merge (*Travel Weekly* 1991i: 47). In 1990 SABRE and AMADEUS signed a cooperation agreement from which both sides hoped to benefit on the technical side and in marketing. But because of irreconcilable differences in the companies' philosophies the cooperation agreement failed. Now both IRSs are looking for a new partner. Shortly before this happened, SAS had already caused hard times for AMADEUS because of its change in status from shareholder to participant. SAS's move to sell its 25 percent stake in AMADEUS was precipitated by the European Economic Community's (EEC) operating rules for IRSs, which are law in the 12 EEC countries, including Denmark and, soon, Sweden and Norway. The CRS rules were designed to make reservations systems "competitively neutral" in how they list airline flight information. In addition to financial reasons (in excess of the originally planned $234 million start-up costs), after the release of the rules SAS decided there would be no strategic value to be an owner of an IRS and therefore withdrew (*Travel Weekly* 1991j: 5). SAS is now a partner airline and remains committed to connecting Scandinavian agencies and its own ticket offices to the AMADEUS system.

Vision for the Future of Airlines IRS's and Conclusions

The airline products of the future will have to differentiate themselves more strongly than they do at present. This includes building product brands that should be understood not only as the communication of a product, but also it should expand the product beyond the mere transport service. IRSs would then function as a department store that makes shelf space available for brand products and sells such space.

Airlines will no longer be able to afford to offer a number of booking classes for air travel segments worldwide in various distribution media and then sit back and hope that they will be booked for optimum profitability. Today, considerations such as

> Where is the flight sold?
> What is the profit on this segment?
> What is the total profit for the airline?
> What is the value of this passenger for the airline?

have to be integrated into a dynamic booking process.

Thanks to IRS it is possible to store this information and to communicate customer-specific data to and from the point of sale. This stored information also serves for a marketing-oriented segmentation of the products and target groups. Increased competitive pressure and neutral distribution infrastructures make customer and agency loyalty important elements of airline distribution strategies. Nowadays IRSs store passenger name records already. A goal for the future could be to create an intelligent airline customer card with a memory chip storing the customer's profile, which could be very useful when selling travel products.

Regarding GALILEO's vision for the future, GALILEO's vice president of product development sees three basic scenarios (Eisele 1990):

- The current number of airlines will remain more or less unchanged and look through ownership in a CRS for the necessary economy of scale in various fields of airline operation automation.
- The current number of airlines will remain more or less unchanged but the airlines will seek the necessary economy of scale in their cooperation and partnership agreements with other airlines.
- There will be mergers and the merged companies will have the necessary size to achieve the necessary economy of scale to handle the various fields of airline operation automation on their own.

The airlines' future distribution elements can be summed up as follows:

- IRSs mean that airlines will have a distribution presence in bigger markets. Competitive pressures will increase. National markets will no longer be owned by national carriers only.
- Production as such will lose much of its importance for the airlines' success.
- The airlines' marketing will become the decisive factor. Brand building, segmentation, new forms of distribution and customer loyalties will form the key to success. Airline marketing will have to develop retail functions and adopt retail philosophies in order not to become dependent on the retail trade. Competition will no longer be based on price alone but also on the quality of the product. This quality must also be communicated to the customer at the distribution level.
- The mere transport product becomes a "travel" product thanks to the integration of other travel elements. This means the airlines are moving into a type of new tour operator market, satisfying demand in the touristic segment.

Travel market and demands are growing; new distribution systems are being developed; new trends such as joint ventures and cooperations are dominating; tourism has become a highranking economic factor with an international radius of action. IRS represents one of the most valuable tools for tourism industry besides the human potential.

Summary

The objective of this entry is to give readers an idea about the global information technologies used by airlines and travel agents. International tourism contains many players: airlines, travel agents, tour companies, hotels, and attractions. In order to deliver a tourism product, it is necessary to have a reliable information and reservation system that integrates all the players.

References

ABACUS Distribution Systems. 1990. ABACUS—the best in travel management. Abacus the evolution of travel. Singapore.

AMADEUS Deutsche Marketing Gesellschaft mbH. 1989. Die Fäden laufen nach Madrid. AMADEUS aktuell 10: 4–10. Frankfurt.

AMADEUS Deutsche Marketing Gesellschaft mbH. 1990. Amadeus update: 1–3. Frankfurt.

Eisele, H. 1990. Paper of a GALILEO presentation at the 1990 IATA Conference (IATA IMC) in Nice: 2–9. Nice.

Fremdenverkehrswirtschaft International, 1990 edition. Speichermedium der Zukunft—Mehr Service durch CD-ROM. No. 7: 26. Hamburg.

Fremdenverkehrswirtschaft International, 1991 edition. EDV & CRS. No. 23: 34. Hamburg.

GALILEO Centre Europe. 1991. *Galileo Fact Sheet, Business Update and Summary Sheet*. 1–9. Swindon.

Kotler, Ph. 1989. *Marketing-Management* 4:629. Stuttgart.

Travel Weekly. 1991i. Continental/EDS pact called favorable to merger of SYSTEM ONE, WORLDSPAN. *Travel Weekly* 40:47.

Travel Weekly, 1991g. Comprehensive data base to be released through SABREVISION. *Travel Weekly* 52:3.

Travel Weekly. 1991e. WORLDSPAN releases reservations software for corporate clients. *Travel Weekly* 40:54.

Travel Weekly. 1991f. WORLD IRIS. *Travel Weekly* 40:55.

Travel Weekly. 1991h. Travel Document Systems Data Base. *Travel Weekly* 60:36.

Travel Weekly. 1991j. SAS confirms role of CRS rules, cost in sale of AMADEUS stake. *Travel Weekly* 68:5.

Travel Weekly. 1991a. Automation marketplace. *Travel Weekly* 78:29–34.

Travel Weekly. 1991b. Air ticketing is low tech in high-tech Japan. *Travel Weekly* 78:37–38.

Travel Weekly. 1991c. Pacific area CRS's hold promise of payoffs for U.S. trade as well. *Travel Weekly* 78:49–51.

Travel Weekly. 1991d. System One goes solo. *Travel Weekly* 78:51.

40

Sources of Information

Charles R. Goeldner

There are two main ways to procure information: (1) ask someone, and (2) find it in a published source. Tourism and hospitality executives, government officials, academicians, and students all need to know where to find pertinent timely information.

The purpose of this article is to identify prime sources of information on travel and tourism. Searching for information can be costly, and effective use of this article can save both money and hours of time. The article supplies useful information that might otherwise be missed.

In the interest of brevity, no attempt has been made to provide a comprehensive list of sources. Rather, the goal was to focus on nine key areas and identify between 10 and 20 valuable sources of information in each area. The nine areas covered in this chapter are (1) Selected List of Libraries and Reference Centers, (2) Selected List of Bibliographies and Finding Guides, (3) Selected List of Yearbooks, Annuals, Handbooks, and so forth, (4) Selected List of Books, (5) Selected List of Editors of Scholarly Tourism Journals, (6) Selected List of Other Publications, (7) Selected List of Trade and Professional Associations, (8) Selected List of University Tourism Research Centers in North America, and (9) Selected List of North American Travel Contacts.

Considerable effort has been made to make these lists short and up-to-date, with enough information to enable users to find information in a library or locate a correct telephone number. Readers should be aware that names, addresses, and prices change frequently.

It is suggested that one look beyond what might be considered "pure" tourism sources because tourism is interdisciplinary. A number of disciplines are very interested in the subject of tourism. Their organizations have set up sections within the discipline to study tourism and have placed the subject on conference programs. Their journals (especially in recreation, leisure, geography, sociology, natural resources, economics, and anthropology) provide valuable information on tourism.

Selected List of Libraries and Reference Centers

Several libraries or special collections of travel and tourism-related materials are important not only for their own usefulness but because they can give a good starting place in the search for information. These collections include

U.S. TRAVEL DATA CENTER, Two Lafayette Centre, 1133 21st Street, N.W., Washington, D.C. 20036. (202) 293-1040.

The Data Center is the national nonprofit center for travel and tourism research. Its resources are devoted to measuring the economic input of travel and monitoring changes in travel markets. The Data Center has become the recognized source of current data used by business and government to develop tourism policies and marketing strategies.

TOURISM REFERENCE AND DOCUMENTATION CENTRE (TRDC), 4th Floor East, 235 Queen Street, Ottawa, Ontario K1A OH6, Canada. (613) 954-3943.

The center maintains Canada's most comprehensive computerized collection of tourism-related information. The holdings—more than 7,000 books and documents—include research papers, statistics, surveys, analyses, journals, conference proceedings, speeches, proposals, feasibility studies, legislation, guide books, bibliographies, and more. Information on this material is held in a data bank accessible by TRDC staff or by users of remote terminals in other parts of the country.

TRAVEL REFERENCE CENTER, Business Research Division, Campus Box 420, University of Colorado, Boulder, Colorado 80309-0420. (303) 492-5056.

The Reference Center was established in 1969 to help the travel industry find information sources and to provide a facility to house a comprehensive collection of travel studies. The Center now houses the largest collection of travel, tourism, and recreation research studies available at any one place in the United States; the present collection, which numbers over 10,000 documents, is growing daily. The collection was computerized in 1985 and the Center can do literature searches using over 900 descriptors. The cost for a literature search is $50.

INFORMATION CENTER, American Hotel & Motel Association, 1201 New York Avenue, N.W., Washington, D.C. 20005-3917. (203) 289-3190.

Information on over 1,300 subjects related to hotel/motel operation is contained in the Information Center. Divided into two divisions, the five-year files (information printed in the last five years) and "historical" files, information is provided on 30 major subject categories.

TRANSPORTATION DEPARTMENT, LIBRARY SERVICES DIVISION, 400 Seventh Street, S.W., Room 2200, Washington, D.C. 20590. (202) 366-0746.

The library contains approximately 500,000 volumes and pamphlets and receives more than 1,700 periodicals. Subject coverage includes highway and bridge engineering, highway economics and finance, soil and soil mechanics, traffic engineering (including traffic safety), traffic surveys, planning and parking, driver studies, general transportation (including planning and policy), urban transportation, railroads, marine engineering, ships and ship building, navigation, oceanography, aeronautics, aviation safety, civil aviation, general aviation, airports, air traffic control, air navigation, aviation statistics, aircraft and airline industries, aviation history, and transportation communications.

AIR TRANSPORTATION OF AMERICA LIBRARY, 1709 New York Avenue, N.W., Washington, D.C. 20006. (202) 626-4000.

The library has approximately 14,000 volumes and 150 periodicals as well as technical reports in the transportation field, with special emphasis on air transport, including its history and economics. Official statistical and administrative reports of regulatory agencies, congressional documents relating to the field, special industry studies and standard transportation texts are also available. The library collects the annual reports and house organs of U.S. scheduled airlines, together with reports of foreign carriers.

AMERICAN AUTOMOBILE ASSOCIATION LIBRARY, 1000 AAA Drive, Heathrow, Florida 32746-5063. (407) 444-7966.

This library contains approximately 14,000 books and reports as well as over 700 periodicals. Coverage includes automobile history, safety, and statistics, traffic engineering, highway safety, driver education, highway development, legislation, planning, motels, campgrounds, travel industry, travel guides, insurance, business, and sales management.

CORNELL UNIVERSITY SCHOOL OF HOTEL ADMINISTRATION LIBRARY, Statler Hall, Cornell University, Ithaca, New York 14853. (607) 255-3673.

Cornell maintains one of the most comprehensive libraries on the hospitality industry. Visitors are welcome to use the collection, but material cannot leave the Cornell campus.

NATIONAL TECHNICAL INFORMATION SERVICE, 5285 Port Royal Road, Springfield, Virginia 22161. (703) 487-4650.

The National Technical Information Service of the Department of Commerce is a central source for the public sale of government sponsored research and other analyses. NTIS announces more than 60,000 new reports annually.

NATIONAL TRUST FOR HISTORIC PRESERVATION LIBRARY, 1785 Massachusetts Avenue, N.W., Washington, D.C. 20036. (202) 673-4219.

The collection covers all subjects related to historic preservation, including archaeology, architecture, fine arts, the building industry, community development, environment, history, historical geography, housing, industrial archaeology, landscape architecture, legislation, museums, planning, properties, real estate, and travel.

CENTRE DES HAUTES ETUDES TOURISTIQUES, Foundation Vasarely 1, Avenue Marcel Pagnol, 13090, Aix-en-Provence, France.

This center maintains a comprehensive collection of the world literature on tourism, which has now been computerized. The center publishes *Touristic Analysis Review* every quarter.

Selected List of Bibliographies and Finding Guides

Leisure, Recreation and Tourism Abstracts (Wallingford, Oxon, UK: CAB International, quarterly). The abstracts, arranged by subject, provide short informative summaries of publications with full bibliographical details and often a symbol for locating the original documents.

"The Travel Research Bookshelf," *Journal of Travel Research* (Boulder: Business Research Division, College of Business and Administration, University of Colorado). A regular feature of the quarterly *Journal of Travel Research*, "The Travel Research Bookshelf" is an annotated bibliography of current travel research materials. Sources and availability of materials are shown for each entry.

The Hospitality Index: An Index for the Hotel, Food Service and Travel Industries (Washington, D.C.: American Hotel and Motel Association, quarterly and annual). Citations of articles, reports, and research from more than 40 different hospitality journals and periodicals comprise this comprehensive data base. Published by the Consortium of Hospitality Research Information Services (CHRIS), the *Index* is a joint effort of Cornell University's School of Hotel Administration, the University of Wisconsin-Stout, the University of Nevada-Las Vegas, and the Information Center of the American Hotel and Motel Association. Information is organized under more than 1,500 subject headings.

Jafari, Jafar, et al. *Bibliographies on Tourism and Related Subjects* (Boulder: Business Research Division, College of Business and Administration, University of Colorado, 1988, 81 pp.). A bibliography of tourism and associated fields, this source offers 271 annotated entries. Information can be accessed in three ways: (1) alphabetical listing, (2) author index, and (3) subject index. Also included is a listing of the tourism bibliographies available from the Centre des Hautes Etudes Touristiques in Aix-en-Provence, France.

Jafari, Jafar, and Dean Aaser, "Tourism as the Subject of Doctoral Dissertations," *Annals of Tourism Research* (Elmsford, New York: Pergamon Press, vol. 15, no. 3, 1988, pp. 407–429). The article discusses tourism as a field of study and presents the results of a computer search of doctoral dissertations on tourism. The search resulted in 157 titles with a touristic focus written between 1951 and 1987. Titles, authors, and schools are given.

Goeldner, C. R., and Karen Dicke. *Bibliography of Tourism and Travel Research Studies, Reports and Articles* (Boulder: Business Research Division, College of Business and Administration, University of Colorado, 1980, 762 pp.). This nine-volume bibliography is a research resource on travel, recreation, and tourism.

Selected List of Yearbooks, Annuals, Handbooks

Travel Industry World Yearbook: The Big Picture (New York: Child and Waters, annual, 158 pp. , $79). This annual issue presents a compact, up-to-date review of the latest happenings in the world of tourism.

National Travel Survey (Washington, D.C.: U.S. Travel Data Center, quarterly and annual). In March 1979, the U.S. Travel Data Center began conducting a monthly national travel survey. Since that time, quarterly and annual summaries of the results have been published to provide researchers with timely, consistent, and relevant data on major trends in U.S. travel activity.

Economic Review of Travel in America, 1989–90 (Washington, D.C.: U.S. Travel Data Center, annual, 70 pp. , $60). This annual report on the role of travel and tourism in the American economy reviews the economic contributions of travel away from home, developments in the travel industry, and the effects of economic changes on travel and tourism.

Air Transport 1990 (Washington, D.C.: Air Transport Association of America, annual, 16 pp. , free). This official annual report on the U.S. scheduled airline industry contains historical and current statistical data on the industry.

Tourism Policy and International Tourism in OECD Member Countries (Paris: The Organization for Economic Cooperation and Development, annual). Annual tourism statistics are reported for Australia, Austria, Belgium, Canada, Denmark, Finland, France, Germany, Greece, Iceland, Ireland, Italy, Japan, Luxembourg, the Netherlands, New Zealand, Norway, Portugal, Spain, Sweden, Switzerland, Turkey, the United Kingdom, and the United States.

PATA Annual Statistical Report (San Francisco: Pacific Asia Travel Association, 112 pp. , $100). Visitor arrival statistics and other relevant data are reported by PATA member governments, especially visitor arrival data for the individual countries by nationality of residence and mode of travel. Selected market sources of visitors to the Pacific area are given, along with data on accommodations, length of stay, visitor expenditures, and national tourist organization budgets.

Yearbook of Tourism Statistics (Madrid: World Tourism Organization, 800 pp., $33). Published in two volumes, this work gives detailed breakdowns of international tourist arrivals and nights by country of residence and nationality and of average foreign tourist expenditure. The yearbook covers 140 countries and territories.

Tourism's Top Twenty (Boulder: Business Research Division, College of Business and Administration, University of Colorado, 1987, 118 pp. , $48). This book, compiled in cooperation with the U.S. Travel Data Center, Washington, D.C., provides facts and figures on travel, tourism recreation, and leisure. Information is presented primarily for the United States; however, some coverage is provided on world tourism. The volume provides fast facts on a wide array of tourism related subjects, including advertising, airlines, attractions, expenditures, hotels and resorts, recreation, world travel, and travel statistics. Sources are given for each table and complete addresses for the sources are provided in an appendix. An index by table number is also included for ease in locating information.

World Travel and Tourism Review (Wallingford, Oxon, UK: CAB International, 250 pp. , $170). This book is an authoritative global guide to indicators, trends, and policy issues. It covers up-to-date figures on travel and tourism flows, forecasts of the most rapidly expanding market sectors, market segment trends, surveys on key travel and tourism sectors, and policy issues.

Selected List of Books

McIntosh, Robert W., and Charles R. Goeldner, *Tourism: Principles, Practices, Philosophies* (New York: John Wiley & Sons, 1990, 534 pp.). The sixth edition of this classic introduction to tourism provides a broad global perspective with emphasis on planning and developing tourism. It investigates the cultural, economic, sociological, and psychological aspects of tourism. The book is divided into five parts: Understanding Tourism: Its Nature, History and Organization; Motivation for Travel and Choosing Travel Products; Tourism Supply, Demand, Economics, and Development; Essentials of Tourism Marketing and Research; and Tourism Practices and Prospects.

Gee, Chuck Y., Dexter J. L. Choy, and James C. Makens, *The Travel Industry* (New York: Van Nostrand Reinhold, 1989, 445 pp.). The emphasis in this text is on introducing concepts about travel as an industry. It provides a basic understanding of travel and tourism and provides insights into the development and operations of the various components of the travel industry.

Mill, Robert C., and Alastair M. Morrison, *The Tourism System* (Englewood Cliffs, N.J.: Prentice-Hall, 1985, 457 pp.). This book presents a comprehensive systems view of tourism and stresses the interrelationships and interdependencies of its various elements. The authors cover all aspects from a marketing point of view and describe how tourism works.

Howell, David W., *Passport, An Introduction to the Travel and Tourism Industry* (Cincinnati: South-Western Publishing Co., 1989, 422 pp.). This book is designed to help the reader understand the roles played by various components of the travel and tourism industry and suggest which of the many different careers might best suit the individual.

Ritchie, J. R. Brent, and Charles R. Goeldner. *Travel, Tourism and Hospitality Research: A Handbook for Managers and Researchers* (New York: John Wiley & Sons, 1986, 512 pp.). This reference handbook provides guidance for travel industry professionals and researchers. Noted scholars and experts in travel, tourism, and hospitality management contributed the book's 43 chapters.

Gunn, Clare A., *Tourism Planning* (New York: Taylor & Francis, 1988, 356 pp.). This text takes a human ecology approach and describes opportunities for greater expansion of tourism on the state and regional scale, without damage to our delicate natural resources. The book provides a unique framework for understanding and regrouping the complicated elements that make up tourism. Planning is related to tourism, and constructive guides for the future are offered.

Gunn, Clare A., *Vacationscope, Designing Tourist Regions* (New York: Van Nostrand Reinhold, 1988, 208 pp.). This volume is a sourcebook of theory, new ideas, and real-world examples for designers, tourism developers, promoters, and students.

Witt, Stephen F., and Luiz Moutinho, *Tourism Marketing and Management Handbook* (Hertfordshire, England: Prentice-Hall International, 1989, 656 pp.). The objective of this handbook is to provide a comprehensive business and academic reference source related to the most crucial issues in tourism marketing and management. Well over one hundred tourism topic entries are included.

Morrison, Alastair M., *Hospitality and Travel Marketing* (Albany: Delmar Publishers, 1989, 532 pp.). This book provides comprehensive coverage of marketing techniques for the hospitality industry. It emphasizes the eight "P's" of hospitality marketing: product, people, packaging and programming, place, promotion, partnership, and pricing.

Lewis, Robert C., and Richard E. Chambers, *Marketing Leadership in Hospitality* (New York: Van Nostrand Reinhold, 1989, 699 pp.). Because marketing is a long-range activity for any organization that seeks survival and growth, this book focuses on a long-range perspective rather than an operational how-to approach. Marketing examples are given from many sources.

Reid, Robert, *Hospitality Marketing Management* (New York: Van Nostrand Reinhold, 1989, 399 pp.). This text covers an introduction to marketing; marketing planning, information, and research; understanding hospitality consumers; advertising and promotion; hospitality group sales; and menu design and pricing strategies.

Krippendorf, Jost, *The Holiday Makers* (London: William Heinemann, 1987, 160 pp.). This book analyzes the different forms of tourism, examines the effects on indigenous countries and their people, and outlines positive steps to reconcile people's holiday requirements with the world's economic and social structures.

Middleton, Victor, *Marketing in Travel and Tourism* (Oxford: Heinemann Professional Publishing, 1988, 308 pp.). Contents include a discussion of the meaning of marketing in the travel and tourism industry as well as aspects that determine and influence modern marketing practice. Customer motivation and segmentation is described, followed by an explanation of the meaning of the marketing mix, with separate chapters on products, prices, promotion, and distribution.

Pearce, Douglas, *Tourism Today: A Geographical Analysis* (Harlow, Essex, UK: Longman Scientific and Technical, 1987, 229 pp.). This book analyzes in a systematic and comprehensive way the geographical dimensions of tourism, and emphasizes general patterns and processes drawn from a wide range of empirical studies, geographical methods of analysis, and theoretical considerations.

Selected List of Editors of Scholarly Tourism Journals

Jafar Jafari, Editor-in-Chief: *Annals of Tourism Research*, Department of Habitational Resources, University of Wisconsin-Stout, Menomonie, Wisconsin 54571.

Charles R. Goeldner, Editor: *Journal of Travel Research*, Business Research Division, College of Business and Administration, University of Colorado, Boulder, Colorado 80309-0419.

Frances Brown, Editor: *Tourism Management*, P.O. Box 63, Westbury House, Bury Street, Guildford, Surrey GU2 5BH, United Kingdom.

Glen Withiam, Executive Editor: *The Cornell Hotel and Restaurant Administration Quarterly*, 20 Thornwood Drive, Ithaca, New York 14850.

John O'Connor, Editor: *Journal of International Hospitality Management*, Pergamon Press Ltd., Headington Hill Hall, Oxford OX3 OBW, United Kingdom.

Claude Kaspar, Editor: *Revenue de Tourisme*, AIEST, Varnbuel strasse 19, CH-9000, St. Gallen, Switzerland.

Francis A. Buttle, Editor: *Journal of Hospitality and Leisure Marketing*. Department of Hotel, Restaurant & Travel Administration, University of Massachusetts at Amherst, Flint Laboratory, Amherst, Massachusetts 01003.

Philip L. Pearce, Editor: *Journal of Tourism Studies*. Department of Psychology, James Cook University, North Queensland, Australia.

G. Akehurst, Editor: *The Services Industries Journal*, Frank Cass & Co. Ltd., Gainsborough House, 11 Gainsborough Road, London, E11 1RS, United Kingdom.

Carolyn Lambert and Carl Riegel, Coeditors: *Hospitality Research Journal*, CHRIE, 1200 17th Street, N.W., Washington, D.C. 20036-3097.

Michael M. Lefever, Editor: *Hospitality and Tourism Educator*, CHRIE, 1200 17th Street, N.W., Washington, D.C. 20036-3097.

K. S. (Kaye) Chon, Editor: *Journal of Travel & Tourism Marketing*, Department of Hotel, Restaurant and Institutional Management, Virginia Polytechnic Institute and State University, Blacksburg, Virginia 24061-0429.

Selected List of Trade Publications

British Hotelier and Restauranteur (Kent, UK: British Hotels, Restaurants and Caterers Association).

Courier (Lexington, Kentucky: National Tour Association, monthly).

Equations (Bangalore, India: Equitable Tourism Options).

Etudes et Memoires (Aix-en-Provence, France: Centre des Hautes Etudes Touristiques, Fondation Vasarely, Universite de Droit, d'Economie et des Sciences).

Hotel & Catering Review (Dublin, Ireland: Jemma Publications).

Hotels (Des Plaines, Illinois: Cahners Publishing, monthly).

International Tourism Reports (London, UK: Economist Publications, Ltd.).

Lodging (Washington, D.C.: American Hotel Association Directory Corporation, monthly except August).

Lodging Hospitality (Cleveland: Penton Publishing, monthly).

Loreto (Brussels, Belgium: Centre de Recherches et de Documentation sur le Loisir, la Recreation et le Tourisme).

Meetings and Conventions (Secaucus, New Jersey: Reed Travel Group, monthly).

Politica del Turismo (Rimini, Italy: Amministrazione Stampa e Diffusione Maggiolo Editore).

Problemy Turystyki (Warsaw, Poland: Instytut Turystyki).

Restaurants USA (Washington, D.C.: National Restaurant Association, monthly except combined June/July issue).

Revue de l'Academie Internationale du Tourisme (Monte Carlo, France: Academie Internationale du Tourisme).

Tour and Travel News (Manhasset, New York: CMP Publications Inc., weekly).

Tourism Research Newsletter (Wellington, New Zealand: New Zealand Tourist and Publicity Department).

The Travel Agent (New York: American Traveler, Fairchild Publications, Capital Cities ABC, Inc., weekly).

Travel & Tourism Analyst (London, UK: Economist Publications, Ltd).

Travel Journalist (Brussels, Belgium: International Travel Documentation Centre).

Travel Trade (New York: Travel Trade Publications, Inc., weekly).

Travel Weekly (Secaucus, New Jersey: Reed Travel Group, twice weekly).

Turista Magazin (Budapest, Hungary).

Turizam (Zagreb, Yugoslavia: Institut za Turizam Zagreb).

Vue Touristique (Brussels, Belgium).

Selected List of Trade and Professional Associations

Travel Industry Association of America, Two Lafayette Centre, 1133 21st Street, N.W., Washington, D.C. 20036.

National Tour Association, 546 East Main Street, P.O. Box 3071, Lexington, Kentucky 40596.

Travel and Tourism Research Association (TTRA), University of Utah, Bureau of Economic and Business Research, P.O. Box 58066, Foothill Station, Salt Lake City, Utah 84158.

Pacific Asia Travel Association (PATA), 71 Stevenson Place, Suite 1425, San Francisco, California 94105.

Air Transport Association of America, 1709 New York Avenue, N.W., Washington, D.C. 20006.

American Hotel and Motel Association, 1201 New York Avenue, N.W., Washington, D.C. 20005.

American Society of Travel Agents, 1101 King Street, Alexandria, Virginia 22314.

Association of Travel Marketing Executives, P.O. Box 43563, Washington, D.C. 20010.

Cruise Lines International Association, 500 Fifth Avenue, Suite 1407, New York, New York 10110.

International Association of Amusement Parks and Attractions, 4230 King Street, Alexandria, Virginia 22302.

International Association of Convention and Visitors Bureaus, P.O. Box 758, Champaign, Illinois 61820.

National Recreation and Park Association, 3101 Part Center Drive, Alexandria, Virginia 22302.

National Restaurant Association, 1200 Seventeenth Street, N.W., Washington, D.C. 20036.

Recreation Vehicle Industry Association, P.O. Box 2999, 1896 Preston White Drive, Reston, Virginia 22090.

Tourism Industry Association of Canada, 130 Albert Street, Ottawa, Ontario, Canada K1P 5G4.

United States Tour Operators Association, 211 East 51st Street, New York, New York 10022.

World Tourism Organization, Calle Capitan Haya 42, E-28020, Madrid, Spain.

Association of European Airlines, 350 avenue Louise, boite 4, B-1050 Brussels, Belgium.

Caribbean Hotel Association, 18 Marseilles Street, Suite 1A, Santurce, Puerto Rico 00907.

East Asia Travel Association, c/o Japan National Tourist Organization, 2-10-1 Yurakucho Chiyoda-Ku, Tokyo 100, Japan.

European Travel Commission, 2 rue Linois, F-75015 Paris, France.

International Bureau of Social Tourism (BITS), 63 rue de la Loi, B-1040 Brussels, Belgium.

Selected List of University Tourism Research Centers in North America

University of Calgary, Division of Travel and Tourism, 2500 University Drive N.W., Calgary, Alberta T2N 1N4, Canada. (403) 220-3800.

University of Colorado-Boulder, Center for Recreation and Tourism Development, College of Business and Administration, Boulder, Colorado 80309-0420. (303) 492-8227.

University of Colorado-Boulder, Travel Reference Center, Business Research Division, College of Business and Administration, Boulder, Colorado 80309-0420. (303) 492-5056.

University of Central Florida, Dick Pope Sr. Institute for Tourism Studies, Orlando, Florida 32816. (407) 275-2982.

University of Hawaii at Manoa, Center for Tourism Research and Policy Study, 346 George Hall, 2560 Campus Road, Honolulu, Hawaii 96822. (808) 948-8946.

University of Massachusetts, Department of Hotel, Restaurant and Travel Administration, Flint Lab, Amherst, Massachusetts 01003. (413) 545-2061.

Michigan State University, Michigan Travel, Tourism and Recreation Resource Center, 131 Natural Resources Building, East Lansing, Michigan 48824-1222. (517) 353-0823.

University of Minnesota, Minnesota Extension Service, Tourism Center, 48 McNeal Hall, 1985 Buford Avenue, St. Paul, Minnesota 55108. (612) 624-4947.

University of Missouri, The Center for Recreational and Leisure Research,

Department of Parks, Recreation and Tourism, 617 Clark Hall, Columbia, Missouri 65211. (314) 882-9511 or (314) 882-3085.

Pennsylvania State University, The Center for Travel and Tourism Research, Department of Recreation and Parks, 267 Recreation Building, University Park, Pennsylvania 16827. (814) 865-1851.

University of South Carolina, Institute for Tourism Research, Department of Hotel, Restaurant and Tourism Administration, Columbia, South Carolina 29201-9980.

Clemson University, Parks, Recreation and Tourism Management, Recreation, Travel and Tourism Institute, 275 Lehotsky Hall, Clemson, South Carolina 29634-1005. (803) 656-2060.

Texas A & M University, Texas Tourism and Recreation Information Program, Department of Recreation, Parks and Tourism Sciences, College Station, Texas 77843-2261. (409) 845-5349.

University of Wisconsin-Extension, Recreation Resources Center, 602 State Street, Madison, Wisconsin 53703. (608) 263-2621.

Selected List of North American Travel Contacts

Canadian Tourism Research Institute, Conference Board of Canada, 255 Smyth Road, Ottawa, Ontario, Canada K1H 8M7.

AMTRAK, 60 Massachusetts Avenue, N.W., Washington, D.C. 20002.

Federal Aviation Administration, 800 Independence Avenue, S.W., Washington, D.C. 20591.

Institute of Certified Travel Agents, 148 Linden Street, Wellesley, Massachusetts 02181.

National Park Service, Statistical Office, P.O. Box 25287, Denver, Colorado 80225.

Tourism Canada, 235 Queen Street, Ottawa, Ontario, Canada K1A 0H6.

U.S. Travel and Tourism Administration, U.S. Department of Commerce, Washington, D.C. 20230.

Travel Industry Association of America, Two Lafayette Centre, 1133 21st Street, N.W., Washington, D.C. 20036.

Author Index

Subject Index

ARIMA. *See* Auto-Regressive Integrated Moving Average
ARR. *See* Average room rate
Arts and tourism, 623–624
ASF. *See* Automatic slip feed
Asia, 600, 843–844
Asia/Pacific reservation systems, 968
ASIS. *See* American Society of Industrial Security
As purchased weight (AP), 117
Assembly/serve foodservice system, 109–110
Asset Revenue Generating Efficiency Index, 344–345
Associations, 380–381
Asymmetrical tourist-host interactions, 619
A Tour through the Whole Island of Britain, 540
Attendance/inventory control software application, 265–266
Attraction and theme parks, 934–943
Attributes, personal, 92
Audit report, 273
Australia, 641, 646–647, 755, 939, 968
Automatic form number reader (AFNR), 260–261
Automatic slip feed (ASF), 260–261
Automation, front office, 430–432
Auto-Regressive Integrated Moving Average (ARIMA), 718. *See also* Box-Jenkins model
Available disposable income (ADI), 88
Average Daily Rate (ADR), 447–451
Average inventory figure, 168
Average room rate (ARR), 447
AXESS reservation system, 968

B & I. *See* Business and industry foodservice
Bacillus cereus, 193–194, 197, 199–200, 205, 212
Back office accounting, 272–275
Back-of-the-house computer applications, 266–275
Back-to-back configuration, 58–59
Bacteria, 139–141, 174–176, 192–194
Bacterial growth, optimal, 201–203
Bactericide, chemical, 145
Bacterium, 139–140
Bakery foods, foodborne illness, 190
Baking area, 60
Balance use, room occupancy, 731
Ballet Folclórico de México, 626
Banker's acceptances, 294
Banquet menu, 110
Bar charts, work loads, 170
Barriers, 21, 51
Baseline knowledge, tourism research, 658
Baskin-Robbins Ice Cream Stores, 251–253

Batters, and doughs, 212–213
Bavarian Oberammergau passion play, 627
Behavioristic approach, cost control, 157–158
Belgium, 939
Bellewaerde Park (Belgium), 939
Benihana of Tokyo, 253
Benzoic acid, 175
Bermuda Blacks Ethnic Clubs, 596
Between-season occupancy, 731
Beverages, foodborne illness, 190
Beverage selection, 99
Bhopal (India) disaster, 186
Bibliographies on Tourism and Related Subjects, 977
Bibliography of Tourism and Travel Research Studies, Reports and Articles, 977
Bill settlement, 483–484
Biochemical spoilage, 176
Bird infestation, 147
Blast chiller, 124
Block format, recipe, 114
Blue Ribbon Services, 250
Board rate, dormitory, 246
Bob's Big Boy, 251
Bonanza Family Restaurants, 7, 251
Bonds, 290–291
Bon Vivant, 186
Bowery Savings Bank, 10, 243
Box-Jenkins model, 680–681, 718
Brainstorming, 861–869
Branding, 246, 390–396
Breach, contract, 573–574, 577–578
Bread selection, 99
Breakfast menu, 99
Britain, 725, 919–920. *See also* England
British Airways, 965–966
British Columbia, Ministry of Regional Economic Development (MRED), 782
British thermal units (BTU), 68
Brochures, 893–895
BTU. *See* British thermal units
Budgeting
    capital, 292–293
    menus, 88–89, 270–272
    multiunit hospitality firms, 304
    operations, 296–304
    preparation process, 298–301
Buffer stock, 70, 75
Buffet, 29, 110
Bulk regeneration ovens, 125
Bureau of Indian Affairs, 767
Bureau of International Transport and Tourism, 766
Bureau of Land Management, 767
Bureau of Reclamation, 767
Burger King, 7, 251–253
Busch Entertainment Corporation, 936
Busch Gardens, 934, 936–937
Buses, 575–576, 578–581, 950. *See also* Transportation

Business and conference tourism, 728
Business cycles, 708
Business format franchise, 252
Business and industry (B & I) foodservice, 243–244. *See also* Institutional foodservice
Business plan, 38–39
Bus Regulatory Reform Act, 576

C. *See* Cycles
CAB. *See* Civil Aeronautics Board
Cable News Network (CNN), 594
Cafeterias, 3–4, 6, 10, 110
Call order system, 29
Calorie, 68
Campbell Soup Company, 186
Campylobacter, 142
Campylobacter jejuni, 178, 183, 191, 194, 197, 199, 201, 204, 208
Canada, 765, 782, 791, 843–844, 927, 947, 952
Canadian Laurentian mountains, 927
Canning industry, 10, 186
Canteen Co., 250
Capacity, contract, 573
Capacity, foodservice, 32, 34
Capital, 289–293
CARA Information Systems Inc., 469
Caribbean region, 597–598, 849
Caribbean Tourism Association, 849
Cash drawers, 262
Cash operations, college foodservice, 228
Cash register polling, remote, 276–277
Cash requirements report, 273
Catering, 4
Cathay Pacific Airways, 967
Catholic Church, and franchising, 252
Causal models, 681–687, 697–698
Caustic soda, 144
Cautionary Platform Research stage, 630
CDC. *See* Centers for Disease Control
CD-ROM. *See* Compact Disc Read Only Memory
CDs. *See* Certificates of deposit
Cedar Point, 937
CEMI. *See* Conventions, expositions, and meetings industry
Census of Selected Services, 936
Centers for Disease Control (CDC), 178–179, 187
Central America, 593
Centralized Reservation Systems (CRS), 475
Central processing unit (CPU), 263
Central States Anthropological Society, 595
Centre des Hautes Etudes Touristiques, 976
Century Travel Club, 631
Cereals, pathogens, 197

Certificates of Deposit (CDs), 294
Certified Protection Professional (CPP), 522
Ceteris paribus condition, 686
CFU. *See* Colony forming units
Chaining recipes, 268
Chain operators, nutrition, 83–84
Chamonix (France), 927
Channels of distribution, 330
Checkout, 482–486
Check tracking software application, 265–266
Chemical spoilage, 176
Chicago Board of Education, 244
Chicago World's Fair, 936
Child Nutrition Act, 8
Children's Aid Society of New York, 8, 244
Child Welfare Act, 245
Chilled food system, 215–217
Chilling variations, 124–125. *See also* Cook-chill process
China Airlines, 967
Chinese Restaurant Syndrome, 176
Chlorine dioxide, 145
Chlorine sanitizers, 145
Choice menus, 95, 110
CHRIS. *See* Consortium of Hospitality Research Information Services
Civil Aeronautics Board (CAB), 575, 577, 854
Civil aviation, 855
Civil law, 570–572
Civil Rights Act, 583
Class sociocentrism, 641
Cleanability, 142
Cleaners, 143–145
Cleaning principles, 143–145
Clerk, receiving, 41, 149, 165–166
  daily report, 165–166
Client type, 25
Clostridium botulinum, 178, 193–194, 197, 199–201, 205, 212, 216
Clostridium perfringens, 142, 177–178, 183, 193–194, 197, 199, 201–203, 205, 208, 210, 213
CM. *See* Contribution margin
CMP. *See* Complete Meeting Package
CNN. *See* Cable News Network
Cobo Hall, 383
Coca Cola, 253
Cockroaches, 146
Code of Federal Regulations, 186
Coffee machine, 10
Coffee shop franchise, 253
Cognition, 653
Cold combination dishes, 213–214
Cold holding, 201–202
Coles Ordinary tavern, 5
College and university foodservice, 226–240, 246
Collinearity, 683

Colony forming units (CFU), 204
Color, food, 93
Combination ovens, 125
Commercial enterprise, 768–769
Commercial foodservice, 3–8, 241, 243
Commerical paper, 294
Commercial relations, 334
Commissary foodservice system, 109
Commissary General, 10
Commoditization, 615
Common law, 569, 583
Commonwealth Games, 948
Communications
  faulty, 620
  mechanistic structure, 328
  multiunit, in restaurants, 275–276
  two-way, 71
Compact Disc Read Only Memory (CD-ROM), 969–971
Compassionate Universe, The, 781
Competition, 20, 22–23, 334, 500. *See also* Marketing
Complaints, 322–323
Complete Meeting Package (CMP), 377
Computerized Lodging Systems, Inc., 469
Computer Reservation Systems (CRS), 965
Computers
  back-of-the-house applications, 266–275
  central processing unit (CPU), 263
  configurations, 263
  converting maps, 763
  electronic cash register (ECR), 258–265, 269–271
  foodservice, 236–237
  hotels, 430–432
  keyboard designs, 259–260
  marketing tool, 891
  menu boards, 259
  menu planning, 99–101, 236, 270–272
  multiunit communications, 275–277
  and PMS, 467–470
  point-of-sale (POS), 258–265, 269–271
  preset keys, 259, 266
  programs, 763
  reservations, 474–475
  seasonality analysis, 717–724
  service-oriented applications, 258–266
  technology, 18
  touch-screen units, 259–260
Concept development, 54, 759–762
Conde Nast Traveler, 890
Coney Island, 935
Confectionery, foodborne illness, 190
Conference centers, 373–377

Conference on Travel and Tourism, United Nations, 542
Consensor, 687
Consistency, food, 93
Consolidated reporting functions, 265, 269–270
Consolidation, 371
Consortium of Hospitality Research Information Services (CHRIS), 977
Constitution, U.S., 568–569
Construction documents, 55
Consumer hazard degree, 191–192
Consumer Health and Nutrition survey, 83
Consumer menu viewpoint, 90–94
Consumer Price Index (CPI), 245, 684
Consumer shows, 382
Contact surfaces, food, 201, 207–208
Contamination protection, 138–139
Contemporaneity, indigenous right, 656
Continental Airlines Holdings, 971
Contract. *See also* Law
  breach, 573–574, 577–578
  of carriage, 577
  foodservice, 24–25, 249–250
  law, 333, 570, 572–573
  renegotiation, 655–656
Contribution margin (CM), 270–271
Conventional study methods, time series, 717
Conventions, 379–387
Conventions, Expositions, and Meetings Industry (CEMI), 379–387
Convention and Visitors Bureau (CVB), 384–385
Conversion, existing building, 52
Conveyor belt production, 124
Cook-chill process
  advantages, 120–121, 126
  chilling variations, 124–125
  components, 123
  cost factors, 121
  defined, 120
  disadvantages, 126
  equipment, 124
  holding stage, 28, 30
  ingredient cooking variations, 123–124
  quality assurance, 121–122
  United Kingdom study, 125–126
  use in U.S., 122–123
Cook-freeze technology, 30
Cook tanks, 123–124
Co-op food buying, 164
Copper, food hazard, 195
Cornell Hotel & Restaurant Administration Quarterly, 223
Cornell University School of Hotel Administration Library, 976

El Al airline, 601, 725
Elder-care centers, 247
Electricity, 67
  grounding, 67–68
Electronic cash register (ECR),
    258–265, 269–271, 273
Electronic mail (E-mail), 277
E-mail. *See* Electronic mail
Emergency action plans, 462–463,
    521–522
Empirical results, tourism, 667–668
Employee
  areas, 61
  files, 264–265
  foodservice. *See* Institutional
    foodservice
  misconduct, 585
  theme parks, 942. *See also* Labor
Employee Assistance Program (EAP),
    222
Employee Polygraph Protection Act,
    222
Employment contracts, 573
Employment multipliers, 664
EMS. *See* Energy management system
Encephalitis, 147
Encountering "the other," 642–644
Encounters, 640–648
Energy Management System (EMS),
    527
Energy sources, 66–68
Engineering, 524–535
England, 246. *See also* Britain
Entrées, 96
Environment
  economic, 18
  food preference factor, 91
  foodservice controls, 207
  hotel management, 409–411
  scanning, 17–19
  types of, 18–19
Environmental Protection Agency
    (EPA), 176, 179
EOQ. *See* Economic order quantity
EP. *See* Edible portion weight
EPA. *See* Environmental Protection
    Agency
EPCOT Center (Disney World), 935
Ephemeral tourist-host interactions,
    620
Equal Employment Opportunity, 222
Equal Employment Opportunity laws
    (EEOC), 516
Equipment
  cold food, 59
  configurations, 57–59
  cost factor formula, 64–65
  design, 66
  functional attributes, 65
  hot food, 59–60
  malfunctioning, 149–150
  needs, 63, 74–75

performance, 66, 152
pre-preparation, 59
profitability, 64–65
selection, 57–59, 63–68
short-order, 60
size, 66
Equity, 291–292
Error magnitude, 702
ESCA. *See* Exposition Service
    Contractors Association
Escherichia coli, 178, 194, 197, 203–204
Estimation, forecasting, 701–702
Ethnic Baja fishing relations, 597
Ethnic boundaries, 626
Ethnic clubs, 596
Ethnic consciousness, 625–627
Ethnic food preferences, 79
Ethnocentrism
  defined, 652
  implications for tourism, 653–657
  malignancies, 648
  measurement, 659–660
  research, 657–660
  scale of operations, 653–654
  tourist encounters, 639–648
Ethnographic interpretation, 659
Euro-American stereotypes, 643
Eurocentricity, 644–645, 654
Euro Disneyland, 937–938
Euromonitor (London), 725
Europe, 334, 601–602, 725, 843–844,
    849, 927, 937–938
European Economic Community
    (EEC), 334, 971
European Travel Commissioner, 849
Events
  customer orientation, 950–951
  economic, tourism impact, 952–953
  multiannual, 708
  tourism roles, 946–948
  planning and marketing, 948–952
Exchange rates (E), 708
Excursionists, 542
Exhibit Designers and Producers
    Association (EDPA), 385
Exhibitions, 382
Existing building, conversion, 52
Exotoxin-forming microorganisms,
    control rules, 205
Expansion, tourism, 636–637
Experiential tourists, 643
Experimental tourists, 643
Explorer's Club (New York), 631
Expoland (Japan), 939
Expositions, 379–387
Exposition Service Contractors
    Association (ESCA), 386
Expressive culture, and tourism, 595
Extended-care facility foodservice, 247
External environment, college
    foodservice, 229
Extra peak accommodation, 731

Extrinsic factors, food preferences,
    91–92

Facility concept determination, 24
Facsimile (FAX), 275
Factor method, recipes, 115–117
Factors, food preference, 78–80, 90–92
Fair market share, 23
Familiarity, food choice, 92
Family influence, food choice, 92
Family style franchise, 253
FANTASIA reservation system, 967
FASB. *See* Financial Accounting
    Standards Board
Fast-food. *See also* Food; Foodservice
  college and university, 246
  educational foodservice, 4
  franchising, 7, 251–253
  healthy menu survey, 84
  production-lining, 33
  restaurants, 3
FAX. *See* Facsimile
FDA. *See* Food and Drug
    Administration
FDI. *See* Foreign direct investment
FDS. *See* Foodservice delivery system
Feasibility, 15, 54–55
Federal Drug Administration, 126
Federal maritime law, 576
Federal Meat Inspection Act, 179
Federal tariff system, 580
Feedback control system, 419
Feet-per-minute (fpm), 209
Festival, defined, 945–946
Festival of Arts (Canada), 952
Festival date variations, 708
Festivals and special events, 945–953
FIFO. *See* First-in/first-out
Final plan, design, 61
Finance, college foodservice, 230
Financial Accounting Standards Board
    (FASB), 288
Financial aid, 751–752
Financial management, 288–295
Financial reporting application, 274
Financing, 55
Fin fish, pathogens, 197
Finland, 915
First American Seaside Resort, 920
First-in/first-out (FIFO), 41, 135, 152,
    167, 236
Fisheries and Wildlife Service, 767
FIT. *See* Free individual traveler
Fixed menu, 94, 110
Flavor, food, 93
Flies, 146
Flight cancellation, liability, 578–579
FLIK International, 250
Florida Sun News, 940
Food
  additives, 195
  adverse reactions, 193, 196

IATA. *See* International Air Transport
  Association
Iberia, 964
IBM, 224
ICAO. *See* International Civil Aviation
  Organization
ICC. *See* Interstate Commerce
  Commission
Ice cream foodservice, 4
Ideas, 861–869
IEA. *See* International Exhibitors
  Associations
IFA. *See* International Franchise
  Association
IFMA. *See* International Foodservice
  Manufacturers Association
Image measurement, 658
Immediate check printing, 260
Immigration laws (IRCA), 516
IMPLAN model, 667
Inactivation curves, 198
Income elasticity, tourism demand,
  675–676
India, 186, 246
Indiana Department of Commerce,
  958
Indiana State park study, 906–907
Indigenous oversight, 654–655
Indirect competitors, 20
Indirect effect, 663
Individual tourist, 614–615
Industrial shows, 382
Industry, 545–546, 561, 743–744
Infant foods, foodborne illness, 190
Infective microorganisms, 199–200,
  204, 213
INFINI reservation system, 967–968
Information Center, 956–962, 975
Information
  hotel services, 427
  influences, 833–834
  pleasure search, 830–835
  products, 956–957
  search strategies, 833
  search timing, 833
  sources, 832–833
Information Center, 956–962, 975
Information and Reservation Systems
  (IRS), 965–969
Information Technology (IT), 965
Infrastructure and development,
  754–770
Ingredients
  control, 110–111
  files, 267–268
  variations, cook-chill process,
    123–124
Inhibitors, 175
Injection (spending), 663
Injury/death, 581
Innkeeper obligations, 582–587
Inns, 581

In-process inventories, 135
In-process storage, 135–136
Input, foodservice, 32, 203
Input, matrix, 666
Input-output analysis (IOA), 663–668
In Search of Excellence, 417
Insect infestation, 146
Inspecting and receiving goods, 151
Institutional foodservice, 4–5, 8–10,
  241–250
Instrumental tourist-host interactions,
  620
Integrated Tour Operating Digital
  Network Services (ITDNS),
  969–970
Interactional tourist, 615–616
Intercultural competencies, 654
Intercultural workshops, 653
Intergenerational equity, dimensions
  of, 782
Intermediate output, foodservice, 32
Internal marketing, 321–322
Internal Revenue Service, 64
International Airline Competition Act,
  853
International Air Transport
  Association, 848
International Air Transport
  Association (IATA), 728
International Association of
  Amusement Parks and Attractions
  (IAAPA), 936, 939–941
International Association of
  Conference Centers (IACC), 376
International Broadcasting, 936
International Civil Aviation
  Organization (ICAO), 855
International Conference on Travel
  and Tourism Statistics, 548–557
International Events Group Inc., 945
International Exhibitors Associations
  (IEA), 385
International Foodservice
  Manufacturers Association
  (IFMA), 242–243
International Franchise Association
  (IFA), 366–367
International House of Pancakes,
  253–254
International relations, 334
International Union of Official Travel
  Organizations (IUOTO), 747, 837
International Union of Tourist
  Organizations (IUOTO), 630
Interstate Commerce Commission
  (ICC), 576, 580
Inti Raymi, 626
Inventory
  application, 274
  counts, 136–137, 168
  estimates, 39–40
  food costs, 161–162, 173

  perpetual, 137, 168
  profile, 774–775
  turnover figure, 168
  types, 168
  verification, 47–48
IOA. *See* Input-output analysis
Iodine sanitizers, 145
Iodophors, 145
IRCA. *See* Immigration laws
Irregularity (I), monthly series, 708,
  711, 724
IRS. *See* Information and Reservation
  Systems
Isolated site, 50
Israel, 726–727
Israeli Ministry of Tourism, 680
Issue of goods, 42
Issues, sales promotion, 890–891
IT. *See* Information Technology
ITDNS. *See* Integrated Tour Operating
  Digital Network Services
Itza Pizza, 239
IUOTO. *See* International Union of
  Official Travel Organization;
  International Union of Tourist
  Organizations

Jack-in-the-Box, 253
Jaguar Sabre Vision, 436
JALCOM reservation system, 968
Japan, 593–594, 766, 843–844, 939,
  948, 969
  Ministry of Transport, 766
Japan Airlines, 967
Japanese language study, 593–594
Japan Ministry of Transport, 766
JCAH. *See* Joint Commission on
  Accreditation of Hospitals
Jerusalem, 822–823
Jet lag, 879–880
Job analysis, 169
Joint Commission on Accreditation of
  Hospitals (JCAH), 248
Jone's Wood, 936
Journal printers, 261
Journal of Travel Research, 976
Junk bond, 291

Kaiser Hospitals, 9
Kansas City Restaurant Association,
  11
Kentucky Fried Chicken, 7, 251, 253
Keyboard designs, computer, 259–260
  Reed style, 259
Key result areas, 35–36
Kings Island, 934, 937
Kitchen planning, 69–75
  configurations, 58–59
KLM airline, 965–966
Knott's Berry Market, 936
Knowledge, baseline, 658
Knowledge-based platform, 630

Knoxville's World's Fair, 947
Korea Ministry of Transportation, 767
Korea National Tourism Corporation, 767

Labeling, nutritional, 90
Labor. *See also* Employee
cook-chill cost, 121
cost control, 169–171, 173
master file, 264
shortage, 255–256
unions, 223–224
Lackman Food Services, 250
LaCrosse Area Convention and
Visitors Bureau study, 776–779
Lactic acid, 146
Lagged dependent variable, 701
Lag phase, 140
Lake Placid, 927
Land costs, 22
Landscaping, 51–52, 913–914
Language, 593, 622–623
Last-in/first-out (LIFO), 41
Latin America, 597–598
Law
accommodation, 581–587
administrative, 569–570
agency, 333
civil, 570–572
common, 569, 583
contract, 333, 570, 572–573
criminal, 570–572
equal employment opportunity, 516
ethics, 334
federal food and drug, 516
hospitality, 332–335
immigration, 516
maritime, 576
private, 570–571
procedural, 571
public, 245, 570–571
regulatory, 333
substantive, 570–571
tourism, 567–587
transportation, 574–581
Law-ethics interplay, 334
Law of Tourism Promotional
Development Fund, The (Korea), 767
Leaders, 418
Leadership, 286, 318
League of Nations, 542
Leakage, 663
Leftover control, 159, 183, 210
Legality, contract, 573
Legislation, complexity of, 749–750
Legumes, pathogens, 197
Leisure, 559–565
Leisure, Recreation and Tourism
(LRT), 564
Leisure, Recreation and Tourism Abstracts, 976

Leptospirosis, 146
Level of expectation, food choice, 92
Levulinic acid, 145
Liability, third party acts, 586
Liability disclaimers, 577
Liability risks, hotels, 585–586
LIFO. *See* Last-in/first-out
Limited choice menu, 110
Line balancing, 75
Lisberg (Sweden), 939
Listeria monocytogenes, 146, 178, 197, 199–200, 202, 204–205, 208
Listeriosis, 142
Lockerbie (Scotland), 593
Lodging. *See also* Hotels
franchising, 366–371
industry, 582
managing, 343–346
marketing, 316–323
operations, 337–346
types, 341–342
Lodgistix, Inc., 469
Logarithmic growth phase, 140
Long-term capital, 290
Lotte World (South Korea), 938–939
Lourdes, pilgrims, 822
Low pathogen count, 211
LRT. *See* Leisure, Recreation and
Tourism
Lufthansa airline, 965
Luggage liability, 579–581
Luxury hotels, 490–491

MM. *See* Menu mix
3M, 224
McCormick Harvesting Machine
Company, 252
McDonald's restaurants, 7, 251–253, 255–256
McKinsey and Company, 930
Magnetic strip readers, 259–260
Maintenance, 524–535
Major destinations, 20, 844
Major tourist flows, 842–843
Major traffic arteries, 20
Malaysia Airline, 968
Malignancies, hospitality, 648
Management
computer applications, 258
current asset, 293–295
engineering, 527–535
financial, 288–295
food production systems, 110–113
food storage procedures, 135–136
hotel, 407–421
information systems, 171–173
maintenance, 527–535
marketing, 324–330
menu, 88–90, 110
organizational, 306–314
participative, 223
reservations, 475–477

safety, 458–464
strategic, 281–286
successful profiles, 38
women, 222–223
Maori culture (New Zealand), 654
MAPE. *See* Mean absolute percentage
error
Maps, 876
Marine foods, foodborne illness, 190
Maritime law, 576
Market
analysis, 15–17
equilibrium, 442
feasibility, 15–25
hotel pricing, 456–457
related factors, 49–50
segmentation, 393
support procedure, 23
tourism, 545
Marketing. *See also* Advertising
Agricultural Marketing Act, 179
American Marketing Association, 324
college/university foodservice, 232–233, 239–240
computer as marketing tool, 891
concept, 317–318
direct, 890–891
event tourism, 948–952
Food Marketing Institute, 82
hospitality marketing mix, 328–330
Hotel Sales and Marketing
Association International
(HSMAI), 384, 435
internal, 321–322
lodging, 316–323
management, 324–330
matrix, 756
relationship, 322
research, 327–328
ski industry, 929–930
target, 327, 949
videos, 891
Marriott Food Service, 226, 250
Maryland, University of, 239
Master-slave computer configuration, 263
Material Safety Data Sheets (MSDS), 461–462
Mathematics, input-output analysis, 664–667
Matrix, marketing, 756
Maximal utilization constrained by
seasonality (MUS), 723, 726–727, 729, 731
Mayan site, 593
MCA Universal Studios, 936
Meal identification card system, 228
Meals-ready-to-eat (MREs), 5
Mean absolute percentage error
(MAPE), 691
Mean square error (MSE), 691

Measurements, statistical, 735–753
Meat
    Federal Meat Inspection Act, 179
    foodborne illness, 190, 211
    pathogens, 197–198
Mechanistic structure, 351
Medicaid, 247
Medicare, 247
Mediterranean region, 601–602
Meetings and Conventions Magazine, 386
Meetings industry, 373–377, 379–387
Meetings Planning International (MPI), 374
Mega-event, 946
Megatrends 2000, 224
Melanesian Explorer, 599
Menu. *See also* Food; Foodservice
    checklist, 100–101
    classification, 110
    college foodservice, 235–236
    computer boards, 259
    computers for planning, 99–101, 236, 270–272
    conceptual plan, 70
    consumer viewpoint, 90–94
    control, 159–160
    cyclical, 159
    defined, 88, 110
    design, 101–102
    engineering software, 270
    equipment needs, 75
    fluctuations, seasonal, 89, 92
    item classifications, 270–271
    item file, 263–264, 269
    management viewpoint, 88–90
    no-choice, 95
    nonselective, 95
    patterns, 94–95
    personnel skills, 90
    planning, 88–94, 96–101
    pricing, 158–159
    reference materials, 95–96
    selective, 95
    single-use, 95, 110
    static, 94, 110
Menu mix (MM), 270–271
Methyl-mercury hazard, 196
Mexico, 246, 583, 626, 843–844
Mice, 147
Microbes, 139
Microbial flora, 139, 197
Microbiological food spoilage, 174–176
Microbiological hazards, 192
Microorganisms, 139–141, 174, 193
    infective, 199–200, 204, 213
Microwave ovens, 125
Middle East, 600–601
Military foodservice, 5, 10–11, 241
Milk
    ordinance, 208
    pathogens, 197

Minnesota, 765
Minor children, 583
Mise-en-place, 32
Mites, 147
MNC, 357, 362
Mobile rethermalization carts, 125
Models
    Box-Jenkins, 680–681, 718
    causal, 681–687, 697–698
    college/university foodservice, 229–230
    delivery service, 402–405
    Delphi, 687–688
    double-log regression, 682
    econometric, 683–685, 697–703
    gravity, 685–687, 698
    IMPLAN, 667
    monthly multiplicative series, 707
    multiple regression, 682
    multiplicative monthly series, 707
    noncausal, 679–689, 697–698
    pleasure travel destination choice, 814–818
    push/pull of motivations, 800–802
    regression, 681–683
    time series forecasting, 680–681
    trip-attraction, 686–687
    trip-generation, 685–687
Modem, 275–276
Modern Maturity, 885
Mold contamination, 139–140, 174–176, 193, 200
Monosodium glutamate (MSG), 176, 194–195
Monthly series, 707–708
Monthly trends, seasonality, 708–716
Montreal Olympic Games, 680
Moods, food choice, 92
Morrill Act, 246
Morrisson's Custom Mge., 250
Motels, 582
Motivation, 655, 896
Moving average, 112
MPI. *See* Meetings Planning International
MREs. *See* Meals-ready-to-eat
MSDS. *See* Material Safety Data Sheets
MSE. *See* Mean square error
MSG. *See* Monosodium glutamate
Multiannual events, 708
Multicollinearity, 683–685
Multifaceted delivery system, 27
Multinational corporation (MNC), 354
Multinational firm, 354–362
Multiple regression model, 682
Multiplicative models, monthly series, 707
Multiplicative seasonality, 711
Multiunit communications, 275–277
Multiunit computers, 275–277
Muriatic acid, 145
Murine typhus, 146

MUS. *See* Maximal utilization constrained by seasonality
Mutual funds, 294–295

NAEM. *See* National Association of Exposition Managers
NASA. *See* National Aeronautics and Space Administration
National Academy of Sciences, 80
National Aeronautics and Space Administration (NASA), 186
National Association of Exposition Managers (NAEM), 382
National Association of Rotary Clubs, 11
National Ballet of Senegal, 626
National Capital Region, 947
National Distribution Companies (NDC), 966
National Foodservice Panel, Incorporated, 122
National Gardening Association (NGA), 913
National Geographic, 644–645
Nationalism, 640, 642
National Marine Fisheries Service, 179
National Park Service, 757, 770
National Research Council's Report on Diet and Health, 82, 203
National Restaurant Association (NRA)
    Consumer Health and Nutrition survey, 83
    consumer nutrition studies, 82
    Education Foundation, 139, 141, 180
    family concept foodservice, 24
    fast-food healthy menus, 7, 84
    history, 11–12
    institutional foodservice, 241, 249
    nutrition information, 85–86
    recruitment, 222
    shows, 382
National Sanitation Foundation, 153
National School Lunch Act, 8, 90, 244
National School Lunch Program (NSLP), 4, 8, 245
National Science Foundation Student Originated Studies grant, 595
National Technical Information Service, 976
National Tourism Agency (NTA), 750
National Tourism Policy Act, 766
National Travel Survey, 977
National Trust for Historical Preservation Library, 976
Nature, encounters, 646–647
NDC. *See* National Distribution Companies
Negative impact, demonstration effect, 632–633
Negligence, 573–574
Negotiated credit, 289